Lecture Notes in Computer Science 11388

Commenced Publication in 1973
Founding and Former Series Editors:
Gerhard Goos, Juris Hartmanis, and Jan van Leeuwen

Editorial Board

Advanced Research in Computing and Software Science
Subline of Lecture Notes in Computer Science

Subline Series Editors

Subline Advisory Board

More information about this series at http://www.springer.com/series/7407

Constantin Enea · Ruzica Piskac (Eds.)

Verification, Model Checking, and Abstract Interpretation

20th International Conference, VMCAI 2019
Cascais, Portugal, January 13–15, 2019
Proceedings

 Springer

Editors
Constantin Enea
IRIF
University Paris Diderot and CNRS
Paris, France

Ruzica Piskac
Yale University
New Haven, CT, USA

ISSN 0302-9743   ISSN 1611-3349   (electronic)
Lecture Notes in Computer Science
ISBN 978-3-030-11244-8   ISBN 978-3-030-11245-5   (eBook)
https://doi.org/10.1007/978-3-030-11245-5

Library of Congress Control Number: 2018966547

LNCS Sublibrary: SL1 – Theoretical Computer Science and General Issues

This Springer imprint is published by the registered company Springer Nature Switzerland AG
The registered company address is: Gewerbestrasse 11, 6330 Cham, Switzerland

Preface

This volume contains the papers presented at VMCAI 2019: the International Conference on Verification, Model Checking, and Abstract Interpretation held during January 13–15, 2019, in Cascais, Portugal, co-located with POPL 2019 (the annual ACM SIGPLAN/SIGACT Symposium on Principles of Programming Languages). Previous meetings were held in Port Jefferson (1997), Pisa (1998), Venice (2002), New York (2003), Venice (2004), Paris (2005), Charleston (2006), Nice (2007), San Francisco (2008), Savannah (2009), Madrid (2010), Austin (2011), Philadelphia (2012), Rome (2013), San Diego (2014), Mumbai (2015), St. Petersburg, Florida (2016), Paris (2017), and Los Angeles (2018).

VMCAI provides a forum for researchers from the communities of verification, model checking, and abstract interpretation to present their research and aims to facilitate interaction, cross-fertilization, and advancement of hybrid methods that combine these and related areas. VMCAI topics include: program verification, model checking, abstract interpretation, program synthesis, static analysis, type systems, deductive methods, decision procedures, theorem proving, program certification, debugging techniques, program transformation, optimization, hybrid and cyber-physical systems.

This year the conference received 62 submissions, of which 27 were selected for publication in the proceedings. Each submission was reviewed by at least three Program Committee members, and the main selection criteria were quality, relevance, and originality. In addition to the presentations of the 27 selected papers, the conference also featured three invited keynote talks by Nuno P. Lopes (Microsoft Research), Kedar Namjoshi (Nokia Bell Labs), Sylvie Putot (Ecole Polytechnique). We warmly thank them for their participation and contributions.

We would like to thank the members of the Program Committee and the external reviewers for their excellent work. We also thank the members of the Steering Committee, and in particular Lenore Zuck and Andreas Podelski, for their helpful advice, assistance, and support. We thank the POPL 2019 Organizing Committee for providing all the logistics for organizing VMCAI. We are also indebted to EasyChair for providing an excellent conference management system.

November 2018

Constantin Enea
Ruzica Piskac

Organization

Program Co-chairs

Constantin Enea   IRIF, University of Paris Diderot and CNRS, France
Ruzica Piskac   Yale University, USA

Program Committee

Miltiadis Allamanis   Microsoft Research
Timos Antonopoulos   Yale University, USA
Domagoj Babic   Google, Inc.
Josh Berdine   Facebook
Ahmed Bouajjani   IRIF, University of Paris Diderot and CNRS, France
Patrick Cousot   New York University, USA
Cezara Dragoi   Inria Paris, ENS, France
Constantin Enea   IRIF, University of Paris Diderot and CNRS, France
Javier Esparza   Technical University of Munich, Germany
Jerome Feret   Inria Paris, ENS, France
Khalil Ghorbal   Inria Rennes, France
Roberto Giacobazzi   University of Verona, Italy
Alberto Griggio   Fondazione Bruno Kessler, Italy
Jan Kretinsky   Technical University of Munich, Germany
Ori Lahav   Tel Aviv University, Israel
Anthony Widjaja Lin   University of Oxford, UK
Ruben Martins   Carnegie Mellon University, USA
Kedar Namjoshi   Nokia Bell Labs
K. Narayan Kumar   Chennai Mathematical Institute, India
Dejan Nickovic   Austrian Institute of Technology AIT, Austria
Jens Palsberg   University of California, Los Angeles, USA
Ruzica Piskac   Yale University, USA
Sylvie Putot   LIX, Ecole Polytechnique
Daniel Schwartz-Narbonne   Amazon Web Services
Martina Seidl   Johannes Kepler University Linz, Austria
Sharon Shoham   Tel Aviv University, Israel
Caterina Urban   ETH Zurich, Switzerland
Lenore Zuck   University of Illinois at Chicago, USA
Damien Zufferey   MPI-SWS

Additional Reviewers

Alpernas, Kalev
Ashok, Pranav
Athaiya, Snigdha
Balatsouras, George
Bardin, Sebastien
Bernardi, Giovanni
Bouaziz, Mehdi
Bozga, Marius
Choi, Wontae
Cox, Arlen
Eilers, Marco
Enea, Constantin
Goubault, Eric
Gurfinkel, Arie
Habermehl, Peter
Hanam, Quinn
Herbreteau, Frédéric
Hollingum, Nicholas
Irfan, Ahmed
Itzhaky, Shachar
Jaax, Stefan
Kaminski, Benjamin Lucien
Krämer, Julia
Laroussinie, François

Le, Xuan Bach
Lefaucheux, Engel
Meggendorfer, Tobias
Meyer, Philipp
Meyer, Roland
Niskanen, Reino
Padon, Oded
Praveen, M.
Rajani, Vineet
Rotar, Alexej
Roveri, Marco
Sankur, Ocan
Sighireanu, Mihaela
Simon, Axel
Sogokon, Andrew
Srinivasan, Venkatesh
Srivathsan, B.
Thibault, Joan
Titolo, Laura
Trabish, David
Vizel, Yakir
Weininger, Maximilian
Welzel, Christoph
Wolf, Karsten

Abstract of Invited Keynote Talks

Semantics for Compiler IRs: Undefined Behavior is not Evil!

Nuno P. Lopes

Microsoft Research
nlopes@microsoft.com

Summary

Building a compiler IR is tricky. First, it should be efficient to compile the desired source language(s) (C, C++, Rust, etc) to this IR. Second, the IR should support all the desired optimizations and analyses, and these should run efficiently. Finally, it should be possible to lower this IR into the desired target(s) assembly efficiently. Striking a good tradeoff in this design space is not easy.

Undefined behavior (UB) has been used in production compilers' IRs for many years, including all of GCC, ICC, LLVM, MSVC. Perhaps surprisingly, even formally verified compilers which target safety-critical systems, such as CompCert [3], have UB in their IR.

In this talk, we will explore what UB is, what it achieves, why it may be a good idea, and why it is not as evil as most people think it is. This is based on work on formalizing LLVM IR's UB semantics [2], a memory model for LLVM supporting UB [1], and work on formal verification of LLVM optimizations that exploit UB [4].

Short Bio: Nuno Lopes is a researcher at MSR Cambridge. He holds a PhD from the University of Lisbon, and has previously interned at MSR Redmond, Apple, Max Planck Institute (MPI-SWS), and the Institute for Systems and Robotics (ISR) Lisbon. Nuno's interests include software verification, compilers, and mixing the two.

References

1. Lee, J., Hur, C.-K., Jung, R., Liu, Z., Regehr, J., Lopes, N.P.: Reconciling high-level optimizations and low-level code in LLVM. In: Proceedings of the ACM on Programming Languages, vol. 2(OOPSLA), November 2018
2. Lee, J., Kim, Y., Song, Y., Hur, C.-K., Das, S., Majnemer, D., Regehr, J., Lopes, N.P.: Taming undefined behavior in LLVM. In: PLDI (2017)
3. Leroy, X.: Formal verification of a realistic compiler. Commun. ACM **52**(7), 107–115 (2009)
4. Lopes, N.P., Menendez, D., Nagarakatte, S., Regehr, J.: Provably correct peephole optimizations with Alive. In: PLDI (2015)

Designing Self-certifying Software Systems

Kedar S. Namjoshi

Bell Labs, Nokia
kedar.namjoshi@nokia-bell-labs.com

Abstract. Large software systems are hard to understand. The size and complexity of the implementation, possibly written in a mix of programming languages, the number of potential configurations, concurrency, distribution, and several other factors contribute to the difficulty of precisely analyzing system behavior. How can one have confidence in the correct working of such a complex system? In this talk, I explore an unusual approach to this challenge. Suppose that a software system is designed so that it produces a mathematical justification (a *certificate*) for the correctness of its result. The behavior of such a *self-certifying* system can then be formally verified at run time, merely by checking the validity of each certificate as it is generated, without having to examine or reason directly about the system implementation. Self-certification thus shrinks the size of the trusted computing base, often by orders of magnitude, as only the certificate checker must be trusted. The central research question is the design of a certificate format that is comprehensive, easy to generate, and straightforward to check. I will sketch how this may be done for a variety of software system types: model checkers and static analyzers, network operating systems, and optimizing compilers. I will also discuss several intriguing open questions and describe some of the unexpected benefits of certification.

Short Bio: Kedar Namjoshi is a member of technical staff at Nokia Bell Labs in Murray Hill, NJ. He received his Ph.D. from the University of Texas at Austin with E. Allen Emerson, and the B.Tech. degree from the Indian Institute of Technology, Madras, both in the Computing Sciences. His research interests include program semantics, specification logics and verification, model checking, static program analysis, distributed computing, and programming methodology.

Under and Over Approximated Reachability Analysis for the Verification of Control Systems

Sylvie Putot

LIX, CNRS and Ecole Polytechnique, Palaiseau, France
putot@lix.polytechnique.fr

Abstract. This talk will present a class of methods to compute under and over approximating flowpipes [1, 2] for differential systems, possibly with delays, systems that are pervasive in the modeling of networked control systems. Computing over-approximations of the reachable states has become a classical tool for the safety verification of control systems. Under-approximations are notoriously more difficult to compute, and their use for verification much less studied. We will discuss the guarantees and properties that can be obtained from the joint use of these under and over-approximations for control systems with inputs and disturbances.

Short Bio: Sylvie Putot is Professor in the Department of Computer Science of Ecole Polytechnique. Her research focuses on set-based methods and abstractions for the verification of numerical programs and more generally cyber-physical systems. She is also one of the main authors of the Fluctuat static analyzer, dedicated to the analysis of floating-point programs.

References

1. Goubault, E., Putot, S.: Forward inner-approximated reachability of non-linear continuous systems. In: Frehse, G., Mitra, S. (eds.) Proceedings of the 20th International Conference on Hybrid Systems: Computation and Control, HSCC 2017, Pittsburgh, PA, USA, 18–20 April 2017. ACM (2017)
2. Goubault, E., Putot, S., Sahlmann, L.: Inner and outer approximating flowpipes for delay differential equations. In: Chockler, H., Weissenbacher, G. (eds.) CAV 2018. LNCS, vol. 10982, pp. 523–541. Springer, Cham (2018)

Contents

On the Semantics of Snapshot Isolation

Azalea Raad[1(✉)], Ori Lahav[2], and Viktor Vafeiadis[1]

[1] MPI-SWS, Kaiserslautern, Germany
{azalea,viktor}@mpi-sws.org
[2] Tel Aviv University, Tel Aviv, Israel
orilahav@tau.ac.il

Abstract. Snapshot isolation (SI) is a standard transactional consistency model used in databases, distributed systems and software transactional memory (STM). Its semantics is formally defined both declaratively as an acyclicity axiom, and operationally as a concurrent algorithm with memory bearing timestamps.

We develop two simpler equivalent operational definitions of SI as lock-based reference implementations that do not use timestamps. Our first locking implementation is prescient in that requires *a priori* knowledge of the data accessed by a transaction and carries out transactional writes eagerly (in-place). Our second implementation is non-prescient and performs transactional writes lazily by recording them in a local log and propagating them to memory at commit time. Whilst our first implementation is simpler and may be better suited for developing a program logic for SI transactions, our second implementation is more practical due to its non-prescience. We show that both implementations are sound and complete against the declarative SI specification and thus yield equivalent operational definitions for SI.

We further consider, for the first time *formally*, the use of SI in a context with racy non-transactional accesses, as can arise in STM implementations of SI. We introduce *robust snapshot isolation* (RSI), an adaptation of SI with similar semantics and guarantees in this mixed setting. We present a declarative specification of RSI as an acyclicity axiom and analogously develop two operational models as lock-based reference implementations (one eager, one lazy). We show that these operational models are both sound and complete against the declarative RSI model.

1 Introduction

Transactions are the *de facto* synchronisation mechanism in databases and geo-replicated distributed systems, and are thus gaining adoption in the shared-memory setting via *software transactional memory* (STM) [20,33]. In contrast to other synchronisation mechanisms, transactions readily provide atomicity, isolation, and consistency guarantees for sequences of operations, allowing programmers to focus on the high-level design of their systems.

However, providing these guarantees comes at a significant cost. As such, various transactional consistency models in the literature trade off consistency

© Springer Nature Switzerland AG 2019
C. Enea and R. Piskac (Eds.): VMCAI 2019, LNCS 11388, pp. 1–23, 2019.
https://doi.org/10.1007/978-3-030-11245-5_1

guarantees for better performance. At nearly the one end of the spectrum, we have *serialisability* [28], which requires transactions to appear to have been executed in some total order. Serialisability provides strong guarantees, but is widely considered too expensive to implement. The main problem is that two conflicting transactions (e.g. one reading from and one updating the same datum) cannot both execute and commit in parallel.

Consequently, most major databases, both centralised (e.g. Oracle and MS SQL Server) and distributed [15,29,32], have opted for a slightly weaker model called *snapshot isolation* (SI) [7] as their default consistency model. SI has much better performance than serialisability by allowing conflicting transactions to execute concurrently and commit successfully as long as they do not have a write-write conflict. This in effect allows reads of SI transactions to read from an earlier memory snapshot than the one affected by their writes, and permits the *write skew anomaly* [11] depicted in Fig. 1. Besides this anomaly, however, SI is essentially the same as serialisability: Cerone et al. [11] provide a widely applicable condition under which SI and serialisability coincide for a given set of transactions. For these reasons, SI has also started gaining adoption in the generic programming language setting via STM implementations [1,8,16,25,26] that provide SI semantics for their transactions.

The formal study of SI, however, has so far not accounted for the more general STM setting in which both transactions and uninstrumented non-transactional code can access the same memory locations. While there exist two equivalent definitions of SI—one declarative in terms of an acyclicity constraint [10,11] and one operational in terms of an optimistic multi-version concurrency control algorithm [7]—neither definition supports *mixed-mode* (i.e. both transactional and non-transactional) accesses to the same locations. Extending the definitions to do so is difficult for two reasons: (1) the operational definition attaches a timestamp to every memory location, which heavily relies on the absence of non-transactional accesses; and (2) there are subtle interactions between the transactional implementation and the weak memory model underlying the non-transactional accesses.

In this article, we address these limitations of SI. We develop two simple lock-based reference implementations for SI that do not use timestamps. Our first implementation is *prescient* [19] in that it requires *a priori* knowledge of the data accessed by a transaction, and performs transactional writes *eagerly* (in-place). Our second implementation is non-prescient and carries out transactional writes *lazily* by first recording them in a local log and subsequently propagating them to memory at commit time. Our first implementation is simpler and may be better suited for understanding and developing a program logic for SI transactions, whilst our second implementation is more practical due to its non-prescience. We show that both implementations are sound and complete against the declarative SI specification and thus yield equivalent operational definitions for SI.

We then extend both our eager and lazy implementations to make them robust under uninstrumented non-transactional accesses, and characterise declaratively the semantics we obtain. We call this extended model *robust snapshot isolation* (RSI) and show that it gives reasonable semantics with mixed-mode accesses.

To provide SI semantics, instead of timestamps, our implementations use *multiple-readers-single-writer* (MRSW) locks. They acquire locks in reader mode to take a snapshot of the memory locations accessed by a transaction and then promote the relevant locks to writer mode to enforce an ordering on transactions with write-write conflicts. As we discuss in Sect. 4, the equivalence of the RSI implementation and its declarative characterisation depends heavily upon the axiomatisation of MRSW locks: here, we opted for the weakest possible axiomatisation that does not order any concurrent reader lock operations and present an MRSW lock implementation that achieves this.

Outline. In Sect. 2 we present an overview of our contributions by describing our reference implementations for both SI and RSI. In Sect. 3 we define the declarative framework for specifying STM programs. In Sect. 4 we present the declarative SI specification against which we demonstrate the soundness and completeness of our SI implementations. In Sect. 5 we formulate a declarative specification for RSI and demonstrate the soundness and completeness of our RSI implementations. We discuss related and future work in Sect. 6.[1]

2 Background and Main Ideas

As noted earlier, the key challenge in specifying STM transactions lies in accounting for the interactions between mixed-mode accesses to the same data. One simple approach is to treat each non-transactional access as a singleton mini-transaction and to provide *strong isolation* [9,27], i.e. full isolation between transactional and non-transactional code. This, however, requires *instrumenting* non-transactional accesses to adhere to same access policies as transactional ones (e.g. acquiring the necessary locks), which incurs a substantial performance penalty for non-transactional code. A more practical approach is to enforce isolation only amongst transactional accesses, an approach known as *weak isolation* [9,27], adopted by the relaxed transactions of C++ [2].

As our focus is on STMs with SI guarantees, instrumenting non-transactional accesses is not feasible. In particular, as we expect many more non-transactional accesses than transactional ones, we do not want to incur any performance degradation on non-transactional code when executed in parallel with transactional code. As such, we opt for an STM with SI guarantees under *weak isolation*. Under weak isolation, however, transactions with explicit abort instructions are problematic as their intermediate state may be observed by non-transactional code. As such, weakly isolated STMs (e.g. C++ relaxed transactions [2]) often forbid explicit aborts altogether. Throughout our development we thus make two simplifying assumptions: (1) transactions are not nested; and (2) there are no explicit abort instructions, following the example of weakly isolated relaxed

---

[1] A full version of this article is available at [31].

T1: $\begin{bmatrix} a := x; \ //\,0 \\ x := a + 1; \end{bmatrix}$ T2: $\begin{bmatrix} b := x; \ //\,0 \\ x := b + 1; \end{bmatrix}$	T1: $\begin{bmatrix} a := x; \ //\,0 \\ y := 1; \end{bmatrix}$ T2: $\begin{bmatrix} b := y; \ //\,0 \\ x := 1; \end{bmatrix}$	T1: $\begin{bmatrix} y := 1; \end{bmatrix}$ T3: $\begin{bmatrix} a := x; \ //\,0 \end{bmatrix}$ T2: $\begin{bmatrix} b := y; \ //\,0 \\ x := 1; \end{bmatrix}$
(LU) Lost Update SI: ✗	(WS) Write Skew SI: ✓	(WS2) Write Skew Variant SI: ✓
T1: $\begin{bmatrix} x := 1; \\ y := 1; \end{bmatrix}$ T3: $\begin{bmatrix} a := y; \ //\,2 \end{bmatrix}$ T2: $\begin{bmatrix} b := x; \ //\,0 \\ y := 2; \end{bmatrix}$	$x := 1;$ T1: $\begin{bmatrix} a := z; \\ b := y; \ //\,0 \end{bmatrix}$ $y := 1;$ T2: $\begin{bmatrix} c := z; \\ d := x; \ //\,0 \end{bmatrix}$	$x := 1;$ $y := 1;$ T2: $\begin{bmatrix} a := y; \ //\,1 \\ b := x; \ //\,0 \end{bmatrix}$
(LU2) Lost Update Variant SI: ✗	(SBT) Store Buffering RSI: ✓	(MPT) Message Passing RSI: ✗

Fig. 1. Litmus tests illustrating transaction anomalies and their admissibility under SI and RSI. In all tests, initially, $x = y = z = 0$. The $//\,v$ annotation next to a read records the value read.

transactions of C++. As we describe later in Sect. 2.3, it is straightforward to lift the latter restriction (2) for our lazy implementations.

For non-transactional accesses, we naturally have to pick some consistency model. For simplicity and uniformity, we pick the release/acquire (RA) subset of the C++ memory model [6,23], a well-behaved platform-independent memory model, whose compilation to x86 requires no memory fences.

Snapshot Isolation (SI). The initial model of SI in [7] is described informally in terms of a multi-version concurrent algorithm as follows. A transaction T proceeds by taking a *snapshot* S of the shared objects. The execution of T is then carried out locally: read operations query S and write operations update S. Once T completes its execution, it attempts to *commit* its changes and succeeds *only if* it is not *write-conflicted*. Transaction T is write-conflicted if another *committed* transaction T′ has written to a location also written to by T, since T recorded its snapshot. If T fails the conflict check it aborts and may restart; otherwise, it commits its changes, and its changes become visible to all other transactions that take a snapshot thereafter.

To realise this, the shared state is represented as a series of *multi-versioned* objects: each object is associated with a history of several versions at different *timestamps*. In order to obtain a snapshot, a transaction T chooses a *start-timestamp* t_0, and reads data from the committed state as of t_0, ignoring updates after t_0. That is, updates committed after t_0 are invisible to T. In order to commit, T chooses a *commit-timestamp* t_c larger than any existing start- or commit-timestamp. Transaction T is deemed write-conflicted if another transaction T′ has written to a location also written to by T *and* the commit-timestamp of T′ is in the execution interval of T ($[t_0, t_c]$).

2.1 Towards an SI Reference Implementation Without Timestamps

While the SI description above is suitable for understanding SI, it is not useful for integrating the SI model in a language such as C/C++ or Java. From a programmer's perspective, in such languages the various threads directly access the *uninstrumented* (single-versioned) shared memory; they do not access their own instrumented snapshot at a particular timestamp, which is loosely related to the snapshots of other threads. Ideally, what we would therefore like is an equivalent description of SI in terms of accesses to uninstrumented shared memory and a synchronisation mechanism such as locks.

In what follows, we present our first lock-based reference implementation for SI that does not rely on timestamps. To do this, we assume that the locations accessed by a transaction can be statically determined. Specifically, we assume that each transaction T is supplied with its *read set*, RS, and *write set*, WS, containing those locations read and written by T, respectively (a static over-approximation of these sets suffices for soundness.). As such, our first reference implementation is *prescient* [19] in that it requires *a priori* knowledge of the locations accessed by the transaction. Later in Sect. 2.3 we lift this assumption and develop an SI reference implementation that is *non-prescient* and similarly does not rely on timestamps.

Conceptually, a candidate implementation of transaction T would (1) obtain a snapshot of the locations read by T; (2) lock those locations written by T; (3) execute T *locally*; and (4) unlock the locations written. The snapshot is obtained via snapshot(RS) in Fig. 3 where the values of locations in RS are recorded in a local array s. The local execution of T is carried out by executing (|T|) in Fig. 3, which is obtained from T by (i) modifying read operations to read locally from the snapshot in s, and (ii) updating the snapshot after each write operation. Note that the snapshot must be obtained *atomically* to reflect the memory state at a particular instance (*cf.* start-timestamp). An obvious way to ensure the snapshot atomicity is to lock the locations in the read set, obtain a snapshot, and unlock the read set. However, as we must allow for two transactions *reading* from the same location to execute in parallel, we opt for *multiple-readers-single-writer* (MRSW) locks.

Let us now try to make this general pattern more precise. As a first attempt, consider the implementation in Fig. 2a written in a simple while language, which releases all the reader locks at the end of the snapshot phase before acquiring any writer locks. This implementation is unsound as it admits the lost update (LU) anomaly in Fig. 1 disallowed under SI [11]. To understand this, consider a scheduling where T2 runs between lines 3 and 4 of T1 in Fig. 2a, which would result in T1 having read a stale value. The problem is that the writer locks on WS are acquired too late, allowing two conflicting transactions to run concurrently. To address this, writer locks must be acquired early enough to pre-empt the concurrent execution of write-write-conflicting transactions. Note that locks have to be acquired early even for locations only written by a transaction to avoid exhibiting a variant of the lost update anomaly (LU2).

1. for (x ∈ RS) lock_r x	1. for (x ∈ WS) lock_w x;	1. for (x ∈ RS ∪ WS) lock_r x
2. snapshot(RS);	2. for (x ∈ RS\WS) lock_r x	2. snapshot(RS);
3. for (x ∈ RS) unlock_r x	3. snapshot(RS);	3. for (x ∈ RS ∪ WS) {
4. for (x ∈ WS) lock_w x	4. for (x ∈ RS\WS) unlock_r x	4. if (x ∈ WS) promote x
5. ⟨T⟩;	5. ⟨T⟩;	5. else unlock_r x; }
6. for (x ∈ WS) unlock_w x	6. for (x ∈ WS) unlock_w x	6. ⟨T⟩;
		7. for (x ∈ WS) unlock_w x
(a)	(b)	(c)
Sound: ✗	Sound: ✓	Sound: ✓
allows (LU), (LU2)	Complete: ✗	Complete: ✗
	disallows (WS)	disallows (WS2)

Fig. 2. Candidate SI implementations of transaction T given read/write sets RS, WS

As such, our second candidate implementation in Fig. 2b brings forward the acquisition of writer locks. Whilst this implementation is sound (and disallows lost update), it nevertheless disallows behaviours deemed valid under SI such as the write skew anomaly (WS) in Fig. 1, and is thus incomplete. The problem is that such early acquisition of writer locks not only pre-empts concurrent execution of *write-write-conflicting* transactions, but also those of *read-write-conflicting* transactions (e.g. WS) due to the exclusivity of writer locks.

To remedy this, in our third candidate implementation in Fig. 2c we first acquire weaker reader locks on all locations in RS or WS, and later *promote* the reader locks on WS to exclusive writer ones, while releasing the reader locks on RS. The promotion of a reader lock signals its intent for exclusive ownership and awaits the release of the lock by other readers before claiming it exclusively as a writer. To avoid deadlocks, we further assume that RS ∪ WS is ordered so that locks are promoted in the same order by all threads.

Although this implementation is "more complete" than the previous one, it is still incomplete as it disallows certain behaviour admitted by SI. In particular, consider a variant of the write skew anomaly (WS2) depicted in Fig. 1, which is admitted under SI, but not admitted by this implementation.

To understand why this is admitted by SI, recall the operational SI model using timestamps. Let the domain of timestamps be that of natural numbers $\mathbb{N}$. The behaviour of (WS2) can be achieved by assigning the following execution intervals for T1: $[t_0^{T_1} = 2, t_c^{T_1} = 2]$; T2: $[t_0^{T_2} = 1, t_c^{T_2} = 4]$; and T3: $[t_0^{T_3} = 3, t_c^{T_3} = 3]$. To see why the implementation in Fig. 2c does not admit the behaviour in (WS2), let us assume without loss of generality that x is ordered before y. Upon executing lines 3–5, (a) T1 promotes y; (b) T2 promotes x and then (c) releases the reader lock on y; and (d) T3 releases the reader lock on x. To admit the behaviour in (WS2), the release of y in (c) must occur before the promotion of y in (a) since otherwise T2 cannot read 0 for y. Similarly, the release of x in (d) must occur before its promotion in (b). On the other hand, since T3 is executed by the same thread after T1, we know that (a) occurs before (d). This however leads to circular execution: (b)→(c)→(a)→(d)→(b), which cannot be realised.

```
0.  LS := ∅;
1.  for (x ∈ RS ∪ WS) lock_r x
2.  snapshot(RS);
3.  for (x ∈ RS\WS) unlock_r x
4.  for (x ∈ WS) {
5.      if (can-promote x) LS.add(x)
6.      else {
7.          for (x ∈ LS) unlock_w x
8.          for (x ∈ WS \ LS) unlock_r x
9.          goto line 0 }
10. }
11. ⟨T⟩;
12. for (x ∈ WS) unlock_w x
```

$$\texttt{snapshot}(RS) \triangleq \texttt{for } (x \in RS) \; s_x := x$$

```
snapshot_RSI(RS) ≜
    start: for (x ∈ RS) s_x := x
        for (x ∈ RS) {
            if (s_x != x) goto start
        }
```

$$(\!|a := x|\!) \triangleq a := s_x$$

$$(\!|x := a|\!) \triangleq x := a; \; s_x := a$$

$$(\!|S_1; S_2|\!) \triangleq (\!|S_1|\!); (\!|S_2|\!)$$

$$(\!|\texttt{while}(e) \; S|\!) \triangleq \texttt{while}(e) \; (\!|S|\!)$$

... and so on...

Fig. 3. SI implementation of transaction T given RS, WS; the code in blue ensures deadlock avoidance. The RSI implementation (Sect. 5) is obtained by replacing snapshot on line 2 with snapshot$_{\text{RSI}}$.

To overcome this, in our final candidate execution in Fig. 3 (ignoring the code in blue), after obtaining a snapshot, we *first* release the reader locks on RS, and *then* promote the reader locks on WS, rather than simultaneously in one pass. As we demonstrate in Sect. 4, the implementation in Fig. 3 is both *sound and complete* against its declarative SI specification.

Avoiding Deadlocks. As two distinct reader locks on x may simultaneously attempt to promote their locks, promotion is done on a 'first-come-first-served' basis to avoid *deadlocks*. A call to `can-promote` x by reader r thus returns a boolean denoting either (i) successful promotion (true); or (ii) failed promotion as another reader r' is currently promoting a lock on x (false). In the latter case, r must release its reader lock on x to ensure the successful promotion of x1 by r' and thus avoid deadlocks. To this end, our implementation in Fig. 3 includes a deadlock avoidance mechanism (code in blue) as follows. We record a list LS of those locks on the write set that have been successfully promoted so far. When promoting a lock on x succeeds (line 5), the LS is extended with x. On the other hand, when promoting x fails (line 6), all those locks promoted so far (i.e. in LS) as well as those yet to be promoted (i.e. in WS \LS) are released and the transaction is restarted.

Remark 1. Note that the deadlock avoidance code in blue does not influence the correctness of the implementation in Fig. 3, and is merely included to make the reference implementation more realistic. In particular, the implementation without the deadlock avoidance code is both sound and complete against the SI specification, provided that the conditional `can-promote` call on line 5 is replaced by the blocking `promote` call.

Avoiding Over-Synchronisation Due to MRSW Locks. Consider the store buffering program (SBT) shown in Fig. 1. If, for a moment, we ignore transactional accesses, our underlying memory model (RA)—as well as all other weak memory models—allows the annotated weak behaviour. Intuitively, placing the two transactions that only *read* z in (SBT) should still allow the weak behaviour since the two transactions do not need to synchronise in any way. Nevertheless, most MRSW lock implementations forbid this outcome because they use a single global counter to track the number of readers that have acquired the lock, which inadvertently also synchronises the readers with one another. As a result, the two read-only transactions act as memory fences forbidding the weak outcome of (SBT). To avoid such synchronisation, in the technical appendix [31] we provide a different MRSW implementation using a separate location for each thread so that reader lock acquisitions do not synchronise.

To keep the presentation simple, we henceforth assume an abstract specification of a MRSW lock library providing operations for acquiring/releasing reader/writer locks, as well as promoting reader locks to writer ones. We require that (1) calls to writer locks (to acquire, release or promote) *synchronise* with all other calls to the lock library; and (2) writer locks provide *mutual exclusion* while held. We formalise these notions in Sect. 4. These requirements do not restrict synchronisation between *two read* lock calls: two read lock calls may or may not synchronise. Synchronisation between read lock calls is relevant only for the completeness of our RSI implementation (handling mixed-mode code); for that result, we further require that (3) read lock calls not synchronise.

2.2   Handling Racy Mixed-Mode Accesses

Let us consider what happens when data accessed by a transaction is modified concurrently by an uninstrumented atomic non-transactional write. Since such writes do not acquire any locks, the snapshots taken may include values written by non-transactional accesses. The result of the snapshot then depends on the order in which the variables are read. Consider the (MPT) example in Fig. 1. In our implementation, if in the snapshot phase y is read before x, then the annotated weak behaviour is not possible because the underlying model (RA) disallows this weak "message passing" behaviour. If, however, x is read before y, then the weak behaviour is possible. In essence, this means that the SI implementation described so far is of little use when there are races between transactional and non-transactional code. Technically, our SI implementation violates *monotonicity* with respect to wrapping code inside a transaction. The weak behaviour of the (MPT) example is disallowed by RA if we remove the transaction block T2, and yet it is exhibited by our SI implementation with the transaction block.

To get monotonicity under RA, it suffices for the snapshots to read the variables in the same order they are accessed by the transactions. Since a static calculation of this order is not always possible, following [30], we achieve this by reading each variable twice. In more detail, our snapshot$_{RSI}$ implementation in Fig. 3 takes *two* snapshots of the locations read by the transaction, and checks that they both return the same values for each location. This ensures that every location is read both before and after every other location in the transaction, and hence all the high-level happens-before orderings in executions of the transactional program are also respected by its implementation. As we demonstrate in Sect. 5, our RSI implementation is both *sound and complete* against our proposed declarative semantics for RSI. There is however one caveat: since equality of values is used to determine whether the two snapshots agree, we will miss cases where different non-transactional writes to a location write the same value. In our formal development (see Sect. 5), we thus assume that if multiple non-transactional writes write the same value to the same location, they cannot race with the same transaction. Note that this assumption cannot be lifted without instrumenting non-transactional writes, and thus impeding performance substantially. That is, to lift this restriction we must instead replace every non-transactional *write* x:=v with lock_w x; x:=v; unlock_w x.

2.3 Non-prescient Reference Implementations Without Timestamps

Recall that the SI and RSI implementations in Sect. 2.1 are prescient in that they require knowledge of the read and write sets of transactions beforehand. In what follows we present alternative SI and RSI implementations that are *non-prescient*.

Non-prescient SI Reference Implementation. In Fig. 4 we present a *lazy* lock-based reference implementation for SI. This implementation is *non-prescient* and does not require *a priori* knowledge of the read set RS and the write set WS. Rather, the RS and WS are computed on the fly as the execution of the transaction unfolds. As with the SI implementation in Fig. 3, this implementation does not rely on timestamps and uses MRSW locks to synchronise concurrent accesses to shared data. As before, the implementation consults a local *snapshot* at s for read operations. However, unlike the eager implementation in Fig. 3 where transactional writes are performed *in-place*, the implementation in Fig. 4 is *lazy* in that it logs the writes in the local array s and propagates them to memory at commit time, as we describe shortly.

Ignoring the code in blue, the implementation in Fig. 4 proceeds with initialising RS and WS with $\emptyset$ (line 1); it then populates the local snapshot array at s with initial value $\perp$ for each location x (line 2). It then executes ⦇T⦈ which is obtained from T as follows. For each *read* operation a:=x in T, first the value of s[x] is inspected to ensure it contains a snapshot of x. If this is not the case (i.e. x $\notin$ RS $\cup$ WS), a reader lock on x is acquired, a snapshot of x is recorded in s[x], and the read set RS is extended with x. The snapshot value in s[x] is subsequently returned in a. Analogously, for each write operation x:=a, the WS is extended with x, and the written value is lazily logged in s[x]. Recall from our candidate executions in Fig. 2 that to ensure implementation correctness, for each written location x, the implementation must first acquire a reader lock on x, and subsequently promote it to a writer lock. As such, for each write operation in T, the implementation first checks if a reader lock for x has been acquired (i.e. x $\in$ RS $\cup$ WS) and obtains one if this is not the case.

```
0.  LS:=∅;
1.  RS:=∅; WS:=∅;
2.  for (x∈Locs) s[x]:=⊥
3.  (|T|);
4.  for (x∈RS\WS) unlock_r x
5.  for (x∈WS) {
6.     if (can-promote x) LS.add(x)
7.     else {
8.        for (x∈LS) unlock_w x
9.        for (x∈WS \ LS) unlock_r x
10.       goto line 0 } }
11. for (x∈WS) x:=s[x]
12. for (x∈WS) unlock_w x
```

$$(|a:=x|) \triangleq \text{if } (x \notin RS \cup WS) \{$$
$$\quad\quad \text{lock\_r } x; \; RS.add(x);$$
$$\quad\quad s[x]:=x;$$
$$\quad \}$$
$$\quad a:=s[x];$$

$$(|x:=a|) \triangleq \text{if } (x \notin RS \cup WS) \; \text{lock\_r } x;$$
$$\quad\quad WS.add(x); \; s[x]:=a;$$

$$(|S_1;S_2|) \triangleq (|S_1|);(|S_2|)$$

$$(|\text{while(e) } S|) \triangleq \text{while(e) } (|S|)$$

… and so on …

Fig. 4. Non-prescient SI implementation of transaction T with RS and WS computed on the fly; the code in blue ensures deadlock avoidance.

Once the execution of $(|T|)$ is completed, the implementation proceeds to *commit* the transaction. To this end, the reader locks on RS are released (line 4), reader locks on WS are promoted to writer ones (line 6), the writes logged in s are propagated to memory (line 11), and finally the writer locks on WS are released (line 12). As we demonstrate later in Sect. 4, the implementation in Fig. 4 is both sound and complete against the declarative SI specification.

Note that the implementation in Fig. 4 is optimistic in that it logs the writes performed by the transaction in the local array s and propagates them to memory at commit time, rather than performing the writes *in-place* as with its pessimistic counterpart in Fig. 3. As before, the code in blue ensures deadlock avoidance and is identical to its counterpart in Fig. 3. As before, this deadlock avoidance code does not influence the correctness of the implementation and is merely included to make the reference implementation more practical.

Non-prescient RSI Reference Implementation. In Fig. 5 we present a *lazy* lock-based reference implementation for RSI. As with its SI counterpart, this implementation is non-prescient and computes the RS and WS on the fly. As before, the implementation does not rely on timestamps and uses MRSW locks to synchronise concurrent accesses to shared data. Similarly, the implementation consults the local *snapshot* at s for read operations, whilst logging write operations lazily in a *write sequence* at wseq, as we describe shortly.

Recall from the RSI implementation in Sect. 2.1 that to ensure snapshot validity, each location is read twice to preclude intermediate non-transactional writes. As such, when writing to a location x, the initial value read (recorded in s) must not be *overwritten* by the transaction to allow for subsequent validation of the snapshot. To this end, for each location x, the snapshot array s contains a *pair* of values, (r, c), where r denotes the snapshot value (initial value read), and c denotes the current value which may have overwritten the snapshot value.

Recall that under weak isolation, the intermediate values written by a transaction may be observed by non-transactional reads. For instance, given the

```
 0. LS:=∅;
 1. RS:=∅; WS:=∅; wseq:=[];
 2. for (x∈Locs) s[x]:=(⊥,⊥)
 3. ⟨T⟩;
 4. for (x∈RS) {(r,-):=s[x];
 5.    if (x!=r) { //read x again
 6.       for (x∈RS∪WS) unlock_r x
 7.          goto line 0 } }
 8. for (x∈RS\WS) unlock_r x
 9. for (x∈WS) {
10.    if (can-promote x) LS.add(x)
11.    else {
12.       for (x∈LS) unlock_w x
13.       for (x∈WS\LS) unlock_r x
14.          goto line 0 } }
15. for ((x,v)∈wseq) x:=v
16. for (x∈WS) unlock_w x
```

$$⟨a:=x⟩ ≜ \text{if } (x∉RS∪WS) \{$$
$$\quad \text{lock\_r } x; \text{ RS.add(x)};$$
$$\quad r:=x; \text{ s[x]}:=(r,r);$$
$$\} (-,c):=s[x]; a:=c;$$

$$⟨x:=a⟩ ≜ \text{if } (x∉RS∪WS) \text{ lock\_r } x$$
$$\text{WS.add(x)};$$
$$(r,-):=s[x]; s[x]:=(r,a);$$
$$\text{wseq}:=\text{wseq}++[(x,a)];$$

$$⟨S_1 ; S_2⟩ ≜ ⟨S_1⟩ ; ⟨S_2⟩$$

$$⟨\text{while}(e) \, S⟩ ≜ \text{while}(e) \, ⟨S⟩$$

... and so on ...

Fig. 5. Non-prescient RSI implementation of transaction T with RS and WS computed on the fly; the code in blue ensures deadlock avoidance.

T: $[x := 1; x := 2 \, || \, a := x$ program, the non-transactional read $a := x$, may read either 1 or 2 for x. As such, at commit time, it is not sufficient solely to propagate the last written value (in program order) to each location (e.g. to propagate only the $x := 2$ write in the example above). Rather, to ensure implementation completeness, one must propagate all written values to memory, in the order they appear in the transaction body. To this end, we track the values written by the transaction as a (FIFO) *write sequence* at location wseq, containing items of the form (x, v), denoting the location written (x) and the associated value (v).

Ignoring the code in blue, the implementation in Fig. 5 initialises RS and WS with ∅, initialises wseq as an empty sequence [] (line 1), and populates the local snapshot array s with initial value $(⊥, ⊥)$ for each location x (line 2). It then executes ⟨T⟩, obtained from T in an analogous manner to that in Fig. 4. For every read a:=x in ⟨T⟩, the current value recorded for x in s (namely c when s[x] holds $(-,c)$) is returned in a. Dually, for every write x:=a in ⟨T⟩, the current value recorded for x in s is updated to a, and the write is logged in the write sequence wseq by appending (x,a) to it.

Upon completion of ⟨T⟩, the snapshot in s is *validated* (lines 4–7). Each location x in RS is thus read again and its value is compared against the snapshot value in s[x]. If validation fails (line 5), the locks acquired are released (line 6) and the transaction is restarted (line 7).

If validation succeeds, the transaction is committed: the reader locks on RS are released (line 8), the reader locks on WS are promoted (line 10), the writes in wseq are propagated to memory in FIFO order (line 15), and finally the writer locks on WS are released (line 16).

As we show in Sect. 5, the implementation in Fig. 5 is both sound and complete against our proposed declarative specification for RSI. As before, the code in blue ensures deadlock avoidance; it does not influence the implementation correctness and is merely included to make the implementation more practical.

Supporting Explicit Abort Instructions. It is straightforward to extend the lazy implementations in Figs. 4 and 5 to handle transactions containing explicit abort instructions. More concretely, as the effects (writes) of a transaction are logged locally and are not propagated to memory until commit time, upon reaching an `abort` in $(\!|T|\!)$ no roll-back is necessary, and one can simply release the locks acquired so far and return. That is, one can extend $(\!|.|\!)$ in Figs. 4 and 5, and define $(\!|\mathsf{abort}|\!) \triangleq$ for $(\mathsf{x} \in \mathrm{RS} \cup \mathrm{WS})$ `unlock_r x; return.`

3   A Declarative Framework for STM

We present the notational conventions used in the remainder of this article, and describe a general framework for declarative concurrency models. Later in this article, we present SI, its extension with non-transactional accesses, and their lock-based implementations as instances of this general definition.

Notation. Given a relation r on a set A, we write $\mathsf{r}^?$, r^+ and r^* for the reflexive, transitive and reflexive-transitive closure of r, respectively. We write r^{-1} for the inverse of r; $\mathsf{r}|_A$ for $\mathsf{r} \cap (A \times A)$; $[A]$ for the identity relation on A, i.e. $\{(a,a) \mid a \in A\}$; irreflexive(r) for $\nexists a.\ (a,a) \in r$; and acyclic(r) for irreflexive(r^+). Given two relations r_1 and r_2, we write $\mathsf{r}_1; \mathsf{r}_2$ for their (left) relational composition, i.e. $\{(a,b) \mid \exists c.\ (a,c) \in \mathsf{r}_1 \land (c,b) \in \mathsf{r}_2\}$. Lastly, when r is a strict partial order, we write $\mathsf{r}|_{\mathrm{imm}}$ for the *immediate* edges in r: $\{(a,b) \in \mathsf{r} \mid \nexists c.\ (a,c) \in \mathsf{r} \land (c,b) \in \mathsf{r}\}$.

Assume finite sets of *locations* Loc; *values* VAL; *thread identifiers* TID, and *transaction identifiers* TXID. We use x, y, z to range over locations, v over values, τ over thread identifiers, and ξ over transaction identifiers.

Definition 1 (Events). *An event is a tuple* $\langle n, \tau, \xi, l \rangle$*, where* $n \in \mathbb{N}$ *is an event identifier,* $\tau \in \mathrm{TID} \uplus \{0\}$ *is a thread identifier (0 is used for initialisation events),* $\xi \in \mathrm{TXID} \uplus \{0\}$ *is a transaction identifier (0 is used for non-transactional events), and* l *is an event label that takes one of the following forms:*

- *A memory access label:* $R(x, v)$ *for reads;* $W(x, v)$ *for writes; and* $U(x, v_r, v_w)$ *for updates.*
- *A lock label:* $RL(x)$ *for reader lock acquisition;* $RU(x)$ *for reader lock release;* $WL(x)$ *for writer lock acquisition;* $WU(x)$ *for writer lock release; and* $PL(x)$ *for reader to writer lock promotion.*

We typically use a, b, and e to range over events. The functions tid, tx, lab, typ, loc, $\mathsf{val_r}$ *and* $\mathsf{val_w}$ *respectively project the thread identifier, transaction identifier, label, type (in* $\{R, W, U, RL, RU, WL, WU, PL\}$*), location, and read/written values of an event, where applicable. We assume only reads and writes are used in transactions* $(\mathsf{tx}(a) \neq 0 \implies \mathsf{typ}(a) \in \{R, W\})$.

Given a relation r on events, we write r_{loc} for $\{(a,b) \in \mathsf{r} \mid \mathsf{loc}(a) = \mathsf{loc}(b)\}$. Analogously, given a set A of events, we write A_x for $\{a \in A \mid \mathsf{loc}(a) = x\}$.

Definition 2 (Execution graphs). *An execution graph, G, is a tuple of the form $(E, \mathsf{po}, \mathsf{rf}, \mathsf{mo}, \mathsf{lo})$, where:*

- *E is a set of events, assumed to contain a set E_0 of initialisation events, consisting of a write event with label $\mathtt{W}(x, 0)$ for every $x \in \mathrm{Loc}$. The sets of read events in E is denoted by $\mathcal{R} \triangleq \{e \in E \mid \mathtt{typ}(e) \in \{\mathtt{R}, \mathtt{U}\}\}$; write events by $\mathcal{W} \triangleq \{e \in E \mid \mathtt{typ}(e) \in \{\mathtt{W}, \mathtt{U}\}\}$; update events by $\mathcal{U} \triangleq \mathcal{R} \cap \mathcal{W}$; and lock events by $\mathcal{L} \triangleq \{e \in E \mid \mathtt{typ}(e) \in \{\mathtt{RL}, \mathtt{RU}, \mathtt{WL}, \mathtt{WU}, \mathtt{PL}\}\}$. The sets of reader lock acquisition and release events, $\mathcal{RL}$ and $\mathcal{RU}$, writer lock acquisition and release events, $\mathcal{WL}$ and $\mathcal{WU}$, and lock promotion events $\mathcal{PL}$ are defined analogously. The set of transactional events in E is denoted by $\mathcal{T}$ ($\mathcal{T} \triangleq \{e \in E \mid \mathtt{tx}(e) \neq 0\}$); and the set of non-transactional events is denoted by $\mathcal{NT}$ ($\mathcal{NT} \triangleq E \setminus \mathcal{T}$).*

- *$\mathsf{po} \subseteq E \times E$ denotes the 'program-order' relation, defined as a disjoint union of strict total orders, each ordering the events of one thread, together with $E_0 \times (E \setminus E_0)$ that places the initialisation events before any other event. We assume that events belonging to the same transaction are ordered by po, and that any other event po-between them also belongs to the same transaction.*

- *$\mathsf{rf} \subseteq \mathcal{W} \times \mathcal{R}$ denotes the 'reads-from' relation, defined between write and read events of the same location with matching read and written values; it is total and functional on reads, i.e. every read is related to exactly one write.*

- *$\mathsf{mo} \subseteq \mathcal{W} \times \mathcal{W}$ denotes the 'modification-order' relation, defined as a disjoint union of strict total orders, each ordering the write events on one location.*

- *$\mathsf{lo} \subseteq \mathcal{L} \times \mathcal{L}$ denotes the 'lock-order' relation, defined as a disjoint union of strict orders, each of which (partially) ordering the lock events to one location.*

In the context of an execution graph $G = (E, \mathsf{po}, \mathsf{rf}, \mathsf{mo}, \mathsf{lo})$—we often use "$G$." as a prefix to make this explicit—the *'same-transaction' relation,* $\mathsf{st} \in \mathcal{T} \times \mathcal{T}$, is the equivalence relation given by $\mathsf{st} \triangleq \{(a, b) \in \mathcal{T} \times \mathcal{T} \mid \mathtt{tx}(a) = \mathtt{tx}(b)\}$. Given a relation $\mathsf{r} \subseteq E \times E$, we write $\mathsf{r_T}$ for lifting r to transaction classes: $\mathsf{r_T} \triangleq \mathsf{st}; (\mathsf{r} \setminus \mathsf{st}); \mathsf{st}$. For instance, when $(w, r) \in \mathsf{rf}$, w is a transaction ξ_1 event and r is a transaction ξ_2 event, then all events in ξ_1 are $\mathsf{rf_T}$-related to all events in ξ_2. Analogously, we write $\mathsf{r_I}$ to restrict r to its *intra-transactional* edges (within a transaction): $\mathsf{r_I} \triangleq \mathsf{r} \cap \mathsf{st}$; and write $\mathsf{r_E}$ to restrict r to its *extra-transactional* edges (outside a transaction): $\mathsf{r_E} \triangleq \mathsf{r} \setminus \mathsf{st}$. Lastly, the 'reads-before' relation is defined by $\mathsf{rb} \triangleq (\mathsf{rf}^{-1}; \mathsf{mo}) \setminus [E]$. Intuitively, rb relates a read r to all writes w that are mo-after the write r reads from; i.e. when $(w', r) \in \mathsf{rf}$ and $(w', w) \in \mathsf{mo}$, then $(r, w) \in \mathsf{rb}$. In the transactional literature, this is known as the *anti-dependency* relation [3,4].

Execution graphs of a given program represent traces of shared memory accesses generated by the program. The set of execution graphs associated with programs written in our while language can be straightforwardly defined by induction over the structure of programs as in e.g. [35]. Each execution of a program P has a particular program *outcome*, prescribing the final values of local variables in each thread. In this initial stage, the execution outcomes are almost unrestricted as there are very few constraints on the rf, mo and lo relations. Such restrictions and thus the permitted outcomes of a program are determined by defining the set of *consistent* executions, which is defined separately for each model we consider. Given a program P and a model M, the set $\text{outcomes}_M(P)$ collects the outcomes of every M-consistent execution of P.

4   Snapshot Isolation (SI)

We present a declarative specification of SI and demonstrate that the SI implementations presented in Figs. 3 and 4 are both sound and complete with respect to the SI specification.

In [11] Cerone and Gotsman developed a declarative specification for SI using dependency graphs [3,4]. Below we adapt their specification to the notation of Sect. 3. As with [11], throughout this section, we take *SI execution graphs* to be those in which $E = \mathcal{T} \subseteq (\mathcal{R} \cup \mathcal{W}) \setminus \mathcal{U}$. That is, the SI model handles transactional code only, consisting solely of read and write events (excluding updates).

Definition 3 (SI consistency [11]**).** *An SI execution* $G = (E, \text{po}, \text{rf}, \text{mo}, \text{lo})$ *is* SI-consistent *if the following conditions hold:*

- $\text{rf}_I \cup \text{mo}_I \cup \text{rb}_I \subseteq \text{po}$ (INT)
- $\text{acyclic}((\text{po}_T \cup \text{rf}_T \cup \text{mo}_T); \text{rb}_T{}^?)$ (EXT)

Informally, (INT) ensures the consistency of each transaction internally, while (EXT) provides the synchronisation guarantees among transactions. In particular, we note that the two conditions together ensure that if two read events in the same transaction read from the same location x, and no write to x is po-between them, then they must read from the same write (known as 'internal read consistency').

Next, we provide an alternative equivalent formulation of SI-consistency which will serve as the basis of our extension with non-transactional accesses in Sect. 5.

Proposition 1. *An SI execution* $G = (E, \text{po}, \text{rf}, \text{mo}, \text{lo})$ *is* SI-consistent *if and only if* INT *holds and the 'SI-happens-before' relation* $\text{si-hb} \triangleq (\text{po}_T \cup \text{rf}_T \cup \text{mo}_T \cup \text{si-rb})^+$ *is irreflexive, where* $\text{si-rb} \triangleq [\mathcal{R}_E]; \text{rb}_T; [\mathcal{W}]$ *and* $\mathcal{R}_E \triangleq \{r \mid \exists w.\ (w, r) \in \text{rf}_E\}$.

Proof. The full proof is given in the technical appendix [31].

Intuitively, SI-happens-before orders events of different transactions; this order is due to either the program order (po_T), or synchronisation enforced by the implementation ($\text{rf}_T \cup \text{mo}_T \cup \text{si-rb}$). By contrast, events of the same transaction are unordered, as the implementation may well execute them in a different order (in particular, by taking a snapshot, it executes external reads before the writes).

In more detail, the $\mathsf{rf_T}$ corresponds to transactional synchronisation due to *causality*, i.e. when one transaction T_2 observes an effect of an earlier transaction T_1. The inclusion of $\mathsf{rf_T}$ ensures that T_2 cannot read from T_1 without observing its *entire* effect. This in turn ensures that transactions exhibit 'all-or-nothing' behaviour: they cannot mix-and-match the values they read. For instance, if T_1 writes to both x and y, transaction T_2 may not read x from T_1 but read y from an earlier (in 'happens-before' order) transaction T_0.

The $\mathsf{mo_T}$ corresponds to transactional synchronisation due to *write-write conflicts*. Its inclusion enforces write-conflict-freedom of SI transactions: if T_1 and T_2 both write to x via events w_1 and w_2 such that $(w_1, w_2) \in \mathsf{mo}$, then T_1 must commit before T_2, and thus its entire effect must be visible to T_2.

To understand si-rb, first note that $\mathcal{R}_\mathsf{E}$ denotes the *external* transactional reads (i.e. those reading a value written by another transaction). That is, the $\mathcal{R}_\mathsf{E}$ are the read events that get their values from the transactional snapshot phases. By contrast, internal reads (those reading a value written by the same transaction) happen only after the snapshot is taken. Now let there be an $\mathsf{rb_T}$ edge between two transactions, T_1 and T_2. This means there exist a read event r of T_1 and a write event w of T_2 such that $(r, w) \in \mathsf{rb}$; i.e. there exists w' such that $(w', r) \in \mathsf{rf}$ and $(w', w) \in \mathsf{mo}$. If r reads internally (i.e. w' is an event in T_1), then T_1 and T_2 are conflicting transactions and as accounted by $\mathsf{mo_T}$ described above, all events of T_1 happen before those of T_2. Now, let us consider the case when r reads externally (w' is not in T_1). From the timestamped model of SI, there exists a start-timestamp $t_0^{T_1}$ as of which the T_1 snapshot (all its external reads including r) is recorded. Similarly, there exists a commit-timestamp $t_c^{T_2}$ as of which the updates of T_2 (including w) are committed. Moreover, since $(r, w) \in \mathsf{rb}$ we know $t_0^{T_1} < t_c^{T_2}$ (otherwise r must read the value written by w and not w'). That is, we know all events in the snapshot of T_1 (i.e. all external reads in T_1) happen before all writes of T_2.[2]

We use the declarative framework in Sect. 3 to formalise the semantics of our implementation. Here, our programs include only non-transactional code, and thus *implementation execution graphs* are taken as those in which $\mathcal{T} = \emptyset$. Furthermore, we assume that locks in implementation programs are used in a *well-formed* manner: the sequence of lock events for *each location*, in each thread (following po), should match (a prefix of) the regular expression $(\mathsf{RL}\cdot\mathsf{RU} \mid \mathsf{WL}\cdot\mathsf{WU} \mid \mathsf{RL}\cdot\mathsf{PL}\cdot\mathsf{WU})^*$. For instance, a thread never releases a lock, without having acquired it earlier in the program. As a consistency predicate on execution graphs, we use the C11 release/acquire consistency augmented with certain constraints on lock events.

Definition 4. *An implementation execution graph* $G = (E, \mathsf{po}, \mathsf{rf}, \mathsf{mo}, \mathsf{lo})$ *is RA-consistent if the following hold, where* $\mathsf{hb} \triangleq (\mathsf{po} \cup \mathsf{rf} \cup \mathsf{lo})^+$ *denotes the 'RA-happens-before' relation:*

- $\forall x. \, \forall a \in \mathcal{WL}_x \cup \mathcal{WU}_x \cup \mathcal{PL}_x, b \in \mathcal{L}_x. \, a = b \lor (a, b) \in \mathsf{lo} \lor (b, a) \in \mathsf{lo}(\mathrm{WSYNC})$
- $[\mathcal{WL} \cup \mathcal{PL}]; (\mathsf{lo} \setminus \mathsf{po}); [\mathcal{L}] \subseteq \mathsf{po}; [\mathcal{WU}]; \mathsf{lo}$ \hfill (WEx)

---

[2] By taking $\mathsf{rb_T}$ instead of si-rb in Proposition 1 one obtains a characterisation of *serialisability*.

- $[\mathcal{RL}]; (\text{lo} \setminus \text{po}); [\mathcal{WL} \cup \mathcal{PL}] \subseteq \text{po}; [\mathcal{RU} \cup \mathcal{PL}]; \text{lo}$ (RSHARE)
- $\text{acyclic}(\text{hb}_{loc} \cup \text{mo} \cup \text{rb})$ (ACYC)

The (WSYNC) states that write lock calls (to acquire, release or promote) *synchronise* with all other calls to the same lock.

The next two constraints ensure the 'single-writer-multiple-readers' paradigm. In particular, (WEX) states that write locks provide *mutual exclusion* while held: any lock event l of thread τ lo-after a write lock acquisition or promotion event l' of another thread τ', is lo-after a subsequent write lock release event u of τ' (i.e. $(l', u) \in \text{po}$ and $(u, l) \in \text{lo}$). As such, the lock cannot be acquired (in read or write mode) by another thread until it has been released by its current owner.

The (RSHARE) analogously states that once a thread acquires a lock in read mode, the lock cannot be acquired in write mode by other threads until it has either been released, or promoted to a writer lock (and subsequently released) by its owner. Note that this does not preclude other threads from simultaneously acquiring the lock in read mode. In the technical appendix [31] we present two MRSW lock implementations that satisfy the conditions outlined above.

The last constraint (ACYC) is that of C11 RA consistency [23], with the hb relation extended with lo.

Remark 2. Our choice of implementing the SI STMs on top of the RA fragment is purely for presentational convenience. Indeed, it is easy to observe that execution graphs of $(\!|P|\!)$ are data race free, and thus, ACYC could be replaced by any condition that implies $\forall x.\ ([\mathcal{W}_x]; (\text{po} \cup \text{lo})^+; [\mathcal{W}_x]; (\text{po} \cup \text{lo})^+; [\mathcal{R}_x]) \cap \text{rf} = \emptyset$ and that is implied by $\text{acyclic}(\text{po} \cup \text{rf} \cup \text{lo} \cup \text{mo} \cup \text{rb})$. In particular, the C11 non-atomic accesses or sequentially consistent accesses may be used.

We next show that our SI implementations in Figs. 3 and 4 are *sound and complete* with respect to the declarative specification given above. The proofs are non-trivial and the full proofs are given in the technical appendix [31].

Theorem 1 (Soundness and completeness). *Let P be a transactional program; let $(\!|P|\!)_E$ denote its eager implementation as given in Fig. 3 and $(\!|P|\!)_L$ denote its lazy implementation as given in Fig. 4. Then:*

$$\text{outcomes}_{\text{SI}}(P) = \text{outcomes}_{\text{RA}}((\!|P|\!)_E) = \text{outcomes}_{\text{RA}}((\!|P|\!)_L)$$

Proof. The full proofs for both implementations is given in the technical appendix [31].

Stronger MRSW Locks. As noted in Sect. 2, for both (prescient and non-prescient) SI implementations our soundness and completeness proofs show that the same result holds for a stronger lock specification, in which reader locks synchronise as well. Formally, this specification is obtained by adding the following to Definition 4:

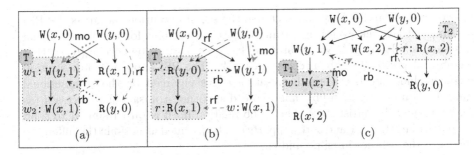

Fig. 6. RSI-inconsistent executions due to (a) rsi-po; (b) $[\mathcal{NT}]$; rf; st; (c) $(\text{mo}; \text{rf})_T$

$$- \;\; \forall x.\, \forall a, b \in \mathcal{RL}_x \cup \mathcal{RU}_x.\, a = b \vee (a, b) \in \text{lo} \vee (b, a) \in \text{lo} \qquad (\text{RSYNC})$$

Soundness of this stronger specification ($\text{outcomes}_{\text{RA}}(\langle\!| P |\!\rangle_x) \subseteq \text{outcomes}_{\text{SI}}(P)$ for $x \in \{E, L\}$) follows immediately from Theorem 1. Completeness ($\text{outcomes}_{\subseteq}(P)$ SIoutcomes$_{\text{RA}}(\langle\!| P |\!\rangle_x)$ for $x \in \{E, L\}$), however, is more subtle, as we need to additionally satisfy (RSYNC) when constructing lo. While we can do so for SI, it is essential for the completeness of our RSI implementations that reader locks not synchronise, as shown by (SBT) in Sect. 2.

In the technical appendix [31] we present two MRSW lock implementations *sound* against the lo conditions in Definition 4. Additionally, the first implementation is *complete* against the conditions of Definition 4 augmented with (RSYNC), whilst the second is complete against the conditions of Definition 4 alone.

5   Robust Snapshot Isolation (RSI)

We explore the semantics of SI STMs in the presence of non-transactional code with *weak isolation* guarantees (see Sect. 2). We refer to this model as *robust snapshot isolation* (RSI), due to its ability to provide SI guarantees between transactions even in the presence of non-transactional code. We propose the first declarative specification of RSI programs and develop two lock-based reference implementations that are both *sound and complete* against our proposed specification.

A Declarative Specification of RSI STMs. We formulate a declarative specification of RSI semantics by adapting the SI semantics in Proposition 1 to account for non-transactional accesses. To specify the abstract behaviour of RSI programs, *RSI execution graphs* are taken to be those in which $\mathcal{L} = \emptyset$. Moreover, as with SI graphs, RSI execution graphs are those in which $\mathcal{T} \subseteq (\mathcal{R} \cup \mathcal{W}) \backslash \mathcal{U}$. That is, RSI transactions comprise solely read and write events, excluding updates.

Definition 5 (RSI consistency). *An execution* $G = (E, \text{po}, \text{rf}, \text{mo}, \text{lo})$ *is* RSI-*consistent iff* INT *holds and* acyclic(rsi-hb$_{loc}$ $\cup$ mo $\cup$ rb), *where* rsi-hb $\triangleq$ (rsi-po $\cup$ rsi-rf $\cup$ mo$_T$ $\cup$ si-rb)$^+$ *is the 'RSI-happens-before' relation, with* rsi-po $\triangleq$ (po $\backslash$ po$_I$) $\cup$ $[\mathcal{W}]$; po$_I$; $[\mathcal{W}]$ *and* rsi-rf $\triangleq$ (rf; $[\mathcal{NT}]$) $\cup$ ($[\mathcal{NT}]$; rf; st) $\cup$ rf$_T$ $\cup$ (mo; rf)$_T$.

As with SI and RA, we characterise the set of executions admitted by RSI as graphs that lack cycles of certain shapes. To account for non-transactional accesses, similar to RA, we require rsi-hb$_{loc}$ ∪ mo ∪ rb to be acyclic (recall that rsi-hb$_{loc}$ ≜ $\{(a,b) ∈ \text{rsi-hb} \mid \text{loc}(a) = \text{loc}(b)\}$). The RSI-happens-before relation rsi-hb includes both the synchronisation edges enforced by the transactional implementation (as in si-hb), and those due to non-transactional accesses (as in hb of the RA consistency). The rsi-hb relation itself is rather similar to si-hb. In particular, the mo$_T$ and si-rb subparts can be justified as in si-hb; the difference between the two lies in rsi-po and rsi-rf.

To justify rsi-po, recall from Sect. 4 that si-hb includes po$_T$. The rsi-po is indeed a strengthening of po$_T$ to account for non-transactional events: it additionally includes (i) po to and from non-transactional events; and (ii) po between two *write* events in a transaction. We believe (i) comes as no surprise to the reader; for (ii), consider the execution graph in Fig. 6a, where transaction T is denoted by the dashed box labelled T, comprising the write events w_1 and w_2. Removing the T block (with w_1 and w_2 as non-transactional writes), this execution is deemed inconsistent, as this weak "message passing" behaviour is disallowed in the RA model. We argue that the analogous transactional behaviour in Fig. 6a must be similarly disallowed to maintain monotonicity with respect to wrapping non-transactional code in a transaction (see Theorem 3). As in SI, we cannot include the entire po in rsi-hb because the write-read order in transactions is not preserved by the implementation.

Similarly, rsi-rf is a strengthening of rf$_T$ to account for non-transactional events: in the absence of non-transactional events rsi-rf reduces to rf$_T$ ∪ (mo; rf)$_T$ which is contained in si-hb. The rf; $[\mathcal{NT}]$ part is required to preserve the 'happens-before' relation for non-transactional code. That is, as rf is included in the hb relation of underlying memory model (RA), it is also included in rsi-hb.

The $[\mathcal{NT}]$; rf; st part asserts that in an execution where a read event r of transaction T reads from a non-transactional write w, the snapshot of T reads from w and so all events of T happen after w. Thus, in Fig. 6b, r' cannot read from the overwritten initialisation write to y.

For the (mo; rf)$_T$ part, consider the execution graph in Fig. 6c where there is a write event w of transaction T_1 and a read event r of transaction T_2 such that $(w, r) ∈ $ mo; rf. Then, transaction T_2 must acquire the read lock of loc(w) after T_1 releases the writer lock, which in turn means that every event of T_1 happens before every event of T_2.

Remark 3. Recall that our choice of modelling SI and RSI STMs in the RA fragment is purely for presentational convenience (see Remark 2). Had we chosen a different model, the RSI consistency definition (Definition 5) would largely remain unchanged, with the exception of rsi-rf ≜ (sw; $[\mathcal{NT}]$) ∪ ($[\mathcal{NT}]$; sw; st) ∪ rf$_T$ ∪ (mo; rf)$_T$, where in the highlighted changes the rf relation is replaced with sw, denoting the 'synchronises-with' relation. As in the RA model sw ≜ rf, we have inlined this in Definition 5.

SI and RSI Consistency. We next demonstrate that in the absence of non-transactional code, the definitions of SI-consistency (Proposition 1) and RSI-consistency (Definition 5) coincide. That is, for all executions G, if $G.\mathcal{NT} = \emptyset$, then G is SI-consistent if and only if G is RSI-consistent.

Theorem 2. *For all executions G, if $G.\mathcal{NT} = \emptyset$, then:*

$$G \text{ is SI-consistent} \iff G \text{ is RSI-consistent}$$

Proof. The full proof is given in the technical appendix [31].

Note that the above theorem implies that for all transactional programs P, if P contains no non-transactional accesses, then $\text{outcomes}_{\text{SI}}(P) = \text{outcomes}_{\text{RSI}}(P)$.

RSI Monotonicity. We next prove the *monotonicity* of RSI when wrapping non-transactional events into a transaction. That is, wrapping a block of non-transactional code inside a new transaction does not introduce additional behaviours. More concretely, given a program P, when a block of non-transactional code in P is wrapped inside a new transaction to obtain a new program P_T, then $\text{outcomes}_{\text{RSI}}(P_T) \subseteq \text{outcomes}_{\text{RSI}}(P)$. This is captured in the theorem below, with its full proof given in the technical appendix [31].

Theorem 3 (Monotonicity). *Let P_T and P be RSI programs such that P_T is obtained from P by wrapping a block of non-transactional code inside a new transaction. Then:*

$$\text{outcomes}_{\text{RSI}}(P_T) \subseteq \text{outcomes}_{\text{RSI}}(P)$$

Proof. The full proof is given in the technical appendix [31].

Lastly, we show that our RSI implementations in Sect. 2 (Figs. 3 and 5) are sound and complete with respect to Definition 5. This is captured in the theorem below. The soundness and completeness proofs are non-trivial; the full proofs are given in the technical appendix [31].

Theorem 4 (Soundness and completeness). *Let P be a program that possibly mixes transactional and non-transactional code. Let $(\!|P|\!)_{\text{E}}$ denote its eager RSI implementation as given in Fig. 3 and $(\!|P|\!)_{\text{L}}$ denote its lazy RSI implementation as given in Fig. 5. If for every location x and value v, every RSI-consistent execution of P contains either (i) at most one non-transactional write of v to x; or (ii) all non-transactional writes of v to x are happens-before-ordered with respect to all transactions accessing x, then:*

$$\text{outcomes}_{\text{RSI}}(P) = \text{outcomes}_{\text{RA}}((\!|P|\!)_{\text{E}}) = \text{outcomes}_{\text{RA}}((\!|P|\!)_{\text{L}})$$

Proof. The full proofs for both implementations are given in the technical appendix [31].

6   Related and Future Work

Much work has been done in formalising the semantics of weakly consistent *database transactions* [3,4,7,10–14,18,34], both operationally and declaratively. On the operational side, Berenson et al. [7] gave an operational model of SI as a multi-version concurrent algorithm. Later, Sovran et al. [34] described and operationally defined the *parallel snapshot isolation* model (PSI), as a close relative of SI with weaker guarantees.

On the declarative side, Adya et al. [3,4] introduced *dependency graphs* (similar to execution graphs of our framework in Sect. 3) for specifying transactional semantics and formalised several ANSI isolation levels. Cerone et al. [10,12] introduced *abstract executions* and formalised several isolation levels including SI and PSI. Later in [11], they used dependency graphs of Adya to develop equivalent SI and PSI semantics; recently in [13], they provided a set of algebraic laws for connecting these two declarative styles.

To facilitate client-side reasoning about the behaviour of database transactions, Gotsman et al. [18] developed a proof rule for proving invariants of client applications under a number of consistency models.

Recently, Kaki et al. [21] developed a program logic to reason about transactions under ANSI SQL isolation levels (including SI). To do this, they formulated an operational model of such programs (parametric in the isolation level). They then proved the soundness of their *logic* with respect to their proposed operational model. However, the authors did not establish the *soundness* or *completeness* of their *operational model* against existing formal semantics, e.g. [11]. The lack of the completeness result means that their proposed operational model may exclude behaviours deemed valid by the corresponding declarative models. This is a particular limitation as possibly many valid behaviours cannot be shown correct using the logic and is thus detrimental to its usability.

By contrast, transactional semantics in the STM setting with mixed (both transactional and non-transactional) accesses is under-explored on both operational and declarative sides. Recently, Dongol et al. [17] applied execution graphs [5] to specify *serialisable* STM programs under weak memory models. Raad et al. [30] formalised the semantics of PSI STMs declaratively (using execution graphs) and operationally (as lock-based reference implementations). Neither work, however, handles the semantics of SI STMs with weak isolation guarantees.

Finally, Khyzha et al. [22] formalise the sufficient conditions on STMs and their programs that together ensure strong isolation. That is, non-transactional accesses can be viewed as singleton transactions (transactions containing single instructions). However, their conditions require *serialisability* for fully transactional programs, and as such, RSI transactions do not meet their conditions. Nevertheless, we conjecture that a DRF guarantee for strong atomicity, similar to [22], may be established for RSI. That is, if all executions of a fully transactional program have no races between singleton and non-singleton transactions, then it is safe to replace all singleton transactions by non-transactional accesses.

In the future, we plan to build on the work presented here by developing reasoning techniques that would allow us to verify properties of STM programs. This can be achieved by either extending existing program logics for weak memory, or developing new ones for currently unsupported models. In particular, we can reason about the SI models presented here by developing custom proof rules in the existing program logics for RA such as [24, 35].

Acknowledgements. We thank the VMCAI reviewers for their constructive feedback. The first author was supported in part by a European Research Council (ERC) Consolidator Grant for the project "RustBelt", under the European Union's Horizon 2020 Framework Programme (grant agreement number 683289). The second author was supported by the Israel Science Foundation (grant number 5166651), and by Len Blavatnik and the Blavatnik Family foundation.

References

1. The Clojure Language: Refs and Transactions. http://clojure.org/refs
2. Technical specification for C++ extensions for transactional memory (2015). http://www.open-std.org/jtc1/sc22/wg21/docs/papers/2015/n4514.pdf
3. Adya, A.: Weak consistency: a generalized theory and optimistic implementations for distributed transactions. Ph.D. thesis, MIT (1999)
4. Adya, A., Liskov, B., O'Neil, P.: Generalized isolation level definitions. In: Proceedings of the 16th International Conference on Data Engineering, pp. 67–78 (2000)
5. Alglave, J., Maranget, L., Tautschnig, M.: Herding cats: modelling, simulation, testing, and data mining for weak memory. ACM Trans. Program. Lang. Syst. **36**(2), 7:1–7:74 (2014)
6. Batty, M., Owens, S., Sarkar, S., Sewell, P., Weber, T.: Mathematizing C++ concurrency. In: Proceedings of the 38th Annual ACM SIGPLAN-SIGACT Symposium on Principles of Programming Languages, pp. 55–66 (2011)
7. Berenson, H., Bernstein, P., Gray, J., Melton, J., O'Neil, E., O'Neil, P.: A critique of ANSI SQL isolation levels. In: Proceedings of the 1995 ACM SIGMOD International Conference on Management of Data, pp. 1–10 (1995)
8. Bieniusa, A., Fuhrmann, T.: Consistency in hindsight: a fully decentralized STM algorithm. In: Proceedings of the 2010 IEEE International Symposium on Parallel and Distributed Processing, IPDPS 2010, pp. 1–12 (2010)
9. Blundell, C., Lewis, E.C., Martin, M.M.K.: Deconstructing transactions: the subtleties of atomicity. In: 4th Annual Workshop on Duplicating, Deconstructing, and Debunking (2005)
10. Cerone, A., Bernardi, G., Gotsman, A.: A framework for transactional consistency models with atomic visibility. In: Proceedings of the 26th International Conference on Concurrency Theory, pp. 58–71 (2015)
11. Cerone, A., Gotsman, A.: Analysing snapshot isolation. In: Proceedings of the 2016 ACM Symposium on Principles of Distributed Computing, pp. 55–64 (2016)
12. Cerone, A., Gotsman, A., Yang, H.: Transaction chopping for parallel snapshot isolation. In: Moses, Y. (ed.) DISC 2015. LNCS, vol. 9363, pp. 388–404. Springer, Heidelberg (2015). https://doi.org/10.1007/978-3-662-48653-5_26
13. Cerone, A., Gotsman, A., Yang, H.: Algebraic laws for weak consistency. In: CONCUR (2017)

14. Crooks, N., Pu, Y., Alvisi, L., Clement, A.: Seeing is believing: a client-centric specification of database isolation. In: Proceedings of the ACM Symposium on Principles of Distributed Computing, PODC 2017, pp. 73–82. ACM, New York (2017). https://doi.org/10.1145/3087801.3087802

15. Daudjee, K., Salem, K.: Lazy database replication with snapshot isolation. In: Proceedings of the 32nd International Conference on Very Large Data Bases, pp. 715–726 (2006)

16. Dias, R.J., Distefano, D., Seco, J.C., Lourenço, J.M.: Verification of snapshot isolation in transactional memory Java programs. In: Noble, J. (ed.) ECOOP 2012. LNCS, vol. 7313, pp. 640–664. Springer, Heidelberg (2012). https://doi.org/10.1007/978-3-642-31057-7_28

17. Dongol, B., Jagadeesan, R., Riely, J.: Transactions in relaxed memory architectures. Proc. ACM Program. Lang. **2**(POPL), 18:1–18:29 (2017). https://doi.org/10.1145/3158106

18. Gotsman, A., Yang, H., Ferreira, C., Najafzadeh, M., Shapiro, M.: 'cause i'm strong enough: reasoning about consistency choices in distributed systems. In: Proceedings of the 43rd Annual ACM SIGPLAN-SIGACT Symposium on Principles of Programming Languages, POPL 2016, pp. 371–384. ACM, New York (2016). https://doi.org/10.1145/2837614.2837625

19. Harris, T., Larus, J., Rajwar, R.: Transactional Memory, 2nd edn. Morgan and Claypool Publishers, San Rafael (2010)

20. Herlihy, M., Moss, J.E.B.: Transactional memory: architectural support for lock-free data structures. In: Proceedings of the 20th Annual International Symposium on Computer Architecture, pp. 289–300 (1993)

21. Kaki, G., Nagar, K., Najafzadeh, M., Jagannathan, S.: Alone together: compositional reasoning and inference for weak isolation. Proc. ACM Program. Lang. **2**(POPL), 27:1–27:34 (2017). https://doi.org/10.1145/3158115

22. Khyzha, A., Attiya, H., Gotsman, A., Rinetzky, N.: Safe privatization in transactional memory. In: Proceedings of the 23rd ACM SIGPLAN Symposium on Principles and Practice of Parallel Programming, pp. 233–245 (2018)

23. Lahav, O., Giannarakis, N., Vafeiadis, V.: Taming release-acquire consistency. In: Proceedings of the 43rd Annual ACM SIGPLAN-SIGACT Symposium on Principles of Programming Languages, pp. 649–662 (2016)

24. Lahav, O., Vafeiadis, V.: Owicki-gries reasoning for weak memory models. In: Halldórsson, M.M., Iwama, K., Kobayashi, N., Speckmann, B. (eds.) ICALP 2015. LNCS, vol. 9135, pp. 311–323. Springer, Heidelberg (2015). https://doi.org/10.1007/978-3-662-47666-6_25

25. Litz, H., Cheriton, D., Firoozshahian, A., Azizi, O., Stevenson, J.P.: SI-TM: reducing transactional memory abort rates through snapshot isolation. SIGPLAN Not. **49**, 383–398 (2014)

26. Litz, H., Dias, R.J., Cheriton, D.R.: Efficient correction of anomalies in snapshot isolation transactions. ACM Trans. Archit. Code Optim. **11**(4), 65:1–65:24 (2015). https://doi.org/10.1145/2693260

27. Martin, M., Blundell, C., Lewis, E.: Subtleties of transactional memory atomicity semantics. IEEE Comput. Archit. Lett. **5**(2), 17 (2006)

28. Papadimitriou, C.H.: The serializability of concurrent database updates. J. ACM **26**(4), 631–653 (1979). https://doi.org/10.1145/322154.322158

29. Peng, D., Dabek, F.: Large-scale incremental processing using distributed transactions and notifications. In: Proceedings of the 9th USENIX Conference on Operating Systems Design and Implementation, pp. 251–264 (2010)

30. Raad, A., Lahav, O., Vafeiadis, V.: On parallel snapshot isolation and release/acquire consistency. In: Ahmed, A. (ed.) ESOP 2018. LNCS, vol. 10801, pp. 940–967. Springer, Cham (2018). https://doi.org/10.1007/978-3-319-89884-1_33
31. Raad, A., Lahav, O., Vafeiadis, V.: The technical appendix for this paper. https://arxiv.org/abs/1805.06196 (2018)
32. Serrano, D., Patino-Martinez, M., Jimenez-Peris, R., Kemme, B.: Boosting database replication scalability through partial replication and 1-copy-snapshot-isolation. In: Proceedings of the 13th Pacific Rim International Symposium on Dependable Computing, pp. 290–297 (2007)
33. Shavit, N., Touitou, D.: Software transactional memory. In: Proceedings of the Fourteenth Annual ACM Symposium on Principles of Distributed Computing, pp. 204–213 (1995)
34. Sovran, Y., Power, R., Aguilera, M.K., Li, J.: Transactional storage for geo-replicated systems. In: Proceedings of the Twenty-Third ACM Symposium on Operating Systems Principles, pp. 385–400 (2011)
35. Vafeiadis, V., Narayan, C.: Relaxed separation logic: a program logic for C11 concurrency. In: Proceedings of the 2013 ACM SIGPLAN International Conference on Object Oriented Programming Systems Languages & Applications, pp. 867–884 (2013)

Program Synthesis with Equivalence Reduction

Calvin Smith[(⊠)] and Aws Albarghouthi

University of Wisconsin–Madison, Madison, WI, USA
`cjsmith@cs.wisc.edu`

Abstract. We introduce *program synthesis with equivalence reduction*, a synthesis methodology that utilizes relational specifications over components of a given synthesis domain to reduce the search space. Leveraging a blend of classic and modern techniques from term rewriting, we use relational specifications to discover a canonical representative per equivalence class of programs. We show how to design synthesis procedures that only consider programs in *normal form*, thus pruning the search space. We discuss how to implement equivalence reduction using efficient data structures, and demonstrate the significant reductions it can achieve in synthesis time.

1 Introduction

Over the past few years, we have witnessed great strides in automated program synthesis, the process of automatic construction of programs that satisfy a given specification—for instance, a logical formula [3], an input-output example [16,24], a type [17], etc. While the underlying algorithmic techniques may appear different, ultimately, a majority of existing algorithms and tools implement a search through the space of programs, be it explicitly through careful enumeration or implicitly through constraint solving.

Of course, the search space in synthesis is enormous—likely infinite. But whenever we are encountered with a large search space, it is often the case that large fractions of the space are redundant. Here, we ask the following question: *How can we exploit operator semantics to efficiently explore large spaces of candidate programs?*

Motivation. Let us consider a generic learner–teacher model, where the learner (the synthesizer) proposes programs and the teacher (the verifier) answers with *yes*/*no*, indicating whether the learner has provided the correct program or not. Our goal is to make the learner *smarter*: we want to reduce the number of questions the learner needs to ask before arriving at the right answer.

Consider the following two string-manipulating programs:

$$p_1 : \ \lambda x.\, \texttt{swap}(\texttt{lower}(x)) \qquad\qquad p_2 : \ \lambda x.\, \texttt{upper}(x)$$

Electronic supplementary material The online version of this chapter (https://doi.org/10.1007/978-3-030-11245-5_2) contains supplementary material, which is available to authorized users.

© Springer Nature Switzerland AG 2019
C. Enea and R. Piskac (Eds.): VMCAI 2019, LNCS 11388, pp. 24–47, 2019.
https://doi.org/10.1007/978-3-030-11245-5_2

where `swap` turns all uppercase characters to lowercase, and vice versa; `lower` and `upper` turn all characters into lowercase or uppercase, respectively. A smart learner would know that turning all characters into lowercase and then applying `swap` is the same as simply applying `upper`. Therefore, the learner would only inquire about one of the programs p_1 and p_2. Formally, the learner knows the following piece of information connecting the three functions:

$$\forall x.\, \texttt{swap}(\texttt{lower}(x)) = \texttt{upper}(x)$$

One could also imagine a variety of other semantic knowledge that a learner can leverage, such as properties of specific functions (e.g., idempotence) or relational properties over combinations of functions (e.g., distributivity). Such properties can be supplied by the developer of the synthesis domain, or discovered automatically using tools like QuickSpec [6] or Bach [37].

Equivalence Reduction. Universally quantified formulas like the one above form *equational specifications* (equations, for short): they define some (but not all) of the behaviors of the *components* (functions in the synthesis domain), as well as relations between them. The equations partition the space of programs into equivalence classes, where each equivalence class contains all equivalent programs with respect to the equations. The learner needs to detect when two programs are in the same equivalence class and only ask the teacher about one *representative* per equivalence class. To do so, we make the observation that we can utilize the equations to define a *normal form* on programs, where programs within the same equivalence class all simplify to the same normal form. By structuring the learner to only consider programs in normal form, we ensure that no redundant programs are explored, potentially creating drastic reductions in the search space. We call this process *program synthesis with equivalence reduction*.

By constraining specifications to be equational (as in the above example), we can leverage standard *completion algorithms*, e.g., Knuth–Bendix completion [21], to construct a *term-rewriting system* (TRS) that is *confluent, terminating*, and *equivalent* to the set of equations. Effectively, the result of completion is a *decision procedure* that checks whether a program p is the representative of its equivalence class—i.e., whether p is in normal form. The difficulty, however, is that constructing such a decision procedure is an *undecidable process*— as equations are rich enough to encode a Turing machine. Nonetheless, significant progress has been made in completion algorithms and *termination proving* (e.g., [15, 41, 43]), which is used for completion.

Given a normalizing TRS resulting from completion, we show how to incorporate it in existing synthesis techniques in order to prune away redundant fragments of the search space and accelerate synthesis. We show how to incorporate equivalence reduction into salient synthesis algorithms that employ *bottom-up*, dynamic-programming-style search—e.g., [2, 3, 28]—and *top-down* search— e.g., [13, 14, 30, 33].

Our primary technical contribution is porting foundational techniques from term rewriting and theorem proving to a contemporary automated program synthesis setting.

Applicability. While our proposed technique is general and orthogonal to much of the progress in program synthesis technology, it is important to note that it is not a panacea. For instance, a number of synthesizers, e.g., the enumerative SyGuS solver [3], prune the search space using *observational equivalence* with respect to a set of input–output examples, which effectively impose a coarse over-approximation of the true equivalence relation on programs. In such settings, equivalence reduction can be beneficial when, for instance, (*i*) evaluating examples is expensive, e.g., if one has to compile the program, simulate it, evaluate a large number of examples; or (*ii*) the verification procedure does not produce counterexamples, e.g., if we are synthesizing separation logic invariants, and one cannot prune through observational equivalence.

Our approach is beneficial in synthesis settings where observational equivalence is not an option or is difficult to incorporate, e.g., in functional program synthesis algorithms like λ^2 [13], Myth [14,30], SynQuid [33], Leon [20], and BIGλ [36]. A number of these tools employ a top-down type-driven search with which observational equivalence is not compatible. Additionally, some of these techniques decompose the problem into multiple subproblems, e.g., a process searching for *mappers* and another searching for *reducers* in BIGλ. In such case, different synthesis subproblems have no *input context* on which to employ observational equivalence. Thus, minimizing the search space is essential.

Contributions. This paper makes a number of contributions:

- *Conceptual.* We present *program synthesis with equivalence reduction*, where a synthesis problem is augmented with domain knowledge in the form of *equational specifications*.
- *Algorithmic.* We demonstrate how to utilize classical and modern techniques from theorem proving and the theory of TRSs to impose a normal form on programs. We demonstrate how to incorporate normal forms in bottom-up and top-down synthesis techniques.
- *Practical.* We implement our approach in an existing synthesis tool for functional, data-parallel programs. To fully exploit equivalence reduction, we discuss the importance of employing efficient data structures used by theorem provers—namely, *perfect discrimination trees* [27]—and fast algorithms for normality checking.
- *Empirical.* We apply our tool to synthesis of *reduction* functions—commutative and associative binary operators that are ubiquitous in modern data-parallel programming. Our thorough empirical evaluation investigates the following important aspects:
  - Speedups gained with equivalence reduction.
  - Overhead of applying equivalence reduction in different algorithms, in relation to program size.
  - Robustness of equivalence reduction to varying the number of equations used.
  - The impact of data structures (perfect discrimination trees) on efficiency.

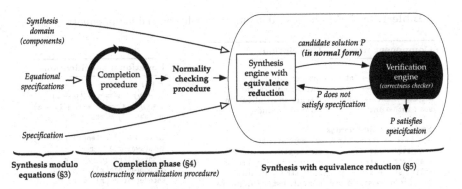

Fig. 1. Overview of synthesis with equivalence reduction

2 Overview and Illustration

2.1 Overview

Figure 1 provides an overview of our proposed synthesis technique. A *synthesis modulo equations problem* is defined by three inputs. First, we are given a *synthesis domain*, which is a set of components (operators) that define the search space of programs. Second, we expect *equational specifications*, which are equations over single components or combinations of components. For example, equations might specify that an operator f is associative, or that two operators, f and g, are inverses of each other. Finally, a synthesis problem also contains a *specification* of the desired program. Below, we describe the various components in Fig. 1 in detail.

2.2 Synthesis Modulo Equations Problem

Synthesis Domain. We will now illustrate the various parts of our approach using a simple example. Consider the synthesis domain shown in Table 1(a). The domain includes basic integer operations as well as a number of functions over strings and *byte arrays* (utf8) that form a subset of Python 3.6's string API.[1] We describe some of the non-standard components. split(x,y) splits string x into a list of strings using the *delimiter* string y, e.g.:

$$\text{split("hizvmcaiz19","z")} = \text{["hi", "vmcai", "19"]}$$

The function join(x,y) concatenates a list of strings x using the delimiter string y. Functions encode/decode transform between strings and UTF-8 byte arrays.

Equational Specifications. Even for such a simple synthesis domain, there is a considerable amount of latent domain knowledge that we can exploit in the synthesis process. Table 1(b) provides a partial view of the equations that we can

---

[1] https://docs.python.org/3/library/stdtypes.html.

Table 1. (a) Left: synthesis domain; (b) Right: partial list of equations

Component name	Description
Integers	
$+$: int $\rightarrow$ int $\rightarrow$ int	integer addition
$-$: int $\rightarrow$ int $\rightarrow$ int	integer subtraction
$*$: int $\rightarrow$ int $\rightarrow$ int	integer multiplication
abs : int $\rightarrow$ int	absolute value
Strings and byte arrays	
$\texttt{++}$: str $\rightarrow$ str $\rightarrow$ str	str concatenation
len : str $\rightarrow$ int	str length
swap : str $\rightarrow$ str	swap upper/lowercase
split : str $\rightarrow$ str $\rightarrow$ [str]	split str w/ delimiter
join : [str] $\rightarrow$ str $\rightarrow$ str	concat. list w/ delimiter
encode : str $\rightarrow$ utf8	encode str as UTF-8
decode : utf8 $\rightarrow$ str	decode UTF-8 into str

Equational specifications

$x + y = y + x$
$(x + y) + z = x + (y + z)$
$x * (y + z) = (x * y) + (x * z)$
$\text{abs}(\text{abs}(x)) = \text{abs}(x)$
$\dots$
$\text{len}(x \mathbin{+\!\!+} y) = \text{len}(x) + \text{len}(y)$
$\text{swap}(\text{swap}(x)) = x$
$\text{join}(\text{split}(x, y), y) = x$
$\text{decode}(\text{encode}(x)) = x$
$\text{encode}(\text{decode}(x)) = x$
$\dots$

utilize for this synthesis domain. The variables x, y, z are implicitly universally quantified. Consider, for instance, the following equation:

$$\forall x, y.\, \text{join}(\text{split}(x, y), y) = x$$

This connects split and join: splitting a string x with delimiter y, and then joining the result using the same delimiter y, produces the string x. In other words, split and join are inverses, assuming a fixed delimiter y.

Other equations specify, e.g., that abs (absolute value of an integer) is idempotent $(\forall x.\, \text{abs}(\text{abs}(x)) = \text{abs}(x))$ or that the function swap is an *involution*—an inverse of itself $(\forall x.\, \text{swap}(\text{swap}(x)) = x)$.

2.3 Completion Phase

Completion Overview. Two programs are equivalent with respect to the equations if we can use the equations to rewrite one into the other—just as a high-school student would apply trigonometric identities to make the two sides of a trigonometric equation identical. Given the set of equations, we would like to be able to partition the space of programs into equivalence classes, where two programs are in the same equivalence class if and only if they are equivalent with respect to the equations. By partitioning the space into equivalence classes, we can ensure that we only consider one representative program per equivalence class. Intuitively, without equations, each program is its own equivalence class. The more equations we add—i.e., the more domain knowledge we have—the larger our equivalence classes are.

Given the set of equations, the completion phase generates a TRS that transforms any program into its normal form—the representative of its equivalence class. It is important to note that the process of determining equality modulo equations is generally undecidable [29], since equations are rich enough to encode transitions of a Turing machine. Completion attempts to generate a decision procedure for equality modulo equations, and as such can fail to terminate.

Nevertheless, advances in automatic termination proving have resulted in powerful completion tools (e.g., [41,43]). Note that completion is a one-time phase for a given synthesis domain, and therefore can be employed offline, not affecting synthesis performance.

The Term Rewriting System. The TRS generated by completion is a set of *rewrite rules* of the form $l \rightarrow r$, which specify that if a (sub)program matches the *pattern* l, then it can be transformed using the pattern r. For instance, completion of the equations in our running example might result in a system that includes the rule $\mathtt{swap}(\mathtt{swap}(x)) \rightarrow x$. In other words, for any program containing the pattern $\mathtt{swap}(\mathtt{swap}(x))$, where x is a variable indicating any completion of the program, we can rewrite it into x.

The above rule appears like a simple syntactic transformation (*orientation*) of the corresponding equation defining that $\mathtt{swap}$ is an involution. However, as soon as we get to slightly more complex equations, the resulting rules can become intricate. Consider, for instance, commutativity of addition. The completion procedure will generate an *ordered* rewrite system to deal with such *unorientable* rules. For example, one rule that completion might generate is $x + y \rightarrow_> y + x$, which specifies that a program of the form $x + y$ can be rewritten into $y + x$ only if $x + y > y + x$, where $>$ is a *reduction ordering*, which is a *well-founded* ordering on programs. (The difficulty in completion is finding a reduction order, just like finding a *ranking function* is the key for proving program termination.)

Normality Checking. Given the TRS generated by the completion procedure, checking whether a program p is in normal formal is a simple process: If any of the rewrite rules in the TRS can be applied to p, then we know that the program is not in normal form, since it can be reduced.

2.4 Synthesis with Equivalence Reduction

Let us now discuss how a synthesis procedure might utilize the TRS generated by completion to prune the search space. For the sake of illustration, suppose our synthesis technique constructs programs in a bottom-up fashion, by combining small programs to generate larger programs, a strategy that is employed by a number of recent synthesis algorithms [2,3,28].

Consider the following simple program,

```
λs, count. len(s ++ "012") + count
```

where s is a string variable and count is an integer variable. The synthesizer constructs this program by applying integer addition to the two smaller expressions: len(s ++ "012") and count. To check if the program is in normal form, the synthesizer attempts to apply all the rules in the TRS generated by completion. If none of the rules apply, the program is *irreducible*, or in normal form. If any rule applies, then we know that the program is not in normal form. In the latter case, we can completely discard this program from the search space. *But what if the end solution uses this program as a subprogram?* By construction of the TRS, if a program p is not in normal form, then all programs p_s, where p appears in p_s as a subprogram, are also *not* in normal form. Intuitively, we can apply the same rewrite rules to p_s as those we can apply to p.

By ensuring that we only construct and maintain programs in normal form, we drastically prune the search space. Figure 2 shows the number of well-typed programs for fixed program size in our running synthesis domain, augmented with two integer and two string variables. The solid (blue) line shows the number of programs (normal forms) for increasing size of the abstract syntax tree (components and variables appearing in the program). When we include the equations in Table 1(b) that only deal with integer components, the number of programs per size shrinks, as shown by the dashed (green) line. Incorpo-

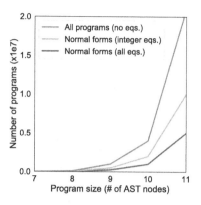

Fig. 2. #normal forms vs. prog. size (Color figure online)

rating the full set of equations (over integer and string components) shrinks the number of normal forms further, as shown by the dotted (red) line. For instance, at 11 AST nodes, there are 21 million syntactically distinct programs, but only about 20% of them are in normal form with respect to the full set of equations.

While the number of programs explodes as we increase the size (unless the synthesis domain is fairly simple), utilizing the equations allows us to delay the explosion and peer deeper into the space of programs. In Sect. 5, we experimentally demonstrate the utility of equations on practical synthesis applications.

3   Synthesis Modulo Equations

We now define synthesis problems with equational specifications.

3.1   Formalizing the Synthesis Problem

Synthesis Domain. A *synthesis domain* $\mathcal{D}$ is a set of *components* $\{f_1, \ldots, f_n\}$, where each component f_i is a function of arity $ar(f_i) \in \mathbb{N}$. The synthesis domain $\mathcal{D}$ induces a set of *candidate programs* $\mathcal{P}_{\mathcal{D}}$, where each $p \in \mathcal{P}_{\mathcal{D}}$ is defined as follows:

$$p := f \qquad\qquad\qquad f \in \mathcal{D} \text{ and } ar(f) = 0$$
$$\mid f(p_1, \ldots, p_n) \qquad f \in \mathcal{D} \text{ and } ar(f) = n > 0$$

When clear from context, we shall use $\mathcal{P}$ to refer to $\mathcal{P}_{\mathcal{D}}$. Components of arity n model functions that take n arguments and return some value; components of arity 0 model constants and input arguments of a program. For simplicity of presentation, we shall restrict our discussion to first-order components and elide types. While our approach can handle higher-order components, the equations we define below are restricted to first-order components.

Synthesis Problems. A *synthesis problem* S is a tuple $(\mathcal{D}, \varphi)$, where $\mathcal{D}$ is a synthesis domain and φ is a *specification*. A *solution* to a synthesis problem S is a program $p \in \mathcal{P}_{\mathcal{D}}$ such that $p \models \varphi$, where $p \models \varphi$ specifies that the program p satisfies the specification φ. We assume that φ is defined abstractly—it can be a Hoare triple that p should satisfy, a reference implementation that p should be equivalent to, a set of input–output examples p should satisfy, etc.

Synthesis Modulo Equations Problems. A *synthesis modulo equations problem* $S^\star$ is a tuple $(\mathcal{D}, \varphi, \mathcal{E})$, where $\mathcal{E}$ defines *equational specifications*. Formally, $\mathcal{E}$ is a set of *equations*, where each equation is a pair $(p_1, p_2) \in \mathcal{P}_{\mathcal{D}}(X) \times \mathcal{P}_{\mathcal{D}}(X)$ and $\mathcal{P}_{\mathcal{D}}(X)$ is the set of programs induced by the domain $\mathcal{D} \cup X$, where $X = \{x, y, z, \ldots\}$ is a special set of variables. An equation (p_1, p_2) denotes the universally quantified formula $\forall X.\, p_1 = p_2$, indicating that programs p_1 and p_2 are semantically equivalent for any substitution of the variables X.

Example 1 (Matrix operations). Suppose that the synthesis domain is defined as follows: $\mathcal{D} = \{t, +_m, i\}$, where t is a unary function that returns the transpose of a matrix, $+_m$ is (infix) matrix addition, and i denotes an input argument. A possible set $\mathcal{E}$ is:

$$t(t(x)) = x \tag{s_1}$$

$$t(x +_m y) = t(x) +_m t(y) \tag{s_2}$$

where x and y are from the set of variables X. Formula s_1 specifies that transposing a matrix twice returns the same matrix; Formula s_2 specifies that transposition distributes over matrix addition. Using $\mathcal{E}$, we can infer that the following programs are semantically equivalent:

$$t(t(i) +_m t(i)) \quad =_{s_2} \quad t(t(i)) +_m t(t(i)) \quad =_{s_1} \quad i +_m i$$

Equivalence Reduction. Given a synthesis problem $S^\star$, the equations $\mathcal{E}$ induce an equivalence relation on candidate programs in $\mathcal{P}$. We shall use $p_1 =_{\mathcal{E}} p_2$ to denote that two programs are *equivalent modulo $\mathcal{E}$* (formally defined in Sect. 3.2). We can partition the set of candidate programs $\mathcal{P}$ into a union of disjoint equivalence classes, $\mathcal{P} = P_1 \uplus P_2 \uplus \ldots$, where for all $p, p' \in \mathcal{P}$,

$$p =_{\mathcal{E}} p' \iff (\exists i \in \mathbb{N} \text{ such that } p, p' \in P_i)$$

For each equivalence class P_i, we shall designate a single program $p_i \in P_i$, called the representative of P_i. A program $p \in \mathcal{P}$ is in *normal form*, denoted $norm(p)$, *iff* it is a representative of some equivalence class P_i.

Solutions of Synthesis Modulo Equations Problems. A solution to a synthesis problem $S^\star = (\mathcal{D}, \varphi, \mathcal{E})$ is a program $p \in \mathcal{P}$ such that (1) $p \models \varphi$ and (2) $norm(p)$ holds. That is, a solution to the synthesis problem is in normal form.

3.2   Term-Rewriting and Completion

We now ground our discussion in the theory of term rewriting systems and discuss using *completion* to transform our equations into a procedure that detects if a program is in normal form. We refer to Baader and Nipkow [4] for a formal exposition of term-rewriting systems.

Rewrite Rules. A *rewrite system* R is a set of *rewrite rules* of the form $(l, r) \in \mathcal{P}_{\mathcal{D}}(X) \times \mathcal{P}_{\mathcal{D}}(X)$, with $vars(r) \subseteq vars(l)$. We will denote a rewrite rule (l, r) as $l \to r$. These rules induce a *rewrite relation*. We say that p rewrites to p', written as $p \to_R p'$, *iff* there exists a rule $l \to r \in R$ that can transform p to p'. We illustrate rewrite rules with an example.

Example 2. Consider the following rewrite rule, $f(x, x) \to g(x)$, where f and g are elements of $\mathcal{D}$ and x is a variable. Consider the program $p = f(f(a, a), b)$, where a and b are two arguments. We can apply the rewrite rule to rewrite p into $p' = f(g(a), b)$, by rewriting the subprogram $f(a, a)$ into $g(a)$.

We will use $\to_R^*$ to denote the reflexive transitive closure of the rewrite relation. The symmetric closure of $\to_R^*$, denoted $\leftrightarrow_R^*$, forms an equivalence relation. We shall drop the subscript R when the TRS is clear from context.

Normal Forms. For a given TRS R, a program p is R-*irreducible iff* there is no program p' such that $p \to_R p'$. For a program p, the set of R-irreducible programs reachable from p via $\to_R$ is its set of *normal forms*. We write $N_R(p) = \{p' \mid p \to^* p', \ p' \text{ is } R\text{-irreducible}\}$ for the normal forms of p.

We say that a TRS R is *normalizing iff* for every program p, $|N_R(p)| \geqslant 1$. A TRS R is *terminating iff* the relation $\to_R$ is *well-founded*; that is, for every program p, there exists $n \in \mathbb{N}$ such that there is no p' where $p \to_R^n p'$ (i.e., no p' reachable from p through n rewrites).

Rewrite Rules and Equations. Recall that equations are of the form $(p_1, p_2) \in \mathcal{P}_{\mathcal{D}}(X) \times \mathcal{P}_{\mathcal{D}}(X)$. It is often convenient to view an equation (p_1, p_2) as two rules: $p_1 \to p_2$ and $p_2 \to p_1$. Let R be the TRS defined by equations in $\mathcal{E}$, then for all programs $p, p' \in \mathcal{P}_{\mathcal{D}}(X)$, we have $p \leftrightarrow_R^* p' \iff p =_{\mathcal{E}} p'$.

R is not terminating by construction, and so cannot be used for determining unique normal forms. For a terminating TRS equivalent to $\mathcal{E}$, we must be more cautious with how rules are generated. The process of generating these rules is known as a *completion procedure*.

Completion Procedures. For our purposes, we only need a declarative view of completion procedures. A completion procedure provides a term rewriting system R_c such that $p \leftrightarrow_{R_c}^* p' \iff p =_{\mathcal{E}} p'$ and for any program p, applying the rules in R_c will always lead to a unique normal form in finitely many rewrites, no matter what the order of application is. Formally, R_c is *terminating and confluent*.

Completion is generally undecidable. Knuth and Bendix are responsible for the first completion procedure [21]; it repeatedly tries to *orient* equations—turn them into rewrite rules—through syntactic transformations. Knuth–Bendix completion, even if it terminates, can still fail to produce a result, as not all equations are orientable. Bachmair et al. neatly side-step this weakness by presenting a completion procedure that cannot fail, called *unfailing completion* [5]. In order to handle the unorientable rules, unfailing completion introduces *ordered rules*:

(a) BOTTOM-UP: Bottom-up synthesis

$$\frac{\quad}{C \leftarrow \emptyset} \text{ INIT} \qquad\qquad \frac{p \in C \qquad p \models \varphi}{p \text{ is a solution}} \text{ VERIFY}$$

$$\frac{f \in \mathcal{D} \qquad \{p_1, \ldots, p_n\} \subseteq C}{p = f(p_1, \ldots, p_n) \qquad norm(p)} \text{ EXPAND}$$

(b) TOP-DOWN: Top-down synthesis

$$\frac{\quad}{C \leftarrow \{\bullet\}} \text{ INIT} \qquad\qquad \frac{p \in C \qquad p \models \varphi}{p \text{ is a solution}} \text{ VERIFY}$$

$$\frac{p \in C \qquad norm(\sigma p) \qquad \bullet \in vars(p) \qquad f \in \mathcal{D}}{\sigma = [\bullet \mapsto f(\bullet_1, \ldots, \bullet_n)] \qquad \{\bullet_i\}_i \text{ are fresh}} \text{ EXPAND}$$

Fig. 3. Synthesis with equivalence reduction algorithms

let $>$ be a *reduction order*, and $r : u \to_> v$ be an ordered rule. (A reduction order is a *well-founded* order that ensures termination of the rewrite system.) Then $p_1 \to p_2$ by rule r *iff* $p_1 \to p_2$ by the unordered rule $u \to v$ and $p_1 > p_2$.

Recall our matrix domain $\mathcal{D} = \{t, +_m, inp\}$ from Example 1, and suppose we have the equation $x +_m y = y +_m x$. Knuth–Bendix completion will not be able to orient this rule. Unfailing completion, when provided with a suitable reduction order $>$, would generate the ordered rule $x +_m y \to_> y +_m x$. Modern completion tools, such as omkbTT [43] and Slothrop [41], are able to simultaneously complete a set of rules and derive an appropriate reduction order.

Knuth–Bendix Order. The *Knuth–Bendix order* (KBO) is a standard family of reduction orders that we will use in our implementation and evaluation. The formal definition of KBO is not important for our exposition, and we thus relegate it to the supplementary material. We will denote a KBO as $>_{\text{KBO}}$, and note that naïvely computing KBO following its standard definition is polynomial in the size of the compared terms. We discuss our linear-time implementation in Sect. 5.3.

4 Synthesis Modulo Equations

We now describe how to incorporate equivalence reduction in *bottom-up* and *top-down* synthesis techniques, and highlight the subtleties involved. An example illustrating both scenarios is provided in the supplementary material.

Bottom-up techniques explore the space of programs in a bottom-up, dynamic-programming fashion, building larger programs from smaller ones. Examples include Escher [2], the enumerative solver of SyGuS [3], and the probabilistic search of Menon et al. [28].

Top-down techniques explore the space of programs in a top-down fashion, effectively, by unrolling the grammar defining the programs. A number of recent synthesis algorithms, particularly for functional programs, employ this methodology, e.g, Myth [30], Myth2 [14], Bigλ [36], λ² [13], and SynQuid [33].

We now present abstract algorithms for these techniques and show how to augment them with equivalence reduction.

4.1   Bottom-Up Synthesis Modulo Equations

We start by describing the bottom-up synthesis algorithm. We would like to find a solution to the synthesis problem $S^* = (\mathcal{D}, \varphi, \mathcal{E})$. We assume that completion has resulted in a procedure $norm(p)$ that checks whether a candidate program p is in normal form.

Figure 3(a) shows a bottom-up synthesis algorithm, BOTTOM-UP, as a set of guarded rules that can be applied non-deterministically. The only state maintained is a set C of explored programs, which is initialized to the empty set in the initialization rule INIT. The algorithm terminates whenever the rule VERIFY applies, in which case a program satisfying the specification φ is found.

The rule EXPAND creates a new program p by applying an n-ary function f to n programs from the set C. Observe, however, that p is only considered if it is in normal form. In other words, the algorithm maintains the invariant that all programs in C are in normal form.

Root-Normality. The invariant that all programs in C are normal can be used to simplify checking $norm(p)$ during the EXPAND step. In synthesizing $p = f(p_1, \ldots, p_n)$, we already know that the subprograms $p_1, \ldots, p_n$ are normal: no rule can apply to any subprogram. Therefore, if p is not normal, it must be due to a rule applying at the root. Checking this property, called *root-normality*, simplifies rule application. Instead of examining all subprogram decompositions of p to see if the rule $l \to r$ applies, it suffices to check whether there exists a substitution σ such that $\sigma p = \sigma l$.

4.2   Top-Down Synthesis Modulo Equations

We now describe how to perform top-down synthesis with equivalence reduction. Top-down synthesis builds programs by unrolling the grammar of programs. We will assume that we have a countable set of variables $X = \{\bullet, \bullet_1, \bullet_2, \ldots\}$, called *wildcards*, which we use as placeholders for extending programs in $\mathcal{P}_\mathcal{D}(X)$.

Figure 3(b) shows the top-down synthesis algorithm, TOP-DOWN, a simplified version of the algorithm in BIGλ [36]. The algorithm maintains a set C of ground (with wildcards) and non-ground programs. C is initialized to the program $\bullet$, using INIT. The rule EXPAND picks a non-ground program from C and substitutes one of its wildcards with a new program. The algorithm terminates when a ground program in C satisfies the specification, as per rule VERIFY.

Normality with Non-ground Programs. The rule EXPAND checks whether p is in normal form before adding it to C. However, note that TOP-DOWN maintains non-ground programs in C, and even if a non-ground program is normal, no ground programs derivable from it through EXPAND need be normal. Therefore, TOP-DOWN may end up exploring subtrees of the search space that are redundant. Deciding if a non-ground program has ground instances in normal form is known as checking *R-ground reducibility*, which is decidable in exponential time [7]. Our formulation avoids exponential checks at the cost of exploring redundant subtrees.

Soundness of both algorithms is discussed in the supplementary material.

5   Implementation and Evaluation

5.1   Implementation and Key Optimizations

We implemented our technique in an existing efficient synthesis tool, written in OCaml, that employs bottom-up and top-down search strategies. Our tool accepts a domain $\mathcal{D}$, defined as typed OCaml functions, along with a set of equations $\mathcal{E}$ over the OCaml functions. As a specification φ for the synthesis problem, we utilize input–output examples (see Sect. 5.2 below).

The implementations of the bottom-up and top-down synthesis algorithms augment the abstract algorithms in Sect. 4 with a deterministic search strategy that utilizes types. Both algorithms explore programs by increasing size—a strategy used in many existing synthesis tools, e.g., [2,13,30], as smaller programs are considered more likely to *generalize*. Both algorithms are type-directed, enumerating only well-typed programs.

Implementing Completion and Reduction Orders. Completions of equations were found using the omkbTT tool [43]—which employs termination provers for completion. All completions used the KBO reduction order (see the supplementary material).

During synthesis, the reduction order can be a performance bottleneck, as we need to compute it for every candidate program. If we were to implement KBO directly from its formal definition (see the supplementary material), evaluating $s >_{\text{KBO}} t$ would be quadratic in $|s| + |t|$. However, program transformation techniques have given us an algorithm linear in the sizes of the terms [26]. In our tool, we implement Löchner's linear-time KBO computation algorithm. The performance impacts of the reduction order will be discussed in Sect. 5.3.

Data Structures for Normalization. Every time a candidate program is considered, we check if it is in normal form using $norm(\cdot)$ (recall algorithms in Fig. 3). More precisely, given a candidate program p, $norm$ attempts to find a substitution σ and a rule $l \rightarrow r \in R$ such that $\sigma(l) = p$. This is a *generalization* problem, which has been studied for years in the field of automated theorem proving. A naïve implementation of *norm* might keep a list of rules in the TRS, and match candidate programs against one rule at a time. Instead, we borrow from the existing literature and use *perfect discrimination trees* [27] to represent our list of rules. Perfect discrimination trees are used in the Waldmeister theorem prover [18] to great effect; *the tree representation lets us match multiple rules at once, and ignore rules that are inapplicable.*

A perfect discrimination tree can be thought of as a *trie*. Figure 4 illustrates the construction for a set of unordered rules (ordered rules can be added analogously). First, rules are rewritten using De Bruijn-like indices [9]. Second, the left-hand side of every rule is converted into a string through a pre-order traversal. Finally, all string representations are inserted into the trie.

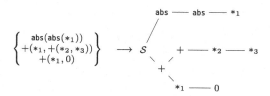

Fig. 4. Building the trie data structure from lhs of rules

To match a candidate program p against the trie, we first convert p to a *flat-term*, which is a linked-list representation of p in pre-order with forward pointers to jump over subterms. For example, the term $+(\text{max}(x, y), 0)$ is converted to:

Now, matching the program against the trie is done using a simple backtracking algorithm, which returns a substitution (if one exists) that converts the left-hand side of a rule in our set to the query program. See [27] for details.

Using perfect discrimination trees in our normalization procedure has several immediate benefits, the most important of which is that unused rules do not impact the performance, as their paths are never followed. In Sect. 5.3, we will evaluate the performance overhead of normalization.

5.2 Synthesis Domain and Benchmarks

A primary inspiration for our work came from applying synthesis to the domain of large-scale, data-parallel programming, where a program is composed of data-parallel combinators, e.g., *map* and *reduce*, which allow programmers to write distributed programs without having to worry about low-level details of distribution. Popular *MapReduce-like* systems, e.g., Apache Spark [45], Hadoop [42], and Dryad [44], provide such high-level interfaces.

Here, we will focus on synthesizing *reducers* in the distributed, data-parallel programming context. Reducers are functions that allow us to *aggregate* large amounts of data by exploiting parallelism. Our long-term goal with synthesis of such aggregation functions from

```
let add-c q1 q2 =
  let real = (fst q1) + (fst q2) in
  let imaginary = (snd q1) + (snd q2) in
  pair real imaginary
```

Fig. 5. Addition of two complex numbers of the form $a + bi$, where a and b are represented as a `pair`

examples is to enable average computer users to construct non-trivial data analyses through examples. We will focus on evaluating our synthesis algorithms in this context.

To synthesize deterministic data-parallel programs, tools like Bigλ ensure that reducers form a *commutative semigroup* (CSG) [36]. This guarantees determinism in the face of data reordering (e.g., *shuffles* [10]). To ensure we only synthesize CSG reducers, we employ the dynamic analysis technique from Bigλ [36].

Synthesis Domain. Our synthesis domain comprises four primary sets of components, each consisting of 10+ components, that focus on different types. These types—integers, tuples, strings, and lists—are standard, and appear as the subject of many synthesis works. See full list in the supplementary material.

Equational Specifications. We manually gathered a set of 50 equations for our synthesis domain. Each class of components has between 3 (lists) and 21 (integers) equations, with a few equations correlating functions over multiple domains (e.g., strings and integers interacting through `length`). Completions of the equations are a mix of ordered and unordered rules describing the interaction of the components. Some equations are described below—full list in the supplementary material.

– *Strings*: In addition to the equations relating `uppercase`, `swap`, and `lowercase` (as defined in Sect. 1), we include equations encoding, e.g., idempotence of `trim`, and the fact that many string operations distribute over concatenation. For instance, we have the equation $\forall x, y. \mathtt{len}(x) + \mathtt{len}(y) = \mathtt{len}(x +\!\!+ y)$.
– *Lists*: We provide equations specifying that operations distribute over list concatenation, as in $\forall x, y. \mathtt{sum}(x) + \mathtt{sum}(y) = \mathtt{sum}(\mathtt{cat}(x, y))$. In addition, we relate constructors/destructors, as in $\forall x, y. \mathtt{head}(\mathtt{cons}(x, y)) = x$.

Benchmarks. Our benchmarks were selected to model common reducers over our domain, and typically require solutions with 10–12 AST nodes—large enough to be a challenge for state-of-the-art synthesizers, as we see later in this Sect. 5.3. A few examples are given below—for a full list, refer to supplementary material.

– *Tuples and integers*: The tuple benchmarks expose several different uses for pairs in reducers—as an encoding for rational numbers (such as in `mult-q`), for complex numbers (in `add-c`), and for points on the plane (as in `distances`). We also treat pairs as intervals over integers (e.g., `intervals` synthesizes *join* in the lattice of intervals [8]). Figure 5 shows the synthesized program for one of those benchmarks.

– *Lists and integers*: Lists are also an interesting target for aggregation, e.g., if we are aggregating values from different scientific experiments, where each item is a list of readings from one sensor. List benchmarks compute a value from two lists and emit the result as a singleton list. For example, `ls-sum-abs` computes absolute value of the sums of two lists, and then adds the two, returning the value as a singleton list.

Like many synthesis tools, we use input–output examples to characterize the desired solution. Examples are used to ensure that the solution (i) matches user expectations and (ii) forms a CSG.

5.3 Experimental Evaluation

Our experiments investigate the following questions:

RQ1. Does equivalence reduction increase the efficiency of synthesis algorithms on the domain described above?

RQ2. What is the overhead of equivalence reduction?

RQ3. How does the performance change with different numbers of equations?

RQ4. Are the data structures used in theorem provers a good fit for synthesis?

To address these questions, we developed a set of 30 synthesis benchmarks. Each benchmark consists of: (i) a specification, in the form of input–output examples (typically no more than 4 examples are sufficient to fully specify the solution); (ii) a set of components from the appropriate domain; (iii) a set of ordered and unordered rewrite rules generated from equations over the provided components.

For each algorithm, bottom-up (BU) and top-down (TD), we created three variations:

– BU and TD: equivalence reduction disabled.
– BU_n and TD_n: equivalence reduction enabled.
– $BU_{\tilde{n}}$ and $TD_{\tilde{n}}$: equivalence reduction without ordered rules. By dropping ordered rules from the generated TRS, we get more normal forms (less pruning).

See Table 2 for the full results. For each experiment, we measure total time taken in seconds. Grey boxes indicate the best-in-category strategy for each benchmark—e.g., the winner of the **sub-c** benchmark is BU_n in the bottom-up category, and $TD_{\tilde{n}}$ in top-down. Values reported are the average across 10 runs.

RQ1: Effects of Equivalence Reduction on Performance. In 2 out of the 3 benchmarks where BU and TD do not terminate, adding equivalence reduction allows the synthesizer to find a solution in the allotted time. For bottom-up, in all benchmarks where BU terminates in under 1 s, both BU_n and $BU_{\tilde{n}}$ outperform the naïve BU, often quite dramatically: in **sum-to-second**, BU takes over 60 s, while BU_n and $BU_{\tilde{n}}$ finish in under 2 s. For top-down, $TD_{\tilde{n}}$ outperforms TD in

Table 2. Experimental results (Mac OS X 10.11; 4 GHz Intel Core i7; 16 GB RAM). We impose a CPU timeout of 300 s and a memory limit of 10 GBs per benchmark. ✗ denotes a timeout.

Benchmark	Bottom-up variations			Top-down variations			Other tools	
	BU	$\mathrm{BU}_{\tilde{n}}$	BU_n	TD	$\mathrm{TD}_{\tilde{n}}$	TD_n	λ^2	SQ
Integers								
add	0.00	0.00	0.00	0.00	0.00	0.00	0.01	0.18
max	0.01	0.01	0.01	0.03	0.05	0.02	0.4	0.6
min	0.01	0.01	0.01	0.05	0.02	0.04	0.01	0.62
Tuples & integers								
add-4	0.05	0.05	0.11	0.12	0.14	1.29	5.35	8.86
mult-q	7.38	0.48	0.44	15.63	1.95	3.03	✗	✗
div-q	7.38	0.48	0.44	14.22	2.12	3.82	✗	✗
add-c	7.39	0.48	0.44	13.51	3.68	8.11	✗	✗
sub-c	7.35	0.48	0.43	31.63	4.51	9.28	✗	✗
add-q-long	✗	44.65	49.51	✗	57.43	95.55	✗	✗
max-pair	32.79	4.02	4.92	40.25	21.53	56.21	✗	✗
intervals	32.76	4.00	4.92	74.77	25.25	21.80	✗	✗
min-pair	32.72	4.03	4.95	81.88	19.55	67.49	✗	✗
sum-to-first	52.74	1.18	0.62	110.35	5.47	15.06	✗	✗
sum-to-second	68.93	1.51	0.70	107.88	5.27	11.22	✗	✗
add-and-mult	7.39	0.48	0.45	26.12	1.51	9.34	✗	✗
distances	✗	7.36	5.58	✗	50.31	100.66	✗	✗
Strings & integers								
str-len	1.40	0.42	0.52	4.47	1.58	2.06	NA	NA
str-trim-len	26.29	6.79	7.14	219.50	52.21	218.61	NA	NA
str-upper-len	5.70	1.78	1.81	26.93	5.64	8.01	NA	NA
str-lower-len	3.86	1.23	1.26	22.48	6.93	4.63	NA	NA
str-add	0.05	0.02	0.03	0.26	0.08	0.07	NA	NA
str-mult	0.05	0.02	0.03	0.17	0.05	0.06	NA	NA
str-max	1.79	0.45	0.54	8.10	1.32	2.99	NA	NA
str-split	✗	✗	✗	✗	✗	✗	NA	NA
Lists & integers								
ls-sum	0.00	0.02	0.03	0.01	0.02	0.11	0.01	10.43
ls-sum2	147.91	88.33	107.02	229.66	✗	254.87	✗	✗
ls-sum-abs	0.08	0.07	0.10	0.22	0.19	0.37	63.00	✗
ls-min	0.00	0.02	0.03	0.01	0.02	0.10	0.01	NA
ls-max	0.00	0.02	0.03	0.01	0.02	0.10	0.01	NA
ls-stutter	27.68	5.12	8.01	50.42	15.90	93.84	✗	NA

nearly all benchmarks that take TD more than 1 s (the exception being ls-sum2). With ordered rules, the exceptions are more numerous. The most egregious is ls-stutter, going from 50 s with TD to 94 s with TD_n. There is still potential for large performance gains: in sum-to-second, we decrease the time from 108 s in TD to under 12 s for TD_n and under 6 s for $\mathrm{TD}_{\tilde{n}}$.

Equivalence Reduction Appears to Drastically Improve the Performance of Bottom-Up and Top-Down Synthesis. In general, the unordered rules outperform the full ordered rules. In the bottom-up case, this performance gap is smaller than 5 s: while the ordered rules are more costly to check, bottom-up synthesis only requires that we check them at the root of a program. In top-down, we must check rule application at all sub-programs. This magnifies the cost of the ordered rules and leads to significant performance differences between TD_n and $\mathrm{TD}_{\tilde{n}}$.

RQ2-a: Overhead of Equivalence Reduction. Figure 6 provides a different look at the benchmarks in Table 2: for each benchmark where BU and TD do not terminate in less that 1 s, we compute (*i*) the *overhead*, the percentage of time spent in the normalization procedure *norm*; and (*ii*) the *reduction*, the percentage of programs visited compared to the un-normalized equivalent, BU or TD. The results are shown as density plots.

Figure 6a and c show the performance characteristics of $BU_{\tilde{n}}$ and $TD_{\tilde{n}}$, respectively. Both have consistent overhead—40% for $BU_{\tilde{n}}$ and 25% for $TD_{\tilde{n}}$—although $TD_{\tilde{n}}$ has a more reliable reduction of over 85%, while $BU_{\tilde{n}}$ ranges from 60% to 90% reduction. Both strategies boast large reductions in the number of candidate programs visited for reasonable overhead, although $TD_{\tilde{n}}$ is the clear winner—$BU_{\tilde{n}}$ dominates $TD_{\tilde{n}}$ in Table 2, suggesting that normalization isn't enough to fully close the gap between BU and TD. In Fig. 6b and d, we see the performance characteristics of BU_n and TD_n, respectively. Compared to Fig. 6a and c, we see a higher overhead with less consistent normalization. Both figures have secondary clusters of benchmarks outside the region of highest density: these contain the benchmarks from the strings and integers domain.

This View of the Data Supports the Conclusion of Table 2 that Unordered Rules Outperform Ordered Rules. While our implementation of KBO is optimized, evaluating the reduction order is still a bottleneck. Our implementation verifies candidate solutions quickly, but **the benefits of high reduction outweigh the large overhead as verification time increases.** For instance, when providing more input-output examples, the verification time increases but not the overhead. In the `ls-stutter` benchmark, $BU_{\tilde{n}}$ visits 1,288,565 programs with an average overhead of 1.07 s, while BU_n visits 792,662 programs with an average overhead of 5.6 s. Increasing the verification cost per program by only 0.0001 s will raise $BU_{\tilde{n}}$'s time by 129 s, while BU_n's time is only raised by 80 s—easily a large enough gap to out-scale the overhead. Indeed, when we instrument our tool with a synthetic delay, this behavior is visible.

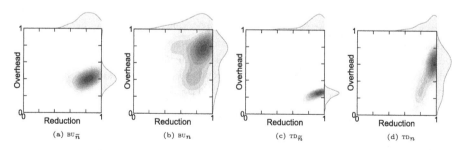

(a) $BU_{\tilde{n}}$ (b) BU_n (c) $TD_{\tilde{n}}$ (d) TD_n

Fig. 6. Equivalence reduction overhead. Benchmarks are converted into (overhead, reduction) pairs and plotted using kernel density estimation (KDE), with marginal distributions projected on to the side. No points lie outside the bounding box (any appearance of such is an artifact of KDE).

RQ2-b: Normalization Overhead w.r.t. Program Size. Experience holds that normalization procedures don't scale as candidate programs become large. To explore how this behavior might impact the effectiveness of equivalence reduction, we instrumented our tool to ignore solutions and explore the space of programs depth-first, during which we record the average overhead of $norm(\cdot)$ at all program sizes. Figure 7 presents the data for the `sum-to-first` benchmark, although the figures are representative of the other benchmarks.

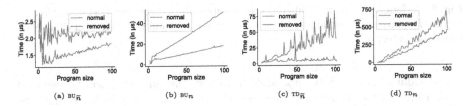

(a) $BU_{\widetilde{n}}$ (b) BU_n (c) $TD_{\widetilde{n}}$ (d) TD_n

Fig. 7. Average performance of $norm(\cdot)$ w.r.t. the size of candidate programs. *Normal* graph represents executions of $norm(\cdot)$ that return `true`; *removed* represents executions that return `false`. Data is average of multiple executions of $norm(\cdot)$ per program size using the `sum-to-first` benchmark. Time is in microseconds—note the difference in scale between graphs.

Unsurprisingly, $norm(\cdot)$ Scales Linearly with Program Size. This Linear Growth Appears Quite Sustainable. Solutions with 100 AST nodes are beyond modern-day synthesis tools, and a 3x slowdown compared to programs of size 40 is manageable.

When we compare the performance of $BU_{\widetilde{n}}$ in Fig. 7a to that of BU_n in Fig. 7b, we observe an order of magnitude loss in performance. This holds as well for $TD_{\widetilde{n}}$ and TD_n in Fig. 7c and d, respectively. Checking KBO is clearly expensive, and so the observed performance in Table 2 of BU_n and TD_n indicate a large amount of search-space reduction occurring.

RQ3 and RQ4: Impact of Rules and Perfect Discrimination Trees. To determine how the number of rules impacts our tool's performance, we completed our entire set of 50 equations to produce 83 unordered rules that we randomly sample subsets from (the results from ordered results are similar). To test the effectiveness of perfect discrimination trees, we compare performance against a naïve algorithm that maintains a list of rules it checks against one by one on a representative benchmark: `str-len`. Not all rules apply to the components used—only 47 out of 83 describe components used for `str-len`. We plot the time taken for synthesis per number of randomly sampled rules, from 0 rules to 150 rules (to clearly show optimal performance). Results are presented in Fig. 8.

We see, for both benchmarks, nearly continuously decreasing graphs; the only exceptions are with low numbers of rules sampled, where it is likely we have mostly unusable rules. The performance levels off at 83 rules, when we are guaranteed to sample all applicable rules. These results are promising: completion

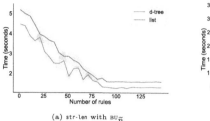
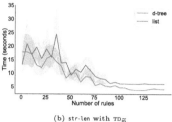

(a) str-len with $BU_{\widetilde{n}}$ (b) str-len with $TD_{\widetilde{n}}$

Fig. 8. Performance versus number of rules sampled for `d-tree` and `list` over 2 benchmarks. The line is the average of 10 samples per x-value, and the lighter band is a 95% confidence interval.

is undecidable, and so it is impossible to predict the rules that will be included from a given set of equations. However, the results in Fig. 8 indicate that—on average—**the more rules we provide the better the algorithm's performance, even when the rules might not be relevant.** Furthermore, we see immediately and clearly that **perfect discrimination trees outperform our list-based implementation.** Performance differences are magnified in the $TD_{\widetilde{n}}$ benchmarks, where checking normality includes checks on every subterm. On the rest of the benchmarks, the naïve implementation results in an average of an 11% increase in time for $BU_{\widetilde{n}}$ and a 144% increase for $TD_{\widetilde{n}}$, which strongly indicates that perfect discrimination trees are an important implementation choice.

Gauging Benchmark Difficulty. We considered related tools as a gauge of benchmark difficulty and a baseline for evaluation. The most similar tool—λ^2 [13]—is top-down, type-directed, uses input–output examples, and searches for programs from smallest to largest. SynQuid (SQ) [33] synthesizes Haskell programs from refinement types, using SMT-driven type-directed synthesis. When able, we encoded specifications of our benchmarks as refinement types.[2]

As seen in Table 2, λ^2 is either not applicable (strings are not supported, and so were ignored) or unable to solve most benchmarks. SQ exhibits similar behavior and performance. We stress that these results are meant as a indication of the difficulty of the benchmarks, and not a head-to-head comparison between our algorithms and those of λ^2 and SQ.

Threats to Validity. We identify two primary threats to the validity of our evaluation. First, we base our evaluation on a single tool in order to evaluate various algorithms and data structures. However, since our bottom-up and top-down strategies are (i) instances of standard synthesis techniques and (ii) comparable to existing implementations (as seen in Table 2), we believe our results can be beneficial to tools like Myth, SynQuid, and λ^2, modulo technical details.

---

[2] We also consider two other works: Bigλ [36] is implemented in Python and not competitive with our baseline, while Myth [30] expects data types to be specified from first principles, and does not have, e.g., integers or strings by default.

Second, the domains considered in our evaluation—integers, lists, etc.—operate over well-behaved algebraic structures. These domains form the core search space of many modern synthesis tools, but one could imagine domains that do not induce many equational specifications, e.g., GUI manipulation and stateful domains.

5.4 Further Discussion

Constructing Equational Specifications. In a large number of recent works on program synthesis, it is assumed that someone designs the synthesis domain by providing a set of components. We additionally assume that we are given a set of equational specifications over the components. In our evaluation, we manually crafted a set of equations for our domain. Alternatively, this process can be automated using tools like QuickSpec [6] and Bach [37].

Rule Preprocessing. The synthesis algorithms we consider search for a program over a regular tree grammar of components. Therefore, one could incorporate equations by rewriting the grammar so as to only generate normal forms. This can be done by encoding the TRS as a regular tree grammar and intersecting it with the search grammar. However, to express a TRS as a regular tree grammar, we require the TRS to be left-linear and unordered [31]. These conditions are too strong to be used as a general technique: most useful equations result in non-left-linear or ordered rules.

Completion and Termination. A key component in our approach is the completion tool that takes our equations and produces a TRS that can be used for pruning the search space. In our evaluation, we found that modern completion procedures were able to complete our equational specifications. In general, however, completion is an undecidable problem. In the supplementary material, we discuss a mechanism to work around this fact, by terminating the completion procedure at any point and salvaging a sub-optimal (non-confluent) TRS.

6   Related Work

Program Synthesis. We are not the first to use normal forms for pruning in synthesis. In type-directed synthesis, Osera and Zdancewic [30] and Frankle et al. [14] restrict the space by only traversing programs in *β-normal form*. Equivalence reduction can be used to augment such techniques with further pruning, by exploiting the semantics of the abstract data types defined. Feser et al. [13] mention that their enumeration uses a fixed set of standard rewrites, e.g., $x + 0 \rightarrow x$, to avoid generating redundant expressions. In contrast, our work presents a general methodology for incorporating equational systems into the search by exploiting completion algorithms.

Techniques that search for fast programs—e.g., *superoptimization* [32,35]—may not be able to directly benefit from equivalence reduction, as it may impose inefficient normal forms. It would be interesting to incorporate a cost model into completion and coerce it into producing minimal-cost normal forms.

In SyGuS [3,39], the synthesizer generates a program encodable in a decidable first-order theory and equivalent to some logical specification. A number of solvers in this category employ a *counter-example-guided synthesis loop* (CEGIS) [38]: they prune the search space using a set of input–output examples, which impose a coarse over-approximation of the true equivalence relation on programs. In the CEGIS setting, equivalence reduction can be beneficial when, for instance, (i) evaluating a program to check if it satisfies the examples is expensive, e.g., if one has to compile the program, simulate it, evaluate a large number of examples; or (ii) the verification procedure does not produce counterexamples, e.g., if we are synthesizing separation logic invariants.

A number of works sample programs from a probabilistic grammar that imposes a probability distribution on programs [11,25,28]. It would be interesting to investigate incorporating equivalence reduction in that context, for instance, by *truncating* the distribution so as to only sample irreducible programs.

Recently, Wang et al. [40] introduced SYNGAR, where abstract transition relations are provided for each component of a synthesis domain. The synthesis algorithm over-approximates equivalence classes by treating two programs equivalent if they are equivalent in the abstract semantics. The abstraction is refined when incorrect programs are found.

Completion and Term-Rewriting Systems. A number of classic works [12, 34] used completion procedures to transform an equational specification into a program—a terminating rewrite system. Our setting is different: we use completion in order to prune the search space in modern inductive synthesis tools.

Kurihara and Kondo's multi-completion [23] sidesteps the issue of picking a reduction order by allowing completion procedures to consider a class of reduction orders simultaneously. Klein and Hirokawa's maximal completion algorithm [19] takes advantage of SMT encodings of reduction orders (such as Zankl et al.'s KBO encoding [46]) to reduce completion to a series of MAXSMT problems in which the parameters of the reduction order are left free. Completion tools like omkbTT [43] and SLOTHROP [41], rely on external termination provers [1,22].

Acknowledgement. This work is supported by the National Science Foundation CCF under awards 1566015 and 1652140.

References

1. Alarcón, B., Gutiérrez, R., Lucas, S., Navarro-Marset, R.: Proving termination properties with MU-TERM. In: Johnson, M., Pavlovic, D. (eds.) AMAST 2010. LNCS, vol. 6486, pp. 201–208. Springer, Heidelberg (2011). https://doi.org/10.1007/978-3-642-17796-5_12

2. Albarghouthi, A., Gulwani, S., Kincaid, Z.: Recursive program synthesis. In: Sharygina, N., Veith, H. (eds.) CAV 2013. LNCS, vol. 8044, pp. 934–950. Springer, Heidelberg (2013). https://doi.org/10.1007/978-3-642-39799-8_67

3. Alur, R., et al.: Syntax-guided synthesis. In: FMCAD (2013)
4. Baader, F., Nipkow, T.: Term Rewriting and All That. Cambridge University Press, Cambridge (1998)
5. Bachmair, L., Dershowitz, N., Plaisted, D.A.: Completion without failure. Resolut. Eqn. Algebraic Struct. **2**, 1–30 (1989)
6. Claessen, K., Smallbone, N., Hughes, J.: QUICKSPEC: guessing formal specifications using testing. In: Fraser, G., Gargantini, A. (eds.) TAP 2010. LNCS, vol. 6143, pp. 6–21. Springer, Heidelberg (2010). https://doi.org/10.1007/978-3-642-13977-2_3
7. Comon, H., Jacquemard, F.: Ground reducibility is EXPTIME-complete. In: Proceedings of the 12th Annual IEEE Symposium on Logic in Computer Science, LICS 1997, pp. 26–34. IEEE (1997)
8. Cousot, P., Cousot, R.: Abstract interpretation: a unified lattice model for static analysis of programs by construction or approximation of fixpoints. In: Proceedings of the 4th ACM SIGACT-SIGPLAN Symposium on Principles of Programming Languages, pp. 238–252. ACM (1977)
9. De Bruijn, N.G.: Lambda calculus notation with nameless dummies, a tool for automatic formula manipulation, with application to the Church-Rosser theorem. In: Indagationes Mathematicae, Proceedings, vol. 75, pp. 381–392. Elsevier (1972)
10. Dean, J., Ghemawat, S.: MapReduce: simplified data processing on large clusters. In: OSDI (2004)
11. Dechter, E., Malmaud, J., Adams, R.P., Tenenbaum, J.B.: Bootstrap learning via modular concept discovery. In: IJCAI (2013)
12. Dershowitz, N.: Synthesis by completion. Urbana **51**, 61801 (1985)
13. Feser, J.K., Chaudhuri, S., Dillig, I.: Synthesizing data structure transformations from input-output examples. In: PLDI (2015)
14. Frankle, J., Osera, P.M., Walker, D., Zdancewic, S.: Example-directed synthesis: a type-theoretic interpretation. In: POPL (2016)
15. Giesl, J., Schneider-Kamp, P., Thiemann, R.: AProVE 1.2: automatic termination proofs in the dependency pair framework. In: Furbach, U., Shankar, N. (eds.) IJCAR 2006. LNCS, vol. 4130, pp. 281–286. Springer, Heidelberg (2006). https://doi.org/10.1007/11814771_24
16. Gulwani, S., Harris, W.R., Singh, R.: Spreadsheet data manipulation using examples. CACM **55**(8), 97–105 (2012)
17. Gvero, T., Kuncak, V., Kuraj, I., Piskac, R.: Complete completion using types and weights. In: PLDI (2013)
18. Hillenbrand, T., Buch, A., Vogt, R., Löchner, B.: Waldmeister-high-performance equational deduction. J. Autom. Reason. **18**(2), 265–270 (1997)
19. Klein, D., Hirokawa, N.: Maximal completion. In: LIPIcs-Leibniz International Proceedings in Informatics, vol. 10. Schloss Dagstuhl-Leibniz-Zentrum fuer Informatik (2011)
20. Kneuss, E., Kuraj, I., Kuncak, V., Suter, P.: Synthesis modulo recursive functions. In: OOPSLA (2013)
21. Knuth, D.E., Bendix, P.B.: Simple word problems in universal algebras. In: Siekmann, J.H., Wrightson, G. (eds.) Automation of Reasoning. SYMBOLIC, pp. 342–376. Springer, Heidelberg (1983). https://doi.org/10.1007/978-3-642-81955-1_23
22. Korp, M., Sternagel, C., Zankl, H., Middeldorp, A.: Tyrolean termination tool 2. In: Treinen, R. (ed.) RTA 2009. LNCS, vol. 5595, pp. 295–304. Springer, Heidelberg (2009). https://doi.org/10.1007/978-3-642-02348-4_21
23. Kurihara, M., Kondo, H.: Completion for multiple reduction orderings. J. Autom. Reason. **23**(1), 25–42 (1999)

24. Lau, T., Wolfman, S.A., Domingos, P., Weld, D.S.: Programming by demonstration using version space algebra. Mach. Learn. **53**(1–2), 111–156 (2003)
25. Liang, P., Jordan, M.I., Klein, D.: Learning programs: a hierarchical Bayesian approach. In: Proceedings of the 27th International Conference on Machine Learning, ICML 2010, pp. 639–646 (2010)
26. Löchner, B.: Things to know when implementing KBO. J. Autom. Reason. **36**(4), 289–310 (2006)
27. McCune, W.: Experiments with discrimination-tree indexing and path indexing for term retrieval. J. Autom. Reason. **9**(2), 147–167 (1992). https://doi.org/10.1007/BF00245458
28. Menon, A.K., Tamuz, O., Gulwani, S., Lampson, B.W., Kalai, A.: A machine learning framework for programming by example. In: ICML (2013)
29. Novikov, P.S.: On the algorithmic unsolvability of the word problem in group theory. Trudy Matematicheskogo Instituta imeni VA Steklova **44**, 3–143 (1955)
30. Osera, P., Zdancewic, S.: Type-and-example-directed program synthesis. In: PLDI (2015)
31. Otto, F.: On the connections between rewriting and formal language theory. In: Narendran, P., Rusinowitch, M. (eds.) RTA 1999. LNCS, vol. 1631, pp. 332–355. Springer, Heidelberg (1999). https://doi.org/10.1007/3-540-48685-2_27
32. Phothilimthana, P.M., Thakur, A., Bodik, R., Dhurjati, D.: Scaling up superoptimization. In: Proceedings of the Twenty-First International Conference on Architectural Support for Programming Languages and Operating Systems, pp. 297–310. ACM (2016)
33. Polikarpova, N., Kuraj, I., Solar-Lezama, A.: Program synthesis from polymorphic refinement types. In: Proceedings of the 37th ACM SIGPLAN Conference on Programming Language Design and Implementation, pp. 522–538. ACM (2016)
34. Reddy, U.S.: Rewriting techniques for program synthesis. In: Dershowitz, N. (ed.) RTA 1989. LNCS, vol. 355, pp. 388–403. Springer, Heidelberg (1989). https://doi.org/10.1007/3-540-51081-8_121
35. Schkufza, E., Sharma, R., Aiken, A.: Stochastic superoptimization. ACM SIGPLAN Not. **48**(4), 305–316 (2013)
36. Smith, C., Albarghouthi, A.: MapReduce program synthesis. In: Proceedings of the 37th ACM SIGPLAN Conference on Programming Language Design and Implementation, pp. 326–340. ACM (2016)
37. Smith, C., Ferns, G., Albarghouthi, A.: Discovering relational specifications. In: Proceedings of the 2017 11th Joint Meeting on Foundations of Software Engineering, pp. 616–626. ACM (2017)
38. Solar-Lezama, A., Tancau, L., Bodík, R., Seshia, S.A., Saraswat, V.A.: Combinatorial sketching for finite programs. In: ASPLOS (2006)
39. Udupa, A., Raghavan, A., Deshmukh, J.V., Mador-Haim, S., Martin, M.M., Alur, R.: TRANSIT: specifying protocols with concolic snippets. ACM SIGPLAN Not. **48**(6), 287–296 (2013)
40. Wang, X., Dillig, I., Singh, R.: Program synthesis using abstraction refinement. Proc. ACM Program. Lang. **2**(POPL), 63 (2017)
41. Wehrman, I., Stump, A., Westbrook, E.: SLOTHROP: Knuth-Bendix completion with a modern termination checker. In: Pfenning, F. (ed.) RTA 2006. LNCS, vol. 4098, pp. 287–296. Springer, Heidelberg (2006). https://doi.org/10.1007/11805618_22
42. White, T.: Hadoop - The Definitive Guide: Storage and Analysis at Internet Scale (2015)

43. Winkler, S., Middeldorp, A.: Termination tools in ordered completion. In: Giesl, J., Hähnle, R. (eds.) IJCAR 2010. LNCS, vol. 6173, pp. 518–532. Springer, Heidelberg (2010). https://doi.org/10.1007/978-3-642-14203-1_43

44. Yu, Y., et al.: DryadLINQ: a system for general-purpose distributed data-parallel computing using a high-level language. In: OSDI (2008)

45. Zaharia, M., et al.: Resilient distributed datasets: a fault-tolerant abstraction for in-memory cluster computing. In: NSDI (2012)

46. Zankl, H., Hirokawa, N., Middeldorp, A.: KBO orientability. J. Autom. Reason. **43**(2), 173–201 (2009)

Minimal Synthesis of String to String Functions from Examples

Jad Hamza[✉] and Viktor Kunčak

LARA, EPFL, Lausanne, Switzerland
{jad.hamza,viktor.kuncak}@epfl.ch

Abstract. We study the problem of synthesizing string to string transformations from a set of input/output examples. The transformations we consider are expressed using a particular class of transducers: functional non-deterministic Mealy machines (f-NDMM). These are machines that read input letters one at a time, and output one letter at each step. The *functionality* constraint ensures that, even though the machine is locally non-deterministic, each input string is mapped to exactly one output string by the transducer.

We suggest that, given a set of input/output examples, the smallest f-NDMM consistent with the examples is a good candidate for the transformation the user was expecting. We therefore study the problem of, given a set of examples, finding a minimal f-NDMM consistent with the examples and satisfying the functionality and totality constraints mentioned above.

We prove that, in general, the decision problem corresponding to that question is NP-complete, and we provide several NP-hardness proofs that show the hardness of multiple variants of the problem.

Finally, we propose an algorithm for finding the minimal f-NDMM consistent with input/output examples, that uses a reduction to SMT solvers. We implemented the algorithm, and used it to evaluate the likelihood that the minimal f-NDMM indeed corresponds to the transformation expected by the user.

1 Introduction

Programming by examples is a form of program synthesis that enables users to create programs by presenting input/output examples. In this paper, we analyze the problem of synthesizing string-to-string transformations from examples.

We consider string transformations that can be represented by finite-state automata, called *functional non-deterministic Mealy machines* (f-NDMM) [17]. f-NDMMs output one letter for each input letter which is read. Non-determinism refers to the fact that f-NDMMs are allowed to have two outgoing transitions from the same state labeled by the same input, while functionality ensures that overall, one input string is mapped to at most one output string. Moreover, if every input string has a corresponding output string, the automaton is called *total*.

© Springer Nature Switzerland AG 2019
C. Enea and R. Piskac (Eds.): VMCAI 2019, LNCS 11388, pp. 48–69, 2019.
https://doi.org/10.1007/978-3-030-11245-5_3

Synthesizing an arbitrary total f-NDMM consistent with input/output examples can be solved in polynomial time, by having the f-NDMM return a default string for the inputs which are not specified in the example. The issue with this basic approach is that the generated automaton might not be what the user had in mind when giving the input/output examples. In other words, input/output examples are not a complete specification, and are ambiguous.

As one of the simplest and robust criteria to rank possible solutions, we propose to synthesize a *minimal* automaton consistent with given input/output examples. For sufficiently long input/output descriptions, the requirement of minimality then forces the automaton to generalize from input/output examples. This rationale is analogous to motivation for Syntax-Guided Synthesis [2]. In our case we use automata minimality as a somewhat application-agnostic criterion. Furthermore, we can in principle leverage the insights from automata theory to improve the synthesis algorithm. Therefore, it is interesting to understand the precise computational complexity of such synthesis problems and to identify directions for promising synthesis approaches. This is the objective of our paper.

Complexity. We prove that the synthesis of minimal automata is in NP, by showing that for a given set of input-output examples E there always exist an f-NDMM consistent with E whose number of states is linear with respect to the size of E. Furthermore, we show how to check in deterministic polynomial time whether a given DFA is a total f-NDMM consistent with E. An NP procedure can iterate for i from 1 to the aforementioned bound, guess a DFA of size i, and check that it is a total f-NDMM consistent with the input/output examples.

We also consider the associated decision problem, which asks, given a set of input/output examples, and a *target* number of states k, whether there exists a total f-NDMM consistent with the examples and which has at most k states. We prove that this problem is NP-hard.

We give three distinct reductions, that apply for different variants of the problem. First, we show that the problem is NP-hard when the target number of states is fixed to 3 (but the input alphabet is part of the problem description). Second, we show that the decision problem is NP-hard when the input and output alphabets are fixed (but the target number of states is part of the problem description).

Third, we study a variant of the problem for *layered* automata for bitvectors, that recognize only words of some fixed length. The name *layered* comes from the fact that their states can be organized into layers that recognize only words of a certain length. We prove that the problem is still NP-hard in that setting, despite the fact that these automata have no cycles.

Algorithm. We provide a reduction to the satisfiability of a logical formula. We implement our reduction, and link it to the Z3 SMT solver. We evaluate our tool and show it can successfully recover simple relations on strings from not too many examples (but scales to many examples as well). We also evaluate the ability of our algorithm to recover a random automaton from a sample set of input-output examples. Our experiments suggest that it is better to give a large number of small examples, rather than a small number of large examples. Moreover, to improve the chance that our algorithm finds a particular automaton, the examples given should generally be at least as long as the number of states.

Contributions of this paper are the following:

- NP-hardness proofs for the decision problem (Sects. 5 and 6),
- Proof that the minimization problem can be solved in NP (Sect. 7),
- A reduction from the minimization problem to a logical formula that can be handled by SMT solvers (Sect. 8),
- An implementation of this reduction and experiments that evaluate the likelihood that minimization finds the automaton the user has in mind (Sect. 9).

Some proofs are deferred to the long version [14].

Note. A preliminary version of this paper, using a different encoding into SMT constraints for the synthesis algorithm, was presented at the SYNT 2018 workshop, without a proceedings entry. SYNT explicitly permits subsequent publication of such papers. Moreover, the present encoding into SMT constraints uses only quantifier-free linear integer arithmetic and is new to this submission.

2   Notation

An *alphabet* Σ is a non-empty finite set of *symbols*. Given a natural number $n \in \mathbb{N}$, we denote by Σ^n the set of sequences (or words) of n symbols of Σ. We denote by Σ^* the set of finite sequences $\bigcup_{n \geq 0} \Sigma^n$. For $u \in \Sigma^*$, $|u|$ denotes the length of the sequence u. A set of words is called a *language*.

A *non-deterministic finite automaton (NFA)* A is a tuple $(\Sigma, Q, q_{init}, \delta, F)$ where Σ is an alphabet, Q is the finite set of states, $q_{init} \in Q$ is the initial state, $\delta \subseteq Q \times \Sigma \times Q$ is the transition function, and $F \subseteq Q$ is the set of *accepting* states. We denote by $\mathcal{L}(A)$ the language accepted by A, i.e. the set of words for which there exists an *accepting run* in A. By an abuse of notation, the set $\mathcal{L}(A)$ is sometimes denoted by A.

An NFA A is *unambiguous* (denoted *UFA*) if every word in Σ^* has at most one accepting run in A. An NFA is *deterministic* (denoted *DFA*) if for every $q_1 \in Q$, $a \in \Sigma$, there exists a unique $q_2 \in Q$ such that $(q_1, a, q_2) \in \delta$. The *size* of an NFA A is its number of states, and is denoted $|A|$.

Let Σ and Γ be two alphabets. For $u \in \Sigma^n$ and $v \in \Gamma^n$ where $u = u_1 \ldots u_n$, $v = v_1 \ldots v_n$, we denote by $u * v$ the sequence in $(\Sigma \times \Gamma)^n$ where $u * v = (u_1, v_1) \ldots (u_n, v_n)$. Note that the operator $*$ is well defined only when $|u| = |v|$.

Given two words $u, v \in \Sigma^*$, we denote by $u \preceq_p v$ the fact that u is a prefix of v. Moreover, *Prefixes*(v) denotes the set of prefixes of v, that is *Prefixes*$(v) = \{u \mid u \preceq_p v\}$.

3   Functional Non-deterministic Mealy Machines

We consider two alphabets, an *input alphabet* Σ and an *output alphabet* Γ. A *functional non-deterministic Mealy machine (f-NDMM)* is a DFA A over $\Sigma \times \Gamma$ satisfying: for all $u \in \Sigma^*$, $v_1, v_2 \in \Gamma^*$ where $|u| = |v_1| = |v_2|$, if $u * v_1 \in \mathcal{L}(A)$ and $u * v_2 \in \mathcal{L}(A)$, then $v_1 = v_2$.

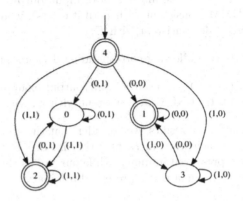

Fig. 1. An automaton that overwrites an input string with 0's or 1's depending on whether the last letter of the input is a 0 or 1.

Remark 1. Note here that we model f-NDMMs with *deterministic* finite automata. The determinism refers to the fact given a state, an input letter and an output letter, there is at most one outgoing transition labeled by those letters. On the other hand, the non-determinism in the f-NDMM refers to the fact that given one state and one input letter, there might be multiple outgoing transitions, each one labeled with a distinct output letter.

Example 1. Figure 1 shows a f-NDMM that outputs a sequence of 0's or a sequence of 1, depending on whether the last letter of the input is a 0 or a 1. Input letters are written on the left-hand-side of the pair, while output letters are on the right-hand-side.

Non-determinism is used in the initial state 4, to guess whether the last letter of the input is a 0 or a 1. In the states 0 and 2, the automaton expects the last letter to be a 1, while in the states 1 and 3, it expects the last letter to be a 0. The sink state is omitted for readability (e.g. reading a 1 and outputting a 1 in state 3 is not allowed).

Remark 2. This example illustrates the higher expressive power of f-NDMMs compared to deterministic Mealy machines, which cannot express this transformation. On the other hand, this transformation can be expressed using more expressive deterministic transducers, such as transducers with look-ahead (that are able to take decisions based by seeking ahead in the input word) or two-way transducers (which are allowed to read the input word multiple times, back and forth).

Due to the functionality restriction described above, an f-NDMM A defines a partial function $\bar{A} \subseteq \Sigma^* \times \Gamma^*$, which is defined for $u \in \Sigma^*$ only when there exists $v \in \Gamma^*$ such that $u * v \in \mathcal{L}(A)$. This unique word v is denoted by $A(u)$. An f-NDMM A is called *total* if the partial function $\bar{A}$ is total. For a set $E \subseteq \Sigma^* \times \Gamma^*$ we say that an f-NDMM A is consistent with E if $E \subseteq \bar{A}$.

Problem 1. Let $E \subseteq (\Sigma \times \Gamma)^*$ be finite a set of input/output examples.

Find a total f-NDMM, consistent with E (if it exists), whose size is minimal (among all total f-NDMMs consistent with E).

We also investigate the following corresponding decision problem.

Problem 2. Let $E \subseteq (\Sigma \times \Gamma)^*$ be a set of input/output examples, and let $n \in \mathbb{N}$. Does there exist a total f-NDMM, consistent with E, with size at most n?

When stating complexity results, we consider that the size of the problem is the sum of the sizes of each word in E, plus the size of n. Our hardness result hold even when n is represented in unary, while our proofs that Problems 1 and 2 belong to NP hold even when n is represented in binary.

3.1   Summary of the Complexity Results

Table 1 summarizes the complexity results proved in this paper. As far as we know, the problem is open when the input alphabet has size one, i.e. $|\Sigma| = 1$. On the other hand, when $|\Gamma| = 1$, the problem becomes trivial as the minimal total f-NDMM consistent with given input/output examples always has a single state with a self-loop.

Layered f-NDMMs are defined in Sect. 6.2, and are f-NDMMs that only recognize words of some particular length. Even in that setting, the problem is NP-complete.

Table 1. Summary of the complexity results

Problem	Layered f-NDMMs	f-NDMMs
Problem 2	NP-complete	NP-complete
With $|\Gamma| = 2$, $n = 3$, $|E| = 1$	$O(1)$ (Remark 4)	NP-complete (Sect. 5)
With $|\Sigma| = 3$, $|\Gamma| = 2$	NP-complete (Sect. 6.2)	NP-complete (Sect. 6.1)
With $|\Sigma| = 3$, $|\Gamma| = 2$, $|E| = 1$	$O(1)$ (Remark 4)	NP-complete (Sect. 6.1)
When Σ, Γ and n are fixed	in P (Remark 3)	in P (Remark 3)

4   Preliminaries for the **NP-Hardness** Proofs

In Sects. 5, 6.1, and 6.2, we prove NP hardness results for Problem 2 and variants. These hardness results carry directly over to Problem 1. Indeed, any algorithm for solving Problem 1 can be adapted to solve Problem 2.

Our proofs rely on reductions from a variant of the boolean satisfiability problem (SAT), called One-In-Three Positive SAT.

Problem 3 (One-In-Three Positive SAT). Given a set of variables V and a set of clauses $C \subseteq V^3$, does there exist an assignment $f : V \to \{\bot, \top\}$ such that for each $(x, y, z) \in C$, exactly one variable out of x, y, z, evaluates to $\top$ through f.

In all reductions, our goal is to build from an instance φ of One-In-Three Positive SAT a set of input/output examples such that φ is satisfiable if and only if there exists a total f-NDMM consistent with the examples (and satisfying the constraints of the minimization problem at hand).

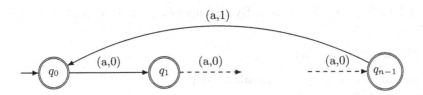

Fig. 2. The form of automata that have an $(a, 0, 1)$-loop.

Our strategy for these reductions is to give input/output examples that constrain the shape of *any* total f-NDMM consistent with these examples. We give input/output examples that ensure that any total f-NDMM consistent with the examples must have certain transitions, and cannot have certain other transitions.

For example, in Sects. 5 and 6.1, we provide input/output examples that restrict the shape of any solution to be of the form given in Fig. 2. Then, knowing that any solution must have this shape, we give additional examples that correspond to our encoding of φ.

We first give a formal definition for automata that are of the shape of the automaton given in Fig. 2.

Definition 1. *Let $A = (\Sigma \times \Gamma, Q, q_{init}, \delta, F)$ be an f-NDMM with $n \in \mathbb{N}$ states, $n \geq 1$. We say that A has an $(a, 0, 1)$-loop if $a \in \Sigma$, and $0, 1 \in \Gamma$, $0 \neq 1$, and the states Q of A can be ordered in a sequence $q_0, \ldots, q_{n-1}$ such that:*

- *$q_{init} = q_0$,*
- *for every $0 \leq i < n - 1$, $(q_i, (a, 0), q_{i+1}) \in \delta$,*
- *$(q_{n-1}, (a, 1), q_0) \in \delta$,*
- *$F = Q$,*

– *there are no transitions in δ labeled with letter a other than the ones mentioned above.*

The following lemma, used in Theorems 1 and 2, shows that we can give an input/output example that forces automata to have an $(a, 0, 1)$-loop. The idea is to give a long example that can only be recognized if the total f-NDMM has an $(a, 0, 1)$-loop.

Lemma 1. *Let $A = (\Sigma \times \Gamma, Q, q_{init}, \delta, F)$ be a total f-NDMM with n states, $n \geq 1$. Let u and v be two words such that:*

$$A(a^{2n} \cdot u) = 0^{n-1}10^{n-1}1 \cdot v.$$

Then A has an $(a, 0, 1)$-loop.

Proof. Consider the run of $a^{2n} * 0^{n-1}10^{n-1}1$ in A, of the form:

$$q_{init} = q_0 \xrightarrow{(a,0)} q_1 \xrightarrow{(a,0)} \cdots \xrightarrow{(a,0)} q_{n-1} \xrightarrow{(a,1)} q_n \xrightarrow{(a,0)} q_{n+1} \cdots \xrightarrow{(a,0)} q_{2n-1} \xrightarrow{(a,1)} q_{2n}$$

where for all $0 \leq i \leq 2n$, $q_i \in Q$. By assumption, we know that from state q_{2n}, A accepts $u * v$.

We want to prove that:

1. the states q_0 to q_{n-1} are all distinct, and
2. $q_n = q_0$, and
3. there are no transitions labeled by a except the ones from the run above, and
4. $F = Q$.

Note that this entails that $q_i = q_{n+i}$ for all $0 \leq i \leq n$.

(1) Assume by contradiction that there exist $0 \leq i < j \leq n-1$ such that $q_i = q_j$. Since A only has n states, we know that there exist $n \leq k < l \leq 2n$ such that $q_k = q_l$. We consider two cases, either $l < 2n$, or $l = 2n$. If $l < 2n$, then the following words are accepted by A, leading to a contradiction to the output-uniqueness property of f-NDMMs.

– $a^{2n-j+i-l+k+(j-i)(l-k)} \cdot u * 0^{n-1-j+i}10^{n-1-l+k+(j-i)(l-k)}1 \cdot v$, by going through
$$q_0 \cdots q_i q_{j+1} \cdots q_{k-1}(q_k \cdots q_{l-1})^{j-i}q_l \cdots q_{2n} \cdots,$$
– $a^{2n-j+i-l+k+(j-i)(l-k)} \cdot u * 0^{n-1-j+i+(j-i)(l-k)}10^{n-1-l+k}1 \cdot v$, by going through
$$q_0 \cdots q_{i-1}(q_i \cdots q_{j-1})^{l-k}q_j \cdots q_k q_{l+1} \cdots q_{2n} \cdots.$$

Similarly, if $l = 2n$, the following words are accepted by A, again leading to a contradiction.

– $a^{2n-j+i-l+k+(j-i)(l-k)} \cdot u * 0^{n-1-j+i}10^{n-l+k}(0^{l-k-1}1)^{(j-i)} \cdot v,$
– $a^{2n-j+i-l+k+(j-i)(l-k)} \cdot u * 0^{n-1-j+i+(j-i)(l-k)}10^{n-l+k} \cdot v.$

We conclude that the states q_0 to q_{n-1} are all distinct.

(2) Since the states q_0 to q_{n-1} are all distinct, we know that $q_n = q_i$ for some $0 \leq i \leq n-1$. Assume by contradiction that $0 < i$. By doing the same case analysis as above (either $l < 2n$, or $l = 2n$), we again find contradictions to the output-uniqueness property of A.
(3) Assume by contradiction that there exist $i \neq j$ with $0 \leq i, j \leq n-1$ and $b \in \Gamma$ such that $\delta(q_i, (a,b)) = q_j$ and this transition is different than the transitions from the run above.

If $i < j$, then there is an alternative loop $q_i, q_j, q_{j+1}, \ldots, q_{n-1}, q_0, q_1, \ldots, q_i$ containing $n - j + i + 1$ transitions labeled by a. In particular, this means that the word $a^{n+n(n-j+i+1)}$ has two different outputs in A. The first one is obtained by going from q_0 to q_i, taking the alternative loop n times, and then going from q_i to q_0 using the $(a, 0, 1)$-loop. The second is obtained by going from q_0 to q_i, taking the $(a, 0, 1)$-loop $(n - j + i + 1)$ times, and then going from q_i to q_0 using the $(a, 0, 1)$-loop. This contradicts the output-uniqueness property of A.

A similar reasoning applies when $j < i$, by using $q_i, q_j, q_{j+1}, \ldots, q_i$ as the alternative loop.

(4) Due to the previous property, the only run labeled whose input is a^i for $0 \leq i \leq n-1$ is the one going through $q_0, q_1, \ldots, q_i$ in the $(a, 0, 1)$-loop. This entails that for $0 \leq i \leq n-1$, q_i is final and $F = Q$.

The following lemma states that multiple input/output examples may be encoded into just one example for f-NDMMs that have an $(a, 0, 1)$-loop.

Lemma 2. *Let $A = (\Sigma \times \Gamma, Q, q_{init}, \delta, F)$ be an f-NDMM with an $(a, 0, 1)$-loop. Let $u, v \in \Sigma^*$ and $u', v' \in \Gamma^*$ such that:*

$$A(u \cdot a \cdot v) = u' \cdot 1 \cdot v'.$$

Then $A(u \cdot a) = u' \cdot 1$ and $A(v) = v'$.

Proof. Using Lemma 1, we know that A has an $(a, 0, 1)$-loop. Therefore, the only transition labeled by $(a, 1)$ is the one leading to the initial state. Therefore, after reading $(u \cdot a) * (u' \cdot 1)$, A must be in the initial state. This entails that $A(u \cdot a) = u' \cdot 1$ and $A(v) = v'$.

5   NP-Hardness of the Minimization Problem with One Input/Output Example and Fixed Number of States

We prove the NP-hardness of Problem 2 by reducing the One-In-Three Positive SAT problem to it. This NP-hardness proof holds even when the target number of states for minimization is fixed to 3, the size of the output alphabet is fixed to 2, and there is single input/output example.

Theorem 1. *Problem 2 is NP-hard when the number of states is fixed, the output alphabet is fixed, and there is a single input/output example.*

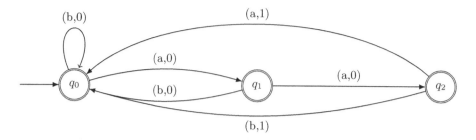

Fig. 3. f-NDMM used in the proof of Theorem 1.

Proof. Consider an instance φ of One-In-Three Positive SAT, with a set of variables V, and a set of clauses $C \subseteq V^3$. We reduce One-In-Three Positive SAT to Problem 2 as follows. We define $\Sigma = V \cup \{a, b\}$, where a and b are fresh symbols and $\Gamma = \{0, 1\}$. Moreover, we define $n = 3$ (fixed number of states).

Then, we define $E = \{w\}$ where w is one input/output example made of the concatenation of all the following words (the word $aaaaaa * 001001$ must go first in the concatenation, but the other words can be concatenated in any order):

- $aaaaaa * 001001$,
- $baaa * 0001$,
- $abaaa * 00001$,
- $aabaaa * 001001$,
- $xbaaa * 00001$ for all $x \in V$,
- $xxxaaa * 000001$ for all $x \in V$,
- $axxxaa * 000001$ for all $x \in V$,
- $aaxxxa * 000001$ for all $x \in V$,
- $xyzaa * 00001$ for all $(x, y, z) \in C$.

We prove that φ has a satisfying assignment if and only if there exists a total f-NDMM A, consistent with E, and with (at most) 3 states.

($\Rightarrow$) Let $f : V \to \{\bot, \top\}$ be a satisfying assignment for φ. We define $A = (\Sigma \times \Gamma, Q, q_{init}, \delta, F)$ following Fig. 3 with $Q = F = \{q_0, q_1, q_2\}$ and $q_{init} = q_0$. The transitions involving $a \in \Sigma$ in A are: $(q_0, (a, 0), q_1), (q_1, (a, 0), q_2) \in \delta$, and $(q_2, (a, 1), q_0) \in \delta$.

Then, for each $x \in V$, if $f(x) = \top$, we add three transitions in δ, called *forward transitions*: $(q_0, (x, 0), q_1)$, $(q_1, (x, 0), q_2)$, and $(q_2, (x, 0), q_0)$. If $f(x) = \bot$, we add three transitions as well, called *looping transitions*: $(q_0, (x, 0), q_0)$, $(q_1, (x, 0), q_1)$, and $(q_2, (x, 0), q_2)$.

A is a total f-NDMM, since all states are final, and for every state and every input in Σ, there is a unique outgoing transition labeled by this input (and some output in Γ). Moreover, we can verify that A is consistent with the input/output example w.

($\Leftarrow$) Let $A = (\Sigma \times \Gamma, Q, q_{init}, \delta, F)$ be a total f-NDMM with 3 states, and consistent with E. Our proofs goes as follows. First, using Lemmas 1 and 2, we deduce that A must have an $(a, 0, 1)$-loop, and must accept all the individual words that constitute the concatenation w. Then, using the facts that $A(baaa) = 0001$, $A(abaaa) = 00001$, $A(aabaaa) = 001001$, we deduce that A must contain the transitions present in Fig. 3, and no other transitions labeled by b.

Then, for each variable $x \in V$, using the facts that $A(xbaaa) = 00001$ and $A(xxxaaa) = A(axxxaa) = A(aaxxxa) = 000001$, we show that x must either have looping transitions, or forward transitions, as described in the first part of the proof. We then use this fact to define f that assigns $\top$ to variables that have forward transitions, and $\bot$ to variables that have looping transitions.

Finally, for each clause $(x, y, z) \in C$, and using $A(xyzaa) = 00001$, we deduce that exactly one variable out of x, y and z must have forward transitions, and conclude that f is a satisfying assignment for φ.

We now give more details for each step of the proof. Our first goal is to prove that A must contain the transitions given in Fig. 3. Since $A(baaa) = 0001$, we know that after reading $(b, 0)$, A must be in state q_0, and therefore there exists a transition $(q, 0, (b, 0), q_0) \in \delta$. Using $A(abaaa) = 00001$ and $A(aabaaa) = 001001$ respectively, we deduce that there exist transitions $(q, 1, (b, 0), q_0)$ and $(q, 2, (b, 1), q_0)$ in δ. Using the output-uniqueness property of A, we can verify that there can be no other transitions labeled by b in A.

Our next goal is to prove that for each variable $x \in V$, x must either have looping transitions or forward transitions.

Since $xbaaa * 00001 \in A$ and the only transitions labeled by $(b, 0)$ are the ones from states q_0 and q_1, we deduce that from the initial state, reading $(x, 0)$ must lead either to q_0 or q_1, and therefore there should either exist a transition $(q_0, (x, 0), q_1) \in \delta$ or a transition $(q_0, (x, 0), q_0) \in \delta$.

Assume $(q_0, (x, 0), q_1) \in \delta$. In that case, we prove that x has forward transitions, in the sense that there are transitions $(q_1, (x, 0), q_2)$ and $(q_2, (x, 0), q_0)$ in δ. We know $xxxaaa * 0000001 \in A$. Since the only state from which the word $aaa * 001$ is accepted is q_0, the automaton A must end in q_0 after reading $xxx * 000$. Moreover, since $(q_0, (x, 0), q_1) \in \delta$, we know A ends in state q_1 after reading $(x, 0)$ in the initial state. Therefore, when reading $xx * 00$ from state q_1, A must end in state q_0. The only way this is possible is by having transitions $(q_1, (x, 0), q_2)$ and $(q_2, (x, 0), q_0)$ in δ.

The other case we consider is when $(q_0, (x, 0), q_0) \in \delta$. Here, we want to prove that x has looping transitions, with $(q_1, (x, 0), q_1)$ and $(q_2, (x, 0), q_2)$ in δ. We know $axxxaa*000001 \in A$. The only state from which $aa*01$ can be accepted is q_1. Moreover, A ends in state q_1 after reading $(a, 0)$. Therefore, A must go from state q_1 to q_1 by reading $xxx * 000$. Due to the self-loop $(q_0, (x, 0), q_0) \in \delta$, the only possibility for this is to have a loop $(q_1, (x, 0), q_1) \in \delta$. Similarly, using $aaxxxa * 000001 \in A$, we deduce there is a loop $(q_1, (x, 0), q_1) \in \delta$.

Overall, we have shown that each variable $x \in V$ either has forward transitions, or looping transitions. We now define the assignment f that assigns $\top$ to variables that have forward transitions, and $\bot$ to variables that have looping transitions. Let $(x, y, z) \in C$. We know $xyzaa * 00001 \in A$. The only state from which $aa * 01$ can be accepted is q_1. Therefore, A must end in state q_1 after reading $xyz * 000$. The only way for this to be the case is that exactly one of x, y, z has forward transitions, while the two others have looping transitions.

6   NP-Hardness Proofs for Other Variants

In this section, we give two other NP-hardness proofs, that cover instances of the problem which are not comparable to the ones treated in Sect. 5.

These proofs also follow the idea of reducing from the One-In-Three Positive SAT problem, but require new encodings. The proofs are deferred to the long version [14].

6.1   NP-Hardness of the Minimization Problem with One Input/Output Example and Fixed Alphabets

Our second NP-hardness proof holds for the case where the sizes of both input and output alphabets are fixed, and there is a single input/output example. When the input and output alphabets are fixed, we can no longer use the encoding given in the previous section, where we could associate to each variable of the SAT formula a letter in our alphabet. Instead, we here rely on the fact that the target number of states is not fixed. As such, this theorem is complementary to Theorem 1.

Theorem 2. *Problem 2 is NP-hard when the alphabets Σ and Γ are fixed, and there is a single input/output example.*

Remark 3. Note that if the input and output alphabets as well as the target number of states are fixed, then Problem 2 can be solved in polynomial time. The reason is that when all these parameters are constants, then there is only a constant number of f-NDMMs to explore.

6.2   NP-Hardness of the Minimization Problem for Layered Automata

In this section, we cover automata that only recognize words of the same length. An NFA $A = (\Sigma, Q, q_{init}, \delta, F)$ is said to be *l-layered* for $l \in \mathbb{N}$ if A only accepts words of length l, i.e. $\mathcal{L}(A) \subseteq \Sigma^l$. An l-layered f-NDMM $A = (\Sigma \times \Gamma, Q, q_{init}, \delta, F)$ is called *l-total* if the domain of the function associated with A is Σ^l.

We then adapt Problem 2 for this setting.

Problem 4. Let Σ be an input alphabet, Γ an output alphabet, and $l \in \mathbb{N}$. Let $u_1 * v_1, \ldots, u_k * v_k$ be a set of input/output examples, with $u_i \in \Sigma^l$ and $v_i \in \Gamma^l$ for all $1 \leq i \leq k$. Let $n \in \mathbb{N}$.

Does there exist an l-layered and l-total f-NDMMs that accepts $u_i * v_i$ for all $1 \leq i \leq k$, and that has at most n states.

The following theorem proves that Problem 4 is NP-hard, even when the alphabets are fixed. In this theorem, we can no longer rely on Lemmas 1 and 2, since layered automata cannot contain cycles. Instead, we have to use multiple input/output examples in our encoding.

Theorem 3. *Problem 4 is NP-hard when the alphabets Σ and Γ are fixed.*

Remark 4. When there is a single input/output example, Problem 4 can be solved in polynomial time. The reason is that, in a layered f-NDMM, we need at least as many states as the size of the example (plus one) to recognize it. Therefore, the minimal layered f-NDMM that recognizes one given input/output example is easy to construct, by using that many states.

7   Solving the Minimization Problem in NP

We now focus on finding an algorithm for solving the minimization Problems 1 and 2. In this section, we propose an approach which solves the problem in non-deterministic polynomial-time. Combined with the proofs in the previous sections, we can deduce that Problem 2 is NP-complete.

The key is to prove (see Lemma 3) that for any valid set of input/output examples, there exists a total f-NDMM, consistent with E, and whose size is at most $2 + \sum_{w \in E} |w|$. Then, a naive minimization approach can iterate through all integers i between 1 and this bound, guess non-deterministically a DFA A of size i, and check whether A is a total f-NDMM consistent with E. We prove that this final check can be done in polynomial time (see Lemma 4), meaning that the whole procedure has non-deterministic polynomial time.

Lemma 3. *Let $E \subseteq (\Sigma \times \Gamma)^*$ be a valid set of input/output examples. There exists a total f-NDMM, consistent with E, with at most $2 + \sum_{w \in E} |w|$ states.*

Proof. We define $T = (\Sigma \times \Gamma, Q^T, q_{init}^T, \delta^T, F^T)$ to be a tree-shaped (partial) f-NDMM consistent with E, as follows:

- Q^T is the set of all prefixes of E,
- $q_{init}^T = \varepsilon$,
- $\delta^T = \{(q_1, (a, b), q_2) \mid q_1, q_2 \in E \land q_2 = q_1 \cdot (a, b)\}$,
- $F^T = E$.

By construction, T has at most $1 + \sum_{w \in E} |w|$ states.

Let $P = Prefixes(dom(E)) \subseteq \Sigma^*$ be the set of all prefixes of $dom(E)$. For each $u \in P$, we choose $v \in \Gamma^*$ as follows:

- if $u \in dom(E)$, choose v as the unique word such that $u * v \in E$,
- otherwise, choose any v such that $u * v \in Prefixes(E)$.

We denote by $P' \subseteq Prefixes(E)$ the set of pairs (u, v) where $u \in P$ and v is the corresponding word, chosen in the previous step. Let $b_0 \in \Gamma$ be a letter of the output alphabet. We define the automaton $A = (\Sigma \times \Gamma, Q, q_{init}, \delta, F)$, which is a total f-NDMM consistent with E, as follows:

- $Q = Q^T \cup \{q_f\}$ where q_f is a new state,
- $q_{init} = q_{init}^T$,
- $\delta = \delta^T \cup$

$$\{(q_f, (a, b_0), q_f) \mid a \in \Sigma\} \cup$$
$$\{(q, (a, b_0), q_f) \mid q \in P' \wedge a \in \Sigma \wedge input(q) \cdot a \notin P\}$$

- $F = P' \cup \{q_f\}$.

It remains to prove three things: (1) A is an f-NDMM, (2) A is total, and (3) $E \subseteq \mathcal{L}(A)$.

1. By construction, A is a DFA. Let $u * v_1 \in A$, and $u * v_2 \in A$, with $u \in \Sigma^*$ and $v_1, v_2 \in \Gamma^*$. Our goal is to prove that $v_1 = v_2$. We consider several cases: (a) $u*v_1$ and $u*v_2$ are both accepted in q_f: By construction of A, q_f is a state from which a run can never get out (a sink state). Consider the accepting run of $u * v_1$ in A and let $q_1 \in Q^T$ be the last state of Q^T before reaching q_f. There is a prefix $u_1 * v_1'$ of $u*v_1$ that corresponds to q_1. Similarly, let $q_2 \in Q^T$ be the last state of Q^T in the run of $u*v_2$ in A, and let $u_2 * v_2'$ be the prefix of $u*v_2$ that corresponds to state q_2. Without loss of generality, we can assume that u_1 is a prefix of u_2.
   Moreover, we prove that u_1 is in fact equal to u_2. Assume by contradiction that u_1 is a strict prefix of u_2, and let $u_2 = u_1 \cdot a \cdot u_1'$. Therefore, there is a transition from q_1 to q_f whose input letter is a, which is not possible since $u_1 \cdot a \in P$. Therefore, $u_1 = u_2$.
   So far, we know $u_1 * v_1'$ goes to state q_1, and $u_1 * v_2'$ goes to state q_2. By construction, the only transitions leading to q_f are from states of P'. So we have $q_1, q_2 \in P'$. We know P' is a function relation, and only associates to each word in Σ^* at most one word in Γ^*. We deduce that $v_1' = v_2'$, and that $q_1 = q_2$.
   Since the runs then join q_f, where the only possible output letter is b_0, we deduce that $v_1 = v_2$.
   (b) $u * v_1$ is accepted in q_f, while $u * v_2$ is accepted in P' (the case where v_1 and v_2 are interchanged is symmetrical): Consider the accepting run of $u * v_1$ in A and let $q_1 \in Q^T$ be the last state of Q^T before reaching q_f. Let $u_1 * v_1'$ be the prefix of $u * v_1$ that corresponds to q_1. Let $u = u_1 \cdot a \cdot u_1'$ with $a \in \Sigma$ and $u_1' \in \Sigma^*$. By construction of q_1, there is a transition from q_1 to q_f whose input letter is a. However, this is a contradiction, as $u_1 \cdot a \in P$.
   (c) $u*v_1$ and $u*v_2$ are both accepted in P'. P' has been built as a functional relation, therefore we must have $v_1 = v_2$.
2. Let $u \in \Sigma^*$. We want to prove that there exists $v \in \Gamma^*$ such that $u*v \in A$. Let $u = u' \cdot u''$ where u' is the longest prefix of u that belongs to P. Let $v' \in \Gamma^*$ be the unique word such that $u' * v' \in P'$. By defining $v = v' \cdot (b_0)^{|u''|}$, and by construction of A, we have $u * v \in A$.
3. Since A is obtained from T by adding one state, some transitions, and by making some states accepting, we have $\mathcal{L}(T) \subseteq \mathcal{L}(A)$. Moreover, by construction of T, we have $E = \mathcal{L}(T)$, so we have $E \subseteq \mathcal{L}(A)$.

Checking whether a DFA A is a total f-NDMM can be done in polynomial time, as shown in Lemma 4. In addition, checking whether an f-NDMM A is consistent with E, can be done by doing membership checks $w \in A$ for each $w \in E$.

Lemma 4. *Let A be a DFA over the alphabet $\Sigma \times \Gamma$. We can check in polynomial time whether A is a total f-NDMM.*

Proof. Let A' be the projection of A over the input part of the alphabet Σ. The output-uniqueness property of A is equivalent to the fact that A' is unambiguous. Checking whether an NFA is unambiguous can be done in polynomial time [23].

For the output existence property, we check whether $\Sigma^* = A'$, which can be done in polynomial time [25] since A' has been verified to be unambiguous.

Using these lemmas, we conclude with the main result of this section.

Theorem 4. *The minimization Problems (1, 2, and 4) can be solved in NP.*

8   Algorithm for Solving the Minimization Problem

8.1   Description of the Algorithm

The algorithm given in the previous section is not applicable in practice, as it requires *guessing* a total f-NDMM that satisfies the constraints. On a computer, this would require enumerating all automata of a certain size until we find one that satisfies the constraints.

In this section, we instead propose to encode the constraints in a logical formula, and let an SMT solver check satisfiability of the formula. More precisely, given a set of input/output examples $E \subseteq (\Sigma \times \Gamma)^*$, and $k \geq 1$, we define a formula $\varphi_{E,k}$ which is satisfiable if and only if there exists a total f-NDMM with k states and that is consistent with E.

Then, in order to find the minimal total f-NDMM with a given set of examples E, our algorithm checks satisfiability of $\varphi_{E,1}$, then $\varphi_{E,2}$, and so on, until one of the formula is satisfiable and the automaton is found.

Encoding all the constraints of the problem in a logical formula is challenging. The main reason is that SMT solver are best suited for dealing with logical formula written in purely existential form, while the constraints that we want to express (totality and output-uniqueness for f-NDMMs) are naturally expressed using alternations between *for all* and *exists* quantifiers. Still, we were able to find a purely existential encoding of the problem, in (quantifier-free) linear arithmetic, which we describe below.

8.2   Encoding

The free variables of $\varphi_{E,k}$ are (bounded) integers and booleans. They are setup so that a valuation of the free variables represent an f-NDMM $(\Sigma \times \Gamma, Q, q_{init}, \delta, F)$

with k states ($Q = \{q_0, \ldots, q_{k-1}\}$). More precisely, $\varphi_{E,k}$ contains for every $q \in Q$ and $\sigma \in \Sigma, \gamma \in \Gamma$, a integer variable

$$0 \leq \delta_{(q,\sigma,\gamma)} < k$$

to represent the value $\delta(q, (\sigma, \gamma))$.

For each state $q \in Q$, $\varphi_{E,k}$ also contains a boolean variable $\mathsf{isFinal}_q$ which is true when state $q \in F$. By convention, q_0 is the initial state, and q_{k-1} is the (non-accepting) sink state.

For states $p, q \in Q$ and input letter $\sigma \in \Sigma$, we also add boolean variables $\delta_{in}^{p,\sigma,q}$ describing the transition relation of the projection A' of A over the input alphabet Σ. The variable δ_{in} is expressed as a relation rather than as a function, since in general, A' can be non-deterministic.

The formula $\varphi_{E,k}$ is then composed of multiple components:

$$\mathsf{AcceptExamples} \wedge \mathsf{Projection} \wedge \mathsf{Unambiguous} \wedge \mathsf{Total}.$$

The formula $\mathsf{AcceptExamples}$ constrains the variables $\delta_{(q,\sigma,\gamma)}$ and $\mathsf{isFinal}_q$ ($q \in Q, \sigma \in \Sigma, \gamma \in \Gamma$) to make sure that every input/output example in E is accepted by A.

The formula $\mathsf{Projection}$ ensures that the variable $\delta_{in}^{p,\sigma,q}$ indeed represents the projection of δ on the input alphabet Σ.

The formulas $\mathsf{Unambiguous}$ and Total correspond to the approach described in Lemma 4. The formula $\mathsf{Unambiguous}$ is a constraint over the variables $\delta_{in}^{p,\sigma,q}$ and $\mathsf{isFinal}_q$. It states that A' is a UFA, which ensures that A accepts every input word at most once. Being unambiguous is naturally stated using quantifiers: for every word w, if w is accepted by two runs r_1 and r_2 in A', then r_1 and r_2 must be identical runs (i.e. going through identical states). However, writing this condition as is would make it hard for the SMT solver to check satisfiability of the formula, due to the universal quantification.

Instead, our formula $\mathsf{Unambiguous}$ is inspired from the algorithm that checks whether a given NFA is unambiguous [23]. This algorithm constructs inductively the pairs of states (q_i, q_j) that are reachable by the same word, but with distinct runs. Then, the NFA is unambiguous if and only if there are no pairs (q, q') in that inductive construction where q and q' are both final states.

The construction starts with the empty set, and adds, for each state q which is reachable, and for every letter $a \in \Sigma$, the pairs (q_1, q_2), with $q_1 \neq q_2$ such that $\delta_{in}(q, a, q_1)$ and $\delta_{in}(q, a, q_2)$ hold. Then, for every (q_i, q_j) and every $a \in \Sigma$, we add the pairs (q_i', q_j') such that $\delta_{in}(q_i, a, q_i')$ and $\delta_{in}(q_j, a, q_j')$ hold.

Therefore, to ensure the unambiguity A', the formula $\mathsf{Unambiguous}$ states that there exists a fixed point (a set of pairs of states represented by boolean variables $r_{q,q'}$ for $q, q' \in Q$) to that construction, i.e. a set which is closed under adding new pairs according to the rules above. Finally, for every $q, q' \in Q$, we add a clause stating that two final states should not belong to the fixed point:

$$\mathsf{isFinal}_q \wedge \mathsf{isFinal}_{q'} \implies \neg r_{q,q'}.$$

The formula Total is also a constraint over the variables $\delta_{in}^{p,\sigma,q}$ and isFinal$_q$., and states that A' recognizes every string in Σ^*. This ensures that the f-NDMM A accepts every input string at least once. Again, this constraint is naturally expressed using quantifiers: for every word w, there exists a run for w in A'. Such formulas are challenging for SMT solvers. Instead, our formula relies on the fact that A' is ensured to be unambiguous by the formula Unambiguous. More precisely, to check that A' accepts every string of Σ^*, it suffices to check that A' has $|\Sigma|^l$ accepting runs, for every $l \geq 0$. Moreover, it was shown that it is enough to do this check for $l \leq |Q|$ (see [25]).

Our formula Total introduces free variables $c_{l,q}$, for each $0 \leq l \leq |Q|$, and $q \in Q$, and constrains them so that they count how many runs of length l end in state q. By definition, the variable c_{0,q_0} equals 1 (only one word of length 0 is accepted in the initial state), and every other c_{0,q_i} ($i > 0$) equals 0 (the empty word is not accepted in non-initial states).

Then, using a linear arithmetic formula, we express every $c_{l,q}$ (with $l > 0$) in terms of the variables $c_{l-1,p}$ for $p \in Q$:

$$c_{l,q} = \sum_{\sigma \in \Sigma, p \in Q} \text{if } \delta_{in}^{p,\sigma,q} \text{ then } c_{l-1,p} \text{ else } 0.$$

Total then states, again using linear constraints, that for every $0 \leq l \leq |Q|$, the number of accepting runs of length l equals $|\Sigma|^l$, i.e.

$$\sum_{q \in Q} \text{if isFinal}_q \text{ then } c_{l,q} \text{ else } 0 = |\Sigma|^l.$$

9   Experimental Evaluation

We implemented our algorithm in Scala, using Z3 [19] as our backend.

9.1   Discovering Small Automata for Common Functions

We give in this section a few examples that we ran using our algorithm. We focus on examples that have small automata, whether or not the input examples are small. Indeed, the combinatorial explosion makes it hard for the SMT solver to find solutions for automata that have more than ~10 states. The results are shown in Fig. 4. The arithmetic examples operate on binary representations of numbers, truncating the output to the length of inputs where needed. We note that simple relations such as addition are recovered from examples without the need to specify any expression grammars as in Syntax-Guided Synthesis [2], because automaton minimality provides the needed bias towards simple solutions. Adding more examples than needed (e.g. 22 examples of length 22) keeps the synthesis time manageable, which is useful for cases of automatically generated examples.

We give in the last column (Time2) of the table the times for an enumeration algorithm which does not use SMT solvers. Our algorithm enumerates all transducers by order of the number of states, and prune the search when it encounters

Problem	#Ex.	Ex.Len.	States	Alphabet	Time (s)	Time2 (s)
$x, y \mapsto x+y$	1	17	3	8	0.23	1.090
$x, y \mapsto x+y$	5	4	3	8	0.20	0.090
$x, y \mapsto x+y$	22	22	3	8	0.19	17.610
xor	1	4	2	8	0.07	0.002
and	1	4	2	8	0.08	0.004
or	1	4	2	8	0.05	0.002
not	1	4	2	4	0.06	0.002
$x \mapsto 2x + 1$	1	5	3	4	0.41	0.160
$(p \vee q) \wedge (r \vee s) \wedge \neg t$	1	32	2	64	0.14	3.960
$(p \vee q) \wedge (r \vee s) \wedge \neg t$	32	1	2	64	0.14	0.240
overwrite	10	2	6	4	0.42	0.150
overwrite (3)	39	3	8	9	4.41	4.310

Fig. 4. Synthesis of some common functions from examples, showing successful discovery of minimal automata and tolerance to many long examples and larger alphabets.

transducers that are not compatible with the input/output examples. When we find a transducer that accepts all input/output examples, we use a *completion* procedure to attempt to make the transducer total by adding transitions. Our implementation should not be considered heavily optimized; we believe that there is space for improvement both in terms of internal data structures and heuristics.

9.2   Evaluating Usefulness of Minimality on Random Automata

The next set of experiments evaluate the likelihood that our algorithm finds the automaton that the user has is mind, depending on the number and size of the input/output examples provided. We generated 100 random minimal total f-NDMMs with 5 states, where the input and output alphabet were both of size 2. For each f-NDMM A, and for every $1 \leq i, j \leq 15$, we generated i random words in Σ^*, of length j. For each such word, we looked up the corresponding output in A, thereby constructing a set of input/output examples E for A. Then, we used our algorithm on E to see whether the obtained automaton would be A. In Table 2, we summarized, for every i and j, out of the 100 automata, how many we were able to reobtain using that method. Overall, the experiments ran for about 3 h, for $15 * 15 * 100 = 22500$ queries. The 3 h also include the time taken to generate the random automata. To generate a random minimal total f-NDMM, we generated a random sample, and applied our algorithm. Then, if the obtained automaton had 5 states, we kept it for our experiment. Our selection for the choice of the random automata is therefore biased, as the automata are found by our tool in the first place.

Discussion. Generally, the results show that the greater the number of examples given, and the longer they are, the more likely we are to find the automaton that we want. More interestingly, we note that we are more likely to find the

Table 2. In a given cell, the number represents, out of 100 random automata, how many we were able to reobtain using our algorithm, with a random sample with i input/output examples of length j.

i \ j	1	2	3	4	5	6	7	8	9	10	11	12	13	14	15
1	0	0	0	0	0	0	0	0	0	0	1	1	1	1	0
2	0	0	0	0	0	0	5	3	8	16	21	16	15	18	22
3	0	0	0	3	1	10	16	32	24	36	35	33	44	44	41
4	0	0	4	7	20	25	37	45	51	53	52	52	51	56	65
5	0	0	6	20	35	46	57	63	59	64	67	62	60	60	64
6	0	0	8	34	43	59	58	67	60	73	75	68	67	66	69
7	0	0	17	37	61	65	70	70	81	76	78	72	75	73	75
8	0	0	22	46	74	79	73	77	78	79	74	77	75	76	78
9	0	0	22	63	67	76	86	80	78	79	82	83	84	82	80
10	0	0	34	59	72	82	86	81	85	80	79	83	84	84	84
11	0	0	36	73	82	86	83	85	85	89	88	86	91	82	83
12	0	0	32	66	86	83	83	86	88	85	86	87	89	88	88
13	0	0	41	83	85	85	89	87	89	85	93	89	88	89	89
14	0	0	41	78	83	88	93	93	92	88	88	87	88	88	91
15	0	0	51	83	87	87	88	84	91	87	91	91	90	87	88

automaton we want with a large number of small examples (e.g. $i = 15, j = 5$) than with a small number of large examples (e.g. $i = 5, j = 15$).

Another interesting observation is that the likelihood of finding the automaton increases sharply when using examples of size $j = 4$ rather than $j = 3$. Without counting the sink state, the automata we considered have 4 states. This suggests that in general, a good strategy is to give multiple examples which are at most as long as the number of states (though the user giving the examples may not know how many states are required for the minimal automaton).

10 Related Work

In [16], we studied the problem of synthesizing tree-to-string transducers from examples. Here, instead of having the user provide input/output examples, we proposed an algorithm that generates particular inputs, and asks the user what are the corresponding outputs. We show that, when the algorithm is allowed to analyze previous answers in order to generate the next question, then the number of questions required to determine the transducer that the user has in mind is greatly reduced (compared to an approach without interaction, where the algorithm would ask for all outputs at once).

The results obtained in [16] do not directly apply here, as they were for single-state transducers. However, some of the techniques are fundamental and could be reused here. In that respect, we could generate questions for the users, and guarantee that the generated f-NDMM is indeed the one that the user had in mind (given some bound on the number of states).

Our paper is similar in spirit to [10], where the author proves that Problem 2 is NP-complete for *deterministic* Mealy machines. Their NP-hardness holds even when the alphabets' sizes are fixed to 2, but the case where the number of states is fixed is not treated. Moroever, even though f-NDMMs are a more general model than deterministic Mealy machines, the NP-hardness of [10] cannot be directly applied to f-NDMMs.

There is a long line of work devoted to learning *deterministic* finite state transducers (see e.g. [1,6,18,20]). Algorithms for learning deterministic finite automata (e.g. [4]) or finite transducers do not directly translate to our setting, since we need to consider functionality and totality constraints, as shown in Sect. 8.2. Methods for learning non-deterministic automata (e.g. [7]) do not directly apply to our setting either, for the same reasons.

A particular case of learning transducers is an interpolation problem, that consists in learning a finite automaton that accepts some given inputs (i.e. outputs 1) and rejects some other inputs (i.e. outputs 0) (see e.g. [8,11,21]).

In [15], the authors present an algorithm for learning *non-deterministic* Mealy machines. They are interested in non-determinism to represent unknown components of reactive systems, and as such do not focus on *functional* non-deterministic Mealy machines. Moreover, their focus is rather on the algorithmic aspect of the problem rather than on complexity classes.

In [12], the author proposes an efficient synthesis procedure from examples for a language that does string transformations, but does not deal with the issue of synthesizing finite-state transducers.

Our algorithm in Sect. 8 is inspired from the bounded synthesis approach of [9]. There, the authors suggest that bounding the number of states is a good strategy to synthesize reactive systems. They also propose a reduction from the bounded synthesis problem for reactive systems to SMT solvers.

In [13], we presented a way to synthesize string-to-string functions given any specification written in weak monadic second-order logic. Using these techniques, it would be possible to synthesize an f-NDMM consistent with input/output examples, by writing the input/output examples as a logical formula. However, this approach would not yield the minimal f-NDMM consistent with the examples. For example, regardless of how many input/output examples we give for the function $(\{0,1\} \times \{0,1\})^* \to \{0,1\}^*$ which xor's two streams of bits, this approach would not yield the 1-state automaton that we are expecting. Instead, the method will generate large automata that are consistent with the given examples, but do not recognize the xor operation for other input strings. On the other hand, our approach can find this automaton with only a few small examples.

The automata we consider in this paper are closely related to the notion of *thin language* (see e.g. [22]). A language L is called thin if for every $n \in \mathbb{N}$, it contains at most one word of length n. Moreover, L is called length-complete if for every $n \in \mathbb{N}$, L contains at least one word of length n. When $|\Sigma| = 1$, i.e. when only the length of the input matters, our minimization problem corresponds exactly to finding a minimal DFA that contains a given set of examples, which is both thin and length-complete. We left this question open in Sect. 3.1, and leave it for future work. This analogy with thin languages breaks when using a non-unary input alphabet.

In [24], the authors encode the problem of learning DFAs in an SMT solver. As is the case with our algorithm, such encodings only perform well for finding automata with a small number of states (up to 10 or 15).

11 Conclusions

f-NDMMs are a form of functional non-deterministic one-way finite-state transducers (see e.g. [5,23]) where each transition is forced to produce exactly one letter (instead of 0 or more in the general case). The term functional corresponds to the output uniqueness property of f-NDMMs, and ensures that despite the non-determinism, at most one output string is produced for each input string. The non-determinism here refers to the input part of the alphabet, and f-NDMMs, even though they are deterministic on $\Sigma \times \Gamma$, can indeed be non-deterministic in the input alphabet Σ. In that sense, f-NDMMs can define transformations that are not captured by deterministic one-way transducers, such as the function that maps a word w to $l^{|w|}$ where l is the last letter of w. On the other hand, deterministic one-way transducers can recognize transformations not recognized by f-NDMMs, since they do not require the output to have the same length as the input. This can be circumvented by padding the input and output strings using a dummy letter. Existing synthesis algorithms generally target classes of deterministic transducers, such as subsequential transducers (see e.g. [26]). Our results about f-NDMMs are a first step towards synthesis algorithm for larger classes of deterministic or functional non-deterministic transducers, such as two-way finite-state transducers, or streaming string transducers [3]. We have shown that most variants of synthesis for f-NDMMs are NP-complete, and presented a promising approach using an encoding into SMT formulas.

Acknowledgement. We thank Rupak Majumdar for references on hardness of the interpolation problem in the settings of automata. We thank anonymous reviewers of previous submissions for their thorough comments and for relevant references related to learning finite automata and regarding the interpolation problem.

References

1. Aarts, F., Kuppens, H., Tretmans, J., Vaandrager, F.W., Verwer, S.: Improving active mealy machine learning for protocol conformance testing. Mach. Learn. **96**(1–2), 189–224 (2014). https://doi.org/10.1007/s10994-013-5405-0
2. Alur, R., et al.: Syntax-guided synthesis. In: Formal Methods in Computer-Aided Design (FMCAD), pp. 1–17. IEEE (2013)
3. Alur, R., Cerný, P.: Expressiveness of streaming string transducers. In: Lodaya, K., Mahajan, M. (eds.) IARCS Annual Conference on Foundations of Software Technology and Theoretical Computer Science, FSTTCS 2010. LIPIcs, Chennai, India, 15–18 December 2010, vol. 8, pp. 1–12. Schloss Dagstuhl - Leibniz-Zentrum fuer Informatik (2010)

4. Angluin, D.: Learning regular sets from queries and counterexamples. Inf. Comput. **75**, 87–106 (1987)

5. Berstel, J.: Transductions and Context-Free Languages. Teubner Studienbücher: Informatik, vol. 38. Teubner, Stuttgart (1979). http://www.worldcat.org/oclc/06364613

6. Bojańczyk, M.: Transducers with origin information. In: Esparza, J., Fraigniaud, P., Husfeldt, T., Koutsoupias, E. (eds.) ICALP 2014. LNCS, vol. 8573, pp. 26–37. Springer, Heidelberg (2014). https://doi.org/10.1007/978-3-662-43951-7_3

7. Bollig, B., Habermehl, P., Kern, C., Leucker, M.: Angluin-style learning of NFA. In: Boutilier, C. (ed.) IJCAI 2009, Proceedings of the 21st International Joint Conference on Artificial Intelligence, Pasadena, California, USA, 11–17 July 2009, pp. 1004–1009 (2009). http://ijcai.org/Proceedings/09/Papers/170.pdf

8. Chen, Y.-F., Farzan, A., Clarke, E.M., Tsay, Y.-K., Wang, B.-Y.: Learning minimal separating DFA's for compositional verification. In: Kowalewski, S., Philippou, A. (eds.) TACAS 2009. LNCS, vol. 5505, pp. 31–45. Springer, Heidelberg (2009). https://doi.org/10.1007/978-3-642-00768-2_3

9. Finkbeiner, B., Schewe, S.: Bounded synthesis. STTT **15**(5–6), 519–539 (2013). https://doi.org/10.1007/s10009-012-0228-z

10. Gold, E.M.: Complexity of automaton identification from given data. Inf. Control **37**(3), 302–320 (1978). https://doi.org/10.1016/S0019-9958(78)90562-4

11. Grinchtein, O., Leucker, M., Piterman, N.: Inferring network invariants automatically. In: Furbach, U., Shankar, N. (eds.) IJCAR 2006. LNCS (LNAI), vol. 4130, pp. 483–497. Springer, Heidelberg (2006). https://doi.org/10.1007/11814771_40

12. Gulwani, S.: Automating string processing in spreadsheets using input-output examples. In: Ball, T., Sagiv, M. (eds.) Proceedings of the 38th ACM SIGPLAN-SIGACT Symposium on Principles of Programming Languages, POPL 2011, Austin, TX, USA, 26–28 January 2011, pp. 317–330. ACM (2011). https://doi.org/10.1145/1926385.1926423

13. Hamza, J., Jobstmann, B., Kuncak, V.: Synthesis for regular specifications over unbounded domains. In: Bloem, R., Sharygina, N. (eds.) Proceedings of 10th International Conference on Formal Methods in Computer-Aided Design, FMCAD 2010, Lugano, Switzerland, 20–23 October, pp. 101–109. IEEE (2010). http://ieeexplore.ieee.org/document/5770938/

14. Hamza, J., Kuncak, V.: Minimal synthesis of string to string functions from examples. CoRR abs/1710.09208 (2017). http://arxiv.org/abs/1710.09208

15. Khalili, A., Tacchella, A.: Learning nondeterministic mealy machines. In: Clark, A., Kanazawa, M., Yoshinaka, R. (eds.) Proceedings of the 12th International Conference on Grammatical Inference, ICGI 2014. JMLR Workshop and Conference Proceedings, Kyoto, Japan, 17–19 September 2014, vol. 34, pp. 109–123. JMLR.org (2014). http://jmlr.org/proceedings/papers/v34/khalili14a.html

16. Mayer, M., Hamza, J., Kuncak, V.: Proactive synthesis of recursive tree-to-string functions from examples. In: Müller, P. (ed.) 31st European Conference on Object-Oriented Programming, ECOOP 2017. LIPIcs, Barcelona, Spain, 19–23 June 2017, vol. 74, pp. 19:1–19:30. Schloss Dagstuhl - Leibniz-Zentrum fuer Informatik (2017). https://doi.org/10.4230/LIPIcs.ECOOP.2017.19

17. Mealy, G.H.: A method for synthesizing sequential circuits. Bell Labs Tech. J. **34**(5), 1045–1079 (1955)

18. Merten, M.: Active automata learning for real life applications. Ph.D. thesis, Dortmund University of Technology (2013). http://hdl.handle.net/2003/29884

19. de Moura, L., Bjørner, N.: Z3: an efficient SMT solver. In: Ramakrishnan, C.R., Rehof, J. (eds.) TACAS 2008. LNCS, vol. 4963, pp. 337–340. Springer, Heidelberg (2008). https://doi.org/10.1007/978-3-540-78800-3_24

20. Oncina, J., García, P., Vidal, E.: Learning subsequential transducers for pattern recognition interpretation tasks. IEEE Trans. Pattern Anal. Mach. Intell. **15**(5), 448–458 (1993). https://doi.org/10.1109/34.211465

21. Pitt, L., Warmuth, M.K.: The minimum consistent DFA problem cannot be approximated within any polynomial. J. ACM **40**(1), 95–142 (1993). https://doi.org/10.1145/138027.138042

22. Păun, G., Salomaa, A.: Thin and slender languages. Discrete Appl. Math. **61**(3), 257–270 (1995). https://doi.org/10.1016/0166-218X(94)00014-5

23. Sakarovitch, J.: Elements of Automata Theory. Cambridge University Press, Cambridge (2009). http://www.cambridge.org/uk/catalogue/catalogue.asp?isbn=9780521844253

24. Smetsers, R., Fiterău-Broștean, P., Vaandrager, F.: Model learning as a satisfiability modulo theories problem. In: Klein, S.T., Martín-Vide, C., Shapira, D. (eds.) LATA 2018. LNCS, vol. 10792, pp. 182–194. Springer, Cham (2018). https://doi.org/10.1007/978-3-319-77313-1_14

25. Stearns, R.E., Hunt III, B.H.: On the equivalence and containment problems for unambiguous regular expressions, regular grammars and finite automata. SIAM J. Comput. **14**(3), 598–611 (1985). https://doi.org/10.1137/0214044

26. Vilar, J.M.: Query learning of subsequential transducers. In: Miclet, L., de la Higuera, C. (eds.) ICGI 1996. LNCS, vol. 1147, pp. 72–83. Springer, Heidelberg (1996). https://doi.org/10.1007/BFb0033343

Automatic Program Repair Using Formal Verification and Expression Templates

Thanh-Toan Nguyen$^{(\boxtimes)}$, Quang-Trung Ta, and Wei-Ngan Chin

School of Computing, National University of Singapore, Singapore, Singapore
{toannt,taqt,chinwn}@comp.nus.edu.sg

Abstract. We present an automated approach to repair programs using formal verification and expression templates. In our approach, an input program is first verified against its formal specification to discover potentially buggy statements. For each of these statements, we identify the expression that needs to be repaired and set up a template patch which is a linear expression composed of the program's variables and unknown coefficients. Then, we analyze the template-patched program against the original specification to collect a set of constraints of the template patch. This constraint set will be solved by a constraint solving technique using Farkas' lemma to identify the unknown coefficients, consequently discovering the actual patch. We implement our approach in a tool called Maple and evaluate it with various buggy programs from a widely used benchmark TCAS, and a synthetic yet challenging benchmark containing recursive programs. Our tool can quickly discover the correct patches and outperforms the state-of-the-art program repair tools.

1 Introduction

The last decade has witnessed the rapid development of automatic program repair, an active research area in computer science [19]. The goal of this research field is to automatically generate patches to fix bugs in software programs. Researchers have applied a common approach which uses test suites to localize bugs, and then generate and validate patches. This test-suite-based method is used by many works, such as [11,14,15,17]. However, this approach might produce *overfitting patches*: fixes that can pass all test cases, but also might break untested yet desired functionality of programs. Therefore, the quality of output patches often depends on the coverage of the provided test suites [22].

To avoid the above limitation of the test-suite-based approach, other researchers proposed to leverage formal specification to guide the repair process. This approach is used in several works like [8,9,13,18,21,25]. In this method, the correctness of a program can be specified by logical formulas, which appear in forms of pre-conditions, post-conditions, assertions, and invariants. Then, a deductive verification system is deployed to check the input program against its provided specifications to localize bugs and generate patches. In comparison to the test-suite-based approach, the formal-specification-based method provides

© Springer Nature Switzerland AG 2019
C. Enea and R. Piskac (Eds.): VMCAI 2019, LNCS 11388, pp. 70–91, 2019.
https://doi.org/10.1007/978-3-030-11245-5_4

better coverage on the relation of the program's input/output. However, the current solutions to generate patches are still limited. For example, Rothenberg and Grumberg [21] use simple code mutations to generate patches while Kneuss et al. [8] need the tests of corner cases to repair functional programs.

In this work, we follow the formal-specification-based approach to repair faulty C programs. We propose a general solution to discover patches by using expression templates and constraint solving. Our method is summarized as follows. We first invoke a deductive system to verify an input program against its specification. If this program fails to meet its specification, we obtain a set of invalid proof obligations, which can be utilized to locate potentially buggy statements. Here, we consider the bug type related to arithmetic expression, which can be the test expression of a branching or a loop statement, or the expression in the right hand side of an assignment. We replace each possibly buggy expression by a template patch which is a linear expression of the program's variables and unknown coefficients to create a template program. This program will be analyzed against the original specification to collect a set of proof obligations containing the template patch. These proof obligations will be solved to determine the actual values of the unknown coefficients, thus discover the repaired program.

Contributions. Our work makes the following contributions.

- We propose an automatic framework to repair programs using formal specification and expression templates. The use of formal verification enables our framework to locate buggy statements faster and more precise than other testing-based approaches.
- We propose a novel method to generate program patches using expression templates and constraint solving. Our solution is more general than existing approaches that perform only simple code mutations.
- We implement the proposed approach in a tool, called Maple, and experiment with it on a widely used benchmark named TCAS and a challenging synthetic benchmark of recursive programs. Our tool can repair a majority of the programs in these benchmarks and outperforms the state-of-the-art program repair tools. Moreover, it does not introduce any overfitting patch.

2   Motivating Example

We consider a simple C program sum which computes the sum of all natural numbers from 0 to a given input number n (Fig. 2). This program is specified by a pair of pre-condition and post-condition, captured by keywords requires/ensures (lines 2, 3). In essence, this specification indicates that given a non-negative input n, or $n \geq 0$, the expected output, represented by the variable res, is $n \cdot (n + 1)/2$.

The body of sum is implemented in a recursive fashion (lines 4–10). In the base case, when the input n is 0, this program returns 0 (line 5). Otherwise, in the recursive case, it first computes the sum s of all natural numbers from 0 to n − 1 (line 7), and adds 2 ∗ n to that sum (line 8). However, this implementation of the recursive case is *buggy*. In line 8, by adding 2 ∗ n to s, the final result of the procedure sum(n) cannot be equal to n · (n + 1)/2, as specified in the post-condition (line 3).

```
1: int sum(int n)
2: //@ requires n ≥ 0
3: //@ ensures res = n·(n + 1)/2
4: {
5:     if (n == 0) return 0;
6:     else {
7:         int s = sum(n − 1);
8:         return 2 ∗ n + s;
9:     }
10: }
```

Fig. 1. A faulty C program

Given the specification in lines 2, 3, existing verification tools such as [1,12] can easily detect the bug at line 8. However, these tools do not support repairing faulty programs. Moreover, repairing this bug is challenging, and the state-of-the-art program repair tools cannot discover a patch that replaces 2 ∗ n by n. There are two reasons as follows. Firstly, this patch cannot be discovered by the technique that performs simple code mutation [21], since it does not consider mutating the variables' coefficients. Even if the coefficient mutation is supported, it is still impractical to discover the correct patch since the number of possible values for these coefficients is infinite. Secondly, the program sum contains a recursive call, which is challenging for the test-suite-based methods [11,15]. For instance, genetic programming operators used by GenProg [11], such as deletion, swap, or insertion, suffer the same difficulty as the mutation-based counterpart in finding the correct coefficients.

We observe that the desired patch should be an expression of some variables in the program. In particular, it can be an expression of at most two variables s and n. Here, we focus on finding the patch in form of a *linear expression*. Therefore, we denote the desired patch by an expression $f(s, n) \triangleq c_1 * s + c_2 * n + c_3$, where c_1, c_2, c_3 are some unknown integer coefficients.

Now, we can apply standard verification techniques [1,12] to collect the proof obligations about $f(s, n)$, which need to be valid so

```
1: int sum(int n)
2: //@ requires n ≥ 0
3: //@ ensures res = n·(n + 1)/2
4: {
5:     if (n == 0) return 0;
6:     else {
7:         int s = sum(n − 1);
8:         return f(s, n); // a template fix
9:     }
10: }
```

Fig. 2. A template fix for the program sum

that the program satisfies its specification. These proof obligations will be solved to discover the actual values of the unknown coefficients c_1, c_2, c_3. We will elaborate the details in Sect. 4.

3 Background

In this section, we represent the background of the formal verification of software. We target to the class of C programs that performs logical and arithmetic computations. The program syntax can be referred to in the C11 standard [6]. In our approach, the functional correctness of a program is represented by a specification, which are logical formulas preceded by the special string "//@", as shown in the motivating example in Fig. 2.

Our specification language is presented in Fig. 3. We write c, x to denote an integer constant, variable, and res is a special variable representing the output of a procedure. The expression e is constructed using basic arithmetic operations: addition, subtraction, multiplication, division. We write P to indicate a first-order logic formula, which is composed of equality and arithmetic constraints, using standard logical connectives and quantifications. Finally, S denotes a specification which is either a pair of pre-condition and post-condition of a procedure (preceded by the keywords **requires** and **ensures**) or an invariant of a loop statement (preceded by the keyword **invariant**).

$$e ::= c \mid x \mid res \mid -e \mid e_1 + e_2 \mid e_1 - e_2 \mid e_1 \cdot e_2 \mid e_1 / e_2$$
$$P ::= \text{true} \mid \text{false} \mid e_1 = e_2 \mid e_1 \neq e_2 \mid e_1 > e_2 \mid e_1 \geq e_2 \mid e_1 < e_2 \mid e_1 \leq e_2$$
$$\mid \neg P \mid P_1 \wedge P_2 \mid P_1 \vee P_2 \mid P_1 \rightarrow P_2 \mid \forall x.P \mid \exists x.P$$
$$S ::= \text{requires } P_1 \text{ ensures } P_2 \mid \text{invariant } P$$

Fig. 3. Syntax of the specification language

We follow the literature to use Hoare logic [4] to verify the functional correctness of a program against its specification. The heart of this logic is a Hoare triple $\{P\}$ C $\{Q\}$ which describes how a program changes its state during the execution. Here P and Q are two assertions, representing the pre-condition and post-condition of the program C. In essence, the Hoare triple $\{P\}$ C $\{Q\}$ states that for a given program state satisfying P, if the program C executes and terminates, then the new program state will satisfy Q.

Hoare logic provides inference rules for all the constructs of an imperative programming language. They include the rules handling assignment, sequential composition of statements, branching statements, function call, etc. These rules are standard and can be found in many works in the field of program verification, such as [4,5]. For example, the rule for the composition of statements and the if statement are presented in Fig. 4. Interested readers can refer to [5] for more Hoare rules.

$$\frac{\{P\}\ \mathtt{C_1}\ \{Q\}\quad \{Q\}\ \mathtt{C_2}\ \{R\}}{\{P\}\ \ \mathtt{C_1;C_2}\ \{R\}}\ \mathtt{composition}\qquad \frac{\{P \wedge R\}\ \mathtt{C_1}\ \{Q\}\quad \{P \wedge \neg R\}\ \mathtt{C_2}\ \{Q\}}{\{P\}\ \mathtt{if}\ (R)\ \mathtt{C_1}\ \mathtt{else}\ \mathtt{C_2}\ \{Q\}}\ \mathtt{if}$$

Fig. 4. Examples of Hoare rules

4 Our Approach to Repair Faulty Programs

We now elaborate our program repair approach. The workflow is illustrated in Fig. 5. Given a program and its specification, we verify the program symbolically, using Hoare logic, to determine whether it behaves correctly w.r.t. its specification. If the verification step fails, we localize the possibly buggy statements and create possible template patches, which are linear expressions of the program's variables with unknown coefficients. Each of the template-patched programs will be verified again to collect a set of constraints (proof obligations) over the corresponding template patch. Then, this constraint set will be solved by a constraint solving technique using Farkas' lemma to discover the unknown coeffients of the template patch. If a solution of these coeffients can be found, then a candidate patch to repair the program is obtained. This candidate will be validated against the specification to determine if it is the actual patch. If the selected buggy statement cannot be repaired, then the next possibly buggy statement will be examined.

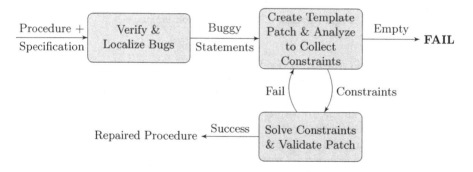

Fig. 5. Overview of Repair Procedure

In the next three Sects. 4.1, 4.2 and 4.3, we will describe the main components of our framework that verify and localize bug, create template patch and collect constraints, and solve constraints. Then, we will summarize our approach using a pseudo code algorithm in Sect. 4.4 and discuss its soundness in Sect. 4.5.

4.1 Verifying Programs and Localizing Bugs

We follow the literature to apply Hoare logic to verify programs and localize bugs. This approach is well-known and has been described in many works, such as [5]. We briefly summarize it as follows.

Program Verification. When symbolically analyzing a procedure of a program against its specification, we first assign its pre-condition to the initial program state of that procedure. Then, the program state after executing each statement of the procedure will be computed using the Hoare rules. Note that for each function call, the callee will not be analyzed directly. Instead, its specification will verified and utilized to update the program state of the caller.

For each loop statement of the procedure, we need to check if the program states at the entry and the exit of the loop imply the loop invariant. Similarly, for each **return** statement, we also need to check if the program state at the returned point implies the post-condition. The procedure is said to be *correct* w.r.t. its specification if all the aforementioned implications (proof obligations) can be proved valid. Otherwise, it is considered *buggy*.

For example, the verification of the program sum in Sect. 2 is presented in Fig. 6. We indicate the program states after executing each statement by the string "//". At the beginning, the initial program state is updated with the given pre-condition $n \geq 0$ (line 5). Then, the program executes the first branch of the if statement and the branching condition $n = 0$ is propagated (line 7).

```
 1: int sum(int n)
 2: //@ requires n≥0
 3: //@ ensures res = n·(n + 1)/2
 4: {
 5:     // n≥0                        (the initial program state is from the pre-condition)
 6:     if (n == 0)
 7:         // n≥0 ∧ n=0
 8:         return 0;
 9:         // n≥0 ∧ n=0 ∧ res=0               (the final program state)
10:         //                             ⇒ need to prove the post-condition:
11:         //                        n≥0 ∧ n=0 ∧ res=0 ⊢ res=n·(n+1)/2
12:     else {
13:         // n≥0 ∧ n≠0
14:         int s = sum(n − 1);
15:         // n≥0 ∧ n≠0 ∧ s=(n−1)·n/2         (use the post-condition of sum)
16:         return 2 ∗ n + s;
17:         // n≥0 ∧ n≠0 ∧ s=(n−1)·n/2 ∧ res=2·n+s     (the final program state)
18:         //                             ⇒ need to prove the post-condition:
19:         //          n≥0 ∧ n≠0 ∧ s=(n−1)·n/2 ∧ res=2·n+s ⊢ res=n·(n+1)/2
20:     }
21: }
```

Fig. 6. Verifying the motivating example

When the program exits (line 8), the constraint of the returned result $res = 0$ is accumulated to obtain the final program state $n \geq 0 \wedge n = 0 \wedge res = 0$. Now, the verification system needs to check if this program state implies the post-condition, that is, to prove the following entailment E_1:

$$E_1 \triangleq n \geq 0 \wedge n = 0 \wedge res = 0 \vdash res = n \cdot (n+1)/2$$

In our approach, the entailment E_1 can be easily proved by invoking an off-the-shelf SMT solver like Z3 [16]. In fact, this entailment is *valid* since the constraint $n = 0 \wedge res = 0$ in its antecedent implies the constraint $res = n \cdot (n + 1)/2$ in its consequent. Hence, this execution path of the if statement is considered correct w.r.t. the specification.

Similarly, when the program executes the else branch (line 12), the branching condition $n \neq 0$ is also propagated to the program state (line 13). When the recursive call sum(n − 1) is performed (line 14), the verification system checks if the current program state $n \geq 0 \wedge n \neq 0$ implies the pre-condition $n - 1 \geq 0$ of this function call. After that, the post-condition $s = (n - 1) \cdot n/2$ of this call will be accumulated into the current program state (line 15). When the program exits (line 16), the final program state is $n \geq 0 \wedge n \neq 0 \wedge s = (n-1) \cdot n/2 \wedge res = 2 \cdot n + s$. Again, the verification system also needs to check whether this program state implies the post-condition, resulting in the following entailment:

$$E_2 \triangleq n \geq 0 \wedge n \neq 0 \wedge s = (n - 1) \cdot n/2 \wedge res = 2 \cdot n + s \vdash res = n \cdot (n + 1)/2$$

However, this entailment is *invalid*, since its antecedent, which can be simplified to $n \geq 0 \wedge res = n \cdot (n+3)/2$, cannot prove its consequent $res = n \cdot (n+1)/2$. Consequently, there is a bug in this execution path of the program sum.

Bug Localization. Once the program is verified, we identify the invalid proof obligation to discover the buggy execution path. For example, the invalid proof obligation for the program sum (Fig. 6) is the entailment E_2 above. Thus, there is a bug in the execution path of the else branch.

In our implementation, we record the correspondence of the constraints in each proof obligation with the program specification and code. This record enables us to identify that the constraint $n \geq 0$ comes from the pre-condition (line 2, Fig. 6), $n \neq 0$ is from the if statement (line 6), etc. Using this record, we can simplify the antecedent of the invalid proof obligation by removing all constraints belonging to the program specification. The remaining constraints which correspond to the program code are the ones that cause the bug. For example, when removing the constraint $n \geq 0$ from E_2, we obtain the constraint F, which corresponds to all possible bugs of the program sum.

$$F \triangleq n \neq 0 \wedge s = (n - 1) \cdot n/2 \wedge res = 2 \cdot n + s$$

To make the bug localization more efficient, we rank the remaining constraints by their likelihood to trigger the bug. Our ranking heuristics are as follows.

– If a constraint has its corresponding program code which belongs to a correct execution path, then this constraint is less likely to cause the bug in other execution paths.

– If a constraint has the corresponding program code belonging to only the buggy execution path, then this constraint is more likely to cause the bug.

For example, the constraint $n \neq 0$ in F corresponds to the conditional statement if (n == 0) (line 6), which also belong the correct execution path related to the proof obligation E_1. Therefore, the likelihood to cause the bug of $n \neq 0$ is low.

The two constraints $s = (n - 1) \cdot n/2$ and $res = 2 \cdot n + s$ correspond to the function call sum(n − 1) (line 14) and the computation $2 * n + s$ (line 16). Since these two statements appear only in the execution path related to the invalid proof obligation E_2, their likelihoods to cause the bug are equally high.

4.2 Creating Template Patches and Analyzing Template Programs

For each possibly buggy expression discovered in the previous step, we substitute it by a linear template patch to create a template-patched program. In essence, a patch is a linear expressions of the program variables in the execution path leading to the bug with unknown coefficients (Definition 1). Then, each template-patched program will be verified against its specification to obtain a set of entailments (proof obligations) related to the expression template.

Definition 1 (Linear Expression Template). *A linear expression template for n variables $x_1, ..., x_n$, denoted as $f(x_1, ..., x_n)$, is an expression of the form $c_1 \cdot x_1 + ... + c_n \cdot x_n + c_{n+1}$, where $c_1, ..., c_n, c_{n+1}$ are unknown integer coefficients.*

For example, given the possibly buggy expression sum(n − 1) discovered in the previous section (line 14, Fig. 6), there exists only 1 variable n in the execution path leading to the function call sum(n − 1). Therefore, we can create a linear expression template $f(n) \triangleq c_1 \cdot n + c_2$, which replaces the expression $n - 1$ to create a patch sum(f(n)).

Similarly, given the possibly buggy expression $2 * n + s$ (line 16, Fig. 6), there exist two variables s, n involved in the corresponding execution path. Hence, we can create a template patch $f(s, n) \triangleq c_1 \cdot s + c_2 \cdot n + c_3$. We illustrate the template-patched program for this bug in Fig. 7.

After analyzing this program against its specification, we obtain a proof obligation set containing one entailment: $n \geq 0 \wedge n \neq 0 \wedge s = (n - 1) \cdot n/2 \wedge res = f(s, n) \vdash res = n \cdot (n + 1)/2$. This entailment can be rewritten as the entailment E_3 below by unfolding the definition of the expression template $f(s, n) \triangleq c_1 \cdot s + c_2 \cdot n + c_3$:

$$E_3 \triangleq n \geq 0 \wedge n \neq 0 \wedge s = (n - 1) \cdot n/2$$
$$\wedge\ res = c_1 \cdot s + c_2 \cdot n + c_3 \vdash res = n \cdot (n + 1)/2$$

```
 1: int sum(int n)
 2: //@ requires n≥0
 3: //@ ensures res = n·(n + 1)/2
 4: {
 5:     // n≥0                                           (the initial program state)
 6:     if (n == 0) return 0;
 7:     else {
 8:         // n≥0 ∧ n≠0
 9:         int s = sum(n − 1);
10:         // n≥0 ∧ n≠0 ∧ s=(n−1)·n/2
11:         return f(s,n);                              // a template patch
12:         // n≥0 ∧ n≠0 ∧ s=(n−1)·n/2 ∧ res=f(s,n)     (the final program state)
13:         //                                ⇒ need to prove the post-condition:
14:         //            n≥0 ∧ n≠0 ∧ s=(n−1)·n/2 ∧ res=f(s,n) ⊢ res=n·(n+1)/2
15:     }
16: }
```

Fig. 7. Verifying the template-patched program

4.3 Solving Constraints to Discover Repaired Programs

In this section, we will describe the underlying constraint solving technique using Farkas' lemma [2]. We first restate Farkas' lemma and then explain how it is applied to solve a set $\mathcal{E}$ of entailments (proof obligations) collected from the verification of template-patched programs.

Theorem 1 (Farkas' Lemma). *Given a system S of linear constraints over real-valued variables $x_1, ..., x_n$:*

$$S \triangleq \bigwedge_{j=1}^{m} \sum_{i=1}^{n} a_{ij} \cdot x_i + b_j \geq 0.$$

When S is satisfiable, it entails the following linear constraint ψ:

$$\psi \triangleq \sum_{i=1}^{n} c_i \cdot x_i + \gamma \geq 0$$

if and only if there exists non-negative numbers $\lambda_1, ..., \lambda_m$ such that

$$\bigwedge_{i=1}^{n} c_i = \sum_{j=1}^{m} \lambda_j \cdot a_{ij} \quad and \quad \sum_{j=1}^{m} \lambda_j \cdot b_j \leq \gamma$$

Given the set $\mathcal{E}$ of entailments, which contain unknown coefficients of the template patch, we can solve it in three steps:

– Normalize the entailments in $\mathcal{E}$ into entailments of the form $S \vdash \psi$, which satisfies the conditions of Farkas' lemma, where S is a conjunction of linear constraints, and ψ is a linear constraint.

- Apply Farkas' lemma to eliminate universal quantification to obtain new constraints with only existential quantification over the unknown coefficients and the factors λ_j.
- Solve the new constraints by an off-the-shelf prover, such as Z3 [16], to find the concrete values of the unknown coefficients in the template patch.

We now illustrate these 3 steps with the entailment E_3 collected in Sect. 4.2 to discover the unknown coefficients c_1, c_2, and c_3 of the expression template $f(s, n) \triangleq c_1 \cdot s + c_2 \cdot n + c_3$.

4.3.1 Normalizing the Entailments

In our work, the entailments obtained from the verification process might contain polynomial terms and equality/inequality relations. Therefore, we need to normalize them into the linear constraint forms satisfying the condition of Farkas' lemma. This normalization includes four steps: (1) linearizing all non-linear expressions, (2) transforming all arithmetic constraints to the form $e \geq 0$, (3) eliminating disjunctions in the antecedent of each entailment, and (4) transforming the consequent of each entailment to contain only one linear constraint. They are explained follows.

1. Linearizing non-linear expressions. We use the associative and distributive properties of arithmetic to unfold and simplify all non-linear expressions into polynomials. Then, we encode each polynomial term whose degree is greater than 1 ($k \cdot x_1^{k_1} \cdot \ldots \cdot x_n^{k_n}$ where $k_1 + \ldots + k_n > 1$) by an expression of its coefficient and a fresh variable ($k \cdot x'$, where x' is a fresh variable). For example, by applying this linearization, we can transform the entailment E_3 into the following entailment E_3', where u is a fresh variable that encodes n^2:

$$E_3' \triangleq n \geq 0 \wedge n \neq 0 \wedge s = \tfrac{1}{2} \cdot u - \tfrac{1}{2} \cdot n$$
$$\wedge\ res = c_1 \cdot s + c_2 \cdot n + c_3 \vdash res = \tfrac{1}{2} \cdot u + \tfrac{1}{2} \cdot n$$

Note that in the linearization above, we do not capture the constraint between the new and the old variables. Hence, once the normalized entailments are solved to discover the unknown coefficients, we will need to validate if the discovered coefficients is also the solution of the original entailments. This detail will be discussed again in Sect. 4.3.3.

2. Transforming arithmetic constraints. We can apply the following equivalence transformations of arithmetic constraints (over integer domain) to obtain the constraints of the form $e \geq 0$, which are required by Farkas' lemma.

$$e_1 = e_2 \equiv (e_1 - e_2 \geq 0) \wedge (e_2 - e_1 \geq 0) \qquad\qquad e_1 \geq e_2 \equiv e_1 - e_2 \geq 0$$
$$e_1 \neq e_2 \equiv (e_1 - e_2 - 1 \geq 0) \vee (e_2 - e_1 - 1 \geq 0) \qquad e_1 < e_2 \equiv e_2 - e_1 - 1 \geq 0$$
$$e_1 > e_2 \equiv e_1 - e_2 - 1 \geq 0 \qquad\qquad\qquad\qquad\qquad e_1 \leq e_2 \equiv e_2 - e_1 \geq 0$$

By applying the above equivalences, we can transform the entailment E_3' into the following entailment E_3'':

$$E_3'' \triangleq n \geq 0 \wedge (n - 1 \geq 0 \vee -n - 1 \geq 0) \wedge s - \frac{1}{2} \cdot u + \frac{1}{2} \cdot n \geq 0 \wedge \frac{1}{2} \cdot u - \frac{1}{2} \cdot n - s \geq 0$$
$$\wedge\ res - c_1 \cdot s - c_2 \cdot n - c_3 \geq 0 \wedge c_1 \cdot s + c_2 \cdot n + c_3 - res \geq 0$$
$$\vdash\ res - \frac{1}{2} \cdot u - \frac{1}{2} \cdot n \geq 0 \wedge \frac{1}{2} \cdot u + \frac{1}{2} \cdot n - res \geq 0$$

3. Eliminating disjunctions in the entailments' antecedents. The disjunction operators in the antecedent of each entailment can be easily eliminated to introduce simpler entailments. In particular, we can replace an entailment like $F_1 \vee F_2 \vdash F_3$ in the entailment set $\mathcal{E}$ by two new entailments $F_1 \vdash F_3$ and $F_2 \vdash F_3$. This disjunction elimination preserves the validity of $\mathcal{E}$, since the entailment $F_1 \vee F_2 \vdash F_3$ is valid if and only if both $F_1 \vdash F_3$ and $F_2 \vdash F_3$ are valid. For example, by applying this transformation to E_3'', we obtain the set of two entailments below:

$$E_{31}'' \triangleq n \geq 0 \wedge n - 1 \geq 0 \wedge s - \frac{1}{2} \cdot u + \frac{1}{2} \cdot n \geq 0 \wedge \frac{1}{2} \cdot u - \frac{1}{2} \cdot n - s \geq 0$$
$$\wedge\ res - c_1 \cdot s - c_2 \cdot n - c_3 \geq 0 \wedge c_1 \cdot s + c_2 \cdot n + c_3 - res \geq 0$$
$$\vdash res - \frac{1}{2} \cdot u - \frac{1}{2} \cdot n \geq 0 \wedge \frac{1}{2} \cdot u + \frac{1}{2} \cdot n - res \geq 0$$

$$E_{32}'' \triangleq n \geq 0 \wedge -n - 1 \geq 0 \wedge s - \frac{1}{2} \cdot u + \frac{1}{2} \cdot n \geq 0 \wedge \frac{1}{2} \cdot u - \frac{1}{2} \cdot n - s \geq 0$$
$$\wedge\ res - c_1 \cdot s - c_2 \cdot n - c_3 \geq 0 \wedge c_1 \cdot s + c_2 \cdot n + c_3 - res \geq 0$$
$$\vdash res - \frac{1}{2} \cdot u - \frac{1}{2} \cdot n \geq 0 \wedge \frac{1}{2} \cdot u + \frac{1}{2} \cdot n - res \geq 0$$

4. Normalize the entailments' consequents. In this final step, we transform all entailments in $\mathcal{E}$ to the form whose consequents contain only 1 linear constraint. This can be done by applying the following transformation rules:

- If the entailment set $\mathcal{E}$ contains an entailment like $F_1 \vdash F_2 \wedge F_3$, then this entailment can be replaced by two new entailments $F_1 \vdash F_2$ and $F_1 \vdash F_3$.
- If $\mathcal{E}$ contains an entailment like $F_1 \vdash F_2 \vee F_3$, then this entailment can be replaced by either $F_1 \vdash F_2$ or $F_1 \vdash F_3$. Here, we derive two new entailment sets $\mathcal{E}_1$ and $\mathcal{E}_2$ which respectively contain $F_1 \vdash F_2$ and $F_1 \vdash F_3$. These two sets $\mathcal{E}_1$ and $\mathcal{E}_2$ will be solved independently, and if one of them has a solution, this solution is also the solution of the original set $\mathcal{E}$.

For example, in the entailment set containing E_{31}'' and E_{32}'', the entailments' consequents have only the conjunction operator ($\wedge$). Hence, we can apply the above transformation rules to derive a set of the following 4 entailments.

$$E_{311}'' \triangleq n \geq 0 \wedge n - 1 \geq 0 \wedge s - \frac{1}{2} \cdot u + \frac{1}{2} \cdot n \geq 0 \wedge \frac{1}{2} \cdot u - \frac{1}{2} \cdot n - s \geq 0$$
$$\wedge\ res - c_1 \cdot s - c_2 \cdot n - c_3 \geq 0 \wedge c_1 \cdot s + c_2 \cdot n + c_3 - res \geq 0$$
$$\vdash res - \frac{1}{2} \cdot u - \frac{1}{2} \cdot n \geq 0$$

$$E''_{312} \triangleq n \geq 0 \wedge n - 1 \geq 0 \wedge s - \tfrac{1}{2} \cdot u + \tfrac{1}{2} \cdot n \geq 0 \wedge \tfrac{1}{2} \cdot u - \tfrac{1}{2} \cdot n - s \geq 0$$
$$\wedge \; res - c_1 \cdot s - c_2 \cdot n - c_3 \geq 0 \wedge c_1 \cdot s + c_2 \cdot n + c_3 - res \geq 0$$
$$\vdash \tfrac{1}{2} \cdot u + \tfrac{1}{2} \cdot n - res \geq 0$$

$$E''_{321} \triangleq n \geq 0 \wedge -n - 1 \geq 0 \wedge s - \tfrac{1}{2} \cdot u + \tfrac{1}{2} \cdot n \geq 0 \wedge \tfrac{1}{2} \cdot u - \tfrac{1}{2} \cdot n - s \geq 0$$
$$\wedge \; res - c_1 \cdot s - c_2 \cdot n - c_3 \geq 0 \wedge c_1 \cdot s + c_2 \cdot n + c_3 - res \geq 0$$
$$\vdash res - \tfrac{1}{2} \cdot u - \tfrac{1}{2} \cdot n \geq 0$$

$$E''_{322} \triangleq n \geq 0 \wedge -n - 1 \geq 0 \wedge s - \tfrac{1}{2} \cdot u + \tfrac{1}{2} \cdot n \geq 0 \wedge \tfrac{1}{2} \cdot u - \tfrac{1}{2} \cdot n - s \geq 0$$
$$\wedge \; res - c_1 \cdot s - c_2 \cdot n - c_3 \geq 0 \wedge c_1 \cdot s + c_2 \cdot n + c_3 - res \geq 0$$
$$\vdash \tfrac{1}{2} \cdot u + \tfrac{1}{2} \cdot n - res \geq 0$$

4.3.2 Generating the New Constraints

Once all the entailments are normalized into the form satisfying the conditions of Farkas' lemma (Theorem 1), we can apply the lemma to eliminate the universal quantification over all variables, and generate the constraints containing only unknown coefficients and factors λ_i. Details about this constraint generation can be referred to in [2]. For instance, given the four entailments above, we can generate the following constraints of the unknown coefficient c_1, c_2, c_3 and the factors λ_i.

$$F_1 \triangleq (-\lambda_3 \cdot c_1 + \lambda_4 \cdot c_1 + \lambda_5 - \lambda_6 = 0)$$
$$\wedge \; (\lambda_1 + \lambda_2 - \lambda_3 \cdot c_2 + \lambda_4 \cdot c_2 + \tfrac{1}{2} \cdot \lambda_5 - \tfrac{1}{2} \cdot \lambda_6 = -\tfrac{1}{2})$$
$$\wedge \; (\lambda_3 - \lambda_4 = 1) \wedge (-\tfrac{1}{2} \cdot \lambda_5 + \tfrac{1}{2} \cdot \lambda_6 = -\tfrac{1}{2})$$
$$\wedge \; (-\lambda_2 - \lambda_3 \cdot c_3 + \lambda_4 \cdot c_3 \leq 0)$$

$$F_2 \triangleq (-\lambda_9 \cdot c_1 + \lambda_{10} \cdot c_1 + \lambda_{11} - \lambda_{12} = 0)$$
$$\wedge \; (\lambda_7 + \lambda_8 - \lambda_9 \cdot c_2 + \lambda_{10} \cdot c_2 + \tfrac{1}{2} \cdot \lambda_{11} - \tfrac{1}{2} \cdot \lambda_{12} = \tfrac{1}{2})$$
$$\wedge \; (\lambda_9 - \lambda_{10} = -1) \wedge (-\tfrac{1}{2} \cdot \lambda_{11} + \tfrac{1}{2} \cdot \lambda_{12} = \tfrac{1}{2})$$
$$\wedge \; (-\lambda_8 - \lambda_9 \cdot c_3 + \lambda_{10} \cdot c_3 \leq 0)$$

$$F_3 \triangleq (-\lambda_{15} \cdot c_1 + \lambda_{16} \cdot c_1 + \lambda_{17} - \lambda_{18} = 0)$$
$$\wedge \; (\lambda_{13} - \lambda_{14} - \lambda_{15} \cdot c_2 + \lambda_{16} \cdot c_2 + \tfrac{1}{2} \cdot \lambda_{17} - \tfrac{1}{2} \cdot \lambda_{18} = -\tfrac{1}{2})$$
$$\wedge \; (\lambda_{15} - \lambda_{16} = 1) \wedge (-\tfrac{1}{2} \cdot \lambda_{17} + \tfrac{1}{2} \cdot \lambda_{18} = -\tfrac{1}{2})$$
$$\wedge \; (-\lambda_{14} - \lambda_{15} \cdot c_3 + \lambda_{16} \cdot c_3 \leq 0)$$

$$F_4 \triangleq (-\lambda_{21} \cdot c_1 + \lambda_{22} \cdot c_1 + \lambda_{23} - \lambda_{24} = 0)$$
$$\wedge \; (\lambda_{19} - \lambda_{20} - \lambda_{21} \cdot c_2 + \lambda_{22} \cdot c_2 + \tfrac{1}{2} \cdot \lambda_{23} - \tfrac{1}{2} \cdot \lambda_{24} = \tfrac{1}{2})$$
$$\wedge \; (\lambda_{21} - \lambda_{22} = -1) \wedge (-\tfrac{1}{2} \cdot \lambda_{23} + \tfrac{1}{2} \cdot \lambda_{24} = \tfrac{1}{2})$$
$$\wedge \; (-\lambda_{20} - \lambda_{21} \cdot c_3 + \lambda_{22} \cdot c_3 \leq 0)$$

4.3.3 Solving the New Constraints

The new constraints obtained from previous steps can be solved by a SMT solver, such as Z3 [16], to discover the actual values of the unknown coefficients. For instance, when solving the aforementioned constraints, we obtain a solution forthe unknown coefficients c_1, c_2, c_3 that $c_1 = 1, c_2 = 1, c_3 = 0$. When replacing these values to the template patch $f(s, n) \triangleq c_1 \cdot s + c_2 \cdot n + c_3$ in E_3, we obtain the following new entailment:

$$\bar{E}_3 \triangleq n \geq 0 \land n \neq 0 \land s = (n-1) \cdot n/2 \land res = s + n \vdash res = n \cdot (n+1)/2$$

Recall that during the linearization of non-linear expressions (Sect. 4.3.1), all polynomial terms are encoded by fresh variables. Since this encoding does not maintain the relations of the old and the new variables, we need to validate if the discovered solution obtained here still satisfies the original entailments. This validation can be easily done by invoking an SMT solver to prove the new entailments (like $\bar{E}_3$).

4.4   The Repair Algorithm

Figure 8 presents our main procedure $\mathsf{Repair}(\mathcal{P}, \mathcal{S})$. Its inputs include a buggy procedure $\mathcal{P}$ and a correct specification $\mathcal{S}$. There are three possible outputs as follows. Firstly, if $\mathcal{P}$ is correct w.r.t. its specification $\mathcal{S}$, then it does not need to be repaired, and the procedure simply returns NONE. Secondly, if $\mathcal{P}$ is buggy and can be repaired, then the procedure returns $\mathsf{PATCH}\langle \bar{\mathcal{P}} \rangle$ to indicate that $\bar{\mathcal{P}}$ is the repaired solution. Finally, the procedure returns FAIL if it cannot repair the buggy procedure $\mathcal{P}$.

The procedure Repair first verifies the input program $\mathcal{P}$ against its specification $\mathcal{S}$ by invoking an auxiliary procedure Verify (line 1). If the verification fails, then there exists a bug in the implementation of $\mathcal{P}$ w.r.t. its specification $\mathcal{S}$. Then, Repair will utilize the invalid proof obligation to discover all possibly

---

Procedure $\mathsf{Repair}(\mathcal{P}, \mathcal{S})$

Input: A procedure $\mathcal{P}$, and its correct specification $\mathcal{S}$.
Output: NONE if $\mathcal{P}$ is correct w.r.t. $\mathcal{S}$, $\mathsf{PATCH}\langle \bar{\mathcal{P}} \rangle$ if $\mathcal{P}$ is buggy and $\bar{\mathcal{P}}$ is the repaired solution, or FAIL if $\mathcal{P}$ is buggy but cannot be repaired.

```
 1: if Verify(P, S) = FAIL then                        //P is buggy w.r.t. to its specs S
 2:     X ← GetInvalidProofObligation(P, S)
 3:     E ← LocalizeBuggyExpressions(P, X)                    //all possible buggy exps
 4:     for E in E do                                    //repair each buggy expression
 5:         T ← CreateTemplatePatch(P, E)
 6:         P' ← CreateTemplateProgram(P, T)
 7:         C ← VerifyAndCollectProofObligations(P', S)
 8:         if HasSolution(C, T) then
 9:             T̄ ← GetSolution(C, T)
10:             P̄ ← CreateRepairedProgram(P', T̄)
11:             if Verify(P̄, S) = SUCCESS then
12:                 return PATCH⟨P̄⟩                        //discover a patch
13:     return FAIL                              //cannot repair any buggy expression
14: else return NONE  //P is correct w.r.t. to its specs S, does not need to be repaired
```

Fig. 8. The repair algorithm

buggy expressions (lines 2, 3). Then, it attempts to repair each of these expressions (lines 4–12).

For each possibly buggy expression E, the procedure Repair creates a template patch T (line 5), which is a linear expression of the program's variables and unknown coefficients, as described earlier in Sect. 4.2. This template patch T will replace E in the original program $\mathcal{P}$ to create a template program $\mathcal{P}'$ (line 6). This template program will be verified again to collect a constraint set $\mathcal{C}$ of proof obligations about the template T. This constraint set will be solved by the technique using Farkas' lemmas (lines 8, 9). If a solution $\bar{T}$ of the template patch T is discovered, it will be used to create a repaired program $\bar{\mathcal{P}}$ (line 10). This repaired program will be validated against the specs $\mathcal{S}$ (line 11), and will be returned by the procedure Repair (line 12) if this validation succeeds.

On the other hand, the procedure Repair returns FAIL if it cannot repair any of the possibly buggy expressions (line 13). It also returns NONE if the original program $\mathcal{P}$ is correct w.r.t. the specification $\mathcal{S}$ (line 14).

4.5 Soundness

We claim that our program repair approach is sound. We formally state this soundness in the following Theorem 2.

Theorem 2 (Soundness). *Given a buggy program $\mathcal{P}$ and a specification $\mathcal{S}$, if the procedure Repair returns a program $\bar{\mathcal{P}}$, then this repaired program satisfies the specification $\mathcal{S}$.*

Proof. In our repair algorithm (Fig. 8), after solving the constraints to discover a candidate program (lines 8–10), we always verify this candidate against its specification $\mathcal{S}$ (line 11). Consequently, if the procedure Repair returns a repaired program $\bar{\mathcal{P}}$, this program always satisfies the specification $\mathcal{S}$.

5   Implementation and Experiment

We implement our program repair approach in a tool, called Maple, using the OCaml programming language. It is built on top of the verification system HIP [1] and the theorem prover Songbird [23,24]. We evaluate the performance of Maple on repairing faulty programs in a literature benchmark TCAS [3], which implements a traffic collision avoidance system for aircrafts. This benchmark is widely used in previous experiments of many program repair tools; it has a correct program of 142 lines of C code and 41 different faulty versions to simulate realistic bugs. However, the benchmark TCAS does not contain any loop or recursive call, a popular feature in modern programming languages. Therefore, we decide to compose a more challenging benchmark, called Recursion, which contain not only non-recursive but also recursive programs.

Our experiment was conducted on a computer with CPU Intel® Core™ i7-6700 (3.4 GHz), 8 GB RAM, and Ubuntu 16.04 LTS. We compare Maple against the state-of-the-art program repair tools for C programs, which are AllRepair

[21], Forensic [9,10], GenProg [11], and Angelix [15]. Among these tools, GenProg and Angelix rely on test suites, while AllRepair and Forensic use specifications (in the form of assertions) to repair programs. The details of our tool Maple and experiments are available online at https://maple-repair.github.io.

5.1 Experiment with the Benchmark TCAS

In this experiment, we evaluate all the tools with 41 faulty programs in the benchmark TCAS [3]. Since this benchmark was used before in the experiment of other tools AllRepair, Forensic, Angelix, and GenProg, we reuse their original settings in our experiment. Particularly, the specification-based tools AllRepair and Forensic keep the correct program along with the faulty versions to check the correctness of the repair candidates. On the other hand, the testing-based tools GenProg and Angelix use different test suites of 50 cases for each faulty program. For our tool Maple, we manually write the specification for the correct program and use this specification to repair the faulty versions.[1]

Table 1 presents the detailed results of our experiment. We report whether a tool can correctly repair a program (denoted by ✓), or repair the program by an overfitted patch (denoted by o)[2], or cannot repair it (denoted by –). We also record the runtime (in seconds) of each tool. Here, we do not set a timeout: a tool can run until either it returns a patch or informs that it fails to find any patch. In the summary rows, we report the total number of the correct and overfitting patches discovered by each tool, and the average time spent by each tool. The best result is highlighted in the **bold** typeface.

Our tool Maple can correctly repair 26/41 faulty programs and does not produce any overfitting patch. This is the *best* result among all participants. The tool AllRepair is the second best, which it can successfully repair 18 programs. Forensic and Angelix are the next best tools, and they can correctly repair 15 and 9 programs, respectively. Note that although Forensic and Angelix can repair in total 23 and 32 programs, respectively, many of them (8 and 23 programs) are repaired by overfitting patches. While these patches pass the test suites used by Angelix and Forensic, they change the desired behaviors of the original program. For instance, in the faulty program v_2, the tool Angelix incorrectly replaces the buggy expression Up_Separation + 300 by Up_Separation + 24, while the expected repaired expression is Up_Separation + 100.

Regarding the execution time, our tool Maple is the *second* fastest when it spends on average 155.3 s to repair a program. It is slower than All-Repair which spends averagely 16.9 s per program. Here, AllRepair uses a simple strategy to mutate operators and constants. In contrast, our tool needs to create a patch template, collect and solve the template's constraints to discover the actual patch. Nonetheless, these heavier computations enable Maple to correctly fix more programs than AllRepair. On

---

[1] Our specification contains 34 lines, while the original program has 142 lines of code.

[2] The correct and the overfitted patches are classified by comparing the similarity in the structures of the repaired and the originally correct programs.

Table 1. Experiment with the benchmark TCAS, where the participants are AllRepair(ARP), Angelix(AGL), GenProg(GPR), Forensic(FRS), and Maple(MPL)

Programs	Repair Result					Repair Time (s)				
	ARP	AGL	GPR	FRS	MPL	ARP	AGL	GPR	FRS	MPL
v_1	✓	✓	o	–	✓	1	46	800	–	104
v_2	–	o	–	✓	✓	–	114	–	28	98
v_3	✓	o	–	–	✓	1	131	–	–	224
v_4	–	✓	o	o	✓	–	11	445	51	139
v_5	–	✓	–	–	–	–	911	–	–	–
v_6	✓	✓	–	✓	✓	1	42	–	52	100
v_7	–	o	–	✓	✓	–	7938	–	43	100
v_8	–	o	–	✓	✓	–	27	–	36	105
v_9	✓	o	o	✓	✓	2	366	149	286	107
v_10	✓	o	o	✓	✓	4	737	487	770	107
v_11	–	o	–	–	✓	–	738	–	–	184
v_12	✓	o	–	–	✓	1	1079	–	–	1264
v_13	–	o	–	–	–	–	926	–	–	–
v_14	–	o	–	–	–	–	230	–	–	–
v_15	–	o	–	–	–	–	1718	–	–	–
v_16	✓	o	–	✓	✓	21	32	–	47	93
v_17	✓	–	–	✓	✓	38	–	–	43	96
v_18	–	–	–	✓	✓	–	–	–	52	97
v_19	–	–	o	✓	✓	–	–	258	35	99
v_20	✓	o	o	✓	✓	1	398	738	224	99
v_21	–	o	–	o	–	–	36	–	452	–
v_22	–	o	–	–	–	–	504	–	–	–
v_23	–	o	o	–	–	–	604	165	–	–
v_24	–	o	–	–	–	–	605	–	–	–
v_25	✓	o	o	✓	✓	1	37	120	364	111
v_26	–	✓	–	–	–	–	1098	–	–	–
v_27	–	✓	–	–	–	–	1179	–	–	–
v_28	✓	✓	–	✓	✓	67	338	–	180	101
v_29	–	–	–	–	✓	–	–	–	–	94
v_30	–	–	–	–	✓	–	–	–	–	98
v_31	✓	o	o	o	✓	1	15	171	491	84
v_32	✓	o	o	o	✓	1	26	62	544	99
v_33	–	–	–	–	–	–	–	–	–	–
v_34	–	o	–	o	–	–	260	–	1420	–
v_35	✓	✓	–	✓	✓	67	175	–	179	111
v_36	✓	–	–	o	–	90	–	–	1501	–
v_37	–	–	–	–	–	–	–	–	–	–
v_38	–	–	–	–	–	–	–	–	–	–
v_39	✓	o	o	✓	✓	1	218	184	367	111
v_40	✓	✓	–	o	✓	4	28	–	514	107
v_41	✓	o	–	o	✓	3	29	–	603	106
Correct (✓)	18	9	0	15	**26**	16.9	3615.0	–	180.4	155.3
Overfit (o)	**0**	23	11	8	**0**	–	729.0	325.4	697.0	–
Total (41)	18	**32**	11	23	26	16.9	1540.7	325.4	360.1	155.3

the other hand, the other tools Forensic, Angelix, and GenProg spend longer time to repair a program, compared to our tool Maple. These performances can be explained as follows. Firstly, Forensic also uses template patches, but its constraint solving technique requires an incremental counter-example-driven template refinement, which is less efficient than our approach of using Farkas' lemma. Secondly, Angelix utilizes a component-based repair synthesis algorithm, which is more costly than our method, in the context of repairing linear expressions. Finally, GenProg needs to heuristically mutate the original programs many times to find correct patches.

5.2 Experiment with the Benchmark Recursion

In this experiment, we evaluate all tools with the synthetic benchmark Recursion, which contains challenging arithmetic programs. This benchmark is presented in Table 2. We classify its programs into two categories: *non-recursive* and *recursive*. The *non-recursive* category includes programs that compute the maximum, the minimum, or the sum of two or three numbers, or the absolute value of a number. On the other hand, programs in the *recursive* category are constructed in a similar fashion to the motivating program sum (Sect. 2). They compute the sums of different sequences of numbers, which can be enumerated by an indexing number i, starting from 0 to a given number n. For example, they include a sequence of n consecutive numbers or a sequence of n products of the form $i \cdot (i+1)$. Although these recursive programs are relatively small (each program contains 5 to 9 lines of code), they are still challenging for the existing state-of-the-art program repair tools.

In order to evaluate GenProg and Angelix, we follow the tools' guidelines to create test suites of 10 cases. Note that these tools require the values of variables for every recursive call of the recursive programs. We also create specifications for the tool AllRepair and Forensic. They follow the same style of using assertions to compare the results of running the correct and buggy programs. For our tool Maple, we create a desired specification for each buggy program. These specifications are small, they contain only 2 lines per program.

Table 2 presents the experimental result with the benchmark Recursion. Our tool Maple can repair all 26 faulty programs and does not generate any overfitting patch. Furthermore, Maple outperforms the second and the third best tools Angelix and Forensic, which could correctly repair only 8 and 5 faulty programs, respectively. On the other hand, the two tools AllRepair and GenProg cannot repair any program. These tools perform only simple code mutations such as alternating Boolean or arithmetic operators, which are insufficient to handle these buggy programs. For the tool Forensic, although it exploits the correct programs to generate test suites to repair the faulty programs, these test suites cannot fully cover the underlying computations of these recursive programs. Consequently, Forensic can discover only overfitting patches, as shown with the *recursive* category in Table 2.

Regarding the runtime, Forensic is the fastest tool when it takes averagely 3.6 s to correctly repair a program. Our tool Maple is the second fastest which spends 5.6 s per correctly repaired program. Note that this average runtime also includes the time spent on recursive programs, which Forensic can produce only overfitting patches. Also, for every program that Forensic can repair correctly (max_2_2, max_3_2, min_2_2, min_3_2, absolute_2), our tool Maple spends less time than Forensic, thanks to the efficiency of the constraint solving technique

Table 2. Experiment with our numeric benchmark, where the participants are AllRepair(ARP), Angelix(AGL), GenProg(GPR), Forensic(FRS), and Maple(MPL)

Programs		Repair Result					Repair Time (s)				
		ARP	AGL	GPR	FRS	MPL	ARP	AGL	GPR	FRS	MPL
non-recursive	max_2_1	−	−	−	o	✓	−	−	−	4	4
	max_2_2	−	✓	−	✓	✓	−	8	−	2	2
	max_3_1	−	−	−	−	✓	−	−	−	−	8
	max_3_2	−	✓	−	✓	✓	−	10	−	5	3
	min_2_1	−	−	−	−	✓	−	−	−	−	4
	min_2_2	−	✓	−	✓	✓	−	8	−	3	2
	min_3_1	−	−	−	−	✓	−	−	−	−	8
	min_3_2	−	✓	−	✓	✓	−	16	−	5	3
	sum_2_1	−	−	−	−	✓	−	−	−	−	2
	sum_2_2	−	−	−	−	✓	−	−	−	−	2
	sum_3_1	−	−	−	−	✓	−	−	−	−	2
	sum_3_2	−	−	−	−	✓	−	−	−	−	2
	absolute_1	−	✓	−	✓	✓	−	15	−	3	2
	absolute_2	−	−	−	−	✓	−	−	−	−	7
recursive	sum_n_1	−	✓	−	−	✓	−	38	−	−	4
	sum_n_2	−	−	−	o	✓	−	−	−	29	7
	sum_n_3	−	−	−	−	✓	−	−	−	−	7
	sum_n_4	−	−	−	o	✓	−	−	−	24	7
	conseq_1	−	✓	−	−	✓	−	35	−	−	4
	conseq_2	−	−	−	o	✓	−	−	−	28	11
	conseq_3	−	−	−	−	✓	−	−	−	−	11
	conseq_4	−	−	−	o	✓	−	−	−	23	11
	increment_1	−	✓	−	−	✓	−	51	−	−	4
	increment_2	−	−	−	−	✓	−	−	−	−	9
	increment_3	−	−	−	−	✓	−	−	−	−	10
	increment_4	−	−	−	−	✓	−	−	−	−	10
Correct	(✓)	**0**	**8**	**0**	5	**26**	−	22.6	−	**3.6**	5.6
Overfit	(o)	**0**	**0**	**0**	5	**0**	−	−	−	21.6	−
Total	(26)	**0**	**8**	**0**	10	**26**	−	22.6	−	12.6	5.6

using Farkas' lemma. In this benchmark, the runtime of all tools is smaller than that of the benchmark TCAS. This is because all programs in this benchmark are shorter: each program contains only 1 procedure of about 5 to 9 lines of code, while each program in the benchmark TCAS contains 8 procedures of totally 142 lines of code.

6 Related Work

There have been many approaches to repair faulty programs, and most of them use test suites to guide the repair process: they are used to localize the bug, then to generate and validate fix candidates. These approaches can be categorized into heuristic-based and semantic-based approaches. Heuristic-based tools, such as

GenProg [11,27], RSRepair [20], traverse programs' abstract syntax trees (AST) using generic programming or random search algorithms, and then modify ASTs by mutation and crossover operations. On the other hand, semantic-based tools such as SemFix [17] and Angelix [15] propose to firstly locate bug locations using ranking methods, such as Tarantula [7]. Then, they employ the symbolic execution technique to generate constraints and solve the collected constraints by a component-based repair synthesis algorithm to generate the repaired programs.

However, there is a major problem that all the test suite-based approaches need to handle is the generation of *overfitting* patches. These patches can easily pass all the test cases, but they also break untested but desired functionality of repaired programs [22]. This problem happens when the test suites, provided by users, contain concrete values, which cannot cover all the functionality of a program. To deal with this problem, the works [28–30] propose methods to automatically generate more test cases. For instance, Yang et al. [19] propose to detect overfitting patches and use fuzzing to generate more test cases to guide the repair tools. However, it is impossible to guarantee that the newly generated test cases can fully cover all behaviours of the original programs.

The works that are closer to ours are [8–10,21], which use formal specification to guide the repair process. In particular, the work [21] uses assertions to compare the output of the correct and the repaired programs. They generate the patch by performing simple code mutations, such as increasing or decreasing numerical constants by 1, or changing logical/arithmetic operators. This approach can fix simple bugs, as demonstrated by the tool AllRepair. The works [9,10] use the provided specifications to generated test cases and use a template-based approach like ours to generate the patches. Since the constraints related to the template fix are resolved by using test cases, these approaches result in many overfitting patches, as shown in our experiments with the tool Forensic.

In contrast to the test-case-based approaches, our work may does not generate overfitting patches, since the utilized specification can captures better symbolic relations of the program input/output, compared to concrete value relations in test suites. This is demonstrated in the experiments that all the patches discovered by our tool Maple are correct patches. Compared to the aforementioned specification-based approaches, our approach to generating the patches is more general. We consider the patches in the form of linear expression templates, and perform symbolic execution to collect and solve constraints over the template patches. Consequently, our tool can repair correctly more faulty programs than other specification-based tools AllRepair and Forensic.

Whereas all the above works, including ours, focus on repairing Boolean and arithmetic properties in C programs, there are works that aim to repair heap properties in C program [25,26], or repair programs in Eiffel [18], Scala [8], and C# [13]. Among these works, the tool AutoFix [18] uses test suites, the work [26] needs programmer's help, while the other works use the specification to guide the repair. Compared to ours, all these works focus on either different fragments of C programs or different programming languages. Therefore, we did not evaluate them in the experiments.

7   Limitations and Future Work

We now discuss the limitations of our work and corresponding planned improvements. There are three limitations as follows. Firstly, our current approach focuses on repairing only linear arithmetic expressions. In the future, we want to extend it to repair more types of expressions, such as arrays, strings, or dynamically allocated data structures like linked lists and trees. Secondly, our tool can fix only one expression each time. Hence, we would like to equip it with the ability of considering multiple buggy expressions at the same time. Thirdly, the tool cannot synthesize missing expressions. Since specifications are used, this problem is equivalent to finding correct code fragments that meet the specifications of the missing expressions. Thus, we can follow the approach of [25] which learns specifications of the existing programs to find the removed program fragments.

8   Conclusions

We have introduced an automated program repair framework using formal verification and expression templates. More specifically, we first utilize a formal verification system to locate and rank the potentially buggy expressions by their likelihood to cause the bug. Then, each buggy expression is replaced by a template patch, which is a linear expression of the program's variables with unknown coefficients, to create a template program. This program will be verified against to collect constraints of the template patch. Finally, we apply a constraint solving technique using Farkas' lemma to solve these constraints to discover the repaired program. In practice, our prototype tool Maple can discover more correct patches than other program repair tools in the widely used benchmark TCAS. It can also fix many challenging programs in the synthetic benchmark Recursion, which cannot be fully repaired by other tools.

Acknowledgements. We are grateful to the anonymous reviewers for their valuable feedback. The first author would like to thank Bat-Chen Rothenberg for her help on the experimentation of AllRepair, and Xianglong Kong for sharing unit tests of the TCAS benchmark. This work is supported by the NRF grant NRF2014NCR-NCR001-030.

References

1. Chin, W.-N., David, C., Nguyen, H.H., Qin, S.: Automated verification of shape, size and bag properties via user-defined predicates in separation logic. Sci. Comput. Program. (SCP) **77**(9), 1006–1036 (2012)
2. Colón, M.A., Sankaranarayanan, S., Sipma, H.B.: Linear invariant generation using non-linear constraint solving. In: Hunt, W.A., Somenzi, F. (eds.) CAV 2003. LNCS, vol. 2725, pp. 420–432. Springer, Heidelberg (2003). https://doi.org/10.1007/978-3-540-45069-6_39
3. Do, H., Elbaum, S.G., Rothermel, G.: Supporting controlled experimentation with testing techniques: an infrastructure and its potential impact. Empirical Softw. Eng. **10**(4), 405–435 (2005)

4. Hoare, C.A.R.: An axiomatic basis for computer programming. Commun. ACM **12**(10), 576–580 (1969)
5. Huth, M., Ryan, M.: Logic in Computer Science: Modelling and Reasoning About Systems. Cambridge University Press, New York (2004). ISBN 052154310X
6. ISO. ISO/IEC 9899: 2011 information technology - programming languages - C. Int. Organ. Stand. **27**, 59 (2011)
7. Jones, J.A., Harrold, M.J., Stasko, J.T.: Visualization of test information to assist fault localization. In: International Conference on Software Engineering (ICSE), pp. 467–477 (2002)
8. Kneuss, E., Koukoutos, M., Kuncak, V.: Deductive program repair. In: Kroening, D., Păsăreanu, C.S. (eds.) CAV 2015. LNCS, vol. 9207, pp. 217–233. Springer, Cham (2015). https://doi.org/10.1007/978-3-319-21668-3_13
9. Könighofer, R., Bloem, R.: Automated error localization and correction for imperative programs. In: International Conference on Formal Methods in Computer-Aided Design (FMCAD), pp. 91–100 (2011)
10. Könighofer, R., Bloem, R.: Repair with on-the-fly program analysis. In: Biere, A., Nahir, A., Vos, T. (eds.) HVC 2012. LNCS, vol. 7857, pp. 56–71. Springer, Heidelberg (2013). https://doi.org/10.1007/978-3-642-39611-3_11
11. Le Goues, C., Nguyen, T., Forrest, S., Weimer, W.: GenProg: a generic method for automatic software repair. IEEE Trans. Softw. Eng. **38**(1), 54–72 (2012)
12. Leino, K.R.M.: Dafny: an automatic program verifier for functional correctness. In: Clarke, E.M., Voronkov, A. (eds.) LPAR 2010. LNCS (LNAI), vol. 6355, pp. 348–370. Springer, Heidelberg (2010). https://doi.org/10.1007/978-3-642-17511-4_20
13. Logozzo, F., Ball, T.: Modular and verified automatic program repair. In: International Conference on Object Oriented Programming Systems Languages and Applications (OOPSLA), pp. 133–146 (2012)
14. Long, F., Rinard, M.: Staged program repair with condition synthesis. In: Joint European Software Engineering Conference and Symposium on the Foundations of Software Engineering (ESEC/FSE), pp. 166–178 (2015)
15. Mechtaev, S., Yi, J., Roychoudhury, A.: Angelix: scalable multiline program patch synthesis via symbolic analysis. In: International Conference on Software Engineering (ICSE), pp. 691–701 (2016)
16. de Moura, L., Bjørner, N.: Z3: an efficient SMT solver. In: Ramakrishnan, C.R., Rehof, J. (eds.) TACAS 2008. LNCS, vol. 4963, pp. 337–340. Springer, Heidelberg (2008). https://doi.org/10.1007/978-3-540-78800-3_24
17. Nguyen, H.D.T., Qi, D., Roychoudhury, A., Chandra, S.: SemFix: program repair via semantic analysis. In: International Conference on Software Engineering (ICSE), pp. 772–781 (2013)
18. Pei, Y., Furia, C.A., Nordio, M., Wei, Y., Meyer, B., Zeller, A.: Automated fixing of programs with contracts. IEEE Trans. Softw. Eng. **40**(5), 427–449 (2014)
19. Program Repair Website (2018). http://program-repair.org/. Accessed 18 Sept 2018
20. Qi, Y., Mao, X., Lei, Y., Dai, Z., Wang, C.: The strength of random search on automated program repair. In: International Conference on Software Engineering (ICSE), pp. 254–265 (2014)
21. Rothenberg, B.-C., Grumberg, O.: Sound and complete mutation-based program repair. In: Fitzgerald, J., Heitmeyer, C., Gnesi, S., Philippou, A. (eds.) FM 2016. LNCS, vol. 9995, pp. 593–611. Springer, Cham (2016). https://doi.org/10.1007/978-3-319-48989-6_36

22. Smith, E.K., Barr, E.T., Le Goues, C., Brun, Y.: Is the cure worse than the disease? Overfitting in automated program repair. In: Joint European Software Engineering Conference and Symposium on the Foundations of Software Engineering (ESEC/FSE), pp. 532–543 (2015)
23. Ta, Q.-T., Le, T.C., Khoo, S.C., Chin, W.N.: Automated lemma synthesis in symbolic-heap separation logic. In: Symposium on Principles of Programming Languages (POPL), pp. 9:1–9:29 (2018)
24. Ta, Q.-T., Le, T.C., Khoo, S.-C., Chin, W.-N.: Automated mutual explicit induction proof in separation logic. In: Fitzgerald, J., Heitmeyer, C., Gnesi, S., Philippou, A. (eds.) FM 2016. LNCS, vol. 9995, pp. 659–676. Springer, Cham (2016). https://doi.org/10.1007/978-3-319-48989-6_40
25. van Tonder, R., Le Goues, C.: Static automated program repair for heap properties. In: International Conference on Software Engineering (ICSE), pp. 151–162 (2018)
26. Verma, S., Roy, S.: Synergistic debug-repair of heap manipulations. In: Joint European Software Engineering Conference and Symposium on the Foundations of Software Engineering (ESEC/FSE), pp. 163–173 (2017)
27. Weimer, W., Forrest, S., Le Goues, C., Nguyen, T.: Automatic program repair with evolutionary computation. Commun. ACM **53**(5), 109–116 (2010)
28. Xin, Q., Reiss, S.P.: Identifying test-suite-overfitted patches through test case generation. In: International Symposium on Software Testing and Analysis, pp. 226–236 (2017)
29. Yang, J., Zhikhartsev, A., Liu, Y., Tan, L.: Better test cases for better automated program repair. In: Joint European Software Engineering Conference and Symposium on the Foundations of Software Engineering (ESEC/FSE), pp. 831–841 (2017)
30. Yu, Z., Martinez, M., Danglot, B., Durieux, T., Monperrus, M.: Test case generation for program repair: a study of feasibility and effectiveness. CoRR abs/1703.00198 (2017)

Lazy but Effective Functional Synthesis

Grigory Fedyukovich[1](✉) ⓘ, Arie Gurfinkel[2], and Aarti Gupta[1]

[1] Princeton University, Princeton, USA
{grigoryf,aartig}@cs.princeton.edu
[2] University of Waterloo, Waterloo, Canada
agurfinkel@uwaterloo.ca

Abstract. We present a new technique for generating a function implementation from a declarative specification formulated as a $\forall\exists$-formula in first-order logic. We follow a classic approach of eliminating existential quantifiers and extracting Skolem functions for the theory of linear arithmetic. Our method eliminates quantifiers *lazily* and produces a synthesis solution in the form of a decision tree. Compared to prior approaches, our decision trees have fewer nodes due to deriving theory terms that can be shared both within a single output as well as across multiple outputs. Our approach is implemented in a tool called AE-VAL, and its evaluation on a set of reactive synthesis benchmarks shows promise.

1 Introduction

The task of generating a function implementation from a specification of an input-output relation is commonly addressed by *functional synthesis*. Many prior approaches have been proposed for functional synthesis [10,13,16,18,20], with applications in various stages of software development, from prototyping to maintaining and repairing existing products. However, there is still a great need to make the synthesizers more robust and scalable, and the synthesized implementations more compact. We build this work on recent advances in *lazy* quantifier elimination methods [3,6,14,17,20] that enabled us to progress in both these dimensions.

Synthesis tasks are often formulated as quantified formulas. We consider formulas of the form $\forall \vec{x} . \exists \vec{y} . \psi(\vec{x}, \vec{y})$ (or $\forall\exists$-formulas in short[1]). A simple example of a synthesis task formulated as a $\forall\exists$-formula to generate a max-function is shown below, where the two input variables x_1 and x_2 are universally quantified and the output y is existentially quantified:

$$\forall x_1, x_2 . \exists y . y \geq x_1 \wedge y \geq x_2 \wedge (x_1 = y \vee x_2 = y)$$

The validity of this formula means that there always exists a maximum between two integers. A witness to the maximum value, i.e., a Skolem function $y = ite(x_1 \geq x_2, x_1, x_2)$, can then be generated (and suitably decoded as a statement in a program). In this paper, we consider the general case of synthesis of *multi-output* programs, i.e., with an arbitrary number of outputs. An

---

[1] Here and later, we use the vector notation to denote multiple variables.

C. Enea and R. Piskac (Eds.): VMCAI 2019, LNCS 11388, pp. 92–113, 2019.
https://doi.org/10.1007/978-3-030-11245-5_5

example task is to generate a program that invokes both max and min-functions at the same time. An encoding of this task as a $\forall\exists$-formula is somewhat bulky, as shown below:

$$\forall x_1, x_2 . \exists y_1, y_2 . y_1 \geq x_1 \wedge y_1 \geq x_2 \wedge (x_1 = y_1 \vee x_2 = y_1) \wedge$$
$$y_2 \leq x_1 \wedge y_2 \leq x_2 \wedge (x_1 = y_2 \vee x_2 = y_2)$$

However, a solution for this synthesis task can still be formulated concisely: $ite(x_1 \geq x_2, y_1 = x_1 \wedge y_2 = x_2, y_1 = x_2 \wedge y_2 = x_1)$. In particular, note that the predicate $x_1 \geq x_2$ is *shared* between the two outputs y_1 and y_2 in the program, which respectively denote the values of the max and min functions.

Our synthesis procedure generates an implementation of a function *while eliminating existential quantifiers* in the formula, similar to prior work by Kuncak et al. [16]. However, quantifier elimination is an expensive iterative procedure in general. To lower the overall cost of functional synthesis, we propose to use a lazy procedure [6] for quantifier elimination in $\forall\exists$-formulas using Model-Based Projection (MBP) for linear arithmetic [14]. Unlike the prior work, our procedure does not require converting the formula into Disjunctive Normal Form (DNF), and thus often produces smaller and non-redundant implementations.

Along with the use of MBPs, we formulate criteria for an *effective decomposition* of a functional synthesis task. In particular, we aim at searching for a *structured* synthesis solution in the form of a decision tree, where each of the synthesis subtasks is defined in terms of a *precondition* and a set of *Skolem constraints* in a grammar, from which a function implementation is generated. While our notion of a precondition is similar to that in prior work [16], our MBP-based procedure results in fewer number of synthesis subtasks, thereby providing performance improvements and smaller implementations.

Our effective decomposition further enables optimization procedures for on-the-fly compaction of the generated function. In particular, we derive Skolem terms that can be re-used across multiple preconditions for a single output, and share the preconditions in a common decision tree across multiple outputs in the program. Our method identifies theory terms that can be shared both within and across outputs. While the motivation for such sharing is similar to optimization of Boolean gate-level circuits in the area of *logic synthesis*, our compaction is enabled by theory-specific reasoning (validity checks), not Boolean optimization at the propositional level. Our evaluation in a tool called AE-VAL demonstrates the benefits of our compaction algorithm, which further reduces the size of the resulting implementations by an average of two.

We have implemented our ideas in AE-VAL on top of our prior work [6], which described a procedure for determining the validity of $\forall\exists$-formulas using MBPs for linear arithmetic [14]. The focus of that effort was on deriving Skolem witnesses for a simulation relation between two given programs. However, there was no method described for functional synthesis, which requires deriving a Skolem *function* rather than a Skolem *relation*. Furthermore, it did not consider minimization or compaction of the generated implementations. Note again, that this minimization/compaction is not at the propositional level, but requires theory-specific reasoning. The required validity checks for compaction are built into the synthesis procedure and use the same MBP-based validity checker recursively. We provide a detailed evaluation of our tool on a selection of public benchmarks from SyGuS-COMP[2] and benchmark examples for reactive synthesis from Assume-Guarantee contracts [13].

We start by providing some background in Sect. 2. Next, in Sect. 3, we describe our criteria for effective decomposition and the MBP-based procedure for formulating the synthesis subtasks. In Sect. 4, we present a method for extracting Skolem functions from Skolem constraints. In Sect. 5, we describe our algorithm for compaction and re-use of theory terms within and across subtasks. We have implemented our procedure for functional synthesis for linear arithmetic and present a detailed evaluation in Sect. 6. Related work is described in Sect. 7 and conclusions in Sect. 8.

2   Background and Notation

A many-sorted first-order theory consists of disjoint sets of sorts $\mathcal{S}$, function symbols $\mathcal{F}$ and predicate symbols $\mathcal{P}$. A set of *terms* is defined recursively as follows:

$$term ::= f(term, \dots, term) \mid const \mid var$$

where $f \in \mathcal{F}$, *const* is an application of some $v \in \mathcal{F}$ of zero arity, and *var* is a variable uniquely associated with a sort in $\mathcal{S}$. A set of quantifier-free *formulas* is built recursively using the usual grammar:

$$formula ::= true \mid false \mid p(term, \dots, term) \mid Bvar \mid$$
$$\neg formula \mid formula \wedge formula \mid formula \vee formula$$

where *true* and *false* are Boolean constants, $p \in \mathcal{P}$, and *Bvar* is a variable associated with sort *Bool*.

In this paper, we consider theories of Linear Rational Arithmetic (LRA) and Linear Integer Arithmetic (LIA). In LRA, $\mathcal{S} \stackrel{\text{def}}{=} \{\mathbb{Q}, Bool\}$, $\mathcal{F} \stackrel{\text{def}}{=} \{+, \cdot\}$, where $\cdot$ is a scalar multiplication (i.e., it does not allow multiplying two terms which both contain variables), and $\mathcal{P} \stackrel{\text{def}}{=} \{=, >, <, \geq, \leq, \neq\}$. In LIA, $\mathcal{C} \stackrel{\text{def}}{=} \{\mathbb{Z}, Bool\}$, $\mathcal{F} \stackrel{\text{def}}{=} \{+, \cdot, div\}$, where *div* is an integer division[3], and $\mathcal{P} \stackrel{\text{def}}{=} \{=, >, <, \geq, \leq, \neq\}$. For both LRA and LIA, we use a shortcut $ite(x, y, z) \stackrel{\text{def}}{=} (x \wedge y) \vee (\neg x \wedge z)$, but do not include *ite* in $\mathcal{F}$.

Formula φ is called satisfiable if there exists an interpretation m, called a model, of each element (i.e., a variable, a function or a predicate symbol), under which φ evaluates to *true* (denoted $m \models \varphi$); otherwise φ is called unsatisfiable. If every model of φ is also a model of ψ, then we write $\varphi \implies \psi$. A formula φ is called *valid* if $true \implies \varphi$.

For existentially-quantified formulas of the form $\exists y \, . \, \psi(\vec{x}, y)$, validity requires that each interpretation for variables in $\vec{x}$ and each function and predicate symbol

---

[2] http://sygus.seas.upenn.edu/SyGuS-COMP2018.html.

[3] We do not consider the modulo operation in this work, but our approach can be extended to support it.

in ψ can be *extended* to a model of $\psi(\vec{x}, y)$. For a valid formula $\exists y \,.\, \psi(\vec{x}, y)$, a term $sk_y(\vec{x})$ is called a *Skolem term*, if $\psi(\vec{x}, sk_y(\vec{x}))$ is valid. More generally, for a valid formula $\exists \vec{y} \,.\, \psi(\vec{x}, \vec{y})$ over a vector of existentially quantified variables $\vec{y}$, there exists a vector of individual Skolem terms for every variable $\vec{y}[j]$, where $0 < j \leq N$ and $N = |\vec{y}|$, such that:

$$true \implies \psi(\vec{x}, sk_{\vec{y}[1]}(\vec{x}), \ldots, sk_{\vec{y}[N]}(\vec{x})) \tag{1}$$

In the paper, we assume that all free variables $\vec{x}$ are implicitly universally quantified. For simplicity, we omit the arguments and simply write φ when the arguments are clear from the context.

3   Decomposing Functional Synthesis

A functional synthesis task aims at generating a function from a given input-output relation. We view this in terms of validity checking of $\forall\exists$-formulas and derive Skolem terms for the existentially-quantified variables. We propose to discover Skolem terms in stages: an original task is decomposed into subtasks, where each of the subtasks is solved in isolation, and the solution to the original problem is obtained as one common *decision tree* that combines the results from the subtasks.

3.1   Illustrative Example

Consider a given formula in Disjunctive Normal Form (DNF) (we defer a discussion of a general case until later in this section). Here, it is intuitively easy to see that the individual Skolem function for each $\vec{y}[j]$ can be represented in the form of a decision tree, as illustrated in the following example.

Example 1. Given a formula $\exists y_1, y_2 \,.\, \psi(x, y_1, y_2)$ in LIA, where

$$\psi(x, y_1, y_2) \stackrel{\text{def}}{=} (x \leq 2 \wedge y_1 > -3 \cdot x \wedge y_2 < x) \vee (x \geq -1 \wedge y_1 < 5 \cdot x \wedge y_2 > x)$$

The formula is valid, which means that for every value of x there exist values of y_1 and y_2 that make either of two disjuncts true. Intuitively, the disjuncts correspond to two cases, when $x \leq 2$ or $x \geq -1$. We call these formulas *preconditions*.

To extract Skolem terms for y_1 and y_2, this example permits considering two preconditions in isolation (however, it may not be true for other formulas, see Sect. 3.3). That is, if $x \leq 2$, then y_1 should satisfy $y_1 > -3 \cdot x$ and y_2 should satisfy $y_2 < x$. In other words, the following two formulas are valid:

$$(x \leq 2) \implies \exists y_1 \,.\, (y_1 > -3 \cdot x)$$
$$(x \leq 2) \implies \exists y_2 \,.\, (y_2 < x)$$

Skolem terms for y_1 and y_2 assuming $x \leq 2$ could be $-3 \cdot x + 1$ and $x - 1$ respectively. Similarly, for the second precondition:

$$(x \geq -1) \implies \exists y_1 \,.\, (y_1 < 5 \cdot x)$$
$$(x \geq -1) \implies \exists y_2 \,.\, (y_2 > x)$$

Assuming $x \geq -1$, a Skolem term for y_1 could again be $-3 \cdot x + 1$, but a Skolem term for y_2 is $x + 1$. Combining these Skolem terms for both preconditions, we get Skolem terms for $\exists y_1, y_2 . \psi(x, y_1, y_2)$:

$$sk_{y_1}(x) \overset{\text{def}}{=} -3 \cdot x + 1$$

$$sk_{y_2}(x) \overset{\text{def}}{=} ite(x \leq 2, x - 1, x + 1)$$

Note that this composition is possible because $(x \leq 2) \vee (x \geq -1)$ is valid. In the next subsection, we describe this process formally.

3.2   Effective Decomposition

Our functional synthesis technique is based on a notion we call *effective decomposition*, defined below.

Definition 1. *A* decomposition *of a valid formula* $\exists \vec{y} . \psi(\vec{x}, \vec{y})$ *is a tuple* $\langle pre, \phi \rangle$, *where* pre *(called* preconditions*) is a vector of formulas of length* M *and* ϕ *(called* Skolem constraints*) is a matrix of dimensions* $M \times |\vec{y}|$, *such that the following three conditions hold.*

$$true \implies \bigvee_{i=1}^{M} pre[i](\vec{x}) \qquad\qquad (i\text{-totality})$$

$$pre[i](\vec{x}) \wedge \bigwedge_{j=1}^{|\vec{y}|} \phi[i, j](\vec{x}, \vec{y}) \implies \psi(\vec{x}, \vec{y}) \qquad\qquad (\text{under-approximation})$$

$$pre[i](\vec{x}) \implies \exists \vec{y} . \bigwedge_{j=1}^{|\vec{y}|} \phi[i, j](\vec{x}, \vec{y}) \qquad\qquad (j\text{-totality})$$

Lemma 1. *For every valid formula* $\exists \vec{y} . \psi(\vec{x}, \vec{y})$, *a decomposition exists.*

Indeed, a decomposition could be constructed by the formula itself and a precondition *true*. We are not interested in such cases because they do not simplify a process of extracting Skolem terms from Skolem constraints ϕ. Instead, we impose additional syntactic restrictions on ϕ. In particular, we call a decomposition $\langle pre, \phi \rangle$ of $\exists \vec{y} . \psi(\vec{x}, \vec{y})$ *$\mathcal{G}$-effective* if all formulas ϕ are expressible in some grammar $\mathcal{G}$.

The task of extracting Skolem terms boils down to developing an algorithm that (1) produces Skolem constraints in $\mathcal{G}$, and (2) exploits $\mathcal{G}$ to extract a matrix of Skolem terms from a matrix of Skolem constraints, i.e., the following holds:

$$\vec{y}[j] = sk[i, j](\vec{x}) \implies \phi[i, j](\vec{x}, \vec{y}) \qquad\qquad (\text{embedding})$$

Theorem 1. *Let* $\langle pre, \phi \rangle$ *be a decomposition of* $\exists \vec{y} . \psi(\vec{x}, \vec{y})$, *and* sk *be a matrix of Skolem terms, such that* (embedding) *holds. Then* Sk_j *is the Skolem term for* $\vec{y}[j]$:

$$Sk_j \overset{\text{def}}{=} ite(pre[1], sk[1, j], \ldots ite(pre[M-1], sk[M-1, j], sk[M, i])) \qquad (2)$$

A straightforward implementation of Sk_j in the form of a decision tree is shown in Fig. 1.

In this work, we restrict $\mathcal{G}$ to be the grammars of LIA/LRA (see Sect. 2) but allow neither disjunctions nor negations. In the next subsection, we outline an algorithm that creates a $\mathcal{G}$-effective decomposition while solving formulas for validity. Then, in Sect. 4, we present an algorithm for extracting Skolem terms from formulas in $\mathcal{G}$.

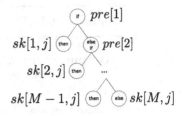

Fig. 1. A decision tree.

3.3 Witnessing Existential Quantifiers with AE-VAL

Obtaining preconditions in general requires quantifier elimination. However, it leads to expensive reasoning, which we would like to improve upon.

Example 2. Consider the following formula:

$$\exists y_1, y_2 . \left(y_1 > x_1 \vee y_2 < -x_2\right) \wedge \left(y_1 < x_2 \vee y_2 > -x_1\right)$$

If we were running the algorithm from [16], we would need to convert this formula into DNF, which would give us four disjuncts. A complete quantifier-elimination procedure would be then required to produce four preconditions and four Skolem constraints.

Our lazy quantifier-elimination method, called AE-VAL, generates both preconditions and Skolem constraints while solving the given formula for validity. In contrast to the DNF translation, for the formula in Example 2, it generates only two preconditions and two Skolem constraints.

The pseudocode of AE-VAL is shown in Algorithm 1 (we refer the reader to [6] for more detail). AE-VAL produces a sequence of Model-Based Projections (MBPs, see the definition below) [14], each of which under-approximates quantifier elimination. It iterates until the disjunction of MBPs is valid and thus avoids a complete quantifier elimination.

Definition 2. *An MBP$_{\vec{y}}$ is a function from models of $\psi(\vec{x}, \vec{y})$ to $\vec{y}$-free formulas if it has a finite image and the following hold:*

$$\text{if } m \models \psi(\vec{x}, \vec{y}) \text{ then } m \models MBP_{\vec{y}}(m, \psi)$$
$$MBP_{\vec{y}}(m, \psi) \implies \exists \vec{y} . \psi(\vec{x}, \vec{y})$$

There are different algorithms for constructing MBPs for different theories. We follow a method from [3] for LIA and present it on the following example. Intuitively, it is based on finding models, testing them on literals of the original formula, and eliminating quantifiers from the conjunctions of literals that passed the test.

Algorithm 1: AE-VAL$\left(\exists \vec{y} . \psi(\vec{x}, \vec{y})\right)$, cf. [6].

Input: $\exists \vec{y} . \psi(\vec{x}, \vec{y})$
Output: Return value $\in \{\text{VALID}, \text{INVALID}\}$ of $\exists \vec{y} . \psi(\vec{x}, \vec{y})$,
        MBPs pre, Skolem constraints ϕ

1 $M \leftarrow 1$;
2 **while** true **do**
3 $\quad$ **if** $true \implies \bigvee_{i=1}^{M} pre[i](\vec{x})$ **then return** $\langle \text{VALID}, pre, \phi \rangle$;
4 $\quad$ $tmp \leftarrow \psi(\vec{x}, \vec{y}) \wedge \bigwedge_{i=1}^{M} \neg pre[i](\vec{x})$;
5 $\quad$ **if** $tmp \implies false$ **then return** $\langle \text{INVALID}, \varnothing, \varnothing \rangle$;
6 $\quad$ $m \leftarrow \text{GETMODEL}(tmp)$;
7 $\quad$ $\langle pre[M], \phi[M, 1], \ldots, \phi[M, |\vec{y}|] \rangle \leftarrow \text{GETMBP}(\vec{y}, m, \psi)$;
8 $\quad$ $M \leftarrow M + 1$;

Example 3. Recall the formula $\exists y_1, y_2 . \psi(x_1, x_2, y_1, y_2)$ from Example 2. Its set of literals is $Lit = \{y_1 > x_1, y_2 < -x_2, y_1 < x_2, y_2 > -x_1\}$. In the first iteration, AE-VAL generates a model m_1 of ψ: $m_1 = \{x_1 \mapsto 0, x_2 \mapsto -2, y_1 \mapsto 0, y_2 \mapsto 1\}$. An MBP of ψ w.r.t. m_1 is then generated iteratively: by eliminating y_1 first, and eliminating y_2 then.

For y_1 and m_1, AE-VAL fills $\phi[1, 1]$ with a set of literals $\{l \in Lit \mid y_1 \in vars(l) \wedge m_1 \models l\}$, i.e., $\{y_1 < x_2\}$. Then AE-VAL eliminates quantifiers from $\exists y_1 . \phi[1, 1]$ and adds the result (i.e., $true$) to the MBP.

For y_2 and m_1, AE-VAL fills $\phi[1, 2]$ with $\{l \in Lit \mid y_2 \in vars(l) \wedge m_1 \models l\}$, i.e., $\{y_2 < -x_2, y_2 > -x_1\}$. It then eliminates quantifiers from $\exists y_2 . \phi[1, 2]$ and adds the result (i.e., $x_1 - x_2 > 1$) to the MBP.

Thus, after the first iteration of AE-VAL, we get the precondition $pre[1] = x_1 - x_2 > 1$, and Skolem constraints $\phi[1, 1]$ and $\phi[1, 2]$. The second iteration proceeds similarly, and AE-VAL outputs $pre[2] = true$, $\phi[2, 1] = y_1 > x_1$, and $\phi[2, 2] = y_2 > -x_1$, and terminates.

Lemma 2. *If* AE-VAL *returns* $\langle \text{VALID}, pre, \phi \rangle$ *for a formula* $\exists \vec{y} . \psi(\vec{x}, \vec{y})$, *then the formula is* effectively decomposable *by pre and* ϕ, *i.e., (i-totality), (under-approximation), and (j-totality) hold.*

Intuitively, the sequence of MBPs provides a *lazy* disjunctive decomposition of the overall problem, where each precondition can capture an arbitrary subspace on the $\vec{x}$ variables (under which it is possible to derive a Skolem term for the $\vec{y}$ variables). It often requires far fewer decompositions than a DNF-based quantifier elimination approach, where each precondition can at best be a *cube*, i.e., a conjunction of predicates on $\vec{x}$. Note that the number of decompositions, M, corresponds directly to the depth of the decision tree in the generated implementations. Thus, our MBP-based procedure for quantifier elimination can potentially perform better and lead to smaller implementations. Our experimental results in Sect. 6 show promising support.

4 Extraction of Skolem Terms

In this section, we describe our procedure for extracting individual Skolem terms from a matrix of Skolem constraints $\phi[i, j]$ in linear arithmetic. As pointed out in (embedding), this procedure is performed independently of a precondition $pre[i]$. We first describe the procedure where each $\phi[i, j]$ has occurrence of only one variable $y = \vec{y}[j]$, and thus has form $\pi(\vec{x}, y)$; and $pre[i](\vec{x}) \implies \exists y . \pi(\vec{x}, y)$ is valid. In Sect. 4.3, we describe how to handle occurrences of multiple $\vec{y}$ variables.

Although the general extraction schema is similar for all background theories, specific algorithmic details of each theory need to be discussed. In the rest of this section, we separately consider algorithms for LRA and LIA.

4.1 Skolem Terms in LRA

In Algorithm 2, we show how to extract a Skolem term for a variable $y \in \vec{y}$ from constraints having form $\pi(\vec{x}, y)$. Intuitively, Algorithm 2 constructs a graph of a function that is embedded in a relation specified by a conjunction of equalities, inequalities, and disequalities over y and $\vec{x}$. Thus, Algorithm 2 takes as input six vectors of clauses extracted from π: E, D, G, GE, L, and LE:

$$E \stackrel{\text{def}}{=} \{y = f_i(\vec{x})\}_i \quad G \stackrel{\text{def}}{=} \{y > f_i(\vec{x})\}_i \quad L \stackrel{\text{def}}{=} \{y < f_i(\vec{x})\}_i$$

$$D \stackrel{\text{def}}{=} \{y \neq f_i(\vec{x})\}_i \quad GE \stackrel{\text{def}}{=} \{y \geq f_i(\vec{x})\}_i \quad LE \stackrel{\text{def}}{=} \{y \leq f_i(\vec{x})\}_i$$

We do not consider constraints having the shape $\alpha \cdot y \sim f(\vec{x})$, because it is safe to normalize it to $y \sim \frac{f(\vec{x})}{\alpha}$ (assuming positive α; a negative α requires swapping the operator $\sim$ between $<$ and $>$, and $\leq$ and $\geq$). Finally, we assume that at least one of the vectors of clauses is non-empty, otherwise a Skolem term could be arbitrary, and there is no need to run Algorithm 2.

Below we present several helper-operators needed to construct a term sk based on a lightweight analysis of clauses in E, D, G, GE, L, and LE (where $\sim \in \{<, \leq, =, \neq, \geq, >\}$):

$$\text{ASSM}(y \sim e(\vec{x})) \stackrel{\text{def}}{=} e \quad \text{ADD}(\ell, c) \stackrel{\text{def}}{=} \ell + c \quad \text{MID}(\ell, u) \stackrel{\text{def}}{=} \frac{\ell + u}{2}$$

In the case when there is at least one conjunct $(y = e(\vec{x})) \in E$ (line 1), the algorithm simply returns the exact term $e(\vec{x})$. Note that there could be two or more equalities in E, which are consistent with each other due to (j-totality). Thus, it does not matter which of them is used for extracting a Skolem term.

In the case when there are lower and upper bounds (lines 2 and 3 respectively), the algorithm extracts expressions that encode the maximal and minimal values that y can take. Technically, it is done by *mapping* sets G and GE (for MAX) and L and LE (for MIN) to results of applications of ASSM to elements of these sets. In the case when $D = \varnothing$ or when ℓ and u are semantically equal, the algorithm has sufficient information to extract a Skolem term. In particular,

---

Algorithm 2: EXTRACTSKLRA($\vec{x}, y, E, D, G, GE, L, LE$)

Input: Variable y, Skolem constraint
$$\pi(\vec{x}, y) = \bigwedge_{\ell \in E \cup D \cup G \cup GE \cup L \cup LE} \ell(\vec{x}, y)$$
Output: Term sk, such that $(y = sk(\vec{x})) \implies \pi(\vec{x}, y)$
1   **if** $E \neq \varnothing$ **then return** ASSM(e), s.t. $e \in E$;
2   **if** $G \cup GE \neq \varnothing$ **then** $\ell \leftarrow max(map(\text{ASSM}, G \cup GE))$;
3   **if** $L \cup LE \neq \varnothing$ **then** $u \leftarrow min(map(\text{ASSM}, L \cup LE))$;
4   **if** $\ell(\vec{x}) = u(\vec{x})$ **then return** ℓ;
5   **if** $D = \varnothing$ **then**
6 | **if** $\ell \neq$ undef $\wedge u \neq$ undef) **then return** MID(ℓ, u);
7 | **if** $\ell =$ undef **then return** ADD($u, -1$);
8 | **if** $u =$ undef **then return** ADD($\ell, 1$);
9   **else**
10 | **if** $\ell =$ undef $\wedge u =$ undef **then** $\ell \leftarrow 1$;
11 | **if** $\ell =$ undef **then** $\ell \leftarrow$ ADD($u, -1$);
12 | **if** $u =$ undef **then** $u \leftarrow$ ADD($\ell, 1$);
13 | **return** BNSR($\ell, u, map(\text{ASSM}, D), |D|$);

---

if both lower and upper bounds are extracted, the algorithm returns a symbolic midpoint (line 6). Otherwise, it returns a symbolic value which differs from the upper or lower bounds (whichever is present) by one (lines 7 and 8).

Example 4. Consider $\pi = (y > 4 \cdot x_1) \wedge (y \geq -3 \cdot x_2 + 1) \wedge (y < x_1 + x_2)$. Algorithm 2 aims at extracting a term sk such that $(y = sk(x_1, x_2)) \implies \pi$. First, the algorithm extracts the lower bound from two inequalities with ">" and "$\geq$": $\ell = max(4 \cdot x_1, -3 \cdot x_2 + 1) = ite(4 \cdot x_1 > -3 \cdot x_2 + 1, 4 \cdot x_1, -3 \cdot x_2 + 1)$. Second, the algorithm extracts the upper bound from the only "<"-inequality: $u = x_1 + x_2$. Finally, the algorithm extracts and returns the symbolic midpoint between ℓ and u. That is, $sk = \frac{ite(4 \cdot x_1 > -3 \cdot x_2 + 1, 4 \cdot x_1, -3 \cdot x_2 + 1) + (x_1 + x_2)}{2}$.

The rest of the algorithm handles disequalities, i.e., in the case when $D \neq \varnothing$ (line 9). It assumes that ℓ and u are extracted, otherwise any suitable ℓ and u could be selected (in lines 10–12, we use some particular but not the only possible choice).

Intuitively, if y is required to differ from some $h(\vec{x})$ and to be in a range (ℓ, u), it is sufficient to pick two distinct terms v_1 and v_2 such that:

$$(y = v_1(\vec{x})) \implies (\ell(\vec{x}) < y < u(\vec{x}))$$
$$(y = v_2(\vec{x})) \implies (\ell(\vec{x}) < y < u(\vec{x}))$$
$$(v_1(\vec{x}) = v_2(\vec{x})) \implies false$$

Since each variable assignment m to $\vec{x}$ makes at most one formula from set $\{h(m) = v_1(m), h(m) = v_2(m)\}$ true, we can always extract a Skolem term $sk = ite(h = v_1, v_2, v_1)$ that satisfies $(y = sk(\vec{x})) \implies (y \neq h(\vec{x}))$.

A similar reasoning is applied to any set D of disequalities: it is enough to consider $|D| + 1$ terms, which are semantically distinct. Our algorithm can be parametrized by any routine that extracts semantically distinct terms belonging to a range between ℓ and u. Two of possible routines are inspired respectively by a binary search (which is used in line 13) and a linear scan.

Definition 3. *Let n be the number of disequalities in D and H be the set of right sides of expressions of D, then the binary-search helper-operator is defined as follows:*

$$
\text{BNSR}(\ell, u, H, n) \stackrel{\text{def}}{=} \begin{cases} \text{MID}(\ell, u) & \text{if } n = 0 \\ ite\Big(\bigvee_{h \in H} \text{MID}(\ell, u) = h, \\ \quad \text{BNSR}\big(l, \text{MID}(\ell, u), H, n-1\big), \text{MID}(\ell, u)\Big) & \text{else} \end{cases}
$$

Example 5. Consider $\pi = (y \neq x_1 \wedge y \neq x_2)$. Since there are no inequalities in π, the lower and upper bounds are obtained from an arbitrary range, say $(0, 1)$. Otherwise, they are computed similarly to as in Example 4. Algorithm 2 uses BNSR and returns the following Skolem term:

$$
sk = ite\Big(\frac{1}{2} = x_1 \vee \frac{1}{2} = x_2, ite\Big(\frac{1}{4} = x_1 \vee \frac{1}{4} = x_2, \frac{1}{8}, \frac{1}{4}\Big), \frac{1}{2}\Big)
$$

Definition 4. *Let s be some number, then*

$$
\text{SCAN}(\ell, s, H, n) \stackrel{\text{def}}{=} \begin{cases} \ell & \text{if } n = 1 \\ ite\Big(\bigvee_{h \in H} \ell = h, \text{SCAN}\big(\ell + s, s, H, n-1\big), \ell\Big) & \text{else} \end{cases}
$$

Example 6. Consider formula π from Example 5, for which $H = \{x_1, x_2\}$, $\ell = 0$, and $u = 1$. A Skolem term can be compiled using the call to $\text{SCAN}(\ell + \frac{u-\ell}{|H|+2}, \frac{u-\ell}{|H|+2}, H, |H|+1)$:

$$
sk = ite\Big(\frac{1}{4} = x_1 \vee \frac{1}{4} = x_2, ite\Big(\frac{1}{2} = x_1 \vee \frac{1}{2} = x_2, \frac{3}{4}, \frac{1}{2}\Big), \frac{1}{4}\Big)
$$

4.2   Skolem Terms in LIA

In this subsection, we present an algorithm for extracting Skolem terms in LIA. Although the flow of the algorithm is similar to the flow of the algorithm for LRA, presented in Sect. 4.1, there are two differences. First, there is no need to calculate a midpoint in the case when both a lower bound ℓ and an upper bound u are given. Instead, because (j-totality) guarantees the existence of at least one integer value for all y, it is enough to choose either the least or the greatest integer value within the range (ℓ, u). Second, there are divisibility constraints, which have to be treated more carefully. Unlike the case of LRA, we consider four vectors of clauses in the Skolem constraints π over LIA:

$$
E \stackrel{\text{def}}{=} \{\alpha \cdot y = f_i(\vec{x})\}_i \quad G \stackrel{\text{def}}{=} \{\alpha \cdot y > f_i(\vec{x})\}_i
$$
$$
D \stackrel{\text{def}}{=} \{\alpha \cdot y \neq f_i(\vec{x})\}_i \quad LE \stackrel{\text{def}}{=} \{\alpha \cdot y \leq f_i(\vec{x})\}_i
$$

Algorithm 3: EXTRACTSKLIA($\vec{x}, y, E, G, LE, D$)

Input: Variable y, Skolem constraint

$$\pi(\vec{x}, y) = \bigwedge_{\ell \in E \cup G \cup LE \cup D} \ell(\vec{x}, y)$$

Output: Term sk, such that $(y = sk(\vec{x})) \implies \pi(\vec{x}, y)$

1 **if** $(E \neq \varnothing)$ **then return** $\text{ASSM}_\mathbb{Z}(e)$, s.t. $e \in E$;
2 **if** $(G \neq \varnothing)$ **then** $\ell \leftarrow max(map(\text{ASSM}_\mathbb{Z}, G))$;
3 **if** $(LE \neq \varnothing)$ **then** $u \leftarrow min(map(\text{ASSM}_\mathbb{Z}, LE))$;
4 **if** $(D = \varnothing)$ **then**
5 $\quad\mid$ **if** $(\ell \neq$ undef$)$ **then return** $\text{ADD}(\ell, 1)$;
6 $\quad\mid$ **if** $(u \neq$ undef$)$ **then return** u;
7 **else**
8 $\quad\mid$ **if** $(\ell =$ undef $\wedge u =$ undef$)$ **then** $\ell \leftarrow 0$;
9 $\quad\mid$ **if** $(\ell =$ undef$)$ **then** $\ell \leftarrow \text{ADD}(u, -1 \cdot |D|)$;
10 $\quad\mid$ **return** $\text{SCAN}_\mathbb{Z}(\ell, D, |D|)$;

We can safely avoid clauses containing $<$ and $\geq$ because of the following transformations:

$$\frac{A < B}{A \leq B - 1} \qquad \frac{A \geq B}{A > B - 1} \qquad\qquad (3)$$

We need these rules to simplify the normalization of inequalities by dividing their right sides by α (assuming positive α; a negative α requires changing the operator $\sim$ accordingly). For example, it would not be correct to normalize an inequality $5 \cdot y \geq 9$ to $y \geq div(9, 5)$. Instead, when $5 \cdot y \geq 9$ is rewritten to $5 \cdot y > 8$, the normalization works correctly: $y > div(8, 5)$. Similarly, an inequality $5 \cdot y < 9$ should be rewritten to $5 \cdot y \leq 8$ and normalized to $y \leq div(8, 5)$.

We also rewrite the divisibility constraints (i.e., $div(y, \alpha) \sim f(\vec{x})$) using the following transformations (in addition to applying (3)):

$$\frac{div(y, \alpha) = f(\vec{x})}{\alpha \cdot f(\vec{x}) \leq y < \alpha \cdot f(\vec{x}) + \alpha} \qquad \frac{div(y, \alpha) > f(\vec{x})}{y > \alpha \cdot f(\vec{x}) + \alpha - 1}$$

$$\frac{div(y, \alpha) \neq f(\vec{x})}{\bigwedge_{i=0}^{\alpha-1} y \neq \alpha \cdot f(\vec{x}) + i} \qquad \frac{div(y, \alpha) \leq f(\vec{x})}{y \leq \alpha \cdot f(\vec{x}) + \alpha - 1}$$

An example for applying the first rule is $div(y, 3) = 0$: y could be either 0, 1, or 2; or in other words $0 \leq y \wedge y < 3$. For the second rule, an example is $div(y, 3) > 0$: y could be anything greater or equal than 3, or alternatively greater than 2. Similarly, $div(y, 3) \leq 0$ is equivalent to $y \leq 2$. Finally, the rule for disequalities enumerates a finite number (equal to α) of disequalities of form $y \neq f(x)$. For instance, $div(y, 3) \neq 1$ is equivalent to $y \neq 3 \wedge y \neq 4 \wedge y \neq 5$.

The pseudocode of the algorithm that extracts a Skolem term for π in LIA is shown in Algorithm 3. It handles constraints using the following helper-operators.

$$\text{ASSM}_\mathbb{Z}(\alpha \cdot y \sim f(\vec{x})) \overset{\text{def}}{=} div(f, \alpha)$$

Definition 5. *Let $h[y/\ell]$ denote the term h with term ℓ substituted for variable y. Then a helper-operator for the linear scan in LIA is implemented as follows.*

$$\text{SCAN}_\mathbb{Z}(\ell, H, n) \overset{\text{def}}{=} \begin{cases} \ell & \text{if } n = 0 \\ ite\Big(\bigwedge_{h \in H} h[y/\ell], \ \ell, \ \text{SCAN}_\mathbb{Z}(\ell + 1, H, n - 1)\Big) & \text{else} \end{cases}$$

For the case when there exists an equality $\alpha \cdot y = e(\vec{x})$ in π, it is sufficient to extract $div(e, \alpha)$ for sk, because requirement (j-totality) guarantees that e is divisible by α. This is implemented in function $\text{ASSM}_\mathbb{Z}$. To handle disequalities, the algorithm can only perform a linear scan, i.e., starting from the lower bound to make the least possible increments (i.e., by one). As opposed to the binary search, the linear scan guarantees that enough semantically distinct terms are considered. We illustrate this in the following example.

Example 7. Consider $\pi = (5 \cdot y \neq 4 \cdot x)$. Since there is no lower bound and no upper bound, we allow $\ell = 0$ (alternatively, any other term can be chosen). Then, since π has only one disequality, we get the final Skolem as a single if-then-else: $ite\Big((5 \cdot 0 \neq 4 \cdot x), 0, 1\Big)$.

4.3 Putting It All Together

Theorem 2. *For some i, let $\phi[i, j](\vec{x}, \vec{y})$ be in LRA (resp. LIA), and $|\vec{y}| = N$. Then for each $j \in [1, N]$, Algorithm 2 (resp. Algorithm 3.) extracts a term $sk[i, j]$, such that* (embedding) *holds.*

For proving this theorem, it remains to show how we obtain $\pi(\vec{x}, \vec{y}[j])$ that Algorithm 2 (resp. Algorithm 3) should take as input with each $\vec{y}[j]$. Indeed, the MBPs constructed in Sect. 3.3 allow occurrences of multiple variables from $\vec{y}$ in a clause in $\phi[i, j]$. However, by construction, a variable $\vec{y}[j]$ can appear in all $\phi[i, k], 1 \leq k \leq j$, but a variable $\vec{y}[j]$ cannot appear in any $\phi[i, k], j < k \leq N$. In particular, term $\phi[i, N]$ is only over the variables $\vec{x}$ and $\vec{y}[N]$. Therefore, we first apply Algorithm 2 (resp. Algorithm 3) to $\phi[i, N]$, to derive the Skolem term $sk[i, N]$. It is then substituted in all appearances of $\vec{y}[N]$ in other constraints $\phi[i, N - 1], \ldots, \phi[i, 1]$. Continuing such reasoning over the remaining variables leads to obtaining suitable inputs for Algorithm 2 (resp. Algorithm 3) and each $\vec{y}[j]$.

5 Synthesis of Compact Skolem Terms

Recall that Theorem 1 gives a way to construct a global Skolem term from preconditions and relations, and Sect. 4 describes algorithms to extract a local term $sk[i,j]$ from a relation $\phi[i,j]$. So far, this provides a procedure that invokes Algorithm 2 or Algorithm 3 as soon as possible, i.e., when $\phi[i,j]$ has just been produced by the MBP-based procedure AE-VAL together with some $pre[i]$. However, for large formulas it is often the case that the number M of generated MBPs is large, and so is a vector of tuples $\langle pre[i], \bigwedge_{0<j\leq N} \phi[i,j] \rangle$ where $0 < i \leq M$.

In this section, we propose to leverage the output of AE-VAL for producing compact Skolem terms. We first describe how to reduce the number of distinct Skolem terms among the tuples generated by AE-VAL for each $y \in \vec{y}$. Next, we aim to reduce the depth of the overall decision tree in case of multiple outputs $\vec{y}$, i.e., extracting a common if-then-else (ite) block which is shared among all outputs.

5.1   Optimizing Decision Trees by Combining Preconditions

Our goal is to decrease the depth of a decision tree that combines Skolem terms for M different preconditions. Recall that at each node i, where $0 < i \leq M$ and for variable $y = \vec{y}[j]$, the Skolem term $sk[i,j]$ and the precondition $pre[i]$ should be connected via (j-totality) and (embedding), i.e.:

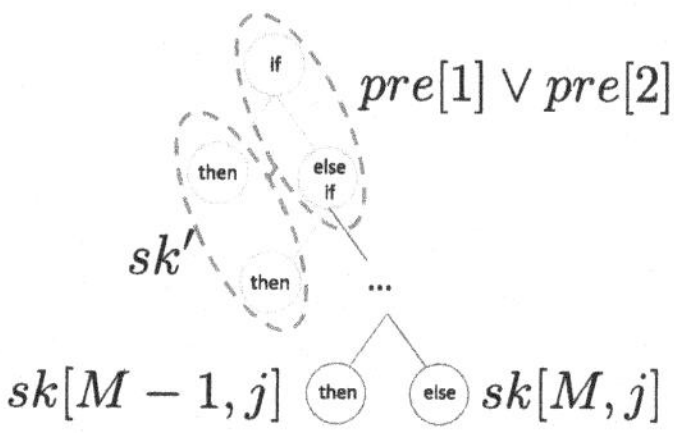

Fig. 2. Optimized decision tree.

$$pre[i](\vec{x}) \implies \exists y \,.\, \phi[i,j](\vec{x},\vec{y})$$
$$y = sk[i,j](\vec{x}) \implies \phi[i,j](\vec{x},\vec{y})$$

Note that preconditions in the decision tree could potentially guard the same Skolem terms, in which case we could compact the size. This is illustrated pictorially in Fig. 2 for the example shown earlier in Fig. 1. In particular, if $sk[1,j]$ and $sk[2,j]$ in Fig. 1 could be replaced by a common sk', then the preconditions $pre[1]$ and $pre[2]$ can be merged using a disjunction, thereby decreasing the depth of the decision tree. The challenge is that sk' might not necessarily be obtained by Algorithm 2 or Algorithm 3, because Skolem constraints $\phi[1,j]$ or $\phi[2,j]$, taken in isolation, are in general not restrictive enough. However, sk' could be produced by Algorithm 2 or Algorithm 3 if $\phi[1,j] \wedge \phi[2,j]$ is given as input.

Generalizing this idea further, we consider an expensive minimization algorithm to search over all partitions of the set $\mathbb{M} \stackrel{def}{=} \{1, \ldots, M\}$ and find the best partition such that each index in a class of the partition can share the same Skolem term. More formally, for each partition $\mathbb{P} \stackrel{def}{=} \{p_1, \ldots p_r\}$ of $\mathbb{M}$, for each class p_k in the partition, we check that:

$$\bigvee_{i \in p_k} pre[i](\vec{x}) \implies \exists y \,.\, \bigwedge_{i \in p_k} \phi[i,j](\vec{x},y) \qquad (4)$$

If all r implications hold, then $\mathbb{P}$ is a valid candidate partition, associated with r Skolem terms $sk', \ldots, sk^{(r)}$ derived from $\bigwedge_{i \in p_1} \phi[i,j](\vec{x},y), \ldots, \bigwedge_{i \in p_r} \phi[i,j](\vec{x},y)$, respectively. We then select the best partition among the valid candidate par-

---

Algorithm 4: GETPARTITIONCLASS($\mathbb{I}, pre, \phi, y = \vec{y}[j]$)

Input: Initial set of indices $\mathbb{I}$, preconditions pre, constraints ϕ

Output: Output set of indices p_k

1 $p_k \leftarrow \mathbb{I}$;

2 **while** $\bigvee\limits_{i \in p_k} pre[i](\vec{x}) \not\Longrightarrow \exists y . \bigwedge\limits_{i \in p_k} \phi[i,j](\vec{x}, y)$ **do**

3 $\quad \big|\quad p_k \leftarrow \{i \in p_k \mid pre[i](\vec{x}) \Longrightarrow \exists y . \bigwedge\limits_{i \in p_k} \phi[i,j](\vec{x}, y)\}$;

4 **for** $i' \in \mathbb{I} \setminus p_k$ **do**

5 $\quad \big|\quad$ **if** $\bigvee\limits_{i \in p_k \cup \{i'\}} pre[i](\vec{x}) \Longrightarrow \exists y . \bigwedge\limits_{i \in p_k \cup \{i'\}} \phi[i,j](\vec{x}, y)$ **then**

6 $\quad \big|\quad \big|\quad p_k \leftarrow p_k \cup \{i'\}$;

7 **return** p_k;

---

titions, based on size of resulting Skolem terms (or other cost criteria). Clearly, examining all possible partitions would have exponential cost, with the check for each partition class also being an expensive validity check.

Instead of the expensive exact minimization, we adopt a greedy strategy for finding a *good* (but not necessarily the best) valid candidate partition, possibly within a predetermined number of iterations. The routine for identifying each partition class p_k is shown in Algorithm 4. First, p_1 is selected from $\mathbb{M}$, then p_2 is selected from $\mathbb{M} \setminus p_1$, and so on.

Algorithm 4 is based on iteratively guessing a set of indices p_k and checking an implication of the form (4). The guessing proceeds in two phases: first it checks if all eligible indices from a set $\mathbb{I} \subseteq \mathbb{M}$ are in p_k. If so, the algorithm terminates. Otherwise, it iteratively tries to strengthen the left side of (4) by removing some of the disjuncts (line 3). After removing a disjunct $pre[i']$ from the left side, the Skolem constraint $\phi[i', j]$ should also be removed from the right side, and the validity check repeats. This way, the algorithm is guaranteed to find the set of indices p_k (possibly, empty) in a finite number of iterations.

The second phase of the guessing aims at strengthening p_k. It simply traverses the set of indices $\mathbb{I} \setminus p_k$ (line 5), adds $pre[i']$ and $\phi[i', j]$ to the left and right sides of 4 respectively and checks validity. The motivation behind the second phase is that the first phase could be too aggressive in practice, thus removing more indices from p_k than needed.

Example 8. Recall our formula from Example 1. For generating a Skolem term for y_1, we create the following $\forall\exists$-formula and check its validity:

$$(x \geq -1 \vee x \leq 2) \Longrightarrow \exists y_1 . (y_1 < 5 \cdot x \wedge y_1 > -3 \cdot x)$$

Since this formula is valid, our algorithm creates a single Skolem term $sk[1,1] = sk[1,2] = -3 \cdot x + 1$.

For generating a Skolem term for y_2, the corresponding $\forall\exists$-formula is invalid, and our algorithm generates two different Skolem terms $sk[2,1]$ and $sk[2,2]$:

$$(x \geq -1 \vee x \leq 2) \Longrightarrow \exists y_2 . (y_2 < x \wedge y_2 > x)$$

5.2 Minimizing the Depth of the Common Decision Tree

To allow re-use of theory terms among multiple outputs $\vec{y}$, a common *ite*-block could be pulled outside of the individual decision trees for each output, denoted $Sk_{\vec{y}}(\vec{x}, \vec{y})$:

$$Sk_{\vec{y}}(\vec{x}, \vec{y}) \stackrel{\text{def}}{=} ite\Big(pre[1](\vec{x}), \bigwedge_{j=1}^{N} \vec{y}[j] = sk[1, j](\vec{x}), \ldots$$

$$ite\big(pre[M-1](\vec{x}), \bigwedge_{j=1}^{N} \vec{y}[j] = sk[M-1, j](\vec{x}), \bigwedge_{j=1}^{N} \vec{y}[j] = sk[M, i](\vec{x})\big)\Big)$$

In general, depending on the cost criteria, it may be advantageous to not have a common *ite*-block at all or to have it be common to a subset of the outputs rather than all outputs. In this section, we consider a simple case where a common *ite*-block is shared among *all* outputs. Then, the remaining goal is to reduce the depth of this block by finding redundant branches.

Recall that Algorithm 4 can be used *per output* to find a good partition among the tuples, i.e., to decide which branches of the *ite*-block can share the same Skolem term. We view the results from this algorithm in the form of a matrix of Skolem terms, with a row for each *ite*-branch and a column for each output. Then, it is straightforward to identify redundant branches, which correspond to identical rows in the matrix. We illustrate this process in an example.

Example 9. Consider a formula with four existentially quantified variables $\vec{y}$ and four preconditions. Suppose the algorithm from Sect. 5 returns the partitions of the set $\{1, 2, 3, 4\}$ for each variable in $\vec{y}$, as shown in the following matrix.

For instance, $\vec{y}[1]$ requires a partition $\{p_1\}$ where $p_1 = \{1, 2, 3, 4\}$. Variable $\vec{y}[2]$ requires partition $\{q_1, q_2\}$ where $q_1 = \{1\}$ and $q_2 = \{2, 3, 4\}$. Variable $\vec{y}[3]$ requires partition $\{r_1, r_2\}$ where $r_1 = \{1, 2, 4\}$ and $q_2 = \{3\}$. Variable $\vec{y}[4]$ requires partition $\{s_1, s_2, s_3\}$ where $s_1 = \{1\}$, $s_2 = \{2, 4\}$ and $s_3 = \{3\}$.

We can easily identify identical rows $A_1, \ldots A_k$ in the matrix, such that for all $0 < j < M$, elements $A_1[j] = A_2[j] = \ldots = A_k[j]$ are equal.

	$\vec{y}[1]$	$\vec{y}[2]$	$\vec{y}[3]$	$\vec{y}[4]$
$pre[1]$	p_1	q_1	r_1	s_1
$pre[2]$	p_1	q_2	r_1	s_2
$pre[3]$	p_1	q_2	r_2	s_3
$pre[4]$	p_1	q_2	r_1	s_2

In this example, row A_1 corresponds to $pre[2]$, and row A_2 corresponds to $pre[4]$. Thus, individual Skolem terms for all variables for $pre[2]$ and $pre[4]$ can be combined, and the depth of the common *ite*-block is reduced by one.

6   Evaluation

We implemented our synthesis algorithms on top of the AE-VAL tool [6] which is in turn built on top of the Z3 SMT solver [5]. Note that the previous implementation of AE-VAL was already able to solve quantified formulas for validity via an iterative MBP construction and to extract Skolem constraints. However, it did not provide procedures to extract Skolem functions (described in Sect. 4) or to compact them (described in Sect. 5). In particular, note that during our compaction procedure, we use AE-VAL recursively to solve subsidiary quantified formulas of the form (4).

6.1   Results on Benchmark Examples

We considered 134 ∀∃-formulas originated from various Assume-Guarantee contracts written in the Lustre programming language [13] [4]. The majority of benchmarks are derived from industrial projects, such as a Quad-Redundant Flight Control System, a Generic Patient Controlled Analgesia infusion pump, as well as a Microwave model, a Cinderella-Stepmother game, and several hand-written examples. Since the original set of benchmarks include minor variations of the same tasks, we identified 80 distinct benchmarks[5] for presentation in Table 1.

All the ∀∃-formulas had more than one existentially-quantified variable. Table 1 presents the statistics and results on the benchmarks. The formulas are over 5–100 universally-quantified variables and 2–49 existentially-quantified variables. The highest depth of the common *ite*-block in the produced Skolem[6] is 7. AE-VAL was able to terminate on all of them within a timeout of 60 s. The solving stage (including construction of MBPs and collecting Skolem constraints) took less than a second for all benchmarks. Compiling **Skolem**$_1$ (i.e., without compaction) took insignificant time, but compacting **Skolem**$_2$ took much longer for 11 outliers (the most crucial one is №16). This can be explained by many iterations for greedily finding a good partition, as explained in Sect. 5.

Figure 3 visualizes the effect of the Skolem compaction. Each point in the plot corresponds to a pair of runs of AE-VAL: the x-axis shows the size of the compacted Skolem (i.e., extracted with the use of both techniques from Sect. 5), and the y-axis shows the size of the naively created Skolem. The geometric mean for the ratio is 2.06, and the largest improvement is 6.95 – seen for the benchmark №38. In nearly half of the cases (35 out of 80), the depth of the *ite*-structure in the Skolem decreased at least by one. However, what proved to be the most effective for compaction is the factoring out of individual Skolem terms for particular variables, i.e., AE-VAL found a function which is good for all preconditions by greedy partitioning.

---

[4] Not to be confused with the evaluation of [13] which applied AE-VAL iteratively, and most of the formulas were invalid. Here, we considered only valid formulas and focused only on the Skolem extraction.

[5] These benchmarks are available at: http://www.cs.princeton.edu/~grigoryf/aeval-benchs.zip.

[6] Without taking into account the individual *ite*-s due to computing greatest and lowest bounds and handling disequalities, as described in Sect. 4.

Table 1. Concrete evaluation data.

∀∃.ψ: Synthesis task; **Skolem₁**: without compaction, **Skolem₂**: with compaction; size: total number of Boolean and arithmetic operators, #∀: number of universally-quantified variables, #∃: number of existentially-quantified variables, #↓: depth of the *ite*-block, **time**: synthesis time (in seconds, for **Skolem₂**, including the compaction).

∀∃.ψ size	#∀	#∃	Skolem₁ size	#↓	time	Skolem₂ size	#↓	time
371	71	25	192	5	0.46	80	4	3.37
337	71	49	116	2	0.31	61	2	0.38
337	70	49	106	2	0.3	64	2	0.27
302	100	30	175	4	0.29	95	4	1.28
296	39	14	180	5	0.29	61	3	2.03
296	98	30	175	4	0.29	95	4	1.34
267	90	49	168	3	0.42	77	3	0.71
247	36	25	126	4	0.33	39	3	0.49
222	39	8	128	4	0.34	54	3	0.79
210	52	7	27	2	0.07	20	2	0.12
201	51	30	231	5	0.39	124	5	4.87
201	50	30	130	3	0.23	77	3	0.45
197	21	14	58	3	0.09	15	1	0.08
195	33	9	199	3	0.24	77	2	0.35
178	30	8	101	3	0.21	44	2	0.34
174	10	7	321	7	0.95	195	6	91.3
166	39	23	552	2	0.3	232	2	0.23
155	52	15	151	2	0.17	67	2	0.16
151	23	20	115	2	0.22	64	2	0.21
149	11	8	240	5	0.73	128	4	3.01
147	24	9	260	4	0.35	87	3	0.75
147	23	9	120	2	0.18	69	2	0.31
140	31	7	34	2	0.07	27	2	0.15
139	30	8	139	3	0.22	37	1	0.24
137	47	20	89	2	0.19	49	2	0.23
134	22	8	210	6	0.44	74	4	12.6
134	21	8	54	2	0.18	36	2	0.25
117	36	15	151	2	0.15	53	1	0.09
105	22	8	290	6	0.44	61	3	9.38
105	21	8	138	3	0.25	66	3	0.42
102	71	30	176	4	0.27	99	4	1.18
102	32	5	21	2	0.11	14	2	0.11
95	20	7	94	4	0.29	39	3	0.76
95	19	7	72	3	0.25	44	3	0.41
84	33	23	552	2	0.3	232	2	0.22
82	26	5	21	2	0.09	14	2	0.11
82	25	5	21	2	0.09	14	2	0.1
78	21	15	431	4	0.35	62	1	0.18
78	20	15	107	2	0.14	41	1	0.09
75	25	4	165	4	0.38	147	4	0.81

∀∃.ψ size	#∀	#∃	Skolem₁ size	#↓	time	Skolem₂ size	#↓	time
71	37	7	26	2	0.07	19	2	0.14
71	37	7	34	2	0.08	27	2	0.11
66	13	7	181	2	0.12	75	2	0.17
62	18	5	21	2	0.1	14	2	0.1
57	17	4	121	3	0.32	109	3	0.62
57	15	5	34	2	0.09	11	1	0.08
51	10	5	36	2	0.09	25	2	0.11
44	13	3	14	2	0.08	11	2	0.1
44	12	3	14	2	0.08	11	2	0.1
40	18	15	429	4	0.34	99	3	0.53
39	12	9	24	2	0.07	18	2	0.1
38	10	4	218	4	0.43	197	4	1.32
38	9	4	88	3	0.31	76	3	0.51
38	13	6	175	5	0.11	28	1	0.14
38	8	5	30	2	0.09	10	1	0.07
38	9	5	44	2	0.08	12	1	0.07
38	12	6	36	2	0.06	17	1	0.06
38	11	5	69	2	0.06	32	1	0.05
38	10	5	51	2	0.06	22	1	0.05
34	12	7	260	3	0.14	75	2	0.24
33	13	4	24	2	0.05	10	1	0.05
28	9	4	47	2	0.09	38	2	0.17
28	8	3	12	2	0.08	9	2	0.09
26	8	3	11	2	0.08	8	2	0.11
26	8	4	42	2	0.07	11	1	0.06
25	5	3	14	2	0.08	11	2	0.12
24	14	11	26	2	0.08	15	2	0.11
22	8	4	28	2	0.05	13	1	0.05
22	7	4	20	2	0.05	9	1	0.05
21	6	5	13	2	0.05	8	2	0.11
21	16	9	24	2	0.06	18	2	0.1
20	13	4	198	4	0.4	177	4	1.47
20	15	6	181	5	0.11	28	1	0.12
20	10	5	44	2	0.09	12	1	0.07
20	14	5	71	2	0.05	32	1	0.06
16	5	2	13	2	0.06	11	2	0.12
15	7	4	47	2	0.1	34	2	0.23
14	9	4	42	2	0.06	11	1	0.06
12	8	5	14	2	0.05	9	2	0.1
12	9	4	30	2	0.05	13	1	0.05

6.2   Comparison with CVC4

We also compared AE-VAL with state-of-the-art tool CVC4 [20], version 1.7-prerelease [git master 464470c3], the winner of the general track of the fifth SyGuS-COMP. Like AE-VAL and unlike most of the synthesizers based on an enumerative search (e.g. [2]), the *refutation-based synthesizer* in CVC4 does not

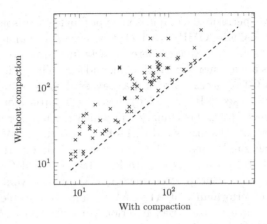

Fig. 3. Size of Skolems terms (i.e., total numbers of Boolean and arithmetic operators).

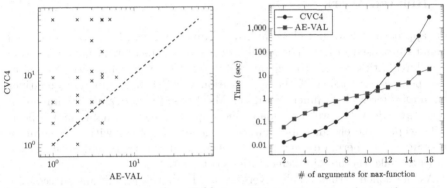

(a) *Ite*-depth for benchmarks from Table 1.   (b) Synthesis time for `max`-functions.

Fig. 4. Benefits of AE-VAL over CVC4.

enforce any syntactic restrictions on its solutions, e.g., formal grammars or templates, and it is more efficient than an enumerative synthesizer also implemented in CVC4.

Among 80 benchmarks from Table 1, CVC4 was able to solve 55, and it exceeded a timeout of 60 s for the remaining 25 benchmarks. In Fig. 4(a), we report the ratio of depths of the *ite*-blocks generated in the implementations. In most of the cases, our implementations have shorter depths.

Note that due to reasonings of encoding [19], CVC4 solved slightly different problems, in which it extracted only individual Skolems for each output variable. It is unable to combine them in one relation or share them, as opposed to what our tool does. Thus, we are unable to compare the overall *size* of the implementations produced by CVC4 and our method.

In addition, we performed comparison experiments on isolated groups of benchmarks from SyGuS-COMP, in which the formal grammars were ignored by both tools. In particular, we considered nearly fifty *single-invocation* benchmarks from groups `array_sum`, `array_search`, and `max`. The performance of both AE-VAL and CVC4 on `array_sum` and `array_search` is similar – both tools converge in less than a second. Figure 4(b) shows a comparison of AE-VAL with CVC4 on a sequence of `max`-benchmarks, in which the number of arguments n for the function `max` being synthesized varies from 2 to 16. AE-VAL and CVC4 both converge with similar results, but the synthesis time varies significantly. Note that for $n < 10$, both tools require less than 1 s (and CVC4 is slightly faster), but for larger n, the performance of CVC4 gets worse almost exponentially, while the performance of AE-VAL remains reasonable. In particular, CVC4 is unable to synthesize a `max` function with 17 inputs after two hours, but AE-VAL synthesizes a solution in just forty seconds.

7   Related Work

Our approach follows the classical flow of functional synthesis for unbounded domains proposed in [16]. Their main idea is to enhance quantifier-elimination procedures with a routine to generate witnesses. However, in practice, it requires an expensive conversion of the specification to DNF and applying quantifier elimination for each disjunct. With our MBP-based lazy quantifier-elimination procedure AE-VAL, we have made the approach more scalable and robust, while keeping the elegance and improving generality of the witness generation procedures. Furthermore, our approach benefits from additional optimization stages to make the final implementations compact.

As mentioned earlier, an older version of AE-VAL was built and successfully used for solving the validity of ∀∃-formulas [6]. It has been successfully used in many applications:

- Realizability checking and synthesis from Assume-Guarantee contracts [13],
- Non-termination checking, and (potentially) synthesis of never-terminating lasso-shaped programs [9],
- Synthesis of simulation relations between pairs of programs [6,7],
- Synthesis of (candidates of) inductive invariants [8].

However, it did not include any procedures to generate terms for a pure functional synthesis setting, or to compact the Skolems and share terms. We believe our new procedures can further improve the above-listed and other applications of AE-VAL.

An alternative way to quantifier elimination for solving functional synthesis tasks is implemented in CVC4 [20]. Their refutation-based approach aims at determining the unsatisfiability of the negated form of ∀∃-formula. A solution is then directly obtained from an unsatisfiable set of ground instances of the negated synthesis conjecture. Similarly to AE-VAL, CVC4 proceeds lazily and creates a decision tree. However, as confirmed by our evaluation, their decision trees are often larger than the decision trees produced by AE-VAL for the same tasks.

Laziness in the search-space exploration allows viewing both AE-VAL and CVC4 as instances of Counterexample-Guided Inductive Synthesis (CEGIS [21]). Typically, the CEGIS-based algorithms, e.g., [1,2,21,22], perform a guided search over the syntax tree of the program being synthesized. Our approach to synthesis, as well as [16] and [20], is driven by the logical structure of a background theory and does not put any restriction on the syntax tree size. This allows generating large and expressive implementations (such as max-functions over dozens of inputs) quickly.

There is a rich body of work on logic synthesis, i.e., synthesis of Boolean gate-level functions from specifications in propositional logic [12]. This considers synthesis of two-level (e.g., sum of products) or multi-level circuits, with minimization of various cost criteria (size, delay, power, etc.), and with sharing Boolean gates across multiple outputs. While our motivation for sharing "logic" is similar, note that we identify theory terms that can be shared within the implementation of an output, and across implementations of multiple outputs. Thus, our minimization/compaction is not at the Boolean-level, but requires theory-specific reasoning (validity checks). Furthermore, most logic synthesis efforts start with functional specifications. There have been some efforts in considering relational specifications [4,15], but these are fairly straightforward extensions of well-known functional techniques.

Finally, a procedure similar to Model-Based Projection has also been used for existential quantification in Boolean formulas [11], where it was called circuit-cofactoring. The application considered there was SAT-based model checking, where a pre-image of a given set of states is computed by existential quantification of a set of variables. The main idea was to use a model on the quantified variables to derive a circuit-cofactor (including disjunctions), which can capture many more states than a generalized cube on the remaining variables. This resulted in far fewer enumerations than cube-based enumeration techniques.

8   Conclusions

We have presented a novel approach to functional synthesis based on lazy quantifier elimination. While checking realizability of the given specification, our algorithm produces a system of synthesis subtasks through effective decomposition. Individual solutions for these subtasks generate a decision tree based implementation, which is further eligible for optimizations. Compared to the existing approaches, our generated solutions are more compact, and the average running time for their synthesis is reasonably small. We have implemented the approach in a tool called AE-VAL and evaluated it on a set of reactive synthesis benchmarks and benchmarks from SyGuS-COMP. We have identified classes of programs when AE-VAL outperformed its closest competitor CVC4 both on running time and on *ite*-depth of implementations. In the future, we wish to extend AE-VAL to other first-order theories, to support (whenever applicable) enumeration-based reasoning, which utilizes grammars and results in even more compact solutions, and to leverage specifications enhanced with input-output examples.

Acknowledgments. We thank Andreas Katis for providing encodings of benchmarks for reactive synthesis from Assume-Guarantee contracts into an SMT-LIB2 format acceptable by AE-VAL.

This work was supported in part by NSF Grant 1525936. Any opinions, findings, and conclusions expressed herein are those of the authors and do not necessarily reflect those of the NSF.

References

1. Alur, R., Černý, P., Radhakrishna, A.: Synthesis through unification. In: Kroening, D., Păsăreanu, C.S. (eds.) CAV 2015. LNCS, vol. 9207, pp. 163–179. Springer, Cham (2015). https://doi.org/10.1007/978-3-319-21668-3_10
2. Alur, R., Radhakrishna, A., Udupa, A.: Scaling enumerative program synthesis via divide and conquer. In: Legay, A., Margaria, T. (eds.) TACAS 2017. LNCS, vol. 10205, pp. 319–336. Springer, Heidelberg (2017). https://doi.org/10.1007/978-3-662-54577-5_18
3. Bjørner, N., Janota, M.: Playing with quantified satisfaction. In: LPAR (short papers), EPiC Series in Computing, vol. 35, pp. 15–27. EasyChair (2015)
4. Brayton, R.K., Somenzi, F.: An exact minimizer for boolean relations. In: ICCAD, pp. 316–319. IEEE (1989)
5. de Moura, L., Bjørner, N.: Z3: an efficient SMT solver. In: Ramakrishnan, C.R., Rehof, J. (eds.) TACAS 2008. LNCS, vol. 4963, pp. 337–340. Springer, Heidelberg (2008). https://doi.org/10.1007/978-3-540-78800-3_24
6. Fedyukovich, G., Gurfinkel, A., Sharygina, N.: Automated discovery of simulation between programs. In: Davis, M., Fehnker, A., McIver, A., Voronkov, A. (eds.) LPAR 2015. LNCS, vol. 9450, pp. 606–621. Springer, Heidelberg (2015). https://doi.org/10.1007/978-3-662-48899-7_42
7. Fedyukovich, G., Gurfinkel, A., Sharygina, N.: Property directed equivalence via abstract simulation. In: Chaudhuri, S., Farzan, A. (eds.) CAV 2016. LNCS, vol. 9780, pp. 433–453. Springer, Cham (2016). https://doi.org/10.1007/978-3-319-41540-6_24
8. Fedyukovich, G., Prabhu, S., Madhukar, K., Gupta, A.: Solving constrained horn clauses using syntax and data. In: FMCAD. ACM (2018)
9. Fedyukovich, G., Zhang, Y., Gupta, A.: Syntax-guided termination analysis. In: Chockler, H., Weissenbacher, G. (eds.) CAV 2018. LNCS, vol. 10981, pp. 124–143. Springer, Cham (2018). https://doi.org/10.1007/978-3-319-96145-3_7
10. Fried, D., Tabajara, L.M., Vardi, M.Y.: BDD-based boolean functional synthesis. In: Chaudhuri, S., Farzan, A. (eds.) CAV 2016. LNCS, vol. 9780, pp. 402–421. Springer, Cham (2016). https://doi.org/10.1007/978-3-319-41540-6_22
11. Ganai, M.K., Gupta, A., Ashar, P.: Efficient SAT-based unbounded symbolic model checking using circuit cofactoring. In: ICCAD, pp. 510–517. IEEE Computer Society/ACM (2004)
12. Hachtel, G.D., Somenzi, F.: Logic Synthesis and Verification Algorithms. Springer, Heidelberg (2006). https://doi.org/10.1007/b117060

13. Katis, A., et al.: Validity-guided synthesis of reactive systems from assume-guarantee contracts. In: Beyer, D., Huisman, M. (eds.) TACAS 2018. LNCS, vol. 10806, pp. 176–193. Springer, Cham (2018). https://doi.org/10.1007/978-3-319-89963-3_10

14. Komuravelli, A., Gurfinkel, A., Chaki, S.: SMT-based model checking for recursive programs. In: Biere, A., Bloem, R. (eds.) CAV 2014. LNCS, vol. 8559, pp. 17–34. Springer, Cham (2014). https://doi.org/10.1007/978-3-319-08867-9_2

15. Kukula, J.H., Shiple, T.R.: Building circuits from relations. In: Emerson, E.A., Sistla, A.P. (eds.) CAV 2000. LNCS, vol. 1855, pp. 113–123. Springer, Heidelberg (2000). https://doi.org/10.1007/10722167_12

16. Kuncak, V., Mayer, M., Piskac, R., Suter, P.: Functional synthesis for linear arithmetic and sets. STTT **15**(5–6), 455–474 (2013)

17. Monniaux, D.: A quantifier elimination algorithm for linear real arithmetic. In: Cervesato, I., Veith, H., Voronkov, A. (eds.) LPAR 2008. LNCS (LNAI), vol. 5330, pp. 243–257. Springer, Heidelberg (2008). https://doi.org/10.1007/978-3-540-89439-1_18

18. Pnueli, A., Rosner, R.: On the synthesis of a reactive module. In: POPL, pp. 179–190. ACM Press (1989)

19. Raghothaman, M., Udupa, A.: Language to specify syntax-guided synthesis problems. CoRR, abs/1405.5590 (2014)

20. Reynolds, A., Deters, M., Kuncak, V., Tinelli, C., Barrett, C.: Counterexample-guided quantifier instantiation for synthesis in SMT. In: Kroening, D., Păsăreanu, C.S. (eds.) CAV 2015. LNCS, vol. 9207, pp. 198–216. Springer, Cham (2015). https://doi.org/10.1007/978-3-319-21668-3_12

21. Solar-Lezama, A., Tancau, L., Bodík, R., Seshia, S.A., Saraswat, V.A.: Combinatorial sketching for finite programs. In: ASPLOS, pp. 404–415. ACM (2006)

22. Torlak, E., Bodík, R.: A lightweight symbolic virtual machine for solver-aided host languages. In: PLDI, pp. 530–541. ACM (2014)

Static Analysis of Binary Code with Memory Indirections Using Polyhedra

Clément Ballabriga[1(✉)], Julien Forget[1(✉)], Laure Gonnord[2(✉)],
Giuseppe Lipari[1(✉)], and Jordy Ruiz[1(✉)]

[1] CRIStAL (Univ. Lille, CNRS, Centrale Lille, UMR 9189), Lille, France
{Clement.Ballabriga,Julien.Forget,Giuseppe.Lipari,
Jordy.Ruiz}@univ-lille.fr
[2] Univ. Lyon, LIP (UMR CNRS/ENS Lyon/UCB Lyon1/INRIA), Lyon, France
laure.gonnord@ens-lyon.fr

Abstract. In this paper we propose a new abstract domain for static analysis of binary code. Our motivation stems from the need to improve the precision of the estimation of the Worst-Case Execution Time (WCET) of safety-critical real-time code. WCET estimation requires computing information such as upper bounds on the number of loop iterations, unfeasible execution paths, etc. These estimations are usually performed on binary code, mainly to avoid making assumptions on how the compiler works. Our abstract domain, based to polyhedra and on two mapping functions that associate polyhedra variables with registers and memory, targets the precise computation of such information. We prove the correctness of the method, and demonstrate its effectiveness on benchmarks and examples from typical embedded code.

1 Introduction

In real time systems, checking that computations complete before their deadlines under all possible contexts is a crucial activity. Worst-Case Execution Time (WCET) analysis consists in computing an upper bound to the longest execution path in the code. It is usually performed on the binary code, because it needs information on the low-level instructions executed by the hardware processor.

In this paper, we propose a static analysis of binary code based on abstract interpretation using a polyhedra-based abstract domain. Our motivation is the need to enhance existing WCET analysis by improving the computation of upper bounds on the number of iterations in loops. However, our abstract domain has other potential applications (not developed in this paper), such as buffer-overflow analysis, unfeasible paths analysis or symbolic WCET computation [6].

Most analyses by abstract interpretation proposed in the literature are performed on *source code*. On the contrary, as it is usually the case for WCET

Partially funded by the French National Research Agency, Corteva project (ANR-17-CE25-0003), and CODAS project (ANR-17-CE23-0004-01).

C. Enea and R. Piskac (Eds.): VMCAI 2019, LNCS 11388, pp. 114–135, 2019.
https://doi.org/10.1007/978-3-030-11245-5_6

```
1   void send_packet(char *buf) {
2       int iphdr_l = ((struct ip*)buf)->hdr_len;
3       int udp_l = ((struct udp*)(buf + iphdr_l))->len;
4       for (int i = 0; i < udp_l; i++) { /* do CRC */ }
5       ethernet_write(buf);
6   }
7
8   void send_request(int iphdr_size, int udp_size) {
9       char buf[1024];
10      if ((iphdr_size >= 20) && (iphdr_size <= 60) &&
11          (udp_size >= 4) && (udp_size <= 100)) {
12          struct ip *h1 = buf;
13          struct udp *h2 = buf + iphdr_size;
14
15          h1->hdr_len = iphdr_size;
16          h2->len = udp_size;
17          fill_packet_payload(buf);
18          send_packet(buf);
19      }
20  }
```

Fig. 1. Network-inspired benchmark

analysis, we propose to analyze *binary code*. There are several important advantages in performing static analysis of binary code: (1) we analyze the code that actually runs on the machine, hence no need for additional assumptions on how the compiler works; (2) in presence of undefined behaviors (of source code), the analysis is more accurate; (3) we can perform the analysis even without access to the source code.

The main problem is that, in higher-level representations, the variables, addresses and values are well identified. In binary code, the notion of program variable is lost, so we can only analyze processor registers and memory locations. We propose to identify the subset of registers and memory locations to be represented in the abstract state as the analysis progresses. This representation enables us to design a relational analysis on binary code, which is the main contribution of the paper.

1.1 Motivating Example

As a motivating example, we present a snippet of C code, inspired from packet processing network drivers in Fig. 1[1]. We remind however that our methodology addresses (disassembled) binary code.

The **send_request** function sends a request in some application-layer protocol that runs over UDP/IP. Lines 12–13 build a packet composed of a variable-length IP header, a fixed-length UDP header, and a variable-length UDP payload

---

[1] The original bench listing is available here: https://pastebin.com/C5UPYRx3.

(some operations on IP or UDP fields have been omitted). Note that the starting address of the UDP header depends on the size of the IP header (h1->hdr_len). At line 17, we call the function responsible for putting the useful data (payload) into the packet. At line 18, the packet is sent using the send_packet function, which belongs to the lower-level network layer API. This function does not take the packet size as parameter, since it can be deduced from the header: in lines 2-3, the function parses the packet to obtain the UDP payload size, and the UDP checksum is computed by iterating over the payload.

To automatically compute a bound on the number of iterations of the loop at line 4, the analysis has to discover that udp_l equals udp_size (due to line 16). This can be done with an appropriate use of a *relational abstract domain*. However, very few of the existing analyses running on binary code use a relational domain, and to the best of our knowledge, none support relations between addresses that are not know statically (udp_l, udp_size). Let us emphasize that such a use of pointers and memory buffers is typical of many embedded systems: for instance in network packet processing, but also in many device drivers.

1.2   Contribution

The contributions of the paper are:

- A new *relational* abstract domain POLYMAP, which consists of a polyhedron and two mappings that track the correspondence between data locations (registers or memory) and polyhedra variables;
- An abstract interpretation procedure, which computes abstract states of POLYMAP for a small assembly language, and which we prove to be sound;
- An experimental evaluation of our prototype called Polymalys. It implements the previous procedure and computes upper bounds to loop iterations. We compare Polymalys with other existing tools on a set of classic benchmarks.

2   Language Definition

In this section, we define the analyzed language, called MEMP, a simplified assembly language where we focus on memory indirection operators.

2.1   Syntax

In order to simplify the presentation, we make the following assumptions: all data locations have the same size, memory accesses are aligned to the word size, there are no integer overflows, and function calls are inlined (these limitations could be lifted using for instance [10,28]). We also reduce the set of instructions to a minimum (Polymalys actually supports the ARM A32 instruction set). The syntax of MEMP is defined in Fig. 2. A program is a sequence of labeled instructions. Instructions operate on registers, labels or constants. Concerning memory instructions, if r contains value c, then $*(r)$ denotes the content at address r (below, we overload the notation and also denote $*(c)$ for this content). OP^c denotes the concrete semantics of operation OP. RAND emulates undefined registers, to represent e.g. function parameters. Other instructions are directly commented in the figure (on the left of each instruction).

$$
\begin{array}{lll}
\text{Programs (P)} & ::= l_1 : I_1, \ l_2 : I_2, \ \ldots, \ l_n : \text{END} \\
\text{Labels (L)} & ::= \{l_1, l_2, \ldots\} \\
\text{Registers (R)} & ::= \{r_1, r_2, \ldots\} \\
\text{Constants (C)} & ::= \{c_1, c_2, \ldots\} \\
\text{Instructions (I)} & ::= \\
\quad r_1 \leftarrow OP^c(r_2, r_3) & | \quad \text{OP r1 r2 r3} \\
\quad r \leftarrow c & | \quad \text{SET r c} \\
\quad \text{Emulate undefined } r & | \quad \text{RAND r} \\
\quad r_1 \leftarrow *(r_2) & | \quad \text{LOAD r1 r2} \\
\quad *(r_1) \leftarrow r_2 & | \quad \text{STORE r1 r2} \\
\quad \text{Branch to } l \text{ if } r = 0 & | \quad \text{BR r l} \\
\quad \text{Halt} & | \quad \text{END}
\end{array}
$$

Fig. 2. Syntax of MEMP

2.2 Formal Semantics

The small-steps semantics of MEMP is defined below. The semantics of data and arithmetic/logic operations is defined in Fig. 3 by function $\xrightarrow{i}$, which operates in a context $(\mathcal{R}, *)$ consisting of two mappings where:

- $\mathcal{R} : R \nrightarrow \mathbb{Z}$ is the *registers content*, which maps registers to their values. We assume that it is initially empty;
- $* : \mathbb{Z} \nrightarrow \mathbb{Z}$ is the *memory content*, which maps memory addresses to their values. We assume that it is also initially empty. Note that integer wrapping could be used to restrain addresses to be in $\mathbb{N}$ instead of $\mathbb{Z}$ [10].

For a given mapping m, we denote $m[x : y]$ the mapping m' such that $m'(x) = y$ and, for every register $x' \neq x$, $m'(x') = m(x')$. In other words, $m[x : y]$ denotes a single mapping substitution (or mapping addition if x was previously unmapped). We also denote $m\backslash(x_1 : x_2)$ the mapping such that the association $x_1 : x_2$ is removed from m.

The semantics of control flow operations is defined in Fig. 4, by the function $\xrightarrow{c}$, which adds a program counter pc to the previous context. We use $\xrightarrow{e}$ to denote the last transition of the program.

3 Abstract Domain

The abstract domain we propose is based on the *polyhedral abstract domain* [12], to which we add information to track relations between polyhedra variables and registers or memory addresses.

$$\frac{}{(\texttt{SET r c}, \mathcal{R}, *) \xrightarrow{i} (\mathcal{R}[r:c], *)} \qquad \frac{c = random()}{(\texttt{RAND r}, \mathcal{R}, *) \xrightarrow{i} (\mathcal{R}[r:c], *)}$$

$$\frac{\mathcal{R}(r_2) = c_2 \qquad \mathcal{R}(r_3) = c_3 \qquad c_1 = \text{OP}^c(c_2, c_3)}{(\texttt{OP r}_1 \texttt{ r}_2 \texttt{ r}_3, \mathcal{R}, *) \xrightarrow{i} (\mathcal{R}[r_1 : c_1], *)}$$

$$\frac{\mathcal{R}(r_2) = c_2 \qquad *(c_2) = c_1}{(\texttt{LOAD r}_1 \texttt{ r}_2, \mathcal{R}, *) \xrightarrow{i} (\mathcal{R}[r_1 : c_1], *)} \qquad \frac{\mathcal{R}(r_1) = c_1 \qquad \mathcal{R}(r_2) = c_2}{(\texttt{STORE r}_1 \texttt{ r}_2, \mathcal{R}, *) \xrightarrow{i} (\mathcal{R}, *[c_1 : c_2])}$$

Fig. 3. Semantics of data and arithmetic operations.

$$\frac{P[pc] = \texttt{BR r l} \qquad \mathcal{R}(r) \neq 0}{P \vdash (pc, \mathcal{R}, *) \xrightarrow{c} (pc + 1, \mathcal{R}, *)} \qquad \frac{P[pc] = \texttt{BR r l} \qquad \mathcal{R}(r) = 0}{P \vdash (pc, \mathcal{R}, *) \xrightarrow{c} (l, \mathcal{R}, *)}$$

$$\frac{P[pc] = \texttt{END}}{P \vdash (pc, \mathcal{R}, *) \xrightarrow{e} (\mathcal{R}, *)} \qquad \frac{P[pc] = I \qquad I \notin \{\texttt{END}, \texttt{BR}\} \qquad (I, \mathcal{R}, *) \xrightarrow{i} (\mathcal{R}', *')}{P \vdash (pc, \mathcal{R}, *) \xrightarrow{c} (pc + 1, \mathcal{R}', *')}$$

Fig. 4. Semantics of control-flow operations.

3.1 Polyhedra

A *polyhedron* p denotes a set of points in a $\mathbb{Z}$ vector space bounded by linear constraints (equalities or inequalities). More formally, let $|S|$ denote the cardinality of set S. Let C_n denote the set of linear constraints in $\mathbb{Z}^n$ on the set of variables $\mathcal{V}_n$, where $|\mathcal{V}_n| = n$. Then $\langle c_1, c_2, ..., c_m \rangle$ denotes the polyhedron p consisting of all the vectors in $\mathbb{Z}^n$ that satisfy constraints $c_1, c_2, ..., c_m$, where $c_i \in C_n$ for $1 \leq i \leq m$ (n and m are unrelated). We denote $dim(p) = n$ the *dimension* of p. In the rest of the paper, the term *variable* implicitly refers to polyhedron variables. We denote:

- $\mathcal{P}$ the set of polyhedra;
- $s \in p$ when s (with $s \in \mathbb{Z}^{dim(p)}$) satisfies the constraints of polyhedron p;
- $p \sqsubseteq_\diamond p'$ iff $\forall s \in p, s \in p'$;
- $p'' = p \sqcup_\diamond p'$ the *convex hull* of p and p';
- $p'' = p \sqcap_\diamond p'$ the union of the constraints of p and p';
- $vars(p)$ the set of variables of p, where $|vars(p)| = dim(p)$ by definition;
- $proj(p, x_1 \ldots x_k)$ the projection of p on space $x_1 \ldots x_k$, with $k < |dim(p)|$;
- $p[x_i/x_j]$ the substitution of variable x_j by x_i in p.

3.2 Abstract States

In polyhedral analysis of source code, variables of the polyhedra are related to variables of the source code. In our case, polyhedra variables are related to registers and memory contents. We use the term *data location* to refer indistinctly to registers or memory addresses. Let $\mathcal{V}$ denote the set of polyhedra variables.

The set of abstract states POLYMAP is defined as $\mathcal{A} = \mathcal{P} \times (R \twoheadrightarrow V) \times (V \twoheadrightarrow V)$. An abstract state $a \in \mathcal{A}$, with $a = (p, \mathcal{R}^\sharp, *^\sharp)$, consists of a polyhedron p, a *register mapping* $\mathcal{R}^\sharp$ and an *address mapping* $*^\sharp$. We have $\mathcal{R}^\sharp(r) = v$ iff variable v represents the value of register r in p. We have $*^\sharp(x_1) = x_2$ iff variable x_2 represents the value at the memory address represented by variable x_1. We denote $vars_R(p)$ the codomain of $\mathcal{R}^\sharp$ (i.e. register content variables), $vars_A(p)$ the domain of $*^\sharp$ (i.e. address variables) and $vars_C(p)$ the codomain of $*^\sharp$ (i.e. address content variables). Sets $vars_R(p)$, $vars_A(p)$ and $vars_C(p)$ are disjoint and are all subsets of $vars(p)$.

Example 1. In the following abstract state, register r_0 contains value 2, and address 2 contains value 1:

$$(\{x_1 = 2, x_2 = x_1, x_3 = 1\}, \{r_0 : x_1\}, \{x_2 : x_3\})$$

The usual operators on the abstract domain (inclusion, join and widening), and its least and greatest elements are presented in Sect. 4.4.

3.3   Aliasing

In a general sense, *aliasing* occurs in a program when a data location can be accessed through several symbolic names. As we will see in Sect. 4, aliases play an important role in our analysis. In fact, we introduce mechanisms that prevent their occurrence in the abstract state (see Sect. 4.2), so as to simplify the analysis. We define the *aliasing relation* between two variables x_1 and x_2 of a polyhedron p as follows:

- Cannot alias: whenever $\langle x_1 = x_2 \rangle \cap p = \emptyset$;
- May alias: whenever $\langle x_1 = x_2 \rangle \cap p \neq \emptyset$;
- Must alias, denoted $x_1 \equiv x_2$: whenever $p \sqsubseteq_\diamond \langle x_1 = x_2 \rangle$.

The aliasing relation between a register r and a variable x is defined by the aliasing relation between $\mathcal{R}^\sharp(r)$ and x. Similarly, the aliasing relation between two registers r_1, r_2 is defined by the aliasing relation between $\mathcal{R}^\sharp(r_1)$ and $\mathcal{R}^\sharp(r_2)$.

To avoid ambiguities with notations on constraints, let $same(x_1, x_2)$ denote the fact that x_1 and x_2 are the same polyhedron variables (not just equivalent variables). There is no need to check register aliases, because a single register cannot be mapped to two different variables ($\mathcal{R}^\sharp$ is a function). The absence of aliases can thus be stated as follows.

Definition 1. Let $s = (p, \mathcal{R}^\sharp, *^\sharp)$ *be an abstract state. We say that s is* alias free *iff:*

$$\forall x_1, x_2 \in vars_A(p), x_1 \equiv x_2 \Rightarrow same(x_1, x_2)$$

4   Computing Abstract States

Our analysis follows the abstract interpretation framework proposed in [12], adapted to our setting with non-local control-flow, following the technique proposed in Astrée [21] and MOPSA [23]. An important singularity of our analysis is that polyhedral variables are progressively created or removed during the analysis. Whenever a new polyhedron variable is introduced, we assume it is a fresh variable that has never been used at any other point during the analysis.

4.1   Interpretation Algorithm

We use $(p', [r_i : x_i], [x_j : x_k])(\cdot)$ as a shorthand for $\lambda(p, \mathcal{R}^\sharp, *^\sharp).(p \sqcap_\diamond p', \mathcal{R}^\sharp[r_i : x_i], *^\sharp[x_j : x_k])$, and denote $-$ when a state component remains unchanged. Procedures to compute the join ($\sqcup$), widening ($\triangledown$) and *antialias* of abstract states, and the transfer function $(I)^\sharp$ of instruction I are detailed in the remainder of this section. The complete interpretation procedure is described in Algorithm 1. It applies to a program P of MEMP. During the interpretation, we keep a subset L of labels of interest. Abstract values are stored in a map M from labels to abstract values. We assume that loop header labels L_W of P have previously been identified using an existing analysis (e.g. Tarjan's algorithm [29]). Figure 5 reports a running example of this analysis, that will be used throughout the rest of the section.

1: RAND r0	5: ADD r3 r0 r1	9: STORE r3 r2
2: RAND r7	6: STORE r3 r1	10: LOAD r6 r3
3: SET r1 4	7: SUB r5 r7 r1	11: END
4: SET r2 5	8: BR r5 10	

Label	Polyhedron	Registers	Memory
5	$p_1 = \langle x_1 = 4, x_2 = 5 \rangle$	$\mathcal{R}_1^\sharp = \{r_0 : x_0, r_1 : x_1, \\ r_2 : x_2, r_7 : x_7\}$	
6	$p_2 = p_1 \sqcap_\diamond \langle x_3 = x_0 + x_1 \rangle$	$\mathcal{R}_2^\sharp = \mathcal{R}_1^\sharp[r_3 : x_3]$	
7	$p_3 = p_2 \sqcap_\diamond \langle x_4 = x_3, x_5 = x_1 \rangle$	$\mathcal{R}_2^\sharp$	$*_1^\sharp = \{x_4 : x_5\}$
8	$p_4 = p_3 \sqcap_\diamond \langle x_8 = x_7 - x_1 \rangle$	$\mathcal{R}_3^\sharp = \mathcal{R}_2^\sharp[r_5 : x_8]$	$*_1^\sharp$
10 (from 9)	$p_5 = p_4 \sqcap_\diamond \langle x_9 = x_2 \rangle$	$\mathcal{R}_3^\sharp$	$*_2^\sharp = \{x_4 : x_9\}$
10' (from 8)	$p_6 = p_4 \sqcap_\diamond \langle x_8 = 0 \rangle$	$\mathcal{R}_3^\sharp$	$*_1^\sharp$
$unify(10, 10')$	$p_7 = p_6[x_9/x_5]$	$\mathcal{R}_3^\sharp$	$*_3^\sharp = \{x_4 : x_9\}$
$10 \sqcup 10'$	$p_8 = p_2 \sqcap_\diamond \langle x_4 = x_3, x_8 = x_7 - x_1, \\ x_1 \leq x_9 \leq x_2 \rangle$	$\mathcal{R}_3^\sharp$	$*_3^\sharp$
11	$p_8 \sqcap_\diamond \langle x_{10} = x_9 \rangle$	$\mathcal{R}_3^\sharp[r_6 : x_{10}]$	$*_3^\sharp$

Fig. 5. Running example of analysis

Algorithm 1. INTERPRET(P)

1: **procedure** UPDATE(ℓ, a, L)   ▷ Auxiliary procedure
2:     $a \leftarrow antialias(a)$
3:     **if** $\ell \in L_W$ **then**   ▷ Check if l is a loop header
4:         $new \leftarrow M[l] \triangledown (M[l] \sqcup a)$
5:     **else**
6:         $new \leftarrow M[\ell] \sqcup a$
7:     **end if**
8:     **if** $new \not\sqsubseteq M[\ell]$ **then**   ▷ Abstract value for ℓ changed, propagate
9:         $M[\ell] \leftarrow new; L \leftarrow L \cup \ell$
10:    **end if**
11: **end procedure**
12:
13: **for all** $(\ell, I) \in P$ **do**   ▷ Start of main procedure
14:    $M[\ell] \leftarrow \bot$ ▷ Begin with empty abstract states
15: **end for**
16: $M[\ell_1] \leftarrow \top; L \leftarrow \{\ell_1\}$ ▷ Program starting label
17: **while** $L \neq \emptyset$ **do**   ▷ Fixpoint iteration
18:    Pick and remove ℓ from L
19:    **match** $P[\ell]$
20:        **with** BR r ℓ'
21:            UPDATE($\ell', (\langle r = 0 \rangle, -, -)(M[\ell]), L$)   ▷ Branching case
22:            UPDATE($\ell + 1, (-, -, -)(M[\ell]), L$)   ▷ Not branching case
23:        **with** END
24:            skip
25:        **with** _
26:            UPDATE($\ell + 1, ((P[\ell])^{\sharp})(M[\ell]), L$)   ▷ Abstract semantics of I
27: **end while**
28: **return** M

4.2   Anti-aliasing

Whenever updating an abstract state, we immediately remove aliases (line 2), because the absence of aliases significantly simplifies the analysis in places where we need to check the equivalence of two variables (LOAD, STORE, $\sqcup$ and $\triangledown$). In practice, aliases are introduced when encountering a conditional branching (see Sect. 4.3). We remove an alias using procedure *antialias*, which relies on the procedure *Merge* defined below. It is based on the following observation: if two addresses are equal, then the values stored at these addresses must be equal too. Let x_1, x_2 be two variables of $vars_A(p)$ such that: $\neg same(x_1, x_2) \wedge x_1 \equiv x_2$.

$$Merge((p, \mathcal{R}^{\sharp}, *^{\sharp}), x_1, x_2) = (p', \mathcal{R}^{\sharp}, *^{\sharp'}) \qquad \begin{array}{l} \text{with } p' = (p[x_1/x_2])[*^{\sharp}(x_1)/*^{\sharp}(x_2)] \\ \text{and } *^{\sharp'} = *^{\sharp} \setminus (x_2 : *^{\sharp}(x_2)) \end{array}$$

Function *antialias* : $\mathcal{A} \rightarrow \mathcal{A}$ applies *Merge* for each pair of distinct equivalent address variables of an abstract state.

Example 2. In state a below, address x_2 is an alias on address x_1. Thus, x_4 must be equal to x_3, so $Merge(a, x_1, x_2)$ replaces x_2 by x_1 and x_4 by x_3. In the result, x_3 is constrained by the original constraints of x_3 and x_4, and the memory mapping $x_2 : x_4$ is discarded.

$$a = (\langle x_1 = x_2, x_3 \geq 4, x_4 \leq 5 \rangle, \; -, \; *^\sharp = \{x_1 : x_3, x_2 : x_4\})$$

$$Merge(a, x_1, x_2) = (\langle 4 \leq x_3 \leq 5 \rangle, \; -, \; *^{\sharp'} = \{x_1 : x_3\})$$

4.3   Transfer Functions

We now define the constraints generated for the analysis of each instruction of our language. We denote $(I)^\sharp : \mathcal{A} \to \mathcal{A}$ the transfer function of instruction I.

Binary Operation. If the relation $r_1 = OP^c(r_2, r_3)$ is linear, we map the target register to a new variable, subject to the corresponding linear constraint in the polyhedron. The memory mapping is unchanged. Otherwise, the target register is mapped to a new unconstrained variable.

$$(\texttt{OP r}_1 \texttt{ r}_2 \texttt{ r}_3)^\sharp = \begin{cases} (\langle x = OP^c(\mathcal{R}^\sharp(r_2), \mathcal{R}^\sharp(r_3)) \rangle, \; [r_1 : x], \; -)(\cdot) & \text{if } linear(OP^c) \\ (-, \; [r_1 : x], \; -)(\cdot) & \text{otherwise} \end{cases}$$

Example 3. In Fig. 5, at label 6 (i.e. the label immediately following the ADD operation) we introduce the constraint $x_3 = x_0 + x_1$ and the register mapping $\mathcal{R}_1^\sharp(r_3) = x_3$.

Set. The impact of the immediate load instruction is straightforward:

$$(\texttt{SET r}_1 \texttt{ c})^\sharp = (\langle x = c \rangle, \; [r_1 : x], -)(\cdot)$$

Rand. The random instruction maps a register to an unconstrained variable:

$$(\texttt{RAND r}_1)^\sharp = (-, \; [r_1 : x], -)(\cdot)$$

Load. If the input state contains a memory address variable that is equivalent to the load address (note that for alias free states, if such a variable exists, it is unique), then in the output state the value of the destination register is the value of the memory value mapped to this address. Otherwise, the value of the destination register is undefined:

$$(\texttt{LOAD r}_1 \texttt{ r}_2)^\sharp = \begin{cases} (\langle x = *^\sharp(a) \rangle, \; [r_1 : x], \; -)(\cdot) & \text{if } a \equiv r_2 \\ (-, \; [r_1 : x], \; -)(\cdot) & \text{otherwise} \end{cases}$$

Example 4. In Fig. 5, at label 10 we have $x_4 \equiv r_3$ and $*^\sharp(x_4) = x_9$, so at label 11 we introduce the constraint $x_{10} = x_9$ and the mapping $\mathcal{R}_3^\sharp[r_6] = x_{10}$.

Store. Again, we need to consider the impact of aliases. If there exists an address variable equivalent to the target register, then there already exists a memory mapping for this address. The previous content at this address is replaced by the content of the source register (see *Replace* below). Otherwise, we create a new memory mapping (see *Create* below). An alias free state contains at most one address variable that must-alias with r_1. It may however contain several may-alias address variables a'. For each such a', this means that a' either equals r_1, which requires a *Replace*, or is different from r_1, which has no impact. We apply operator $\sqcup$ on both cases to manage this uncertainty, and add the constraints for each may-alias address (see *May* below).

$$(\text{STORE } \mathbf{r_1 \ r_2})^\sharp = \begin{cases} \lambda s.Replace(a)(May(s)) & \text{if } \exists a \in vars_A(p), a \equiv r_1 \\ \lambda s.Create(May(s)) & \text{otherwise} \end{cases}$$

With ($\bigcirc$ denotes function composition):

$$Replace(a) = (\langle x = \mathcal{R}^\sharp(r_2) \rangle, \ -, \ [a : x])(\cdot)$$
$$Create = (\langle x_i = \mathcal{R}^\sharp(r_1), x_j = \mathcal{R}^\sharp(r_2) \rangle, -, [x_i : x_j])(\cdot)$$
$$May = \bigcirc_{\{a \in A | a \text{ may-alias } r_1\}} \lambda s.(Replace(a)(s) \sqcup s)$$

Example 5. In Fig. 5, at label 7, we create a new memory mapping $*_1^\sharp(x_4) = x_5$ and we introduce the constraints $x_4 = x_3$, $x_5 = x_1$.

Example 6. In Fig. 5, at label 10, when coming from label 9, we replace a previous mapping, x_4 is mapped to x_9 (instead of x_5 previously), and we introduce the constraint $x_9 = x_2$.

Branching. In Algorithm 1, when branching to a target label (ℓ') the branching condition holds ($r = 0$). We add no constraint for the otherwise case because it cannot be encoded using a linear relation.

Example 7. In Fig. 5, at label 10, when coming from label 6, we add the constraint $x_8 = 0$.

4.4 Abstract Domain Operators, Least and Greatest Elements

Our analysis introduces new variables and removes old ones as it progresses. There is no predefined correspondence between variables and data locations, because the set of data locations used by the program is unknown a priori. As a consequence, it may happen that two abstract states use different variables to designate the same data location. This implies that to compare two states we first need to check whether some variables of the two states actually correspond to the same data location. This verification relies on a *unification* procedure, presented below. Unification is used for inclusion testing, and also in the join and widening operators.

Unification. Unification checks for the equivalence of two variables in two polyhedra, p_1 and p_2. Intuitively, we try to express each variable as a linear expression of a well-chosen set of variables to conveniently check their equivalence.

Let $V_c = vars(p_1) \cap vars(p_2)$ and $p' = proj(p_1, V_c) \sqcup_\diamond proj(p_2, V_c)$. We denote $npiv(p')$ the set of non-pivot variables discovered by Gauss-Jordan elimination performed on the system of equality constraints of p' (we exclude inequalities). Then, $npiv(p')$ is such that, in p':

- no variable in $npiv(p')$ is equivalent to a linear expression of other variables of $npiv(p')$;
- each variable in $vars(p') \setminus npiv(p')$ is equivalent to a linear expression of variables from $npiv(p')$.

Let $linexpr(x, p_1, npiv(p'))$ denote the linear expression representation of variable $x \in vars(p_1)$ in terms of variables in $npiv(p')$, represented as the vector of the linear expression coefficients. Let C' be the constraint system of $proj(p_1, x \cup npiv(p'))$. If C' contains an equality constraint involving x, then computing $linexpr(x, p_1, npiv(p'))$ is straightforward. Otherwise, the empty vector is returned. If several (non-equivalent) equality constraints appear, we arbitrarily pick one. Note that, even though our unification can miss equivalent variables, this does not jeopardize the soundness of the analysis (see Sect. 5.3 and in particular Lemma 3).

Algorithm 2 describes our unification procedure. We directly modify the second state to unify it with the first one. First, we compute set of non-pivot variables (line 4). Then, we check for the equivalence of address variables according to their linear expression representation, and we perform variable substitutions in p_2', $\mathcal{R}_2^{\sharp'}$ and $*_2^{\sharp'}$ in case of equivalence (line 8). Register unification is simpler, we just replace the bindings in $\mathcal{R}_2^{\sharp}$ by those of $\mathcal{R}_1^{\sharp}$ (line 12).

Algorithm 2. $unify((p_1, \mathcal{R}_1^\sharp, *_1^\sharp), (p_2, \mathcal{R}_2^\sharp, *_2^\sharp))$

1: $(p_2', \mathcal{R}_2^{\sharp'}, *_2^{\sharp'}) \leftarrow (p_2, \mathcal{R}_2^\sharp, *_2^\sharp)$
2: $V_c \leftarrow vars(p_1) \cap vars(p_2)$ ▷ common variables
3: $p' \leftarrow proj(p_1, V_c) \sqcup_\diamond proj(p_2, V_c)$
4: $B \leftarrow npiv(p')$
5: **for all** $(x_i, x_j) \in vars_A(p_1) \times vars_A(p_2)$ **do**
6:     $v_i = linexpr(x_i, p_1, B)$; $v_j = linexpr(x_j, p_2, B)$
7:     **if** $v_i \neq []$ and $v_j \neq []$ and $v_i = v_j$ **then**   ▷ variables are equivalent
8:         Replace x_j by x_i and $*^\sharp(x_j)$ by $*^\sharp(x_i)$ in p_2', $\mathcal{R}_2^{\sharp'}$, and $*_2^{\sharp'}$
9:     **end if**
10: **end for**
11: **for all** $r \in Dom(\mathcal{R}_1^\sharp) \cap Dom(\mathcal{R}_2^\sharp)$ **do**   ▷ variables are trivially equivalent
12:     Replace $\mathcal{R}_2^\sharp(r)$ by $\mathcal{R}_1^\sharp(r)$ in p_2', $\mathcal{R}_2^{\sharp'}$, and $*_2^{\sharp'}$
13: **end for**
14: **return** $(p_2', \mathcal{R}_2^{\sharp'}, *_2^{\sharp'})$

Example 8. In Fig. 5, when computing $unify(10, 10')$, s_1 corresponds to the state of 10 and s_2 to the state of $10'$. A possible set of non-pivot variables is $\{x_0, x_7\}$. In s_1 (and in s_2), we have $x_4 - x_0 + 0 \cdot x_7 - 4 = 0$, so $linexpr(x_4) = [1; -1; 0; -4]$ (corresponding, respectively, to the coefficients of x_4, x_0, x_7, and the constant). Since $*_2^\#(x_4) = x_9$ (in s_1) and $*_1^\#(x_4) = x_5$ (in s_2), we replace x_5 by x_9 in s_2.

Inclusion. Let us now define formally the partially ordered set $(\mathcal{A}, \sqsubseteq)$. Given two functions f and g, we denote $f \subseteq g$ when $Dom(f) \subseteq Dom(g)$ and $\forall x \in Dom(f) : f(x) = g(x)$. Introducing new mappings in $\mathcal{R}^\#$ or $*^\#$ (i.e. enlarging their domains) actually removes feasible concrete states, thus we define abstract states inclusion as follows (see Lemma 4 for more details):

Definition 2. *Let $a_1 = (p_1, \mathcal{R}_1^\#, *_1^\#)$ and $a_2 = (p_2, \mathcal{R}_2^\#, *_2^\#)$. The ordering operator $\sqsubseteq$ is defined as follows:*

$$a_1 \sqsubseteq a_2 \Leftrightarrow p_1' \sqsubseteq_\diamond p_2 \wedge \mathcal{R}_2^\# \subseteq \mathcal{R}_1^{\#'} \wedge *_2^\# \subseteq *_1^{\#'}$$
$$with \ (p_1', \mathcal{R}_1^{\#'}, *^{\#'}) = unify(a_2, a_1)$$

There exists several equivalent representations of the greatest and least elements of $(\mathcal{A}, \sqsubseteq)$. We define them as follows:

Definition 3. *The greatest element of $(\mathcal{A}, \sqsubseteq)$ is denoted $\top$, with $\top = (\langle\rangle, \emptyset, \emptyset)$.*

Definition 4. *The least element of $(\mathcal{A}, \sqsubseteq)$ is denoted $\bot$ and defined as $\bot = (p_\bot, \mathcal{R}_\bot^\#, *_\bot^\#)$, where $p_\bot$ is the empty polyhedron and $\mathcal{R}_\bot^\#, *_\bot^\#$ are such that every data location is mapped to a variable.*

Join. Algorithm 3 describes our join procedure. It unifies the input states (line 1), then computes the convex hull on the unified states (line 2). Then, if a memory location or register is bound in one input state and unbound in the other, it is unbound in the result state.

Example 9. In Fig. 5, when computing $10 \sqcup 10'$, we obtain identical register and memory mappings for 10 and $unify(10, 10')$. The convex hull $p_5 \sqcup_\diamond p_7$ groups the constraints on x_9 ($x_1 \leq x_9 \leq x_2$) and lifts those on x_8.

Widening. Due to the presence of loops, the widening operator ∇ is used to ensure that our analysis reaches a fixpoint. ∇ is defined just like $\sqcup$, except that we use a polyhedra widening operator $\nabla_\diamond$ in place of $\sqcup_\diamond$.

4.5   Loop Bounds

To compute loop bounds, for each loop header label ℓ we create a "virtual" register r_ℓ, to count the number of iterations of ℓ. We instrument the program

Algorithm 3. $(p_1, \mathcal{R}_1^\sharp, *_1^\sharp) \sqcup (p_2, \mathcal{R}_2^\sharp, *_2^\sharp)$

1: $(p_2', \mathcal{R}_2^{\sharp'}, *_2^{\sharp'}) = unify((p_1, \mathcal{R}_1^\sharp, *_1^\sharp), (p_2, \mathcal{R}_2^\sharp, *_2^\sharp))$
2: $p \leftarrow p_1 \sqcup_\diamond p_2'$
3: $\mathcal{R}^\sharp \leftarrow \emptyset;\ *^\sharp \leftarrow \emptyset$
4: **for all** $r \in Dom(\mathcal{R}_1^{\sharp'})$ **do**
5:     **if** $\mathcal{R}_1^\sharp(r) = \mathcal{R}_2^{\sharp'}(r)$ **then** $\mathcal{R}^\sharp(r) \leftarrow \mathcal{R}_1^\sharp(r)$ **end if**
6: **end for**
7: **for all** $a \in Dom(*_1^{\sharp'})$ **do**
8:     **if** $*_1^\sharp(a) = *_2^{\sharp'}(a)$ **then** $*^\sharp(a) \leftarrow *_1^\sharp(a)$ **end if**
9: **end for**
10: **return** $(p, \mathcal{R}^\sharp, *^\sharp)$

so that the register r_ℓ is set to 0 when entering loop ℓ, and incremented at each iteration of ℓ (which is fairly classic, see e.g. [15]).

Finally, let P a program of MEMP and $M = interpret(P)$. Let ℓ_e be the label of instruction END in P. Let $(p_f, \mathcal{R}_f^\sharp, *_f^\sharp) = M[\ell_e]$. Then the loop bound for a loop header ℓ is computed as $\max(p_f, \mathcal{R}_f^\sharp[r_\ell])$ (where $\max(p, x)$ denotes the greatest value of variable x satisfying the constraints of p).

5   Soundness

In this section, we prove the soundness of our analysis. We first establish a set of important lemmas on our abstract domain operators, and then prove soundness with respect to the concretization function.

5.1   Join

Operator $\sqcup$ is not commutative. We establish that it does however compute an upper bound of its operands, with respect to our inclusion definition (Lemma 1). The proof is based on two auxiliary properties on mapping inclusions:

Property 1. Let $a_1 = (p_1, \mathcal{R}_1^\sharp, *_1^\sharp)$, $a_2 \in \mathcal{A}$, $a_3 = (p_3, \mathcal{R}_3^\sharp, *_3^\sharp) = a_1 \sqcup a_2$. We have:

$$(p_1 \sqsubseteq_\diamond p_3) \wedge (\mathcal{R}_3^\sharp \subseteq \mathcal{R}_1^\sharp) \wedge (*_3^\sharp \subseteq *_1^\sharp)$$

Proof. Considering Algorithm 3: $(p_1 \sqsubseteq_\diamond p_3)$ follows from line 2, $(\mathcal{R}_3^\sharp \subseteq \mathcal{R}_1^\sharp)$ from line 5, and $(*_3^\sharp \subseteq *_1^\sharp)$ from line 8.   □

Property 2. Let $a_1, a_2, a_1' \in \mathcal{A}$, with $a_1' = (p_1', \mathcal{R}_1^{\sharp'}, *_1^{\sharp'}) = unify(a_2, a_1)$. Then:

$$(\mathcal{R}_2^\sharp \subseteq \mathcal{R}_1^\sharp) \wedge (*_2^\sharp \subseteq *_1^\sharp) \Rightarrow (\mathcal{R}_2^\sharp \subseteq \mathcal{R}_1^{\sharp'}) \wedge (*_2^\sharp \subseteq *_1^{\sharp'})$$

Proof. Obvious from Algorithm 2.

Lemma 1. Let $a_1, a_2 \in \mathcal{A}$. We have: $(a_1 \sqsubseteq a_1 \sqcup a_2) \wedge (a_2 \sqsubseteq a_1 \sqcup a_2)$.

Proof. Polyhedron inclusion follows from the polyhedra join operator. We must also prove the inclusion of register and memory mappings (after unification).

Case for a_1 follows from Properties 1 and 2. Concerning the case for a_2, let $a_3 = a_1 \sqcup a_2$. When computing a_3, a variable v of a_2 falls into one of three categories: (1) v is also in $vars(p_1)$, it remains in a_3; (2) v is equivalent to a variable v_1 of $vars(p_1)$, it is replaced by v_1 in a_3 (Algorithm 2, line 8); (3) otherwise, it is removed (Algorithm 3). Then, let $a'_2 = unify(a_3, a_2)$. When computing a'_2, variables that fell in category 2 at the previous step (when computing a_3) will be replaced by their equivalent in a_3, because they fall again in category 2. Thus we obtain $\mathcal{R}_3^\sharp \subseteq \mathcal{R}_2^{\sharp'}$, $*_3^\sharp \subseteq *_2^{\sharp'}$, which concludes the proof. □

5.2 Widening

Lemma 2 establishes that operator $\triangledown$ is indeed a widening operator.

Property 3. Let $a_1, a_2 \in \mathcal{A}$. We have: $(a_1 \sqcup a_2) \sqsubseteq (a_1 \triangledown a_2)$.

Proof. The property holds because $\sqcup$ and $\triangledown$ use the same unification procedure, and because we assume that $\triangledown_\diamond$ is a valid polyhedra widening operator. □

Property 4. Let $a_1 = (p_1, \mathcal{R}_1^\sharp, *_1^\sharp)$, $a_2 \in \mathcal{A}$, $a_3 = (p_3, \mathcal{R}_3^\sharp, *_3^\sharp) = a_1 \triangledown_\diamond a_2$. We have: $(p_1 \sqsubseteq_\diamond p_3) \wedge (\mathcal{R}_3^\sharp \subseteq \mathcal{R}_1^\sharp) \wedge (*_3^\sharp \subseteq *_1^\sharp)$

Proof. Same as for Property 1.

Property 5. Let $(b_n)_{n\in\mathbb{N}}$ be a non decreasing infinite sequence in $\mathcal{A}$. Then, the sequence $a_0 = b_0$ and $a_{n+1} = a_n \triangledown b_{n+1}$ converges in a finite number of steps.

Proof. Thanks to Property 4, and considering that there is a finite quantity of data locations, there exists $N \in \mathbb{N}$ such that for all $i > N$, $\mathcal{R}_{i+1}^\sharp = \mathcal{R}_i^\sharp$ and $*_{i+1}^\sharp = *_i^\sharp$. Thus, $a_{i+1} = (p_i \triangledown_\diamond q_{i+1}, \mathcal{R}_i^\sharp, *_i^\sharp)$, where q_{i+1} is the polyhedron of b_{i+1} and p_i that of a_i.

Assuming that $\triangledown_\diamond$ is a valid polyhedra widening operator, there exists $m > N$ such that $p_{m+1} = p_m$. Since $m > N$ we also have $\mathcal{R}_{m+1}^\sharp = \mathcal{R}_m^\sharp$ and $*_{m+1}^\sharp = *_m^\sharp$, which concludes the proof. □

Lemma 2. *Operator $\triangledown$ is a widening operator.*

Proof. Follows from Properties 3 and 5.

5.3 Concrete and Abstract States

Let $\mathcal{C} = ((R \nrightarrow \mathbb{Z}) \times (\mathbb{Z} \nrightarrow \mathbb{Z}))$ denote the set of concrete states (pairs of registers contents and memory contents). Data locations are mapped to values in a concrete state, while they are mapped to polyhedra variables in the abstract state. The concretization function γ relates data location values to data location variables as follows:

Definition 5. *Let $a = (p, \mathcal{R}^\sharp, *^\sharp)$ be an abstract state. The concretization function γ is defined as follows:*

$$\gamma : \mathcal{A} \longrightarrow \mathcal{P}(\mathcal{C})$$

$$(p, \mathcal{R}^\sharp, *^\sharp) \longmapsto \Big\{ (*, \mathcal{R}) \mid \exists f : Dom(*^\sharp) \to Dom(*),$$

$$\left(\overset{\diamond}{\underset{r \in Dom(\mathcal{R}^\sharp)}{\bigcap}} \langle \mathcal{R}^\sharp(r) = \mathcal{R}(r) \rangle \;\; \sqcap_\diamond \;\; \overset{\diamond}{\underset{x \in Dom(*^\sharp)}{\bigcap}} \langle x = f(x), *^\sharp(x) = *(f(x)) \rangle \right) \sqsubseteq_\diamond p \Big\}$$

More intuitively, we build a polyhedron p' with the following constraints: (1) register values of the concrete state ($\mathcal{R}(r)$) must be equal to the corresponding variable in the abstract state ($\mathcal{R}^\sharp(r)$); (2) we try to find a function f that maps address variables to addresses ($x = f(x)$), then the content of each address variables ($*^\sharp(x)$) must be equal to the memory value ($*(f(x))$). If $p' \sqsubseteq_\diamond p$ then the concrete state satisfies the constraints of p and belongs to the concretization.

Example 10.

$$a = (\{1 \leq x_1 \leq 2, x_2 = x_1, x_3 = 1\}, \{r_0 : x_1\}, \{x_2 : x_3\})$$

$$\gamma(a) = \{(\{r_0 = 1\}, \{*(1) = 1\}), \qquad\qquad\qquad (f(x_2) = 1)$$

$$(\{r_0 = 2\}, \{*(2) = 1\})\} \qquad\qquad\qquad\qquad (f(x_2) = 2)$$

Let $\overset{c}{\to}^*$ denote the transitive closure of $\overset{c}{\to}$. The soundness of our abstract interpretation is established as follows:

Theorem 1. *Let P be a MEMP program. Let $M = Interpret(P)$. Then, for any concrete state s_{init}: $(P \vdash (l_1, s_{init}) \overset{c}{\to}^* (\ell, s)) \implies (s \in \gamma(M[\ell]))$.*

Proof. The proof of soundness follows from the structure of Algorithm 1, and from the following lemmas, which establish the soundness of each operator used in the algorithm.

Lemma 3. *Let $a_1, a_2 \in \mathcal{A}$. We have: $\gamma(a_1) = \gamma(unify(a_2, a_1))$.*

Proof. Let $a_1' = unify(a_2, a_1)$. Since we assume that a_1 and a_2 are alias free (recall Sect. 4.2), any two non-equivalent variables in a_1 are also replaced by non-equivalent variables in a_1' (or unchanged). Thus a_1' is a simple renaming of a_1, and so a_1 and a_1' have the same concretization. □

Lemma 4. *Let $a_1, a_2 \in \mathcal{A}$. We have: $(a_1 \sqsubseteq a_2) \Rightarrow \gamma(a_1) \subseteq \gamma(a_2)$.*

Proof. Let $s \in \gamma(a_1)$. Let $a_1' = (p_1', \mathcal{R}_1^{\sharp'}, *_1^{\sharp'}) = unify(a_2, a_1)$. From Lemma 3, $s \in \gamma(a_1')$, thus there exists a function f for s satisfying the property of Definition 5 with $a = a_1$. Now, assume that $p_1' \sqsubseteq_\diamond p_2 \wedge \mathcal{R}_2^\sharp \subseteq \mathcal{R}_1^{\sharp'} \wedge *_2^\sharp \subseteq *_1^\sharp$ (i.e. $a_1 \sqsubseteq a_2$). Then there exists a function f' for s that satisfies Definition 5, with $a = a_2$: just take f' such that it is the restriction of f to $Dom(*_2^\sharp)$. So $s \in \gamma(a_2)$. □

Lemma 5. *Let a_1, $a_2 \in \mathcal{A}$. We have: $\gamma(a_1) \cup \gamma(a_2) \subseteq \gamma(a_1 \sqcup a_2)$.*

Proof. From Lemmas 1 and 4.

Lemma 6. *Let a_1, $a_2 \in \mathcal{A}$. We have: $\gamma(a_1) \cup \gamma(a_2) \subseteq \gamma(a_1 \triangledown a_2)$.*

Proof. From Lemmas 5, 4 and Property 3.

Lemma 7. *Let $a \in \mathcal{A}$. We have: $\gamma(a) \subseteq \gamma(antialias(a))$.*

Proof. Let $(p, \mathcal{R}^\sharp, *^\sharp) = a$. Let x_1, $x_2 \in vars_A(p)$ be such that $\neg same(x_1, x_2) \wedge x_1 \equiv x_2$. Then:

$$
\begin{aligned}
s \in \gamma(a) &\Rightarrow s \in \gamma(p \sqcap_\diamond \langle x_1 = x_2, *^\sharp(x_1) = *^\sharp(x_2) \rangle, \mathcal{R}^\sharp, *^\sharp) \\
&\Rightarrow s \in \gamma((p[x_1/x_2])[*^\sharp(x_1)/ *^\sharp (x_2)], \mathcal{R}^\sharp, *^\sharp) \\
&\Rightarrow s \in \gamma(Merge(a_1, x_1, x_2))
\end{aligned}
$$

The soundness of *antialias* follows. □

Lemma 8. *Let P be a MEMP program. Let $M = Interpret(P)$. Then, for all labels ℓ, ℓ' of P:*

$$(P \vdash (\ell, \mathcal{R}, *) \xrightarrow{c} (\ell', \mathcal{R}', *')) \Longrightarrow ((\mathcal{R}, *) \in \gamma(M[\ell]) \Rightarrow (\mathcal{R}', *') \in \gamma(M[\ell']))$$

Proof. Trivially follows from the formal semantics and from the definition of transfer functions, except for STORE. Let $a' = (p', \mathcal{R}^{\sharp'}, *^{\sharp'}) = (\text{STORE } r_1 \ r_2)^\sharp(a)$. The proof follows from noting that: (1) Both in the *Create* and *Replace* cases, we obtain $*^{\sharp'}(\mathcal{R}^{\sharp'}(r_1)) = \mathcal{R}^{\sharp'}(r_2)$, which is coherent with the formal semantics of STORE; (2) The soundness of *May* follows from the soundness of $\sqcup$ and *Replace*. □

Lemma 9. *Algorithm 1 terminates.*

Proof. Because $\triangledown$ is applied on loop headers and $\triangledown$ is a valid widening operator. □

6 Related Works

Abstract interpretation using polyhedra has been first described in [12]. Static analysis tools such as Astree [21], Frama-C [11] or PAGAI [18] use various abstract domains (including polyhedra) to generate invariants for proving various properties, such as the absence of array out-of-bounds accesses for instance.

While Astree and Frama-C work on the Abstract Syntax Tree, PAGAI processes LLVM Intermediate Representation (IR). Compared to our approach, both the AST and LLVM representations are closer to the source code, and contain information on variables and their types, and also a precise control flow. This makes the analysis easier to design, but less precise as far as WCET is concerned.

Several other abstract domains other that polyhedra, capable of representing linear constraints between variables, have been proposed, such as for instance [20, 24, 30]. Choosing the most appropriate domain boils down to a trade-off between the execution time and the precision of the analysis. In our work we chose the polyhedra domain and thus favored precision. However, we think that it would be simple to adapt our work to another domain (e.g. to reduce analysis time), because our computation of memory and register mappings does not depend on how constraints between variables are represented and computed.

Several works address static analysis of binary code [4, 7, 13, 26, 27], however they do not consider the problem of identifying memory locations of interest. In contrast, we identify these locations during the analyses.

An important problem when dealing with binary code analysis is to figure out the set of interesting data locations used by the program. This is related to pointer analysis (the so-called *aliasing* problem), and has been extensively studied [17, 19]. While the majority of pointer analyses have been proposed in the context of compiler optimizations, a certain number of ideas can be borrowed and applied to binary code analysis.

In this paper, our approach is applied to static loop bound estimation, in the context of WCET analysis, so we compare our results with other loop bound estimation tools. The oRange tool [8] is based on an abstract interpretation method defined in [2]. It provides a very fast estimation of loop bounds, but it is restricted to C source code. SWEET [14] features a loop bound estimator, which works on an intermediary representation (ALF format). The approach is based on slicing and abstract interpretation and it generally provides very tight loop bounds even in complex cases, but the running time of the analysis seems to depend on the loop bound values, and in our experience for large loop bounds the analysis did not terminate.

KTA [9] is a static WCET analysis tool based on abstract interpretation and path exploration of binary code. As its purpose is to compute a WCET, it does not directly provide information on loop bounds and we could not find documentation on the method used to compute these bounds. Thus, KAT was not included in our benchmarks. Furthermore, the analysis time seems to depend on the loop bound values.

Compared to these existing works, our approach combines the polyhedral domain with binary code analysis, taking into account memory accesses and supporting analysis of relations between unknown memory addresses; moreover our method is proved to be sound and to always terminate.

7   Experimental Results

Our methodology is implemented in a prototype called Polymalys. Our experiments consist of two parts. First, we validate our approach by comparing Polymalys with other existing loop bound analysis tools on classic benchmarks. Then, we provide detailed examples of programs for which Polymalys successfully estimates loops bounds, while the other tools fail to do so.

7.1 Implementation

Polymalys is implemented as a plugin of OTAWA (version 2.0), an open source WCET computation tool [5]. Polymalys relies on OTAWA for control-flow analysis and manipulation, and on PPL [3] for polyhedra operations. Polymalys implements several optimizations to reduce the number of variables and constraints of an abstract state $(p, \mathcal{R}^\sharp, *^\sharp)$, most notably:

- *Unmapped variables*: any variable that is not in $\mathcal{R}^\sharp$ or in $*^\sharp$ can be safely removed from the polyhedron by performing a projection on the remaining (used) variables;
- *Dead registers*: we remove *dead register* variables by perform a preliminary *liveness analysis*, using classic data-flow analysis methods [1];
- *Out-of-scope variables*: whenever modifying the stack pointer register (SP), assuming that the stack grows downwards, for each pair of variables (x_i, x_j) such that $*^\sharp(x_i) = x_j$, if $p \sqsubseteq_\diamond \langle x_i < \mathcal{R}^\sharp[SP] \rangle$ then x_i and x_j can be removed.

7.2 Benchmarks

The analyses have been executed on a PC with an Intel core i5 3470 at 3.2 Ghz, with 8 GB of RAM. Every benchmark has been compiled with ARM crosstool-NG 1.20.0 (gcc version 4.9.1), using the -O1 optimization level.

First, we report the results of our experiments on the Mälardalen benchmarks [16] and on PolyBench [25] in Table 1. The benchmarks *gemver*, *covariance*, *correlation*, *nussinov* and *floyd-warshall* are from PolyBench, while the others are from Mälardalen. We exclude benchmarks that are not supported by OTAWA, mainly due to floating point operations or indirect branching (e.g. switch). We compare Polymalys with SWEET [22], PAGAI [18] and oRange [8]. For each benchmark, we report: the number of lines of code (in the C source), the total number of loops, the number of loops that are correctly bounded by each tool, and the computation time. We do not report the computation time for SWEET because we only had access to it through an online applet. For oRange, computation time is below the measurement resolution (10 ms), except for *edn*, where it reaches 50 ms. We ran PAGAI with the -d pk -t lw+pf options. For the PolyBench benchmarks, we did not succeed in running them with SWEET due to the online applet limitation. For the *correlation* benchmark, we did not succeed in running it with PAGAI, it terminates without giving any result.

The execution time of Polymalys is typically higher than that of PAGAI because we introduce more variables and constraints. We believe that we can reduce the gap with additional optimizations, however Polymalys will probably remain more costly , because it works at a lower level of abstraction.

Cases where tools fail to analyze some loop bounds are depicted in bold. There is only one benchmark for which Polymalys did not find a loop bound: for janne_complex. The difficulty is that it contains complex loop index updates inside a if-then-else. On the contrary, there are several cases where Polymalys successfully estimates loops bounds, while the other tools fail to do so. Note that PAGAI does not specifically compute loop bounds, instead it computes loop invariants. We deduced loop bounds from these invariants.

Table 1. Benchmark results.

Benchmark	LoC	Loops	Loops correctly bounded				Time (ms)	
			Polymalys	SWEET	PAGAI	oRange	Polymalys	PAGAI
crc	16	1	1	1	1	1	150	40
fibcall	22	1	1	1	1	1	230	50
janne_complex	26	2	**1**	2	**1**	**1**	870	140
expint	56	3	3	**2**	3	3	732	9140
matmult	84	5	5	5	5	5	3455	1380
fdct	149	2	2	2	2	2	7421	2150
jfdctint	165	3	3	3	3	3	10660	1960
fir	189	2	2	2	2	1	4989	390
edn	198	12	12	12	**9**	12	21356	15660
ns	414	4	4	4	4	4	1700	380
gemver	186	10	10	**N/A**	10	10	12136	6029
covariance	138	11	11	**N/A**	11	11	7248	836
correlation	168	13	13	**N/A**	**N/A**	13	9129	25062
nussinov	143	8	8	**N/A**	8	8	7272	2811
floyd-warshall	112	7	7	**N/A**	**2**	7	2904	468

7.3   Loop Bounds Examples

We further illustrate the differences between tool capabilities on some synthetic program examples.

Example 11. The following example contains pointer aliasing and pointer arithmetic:

```
foo() {
  int i, bound = 10;
  int *ptr = &bound;
  ptr++; ptr--; *ptr = 15; k = 0;
  for (i = 0; i < bound; i++);
}
```

PAGAI does not find the loop bound (the loop is considered unbounded), because it does not infer that `ptr = &bound` when executing the instruction `*ptr=15`. Other tools bound the loop correctly (15 iterations).

Example 12. The following example contains an off-by-one array access:

```
1   #define SIZE 10
2   foo(int offset) {
3     int i, bound = 10;
4     int tab[SIZE];
5     if ((offset > SIZE) || (offset < 0))
6       return -1;
7     tab[offset] = 100;
8     for (i = 0; i < bound; i++);
9   }
```

The off-by-one error (lines 5–6) may cause the array cell assignment (line 7) to overwrite the bound variable with the value 100. Polymalys correctly detects that the loop may iterate 100 times, while oRange and SWEET detect a maximum of 10 iterations. PAGAI also bounds to 10 iterations, but warns about a possible undefined behavior and unsafe result. Note that the bound depends on the stack variable allocation layout. In our experiments, the compiler allocates the bound variable next to the array. Such an information is much easier to analyze at the binary code level than at the source code level.

Example 13. The following example shows the benefits of a relational domain:

```
1   #define MAXSIZE 10
2   foo() {
3     int base, end, i;
4     if (end - base > MAXSIZE)
5       end = base + MAXSIZE;
6     for (i = base; i < end; i++);
7   }
```

Here, we do not know statically the value of end and base. However, due to the *if* statement (line 4), Polymalys introduces the constraint $end - base \leq 10$. Thus, Polymalys bounds the loop correctly (10 iterations), while PAGAI, oRange and SWEET do not.

Example 14. Finally, we report analysis results for the motivational example of Fig. 1. Polymalys correctly finds that the loop bound is equal to the maximum size of the UDP payload; PAGAI, oRange and SWEET fail to provide any bound.

8   Conclusion

In this paper we propose a novel technique for performing abstract interpretation of binary code using polyhedra. It consists in adding new variables to the polyhedra as the analysis progresses, and maintaining a correspondence with registers and memory addresses. Thanks to the relational properties of polyhedra, our technique naturally provides information on pointer relations when compared to other techniques based on non-relational domains. While the complexity of our method is currently still higher than other existing techniques, we believe that there is room for improvement. In particular, we are planning to extend our work with a modular procedure analysis and a data-structure analysis.

References

1. Aho, A.V., Lam, M.S., Sethi, R., Ullman, J.D.: Compilers: Principles, Techniques, and Tools, 2nd edn. Addison-Wesley Longman Publishing Co. Inc., Boston (2006)
2. Ammarguellat, Z., Harrison, III, W.L.: Automatic recognition of induction variables and recurrence relations by abstract interpretation. In: Proceedings of the ACM SIGPLAN 1990 Conference on Programming Language Design and Implementation, PLDI 1990, pp. 283–295. ACM, New York (1990)
3. Bagnara, R., Hill, P.M., Zaffanella, E.: The Parma Polyhedra Library: toward a complete set of numerical abstractions for the analysis and verification of hardware and software systems. Sci. Comput. Program. **72**(1), 3–21 (2008)
4. Balakrishnan, G., Reps, T.: Analyzing memory accesses in x86 executables. In: Duesterwald, E. (ed.) CC 2004. LNCS, vol. 2985, pp. 5–23. Springer, Heidelberg (2004). https://doi.org/10.1007/978-3-540-24723-4_2
5. Ballabriga, C., Cassé, H., Rochange, C., Sainrat, P.: OTAWA: an open toolbox for adaptive WCET analysis. In: Min, S.L., Pettit, R., Puschner, P., Ungerer, T. (eds.) SEUS 2010. LNCS, vol. 6399, pp. 35–46. Springer, Heidelberg (2010). https://doi.org/10.1007/978-3-642-16256-5_6
6. Ballabriga, C., Forget, J., Lipari, G.: Symbolic WCET computation. ACM Trans. Embed. Comput. Syst. (TECS) **17**(2), 39 (2018)
7. Bardin, S., Herrmann, P., Védrine, F.: Refinement-based CFG reconstruction from unstructured programs. In: Jhala, R., Schmidt, D. (eds.) VMCAI 2011. LNCS, vol. 6538, pp. 54–69. Springer, Heidelberg (2011). https://doi.org/10.1007/978-3-642-18275-4_6
8. Bonenfant, A., de Michiel, M., Sainrat, P.: oRange: a tool for static loop bound analysis. In: Workshop on Resource Analysis, University of Hertfordshire, Hatfield, UK (2008)
9. Broman, D.: A brief overview of the KTA WCET tool. arXiv preprint arXiv:1712.05264 (2017)
10. Bygde, S., Lisper, B., Holsti, N.: Fully bounded polyhedral analysis of integers with wrapping. Electron. Notes Theor. Comput. Sci. **288**, 3–13 (2012)
11. Correnson, L., Signoles, J.: Combining analyses for C program verification. In: Stoelinga, M., Pinger, R. (eds.) FMICS 2012. LNCS, vol. 7437, pp. 108–130. Springer, Heidelberg (2012). https://doi.org/10.1007/978-3-642-32469-7_8
12. Cousot, P., Halbwachs, N.: Automatic discovery of linear restraints among variables of a program. In: Proceedings of the 5th ACM SIGACT-SIGPLAN Symposium on Principles of Programming Languages (POPL), pp. 84–96. ACM (1978). https://doi.org/10.1145/512760.512770
13. Djoudi, A., Bardin, S.: BINSEC: binary code analysis with low-level regions. In: Baier, C., Tinelli, C. (eds.) TACAS 2015. LNCS, vol. 9035, pp. 212–217. Springer, Heidelberg (2015). https://doi.org/10.1007/978-3-662-46681-0_17
14. Ermedahl, A., Sandberg, C., Gustafsson, J., Bygde, S., Lisper, B.: Loop bound analysis based on a combination of program slicing, abstract interpretation, and invariant analysis. In: Rochange, C. (ed.) 7th International Workshop on Worst-Case Execution Time Analysis (WCET 2007). OpenAccess Series in Informatics (OASIcs), vol. 6. Schloss Dagstuhl-Leibniz-Zentrum fuer Informatik, Dagstuhl, Germany (2007)
15. Gulwani, S., Mehra, K.K., Chilimbi, T.: Speed: precise and efficient static estimation of program computational complexity. In: ACM SIGPLAN-SIGACT Symposium on Principles of Programming Languages (POPL 2009), pp. 127–139. ACM (2009)

16. Gustafsson, J., Betts, A., Ermedahl, A., Lisper, B.: The Mälardalen WCET benchmarks: past, present and future. In: OASIcs-OpenAccess Series in Informatics, vol. 15. Schloss Dagstuhl-Leibniz-Zentrum fuer Informatik (2010)

17. Hardekopf, B., Lin, C.: The ant and the grasshopper: fast and accurate pointer analysis for millions of lines of code. ACM SIGPLAN Not. **42**(6), 290–299 (2007)

18. Henry, J., Monniaux, D., Moy, M.: Pagai: a path sensitive static analyser. Electron. Notes Theor. Comput. Sci. **289**, 15–25 (2012)

19. Hind, M.: Pointer analysis: haven't we solved this problem yet? In: ACM SIGPLAN-SIGSOFT Workshop on Program Analysis for Software Tools and Engineering (PASTE 2001), pp. 54–61. ACM, New York (2001)

20. Karr, M.: Affine relationships among variables of a program. Acta Inform. **6**(2), 133–151 (1976)

21. Kästner, D., et al.: Astrée: proving the absence of runtime errors. In: Embedded Real Time Software and Systems (ERTS2 2010), p. 9, May 2010

22. Lisper, B.: SWEET – a tool for wcet flow analysis (extended abstract). In: Margaria, T., Steffen, B. (eds.) ISoLA 2014. LNCS, vol. 8803, pp. 482–485. Springer, Heidelberg (2014). https://doi.org/10.1007/978-3-662-45231-8_38

23. Tamburini, P., Stagni, R., Cappello, A.: Design of a modular platform for static analysis. In: Spoto, F. (ed.) 9th Workshop on Tools for Automatic Program Analysis (TAPAS 2018). Lecture Notes in Computer Science (LNCS). Springer, Cham, p. 4, August 2018

24. Miné, A.: Field-sensitive value analysis of embedded C programs with union types and pointer arithmetics. In: ACM SIGPLAN/SIGBED Conference on Languages, Compilers, and Tools for Embedded Systems (LCTES 2006), pp. 54–63 (2006)

25. Pouchet, L.N.: Polybench: the polyhedral benchmark suite (2012). http://www.cs.ucla.edu/pouchet/software/polybench

26. Reps, T., Balakrishnan, G.: Improved memory-access analysis for x86 executables. In: Hendren, L. (ed.) CC 2008. LNCS, vol. 4959, pp. 16–35. Springer, Heidelberg (2008). https://doi.org/10.1007/978-3-540-78791-4_2

27. Sepp, A., Mihaila, B., Simon, A.: Precise static analysis of binaries by extracting relational information. In: 18th Working Conference on Reverse Engineering (WCRE 2011). IEEE (2011)

28. Sharir, M., Pnueli, A.: Two approaches to interprocedural data flow analysis. Technical report, New York University. Courant Institute of Mathematical Sciences. Computer Science Department (1978)

29. Tarjan, R.: Depth-first search and linear graph algorithms. SIAM J. Comput. **1**(2), 146–160 (1972)

30. Venet, A.: The gauge domain: scalable analysis of linear inequality invariants. In: 24th International Conference on Computer Aided Verification (CAV 2012), pp. 139–154 (2012)

Disjunctive Relational Abstract Interpretation for Interprocedural Program Analysis

Rémy Boutonnet[(⊠)] and Nicolas Halbwachs

University of Grenoble Alpes, CNRS, Grenoble INP
(Institute of Engineering Univ. Grenoble Alpes), VERIMAG,
38000 Grenoble, France
`{remy.boutonnet,nicolas.halbwachs}@univ-grenoble-alpes.fr`

Abstract. Program analysis by abstract interpretation using relational abstract domains—like polyhedra or octagons—easily extends from state analysis (construction of reachable states) to relational analysis (construction of input-output relations). In this paper, we exploit this extension to enable interprocedural program analysis, by constructing relational summaries of procedures. In order to improve the accuracy of procedure summaries, we propose a method to refine them into disjunctions of relations, these disjunctions being directed by preconditions on input parameters.

1 Introduction

Linear Relation Analysis (LRA [17])—or polyhedral abstract interpretation—is a classical method for discovering invariant linear inequalities among the numerical variables of a program. This method is still one of the most powerful numerical program analysis techniques, because of the expressivity of the discovered properties. However, it is not applicable to large monolithic programs, because of its prohibitive complexity, in terms of number of involved variables—in spite of recent progress in polyhedra algorithmics [22,37,49]. An obvious solution consists in using it in a modular way: the analysis of reasonably small procedures can provide, once and for all, a *summary* as an input-output relation; this summary can be reused in the analysis of programs calling the procedure. The *relational* nature of LRA is, of course, beneficial in this process.

On the other hand, the numerous works on interprocedural analysis, often concluded that such a "bottom-up" approach—where a procedure is analyzed before its callers—generally results in very imprecise summaries, because the procedure is considered independently of its calling context. One can object that

---

This work has been partially supported by the European Research Council under the European Union's Seventh Framework Programme (FP/2007-2013)/ERC Grant Agreement nr. 306595 "STATOR0".

© Springer Nature Switzerland AG 2019
C. Enea and R. Piskac (Eds.): VMCAI 2019, LNCS 11388, pp. 136–159, 2019.
https://doi.org/10.1007/978-3-030-11245-5_7

this imprecision can be also due to the poor expressivity of the used domains, in particular those commonly used in compilers (e.g., data-flow analysis [32]).

So interprocedural analysis can provide a solution to the prohibitive cost of LRA, which, in turn, can provide a convenient expressive power for expressing more accurate procedure summaries.

This idea of using LRA to synthesize input-output relations is quite straightforward and not new. In particular, it is systematically applied in the tool PIPS [3,23], which considers each basic statement as an elementary relation, and synthesizes the input-output relation of a full program by composing these relations bottom-up. In this paper, we specialize the approach to the synthesis of procedure summaries. An easy way for building a relational summary of a procedure consists in duplicating the parameters to record their initial value, then performing a standard LRA of the body, which provides the summary as the least upper bound (convex hull) of the results at return points of the procedure.

However, it appears that conjunctions of linear constraints, i.e., convex polyhedral relations, are too restrictive. Obviously, procedures may exhibit very different and irregular behaviors according to the values of conditions appearing in tests. For instance,

- in many cases, whether an outermost loop is entered at least once or not is very relevant for the global behavior of the procedure;
- when a procedure has several return points, they are likely to correspond to quite different behaviors;
- for a simple recursive procedure, the base case(s) should be distinguished from those which involve recursive calls.

So it is natural to look for summaries that are *disjunctions* of polyhedral relations. However, algorithms for manipulating polyhedra do not extend easily to general disjunctions of polyhedra. A solution consists in using *trace partitioning* [9,28,38,47]. This solution is used in [24,26], where the partitioning is directed by formulas on Boolean variables. Here, we will propose such a partitioning directed by well-chosen *preconditions* on input parameters.

Contributions: While being mainly interested in LRA, we consider a more general framework. We provide a general formalization of relational abstract interpretation, that we didn't find elsewhere. As its use for computing procedure summaries often provides too rough results, we propose an approach to build disjunctive summaries, based on precondition partitioning. The choice of partitions is a heuristic process. We propose a method based on successive partition refinements, guided, on one hand, by the reachability of control points, and on the other hand, by the partitioning of summaries of called procedures. The method has been implemented in a prototype analyzer. Our experiments give encouraging results.

The paper is organized as follows. To situate our work, we first survey the abundant literature on interprocedural program analysis (Sect. 2). Since our approach can be applied in a more general context than LRA, we will develop each aspect in a stratified fashion: first, we consider the very general framework, then we present a specialization to LRA, before an application on a running example. Section 3 is concerned with concrete relational semantics of programs, and introduces the notations in the general framework and for numerical programs, together with our running example. Sections 4 and 5 deal with relational abstract interpretation and its use for building procedure summaries relative to a precondition. In view of the results on our example, in Sect. 6, we propose to compute disjunctive summaries directed by a partition of preconditions. In Sect. 7, we present a way of partitioning preconditions by successive refinements. The application of our method to recursive procedures is illustrated in Sect. 8. Section 9 briefly presents our prototype implementation, and some experiments are described in Sect. 10. Section 11 gives the conclusion and sketches some future work.

2   Related Work

Interprocedural analysis originated in side-effects analysis, from works of Spillman [51], Allen [1, 2] and Barth [6].

Interprocedural analyses can be distinguished according to the order in which procedures are traversed. In top-down analyses, procedures are analyzed following their invocation order [2], from callers to callees, while in bottom-up analyses, procedures are analyzed according to the inverse invocation order, from the callees up to the callers, by computing procedure summaries. Hybrid analyses [53] combine top-down and bottom-up analyses. We are interested in bottom-up approaches since each procedure is analyzed only once, regardless of the calling contexts, in possibly much smaller variable environments, thereby allowing a modular analysis with potential scalability improvements for numerical analyses such as LRA.

Sharir and Pnueli [48] introduced the functional approach and the call strings approach for distributive data flow frameworks. The functional approach computes procedure summaries, either from the bottom-up composition of individual propagation functions or by propagating data flow properties in a top-down fashion and by tabulating properties obtained at the exit node of a procedure with the associated property at entry. In the call strings approach, data flow properties are tagged by a finite string which encodes the procedure calls encountered during propagation. Call strings are managed as stacks and updated during propagation through a procedure call or return.

Reps et al. [46] proposed an algorithm belonging to the family of functional approaches to solve data flow problems with finite semilattices and distributive propagation functions in polynomial time, by recasting these data flow problems into graph reachability problems. Jeannet et al. [30,50] proposed a method reminiscent of the call strings approach, for the relational numerical analysis of programs with recursive procedures and pointers to the stack. It is a top-down approach based on an abstraction of the stack. An implementation is available in the Interproc tool [25]. Abstract states are partitioned according to Boolean conditions, but not according to possible input abstract states of a procedure. Yorsh et al. [52] proposed a bottom-up approach for finite distributive data flow properties and described how precise summaries for this class of properties can be constructed by composition of summaries of individual statements.

A relational abstraction of sets of functions for shape analysis is proposed in [27], considering functions of signature $D_1 \rightarrow D_2$, provided that abstractions A_1 of $\mathcal{P}(D_1)$ and A_2 of $\mathcal{P}(D_2)$ exist, and that A_1 is of finite cardinality. This abstraction is relational since it is able to express relations between images of abstract elements mapped by a set of functions, but the abstraction A_1 is required to be of finite cardinality, thus excluding numerical abstract domains such as convex polyhedra.

Gulwani et al. [20] proposed a backward analysis to compute procedure summaries as constraints that must be satisfied to guarantee that some generic assertion holds at the end of a procedure. A generic assertion is an assertion with context variables which can be instantiated by symbols of a given theory. Procedure summaries are obtained by computing weakest preconditions of generic assertions. These generic assertions must be given prior to the analysis, thus forbidding the automatic discovery of procedure properties.

Cousot and Cousot [15,16] describe the symbolic relational separate analysis for abstract interpretation, which uses relational domains, relational semantics and symbolic names to represent initial values of variables modified by a procedure. When instantiated with the convex polyhedra abstract domain, this approach computes procedure summaries which are input-output relations represented by a single convex polyhedron, with no ability to capture disjunctive behaviors in procedures. Recursive procedures are supported, as presented earlier in [13,14,21].

Müller-Olm et al. [40,42] proposed an interprocedural bottom-up analysis to discover all Herbrand equalities between program variables in polynomial time. This approach was extended to linear two-variables equalities [18] and to affine relations [41]. This approach considers only abstracted programs with affine assignments, ignoring conditions on branches and dealing conservatively with other assignments. We are proposing a more general approach, which is also able to capture some disjunctive behaviors.

In the PIPS tool [3,23], statements are abstracted by affine transformers [35,36] which are input-output relations represented by convex polyhedra. The summary of a whole procedure is obtained from the composition of statement transformers, in a bottom-up fashion. Recursive procedures are not supported and each procedure summary is a single affine input-output relation, preventing the expression of disjunctive behaviors.

Popeea et al. [43–45] presented an analysis to both prove user-supplied safety properties and to find bugs by deriving conditions leading either to success or failure in each procedure. Disjunctive numerical properties are handled by a complete decision procedure for linear arithmetic provided by the Omega Test [31]. Our approach is able to discover automatically some disjunctive behaviors of procedures without requiring user-provided assertions.

Kranz et al. [33] proposed a modular analysis of executables based on Heyting completion [19]. Unfortunately, in the convex polyhedra abstract domain, the pseudo-complement $a \Rightarrow b = \sqcup \{d \mid a \sqsubseteq d \sqsubseteq b\}$ of a relative to b is not available in general.

3   Concrete Relational Semantics

3.1   General Framework

In our general framework, a program or a procedure is just a transition system. We introduce below a few definitions and notations.

States and Relations: Let S be a set of states. Let 2^S be the powerset of S. Let $\mathcal{R} = 2^{S \times S}$ be the set of binary relations on S.

- We define src, tgt the projection functions $\mathcal{R} \mapsto 2^S$ such that: $\forall r \in \mathcal{R}$,

$$src(r) = \{s_0 \in S \mid \exists s_1 \in S, (s_0, s_1) \in r\}, \ tgt(r) = \{s_1 \in S \mid \exists s_0 \in S, (s_0, s_1) \in r\}$$

- If $U \subseteq S$, we define Id_U the relation $\{(s, s) \mid s \in U\}$.
- If $r_1, r_2 \in \mathcal{R}$, we denote by $r_1 \circ r_2$ their composition:

$$r_1 \circ r_2 = \{(s, s') \mid \exists s'', (s, s'') \in r_1 \text{ and } (s'', s') \in r_2\}$$

Forward, Backward Relational Semantic Equations: Let $\rho \in \mathcal{R}$ be a transition relation on S. We are interested in computing an upper approximation of its transitive closure ρ^*, which can be defined as a least fixpoint:

$$\rho^* = \mu r. Id_S \cup (r \circ \rho) \quad \text{(forward equation)}$$
$$= \mu r. Id_S \cup (\rho \circ r) \quad \text{(backward equation)}$$

Trace Partitioning: We use the classical "trace partitioning" technique [38,47]. Assume that the set S is finitely partitioned: $S = S_1 \oplus S_2 \oplus \ldots \oplus S_n$. This partitioning can reflect the control points in a program or a control-flow graph, but it can also be more "semantic", and express state properties, like preconditions. If $r \in \mathcal{R}$, for each $i, j \in \{1, \ldots, n\}$, we define $r(S_i, S_j) = r \cap (S_i \times S_j)$.

With these notations, the relations $\rho^*(S_i, S_j)$ can be defined by the following system of fixpoint equations (henceforth, we consider only forward computation, backward computation is symmetrical):

$$\forall j \neq i, \rho^*(S_i, S_j) = \bigcup_{k=1}^{n} \rho^*(S_i, S_k) \circ \rho(S_k, S_j)$$

$$\rho^*(S_i, S_i) = Id_{S_i} \cup \bigcup_{k=1}^{n} \rho^*(S_i, S_k) \circ \rho(S_k, S_i)$$

Concrete Relational Summaries: Let p be a procedure, $S, \rho, \mathcal{I}, \mathcal{E}$, respectively, its set of states, its transition relation, its sets of initial states (global precondition) and exit states. We assume that S is partitioned, and that $\mathcal{I}, \mathcal{E}$ belong to the partition. The *concrete relational summary* of p is $\sigma_p = \rho^*(\mathcal{I}, \mathcal{E})$. So, for the forward computation of the summary, we are concerned with the computation of $\rho^*(\mathcal{I}, S_j)$, $j = 1...n$, according to the equations

$$\rho^*(\mathcal{I}, S_j) = \left(\bigcup_{k=1}^{n} \rho^*(\mathcal{I}, S_k) \circ \rho(S_k, S_j) \right) \cup \left\{ \begin{array}{l} Id_{\mathcal{I}} \text{ if } S_j = \mathcal{I} \\ \emptyset \quad \text{ otherwise} \end{array} \right\}$$

Concrete Semantics of Procedure Calls: Let S be the set of states of a procedure p, T be the set of states of a program calling p. For a given call to p, let us write π the mapping $\in 2^{S \times S} \mapsto 2^{T \times T}$ representing the parameter passing mechanism (generally, a renaming of formal parameters into actual ones). Then, if T_i (resp. T_j) represents the sets of states just before (resp., just after) the call, the elementary relation corresponding to the call is $\rho(T_i, T_j) = \pi(\sigma_p)$.

3.2 Numerical Programs and Procedures

Procedures: For simplicity, and without loss of generality, the following assumptions are taken:

– All procedure parameters are supposed to be passed by reference. However, we are not concerned with pointer manipulation, and we entrust existing analyses to detect aliasing problems.
– Global variables are dealt with as additional parameters.
– For clarity, we will consider that all variables are parameters, since local variables don't raise any problem, but complicate the presentation.

In LRA, only numerical variables—taking their values in a numerical domain $\mathcal{N}$ ($= \mathbb{Z}$ or $\mathbb{Q}$)—are considered. A state of a numerical procedure with n variables is thus a pair (c, V), where $c \in C$ is a control point (a line, a statement, a block in a control-flow graph, ...), and $V = (v_1, ..., v_n) \in \mathcal{N}^n$ is a vector of numerical values. Control points provide a natural partitioning of such a set of states: $S_c = \{(c, V) \mid V \in \mathcal{N}^n\}$. The set of initial states $\mathcal{I}$ of a procedure with entry point $c_{\mathcal{I}}$ is such an $S_{c_{\mathcal{I}}}$, possibly restricted by a precondition $A_{\mathcal{I}} \subseteq \mathcal{N}^n$ on parameter values: $\mathcal{I} = \{(c_{\mathcal{I}}, V) \mid V \in A_{\mathcal{I}}\}$.

From State to Relational Collecting Semantics: Given such a partition $\{S_c \mid c \in C\}$, the usual collecting semantics defines the set A_c of reachable variable valuations in each S_c, such that $A_c = \{V \mid (c, V) \text{ is a reachable state from } \mathcal{I}\}$, as the least solution of a system of fixpoint equations:

$$A_c = F_c\left(\{A_{c'} \mid c' \in C\}\right) \cup \begin{cases} A_{\mathcal{I}} & \text{if } c = c_{\mathcal{I}} \\ \emptyset & \text{otherwise} \end{cases}$$

where the semantic function F_c expresses how the states in S_c depends on the states at other control points. This state semantics can be straightforwardly extended to relational semantics as follows: for each variable v_i, a new variable v_i^0 is introduced to record the initial value of v_i. The new set of states is thus $C \times \mathcal{N}^{2n}$, and the new initial state is

$$\mathcal{I} = \{(c_{\mathcal{I}}, (v_1^0, \ldots v_n^0, v_1, \ldots, v_n)) \mid (v_1^0, \ldots, v_n^0) \in A_{\mathcal{I}} \wedge v_i = v_i^0, i = 1...n\}$$

The relational semantics is equivalent to the state semantics of the same procedure, initialized with the assignments $v_i^0 = v_i$ for each $i = 1...n$.

Concrete Relational Summary: Let $\mathcal{E} \subset C$ be the set of exit points of the procedure. Then, $\bigcup_{c \in \mathcal{E}} A_c$ is the concrete summary of the procedure. In presence of local variables, they should be eliminated from this expression by existential quantification.

3.3   A Very Simple Example

Our example program is the classical Euclidean division, shown below with its relational semantic equations:

```
  void div (int a, b, *q, *r){
      assume (a ≥ 0 && b ≥ 1);
1     *q=0; *r=a;
2     while
3          (*r ≥ b) {
4          *r = *r-b; *q = *q+1;
5     }
6  }
```

$$A_1 = \{(a^0, b^0, q^0, r^0, a, b, q, r) \mid$$
$$a^0 \geq 0 \wedge b^0 \geq 1 \wedge a = a^0 \wedge$$
$$b = b^0 \wedge q = q^0 \wedge r = r^0\}$$
$$A_2 = A_1[q \leftarrow 0][r \leftarrow a]$$
$$A_3 = A_2 \cup A_5$$
$$A_4 = A_3 \cap (r \geq b)$$
$$A_5 = A_4[r \leftarrow r - b][q \leftarrow q + 1]$$
$$A_6 = A_3 \cap (r \leq b - 1)$$

The least solution for A_6, the unique exit point, is the concrete summary of the procedure: $a = a^0 \wedge b = b^0 \wedge a = bq + r \wedge q \geq 0 \wedge b - 1 \geq r \geq 0$. Notice that it contains a non linear relation, so it cannot be precisely obtained by LRA. For simplicity, we pretended to duplicate all parameters. Of course, in practice, pure input parameters ("value" parameters, whose value is not changed in the procedure) as well as pure output parameters ("result" parameters, whose initial value is not used in the procedure) don't need to be duplicated.

4   Relational Abstract Interpretation

4.1   General Framework

Relational Abstract Domains: A *relational abstract domain* is a complete lattice $(\mathcal{R}^\sharp, \sqsubseteq, \bot, \top, \sqcap, \sqcup)$ related to $\mathcal{R}$ by a Galois connection, i.e., a pair of increasing functions: $\alpha_\mathcal{R} : \mathcal{R} \mapsto \mathcal{R}^\sharp$ (abstraction), $\gamma_\mathcal{R} : \mathcal{R}^\sharp \mapsto \mathcal{R}$ (concretization), such that $\forall r \in \mathcal{R}, r^\sharp \in \mathcal{R}^\sharp, \alpha(r) \sqsubseteq r^\sharp \Leftrightarrow r \subseteq \gamma(r^\sharp)$.

If $U \subseteq S$, we denote by $Id_U^\sharp$ the abstract relation $\alpha_\mathcal{R}(Id_U)$. If $r_1^\sharp, r_2^\sharp \in \mathcal{R}^\sharp$, we define $r_1^\sharp \circ r_2^\sharp$ their composition as $\alpha_\mathcal{R}(\gamma_\mathcal{R}(r_1^\sharp) \circ \gamma_\mathcal{R}(r_2^\sharp))$. A relational abstract domain induces two abstract domains, $S_\rightarrow^\sharp$ and $S_\leftarrow^\sharp$ on 2^S:

$$\forall U \subseteq S, \alpha_{S_\rightarrow}(U) = \alpha_\mathcal{R}(U \times S), \quad \alpha_{S_\leftarrow}(U) = \alpha_\mathcal{R}(S \times U)$$

Notice that both $S_\rightarrow^\sharp$ and $S_\leftarrow^\sharp$ are included in $\mathcal{R}^\sharp$. We can define the abstract projections $src^\sharp : \mathcal{R}^\sharp \mapsto S_\rightarrow^\sharp$ and $tgt^\sharp : \mathcal{R}^\sharp \mapsto S_\leftarrow^\sharp$ by:

$$src^\sharp(r^\sharp) = \alpha_{S_\rightarrow}(src(\gamma_\mathcal{R}(r^\sharp))), \quad tgt^\sharp(r^\sharp) = \alpha_{S_\leftarrow}(tgt(\gamma_\mathcal{R}(r^\sharp)))$$

Relational Abstract Analysis: Let ρ be a transition relation, and $\rho^\sharp$ be an upper bound of its abstraction. We assume the availability of both a widening and a narrowing operation $\nabla, \Delta : \mathcal{R}^\sharp \times \mathcal{R}^\sharp \mapsto \mathcal{R}^\sharp$. Classically [12], an upper approximation of $\rho^{\sharp*}$ can be obtained by computing the limit $r^{\sharp\nabla}$ of an increasing approximation sequence:

$$r_0^\sharp = \bot, \ r_{n+1}^\sharp = r_n^\sharp \nabla (r_n^\sharp \circ \rho^\sharp)$$

then the limit $r^{\sharp\nabla\Delta}$ of a decreasing sequence:

$$r_0'^\sharp = r^{\sharp\nabla}, r_{n+1}'^\sharp = r_n'^\sharp \Delta (r_n'^\sharp \circ \rho^\sharp)$$

The result $r^{\sharp\nabla\Delta}$ is an abstract approximation of ρ^*, i.e., $\rho^* \subseteq \gamma(r^{\sharp\nabla\Delta})$.

Abstract Partition: For $\leftrightarrow \in \{\leftarrow, \rightarrow\}$, we define an abstract partition of $S_\leftrightarrow^\sharp$ as a finite set $\{S_0^\sharp, ..., S_n^\sharp\} \subseteq S_\leftrightarrow^\sharp$, such that $\{S_i = \gamma_{S_\leftrightarrow}(S_i^\sharp) \mid i = 1...n\}$ is a partition of S. More generally, if $U \subseteq S$, an abstract partition of $U_\leftrightarrow^\sharp = \alpha_{S_\leftrightarrow}(U)$ is a finite set $\{U_0^\sharp, ..., U_n^\sharp\} \subseteq U_\leftrightarrow^\sharp$, such that $\{U_i = \gamma_{S_\leftrightarrow}(U_i^\sharp) \mid i = 1...n\}$ is a partition of U.

Partitioned Relational Abstract Analysis: Let $\{S_i = \gamma(S_i^\sharp) \mid i = 1...n\}$ be a partition of S, let ρ be a transition relation, $\rho(S_i, S_j)$ be defined as before for $i, j = 1...n$, and $\rho^\sharp(S_i^\sharp, S_j^\sharp)$ be (an upper bound of) the abstraction of $\rho(S_i, S_j)$. An upper approximation of the vector $\{\rho^{\sharp*}(S_i^\sharp, S_j^\sharp) \mid i, j = 1...n\}$ can be obtained as the limit of (vectorial) increasing-decreasing sequences corresponding to the system of fixpoint equations:

$$\forall i = 1...n, \forall j \neq i, \ \rho^{\sharp*}(S_i^\sharp, S_j^\sharp) = \bigsqcup_{k=1}^{n} \rho^{\sharp*}(S_i^\sharp, S_k^\sharp) \circ \rho^\sharp(S_k^\sharp, S_j^\sharp)$$

$$\rho^{\sharp*}(S_i^\sharp, S_i^\sharp) = Id_{S_i^\sharp}^\sharp \sqcup \bigsqcup_{k=1}^{n} \rho^{\sharp*}(S_i^\sharp, S_k^\sharp) \circ \rho^\sharp(S_k^\sharp, S_i^\sharp)$$

Abstract Summary and Abstract Effect of a Procedure Call: Let p be a procedure, $\mathcal{I}, \mathcal{E}$ its set of initial and exit states. The abstract summary of p is $\sigma_p^\sharp = \rho^{\sharp*}(\mathcal{I}^\sharp, \mathcal{E}^\sharp)$. The abstract effect of a call to p, with parameter passing π, situated between $T_i^\sharp$ and $T_j^\sharp$ is $\rho^\sharp(T_i^\sharp, T_j^\sharp) = \pi(\sigma_p^\sharp)$.

4.2 Building Summaries Using LRA

LRA makes use of the lattice of convex polyhedra [5,17]. It abstracts a set of numerical vectors by its convex hull (i.e., its least convex superset). Notice that the convex hull of an infinite set of vectors is not necessarily a polyhedron, but the finiteness of the analysis—thanks to the use of a widening operation—ensures that all the computed approximations are polyhedra, i.e., sets of solutions of a finite system of affine inequalities.

Intersection $(P_1 \sqcap P_2)$, convex hull $(P_1 \sqcup P_2)$, projection $(\exists X.P)$, effect of variable assignment $(P[x \leftarrow exp]$, widening $(P_1 \nabla P_2)$, test for inclusion $(P_1 \sqsubseteq P_2)$

and emptiness $(P = \emptyset)$ are available. Instead of using a narrowing operator to ensure the finiteness of the decreasing sequence, a limited number of iterations of the abstract function is generally applied.

Polyhedra can be used for representing input-output relations, as an abstraction of the relational semantics described in Sect. 3.2. We write $P(X^0, X)$ a polyhedron involving initial values X^0 and current values X. Notice that the source and the target of the relation r expressed by $P(X^0, X)$ can be obtained by polyhedron projections:

$$src^\sharp(r) = \exists X.P(X^0, X), \ tgt^\sharp(r) = \exists X^0.P(X^0, X)$$

4.3   Example

Let us apply LRA to our Euclidean division example. The abstract equations are as follows:

$$P_1 = (a^0 \geq 0, b^0 \geq 1, a = a^0, b = b^0, q = q^0, r = r^0)$$

$$
\begin{aligned}
P_2 &= P_1[q \leftarrow 0][r \leftarrow a] & P_4 &= P_3 \sqcap (r \geq b) \\
P_3 &= P_2 \sqcup P_5 & P_5 &= P_4[r \leftarrow r - b][q \leftarrow q + 1] \\
P_6 &= P_3 \sqcap (r \leq b - 1)
\end{aligned}
$$

P_6 corresponds to the unique exit point of the procedure, so it is the summary. The standard analysis—where the widening is applied on P_3 during the increasing sequence, and the decreasing sequence is limited to 2 steps—provides:

$$P_6 = (a = a^0, \ b = b^0, \ r \geq 0, \ q \geq 0, \ b \geq r + 1)$$

It is a rather weak summary, all the more as the precondition $a^0 \geq 0$ has been lost. This suggests that preconditions should be considered more carefully.

5   Preconditions

For closed programs, the initial state is generally not relevant, since, normally, the variables are explicitly assigned an initial value before being used. When considering procedures, the initial state is implicitly defined by the initial values of parameters. Therefore, it is essential to take it into account. In particular, the correct behavior of a procedure often depends on (user-defined) preconditions on parameter values. We will call *global precondition* the abstraction of the set of legal initial states of a procedure: $\mathcal{I}_p^\sharp = \alpha_{S_\rightarrow}(\mathcal{I}_p)$. Notice that we already took into account the global precondition $a \geq 0, b \geq 1$ in our example. Such global precondition may be given by the user, or deduced from another analysis of the calling contexts, or simply $\top$.

Moreover, preconditions can be used to differentiate cases of input values (calling contexts) that should be considered separately. These preconditions will be obtained by refining the global precondition. This is the way we intend to build disjunctive summaries.

Widening under a Precondition: In relational analysis, a precondition provides an obvious invariant: a procedure may not change its initial state, so any concrete relation $\rho^*(\mathcal{I}_p, S_i)$ has its source within $\mathcal{I}_p$. However, it is not as obvious with abstract analysis: because of the use of widening, it may happen that the result $r^{\#\nabla\triangle}$ does not satisfy this invariant, i.e., $\gamma_{\mathcal{R}}(r^{\#\nabla\triangle})$ is not included in $\mathcal{I}_p \times S$. This is what happened in our example (Sect. 4.3). As a consequence, it is sound and interesting to make use of a "limited widening" when computing $r^{\#\nabla}$: we define this more precise widening by $r\nabla_{\mathcal{I}_p^{\#}} r' = (r\nabla r') \sqcap \mathcal{I}_p^{\#}$.

Example: Coming back to our example in Sect. 4.3, the widening is performed on P_3. Instead of applying the widening classically, i.e., computing $P_3 = P_3\nabla(P_2 \sqcup P_5)$, we limit it with the precondition, i.e., compute $P_3 = (P_3\nabla(P_2 \sqcup P_5)) \sqcap (a^0 \geq 0, b^0 \geq 1)$. The summary we obtain

$$P_6 = (a = a^0,\ b = b^0,\ r \geq 0,\ q \geq 0,\ b \geq r+1,\ a \geq q+r)$$

recovers more than just the precondition. Instead of gaining just $a \geq 0$, we get the stronger $a \geq q + r$.

6   Disjunctive Summaries

Up to now, we described the classical analysis by abstract interpretation, with an emphasis on relational analysis, use of trace partitioning, and taking care of preconditions. In this section, we propose to refine the partitioning by distinguishing the calling contexts of a procedure, defined as preconditions.

Abstract domains are generally not closed under disjunction (in some sense, it is the essence of abstraction). In order to build more precise procedure summaries, it is natural to consider disjunctions of abstract relations. However, some restrictions must be applied to be able to compute on such disjunctions. Moreover, in order to be able to exploit such a disjunctive procedure summary when using it on a procedure call, the values of the actual parameters should determine which disjunct must apply. Thus, different disjuncts should have disjoint sources.

6.1   Disjunctive Refinements of an Abstract Relation

If p is a procedure with global precondition $\mathcal{I}$, a disjunctive refinement of the abstract relation $\rho^{\#*}(\mathcal{I}^{\#}, S_i^{\#})$ will be a finite set $r_1^{\#*}, ..., r_m^{\#*}$ of abstract relations, such that

(1) $\forall k = 1...m, r_k^{\#*} \sqsubseteq \rho^{\#*}(\mathcal{I}^{\#}, S_i^{\#})$

(2) $\forall k_1, k_2 = 1...m, k_1 \neq k_2 \Rightarrow \gamma(src^{\#}(r_{k_1}^{\#*})) \cap \gamma(src^{\#}(r_{k_2}^{\#*})) = \emptyset$

(3) $\displaystyle\bigcup_{k=1}^{m} \gamma(src^{\#}(r_k^{\#*})) = \gamma(\mathcal{I}^{\#})$

In other words, $\{src^{\sharp}(r_k^{\sharp *})\}_{k=1...m}$ forms an abstract partition of $\mathcal{I}^{\sharp}$. Notice that, with this definition, the disjunctive summary of a procedure can also be seen as a conjunction of implications:

$$\bigvee_{k=1}^{m} r_k^{\sharp *} \iff \bigwedge_{k=1}^{m} \left(src^{\sharp}(r_k^{\sharp *}) \Rightarrow r_k^{\sharp *} \right)$$

emphasizing the fact that the partitioning is directed by properties of input parameters. Conversely, given an abstract partition $\{\mathcal{I}_k^{\sharp}\}_{k=1...m}$ of $\mathcal{I}^{\sharp}$, one can compute a disjunctive refinement of the abstract relation $\rho^{\sharp *}(\mathcal{I}^{\sharp}, S_i^{\sharp})$ simply by computing $r_k^{\sharp *} = \rho^{\sharp *}(\mathcal{I}_k^{\sharp}, S_i^{\sharp})$ for each $k = 1...m$.

6.2 Disjunctive Abstract Summary and Abstract Effect of a Call

Given a disjunctive refinement $\{r_k^{\sharp *}\}_{k=1...m}$ of an abstract relation, the corresponding abstract summary of a procedure is a set of disjuncts:

$$\{\sigma_k^{\sharp} = r_k^{\sharp *}(\mathcal{I}_p^{\sharp}, \mathcal{E}_p^{\sharp})\}_{k=1...m}$$

Given such a disjunctive summary, the abstract effect of a call to p, with parameter passing π, situated between $T_i^{\sharp}$ and $T_j^{\sharp}$ is

$$\rho^{\sharp}(T_i^{\sharp}, T_j^{\sharp}) = \bigsqcup_{k=1}^{m} \pi(\sigma_k^{\sharp})$$

6.3 Application to LRA

Disjunctive Polyhedral Summaries: Let p be a procedure, X be its vector of variables, and $\mathcal{I}^{\sharp}$ be its polyhedral global precondition. A disjunctive polyhedral summary of p is a disjunction of input-output relations expressed by a set of polyhedra $\{R_1, ..., R_m\}$, and such that, if we define $\mathcal{I}_k^{\sharp} = src^{\sharp}(R_k) = \exists X.R_k$ ($k = 1...m$), the set $\{\mathcal{I}_k^{\sharp}\}_{k=1...m}$ forms an abstract partition of $\mathcal{I}^{\sharp}$.

Polyhedron Transformer of a Procedure Call: With the same notations concerning the procedure p and its disjunctive polyhedral summary, assume that $X = (x_1, ..., x_n)$ is the list of formal parameters. Let q be a caller to p, $A = (a_1, ..., a_n)$ be the actual parameters of a call to p situated between control points c and c' in q. Let Q_c be the polyhedron associated with c in q. Then the polyhedron associated with the return point c' is

$$Q_{c'} = \bigsqcup_{k=1}^{m} \left(\exists A^1.Q_c[A/A^1] \sqcap R_k[X^0/A^1][X/A] \right)$$

where

- $Q_c[A/A^1]$ is the result of renaming, in Q_c, each variable a_i as a_i^1

- $R_k[X^0/A^1][X/A]$ is the result of renaming, in R_k, each variable x_i^0 as a_i^1, and each variable x_i as a_i (this term is what we wrote $\pi(\sigma_k^\sharp)$ in the general framework Sect. 6.2).

In other words, the auxiliary variables $A^1 = (a_1^1, \ldots, a_n^1)$ represent the values of actual parameters before the call, so they are substituted for A in the calling context Q_c and to X^0 in the summary; the values A of the actual parameters after the call, are substituted for X in the summary.

7   Partition Refinement

7.1   General Framework

Given an abstract partition of the global precondition of a procedure, we know how to compute and use a disjunctive summary based on this partition. In this section, we propose a heuristic method to choose the abstract partition.

Complementable Abstract Values: An abstract value $r^\sharp$ is said to be complementable, if there exists an abstract value $\overline{r^\sharp}$ (its complement) such that $r^\sharp \sqcap \overline{r^\sharp} = \bot$ and $\gamma(r^\sharp) \cup \gamma(\overline{r^\sharp}) = \mathcal{R}$. For instance, complementable convex polyhedra are half-spaces, i.e., polyhedra defined by a single inequality.

Refinement According to Local Reachability: Let $\{r^{\sharp \nabla \Delta}(\mathcal{I}^\sharp, S_i^\sharp)\}_{i=1\ldots n}$ be the result of a classic analysis from a precondition $\mathcal{I}^\sharp$. For a given $i \in \{1\ldots n\}$, $\mathcal{I}_i^\sharp = src^\sharp(r^{\sharp \nabla \Delta}(\mathcal{I}^\sharp, S_i^\sharp))$ is a necessary condition for $S_i^\sharp$ to be reachable. As a consequence, if $s^\sharp$ is a complementable abstract value such that

- $\mathcal{I}_i^\sharp \sqsubseteq s^\sharp$
- $\mathcal{I}'^\sharp = \mathcal{I}^\sharp \sqcap s^\sharp \neq \bot$ and $\mathcal{I}''^\sharp = \mathcal{I}^\sharp \sqcap \overline{s^\sharp} \neq \bot$

then $(\mathcal{I}'^\sharp, \mathcal{I}''^\sharp)$ is a good candidate for refining the precondition $\mathcal{I}^\sharp$. As a matter of fact, $\mathcal{I}''^\sharp$ is a sufficient precondition for $S_i^\sharp$ to be unreachable.

Refinement According to the Summary of a Called Procedure: The effect of a call to a procedure with a partitioned summary $\{\sigma_k^\sharp\}_{k=1\ldots m}$ (as defined in Sect. 6.2) involves a least upper bound $\bigsqcup_{k=1}^m \pi(\sigma_k^\sharp)$, which is likely to lose precision. So it is interesting to refine the partition in the caller in order to split this least upper bound. Let us denote by $\mathcal{J}_k^\sharp = \pi(src^\sharp(\sigma_k^\sharp))$, i.e., the condition on actual parameters for $\sigma_k^\sharp$ to be applicable. Then, in the caller, $\mathcal{I}_k^\sharp = src^\sharp(r^{\sharp \nabla \Delta}(\mathcal{I}^\sharp, \mathcal{J}_k^\sharp))$, is a necessary precondition for $\mathcal{J}_k^\sharp$ to be satisfiable. As a consequence, if $s^\sharp$ is a complementable abstract value such that

- $\mathcal{I}_k^\sharp \sqsubseteq s^\sharp$
- $\mathcal{I}'^\sharp = \mathcal{I}^\sharp \sqcap s^\sharp \neq \bot$ and $\mathcal{I}''^\sharp = \mathcal{I}^\sharp \sqcap \overline{s^\sharp} \neq \bot$

then $(\mathcal{I}'^\sharp, \mathcal{I}''^\sharp)$ is a good candidate for refining the precondition $\mathcal{I}^\sharp$. As a matter of fact, $\mathcal{I}''^\sharp$ is a sufficient precondition for $\mathcal{J}_k^\sharp$ to be unsatisfiable at the call.

Iterative Refinements: Our proposal is to build the summary of a procedure as the result of a sequence of analyses, working on more and more refined partitions. We define $\mathcal{P}^{(\ell)} = \{\mathcal{I}_k^{\#(\ell)}\}_{k=1...m_\ell}$ the partition of abstract preconditions considered at ℓ-th analysis. Starting with $\mathcal{P}^{(0)} = \{\mathcal{I}^{\#}\}$ (the singleton made of the global precondition of the procedure), for each ℓ, we compute from $\mathcal{P}^{(\ell)}$ the corresponding disjunctive abstract relation $\{r_k^{\#(\ell)}\}_{k=1...m_\ell}$, which is used to refine $\mathcal{P}^{(\ell)}$ into $\mathcal{P}^{(\ell+1)}$, using one of the refinement techniques presented above. This process is not guaranteed to terminate, but may be stopped at any step. In practice, the size of the partition will be limited by a constant parameter of the analysis.

Ensuring the Monotonicity of the Refinement: Refining a precondition is intended to provide a more precise summary. However, this is not guaranteed because of the non-monotonicity of the widening operator. So at step ℓ, when precondition $\mathcal{I}_k^{\#(\ell)}$ has been split into a pair $(\mathcal{I}_{k'}^{\#(\ell+1)}, \mathcal{I}_{k''}^{\#(\ell+1)})$ of new preconditions, the analyses performed at step $\ell+1$ from these new preconditions should use a widening limited by $r_k^{\#(\ell)}$. The monotonicity of the refinement is especially important when dealing with recursive procedures, and avoids the difficulties tackled by [4].

7.2   Application to LRA

Complementable Polyhedra: As said before, complementable polyhedra are those defined by a single inequality. So any polyhedron is the intersection of a finite number of complementable polyhedra. The complement of "$aX \leq b$" is obtained either with the converse *strict* inequality "$aX > b$" (strict inequalities are handled in the PPL [5,8] and in Apron [29]), or, in case of integer variables, by the inequality "$aX \geq b+1$".

Precondition Refinement: From a precondition $\mathcal{I}^{\#}$, a standard analysis by LRA provides, at each control point c of the program, a polyhedron $P_c(\mathcal{I}^{\#})$. From these solutions, we can try to refine the precondition:

– For each control point c, let $Q_c = \exists X.P_c(\mathcal{I}^{\#})$ be the projection of $P_c(\mathcal{I}^{\#})$ on initial variables. Then, if $Q_c \neq \mathcal{I}^{\#}$, any constraint χ of Q_c not satisfied by $\mathcal{I}^{\#}$ can be used to separate $\mathcal{I}^{\#}$ into $\mathcal{I}_1^{\#} = \mathcal{I}^{\#} \cap \chi$ and $\mathcal{I}_2^{\#} = \mathcal{I}^{\#} \cap \overline{\chi}$, since the point c is unreachable by any execution starting in $\mathcal{I}_2^{\#}$. Obviously, this should be tried on control points following a test, and especially those corresponding to loop conditions.
– For each control point c corresponding to a call to a procedure, say $p(A)$, let $\{R_1, ..., R_m\}$ be the polyhedral summary of p, and for each $k = 1...m$, $\mathcal{J}_k^{\#}(p) = src^{\#}(R_k)[X^0/A]$ (i.e., $\mathcal{J}_k^{\#}(p)$ is the precondition of R_k, expressed on actual parameters). Then, let $Q_{c,k} = \exists X.P_c(\mathcal{I}^{\#}) \sqcap \mathcal{J}_k^{\#}(p)$ be the projection of $P_c(\mathcal{I}^{\#}) \sqcap \mathcal{J}_k^{\#}(p)$ on the initial variables of the caller. Then, as before, if $Q_{c,k} \neq \mathcal{I}^{\#}$, any constraint χ of $Q_{c,k}$ not satisfied by $\mathcal{I}^{\#}$ can be used to separate

$\mathcal{I}^\sharp$ into $\mathcal{I}_1^\sharp = \mathcal{I}^\sharp \cap \chi$ and $\mathcal{I}_2^\sharp = \mathcal{I}^\sharp \cap \overline{\chi}$, and it is interesting since starting the caller in $\mathcal{I}_2^\sharp$ makes empty the precondition $\mathcal{J}_k^\sharp(p)$.

Notice that, in both cases, the choice of the constraint χ is arbitrary, and that several such constraints can be used in turn. So the fact that the refinement is done according to one single constraint is not a limitation.

7.3 Example

The analysis of the example in Sect. 4.3, from the precondition $\mathcal{I}^{\sharp(0)} = (a^0 \geq 0, b^0 \geq 1)$, as done in Sect. 5, provides, on the branches of the loop condition $(r \geq b)$, the solutions:

$$P_4(\mathcal{I}^{\sharp(0)}) = (a^0 = a, b^0 = b, r \geq b, q \geq 0, b \geq 1, a \geq q + r)$$
$$P_6(\mathcal{I}^{\sharp(0)}) = (a^0 = a, b^0 = b, r \geq 0, q \geq 0, b \geq r + 1, a \geq q + r)$$

The projections of these solutions on the initial values are:

$$src^\sharp(P_4(\mathcal{I}^{\sharp(0)})) = (a^0 \geq b^0 \geq 1) \quad src^\sharp(P_6(\mathcal{I}^{\sharp(0)})) = (a^0 \geq 0, b^0 \geq 1)$$

$src^\sharp(P_6(\mathcal{I}^{\sharp(0)})) = \mathcal{I}^{(0)}$, so it does not induce any refinement. However, $src^\sharp(P_4(\mathcal{I}^{\sharp(0)})) \neq \mathcal{I}^{\sharp(0)}$, since $\mathcal{I}^{\sharp(0)}$ does not imply $a^0 \geq b^0$. We can refine $\mathcal{I}^{\sharp(0)}$ into

$$\mathcal{I}_1^{\sharp(1)} = (a^0 \geq b^0 \geq 1) \text{ and } \mathcal{I}_2^{\sharp(1)} = (b^0 - 1 \geq a^0 \geq 0)$$

i.e., separate the cases where the loop is entered at least once or not. New analyses from these refined preconditions provide:

$$P_4(\mathcal{I}_1^{\sharp(1)}) = (a^0 = a, b^0 = b, r \geq b, q \geq 0, b \geq 1, a \geq q + r)$$
$$P_6(\mathcal{I}_1^{\sharp(1)}) = (a^0 = a, b^0 = b, r \geq 0, q \geq 0, q + r >= 1, b \geq r + 1,$$
$$a + 1 \geq b + q, a \geq b)$$
$$P_4(\mathcal{I}_2^{\sharp(1)}) = \bot$$
$$P_6(\mathcal{I}_2^{\sharp(1)}) = (a^0 = a, b^0 = b, b - 1 \geq a \geq 0, q = 0, r = a)$$

The projections of these solutions on the initial values are:

$$src^\sharp(P_4(\mathcal{I}_1^{\sharp(1)})) = (a^0 \geq b^0 \geq 1) = \mathcal{I}_1^{\sharp(1)})$$
$$src^\sharp(P_6(\mathcal{I}_1^{\sharp(1)})) = (a^0 \geq b^0 \geq 1) = \mathcal{I}_1^{\sharp(1)})$$
$$src^\sharp(P_4(\mathcal{I}_2^{\sharp(1)})) = \bot$$
$$src^\sharp(P_6(\mathcal{I}_2^{\sharp(1)})) = (b^0 - 1 \geq a^0 \geq 0) = \mathcal{I}_2^{\sharp(1)}$$

so, according to our criteria, the preconditions cannot be further refined, and we get the summary

$$R_1 = (a^0 = a, b^0 = b, a^0 \geq b^0 \geq 1,$$
$$r \geq 0, q \geq 0, q + r >= 1, b \geq r + 1, a + 1 \geq b + q)$$
$$R_2 = (a^0 = a, b^0 = b, b^0 - 1 \geq a^0 \geq 0, q = 0, r = a)$$

directed by input conditions $R_1^0 = (a^0 \geq b^0 \geq 1)$ and $R_2^0 = (b^0 - 1 \geq a^0 \geq 0)$.

7.4   A Last Improvement: Postponing Loop Feedback

The previous example shows a weakness of the analysis: the summary has been partitioned according to whether the loop is entered at least once (R_1) or not (R_2). However, in the former case, since the loop body is executed at least once, we should obtain $q \geq 1$, a fact which is missed by the analysis. We could recover this fact by systematically unrolling once each loop that gives raise to such a partitioning. We propose another, cheaper solution. The problem comes from the least upper bound computed at loop entry ($P_3 = P_2 \sqcup P_5$ in the abstract equations of Sect. 4.3), before the test on the loop condition ($P_6 = P_3 \sqcap (r \leq b - 1)$). The solution consists in permuting the least upper bound and the test, computing instead $P_6 = (P_2 \sqcap (r \leq b - 1)) \sqcup (P_5 \sqcap (r \leq b - 1))$[1].

Back to the Example: Computing $R_1 = P_6(\mathcal{I}_1^{\sharp(1)})$ with this new equation, since $P_2 \sqcap (r \leq b - 1) = \bot$, we get

$$R_1 = \left(a^0 = a, b^0 = b, a^0 \geq b^0 \geq 1, r \geq 0, q \geq 1, b \geq r + 1, a + 1 \geq b + q + r\right)$$

Once again, we recover more precision than expected, since, in addition to finding $q \geq 1$, $a + 1 \geq b + q$ is strengthened into $a + 1 \geq b + q + r$.

8   Recursive Procedures

The relational abstract interpretation of recursive procedures was proposed a long time ago [13,15,21]. It involves the use of widening, since the summary of a recursive procedure depends on itself. Moreover, a group of mutually recursive procedures must be analyzed jointly, with widening applied on a cutset of their call graph. In this section, we only show a simple example of how our technique can be applied to build a disjunctive summary of a recursive procedure. It will also illustrate the refinement according to the summary of a called procedure.

Example: McCarthy's 91 Function. The opposite procedure is the well-known "91 function" defined by John McCarthy. For simplicity, we don't duplicate parameters, knowing that x is a value parameter and y is a result parameter. The polyhedral summary of the procedure can be defined by the following equations:

$R(x, y) = P_2 \sqcup P_7$
$P_2 = (x \geq 101, y = x - 10)$
$P_7 = (x \leq 100 \sqcap (\exists t. R(x + 11, t) \sqcap R(t, y)))$

```
void f91 (int x,*y) {
    int z, t ;
1   if (x > 100) *y = x -10 ;
2
3   else {   z = x + 11 ;
4            f91 (z, &t) ;
5            f91 (t, y) ;
6   }
}
```

---

[1] This change in the abstract equations could also be obtained by transforming each loop "*while c do B*" into "*if c {do B while c}*", a transformation called "loop inversion" often applied by compilers.

A first, standard analysis, without partitioning, reaches the following fixpoint after one widening step:

$$P_2 = (x \geq 101, y = x - 10), \quad P_6 = (x \leq 100, y + 9 \geq x, y \geq 91)$$
$$R^{(0)} = (x \leq y + 10, y \geq 91)$$

Since $src^{\#}(P_2) = (x \geq 101)$ splits the global precondition $\mathcal{I}^{\#} = \top$, we refine the precondition into $\mathcal{I}_1^{\#(1)} = (x \geq 101)$ and $\mathcal{I}_2^{\#(1)} = (x \leq 100)$. From this (obvious) partition, the results are not much better:

$$P_2(\mathcal{I}_1^{\#(1)}) = (x \geq 101, y = x - 10), \quad P_2(\mathcal{I}_2^{\#(1)}) = \bot$$
$$P_6(\mathcal{I}_1^{\#(1)}) = \bot, \quad P_6(\mathcal{I}_2^{\#(1)}) = (x \leq 100, y \geq 91)$$
$$R^{(1)}(\mathcal{I}_1^{\#(1)}) = (x \geq 101, y = x - 10), \quad R^{(1)}(\mathcal{I}_2^{\#(1)}) = (x \leq 100, y \geq 91)$$

But now, the partitioned precondition involves a refinement of $\mathcal{I}_2^{\#(1)}$ at the first recursive call, according to the condition $x + 11 \geq 101$. We get $\mathcal{I}_1^{\#(2)} = (90 \leq x \leq 100)$ and $\mathcal{I}_2^{\#(2)} = (x \leq 89)$. The final result is

$$R^{(1)}(\mathcal{I}_1^{\#(1)}) = (x \geq 101, y = x - 10)$$
$$R^{(2)}(\mathcal{I}_1^{\#(2)}) = (90 \leq x \leq 100, y = 91)$$
$$R^{(2)}(\mathcal{I}_2^{\#(2)}) = (x \leq 89, y = 91)$$

which is the most precise summary.

9 Implementation

This approach has been implemented in a prototype static analyzer . Organized as a collection of tools, the analyzer computes numerical invariants on programs written in a significant subset of C. A front-end tool based on Clang [34] and LibTooling translates the abstract syntax tree of a C program into an intermediate representation. The analyzer tool then computes numerical invariants on the intermediate representation. Abstract domains, such as convex polyhedra, are provided by the Apron [29] library. The analyzer can either consider an inlined version of the program, or construct and use procedure summaries as described in the paper, with some restrictions: for the time being, recursive procedures are not yet taken into account, and postponing the loop feedback is not performed as described in Sect. 7.4, but makes use of "loop inversion".

Procedures are analyzed only once, regardless of the number of call sites, in a bottom-up fashion according to the inverse invocation order, with respect to the dependencies induced by the program call graph.

In order to limit the number of additional variables, the tool does not duplicate all procedure parameters, but applies a simple dataflow analysis before summary construction to identify procedure parameters which are either pure input parameters or pure output parameters, and thus which do not need to be duplicated.

Refinement according to local reachability is performed by the analyzer only at direct successors of test nodes and particularly at loop entry and loop exit. Candidate nodes for refinement are examined during each refinement step using a breadth-first traversal of the program graph. For practical reasons, in order to guarantee the termination of the refinement process and to limit procedure summaries to a reasonable size, an upper-bound θ on the refinement depth for a given procedure is set to $\theta = 2$. This limits procedure summaries to a maximum size of 4.

10   Experiments

Up to now, to illustrate our approach, we presented only tiny examples, for which the precondition partitioning is obvious. However, in presence of more complex control structures—nested and/or successive loops—and when preconditions result from more involved invariants, the usefulness of our method for discovering relevant preconditions is more convincing. Several more complex ad-hoc examples can be found on the repository github.com/programexamples/programexamples.

More thorough experiments are necessary to validate our approach, and in particular to answer the following questions:

- Since we analyze a procedure several times to construct its summary, it is likely to be time-consuming. So it is interesting to measure the cost of summary construction with respect to the time hopefully saved by using the summary.
- Precondition partitioning is a heuristic process, so it is important to evaluate the precision lost or gained by using a disjunctive summary instead of analyzing again the procedure for each calling context.

So our experiments consists in comparing our bottom-up approach with an analysis of inlined programs, both with respect to the analysis time and the precision of results. Several difficulties must be addressed first:
- Most public benchmarks are not usable, since they contain very few numerical programs with procedures. For instance, in the SV-COMP benchmark[2], most numerical examples are inlined; the ALICe benchmark[3] also contains only monolithic programs. For our assessment, we used the benchmark of the Mälardalen[4] WCET research group, which contains various small and middle-sized programs, such as sorts, matrix computations, fft, etc. Moreover, some programs of this benchmark were sometimes extended with auxiliary variables counting the number of executions of each block to help the evaluation of the execution time [10]; these extensions—the name of which are prefixed with "cnt_" below—are interesting for us, since they contains more numeric variables.

---

[2] sv-comp.sosy-lab.org/2018/benchmarks.php.
[3] alice.cri.mines-paristech.fr/models.html.
[4] www.mrtc.mdh.se/projects/wcet/benchmarks.html.

- The comparison of polyhedral results is not straightforward:
  - On one hand, we must decide which polyhedra to compare. The correspondence of control points between the inlined program and the structured one is not easy to preserve. In our experiments, we only compared the results at the end of the main program. Of course, for the comparison to be meaningful, the results on the inlined program must be first projected on the variables of the main program.
  - On the other hand, while a qualitative comparison of two polyhedra is easy—by checking their inclusion in both directions—, a quantitative comparison is more difficult: it could be precisely achieved by comparing their volumes—algorithms are available for that [7,11]—but it is only possible for bounded polyhedra. In our assessment, besides a qualitative comparison, we only compared the number of constraints.

All our experiments are done using the convex polyhedra abstract domain. Widening is never delayed and decreasing sequences are limited to 7 terms. The analysis times are those obtained on an Intel Xeon E5-2630 v3 2.40 Ghz machine with 32 GB of RAM and 20MB of L3 cache running Linux.

Table 1 compares our method with a standard LRA on inlined programs, in terms of analysis time, qualitative precision and number of constraints of results found at the exit points of the main procedures. The "# procs" column gives the number of procedures in each program and the "max. # calls" column gives the maximum number of call sites per procedure in a program. We define:

- t_{IL} (resp. t_{IP}) the time (in seconds) for analyzing the inlined program (resp. the time for interprocedural analysis)
- P_{IL} (resp. P_{IP}) the polyhedron result of the inlined analysis (resp., of the interprocedural analysis)
- C_{IL} (resp. C_{IP}) the number of constraints of P_{IL} (resp. of P_{IP}).

The qualitative results comparison is shown by column "cmp. res." which indicates whether the result P_{IP} is better ($\sqsupseteq$), worse ($\sqsubseteq$), equal ($=$) or incomparable ($<>$) w.r.t. P_{IL}. The S column gives for each program the speedup of our method defined as $S = t_{\mathrm{IL}}/t_{\mathrm{IP}}$. Our method is significantly faster than standard LRA using inlining for 13 over 19 programs ($\approx 68\%$ of programs), with an average speedup of 2.9. The loss of precision is very moderate since only 1 over 19 programs, namely **minver**, has a less precise convex polyhedra at the exit node of the main procedure.

Interestingly, our method also leads to precision improvements for some programs, such as **janne_complex**, **my_sin** and **cnt_minver**, due to the use of disjunction, enabling a more accurate analysis of procedure behaviors. Moreover, those precision improvements are not necessarily obtained at the expense of analysis time, since the **janne_complex** program has a more precise convex polyhedra at the exit of the main procedure, with a 60% increase in the number of constraints and has also the highest speedup with $S = 15.34$.

Table 2 reports the computation times of the summary of each procedure in each program. The τ_c column gives the fraction of the analysis time using our method spent during the computation of each procedure summary, defined as $\tau_c = $ Procedure summary comp. time/Program analysis time using rel. summ.

Table 1. Experimental results.

Program	# procs	max. # calls	Inlining		Interprocedural		cmp. res.	S
			t_{IL}	C_{IL}	t_{IP}	C_{IP}		
fabs	2	1	0.013	4	0.015	4	=	0.87
fdct	2	1	0.084	0	0.069	0	=	1.22
fft1	6	3	0.742	4	0.465	3	<>	1.59
fir	2	1	0.040	1	0.072	1	=	0.55
janne_complex	2	1	0.948	5	0.062	8	⊐	15.34
minver	4	2	0.155	1	0.686	2	⊏	0.23
my_sin	2	1	0.032	1	0.028	5	⊐	1.14
jfdctint	2	1	0.082	3	0.060	3	=	1.38
ludcmp	3	1	0.074	3	0.102	3	=	0.73
ns	2	1	0.057	0	0.051	0	=	1.13
qurt	4	1	0.057	1	0.028	1	=	2.06
select	2	1	0.097	0	0.057	0	=	1.69
ud	2	1	0.093	3	0.118	3	=	0.79
cnt_fdct	2	1	0.098	1	0.075	1	=	1.31
cnt_fft1	6	3	33.417	5	2.646	3	<>	12.63
cnt_jfdctint	2	1	0.102	5	0.070	5	=	1.46
cnt_ns	2	1	0.085	0	0.067	0	=	1.25
cnt_qurt	4	1	0.601	2	0.063	2	=	9.54
cnt_minver	4	2	1.008	1	3.424	6	⊐	0.29

The summary construction time for small utility procedures, such as the **my_fabs**, **my_sin**, **my_cos** and **my_log** procedures, in the **fft1** and **cnt_fft1** programs, are very small (lower than 4 ms) and often individually negligible with respect to the analysis time of the entire program (with τ_c often lower than 1%). This suggests that our method could be particularly beneficial, in terms of analysis performance, for programs built on top of a collection of utility procedures or a library of such procedures, each procedure summary being computed only once and possibly used in many call contexts.

Our last experiment concerns the speedup of our interprocedural analysis with respect to the number of calls. Notice that the Mälardalen benchmark is not very favorable in this respect, since most procedures are called only once. Our analysis on the **cnt_ns** program has a moderate speedup of 1.25. In order to observe the evolution of the speedup with the number of calls, we increase the number of calls to the *foo* procedure in the main procedure of the **cnt_ns** program. The opposite

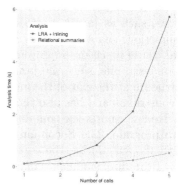

Table 2. Summaries computation times.

Program	Function	Time (s)	τ_c
fabs	fabs	0.001	0.067
fdct	fdct	0.050	0.588
fft1	my_fabs	< 0.001	0.001
	my_sin	0.002	0.004
	my_cos	< 0.001	0.001
	my_log	< 0.001	< 0.001
	fft1	0.350	0.753
fir	fir	0.019	0.267
janne	janne	0.037	0.602
minver	mmul	0.047	0.069
	minver_fabs	< 0.001	< 0.001
	minver	0.616	0.897
my_sin	my_sin	0.003	0.098
jfdctint	jpeg_fdct_islow	0.031	0.528
ludcmp	fabs	< 0.001	0.002
	ludcmp	0.055	0.540
ns	foo	0.011	0.215

qurt	qurt_fabs	< 0.001	0.007
	qurt_sqrt	0.004	0.138
	qurt	0.002	0.066
select	select	0.042	0.730
ud	ludcmp	0.050	0.425
cnt_fdct	fdct	0.070	0.941
cnt_fft1	my_fabs	0.001	< 0.001
	my_sin	0.004	0.001
	my_cos	< 0.001	< 0.001
	my_log	< 0.001	< 0.001
	fft1	1.750	0.661
cnt_jfdctint	jpeg_fdct_islow	0.035	0.500
cnt_ns	foo	0.026	0.382
cnt_qurt	qurt_fabs	0.001	0.010
	qurt_sqrt	0.019	0.308
	qurt	0.003	0.047
cnt_minver	mmul	0.126	0.037
	minver_fabs	< 0.001	< 0.001
	minver	2.925	0.854

graphic shows the evolution of the analysis times of these successive versions, comparing our analysis with respect to standard LRA with inlining.

The analysis of the **cnt_ns** program using our disjunctive relational summaries analysis becomes significantly faster than standard LRA with inlining when there are more than 2 calls to the *foo* procedure in the main procedure.

11   Conclusion and Future Work

In this paper, we proposed a method for interprocedural analysis as a solution to the cost of using expressive relational abstract domains in program analysis. An analysis using a relational domain can be straightforwardly transformed into a relational analysis, computing an input-output relation. Such relations can be used as procedure summaries, computed once and for all, and used bottom-up to compute the effect of procedure calls. Applying this idea with linear relation analysis, we concluded that the obtained polyhedral summaries are not precise enough, and deserve to be refined disjunctively. The main ideas of the paper are as follows. First, we used precondition partitioning as a basis of disjunctive summaries. Then, we proposed a heuristic method for refining a summary according to reachability of control points or calling contexts of called procedures. We also identified some technical improvements, like widening limited by preconditions and previously computed relations, and more precise computation of results at loop exit points. Our experiments show that using summaries built in this way can significantly reduce the analysis time, especially for procedures used several times. On the other hand, the precision of the results is not dramatically damaged, and can even be improved, due to disjunctive analysis.

Future work should be devoted to applying the method with other relational domains. In particular, octagons [39] would be interesting since they permit a better quantitative comparison of results: apart from infinite bounds, two octagons on the same variables can be precisely compared by comparing their constant vectors. Another, longer-term, perspective is to use disjunctive relational summaries for procedures acting on remanent memories, like methods in object-oriented programming or reaction functions in reactive programming. Our precondition partitioning could result in partitioning memory states, and allow disjunctive memory invariants to be constructed modularly.

References

1. Allen, F.E.: Interprocedural analysis and the information derived by it. In: Hackl, C.E. (ed.) IBM 1974. LNCS, vol. 23, pp. 291–321. Springer, Heidelberg (1975). https://doi.org/10.1007/3-540-07131-8_31
2. Allen, F.E.: Interprocedural data flow analysis. In: IFIP Congress, pp. 398–402 (1974)
3. Ancourt, C., Coelho, F., Irigoin, F.: A modular static analysis approach to affine loop invariants detection. Electron. Notes Theor. Comput. Sci. **267**(1), 3–16 (2010)
4. Apinis, K., Seidl, H., Vojdani, V.: How to combine widening and narrowing for non-monotonic systems of equations. In: ACM SIGPLAN Conference on Programming Language Design and Implementation, PLDI 2013, Seattle, WA, pp. 377–386, June 2013
5. Bagnara, R., Ricci, E., Zaffanella, E., Hill, P.M.: Possibly not closed convex polyhedra and the parma polyhedra library. In: Hermenegildo, M.V., Puebla, G. (eds.) SAS 2002. LNCS, vol. 2477, pp. 213–229. Springer, Heidelberg (2002). https://doi.org/10.1007/3-540-45789-5_17
6. Barth, J.M.: An interprocedural data flow analysis algorithm. In: Proceedings of the 4th ACM SIGACT-SIGPLAN Symposium on Principles of Programming Languages, pp. 119–131. ACM (1977)
7. Barvinok, A.I.: A polynomial time algorithm for counting integral points in polyhedra when the dimension is fixed. Math. Oper. Res. **19**(4), 769–779 (1994). https://doi.org/10.1287/moor.19.4.769. https://doi.org/10.1287/moor.19.4.769
8. Becchi, A., Zaffanella, E.: An efficient abstract domain for not necessarily closed polyhedra. In: Podelski, A. (ed.) SAS 2018. LNCS, vol. 11002, pp. 146–165. Springer, Cham (2018). https://doi.org/10.1007/978-3-319-99725-4_11
9. Bourdoncle, F.: Abstract interpretation by dynamic partitioning. J. Funct. Program. **2**(4), 407–435 (1992)
10. Boutonnet, R., Asavoae, M.: The WCET analysis using counters - a preliminary assessment. In: Proceedings of 8th JRWRTC, in Conjunction with RTNS14, Versailles, France, October 2014
11. Clauss, P.: Counting solutions to linear and nonlinear constraints through Ehrhart polynomials: applications to analyze and transform scientific programs. In: Proceedings of the 10th International Conference on Supercomputing, ICS 1996, Philadelphia, PA, USA, 25–28 May 1996, pp. 278–285 (1996). http://doi.acm.org/10.1145/237578.237617

12. Cousot, P., Cousot, R.: Abstract interpretation: a unified lattice model for static analysis of programs by construction or approximation of fixpoints. In: 4th ACM Symposium on Principles of Programming Languages, POPL 1977, Los Angeles, January 1977
13. Cousot, P., Cousot, R.: Static determination of dynamic properties of recursive procedures. In: IFIP Conference on Formal Description of Programming Concepts, St. Andrews, NB, Canada. North-Holland Publishing Company (1977)
14. Cousot, P., Cousot, R.: Relational abstract interpretation of higher order functional programs (extended abstract). In: Proceedings of Actes JTASPEFL 1991 (Bordeaux), Laboratoire Bordelais de Recherche en Informatique (LaBRI), October 1991, pp. 33–36 (1991)
15. Cousot, P., Cousot, R.: Compositional separate modular static analysis of programs by abstract interpretation. In: Proceedings of SSGRR, pp. 6–10 (2001)
16. Cousot, P., Cousot, R.: Modular static program analysis. In: Horspool, R.N. (ed.) CC 2002. LNCS, vol. 2304, pp. 159–179. Springer, Heidelberg (2002). https://doi.org/10.1007/3-540-45937-5_13
17. Cousot, P., Halbwachs, N.: Automatic discovery of linear restraints among variables of a program. In: Proceedings of the 5th ACM SIGACT-SIGPLAN Symposium on Principles of Programming Languages, pp. 84–96. ACM (1978)
18. Flexeder, A., Müller-Olm, M., Petter, M., Seidl, H.: Fast interprocedural linear two-variable equalities. ACM Trans. Programm. Lang. Syst. (TOPLAS) 33(6), 21 (2011)
19. Giacobazzi, R., Scozzari, F.: A logical model for relational abstract domains. ACM Trans. Programm. Lang. Syst. (TOPLAS) 20(5), 1067–1109 (1998)
20. Gulwani, S., Tiwari, A.: Computing procedure summaries for interprocedural analysis. In: De Nicola, R. (ed.) ESOP 2007. LNCS, vol. 4421, pp. 253–267. Springer, Heidelberg (2007). https://doi.org/10.1007/978-3-540-71316-6_18
21. Halbwachs, N.: Détermination automatique de relations linéaires vérifiées par les variables d'un programme. Ph.D. thesis, Université Scientifique et Médicale de Grenoble (1979)
22. Howe, J.M., King, A.: Polyhedral analysis using parametric objectives. In: Miné, A., Schmidt, D. (eds.) SAS 2012. LNCS, vol. 7460, pp. 41–57. Springer, Heidelberg (2012). https://doi.org/10.1007/978-3-642-33125-1_6
23. Irigoin, F., Jouvelot, P., Triolet, R.: Semantical interprocedural parallelization: an overview of the pips project. In: ACM International Conference on Supercomputing 25th Anniversary Volume, pp. 143–150. ACM (2014)
24. Jeannet, B.: Dynamic partitioning in linear relation analysis: application to the verification of reactive systems. Formal Methods Syst. Des. 23(1), 5–37 (2003)
25. Jeannet, B.: INTERPROC analyzer for recursive programs with numerical variables. INRIA. http://pop-art.inrialpes.fr/interproc/interprocweb.cgi. Accessed 06 Nov 2010
26. Jeannet, B.: Relational interprocedural verification of concurrent programs. Softw. Syst. Model. 12(2), 285–306 (2013)
27. Jeannet, B., Gopan, D., Reps, T.: A relational abstraction for functions. In: Hankin, C., Siveroni, I. (eds.) SAS 2005. LNCS, vol. 3672, pp. 186–202. Springer, Heidelberg (2005). https://doi.org/10.1007/11547662_14
28. Jeannet, B., Halbwachs, N., Raymond, P.: Dynamic partitioning in analyses of numerical properties. In: Cortesi, A., Filé, G. (eds.) SAS 1999. LNCS, vol. 1694, pp. 39–50. Springer, Heidelberg (1999). https://doi.org/10.1007/3-540-48294-6_3

29. Jeannet, B., Miné, A.: APRON: a library of numerical abstract domains for static analysis. In: Bouajjani, A., Maler, O. (eds.) CAV 2009. LNCS, vol. 5643, pp. 661–667. Springer, Heidelberg (2009). https://doi.org/10.1007/978-3-642-02658-4_52
30. Jeannet, B., Serwe, W.: Abstracting call-stacks for interprocedural verification of imperative programs. In: Rattray, C., Maharaj, S., Shankland, C. (eds.) AMAST 2004. LNCS, vol. 3116, pp. 258–273. Springer, Heidelberg (2004). https://doi.org/10.1007/978-3-540-27815-3_22
31. Kelly, W., Maslov, V., Pugh, W., Rosser, E., Shpeisman, T., Wonnacott, D.: The Omega calculator and library, version 1.1. 0. College Park, MD 20742, 18 (1996)
32. Khedker, U., Sanyal, A., Sathe, B.: Data Flow Analysis: Theory and Practice. CRC Press, Boca Raton (2009)
33. Kranz, J., Simon, A.: Modular analysis of executables using on-demand heyting completion. Verification, Model Checking, and Abstract Interpretation. LNCS, vol. 10747, pp. 291–312. Springer, Cham (2018). https://doi.org/10.1007/978-3-319-73721-8_14
34. Lattner, C., Adve, V.: LLVM: a compilation framework for lifelong program analysis & transformation. In: Proceedings of the 2004 International Symposium on Code Generation and Optimization (CGO 2004), Palo Alto, California, March 2004
35. Maisonneuve, V.: Convex invariant refinement by control node splitting: a heuristic approach. Electron. Notes Theor. Comput. Sci. **288**, 49–59 (2012)
36. Maisonneuve, V., Hermant, O., Irigoin, F.: Computing invariants with transformers: experimental scalability and accuracy. Electron. Notes Theor. Comput. Sci. **307**, 17–31 (2014)
37. Maréchal, A., Monniaux, D., Périn, M.: Scalable minimizing-operators on polyhedra via parametric linear programming. In: Ranzato, F. (ed.) SAS 2017. LNCS, vol. 10422, pp. 212–231. Springer, Cham (2017). https://doi.org/10.1007/978-3-319-66706-5_11
38. Mauborgne, L., Rival, X.: Trace partitioning in abstract interpretation based static analyzers. In: Sagiv, M. (ed.) ESOP 2005. LNCS, vol. 3444, pp. 5–20. Springer, Heidelberg (2005). https://doi.org/10.1007/978-3-540-31987-0_2
39. Miné, A.: The octagon abstract domain. In: AST 2001 in WCRE 2001, pp. 310–319. IEEE/IEEE CS Press, October 2001
40. Müller-Olm, M., Rüthing, O., Seidl, H.: Checking herbrand equalities and beyond. In: Cousot, R. (ed.) VMCAI 2005. LNCS, vol. 3385, pp. 79–96. Springer, Heidelberg (2005). https://doi.org/10.1007/978-3-540-30579-8_6
41. Müller-Olm, M., Seidl, H.: Computing interprocedurally valid relations in affine programs. Princ. Prog. Lang. (2004)
42. Müller-Olm, M., Seidl, H., Steffen, B.: Interprocedural analysis (almost) for free. Univ. Dekanat Informatik (2004)
43. Popeea, C., Chin, W.-N.: Inferring disjunctive postconditions. In: Okada, M., Satoh, I. (eds.) ASIAN 2006. LNCS, vol. 4435, pp. 331–345. Springer, Heidelberg (2007). https://doi.org/10.1007/978-3-540-77505-8_26
44. Popeea, C., Chin, W.N.: Dual analysis for proving safety and finding bugs. In: Proceedings of the 2010 ACM Symposium on Applied Computing, pp. 2137–2143. ACM (2010)
45. Popeea, C., Chin, W.N.: Dual analysis for proving safety and finding bugs. Sci. Comput. Program. **78**(4), 390–411 (2013)
46. Reps, T., Horwitz, S., Sagiv, M.: Precise interprocedural dataflow analysis via graph reachability. In: Proceedings of the 22nd ACM SIGPLAN-SIGACT Symposium on Principles of Programming Languages, pp. 49–61. ACM (1995)

47. Rival, X., Mauborgne, L.: The trace partitioning abstract domain. ACM Trans. Program. Lang. Syst. (TOPLAS) **29**(5), 26 (2007)
48. Sharir, M., Pnueli, A.: Two approaches to interprocedural data flow analysis. New York University, Courant Institute of Mathematical Sciences, Computer Science Department (1978)
49. Singh, G., Püschel, M., Vechev, M.T.: Fast polyhedra abstract domain. In: POPL, pp. 46–59 (2017)
50. Sotin, P., Jeannet, B.: Precise interprocedural analysis in the presence of pointers to the stack. In: Barthe, G. (ed.) ESOP 2011. LNCS, vol. 6602, pp. 459–479. Springer, Heidelberg (2011). https://doi.org/10.1007/978-3-642-19718-5_24
51. Spillman, T.C.: Exposing side-effects in a PL/I optimizing compiler. In: IFIP Congress, vol. 1, pp. 376–381 (1971)
52. Yorsh, G., Yahav, E., Chandra, S.: Generating precise and concise procedure summaries. In: ACM SIGPLAN Notices, vol. 43, pp. 221–234. ACM (2008)
53. Zhang, X., Mangal, R., Naik, M., Yang, H.: Hybrid top-down and bottom-up interprocedural analysis. In: ACM SIGPLAN Notices, vol. 49, pp. 249–258. ACM (2014)

Exploiting Pointer Analysis in Memory Models for Deductive Verification

Quentin Bouillaguet[1,2]([envelope]), François Bobot[1], Mihaela Sighireanu[2][ID], and Boris Yakobowski[1,3]

[1] CEA, LIST, Software Reliability Laboratory, Gif-sur-Yvette, France
{quentin.bouillaguet,francois.bobot,boris.yakobowski}@cea.fr
[2] IRIF, University Paris Diderot and CNRS, Paris, France
[3] AdaCore, Paris, France

Abstract. Cooperation between verification methods is crucial to tackle the challenging problem of software verification. The paper focuses on the verification of C programs using pointers and it formalizes a cooperation between static analyzers doing pointer analysis and a deductive verification tool based on first order logic. We propose a framework based on memory models that captures the partitioning of memory inferred by pointer analyses, and complies with the memory models used to generate verification conditions. The framework guided us to propose a pointer analysis that accommodates to various low-level operations on pointers while providing precise information about memory partitioning to the deductive verification. We implemented this cooperation inside the Frama-C platform and we show its effectiveness in reducing the task of deductive verification on a complex case study.

1 Introduction

Software verification is a challenging problem for which different solutions have been proposed. Two of these solutions are deductive verification (DV) and static analysis (SA). Deductive verification is interested in checking precise and expressive properties of the input code. It requires efforts from the user that has to specify the properties to be checked, plus other annotations – e.g., loop invariants. Using these specifications, DV tools build verification conditions which are formulas in various logic theories and send them to specialized solvers. For C programs with pointers, DV has been boosted by the usage of Separation Logic [29], which leads to compact proofs due to the local reasoning allowed by the separating conjunction operator. However, for programs with low-level operations on pointers (e.g., pointer arithmetics and casting), this approach is actually limited by the theoretical results on the fragment of separation logic employed [7] and on the availability of solvers. Therefore, this class of programs is most commonly dealt using classic approaches based on memory models *à la*

This work was partially supported by grant ANR-14-CE28-0018-03.

C. Enea and R. Piskac (Eds.): VMCAI 2019, LNCS 11388, pp. 160–182, 2019.
https://doi.org/10.1007/978-3-030-11245-5_8

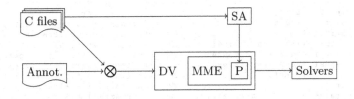

Fig. 1. Verification using memory partitioning inferred by pointer analysis

Burstall-Bornat [6,9], which may be adapted to be sound in presence of low-level operations [31] and dynamic allocation [36]. The memory model is chosen in general by the DV engine which may employ some heuristics to guide the choice [20]. Indeed, changing the memory model may result in an increase of the number of proofs discharged automatically [35]. However, annotations on non aliasing between pointers and memory partitioning complicates the task of users and of underlying solvers.

On the other hand, static analysis targets checking a fixed class of properties. This loss in the expressivity of properties is counterbalanced by a high degree of automation. For example, static pointer analysis for C programs usually computes over-approximations of the set of values (addresses) for each pointer expression at each control point. These abstractions do not speak about concrete memory addresses, but refer to symbolic memory regions provided by the memory allocated to program variables and in heap by dynamic allocation methods.

The information obtained by static analysis may help to infer partitioning of the memory in disjoint regions which can then be used by DV tools. The success of this collaboration between SA and DV tool strongly depends on the coarseness of the abstraction used by SA to keep track of the locations scanned by a pointer inside each memory region. For example, consider p a pointer to integer and a variable s of type record with five integer fields, struct {int m,n,o,p,q;}, such that p scans locations of all fields of s except o (i.e., &s.m, &s.n, &s.p and &s.q). Pointer analyses (e.g., Sect. 5.2 of [28]) over-approximate the location of p to any location in the memory region of s which is multiple of an integer, thus including the spurious o field. Therefore, it is important to be able to try several SA algorithms to gather precise information about the memory partitioning.

Our contribution targets this specific cooperation of SA and DV methods in the context of first-order logic solvers. The verification process we propose is summarized by the flow diagram in Fig. 1. The code to be verified is first given to the static analyzer to produce state invariants including a sound partitioning P of the program's memory. The partitioning P is exploited by a functor M which produces a memory model environment MME used by the DV tool to generate verification conditions into a logic theory supported by automatic solvers. Our first contribution is the formalization of the functor M and of the information it needs from the static analysis. Secondly, we demonstrate that several existing pointer analyses may be used in this general framework. Thirdly, we implemented this functor in the Frama-C platform [22] between the plug-ins Eva for static

```
1│typedef int32_t data_t;              22│  pos_t **posArr =
2│typedef uint8_t pos_t;               23│    (pos_t **) &(args->pos1);
3│typedef struct {                     24│  /** init arrays from inputs */
4│  data_t *in1, *in2, *in3, *in4;     25│  int32_t sortArr[4]; // values
5│  data_t *out1,*out2,*out3,*out4;    26│  uint8_t permArr[4]; // permutation
6│  pos_t  *pos1,*pos2,*pos3,*pos4;    27│  /*@ loop invariant: ... */
7│         } intf4_t;                  28│  for (int i = 0; i < 4; i++) {
8│/*@ requires:                        29│    sortArr[i] = *inArr[i];
9│ *    sep({args->in1,...,args->in4}, 30│    permArr[i] = i;
10│ *        args->out1,...,args->out4,31│  }
11│ *        args->pos1,...,args->pos4);32│
12│ *  ensures:                        33│  /* sorting algorithm on sortArr
13│ *    sorted_vals(&(args->out1),4); 34│   * with permutation in permArr */
14│ *  ensures:                        35│
15│ *    perm(&(args->in1),&(args->out1),36│ /** copy results to outputs */
16│ *        &(args->pos1),4); */       37│  /*@ loop invariant: ... */
17│void sort4(intf4_t *args) {          38│  for (int i = 0; i < 4; i++) {
18│  data_t **inArr   =                 39│    (*outArr[i]) = sortArr[i];
19│    (data_t **) &(args->in1);        40│    (*posArr[i]) = permArr[i];
20│  data_t **outArr  =                 41│  }
21│    (data_t **) &(args->out1);       42│}
```

Fig. 2. Sorting function for **N** = 4 inputs and outputs

analysis and WP for deductive verification. Finally, we propose a new pointer analysis exploiting a value analysis based on abstract interpretation; this analysis is able to produce the memory model that reduces the verification effort of a relevant benchmark.

2   A Motivating Example

We overview the issues targeted and the solution proposed in this work using the C code given in Fig. 2. This code is extracted from the C code generated by the compiler of a high level data flow language. It combines at least three complex features of pointers in C.

The first feature is the duality of records and arrays, which is used here to interpret the (large) list of arguments for a function as individual fields in a compound (record) type or as cells of an array. Thus, the read of the k-th field ($k \geq 0$) named fk of a record stored at location s and using only fields of type τ may be written s->fk or *(&(s->f0)+k), where f0 is the first field. It is debatable whether the C standard actually permits this form of dual indexing between records with fields of the same type and arrays [34], but some programs, including this one, use this feature with success. In our example, this duality is used in function sort4 to ease the extraction of numerical values from the inputs and the storage of the sorted values in the outputs. This first feature makes our running example more challenging, but the technique we propose is also effective when the parameters are encapsulated in arrays of pointers, e.g., when inputs and outputs are declared as a field of type array by data_t* in[4]. The second feature is precisely the usage of arrays of pointers which is notoriously difficult to be dealt precisely by pointer analyses. The third feature is the complex separation constraints between pointers stored in arrays, which leads to a quadratic number of constraints on the size of the array and complicates the task of DV tools. In the following, we discuss in detail these issues and our approach to deal with them.

Inputs and outputs of sort4 have the same type, data_t, which shall encapsulate a numerical value to be sorted. For simplicity, we consider only one field of int32_t type for data_t. Type pos_t models an element of the permutation and denotes the destination position (an unsigned integer) of the value sorted. The parameters of sort4 are collected by type intf4_t: four pointers to data_t for input values, four pointers to data_t for output values, and four pointers to pos_t for the new positions of input values.

The function is annotated with pre/post conditions and with loop invariants. The pre-condition requires (predicate sep) that (1) all pointers in *args are valid, i.e. point to valid memory locations, (2) the pointers in fields in are disjoint from any pointer in fields out and pos, and (3) pointers in fields out and pos are pairwise disjoint. Notice that the in fields may alias. The post-condition states that the values pointed by the fields out are sorted (predicate sorted_vals) and, for each output i, the value of this output is equal to the value of the input j such that pos[j] is i (predicate perm).

The separation pre-condition is necessary for the proof of the post-condition because any aliasing between fields out may crush the results of the sorting algorithm. The encoding of this pre-condition in FOL is done by a conjunction of dis-equalities which is quadratic on the number of pointers concerned. More precisely, for n inputs (and so n outputs and n positions), there are $O(n^2)$ such constraints. (In SL, this requirement is encoded in linear formulas.) The original code from which our example is inspired instantiate n with 24 and therefore generates a huge number of dis-equalities. Several techniques have been proposed to reduce the number of dis-equalities generated by the separation constraints. For example, a classic technique is assigning a distinct logic value (a color) to each pointer in the separated set. This technique does not apply in our example if the type data_t is a record with more than one field because the color shall concern only the numerical value to be sorted.

As an alternative, we propose to use precise points-to analyses to lift out such constraints and to simplify the memory model used for the proof of the function. Importantly, we perform a per-call proof of sort4, instead of a unitary proof. For each call of sort4, the static analysis tries to check that the separation pre-condition is satisfied and provides a model for the memory where the pointers are dispatched over disjoint zones. Unfortunately, the precision of the points-to analyses (and consequently the number of separation constraints discharged) may change radically with the kind of initialization done for the arguments of sort4. We will illustrate this behavior for two calls of sort4 given in Fig. 3: the call in listing (a) uses variables and the one in listing (b) uses arrays. Notice that each call satisfies the separation pre-condition of sort4.

Typed Memory Model: For completeness, we quickly present first how DV tools using FOL deal with our example using the Burstall-Bornat model. In this model, the memory is represented by a set of array variables, each array corresponding to a (pre-defined, basic) type of memory locations. For our

Listing 1.1: (a) using variables

```
1   data_t   df_1,df_2,...,df_8;
2   pos_t    pf_1,pf_2,pf_3,pf_4;
3   intf4_t SORT = {
4    .in1=&df1,    .in2=&df2,
5    .in3=&df3,    .in4=&df4,
6    .out1=&df5,   .out2=&df6,
7    .out3=&df7,   .out4=&df8,
8    .pos1=&pf1,   .pos2=&pf2,
9    .pos3=&pf3,   .pos4=&pf4 };
10
11  df_1 = nondet_data();
12  df_2 = nondet_data();
13  df_3 = nondet_data();
14  df_4 = nondet_data();
15
16  sort4(&SORT);
```

Listing 1.2: (b) using arrays

```
1   data_t   df[8];
2   pos_t    pf[4];
3   intf4_t SORT = {
4    .in1=df+1,    .in2=df+2,
5    .in3=df+3,    .in4=df+4,
6    .out1=df+5,   .out2=df+6,
7    .out3=df+7,   .out4=df,
8    .pos1=pf,     .pos2=pf+1,
9    .pos3=pf+2,   .pos4=pf+3 };
10
11  df[1] = nondet_data();
12  df[2] = nondet_data();
13  df[3] = nondet_data();
14  df[4] = nondet_data();
15
16  sort4(&SORT);
```

Fig. 3. Two calls for the sorting function using different initialization

example, the memory model includes six array variables: M_int32, M_uint8, M_int32_ref, M_uint8_ref, M_int32_ref_ref, M_uint8_ref_ref storing values of type respectively int32_t, uint8_t, int32_t*, uint8_t*, int32_t** and uint8_t**. Program variables are used as indices in these arrays, e.g., variable inArr is an index in array M_int32_ref_ref and sortArr is index of M_int32.

The separation pre-condition of sort4 is encoded by dis-equalities, e.g., M_int32_ref[args_in4] <> M_int32_ref[args_out1] where args_in4 is bound to the term $shift$(M_int32_ref_ref[args], in4) which encodes the access to the memory location &(args->in4) using the logic function $shift$;args_out1 is defined similarly. However, these dis-equalities are not propagated through the assignments at lines 18–23 in Fig. 2, which interpret the sequence of (input/output/position) fields as arrays. Therefore, additional annotations are required to prove the correct initialization of the output at lines 39–41. Some of these annotations may be avoided using our method that employs pointer analyses to infer precise memory models, as we show below.

Base-Offset Pointer Analysis: Consider now a pointer analysis which is field and context sensitive, and which computes an over-approximation of the value of each pointer expression at each program statement. The over-approximation, that we name *abstract location*, is built upon the standard concrete memory model of C [25]. An abstract location is *a partial map* between the set of program's variables and the set of intervals in $\mathbb{N}$. An element of this abstraction, $(v, i^\#)$, denotes the symbolic (i.e., not related with the locations in the virtual memory space used during the concrete execution) memory block that starts at the location of the program variable v (called also *base*), and the abstraction by an interval $i^\#$ of the set of possible offsets (in bytes) inside the symbolic block of v to which the pointer expression may be evaluated. In this memory model, symbolic blocks of different program variables are implicitly separated: it is impossible to move from the block of one variable to another using pointer arithmetic. The memory model is modeled by a set of logic arrays, one for each symbolic block. The over-approximation computed by the analysis allows to dispatch a pointer expression used in a statement on these arrays.

In our example, for the call of sort4 in Fig. 3(a), the memory model includes the symbolic blocks for program's variable df$i$, pf$i$ and SORT. The above analysis computes for the pointer expressions args->in1 and *(args->in1) at the start of sort4, the abstract location $\{(\text{SORT}, [0, 0])\}$ and $(\text{df1}, [0, 0])$ respectively. The abstract locations for the pointer expressions involving other fields of args are computed similarly. The separation pre-condition of sort4 is implied by these abstract locations. After the fields of args are interpreted as arrays (lines 18–23 of sort4), the pointer expression outArr+i at line 39, where i is restricted to the interval $[0, 3]$, is over-approximated to the abstract location $\{(\text{SORT}, [16, 31])\}$. Similarly, inArr+i is abstracted by $\{(\text{SORT}, [0, 15])\}$. Therefore, the left value given by the pointer expression outArr[i] (at line 39) is (precisely) computed to be $\{(\text{df5}, [0, 0]), ..., (\text{df8}, [0, 0])\}$. This allows proving the correctness of the output computed by sort4.

For the call in Fig. 3(b), the memory model includes symbolic blocks for program's variable df, pf and SORT. The analysis computes for pointer expressions args->in1 and *(args->in1) (used at the start of sort4), the abstract location $\{(\text{SORT}, [0, 0])\}$ resp. $(\text{df}, [0, 3])$, which also allows to prove the separation pre-condition. The interpretation of fields as arrays (lines 18–23) leads to the abstract location $\{(\text{df}, [1, 4])\}$ for inArr+i, which is very precise. However, because the initialization of the field SORT.out4 at line 18 in Fig. 3(b) breaks the uniformity of the interval, the pointer expression outArr+i (at line 39) is over-approximated to $\{(\text{df}, [0, 7])\}$. This prevents the proof of the post-condition.

In conclusion, such an analysis is able to infer a sound memory model that offers a finer grain of separation than the typed memory model. However, it is not precise enough to deal with the array of pointers and field duality in records.

Partitioning Analysis: Based on the base-offset pointer analysis above, we define in Sect. 5.3 a new analysis that computes for each pointer expression an abstract location that collects a finite set of *slices of symbolic blocks*, i.e., the abstraction is a partial mapping from program's variables to sets of intervals representing offsets in the block. With this analysis, the abstract location computed for outArr+i (at line 39 of sort4, call in Fig. 3(b)) is more precise, i.e., $\{\text{df} \mapsto \{[5, 7], [0, 0]\}\}$, and it allows to prove the post-condition for sort4. Notice that the analysis computes *a finite set of slices* in symbolic blocks whose concretizations (sets of locations) are pairwise disjoint. For this reason, this analysis may be imprecise if its parameter fixing the maximum size of this set is exceeded. This analysis also deals precisely with the call of sort4 in Fig. 3(a).

Dealing with Different Analyses: The above comments demonstrate the diversity of results obtained for the memory models for different points-to analysis algorithms. One of our contributions is to define a generic interface for the definition of the memory model for the DV based on the results obtained by static analyses doing points-to analysis (SPA). This interface eases the integration of a new SPA algorithm and the comparison of results obtained with different SPA

$n \in \mathbb{N}, k \in \mathbb{Z}$ integer constants		num	integer type in $\{i8, u8, i16, \dots, u64\}$
$rt \in \text{Rtyp}$	record type names	$f \in \text{Fld}$	field names
$v \in \text{Cvar}$	program variables	$op \in O$	unary and binary arithmetic operators

scalar types	$\text{Styp} \ni u ::= \text{num} \mid t \text{ ptr}$
program types	$\text{Ctyp} \ni t ::= u \mid rt \mid u[n]$
expressions	$\text{Expr} \ni e ::= ie \mid a$
integer expressions	$\text{Iexpr} \ni ie ::= k \mid lv \mid op \; ie \mid ie \; op \; ie'$
address expressions	$\text{Aexpr} \ni a ::= \text{null} \mid lv \mid \&lv \mid a + ie$
left-values	$\text{Lval} \ni lv ::= v \mid lv.f \mid *a$
statements	$\text{Stmt} \ni s ::= lv{=}e \mid \text{assert } e$

Fig. 4. Syntax of our Clight fragment

algorithms. We formalize this interface in Sect. 4 and instantiate it for different SPA algorithms in Sect. 5. Our results are presented in Sect. 6.

3   Generating Verification Conditions

To fix ideas, we recall the basic principles of generating verification conditions (VC) using a memory model by means of a simple C-like language.

3.1   A Clight Fragment

We consider a fragment of Clight [4] that excludes casts, union types and multi-dimensional arrays. We also restrict the numerical expressions to integer expressions. The syntax of expressions, types and atomic statements is defined by the grammar in Fig. 4. This fragment is able to encode all assignment statements in Figs. 2 and 3 using classic syntax sugar (e.g., `**(arr + i)` for `*arr[i]`, `&((*args).in1)` for `&(args->in1)`). Complex control statements can be encoded using the standard way. User defined types are pointer types, static size array types, and record types. A record type declares a list of typed fields with names from a set `Fld`; for simplicity, we suppose that each field has a unique name. We split expressions into integer expressions and address expressions to ease their typing. Expressions are statically typed by a type t in `Ctyp`. When this information is needed, we write e^t.

We choose to present our work on this simple fragment for readability. However, our framework may be extended to other constructs. For example, our running example contains struct initialization. Struct assignment may be added by explicit assignment of fields. Type casting for arithmetic and compatible pointer types (i.e., aligned on the same type) may be dealt soundly in DV tools employing array-based memory models using the technique in [31]. Functions calls may be also introduced if we choose context-sensitive SA. In general, DV

---

sig *AMM* :
    type $Loc \triangleq \mathtt{Cvar} \times \mathbb{N}$ **types** $Mem, \quad Val \triangleq Vint(\mathbb{Z}) \mid Vptr(Loc)$
      ops $base : \mathtt{Cvar} \to Loc$ **ops** $load : Mem \to \mathtt{Styp} \to Loc \to Val_{\perp}$
          $shift : Loc \to \mathbb{N} \to Loc$ $store : Mem \to \mathtt{Styp} \to Loc \to Val \to Mem_{\perp}$

Fig. 5. Abstract signature for the concrete memory model

tools conduct unit proofs for functions. We restrict this work to whole-program proofs, because it avoids the requirement that SA is able to conduct analyses starting with function's pre-conditions. Our memory model could however be instantiated with an inter-procedural SA, thus enabling unit proof of functions.

3.2 Memory Model

We define the denotational semantics of our language using an environment called *abstract memory model* (AMM). (This name is reminiscent of the first abstract memory model defined in [24,25] for CompCert. We enriched it with some notations to increase readability of our presentation.) Figure 5 summarizes the elements of this abstract memory model. The link between abstract and concrete standard memory models is provided in the extended version.

The states of the memory are represented by an abstract data type *Mem* which associates locations of type *Loc* to values in the type *Val*. Locations are pairs (b, o) where b is the identifier of a symbolic block and o is an integer giving the offset of the location in the symbolic block of b. Because we are not considering dynamic allocation, symbolic blocks are all labeled by program's variables. Thus we simplify the concrete memory model by replacing block identifiers by program variables. Values of type *Loc* are built by two operations of *AMM*: $base(\mathtt{v})$ gives the location of a program variable $\mathtt{v}$ and $shift(\ell, n)$ computes the location obtained by shifting the offset of location ℓ by n bytes. The shift operation abstracts pointer arithmetics. The typing function $\mathtt{cty}(.)$ is extended to elements of *Loc* based on the typing of expressions used to access them. Some operations are partial and we denote by $\perp$ the undefined value. A set A extended with the undefined value is denoted by $A_{\perp}$. The axiomatization of loading and storing operations is similar to the one in [24,25].

3.3 Semantics

Figure 6 defines the rules of the semantics using the abstract memory model, via the overloaded functions $[\![\cdot]\!]$. The semantic functions are partial: the undefined case $\perp$ cuts the evaluation. The operators $\widehat{\mathtt{op}}$ are interpretations of operations $\mathtt{op}$ over integer types $\mathtt{num}$. The functions $\mathtt{offset}(\cdot)$ and $\mathtt{sizeof}(\cdot)$ are defined by the Application Binary Interface (ABI) and depend on the architecture. Conversions between integer values are done using function $\mathtt{cast}(\cdot, \cdot)$.

$$[\![\cdot]\!] : \mathtt{Stmt} \rightarrow Mem \rightarrow Mem_\perp$$

$[\![\mathtt{lv}^\mathtt{u}\mathtt{=e}]\!](m)$	$\triangleq store(m, \mathtt{u}, [\![\mathtt{lv}]\!](m), [\![\mathtt{e}]\!](m))$
$[\![\mathtt{assert}\ \mathtt{e}]\!](m)$	$\triangleq$ if $[\![\mathtt{e}]\!](m) \not\sim 0$ then m else $\perp$

$$[\![\cdot]\!] : \mathtt{Expr} \rightarrow Mem \rightarrow Val_\perp$$

$[\![\mathtt{ie}]\!](m)$	$\triangleq Vint([\![\mathtt{ie}]\!](m))$
$[\![\mathtt{a}]\!](m)$	$\triangleq Vptr([\![\mathtt{a}]\!](m))$

$$[\![\cdot]\!] : \mathtt{Iexpr} \rightarrow Mem \rightarrow \mathbb{Z}_\perp$$

$[\![\mathtt{i}]\!](m)$	$\triangleq \mathtt{i}$
$[\![\mathtt{lv}^\mathtt{num}]\!](m)$	$\triangleq i,\ Vint(i) = load(m, \mathtt{num}, [\![\mathtt{lv}]\!](m))$
$[\![\mathtt{op\ ie}]\!](m)$	$\triangleq \widehat{op}([\![\mathtt{ie}]\!](m))$

$$[\![\cdot]\!] : \mathtt{Lval} \rightarrow Mem \rightarrow Loc_\perp$$

$[\![\mathtt{v}]\!](m)$	$\triangleq base(\mathtt{v})$
$[\![\mathtt{lv.f}]\!](m)$	$\triangleq shift([\![\mathtt{lv}]\!](m), \mathtt{offset(f)})$
$[\![\mathtt{*a}]\!](m)$	$\triangleq [\![\mathtt{a}]\!](m)$

$$[\![\cdot]\!] : \mathtt{Aexpr} \rightarrow Mem \rightarrow Loc_\perp$$

$[\![\mathtt{null}]\!](m)$	$\triangleq base(\mathtt{null})$
$[\![\mathtt{lv}^{\mathtt{u}[n]}]\!](m)$	$\triangleq [\![\mathtt{lv}]\!](m)$
$[\![\mathtt{lv^{t\ ptr}}]\!](m)$	$\triangleq \ell$ where $load(m, \mathtt{t\ ptr}, [\![\mathtt{lv}]\!](m)) = Vptr(\ell)$
$[\![\mathtt{\&lv}]\!](m)$	$\triangleq [\![\mathtt{lv}]\!](m)$
$[\![\mathtt{a^{t\ ptr} + ie}]\!](m)$	$\triangleq shift([\![\mathtt{a}]\!](m), \mathtt{sizeof(t)} \times \mathtt{cast}([\![\mathtt{ie}]\!](m), \mathtt{u32}))$

Fig. 6. Semantics of our Clight fragment

3.4 Generating Verification Conditions

Verification conditions (VC) are generated from Hoare's triple $\{P\}$ s $\{Q\}$ with P and Q formulas in some logic theory $\mathcal{T}$ used for program annotations and s a program statement. The classic method [18,23] is built on the computation of a formula $R_\mathtt{s}(\boldsymbol{v}_b, \boldsymbol{v}_e)$ in $\mathcal{T}$ specifying the relation between the states of the program before and after the execution of s, which are represented by the set of logic variables $\boldsymbol{v}_b$ resp. $\boldsymbol{v}_e$. The VC built for the above Hoare's triple is $\forall \boldsymbol{v}_b, \boldsymbol{v}_e.\ (P(\boldsymbol{v}_b) \wedge R(\boldsymbol{v}_b, \boldsymbol{v}_e)) \implies Q(\boldsymbol{v}_e)$ and it is given to solvers for $\mathcal{T}$ to check its validity. In the following, we denote by $\mathcal{E}$ the set of logic terms built in the logic theory $\mathcal{T}$ using the constants, operations, and variables in a set $\mathcal{X}$. For a logic sort τ, we designate by $\mathcal{E}_\tau$ the terms of type τ.

Compilation Environment: Formula $R_\mathtt{s}(\cdot, \cdot)$ is defined based on the dynamic semantics of statements, like the one given in Fig. 6 for our language. The compilation of this semantics into formulas $\mathcal{T}$ uses a *memory model environment* (called simply environment) that implements the interface of the abstract memory model given in Fig. 5. This environment changes at each context call and keeps the information required by the practical compilation into formulas, e.g., the set of variables used for modeling the state at the current control point of this specific context call. Figure 7 defines the signature of memory environments.

```
sig MME :
    type Loc                          types Mem, Val ≜ Vint(𝓔_I) | Vptr(Loc)
    ops base : Cvar → Loc               ops load : Mem → Styp → Loc → Val_⊥
        shift : Mem → Loc → 𝓔_I → Loc_⊥       store : Mem → Styp → Loc → Val → (Mem × 𝓔_B)_⊥
```

Fig. 7. Signature of the memory model environments

The types Mem and Loc encapsulate information about the program states and memory locations respectively. Notice that the logical representation of locations is hidden by this interface, which allows to capture very different memory models. The compilation information about the values stored is given by the type Val, which represent integers by integer terms in $\mathcal{T}$, i.e., in the set $\mathcal{E}_{\mathbb{I}}$. Operation shift implements arithmetics on locations by an integer term. Operation store encapsulates the updating of the environment by an assignment and produces a new environment and a term in $\mathcal{E}_{\mathbb{B}}$, i.e., a formula of $\mathcal{T}$.

Prerequisites on the Logic Theory: For DV tools based on first order logic, the theory $\mathcal{T}$ is a multi-sorted FOL that embeds the logic theory used to annotate programs (which usually includes boolean and integer arithmetics theories) and the McCarthy's array theory [26] employed by the Burstall-Bornat memory model [6] to represent atomic memory blocks. The memory model environment associates to each memory blocks a set of logic array variables using base operations. It encodes the operations $load(m, t, \ell)$ resp. $store(m, t, \ell, v)$ into logic array operations $read(a, o)$ resp. $store(a, o, v)$, where a is the array variable for the symbolic block b of location ℓ that stores values of type t and o is the offset of ℓ in b. $\mathcal{T}$ also embeds abstract data types (or at least polymorphic pairs with component selection by *fst* and *snd*), and uninterpreted functions. Polymorphic conditional expression "$(e_{cond})?e_{true} : e_{false}$" are also needed.

In the following, we use the logic theory above $\mathcal{T}$ and suppose that an infinite number of fresh variables can be generated. To ease the reading of environment definitions, we distinguish the logic terms by using the mathematical style and by underlining the terms of $\mathcal{T}$, e.g., $\underline{x + x}$. For example, the logic term $\underline{read}(m(b), \underline{4 + x})$ is built from a VC generator term $m(b)$ that computes a logic term of array type and the logic sub-term $\underline{read}(\cdot, 4 + x)$.

Example: Consider the Hoare's triple $\{P\}\ (*(\&r.f))^{i8} = 5\ \{Q\}$. Let l_0 be shift(m_0, base(r), offset(f)), where m_0 (resp. m_1) is the environment for the source state (resp. modified by the store for the destination state); that is $m_1, \phi_1 \triangleq$ store(m_0, i8, l_0, Vint(5)). The formula $\underline{P}$ (resp. $\underline{Q}$) is generated from P (resp. Q) using compilation environment m_0 (resp. m_1). Then the VC generated by the above method is $\underline{P} \wedge \phi_1 \implies \underline{Q}$. Notice that the above calls of the environment's operations follow the order given by the semantics in Fig. 6, except for the failure cases. Indeed, to simplify our presentation, we consider that statement's pre-condition includes the constraints that eliminate runs leading to undefined behaviors. Therefore, the VC generation focuses on encoding in $R_s(\cdot, \cdot)$ the correct executions of statements.

4   Partition-Based Memory Model

We define a functor that produces memory models environments implementing the interface on Fig. 7 from the information inferred by a pointer analysis. The main idea is that the SA produces a finite partitioning of symbolic blocks into

sig PA :
   type $\mathcal{L}$ type $\mathcal{S}$ type $\mathcal{B}$
   ops base : $\mathsf{Cvar} \to \mathcal{L}$ ops load : $\mathcal{S} \to \mathsf{Ptr} \to \mathcal{L} \to \mathcal{L}$ ops base : $\mathcal{B} \to \mathsf{Cvar}$
       domain : $\mathcal{L} \to 2^{\mathcal{B}}$ shift : $\mathcal{S} \to \mathcal{L} \to \mathcal{E}_{\mathbb{I}} \to \mathcal{L}$ slice : $\mathcal{B} \to \mathcal{E}_{\mathbb{I}} \to \mathcal{E}_{\mathbb{B}}$

disjointness: $\quad \forall b_1^{\#}, b_2^{\#} \in \mathcal{B} \cdot b_1^{\#} \neq b_2^{\#} \Rightarrow \gamma(b_1^{\#}) \cap \gamma(b_2^{\#}) = \emptyset \qquad\qquad\qquad (1)$

completeness: $\quad \forall v \in \mathsf{Cvar} \; \forall i \in [0, \mathtt{sizeof}(\mathsf{cty}(v)) - 1] \; \exists b^{\#} \in \mathcal{B} \cdot (v, i) \in \gamma(b^{\#}) \quad (2)$

unique base: $\quad \forall b^{\#} \in \mathcal{B} \; \exists! v \in \mathsf{Cvar} \cdot \gamma(b^{\#}) \subset \{(v, i) \mid i \in \mathbb{N}\} \qquad\qquad\quad (3)$

sound $\mathcal{B}$ ops: $\quad \forall b^{\#} \in \mathcal{B} \cdot \gamma(b^{\#}) = \{(v, i) \in Loc \mid v = \mathsf{base}(b^{\#}) \wedge \mathsf{slice}(b^{\#}, \underline{i}) = true\} \quad (4)$

sound $\mathcal{L}$ ops: $\quad \forall \ell^{\#} \in \mathcal{L} \; \forall \ell \in \gamma(\ell^{\#}) \; \exists b^{\#} \in \mathsf{domain}(\ell^{\#}) \cdot \ell \in \gamma(b^{\#}) \qquad\qquad (5)$

sound $\mathcal{S}$ ops: $\quad \forall s \; \forall s^{\#} \in \mathcal{S}(s) \; \forall \ell^{\#} \in s^{\#} \cdot$

$$\gamma(\mathsf{shift}(s^{\#}, \ell^{\#}, e)) \supseteq \{shift(\ell, i) \mid \ell \in \gamma(\ell^{\#}), m \in \gamma(s^{\#}), i \in [\![e]\!](m)\} (6)$$

$\qquad\qquad\qquad \forall s \; \forall s^{\#} \in \mathcal{S}(s) \; \forall \ell^{\#} \in s^{\#} \cdot$

$$\gamma(\mathsf{load}(s^{\#}, \mathtt{t\ ptr}, \ell^{\#})) \supseteq \{load(m, \mathtt{t\ ptr}, \ell) \mid \ell \in \gamma(\ell^{\#}), m \in \gamma(s^{\#})\} (7)$$

Fig. 8. A signature for pointer analysis and its properties

a set of pairwise disjoint sub-blocks and each sub-block is mapped to a specific set of array logic variables by the compilation environment. We first formalize the pre-requisites for the pointer analysis using a signature constrained by well-formed properties. Then, we define the functor by providing an implementation for each element of the interface on Fig. 7.

4.1 Pointer Analysis Signature

A necessary condition on the pointer analysis is its soundness. To ease the reasoning about this property of analysis, we adopt the abstract interpretation [16] framework. In this setting, a SA computes an abstract representation $s^{\#}$ of the set of concrete states reached by the program's executions before the execution of each statement. The abstract states $s^{\#}$ belong to a complete lattice $(S^{\#}, \sqsubseteq^{\#})$ which is related to the set of concrete program configurations $State$ by a pair of functions $\alpha : 2^{State} \to S^{\#}$ (abstraction) and $\gamma : S^{\#} \to 2^{State}$ (concretization) forming a Galois connection. In the following, we overload the symbol γ to denote concretization functions for other abstract objects.

Aside being sound, the SA shall be context sensitive and provide, for each context call, an implementation of the signature on Fig. 8. The values of $\mathcal{S}$ provides, for each statement of the current context, the abstract state in $S^{\#}$ computed by the analysis. The type $\mathcal{L}$ represents the domain of abstract values computed for the pointer expressions in abstract states. The concretization function $\gamma : \mathcal{L} \to 2^{Loc}$ maps abstract locations to sets of concrete locations.

The type $\mathcal{B}$ stands for the set of pairwise disjoint abstract blocks partitioning the symbolic memory blocs, for the fixed specific context call. The concretization function for abstract blocks $\gamma : \mathcal{B} \to 2^{Loc}$ maps blocks to set of concrete locations. Equations (1) and (2) in Fig. 8 specify that abstract blocks in $\mathcal{B}$ shall form a partition of the set of concrete locations available in symbolic blocks such that an abstract block belongs to a unique symbolic block.

The operation $\mathsf{base}(b^\#)$ returns the symbolic block to which $b^\#$ belongs, represented by the program variable labeling this symbolic block. The range of an abstract block $b^\#$ inside its symbolic block is specified by the operation $\mathsf{slice}(b^\#, e)$, which returns a formula (boolean term in $\mathcal{E}_\mathbb{B}$) that constrains e to be in this range. The soundness of the base and slice operations is specified by Eq. (4). The set of abstract blocks covered by an abstract location is provided by the operation domain, whose soundness is specified by Eq. (5). The operation base abstracts the offset 0 of a program variable. Abstract locations may be shifted by an integer term using operation shift. Operation $\mathsf{load}(s, \mathsf{t}\ \mathsf{ptr}, \ell^\#)$ computes the abstract location stored at $\ell^\#$ in some context s, i.e., it dereferences $\ell^\#$ of type $\mathsf{t}\ \mathsf{ptr}\ \mathsf{ptr}$ for some t. (We denote by Ptr the set of all pointer types in the program.) The last two operations shall be sound abstract transformers on abstract locations, as stated in Eqs. (6) resp. (7).

4.2   A Functor for Memory Model Environments

We define now our functor that uses the signature PA to define the elements of the memory model environment MME defined in Fig. 7. To disambiguate symbols, we prefix names of types and operations by the name of the signature or logic theory when necessary.

Environment's Type: A compilation environment $\mathsf{m} \in \mathsf{Mem}$ stores the mapping to abstract states from PA and and a total function that associates to each abstract block in $\mathsf{PA}.\mathcal{B}$ a logic variable in $\mathcal{X}$:

$$\mathsf{MME}.\mathsf{Mem} \triangleq \mathsf{PA}.\mathcal{S} \times [\mathsf{PA}.\mathcal{B} \to \mathcal{T}.\mathcal{X}] \tag{8}$$

where $[A \to B]$ denotes the set of total functions from A to B, i.e., B^A. We designate by m_s and m_ϵ the first and second component of some $\mathsf{m} \in \mathsf{Mem}$.

If an abstract block $b^\#$ stores only one type of values, the logic variable $\mathsf{m}_\epsilon(b^\#)$ has type $array(\mathbb{Z}, \tau)$ where τ is the logic type for the values stored. For blocks storing integer values (i.e., num), τ is naturally (logical) $\mathbb{Z}$ or $\mathbb{N}$. For blocks storing pointer values, τ is $\mathbb{Z} \times \mathbb{Z}$, (b, o) where the b denotes the abstract block of the location and o represents the location's offset. We denote by $\underline{b^\#}$ the integer constant that uniquely identifies $b^\# \in \mathcal{B}$. If an abstract block $b^\#$ stores values of both kinds of scalar types (notice that only scalar values are stored in array-based models), the logic variable $\mathsf{m}_\epsilon(b^\#)$ has the type pair of arrays, $(array(\mathbb{Z}, \mathbb{Z}), array(\mathbb{Z}, \mathbb{Z} \times \mathbb{Z}))$ where the first array is used for integer values and the second one for pointer values. For readability, we detail here only the case of homogeneously typed blocks. Notice that the mapping m_ϵ binds fresh array variable names to abstract blocks changed by store operation.

Locations' Type: The type $\mathsf{MME}.\mathsf{Loc}$ collects the logic encoding of locations as a pair of integer terms $(e_b, e_o) \in \mathcal{E}_\mathbb{I} \times \mathcal{E}_\mathbb{I}$ together with the abstract location ℓ

provided by the static analysis, i.e., $\mathsf{MME.Loc} \triangleq \mathcal{E}_{\mathbb{I} \times \mathbb{I}} \times \mathsf{PA}.\mathcal{L}$. Intuitively, in the logic pair (e_b, e_o), e_b is interpreted as an abstract block identifier and e_o models the offset of the location in the *symbolic block of the abstract block* e_b, i.e., an integer in the slice of e_b.

Locations' Operations: The values of $\mathsf{MME.Loc}$ are built by two operations $\mathsf{MME.base}$ and $\mathsf{MME.shift}$ defined as follows. For a program variable v, $\mathsf{MME.base}(\mathrm{v})$ is based on the abstract location $\ell^{\#}$ returned by $\mathsf{PA.base}(\mathrm{v})$. The domain of $\ell^{\#}$ shall have only one abstract block $b^{\#}$ because program variables are located at the start of symbolic blocks. Moreover, the term denoting the offset shall be the constant 0. Formally:

$$\mathsf{MME.base}(\mathrm{v}) \triangleq \langle(\underline{b^{\#}}, 0), \ell^{\#}\rangle \text{ where } \mathsf{PA.base}(\mathrm{v}) = \ell^{\#}, \mathsf{domain}(\ell^{\#}) = \{b^{\#}\} \quad (9)$$

The shifting of a location in Loc by an expression e is computed based on the abstract shift operation as follows:

$$\mathsf{MME.shift}(\mathrm{m}, \langle(\underline{e_b}, e_o), \ell^{\#}\rangle, e) \triangleq \langle(\underline{e'_b}, e_o + e), \ell_s^{\#}\rangle \quad (10)$$

where $\ell_s^{\#} = \mathsf{PA.shift}(\mathrm{m}_s, \ell^{\#}, e)$ and the new logic base e'_b selects (using a conditional expression) the base $b_i^{\#}$ from the ones of $\ell_s^{\#}$. Let us denote by $\mathsf{fits}(e_b, \ell^{\#}, b^{\#})$ the boolean term testing that the block identifier in e_b is one of the blocks identifiers in $\mathsf{PA.domain}(\ell^{\#})$ which has the same symbolic block (i.e., base) as $b_i^{\#}$, i.e.:

$$\mathsf{fits}(e_b, \ell^{\#}, b^{\#}) \triangleq \bigvee_{b_j^{\#} \in \mathsf{PA.domain}(\ell^{\#}) \text{ s.t. } \mathsf{PA.base}(b_j^{\#}) = \mathsf{PA.base}(b^{\#})} e_b = b_j^{\#} \quad (11)$$

Using fits, if $\mathsf{PA.domain}(\ell_s^{\#})$ is $\{b_1^{\#}, \ldots, b_n^{\#}\}$, the formal definition of e'_b is:

$$e'_b \triangleq \begin{pmatrix} \mathsf{fits}(e_b, \ell^{\#}, b_1^{\#}) \wedge \mathsf{PA.slice}(b_1^{\#}, \underline{e_o + e}) \; ? \; b_1^{\#} \; : \\ \ddots \; \mathsf{fits}(e_b, \ell^{\#}, b_{n-1}^{\#}) \wedge \mathsf{PA.slice}(b_{n-1}^{\#}, \underline{e_o + e}) \; ? \; b_{n-1}^{\#} \; : \; b_n^{\#} \end{pmatrix} \quad (12)$$

Indeed, since the shift operation can not change the symbolic block, we have to test, using fits, that each resulting block identifier $b_i^{\#}$ has the same symbolic block as e_b.

The size of the expression encoding $\mathsf{MME.shift}$ depends on the product of sizes of domains computed by PA for $\ell^{\#}$ and $\ell_s^{\#}$. If the abstract locations have a singleton domain, i.e. $\mathsf{PA.domain}(\ell_s^{\#}) = \{b_1^{\#}\}$, then e'_b is simply $b_1^{\#}$. When the precision of the SA does not enable such simplification, we could soundly avoid big expressions generated by $\mathsf{MME.shift}$ by using in $\mathsf{MME.load}$ and $\mathsf{MME.store}$ operations only the component abstract location of an environment's location.

Loading from Memory: Reading an integer value in the environment m at a location $\mathsf{l} = \langle(e_b, e_o), \ell^{\#}\rangle$ is compiled into a read operation (denoted by $a[e]$ for concision) from an array variable obtained by statically dispatching the logical base e_b of I among the possible base identifiers in PA.domain$(\ell^\#) = \{b_1^\#, \ldots, b_n^\#\}$ as follows:

$$\mathsf{MME.load}(\mathsf{m}, \mathtt{num}, \langle (e_b, e_o), \ell^\# \rangle) \triangleq \mathsf{Vint}\,(e) \tag{13}$$

where

$$e \triangleq \begin{pmatrix} e_b = b_1^\# \;?\; \mathsf{m}_\epsilon(b_1^\#)[e_o] \;:\; \\ \ddots \; e_b = b_{n-1}^\# \;?\; \mathsf{m}_\epsilon(b_{n-1}^\#)[e_o] \;:\; \mathsf{m}_\epsilon(b_n^\#)[e_o] \end{pmatrix} \tag{14}$$

The size of the expression above may be reduced by asking to SA an over-approximation $o^\#$ of the values of expression e_o in the current state. If SA is able to produce a precise result for $o^\#$, we could remove from the expression above the cases for abstract blocks $b_j^\#$ for which PA.slice$(b_j^\#, o^\#) = \mathit{false}$ (i.e., the formula is invalid for the values in $o^\#$).

The expression in Eq. (14) is also used for reading pointer values. In this case, the expression obtained is a tuple. The abstract location corresponding to this logic expression is obtained using the abstract PA.load operation in the abstract state component m_s of the environment:

$$\mathsf{MME.load}(\mathsf{m}, \mathtt{t\ ptr}, \langle (b, o), \ell^\# \rangle) \triangleq \mathsf{Vptr}\left(e, \mathsf{PA.load}(\mathsf{m}_s, \mathtt{t\ ptr}, \ell^\#)\right) \tag{15}$$

Storing in Memory: The compilation of *store* semantic operation is done by the MME.store operation that produces a new environment m′ and a boolean term (formula) e' encoding the relation between the logic arrays associated to blocks before and after the assignment as follows:

$$\mathsf{MME.store}(\mathsf{m}, \mathtt{t}, \langle (e_b, e_o), \ell^\# \rangle, \mathsf{v}) \triangleq \mathsf{m}', \underline{e}' \text{ for } \mathsf{v} \in \{\mathsf{Vint}(\underline{e}), \mathsf{Vptr}(\langle \underline{e}, \ell_v^\# \rangle)\} \tag{16}$$

where $\mathsf{m}' = \langle s'^\#, \mathsf{m}_\epsilon' \rangle$ with $s'^\#$ the abstract state computed by the analysis for the control pointer after the assignment compiled. The new block mapping m_ϵ' uses fresh logic variables for the abstract blocks in the domain PA.domain$(\ell^\#) = \{b_1^\#, \ldots, b_n^\#\}$ of the abstract location $\ell^\#$ at which is done the update:

$$\mathsf{m}_\epsilon' \triangleq \mathsf{m}[b_1^\# \longleftarrow \alpha_1, \cdots, b_n^\# \longleftarrow \alpha_n] \tag{17}$$

The fresh variables are related with the old ones using the store operator on logic arrays, denoted by $a[i \longleftarrow e]$, in the generated formula e' defined as follows:

$$e' \triangleq \bigwedge_{i=1}^n \left((e_b = b_i^\#) \;?\; \alpha_i = \mathsf{m}[b_i^\#][e_o \longleftarrow e] \;:\; \alpha_i = \mathsf{m}[b_i^\#]\right) \tag{18}$$

The size of this expression may be reduced using the SA results in a similar way as for load. In general, the size of expressions generated by the compilation in Eqs. (12), (14) and (18) depends on size of the domain for the abstract locations computed by the static analysis. Indeed, if the analysis always provides abstract locations with a singleton domain, the compilation produces expressions with only one component, while proving most separation annotations. However, if the analysis computes a small set $\mathcal{B}$ (however bigger or equal to the number of program variables), the VC generated does not win any concision (we are falling back to the separation given by the typed model).

Functor's Properties: The requirements on the signature PA ensure that the operations domain, load and shift are sound. This enforces the soundness of definitions for the MME's operations. Based on this observation, we conjecture that these operations compute a sound post-condition relation, although this relation maybe not the strongest post-condition. A formal proof is left for future work.

5   Instances of Pointer Analysis Signature

The signature PA may be implemented by several existing pointer analyses. We consider three of them here and we show how they fulfill the requirements of PA. We also define an analysis which exploits the results of a precise pointer analysis to provide an appropriate partitioning of the memory in PA.$\mathcal{B}$.

All pointer analyses we consider computes statically the possible values (i) of an address expression, i.e., an over-approximation of $[\![a]\!]$ ($a \in$ Aexpr from Fig. 4) and (ii) of an address dereference, i.e., an over-approximation of $[\![*a]\!]$. For these reason, these analyses belong to the points-to analyses class [19].

5.1   Basic Analyses (B and B$_\top$)

The first points-to analysis abstracts locations by a finite set of pairs $(v, I^\#)$ built from a symbolic block identifier v and an abstraction for sets of integers $I^\#$ collecting the possible offsets of the location in the symbolic block. If we fix $\mathcal{I}^\#$ to be the abstract domain used to represents sets of integers, then the abstract domain for locations is defined by $Loc^\# \triangleq 2^{\mathtt{Cvar} \times \mathcal{I}^\#}$.

Many abstract domains have been proposed to deal with integer sets in abstract interpretation framework. For points-to analysis, most approaches use the classic domain of intervals [16]. To obtain more precise results, we consider here the extension of the interval domain which also keeps modulo constraints and small sets of integers. This domain is implemented in the Eva plugin of Frama-C [22]. Then, the abstract sets in $\mathcal{I}^\#$ are defined by the following grammar:

$$\mathcal{I}^\# \ni I^\# ::= \top \mid [i_\infty..i'_\infty]r\%n \mid \{i_1, \ldots, i_n\} \tag{19}$$

where $r, n \in \mathbb{N}$ are natural constants, $i_1, \ldots, i_n \in \mathbb{Z}$ are integer constants and $i_\infty, i'_\infty \in \mathbb{Z} \cup \{+\infty, -\infty\}$ are integer constants extended with two symbols to capture unspecified bounds. We wrote $[i_\infty..i'_\infty]$ for $[i_\infty..i'_\infty]0\%1$. The concretization of a value $I^\#$ in $\mathcal{I}^\#$, $\gamma : \mathcal{I}^\# \to 2^\mathbb{Z}$ maps $[i_\infty..i'_\infty]r\%n$ to the set of integers $k \in [i, i']$ such that $k\%n = r$. Because the abstract intervals are used to capture offsets in symbolic blocks which have a known size (given by the ABI), the concrete offsets are always bounded, but they may be very large. We obtain independence of the ABI by introducing unspecified bounds for intervals and the $\top$ value. For efficiency, the size of explicit sets $\{i_1, \ldots, i_n\}$ is kept bounded by a parameter of the analysis, denoted in the following **ilvl**. The domain $\mathcal{I}^\#$ comes with lattice operators (e.g., join $\sqcup^\#$) and abstract transformers for operations on integers. Our work requires a sound abstract transformer for addition, $+^\#$.

$$\mathcal{L} \triangleq Loc^{\#} \qquad \mathcal{S} \triangleq \texttt{Stmt} \to S^{\#} \tag{20}$$

$$\mathcal{B} \triangleq \texttt{Cvar} \qquad \texttt{base}(\texttt{v}) \triangleq \{(\texttt{v}, \{0\})\} \qquad \texttt{slice}(\texttt{v}, e) \triangleq 0 \le e < \texttt{sizeof}(\texttt{cty}(\texttt{v})) \tag{21}$$

$$\texttt{domain}(\ell^{\#}) \triangleq \{\texttt{v} \mid (\texttt{v}, I^{\#}) \in \ell^{\#}\} \tag{22}$$

$$\texttt{shift}(\texttt{s}, \ell^{\#}, e) \triangleq \sqcup^{\#}_{(\texttt{v}_k, I^{\#}_k) \in \ell^{\#}} \{(\texttt{v}_k, I^{\#}_k +^{\#} [\![e]\!]^{\#}(\texttt{s}))\} \tag{23}$$

$$\texttt{load}(\texttt{s}, \texttt{t ptr}, [\![\texttt{a}]\!]^{\#}(\texttt{s})) \triangleq [\![*\texttt{a}]\!]^{\#}(\texttt{s}) \tag{24}$$

Fig. 9. Implementation of PA by analyses **B** and **B**$_\top$

*Precise Offsets (**B**):* Let us consider a precise instance of such an analysis, i.e. field-sensitive and employing the abstract domain of intervals $\mathcal{I}^{\#}$ defined above. Let $S^{\#}$ be the abstract domain for program's states implemented in this analysis. This domain captures the abstract values for all program's variables. We denote by $[\![\texttt{a}]\!]^{\#}(\texttt{s})$ the abstract location (in $Loc^{\#}$) computed by the analysis for the address expression a at statement s. For address expressions typed as pointer to pointer types, the abstract value of the address expression $[\![*\texttt{a}]\!]^{\#}(\texttt{s})$ is also an element of $Loc^{\#}$ and computes the points-to information.

The types and operations of PA are shown in Fig. 9. The symbolic blocks are not partitioned, since $\mathcal{B} \triangleq \texttt{Cvar}$. Then, the slice for a block is the set of valid offsets for the symbolic block and the generated constraint is very simple. Abstract locations are shifted precisely using the abstract transformer for addition in $\mathcal{I}^{\#}$. It is usually precise when e is a constant. The soundness properties required by PA are trivially satisfied due to the simple form of abstract blocks' type and the soundness of operations on the abstract domains used.

*Imprecise Offsets (**B**$_\top$):* We also consider an instance of the points-to analysis which is not field-sensitive. For example, the **B**$_\top$ analysis computes for $[\![\texttt{\&SORT.out2}]\!]^{\#}(\texttt{s}_3)$, where $\texttt{s}_3$ is the assignment at line 3 of listing in Fig. 3(a), the set of abstract location $\{(\texttt{df}i, \top), \ldots, (\texttt{pf}j, \top) \mid 1 \le i \le 8, 1 \le j \le 4\}$. The definition of the elements of the signature PA is exactly the one given in Fig. 9.

5.2 Partitioning by Cells (C)

Analyzers that do not handle aggregate types (arrays and structs) decompose the symbolic blocks of variables having aggregate types into atomic blocks that all have a scalar type. We call these blocks *cells*. For examples, the symbolic block of variable pf in Fig. 3(b) is split into four cells of type pos_t. For this analysis, the definitions for PA are those given in Fig. 9 except for the type $\mathcal{B}$ and the operations using this type slice and domain. To define $\mathcal{B}$, we first define the set $\mathcal{C}(\texttt{t})$ of *cells-paths* of type t by induction on the syntax of t as follows:

$$\mathcal{C}(\texttt{t}) \triangleq \begin{cases} \{\epsilon\} & \text{if } \texttt{t} \in \texttt{Styp} \\ \bigcup_{1 \le i \le n} \texttt{f}_i \cdot \mathcal{C}(\texttt{t}_i) & \text{if } \texttt{t} \text{ is the record type } \{\texttt{f}_1 : \texttt{t}_1, \ldots, \texttt{f}_n : \texttt{t}_n\} \\ \bigcup_{0 \le i < n} [i] \cdot \mathcal{C}(\texttt{t}_e) & \text{if } \texttt{t} \text{ is the array type } \texttt{t}_e[n] \end{cases}$$

where the operator "." prefixes each path of its second operand by its first operand. For a variable v, we define $\mathcal{C}(\mathtt{v}) = \mathtt{v} \cdot \mathcal{C}(\mathtt{cty}(v))$. For example in Fig. 3(b), $\mathcal{C}(\mathtt{df}) = \{\mathtt{df} \cdot [0], \ldots, \mathtt{df} \cdot [7]\}$. Given a cell-path c, we denote by $r(c)$ the range of offsets (in bytes) that correspond to the path and which is computed using ABI. Then, we replace definitions in Eqs. (21–22) from Fig. 9 by:

$$\mathcal{B} \triangleq \{\mathcal{C}(\mathtt{v}) \mid \mathtt{v} \in \mathtt{Cvar}\} \qquad \mathrm{slice}(\mathtt{v} \cdot c, e) \triangleq e \in r(c)$$
$$\mathrm{domain}(\ell^{\#}) \triangleq \{\mathtt{v} \cdot c \in \mathcal{B} \mid \exists i \in \mathbb{N}, (\mathtt{v}, i) \in \gamma(\ell^{\#}) \wedge i \in r(c)\}$$

meaning that the slice of a cell-path is given by the range of bytes corresponding to the cell, and the domain of an abstract location is defined by enumerating all cells that intersect with abstract location's abstract offsets.

5.3   Partitioning by Dereference Analysis (P)

We have seen in Sect. 4.2 that the size of generated VC strongly depends on two factors: the size of $\mathcal{B}$ and the number of abstract blocks in the domain of abstract locations. This section defines an analysis which, based on the results of **B**, aims to minimize these two factors while still producing sound results. Roughly, the idea is to group cells that are accessed by a set of left values which is upwards-closed w.r.t. the relation "points-to" computed by **B**. Therefore, two different abstract blocks will never be pointed-to by the same left value, i.e., if the domains of abstract locations $[\![*a_1]\!]^{\#}(\mathtt{s}_1)$ and $[\![*a_2]\!]^{\#}(\mathtt{s}_2)$ share an abstract block $b^{\#}$, then $[\![a_1]\!]^{\#}(\mathtt{s}_1)$ and $[\![a_2]\!]^{\#}(\mathtt{s}_2)$ belong to the same block.

For this, we define a partition P of *pointer-typed left-values* used by statements of the current context call using the equivalence relation $\simeq$ defined as follows. We denote by $\ell^{\#} \downarrow_n$ the set of concrete locations $\gamma(\ell^{\#} +^{\#} 0) \cup \ldots \cup \gamma(\ell^{\#} +^{\#} n - 1)$. Then, two left-values appearing in some statements are related by $\simeq$ if the concretization of the abstract locations computed by **B** for their addresses on the corresponding statements overlap. Formally, for any left-values $\mathtt{lv}_1$ and $\mathtt{lv}_2$ used in statements $\mathtt{s}_1$ resp. $\mathtt{s}_2$,

$$\left([\![(\&\mathtt{lv}_1)^{\mathtt{t}_1}]\!]^{\#}(\mathtt{s}_1) \downarrow_{n_1}\right) \bigcap \left([\![(\&\mathtt{lv}_2)^{\mathtt{t}_2}]\!]^{\#}(\mathtt{s}_2) \downarrow_{n_2}\right) \neq \emptyset \implies (\mathtt{lv}_1, \mathtt{s}_1) \simeq (\mathtt{lv}_2, \mathtt{s}_2)$$

where $n_i = \mathtt{sizeof}(\mathtt{t}_i)$. By definition, this relationship is reflexive and symmetric, and we close it transitively. It is computed by a simple iterative process on top of the results of **B** analysis. For a given element $p \in P$, we compute the set of concrete locations pointing to left-values in p:

$$B(p) \triangleq \bigcup_{(\mathtt{lv}_i, \mathtt{s}_i) \in p} \gamma([\![\&\mathtt{lv}_i]\!]^{\#}(\mathtt{s}_i))$$

Analysis **P** implements signature PA using the definitions in Fig. 9 except for (21–22) that are replaced by:

$$\mathcal{B} \triangleq \{\langle \mathtt{v}, s \rangle \mid \exists p \in P \wedge s = \{i \mid (\mathtt{v}, i) \in B(p)\}\}$$
$$\mathrm{slice}(\langle \mathtt{v}, s \rangle, e) \triangleq e \in s$$
$$\mathrm{domain}(\ell^{\#}) \triangleq \{\langle \mathtt{v}, s \rangle \in \mathcal{B} \mid \exists i \in \mathbb{N}, (\mathtt{v}, i) \in \gamma(\ell^{\#}) \wedge i \in s\}$$

In the example on Fig. 3(b), if **B** is precise enough, **P** computes a $\mathcal{B}$ which splits the symbolic block labeled by the array variable df into (only) two abstract blocks: one for the bytes located at indexes [1..4] (whose addresses are stored in input fields) and another for indexes $\{0\} \cup [5..7]$ (stored in output fields).

6 Experimental Results

6.1 Implementation

We implemented our framework in Frama-C [22], an extensible and modular platform for the analysis of software written in C. Frama-C includes various plug-ins, interacting with each other through interfaces defined by the platform.

The plug-in Eva is a context-sensitive static analyzer based on abstract interpretation; it employs several numerical abstract domains, including the one defined in Eq. (19) for sets of integers. On top of the value analysis provided by Eva, which includes the **B** analysis from Sect. 5, we coded new partition analyses to obtain analyses $\mathbf{B_T}$, **C** and **P**.

The WP plug-in of Frama-C is a DV tool which also includes a built-in simplifier for formulae, Qed [14], a driver to call SMT solvers and the signature MME for memory model environments [15]. We coded in WP the signature PA, the functor defined in Sect. 4.2, and each implementation of PA for the above static analyses. The full development represents 1680 LoC of Ocaml.

6.2 Experimental Setup

Case Study: We consider a case study which extends our running example from Fig. 2 such that the type data_t is a record which encapsulates numerical values to be sorted and other information. We attempt to prove the functional correctness of the sort function for various number of inputs $\mathbf{N} \in \{4, 8, 16, 32\}$. The specification of sort consists of 40 ACSL properties, which WP transforms into 62 VC for each memory model. We also consider 3 different context calls for sort as the entry point for the analysis. They initialize the fields of the SORT variable using pointers to: variables on the stack similar to Fig. 3(a) (**vars**), fields of a single record (**strct**) and two arrays (for values and permutations) (**arrs**). In addition, we consider two variants for contexts **strct** and **arrs**. In the (**grp**) variant, all input and output fields are grouped together, i.e., inputs point to the first **N** fields/indexes in a regular way and outputs to the remainder. For the (**rdn**) variant, inputs and outputs are initialized in a randomized order, as in Fig. 3(b) for **arrs**. The latter case is designed to defeat points-to analyses where offsets are abstracted solely by intervals plus congruences.

Variants of Memory Models: For comparison with the basic DV tools, we also conduct proof using the default memory model of WP (case **Typed**). To observe the influence of the precision of points-to analysis **B** on the generated memory models environments, we vary the parameter **ilvl** which gives the upper limit for

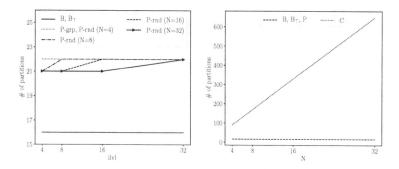

Fig. 10. Comparison between analyses on number of partitions

the size of small sets kept by the abstract domain $\mathcal{I}^{\#}$ in Sect. 5.1. We apply **B** for **ilvl** in $\{4, 8, 16, 32\}$ to generate its memory model environment and the VC. For the same values, we launch the **C** (resp. **P**) analysis after **B** and generate the corresponding environments.

Proving VCs: WP generates VC using the library for many sorted first-order logic provided by Qed. After applying on-the-fly simplifications of VCs, Qed exports the VC to back-end solvers. We configure WP to discharge simplified VCs to the Alt-ergo prover and the remaining unproved VCs to be sent to CVC4. Those experiments ran on an Intel(R) Xeon(R) CPU E5-2660 v3 @ 2.60 GHz with a timeout of 10 s per goal for each solver.

6.3   Results

Figure 10 shows the number of partitions (size of PA.$\mathcal{B}$) inferred by the various analysis for a given call context. Recall that the partitioning generated by **B** is always constant, since fixed by the program variables. As expected, **C**'s result is linear in the number of inputs (right plot in Fig. 10). The partitioning by **P** creates fewer abstract blocks when **N** is less than **ilvl** (left plot in Fig. 10). Fewer blocks means a less precise analysis: in our example, the two equivalence classes that get merged are those corresponding to inputs and outputs.

Figure 11 (left) shows that **B** partitioning is sufficient to prove all goals for the **vars** context, since all values are implicitly separated onto different symbolic bases. However, for contexts **strct** and **arrs**, inputs and outputs share the same symbolic base which is too imprecise to prove all goals. Analysis **B**⊤ infers that the fields of SORT point to all possible inputs and outputs, which yields even worse results. The results for **C** partitioning worsen with the increase in the number of inputs due to the complexity of the VCs generated. For **P** partitioning, we are not interested in the **vars** context considering it is but a small refinement of **B** in that context. In our experiments, we were able to identify two classes of experiments giving similar results in term of provability and time: $\mathbf{P}_{max}$ are results for experiments where partitions are maximal and conversely for $\mathbf{P}_{few}$. For readability reasons, we display only the worse results of those two classes.

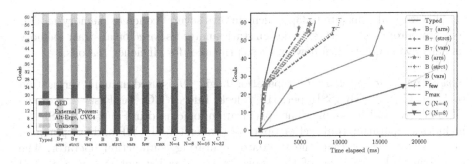

Fig. 11. Results for solving generated VC

Figure 11 (right) shows for each model the total time spent on the VCs that get proven (i.e., do not timeout), and the total number of proven goals. For an equal number of proven goals, shorter times are better. We observe that more partitions lead to bigger VCs which take more time to be proven, especially for **C** partitioning. Refining **B** partitioning within **P** leads to a better provability at the cost of a negligible increase in time in provers. Indeed, we are interested in proving all VCs since some goals (shown as valid) implicitly assume that other goals are verified. These results demonstrate that **P** analysis offers the best trade-off between partition's granularity and provability in reasonable time, regardless of the context. Moreover, all verification conditions are proved for the regular context; for randomized contexts, better results are obtained by increasing the precision of points-to analysis **B**. The improvement of **P** is real because **B** exhibits the same performance only for the **vars** context.

7   Related Work and Conclusion

Memory Model for C: Program verification and certified compilation have proposed several memory models to capture the semantics of C pointers. All these models view the memory as a collection of disjoint regions. Two main classes may be distinguished: (i) the regions are typed by the value stored, therefore regions storing values of different types are disjoint and (ii) the regions are seen as raw arrays of bytes to capture low-level manipulations of memory in C. The first class provides a good abstraction for verification of type-safe languages, (e.g., Java-like [1,2], HOL [27]) or type-safe C programs (GRASSHoper [30], HIP/Sleek [13]). The second class is mainly used inside static analyzers for C (Infer [10], MemCAD [11], Eva [8]) or deductive verifiers (Caduceus [17], HAVOC [12], SMACK [31], VCC [5], VeriFast [21]). Hybrid memory models either introduce typing in raw memory models for efficiency, or introduce raw models in typed ones for precision. WP supports both classes of models and provides instances of the environment MME for them [15].

The CompCert project [24,25] employs an abstract memory model to capture in an uniform way refinements of memory models for the certified compilation of

C. This work also inspired [33], which surveys several concrete memory models for C and proposes a method to design static analyzers based on abstract memory models. Eva is not built following these principles for efficiency reasons.

Separation Logic versus FOL: Separation Logic [29] is used in many verification tools for C (e.g., GRASSHoper, HIP/Sleek, Infer, VCC, VeriFast) due to the efficiency of local reasoning. The specification logic used in Frama-C, ACSL [3], includes a separating conjunction operator (understood by WP and Eva plugins), but it is far weaker than the standard separating conjunction operator. The underlying solvers for SL of the above tools are either not available or deal with the type safe fragment of C. The recent SL-COMP initiative motivated the development of several independent solvers for type safe fragments of SL, one of them included in the CVC4 [32] solver. Our work focuses on DV tools using FOL and infers separation properties between memory regions. Our pointer analyses may be used in SL-based tools to obtain precise properties on arrays of pointers.

Pointer Analyses for DV: Static analysis based on region inference is used in [20] to partition a typed memory model. The analysis is less precise than the points-to analysis in Eva because the loss of precision for one location could force many precise locations to be collapsed in the same region. [31] employs pointer analysis to ensure a sound usage of the typed memory model in presence of casts. This work may be applied to extend the class of programs we deal with, but our focus is on improving efficiency of DV, not its realm. Recent work [36] proposes a precise points-to analysis to infer separation information in order to decrease the size of VCs. Although Eva is doing a less precise analysis, it is still able to infer such separation properties. In addition, we define a formalized channel to transfer such information to DV tools. The authors of [5] explore different memory models to generate with VCC a benchmark of problems for SMT solvers. By implementing various memory models for WP, we increase such benchmark.

Conclusion: We have formalized the collaboration of a pointer analysis tool and a deductive verification tool by a functor which exploits the results of the pointer analysis to define sound and precise memory model environments used in the generation of verification conditions in first order logic theories. We applied this functor to several pointer analyses, including classic analyses (points-to analysis) and a new analysis that allows to obtain precise partitioning information of the program's memory. We reported on the implementation of the functor in Frama-C and on the results obtained by different analyses on a benchmark of C programs that exhibit complex features of pointers in C (arrays of pointers, duality of fields) and complex separation annotations. The results obtained show the interest of our functor for the automatization of deductive verification.

References

1. Barnett, M., Chang, B.-Y.E., DeLine, R., Jacobs, B., Leino, K.R.M.: Boogie: a modular reusable verifier for object-oriented programs. In: de Boer, F.S., Bonsangue, M.M., Graf, S., de Roever, W.-P. (eds.) FMCO 2005. LNCS, vol. 4111, pp. 364–387. Springer, Heidelberg (2006). https://doi.org/10.1007/11804192_17
2. Barnett, M., Leino, K.R.M., Schulte, W.: The Spec# programming system: an overview. In: Barthe, G., Burdy, L., Huisman, M., Lanet, J.-L., Muntean, T. (eds.) CASSIS 2004. LNCS, vol. 3362, pp. 49–69. Springer, Heidelberg (2005). https://doi.org/10.1007/978-3-540-30569-9_3
3. Baudin, P., et al.: ACSL: ANSI C Specification Language (preliminary design V1.2), preliminary edition, May 2008
4. Blazy, S., Leroy, X.: Mechanized semantics for the clight subset of the C language. J. Autom. Reasoning 43(3), 263–288 (2009)
5. Böhme, S., Moskal, M.: Heaps and data structures: a challenge for automated provers. In: Bjørner, N., Sofronie-Stokkermans, V. (eds.) CADE 2011. LNCS (LNAI), vol. 6803, pp. 177–191. Springer, Heidelberg (2011). https://doi.org/10.1007/978-3-642-22438-6_15
6. Bornat, R.: Proving pointer programs in hoare logic. In: Backhouse, R., Oliveira, J.N. (eds.) MPC 2000. LNCS, vol. 1837, pp. 102–126. Springer, Heidelberg (2000). https://doi.org/10.1007/10722010_8
7. Brotherston, J., Kanovich, M.: On the Complexity of Pointer Arithmetic in Separation Logic (an extended version). arXiv:1803.03164 [cs], March 2018
8. Bühler, D.: Structuring an abstract interpreter through value and state abstractions. Ph.D. thesis, University of Rennes (2017)
9. Burstall, R.M.: Some techniques for proving correctness of programs which alter data structures. Mach. Intell. 7, 23–50 (1972)
10. Calcagno, C., Distefano, D., O'Hearn, P.W., Yang, H.: Beyond reachability: shape abstraction in the presence of pointer arithmetic. In: Yi, K. (ed.) SAS 2006. LNCS, vol. 4134, pp. 182–203. Springer, Heidelberg (2006). https://doi.org/10.1007/11823230_13
11. Chang, B.-Y.E., Rival, X., Necula, G.C.: Shape analysis with structural invariant checkers. In: Nielson, H.R., Filé, G. (eds.) SAS 2007. LNCS, vol. 4634, pp. 384–401. Springer, Heidelberg (2007). https://doi.org/10.1007/978-3-540-74061-2_24
12. Chatterjee, S., Lahiri, S.K., Qadeer, S., Rakamarić, Z.: A low-level memory model and an accompanying reachability predicate. STTT 11(2), 105–116 (2009)
13. Chin, W., David, C., Nguyen, H.H., Qin, S.: Automated verification of shape, size and bag properties via user-defined predicates in separation logic. Sci. Comput. Program. 77(9), 1006–1036 (2012)
14. Correnson, L.: Qed. Computing what remains to be proved. In: Badger, J.M., Rozier, K.Y. (eds.) NFM 2014. LNCS, vol. 8430, pp. 215–229. Springer, Cham (2014). https://doi.org/10.1007/978-3-319-06200-6_17
15. Correnson, L., Bobot, F.: Exploring memory models with Frama-C/WP (2017). Personal communication
16. Cousot, P., Cousot, R.: Abstract interpretation: a unified lattice model for static analysis of programs by construction or approximation of fixpoints. In: POPL, pp. 238–252. ACM (1977)
17. Filliâtre, J.-C., Marché, C.: The Why/Krakatoa/Caduceus platform for deductive program verification. In: Damm, W., Hermanns, H. (eds.) CAV 2007. LNCS, vol. 4590, pp. 173–177. Springer, Heidelberg (2007). https://doi.org/10.1007/978-3-540-73368-3_21

18. Flanagan, C., Saxe, J.B.: Avoiding exponential explosion: generating compact verification conditions. SIGPLAN Not. **36**(3), 193–205 (2001)
19. Hind, M.: Pointer analysis: haven't we solved this problem yet? In: Proceedings of PASTE, Snowbird, Utah, United States, pp. 54–61. ACM Press (2001)
20. Hubert, T., Marché, C.: Separation analysis for deductive verification. In: Proceedings of HAV, Braga, Portugal, pp. 81–93, March 2007
21. Jacobs, B., Piessens, F.: The VeriFast program verifier. Technical report CW-520, Department of Computer Science, Katholieke Universiteit Leuven (2008)
22. Kirchner, F., Kosmatov, N., Prevosto, V., Signoles, J., Yakobowski, B.: Frama-C: a software analysis perspective. Formal Asp. Comput. **27**(3), 573–609 (2015)
23. Leino, K.R.M.: Efficient weakest preconditions. Inf. Process. Lett. **93**(6), 281–288 (2005)
24. Leroy, X., Appel, A.W., Blazy, S., Stewart, G.: The CompCert Memory Model, Version 2. Research report RR-7987, INRIA, June 2012
25. Leroy, X., Blazy, S.: Formal verification of a C-like memory model and its uses for verifying program transformations. J. Autom. Reasoning **41**(1), 1–31 (2008)
26. McCarthy, J.: Towards a mathematical science of computation. In: IFIP Congress, pp. 21–28 (1962)
27. Mehta, F., Nipkow, T.: Proving pointer programs in higher-order logic. In: Baader, F. (ed.) CADE 2003. LNCS (LNAI), vol. 2741, pp. 121–135. Springer, Heidelberg (2003). https://doi.org/10.1007/978-3-540-45085-6_10
28. Miné, A.: Static analysis by abstract interpretation of concurrent programs. Technical report, École normale supérieure, May 2013. http://www-apr.lip6.fr/~mine/hdr/hdr-compact-col.pdf
29. O'Hearn, P., Reynolds, J., Yang, H.: Local reasoning about programs that alter data structures. In: Fribourg, L. (ed.) CSL 2001. LNCS, vol. 2142, pp. 1–19. Springer, Heidelberg (2001). https://doi.org/10.1007/3-540-44802-0_1
30. Piskac, R., Wies, T., Zufferey, D.: Automating separation logic with trees and data. In: Biere, A., Bloem, R. (eds.) CAV 2014. LNCS, vol. 8559, pp. 711–728. Springer, Cham (2014). https://doi.org/10.1007/978-3-319-08867-9_47
31. Rakamarić, Z., Hu, A.J.: A scalable memory model for low-level code. In: Jones, N.D., Müller-Olm, M. (eds.) VMCAI 2009. LNCS, vol. 5403, pp. 290–304. Springer, Heidelberg (2008). https://doi.org/10.1007/978-3-540-93900-9_24
32. Reynolds, A., Iosif, R., Serban, C., King, T.: A decision procedure for separation logic in SMT. In: Artho, C., Legay, A., Peled, D. (eds.) ATVA 2016. LNCS, vol. 9938, pp. 244–261. Springer, Cham (2016). https://doi.org/10.1007/978-3-319-46520-3_16
33. Sotin, P., Jeannet, B., Rival, X.: Concrete memory models for shape analysis. Electr. Notes Theor. Comput. Sci. **267**(1), 139–150 (2010)
34. Stackoverflow. Is it legal to access struct members via offset pointers from other struct members? https://stackoverflow.com/questions/51737910/. Accessed 5 Oct 2018
35. Tuch, H., Klein, G., Norrish, M.: Types, bytes, and separation logic. In: POPL, pp. 97–108. ACM (2007)
36. Wang, W., Barrett, C., Wies, T.: Partitioned memory models for program analysis. In: Bouajjani, A., Monniaux, D. (eds.) VMCAI 2017. LNCS, vol. 10145, pp. 539–558. Springer, Cham (2017). https://doi.org/10.1007/978-3-319-52234-0_29

Small Faults Grow Up - Verification of Error Masking Robustness in Arithmetically Encoded Programs

Anja F. Karl[1]([⊠]), Robert Schilling[1,2], Roderick Bloem[1], and Stefan Mangard[1]

[1] Graz University of Technology, Inffeldgasse 16A, 8010 Graz, Austria
{anja.karl,robert.schilling,roderick.bloem,stefan.mangard}@iaik.tugraz.at
[2] Know-Center GmbH, Inffeldgasse 13/6, 8010 Graz, Austria

Abstract. The increasing prevalence of soft errors and security concerns due to recent attacks like rowhammer have caused increased interest in the robustness of software against bit flips.

Arithmetic codes can be used as a protection mechanism to detect small errors injected in the program's data. However, the accumulation of propagated errors can increase the number of bits flips in a variable - possibly up to an undetectable level.

The effect of error masking can occur: An error weight exceeds the limitations of the code and a new, valid, but incorrect code word is formed. Masked errors are undetectable, and it is crucial to check variables for bit flips before error masking can occur.

In this paper, we develop a theory of provably robust arithmetic programs. We focus on the interaction of bit flips that can happen at different locations in the program and the propagation and possible masking of errors. We show how this interaction can be formally modeled and how off-the-shelf model checkers can be used to show correctness. We evaluate our approach based on prominent and security relevant algorithms and show that even multiple faults injected at any time into any variables can be handled by our method.

Keywords: Formal verification · Fault injection
Error detection codes · Arithmetic codes · Error masking

This project has received funding from the European Research Council (ERC) under the European Unions Horizon 2020 research and innovation programme (grant agreement No. 681402), by the Austrian Science Fund (FWF) through the research network RiSE (S11406-N23), and by the Austrian Research Promotion Agency (FFG) via the competence center Know-Center, which is funded in the context of COMET Competence Centers for Excellent Technologies by BMVIT, BMWFW, and Styria. The authors would like to especially thank Karin Greiml and Bettina Könighofer for their support.

© Springer Nature Switzerland AG 2019
C. Enea and R. Piskac (Eds.): VMCAI 2019, LNCS 11388, pp. 183–204, 2019.
https://doi.org/10.1007/978-3-030-11245-5_9

1 Introduction

A typical assumption when writing software is that registers and memory content do not change unless the software performs a write operation on these locations. However, in practice, this assumption is challenged in several ways. On the one hand, the feature size of transistors in processors and memories keeps shrinking and shrinking, which allows natural phenomena like cosmic radiation to sporadically flip bits in memories and processors [4]. On the other hand, there exist attack techniques that aim at overcoming security mechanisms of systems by inducing targeted faults into a system. There is a wide range of publications on how to induce faults in systems using for example voltage glitches [3] or lasers [29]. The rowhammer effect [15] even allows attackers to cause bit flips remotely without any physical access to the target device.

Independent of whether a fault is caused by a natural phenomenon or an attacker, we refer to any change of a system state that is not caused by the software itself as a fault. Faults have huge implications on the security and safety of a system. Even a single bit flip, can lead to a critical system failure or reveal secret cryptographic keys (e.g. [1,7]). Consequently, appropriate mechanisms for detecting and handling faults are necessary.

The first error detection codes have been invented by Golay [13] and Hamming [14]. They proposed to add redundancy to every number, to increase the Hamming Distance [14] between encoded numbers. The higher the size of redundancy, the more bit flips can be detected. In the subsequent years, a special form of error detection codes have been discovered: Arithmetic codes do not only detect up to a fixed number of bit flips, the code words also remain valid over a certain set of arithmetic operations, e.g. $\text{encode}(a) +_{enc} \text{encode}(b) = \text{encode}(a + b)$. The number of detectable bit flips depends on the minimum arithmetic distance between valid code words [17], referred to as d_{min}. Examples for arithmetic error detection codes are AN, AN+B and residue codes [9,10,22].

1.1 Error Masking

In this work, we build up on the theory of arithmetic distance between arithmetic code words [17] and extend it to describe the propagation of errors and their arithmetic weights over an arithmetic program.

Listing 1.1. Copy of an invalid code word, resulting in two faulted variables a and b.

```
1 a  := encode(0)
2 a  := flip(a, 0ᵗʰ bit)
3 b  := a
```

Every typical program contains data dependencies. If a value depends on a faulted one, it is influenced by that fault and is unlikely to be correct – the error propagated to the new variable. Listing 1.1 shows a simple example of an error propagating from one faulted variable to another one.

Listing 1.2. The sum of two invalid code words a and b, yields a faulted code word c containing two flipped bits.

```
1 a := encode(0)
2 a := flip(a, 0ᵗʰ bit)
3 b := a + a
4 c := a + b
```

As soon as an instruction has two faulted operands, the arithmetic weight of the errors can accumulate, and as a result the new error's weight can exceed the detection limit d_{min} of the code. In Listing 1.2, the flip of the 0th bit in a results in a flip of the 1st bit in b. Both errors accumulate to two bit flips in c.

Definition 1 (Error Masking). *Error masking is the effect of a new, valid, but incorrect code word emerging from an operation with two faulted operands.*

Listing 1.3. The injected fault is detected before errors can accumulate.

```
1 a := encode(0)
2 a := flip(a, 0ᵗʰ bit)
3 b := a + a
4 check(b)
5 c := a + b
```

A countermeasure for error masking is to check variables for errors at intermediate program locations, like in the example in Listing 1.3. However, it is non-trivial to determine where to place these checks: on the one hand, too many checks increase the run time of a program significantly, on the other hand, missing checks can lead to error masking.

1.2   Contribution

Within this work, we present a technique to prove that a program is robust against error masking. The following three points summarize our contribution:

1. We introduce the theory behind the effect of error masking based on the concept of error propagation over arithmetically encoded programs.
2. We use these insights to define the property of error masking robustness and present a novel technique to prove that the checks inside a program are sufficient to prevent error masking.
3. We demonstrate the capabilities of our approach based on real world programs. We were able to detect error masking vulnerabilities in cryptography algorithms and propose verifiable robust adaptions of these algorithms containing intermediate checks.

The core idea of our proposed method is the translation of an input program into a model of its worst-case error propagation, and to evaluate the model using an off-the-shelf model checker. With our method, we are not limited to detect robustness violations, but also receive indications of the problematic statements.

Furthermore, our approach is generic for all arithmetic encoding schemes, as long as there is a minimum arithmetic distance d_{min} between valid code words.

The flexibility of the technique allows us to use fault specifications of varying complexity. In contrast to other approaches, our method allows us to evaluate a program in the presence of *multiple faults* distributed over *all possible locations*!

1.3   Outline

The remainder of this paper is organized as follows: First, Sect. 2 describes the state of the art and related work. Next, Sect. 3 states the preliminaries and explains the concept of arithmetic codes and its most prominent examples. Our proposed approach to detect error masking is presented in Sects. 4 and 5: Sect. 4 describes the input language and the fault model, and Sect. 5 states the process to create a verifiable abstraction of the program under verification. Following, we prove the correctness of our approach in Sect. 6 and present our experimental results in Sect. 7. Finally, we conclude with a discussion of (dis-)advantages of our approach in Sect. 8 and a summary in Sect. 9.

2   Related Work

The first papers on arithmetic codes can be dated back to the 1950's and 1960's [9,10,17,22]. They describe a class of error detection codes that natively supports arithmetic operations without decoding the code word. While arithmetic codes have been developed to detect and correct bit flips during data transmission, they turned out to be also well suited as protection mechanism against a more recent concern: Using modern technology, adversaries are able to intentionally inject faults during program execution and thus reveal secret information [18].

In the recent years, researchers developed methods to automatically encode programs at compile time [11,25,26]. Although some of the required checks can be inserted automatically, they are insufficient for the prevention of error masking, and the user needs to specify further check locations himself. However, there is currently no exact theory to decide where necessary checks are required. This paper addresses this problem by introducing a method to automatically evaluate the placement of checks inside a program.

The idea of applying formal methods to verify the robustness of programs against faults is shared with multiple related papers: Pattabiraman et al. [21] and Larsson and Hähnle [16] both propose to use symbolic execution. The first of these two papers describes a method, where registers and memory locations are symbolically tagged with an *err* label, and error propagation is modelled through duplication of this label. The framework runs user defined error detectors to identify and report problems. However, the authors do not consider the exact number of bit flips on a variable, which prevents the tool from identifying error masking. The second publication focuses on the symbolic injection of multiple bit flips at fixed fault locations. In contrast to our work, it proposes a method tailored to the principle of code duplication as countermeasure. This method compares the result of two versions of the same code, where one is based on faulted data. The effectiveness of code multiplication requires a strict independence of all redundant data paths. Walker et al. [31] introduce a method to identify such dependencies inside programs.

The idea of using LLVM bitcode transformations to add explicit fault injections to the source code is shared with the papers [30] and [12]. The idea of [30] is to execute two versions of a program - the original and a faulted version - and to evaluate user defined predicates. Every combination of the program counter and the state of these predicates form a node in a transition diagram. If an execution ever reaches a node unreachable in the fault-free transition diagram their tool reports an error. In the second paper, mutated binaries are model checked against a given specification. The results are then compared with the results of a fault-free verification run to identify differences. All those papers share similarities with our work, but they apply to different countermeasures and are not designed to detect error masking.

On the side of formal verification of programs using error detection codes, as to our knowledge, only few publications exist so far. Meola [20] formally proved the robustness of a small encoded program using Hoare Logic, and Schiffel [27] investigates the soundness and completeness of arithmetic codes using formal methods. Schiffel posits that the formal verification of AN-encoded programs using model checkers is impossible due to the exponential increase of verification time. We address this challenge by creating an abstraction of the program, only considering the error's weight instead of a variable's value.

3   Arithmetic Error Detecting Codes

Error detecting codes are a well-known way to detect errors during storage or computation. They can be divided into multiple sub-classes, among them the class of arithmetic error detection codes. These codes do not only guarantee a detection of all errors with an arithmetic weight smaller a constant d_{min}, they also remain valid over certain arithmetic operations, like additions.

3.1   Examples for Arithmetic Codes

One prominent example for an arithmetic code is the AN-code [9,10,26]. All valid AN code words are multiples of an user-defined constant A, with $\mathtt{encode}(x) = x \cdot A$. To check a code word for validity, the remainder of the code word divided by A is calculated. For all valid code words, this remainder must be 0, otherwise the check detects an error and aborts execution. In the case of AN codes the check aborts, if a code word is not a multiple of A, $var_{enc} \bmod A \neq 0$.

A second class of arithmetic codes are residue codes [17]. A residue code word is defined by x concatenated with $x \bmod M$, given a constant modulus M, $\mathtt{encode}(x) = (x \mid x \bmod M)$. This code separates the redundancy part from the functional value x, thus the name *separate code*. Although the robustness of the code is defined by the modulus M, residue codes only guarantee detection of a single bit flip. To overcome this limitation, the redundancy part can be increased by using more than one residue [23,24], yielding a multi-residue code.

3.2   Arithmetic Weight and Distance

Both, AN-codes and (multi-) residue codes use the arithmetic weight and the arithmetic distance to quantify the robustness of the instantiated code. These properties are similar to the Hamming weight and Hamming distance [14] used for binary linear codes. The arithmetic weight $W(|x|)$ of the integer value x is defined as the minimum number of non-zero coefficients in the signed digit representation of x.

$$W(|x|) = \min \left\{ \sum_{i=0}^{\infty} |b_i| \ \middle| \ b_i \in \{-1, 0, 1\}, x = \sum_{i=0}^{\infty} b_i 2^i \right\}$$

The arithmetic distance $d(x_1, x_2)$ between the two integers x_1 and x_2 is equal to the arithmetic weight of the absolute difference between x_1 and x_2.

$$d(x_1, x_2) = W(|x_1 - x_2|)$$

The constant d_{min} is the only information about the encoding our method requires. It is defined as the minimum arithmetic distance between any two valid code words x_{enc1} and x_{enc2}. All errors with a weight up to d_{min} are guaranteed to be detected by a properly implemented check. This property is essential to verify the error masking robustness, as described in the subsequent sections.

$$d_{min} = \min_{x_{enc1} \neq x_{enc2}} d(x_{enc1}, x_{enc2})$$

4   Error Masking Robust Programs

In this section, we first describe the input program's language and define the fault model considered in our approach. Next, we explain, how to derive a program P_f containing explicit fault injections. Finally, we present a formal definition of robustness against error masking based on an explicitly faulted program P_f.

4.1   Programs

Our robustness verification method is applicable for arithmetic programs of the following form.

Definition 2 (Input Programs). *An input program P is a directed graph $P = (V, E, \lambda, v_0, Var)$, where V is a set of vertices, $E \subseteq V \times V$ is a set of edges, $\lambda : V \rightarrow S$ is a mapping of vertices to statements, $v_0 \in V$ is a start vertex, and $Var = Var^{loc} \cup Var^{arg}$ is a set of local variables and program arguments.*

All variables $var \in Var$ and constants $const_{enc} \in Const_{enc} = \{\texttt{encode}(n) \mid n \in \mathbb{N}\}$ are arithmetically encoded natural numbers. All statements $s \in S$ are either arithmetic instructions $s \in S_{arith}$ or control-flow directives $s \in S_{cf}$, i.e., $S = S_{arith} \cup S_{cf}$. Arithmetic instructions $s \in S_{arith}$ can either be assignments of constants $s \in S_{assign}$, additions $s \in S_{add1} \cup S_{add2}$, or subtractions $s \in S_{sub}$. We distinguish between additions with the same variable for both operands, $s \in S_{add1}$, and additions with different variables, $s \in S_{add2}$. Formally, we have $S_{arith} = S_{assign} \cup S_{add1} \cup S_{add2} \cup S_{sub}$, with

$$S_{assign} = \{var := const_{enc} \mid var \in Var, const_{enc} \in Const_{enc}\},$$
$$S_{add1} = \{var := var_1 + var_1 \mid var, var_1 \in Var\},$$
$$S_{add2} = \{var := var_1 + var_2 \mid var, var_1, var_2 \in Var\}, \text{ and}$$
$$S_{sub} = \{var := var_1 - var_2 \mid var, var_1, var_2 \in Var\}.$$

Control-flow directives $s \in S_{cf}$ include direct jumps $s \in S_{jump}$, conditional branches $s \in S_{cbranch}$, checks $s \in S_{check}$ and terminators $s \in S_{ret}$. We have $S_{cf} = S_{jump} \cup S_{cbranch} \cup S_{check} \cup S_{ret}$, with

$$S_{jump} = \{\texttt{goto } v \mid v \in V\},$$
$$S_{cbranch} = \{\texttt{if } (c) \texttt{ goto } v_1 \texttt{ else goto } v_2 \mid v_1, v_2 \in V, c \in C\},$$
$$S_{check} = \{\texttt{check}\,(var) \mid var \in Var\}, \text{ and}$$
$$S_{ret} = \{\texttt{return } var \mid var \in Var\}.$$

Boolean conditions $c \in C$ are either comparisons val_1 **op** val_2, with $val_1, val_2 \in Const_{enc} \cup Var$ and **op** $\in \{<, \leq, =, \neq, \geq, >\}$, or boolean combinations of comparisons. In the fault-free case, conditional branches continue with the first target vertex, if the condition c evaluates to true, and with the second vertex otherwise. Every conditional branch performs an implicit check on all operands in c. To avoid flipping the boolean value of c itself, we propose to use branch protection algorithms like [28]. The execution of a conditional branch can fall into one of three cases: (1) Every operand is correct and the execution jumps to the correct vertex. (2) Any operand in the condition is faulted, but contains a detectable fault. In this case, the conditional branch statement aborts execution and enters a safe state. (3) The error weight on the compared operands exceeds $d_{min} - 1$, and the branch protection mechanism can miss the fault. The statement continues with either of both **goto** statements and executes a possibly invalid path. This behavior is a consequence of error masking and will be detected by our method.

A runtime assertion **check**(var) checks a code word var for validity, aborts execution and enters a safe state if it detects a fault on this variable. However, checks are not able to detect masked errors and only guarantee to disclose errors with a maximum arithmetic weight of $d_{min} - 1$. The actual implementation of a check depends on the encoding scheme of the program and is both possible in hardware and in software.

Every vertex v_i with a statement $\lambda(v_i) \in S_{arith} \cup S_{check} \cup S_{jump}$ has exactly one successor v_{i+1}. If $\lambda(v_i) = \texttt{goto } v_j$, the destination vertex v_j must be the single successor of v_i. All vertices v_i with conditional branch statements $\lambda(v_i) = $ if (c) goto v_j else goto v'_j have exactly two outgoing edges to v_j and v'_j, and all vertices v_i with return statements $\lambda(v_i) \in S_{ret}$ have zero successors.

Our method requires the whole program to be encoded using the same encoding scheme and the same encoding constants. As a consequence, there is a value $d_{min} > 1$, which is smaller or equal to the arithmetic distance of any two valid code words. The constant $d_{min} - 1$ forms the upper limit for the number of guaranteed detectable bit flips and needs to be known in order to evaluate a program using our method. The programmer is responsible for choosing an appropriate encoding scheme, such that all operations in the program are possible in the encoded domain and no overflows can occur.

Listing 1.4. Running example.

```
1  toy():
2      a := encode(0)
3      b := a + a
4      check(b)
5      c := a + b
6      return c
```

As running example we use our small toy program from Listings 1.2 and 1.3. The flip in both programs was not intended and occurred due to either an attacker or environmental influences during execution. Listing 1.4 shows the original program, as it was written by the programmer.

4.2 Fault Model

This work focuses on faults in memory, where bits of variable values are flipped. Every fault consists of a (possibly negative) error Err of an arithmetic weight $W(|Err|) < d_{min}$ added to a variable var at any point in time during program execution. A special case of faults are bit flips. A single bit flip in the ith bit corresponds to an error $Err = b_i 2^i$, with $b_i = 1$ if the flip sets the bit, and $b_i = -1$ otherwise. Therefore, the arithmetic weight of a single bit flip is $W(|Err|) = 1$. All faults injected into a variable var remain present until a new value is assigned to var and overwrites the fault. In this work, we do not consider control-flow attacks as there are already promising countermeasures [28,32] to protect this attack vector. We assume that an integrity mechanism is present such that all instructions as well as the control-flow of the program are protected.

4.3 Explicitly Faulted Programs

In order to verify the robustness of a program, we need to make faults in the input program visible to the model checker. Therefore, we define a derived program with explicit fault injections. The derived program contains a copy of every vertex $v \in V$ called v'_f with the same statement; i.e., $\lambda_f(v'_f) = \lambda(v)$. Additionally, we add a vertex v''_f before every v'_f. The statement of v''_f injects faults explicitly into the operands of the statement $\lambda_f(v'_f)$. Formally, we define P_f as:

Definition 3 (Explicitly Faulted Program P_f). *Let* $P = (V, E, \lambda, v_0, Var)$ *be a program, let* $V_f' = V \times \{1\}$ *and* $V_f'' = V \times \{2\}$ *be two copies of* V, *and let* $V_f = V_f' \cup V_f''$. *The explicitly faulted program* $P_f = (V_f, E_f, \lambda_f, v_{0f}, Var_f)$ *is a graph, where* $E_f = E_{f_1} \cup E_{f_2}$ *is the set of edges with* $E_{f_1} = \{(v_f'', v_f') \mid v_f'' = (v, 2), v_f' = (v, 1), v \in V\}$ *and* $E_{f_2} = \{(v_{1_f}', v_{2_f}'') \mid v_{1_f}' = (v_1, 1), v_{2_f}'' = (v_2, 2), (v_1, v_2) \in E\}$, *and* $Var_f = Var$ *is the set of variables. The start vertex* v_{0f} *is defined by* $v_{0f} = (v_0, 2)$ *and the statement function* λ_f *as*

$$
\lambda_f((v, i)) = \begin{cases}
\lambda(v) & \text{if} \quad i = 1 \\
var := var + Err_v & \text{if} \quad i = 2 \text{ and } \lambda(v) = \textbf{return } var \\
\begin{aligned} var_1 &:= var_1 + Err1_v \\ var_2 &:= var_2 + Err2_v \end{aligned} & \text{if} \quad i = 2 \text{ and } \lambda(v) = var := var_1 \pm var_2 \\
\epsilon & \text{else.}
\end{cases}
$$

In this formula, Err_v denotes the error injected before execution of the statement of v into its operand. In the case of two operands, the $Err1_v$ is the error injected into the first operand and $Err2_v$ is the error injected into the second operand. If $\lambda(v)$ has no operands, the statement $\lambda_f((v, 2))$ is empty. The explicitly faulted version of our toy example is depicted in Listing 1.5.

Listing 1.5. P_f of the running example in Listing 1.4.

```
1    toy():
2          a := encode(0)

4          a := a + Err1_{v1}
5          a := a + Err2_{v1}
6          b := a + a

8          check(b)

10         a := a + Err1_{v3}
11         b := b + Err2_{v3}
12         c := a + b

14         c := c + Err_{v4}
15         return c
```

4.4   Robustness Condition

The explicit faults in P_f allow us to name the errors on every variable during execution. Therefore, we can introduce the following terms and define the condition for robustness of a program against error masking.

Definition 4 (Execution Path). *A path* $\pi = \pi[0], \ldots, \pi[n]$ *is a sequence of* $n + 1$ *vertices with* $\pi[i] \in V$, *where the program graph* P *has a directed edge between any two subsequent elements* $(\pi[i], \pi[i+1]) \in E$.

Definition 5 (Execution Trace). *An execution trace $\pi^{exec} = \pi[0], \dots, \pi[n]$ of a program P is an execution path through the program starting at $\pi[0] = v_0$ and ending with a vertex $\pi[n]$, with $\lambda(\pi[n]) \in S_{ret}$.*

Definition 6 (Feasible Execution Trace). *An execution path π is contained in an execution trace π^{exec}, if all elements of π are also included in π^{exec} and their order is preserved. An execution trace π^{exec} of a program P is feasible in an explicitly faulted program P_f, iff there is an execution trace π_f^{exec}, such that π^{exec} is contained in π_f^{exec}.*

Definition 7 (Fault-Free Program). *Given a program P_f, the fault-free program P_f^0 is defined as P_f with no errors injected at any vertex, i.e. for all $v \in V$ it holds that $Err_v = 0$, $Err1_v = 0$, and $Err2_v = 0$.*

Definition 8 (Program State). *Given a deterministic, explicitly faulted program P_f and fixed values for every program argument and injected errors, there is only one feasible execution trace π. We define the program state $\Pi[t]$ of π as the mapping from all variables to their value at execution step t. The function $[\![\Pi[t] \mid var]\!]$ returns the value of the variable var in this execution state, and $[\![\Pi[t]]\!]_\pi$ returns the execution path $\pi[0], \dots, \pi[t]$ up to $\pi[t]$.*

Definition 9 (Error on a variable). *Given an execution state Π_f of P_f and the corresponding execution state Π_f^0 of P_f^0, the error $[\![\Pi_f[t] \mid Err(var)]\!]$ on a variable var is the difference between $[\![\Pi_f[t] \mid var]\!]$ and $[\![\Pi_f^0[t] \mid var]\!]$.*

Definition 10 (Robustness of an explicitly faulted program). *A faulted program P_f is error masking robust if every feasible execution trace is also feasible in the fault-free program P_f^0 and all its executions return either a fault-free value $[\![\Pi_f[k] \mid Err(var)]\!] = 0$ or any fault on the returned value $[\![\Pi_f[k] \mid var]\!]$ is smaller than d_{min} and therefore guaranteed detectable.*

Definition 11 (Robustness of an program). *A program P is robust against error masking iff the explicitly faulted program P_f is robust against error masking.*

To guarantee the robustness against error masking, the properties stated in Definition 10 are required to hold on the explicitly faulted program. The first condition can be ensured by preventing error masking on any variables compared in a branch condition, while the latter requires the absence of error masking on the return value. Both problems are detected by the method described in the next section.

5   Proving a Program Robust Against Error Masking

This section describes the verification of the error masking robustness of a program, as defined in Sect. 4. Figure 1 depicts the verification process: starting from an input program P, we create the explicitly faulted program P_f and derive an abstract model of the worst case error weight propagation P_w. This model is

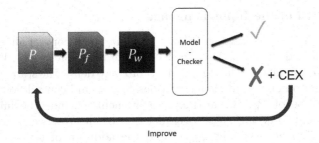

Fig. 1. The work flow of the verification process.

then model checked for error masking robustness. In the case of error masking possibilities, the model checker generates a counterexample, which can be used to improve P by inserting additional checks. If the model checker reports no errors, the program is guaranteed to be error masking robust.

The main idea behind our method is to track the maximum error weight on each variable and to ensure this error weight never exceeds $d_{min} - 1$. In this case, errors can never mask each other and are always detectable. Our technique to prove error masking robustness involves three main steps: (1) We derive the explicitly faulted program $P \rightsquigarrow P_f$ from the input program P, as described in Sect. 4. (2) We transforms the faulted program P_f into an error weight counting program $P_f \rightsquigarrow P_w$. The program P_w is a model of the worst case error weight propagation and contains assertions for ensuring P to be robust. (3) We apply an off-the-shelf model checker to evaluate the new program P_w. The model checker proves the absence of error masking or provides a counterexample in case of any violations of the robustness assertions.

In order to define the error weight counting program P_w, we first introduce the concept of fault specifications and afterwards explain the language of P_w and its construction.

5.1 Fault Specification

The fault specification FS constraints the maximum arithmetic weight of any injected error and is provided by the user.

Definition 12 (Maximum Injected Error Weight). *The maximum injected error weight W_v denotes the maximum weight of errors injected over all visits to a vertex v into the operand of $\lambda(v)$. In the case of two operands, $W1_v$ and $W2_v$ are the maximum injected error weights of the first and the second operand.*

Definition 13 (Fault Specification). *A fault specification FS is a Boolean expression over predicates $\sum(W_v)$ op n, with op $\in \{<, \leq, =, \geq, >, \neq\}$ and a constant $n \leq d_{min}$, such that FS restricts every injected error weight to an upper limit of $d_{min} - 1$.*

A simple example for a fault specification is to limit the sum of all maximum injected error weights to a constant $n < d_{min}$; i.e.: $\sum W_v + \sum W1_v + \sum W2_v \leq n$.

5.2   Adaption of the Input Language

The language of P_w is defined as follows. Let Var_w be a copy of all variables of Var. For every node $v \in V$ we have an error weight injection variable W_v for each operand of $\lambda(v)$. Similar to the statements S of P, we define the statements S_w of P_w as combination of arithmetic instructions S_{arith_w} and control-flow directives S_{cf_w}. In the case of P_w, the arithmetic statements include the initialization of an error weight inject $S_{init\_inj_w}$, the deletion of an error weight S_{zero_w}, the duplication of an error weight S_{dupl_w} and the addition of two error weights S_{add_w}. Formally, these statements are defined as:

$$S_{init\_inj_w} = \{W_v := * \mid v \in V\},$$
$$S_{zero_w} = \{var_w := 0 \mid var_w \in Var_w\},$$
$$S_{dupl_w} = \{var_w := var_{1w} \mid var_w, var_{1w} \in Var_w\}, \text{ and}$$
$$S_{add_w} = \{var_w := var_{1w} + var_{2w} \mid var_w, var_{1w}, var_{2w} \in Var_w\}.$$

Control-flow directives S_{cf_w} include jumps S_{jump_w}, conditional branches $S_{cbranch_w}$, terminators S_{ret_w}, assertions S_{assert_w} and assumptions S_{assume_w}, i.e. $S_{cf_w} = S_{jump_w} \cup S_{cbranch_w} \cup S_{ret_w} \cup S_{assert_w} \cup S_{assume_w}$. Let V_w be the set of vertices in P_w, Var_w a set of variables, and fs a fault specification. We can define the different kinds of control-flow directives of P_w as:

$$S_{jump_w} = \{\texttt{goto } v_w \mid v_w \in V_w\},$$
$$S_{cbranch_w} = \{\texttt{if } (*) \texttt{ goto } v_{1w} \texttt{ else goto } v_{2w} \mid v_{1w}, v_{2w} \in V_w\},$$
$$S_{ret_w} = \{\texttt{return}\},$$
$$S_{assert_w} = \{\texttt{assert}\,(var_w < d_{min}) \mid var_w \in Var_w\}, \text{ and}$$
$$S_{assume_w} = \{\texttt{assume}\,(var_w == 0) \mid var_w \in Var_w\} \cup \{\texttt{assume}\,(FS)\}$$

In this syntax, the $*$ symbol denotes non-deterministic value. The task of the model checker is to prove that for any value as $*$ the assertions inside P_w are never violated, given that all assumptions are fulfilled.

5.3   Translation of the Explicitly Faulted Program into a Weight Counting Program

The error weight counting program P_w can be derived from an explicitly faulted program P_f, via the transformation $P_f \rightsquigarrow P_w$. P_w is an abstraction of the program P_f, which stores only the upper bound of the error weight on the corresponding variables' value. Therefore, P_w contains one error weight counter $var_w \in Var_w$ for every variable of Var_f. All error weight counters in $Var_w = Var_f$ are unsigned variables, which are initialized to zero. In addition to the two copies of V in P_f, P_w contains a third copy $V_w''' = V \times \{3\}$, where assertions are added. Furthermore, P_w starts with multiple initialization vertices, namely $v_w^{ew\_init}$, $v_w^{W\_init}$, and v_w^{fs}. The vertex $v_w^{ew\_init}$ is the first vertex of the program with the following statements:

$$\lambda_w(v_w^{ew\_init}) = \{var_w := 0 \mid var_w \in Var_w\}.$$

Next, within the node $v_w^{W\text{-}init}$, every maximum injected error weight W_v is set to a non-deterministic, positive integer:

$$\lambda_w(v_w^{W\text{-}init}) = \{W_v := * \mid v \in V\} \cup \{W1_v := * \mid v \in V\} \cup \{W2_v := * \mid v \in V\}.$$

As final initialization step, the node v^{fs} limits the maximum injected error weights according to the fault specification:

$$\lambda_w(v_w^{fs}) = \texttt{assume}(fs).$$

Let v_f' be a vertex in V_f', and v_w' be the corresponding copy in V_w'. Furthermore, let each var_w be the error weight counter for the variable var_f. Every arithmetic statement $\lambda_f(v_f') \in S_{arith}$ is transformed into a new statement $\lambda_w(v_w')$ by the following rules:

$$\lambda_w(v_w') = \begin{cases} var_w := 0 & \text{if } \lambda_f(v_f') = var := const_{enc} \\ var_w := var_{1w} & \text{if } \lambda_f(v_f') = var := var_1 + var_1 \\ var_w := var_{1w} + var_{2w} & \text{if } \lambda_f(v_f') = var := var_1 + var_2 \\ var_w := var_{1w} + var_{2w} & \text{if } \lambda_f(v_f') = var := var_1 - var_2 \end{cases}.$$

Assigning a constant to a variable var_f is equivalent to erasing the error that was stored in var_f before execution of the assignment. Therefore, the error weigh counter is erased. When the same variable is added to itself, the error itself is multiplied by two, but its weight remains the same. Therefore, the addition of the same variables $var := var_1 + var_1$ is the same as copying the error weight counter var_{1w} to var_w. Finally, every addition and subtraction has the worst case error propagation $var_w := var_{1w} + var_{2w}$, as modelled by the last two cases.

Let c_{iw} be all operands of a condition c. Similarly to $\lambda_f(v_f') \in S_{arith}$, every control-flow directive $\lambda_f(v_f') \in S_{cf}$ is translated according to

$$\lambda_w(v_w') = \begin{cases} \texttt{goto } v_{1w} & \text{if } \lambda_f(v_f') = \texttt{goto } v_{1f} \\[2ex] \begin{aligned} &\texttt{assume } (c_{iw} = 0) \\ &\texttt{if } (*) \texttt{ goto } v_{1w}' \\ &\texttt{else goto } v_{2w}' \end{aligned} & \text{if } \lambda_f(v_f') = \begin{aligned} &\texttt{if } (c) \texttt{ goto } v_{1f}' \\ &\texttt{else goto } v_{2f}' \end{aligned} \\[3ex] \texttt{assume } (var_w = 0) & \text{if } \lambda_f(v_f') = \texttt{check } (var) \\[2ex] \begin{aligned} &\texttt{assert } (var_w < d_{min}) \\ &\texttt{return} \end{aligned} & \text{if } \lambda_f(v_f') = \texttt{return } var_f \end{cases}.$$

Every unconditional jump in P_f corresponds to the same jump in P_w. However, every conditional branch is transformed into a non-deterministic branch, regardless of the previous branch condition. This transformation guarantees independence of actual variable values and brings along both advantages and restrictions. These matters are further discussed in Sect. 8. As all variables accessed by c are implicitly checked by a branch protection algorithm as described in Subsect. 4.1, the new statement begins with the assumptions that all c_{iw} are fault-free. When a check(var) statement of P_f is executed, exactly one of the following cases must apply:

1. $0 < var < d_{min}$: In this case, an error is detected for sure and the execution is aborted. There cannot be any further error masking and therefore this case can be neglected.
2. $var \geq d_{min}$: In this case the program could either be terminated or continued. This case violates the robustness property and is reported by the assertion assert($var_w < d_{min}$).
3. $var = 0$: The only remaining case is the error free case, which can be assumed, once the robustness assertion has been passed.

Eventually, a return statement quits execution of a program and no further error masking can occur. Every return in P_f corresponds to a return in P_w.

Like in P_f, all fault injections are explicit. A fault injection in P_w is represented by an increment of the error weight counter by the maximum injectable error weight. After the error has been injected, there are no bit flips left for this location and the remaining error weight is set to 0.

$$\lambda_w(v_w'') = \begin{matrix} var_w := var_w + W_v \\ W_v := 0 \end{matrix} \qquad \text{if } \lambda_f(v_f'') = var_f := var_f + Err_v$$

Finally, a model checker requires a definition of the correctness for a program. As defined in Definition 10, the correctness of the program can be guaranteed if all variables' error weights remain below d_{min}. If there is any chance this property is ever violated, the model checker should prompt a warning and give a violating counterexample. Within the program P_w, the correctness is assured by calls to the assert function. Let $v_w''' \in V_w'''$ be a node of the third vertex copy of V, and var_w be the error weight counter modified by $\lambda_w(v_w'')$. Then $\lambda_w(v_w''')$ is given as

$$\lambda_w(v_w''') = \texttt{assert}\,(var_w < d_{min} \mid var_w \in Var_w).$$

Given the previously defined construction, we can define P_w as follows.

Definition 14 (Error Weight Counting Program P_w). *Let* $V_w = \{v_w^{ew\_init}, v_w^{W\_init}, v_w^{fs}\} \cup V_w' \cup V_w'' \cup V_w'''$ *be a set of vertices and* $E_w = \{(v_w^{ew\_init}, v_w^{W\_init}), (v_w^{W\_init}, v_w^{fs})\} \cup \{(v_w'', v_w') \mid v_f' \in V_f\} \cup \{(v_w', v_w''') \mid v_f \in V_f\} \cup \{(v_{1w}''', v_{2w}'') \mid v_{1w}''' = (v_1, 3), v_{2w}'' = (v_2, 2), (v_1, v_2) \in E_f\}$ *a set of edge between the nodes. Then* P_w *is defined as* $P_w = (V_w, E_w, \lambda_w, v_{0w}, Var_w)$, *with* $v_{0w} = v_w^{ew\_init}$ *and* $Var_w = Var$.

After performing the steps described above, the transformation is complete. The resulting program P_w models the worst case error propagation and any potential error masking in P is present as an assertion violation in P_w.

Listing 1.6. P_w of the toy example.

```
1    toy():
2        a, b, c := 0
3        W1_{v_1}, W2_{v_1}, W1_{v_3}, W2_{v_2}, W^{v_4} := *
4        assume(W1_{v_1} + W2_{v_1} + W1_{v_3} + W2_{v_2} + W^{v_4} ≤ 2)

6        a := 0
7        assert(a < d_{min})

9        a := a + W1_{v_1}
10       a := a + W2_{v_1}
11       b := a
12       assert(b < d_{min})

14       assume(b = 0)

16       a := a + W1_{v_3}
17       b := b + W2_{v_3}
18       c := a + b
19       assert(c < d_{min})

21       c := c + W_{v_4}
22       assert(c < d_{min})
23       return
```

The weight counting program of our toy example can be seen in Listing 1.6. Within the first line, it sets every error weight counter (a, b, and c) to zero. The next line initializes all error weight injections to arbitrary values before they are restricted according to the fault specification, in this case to at most two bit flips in total. The next lines (lines 6–22) consist of each the injection of the error weight into the operands, followed by the error propagation and the robustness assertions. The check on b in the middle of the program has been transformed to an `assume` and finally P_w ends with the transformed `return` statement.

5.4   Applying a Model Checker to Prove Correctness

As third step, we use a model checker to verify the resulting program P_w. For our running example, we are able to verify its error masking robustness, giving the fault specification $\sum(W_v) \leq 2$ with $d_{min} = 3$. However, without the line `check(b)`, the model checker successfully reports a vulnerability within the instruction c := a + b, if a contains an error of weight 2. This result corresponds to the expected outcome as illustrated in Sect. 1.

The next section will give a proof of correctness of our method, followed by an evaluation of the method using real world examples.

6   Proof of Correctness

We can show that for every potential error masking in P, P_w contains an assertion violation. For this, we use the following definitions.

Definition 15 (Mapping of a Program State). *Given a program state $\Pi_f[t]$ of the explicitly faulted program P_f, we define $\Pi_w(\Pi_f[t])$ as the corresponding program state of P_w, where for all Err_v it holds that $W(\|[\Pi_f[0] \mid Err_v]\|) = [\![\Pi_w(\Pi_f[0]) \mid W_v]\!]$ and $[\![\Pi_w(\Pi_f[t])]\!]_\pi$ is the smallest execution trace containing $[\![\Pi_f[t]]\!]_\pi$.*

Theorem 1. *Let $\Pi_f[t]$ be a program state, where every variable is smaller or equal to its corresponding error weight counter in $\Pi_w(\Pi_f[t])$. After any statement $\lambda_f(v_f) \in S_{arith}$, the error of the variable var_f modified by $\lambda_f(v_f)$ is smaller or equal to the error weight counter var_w belonging to this variable.*

Proof. All arithmetic statements fall into one of the following cases: (1) In the case of $\lambda_f(v_f) = var_f := \texttt{encode}(c)$, a variable is set to a encoded constant, which originally contains no fault. $W(\|Err(\texttt{encode}(c))\|) = 0 \to var_w = 0 \geq W(\|Err(var_f)\|)$. (2) In the case of addition of the same variable with itself, $\lambda_f(v_f) = var_f := var_{f_1} + var_{f_1}$, we get $D(var_{f_1} + var_{f_1}, var_{f_1}^0 + var_{f_1}^0) = W(|2Err(var_{f_1})|) = W(|Err(var_{f_1})|)$, such that $var_w = W(\|Err(var_{f_1})\|) = W(\|Err(var_f)\|)$. (3) If two different variables are added or subtracted, $\lambda_f(v_f) = var_f := var_{f_1} \pm var_{f_2}$, the new error weight fulfills the following inequality: $D(var_{f_1} + var_{f_2}, var_{f_1}^0 + var_{f_2}^0) = W(|Err(var_{f_1}) - Err(var_{f_2})|) \leq W(\|Err(var_{f_1})\|) + W(\|Err(var_{f_2})\|)$. Therefore it holds that $var_w = W(\|Err(var_{f_1})\|) + W(\|Err(var_{f_2})\|) \geq W(\|Err(var_f)\|)$.

Theorem 2. *In any program state $\Pi_f[t]$ of P_f with $\Pi_w(\Pi_f[t])$ fulfilling all assumed conditions, the error of a variable $[\![\Pi_f[t] \mid Err(var_f)]\!]$ has at most the arithmetic weight stored in the corresponding error weight variable, i.e., var_w, $[\![\Pi_f[t] \mid Err(var_f)]\!] \leq [\![\Pi_w(\Pi_f[t]) \mid var_w]\!]$.*

Proof. Every execution trace π_f starts with the same vertex $\pi_f[0] = v_{0_f}$, where no errors could have been injected yet. Therefore, it is correct to assume that all variable's error weight are 0. Suppose all error weights in every program state $\Pi_w(\Pi_f[i])$ with $i < t$ are correct. $\forall i < t.\forall var_f [\![\Pi_f[i] \mid Err(var_f)]\!] \leq [\![\Pi_w(\Pi_f[i]) \mid var_w]\!]$. We can show that after any further step with $\pi_f[t+1] = v_f$, the variable modified by $\lambda_f(v_f)$ has an error weight $[\![\Pi_f[t+1] \mid Err(var_f)]\!] \leq [\![\Pi_w(\Pi_f[t+1]) \mid var_w]\!]$: The statement $\lambda_f(v_f)$ can be either an arithmetic statement, an control-flow directive or an error injection. Theorem 1 proves that this property is fulfilled for every statement $\lambda_f(v_f) \in S_{arith}$. In contrast to that, control-flow directives do not modify the error weights directly. As long as the execution follows the same path through the program $\forall t \Pi_f[t] = w(\Pi_f[t])$, the control-flow directives will not influence any error weights. Finally, given Definition 15 defines that all for all E_v it holds that $W(\|[\Pi_f[0] \mid E_v]\|) = [\![\Pi_w(\Pi_f[0]) \mid W_v]\!]$. This guarantees that $[\![\Pi_f[t+1] \mid Err(var_f)]\!] \leq [\![\Pi_w(\Pi_f[t+1]) \mid var_w]\!]$.

This shows, that the weight of the error on all variables remains smaller or equal the value of the corresponding weight variables.

Theorem 3 (Transformation of Checks). *Every passed $\texttt{check}(var_f)$ either implies a violation of the assertion $\texttt{assert}(var_w < d_{min})$ or that $Err(var_f) = 0$.*

Proof. There are three cases for the execution of every check:

1. $0 < W(|Err(var_f)|) < d_{min}$: In this case, the check is not passed and the execution is aborted. No further error masking can occur.
2. $W(|Err(var_f)|) \geq d_{min}$: If the error weight exceeds the minimum arithmetic distance, Theorem 2 proves that $var_w \geq W(|Err(var_f)|)$, and the assertion $\texttt{assert}(var_w < d_{min})$ is violated.
3. $W(|Err(var_f)|) = 0$: The only remaining case is the error free case, which can be assumed, once the robustness assertion has been passed.

Theorem 4. *Given a program P_w containing loops, where all error weights are injected in the first iteration, and a program P'_w abstracting the same program P, with all error weight injections distributed over all infinite loop iterations, it is always true that if P_w is correct, then P'_w also is correct.*

Proof. The value of an error weight counter in a program state $\Pi_w[t]$ can be represented as the sum of multiple error weight injections. $[\![\Pi_w[t] \mid var_w]\!] = \sum_{j=0}^{\infty} k_v[j] W_v[j]$, where the factor k_v indicates the number of times the injected error weight has accumulated in an error weight counter, and $W_v[j]$ is the error weight injected in loop iteration j. In the case of P_w, $W_v[0] = W_v$ and $\forall j > 0 : W_v[j] = 0$, while all $W_v[j]$ of P'_w are smaller or equal those of P_w. Furthermore, $\forall j > 0 : k_v[0] = 0 \lor k_v[0] > k_v[j]$, therefore, the only way that $[\![\Pi_w[t] \mid var_w]\!] < [\![\Pi'_w[t] \mid var_w]\!]$ can be achieved is, if var_w is overwritten after injecting $W_v[0]$ ($k_v[0] = 0$), and j is the current loop iteration. However, in the next loop iteration, this error weight will be overwritten again ($k_v[j] = 0$). The maximum value during the first loop iteration will never be exceeded.

Theorem 5 (Correctness of P_w). *If P_w is correct, P_f is correct and P is robust against error masking.*

Proof. Assume P_f is incorrect. Let $\Pi_f[k]$ be the last execution state of a program run violating the correctness of P_f, and var_{ret} be the returned value. A program run Π_f can violate the correctness condition in two ways: (1) The return value is a faulted code word $[\![\Pi_f[k] \mid var_{ret}]\!] \neq [\![\Pi_f^0[k] \mid var_{ret}]\!]$, with its error weight undetectable $[\![\Pi_f[k] \mid W(|Err(var_{ret})|)]\!] \geq d_{min}$, or (2), an invalid path through the program is taken. In case (1), Theorem 2 provides a proof, that $[\![\Pi_f[k], Err(var_{ret})]\!] > d_{min} \rightarrow [\![\Pi_w(\Pi_f[k]) \mid var_{wret}]\!] > d_{min}$. Therefore, at least the last assertion in P_w is violated and P_w is incorrect. Case (2) can only be caused, if the execution of a statement of the form $\texttt{if } (cond) \texttt{ goto } v_{1_f} \texttt{ else goto } v_{2_f}$ continues with the wrong branch. An appropriate branch protection mechanism will abort execution as long as it detects any fault in either the compared operands or in the comparison result. This leaves the remaining situations where (2) is possible, as those, where a fault on the comparison operands contains a masked error. However, Theorem 2 proves that the assertions in P_w detect this case as well, and therefore P_w is incorrect in this case too. This shows, that any violation of P_f will always result in a violation of P_w, and if P_w is correct, that implies that P_f is robust.

Theorem 6 (Decidability). *The correctness of every error counting program* P_w *is decidable, even in the case of an extended version with recursive function calls.*

Every possible value range of the error counting variables is limited by the constant d_{min}. After all modifications of all error counting variables, the model checker evaluates the correctness assertions and returns a counterexample in the case of a violation. Therefore, in every program P_w no variable value ever exceeds $2 \cdot (d_{min} - 1)$. The domain of all variables is finite. Therefore, the resulting programs are effectively Boolean programs and the problem is reducible to solving a Boolean program. According to Ball and Rajamani [2], Boolean programs are equivalent to push-down automatons and therefore decidable [8].

7 Evaluation

The former sections described our method to verify the error masking robustness of encoded programs. Using this technique, we were able to identify real error masking vulnerabilities of real world, security relevant algorithms. Our set of algorithms under verification contains (among others) the following algorithms, which we want to describe in further detail: (1) Fibonacci Number Generator, (2) Euclidean Algorithm, (3) Extended Euclidean Algorithm, (4) Square & Multiply Exponentiation Algorithm and (5) Exponentiation in $\mathbb{Z}_n$. All of these iterative algorithms can be expressed in our toy language, with multiplication, division and modulo replaced by repeated addition and all function calls inlined. For further details on the algorithms, we refer to [19].

In our experiments, we used algorithms in the form of C source code, compiled them to LLVM bitcode, and generated the weight counting programs using a tool based on the LLVM compiler framework. Afterwards, we evaluated both a checkless version and a version containing correctly placed checks using the model checker CPAChecker [6]. Table 1 shows the verification time given different fault specifications. As configuration, we choose an iterative bounded model checking approach, where the loop bound is incremented if no error was found up to a limit of 5 loop iterations. This allowed us to calculate the exact loop bound where error masking occurs for the given specification. If the result is still unsound after a bounded model checking with an unroll bound of 5, we run a predicate analysis [5] algorithm to conclude the evaluation. Table 1 shows the verification time of the first algorithm with a sound result, on a machine with up to 16 threads running in parallel.

Table 1 shows that the complexity of the evaluation depends less on the number of injected bit flips, but more on the number of loop iterations necessary until error masking occurs, as well as the complexity (number and depth of nested loops) of P. Especially in the case of the last fault specification, d_{min} was greater than three times the maximum injectable error weight. In practise such a ratio and therefore this problem is quite unlikely, because a high d_{min} is costly (more redundant bits are necessary) and will not be chosen as protection against the injection of a way smaller number of bit flips.

Table 1. Verification times for different fault specifications.

d_{min}	FaultSpec	Program	Without checks			With correct checks	
			Ver. time	Iter.	Robust?	Ver. time	Robust?
2	$\sum W_i^v \leq 1$	(1) Fibonacci	1 s	2	✗	1 s	✓
		(2) Euclid	1 s	–	✓	–	–
		(3) Extended Euclid	8 s	2	✗	241 s	✓
		(4) Square & Multiply	16 s	2	✗	152 s	✓
		(5) Exp in $\mathbb{Z}_n$	53 s	2	✗	43 s	✓
20	$\sum W_i^v \leq 10$	(1) Fibonacci	1 s	2	✗	1 s	✓
		(2) Euclid	1 s	–	✓	–	–
		(3) Extended Euclid	11 s	2	✗	271 s	✓
		(4) Square & Multiply	11 s	2	✗	159 s	✓
		(5) Exp in $\mathbb{Z}_n$	48 s	2	✗	43 s	✓
300	$\sum W_i^v \leq 100$	(1) Fibonacci	1 s	3	✗	1 s	✓
		(2) Euclid	1 s	–	✓	–	–
		(3) Extended Euclid	70 s	3	✗	1497 s	✓
		(4) Square & Multiply	161 s	3	✗	547 s	✓
		(5) Exp in $\mathbb{Z}_n$	t/o 1800 s	?	?	28 s	✓
40	$\sum W_i^v \leq 10$	(1) Fibonacci	2 s	4	✗	1 s	✓
		(2) Euclid	1 s	–	✓	–	–
		(3) Extended Euclid	1528 s	4	✗	t/o (1800 s)	?
		(4) Square & Multiply	1043 s	3	✗	561 s	✓
		(5) Exp in $\mathbb{Z}_n$	t/o 1800 s	?	?	28 s	✓

Table 2. Comparison of evaluated programs.

Program	# Checks P	# Instr. P	# W_i^v in $P_{weights}$	# Instr. $P_{weights}$
(1) Fibonacci	1	70	12	219
(2) Euclid	0	68	11	186
(3) Extended Euclid	5	162	61	943
(4) Square & Multiply	2	136	51	765
(5) Exp in $\mathbb{Z}_n$	2	211	78	1126

Therefore, more iterations were necessary to detect error masking and the verification task was more difficult. More details about the programs under test can be found in Table 2.

As the results show, the complexity of the verification depends less on the number of injected bit flips, than on the complexity of the programs. The high number of bit flips is possible through abstracting the concrete variable values away and comes with advantages and drawbacks alike. The next section further discusses these challenges and gives ideas for future work.

8   Discussion and Future Work

Our technique to prove the absence of error masking brings along advantages but also holds potential for future work. Most important is the fact, that we evaluate abstraction of the original program. There are two main drawbacks of this: (1) Not every error with an arithmetic weight $\geq d_{min}$ automatically allows to form a new valid code word, this also depends on the actual encoded data. (2) Due to the discarded branch conditions, we might report spurious errors on infeasible paths through the program.

Nevertheless, there are important reasons and advantages of this decision: First, the abstraction gives us independence of the program argument's values. Therefore the search space for variable values is way smaller. Second, by storing the weights instead of the exact errors, the model checker does not need to calculate any arithmetic weight. This significantly reduces the complexity of the verification problem. Furthermore, the abstraction of the branch condition reduces the length of the path conditions and the algorithm *Predicate Analysis* solves the tasks independently of loop iterations. All these advantages help to decrease the verification effort.

However, this method just builds one step towards complete verification of robustness against injected faults. Both, the language and the fault model can be further extended. Including pointers and support for other encoding schemes (e.g. linear codes) may introduce new challenges and poses an interesting problem for the future.

9   Conclusion

In this article, we presented a novel method to verify the robustness against error masking of arithmetically encoded programs. This property guarantees that all faults according to the predefined fault model are detectable. The described technique applies formal methods to either prove the absence of error masking or calculate a counterexample. We provided a proof for the correctness of our approach and evaluated it using the model checker CPAChecker. Finally, a demonstration based on a real-world example multiplication algorithm shows the feasibility of our method.

References

1. Ali, S., Mukhopadhyay, D., Tunstall, M.: Differential fault analysis of AES: towards reaching its limits. J. Cryptogr. Eng. **3**, 73–97 (2013). https://doi.org/10.1007/s13389-012-0046-y
2. Ball, T., Rajamani, S.K.: Bebop: a symbolic model checker for boolean programs. In: Havelund, K., Penix, J., Visser, W. (eds.) SPIN 2000. LNCS, vol. 1885, pp. 113–130. Springer, Heidelberg (2000). https://doi.org/10.1007/10722468_7
3. Bar-El, H., Choukri, H., Naccache, D., Tunstall, M., Whelan, C.: The sorcerer's apprentice guide to fault attacks. Proc. IEEE **94**, 370–382 (2006). https://doi.org/10.1109/JPROC.2005.862424

4. Baumann, R.C.: Radiation-induced soft errors in advanced semiconductor technologies. IEEE Trans. Device Mater. Reliab. **5**(3), 305–316 (2005)
5. Beyer, D., Dangl, M., Wendler, P.: A unifying view on SMT-based software verification. J. Autom. Reason. **60**(3), 299–335 (2018)
6. Beyer, D., Keremoglu, M.E.: CPACHECKER: a tool for configurable software verification. In: Gopalakrishnan, G., Qadeer, S. (eds.) CAV 2011. LNCS, vol. 6806, pp. 184–190. Springer, Heidelberg (2011). https://doi.org/10.1007/978-3-642-22110-1_16
7. Boneh, D., DeMillo, R.A., Lipton, R.J.: On the importance of eliminating errors in cryptographic computations. J. Cryptol. **14**, 101–119 (2001). https://doi.org/10.1007/s001450010016
8. Bouajjani, A., Esparza, J., Maler, O.: Reachability analysis of pushdown automata: application to model-checking. In: Mazurkiewicz, A., Winkowski, J. (eds.) CONCUR 1997. LNCS, vol. 1243, pp. 135–150. Springer, Heidelberg (1997). https://doi.org/10.1007/3-540-63141-0_10
9. Brown, D.T.: Error detecting and correcting binary codes for arithmetic operations. IRE Trans. Electron. Comput. **9**, 333–337 (1960). https://doi.org/10.1109/TEC.1960.5219855
10. Diamond, J.M.: Checking codes for digital computers. Proc. IRE **43**(4), 483–490 (1955). https://doi.org/10.1109/JRPROC.1955.277858
11. Fetzer, C., Schiffel, U., Süßkraut, M.: AN-encoding compiler: building safety-critical systems with commodity hardware. In: Buth, B., Rabe, G., Seyfarth, T. (eds.) SAFECOMP 2009. LNCS, vol. 5775, pp. 283–296. Springer, Heidelberg (2009). https://doi.org/10.1007/978-3-642-04468-7_23
12. Given-Wilson, T., Heuser, A., Jafri, N., Lanet, J.L., Legay, A.: An automated and scalable formal process for detecting fault injection vulnerabilities in binaries (2017). https://hal.inria.fr/hal-01629135, working paper or preprint
13. Golay, M.: Notes on digital coding. Proc. IRE **37**(6), 657–657 (1949). https://doi.org/10.1109/JRPROC.1949.233620
14. Hamming, R.W.: Error detecting and error correcting codes. Bell Labs Tech. J. **29**(2), 147–160 (1950)
15. Kim, Y., et al.: Flipping bits in memory without accessing them: an experimental study of DRAM disturbance errors. In: International Symposium on Computer Architecture – ISCA 2014, pp. 361–372 (2014)
16. Larsson, D., Hähnle, R.: Symbolic fault injection. In: Beckert, B. (ed.) Proceedings of 4th International Verification Workshop in connection with CADE-21. CEUR Workshop Proceedings, Bremen, Germany, 15–16 July 2007, vol. 259. CEUR-WS.org (2007). http://ceur-ws.org/Vol-259/paper09.pdf
17. Massey, J.L.: Survey of residue coding for arithmetic errors. Int. Comput. Cent. Bull. **3**(4), 3–17 (1964)
18. Medwed, M., Schmidt, J.-M.: Coding schemes for arithmetic and logic operations - how robust are they? In: Youm, H.Y., Yung, M. (eds.) WISA 2009. LNCS, vol. 5932, pp. 51–65. Springer, Heidelberg (2009). https://doi.org/10.1007/978-3-642-10838-9_5
19. Menezes, A., van Oorschot, P.C., Vanstone, S.A.: Handbook of Applied Cryptography. CRC Press, Boca Raton (1996)
20. Meola, M.L., Walker, D.: Faulty logic: reasoning about fault tolerant programs. In: Gordon, A.D. (ed.) ESOP 2010. LNCS, vol. 6012, pp. 468–487. Springer, Heidelberg (2010). https://doi.org/10.1007/978-3-642-11957-6_25

21. Pattabiraman, K., Nakka, N., Kalbarczyk, Z.T., Iyer, R.K.: SymPLFIED: symbolic program-level fault injection and error detection framework. IEEE Trans. Comput. **62**(11), 2292–2307 (2013). https://doi.org/10.1109/TC.2012.219
22. Peterson, W.W.: Error-Correcting Codes. MIT Press, Cambridge (1961)
23. Rao, T.R.N.: Biresidue error-correcting codes for computer arithmetic. IEEE Trans. Comput. **19**(5), 398–402 (1970)
24. Rao, T.R.N., Garcia, O.N.: Cyclic and multiresidue codes for arithmetic operations. IEEE Trans. Inf. Theory **17**(1), 85–91 (1971)
25. Rink, N.A., Castrillón, J.: Extending a compiler backend for complete memory error detection. In: Dencker, P., Klenk, H., Keller, H.B., Plödereder, E. (eds.) Automotive - Safety and Security 2017 - Sicherheit und Zuverlässigkeit für automobile Informations technik. LNI, Stuttgart, Germany, 30–31 Mai 2017, vol. P-269, pp. 61–74. Gesellschaft für Informatik, Bonn (2017). https://dl.gi.de/20.500.12116/147
26. Schiffel, U.: Hardware error detection using AN-codes. Ph.D. thesis, Dresden University of Technology (2011). http://nbn-resolving.de/urn:nbn:de:bsz:14-qucosa-69872
27. Schiffel, U.: Safety transformations: sound and complete? In: Bitsch, F., Guiochet, J., Kaâniche, M. (eds.) SAFECOMP 2013. LNCS, vol. 8153, pp. 190–201. Springer, Heidelberg (2013). https://doi.org/10.1007/978-3-642-40793-2_18
28. Schilling, R., Werner, M., Mangard, S.: Securing conditional branches in the presence of fault attacks. In: Design, Automation and Test in Europe Conference and Exhibition – DATE 2018, pp. 1586–1591 (2018)
29. Selmke, B., Brummer, S., Heyszl, J., Sigl, G.: Precise laser fault injections into 90 nm and 45 nm SRAM-cells. In: Homma, N., Medwed, M. (eds.) CARDIS 2015. LNCS, vol. 9514, pp. 193–205. Springer, Cham (2016). https://doi.org/10.1007/978-3-319-31271-2_12
30. Sharma, V.C., Haran, A., Rakamaric, Z., Gopalakrishnan, G.: Towards formal approaches to system resilience. In: IEEE 19th Pacific Rim International Symposium on Dependable Computing, PRDC 2013, Vancouver, BC, Canada, 2–4 December 2013, pp. 41–50. IEEE Computer Society (2013). https://doi.org/10.1109/PRDC.2013.14
31. Walker, D., Mackey, L.W., Ligatti, J., Reis, G.A., August, D.I.: Static typing for a faulty lambda calculus. In: Reppy, J.H., Lawall, J.L. (eds.) Proceedings of the 11th ACM SIGPLAN International Conference on Functional Programming, ICFP 2006, Portland, Oregon, USA, 16–21 September 2006, pp. 38–49. ACM (2006). https://doi.org/10.1145/1159803.1159809
32. Werner, M., Unterluggauer, T., Schaffenrath, D., Mangard, S.: Sponge-based control-flow protection for IoT devices. CoRR abs/1802.06691 (2018). http://arxiv.org/abs/1802.06691

Relatively Complete Pushdown Analysis of Escape Continuations

Kimball Germane[1(✉)] and Matthew Might[2]

[1] Brigham Young University, Provo, USA
kimball@cs.byu.edu
[2] University of Alabama, Birmingham, USA

Abstract. Escape continuations are weaker than full, first-class continuations but nevertheless can express many common control operators. Although language and compiler designs profitably leverage escape continuations, all previous approaches to analyze them statically in a higher-order setting have been ad hoc or imprecise. We present MCCFA2, a generalization of CFA2 that analyzes them with pushdown precision in their most-general form. In particular, the summarization algorithm of MCCFA2 is both sound and complete with respect to a conservative extension of CFA2's abstract semantics. We also present an *continuation age* analysis as a client of MCCFA2 that reveals critical function call optimizations.

1 Introduction

Continuations are a powerful tool in the hands of programmers, whether handled as a naked reference provided by `call/cc` or through the veneer of the exceptional `raise`, the logical `fail`, the cooperative `yield`, or the primitive `longjmp`.[1] On the other side of the language, compiler writers unify their implementations of these and other control constructs by expressing them directly via continuations [1,2,9]. While this unification has the effect of simplifying the compiler, it also amplifies the effect the compiler's power to reason about continuations has on the quality of the code it generates. Here, static analysis tools that provide maximal insight into a program's continuation use become critical.

CFA2 [19] was the first abstract interpretation of higher-order programs to model the continuation with a pushdown automaton, allowing it to precisely match calls and returns. Compared to that of finite-state models as in k-CFA [13,15], this choice of model greatly increased the precision with which continuation use could be reasoned, but at the cost of the ability to reason about any non-trivial continuation use—including any of the control constructs mentioned above. Vardoulakis and Shivers [21] extend CFA2 to soundly reason about `call/cc` but their technique sacrifices completeness w.r.t. the abstract semantics (a point we discuss further in Sect. 8.4). Vardoulakis and Shivers [21] also

---

[1] Of course, even `return` calls the current continuation, but we consider such uses essentially trivial.

© Springer Nature Switzerland AG 2019
C. Enea and R. Piskac (Eds.): VMCAI 2019, LNCS 11388, pp. 205–225, 2019.
https://doi.org/10.1007/978-3-030-11245-5_10

propose two ad-hoc extensions to CFA2 to reason about exceptions. Integrating either of these proposals unduly complicates the summarization algorithm. In contrast, our approach subsumes and generalizes these proposals and yields a simpler and more coherent summarization algorithm relative to CFA2. We discuss the details of our relationship to these proposals in Sect. 11.

Although `call/cc` is a highly-expressive control construct, the power of the first-class continuations it furnishes isn't always necessary: many uses of continuations require only second-class *escape continuations*, of which `raise`, `fail`, `longjmp`, and others are thinly-masked expressions. This paper presents MCCFA2, an alternative extension to CFA2 that can reason about escape continuations both soundly and completely w.r.t. the abstract semantics and in a general, principled way.

MCCFA2 extends each of CFA2's three stages: the core language and concrete semantics, the abstract semantics, and the summarization algorithm.

1. CFA2 operates over a CPS λ-calculus statically restricted to preclude any non-trivial continuation behavior (let alone `call/cc`). We conservatively extend [4] this language to allow function calls to provide and procedures to receive and bind multiple continuations. This capability allows the language to express escape continuations generally but so regulates their lifetimes that they can be allocated on the stack [20]. To underscore this fact, our concrete semantics allocates continuations on a stack rather than a heap.
2. CFA2's abstract semantics is sound but not complete w.r.t. its concrete semantics. We extend CFA2's abstract semantics to accommodate multiple continuations. This extended abstract semantics is sound w.r.t. the extended concrete and, again, conservatively extends CFA2's. That is, MCCFA2's abstract semantics of a program in CFA2's core language are exactly as precise as CFA2's. The primary distinction between the two abstract semantics is that MCCFA2's walks the stack at each call to find the return point whereas CFA2's can determine the return point by the syntactic form of the continuation at the call site.
3. CFA2's summarization algorithm is both sound and complete w.r.t. its abstract semantics. Similarly, MCCFA2's summarization algorithm is both sound and complete w.r.t. *its* abstract semantics. To accommodate multiple continuations, MCCFA2's algorithm unifies and generalizes CFA2's by treating every continuation call as a potential escape: continuation calls that represent local returns are immediately identified as such, while those that represent non-local returns (escapes) are discovered as the algorithm walks the abstract stack.

In summary, MCCFA2 offers sound and relatively complete account of escape continuations in a general, higher-order setting. Additionally, MCCFA2 can be combined with Vardoulakis and Shivers' extension to handle first-class control which yields an analysis that forfeits precision only when continuations are used in a genuinely first-class way (Sect. 8.4).

In the next section, we discuss the MCCFA2 extension in more depth. We then establish notation (Sect. 3) and proceed to formally introduce MCPS

(Sect. 4) and its concrete (Sect. 5) and abstract (Sect. 6) semantics, connected by a sound abstraction (Sect. 7). We then present summarization (Sect. 8), by way of an algorithm (Sect. 8.2) and its correctness (Sect. 8.5). We then walk through an example MCPS program analysis (Sect. 9). Finally, we sketch how to integrate Vardoulakis and Shivers' technique to handle first-class control into MCCFA2 (Sect. 8.4) and compare MCCFA2 to other proposals to handle exceptions, as well as other related work (Sect. 11).

2   Overview

In this section, we overview MCCFA2 and discuss some significant aspects of its design.

2.1   Core Language

CFA2 considers programs to have originated in some direct-style source language before CPS conversion into its core language. Accordingly, CFA2 operates over a CPS λ-calculus partitioned into *user-world* and *continuation-world* terms [20,21]. User-world terms are those that have a direct correspondent in the source program whereas continuation-world terms are those introduced directly by the CPS transform. For instance, for a continuation reference k, the CPS term $(f\,x\,k)$ is a user-world call as it directly corresponds to the call $(f\,x)$ in the source program, whereas the CPS term $(k\,x)$ is a continuation-world call as it was synthesized from the tail-position appearance of the reference x in the source program. This static partition allows CFA2 to distinguish source-level uses of the continuation from regular function calls and thereby model such uses more precisely. CFA2's core language includes the additional restriction that continuation references may not appear free under a user-world λ-term, making it impossible to encode any control construct that interacts non-trivially with its context, let alone call/cc.

CFA2 is able to so precisely model the continuation behavior of the programs in its core language in part because its core language is statically limited to offer no interesting continuation behavior. MCCFA2 extends the CFA2's core language of the CPS λ-calculus to the *multiple continuation-passing style* (MCPS) λ-calculus in which function calls can provide and procedures can receive and bind multiple continuations. This ability allows the MCPS λ-calculus (or simply MCPS) to express escape continuations generally. MCPS retains the restriction that continuation references may not appear free under a user-world λ-term, which precludes it from encoding call/cc.

MCPS is a conservative extension [4] of single CPS that can be found in several continuation-aware compilers. For instance, MCPS limited to two continuations—"double-barreled" CPS—has been used frequently to encode exceptions and other control constructs [2,9–11,17]. MCPS is also the intermediate language of the multi-return λ-calculus (MRLC) [16] (which we revisit in Sect. 9).

The static restriction of MCPS on where continuation references may occur regulates continuation lifetimes to strictly follow a stack discipline. Thus, MCPS offers compiler writers an efficient implementation of continuations allocated on the run-time stack [7,20]. We underscore this fact by stack-allocating continuations in MCCFA2's concrete semantics (Sect. 5), deviating from CFA2's concrete semantics which heap-allocates them.

2.2   Summarization Algorithm

As it runs, CFA2's summarization algorithm records summaries of the form $(entry, exit)$ which expresses that the entry state $entry$ reaches the corresponding $exit$ state. In the presence of multiple continuations, this form of summary doesn't adequately capture the flow of $entry$ and $exit$ as $exit$ applies one of the multiple continuations that may be in scope at $entry$. To accommodate this fact, the summarization algorithm of MCCFA2 uses summaries of the form $(entry, exit, n)$ which include the index of the continuation (w.r.t. $entry$) called in $exit$.

In CFA2's core language, proper and tail calls in the source program are syntactically distinguished by the form of continuation: a user-world call which constructs a continuation (via a continuation-world λ-term) is a proper call whereas a user-world call which references the continuation is a tail call. CFA2's summarization algorithm exploits this knowledge by separately tracking proper callers and tail callers. When a procedure calls its continuation (i.e. *returns* in the source program), the tail callers are used to extend summaries and the proper callers are used as return points. In the presence of multiple continuations, proper and tail calls cannot in general be distinguished at the time of the call since, for the purposes of extending summaries or offering return points, the type of call is not known until the continuation is called. To accommodate this fact, the summarization algorithm of MCCFA2 (1) does not separately track proper and tail calls and (2) treats every continuation call as a potential escape. Accordingly, each continuation call instigates a phase of the algorithm which walks the abstract stack in search of return points, extending summaries as it goes.

Altogether, these changes simplify and generalize the summarization algorithm of CFA2.

3   Notation

We leverage metavariables heavily and try to be extremely careful in their use. For an arbitrary metavariable x, a bolded metavariable $\boldsymbol{x}$ represents a vector of x and a bolded, superscripted metavariable $\boldsymbol{x}^+$ represents a non-empty vector of x. The quantity $\pi_i(\boldsymbol{x})$ is the ith element of $\boldsymbol{x}$ indexed from 1. Vectors will sometimes be treated as sets and functions will sometimes be lifted over vectors. For a multi-argument function of vectors and scalars, the scalars are lifted appropriately as well. For example, $f(\boldsymbol{x}, y) = \langle f(x_1, y), \ldots, f(x_n, y) \rangle$ for $\boldsymbol{x} = \langle x_1, \ldots, x_n \rangle$. The empty vector is denoted $\langle\rangle$. We often use head–tail notation both to construct and deconstruct vectors, writing $\langle x_1, x_2, \ldots, x_n\rangle$ as $x_1 :: \langle x_2, \ldots, x_n\rangle$.

Throughout the paper, a definition's left side is a pattern which deconstructs and binds subvalues of the value of the expression on its right.

4   Partitioned CPS λ-Calculus

We view MCPS programs as being obtained by a CPS transformation of a direct-style source program. Hence, we maintain a distinction between user-world and continuation-world terms where a user-world term directly corresponds to a term in the source program and a continuation-world term is introduced by the CPS transformation. Both worlds contain λ terms, calls, and variable references. A user-world λ term *ulam* has a user parameter vector $\boldsymbol{u}$, a non-empty continuation parameter vector $\boldsymbol{k}$, and a call *call*. Given *lam* or *call*, the continuation parameter function CP retrieves the vector $\boldsymbol{k}$ of the innermost-enclosing *ulam* of *lam* or *call* (where a *ulam* encloses itself for this definition). A user-world call *ucall* has a user operator expression f, an argument expression vector $\boldsymbol{e}$, and a non-empty continuation expression vector $\boldsymbol{q}$. The continuation argument function LC retrieves the vector $\boldsymbol{q}$ of a given *ucall* or the surrounding $\boldsymbol{q}$ of a given *clam*. A user-world variable u will be bound only to user-world values. A continuation-world λ term *clam* has a user parameter vector $\boldsymbol{u}$ and a call *call*. A continuation-world call *ccall* has a continuation operator expression q and an argument expression vector $\boldsymbol{e}$. A continuation-world variable k will be bound only to continuations (Fig. 1).

All λ terms and calls are labelled uniquely in a given program to distinguish otherwise identical terms. We will sometimes identify a term with its label but the meaning should be clear from context.

Programs are closed *ulam*s with a single continuation parameter and continuation variables may not appear free within a *ulam* term.

$$pr \in Pr = \{ulam : ulam \in ULam, ulam \text{ is closed and } |CP(ulam)| = 1\}$$

$\gamma \in Lab$	= a set of labels	$call \in Call$	$= UCall + CCall$
$u \in UVar$	= a set of identifiers	$ucall \in UCall$	$::= (f\,\boldsymbol{e}\,\boldsymbol{q}^{+})_\gamma$
$k \in CVar$	= a set of identifiers	$ccall \in CCall$	$::= (q\,\boldsymbol{e})_\gamma$
$lam \in Lam$	$= ULam + CLam$	$e, f \in UExp$	$= UVar + ULam$
$ulam \in ULam$	$::= (\lambda_\gamma\,(\boldsymbol{u}\,\boldsymbol{k}^{+})\,call)$	$q \in CExp$	$= CVar + CLam$
$clam \in CLam$	$::= (\lambda_\gamma\,(\boldsymbol{u})\,call)$		

Fig. 1. Partitioned CPS λ-calculus syntax

5   Concrete Semantics

We start by defining an abstract machine to evaluate MCPS programs which will serve as the ground truth of evaluation. Like many real-world runtimes, this machine uses a stack to house both local environments and return-point information. (A stack is not necessary however; an MCPS machine that heap-allocates continuations works as well.) A value environment serves as a heap and all values are heap-allocated.

$$\varsigma \in State = Eval + Apply$$
$$\mathrm{E} \in Eval = Call \times BEnv \times CEnv \times Stack \times VEnv \times Time$$
$$Apply = UApply + CApply$$
$$\mathrm{UA} \in UApply = Proc \times \boldsymbol{D} \times \boldsymbol{Cont}^+ \times Stack \times VEnv \times Time$$
$$\mathrm{CA} \in CApply = CodeP \times \boldsymbol{D} \times Stack \times VEnv \times Time$$

$$\beta_u \in BEnv = UVar \rightharpoonup Time \qquad \beta_k \in CEnv = CVar \rightharpoonup Cont$$
$$d \in D = Proc \qquad st \in Stack = \boldsymbol{Frame}$$
$$proc \in Proc = Clos \qquad fr \in Frame = BEnv \times CEnv$$
$$Clos = ULam \times BEnv \qquad c \in Cont = CodeP \times FrameP$$
$$ve \in VEnv = UVar \times Time \rightharpoonup D \qquad cp \in CodeP = CLam + \{halt\}$$
$$t \in Time = \text{a countably-infinite set} \qquad fp \in FrameP = \mathbb{N}$$

Fig. 2. Concrete state space

Figure 2 presents the concrete state space *State* of this machine. Each state in *State* has a stack *st*, a value environment *ve* serving as the heap, and a timestamp *t*. *State* is partitioned into two domains, *Eval* and *Apply*. An *Eval* state focuses on a call *call* in the context of a user environment β_u and continuation environment β_k. *Apply* is further partitioned into the user domain *UApply* and continuation domain *CApply*. A *UApply* state holds a procedure *proc* ready to apply to an argument vector $\boldsymbol{d}$ and non-empty continuation vector $\boldsymbol{c}$. A *CApply* state, on the other hand, holds a code pointer *cp* and result vector $\boldsymbol{d}$. We also make finer distinctions between states: an *Eval* state with a user call is a *UEval* state, denoted UE; a *Eval* state with a continuation call with a *CVar* operator is a *CEvalExit* state, denoted CEE, and a *CLam* operator is a *CEvalInner* state, denoted CEI.

Figure 3 presents the concrete machine's evaluation relation $\rightarrow$ as the union of four relations. The side conditions of each relation are divided so that user-world conditions are on the left and continuation-world on the right. (An overarching, implicit side condition is that, when a function is lifted over two different vectors, those vectors must have the same length.) The concrete machine evaluates programs by alternating between two modes: evaluating operators/arguments and applying an evaluated operator to its arguments, corresponding precisely to *Eval* and *Apply* states.

UEval

$$((f\, e\, q^+)_\gamma, \beta_u, \beta_k, st, ve, t) \to_{UE} (proc, d, c, st', ve, t'), \text{ where}$$

$$
\begin{aligned}
proc &= \mathcal{A}_u(f, \beta_u, ve), & st' &= pop(c, (\beta_u, \beta_k) :: st), \text{ and} \\
d &= \mathcal{A}_u(e, \beta_u, ve), & c &= \mathcal{A}_k(q, \beta_k, st) \\
t' &= tick(t),
\end{aligned}
$$

CEval

$$((q\, e)_\gamma, \beta_u, \beta_k, st, ve, t) \to_{CE} (cp, d, st', ve, t'), \text{ where}$$

$$
\begin{aligned}
d &= \mathcal{A}_u(e, \beta_u, ve), & st' &= pop(\langle c \rangle, (\beta_u, \beta_k) :: st), \text{ and} \\
t' &= tick(t), & (cp, fp) &= c = \mathcal{A}_k(q, \beta_k, st)
\end{aligned}
$$

UApply

$$(proc, d, c, st, ve, t) \to_{UA} (call, \beta'_u, \beta_k, st, ve', t'), \text{ where}$$

$$
\begin{aligned}
((\lambda_\gamma\, (u\, k^+)\, call), \beta_u) &= proc, \\
\beta'_u &= \beta_u[u \mapsto t'], & \beta_k &= [k \mapsto c] \\
ve' &= ve[(u, t') \mapsto d], \\
t' &= tick(t), \text{ and}
\end{aligned}
$$

CApply

$$((\lambda_\gamma\, (u)\, call), d, (\beta_u, \beta_k) :: st, ve, t) \to_{CA} (call, \beta'_u, \beta_k, st, ve', t'), \text{ where}$$

$$
\begin{aligned}
\beta'_u &= \beta_u[u \mapsto t'], \\
ve' &= ve[(u, t') \mapsto d], \text{ and} \\
t' &= tick(t)
\end{aligned}
$$

Argument Evaluation

$$
\begin{aligned}
\mathcal{A}_u(u, \beta_u, ve) &= ve(u, \beta_u(u)) & \mathcal{A}_k(k, \beta_k, st) &= \beta_k(k) \\
\mathcal{A}_u(ulam, \beta_u, ve) &= (ulam, \beta_u) & \mathcal{A}_k(clam, \beta_k, st) &= (clam, |st| + 1)
\end{aligned}
$$

pop Metafunction

$$pop(c, st) = st|_{\max(height(c))} \text{ where } height(cp, fp) = fp$$

Program Injection

$$\mathcal{I}(pr, d) = ((pr, \bot), d, \langle(halt, 0)\rangle, \langle\rangle, \bot, t_0)$$

Fig. 3. The concrete semantics

For *Eval* states, the metafunction $\mathcal{A}_u$ evaluates atomic user–world expressions, dereferencing variables and constructing closures. Likewise, $\mathcal{A}_k$ evaluates continuation expressions, dereferencing variables and constructing code–frame pointer pairs. As part of each call—user or continuation—the evaluated continuations are used to determine the youngest live frame on the stack. If a call doesn't reference some continuations in scope, the frames unique to them become dead. The *pop* metafunction discards all such frames that reside at the top of the stack as part of the transition (where the notation $st|_{fp}$ indicates the oldest fp frames of st). Hence, arbitrarily many frames may be popped when a call is made. This stack management policy follows Might and Shivers' generalization [14] of the stack management policy of the Orbit compiler [1].

Apply states precipitate the procedure entry or re-entry, depending on whether a user procedure or continuation is applied. Application of a user procedure *proc* extends its environment β_u with bindings for the arguments and the heap *ve* with their values, as well as constructing a continuation environment β_k. New user bindings use the timestamp t' to ensure freshness; in this work, this is the sole use of timestamps. Continuation application entails popping the stack to c's frame pointer fp, jumping to c's code pointer cp, and extending the local environment β_u with bindings and the heap *ve* with the result values.

A program *pr* and its arguments $\boldsymbol{d}$ are injected into a *UApply* state with a single *halt* continuation pointing to the base of the stack, empty stack, empty value environment, and epoch time.

6   Abstract Semantics

The next stage of MCCFA2 is the definition of an abstract semantics. The abstract state space $\widehat{State}$, seen in Fig. 4, is partitioned identically to *State*. However, abstract states themselves and their components differ nontrivially from their concrete counterparts. Following CFA2, abstract states lack timestamps,

$$\hat{\varsigma} \in \widehat{State} = \widehat{Eval} + \widehat{Apply}$$

$$\hat{E} \in \widehat{Eval} = Call \times \widehat{Stack} \times Heap$$

$$\widehat{Apply} = \widehat{UApply} + \widehat{CApply}$$

$$\hat{\mathsf{UA}} \in \widehat{UApply} = \widehat{Proc} \times \widehat{\boldsymbol{D}} \times \widehat{\boldsymbol{CExp}}^+ \times \widehat{Stack} \times Heap$$

$$\hat{\mathsf{CA}} \in \widehat{CApply} = CodeP \times \widehat{\boldsymbol{D}} \times \widehat{Stack} \times Heap$$

$$\widehat{proc} \in \widehat{Proc} = \widehat{Clos}$$

$$\hat{d} \in \widehat{D} = \mathcal{P}(\widehat{Proc})$$

$$\widehat{Clos} = ULam$$

$$h \in Heap = UVar \rightharpoonup \widehat{D}$$

$$\hat{st} \in \widehat{Stack} = \widehat{Frame}$$

$$\widehat{Frame} = SyntaxMap$$

$$sm \in SyntaxMap = CVar \rightharpoonup \widehat{CExp}$$

$$\hat{q} \in \widehat{CExp} = CExp + \{halt\}$$

Fig. 4. Abstract state space

$\widetilde{UEval}$

$$((f\,e\,q^+)_\gamma, \widehat{st}, h) \rightsquigarrow_{UE} (ulam, \hat{d}, \hat{q}, \widehat{st}', h), \text{ where}$$

$$ulam \in \hat{\mathcal{A}}(f, h), \qquad\qquad (\hat{q}, \widehat{st}') = \widehat{pop}(q, \widehat{st})$$
$$\hat{d} = \hat{\mathcal{A}}(e, h), \text{ and}$$

$\widetilde{CEval}$

$$((q\,e)_\gamma, \widehat{st}, h) \rightsquigarrow_{CE} (cp, \hat{d}, \widehat{st}', h), \text{ where}$$

$$\hat{d} = \hat{\mathcal{A}}(e, h) \text{ and} \qquad\qquad (\langle cp \rangle, \widehat{st}') = \widehat{pop}(\langle q \rangle, \widehat{st})$$

$\widetilde{UApply}$

$$((\lambda_\gamma\,(u\,k^+)\,call), \hat{d}, \hat{q}, \widehat{st}, h) \rightsquigarrow_{UA} (call, \widehat{st}', h'), \text{ where}$$

$$h' = h \sqcup [u \mapsto \hat{d}] \text{ and} \qquad\qquad \widehat{st}' = [k \mapsto \hat{q}] :: \widehat{st}$$

$\widetilde{CApply}$

$$((\lambda_\gamma\,(u)\,call), \hat{d}, \widehat{st}, h) \rightsquigarrow_{CA} (call, \widehat{st}, h'), \text{ where}$$

$$h' = h \sqcup [u \mapsto \hat{d}]$$

Argument Evaluation

$$\hat{\mathcal{A}}(ulam, h) = \{ulam\} \qquad\qquad \hat{\mathcal{A}}(u, h) = h(u)$$

$\widehat{pop}$ **Metafunction**

$$\widehat{pop}(k, sm :: \widehat{st}') = \widehat{pop}(sm(k), \widehat{st}')$$
$$\widehat{pop}(\hat{q}, \widehat{st}) = (\hat{q}, \widehat{st}) \text{ if } \pi_i(\hat{q}) \in CodeP \text{ for some } i$$

Program Injection

$$\hat{\mathcal{I}}(pr, \hat{d}) = (pr, \hat{d}, \langle halt \rangle, \langle \rangle, \bot)$$

Fig. 5. The abstract semantics

an abstract denotable $\hat{d}$ is a superposition of procedures $\widehat{proc}$; and closures no longer include an environment.[2]

MCCFA2 summarization crucially relies on a non-standard abstraction for continuation environments: the *syntax map*. A syntax map is a finite mapping from continuation variables to continuation expression syntax, i.e., the syntax of the continuation arguments in a call expression. Each stack frame houses a syntax map and a stack of these frames comprises the program's control linkage information. The particular maintenance of this stack, which we describe shortly, allows us to omit frame pointers from continuations—they consist of merely a code pointer.

---

[2] Deviating from CFA2, we omit environments from stack frames as well. This is only to simplify the presentation; they can be reintroduced without difficulty.

We define the abstract semantics as a union of the four relations defined in Fig. 5. Once again, user-world conditions are sequestered to the left column and continuation-world to the right. Because multiple procedure values may be in superposition as a call's operator, the target procedure is chosen nondeterministically. Just as in the concrete semantics, the stack is popped at both user and continuation calls according to the generalized Orbit policy. However, the mechanism by which this policy is upheld is significantly different.

When a user call is made, the $\widehat{pop}$ metafunction uses the call's continuation expressions q and the stack $\widehat{st}$ to determine the dead frames (if any) to pop from the stack. If there is some $clam$ within q, then the caller frame is live (since a nested call may return to it) and no dead frames can be popped. On the other hand, if $q = k$ for some k, the call is a tail call and at least one dead frame (the caller's) can be popped. Thus, each step of $\widehat{pop}$ determines whether the top frame of the provided stack is dead and, if so, pops it. It may be that such a step results in some syntax vector k' which indicates that the newly-revealed top frame is dead also, a situation that occurs when a call doesn't reference the only continuations on which multiple frames atop the stack depend. For this reason, $\widehat{pop}$ is recursive and can pop arbitrarily-many frames in a given transition.

The $\widehat{pop}$ metafunction is used to implement continuation calls as well. When used in this way, the continuation operator q is provided to $\widehat{pop}$ along with the stack. If $q \in CLam$, the call represents a $\mathtt{let}$-continuation, a local binding construct in the source program. In this case, $\widehat{pop}$ correctly determines that the top frame is live and preserves the stack. If $q \in CVar$, the call represents a return to some continuation in scope. In this case, the recursive definition of $\widehat{pop}$ effects the popping of the stack and discovery of the return point.

The $\widehat{\mathcal{I}}$ metafunction injects a program and abstract argument vector into an initial machine state.

7   Abstraction

With machines for both the concrete and abstract semantics defined, we need to ensure that the abstract semantics *simulates* the concrete semantics. To obtain this assurance, we first need to establish a correspondence between their state spaces and introduce a notion of precision into the abstract state space. Figure 6 presents this correspondence via the concrete–abstract abstraction map $|\cdot|_{ca}$ and the abstraction refinement relation $\sqsubseteq$.

The bulk of $|\cdot|_{ca}$ is contained in the mutually-inductive metafunctions *reconstruct* and *reconstruct** which reconstruct an abstract stack and continuations from a concrete stack and continuations. If the stack st given to *reconstruct** is empty, the given argument vector c must be **halt** and the result is its abstraction **halt** paired with the empty stack. Otherwise, the code pointer $clam$ of the *height*-maximum continuation c is determined and the continuation argument syntax vector q in which it's found is paired with the *reconstruct*ion of the continuation parameter vector k of its enclosing λ-term and the rest of the stack. The *reconstruct* metafunction uses *reconstruct** to reconstruct all but the top

Abstraction

$$|((ulam, \beta_u), \boldsymbol{d}, \boldsymbol{c}, st, ve, t)|_{ca} = (ulam, |\boldsymbol{d}|_{ca}, \hat{\boldsymbol{q}}, \widehat{st}, |ve|_{ca}) \text{ where } (\hat{\boldsymbol{q}}, \widehat{st}) = reconstruct^*(\boldsymbol{c}, st)$$

$$|(cp, \boldsymbol{d}, st, ve, t)|_{ca} = (cp, |\boldsymbol{d}|_{ca}, \widehat{st}, |ve|_{ca}) \text{ where } (\langle cp \rangle, \widehat{st}) = reconstruct^*(\langle\langle cp, |st| \rangle\rangle, st)$$

$$|(call, \beta_u, \beta_k, st, ve, t)|_{ca} = (call, \widehat{st}, |ve|_{ca}) \text{ where } \widehat{st} = reconstruct(CP(call), \beta_k, st)$$

$$|(ulam, \beta_u)|_{ca} := \{ulam\}$$

$$|(cp, fp)|_{ca} := cp$$

$$|ve|_{ca} := \{(u, \bigsqcup_t |ve(u, t)|_{ca})\}$$

Stack Reconstruction

$$reconstruct^*(\boldsymbol{c}, st) = \begin{cases} (|\boldsymbol{c}|_{ca}, \langle\rangle) \text{ if } st = \langle\rangle \\ (\boldsymbol{q}, reconstruct(\boldsymbol{k}, \beta_k, st')) \text{ if } st = (\beta_u, \beta_k) :: st' \end{cases}$$

where $\boldsymbol{k} = CP(clam)$ and $\boldsymbol{q} = LC(clam)$ for $(clam, fp) = \text{argmax}(height(\boldsymbol{c}))$

$$reconstruct(\boldsymbol{k}, \beta_k, st) = sm :: \widehat{st} \text{ where } sm = [\boldsymbol{k} \mapsto \hat{\boldsymbol{q}}] \text{ and } (\hat{\boldsymbol{q}}, \widehat{st}) = reconstruct^*(\beta_k(\boldsymbol{k}), st)$$

Refinement

$$(ulam, \hat{\boldsymbol{d}}_1, \hat{\boldsymbol{q}}, \widehat{st}, h_1) \sqsubseteq (ulam, \hat{\boldsymbol{d}}_2, \hat{\boldsymbol{q}}, \widehat{st}, h_2) \text{ iff } \hat{\boldsymbol{d}}_1 \sqsubseteq \hat{\boldsymbol{d}}_2 \text{ and } h_1 \sqsubseteq h_2$$

$$(cp, \hat{\boldsymbol{d}}_1, \widehat{st}, h_1) \sqsubseteq (cp, \hat{\boldsymbol{d}}_2, \widehat{st}, h_2) \text{ iff } \hat{\boldsymbol{d}}_1 \sqsubseteq \hat{\boldsymbol{d}}_2 \text{ and } h_1 \sqsubseteq h_2$$

$$(call, \widehat{st}, h_1) \sqsubseteq (call, \widehat{st}, h_2) \text{ iff } h_1 \sqsubseteq h_2$$

$$\langle \hat{\boldsymbol{d}}_{1,1}, \ldots, \hat{\boldsymbol{d}}_{1,n} \rangle \sqsubseteq \langle \hat{\boldsymbol{d}}_{2,1}, \ldots, \hat{\boldsymbol{d}}_{2,n} \rangle \text{ iff } \hat{\boldsymbol{d}}_{1,i} \sqsubseteq \hat{\boldsymbol{d}}_{2,i} \text{ for } i = 1, \ldots, n$$

$$\hat{\boldsymbol{d}}_1 \sqsubseteq \hat{\boldsymbol{d}}_2 \text{ iff } \hat{\boldsymbol{d}}_1 \subseteq \hat{\boldsymbol{d}}_2$$

Fig. 6. Abstraction map and refinement relation

frame of the stack. It uses the given continuation parameter vector $\boldsymbol{k}$ and the resultant continuation argument syntax vector $\hat{\boldsymbol{q}}$ to build the top frame.

The abstraction refinement relation $\sqsubseteq$ is standard.

Theorem 1 (Simulation).
If $\varsigma \rightarrow \varsigma'$ and $|\varsigma|_{ca} \sqsubseteq \hat{\varsigma}$, then there exists $\hat{\varsigma}'$ such that $\hat{\varsigma} \rightsquigarrow \hat{\varsigma}'$ and $|\varsigma'|_{ca} \sqsubseteq \hat{\varsigma}'$.

The soundness of the *Eval–Apply* transitions are non-trivial as they must establish that equivalent frames are popped from the stack in the transitions. To establish it, we use the following lemma.

Lemma 1. *Suppose $|\text{UE}|_{ca} \sqsubseteq \hat{\text{UE}}$ where $\text{UE} = ((f \, e \, q^+)_\gamma, \beta_u, \beta_k, st, ve, t)$. If $\boldsymbol{k} = CP(\gamma)$, $\mathcal{A}_k(\boldsymbol{q}, \beta_u, st) = \boldsymbol{c}$, $reconstruct(\boldsymbol{k}, \beta_k, st) = \widehat{st}$, and $pop(\boldsymbol{c}, (\beta_u, \beta_k) :: st) = st'$, then $reconstruct^*(\boldsymbol{c}, st') = \widehat{pop}(\boldsymbol{q}, \widehat{st})$.*

This lemma establishes that *pop* and $\widehat{pop}$ commute with *reconstruct* and *reconstruct*. That is, given a concrete stack st, one can *reconstruct* an abstract stack $\widehat{st}$ and $\widehat{pop}$ it to $\widehat{st}'$ or *pop* it to st' and *reconstruct** to obtain $\widehat{st}'$. This lemma is established by proving that *reconstruct/reconstruct** yield stacks that preserve the behavior of *pop* in $\widehat{pop}$. A proof is given in a technical report [5].

$$\tilde{\varsigma} \in \widetilde{State} = \widetilde{Eval} + \widetilde{Apply}$$

$$\widetilde{Eval} = \widetilde{UEval} + \widetilde{CEval} \qquad\qquad \widetilde{Apply} = \widetilde{UApply} + \widetilde{CApply}$$

$$\tilde{u}_E \in \widetilde{UEval} = UCall \times Heap \qquad \tilde{u}_A \in \widetilde{UApply} = \widetilde{UProc} \times \hat{D}^* \times Heap$$

$$\tilde{c}_E \in \widetilde{CEval} = CCall \times Heap \qquad \tilde{c}_A \in \widetilde{CApply} = \widetilde{CProc} \times \hat{D}^* \times Heap$$

Fig. 7. Local state space

8 Summarization

Because abstract stacks are unbounded, the abstract state space is infinite. Hence, we can't perform abstract interpretation simply by enumerating the states reachable from the program entry state. Instead, we'll perform it using a summarization algorithm similar to that of CFA2.

Summarization algorithms are so-called because they discover and summarize reachability facts between system states. CFA2's summarization algorithm summarizes the fact that *exit* is reachable from *entry* in a stack-respecting way with a pair (*entry*, *exit*). This form of summary is inadequate for MCPS. Instead, we use a summary (*entry*, *exit*, *n*) to record the fact that both *exit* is reachable from *entry* in a stack-respecting way and *exit* is returning to the *n*th continuation of *entry*.

In Sect. 8.5, we show that the summarization algorithm inherently respects the stack. Consequently, the stack component of abstract states is unnecessary and the summarization algorithm operates over the *local semantics*, the stack-free residue of the abstract semantics.

$$((f \, e \, q^+)_\ell, h) \Rrightarrow_{UE} (ulam, \hat{d}, h) \qquad\qquad ((clam \, e), h) \Rrightarrow_{CE} (clam, \hat{d}, h)$$

$$ulam \in \hat{A}(f, h) \qquad\qquad\qquad \hat{d} = \hat{A}(e, h)$$
$$\hat{d} = \hat{A}(e, h)$$

$$((\lambda_\gamma \, (u \, k^+) \, call), \hat{d}, h) \Rrightarrow_{UA} (call, h') \qquad ((\lambda_\gamma \, (u) \, call), \hat{d}, h) \Rrightarrow_{CA} (call, h')$$

$$h' = h \sqcup [u \mapsto \hat{d}] \qquad\qquad\qquad h' = h \sqcup [u \mapsto \hat{d}]$$

Fig. 8. The local semantics

8.1 Local Semantics

The local semantics describes segments of evaluation that don't require the return-point information of the stack. Figure 7 contains the local state space, which is simply the abstract state space with stacks excised. Accordingly, the local abstraction map $|\cdot|_{al}$ merely performs the excision:

$Summary, Call, Final = \emptyset$
$Seen, Work = \{(\tilde{\mathcal{I}}(pr, \hat{d}), \tilde{\mathcal{I}}(pr, \hat{d}))\}$

while $Work \neq \emptyset$:
  remove $(\tilde{\text{UA}}, \tilde{\varsigma})$ from $Work$
  switch $\tilde{\varsigma}$:
    case $\tilde{\text{UA}}, \tilde{\text{CA}}, \tilde{\text{CEI}}$:
      for $\tilde{\varsigma}' \in succ(\tilde{\varsigma})$:
        Propagate$(\tilde{\varsigma}, \tilde{\varsigma}')$
    case $\tilde{\text{UE}}$:
      for $\tilde{\varsigma}' \in succ(\tilde{\varsigma})$:
        Propagate$(\tilde{\varsigma}', \tilde{\varsigma}')$
        insert $(\tilde{\text{UA}}, \tilde{\varsigma}, \tilde{\varsigma}')$ into $Call$
        for $(\tilde{\varsigma}', \tilde{\text{CEE}}, n) \in Summary$:
          Link$(\tilde{\text{UA}}, \tilde{\varsigma}, \tilde{\varsigma}', \tilde{\text{CEE}}, n)$
    case $\tilde{\text{CEE}}$:
      Return$(\tilde{\text{UA}}, \tilde{\varsigma}, CP(\tilde{\text{UA}}, CV(\tilde{\text{CEE}})))$

Propagate$(\tilde{\text{UA}}, \tilde{\varsigma})$:=
  if $(\tilde{\text{UA}}, \tilde{\varsigma}) \notin Seen$:
    insert $(\tilde{\text{UA}}, \tilde{\varsigma})$ into $Seen$
    insert $(\tilde{\text{UA}}, \tilde{\varsigma})$ into $Work$

Return$(\tilde{\text{UA}}, \tilde{\text{CEE}}, n)$:=
  if $(\tilde{\text{UA}}, \tilde{\text{CEE}}, n) \notin Summary$:
    insert $(\tilde{\text{UA}}, \tilde{\text{CEE}}, n)$ into $Summary$
  if $\tilde{\text{UA}} = \tilde{\mathcal{I}}(pr, \hat{d})$:
    Final$(\tilde{\text{CEE}})$
  for $(\tilde{\text{UA}}^*, \tilde{\text{UE}}, \tilde{\text{UA}}) \in Call$:
    Link$(\tilde{\text{UA}}^*, \tilde{\text{UE}}, \tilde{\text{UA}}, \tilde{\text{CEE}}, n)$

Link$(\tilde{\text{UA}}, \tilde{\text{UE}}, \tilde{\text{UA}}^*, \tilde{\text{CEE}}, n)$:=
  switch $CA(\tilde{\text{UE}}, n)$:
    case k:
      Return$(\tilde{\text{UA}}, \tilde{\text{CEE}}, CP(\tilde{\text{UA}}, k))$
    case $clam$:
      Update$(\tilde{\text{UA}}, clam, \tilde{\text{CEE}},,$
)

Update$(\tilde{\text{UA}}, clam, \tilde{\text{CEE}}, , :=)$
  $\tilde{\text{CEE}}$ of form $((k\, e), h)$
  $\hat{d} = \mathcal{A}_u(e, h)$
  Propagate$(\tilde{\text{UA}}, (clam, \hat{d}, h))$

Final$(\tilde{\varsigma})$:=
  $\tilde{\varsigma}$ of form $((k\, e), h)$
  insert $(halt, \mathcal{A}_u(e, h), h)$ into $Final$

Fig. 9. The summarization algorithm

$$|(ulam, \hat{d}, \hat{q}, \widehat{st}, h)|_{al} = (ulam, \hat{d}, h)$$

$$|(clam, \hat{d}, \widehat{st}, h)|_{al} = (clam, \hat{d}, h)$$

$$|(call, \widehat{st}, h)|_{al} = (call, h)$$

We define the local semantics as the union of four relations over local states, seen in Fig. 8. This semantics is similar to the abstract semantics except that it is not defined over continuation calls that exit the procedure, which requires the return-point information of the stack. The summarization algorithm is tasked with linking exits to their return points.

The *local successors* $succ(\tilde{\varsigma})$ of a state $\tilde{\varsigma}$ is defined $succ(\tilde{\varsigma}) = \{\tilde{\varsigma}' : \tilde{\varsigma} \approx \tilde{\varsigma}'\}$.

8.2 Summarization Algorithm

Figure 9 presents the summarization algorithm. The product of running the algorithm is three relations: the ternary relations *Summary* and *Call*, and the unary relation *Final*. A summary $(\tilde{\text{UA}}, \tilde{\text{CEE}}, n) \in Summary$ records the fact that $\tilde{\text{CEE}}$ exits the procedure entered by $\tilde{\text{UA}}$ through its nth continuation (by position). A call edge $(\tilde{\text{UA}}_0, \tilde{\text{UE}}, \tilde{\text{UA}}) \in Call$ records the fact that, in the invocation $\tilde{\text{UA}}_0$ heads, the call $\tilde{\text{UE}}$ yields the entry $\tilde{\text{UA}}$. A state $\tilde{\text{UA}} \in Final$ is simply a terminal state of evaluation.

We define the summarization algorithm imperatively and based on a workset, after the style of CFA2's. The workset consists of pairs of states of form $(\tilde{u}_{A}, \tilde{\varsigma})$ where $\tilde{u}_{A}$ is entry state of the procedure invocation containing $\tilde{\varsigma}$. The workset is initialized with $\tilde{\mathcal{I}}(pr, \hat{d})$ paired with itself (where $\tilde{\mathcal{I}}(pr, \hat{d}) = |\hat{\mathcal{I}}(pr, \hat{d})|_{al}$).

When $\tilde{\varsigma}$ has local successors (as determined by $\widetilde{succ}$), these are Propagated to the workset. When $\tilde{\varsigma} \in \widetilde{UEval}$, its successors are $\widetilde{UApply}$ states which are their own corresponding entries. Thus, each successor $\tilde{\varsigma}'$ is Propagated with itself and the call is recorded in $Call$. Each summary that begins with $\tilde{\varsigma}'$ is Linked with the caller. Link searches for the return point of a call by looking at the continuation expression at the position the summary exited. If that continuation expression is some k, Return searches deeper in the stack with that continuation position mapped through the formal parameters. If that continuation expression is some $clam$, Update synthesizes the return point and Propagates it.

Finally, when $\tilde{\varsigma} \in \widetilde{CEvalExit}$, its continuation position with respect to $\tilde{u}_{A}$ is determined by CP and passed to Return. If the entry–exit–position triple is already recorded in $Summary$, the path is sure to be explored and the search is cut off. Otherwise, the triple is recorded in $Summary$. If $\tilde{u}_{A}$ is the program entry state, then $\tilde{\varsigma}$ is a program exit state and Final uses it to synthesize a state to record in $Final$. The last step of Return Links every caller of $\tilde{u}_{A}$ with the triple.

8.3   Comparison with CFA2

The MCCFA2 summarization algorithm simplifies and generalizes that of CFA2.

To simplify, MCCFA2's algorithm builds a single $Call$ relation where CFA2 builds the $Callers$ relation for proper callers and $TCallers$ relation for tail callers. Our consolidation of these relations was due to expediency: with multiple continuations, one can't in general determine whether a call's particular continuation will be invoked at the point of the call and hence the type of call cannot be known a priori. However, the result is a more uniform treatment of calls which is both simpler and more general.

MCCFA2's algorithm also operates over a more general language than CFA2's—the MCPS λ-calculus. The presence of multiple continuations means the return point of a call is no longer guaranteed to be at the top of the stack. To reflect this, MCCFA2's algorithm essentially has two phases: the first drives the workset loop and explores the state space; the second is activated when a procedure exits and the stack is walked to find the return point.

8.4   Integrating First-Class Control

Vardoulakis and Shivers [21] extend CFA2 to handle call/cc by allowing free continuation references in operator position. The similarly-extended summarization algorithm keeps track of two additional unary relations: $EntriesEsc$ contains entry states of procedures that bind escaping continuations (that is, continuations with free references) and $Escapes$ contains exit states in which escaped continuations are applied. When the algorithm encounters an entry state over a procedure *ulam* that binds an escaping continuation k, that state is added to *EntriesEsc* and linked (by summary) to any *Escapes* states that apply k. On the other end, when it encounters an exit state that applies an escaped continuation bound to k, that state is added to *Escapes* and linked to any *EntriesEsc* states that bind k.

Because the non-local linking it performs ignores path realizability, the extended summarization algorithm is incomplete with respect to the CFA2's abstract semantics. Thus, summarization introduces spurious paths for even morally second-class uses of `call/cc`, such as exceptions. The present work has demonstrated that such uses can be treated completely with respect to the abstract semantics. Furthermore, we can integrate this extension into MCCFA2 and pay-as-we-go for analysis of bonafide first-class control but enjoy complete analysis otherwise.

To integrate this technique, we also keep track of *EntriesEsc* and *Escapes*. We add an entry state to *EntriesEsc* when any of the continuations it binds escape and link it to *Escapes* states that invoke any escaped continuation under those bound names. We add an exit state to *Escapes* when it applies an escaped continuation and link it to *EntriesEsc* states that bind the continuation's name. We include the binding continuation of the escaped continuation in the synthesized link to let `Return` propagate the control transfer.

In Sect. 11, we consider specific extensions to CFA2 and how this work subsumes or enhances them.

8.5   Summarization Correctness

Our summarization algorithm is sound and complete with respect to the abstract semantics. Before we formally define those properties, we need to introduce some auxiliary definitions.

A *path* p is a sequence of abstract states $\hat{\varsigma}_0, \hat{\varsigma}_1, \ldots, \hat{\varsigma}_n$ where $\hat{\varsigma}_0 \rightsquigarrow \hat{\varsigma}_1 \rightsquigarrow \ldots \rightsquigarrow \hat{\varsigma}_n$. We denote by $p_0 \rightsquigarrow p_1$ the concatenation of paths p_0 and p_1. The smallest reflexive relation over $\widehat{State}$ is denoted by $\rightsquigarrow^0$, the transitive closure of $\rightsquigarrow$ by $\rightsquigarrow^+$, and the reflexive, transitive closure of $\rightsquigarrow$ by $\rightsquigarrow^*$.

To extract the continuation variable from $\hat{\text{CE}} = ((k\,e)_\gamma, \widehat{st}, h)$, let $CV(\hat{\text{CE}}) = k$. To determine the continuation position of a continuation from the operator of $\hat{\text{UA}} = ((\lambda_\gamma\,(u\,k^+)\,call), \hat{d}, \hat{q}, \widehat{st}, h)$, let $CP(\hat{\text{UA}}, k) = i$ where $\pi_i(k) = k$. Finally, to extract the ith continuation argument (by position) from $\hat{\text{UE}} = ((f\,e\,q^+)_\gamma, \widehat{st}, h)$, let $CA(\hat{\text{UE}}, i) = \pi_i(q)$.

The *corresponding entry* of an abstract state is the entry state of the invocation of which it's a part.

Definition 1 (Corresponding Entry). *Let* $CE_p(\hat{\varsigma})$ *denote the* corresponding entry *of a state* $\hat{\varsigma}$ *in path* p. *For path* $p \equiv \hat{\text{UA}} \rightsquigarrow^* \hat{\varsigma}$, $CE_p(\hat{\varsigma}) = \hat{\text{UA}}$ *if:*

1. $p \equiv \hat{\text{UA}} \rightsquigarrow^0 \hat{\varsigma}$;
2. $p \equiv \hat{\text{UA}} \rightsquigarrow^* \hat{\varsigma}' \rightsquigarrow \hat{\varsigma}$, $\hat{\text{UA}} = CE_p(\hat{\varsigma}')$, $\hat{\varsigma}' \notin \widehat{UEval}$, *and* $\hat{\varsigma}' \notin \widehat{CEvalExit}$; *or*

3. $p \equiv \hat{\textsc{ua}} \leadsto^+ \hat{\textsc{ue}} \leadsto \hat{\textsc{ua}}' \leadsto^+ \hat{\textsc{cee}} \leadsto \hat{\varsigma}$, $\hat{\textsc{ua}} = CE_p(\hat{\textsc{ue}})$, $CA(\hat{\textsc{ue}}, n) \in CLam$, and $\hat{\textsc{ua}}' \equiv_p \hat{\textsc{cee}}$ by n.

For a path $p \equiv \hat{\textsc{ua}} \leadsto^+ \hat{\textsc{cee}}$, we say $\hat{\textsc{ua}} \equiv_p \hat{\textsc{cee}}$ by n if:

1. $\hat{\textsc{ua}} = CE_p(\hat{\textsc{cee}})$ and $CP(\hat{\textsc{ua}}, CV(\hat{\textsc{cee}})) = n$; or
2. $p \equiv \hat{\textsc{ua}} \leadsto^+ \hat{\textsc{ue}} \leadsto \hat{\textsc{ua}}' \leadsto^+ \hat{\textsc{cee}}$, $\hat{\textsc{ua}} = CE_p(\hat{\textsc{ue}})$, $\hat{\textsc{ua}}' \equiv_p \hat{\textsc{cee}}$ by n', $CA(\hat{\textsc{ue}}, n') = k$, and $CP(\hat{\textsc{ua}}, k) = n$.

The first case of CE_p says that, in path p, a procedure entry state $\hat{\textsc{ua}}$ is its own corresponding entry. The second says that the corresponding entry is preserved across an intraprocedural transition. The third says that a return state $\hat{\textsc{ca}}$ has the corresponding entry of a user call state $\hat{\textsc{ue}}$ if its nth continuation argument is some *clam* and that $\hat{\textsc{ua}}' \equiv_p \hat{\textsc{cee}}$ by n holds for the intervening path $\hat{\textsc{ua}}' \leadsto^+ \hat{\textsc{cee}}$. Two states with the same corresponding entry are part of the same abstract procedure invocation.

The ternary "same-level" relation $\cdot \equiv_p \cdot$ by $\cdot$ captures the fact that an exit state $\hat{\textsc{cee}}$ returns through a sequence of tail calls through $\hat{\textsc{ua}}$'s nth continuation. The base case relates an entry state $\hat{\textsc{ua}}$ and an exit state $\hat{\textsc{cee}}$ in the same invocation that returns through the nth continuation of $\hat{\textsc{ua}}$. The inductive case assumes that $\hat{\textsc{cee}}$ returns through the n'th continuation of $\hat{\textsc{ua}}'$ and, if the n'th continuation of its caller $\hat{\textsc{ue}}$ is a reference, extends it by $\hat{\textsc{ue}}$'s corresponding entry $\hat{\textsc{ua}}$ and the position n of the referenced continuation with respect to $\hat{\textsc{ua}}$.

Summarization Soundness. Soundness is the property that any abstract path p initiated by $\hat{\mathcal{I}}(pr, \hat{d})$ is contained in the results of summarization. Formally, we have the following:

Theorem 2 (Soundness).
After summarization,

1. *if* $p \equiv \hat{\mathcal{I}}(pr, \hat{d}) \leadsto^* \hat{\textsc{ua}} \leadsto^+ \hat{\textsc{cee}}$ *such that* $\hat{\textsc{ua}} \equiv_p \hat{\textsc{cee}}$ *by* n, *then* $(|\hat{\textsc{ua}}|_{al}, |\hat{\textsc{cee}}|_{al}, n) \in Summary$; *and*
2. *if* $p \equiv \hat{\mathcal{I}}(pr, \hat{d}) \leadsto^* \hat{\textsc{ua}} \leadsto^+ \hat{\textsc{ue}} \leadsto \hat{\textsc{ua}}'$ *such that* $\hat{\textsc{ua}} = CE_p(\hat{\textsc{ue}})$, $(|\hat{\textsc{ua}}|_{al}, |\hat{\textsc{ue}}|_{al}, |\hat{\textsc{ua}}'|_{al}) \in Call$;
3. *if* $p \equiv \hat{\mathcal{I}}(pr, \hat{d}) \leadsto^+ \hat{\varsigma}$ *such that* $\hat{\varsigma}$ *is a final state, then* $|\hat{\varsigma}|_{al} \in Final$.

The proof of this theorem is the same as that of CFA2 modulo our definitions of corresponding entry and "same-level" states (and our omission of local environments from stack frames). The key step is ensuring that each called continuation is properly identified on the stack. In CFA2, where only a single continuation is possible, the continuation resides at the penultimate stack frame. In MCCFA2, the continuation could reside arbitrarily-deep in the stack. We address this possibility by connecting the path structure induced by corresponding entries and "same-level" states to stack behavior. The proof appears in a technical report [5].

Summarization Completeness. Completeness is the property that only abstract paths p initiated by $\hat{\mathcal{I}}(pr, \hat{d})$ are contained in the results of summarization. Formally, we have the following:

Theorem 3 (Completeness).
After summarization,

1. *if* $(\tilde{\mathrm{UA}}, \tilde{\mathrm{CEE}}, n) \in Summary$ *then there exists* $p \equiv \hat{\mathcal{I}}(pr, \hat{d}) \rightsquigarrow^* \hat{\mathrm{UA}} \rightsquigarrow^+ \hat{\mathrm{CEE}}$ *such that* $\tilde{\mathrm{UA}} = |\hat{\mathrm{UA}}|_{al}$, $\tilde{\mathrm{CEE}} = |\hat{\mathrm{CEE}}|_{al}$, *and* $\hat{\mathrm{UA}} \equiv_p \hat{\mathrm{CEE}}$ *by* n; *and*
2. *if* $(\tilde{\mathrm{UA}}, \tilde{\mathrm{UE}}, \tilde{\mathrm{UA}}') \in Call$, *then there exists* $p \equiv \hat{\mathcal{I}}(pr, \hat{d}) \rightsquigarrow^* \hat{\mathrm{UA}} \rightsquigarrow^+ \hat{\mathrm{UE}} \rightsquigarrow \hat{\mathrm{UA}}'$ *such that* $\tilde{\mathrm{UA}} = |\hat{\mathrm{UA}}|_{al}$, $\tilde{\mathrm{UE}} = |\hat{\mathrm{UE}}|_{al}$, $\tilde{\mathrm{UA}}' = |\hat{\mathrm{UA}}'|_{al}$, *and* $\hat{\mathrm{UA}} = CE_p(\hat{\mathrm{UE}})$;
3. *if* $\tilde{\varsigma} \in Final$, *then there exists* $p \equiv \hat{\mathcal{I}}(pr, \hat{d}) \rightsquigarrow^+ \hat{\varsigma}$ *such that* $\tilde{\varsigma} = |\hat{\varsigma}|_{al}$ *and* $\hat{\varsigma}$ *is a final state.*

The proof of this theorem strongly resembles the corresponding proof for CFA2 except for the use of summaries to extend paths; it appears in a technical report [5].

A CFA2-produced summary $(entry, exit)$ records not only that $exit$ is reachable from $entry$ but also such that the intervening evaluation perfectly balances proper calls and returns. The path segments represented by these summaries exhibit the property of *stack irrelevance*, that is, that the evaluation of these path segments is not influenced by nor influences the stack of the $entry$ state. This property allows abstract paths to be synthesized by replacing irrelevant suffixes of the stack.

When multiple continuations are present, user and continuation calls can pop arbitrary portions of the stack, even below the stack of the $entry$ state. Hence, a summary $(entry, exit, n)$ subject to the same call–return balance restriction does not enjoy this property. However, such paths can be *normalized*, removing irrelevant suffixes of each constituent invocation, so that summaries can be employed in the same way. This ability is critical to demonstrating completeness, one of our technical contributions.

9   Multi-return λ-Calculus

Shivers and Fisher [16] introduce the multi-return λ-calculus (MRLC) as an extension of a direct-style λ-calculus in which return points become an explicit (though second-class) language construct. With this mechanism, MRLC essentially provides user-level access to multiple escape continuations without the severe notational overhead of CPS. This access makes MRLC adept at expressing programs from particular control-heavy domains such as LR parsing, backtracking search, and functional tree transformations [20]. MRLC is designed to translate into MCPS so our analysis framework is keenly poised to handle these domains as well.

Shivers and Fisher illustrate the utility of MRLC with a parsimonious `filter` program which employs multiple return points to reuse as much of the input list as possible. We consider MCCFA2 applied to the MCPS transformation of this program:

```
(λ0 (? ws k0)
  (define1 (recur xs k1 k2)
    (case xs k1
          (λ3 (y ys)
             (? y (λ5 (t)
                     (if t
                       (λ7 () (recur ys k1 (λ9 (zs) (cons y zs k2)10))8)
                       (λ11 () (recur ys (λ13 () (k2 ys)14) k2)12))6))4))2)
    (recur ws (λ16 () (k0 ws)17) k0)15)
```

The primitive case procedure performs case analysis on its first argument, deconstructs it, and invokes one of its continuations on the subparts. To exercise the full behavior of this program, we apply it to $\langle$<havoc>, $\top_{list}\rangle$ where <havoc> is an arbitrary primitive predicate.

The table in Fig. 10 presents the destination and content of each analysis fact MCCFA2 discovers, in a possible order of discovery. Each call is a triple consisting of the calling procedure entry, the call site, and the called procedure entry. Primitive procedures have opaque representations of the form <name>. Each summary is a triple consisting of a procedure entry, procedure exit, and continuation index. A procedure exit is merely the exit site with the result values implicit. Primitive procedure exit sites are not represented in the program so we denote them with a pair ($<name>$, n) of primitive identifier and continuation index, The final state is simply the program result value.

1	CALL	$(\lambda_0, call_{15}, \lambda_1)$	11	SUMMARY	$(<if>,(<if>,1),1)$
2	CALL	$(\lambda_1, call_2, <case>)$	12	CALL	$(\lambda_1, call_8, \lambda_1)$
3	SUMMARY	$(<case>,(<case>,1),1)$	13	SUMMARY	$(<if>,(<if>,2),2)$
4	SUMMARY	$(\lambda_1,(<case>,1),1)$	14	CALL	$(\lambda_1, call_{12}, \lambda_1)$
5	SUMMARY	$(\lambda_0, exit_{17}, 1)$	15	SUMMARY	$(\lambda_1, exit_{14}, 2)$
6	FINAL	$(\top_{list})$	16	CALL	$(\lambda_1, call_{10}, <cons>)$
7	SUMMARY	$(<case>,(<case>,2),2)$	17	SUMMARY	$(\lambda_0, exit_{14}, 2)$
8	CALL	$(\lambda_1, call_4, <?>)$	18	SUMMARY	$(<cons>,(<cons>,1),1)$
9	SUMMARY	$(<?>,(<?>,1),1)$	19	SUMMARY	$(\lambda_1,(<cons>,1),2)$
10	CALL	$(\lambda_1, call_6, <if>)$	20	SUMMARY	$(\lambda_0,(<cons>,1),1)$

Fig. 10. An MCCFA2 analysis

10   Continuation Age Analysis

When a user call is made with multiple continuations, Might and Shivers' generalization of Orbit's stack-management policy [14] dictates that all dead frames are popped from the stack before the target procedure is entered. Dead frames are typically determined dynamically by comparing the frame pointers of the call's continuations (as seen in the *UEval* rule of our concrete semantics) which requires an MCPS-based compiler to emit comparison code at each call site.

Vardoulakis and Shivers [20] introduced *continuation age* analysis which attempts to statically determine the relative ages among each call's continuations. They build their analysis into a pre-existing finite-state k-CFA [15,18] analysis framework. We can perform continuation age analysis directly on the pushdown model MCCFA2 constructs without modifying the MCCFA2 implementation.

For each call site $ucall = (f\, e\, k^+)_\gamma$ where $|k| > 1$, let

$$\phi_0 = \{(\tilde{\mathrm{U}}\mathrm{A}_0, \tilde{\mathrm{U}}\mathrm{E}_0, k) : (\tilde{\mathrm{U}}\mathrm{A}_0, \tilde{\mathrm{U}}\mathrm{E}_0, \tilde{\mathrm{U}}\mathrm{A}) \in Call, \tilde{\mathrm{U}}\mathrm{E}_0 = (ucall, h) \text{ for some } h\}.$$

That is, ϕ_0 is a set of triples where each triple contains a $\widetilde{UEval}$ state focused on $ucall$, its corresponding entry, and its continuation argument vector (comprising only continuation references). Find the fixed point of $f(\phi_0)$ defined as

$$
\begin{aligned}
f(\phi_0)(\phi) = \phi_0 \cup \{(\tilde{\mathrm{U}}\mathrm{A}_0, \tilde{\mathrm{U}}\mathrm{E}_0, q') &: (\tilde{\mathrm{U}}\mathrm{A}, \tilde{\mathrm{U}}\mathrm{E}, q) \in \phi, \\
& q \in CVar^+, \\
& (\tilde{\mathrm{U}}\mathrm{A}_0, \tilde{\mathrm{U}}\mathrm{E}_0, \tilde{\mathrm{U}}\mathrm{A}) \in Call, \\
& k = CP(ulam) \text{ where } \tilde{\mathrm{U}}\mathrm{A} = (ulam, \hat{d}, h) \text{ for some } \hat{d} \text{ and } h, \\
& q_0 = LC(ucall) \text{ where } \tilde{\mathrm{U}}\mathrm{E}_0 = (ucall, h) \text{ for some } h, \\
& q' = [k \mapsto q_0](q)\,\}.
\end{aligned}
$$

The function f considers all triples in its argument ϕ that have a continuation argument vector q consisting solely of continuation references. The callers of each such triple's entry state are used to construct new triples containing that caller, its corresponding entry, and q mapped over $[k \mapsto q_0]$ which permutes the outer caller's continuation vector to match the inner caller's.

By MCCFA2 soundness, this process will accumulate all continuation argument vectors that contain some *clam* that is eventually bound to a reference at the original *ucall*. Given a fixed point ϕ of $f(\phi_0)$, we can consider only the continuation vectors that contain a *clam*. One of the many ways to use the resultant vectors is to map each to the set of indices at which a *clam* is found. Any indices in the intersection of these sets are those of the youngest continuation. If the intersection is empty, the union contains indices that *may* be the youngest. This information may decrease the number of comparisons necessary to determine the youngest at run time.

11   Related Work

There are many instances of pushdown control-flow analysis for higher-order languages [3,6,8,19]. This work is framed around CFA2. In their extension of CFA2 to handle first-class control [21], Vardoulakis and Shivers outline two approaches to extend CFA2 to support exceptions without sacrificing precision:

1. Outlined in [21, Sect. 2.4], they propose to let exit points encapsulate a pair of values, the first representing the result of standard control flow and the second of exceptional control flow. Since procedures don't exit naturally and

exceptionally simultaneously, this pair behaves as a sum with the position of the value providing an additional bit of information. Our approach generalizes this approach in a sense by providing as many bits as the continuation position takes to encode.

2. Outlined in [21, Sect. 5.5], they propose translating the program into 2CPS, using the first continuation for standard control flow and the second for exceptional—the standard "double-barrelled" CPS. In this approach, two distinct summary relations must be maintained by the summarization algorithm "to not confuse exceptional with ordinary control flow". As in the previous approach, the caller syntax is inspected to determine whether it can handle the type of return the summary represents, this time looking for a literal λ term in the appropriate continuation position. Our approach extends this approach in the obvious way, generalizing to arbitrarily many continuations and using indices to distinguish summaries. This generalization is not free, however, as we have made significant modifications to the summarization algorithm and soundness/completeness arguments, in turn.

Pushdown exception-flow analysis has also been applied in the context of object-oriented programs [12]. Like extended CFA2, the treatment is specialized to exceptions and not the multiple continuations in general.

Acknowledgments. This material is partially based on research sponsored by DARPA under agreement number AFRL FA8750-15-2-0092 and by NSF under CAREER grant 1350344. The U.S. Government is authorized to reproduce and distribute reprints for Governmental purposes notwithstanding any copyright notation thereon.

References

1. Adams, N., Kranz, D., Kelsey, R., Rees, J., Hudak, P., Philbin, J.: ORBIT: an optimizing compiler for scheme. In: SIGPLAN 1986. ACM, New York (1986)
2. Appel, A.W.: Compiling with Continuations. Cambridge University Press, Cambridge (2007)
3. Earl, C., Might, M., Van Horn, D.: Pushdown control-flow analysis of higher-order programs. In: Workshop on Scheme and Functional Programming (2010)
4. Felleisen, M.: On the expressive power of programming languages. Sci. Comput. Program. **17**(1), 35–75 (1991)
5. Germane, K., Might, M.: Multi-continuation pushdown analysis. Technical report, January 2019. http://kimball.germane.net/germane-mccfa2-techreport.pdf
6. Gilray, T., Lyde, S., Adams, M.D., Might, M., Van Horn, D.: Pushdown control-flow analysis for free. In: Proceedings of the 43rd Annual ACM Symposium on Principles of Programming Languages. POPL 2016, pp. 691–704. ACM, New York (2016)
7. Hieb, R., Dybvig, R.K., Bruggeman, C.: Representing control in the presence of first-class continuations. In: Proceedings of the ACM SIGPLAN 1990 Conference on Programming Language Design and Implementation. PLDI 1990, pp. 66–77. ACM, New York (1990)

8. Johnson, J.I., Van Horn, D.: Abstracting abstract control. In: Proceedings of the 10th ACM Symposium on Dynamic languages, pp. 11–22. ACM (2014)

9. Kennedy, A.: Compiling with continuations, continued. In: Proceedings of the 12th ACM International Conference on Functional Programming. ICFP 2007, pp. 177–190. ACM, New York (2007)

10. Kim, J., Yi, K., Danvy, O.: Assessing the overhead of ML exceptions by selective CPS transformation, vol. 5, January 1998

11. Ley-Wild, R., Fluet, M., Acar, U.A.: Compiling self-adjusting programs with continuations. In: Proceedings of the 13th ACM International Conference on Functional Programming. ICFP 2008, pp. 321–334. ACM, New York (2008)

12. Liang, S., Sun, W., Might, M., Keep, A., Horn, D.V.: Pruning, pushdown exception-flow analysis. In: Proceedings of the 2014 IEEE 14th International Working Conference on Source Code Analysis and Manipulation, pp. 265–274. IEEE Computer Society (2014)

13. Might, M.: Environment analysis of higher-order languages (2007)

14. Might, M., Shivers, O.: Environment analysis via ΔCFA. In: Conference Record of the 33rd ACM Symposium on Principles of Programming Languages. POPL 2006, pp. 127–140. ACM, New York (2006)

15. Shivers, O.: Control-flow analysis of higher-order languages. Ph.D. thesis. Carnegie Mellon University (1991)

16. Shivers, O., Fisher, D.: Multi-return function call. J. Funct. Program. **16**(4), 547–582 (2006)

17. Thielecke, H.: Comparing control constructs by double-barrelled CPS. Higher-Order Symb. Comput. **15**(2), 141–160 (2002)

18. Van Horn, D., Might, M.: Abstracting abstract machines. In: Proceedings of the 15th ACM International Conference on Functional Programming. ICFP 2010, pp. 51–62. ACM, New York (2010)

19. Vardoulakis, D., Shivers, O.: CFA2: a context-free approach to control-flow analysis. In: Gordon, A.D. (ed.) ESOP 2010. LNCS, vol. 6012, pp. 570–589. Springer, Heidelberg (2010). https://doi.org/10.1007/978-3-642-11957-6_30

20. Vardoulakis, D., Shivers, O.: Ordering multiple continuations on the stack. In: Proceedings of the 20th ACM Workshop on Partial Evaluation and Program Manipulation. PEPM 2011, pp. 13–22. ACM, New York (2011)

21. Vardoulakis, D., Shivers, O.: Pushdown flow analysis of first-class control. In: Proceedings of the 16th ACM International Conference on Functional Programming. ICFP 2011, pp. 69–80. ACM, New York (2011)

Demand Control-Flow Analysis

Kimball Germane[1]([⊠]), Jay McCarthy[2], Michael D. Adams[3],
and Matthew Might[4]

[1] Brigham Young University, Provo, USA
kimball@cs.byu.edu
[2] University of Massachusetts Lowell, Lowell, USA
[3] University of Utah, Salt Lake City, USA
[4] University of Alabama, Birmingham, USA

Abstract. Points-to analysis manifests in a functional setting as
control-flow analysis. Despite the ubiquity of *demand* points-to analyses, there are no analogous demand control-flow analyses for functional
languages in general. We present demand 0CFA, a demand control-flow
analysis that offers clients in a functional setting the same pricing model
that demand points-to analysis clients enjoy in an imperative setting. We
establish demand 0CFA's correctness via an intermediary exact semantics, demand evaluation, that can potentially support demand variants
of more-precise analyses.

1 Introduction

Points-to analysis is a fundamental program analysis over languages that exhibit
imperative or object-oriented features. A particular points-to analyses is specified
as *exhaustive* or *demand*. An exhaustive points-to analysis calculates points-to
facts for *every* variable reference in the program or component. In contrast,
a demand points-to analysis calculates points-to facts for a client-specified set
of variable references. A demand analysis that obtains points-to facts about a
specified set and avoids analysis work that doesn't contribute thereto presents
a pricing model to clients distinct from that of exhaustive analyses. As we discuss in the next section, this pricing model offers advantages to clients such as
compilers and IDEs.

Control-flow analysis (CFA) is the analogue of points-to analysis in languages
that offer first-class functions [12]. Unlike those of points-to analysis, however,
the specifications of essentially all modern CFAs define *exhaustive* analyses that
produce a comprehensive account of control flow for a target program or component. However, a demand CFA would offer clients in the functional setting many
of the same advantages that a demand points-to analysis offers its clients in an
imperative or object-oriented setting. This paper introduces *demand 0CFA*, a
specification of a demand CFA. As a demand analysis, demand 0CFA resolves
the (potentially higher-order) control flows of arbitrary client-specified subexpressions while avoiding analysis work that doesn't pertain to them. Previous demand analyses for functional languages offer limited demand behavior

© Springer Nature Switzerland AG 2019
C. Enea and R. Piskac (Eds.): VMCAI 2019, LNCS 11388, pp. 226–246, 2019.
https://doi.org/10.1007/978-3-030-11245-5_11

in higher-order settings [15] or apply only in limited higher-order settings [8]; in contrast, demand 0CFA offers full demand behavior in a general higher-order setting.

To a first approximation, demand 0CFA is achieved by extending exhaustive 0CFA with another mode of operation. Rather than (abstractly) evaluating every expression to its values as exhaustive 0CFA does, demand 0CFA in one mode evaluates some expressions to their values and in another traces some values to the expressions that take them on. At various points in analysis, the operation of each of these modes is informed by results of the other. To provide context for the additional tracing mode, we review exhaustive 0CFA in Sect. 4 before formally introducing demand 0CFA in Sect. 5; we briefly review the call-by-value λ calculus (their common language) in Sect. 3. We report on an evaluation of the efficiency and precision of demand 0CFA relative to 0CFA in Sect. 6. The connection between demand 0CFA and a ground-truth exact semantics is not as direct as that of exhaustive 0CFA; in Sect. 7, we bridge this connection with *demand evaluation*, a demand specification of *exact* evaluation. We discuss related work in Sect. 8 and future work in Sect. 9. In the next section, we overview the utility and operation of demand 0CFA.

2   Overview

Palsberg characterizes higher-order program analysis as the combination of first-order program analysis and control-flow analysis (under the name *closure analysis*) [16]. That is, in order to apply a first-order analysis to a higher-order program, one must be able to contend with higher-order control flow.

However, control-flow analysis is expensive. Even the least-expensive "full-precision" CFA—0CFA—has time complexity cubic in program size and this bound is unlikely to be decreased [20]. And, for some clients, control-flow information may be quickly obsoleted. For instance, both the transformations that optimizing compilers perform and the user edits made within a client IDE can invalidate analysis results [4]. This dynamic discourages potential clients of CFA, such as compilers and IDEs, even when the program insight it offers would be useful.

However, this dynamic is not rooted solely in the raw cost of CFA, but also in the pricing model it offers clients. Under this model, clients purchase an (exhaustive) conglomeration of control-flow facts for a large sum up front. For potential clients that forego CFA, the average utility (to the client) of a constituent control-flow fact must not outweigh the average cost (to the client). However, the fact that neither utility nor cost is constant across facts suggests that these clients could be better-served by an alternative pricing model. Before we discuss this pricing model in more detail, we will briefly discuss why neither the (1) utility nor (2) cost would be constant:

1. For clients that don't need *all* control-flow information to be effective, some control-flow facts are more valuable than others. For instance, optimizing compilers likely value facts regarding a critical path in the program at a

premium over run-once code. Similarly, an IDE attempting to provide the user with insight into a particular program part values information about that part higher than other parts.

2. The control flow at a particular program point has a kind of locality and not all program points exhibit the same locality. For instance, the target of f in the fragment $(\lambda f.(f\,x)\,\lambda y.e)$ has higher locality than it does in $(\lambda f.(f\,x)\,g)$. This locality can translate into the amount of analysis required to resolve the control flow [1]. This variation makes little difference to an exhaustive analysis, however, since such an analysis cannot selectively omit expensive facts.

2.1   The Demand Pricing Model

The demand pricing model allows clients to purchase analysis facts selectively. To illustrate some of the advantages of the demand pricing model for a functional language, let's consider super-β inlining [17]. Super-β inlining is the higher-order analogue of procedure inlining. Super-β inlining syntactically replaces the operator f in the call $(f\,x)$ with the target code (in terms of λ). For instance, if f always evaluates to a closure over $\lambda y.e$, the super-β inline of the call is $(\lambda y.e\,x)$, a form susceptible to further optimizations.

For the purposes of super-β inlining, the demand pricing model has several distinct advantages over the exhaustive pricing model; we discuss two:

1. Super-β inlining is not an essential optimization but also cannot be performed without flow information. Under an exhaustive pricing model, one inlining opportunity is revealed only if all inlining opportunities are revealed. In contrast, a demand pricing model allows clients to obtain control-flow information about individual program expressions without necessarily analyzing all other expressions.
2. Super-β inlining unlocks a potential cascade of optimizations as an inlined call site is simplified. In transforming the program, these optimizations can invalidate the CFA results of the original program. Under an exhaustive pricing model, these results were likely both comprehensive and expensive, resulting in a significant loss. In constraint, under the demand pricing model, the set of results invalidated is both small and relatively inexpensive.

In Sect. 6, we evaluate the fitness of demand 0CFA to super-β inlining in terms of its precision relative to exhaustive 0CFA.

2.2   Alternative Sources of the Demand Pricing Model

Demand analyses are confined to limited higher-order settings. For instance, demand points-to analysis for object-oriented languages has a rich literature (e.g. [18,19]) but, especially as the same specification can have strikingly different manifestations in the object-oriented and functional settings [12], it is not clear that current techniques could port directly. The few demand analyses that have targeted functional languages directly each suffer from their own limitations. For instance, Demand-Driven Program Analysis [15] constructs a call graph rooted at program entry and the subtransitive CFA of Heintze and McAllester [8] applies to typed programs with bounded types. In order to enable the whole host of demand first-order program analyses in a higher-order setting, general higher-order control flow must be directly addressed.

While not offering pure demand analysis, the CFA community has recognized the utility of and offered more-selective CFAs. Both Shivers' escape technique [17, Chap. 3] and Ashley and Dybvig's sub-0CFA [1] allow the client to delimit a region of the program to be analyzed. This option comes with its own difficulties: because each analysis is (willfully) blind to the actual control flow outside the region, selecting an appropriate region is critical but not straightforward. For instance, a region that is too small could omit some or even all of the sources of dependent value and control flow; on the other hand, a region that is too large wastes analysis effort obtaining irrelevant (to a particular question) control-flow facts. Exasperatingly, approaching optimal region selection in general likely requires control-flow analysis itself.

In a demand analysis, however, the region-selection problem is non-existent because the analyzer will traverse as much of the program as necessary to resolve the desired control flow. Because the reason the client initially was going to delimit a region was to minimize the analysis time, clients of demand analyses may impose time limits on the demand analyzer. Imposing a time limit rather than a region limit is a much better fit for the client as it was selecting the region to optimize for time, whereas in this arrangement it can optimize for time directly.

2.3   How Demand CFA Operates

An exhaustive CFA, regardless of whether it is based on abstract interpreters or flow constraints, proceeds in a kind of evaluation mode. To analyze a program, it starts at the top level and, like an evaluator, dispatches on the type of expression under focus. The analysis of each expression shadows its concrete evaluation: variable references bring the environment and result value into accord; λ-terms produce values themselves; and applications cause the analyzer to descend on the operator and argument and then operator body, once it's known. As we'll see, an evaluation-centric mode is inadequate to achieve a demand CFA. The key idea behind demand CFA is to introduce an additional *tracing* mode to the analyzer which performs the dual function of evaluation: where evaluation seeks the values to which an expression can evaluate, tracing seeks the expressions which evaluate to a particular value.

Clients specify a particular fact of interest to an analyzer by issuing a query. In the setting of an applicative functional language, queries take the form of subexpressions for which the client would like control-flow information. Issues arise, however, because a query may be an arbitrary subexpression and, in particular, depend on the resolution of a free reference to a variable x. In an exhaustive analysis, the flows to the binding of x are established before the evaluation of any reference to it (which we discuss further in Sect. 4.1). A demand analysis has no such guarantee and must be prepared to establish the flows from this point. To do so, it first considers the way in which x is bound, which, in a lexically-scoped language, is syntactically apparent. For this example, suppose that it is bound by application of a closure over $\lambda x.e$. Next, it traces the flow of the closure over $\lambda x.e$ to each call site which applies it. Since x is bound by its application, the values of the arguments at those call sites constitute its value flows. The analyzer obtains these values by issuing evaluation subqueries for each argument expression.

Let's consider the resolution of the query y in the context of the program $(\lambda f\, x.(f\, x)\, \lambda y.y\, \lambda z.z)$. (In other words, we'll look at a demand approach to determining the values that the reference y can take on.) In order to resolve an evaluation query, the analyzer assumes evaluation mode and, accordingly, attempts to evaluate y. Since y is a variable reference and the analyzer doesn't have its binding available to it, it inspects the program to discover that it is the binder of $\lambda y.y$, bound when a closure over $\lambda y.y$ is applied. At this point, the analyzer enters tracing mode, following the value of $\lambda y.y$ to all of the places where it is applied. The way it traces a value flow manifests its duality to evaluation once again: evaluation dispatches on the type of expression but tracing dispatches on the type of syntactic context of the expression under focus. The analyzer observes that $\lambda y.y$ is in an argument context and its value will be bound to an operator parameter. Its next task, then, is to obtain the operator value by shifting back into evaluation mode. Once it discovers the operator value to be a closure over $\lambda f\, x.(f\, x)$, it can continue tracing the value of $\lambda y.y$ through references to f. The only reference to f is in operator position in $(f\, x)$ and $(f\, x)$ constitutes a call site of the value of $\lambda y.y$. From here, the value bound to y can be obtained as the value of x. To resolve the value bound to x, the analyzer follows the same process as it did to resolve y, discovering the entire expression as a call site for the binding λ-term of x and $\lambda z.z$ in the corresponding argument position. With $\lambda z.z$, the analyzer has determined that each reference to y evaluates to a closure over $\lambda z.z$.

In this example, the demand approach appears especially indirect since an exhaustive analysis that "evaluated" the call would shortly discover the value of y. Exhaustive analyses typically enjoy an economy of scale: they perform less work to obtain an analysis fact, on average, than a demand analysis [9]. Nevertheless, the selective nature of demand analyses can more than compensate for this overhead.

3   The Call-by-Value λ-Calculus

In this section, we formally present the language that both 0CFA and demand 0CFA operate on. Its semantics serve as the ground truth for the correctness theorems of demand 0CFA in Sect. 7.

Following Nielson *et al.*, expressions e in our language are labelled terms t^ℓ and terms take the form of variable references x, λ-abstractions $\lambda x.e$, and applications $(e_0\, e_1)$. Formally, we have

$$x \in \mathbf{Var} \qquad \ell \in \mathbf{Lab}$$
$$e \in \mathbf{Exp} \qquad t \in \mathbf{Term}$$

$$e ::= t^\ell \qquad t ::= x \mid \lambda x.e \mid (e_0\, e_1)$$

Variables and labels are drawn from the disjoint infinite sets **Var** and **Lab**, respectively. Labels are unique and therefore distinguish otherwise identical terms; we omit them when unnecessary.

We define an environment-based call-by-value semantics in big-step style which relates *configurations* (ρ, e, c) to values v when an expression e evaluates to a value v under an environment ρ and calling context c. We denote this relationship by the judgment $\rho, c \vdash e \Downarrow v$. In this simple language, the only form of value is that of a closure $(\lambda x.e, \rho)$, a pair of a λ-abstraction and its closing environment, where environments are a finite map from variables x to values v. Calling contexts are finite sequences of labels. Formally, values, environments, and calling contexts are given as

$$v ::= (\lambda x.e, \rho) \qquad \rho ::= \bot \mid \rho[x \mapsto v] \qquad c ::= \langle\rangle \mid \ell :: c$$

The semantic relation over configurations and values is defined by three rules, one for each type of syntactic expression.

$$\text{REF}\frac{}{\rho, c \vdash x^\ell \Downarrow \rho(x)} \qquad \text{LAM}\frac{}{\rho, c \vdash (\lambda x.e)^\ell \Downarrow (\lambda x.e, \rho)}$$

$$\text{APP}\frac{\rho, c \vdash e_0 \Downarrow (\lambda x.e, \rho') \quad \rho, c \vdash e_1 \Downarrow v' \quad \rho'[x \mapsto v'], \ell :: c \vdash e \Downarrow v}{\rho, c \vdash (e_0\, e_1)^\ell \Downarrow v}$$

These rules are standard: the REF rule states that a variable reference evaluates to the value bound to that variable in the environment; the LAM rule states that a λ-abstraction evaluates to a closure, pairing it with its environment; and the APP rule states that an application evaluates to the body of the operator value under the operator environment extended to bind the operator parameter to the argument value. We also assume that premises are established from the left to right.

4   Background: 0CFA

In this section, we review the core of the constraint-based formulation of 0CFA presented by Nielson *et al.* [14]. We consider the analysis over only the unary λ-calculus presented in the previous section but it is straightforward to extend it to a richer language (see Nielson *et al.* [14]).

A 0CFA analysis is a pair $(\hat{C}, \hat{\rho})$ where $\hat{C}$ is an *abstract cache* that associates to each expression e an abstract value and $\hat{\rho}$ is an *abstract environment* that associates to each variable x an abstract value. The intent is that $\hat{C}$ associates to each expression e an abstraction of those values to which e can evaluate and that $\hat{\rho}$ associates to each variable x an abstraction of those values to which x can be bound during evaluation. An abstract value $\hat{v}$ is a set of λ-terms which yields the following functionalities

$$\hat{v} \in \widehat{\mathbf{Val}} \quad = \mathcal{P}(\mathbf{Lam}) \quad \text{abstract values}$$
$$\hat{\rho} \in \widehat{\mathbf{Env}} \quad = \mathbf{Var} \to \widehat{\mathbf{Val}} \quad \text{abstract environments}$$
$$\hat{\mathcal{C}} \in \widehat{\mathbf{Cache}} = \mathbf{Lab} \to \widehat{\mathbf{Val}} \quad \text{abstract caches}$$

where **Var**, **Lab**, and **Lam** are the variables, labels, and λ-terms of the analyzed program and, hence, are finite.

[REF]	$(\hat{\mathcal{C}}, \hat{\rho}) \models_{fs} x^\ell$	iff $\hat{\rho}(x) \subseteq \hat{\mathcal{C}}(\ell)$
[LAM]	$(\hat{\mathcal{C}}, \hat{\rho}) \models_{fs} (\lambda x.e)^\ell$	iff $\{\lambda x.e\} \subseteq \hat{\mathcal{C}}(\ell)$

$$[\text{APP}] \; (\hat{\mathcal{C}}, \hat{\rho}) \models_{fs} (t_0^{\ell_0} \; t_1^{\ell_1})^\ell \; \textit{iff} \; \begin{array}{l} (\hat{\mathcal{C}}, \hat{\rho}) \models_{fs} t_0^{\ell_0} \wedge (\hat{\mathcal{C}}, \hat{\rho}) \models_{fs} t_1^{\ell_1} \wedge \\ \forall \lambda x.t^{\ell_2} \in \hat{\mathcal{C}}(\ell_0), (\hat{\mathcal{C}}, \hat{\rho}) \models_{fs} t^{\ell_2} \wedge \hat{\mathcal{C}}(\ell_2) \subseteq \hat{\mathcal{C}}(\ell) \wedge \hat{\mathcal{C}}(\ell_1) \subseteq \hat{\rho}(x) \end{array}$$

Fig. 1. The $\models_{fs}$ relation

What constitutes a 0CFA analysis of a program is defined by a relation over analyses and programs; Fig. 1 defines one such relation by means of a set of clauses, one for each category of expression:

The REF *Clause.* The REF clause relates $(\hat{\mathcal{C}}, \hat{\rho})$ to a reference x^ℓ if $\hat{\rho}(x) \subseteq \hat{\mathcal{C}}(\ell)$. For a closed program, the $\models_{fs}$ relation only considers a reference x^ℓ after it has ensured that $\hat{\rho}(x)$ abstracts all of the values to which x could be bound.

The LAM *Clause.* The LAM clause relates $(\hat{\mathcal{C}}, \hat{\rho})$ to a λ-term $(\lambda x.e)^\ell$ if $\{\lambda x.e\} \subseteq \hat{\mathcal{C}}(\ell)$. This clause leaves implicit the fact that, prior to ensuring that this constraint holds, the $\models_{fs}$ specification ensures that $\hat{\rho}(x)$ is populated appropriately for every variable y with a free reference in $\lambda x.e$.

The APP *Clause.* The work of $\models_{fs}$ is done by the APP clause, which relates $(\hat{\mathcal{C}}, \hat{\rho})$ to an application $(t_0^{\ell_0} \; t_1^{\ell_1})^\ell$ if several conditions hold. First, $\models_{fs}$ must relate $(\hat{\mathcal{C}}, \hat{\rho})$ to both the operator $t_0^{\ell_0}$ and argument $t_1^{\ell_1}$. Second, for every $\lambda x.e$ in the operator cache $\hat{\mathcal{C}}(\ell_0)$, the constraint $\hat{\mathcal{C}}(\ell_2) \subseteq \hat{\mathcal{C}}(\ell)$, ensuring that values of the call include those of the function body, and the constraint $\hat{\mathcal{C}}(\ell_1) \subseteq \hat{\rho}(x)$, ensuring that the values bound to x include those of the argument, must both hold.

When $(\hat{\mathcal{C}}, \hat{\rho}) \models_{fs} pr$ holds, we say that $(\hat{\mathcal{C}}, \hat{\rho})$ is *acceptable* with respect to pr. Acceptability implies soundness, so, for an acceptable analysis $(\hat{\mathcal{C}}, \hat{\rho})$, for every label ℓ of a term t, $\hat{\mathcal{C}}(\ell)$ abstracts every value to which t evaluates and, for every variable x, $\hat{\rho}(x)$ abstracts every value to which x becomes bound. We will not review how to arrive at an acceptable analysis, but the interested reader may consult Nielson *et al.* [14].

4.1   An Inherently-Exhaustive Specification

The $\models_{fs}$ relation inherently specifies an exhaustive analysis. The crux is essentially that the notion of acceptability it defines (which entails soundness) holds only for closed programs; it cannot make guarantees about an analysis related to an open expression. For instance, what analyses are related to the lone free variable x^2? According to the specification, $(\bot, \bot) \models_{fs} x^2$ holds since $\bot(x) = \emptyset \subseteq \emptyset = \bot(2)$. But the analysis $(\bot, \bot)$ doesn't capture the flow behavior of x^2 as it appears in $((\lambda x.x^2)^1 \, (\lambda y.y^4)^3)^0$. The $\models_{fs}$ relation relies on previously-imposed constraints to populate the environment mapping of x and thus appropriately constrain x^2. Without special provision, this occurs only if the binding term of x is processed before the reference x^2 is encountered. Since $\models_{fs}$ relies on this for every variable, it accurately defines acceptability for only closed programs in general.

5 Demand 0CFA

Demand 0CFA specifies what it means for an analysis to be acceptable with respect to a (possibly open) program subexpression. In other words, this specification ensures that an analysis accounts for all values to which a subexpression may evaluate, even if that subexpression has free variables. Demand 0CFA strives to analyze only those parts of the program needed to obtain a sound result for the target subexpression, though additional expressions are often implicated by control or value dependencies.

A *demand 0CFA analysis* is a pair $(\hat{\mathcal{C}}, \hat{\mathcal{E}})$ where $\hat{\mathcal{C}}$ has the same form as in 0CFA and $\hat{\mathcal{E}}$ is an *abstract callers* relation which associates to λ-term body expressions e a set of call sites $(e_0 \, e_1)$. In demand 0CFA, $\hat{\mathcal{C}}$ does not necessarily (nor typically) associate every expression to an abstract value but only those necessary to determine the control flow of a externally-selected expression. The intent is that $\hat{\mathcal{E}}$ associates to each of certain λ-terms (also determined by an externally-selected expression) the set of call sites that apply (closures over) it. As in Nielson *et al.* [14], an abstract value $\hat{v}$ is a set of λ-terms, yielding the following functionalities:

$$
\begin{aligned}
\hat{v} \in \widehat{\mathbf{Val}} &= \mathcal{P}(\mathbf{Lam}) \\
\hat{c} \in \widehat{\mathbf{App}} &= \mathcal{P}(\mathbf{App}) \\
\hat{\mathcal{C}} \in \widehat{\mathbf{Cache}} &= \mathbf{Lab} \to \widehat{\mathbf{Val}} \\
\hat{\mathcal{E}} \in \widehat{\mathbf{Calls}} &= \mathbf{Exp} \to \widehat{\mathbf{App}}
\end{aligned}
$$

Just as with exhaustive 0CFA, there is the notion of *acceptability* for a demand 0CFA analysis. Rather than being acceptable w.r.t. a program, however, a demand 0CFA analysis is acceptable w.r.t. a query. The relation $\models_{fs\,eval}$ relates an analysis $(\hat{\mathcal{C}}, \hat{\mathcal{E}})$ to an expression e when $(\hat{\mathcal{C}}, \hat{\mathcal{E}})$ is acceptable for the evaluation of e. This means that $(\hat{\mathcal{C}}, \hat{\mathcal{E}})$ entails the evaluation and tracing necessary to evaluate e. Similarly, the relation $\models_{fs\,call}$ relates an analysis $(\hat{\mathcal{C}}, \hat{\mathcal{E}})$ to an occurrence $(\lambda x.e_0, e)$ when $(\hat{\mathcal{C}}, \hat{\mathcal{E}})$ is acceptable for the trace of $\lambda x.e_0$ from e. This means that $(\hat{\mathcal{C}}, \hat{\mathcal{E}})$ entails the evaluation and tracing necessary to trace $\lambda x.e_0$ from e. We discuss each relation in more detail below.

The demand 0CFA specification makes use of the *syntactic context* of expressions provided by a function $\mathbb{K}_{pr} : \textbf{Exp} \to \textbf{Ctx}$ where

$$\textbf{Ctx} \ni ctx ::= \Box \mid (\Box\,e)^\ell \mid (e\,\Box)^\ell \mid (\lambda x.\Box)^\ell$$

That is, the syntactic context ctx of an expression e within a program pr is either the top-level context $\Box$, an operator context $(\Box\,e_1)^\ell$, an argument context $(e_0\,\Box)^\ell$, or an abstraction body context $(\lambda x.\Box)^\ell$. (From now on, we will leave pr implicit.) The syntactic context can also be seen as an inherited attribute at the node of an expression e within a program's abstract syntax tree.

5.1 The $\models_{fseval}$ Relation

The relation $\models_{fseval}$ relates an analysis $(\hat{\mathcal{C}}, \hat{\mathcal{E}})$ to an expression t^ℓ. Its purpose is to ensure that $\hat{\mathcal{C}}(\ell)$ contains an abstraction of all the values to which t^ℓ can evaluate; in this sense, it corresponds to the $\models_{fs}$ relation of exhaustive 0CFA. The definition of $\models_{fseval}$ can be seen in Fig. 2 and, like $\models_{fs}$, includes a clause for each syntactic category of the λ-calculus.

[REF]	$(\hat{\mathcal{C}}, \hat{\mathcal{E}}) \models_{fseval} x^\ell$	*iff*	$(\lambda x.e)^{\ell_b} = \mathrm{bind}_{fs}(x, x^\ell) \wedge (\hat{\mathcal{C}}, \hat{\mathcal{E}}) \models_{fscall} (\lambda x.e, (\lambda x.e)^{\ell_b}) \wedge$ $\forall (t_0^{\ell_0}\,t_1^{\ell_1})^{\ell_2} \in \hat{\mathcal{E}}(e), (\hat{\mathcal{C}}, \hat{\mathcal{E}}) \models_{fseval} t_1^{\ell_1} \wedge \hat{\mathcal{C}}(\ell_1) \subseteq \hat{\mathcal{C}}(\ell)$
[LAM]	$(\hat{\mathcal{C}}, \hat{\mathcal{E}}) \models_{fseval} (\lambda x.e)^\ell$	*iff*	$\{\lambda x.e\} \subseteq \hat{\mathcal{C}}(\ell)$
[APP]	$(\hat{\mathcal{C}}, \hat{\mathcal{E}}) \models_{fseval} (t_0^{\ell_0}\,t_1^{\ell_1})^\ell$	*iff*	$(\hat{\mathcal{C}}, \hat{\mathcal{E}}) \models_{fseval} t_0^{\ell_0} \wedge$ $\forall \lambda x.t_2^{\ell_2} \in \hat{\mathcal{C}}(\ell_0), (\hat{\mathcal{C}}, \hat{\mathcal{E}}) \models_{fseval} t_2^{\ell_2} \wedge \hat{\mathcal{C}}(\ell_2) \subseteq \hat{\mathcal{C}}(\ell)$

Fig. 2. The $\models_{fseval}$ relation

The REF Clause. To determine the values to which a reference x may evaluate, the REF clause uses the bind_{fs} metafunction, defined in Fig. 3, to reconstruct the binding λ-term $\lambda x.e$. It then relies on the $\models_{fscall}$ relation to ensure that each call site of (closures over) $\lambda x.e$ is known. For each such call site, the REF clause constrains the reference x to evaluate to each value to which the argument may evaluate.

The LAM Clause. A λ-term $\lambda x.e$ evaluates to only closures over itself, so the LAM clause of $\models_{fseval}$ is the same as the LAM clause of $\models_{fs}$. However, unlike $\models_{fs}$, the $\models_{fseval}$ relation does not assume at this point that the free variables of $\lambda x.e$ are subject to any constraints to ensure they're bound.

The APP Clause. The APP clause ensures that the operator is evaluated, that the body of each of its values is evaluated, and that the application itself takes on each of the body values. Unlike the APP clause of $\models_{fs}$, the APP clause of $\models_{fseval}$ doesn't evaluate the argument nor bind its values in the operator's. If the argument value is needed, the REF clause will obtain it.

$$\text{bind}_{fs}(x,e) = \text{bind}_{fs}(x,(e\,e')^\ell) \quad \text{if } \mathbb{K}(e) = (\square\,e')^\ell$$
$$\text{bind}_{fs}(x,e) = \text{bind}_{fs}(x,(e'\,e)^\ell) \quad \text{if } \mathbb{K}(e) = (e'\,\square)^\ell$$
$$\text{bind}_{fs}(x,e) = (\lambda x.e)^\ell \quad\quad\quad\; \text{if } \mathbb{K}(e) = (\lambda x.\square)^\ell$$
$$\text{bind}_{fs}(x,e) = \text{bind}_{fs}(x,(\lambda y.e)^\ell) \; \text{if } \mathbb{K}(e) = (\lambda y.\square)^\ell \text{ where } x \neq y$$

Fig. 3. Given a variable x and an expression e in which x appears free, the bind_{fs} metafunction reconstructs the binding λ-term of x (of which e is a subexpression) by walking upward on the program syntax tree until it encounters the binder of x. Because whole programs are closed (and, we assume, demand 0CFA has access to them), bind_{fs} will always encounter the binder of x before it reaches the program top level. To perform demand 0CFA over components with free variables, bind_{fs} could be altered to signal the occurrence of one to the analyzer, which might apply, e.g., Shivers' escape technique [17].

5.2 The $\models_{fscall}$ Relation

The relation $\models_{fscall}$ relates an analysis $(\hat{\mathcal{C}}, \hat{\mathcal{E}})$ to an *occurrence* $(\lambda x.e, t^\ell)$ which denotes that t^ℓ evaluates (in some context) to a closure over $\lambda x.e$. Its purpose is to ensure that $\hat{\mathcal{E}}(e)$ contains every call site $(t_0^{\ell_0}\, t_1^{\ell_1})^{\ell_2}$ which may apply a closure over $\lambda x.e$, as it flowed from t^ℓ. In order to trace the value flow from t^ℓ, $\models_{fscall}$ considers the syntactic context of t^ℓ, which reveals its next occurrence. Accordingly, the definition of $\models_{fscall}$, seen in Fig. 4, includes a clause for each syntactic (expression) context: operator, argument, λ-term body, and top-level.

[RATOR]	$(\hat{\mathcal{C}}, \hat{\mathcal{E}}) \models_{fscall} (\lambda x.e, t_0^{\ell_0})$ for $\mathbb{K}(t_0^{\ell_0}) = (\square\, t_1^{\ell_1})^{\ell_2}$	iff	$\{(t_0^{\ell_0}\, t_1^{\ell_1})^{\ell_2}\} \subseteq \hat{\mathcal{E}}(e)$
[RAND]	$(\hat{\mathcal{C}}, \hat{\mathcal{E}}) \models_{fscall} (\lambda x.e, t_1^{\ell_1})$ for $\mathbb{K}(t_1^{\ell_1}) = (t_0^{\ell_0}\, \square)^{\ell_2}$	iff	$(\hat{\mathcal{C}}, \hat{\mathcal{E}}) \models_{fseval} t_0^{\ell_0} \,\wedge$ $\forall \lambda y.e' \in \hat{\mathcal{C}}(\ell_0), \forall \ell \in \text{find}_{fs}(y, e'), (\hat{\mathcal{C}}, \hat{\mathcal{E}}) \models_{fscall} (\lambda x.e, y^\ell)$
[BODY]	$(\hat{\mathcal{C}}, \hat{\mathcal{E}}) \models_{fscall} (\lambda x.e, t^\ell)$ for $\mathbb{K}(t^\ell) = (\lambda y.\square)^{\ell_y}$	iff	$(\hat{\mathcal{C}}, \hat{\mathcal{E}}) \models_{fscall} (\lambda y.t^\ell, (\lambda y.t^\ell)^{\ell_y}) \,\wedge$ $\forall (e_0\, e_1)^{\ell_2} \in \hat{\mathcal{E}}(t^\ell), (\hat{\mathcal{C}}, \hat{\mathcal{E}}) \models_{fscall} (\lambda x.e, (e_0\, e_1)^{\ell_2})$
[TOP]	$(\hat{\mathcal{C}}, \hat{\mathcal{E}}) \models_{fscall} (\lambda x.e, t^\ell)$ for $\mathbb{K}(t^\ell) = \square$	iff	always

Fig. 4. The $\models_{fscall}$ relation

The RATOR *Clause.* When $\lambda x.e$ occurs at the operator $t_0^{\ell_0}$ of the application $(t_0^{\ell_0}\, t_1^{\ell_1})^{\ell_2}$, $(t_0^{\ell_0}\, t_1^{\ell_1})^{\ell_2}$ is a caller of a closure over $\lambda x.e$. The RATOR clause ensures that, in such cases, $(t_0^{\ell_0}\, t_1^{\ell_1})^{\ell_2} \in \hat{\mathcal{E}}(e)$.

The RAND *Clause.* When $\lambda x.e$ occurs at the argument $t_1^{\ell_1}$ of the application $(t_0^{\ell_0}\, t_1^{\ell_1})^{\ell_2}$, it will be bound to x_2 for each closure over $\lambda y.e'$ to which $t_0^{\ell_0}$ evaluates. The RAND clause ensures that $t_0^{\ell_0}$ is evaluated and, for each closure over $\lambda y.e'$ to which it evaluates, uses the find_{fs} metafunction, defined in Fig. 5, to locate references to y in e'. The RAND clause then ensures that $\lambda x.e$ occurs at each such reference.

$$\begin{aligned}
\mathrm{find}_{fs}(x, x^\ell) &= \{\ell\} \\
\mathrm{find}_{fs}(x, y^\ell) &= \emptyset && \text{if } x \neq y \\
\mathrm{find}_{fs}(x, (\lambda x.e)^\ell) &= \emptyset \\
\mathrm{find}_{fs}(x, (\lambda y.e)^\ell) &= \mathrm{find}_{fs}(x, e) && \text{if } x \neq y \\
\mathrm{find}_{fs}(x, (f\ e)^\ell) &= \mathrm{find}_{fs}(x, f) \cup \mathrm{find}_{fs}(x, e)
\end{aligned}$$

Fig. 5. Given a variable x and an expression e in its scope, the find_{fs} metafunction gathers the references to x within e by descending downward on the program syntax tree.

The BODY Clause. When $\lambda x.e$ occurs at the body t^ℓ of a λ-term $(\lambda y.t^\ell)^{\ell_y}$, a closure over $\lambda x.e$ will be the result of a call to a closure over $\lambda y.t^\ell$. In other words, $\lambda x.e$ will also occur at each caller $(e_0\ e_1)^{\ell_2}$ of $\lambda y.t^\ell$. The BODY clause ensures that the callers of $\lambda y.t^\ell$ are known and that $\lambda x.e$ occurs at each of them.

The TOP Clause. When $\lambda x.e$ occurs at an expression t^ℓ with context $\square$, it has reached the top level of the program or component. If this top level is of the entire program, such an occurrence means that the result of the program is a closure over $\lambda x.e$ and that it is not applied along this flow. If this top level is of only a component, such an occurrence means that a closure over $\lambda x.e$ escapes the component and can signal the analyzer to respond appropriately.

5.3 Constraint Generation

The constraint generation process of demand 0CFA is very similar to that of exhaustive 0CFA: it proceeds by recursion over the definitions of $\models_{fseval}$ and $\models_{fscall}$ using memoization to avoid revisiting any particular relation. The constraints themselves, however, differ substantially. Evaluation of x^ℓ with x bound as $\lambda x.e$ generates the constraint $(t_0^{\ell_0}\ t_1^{\ell_1})^{\ell_2} \in \hat{\mathcal{E}}(e) \implies \hat{\mathcal{C}}(\ell_1) \subseteq \hat{\mathcal{C}}(\ell)$. Like exhaustive 0CFA, evaluation of $(\lambda x.e)^\ell$ generates the constraint $\{\lambda x.e\} \subseteq \hat{\mathcal{C}}(\ell)$. Evaluation of $(t_0^{\ell_0}\ t_1^{\ell_1})^{\ell_2}$ generates the constraint $\lambda x.t^\ell \in \hat{\mathcal{C}}(\ell_0) \implies \hat{\mathcal{C}}(\ell) \subseteq \hat{\mathcal{C}}(\ell_2)$. Evaluation of $t_0^{\ell_0}$ to a closure over $\lambda x.e$ in syntactic context $(\square\ t_1^{\ell_1})^{\ell_2}$ generates the constraint $\{(t_0^{\ell_0}\ t_1^{\ell_1})^{\ell_2}\} \subseteq \hat{\mathcal{E}}(e)$.

6 Evaluation

In this section, we evaluate whether

1. demand 0CFA is essentially as precise as exhaustive 0CFA, and
2. a non-trivial fraction of control-flow information is available for relatively low cost.

In each evaluation, we use the same corpus of 30 programs. The corpus was obtained by using a random program generator and filtering to include only those programs (1) consist of between 2,500 and 10,000 expressions and (2) take (individually) over five seconds for exhaustive 0CFA to analyze. The corpus consists of the first 30 programs encountered by this technique. While this corpus may not be representative of real-world programs, the second criterion ensures that all programs within it exhibit non-trivial control flow (at least from the perspective of 0CFA). The time that exhaustive 0CFA takes to analyze each program is used as that program's baseline in proceeding evaluations.

6.1   The Relative Precision of Demand 0CFA

Control-flow analysis is necessary to justify valuable optimizations such as super-β inlining [17]. This particular optimization, when applied at a call site $(f\,e)$, requires that f evaluates to closures over only a single λ-term. A CFA demonstrates this condition when it calculates a singleton flow set for f.

Demand 0CFA sometimes considers unreachable code and therefore calculates a larger control-flow relation than exhaustive 0CFA does. (We discuss this further in Sect. 7.) This could undermine its ability to justify optimizations relative to exhaustive 0CFA if exhaustive 0CFA calculates a singleton flow set for an expression but demand 0CFA fails to. We compare, for each program, the number of reachable non-λ-term expressions for which exhaustive 0CFA calculates a singleton flow set to the number of those for which demand 0CFA calculates a singleton flow set. We omit an (uninteresting) table as data shows that, for our corpus, there are very few cases in which demand 0CFA doesn't calculate a singleton flow set when exhaustive 0CFA does: for two programs, it does so in about 98% of cases; for the remaining 28 programs, it does so in at least 99% of cases; and for six programs, it does so for 100% of cases. If λ-term expressions were included in these counts, theses percentages would uniformly increase since both exhaustive 0CFA and demand 0CFA always calculate a singleton set for them. These results demonstrate the demand 0CFA is essentially as precise as exhaustive 0CFA.

6.2   The Existence of Cheap Control-Flow Information

With an exhaustive CFA, it doesn't make sense to talk about the cost to obtain any given piece of control-flow information since, by design, exhaustive CFA bundles all control-flow information together. We can however talk about the *MCE*, the mean cost per expression as the quotient of the cost of the bundle and the number of program expressions whose control-flow information it includes. For example, Program 5 has 5,338 expressions and takes exhaustive 0CFA 5.84 seconds to analyze, so its MCE in terms of time is 5.84 s/5338 $\approx$ 1.09 ms.

The intuition presented in Sect. 2 suggests that the locality of control flow varies across expressions. If the locality of control flow is a proxy for the cost of obtaining it, then this cost varies across expressions as well. In turn, a varying cost means that the control-flow information for some expressions may be obtainable at sub-MCE cost. In real terms, if these assumptions hold, we would expect that the control-flow information of some of the expressions in Program 5 would be obtainable for less than 1.09 ms.

For this evaluation, we limit the running time of demand 0CFA to a fraction α of the MCE for each program. We then dispatch demand 0CFA on each program expression in succession with analysis of each expression subject to this limit. The analysis of an expression either succeeds, yielding a sound account of its control-flow information, or reaches the limit, yielding no information, before we dispatch demand 0CFA on a successive expression. Figure 6 shows the percentage of expressions for which demand 0CFA succeeds in this manner under time limits determined by various fractions α.

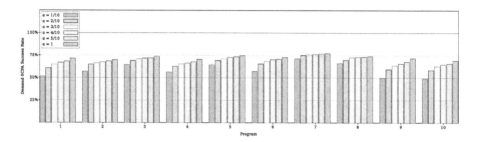

Fig. 6. This graph shows the demand 0CFA success rate for fractions $\alpha = 1/10, 2/10, 3/10, 4/10, 5/10, 1$ of the MCE for 10 programs randomly selected from our corpus. These data show that demand 0CFA can obtain the control flow for a significant fraction of expressions—on average over 50%—when time-limited to 1/10 of MCE. As expected, this fraction increases as the fraction of MCE increases, nearing 75% at when demand 0CFA is time-limited MCE itself. These results imply that nearly 75% of a program's control flow is obtainable for an order-of-magnitude less time than taken by exhaustive 0CFA. (See text.)

We report the median percentage of three runs for 10 programs programs randomly selected from our corpus and for $\alpha = 1/10, 2/10, 3/10, 4/10, 5/10, 1$. As the graph shows, demand 0CFA can obtain the control flow for a significant fraction of expressions—on average over 50%—when time-limited to 1/10 of MCE. As expected, this fraction increases as the fraction of MCE increases, nearing 75% at when demand 0CFA is time-limited MCE itself.

A first-order upper bound to demand 0CFA's relative running time is its fraction α. If demand 0CFA is time-limited to 1/10 of MCE, then, even if it is dispatched on every program expression, it will not take more than 1/10 of the time of exhaustive 0CFA. However, as the data show, the vast majority of expressions analyzable in 2/10 of MCE are analyzable in 1/10 of MCE, and similarly for 3/10 relative to 2/10, etc. Using this fact, we can obtain a second-order upper bound A to demand 0CFA's relative running time via the formula

$$A = \sum_{i=1}^{n} \alpha_i(f_i - f_{i-1})$$

given a sequence of fractions $\alpha_1, \alpha_2, \ldots, \alpha_n$ of MCE and corresponding fractions $f_1, f_2, \ldots, f_n$ of demand 0CFA success rates, where $\alpha_0 = 0$ and $f_0 = 0$. By this estimate, when $\alpha = 1$, demand 0CFA on average obtains nearly 75% of a program's control flow in approximately 11% of the time taken by exhaustive 0CFA.

In practice, compilers can't limit demand 0CFA to a fraction of MCE, because the MCE is determined only by running an exhaustive 0CFA analysis. For instance, a compiler of Program 5 would not know that its MCE was $1.01\,ms$ since it would not know the time taken by exhaustive 0CFA was $5.84\,$s. Instead, it might know simply that it has $0.5\,$s to budget to demand 0CFA. To increase effectiveness, it might allocate this budget non-uniformly across the program, using program knowledge to concentrate it on performance-critical program parts.

These results demonstrate not only that some pieces of control-flow information indeed cost less than MCE to obtain but also that

1. a significant fraction cost an order of magnitude less than MCE to obtain and
2. demand 0CFA can efficiently obtain them taking an order of magnitude less than MCE.

7   Demand 0CFA Correctness

The purpose of this section is to establish that demand 0CFA is sound w.r.t. an exact forward semantics. To do so, we will establish that demand 0CFA is sound w.r.t. an exact *demand* semantics and that this demand semantics has a formal correspondence to an exact forward semantics.

We term the exact demand semantics we define *demand evaluation*. To a first approximation, demand evaluation computes a subderivation of a full derivation of a program's evaluation, where the particular subderivation computed is determined in part by the program subexpression. This is only an approximate description of the action of demand evaluation for a few reasons: first, one may successfully apply demand evaluation to unreachable program subexpressions, computing derivations that don't appear in the derivation of the whole program's evaluation; second, the product of demand evaluation isn't necessarily a single contiguous subderivation but may instead be a set of related subderivations obtained (conceptually) by removing irrelevant judgments from a larger derivation.

Although our intuition is rooted in derivations, we formalize demand evaluation as exact demand analyses related to program configurations, analogous to how we formalized demand 0CFA as approximate demand analyses related to program expressions. Doing so decreases the conceptual distance between demand 0CFA and demand evaluation, making soundness easier to establish. In order to connect demand evaluation to forward evaluation, we reify derivations from exact demand analyses and formally establish a correspondence between those derivations and forward derivations in a technical report [6].

7.1   Demand Evaluation

We define demand evaluation in the same way that we define demand 0CFA: namely, we define an *exact analysis* $(C, \mathcal{E})$ that records exact evaluation facts and two (undecidable) relations, $\models_{eval}$ and $\models_{call}$, over exact analyses and configurations (ρ^d, e, n_c). Both $\models_{eval}$ and $\models_{call}$ relate analyses and configurations in an analogous way to $\models_{fseval}$ and $\models_{fscall}$.

Figure 7 contains formal definitions for the domains of demand evaluation. An exact analysis $(C, \mathcal{E})$ consists of a *cache* C and a caller relation $\mathcal{E}$. In the exact semantics, a caller relation $\mathcal{E}$ is actually a function from called contexts to caller contexts. A cache C is itself a triple $(\$, \sigma, \nu)$ of three functions: $\$$ associates configurations with *names*, σ associates names with values, and ν associates names with calling contexts. A name n serves the function of an address that can be known and transmitted before anything is bound to it; it can be used to obtain the value that may eventually be bound to it in σ. The domain **Name** can be any countably-infinite set; when we must be concrete, it will assume the set of natural numbers $\mathbb{N}$. Demand evaluation environments map variables to names (and not to values contra environments in the exact, big-step semantics presented in Sect. 2) which are resolved in the store σ. Similarly, calling contexts are indirected by names which are resolved in the context store ν. (Names within environments and names in contexts come from different address spaces and never interact.) Closures remain the only type of value and remain a pair $(\lambda x.e, \rho^d)$ of a λ-term $\lambda x.e$ and an enclosing environment ρ^d. Configurations are a triple (ρ^d, e, n) of an environment ρ^d closing an expression e in a calling context named by n (and resolved through ν). In the exact semantics, an occurrence is merely a configuration, but we ensure that every configuration treated as such has a value in C.

$$
\begin{aligned}
n &\in \textbf{Name} & & \text{a countably-infinite set} \\
\rho^d &\in \textbf{Env}_d & ::= & \quad \bot \mid \rho^d[x \mapsto n] \\
(\lambda x.e, \rho^d) &\in \textbf{Value} & = & \quad \textbf{Lam} \times \textbf{Env}_d \\
c^d &\in \textbf{CCtx}_d & ::= & \quad \text{mt} \mid \ell :: n \\
(\rho^d, e, n) &\in \textbf{Config} & = & \quad \textbf{Env}_d \times \textbf{Exp} \times \textbf{Name} \\
& \textbf{Occur} & = & \quad \textbf{Config} \\
\$ &\in \textbf{Names} & = & \quad \textbf{Config} \to \textbf{Name} \\
\sigma &\in \textbf{Store} & = & \quad \textbf{Name} \to \textbf{Value} \\
\nu &\in \textbf{CStore} & = & \quad \textbf{Name} \to \textbf{CCtx}_d \\
C &\in \textbf{Cache} & = & \quad \textbf{Names} \times \textbf{Store} \times \textbf{Store} \\
\mathcal{E} &\in \textbf{Calls} & = & \quad \textbf{Config} \to \textbf{Config}
\end{aligned}
$$

Fig. 7. Demand evaluation domains

An exact demand analysis encapsulates the evaluation of a given configuration. However, because configuration environments and calling contexts are threaded through stores, all configurations for a given expression have the same shape. In consequence, a configuration does not uniquely identify a particular evaluation for an expression—that is, the evaluation of a particular instance of the expression in evaluation. Instead, we will define our acceptability relations

$\models_{eval}$ and $\models_{call}$ to admit analyses that encapsulate *some* evaluation of the given configuration.

7.2   The $\models_{eval}$ Relation

The $\models_{eval}$ relation relates an analysis $(C, \mathcal{E})$ to a judgment $\rho^d, n_c \vdash e \Downarrow^d v^d$ when $(C, \mathcal{E})$ entails the evaluation of the configuration (ρ^d, e, n_c) to the value v^d. Its definition, seen in Fig. 8, contains a clause for each type of expression. Each of these clauses functions essentially as its counterpart does in $\models_{fseval}$.

$$(C, \mathcal{E}) \models_{eval} \rho^d, n_c \vdash x^\ell \Downarrow^d v^d$$
$$\textit{iff}$$

[REF]
$$
\begin{aligned}
&C_\$(\rho^d, x^\ell, n_c) = \rho^d(x) \\
&(\rho_0^d[x \mapsto n], e, n_{c'}) = \mathrm{bind}(x, \rho^d, x^\ell, n_c) \\
&C(\rho_0^d, \lambda x.e, n_{c''}) = (\lambda x.e, \rho_0^d) \\
&(C, \mathcal{E}) \models_{call} (\rho_0^d, \lambda x.e, n_{c''}) \Rightarrow_d (\rho_1^d, (e_0\, e_1)^{\ell_0}, n_{c'''}) \implies \\
&\quad C_\$(\rho_1^d, e_1, n_{c'''}) = n \\
&\quad \mathcal{E}(\rho_0^d[x \mapsto n], e, n_{c'}) = (\rho_1^d, (e_0\, e_1)^{\ell_0}, n_{c'''}) \\
&\quad \rho^d(x) = C_\$(\rho_1^d, e_1, n_{c'''}) \\
&\quad (C, \mathcal{E}) \models_{eval} \rho_1^d, n_{c'''} \vdash e_1 \Downarrow^d v^d
\end{aligned}
$$

$$(C, \mathcal{E}) \models_{eval} \rho^d, n_c \vdash (\lambda x.e)^\ell \Downarrow^d (\lambda x.e, \rho^d)$$
$$\textit{iff}$$

[LAM]
$$C(\rho^d, (\lambda x.e)^\ell, n_c) = (\lambda x.e, \rho^d)$$

$$(C, \mathcal{E}) \models_{eval} \rho^d, n_c \vdash (e_0\, e_1)^\ell \Downarrow^d v^d$$
$$\textit{iff}$$

[APP]
$$
\begin{aligned}
&(C, \mathcal{E}) \models_{eval} \rho^d, n_c \vdash e_0 \Downarrow^d (\lambda x.e, \rho_0^d) \implies \\
&\rho_1^d = \rho_0^d[x \mapsto C_\$(\rho^d, e_1, n_c)] \\
&C_\nu(n_{c'}) = \ell :: n_c \\
&\mathcal{E}(\rho_1^d, e, n_{c'}) = (\rho^d, (e_0\, e_1)^\ell, n_c) \\
&C_\$(\rho_1^d, e, n_{c'}) = C_\$(\rho^d, (e_0\, e_1)^\ell, n_c) \\
&(C, \mathcal{E}) \models_{eval} \rho_1^d, n_{c'} \vdash e \Downarrow^d v^d
\end{aligned}
$$

Fig. 8. The $\models_{eval}$ relation

The REF *Clause.* The REF clause specifies that an analysis $(C, \mathcal{E})$ entails the evaluation of a variable reference configuration (ρ^d, x^ℓ, n_c). It ensures that such a configuration evaluates to a value v^d when (1) the name of the configuration reflects the name of the environment binding, (2) the closure that created that binding when applied (furnished by bind) is called at a call site, (3) the name of the argument configuration at that call site is consistent with the new environment binding, and (4) the argument configuration evaluates to v^d.

The bind metafunction (defined in Fig. 9) reconstructs not simply the binding λ-term $\lambda x.e$ of x but the configuration at which the particular closure over $\lambda x.e$ first appears.

$$\begin{aligned}
\mathrm{bind}(x, \rho^d, e, n) &= \quad (\rho_0^d, (\lambda x.e)^\ell, n_0) \quad\quad \text{where} \quad\quad \mathbb{K}(e) = (\lambda x.\square)^\ell \text{ and } \rho^d = \rho_0^d[x \mapsto n] \\
\mathrm{bind}(x, \rho^d, e, n) &= \mathrm{bind}(x, \rho_0^d, (\lambda x.y)^\ell, n_0) \text{ where } \mathbb{K}(e) = (\lambda y.\square)^\ell, \, x \neq y, \text{ and } \rho^d = \rho_0^d[y \mapsto n] \\
\mathrm{bind}(x, \rho^d, e, n) &= \quad \mathrm{bind}(x, \rho^d, (e\, e_1)^\ell, n) \quad \text{where} \quad\quad\quad\quad \mathbb{K}(e) = (\square\, e_1)^\ell \\
\mathrm{bind}(x, \rho^d, e, n) &= \quad \mathrm{bind}(x, \rho^d, (e_0\, e)^\ell, n) \quad \text{where} \quad\quad\quad\quad \mathbb{K}(e) = (e_0\, \square)^\ell
\end{aligned}$$

Fig. 9. Given a variable x and an expression e in which x appears free, along with its closing environment and calling context, the bind metafunction reconstructs the "birth" context of the closure which yields this binding of x when applied. The resultant name of the calling context must be consistent with (and is uniquely identified by) the calling context discovered for this closure.

The LAM *Clause.* The LAM clause of $\models_{eval}$ specifies that an analysis $(C, \mathcal{E})$ entails the evaluation of a λ-term configuration $(\rho^d, (\lambda x.e)^\ell, n_c)$ if $C(\rho^d, (\lambda x.e)^\ell, n_c) = (\lambda x.e, \rho^d)$ meaning that $C_\$(\rho^d, (\lambda x.e)^\ell, n_c) = n$ and $\sigma(n) = (\lambda x.e, \rho^d)$ for some n.

The APP *Clause.* The APP clause applies to configurations focused on an application expression $(e_0\, e_1)^\ell$. It ensures that such a configuration evaluates to a value v^d when (1) the operator e_0 is evaluated (within its configuration) to some value $(\lambda x.e, \rho_0^d)$, (2) the environment ρ_0^d and calling context n_c are defined appropriately in the configuration of e, (3) the caller of that configuration is defined in $\mathcal{E}$, and (4) that configuration evaluates to v^d.

7.3   The $\models_{call}$ Relation

The $\models_{call}$ relation relates an analysis $(C, \mathcal{E})$ to a judgment $(\rho^d, e, n_c) \Rightarrow_d (\rho_0^d, (e_0\, e_1)^\ell, n_{c'})$ when $(C, \mathcal{E})$ entails that the value of the configuration (ρ^d, e, n_c) is applied at the configuration $(\rho_0^d, (e_0\, e_1)^\ell, n_{c'})$. Its definition, seen in Fig. 10, contains a clause for each type of expression context. Each of these clauses functions essentially as its counterpart does in $\models_{fs\,call}$.

The RATOR *Clause.* The resultant value of a configuration (ρ^d, e_0, n_c) where e_0 has context $(\square\, e_1)^\ell$ is applied at $(e_0\, e_1)^\ell$ (assuming the convergence of evaluation of e_1) so its caller configuration is $(\rho^d, (e_0\, e_1)^\ell, n_c)$.

The RAND *Clause.* The resultant value of a configuration (ρ^d, e_1, n_c) where e_1 has context $(e_0\, \square)^\ell$ is bound to the parameter x of the value $(\lambda x.e, \rho_0^d)$ of e_0 and appears at every reference to x in e. The RAND clause ensures that the argument value is called at configuration $(\rho_0^d, (e_2\, e_3)^{\ell_0}, n_{c'})$ when (1) the operator expression is evaluated to a value, (2) the environment of that value is extended with the name of the argument and the calling context is extended with the call-site label, and (3) the find metarelation furnishes a configuration whose value is called at $(\rho_0^d, (e_2\, e_3)^{\ell_0}, n_{c'})$.

The find metarelation, defined in Fig. 11, relates references to x in a configuration (ρ^d, e, n_c) to configurations $(\rho_0^d, x^\ell, n_{c'})$ wich constitute references to x.

The BODY *Clause.* If a configuration is in a body context, its result becomes the result of the caller of the closure over its enclosing λ-term. The BODY clause ensures that the resultant value of a configuration $(\rho^d[x \mapsto n], e, n_c)$ such that

[RATOR]
$$(C, \mathcal{E}) \models_{call} (\rho^d, e_0, n_c) \Rightarrow_d (\rho^d, (e_0\, e_1)^\ell, n_c) \text{ for } \mathbb{K}(e_0) = (\square\, e_1)^\ell$$
$$iff$$
$$\textbf{always}$$

[RAND]
$$(C, \mathcal{E}) \models_{call} (\rho^d, e_1, n_c) \Rightarrow_d (\rho^d_0, (e_2\, e_3)^{\ell_0}, n_{c'}) \text{ for } \mathbb{K}(e_1) = (e_0\, \square)^\ell$$
$$iff$$
$$(C, \mathcal{E}) \models_{eval} \rho^d, n_c \vdash e_0 \Downarrow^d (\lambda x.e, \rho^d_1) \implies$$
$$\rho^d_2 = \rho^d_1[x \mapsto C_\$(\rho^d, e_1, n_c)]$$
$$C_\nu(n_{c''}) = \ell :: n_c$$
$$(\rho^d_3, x^{\ell_1}, n_{c'''}) \in \text{find}(x, \rho^d_2, e, n_{c''}) \implies$$
$$(C, \mathcal{E}) \models_{call} (\rho^d_3, x^{\ell_1}, n_{c'''}) \Rightarrow_d (\rho^d_0, (e_2\, e_3)^{\ell_0}, n_{c'})$$

[BODY]
$$(C, \mathcal{E}) \models_{call} (\rho^d[x \mapsto n], e, n_c) \Rightarrow_d (\rho^d_0, (e_0\, e_1)^{\ell_0}, n_{c'}) \text{ for } \mathbb{K}(e) = (\lambda x.\square)^\ell$$
$$iff$$
$$(C, \mathcal{E}) \models_{call} (\rho^d, (\lambda x.e)^\ell, n_{c''}) \Rightarrow_d (\rho^d_1, (e_2\, e_3)^{\ell_1}, n_{c''}) \implies$$
$$(C, \mathcal{E}) \models_{call} (\rho^d_1, (e_2\, e_3)^{\ell_1}, n_{c''}) \Rightarrow_d (\rho^d_0, (e_0\, e_1)^{\ell_0}, n_{c'})$$

[TOP]
$$(C, \mathcal{E}) \models_{call} (\rho^d, e, n_c) \Rightarrow_d (\rho^d_0, (e_0\, e_1)^\ell, n_{c'}) \text{ for } \mathbb{K}(e) = \square$$
$$iff$$
$$\textbf{never}$$

Fig. 10. The $\models_{call}$ relation

$$(\rho^d, x^\ell, n_c) \in \text{find}(x, \rho^d, x^\ell, n_c) \quad iff \quad \textbf{always}$$
$$(\rho^d_0, x^\ell, n_{c'}) \in \text{find}(x, \rho^d, \lambda y.e^\ell, n_c) \quad iff \quad (\rho^d_0, x^\ell, n_{c'}) \in \text{find}(x, \rho^d[y \mapsto n], e, n_{c''})$$
$$\text{where } x \neq y \text{ and for some } n, n_{c''}$$
$$(\rho^d_0, x^\ell, n_c) \in \text{find}(x, \rho^d, (e_0\, e_1)^\ell, n_c) \; iff \quad (\rho^d_0, x^\ell, n_c) \in \text{find}(x, \rho^d, e_0, n_c)$$
$$(\rho^d_0, x^\ell, n_c) \in \text{find}(x, \rho^d, (e_0\, e_1)^\ell, n_c) \; iff \quad (\rho^d_0, x^\ell, n_c) \in \text{find}(x, \rho^d, e_1, n_c)$$

Fig. 11. The find relation

e has syntactic context $(\lambda x.\square)^\ell$ is called at a configuration $(\rho^d_1, (e_2\, e_3)^{\ell_1}, n_{c'''})$ when (1) the enclosing value is called at configuration $(\rho^d_1, (e_2\, e_3)^{\ell_1}, n_{c'''})$, and (2) the resultant value of $(\rho^d_1, (e_2\, e_3)^{\ell_1}, n_{c'''})$—the value of the initial configuration over e—is called at configuration $(\rho^d_1, (e_2\, e_3)^{\ell_1}, n_{c'''})$.

The TOP *Clause.* A closure that reaches the top level of the program is not called at any configuration within evaluation.

7.4 Soundness

We can now formally state the correctness of demand 0CFA relative to demand evaluation. Correctness is expressed by two lemmas which each relate a demand evaluation relation to its demand 0CFA counterpart.

Lemma 1. *If* $(C, \mathcal{E}) \models_{eval} \rho^d, n_c \vdash t^\ell \Downarrow^d (\lambda x.e, \rho^d_0)$ *then, if* $(\hat{C}, \hat{\mathcal{E}}) \models_{fs\,eval} t^\ell$, $\lambda x.e \in \hat{C}(\ell)$.

Lemma 2. *If* $(C, \mathcal{E}) \models_{call} (\rho^d, t^\ell, n_c) \Rightarrow_d (\rho^d_0, (e_0\, e_1)^{\ell_0}, n_{c'})$ *where* $C(\rho^d, t^\ell, n_c) = (\lambda x.e, \rho^d_0)$ *then, if* $(\hat{C}, \hat{\mathcal{E}}) \models_{fs\,call} (\lambda x.e, t^\ell)$, $(e_0\, e_1)^{\ell_0} \in \hat{\mathcal{E}}(e)$.

Lemma 1 states that a demand 0CFA analysis $(\hat{\mathcal{C}}, \hat{\mathcal{E}})$ acceptable by $\models_{fseval}$ for an expression e contains an abstraction of every value for which there is an acceptable (by $\models_{eval}$) exact analysis $(C, \mathcal{E})$. Lemma 2 says that the demand 0CFA specification $\models_{fseval}$ will always include abstractions of calling configurations discovered by the demand evaluation specification $\models_{call}$. Because we took great pains to keep exact demand evaluation close to approximate demand evaluation, the proofs of these lemmas proceed straightforwardly by mutual induction on the definitions of $\models_{eval}$ and $\models_{call}$. The coinductive step proceeds by cases over expressions, in the case of Lemma 1, and syntactic contexts, in the case of Lemma 2. The corresponding clauses in the exact and approximate relations themselves tightly correspond, so each case proceeds without impediment.

8   Related Work

Palmer and Smith's Demand-Driven Program Analysis (DDPA) [15] is most-closely related to this work, being both demand-driven and a control-flow analysis. DDPA differs from demand 0CFA in that it must construct a call graph from the program entry point, using its demand lookup facilities to resolve targets along the way. In contrast, demand 0CFA is able to construct the call graph on demand from an arbitrary control point.

There are three nominal higher-order demand-driven analyses that use the term *demand* in a different sense than we do. The first is a "demand-driven 0-CFA" derived by using a calculational approach to abstract interpretation [11]. The derived analysis is not demand in our sense in that one cannot specify an arbitrary program expression to be analyzed but instead refers to an analyzer that attempts to analyze only those parts of the program that influence the final result. In this very loose sense, demand 0CFA is a generalization of demand-driven 0CFA. The authors relate their work to the second nominally demand analysis, Biswas [2] which uses the term *demand* in a similar way for first-order functional programs. Heintze and McAllester's [8] "subtransitive CFA" computes an underapproximation of control-flow in linear time which can be transitively closed at quadratic cost (for cubic total cost) and is described by the authors as "demand-driven". Their analysis operates over typed programs with bounded type; in contrast, demand 0CFA operates over untyped programs.

The CFA aspect of this work is related to the myriad exhaustive specifications of CFA [3,5,7,10,13,17,21,22]. The most significant difference of this work is its demand-driven nature. However, other differences remain: modern conceptions of CFA are based on small-step abstract machines [21] or big-step definitional interpreters [3,23] which offer flow, context, and path sensitivity; we have presented demand 0CFA as a constraint-based analysis that is flow-, context-, and path-*insensitive*.

Control-flow analysis is the higher-order analogue of points-to analysis. Even object-oriented programs exhibit higher-order control flow in that the destination of a method call depends on the class of the dynamic target. While earlier work [19] leveraged only the class hierarchy to approximate the call graph, later work used it merely as a foothold to a more-precise construction of it [18].

9   Conclusion and Future Work

In this paper, we introduced demand 0CFA, a monovariant, context-insensitive, constraint-based, demand-driven control-flow analysis, and discussed how it is well-suited to many CFA clients. Future work includes enhancing demand 0CFA with both polyvariance and context-sensitivity, arriving at a demand-driven k-CFA hierarchy [17]. While flow insensitivity is fundamental to our formalism, context- and even path-insensitivity are not. However, the constraint-based framework which underlies demand 0CFA is likely not essential to it and it may be possible to port the approach to a small-step abstract machine-based framework (e.g. [21]) to achieve flow sensitivity. Applying the insight of Gilray *et al.* [7], introducing an environment may provide the leverage needed to obtain a pushdown abstraction of control flow.

Acknowledgement. This material is partially based on research sponsored by DARPA under agreement number AFRL FA8750-15-2-0092 and by NSF under CAREER grant 1350344. The U.S. Government is authorized to reproduce and distribute reprints for Governmental purposes notwithstanding any copyright notation thereon.

References

1. Ashley, J.M., Dybvig, R.K.: A practical and flexible flow analysis for higher-order languages. ACM Trans. Program. Lang. Syst. **20**, 845–868 (1998)
2. Biswas, S.K.: A demand-driven set-based analysis. In: Proceedings of the 24th ACM SIGPLAN-SIGACT Symposium on Principles of Programming Languages, POPL 1997. ACM (1997)
3. Darais, D., Labich, N., Nguyen, P.C., Van Horn, D.: Abstracting definitional interpreters (functional pearl). Proc. ACM Program. Lang. **1**(ICFP), 12 (2017)
4. Duesterwald, E., Gupta, R., Soffa, M.L.: A practical framework for demand-driven interprocedural data flow analysis. ACM Trans. Program. Lang. Syst. (TOPLAS) **19**(6), 992–1030 (1997)
5. Earl, C., Might, M., Van Horn, D.: Pushdown control-flow analysis of higher-order programs. In: Workshop on Scheme and Functional Programming (2010)
6. Germane, K., Might, M.: Demand control-flow analysis. Technical report, January 2019. http://kimball.germane.net/germane-dcfa-techreport.pdf
7. Gilray, T., Lyde, S., Adams, M.D., Might, M., Van Horn, D.: Pushdown control-flow analysis for free. In: Proceedings of the 43rd Annual ACM SIGPLAN Symposium on Principles of Programming Languages, POPL 2016. ACM (2016)
8. Heintze, N., McAllester, D.: Linear-time subtransitive control flow analysis. In: Proceedings of the ACM SIGPLAN 1997 Conference on Programming Language Design and Implementation, PLDI 1997. ACM Press (1997)
9. Heintze, N., Tardieu, O.: Demand-driven pointer analysis. In: ACM SIGPLAN Notices, vol. 36, pp. 24–34. ACM (2001)
10. Johnson, J.I., Van Horn, D.: Abstracting abstract control. In: Proceedings of the 10th ACM Symposium on Dynamic Languages. ACM (2014)

11. Midtgaard, J., Jensen, T.: A calculational approach to control-flow analysis by abstract interpretation. In: Alpuente, M., Vidal, G. (eds.) SAS 2008. LNCS, vol. 5079, pp. 347–362. Springer, Heidelberg (2008). https://doi.org/10.1007/978-3-540-69166-2_23

12. Might, M., Smaragdakis, Y., Van Horn, D.: Resolving and exploiting the k-CFA paradox: illuminating functional vs. object-oriented program analysis. In: Proceedings of the 2010 ACM SIGPLAN Conference on Programming Language Design and Implementation, PLDI 2010. ACM Press (2010)

13. Nielson, F., Nielson, H.R.: Infinitary control flow analysis: a collecting semantics for closure analysis. In: Proceedings of the 24th ACM SIGPLAN Symposium on Principles of Programming Languages, POPL 1997. ACM Press (1997)

14. Nielson, F., Nielson, H.R., Hankin, C.: Principles of Program Analysis. Springer, Heidelberg (1999). https://doi.org/10.1007/978-3-662-03811-6

15. Palmer, Z., Smith, S.F.: Higher-order demand-driven program analysis. In: 30th European Conference on Object-Oriented Programming (2016)

16. Palsberg, J.: Closure analysis in constraint form. ACM Trans. Program. Lang. Syst. **17**(1), 47–62 (1995)

17. Shivers, O.: Control-flow analysis of higher-order languages. Ph.D. thesis, Carnegie Mellon University (1991)

18. Sridharan, M., Bodík, R.: Refinement-based context-sensitive points-to analysis for Java. In: Proceedings of the 27th ACM SIGPLAN Conference on Programming Language Design and Implementation, PLDI 2006, pp. 387–400. ACM, New York (2006)

19. Sridharan, M., Gopan, D., Shan, L., Bodík, R.: Demand-driven points-to analysis for Java. In: Proceedings of the 20th Annual ACM SIGPLAN Conference on Object-Oriented Programming, Systems, Languages, and Applications, OOPSLA 2005, pp. 59–76. ACM, New York (2005)

20. Van Horn, D., Mairson, H.G.: Flow analysis, linearity, and PTIME. In: Alpuente, M., Vidal, G. (eds.) SAS 2008. LNCS, vol. 5079, pp. 255–269. Springer, Heidelberg (2008). https://doi.org/10.1007/978-3-540-69166-2_17

21. Van Horn, D., Might, M.: Abstracting abstract machines. In: Proceedings of the 15th ACM International Conference on Functional Programming, ICFP 2010, pp. 51–62. ACM, New York (2010)

22. Vardoulakis, D., Shivers, O.: CFA2: a context-free approach to control-flow analysis. Logical Methods Comput. Sci. (2011)

23. Wei, G., Decker, J., Rompf, T.: Refunctionalization of abstract abstract machines: bridging the gap between abstract machines and abstract definitional interpreters (functional pearl). Proc. ACM Program. Lang. **2**(ICFP), 105:1–105:28 (2018)

Effect-Driven Flow Analysis

Jens Nicolay[(⊠)], Quentin Stiévenart[(⊠)], Wolfgang De Meuter[(⊠)],
and Coen De Roover[(⊠)]

Software Languages Lab, Vrije Universiteit Brussel, Brussels, Belgium
{jnicolay,qstieven,wdmeuter,cderoove}@vub.ac.be

Abstract. Traditional machine-based static analyses use a worklist algorithm to explore the analysis state space, and compare each state in the worklist against a set of seen states as part of their fixed-point computation. This may require many state comparisons, which gives rise to a computational overhead. Even an analysis with a global store has to clear its set of seen states each time the store updates because of allocation or side-effects, which results in more states being reanalyzed and compared.

In this work we present a static analysis technique, MODF, that does not rely on a set of seen states, and apply it to a machine-based analysis with global-store widening. MODF analyzes one function execution at a time to completion while tracking read, write, and call effects. These effects trigger the analysis of other function executions, and the analysis terminates when no new effects can be discovered.

We compared MODF to a traditional machine-based analysis implementation on a set of 20 benchmark programs and found that MODF is faster for 17 programs with speedups ranging between 1.4x and 12.3x. Furthermore, MODF exhibits similar precision as the traditional analysis on most programs and yields state graphs that are comparable in size.

Keywords: Program analysis · Static analysis
Abstract interpretation · Effects

1 Introduction

1.1 Motivation

Traditional machine-based analyses [25] use a worklist algorithm to explore the analysis state space. The worklist contains the program states that still have to be explored by the fixed-point computation. In order to reach a fixed point, every state that is pulled from the worklist has to be checked against a set of seen states. If the state was already analyzed, then it must not be reanalyzed to ensure termination of the analysis.

Comparing states in this manner gives rise to a computational overhead, especially if the store is contained in the program states. To accelerate the fixed-point computation, global-store widening can be applied [22]. Global-store widening

© Springer Nature Switzerland AG 2019
C. Enea and R. Piskac (Eds.): VMCAI 2019, LNCS 11388, pp. 247–274, 2019.
https://doi.org/10.1007/978-3-030-11245-5_12

lifts the store out of individual states and turns it into a global analysis component, making it a shared component of each state that the analysis produces. This reduces the number of times states have to be reanalyzed and compared, and state comparison itself also becomes cheaper.

Yet, despite improved tractability, an analysis with a global store may still require many state comparisons. Moreover, each time the global store is updated, the set of seen states has to be cleared because all states explored so far were computed with a previous version of the store that is different from the latest one. Although clearing the set of seen states makes checking for membership of this set cheaper, naive approaches do so in an indiscriminate manner. Seen states that are not dependent on a particular store update will still be removed from the set of seen states, and will be reanalyzed without the analysis discovering new information (new states, new store updates, ...). This causes the analysis to reanalyze and compare states unnecessarily.

Therefore, the impact of maintaining a set of seen states on the performance, which is unpredictable in general, motivated the following two research questions.

1. *How to design a static analysis that does not require a set of seen states to reach a fixed point?* and
2. *What are the implications on performance and precision when compared to a traditional technique?*

As the set of seen states plays an important role in ensuring termination of the analysis, our answer focuses on its fixed-point mechanism while assuming regular semantics and configurability (lattices, context-sensitivity, ...).

1.2   Approach

In this work we present a static analysis technique for higher-order, side-effecting programs, called MODF, that does not rely on a set of seen states for computing a fixed point. MODF analyzes one single function execution at a time to completion while tracking read, write, and call effects. These effects trigger the analysis of other function executions, and the analysis terminates when no new effects can be discovered. This means that, unlike existing analyses that rely on effects, MODF uses the effects discovered during analysis to drive the analysis itself. The result of the analysis is a flow graph that can be queried by client analyses for obtaining information about fundamental program properties such as control flow and value flow.

Whenever during a function execution another function is called, a call effect is generated and the cached return value of the called function is retrieved from the store and used as return value. If it is the first call to a particular function, then the called function is added to the worklist for future analysis. Whenever a function reads from the global store, this read dependency is tracked. Upon a write to an address in the store, all read-dependent functions are added to the worklist for reanalysis. When a function returns, its return value is written to the store using the function as the address. Calls beyond the initial one to a particular function do not by themselves trigger that function's reanalysis. Because both the arguments and the return value are stored, writing the argument values at call time and writing the return value at return time ensures that the required (dependent) functions are reanalyzed, thereby honoring the call/return pattern.

By not relying on a set of seen states, MODF avoids the associated state comparisons, and by tracking read and write effects MODF is more selective in reanalyzing program states. The goal of this design is to remove an important source of overhead in naive implementations of machine-based techniques such as AAM [25]. In addition, caching of return values in combination with selective reanalysis acts as a memoization mechanism that a MODF analysis can benefit from.

We applied MODF to a traditional AAM analyzer with global-store widening, and our evaluation shows that for many benchmark programs the MODF analyzer is indeed faster while maintaining precision (Sect. 4).

Contributions

- The formal definition of a function-modular static analysis design for higher-order, side-effecting programs that does not rely on a set of seen states (MODF).
- The application of MODF to AAM, a well-known and widely used analysis approach.
- The implementation of an AAM-based MODF analyzer and its evaluation in terms of performance and precision.

Overview of the Paper. We first introduce MODF (Sect. 2) and formalize our approach (Sect. 3). We then compare a MODF analyzer to an AAM analyzer in terms of performance and precision (Sect. 4). We discuss related work (Sect. 5) and conclude by presenting open questions for future research (Sect. 6).

2   Overview of the Approach

We illustrate MODF through a number of examples involving (recursive) function calls, higher-order functions, and side-effects.

Function execution occurs in a particular execution *context*, and the combination of a function f and its execution context is denoted by κ_f. The program itself is executed in an initial context denoted by κ_0, but in the remainder of this paper we treat it like any other function execution context and refer to it as such (conceptually a program can be thought of as representing the body of an implicit main function that is called to start the execution of the program). MODF analyzes each function execution separately from other executions, tracking function calls and accesses to the global store. When an address is read from the store, a *read effect* is generated by the analysis: $\mathbf{r}(\mathbf{x})$ denotes a read effect on variable x (we use variable names as addresses for simplicity). Similarly, when a value is added or modified in the store, a *write effect* is generated: $\mathbf{w}(\mathbf{x})$ denotes a write effect on variable x. MODF does not immediately step into a function when it is called, but rather models these calls through *call effects*: $c(\kappa)$ denotes a call effect on the context κ. Tracking read, write, and call effects enables detecting how changes made by the execution of one function affect other function executions.

2.1 Simple Function

Consider the following Scheme program, which defines a function f and calls it twice.

```
(define (f) 3)
(f)
(f)
```

MODF starts by analyzing the initial context κ_0. When encountering the first call to f, MODF produces a call effect $c(\kappa_f)$ and looks up the return value of f in the store at address κ_f (contexts are used as addresses in the store). Because f has not yet produced a return value, the lookup results in the bottom value $\bot$, which denotes the absence of information. Looking up this return value produces a read effect $r(\kappa_f)$. The presence of this effect results in κ_0 having a read dependency on address κ_f.

The second call to f is treated in the same manner, so that context κ_0 is now fully analyzed. This is represented by the following graph, where green nodes correspond to expressions that have to be evaluated by the program, and red nodes correspond to values reached by evaluating the preceding green node. The edges correspond to transitions in the evaluation of the program and may be annotated with one or more effects. For clarity, we omit some of the read effects in the graphs that follow.

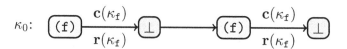

Because the analysis of context κ_0 yielded a function call with context κ_f, and context κ_f was not encountered before, MODF proceeds by analyzing it. This produces an abstract return value **int** (assuming a type lattice as the abstract domain for values), which is written in the store at location κ_f, thereby producing a write effect $w(\kappa_f)$.

$$\kappa_f: \quad \boxed{3} \xrightarrow[w(\kappa_f)]{} \boxed{\textbf{int}}$$

Because context κ_f updates address κ_f, and κ_0 has a read dependency on this address, the analysis of the context κ_0 is retriggered with the updated store, during which the resulting values of function calls to f are now correctly resolved. No new effects are discovered.

κ_0: (f) $\xrightarrow[r(\kappa_f)]{c(\kappa_f)}$ int $\longrightarrow$ (f) $\xrightarrow[r(\kappa_f)]{c(\kappa_f)}$ int

Because all discovered contexts have been analyzed and no new store-changing effects were detected, MODF has reached a fixed point.

2.2 Higher-Order Function

The following example illustrates the analysis of higher-order functions. Function g returns a closure f which is called on the last line.

```
(define (f) 3)
(define (g) f)
(define x (g))
(x)
```

The first iteration of MODF analyzes the initial context κ_0 and detects the call to function g, immediately followed by the assignment of value $\perp$ to variable x because no return value was previously computed for g. The call to variable x therefore results in a $\perp$ value as well.

κ_0: (g) $\xrightarrow[r(\kappa_g)]{c(\kappa_g)}$ $\perp$ $\longrightarrow$ (x) $\longrightarrow$ $\perp$

In the next iteration MODF analyzes context κ_g, as it was encountered for the first time during the previous iteration. The analysis detects that g returns function f, and this return value is stored at address κ_g.

κ_g: f $\xrightarrow[w(\kappa_g)]{}$ f

The third iteration reanalyzes κ_0 as one of the addresses read by this context (κ_g) has been written to. The value of variable x now is function f, and a call effect is generated on context κ_f that immediately returns value $\perp$ because f has not been analyzed previously.

κ_0: (g) $\xrightarrow[r(\kappa_g)]{c(\kappa_g)}$ f $\longrightarrow$ (x) $\xrightarrow[r(\kappa_f)]{c(\kappa_f)}$ $\perp$

The fourth iteration analyzes newly discovered context κ_f and discovers abstract return value **int**, which is stored at address κ_f, generating a write effect.

κ_f: 3 $\xrightarrow[w(\kappa_f)]{}$ int

The fifth and final iteration reanalyzes the initial context, for which the call (x) produces the return value **int** residing at address κ_f, and MODF reaches a fixed point.

$$\kappa_0: \quad \boxed{(g)} \xrightarrow[r(\kappa_g)]{c(\kappa_g)} \boxed{f} \longrightarrow \boxed{(x)} \xrightarrow[r(\kappa_f)]{c(\kappa_f)} \boxed{int}$$

Although this example only considers a program in which a function is returned by another function, MODF supports closures as arguments to or return values of function calls.

2.3   Recursion and Function Arguments

The next example features a recursive function **sum** which computes the sum of natural numbers between 1 and **n**.

```
(define (sum n acc)
  (if (= n 0)
    acc
    (sum (- n 1) (+ acc n))))
(sum 5 0)
```

First, the initial context κ_0 is analyzed, and the call to **sum** immediately results in value $\bot$, generating a call effect for context κ_{sum}. During this iteration (i.e., at the call site), the analysis binds the argument values in the store, generating the corresponding write effects. The store itself is global to the analysis, and only grows monotonically. In our examples we use the name of a variable as the address at which we store its value, so that a particular function parameter is always stored at the same address and multiple calls to **sum** cause the different arguments values to become joined in the store.

$$\kappa_0: \quad \boxed{(\text{sum } 5 \text{ } 0)} \xrightarrow[r(\kappa_{sum}), \text{ } w(n), \text{ } w(acc)]{c(\kappa_{sum})} \boxed{\bot}$$

The second iteration of MODF proceeds with the analysis of context κ_{sum} and the possible return value **int**, stemming from expression **acc** in the then-branch, is detected. The value corresponding to the recursive call in the else-branch is $\bot$ as the address κ_{sum} is not yet bound in the store at this point.

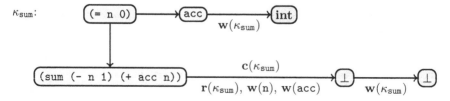

In the third iteration, the analysis has to consider either κ_0 or κ_{sum}, because both contexts have a read dependency on address κ_{sum}, which was written during the previous iteration. Although the order in which contexts are analyzed may influence the convergence speed of a MODF analysis, it will not influence its end result. For this example's sake, we assume MODF reanalyzes κ_0 first, in which the call to sum now produces return value **int** by reading address κ_{sum} in the store.

$$\kappa_0: \quad \boxed{(\text{sum 5 0})} \xrightarrow[\mathbf{r}(\kappa_{\text{sum}}),\ \mathbf{w}(\text{n}),\ \mathbf{w}(\text{acc})]{\mathbf{c}(\kappa_{\text{sum}})} \boxed{\text{int}}$$

Finally, context κ_{sum} is reanalyzed, and the recursive call now also results in the expected abstract value **int**. Because the return value of the sum function was already determined to be **int**, the store does not change and no additional contexts have to be analyzed, concluding the analysis.

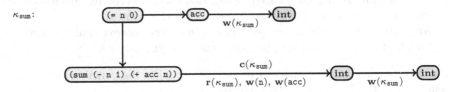

2.4   Mutable State

In this final example we mutate state using the set! construct. Variable x in the program below initially holds an integer value. After evaluating x a first time, function f is called, which changes the value of x to a string, and variable x is evaluated again.

```
(define x 0)
(define (f) (set! x "foo"))
(display x)
(f)
(display x)
```

A first analysis of initial context κ_0 correctly infers the first value for x (**int**) but incorrectly infers its second value as execution context κ_f has not yet been analyzed. However, the read dependency of κ_0 on the address of variable x is inferred as a read effect.

$$\kappa_0: \quad \boxed{\text{x}} \xrightarrow[\mathbf{r}(\text{x})]{} \boxed{\text{int}} \longrightarrow \boxed{(\text{f})} \xrightarrow[\mathbf{r}(\kappa_f)]{\mathbf{c}(\kappa_f)} \boxed{\bot} \longrightarrow \boxed{\text{x}} \xrightarrow[\mathbf{r}(\text{x})]{} \boxed{\text{int}}$$

In the next iteration, context κ_f is analyzed. It writes to the address of variable x and to return location κ_f.

$\kappa_{\mathtt{f}}$:

$$\boxed{\texttt{(set! x "foo")}} \xrightarrow[\mathbf{w}(\mathbf{x})]{} \boxed{\mathbf{str}} \xrightarrow[\mathbf{w}(\kappa_{\mathtt{f}})]{} \boxed{\mathbf{str}}$$

Finally, the reanalysis of context κ_0 is triggered due to changes on addresses on which it depends ($\mathbf{x}$ and $\kappa_{\mathtt{f}}$), and a sound over-approximation of the possible value of $\mathbf{x}$ is obtained.

κ_0:

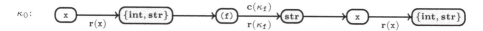

3   Formal Definition

We formally define MODF for a higher-order, side-effecting language as a process that alternates between two phases:

1. An *intra-context* analysis analyzes a function execution context given an input store, and tracks the effects performed within this context.
2. An *inter-context* analysis triggers subsequent intra-context analysis based on the effects observed during previous intra-context analyses.

Before introducing these analysis phases, we provide the concrete operational semantics of the language under analysis.

3.1   Input Language

As input language for the formal definition of MODF, we use the untyped λ-calculus in A-Normal Form with support for side-effects through `set!`. A-Normal Form, or ANF, is a restricted syntactic form for λ-calculus programs in which operators and operands are restricted to *atomic expressions*. Atomic expressions *ae* are expressions that can be evaluated immediately without impacting the program state, as opposed to non-atomic expressions that may impact the program state. This syntactic simplification of the language does not limit its expressiveness, as any λ-calculus program can be automatically rewritten into its A-Normal Form [4]. We assume the domain of expressions (Exp) to be finite, as any program contains a finite number of expressions and we only consider expressions appearing in the analyzed program.

We include atomic expressions that denote integer and string primitive values in the language for consistency with the examples given previously and to illustrate that they do not present any complications with respect to the analysis. Other primitive values can be added in a similar fashion.

The `set!` operator modifies the value of a variable x to the value resulting from the evaluation of an atomic expression *ae*. While the presentation in this paper focuses on a functional language with only `set!` as an imperative construct, nothing prevents the MODF approach from being applied to languages with other and additional imperative constructs.

$$e \in \mathsf{Exp} ::= ae \mid (f\ ae) \qquad\qquad lam \in \mathsf{Lam} ::= (\lambda\ (x)\ e)$$
$$\mid (\texttt{set!}\ x\ ae) \qquad\qquad x \in \mathsf{Var}\ \text{a finite set of identifiers}$$
$$\mid (\texttt{let}\ ((x\ e))\ e) \qquad\qquad n \in \mathbb{Z}\ \text{the set of finite integers}$$
$$f, ae \in \mathsf{AExp} ::= x \mid lam \mid n \mid s \qquad s \in \mathbb{S}\ \text{the set of finite strings}$$

3.2 Concrete Semantics

The concrete semantics of the input language is defined as a transition relation, denoted $\varsigma, \sigma \to \varsigma', \sigma'$. It acts on a state ς and a store σ, producing a successor state and store.

State Space. A state is composed of a control component c, which can either contain an expression to evaluate in an environment ($\mathbf{ev}(e, \rho)$) or a value ($\mathbf{val}(v)$), and a stack ι, which itself is a sequence of frames representing the continuation of the execution. The values (v) in this language are primitive values such as integers ($\mathbf{int}$) and strings ($\mathbf{str}$), and closures ($\mathbf{clo}$) that bind lambda-expressions with their defining environments. Environments map variables to addresses, and stores map addresses to values. We leave addresses undefined for the sake of generality, but we assume that there are infinitely many concrete addresses.

$$\varsigma \in \Sigma ::= \langle c, \iota \rangle \qquad\qquad \phi \in Frame ::= \mathbf{let}(a, e, \rho)$$
$$c \in Control ::= \mathbf{ev}(e, \rho) \mid \mathbf{val}(v) \qquad\qquad \rho \in Env = \mathsf{Var} \to Addr$$
$$v \in Val ::= \mathbf{clo}(lam, \rho) \mid \mathbf{int}(n) \mid \mathbf{str}(s) \qquad\qquad \sigma \in Store = Addr \to Val$$
$$\iota \in Stack ::= \phi : \iota \mid \epsilon \qquad\qquad a \in Addr\ \text{an infinite set of addresses}$$

Atomic Evaluation. Atomic expressions are evaluated by the atomic evaluation function $\mathcal{A} : \mathsf{AExp} \times Env \times Store \to Val$ that, given an environment and a store, computes the value of the atomic expression. Variable references x are evaluated by looking up the address of that variable in the environment and returning the value that resides in the store at that address. The evaluation of a lambda expression results in a closure that pairs the lambda expression with the current environment. Integers and strings are tagged with their respective type during atomic evaluation.

$$\mathcal{A}(x, \rho, \sigma) = \sigma(\rho(x)) \qquad \mathcal{A}(lam, \rho, \sigma) = \mathbf{clo}(lam, \rho) \qquad \mathcal{A}(n, \rho, \sigma) = \mathbf{int}(n) \qquad \mathcal{A}(s, \rho, \sigma) = \mathbf{str}(s)$$

Transition Relation. The transition relation is defined using 5 rules.

Function $\mathcal{A}$ is used by the transition relation to evaluate an atomic expression into a value, leaving the stack and the store unmodified.

$$\frac{v = \mathcal{A}(ae, \rho, \sigma)}{\langle \mathbf{ev}(ae, \rho), \iota \rangle, \sigma \to \langle \mathbf{val}(v), \iota \rangle, \sigma}$$

For a function call, first the operator f and the operand ae are evaluated atomically. Evaluation then continues by stepping into the body e' of the called function with the environment and store extended with the value v of the argument x at a fresh address generated by the allocation function $alloc : \mathsf{Var} \to Addr$.

$$\frac{\mathbf{clo}((\lambda(x)e'), \rho') = \mathcal{A}(f, \rho, \sigma) \qquad v = \mathcal{A}(ae, \rho, \sigma) \qquad a = alloc(x) \qquad \rho'' = \rho'[x \mapsto a]}{\langle \mathbf{ev}((f\ ae), \rho), \iota \rangle, \sigma \to \langle \mathbf{ev}(e', \rho''), \iota \rangle, \sigma[a \mapsto v]}$$

A $\mathtt{set!}$ expression is evaluated by first evaluating the atomic expression ae to obtain the new value v for x, and then updating the value of x in the store.

$$\frac{v = \mathcal{A}(ae, \rho, \sigma)}{\langle \mathbf{ev}((\mathtt{set!}\ x\ ae), \rho), \iota \rangle, \sigma \to \langle \mathbf{val}(v), \iota \rangle, \sigma[\rho(x) \mapsto v]}$$

A $\mathtt{let}$ expression is evaluated in two steps. A first rule pushes a continuation on the stack and evaluates the expression for which x has to be bound to the result. The environment is extended at this point to enable recursion, so that a function can refer to itself in its body (meaning that this $\mathtt{let}$ is equivalent to Scheme's $\mathtt{letrec}$).

$$\frac{a = alloc(x) \qquad \rho' = \rho[x \mapsto a] \qquad \iota' = \mathbf{let}(a, e_2, \rho') : \iota}{\langle \mathbf{ev}((\mathtt{let}\ ((x\ e_1))\ e_2), \rho), \iota \rangle, \sigma \to \langle \mathbf{ev}(e_1, \rho'), \iota' \rangle, \sigma}$$

A second rule then acts when a value has been computed for the variable x by evaluating the body of the $\mathtt{let}$ after binding the address of x to its value in the store.

$$\frac{\sigma' = \sigma[a \mapsto v]}{\langle \mathbf{val}(v), \mathbf{let}(a, e, \rho) : \iota \rangle, \sigma \to \langle \mathbf{ev}(e, \rho), \iota \rangle, \sigma'}$$

This completes the rules for the concrete semantics of the input language.

Allocation. The *alloc* function for allocating addresses in the store is a parameter of the analysis. For defining concrete semantics, natural numbers can be used as concrete addresses, i.e., we take $Addr = \mathbb{N}$ and have *alloc* generate fresh addresses each time it is called.

Collecting Semantics. The concrete collecting semantics of a program e is the set of states that the program may reach during its execution. It is defined as the fixed point of a transfer function $\mathcal{F}^e : \mathcal{P}(\Sigma \times Store) \to \mathcal{P}(\Sigma \times Store)$, where function $\mathcal{I}(e) : \mathsf{Exp} \to \Sigma$ injects a program represented by an expression into an initial state.

$$\mathcal{F}^e(S) = \{(\mathcal{I}(e), [])\} \cup \bigcup_{\substack{\varsigma, \sigma \in S \\ \varsigma, \sigma \to \varsigma', \sigma'}} (\varsigma', \sigma') \qquad\qquad \mathcal{I}(e) = \langle \mathbf{ev}(e, []), \epsilon \rangle$$

In the remainder of this section, we discuss approaches to soundly over-approximate the set of concrete states formed by $\mathrm{lfp}(\mathcal{F}^e)$. First, we abstract all elements of the state space except for the stack (Sect. 3.3), resulting in an infinite abstract interpretation. We then examine and compare different existing approaches for abstracting the stack and introduce and discuss the approach taken by MODF (Sect. 3.4).

3.3 Abstracting Values

Similar to Earl et al. [3], we perform a first abstraction of the concrete semantics to obtain a baseline abstract interpretation to illustrate the similarities and differences between MODF and related work. In this abstraction, we render the set of values and the set of addresses finite but leave the stack untouched.

State Space. This first abstraction consists of rendering the set of addresses finite, which implies that stores now map to *sets of values* rather than a single value. To ensure that the set of values is finite, we also abstract primitive values into their type, although other finite abstractions would work as well. As a result, all components of this state space are finite with the exception of the stack, which can grow infinitely (something we address in the next sections). We highlight the main changes in the formalism in gray.

$$\varsigma \in \Sigma ::= \langle c, \iota \rangle \qquad \qquad \phi \in Frame ::= \mathbf{let}(a, e, \rho)$$

$$c \in Control ::= \mathbf{ev}(e, \rho) \mid \mathbf{val}(\ \{v, \dots\}\ ) \qquad \rho \in Env = \mathsf{Var} \to Addr$$

$$v \in Val ::= \mathbf{clo}(lam, \rho) \mid \boxed{\mathbf{int}} \mid \boxed{\mathbf{str}} \qquad \sigma \in Store = Addr \to \boxed{\mathcal{P}(Val)}$$

$$\iota \in Stack ::= \phi : \iota \mid \epsilon \qquad \qquad a \in Addr \ \text{a} \ \boxed{\text{finite}} \ \text{set of addresses}$$

Atomic Evaluation. The changes in the state space propagate to the atomic evaluation function. The atomic evaluation function $\mathcal{A} : \mathsf{AExp} \times Env \times Store \to \mathcal{P}(Val)$ now evaluates to a set of abstract values, losing information about concrete values of integers and strings.

$$\mathcal{A}(x, \rho, \sigma) = \sigma(\rho(x)) \qquad \mathcal{A}(lam, \rho, \sigma) = \{\ \mathbf{clo}(lam, \rho)\ \} \qquad \mathcal{A}(n, \rho, \sigma) = \{\mathbf{int}\} \qquad \mathcal{A}(s, \rho, \sigma) = \{\mathbf{str}\}$$

Transition Relation. The rules of the transition relation are updated to account for the changes in the store and atomic evaluation function. Because multiple values can be bound at the same address in the store, it is crucial that store updates become store *joins* instead for the sake of soundness. Store joins are defined as the pointwise lift of the join operation of abstract values (which in our case, is the set union). To avoid unnecessary non-determinism, we introduce the $V \in \mathcal{P}(Val)$ metavariable to denote a set of values.

$$\frac{V = \mathcal{A}(ae, \rho, \sigma)}{\langle \mathbf{ev}(ae, \rho), \iota \rangle, \sigma \rightarrow \langle \mathbf{val}(\,V\,), \iota \rangle, \sigma}$$

$$\frac{\mathbf{clo}((\lambda(x)e'), \rho') \in \mathcal{A}(f, \rho, \sigma) \quad V = \mathcal{A}(ae, \rho, \sigma) \quad a = alloc(x) \quad \rho'' = \rho'[x \mapsto a]}{\langle \mathbf{ev}((f\ ae), \rho), \iota \rangle, \sigma \rightarrow \langle \mathbf{ev}(e', \rho''), \iota \rangle, \sigma \sqcup [a \mapsto V\,]}$$

$$\frac{V = \mathcal{A}(ae, \rho, \sigma)}{\langle \mathbf{ev}((\mathtt{set!}\ x\ ae), \rho), \iota \rangle, \sigma \rightarrow \langle \mathbf{val}(V), \iota \rangle, \sigma \sqcup [\rho(x) \mapsto V\,]}$$

$$\frac{a = alloc(x) \quad \rho' = \rho[x \mapsto a] \quad \iota' = \mathbf{let}(a, e_2, \rho') : \iota}{\langle \mathbf{ev}((\mathtt{let}\ ((x\ e_1))\ e_2), \rho), \iota \rangle, \sigma \rightarrow \langle \mathbf{ev}(e_1, \rho'), \iota' \rangle, \sigma} \qquad \frac{\sigma' = \sigma \sqcup [a \mapsto V\,]}{\langle \mathbf{val}(\,V\,), \mathbf{let}(a, e, \rho) : \iota \rangle, \sigma \rightarrow \langle \mathbf{ev}(e, \rho), \iota \rangle, \sigma'}$$

Allocation and Context Sensitivity. The choice for the abstraction of the set of addresses and for the definition of the *alloc* function influences the context-sensitivity of the abstract interpretation. For example, abstracting addresses to variable names ($Addr = \mathsf{Var}$, with $alloc(x) = x$) results in a context-insensitive 0-CFA analysis. Any allocation function is sound [12], and it is possible to introduce more precise context-sensitivities. We refer to Gilray et al. [7] for a discussion of the impact of allocation on the precision of analyses.

Collecting Semantics. Using the abstraction defined here, the abstract collecting semantics of a program e is defined similarly to the concrete collecting semantics. The abstract transfer function $\mathcal{F}^e$ uses the abstract transition relation instead of the concrete one.

$$\mathcal{F}^e(S) = \{(\mathcal{I}(e), [])\} \cup \bigcup_{\substack{\varsigma, \sigma \in S \\ \varsigma, \sigma \rightarrow \varsigma', \sigma'}} (\varsigma', \sigma')$$

The fixed point of the abstract transfer function defines the abstract collecting semantics. However, the set defined by $\mathrm{lfp}(\mathcal{F}^e)$ may not be computable as we have not performed abstraction of the stack. It is therefore not suitable for static analysis without additional abstractions as discussed in the following sections.

3.4 Abstracting the Stack

We left the stack untouched until now, which means it can grow infinitely, resulting in an abstract interpretation that may not terminate. Multiple approaches for abstracting the stack have been proposed, which we summarize here before detailing our own approach in MODF.

AAM Abstraction. AAM (Abstracting Abstract Machines [25]) is a technique for finitely abstracting machine-based interpreters. AAM eliminates potentially infinite recursion by allocating recursive components in the store and—as we did in Sect. 3.3—making the set of store addresses finite. With a finite number of addresses in the store the store cannot grow infinitely, and therefore AAM provides a suitable foundation for static analysis. The solution proposed in AAM to abstract the stack therefore is to thread the potentially infinite sequence of stack frames through the store, rendering the stack finite.

State Space. The components of the state space that require adaptation are the store, which now also contains stacks, and the stacks themselves, which contain at most a single continuation frame and the address at which the rest of the stack resides in the store. To differentiate between stack addresses and value addresses in the store, we introduce contexts (κ) to represent stack addresses.

$$\varsigma \in \Sigma ::= \langle c, \iota \rangle$$
$$c \in Control ::= \mathbf{ev}(e, \rho) \mid \mathbf{val}(\{v, \dots\})$$
$$v \in Val ::= \mathbf{clo}(lam, \rho) \mid \mathbf{int} \mid \mathbf{str}$$
$$\iota \in Stack ::= \phi : \kappa \mid \epsilon$$
$$\phi \in Frame ::= \mathbf{let}(a, e, \rho)$$

$$\rho \in Env = Var \rightharpoonup Addr$$
$$\sigma \in Store = (Addr + K) \rightarrow \mathcal{P}(Val + Stack)$$
$$a \in Addr \text{ a finite set of addresses}$$
$$\kappa \in K \text{ a finite set of contexts}$$

Transition Relation. The only rules of the transition relation impacted by these changes are the rules that push and pop continuation frames from the stack.

To evaluate a `let` binding, a continuation frame is pushed onto the stack. First a stack address is allocated using stack allocation function *allocCtx*. The store can then be extended at the address returned by the stack allocator to contain the current continuation, and a new stack is used in the resulting state. When the **let** continuation has to be popped from the stack, the rest of the stack is looked up in the store at address κ.

$$\frac{V = \mathcal{A}(ae, \rho, \sigma)}{\langle \mathbf{ev}(ae, \rho), \iota \rangle, \sigma \rightsquigarrow \langle \mathbf{val}(V), \iota \rangle, \sigma}$$

$$\frac{\mathbf{clo}((\lambda(x)e'), \rho') \in \mathcal{A}(f, \rho, \sigma) \quad V = \mathcal{A}(ae, \rho, \sigma) \quad a = alloc(x) \quad \rho'' = \rho'[x \mapsto a]}{\langle \mathbf{ev}((f\ ae), \rho), \iota \rangle, \sigma \rightsquigarrow \langle \mathbf{ev}(e', \rho''), \iota \rangle, \sigma \sqcup [a \mapsto V]}$$

$$\frac{V = \mathcal{A}(ae, \rho, \sigma)}{\langle \mathbf{ev}((\mathbf{set!}\ x\ ae), \rho), \iota \rangle, \sigma \rightsquigarrow \langle \mathbf{val}(v), \iota \rangle, \sigma \sqcup [\rho(x) \mapsto V]}$$

$$\frac{a = alloc(x) \quad \rho' = \rho[x \mapsto a] \quad \iota' = \mathbf{let}(a, e_2, \rho') : \kappa \quad \kappa = allocCtx(e_1, \rho) \quad \sigma' = \sigma \sqcup [\kappa \mapsto \{\iota\}]}{\langle \mathbf{ev}((\mathbf{let}\ ((x\ e_1))\ e_2), \rho), \iota \rangle, \sigma \rightsquigarrow \langle \mathbf{ev}(e_1, \rho'), \iota' \rangle, \sigma'}$$

$$\frac{\sigma' = \sigma \sqcup [a \mapsto V] \quad \iota \in \sigma(\kappa)}{\langle \mathbf{val}(V), \mathbf{let}(a, e, \rho) : \kappa \rangle, \sigma \rightsquigarrow \langle \mathbf{ev}(e, \rho), \iota \rangle, \sigma'}$$

Allocation and Context Sensitivity. Like function *alloc*, function *allocCtx* is a parameter of the analysis that can be used to influence the context sensitivity of the analysis. To facilitate comparison with MODF (see Sect. 3.4), we take $K = \mathsf{Exp} \times Env$ and $allocCtx : \mathsf{Exp} \times Env \rightarrow K$ with $allocCtx(e, \rho) = (e, \rho)$. With this definition of *allocCtx*, and because environments contain addresses, any context sensitivity introduced by the value address allocator *alloc* will also influence the context-sensitivity of stack addresses.

Collecting Semantics. The abstract transfer function for computing the abstract collecting semantics needs to be adapted to use the transition relation developed here. In contrast to the abstract transfer function of Sect. 3.3, the resulting abstract collecting semantics is guaranteed to be computable, as the abstraction is finite. This therefore results in an abstract interpretation suitable for a static analysis, although the resulting analysis may not be efficient. If the fixed point is computed with the usual fixed-point computation techniques, such as the commonly used worklist algorithm [19], this requires maintaining a set of states that have been visited in order to avoid re-visiting a state more than once. This in turn ensures that the algorithm terminates.

Because traditional, unoptimized AAM is inefficient, a common performance optimization technique is widening of the global store [25]. Global-store widening widens all reachable stores into a single global store, in effect removing the store as component from individual states.

$$\mathcal{F}^e(S, \sigma) = (\{\mathcal{I}(e)\}, []) \cup (\bigcup_{\substack{\varsigma \in S \\ \varsigma, \sigma \rightsquigarrow \varsigma', \sigma'}} \varsigma', \quad \bigsqcup_{\substack{\varsigma \in S \\ \varsigma, \sigma \rightsquigarrow \varsigma', \sigma'}} \sigma')$$

Although global store-widening improves the performance of the analysis (at the cost of precision), the fixed-point computation of the transfer function using a worklist algorithm has to carefully clear the set of seen states when changes are performed on the global store, as the store is shared with all explored states and changes therefore may impact states that have already been visited. While clearing this set of seen states is crucial for soundness, it does however cause a significant cost, as many of the states present in the set of seen states may not be impacted by the store changes, but will still have to be visited. Our experiments, described in Sect. 4 and in which we observed that 80% of the reanalyzed states in AAM do not yield new states, confirm this. The worst-case complexity of AAM for computing the context-insensitive 0-CFA analysis is $O(n^3)$ [25], with n representing the size of the program.

Pushdown Abstraction. CFA2 [26] and PDCFA [3] are two approaches that use a pushdown automaton instead of a finite state machine to approximate the behavior of a program. However, besides requiring significant engineering effort, using these two techniques as the foundation for static analysis yields a computational costs in $O(2^n)$ for CFA2 and in $O(n^6)$ for PDCFA, resp. [8]. Additionally, CFA2 only supports programs that are written in continuation-passing style.

AAC Abstraction. Johnson et al. [10] proposes a variation on stack abstraction found in AAM called AAC (Abstracting Abstract Control). AAC does not allocate stacks in the value store, but instead introduces a different "stack store" for this purpose. This enables the allocation of stack addresses that consist of all components that influence the outcome of a procedure application (assuming the absence of first-class control), i.e., the entire calling context including the value store. This in turn leads to full call/return precision under a given value abstraction, but without requiring the complex implementation of pushdown automata. In AAC the continuation is also split into a local continuation and a meta-continuation. The local continuation represents the intraprocedural stack and is represented as a sequence of frames, i.e., with maximal precision. A local continuation is bounded by a meta-continuation which is allocated in the store at function calls and therefore represents the interprocedural (call) stack. Although AAC offers high precision, the worst-case computational cost of a context-insensitive AAC flow analysis [10] was found to be $O(n^8)$ [8], where n is the size of the input program. P4F [8] is the name for the technique of choosing AAC stack addresses consisting only of an expression and an environment. While this results in a reduced computational cost of $O(n^3)$ for a context-insensitive analysis, maximal (pushdown) call/return precision for side-effecting programs is lost because the store is not a component of the stack address.

Modular Abstraction. Rather than abstracting the stack, MODF, the approach presented in this paper, modifies the fixed-point computation to ensure that the stack cannot grow infinitely. Similarly to AAC, during the execution of the body of a function, the stack is modeled as a sequence of frames that can grow. By modifying the fixed-point computation to compute local fixed points for each function call, and because the only means of looping in the input language is recursion, the stack cannot grow infinitely, ensuring the termination of the abstract semantics with MODF. In the next section we describe changes made to the abstract semantics introduced in Sect. 3.3 in order to obtain a MODF analysis.

3.5   Intra-context Abstract Semantics for Modf

We first describe changes made to the state space and the abstract transition relation to accomodate for the fixed point computation of MODF.

State Space. Contrary to AAM, MODF leaves the stack untouched and preserves its concrete nature. Instead it is the fixed-point computation that ensures that the stack cannot grow infinitely. Two extra components are necessary to approximate the semantics of a program using MODF.

1. Transition relations are annotated with effects (*eff*) in order to denote operations performed during a transition: a write effect ($\mathbf{w}(a)$) indicates that the store has been modified at address a, a read effect ($\mathbf{r}$) indicates that the store has been accessed at address a, and a call effect ($\mathbf{c}(\kappa)$) indicates that there has been a function call to the function denoted by context κ. These effects are used to detect dependencies between the analyzed contexts.
2. The $\mathbf{ret}(\kappa)$ continuation frame is introduced to represent the end of the execution of a function body. Results of function calls are written in the store at addresses that correspond to execution contexts.

$$
\begin{array}{ll}
\varsigma \in \Sigma ::= \langle c, \iota \rangle & \rho \in Env = \mathsf{Var} \to Addr \\
c \in Control ::= \mathbf{ev}(e, \rho) \mid \mathbf{val}(\{v, \dots\}) & \mathit{eff} \in \mathit{Eff} ::= \mathbf{w}(a) \mid \mathbf{r}(a) \mid \mathbf{c}(\kappa) \\
v \in Val ::= \mathbf{clo}(lam, \rho) \mid \mathbf{int} \mid \mathbf{str} & \sigma \in Store = (Addr + K) \to \mathcal{P}(Val) \\
\iota \in Stack ::= \phi : \iota \mid \epsilon & a \in Addr \text{ a finite set of addresses} \\
\phi \in Frame ::= \mathbf{let}(a, e, \rho) \mid \mathbf{ret}(\kappa) & \kappa \in K \text{ a finite set of contexts}
\end{array}
$$

Atomic Evaluation. The atomic evaluation function $\mathcal{A} : \mathsf{AExp} \times \mathit{Env} \times \mathit{Store} \rightarrow$ $\mathcal{P}(\mathit{Val}) \times \mathcal{P}(\mathit{Eff})$ may read from the store, and therefore now returns a set of effects indicating whether this was the case.

$$\mathcal{A}(x, \rho, \sigma) = \sigma(\rho(x)), \{\mathbf{r}(\rho(x))\} \qquad \mathcal{A}(lam, \rho, \sigma) = \{\mathbf{clo}(lam, \rho)\}, \{\}$$

$$\mathcal{A}(n, \rho, \sigma) = \{\mathbf{int}\}, \{\} \qquad \mathcal{A}(s, \rho, \sigma) = \{\mathbf{str}\}, \{\}$$

Transition Relation. The transition relation is annotated with effects too: $\varsigma, \sigma \xrightarrow{E} \varsigma', \sigma'$ indicates that the transition has generated the set of effects in E. When evaluating an atomic expression, the transition relation is annotated with the effects generated by the atomic evaluation function.

$$\frac{V, E = \mathcal{A}(ae, \rho, \sigma)}{\langle \mathbf{ev}(ae, \rho), \iota \rangle, \sigma \xrightarrow{E} \langle \mathbf{val}(V), \iota \rangle, \sigma}$$

Function calls are evaluated differently than in the AAM semantics and its variant discussed so far. In MODF each function execution is analyzed in isolation from other function executions. The evaluation of a function call therefore does not step into the body of the called function, but rather generates a call effect **c** that will be used by the fixed-point computation to trigger additional intra-context analyses. Immediately after generating a call effect, the return value for the execution context is read from the store, thereby also generating a read effect $\mathbf{r}(\kappa)$. If execution context κ was not analyzed before, then $\sigma(\kappa) = \bot$ and the result of the function call is $\bot$. A function call also results in a write effect $\mathbf{w}(a)$ being generated at address a of the parameter of the function call.

$$\frac{\begin{array}{c} V_f, E_1 \in \mathcal{A}(f, \rho, \sigma) \quad \mathbf{clo}((\lambda(x)e'), \rho') \in V_f \quad V, E_2 = \mathcal{A}(ae, \rho, \sigma) \quad a = alloc(x) \\ \rho'' = \rho'[x \mapsto a] \quad \kappa = allocCtx(e', \rho'') \quad V' = \sigma(\kappa) \quad E = E_1 \cup E_2 \cup \{\mathbf{w}(a), \mathbf{c}(\kappa), \mathbf{r}(\kappa)\} \end{array}}{\langle \mathbf{ev}((f\ ae), \rho), \iota \rangle, \sigma \xrightarrow{E} \langle \mathbf{val}(V'), \iota \rangle, \sigma \sqcup [a \mapsto v]}$$

When evaluating a `set!`, a write effect is generated for the address being modified.

$$\frac{V, E_1 = \mathcal{A}(ae, \rho, \sigma) \qquad E = E_1 \cup \{\mathbf{w}(\rho(x))\}}{\langle \mathbf{ev}((\mathtt{set!}\ x\ ae), \rho), \iota \rangle, \sigma \xrightarrow{E} \langle \mathbf{val}(V), \iota \rangle, \sigma \sqcup [\rho(x) \mapsto V]}$$

Rules for evaluating a `let` remain the same, with the exception that a write effect is generated when the value is bound into the store.

$$\frac{a = alloc(x) \quad \rho' = \rho[x \mapsto a] \quad \iota' = let(a, e_2, \rho') : \iota}{\langle \mathbf{ev}((\mathtt{let}\ ((x\ e_1))\ e_2), \rho), \iota \rangle, \sigma \xrightarrow{\{\}} \langle \mathbf{ev}(e_1, \rho'), \iota' \rangle, \sigma} \qquad \frac{E = \{\mathbf{w}(a)\} \quad \sigma' = \sigma \sqcup [a \mapsto V]}{\langle \mathbf{val}(V), let(a, e, \rho) : \iota \rangle, \sigma \xrightarrow{E} \langle \mathbf{ev}(e, \rho), \iota \rangle, \sigma'}$$

A new rule is added to account for the **ret** frame, which is reached at the end of a function execution. When a function call with context κ reaches the end of its execution, the resulting value is allocated in the store at address κ and a write effect $\mathbf{w}(\kappa)$ is generated.

$$\frac{E = \{\mathbf{w}(\kappa)\}}{\langle \mathbf{val}(V), \mathbf{ret}(\kappa) : \epsilon \rangle, \sigma \xrightarrow{E} \langle \mathbf{val}(V), \epsilon \rangle, \sigma \sqcup [\kappa \mapsto v]}$$

Allocation and Context Sensitivity. Similarly to previous stack abstractions, in MODF the definition of the allocation strategy will influence the context sensitivity of the resulting analysis. While the semantics of MODF is different, the existing allocation strategies for the value store (function *alloc*) developed in the context of AAM [7] can be reused in order to obtain analyses with various context sensitivities.

MODF also requires an allocator for function execution contexts (function *allocCtx*). Unlike in AAM or AAC, however, in MODF contexts are not considered to be stack addresses because they are not used to store continuations (although contexts *are* used as addresses to store return values). Similar to existing approaches that require one, context allocator *allocCtx* in MODF can be used to tune the precision of the analysis. However, because the inter-context analysis must be able to analyze execution contexts, at least the following information must be determinable from a function execution context in MODF: (i) the syntactic function, and (ii) the argument values. For the argument values, one option would be to include the argument values as part of the context. We opt for including the extended environment (the environment after binding function parameters) instead, so that the signature of *allocCtx* is *allocCtx* : $\mathsf{Exp} \times \mathit{Env} \to K$ with $\mathit{allocCtx}(e, \rho) = (e, \rho)$. With this choice of context allocator, the single mechanism of read-dependency tracking (also of the addresses of the function parameters) suffices to trigger the reanalysis of function executions when they are called with different argument values.

Note that when taking a context-insensitive *alloc* function (0-CFA), then taking only a function as execution context (as we did in the examples in Sect. 2) is sound, since each parameter is its own address and a function therefore corresponds with a single and unique set of parameter addresses.

3.6   Intra-context Analysis

Contrary to AAM-style analyses, MODF cannot be used with a traditional transfer function for computing the abstract collecting semantics. Instead, MODF performs local fixed-point computations for each function execution context through an *intra-context analysis*, which will be used by an *inter-context analysis* (presented in the next section) in order to obtain the abstract collecting semantics. The intra-context analysis is defined as a function $\mathit{Intra} : K \times \mathit{Store} \to A \times \mathit{Store} \times \mathcal{P}(\mathit{Eff})$ which, given a context κ and a store σ, provides:

- Some information computed by the analysis, represented by an element of A; we define A as the set of reachable states within a context ($A = \mathcal{P}(\Sigma)$) because it most closely resembles the collecting semantics computed by a machine-based analysis such as AAM.

- The resulting store, which has to contain the return value of the context at address $\mathbf{ret}(\kappa)$, i.e., for the resulting store σ' we should have $\mathbf{ret}(\kappa) \in \text{dom}(\sigma')$.
- The set of effects generated by the transition relation during the analysis of context κ.

With the definition of the abstract transition relation $\overset{E}{\leadsto}$, we define the intra-context analysis as the fixed-point computation of a transfer function $\mathcal{F}_{\sigma_0}^{\kappa}$, acting on elements of the domain $A \times \textit{Store} \times \mathcal{P}(\textit{Eff})$. For a context under analysis κ and for an initial store σ_0, this domain consists of the set of reachable states, the store, and the set of generated effects.

$$\mathcal{F}_{\sigma_0}^{(e,\rho)}(S,\sigma,E) = \langle \{\varsigma_0\}, \sigma_0, \varnothing \rangle \cup \bigcup_{\substack{\varsigma \in S \\ \varsigma,\sigma \overset{E'}{\leadsto} \varsigma',\sigma'}} \langle \{\varsigma'\}, \sigma', E' \rangle$$

$$\text{where } \varsigma_0 = \langle \mathbf{ev}(e,\rho), \mathbf{ret}((e,\rho)) : \epsilon \rangle$$

This transfer function deems as reachable the initial state ς_0, and any state ς' that can be reached in one abstract transition from a reachable state ς. The initial stack consists of a single stack frame $\mathbf{ret}$ to mark the boundary of the function execution. Effects detected during transitions are collected and will be used by the inter-context analysis to detect contexts that need to be reanalyzed. The intra-context analysis is defined as the least fixed point of the transfer function: $\textit{Intra}(\kappa, \sigma) = \text{lfp}(\mathcal{F}_{\sigma}^{\kappa})$. The only way a state could be reachable from itself would be through a recursive call, but this is delegated to the inter-context analysis. Therefore the computation of this fixed point does not require a set of seen states and associated state comparisons.

3.7 Inter-context Analysis

The inter-context analysis operates on a worklist of execution contexts, analyzing one execution context until completion before moving on to the next one. A MODF analysis starts with the inter-context analysis on a worklist containing the root context as sole element. The root context represents the initial context in which the input program is evaluated. The inter-context analysis terminates when its worklist is empty, returning the mapping from contexts to intra-context analysis results. The inter-context analysis also keeps track of the read dependencies of contexts on addresses to support the mechanism of reanalyzing contexts when an address they depend on is written to.

Formally speaking, the inter-context analysis is defined by the function $\textit{Inter}$: $\mathcal{P}(K) \times (\textit{Addr} \to \mathcal{P}(K)) \times \textit{Store} \times (K \to A) \to (K \to A)$. It acts on a worklist of contexts $(\mathcal{P}(K))$, a map that tracks which addresses are read from by which context $(\textit{Addr} \to \mathcal{P}(K))$, a global store $(\textit{Store})$, and a map S that stores the most recent results from intra-context analyses $(K \rightarrow A)$. Since we compute collecting semantics, we have $A = \mathcal{P}(\Sigma)$.

$$Inter(\varnothing, \_, \_, S) = S$$

$$Inter(\kappa \uplus \kappa s, R, \sigma, S) = Inter(\kappa s \ \cup \bigcup_{\substack{\mathbf{c}(\kappa') \in E \\ \kappa' \notin \mathrm{dom}(\sigma)}} \kappa' \cup \bigcup_{\substack{\mathbf{w}(a) \in E \\ \kappa' \in R(a) \\ \sigma(a) \neq \sigma'(a)}} \kappa', R \sqcup \bigsqcup_{\mathbf{r}(a) \in E} [a \mapsto \{\kappa\}], \sigma', S[\kappa \mapsto S'])$$

where $\langle S', \sigma', E \rangle = Intra(\kappa, \sigma)$

If the worklist is empty, map S is returned. Otherwise, the inter-context analysis pulls a context κ from its worklist and performs an intra-context analysis. Based on the results of the intra-context analysis, additional contexts may be added to the worklist. Adding contexts to the worklist requires comparing contexts which is cheaper than comparing states in a traditional analysis where the worklist contains program states. Also note the absence of a set of seen states, which is needed in traditional algorithms to ensure termination. A context κ' is added to the worklist if at least one of the following two conditions is met.

1. Context κ' was called ($\mathbf{c}(\kappa') \in E$) and has not yet been analyzed (modelled as $\kappa' \notin \mathrm{dom}(\sigma)$).
2. Context κ' has a read dependency on an address a ($\kappa' \in R(a)$) and a was written to ($\mathbf{w}(a) \in E$) in a way that changes the store ($\sigma(a) \neq \sigma'(a)$).

Any address a' that was read during the intra-context analysis of context κ (i.e., $\mathbf{r}(a') \in E$) is registered as being depended upon by κ by updating the mapping of read dependencies R accordingly. The global store is also updated and the result S' of the intra-context analysis is stored in S.

Collecting Semantics. Let $\kappa_0 = allocCtx(e, [])$ be the root context for program e. The abstract collecting semantics of program e is obtained by computing $Inter(\kappa_0, \varnothing, \varnothing, \varnothing, \varnothing)$, which results in a mapping $S \in K \rightarrow A$ from contexts to the set of states that may be reachable in that context.

3.8 Soundness

Soundness of the Abstract Semantics. Except from the rule for function calls, our abstraction of the transition relation rules follows the usual AAM recipe. Their soundness is proven by a case analysis [25]. As our function call rule does not step into the body of the called function, its soundness solely relies on the fact that $\sigma(\kappa)$ holds a sound approximation of the result of a function call—which is proven in the last paragraph of this section.

Soundness of the Intra-context Analysis. We have to show that given an approximation of the store σ, our intra-context analysis $Intra(\kappa, \sigma)$ yields a sound over-approximation for the reachable states, the store, and the effects returned. This is the case because all states reachable from its input store and context will be analyzed, by definition. The soundness of the intra-context analysis therefore also relies on the fact that the given input store is sound.

Soundness of the Inter-context Analysis. The soundness proof for the inter-context analysis amounts to showing that the considered store eventually becomes a sound over-approximation of all possible stores reached by the concrete semantics, and contains an over-approximation of all return values of each function at the address corresponding to their context. This is shown by the fact that intra-context analyses are sound for the store with which they are executed, hence the resulting store is completed with information coming from the analysis of a context given an input store. This in turn will trigger other analyses based on the discovered read dependencies and function calls. We note that a discovered context that has not yet been analyzed will be analyzed by the intra-context analysis, and that a context that has already been analyzed will be analyzed upon changes to values in the store. Eventually, all reachable contexts will be analyzed for all possible changes to the values they depend on, resulting in a sound over-approximation of the store and a sound over-approximation of all possible return values of these contexts. Hence, the inter-context analysis is sound.

3.9   Termination

Termination of the Intra-context Analysis. The intra-context analysis, defined as a fixed-point computation, always terminates. All components of the abstract state space are finite, except for the stack: the abstract address domain *Addr* itself is made finite by the abstraction, and this propagates to the other components of the state space. The resulting set of abstract environments is finite, as there is a finite number of variable names and a finite number of abstract addresses to compose them from. The set of abstract values (*Val*) is finite as there is a finite number of abstract environments from which closures can be composed. The sets of stores (*Store*), effects (*Eff*), and contexts (*K*) become finite too.

Even though the *Stack* abstract domain is not finite, the intra-context analysis cannot construct an infinite stack. Stacks only grow when analyzing `let` expressions, and there can only be a finite number of such expressions within a function body. Constructing an infinite stack requires loops in the analysis, which is precluded by our use of the value cached in the store for a (potentially recursive) function call. The fixed-point computation for the intra-context analysis will therefore always terminate.

Termination of the Inter-context Analysis. The inter-context analysis terminates when its worklist is empty. This worklist grows in two cases.

First, when a function call with context κ is encountered for the first time (i.e., a $\mathbf{c}(\kappa)$ effect is discovered), κ is added to the worklist. There is a finite number of syntactic function calls, and once a function call has already been considered (modelled as $\kappa \in \mathrm{dom}(\sigma)$), it will not be considered again. The worklist can hence not grow indefinitely through function calls.

Second, when a write effect $\mathbf{w}(a)$ is discovered for an address that is read by a context κ, this context is added to the worklist under the condition that the value residing at address a in the store has itself changed ($\sigma(a) \neq \sigma'(a)$). The store being monotone and the number of possible values associated with each address in the store being finite, values will eventually stabilize. This ensures that a given context can be considered for reanalysis only a finite number of times.

Altogether, each context κ will only be analyzed a finite number of times, and there can only be a finite number of contexts for a given program. This ensures that the inter-context analysis always terminates.

3.10   Complexity

Complexity of the Intra-context Analysis. The intra-context analysis can execute at most a number of transitions equal to the number of expressions in the context under analysis. Hence, the complexity of the intra-context analysis given a specific context and specific store is in $\mathcal{O}(|\mathsf{Exp}|)$, where $|\mathsf{Exp}|$ is the size of the program under analysis.

Complexity of the Inter-context Analysis. Each context managed by the inter-context analysis can be analyzed for each change in the store to each of the addresses read in that context. An address can have at most $|\mathsf{Exp}|$ different values, hence the number of changes to an address is bounded by $|\mathsf{Exp}|$. Similarly, with our address allocation strategy, there are at most $|\mathsf{Exp}|$ addresses in the store, hence each context can be analyzed at most $|\mathsf{Exp}|^2$ times.

The inter-context analysis manages at most $|\mathsf{Exp}|$ contexts. With these bounds, one derives a worst-case time complexity of $\mathcal{O}(|\mathsf{Exp}|^4)$: there are at most $|\mathsf{Exp}|$ contexts, each analyzed at most $|\mathsf{Exp}|^2$ times, and the complexity of the analysis of one context being bounded by $|\mathsf{Exp}|$. However, note that for a given program, the number of contexts is inversely proportional to the size of each context: a program with the worst-case context length ($|\mathsf{Exp}|$) can have only one context, as its number of expressions is equal to the size of the program. Conversely, a program with the worst-case number of contexts ($|\mathsf{Exp}|$) has the minimal size for each context. In fact, the number of contexts is related to the size of the contexts in such a way that the worst-case of their multiplication is $|\mathsf{Exp}|$. Hence, MODF has a worst-case time complexity of $\mathcal{O}(|\mathsf{Exp}|^3)$, which is equal to the worst-case time-complexity of a 0-CFA AAM analysis widened with a global store [25]. In practice, as we evaluate in Sect. 4, MODF executes in a lower analysis time than the equivalent AAM analysis.

4   Evaluation

We implemented an AAM analyzer and a MODF analyzer in the Racket dialect of Scheme, and evaluated them on several Scheme benchmark programs. Compared to the descriptions and formalizations presented in this paper, the analyzers support a more extensive input language and semantics featuring conditionals, lists, vectors, and additional primitives. Our AAM analyzer is a faithful implementation of an AAM analysis, more specifically the AAC variant introduced by

Johnson and Van Horn [10], configured with 0-CFA store value allocators and a stack value allocator identical to that of MODF.

To make the comparison possible and fair, we actually derived MODF from the AAM implementation, only changing what was necessary. Therefore both implementations share infrastructure for ASTs, lattices, machine semantics (the intra-context small-step relation), primitives, and so on. We did not optimize the AAM and MODF analyzer and will address applying and evaluating different optimization strategies as future work (also see Sect. 5). The worklist strategy used by the inter-context analysis of MODF and by the AAM analysis both follow a last-in first-out strategy. The analyzers' implementation and test setup, including benchmark programs, are publicly available[1].

Our set of benchmark programs consists of 20 Scheme programs coming from a variety of sources, including the Gabriel performance benchmarks [6], benchmarks from related work typically used to challenge control-flow analyses (see Sect. 5), and benchmarks from the Computer Language Benchmarks Game [5]. In the remainder of this section we report on the soundness, precision, and performance of our implementations on these programs.

4.1   Soundness Testing

We first established the correctness of our AAM-based semantics by running each benchmark program under concrete semantics and checking that it produced a single answer equivalent to the answer computed by Racket for the same program. We then mechanically checked that, for each program and under abstract semantics, the abstract values for all variables produced by our AAM and MODF implementations subsume their corresponding concrete values after abstraction [1]. From these experiments we conclude that both analyzers are sound w.r.t. to our set of benchmark programs.

4.2   Precision Evaluation

We measured the overall precision of each analysis by counting the number of abstract values in all states of the results of each analysis. Because we use a set lattice, set size can be used as a measure of precision: the more elements are in a set representing an abstract value, the lower the precision. Column *Values* in Table 1 lists the results of this experiment (lower is better). In comparison to AAM, MODF may lose precision with respect to function argument values and the return value for a function execution context, as under our test configuration (0-CFA) these values are joined in the store. Upon reanalysis of a context, this may introduce spurious results. In contrast, AAM will not have spurious results for a first call to a function, but may have spurious results for subsequent calls. As seen from the numbers in Table 1, we conclude that in practice the AAM and MODF analyzers are similar in precision for the majority of our benchmark programs.

---

[1] https://github.com/jensnicolay/modf.

Table 1. Precision comparison between AAM and MODF. |Exp| is the number of atoms present in the program under analysis. *Values* is the sum of the set of abstract values (lower is better), and *Mono* is the number of monomorphic call sites detected by the analysis (higher is better). The *Difference* columns indicate the difference in percentage of the results for AAM and MODF: a positive percentage indicates that MODF has detected more elements. For *Values*, lower percentages are better, and for *Mono*, higher percentages are better.

Program	|Exp|	AAM		MODF		Difference	
		Values	Mono	Values	Mono	Values	Mono
primtest	281	66	55	66	55	+0%	+0%
partialsums	326	86	73	86	73	+0%	+0%
treeadd	354	123	57	128	57	+5%	+0%
spectralnorm	400	109	89	109	89	+0%	+0%
matrix	351	106	77	109	74	+2%	−4%
classtree	430	439	97	441	91	+0%	−6%
fankuch	415	131	98	133	97	+2%	−1%
destruct	356	167	48	163	48	−2%	+0%
supermerge	202	972	21	990	18	+2%	−14%
churchnums	194	403	19	403	19	+0%	+0%
deriv	331	735	46	756	47	+3%	+2%
regex	540	426	69	423	69	−1%	+0%
triangl	448	698	40	659	40	−6%	+0%
graphs	1407	657	198	657	197	+0%	−1%
mazefun	1100	2587	117	2615	116	+1%	−1%
dderiv	449	2463	49	2457	49	+0%	+0%
scm2java	1769	5908	266	5956	265	+1%	−1%
browse	1251	8935	129	8606	129	−4%	+0%
mceval	1390	13178	159	13049	159	−1%	+0%
boyer	2260	115365	86	115574	86	+0%	+0%

Although the measurements of the number of values give a good indication of the overall precision of the analysis results, they do not reveal much about "useful" precision. Therefore we also counted the number of singleton sets computed by each abstract analysis (column *Mono* in Table 1, higher is better). Singleton sets indicate abstract values that, in our configuration, represent either a single primitive type, a single closure, or a single address (list or vector). Therefore, this measure of precision is interesting for client analyses such as type analysis, call graph reachability, and monomorphic call inference (a single closure value for an operator position corresponds to a monomorphic function call). We conclude again that the precision of the AAM analyzer and MODF analyzer are comparable in this respect for the majority of the benchmark programs.

4.3   Performance Evaluation

We measured the time it takes for the analyses to complete, and how many abstract states are computed in this time. Table 2 depicts the results sorted in ascending order by AAM analysis time. The results show an average speedup of 3.7 for MODF over AAM on our set of 20 benchmark programs. MODF finished the analysis faster in 17 out of 20 programs, with speedup factors ranging between 1.4 and 12.3. We registered a slowdown for 3 out of 20 programs, with a doubling of analysis time for one smaller benchmark. The higher the AAM analysis time for a program, the better MODF performs: in Table 2 MODF generally results in a speedup.

Table 2. Performance comparison between AAM and MODF. For AAM and MODF, column *States* is the number of states that the analysis has explored, and *Time* is the time taken by the analysis to run to completion, in milliseconds. The *Reduction* columns indicate the improvement in number of states and in time resulting from MODF, as a factor of the number of states explored (resp. the time taken) by AAM over the number of states explored (resp. the time taken) by MODF. A higher reduction factor shows more improvement resulting from MODF.

Program	|Exp|	AAM		MODF		Reduction	
		States	Time	States	Time	States	Time
primtest	281	178	18	183	7	1.0×	**2.6×**
partialsums	326	223	18	225	7	1.0×	**2.6×**
treeadd	354	263	28	292	35	0.9×	0.8×
spectralnorm	400	256	31	269	10	1.0×	**3.1×**
matrix	351	237	44	256	27	0.9×	**1.6×**
classtree	430	352	72	465	137	0.8×	0.5×
fankuch	415	308	73	338	54	0.9×	**1.4×**
destruct	356	274	95	306	58	0.9×	**1.6×**
supermerge	202	356	295	212	63	**1.7×**	**4.7×**
churchnums	194	428	309	318	82	**1.3×**	**3.8×**
deriv	331	419	313	400	118	1.0×	**2.7×**
regex	540	579	558	491	86	**1.2×**	**6.5×**
triangl	448	371	861	373	205	1.0×	**4.2×**
graphs	1407	918	2020	898	347	1.0×	**5.8×**
mazefun	1100	1066	2655	1140	3379	0.9×	0.8×
dderiv	449	750	3003	546	889	**1.4×**	**3.4×**
scm2java	1769	2446	24925	1602	2356	**1.5×**	**10.6×**
browse	1251	1565	41478	1510	10621	1.0×	**3.9×**
mceval	1390	2333	46483	2478	23040	0.9×	**2.0×**
boyer	2260	13048	5241215	2154	425915	**6.1×**	**12.3×**

To gain insights to why MODF is faster on these programs, we performed some additional measurements with the following averaged results:

1. 8% of the running time of the AAM analyzer is spent checking seen states, which is avoided by MODF.
2. Adding return value merging to the AAM analyzer—something inherently present in MODF—only improves its running time by 2%.
3. 80% of reanalyzed states by the AAM analyzer do not yield new states, while this is the case for 63% of reanalyzed states by the MODF analyzer.

Considering that, apart from the effect tracking and the fixed-point computation, both analyzers share the same implementation, we can conclude that (i) avoiding the cost of checking for seen states, and (ii) profiting of a worklist strategy that can selectively reanalyze states upon store updates in combination with memoization of return values are the two major factors in explaining why MODF outperforms AAM on our set of benchmark programs.

MODF also tends to produce smaller flow graphs than AAM as analysis time increases, although for the smaller benchmarks MODF slightly outputs more program states. The reason is that MODF immediately continues after a function call with the cached result fetched from the store, even if the function was not previously analyzed. In the latter case, a ⊥ return value results, which does not occur in AAM. However, for the larger benchmarks, the advantages of MODF and especially its return value memoization outweigh these ⊥ return flows, and MODF often produces flow graphs with less states than AAM. It is also worth noting that MODF often is faster even when producing more states.

In conclusion, while MODF loses some precision for some programs when compared with AAM, we believe that the tradeoff our technique proposes between performance and precision is worthwhile.

5 Related Work

Modular Analysis. MODF can be regarded as a modular analysis in that function execution contexts are analyzed one at a time and to completion. The concept of a modular analysis was formalized by Cousot and Cousot [2], which presents different general-purpose techniques. Sharir and Pnueli [21] introduces a program analysis that integrates an interprocedural analysis with intraprocedural analysis, similarly to MODF. The result of the intraprocedural analysis is a summary that is used by the interprocedural analysis. However, this approach remains limited to a first-order setting while MODF was explicitly designed with support for higher-order, side-effecting programs. Moreover, unlike modular summary-based analyses, MODF *does* reanalyze function execution contexts as new contexts and effects are discovered.

Abstract Machines. In this paper we compare a MODF analyzer against an implementation of a variation of AAM, a well-known machine-based analysis approach [10,25] Related work has produced different techniques and extensions for AAM with varying trade-offs between precision and performance, of which a summary can be found in Gilray et al. [8]. MODF itself also uses AAM-style semantics for its small-step analysis of functions, which makes the comparison with the AAM analyzer justified and straightforward, the latter also on a technical level by maximizing code reuse. Applications of AAM are found in various domains, such as detecting function purity [18], performing symbolic execution for contracts [15], analyzing concurrent programs [14,23,24], determining function coupling [16], discovering security vulnerabilities [17] or performing malware analysis [11]. The approach used by MODF could improve the performance of such applications and other client analyses without impacting their precision.

Might and Shivers [13] introduced abstract garbage collection and abstract counting as techniques for increasing the performance and precision of a store-based abstract interpretation. Abstract garbage collection reclaims unused store addresses, but is not straightforward to adapt for MODF because of the per-context analysis in combination with a global store. Abstract counting keeps track of whether an address is allocated exactly once or multiple times in the store. If the address has only been allocated once, a strong update can be used instead of a weak update. Abstract counting is orthogonal to MODF and incorporating it into our approach and evaluating its effects is future work.

In this paper we compare unoptimized implementations of a MODF and an AAM analyzer. Johnson et al. [9] presents OAAM, a series of 6 steps that can be applied to optimize naive global-store AAM implementations for higher-order, functional languages, resulting in two to three order of magnitude speedups. However, OAAM requires heavy semantics and implementation engineering, while MODF is a simple technique that can be applied to side-effecting semantics as well. Some OAAM optimizations can be applied to MODF (e.g., store pre-allocation), while others clearly cannot (e.g., optimizations that rely on the absence of side effects, or those that involve the set of seen states).

Effect Systems. MODF relies on effects to drive the inter-context analysis. This however differs from typical usages of effect systems [20]. A first difference is that effect systems usually extend a static type system, while MODF does not make any assumptions about the type system of the analyzed language. Another major difference is that effect systems are used to *reason* about the effects performed in the program under analysis, while MODF *relies* on effects during the analysis to perform a general-purpose static analysis that can serve a number of client applications. Hence, while both MODF and effect systems use effects, the way effects are used is entirely different.

6   Conclusion

We presented MODF, a technique for the static analysis of higher-order, side-effecting programs in a modular way. MODF analyzes one single function execution at a time to completion while tracking read, write, and call effects. These effects trigger the analysis of other function executions, and the analysis terminates when no new effects can be discovered.

The goal of MODF's design is to reduce the overhead associated with maintaining a set of seen states while exploring the state space. By not relying on a set of seen states, MODF avoids many state comparisons, and by tracking read and write effects MODF is more selective in reanalyzing program states than traditional implementations of machine-based static analyses such as AAM.

We implemented an AAM analyzer and derived a MODF analyzer from it by adding effect tracking and changing the fixed point computation, and evaluated the two implementations on 20 benchmark programs. Our experiments show an average speedup of 3.7 for MODF over AAM on our set of benchmark programs. MODF finished the analysis faster in 17 out of 20 programs, with speedup factors ranging between 1.4 and 12.3. We also found that the AAM and MODF analyzer are similar in precision for the majority of our benchmark programs, while computing flow graphs of similar size or smaller.

In future research we will experiment with different concepts of modules and context sensitivities for analyzing modules, and will also examine opportunities to incrementalize and parallelize the approach. Although MODF is already inherently incremental in the sense that upon a change in the input program initially only the directly affected execution contexts can be (or should be) reanalyzed, the monotonicity of the global store complicates matters in terms of precision. The modular nature of MODF and the fact that the approach tracks interference between modules by design should facilitate its parallelization.

Acknowledgments. Jens Nicolay is funded by the SeCloud project sponsored by Innoviris, the Brussels Institute for Research and Innovation.

References

1. Andreasen, E.S., Møller, A., Nielsen, B.B.: Systematic approaches for increasing soundness and precision of static analyzers. In: Proceedings of the 6th ACM SIGPLAN International Workshop on State of the Art in Program Analysis, SOAP@PLDI 2017, pp. 31–36 (2017)
2. Cousot, P., Cousot, R.: Modular static program analysis. In: Horspool, R.N. (ed.) CC 2002. LNCS, vol. 2304, pp. 159–179. Springer, Heidelberg (2002). https://doi.org/10.1007/3-540-45937-5_13
3. Earl, C., Might, M., Van Horn, D.: Pushdown control-flow analysis of higher-order programs. In: Proceedings of the 2010 Workshop on Scheme and Functional Programming (Scheme 2010) (2010)
4. Flanagan, C., Sabry, A., Duba, B., Felleisen, M.: The essence of compiling with continuations. ACM SIGPLAN Not. **28**(6), 237–247 (1993)
5. Fulgham, B., Gouy, I.: The computer language benchmarks game (2009). http://shootout.alioth.debian.org
6. Gabriel, R.P.: Performance and Evaluation of LISP Systems, vol. 263. MIT press, Cambridge (1985)
7. Gilray, T., Adams, M.D., Might, M.: Allocation characterizes polyvariance: a unified methodology for polyvariant control-flow analysis. In: Proceedings of the 21st ACM SIGPLAN International Conference on Functional Programming, ICFP 2016, Nara, Japan, 18–22 September 2016, pp. 407–420 (2016)
8. Gilray, T., Lyde, S., Adams, M.D., Might, M., Horn, D.V.: Pushdown control-flow analysis for free. In: Proceedings of the 43th Annual ACM Symposium on the Principles of Programming Languages (POPL 2016) (2016)

9. Johnson, J.I., Labich, N., Might, M., Van Horn, D.: Optimizing abstract abstract machines. In: ACM SIGPLAN International Conference on Functional Programming, ICFP 2013, Boston, MA, USA, 25–27 September 2013, pp. 443–454 (2013)
10. Johnson, J.I., Van Horn, D.: Abstracting abstract control. In: Proceedings of the 10th ACM Symposium on Dynamic languages, pp. 11–22. ACM (2014)
11. Liang, S., Might, M., Horn, D.V.: Anadroid: Malware analysis of android with user-supplied predicates. Electr. Notes Theor. Comput. Sci. **311**, 3–14 (2015)
12. Might, M., Manolios, P.: *A posteriori* soundness for non-deterministic abstract interpretations. In: Jones, N.D., Müller-Olm, M. (eds.) VMCAI 2009. LNCS, vol. 5403, pp. 260–274. Springer, Heidelberg (2008). https://doi.org/10.1007/978-3-540-93900-9_22
13. Might, M., Shivers, O.: Improving flow analyses via γCFA: abstract garbage collection and counting. ACM SIGPLAN Not. **41**, 13–25 (2006)
14. Might, M., Van Horn, D.: A family of abstract interpretations for static analysis of concurrent higher-order programs. In: Yahav, E. (ed.) SAS 2011. LNCS, vol. 6887, pp. 180–197. Springer, Heidelberg (2011). https://doi.org/10.1007/978-3-642-23702-7_16
15. Nguyen, P.C., Gilray, T., Tobin-Hochstadt, S., Horn, D.V.: Soft contract verification for higher-order stateful programs. PACMPL **2**(POPL), 51:1–51:30 (2018)
16. Nicolay, J., Noguera, C., Roover, C.D., Meuter, W.D.: Determining dynamic coupling in JavaScript using object type inference. In: Proceedings of the Thirteenth IEEE International Working Conference on Source Code Analysis and Manipulation (SCAM 2013), pp. 126–135 (2013)
17. Nicolay, J., Spruyt, V., De Roover, C.: Static detection of user-specified security vulnerabilities in client-side JavaScript. In: Proceedings of the 2016 ACM Workshop on Programming Languages and Analysis for Security, pp. 3–13. ACM (2016)
18. Nicolay, J., Stiévenart, Q., De Meuter, W., De Roover, C.: Purity analysis for JavaScript through abstract interpretation. J. Softw. Evol. Process (2017). https://doi.org/10.1002/smr.1889
19. Nielson, F., Nielson, H.R., Hankin, C.: Algorithms. Principles of Program Analysis, pp. 365–392. Springer, Heidelberg (1999). https://doi.org/10.1007/978-3-662-03811-6_6
20. Nielson, F., Nielson, H.R., Hankin, C.: Type and effect systems. Principles of Program Analysis, pp. 283–363. Springer, Heidelberg (1999). https://doi.org/10.1007/978-3-662-03811-6_5
21. Sharir, M., Pnueli, A.: Two approaches to interprocedural data flow analysis. Technical report, New York University, Department of Computer Science (1978)
22. Shivers, O.: Control-flow analysis of higher-order languages. Ph.D. thesis, Carnegie Mellon University Pittsburgh, PA (1991)
23. Stievenart, Q., Nicolay, J., De Meuter, W., De Roover, C.: Detecting concurrency bugs in higher-order programs through abstract interpretation. In: Proceedings of the 17th International Symposium on Principles and Practice of Declarative Programming, pp. 232–243. ACM (2015)
24. Stiévenart, Q., Nicolay, J., De Meuter, W., De Roover, C.: Mailbox abstractions for static analysis of actor programs. In: 31st European Conference on Object-Oriented Programming, ECOOP 2017, pp. 25:1–25:30 (2017)
25. Van Horn, D., Might, M.: Abstracting abstract machines. ACM SIGPLAN Not. **45**, 51–62 (2010)
26. Vardoulakis, D., Shivers, O.: CFA2: a context-free approach to control-flow analysis. In: Gordon, A.D. (ed.) ESOP 2010. LNCS, vol. 6012, pp. 570–589. Springer, Heidelberg (2010). https://doi.org/10.1007/978-3-642-11957-6_30

Type-Directed Bounding of Collections in Reactive Programs

Tianhan Lu[(⊠)], Pavol Černý, Bor-Yuh Evan Chang, and Ashutosh Trivedi

University of Colorado Boulder, Boulder, USA
{tianhan.lu,pavol.cerny,bec,ashutosh.trivedi}@colorado.edu

Abstract. Our aim is to statically verify that in a given reactive program, the length of collection variables does not grow beyond a given bound. We propose a scalable type-based technique that checks that each collection variable has a given refinement type that specifies constraints about its length. A novel feature of our refinement types is that the refinements can refer to *AST counters* that track how many times an AST node has been executed. This feature enables type refinements to track limited flow-sensitive information. We generate verification conditions that ensure that the AST counters are used consistently, and that the types imply the given bound. The verification conditions are discharged by an off-the-shelf SMT solver. Experimental results demonstrate that our technique is scalable, and effective at verifying reactive programs with respect to requirements on length of collections.

1 Introduction

Collections are widely used abstract data types in programs. Collections, by providing a layer of abstraction, allow a programmer to flexibly choose different implementations leading to better modularity essential for developing good quality software. Since collections are extensively used, related performance issues have attracted considerable attention [20,29,30]. Besides performance issues, improper usage of collections may lead to security vulnerabilities such as denial-of-service (DoS) attacks. The performance and security issues are more pronounced in reactive programs such as service threads in operating systems or web applications. An important category of DoS vulnerabilities is out-of-memory error caused by collections with excessively large lengths.

Problem. The goal of this paper is to verify bounds on collection lengths using a scalable type-directed approach. Given constraints on inputs, our technique statically verifies at any point of execution total length of collection variables is less than a given bound. Verifying bound on collection lengths for reactive programs brings the following *challenges*:

Non-termination. Reactive programs do not terminate. The most common method for resource bound analysis is based on finding loop bounds [8,14,15, 17,24,31]. This method therefore does not directly apply to reactive programs.

© Springer Nature Switzerland AG 2019
C. Enea and R. Piskac (Eds.): VMCAI 2019, LNCS 11388, pp. 275–296, 2019.
https://doi.org/10.1007/978-3-030-11245-5_13

Scalability. We need a scalable and modular solution, because real world reactive programs such as web servers are large (e.g. up to $30kloc$).

Non-inductiveness of invariants. The necessary safety invariants might be *non-inductive*. For instance, collection lengths of a program may be bounded, but this is at first glance not provable by checking each statement in isolation, because a particular statement might simply add an element to a collection, thus breaking an invariant that is naively constructed to help verifying boundedness.

Approach. We now describe our approach, with a focus on how the three challenges are addressed. We develop a refinement type system, where the user is able to specify bounds on collection lengths, as well as an overall guarantee on the total length of all collections. These bounds might be symbolic, referring to for instance to bounds on lengths of input collections. Our tool QUANTM then type checks the program, and proves (or refutes) the overall guarantee.

First, to address the challenges of non-termination, our system relies purely on *safety properties*, never requiring a liveness property such as termination. We also do not require finding loop bounds.

Second, to address the challenge of scalability, we use type-based reasoning only. This entails checking at most one invariant per collection, as opposed to one invariant per each code location (as the approaches based on abstract interpretation [15,17] might need).

Third, to address the challenge of non-inductiveness of invariants, we allow the refinement refer to *AST counters* that count how many times an Abstract Syntax Tree (AST) node has been executed. For instance, consider the fragment:

```
while (true) { if (*) { C: s.add(r1);...;D: t.add(r2); }  }
```

and suppose we are interested in the invariant $|\text{len}(s) - \text{len}(t)| \leq 1$, that is, the difference between lengths of the two collections s and t is at most 1. The invariant is not inductive, the statement s.add(r) breaks it. However, let C be a counter associated with the AST node of s.add(r1), and D with t.add(r2). The invariant $\text{len}(s) + D = \text{len}(t) + C$ holds. We can then add a counter axiom $(D + 1 \equiv C) \vee (C \equiv D)$ as the two statements are inside a same basic block. Counter axioms are the place where the limited amount of flow-sensitive information that our system uses is captured. The inductive invariant and the axiom together imply the property we are interested in: $|\text{len}(s) - \text{len}(t)| \leq 1$.

Contributions. The main contributions of this paper are

– **Refinement types for collection lengths.** We propose to encode the total length of collection variables as safety properties of all reachable program states, as opposed to relying on analyzing time bounds. We develop a refinement type system where the refinements allow reasoning about collection lengths.

– **AST counters for inductive invariants.** A novel feature of our refinement types is that the refinements can refer to *AST counters* that track how many times an AST node has been executed. This feature enables type refinements to track limited flow-sensitive information.

- **Empirical evaluation.** Experimental results show that our approach scales to programs up to $30kloc$ ($180kloc$ in total), within 52 s of analysis time per benchmark. Moreover, we discovered a Denial-of-Service vulnerability in one of our benchmarks because of correctly not being able to verify boundedness.

2   Overview

We demonstrate our approach for verifying the total collection lengths for reactive programs on a motivating example in Fig. 1.

2.1   Using Quantm

Overall, a user interacts with our tool QUANTM as follows. First, they write a driver that encodes a particular usage pattern that they are interested in. Then they specify invariants as type annotations. After these two steps, our type system will take care of the rest by automatically checking if the invariant relations are valid. If the invariants are indeed valid, QUANTM will automatically discharge a query to an off-the-shelf SMT solver, returning the result "verified" or "not verified". The "verified" answer is conclusive, as our method is sound. The "not verified" is inconclusive: either the bound does not hold, or the user has not provided sufficient invariants to answer the verification problem.

Example (Blogging Server). We simplified code from a Java web server based on the Spring framework that allows users to upload a blog post, delete a blog post and render a list of posts as an html page. Callback methods `postNewBlog`, `deleteBlog`, and `showBlogs` implement these functionalities. Method `driver` encodes an infinite input sequence that a user of our tool is interested in: it first reads a blog from input and appends it to the database, then renders the blog as an HTML page, and finally removes the blog from database. Our goal is to verify the boundedness of total collection lengths in every method separately, when input variables satisfy given constraints (e.g., inputs can have upper bounds on their length). In particular, callback methods `postNewBlog` and `deleteBlog` do not declare collection-typed variables and therefore they are vacuously bounded. More interestingly, we would like to verify the following bounding predicates denoted by `@Guarantee` in Fig. 1.

- The total length of collection variables in method `driver` is less than 2, i.e. $\text{len}(blogDB) < 2$
- Total length of collection variables in method `showBlogs` is less than or equal to length of input variable `blogDB`, i.e. $\text{len}(toShow) \leq \text{len}(blogDB) + 2$

We emphasize that our approach is able to verify above bounds when there exist neither time bounds nor input bounds, because input variables `input` and `blogDB` have no constraint at all, i.e. a `true` constraint.

The notation `@Inv` in Fig. 1 denotes a refinement type. The content inside the brackets following `@Inv` is the refinement of that particular type. For example, $\text{len}(blogDB) = c8 - c10$ is a type refinement on variable `blogDB`.

```
1  void driver(@Inv("true") List<String> input) {
2      @Guarantee("len(blogDB)<2")
3      @Inv("len(blogDB)=c8-c10") List<String> blogDB = new List<String>();
4      @Inv("iterOf(input)") Iterator<String> it = input.iterator();
5      String blog;
6      while(*) {
7          blog = it.next();
8          c8:     postNewBlog(blog, blogDB);
9          c9:     showBlog(blogDB);
10         c10:    deleteBlog(blogDB);
11 } }
12 @Summary{"len(blogDB')=len(blogDB)+1"}
13 void postNewBlog(String blog, List<String> blogDB) {//callback: add post
14     blogDB.add(blog);
15 }
16 @Summary{"len(blogDB')=len(blogDB)-1"}
17 void deleteBlog(List<String> blogDB) { //callback: delete last post
18     blogDB.remove();
19 }
20 @Summary{"len(blogDB')=len(blogDB)"}
21 void showBlogs(@Inv("true") List<String> blogDB) {
22     @Guarantee("len(toShow)<=len(blogDB)+2")
23     //callback: display blog contents
24     @Inv("len(toShow)-idx(it)=c28+c30+c33-c32") List<String> toShow = new
          List<String>();
25     @Inv("iterOf(blogDB)")Iterator<String> it = blogDB.iterator();
26     String blog;
27     blog = "Welcome!\n";
28     c28:  toShow.add(b);
29     blog = "Blog begins:\n";
30     c30:  toShow.add(b);
31     while(*) {
32         c32:    blog = it.next();
33         c33:    toShow.add(blog);
34     }
35 // render toShow as an HTML page
36 }
```

Fig. 1. Motivating example: a simplified version of a blogging server.

Specifying Invariants with AST Counters. We now explain the role of the AST counters in the invariant. For example, if we look at the inner loop at line 31–34 in Fig. 1, the property we most likely need for list `toShow` is $\mathtt{len}(toShow) \leq \mathtt{idx}(it)+2$, where $\mathtt{idx}(it)$ represents the number of elements that has been visited using iterator it. However, this property is actually not inductive because it breaks after line 28(as well as line 30), as $\mathtt{len}(toShow)$ is incremented by 1 but nothing else is updated in the invariant. However, we can add AST counters to the invariant, and obtain $\mathtt{len}(toShow) - \mathtt{idx}(it) = c28 + c30 + c33 - c32$. We thus obtain an inductive invariant that is then used as the type of `toShow`.

The purpose of these counters is to enable writing expressive invariants. The interesting invariants usually do not depend on the value of the counters (the value grows without bound for nonterminating programs), just on relations between counters of different AST nodes. These could be seen on the example in the previous section.

As another example, consider how we reason about the non-terminating loop at line 6–11, we first summarize the effects of callback `postNewBlog` and `deleteBlog` on any collection variable passed in as argument(s), which is to add 1 element to or remove 1 element from list `blogDB`. Method summaries are automatically applied at invocation sites. Next, since we have AST counters, we are now able to easily define the length of variable blogDB as an inductive invariant $\text{len}(blogDB) = \text{c8} - \text{c10}$ (shown at line 2) that hold at before and after every execution step. Note that this invariant serves as a safety property of all program states under the existence of non-terminating executing traces, which is the root cause of the mainstream approach in resource bound analysis to fail under the scenario of reactive programs.

2.2 Inside Quantm

Typechecking. Our type system is based on Liquid types [22], where the refinements can express facts about collections and AST counters. Our type checking rules are standard, with added rules that capture the semantics of collections (lists) and counters.

Constraints on AST Counters. Constraints on AST counters are generated from the Abstract Syntax Tree structure of the program. For instance, AST counter c32 is always either greater than (by 1) AST counter c33 (after executing line 32) or equal to it (after executing line 33) at any time during an execution. We formalize this and other relations on counters in a set of axioms.

Verification Condition Generation. We generate verification conditions that ensure that the AST counters are used consistently, and that the types imply the given bound. For instance, now that we have invariants describing lengths of list blogDB and toShow in the method showBlogs, we can plug in counter axioms and check the required implications. For instance, the type of toShow is $\text{len}(toShow) - \text{idx}(it) = \text{c28} + \text{c30} + \text{c33} - \text{c32}$. From the counter axioms, we have that $\text{c28} \leq 1 \wedge \text{c30} \leq 1$ (as the corresponding statements are executed once at most) and $(\text{c32} \equiv \text{c33} + 1) \vee (\text{c32} \equiv \text{c33})$ (as the corresponding statements are sequentially executed). We then use an off-the-shelf SMT solver to check that the inductive invariant and the counter axioms imply the guarantee that the user specified: $\text{len}(toShow) \leq \text{len}(blogDB) + 2$.

3 Quantm Type System

In this section, we present the core calculus of our target program along with the types and refinements, and operational semantics. As usual, we write $\mathbb{B}$ and $\mathbb{Z}$ for the Boolean and integer domains. We write $\bar{v}$ to denote a list of syntactic elements separated either by comma or semicolon: $v_1, v_2, \ldots, v_k$ or $v_1; v_2; \ldots; v_k$. We also write $(\bar{v} :: v_{k+1})$ for the list value $(v_1, v_2, \ldots, v_k, v_{k+1})$. We model other types of collection data types (such as sets and maps) as lists because of being only interested in sizes of collection-typed variables.

3.1 Syntax and Refinement Types

Core Calculus. Our core calculus focuses on methods manipulating collections as shown in Fig. 2a. A method M is composed of a sequence of input-variable declarations $\overline{\tau\, u}$, a sequence of initialized local-variables declarations $\overline{\tau\, x = e}$, and a

Method definition	M	$::= \overline{\tau\,u}\,\overline{\tau\,x} = e\;s$
Compound statements	s	$::= s_{\mathrm{B}} \mid \{\overline{s}\} \mid \texttt{if}(e)\texttt{ then } s_1 \texttt{ else } s_2 \mid \texttt{while}(e)\;s$
Basic statements	s_{B}	$::= x = e \mid x = z.\texttt{next}() \mid y.\texttt{rmv}() \mid y.\texttt{add}(x) \mid \texttt{skip}$
Expressions	e	$::= x \in X \mid u \in U \mid n \in \mathbb{Z} \mid b \in \mathbb{B} \mid y.\texttt{iter}()$
		$\mid \texttt{new List}[\tau_{\mathrm{B}}] \mid e_1 \oplus e_2 \mid e_1 \bowtie e_2 \mid e_1 \vee e_2 \mid \neg e$
Variables	u, x, y, z	$::= x \in X \mid u \in U \mid y, z \in X \cup U$

(a) The core calculus.

Base types	τ_{B}	$::= \texttt{Int} \mid \texttt{Bool} \mid \texttt{Iter}[\tau_{\mathrm{B}}] \mid \texttt{List}[\tau_{\mathrm{B}}]$
Refinement types	τ	$::= [\![\tau_{\mathrm{B}} \mid r]\!]$
Refinements	r	$::= b \in \mathbb{B} \mid x_{\mathrm{bool}} \mid \texttt{iterOf}(x_{\mathrm{list}}) \mid e_1^\tau \bowtie e_2^\tau \mid r_1 \vee r_2 \mid \neg r$
Refinement expressions	e^τ	$::= n \in \mathbb{Z} \mid \nu_{\mathrm{int}} \mid x_{\mathrm{int}} \mid \texttt{len}(e_{\mathrm{list}}^\tau) \mid \texttt{idx}(e_{\mathrm{iter}}^\tau) \mid e_1^\tau \oplus e_2^\tau \mid c \in C$
List expressions	e_{list}^τ	$::= \nu_{\mathrm{list}} \mid x_{\mathrm{list}}$
Iterator expressions	e_{iter}^τ	$::= \nu_{\mathrm{iter}} \mid x_{\mathrm{iter}}$
Typing context	Γ	$::= \cdot \mid \Gamma, x : \tau$

(b) Types and refinements.

Fig. 2. (a) The core calculus for methods manipulating collections. The operator $\oplus$ stands for arithmetic operators, while $\bowtie$ stands for comparison operators. (b) The types and corresponding refinements. The subscripts in variables $x_{\mathrm{bool}}, x_{\mathrm{int}}, x_{\mathrm{list}}, x_{\mathrm{iter}} \in X \cup U$ are used to emphasize their types, $\oplus$ is arithmetic operator restricted to linear arithmetic, and $\bowtie$ is a comparison operator.

method body s that is composed of basic and compound statements. We denote the set of input variables and local variables by U and X, respectively. The basic statements $x = z.\texttt{next}()$, $y.\texttt{rmv}()$, and $y.\texttt{add}(x)$ provide standard operations on iterator variable z and collection variable y. In addition, we have standard assignment statement $x = e$, where e is an expression without side effects.

Refinement Type System. Our type system, shown in Fig. 2b, permits type refinements over base types integer $\texttt{Int}$, boolean $\texttt{Bool}$, iterator $\texttt{Iter}$ and list $\texttt{List}$. A refinement type $[\![\tau_{\mathrm{B}} \mid r]\!]$ further qualifies variables by providing an assertion over the values of the variable using a predicate r. A unique feature of our refinement predicates is that, the predicates can refer to AST counters $c \in C$ to track limited flow-sensitive information. Moreover, predicate can refer to the variable on which the refinement is expressed using the self-reference variable ν. A refinement can be expressed as an arbitrary Boolean combination of Boolean values b, Boolean-typed program variables x_{bool}, predicates $\texttt{iterOf}(x_{\mathrm{list}})$ (expressing that the variable is an iterator of a list variable x_{list}), and comparisons between *refinement expressions*. A refinement expression e^τ is integer-typed and can be composed of integer values n, integer-typed variable x_{int}, length expressions $\texttt{len}(e_{\mathrm{list}}^\tau)$ (representing the length of list expression e_{list}^τ), index expressions $\texttt{idx}(e_{\mathrm{iter}}^\tau)$ (representing the current index of an iterator expression e_{iter}^τ), *AST counter variables*, and arithmetic operations over other refinement expressions. An AST counter variable $c \in C$ is associated with an AST node. Intuitively, it counts the number of times an AST node has been executed. List expressions e_{list}^τ could be ν_{list} (which refers to the refined variable itself) or a list-typed program variable x_{list}. Explanation for the iterator expression e_{iter}^τ is analogous. Typing context Γ is a mapping from variables to their types. Overall, our refinement language is in a decidable logic fragment EUFLIA ($\overline{\text{E}}$quality, $\overline{\text{U}}$ninterpreted $\overline{\text{F}}$unctions and $\overline{\text{LI}}$near $\overline{\text{A}}$rithmetic) where $\text{len}(e_{\text{list}}^\tau)$, $\text{idx}(e_{\text{iter}}^\tau)$ and $\text{iterOf}(e_{\text{iter}}^\tau)$ are treated as uninterpreted functions.

3.2 Operational Semantics

We define small-step operational semantics of our core calculus as well as semantics of type refinements in Figs. 3 and 4. An environment (or equivalently, a state) η is a mapping from program variables to values, which intuitively serves as a stack activation record. The domain of variable values include integers, booleans, iterators, and list values. The calculus also supports lists of lists. We denote the initial environment as η_{init}. Environment η_{init} initializes counters as zero, input variables as concrete input values, and local variables as their initial values specified in the method.

Figure 3 defines the small-step operational semantics for our core calculus. We use the following three judgment forms:

1. Judgment form $\langle \eta, e \rangle \rightsquigarrow e'$ states that expression e is evaluated to expression e' in one evaluation step under environment η,
2. Judgment form $\langle \eta, s \rangle \rightsquigarrow \langle \eta', s' \rangle$ states that after one evaluation step of executing statement s under environment η, the environment changes to η' and the next statement to be evaluated is s', and
3. Judgment form $\langle \eta, s \rangle \twoheadrightarrow \eta'$ expresses the AST counter state transitions by modifying η to increment the counter value associated with statement s.

Compared with standard operational semantics (IMP language [28]), there are two main differences. The first difference is that we introduce collections into our core calculus. The semantics of collection operations is straightforward as shown in Fig. 3. The other significant difference is due to the use of AST counters in refinement types. Most of the differences from non-standard semantics is related to handling of these counters. The function $\kappa(s, M)$ returns the unique counter c associated with the statement s in the method M. Notice that the intermediate derivations of the rules may produce auxiliary statements that are not present in the original program. Since the refinement types may not refer to these counters, we ignore counter values for these auxiliary statements by associating them with a same special counter $\perp$, whose value we do not care about. E.g., The conclusion of the rule E-IFEXPR introduces a new $^\perp$if statement along with original statements s_1 and s_2, associating this new if-else statement with counter $\perp$. Rules E-COUNTER and E-COUNTER-AUX are mainly concerned with AST counter bookkeeping. The explanation of other rules is straightforward.

Types and Refinements. Figure 4 defines semantics of types and refinements. Judgment form $v \vDash_\eta \tau$ states that the value v conforms to a type τ under environment η. The semantics of the base-types $\eta[x] \vDash_\eta \tau_B$ is straightforward and hence omitted. The judgment form $\vDash_\eta x : r$ states that variable x to which

$$\text{Environment } \eta ::= \cdot \mid \eta[x \to v] \mid \eta[u \to v] \mid \eta[c \hookrightarrow n]$$
$$\text{Values} \qquad v ::= n \in \mathbb{Z} \mid b \in \mathbb{B} \mid \texttt{Iter}(n \in \mathbb{N}, x \in X \cup U) \mid (v_1, v_2, \ldots, v_n)$$

(a) Environment and Values

E-VAR
$$\langle \eta, x \rangle \rightsquigarrow \eta[x]$$

E-ARITHL
$$\frac{\langle \eta, e_1 \rangle \rightsquigarrow e_1'}{\langle \eta, e_1 \oplus e_2 \rangle \rightsquigarrow e_1' \oplus e_2}$$

E-ARITHR
$$\frac{\langle \eta, e_2 \rangle \rightsquigarrow e_2'}{\langle \eta, v \oplus e_2 \rangle \rightsquigarrow v \oplus e_2'}$$

E-NEG
$$\frac{\langle \eta, e \rangle \rightsquigarrow e'}{\langle \eta, \neg e \rangle \rightsquigarrow \neg e'}$$

E-COMPL
$$\frac{\langle \eta, e_1 \rangle \rightsquigarrow e_1'}{\langle \eta, e_1 \bowtie e_2 \rangle \rightsquigarrow e_1' \bowtie e_2}$$

E-COMPR
$$\frac{\langle \eta, e_2 \rangle \rightsquigarrow e_2'}{\langle \eta, v \bowtie e_2 \rangle \rightsquigarrow v \bowtie e_2'}$$

E-ORL
$$\frac{\langle \eta, e_1 \rangle \rightsquigarrow e_1'}{\langle \eta, e_1 \vee e_2 \rangle \rightsquigarrow e_1' \text{ or } e_2}$$

E-ORR
$$\frac{\langle \eta, e_2 \rangle \rightsquigarrow e_2'}{\langle \eta, v \vee e_2 \rangle \rightsquigarrow v \vee e_2'}$$

E-COUNTER
$$\frac{\kappa(s, M) = c}{\langle \eta, s \rangle \twoheadrightarrow \eta[c \hookrightarrow \eta[c] + 1]}$$

E-COUNTER-AUX
$$\frac{\kappa(s, M) = \bot}{\langle \eta, s \rangle \twoheadrightarrow \eta}$$

E-ITERATOR
$$\langle \eta, y.\texttt{iter}() \rangle \rightsquigarrow \texttt{Iter}(0, y)$$

E-NEWLIST
$$\langle \eta, \texttt{new List}[\tau_B] \rangle \rightsquigarrow ()$$

E-ASSIGN
$$\frac{\langle \eta, x = e \rangle \twoheadrightarrow \eta' \qquad \langle \eta, e \rangle \rightsquigarrow^* v}{\langle \eta, x = e \rangle \rightsquigarrow \langle \eta'[x \to v], \texttt{skip} \rangle}$$

E-NEXT
$$\frac{\langle \eta, x = z.\texttt{next}() \rangle \twoheadrightarrow \eta' \quad \eta[z] = \texttt{Iter}(i, y)}{\eta[y] = (v_1, \ldots, v_n) \qquad i < n-1}{\langle \eta, x = z.\texttt{next}() \rangle \rightsquigarrow \langle \eta'[z \to \texttt{Iter}(i+1, y)][x \to v_{i+1}], \texttt{skip} \rangle}$$

E-ADD
$$\frac{\langle \eta, y.\texttt{add}(x) \rangle \twoheadrightarrow \eta' \quad \eta[y] = (\overline{v}) \quad \langle \eta, x \rangle \rightsquigarrow v}{\langle \eta, y.\texttt{add}(x) \rangle \rightsquigarrow \langle \eta'[y \to (\overline{v} :: v)], \texttt{skip} \rangle}$$

E-REMOVE
$$\frac{\langle \eta, y.\texttt{rmv}() \rangle \twoheadrightarrow \eta' \quad \eta[y] = (\overline{v} :: v)}{\langle \eta, y.\texttt{rmv}() \rangle \rightsquigarrow \langle \eta'[y \to (\overline{v})], \texttt{skip} \rangle}$$

E-IFEXPR
$$\frac{\langle \eta, \texttt{if}(e) \texttt{ then } s_1 \texttt{ else } s_2 \rangle \twoheadrightarrow \eta' \quad \langle \eta, e \rangle \rightsquigarrow e'}{\langle \eta, \texttt{if}(e) \texttt{ then } s_1 \texttt{ else } s_2 \rangle \rightsquigarrow \langle \eta', {}^\bot\texttt{if}(e') \texttt{ then } s_1 \texttt{ else } s_2 \rangle}$$

E-IFTRUE
$$\frac{\langle \eta, \texttt{if}(\texttt{true}) \texttt{ then } s_1 \texttt{ else } s_2 \rangle \twoheadrightarrow \eta'}{\langle \eta, \texttt{if}(\texttt{true}) \texttt{ then } s_1 \texttt{ else } s_2 \rangle \rightsquigarrow \langle \eta', s_1 \rangle}$$

E-IFFALSE
$$\frac{\langle \eta, \texttt{if}(\texttt{false}) \texttt{ then } s_1 \texttt{ else } s_2 \rangle \twoheadrightarrow \eta'}{\langle \eta, \texttt{if}(\texttt{false}) \texttt{ then } s_1 \texttt{ else } s_2 \rangle \rightsquigarrow \langle \eta', s_2 \rangle}$$

E-WHILE
$$\frac{\langle \eta, \texttt{while}(e) \ s \rangle \twoheadrightarrow \eta'}{\langle \eta, \texttt{while}(e) \ s \rangle \rightsquigarrow \langle \eta', {}^\bot\texttt{if}(e) \texttt{ then } {}^\bot\{s; {}^\bot\texttt{while}(e) \ s\} \texttt{ else skip} \rangle}$$

E-BLOCK
$$\frac{\langle \eta, \{\overline{s}\} \rangle \twoheadrightarrow \eta' \quad \overline{s} = s_1; s_2; \ldots; s_n}{\langle \eta', s_1 \rangle \rightsquigarrow \langle \eta'', s_1' \rangle \quad \overline{s'} = {}^\bot s_1'; s_2; \ldots; s_n}{\langle \eta, \{\overline{s}\} \rangle \rightsquigarrow \langle \eta'', {}^\bot\{\overline{s'}\} \rangle}$$

E-BLOCKSKIP
$$\frac{\overline{s} = \texttt{skip}; s_2; \ldots; s_n \qquad \overline{s'} = s_2; \ldots; s_n}{\langle \eta, \{\overline{s}\} \rangle \rightsquigarrow \langle \eta, {}^\bot\{\overline{s'}\} \rangle}$$

(b) Operational semantics

Fig. 3. Environment, values, and small-step operational semantics.

$$\eta[x] \models_\eta \llbracket \tau_\mathsf{B} \mid r \rrbracket \quad \text{iff} \quad \eta[x] \models_\eta \tau_\mathsf{B} \text{ and } \models_\eta x : r$$
$$\models_\eta b \quad \text{iff} \quad b \equiv \mathbf{true}$$
$$\models_\eta x : y_\mathsf{bool} \quad \text{iff} \quad \models_\eta \eta[y_\mathsf{bool}]$$
$$\models_\eta x : \neg r \quad \text{iff} \quad (\models_\eta x : r) \neq \mathbf{true}$$
$$\models_\eta x : r_1 \lor r_2 \quad \text{iff} \quad \models_\eta x : r_1 \text{ or } \models_\eta x : r_2$$
$$\models_\eta x : \mathtt{iterOf}(y) \quad \text{iff} \quad \text{for some } i \geq 0 \text{ we have } \eta[x] = \mathtt{Iter}(i, y)$$
$$\models_\eta x : e_1^\tau \bowtie e_2^\tau \quad \text{iff} \quad \mathtt{eval}(x : e_1^\tau)_\eta \bowtie \mathtt{eval}(x : e_2^\tau)_\eta$$
$$\mathtt{eval}(x : e^\tau)_\eta \quad = \quad v, \text{ where } e = \mathtt{subst}(x : e^\tau)_\eta \land \langle \eta, e \rangle \rightsquigarrow^* v$$
$$\mathtt{subst}(x : e^\tau)_\eta \quad = \quad (e^\tau[x/\nu])[n_i/\mathtt{len}(x_\mathsf{list}^i), k_j/\mathtt{idx}(y_\mathsf{iter}^j)]_{\forall x_\mathsf{list}^i, y_\mathsf{iter}^j}$$
$$\text{where } \eta[x_\mathsf{list}^i] = (v_1, \dots, v_{n_i}) \text{ and } \eta[y_\mathsf{iter}^j] = \mathtt{Iter}(k_j, *)$$

Fig. 4. Refinement semantics.

expression ν in refinement r refers, conforms to the refinement under the environment η. We exploit helper functions $\mathtt{eval}(x : e^\tau)_\eta$ and $\mathtt{subst}(x : e^\tau)_\eta$ in refinement semantics defined in the following fashion:

– Function $\mathtt{eval}(x : e^\tau)_\eta$ takes a refinement expression e^τ, a variable x (to which self-reference ν in e^τ refers), and an environment η as inputs and then returns the evaluation of refinement expression.
– Function $\mathtt{subst}(x : e^\tau)_\eta$ takes as inputs refinement expression e^τ, variable x (to which expression ν refers), and environment η, and returns an expression that is the result of first substituting self-reference ν with variable x and then substituting every $\mathtt{len}(x_\mathsf{list})$ in e^τ with length of list-typed variable x_list, as well as every $\mathtt{idx}(y_\mathsf{iter})$ with index value of iterator-typed variable y_iter.

We write $\rightsquigarrow^*$ for the transitive closure of $\rightsquigarrow$. Most of the refinement semantics are straightforward. In particular, the semantics of $\mathtt{iterOf}(y)$ is that variable x, to which ν refers, is an iterator for list-typed variable y.

3.3 Well-Typed Methods

We say that an environment η is *reachable* in a method M if $\langle \eta_\mathsf{init}, M \rangle \rightsquigarrow^* \langle \eta, s \rangle$. We write $\mathsf{ReachEnv}(M)$ for the set of all reachable environments of M. We say that an environment η is *well-typed* in M if all of the variables conform to their types, i.e. for all $x \in X \cup U$ with type $\llbracket \tau_\mathsf{B} \mid r \rrbracket$, we have that $\eta[x] \models_\eta \llbracket \tau_\mathsf{B} \mid r \rrbracket$. We write $\mathsf{WellTyped}(M)$ for the set of all well-typed environments in M. We say that a method M is *well-typed* if all of the reachable states of M are well-typed, i.e. $\mathsf{ReachEnv}(M) \subseteq \mathsf{WellTyped}(M)$.

4   Collection Bound Verification Problem

Given a method M, our goal is to verify that if the inputs to the method satisfy a given assumption $\phi_\mathcal{A}$, then the method M guarantees that the collection lengths remain bounded. The guarantee requirements $\phi_\mathcal{G}$ can be expressed as a predicate constructed using the refinement language introduced in Fig. 2b Observe that, since this verification condition is not attached to any particular variable, it is free from predicates $\texttt{iterOf}(x_{\text{list}})$ and self-reference ν. We further assume that the assumptions on the input variables are expressed using type refinements on the input variables. Formally, we are interested in the following problem:

Definition 1 (Collection Bound Verification Problem). *Given a method M along with its input variables with types and refinements $u_i : \tau_i$, and a guarantee requirement $\phi_{\mathcal{G}}$, verify that every reachable environment satisfies $\phi_{\mathcal{G}}$, i.e. for all $\eta \in \mathsf{ReachEnv}(M)$ we have that $\vDash_\eta \phi_{\mathcal{G}}$.*

We present a type-directed approach to solve this problem. We first propose type-checking rules to verify if the method is well-typed. Then, we discuss how to automatically derive AST counter relation axioms in Sect. 4.2. Finally, we reduce solving the verification problem into issuing SMT queries, in Sect. 4.3, using as constraints the type refinements verified in Sect. 4.1 as well as AST counter relation axioms extracted from Sect. 4.2.

4.1   Type Checking

Our key analysis algorithm is encoded into refinement type checking rules shown in Fig. 5. Subtyping between two refinement types is defined as the implication relation between two refinements using the following rule:

$$\frac{\tau_{B1} <: \tau_{B2} \qquad r_1 \implies r_2}{[\![\tau_{B1} \mid r_1]\!] <: [\![\tau_{B2} \mid r_2]\!]} \text{ <:-REFINEMENTTYP}$$

Figure 5 defines type-checking rules for refinement types, while the rules for base types are standard and thus presented in companion paper [27]. Notation $\tau[e^{\tau'}/e^\tau]$ denotes substituting expression e^τ with $e^{\tau'}$ in the refinement of type τ.

The Judgment form $\Gamma \vdash s$ states that the statement s is successfully type checked under typing context Γ if premises are satisfied. We case split on the right hand side of assignment statement $x = e$ into: Rule T-ASSIGNITER, T-ASSIGN, T-ASSIGNLIST, and T-ASSIGNNEWLIST. Intuitively, type checking rules check that after applying each corresponding evaluation rule, type refinements should still be valid. More specifically, in each type checking rule we check for all refinements, if its validity before applying a corresponding evaluation rule implies its validity afterwards. For example, after applying Rule E-ADD, the environment has the following updates: length of collection variable y is incremented by 1 and the associated AST counter's value is incremented by 1. Therefore Rule T-ADD checks the implication of validity between a type $\tau_w[w/\nu]$ and the result after applying to it a substitution $(\tau_w[w/\nu])[(\texttt{len}(y)+1)/\texttt{len}(y), (c+1)/c]$, which precisely expresses the actual value of type $\tau_w[w/\nu]$ after applying Rule E-ADD in terms of its value beforehand. Rule T-REMOVE is dual to Rule T-ADD. In Rule T-ASSIGNITER, in addition to subtyping checking, we also check for variable z if its refinement will still hold true after substituting `iterOf(*)` with `iterOf(y)`. The intuition behind is that after evaluating statement $z = y.\text{iter}()$, variable z will become an iterator for variable y, no matter what list it was an iterato for. For a reader interested in why we must treat refinement `iterOf(x)` differently, the root cause here is that unlike `idx(z)` specifying a property of **one** variable, `iterOf(x)` actually specifies a relation between **two** variables. Rule T-ASSIGN checks if refinements will still hold true when x becomes e, no matter if variable x is integer-typed, boolean-typed or iterator-typed (where `idx(x)` becomes `idx(e)`). Rule T-ASSIGNLIST and Rule T-ASSIGN are similar, except that in Rule T-ASSIGNLIST we check if refinements will still hold true when `len(x)` becomes `len(e)`. We split Rule T-ASSIGNLIST from Rule T-ASSIGN, avoiding simply checking if x becoming e will break any refinement, because assignment $x = e$ does not make refinement `iterOf(x)` become `iterOf(e)`. In Rule T-NEXT, besides checking the validity of implication, we also check if every type refinement is logically equivalent to itself being existentially quantified by variable x. Intuitively, this ensures soundly that the assignment in statement $x = z.\text{next}()$ will not break any refinement, since there is no constraint on list elements retrieved from list variable z by invoking $z.\text{next}()$. Just like Rule E-COUNTER interleaves with every evaluation rule in Fig. 3, Rule T-COUNTER serves as a premise for every type checking rule of compound statements. For every type checking rule of basic statements, Rule T-COUNTER is embedded into subtyping checking. Rule T-DECL checks that all local variables' type refinements are valid, given their initial values. We also define a helper function $\langle\!\langle s_1 \rangle\!\rangle \subseteq \langle\!\langle s_2 \rangle\!\rangle$ that is used in Rule T-DECL, which describes AST sub-node relations between AST node s_2 and its sub-node s_1.

SUBNODE-BLOCK
$$\overline{s} = s_1; \ldots; s_n$$
$$\overline{\langle\!\langle s_i \rangle\!\rangle \subseteq \langle\!\langle \{\overline{s}\} \rangle\!\rangle}, \text{ for all } i \in \{1, \cdots, n\}$$

SUBNODE-WHILE
$$\langle\!\langle s \rangle\!\rangle \subseteq \langle\!\langle \text{while}(e) \ s \rangle\!\rangle$$

SUBNODE-IF
$$\overline{\langle\!\langle s_i \rangle\!\rangle \subseteq \langle\!\langle \text{if}(e) \text{ then } s_1 \text{ else } s_2 \rangle\!\rangle}, \text{ for } i \in \{1, 2\}$$

4.2   AST Counter Axioms

We next present the AST counter relation axioms. The goal of deriving counter relation axioms is to improve verification precision by having additional constraints when encoding the problem statement into SMT queries. We let counter relations precisely correspond to abstract syntax tree structure of a program. Respecting semantics of counters, these counters keep record of the number of times a particular AST node has been executed at runtime.

The function $\Delta(s)$ takes as input a statement s and statically outputs a predicate about the relations on all AST sub nodes of statement s, as well as counter relation axioms derived from all AST sub nodes themselves. For example, Rule R-BLOCK extracts counter relations from a block of statements $\{\overline{s}\}$.

For $1 \leq j \leq n-1$, in the constraint d_j the counter c_i associated with statement s_i is either: (a) equal to counter c_{i+1} associated with statement s_{i+1}, when statement s_i and s_{i+1} have both been executed; or (b) the counter c_i is equal to $c_{i+1}+1$, when statement s_i has been executed, but not statement s_{i+1}. Intuitively, constraint d_j describes a set of valid counter relations at one program state, which is immediately after executing statement s_j but before executing statement s_{j+1}. Constraint d_n denotes the counter relations right after finishing executing block statement $\{\bar{s}\}$. Additionally, the value of counter c_0 (associated with block statement $\{\bar{s}\}$ itself) is always equivalent to the value of counter c_1 (associated with the first statement s_1 in the block), respecting operational semantics of $\{\bar{s}\}$ defined in Rule E-BLOCK of Fig. 3. Furthermore, the constraints C_i, for $1 \leq i \leq n$, are recursively generated from every statement s_i. Intuitively, these relations describes counter relations when flow-sensitively executing the code block $\{\bar{s}\}$ (Fig. 6).

As another example, Rule R-WHILE extracts counter relations from a while loop. Note that we cannot conclude any relations between counter c_b (associated with loop body s) and counter c_0 (associated with loop $\texttt{while}(e)\ s$), because although loop body s may be executed for a positive number times or may not be executed, loop $\texttt{while}(e)\ s$ will always be executed for one more time whenever executing this AST node, according to Rule E-WHILE in Fig. 3. Other rules are straightforward. Proof of soundness for above counter relations is straightforward and hence omitted.

4.3   Collection Bound Verification

We formalize our approach that solves the collection bound verification problem for method M by constructing an SMT query. We first obtain constraints from type refinements and AST counter axioms, and then generate the following SMT query that searches for counterexamples for the guarantee $\phi_{\mathcal{G}}$:

$$\Psi_{\text{ast}} \wedge \bigwedge_{\langle\!\langle \tau\, u \rangle\!\rangle \subseteq \langle\!\langle M \rangle\!\rangle} \Phi(u : \tau) \wedge \bigwedge_{\langle\!\langle \tau\, x \rangle\!\rangle \subseteq \langle\!\langle M \rangle\!\rangle} \Phi(x : \tau) \wedge \neg\phi_{\mathcal{G}},$$

where Ψ_{ast} are the constraints generated from functions $\Delta(s)$ defined in Sect. 4.2. The helper function $\Phi(x : \tau)$, defined in Fig. 7 takes as input a variable x together with its type τ, and returns refinement constraints from type τ. Intuitively, constraint Ψ_{ast} soundly constrains the possible values that AST counters could take when flow-sensitively executing a program. Constraints $\Phi(u : \tau)$ encode assumptions on the inputs to the method, and constraints $\Phi(x : \tau)$ soundly constrain the values that local variables could take. Together they constitute a constraint on all reachable program states (which is proven in Sect. 5). In other words, the conjunction of constraints defines a set of program states that is a sound over-approximation of every actual reachable program states of method M. Therefore, the answer to the query provides a sound solution to the collection bound verification problem.

T-ADD

$$\kappa(y.\mathbf{add}(x), M) = c$$
$$\forall(w : \tau_w) \in \Gamma.(\tau_w[w/\nu]) <: (\tau_w[w/\nu])[(\mathbf{len}(y)+1)/\mathbf{len}(y), (c+1)/c]$$
$$\overline{\Gamma \vdash y.\mathbf{add}(x)}$$

T-REMOVE

$$\kappa(y.\mathbf{rmv}(), M) = c$$
$$\forall(w : \tau_w) \in \Gamma.(\tau_w[w/\nu]) <: (\tau_w[w/\nu])[(\mathbf{len}(y)-1)/\mathbf{len}(y), (c+1)/c]$$
$$\overline{\Gamma \vdash y.\mathbf{rmv}()}$$

T-ASSIGNITER

$$\kappa(z = y.\mathbf{iter}(), M) = c \qquad \forall(w : \tau_w) \in \Gamma.(\tau_w[w/\nu]) <: (\tau_w[w/\nu])[0/\mathbf{idx}(z), (c+1)/c]$$
$$\Gamma \vdash z : \tau_z \qquad (\tau_z[z/\nu]) <: (\tau_z[z/\nu])[0/\mathbf{idx}(z), (c+1)/c, \mathbf{iterOf}(y)/\mathbf{iterOf}(*)]$$
$$\overline{\Gamma \vdash z = y.\mathbf{iter}()}$$

T-ASSIGN

$$\kappa(x = e, M) = c \qquad \Gamma \vdash x : [\![\tau_B \lfloor r_x]\!] \qquad \tau_B \text{ is not a list type}$$
$$\forall(w : \tau_w) \in \Gamma.(\tau_w[w/\nu]) <: (\tau_w[w/\nu])[e/x, (c+1)/c]$$
$$\overline{\Gamma \vdash x = e}$$

T-ASSIGNLIST

$$\kappa(x = e, M) = c \qquad \Gamma \vdash x : [\![\tau_B \lfloor r_x]\!] \qquad \tau_B \text{ is a list type}$$
$$\forall(w : \tau_w) \in \Gamma.(\tau_w[w/\nu]) <: (\tau_w[w/\nu])[\mathbf{len}(e)/\mathbf{len}(x), (c+1)/c]$$
$$\overline{\Gamma \vdash x = e}$$

T-ASSIGNNEWLIST

$$\kappa(x = \mathbf{new\ List}[\tau_B], M) = c$$
$$\forall(w : \tau_w) \in \Gamma.(\tau_w[w/\nu]) <: (\tau_w[w/\nu])[0/\mathbf{len}(x), (c+1)/c]$$
$$\overline{\Gamma \vdash x = \mathbf{new\ List}[\tau_B]}$$

T-COUNTER

$$s \neq s_B \qquad \kappa(s, M) = c$$
$$\forall(w : \tau_w) \in \Gamma.(\tau_w[w/\nu]) <: (\tau_w[w/\nu])[(c+1)/c]$$
$$\overline{\Gamma \vdash_c s}$$

T-NEXT

$$\kappa(x = z.\mathbf{next}(), M) = c$$
$$\forall(w : \tau_w) \in \Gamma.(\tau_w[w/\nu]) <: (\tau_w[w/\nu])[(\mathbf{idx}(z)+1)/\mathbf{idx}(z), (c+1)/c]$$
$$\forall(w : [\![\tau_w \lfloor r_w]\!]) \in \Gamma.r_w \Longleftrightarrow \exists x.r_w$$
$$\overline{\Gamma \vdash x = z.\mathbf{next}()}$$

T-BLOCK

$$\overline{s} = s_1; \ldots; s_n$$
$$\Gamma \vdash_c \{\overline{s}\}$$

T-DECL

$$\langle \eta_{\text{init}}, e \rangle \rightsquigarrow v \qquad \Gamma \vdash s \qquad \forall \langle\!\langle \tau\ x = e \rangle\!\rangle \subseteq \langle\!\langle M \rangle\!\rangle.v \vDash_{\eta_{\text{init}}} \tau \qquad \Gamma \vdash s_i, \text{ for all } i \in \{1, \cdots, n\}$$
$$\overline{\Gamma \vdash \overline{\tau\ u\ \tau\ x = e}\ s} \qquad\qquad\qquad \overline{\Gamma \vdash \{\overline{s}\}}$$

T-WHILE

$$\frac{\Gamma \vdash_c \mathbf{while}(e)\ s \qquad \Gamma \vdash s}{\Gamma \vdash \mathbf{while}(e)\ s}$$

T-SKIP

$$\frac{}{\Gamma \vdash \mathbf{skip}}$$

T-IF

$$\frac{\Gamma \vdash_c \mathbf{if}(e)\ \mathbf{then}\ s_1\ \mathbf{else}\ s_2 \qquad \Gamma \vdash s_1 \qquad \Gamma \vdash s_2}{\Gamma \vdash \mathbf{if}(e)\ \mathbf{then}\ s_1\ \mathbf{else}\ s_2}$$

Fig. 5. Type checking rules

R-BLOCK

$$\overline{s} = s_1; \ldots; s_n \qquad \Delta(s_i) = C_i \text{ and } \kappa(s_i, M) = c_i, \text{ for all } i \in \{1, \cdots, n\}$$

$$d_j = (\bigwedge_{i=1}^{j} c_i \equiv c_{i-1} \wedge c_{j+1}+1 \equiv c_j), \text{ for all } j \in \{1, \cdots, n-1\}$$

$$\frac{\kappa(\{\overline{s}\}, M) = c_0 \qquad d_n = (c_0 \equiv \cdots \equiv c_n)}{\Delta(\{\overline{s}\}) = \bigwedge_{i=1}^{n} C_i \wedge \bigvee_{i=1}^{n} d_i}$$

R-WHILE

$$\frac{\Delta(s) = C \qquad \kappa(\texttt{while}(e)\ s, M) = c_0 \qquad \kappa(s, M) = c_b}{\Delta(\texttt{while}(e)\ s) = C}$$

R-BASIC

$$\frac{}{\Delta(s_{\mathrm{B}}) = \mathbf{true}}$$

R-IF

$$\frac{\Delta(s_i) = C_i \text{ and } \kappa(s_i, M) = c_i, \text{ for } i \in \{1, 2\} \qquad \kappa(\texttt{if}(e)\ \texttt{then}\ s_1\ \texttt{else}\ s_2, M) = c_0}{\Delta(\texttt{if}(e)\ \texttt{then}\ s_1\ \texttt{else}\ s_2) = (c_0 \equiv c_1 + c_2) \wedge C_1 \wedge C_2}$$

Fig. 6. AST counter axioms

$$
\begin{aligned}
\Phi(x : \tau_{\mathrm{B}}) &\overset{\text{def}}{=\!=} \mathbf{true} \\
\Phi(x : \llbracket \tau_{\mathrm{B}} \mathord{\downarrow} x_{\text{bool}} \rrbracket) &\overset{\text{def}}{=\!=} x_{\text{bool}}[x/\nu] \\
\Phi(x : \llbracket \tau_{\mathrm{B}} \mathord{\downarrow} e_1^\tau \bowtie e_2^\tau \rrbracket) &\overset{\text{def}}{=\!=} e_1^\tau[x/\nu] \bowtie e_2^\tau[x/\nu] \\
\Phi(x : \llbracket \tau_{\mathrm{B}} \mathord{\downarrow} r_1 \vee r_2 \rrbracket) &\overset{\text{def}}{=\!=} r_1[x/\nu] \vee r_2[x/\nu] \\
\Phi(x : \llbracket \tau_{\mathrm{B}} \mathord{\downarrow} \neg r \rrbracket) &\overset{\text{def}}{=\!=} \neg r[x/\nu] \\
\Phi(x : \llbracket \tau_{\mathrm{B}} \mathord{\downarrow} \texttt{iterOf}(y) \rrbracket) &\overset{\text{def}}{=\!=} 0 \leq \texttt{idx}(x) \leq \texttt{len}(y)
\end{aligned}
$$

Fig. 7. The helper function Φ for extracting refinement constraints.

5   Soundness

In this section, we present theorems on refinement preservation and refinement progress. Intuitively, refinement preservation guarantees that if a program passes refinement type checking (Sect. 4.1), then it will always end up in a well-typed environment (Sect. 3.3), under which we perform bound verification (Sect. 4.3). Refinement progress states that a program that passes type checking will not get stuck. Refinement preservation is the core theorem, we prove it below.

Theorem 1 (Refinement preservation). *If we have that* $\eta \vDash \Gamma$, $\Gamma \vdash s$, *and* $\langle \eta, s \rangle \rightsquigarrow \langle \eta', s' \rangle$, *then* $\eta' \vDash \Gamma$ *and* $\Gamma \vdash s'$.

Proof. Given $\eta \vDash \Gamma$ and $\Gamma \vdash s$ and $\langle \eta, s \rangle \rightsquigarrow \langle \eta', s' \rangle$, we focus on proving $\eta' \vDash \Gamma$, because the validity of $\Gamma \vdash s'$ is directly implied from the premises in Fig. 5. The goal is to prove for every variable x_i with type τ_i in $\mathrm{Dom}(\eta)$, we have $\eta'[x_i] \vDash_{\eta'} \tau_i[x_i/\nu]$.

- **Rule E-Add**: We need to prove that if $\eta \vDash \Gamma$ and $\langle \eta, y.\texttt{add}(x) \rangle \rightsquigarrow \langle \eta', \texttt{skip} \rangle$, then $\eta' \vDash \Gamma$. From the Rule T-ADD, we have

(Fact 1): $\eta \models \Gamma$ implies that $\eta \models \Gamma[(\text{len}(y)+1)/\text{len}(y), (c+1)/c]$, where we define $\Gamma[(\text{len}(y)+1)/\text{len}(y), (c+1)/c]$ as performing substitution $[(\text{len}(y)+1)/\text{len}(y), (c+1)/c]$ for all types in typing context Γ.

From the Rule E-ADD, we can infer that if $\langle \eta, y.\text{add}(x) \rangle \rightsquigarrow \langle \eta', \text{skip} \rangle$, then $\eta'(z) = \eta(z)$ for variables other than c and y. Furthermore, $\eta'[c] = \eta[c] + 1$ an $\text{len}(\eta'[y]) = \text{len}(\eta[y]) + 1$. Based on these properties of η', we prove by a simple induction on the structure of refinements that (Fact 2): if $\eta \models \Gamma[(\text{len}(y)+1)/\text{len}(y), (c+1)/c]$ then $\eta' \vdash \Gamma$.

By chaining Fact 1 and Fact 2, we can conclude the proof.

The other cases are similar or simpler, and can be found in the companion paper [27]. □

Corollary 1 states that all reachable program states are well-typed (Sect. 3.3). The proof immediately follows from Theorem 1.

Corollary 1. *If $\Gamma \vdash M$ and $\eta \in \textsf{ReachEnv}(M)$ then $\eta \models \Gamma$.*

Theorem 2 (Refinement progress). *If $\eta \models \Gamma$ and $\Gamma \vdash s$, then either statement s is skip, or there exist η' and s' such that $\langle \eta, s \rangle \rightsquigarrow \langle \eta', s' \rangle$*

The proof of Theorem 2 is standard and hence omitted.

6   Experiment

We implemented our tool QUANTM in Scala using the Checker Framework [12, 21], Microsoft Z3 [11] and Scala SMT-LIB [2]. QUANTM is implemented as a Java annotation processor, relying on the Checker Framework to extract type annotations and perform type checking. Microsoft Z3 served as an off-the-shelf SMT solver. We also used Scala SMT-LIB for parsing string-typed annotations. We chose several web applications as benchmarks (180k lines of code in total), each of which supports various functionalities. Benchmarks were collected from different sources, including GitHub (jforum3 with 218 stars and SpringPetClinic with 2325 stars), Google Code Archive (jRecruiter[1]), and DARPA STAC project [1] (TextCrunchr, Braidit, WithMi, Calculator, Battleboats, Image_processor, Smartmail, Powerbroker, and Snapbuddy). To set up the experiments, we created drivers invoking callback methods in patterns that imitate standard usage. To support the Object-Oriented feature (which is orthogonal to the problem and approach in the paper), we not only annotate collection-typed local variables, but also annotate collection-typed object fields that are reachable from local variables. Then we gave bounds to each method as tight as possible and used Microsoft Z3 to verify the bounds.

6.1   Research Questions

We evaluated our technique by answering the following research questions

RQ1. **Bound verification.** How effective is *AST Counter Instrumentation*? That is, what percentage of methods and collection variables were verified w.r.t. their specifications.

RQ2. **Analysis speed.** How fast/scalable is our verification technique?

---

[1] https://code.google.com/archive/p/jrecruiter/.

Table 1. Benchmark results. "Lines of code" counts the total lines of code in projects. "Verified methods" gives number of verified methods and unverified methods. Number of verified methods is split into *non-vacuously* and *vacuously* verified, where being vacuously verified means not declaring any local collection variables. "Verified/Unverified collections" gives the number of collection variables that are verified versus unverified. "Callbacks" gives the number of invoked callbacks in drivers. "Method summaries" gives the number of method summaries supporting verifying collection variables that are inter-procedurally mutated. "Analysis time" indicates the speed of our analysis on each benchmark. Experiments were conducted on a 4-core 2.9 GHz Intel Core i7 MacBook with 16 GB of RAM running OS X 10.13.6.

Benchmarks	Lines of code	Verified/Unverified methods	Verified/Unverified collections	Call-backs	Summaries	Analysis time (s)
TextCrunchr	2, 150	$(13 + 190)/5$	23/5	4	9	14.7
Braidit	20, 835	$(8 + 2114)/0$	50/0	8	8	84.2
jforum3	22, 813	$(35 + 1675)/8$	54/10	24	27	69.8
jRecruiter	13, 936	$(29 + 933)/5$	40/4	10	7	45.1
SpringPetClinic	1, 429	$(6 + 98)/0$	11/1	9	12	15.8
WithMi	24, 927	$(30 + 2515)/5$	35/2	5	4	82.0
Calculator	5, 378	$(20 + 316)/2$	25/6	5	3	18.2
Battleboats	21, 525	$(8 + 2171)/6$	12/2	5	2	75.6
Image_processor	1, 365	$(4 + 110)/0$	5/0	0	0	7.8
Smartmail	1, 977	$(7 + 137)/4$	11/3	0	0	10.9
Powerbroker	29, 374	$(22 + 3015)/8$	27/3	3	8	91.6
Snapbuddy	34, 797	$(57 + 2940)/8$	88/9	5	2	107.0
Total	180, 506	$(239 + 16214)/51$	381/45	78	82	622.6

RQ1: Bound Verification. We verified 16453 methods in total, 239 of which are non-vacuously verified (who declares at least one collection variable) and the rest are vacuously verified (who declares no collection variable). If not considering vacuously verified methods, then we verified 239 out of 290 (82.4%) methods. In order to verify method boundedness, we also wrote and verified global invariants on 381 collection variables out of a total of 426 (89.4%), as well as provided 82 method summaries. We invoked 78 callbacks from drivers. We believe this result demonstrates that our technique is effective at verifying method and variable specifications. Our technique works very well when there is no statement reading a list-typed element from a collection, which if it happens, constitutes the vast majority of the causes of the 51 unverified methods and 45 unverified collections, because to ensure soundness we had to enforce no constraint on these list-typed variables read from collections, leading to unboundedness. We currently do not support this feature in the type system and we will leave it for future work. Note that in the table we did not include unverified methods and variables caused by orthogonal problems such as Java features (e.g. dynamic dispatch) discussed in Sect. 6.2.

We attribute the effectiveness of *AST Counter Instrumentation* to the scalable type checking approach and our AST counter-base approach. Also note that without *AST Counter Instrumentation*, it would have not been possible to **flow-insensitively** verify the desired properties. The detailed results from each benchmark are in Table 1.

Alias. Note that the operational semantics defined in Fig. 3 does not support aliasing among collection-typed variables. This is because aliasing is orthogonal to the problem and approach in the paper. To demonstrate that this is indeed the case, we extend our framework with aliasing, which we present in the companion paper [27]. The implementation uses the framework from the appendix.

Case Studies. We present an interesting loop that we found and simplified from the jforum3 benchmark. In the while loop at line 4–17, line 5 reads in a String with `readLine` and line 14 adds an element to list `comments`. Although the while loop may not terminate, the inductive invariant $len(comments) - idx(reader) = c5\text{-}c14$ is preserved before and every execution step. Here we consider variable `reader` as an iterator, respecting the semantics of the `readLine` API.

```
1 @Inv("len(comments)-idx(reader)=c5-c14") List<String> comments = new
    ArrayList<>();
2 // ...
3 String s;
4 while (true) {
5 c5: s = reader.readLine();
6     if (s != null) {
7         s = s.trim();
8     }
9     if (s == null || s.length() < 1) {
10         continue;
11     }
12     if (s.charAt(0) == '#') { // comment
13         if (collectComments && s.length() > 1) {
14             c14: comments.add(s.substring(1));
15         }
16     continue;
17 }
```

We also discovered a Denial-of-Service bug from benchmark TextCrunchr that is caused by a collection variable with an excessively large length. TextCrunchr is a text analysis program that is able to perform some useful analysis (word frequency, word length, etc.), as well as process plain text files and compressed files, which it will uncompress to analyze the contents. The vulnerability is in the decompressing functionality where it uses a collection variable `queue` to store files to be decompressed. Our tool QUANTM correctly did not verify the boundedness of variable `queue` and we believe this leads to TextCrunchr's being vulnerable to a Zip bomb attack, because variable `queue` may store an exponential number of files that is caused by a carefully crafted zip file, which contains other carefully crafted zip files inside, thus leading to an exponential number of files to be stored in variable `queue` and to be decompressed.

RQ2: Analysis Speed. On average, it takes 51.9 s to analyze a 15k lines of code benchmark program (including vacuously verified methods) with QUANTM. The detailed results from each benchmark are in Table 1. Given the lines of code of our benchmarks, we believe this result indicates that the speed of our analysis benefits from being type-based and flow-insensitive, exhibiting the potential of scaling to even larger programs.

6.2   Limitations, Future Work and Discussion

In experiments, we encountered collection variables that could not be annotated, leaving QUANTM unable to verify boundedness of methods that declare them. We next categorize the reasons and discuss future work for improvements:

- To ensure soundness, we enforce no constraint on a collection-typed variable's length (i.e. allow it to be infinitely long), when it is the result of reading a list-typed element from a collection. The reason is that the type system does not yet support annotating lengths of inner lists. This extension of our type system is left for future work.
- Not discovering the right global invariants. In the future we plan to automate the invariant discovery process with abstract interpretation, which will hopefully help uncover more invariants.
- Imprecision and "soundiness" caused by Java features such as aliasing, dynamic dispatch, inner class, class inheritance and multi-threading. We regard these as orthogonal problems to our problem statement and we could extend our type system to support them.

Integration with Building Tools. To evaluate how user-friendly QUANTM is for a developer, we also evaluated how QUANTM integrates with open source repositories (i.e. jforum3, jRecruiter and SpringPetClinic) that use popular building tools (e.g. Maven). We discovered that the configuration is reasonably easy: Developers only need to add several Maven dependencies (including QUANTM, Checker framework, Scala library, Scala SMT-LIB and Microsoft Z3's Java bindings) into `pom.xml` and specify QUANTM as an additional annotation processor. After that, a developer could immediately start using our tool!

Annotation Workflow. The typical annotation workflow of a user is to first configure QUANTM as an annotation processor, and then compile the target code/project without any annotations. Note that errors and warnings are expected if QUANTM cannot prove boundedness of a procedure, which is intrinsically caused by insufficient annotations (i.e. type refinements). In the end, a user will fix the errors and warnings by annotating collection variables. In the case of a method returning a locally allocated collection variable, we inlined the method into its caller to ensure soundness. Additionally, to perform interprocedural analysis, we introduce method summaries to describe changes in lengths of collection-typed variables caused by method invocation. Method summaries are expressed in the refinement language defined in Fig. 2b, together with variables in their primed version, which denotes the values after method invocation. Method summaries are automatically applied when type checking a method invocation statement. The annotation burden for method summaries was light (6.8 methods on average) in the experiments.

7   Related Works

Type Systems for Resource Analysis. Type-based approaches have been proposed for resource analysis [9,25,26]. These works verify size relations between input and output list variables as a function specification. Additionally, there is a line of works that combines a type-based approach with the idea of amortized analysis [18,19] to analyze resource usage. These approaches are not able to analyze programs with mutation and it is also unclear how to adapt them into a setting with mutation. The reason is the need for the analysis to be flow-sensitive in the presence of mutation, because mutation causes program variables' sizes to change. In contrast, we emphasize that it is our novelty to introduce *AST Counter Instrumentation*, making it possible to write flow-insensitive types in the presence of mutation, and thus enjoy the benefits of a type-based approach—being compositional and scalable. We put back the limited flow-sensitive information (in the form of counter axioms) only after the type checking phase.

Resource Analysis by Loop-Bound Analysis. Bound analysis techniques [8, 14,15,17,24,31] emphasize that time bounds (especially loop bounds) are necessary for resource bound analysis and therefore they focus on obtaining loop bounds. However, time boundedness is actually only a sufficient condition for resource boundedness. In contrast, our approach verifies resource bounds even when time bounds are not available. The other difference is that, Gulwani et al. and Zuleger et al.'s works [15,17,31] generate invariants at different program locations, as opposed to our approach of using same invariants at all program locations. In more detail, Carbonneaux et al. [8] use a Hoare logic style inter-procedural reasoning to derive constraints on unknown coefficients of loop bounds, who are in the form of pre-defined templates consisting of multivariate intervals. Gulwani et al. [15] introduce a technique to first transform multi-path loops into loop paths who interleave in an explicit way, and then generate different invariants at different program locations. In another work, Gulwani et al. [17], compute the transitive closure of inner loops, which are invariants only hold true at the beginning of loops. It also utilizes several common loop patterns to obtain ranking functions, which are eventually used to compute loop bounds. Sinn et al. [24] flatten multi-path loops into sets of mutual independent loop paths and uses global lexicographic ranking functions to derive loop bounds. Similarly, Giesl et al. [14] use a standard ranking function approach to obtain loop bounds for its bound analysis, which is a component of its interleaving of size analysis and bound analysis. Zuleger et al. [31] txake size-change abstraction approach from termination analysis domain into bound analysis. Size-change abstraction relates values of variables before and after a loop iteration at the beginning of a loop, which are eventually used to obtain loop bounds. Additionally, although Gulwani et al. [16] also adopt a counter approach by instrumenting loops with counters, the functionalities of counters are different. In our *AST Counter Instrumentation* approach, counters enable writing flow-insensitive global invariants under the scenario of mutation. In contrast, the functionality of counters in Gulwani et al.'s work [16] is to make it explicit if one loop is semantically (instead of syntactically) nested in another loop: each loop is associated with a counter and this work encodes loop nest relations as counter dependencies.

Resource Analysis by Cost-Recurrence Relations. A classical approach to cost analysis [3–7,13] is to derive a set of cost recurrence relations from the original program, whose closed-form solutions will serve as an over-approximation of the cost usage. As pointed out by Alonso et al. [7], one of the limitations in recurrence relation approach is that it poorly supports mutation, because of ignoring the side effects of a callee that may have on its caller. Since collection APIs typically have side effects, recurrence relation may not be the best approach to reason about collection variables' lengths. Additionally, we believe our approach applies to a wider class of programs, because it is more difficult to find closed-form solutions than our approach of checking if a set of constraints implies the desired property.

Refinement Types. Our type system is inspired by Rondon et al. [22]. The subsequent work by Rondon et al. [23] propose a flow-sensitive refinement type system to reason about programs with mutation. Similarly, Coughlin et al.'s work [10] handles mutation via a flow-sensitive approach, allowing type refinements to temporarily break and then get re-established later at some other control locations. It adopts flow-sensitive analysis between control locations who break and re-establish the invariant, respectively. Compared with Rondon et al. [23] and Coughlin et al. [10], our work is different because it separates types and refinements from counter relation axioms, where types and refinements are flow-insensitive but counter relation axioms are flow-sensitive. The advantage of our approach over Coughlin et al.'s work is that, to verify a given property, Coughlin et al.'s work is more expensive because it is sensitive to the distance (in terms of lines of code) between any two relevant control locations (i.e., where the first location breaks an invariant and the second location potentially restores the invariant). More specifically, Coughlin et al.'s work has to perform flow-sensitive and path-sensitive symbolic execution between any two relevant control locations. In comparison, our approach is insensitive to the distance between any two relevant control locations.

8   Conclusion

We proposed a technique that statically verifies the boundedness of total length of collection variables when given constraint(s) on input(s). Our technique is able to verify the above property for non-terminating reactive programs. To ensure scalability, we take a type-based approach and enforce using global inductive invariants, as opposed to different invariants at different program locations. To design global invariants for programs supporting mutation, we introduce AST counters, which track how many times an AST node was executed. We then add axioms on relations of the counter variables. Experimental results demonstrate that our technique is scalable, and effective at verifying bounds.

We plan to build on this work in at least the following two directions: (i) extending from collection lengths to general memory usage, (ii) generalizing the AST counter technique and applying it in different contexts.

References

1. DARPA space-time analysis for cybersecurity program (STAC). http://www. darpa.mil/program/space-time-analysis-for-cybersecurity
2. Scala library for parsing and printing the SMT-LIB format. https://github.com/ regb/scala-smtlib
3. Albert, E., Arenas, P., Genaim, S., Puebla, G., Zanardini, D.: Cost analysis of Java bytecode. In: De Nicola, R. (ed.) ESOP 2007. LNCS, vol. 4421, pp. 157–172. Springer, Heidelberg (2007). https://doi.org/10.1007/978-3-540-71316-6_12
4. Albert, E., Genaim, S., Gomez-Zamalloa, M.: Heap space analysis for Java bytecode. In: Proceedings of the 6th International Symposium on Memory Management, pp. 105–116. ACM (2007)
5. Albert, E., Genaim, S., Gómez-Zamalloa Gil, M.: Live heap space analysis for languages with garbage collection. In: Proceedings of the 2009 International Symposium on Memory Management, pp. 129–138. ACM (2009)
6. Albert, E., Genaim, S., Masud, A.N.: More precise yet widely applicable cost analysis. In: Jhala, R., Schmidt, D. (eds.) VMCAI 2011. LNCS, vol. 6538, pp. 38–53. Springer, Heidelberg (2011). https://doi.org/10.1007/978-3-642-18275-4_5
7. Alonso-Blas, D.E., Genaim, S.: On the limits of the classical approach to cost analysis. In: Miné, A., Schmidt, D. (eds.) SAS 2012. LNCS, vol. 7460, pp. 405–421. Springer, Heidelberg (2012). https://doi.org/10.1007/978-3-642-33125-1_27
8. Carbonneaux, Q., Hoffmann, J., Shao, Z.: Compositional certified resource bounds. ACM SIGPLAN Not. **50**(6), 467–478 (2015)
9. Chin, W.N., Khoo, S.C.: Calculating sized types. High.-Order Symb. Comput. **14**(2–3), 261–300 (2001)
10. Coughlin, D., Chang, B.Y.E.: Fissile type analysis: modular checking of almost everywhere invariants. ACM SIGPLAN Not. **49**, 73–85 (2014)
11. de Moura, L., Bjørner, N.: Z3: an efficient SMT solver. In: Ramakrishnan, C.R., Rehof, J. (eds.) TACAS 2008. LNCS, vol. 4963, pp. 337–340. Springer, Heidelberg (2008). https://doi.org/10.1007/978-3-540-78800-3_24
12. Dietl, W., Dietzel, S., Ernst, M.D., Muşlu, K., Schiller, T.W.: Building and using pluggable type-checkers. In: Proceedings of the 33rd International Conference on Software Engineering, pp. 681–690. ACM (2011)
13. Flores-Montoya, A., Hähnle, R.: Resource analysis of complex programs with cost equations. In: Garrigue, J. (ed.) APLAS 2014. LNCS, vol. 8858, pp. 275–295. Springer, Cham (2014). https://doi.org/10.1007/978-3-319-12736-1_15
14. Giesl, J., et al.: Proving termination of programs automatically with AProVE. In: Demri, S., Kapur, D., Weidenbach, C. (eds.) IJCAR 2014. LNCS (LNAI), vol. 8562, pp. 184–191. Springer, Cham (2014). https://doi.org/10.1007/978-3-319-08587-6_13
15. Gulwani, S., Jain, S., Koskinen, E.: Control-flow refinement and progress invariants for bound analysis. ACM SIGPLAN Not. **44**, 375–385 (2009)
16. Gulwani, S., Mehra, K.K., Chilimbi, T.: Speed: precise and efficient static estimation of program computational complexity. ACM SIGPLAN Not. **44**, 127–139 (2009)
17. Gulwani, S., Zuleger, F.: The reachability-bound problem. ACM SIGPLAN Not. **45**, 292–304 (2010)
18. Hoffmann, J., Aehlig, K., Hofmann, M.: Multivariate amortized resource analysis. ACM SIGPLAN Not. **46**, 357–370 (2011)

19. Hoffmann, J., Das, A., Weng, S.C.: Towards automatic resource bound analysis for OCaml. ACM SIGPLAN Not. **52**, 359–373 (2017)
20. Olivo, O., Dillig, I., Lin, C.: Static detection of asymptotic performance bugs in collection traversals. ACM SIGPLAN Not. **50**, 369–378 (2015)
21. Papi, M.M., Ali, M., Correa Jr., T.L., Perkins, J.H., Ernst, M.D.: Practical pluggable types for Java. In: Proceedings of the 2008 International Symposium on Software Testing and Analysis, pp. 201–212. ACM (2008)
22. Rondon, P.M., Kawaguci, M., Jhala, R.: Liquid types. ACM SIGPLAN Not. **43**, 159–169 (2008)
23. Rondon, P.M., Kawaguchi, M., Jhala, R.: Low-level liquid types. ACM SIGPLAN Not. **45**, 131–144 (2010)
24. Sinn, M., Zuleger, F., Veith, H.: A simple and scalable approach to bound analysis and amortized complexity analysis. In: Computer Aided Verification-26th International Conference (CAV 14), pp. 743–759 (2014)
25. Vasconcelos, P.B.: Space cost analysis using sized types. Ph.D. thesis, University of St Andrews (2008)
26. Vasconcelos, P.B., Hammond, K.: Inferring cost equations for recursive, polymorphic and higher-order functional programs. In: Trinder, P., Michaelson, G.J., Peña, R. (eds.) IFL 2003. LNCS, vol. 3145, pp. 86–101. Springer, Heidelberg (2004). https://doi.org/10.1007/978-3-540-27861-0_6
27. Lu, T., Cerný, P., Chang, B.-Y.E., Trivedi, A.: Type-directed bounding of collections in reactive programs. CoRR abs/1810.10443 (2018)
28. Winskel, G.: The Formal Semantics of Programming Languages: An Introduction. MIT Press, Cambridge (1993)
29. Xu, G., Rountev, A.: Precise memory leak detection for Java software using container profiling. In: Proceedings of the 30th International Conference on Software Engineering, pp. 151–160. ACM (2008)
30. Xu, G., Rountev, A.: Detecting inefficiently-used containers to avoid bloat. ACM SIGPLAN Not. **45**, 160–173 (2010)
31. Zuleger, F., Gulwani, S., Sinn, M., Veith, H.: Bound analysis of imperative programs with the size-change abstraction. In: Yahav, E. (ed.) SAS 2011. LNCS, vol. 6887, pp. 280–297. Springer, Heidelberg (2011). https://doi.org/10.1007/978-3-642-23702-7_22

Solving and Interpolating Constant Arrays Based on Weak Equivalences

Jochen Hoenicke[✉] and Tanja Schindler[✉]

University of Freiburg, Freiburg im Breisgau, Germany
{hoenicke,schindle}@informatik.uni-freiburg.de

Abstract. We present a new solver and interpolation algorithm for the theory of arrays with constant arrays. It is based on our previous work on weakly equivalent arrays. Constant arrays store the same value at every index, which is useful for model checking of programs with initialised memory. Instead of using a store chain to explicitly initialise the memory, using a constant array can considerably simplify the queries and thus reduce the solving and interpolation time. We show that only a few new rules are required for constant arrays and prove the correctness of the decision procedure and the interpolation procedure. We implemented the algorithm in our interpolating solver SMTINTERPOL.

1 Introduction

This paper presents a new solver and interpolation algorithm for the theory of arrays with constant arrays. It is a direct extension of the algorithms presented in [4, 10].

Interpolation based model checking is a successful technique for proving correctness of programs. In the Software Verification Competition (SV-COMP) [1] the winners of the last three years are using interpolants to generate candidate invariants [6, 9]. These programs use SMT solvers with different theories. For example, to represent heap memory with pointer arithmetic or static arrays in C the tools usually use the theory of arrays. Often, allocated memory is either explicitly or implicitly initialised with a default value. For example in C programs statically allocated memory is guaranteed to be initialised to be zero at start-up. Without the feature of constant arrays, the initialisation has to be done explicitly in the formula. This can lead to a huge store term that stores thousands of zeros into a large static block. This store term has to be carried around by the model checker and provided with each query of the solver. It may also slow down the solving process, especially when counter-examples have to be generated, or when the initialisation is crucial for showing unsatisfiability.

In this paper we describe an extension of the array theory for constant arrays. Constant arrays are simply arrays that store the same given constant at all indices. They have already been described in [14] where a decision procedure was

This work is supported by the German Research Council (DFG) under HO 5606/1-1.

C. Enea and R. Piskac (Eds.): VMCAI 2019, LNCS 11388, pp. 297–317, 2019.
https://doi.org/10.1007/978-3-030-11245-5_14

given, but so far no interpolation algorithm exists. We present a new decision procedure based on weakly equivalent arrays that is interpolation-friendly, and an interpolation algorithm for proofs generated by this decision procedure.

The decision procedure and interpolation algorithm are implemented in our interpolating SMT solver SMTINTERPOL. The new rules necessary for constant arrays are only triggered if constant arrays exist in the input formula. Thus, the performance of the decision procedure is not negatively affected for the previously supported formulas. Furthermore, the new lemmas can quickly be found using the existing data structures for weak equivalence. Our preliminary evaluation shows that using constant arrays instead of explicitly initialised arrays significantly reduces the query size and solving time.

The contributions of this paper are:

- a decision procedure for constant arrays based on weakly equivalent arrays,
- an interpolation procedure for constant arrays that also allows for combining equality interpolating theories,
- correctness proofs for the decision procedure and the produced interpolants.

2 Preliminaries

In this section we define our variant of the theory of arrays with constant arrays and give a short summary of Craig interpolation.

2.1 Theory of Arrays

We assume standard sorted first-order logic with equality. We use $\top$ for the formula that is always true and $\bot$ for false. Theories are defined by the signature and a set of axioms for their interpreted symbols. The theory of arrays $\mathcal{T}_A$ uses a parametric sort $(\sigma \Rightarrow \tau)$, which denotes the arrays with the index sort σ and the element sort τ. The signature Σ_A contains a select function $\cdot[\cdot] : (\sigma \Rightarrow \tau) \times \sigma \to \tau$ and a store function $\cdot\langle \cdot \lhd \cdot \rangle : (\sigma \Rightarrow \tau) \times \sigma \times \tau \to (\sigma \Rightarrow \tau)$. For array a, index i and element v, $a[i]$ returns the element stored in a at index i, and $a\langle i \lhd v \rangle$ returns a fresh array that is a copy of a where the element at i is replaced by v.

These functions are defined by the following axioms by McCarthy [11].

$$\forall\, a : (\sigma \Rightarrow \tau)\ i : \sigma\ v : \tau.\ a\langle i \lhd v \rangle[i] = v \tag{idx}$$

$$\forall\, a : (\sigma \Rightarrow \tau)\ i : \sigma\ j : \sigma\ v : \tau.\ i \neq j \to a\langle i \lhd v \rangle[j] = a[j] \quad \text{(read-over-write)}$$

To get an extensional array theory, we include in the signature Σ_A the function $\mathrm{diff}(\cdot, \cdot) : (\sigma \Rightarrow \tau) \times (\sigma \Rightarrow \tau) \to \sigma$, which was proposed by Bruttomesso et al. [3]. For distinct arrays a and b, it returns an index where a and b differ, and an arbitrary index otherwise. This is ensured by the following axiom (which implies extensionality).

$$\forall\, a : (\sigma \Rightarrow \tau)\ b : (\sigma \Rightarrow \tau).\ a[\mathrm{diff}(a, b)] = b[\mathrm{diff}(a, b)] \to a = b. \tag{ext-diff}$$

The theory of arrays with constant arrays, proposed by Stump et al. [14], additionally defines a function $\text{const}_\sigma(\cdot) : \tau \to (\sigma \Rightarrow \tau)$. For an element v, the function application $\text{const}_\sigma(v)$ returns an array that contains the element v at all indices i, which is formalised by the following axiom:

$$\forall\, i : \sigma\ v : \tau.\ \text{const}_\sigma(v)[i] = v \qquad\qquad \text{(const)}$$

For simplicity we often write $\text{const}(v)$ for $\text{const}_\sigma(v)$ if the index type can be deduced from context or is not important.

To facilitate Nelson–Oppen theory combination, we need a stably infinite array theory. To achieve this, we require that the index sort is stably infinite and that the element sort has a model containing at least two elements (we allow Booleans as the element sort). However, simply adding the axiom for constant arrays renders the resulting array theory non-stably infinite. As an example, the formula $\text{const}_\sigma(v)\langle i \lhd w \rangle = \text{const}_\sigma(w) \wedge v \neq w$ is satisfiable, but only if the sort σ contains only one element. To avoid this problem, Stump et al. assume that the index set is always infinite. We make this explicit by adding infinity axioms, i.e., for every sort σ for which $\text{const}_\sigma(\cdot)$ is used and for every natural number n, we add the axiom

$$\forall\, i_1 : \sigma \dots i_n : \sigma.\ \exists\, j : \sigma.\ j \neq i_1 \wedge \cdots \wedge j \neq i_n \qquad\qquad \text{(infinity)}$$

To avoid unsoundness in our solver for SMTLIB, which does not mandate the infinity axiom, we only allow constant arrays for index domains that are known to be infinite, e.g., integers and reals.

2.2   Interpolation

An interpolation problem with respect to a given background theory $\mathcal{T}$ is a pair of formulas (A, B) such that $A \wedge B$ is unsatisfiable in $\mathcal{T}$. We also say that A and B form a partitioning of $F : A \wedge B$. A *Craig interpolant* for (A, B) is a formula I such that (i) A implies I in the theory $\mathcal{T}$, (ii) I and B are unsatisfiable in $\mathcal{T}$ and (iii) all non-theory symbols in I occur in both A and B.

We call a non-theory symbol *shared* if it occurs in both A and B, *A-local* if it occurs only in A, and *B-local* if it occurs only in B. This definition is naturally extended to terms and literals. In addition, a term or literal is called *mixed* if it contains both A-local and B-local symbols.

Given a resolution proof for unsatisfiability of a formula $F : A \wedge B$, an interpolant for (A, B) can be derived inductively from the proof tree. We use the proof tree preserving interpolation scheme by Christ et al. [5]. This is an extension to Pudlák's [13] and McMillan's [12] interpolation algorithms and also supports SMT and theory combination with equality interpolating theories.

For proof tree preserving interpolation, each theory has to compute interpolants for its theory conflicts. An interpolant for a theory conflict C is computed as an interpolant of $(C \restriction A, C \restriction B)$ where $\restriction A$ and $\restriction B$ are projection functions that split the literals of the conflict C into A- and B-parts. If a literal ℓ is A-local, its projections are defined as $\ell \,\lfloor\, A \equiv \ell$ and $\ell \,\lfloor\, B \equiv \top$, and analogously for B-local literals. Shared literals are projected to both partitions: $\ell \,\lfloor\, A \equiv \ell \,\lfloor\, B \equiv \ell$. The projection of a conjunction is the conjunction of the projections.

The crucial part of proof tree preserving interpolation is the extension of the projections to mixed equality and disequality literals. We introduce an uninterpreted binary predicate EQ and, for each atom $a = b$ where a is A-local and b is B-local, a fresh variable x_{ab}. The projections for the literals $a = b$ and $a \neq b$ are defined as follows.

$$(a = b) \,\lfloor\, A \equiv (a = x_{ab}) \qquad (a = b) \,\lfloor\, B \equiv (x_{ab} = b)$$
$$(a \neq b) \,\lfloor\, A \equiv \mathrm{EQ}(x_{ab}, a) \qquad (a \neq b) \,\lfloor\, B \equiv \neg\,\mathrm{EQ}(x_{ab}, b)$$

An interpolant of a conflict containing the literal $a = b$ may contain the auxiliary variable x_{ab} at any place. For an interpolant of a conflict containing $a \neq b$, proof tree preserving interpolation requires that the auxiliary variable x_{ab} occurs only as first parameter of a positively occurring EQ predicate, i.e., the interpolant has the form $I[\mathrm{EQ}(x_{ab}, s_1)] \ldots [\mathrm{EQ}(x_{ab}, s_n)]$ for shared terms $s_1, \ldots, s_n$. This is usually automatically the case. As an example, an interpolant of the theory conflict $a = b \wedge f(a) \neq f(b)$ where a is A-local, b is B-local and f is shared, is defined as an interpolant of the problem

$$(a = x_{ab} \wedge \mathrm{EQ}(x_{f(a)f(b)}, f(a)), \quad x_{ab} = b \wedge \neg\,\mathrm{EQ}(x_{f(a)f(b)}, f(b))).$$

Such an interpolant is $I = \mathrm{EQ}(x_{f(a)f(b)}, f(x_{ab}))$.

3   Decision Procedure for Arrays

In this section we present the decision procedure for the theory of arrays with constant arrays. It extends our decision procedure based on weakly equivalent arrays, which we summarise in the next subsection. In Sect. 3.2, we present the necessary changes for constant arrays and prove the correctness of the decision procedure.

Our decision procedure is compatible with proof tree preserving interpolation presented in the previous section. It can propagate equalities and disequalities between terms from different parts of the interpolation problem, but it does not create new mixed terms. Most existing procedures create mixed select terms, e.g, when instantiating (read-over-write) on an A-local store term and a B-local index.

3.1   Weakly Equivalent Arrays

Our solver for the array theory fits into the Nelson–Oppen theory combination framework. For a formula F, we define the set of shared terms V. In the original presentation of Nelson–Oppen, shared variables are introduced for every term shared between different theories, e.g. for every select term $a[i]$, shared variables $v_a, v_i, v_{a[i]}$ are created, the formula $v_{a[i]} = v_a[v_i]$ is added to the array theory and $a[i]$ in the original formula is replaced by $v_{a[i]}$. Each theory then propagates equality constraints on these shared variables in the form of a disjunction of equalities and disequalities. We find it simpler to work directly with the shared terms and treat in each theory the terms whose head symbol is from a foreign theory as an uninterpreted constant. The reader who prefers the variable view can replace in the remainder of the paper every term t by its auxiliary variable v_t.

Our algorithm starts with a preprocessing phase. In the preprocessing phase, we instantiate for each store term $a\langle i \lhd v\rangle$ the axiom (idx) $a\langle i \lhd v\rangle[i] = v$ and for each diff term $\text{diff}(a, b)$ the axiom (ext-diff) $a[\text{diff}(a,b)] = b[\text{diff}(a,b)] \to a = b$. Note that this preprocessing step can be done for each input formula separately and that an interpolant for the preprocessed formulas is also an interpolant for the original formulas. We then compute the set of shared terms V as the set of all terms in the (preprocessed) formula of array type as well as for each select term $a[i]$ the terms $a[i]$ and i and for every store term $a\langle i \lhd v\rangle$ the terms $i, a[i], a\langle i \lhd v\rangle[i]$. Note that this step creates a new term $a[i] \in V$ for a store term $a\langle i \lhd v\rangle$.

The main algorithm of our solver is the DPLL(T) algorithm that generates partial models by assigning truth values to literals and asks each theory for conflicts. In the case of the theory of arrays, the literals are the equalities on V. The theory solver takes as input a candidate equality relation $\sim$ on V (it assumes that terms are not equal unless the corresponding equality literal is set). If the equality relation $\sim$ is satisfiable for the theory of arrays and is compatible with all other theories and the input formula, we found a satisfying model. Otherwise the theory solver returns a conflict, i.e., a (small) conjunction of equalities and disequalities that are part of $(V, \sim)$ and contradict the array axioms.

To find these conflicts, our array solver uses the notion of weak equivalence over $(V, \sim)$. The *weak equivalence graph* G is defined by its vertices, the array-valued terms in V, and its undirected edges of the form (i) $s_1 \leftrightarrow s_2$ if $s_1 \sim s_2$ and (ii) $s_1 \overset{i}{\leftrightarrow} s_2$ if s_1 has the form $s_2\langle i \lhd \cdot\rangle$ or vice versa. If two arrays a and b are connected in G by a path P, they are called *weakly equivalent*. This is denoted by $a \overset{P}{\Leftrightarrow} b$. Weakly equivalent arrays can differ only at finitely many indices given by $\text{Stores}(P) := \{i \mid \exists s_1\, s_2.\ s_1 \overset{i}{\leftrightarrow} s_2 \in P\}$. Two arrays a and b are called *weakly equivalent on i*, denoted by $a \approx_i b$, if they are connected by a path P such that $k \not\sim i$ holds for each $k \in \text{Stores}(P)$. Two arrays a and b are called *weakly congruent on i*, $a \sim_i b$, if they are weakly equivalent on i, or if there exist $a'[j], b'[k] \in V$ with $a'[j] \sim b'[k]$ and $j \sim k \sim i$ and $a \approx_i a'$, $b' \approx_i b$. If a and b are weakly congruent on i, they must store the same value at i. For example, if $a\langle i + 1 \lhd v\rangle \sim b$ and $b[i] \sim c[i]$, arrays a and b are weakly equivalent on i, but a and c are only weakly congruent on i.

For the theory of arrays without constant arrays the following two patterns are sufficient to detect all conflicts.

$$\frac{a \approx_i b}{a \overset{P}{\Leftrightarrow} b} \quad \frac{i \sim j}{\bigwedge_{i \in \text{Stores}(P)} a \sim_i b} \quad \frac{a[i] \not\sim b[j]}{a \not\sim b} \qquad \begin{array}{l} \text{(read-over-weakeq)} \\[2ex] \text{(weakeq-ext)} \end{array}$$

The first pattern, based on (read-over-write), checks if a disequality between select terms $a[i]$ and $b[j]$ with $i \sim j$ contradicts a weak equivalence between a and b. The second pattern detects inequalities on array terms that contradict the fact that they are weakly equivalent on every index. These patterns are complete for the quantifier-free theory of arrays [4], i.e., if no pattern is applicable, there is a model for the array theory compatible with $\sim$.

If a pattern is detected, the solver returns a conflict, which is the conjunction of equalities and disequalities that contradict the array axioms. We use $\mathrm{Cond}(a \overset{P}{\Leftrightarrow} b), \mathrm{Cond}(a \approx_i b), \mathrm{Cond}(a \sim_i b)$ to denote the conjunction of the literals $v = v'$ (resp. $v \neq v'$), $v, v' \in V$, such that $v \sim v'$ (resp. $v \not\sim v'$) is necessary to show the corresponding property. The conflict for (read-over-weakeq) can then be written as $\mathrm{Cond}(a \approx_i b) \wedge i = j \wedge a[i] \neq b[j]$ and similarly for the other pattern. The negated conflict is inserted into the DPLL engine as a theory lemma clause.

3.2   Extension for Constant Arrays

For every constant array $\mathrm{const}(v)$ in the formula, we add $\mathrm{const}(v)$ and v to the set V of shared terms. We extend the decision procedure from [4] in two ways. On the one hand, we define two new patterns to treat constant arrays, on the other hand, we extend the definition of weak congruence to treat extensionality.

The first pattern is applicable if any two constant arrays are weakly equivalent: if two constant arrays $\mathrm{const}(v), \mathrm{const}(w)$ are connected by a weak path, they can differ only at finitely many indices. But as they are constant and the index sort is infinite, the arrays must already be equal, which means that the constant element values v and w must be equal. The second pattern, which is very similar to (read-over-weakeq), is applicable if an array a is weakly equivalent on i to a constant array $\mathrm{const}(v)$ and there is a select term $a[i]$. Then it must store the same value at position i as the constant array, which is constantly v, independently of i. Formally, the patterns are as follows:

$$\mathrm{const}(v) \overset{P}{\Leftrightarrow} \mathrm{const}(w) \qquad v \not\sim w \qquad \text{(const-weakeq)}$$
$$a \approx_i \mathrm{const}(v) \qquad a[i] \not\sim v \qquad \text{(read-const-weakeq)}$$

For extensionality, pattern (weakeq-ext) can be used, but we need to update the definition of weak congruence on i. In addition to the previous definition, two arrays a and b are also weakly congruent on i if the following holds: a is weakly equivalent to an array s, b is weakly equivalent to a constant array $\mathrm{const}(v)$, and $s[j]$ is equal to v at an index j that is equal to i, or symmetrically with a and b switched. Formally, the new definition is as follows.

Definition 1 (Weak congruence on i with constant arrays). *Two arrays a and b are weakly congruent on i, denoted by $a \sim_i b$, if either*

1. they are weakly equivalent on i, i.e., $a \approx_i b$, or

2. *there exist* $a'[j], b'[k] \in V$ *with* $a'[j] \sim b'[k]$ *and* $j \sim k \sim i$ *and* $a \approx_i a'$, $b' \approx_i b$, *or*

3. *there exist* $s[j], \text{const}(v) \in V$ *with* $s[j] \sim v$ *and* $i \sim j$ *and either* $a \approx_i s$, $\text{const}(v) \approx_i b$ *or* $a \approx_i \text{const}(v)$, $s \approx_i b$.

Theorem 1. *The conflict patterns (read-const-weakeq), (const-weakeq) as well as (weakeq-ext) with the updated definition of weak congruence are sound, i.e., the corresponding conflict contradicts the theory of arrays.*

Proof. For (const-weakeq), consider the path P with $\text{const}(v) \overset{P}{\nleftrightarrow} \text{const}(w)$. Let $\text{Stores}(P) = \{i_1, \ldots, i_n\}$ be the set of store indices. By the axiom (infinity) there is an index j with $j \neq i_1, \ldots, j \neq i_n$. By induction over the length of the weak path P, it holds that $\text{Cond}(\text{const}(v) \overset{P}{\nleftrightarrow} \text{const}(w))$ implies $\text{const}(v)[j] = \text{const}(w)[j]$. With the axiom (const) this contradicts $v \neq w$.

For (read-const-weakeq), induction over the length of the weak path shows that $\text{Cond}(a \approx_i \text{const}(v))$ implies $a[i] = \text{const}(v)[i]$. Using the axiom (const) this gives a conflict with $a[i] \neq v$.

For (weakeq-ext), we refer to the proof in [4]. It remains to show that $\text{Cond}(a \sim_i b)$ implies $a[i] = b[i]$ also in case 3. of Definition 1. If $\text{Cond}(a \approx_i s) \wedge \text{Cond}(b \approx_i \text{const}(v)) \wedge i = j \wedge s[j] = v$ hold, then induction over the paths for $a \approx_i s$ and $b \approx_i \text{const}(v)$ shows that this implies $a[i] = s[i]$ and $b[i] = \text{const}(v)[i]$. With $i = j \wedge s[j] = v$, congruence, and the axiom (const) this implies $a[i] = b[i]$ as desired. The other case with $a \approx_i \text{const}(v)$, $s \approx_i b$ is symmetric. □

Theorem 2. *The patterns (read-const-weakeq), (const-weakeq), together with the patterns in Sect. 3.1 and the updated definition for weak congruence, are complete for the theory of arrays with extensionality and constant arrays.*

Proof. We show for a given equivalence relation $\sim$ on V where no pattern matches that there is an array model $\mathcal{M}$ compatible with $\sim$. We build $\mathcal{M}$ for all sorts inductively over the structure of the sort, such that for $t, t' \in V$, $\mathcal{M}[t] = \mathcal{M}[t']$ holds if and only if $t \sim t'$. The base case is a non-array sort σ, for which we define the domain $\mathcal{D}_\sigma$ as the set containing at least the equivalence classes $V_\sigma/\sim$ of terms. In the case of σ being an index sort, $\mathcal{D}_\sigma$ also contains an infinite number of unique elements (to ensure the infinity axiom). For a term $t \in V$ of type σ that is not an array we define $\mathcal{M}[t] = \{t' \in V | t' \sim t\}$. The domain of an array sort $\mathcal{D}_{(\sigma \Rightarrow \tau)}$ is defined as the set of total functions $\mathcal{D}_\sigma \to \mathcal{D}_\tau$. Since $\mathcal{D}_\sigma$ is infinite, we can assume that there is a function $\ulcorner \cdot \urcorner$ that returns for every weak equivalence class a unique element from $\mathcal{D}_\sigma$ different from any element $\mathcal{M}[i]$ for $i \in V_\sigma$. For τ our assumption is that there are at least two distinct elements $Fst_\tau, Snd_\tau \in \mathcal{D}_\tau$ (which can be equal to some $\mathcal{M}[v]$ for $v \in V_\tau$). We define the valuation of all terms $a \in V$ that have an array sort $(\sigma \Rightarrow \tau)$ as follows:

$$\mathcal{M}[a](\mathtt{J}) = \begin{cases} \mathcal{M}[a'[i]] & \text{if there is } a'[i] \in V \text{ with } \mathcal{M}[i] = \mathtt{J}, \text{ and } a \approx_i a' \\ \mathcal{M}[v] & \text{if there is } \mathrm{const}(v) \in V \text{ with a } \overset{P}{\leftrightsquigarrow} \mathrm{const}(v), \\ & \text{and } \mathcal{M}[i] \neq \mathtt{J} \text{ for all } i \in \mathrm{Stores}\,(P) \\ Snd_\tau & \text{if } \mathtt{J} = \ulcorner \mathrm{WeakEQ}(a) \urcorner \text{ and no } \mathrm{const}(v) \in \mathrm{WeakEQ}(a) \\ Fst_\tau & \text{otherwise} \end{cases}$$

The first two cases ensure that the valuation for the array a is compatible with the $a[i]$ terms in the formula and that an array $\mathrm{const}(v)$ stores only the value v. The last two cases ensure that arrays from different weak equivalence classes store different values at some index.

First, the definition is well-defined: if there are two terms $a_1[i_1], a_2[i_2] \in V$ for which the first case applies, then $i_1 \sim i_2$, $a_1 \approx_{i_1} a_2$, and the pattern (read-over-weakeq) ensures that $a_1[i_1] \sim a_2[i_2]$. By induction hypothesis, $\mathcal{M}[a_1[i_1]] = \mathcal{M}[a_2[i_2]]$. If there are two terms v_1, v_2 for which the second case applies, then there are weak paths $a \overset{P_1}{\leftrightsquigarrow} \mathrm{const}(v_1)$ and $a \overset{P_2}{\leftrightsquigarrow} \mathrm{const}(v_2)$. Hence, there is a path $\mathrm{const}(v_1) \overset{P}{\leftrightsquigarrow} \mathrm{const}(v_2)$ and the pattern (const-weakeq) ensures that $v_1 \sim v_2$. If there is a term $a'[i_1]$ for which the first case applies and $\mathrm{const}(v)$ for which the second case applies, then $a' \approx_{i_1} \mathrm{const}(v)$ holds. The pattern (read-const-weakeq) ensures that $a'[i_1] \sim v$. The third case cannot apply if the first case applies by the definition of $\ulcorner \cdot \urcorner$. The third case also cannot apply when the second case applies. The last case only applies if the other cases do not apply.

Next we show that for every $a\langle i \triangleleft v\rangle \in V$, the above definition assigns to $\mathcal{M}[a\langle i \triangleleft v\rangle](\mathtt{J})$ the value $\mathcal{M}[a](\mathtt{J})$ if $\mathcal{M}[i] \neq \mathtt{J}$ and $\mathcal{M}[v]$ if $\mathcal{M}[i] = \mathtt{J}$. The latter holds because the preprocessing step adds $a\langle i \triangleleft v\rangle[i] = v$ to the formula and $a' = a\langle i \triangleleft v\rangle$ fulfils the first case. Hence, $\mathcal{M}[a\langle i \triangleleft v\rangle](\mathtt{J}) = \mathcal{M}[a\langle i \triangleleft v\rangle[i]] = \mathcal{M}[v]$. For $\mathtt{J}$ with $\mathcal{M}[i] \neq \mathtt{J}$, one can show $\mathcal{M}[a\langle i \triangleleft v\rangle](\mathtt{J}) = \mathcal{M}[a](\mathtt{J})$ by case distinction over which case applies in the definition of $\mathcal{M}[a](\mathtt{J})$. It is easy to see that the same case also applies for $\mathcal{M}[a\langle i \triangleleft v\rangle](\mathtt{J})$ if $\mathcal{M}[i] \neq \mathtt{J}$ holds and that the defined value is the same.

Finally, we show extensionality, i.e., we show for $a, b \in V$ that $\mathcal{M}[a]$ and $\mathcal{M}[b]$ differ or $a \sim b$ holds. If a and b are not weakly equivalent, then they differ at either $\mathtt{J} = \ulcorner \mathrm{WeakEQ}(a) \urcorner$ or $\mathtt{J} = \ulcorner \mathrm{WeakEQ}(b) \urcorner$: if both arrays are not weakly equivalent to any $\mathrm{const}(v)$, then values $Fst_\tau \not\sim Snd_\tau$ are different and if w.l.o.g. a is weakly equivalent to some $\mathrm{const}(v)$ then $\mathcal{M}[a](\mathtt{J}) = \mathcal{M}[v]$, but $\mathcal{M}[b](\mathtt{J})$ is either equal to a different constant value or is alternating between Fst_τ and Snd_τ. If a and b are weakly equivalent, i.e., $a \overset{P}{\leftrightsquigarrow} b$, and $a \sim_i b$ for some $i \in \mathrm{Stores}\,(P)$ does not hold, then we can show that $\mathcal{M}[a](\mathcal{M}[i]) \neq \mathcal{M}[b](\mathcal{M}[i])$ holds as follows. Take i_1 to be the first store index on the path from a to b with $i_1 \sim i$ ($i \in \mathrm{Stores}\,(P)$ guarantees its existence). Then for the array a' on the left of this store edge $a \approx_i a'$ holds, and the preprocessing step created the select term $a'[i_1] \in V$. Similarly we find i_2 and b' with $b \approx_i b'$ and $b'[i_2]$. Since $a \not\sim_i b$, we have $a'[i_1] \not\sim b'[i_2]$ and the values differ. Finally, if $a \overset{P}{\leftrightsquigarrow} b$, and $a \sim_i b$ holds for all $i \in \mathrm{Stores}\,(P)$, then $a \sim b$ by pattern (weakeq-ext). $\qquad \square$

Remark 1. If the element sort is known to be stably infinite, it is not necessary to create a $a[i]$ term for every $a\langle i \lhd v\rangle$ term. In this case, one can always find a fresh value for every $\text{WeakEQ}_i(a)$ class as model value for $a[i]$. This slightly complicates the extensionality proof, as the preprocessor does not create the $a[i]$ terms, see [4] for details.

It turns out that adding the select terms in the preprocessor makes the case 3. of Definition 1 superfluous, as there is always a select term that is equal because of the pattern (read-const-weakeq) and case 2. can be used instead. Nonetheless we decided to include this case to allow using the more efficient procedure that does not add the select terms in the preprocessor.

3.3 Implementation Details

First we note that our algorithm can also be easily adapted to not only find conflicts but also propagate new equalities. In our implementation we build $(V, \sim)$ incrementally and the array solver assumes that all elements that are not explicitly equal are not equal. Thus the produced conflicts can still have undefined literals. If there is only one undefined literal, the conflict can be used to propagate a new equality. If there are more undefined literals the conflict will tell the DPLL engine, which undecided equalities can potentially cause a conflict and need to be decided.

We use an efficient data structure to represent the weak equivalence classes [4]. For each equivalence class of $(V, \sim)$ a node is created. Each node has at most two outgoing edges, a primary and a secondary, which correspond to the store edges in the weak equivalence graph and are labelled by the corresponding index. The primary edges form a tree, where each edge points in the direction of the root of the tree, which is the representative of the whole weak equivalence class. The secondary edges are used to find the representative of $\approx_i$ in the case that i is equal to the label of the primary edge. The representative of $\approx_i$ is either the root node or a node with a primary but no secondary edge.

For the representative of a weak equivalence class we remember the constant arrays in this class. For the representative of $\approx_i$ we remember the select term involving i. This means that the root node has a map from index i to the corresponding select term and the other nodes without a secondary edge only store the select term for the index on the label of the primary edge. This allows to quickly identify instantiations for the patterns (read-over-weakeq), (const-weakeq), and (read-const-weakeq). For example, if two weak equivalence classes both containing constant arrays are merged, we can instantiate the (const-weakeq) pattern.

To find instances of (weakeq-ext) we compute the model in a similar way as described in the proof of Theorem 2 and use a hash set to detect two arrays which are extensionally equal. We then use our data structure to find the weak equivalence paths needed for the conflict.

The problem of solving quantifier-free formulas over arrays is NP-complete, and the overall algorithm including the DPLL engine is exponential. In [4], we showed that identifying the instances of the (read-over-weakeq) pattern is cubic in the size of the formula. Adding constant arrays and the new patterns does not change the overall complexity.

4   Interpolation

In the following, we present an interpolation algorithm for the extensional theory of arrays with constant arrays. It computes quantifier-free interpolants for the theory conflicts described in Sect. 3. The algorithm extends our algorithm presented in [10].

We first describe the basic concepts needed to compute interpolants in the presence of weak equivalences and weak congruences and shortly outline the interpolation algorithm for (read-over-weakeq) and (weakeq-ext) conflicts. Afterwards, we show how to extend the algorithm to the new conflicts (const-weakeq) and (read-const-weakeq) and how to modify the algorithm for (weakeq-ext) with the updated definition of weak congruence.

4.1   Interpolation for the Theory of Arrays

Our interpolation algorithm for the theory of arrays follows a colour-based approach [8]: each conflict contains weak paths that are subdivided into A- and B-coloured subpaths as follows. Equality edges $\leftrightarrow$ are A- or B-coloured if the corresponding equality literal is in A or B, respectively. For shared literals, the edge can be either A- or B-coloured, whatever is more convenient. If the corresponding literal is a mixed equality $a' = b'$, the edge is split into an A- and a B-coloured edge $a' \leftrightarrow x_{a'b'} \leftrightarrow b'$ using the auxiliary variable $x_{a'b'}$ of the literal. Store edges $\overset{i}{\leftrightarrow}$ are assigned to the part that contains the store term. The boundary term between an A- and a B-path is shared and may be used in the interpolant.

A (read-over-weakeq) conflict consists of a weak path $a \approx_i b$ showing that a and b store the same value at i, which together with the index equality $i = j$ contradicts the main disequality $a[i] \neq b[j]$. Depending on the main disequality $a[i] \neq b[j]$ the algorithm distinguishes four base cases: (r-i) there exists a shared term representing the index equality $i = j$ and $a[i] \neq b[j]$ is in B or mixed, (r-ii) there exists a shared term for $i = j$ and $a[i] \neq b[j]$ is A-local, (r-iii) i, j and $a[i] \neq b[j]$ are all B-local, or (r-iv) i, j and $a[i] \neq b[j]$ are A-local.

In case (r-i), the shared term x for the index equality $i = j$ can either be i or j, if one of them is shared, or the auxiliary variable x_{ij}. For simplicity of the presentation, we focus here on the cases where i or x_{ij} is the shared term, and j and therefore $b[j]$ are B-local.

The basic idea is to summarise maximal A-paths by equalities between shared select terms over the path ends, which must be shared. A path $\pi : s_1 \approx_i s_2$ together with $i = x$ implies $s_1[x] = s_2[x]$ for the shared term x. As some store index disequalities contained in an A-path may be B-local or mixed, an interpolant formula for this A-path also needs to contain the negated B-projections of

B-local and mixed store index disequalities. An interpolant for an inner A-path $\pi : s_1 \approx_i s_2$ is given by

$$I_\pi : s_1[x] = s_2[x] \vee F_\pi^A(x)$$

where F_π^A is defined as

$$F_\pi^A(x) \equiv \bigvee_{\substack{k \in \text{Stores}(\pi) \\ i \neq k \ B\text{-local}}} x = k \ \vee \bigvee_{\substack{k \in \text{Stores}(\pi) \\ i \neq k \ \text{mixed}}} \text{EQ}(x_{ik}, x).$$

For the outer A-path $\pi : a \approx_i s_1$ in the mixed case, where $a[i]$ is A-local, the select equality in the interpolant must be replaced by the corresponding EQ predicate, i.e., the resulting path interpolant is $\text{EQ}(x_{a[i]b[j]}, s_1[x]) \vee F_\pi^A(x)$.

For B-paths, the interpolant only needs to collect the A-projections of A-local and mixed index disequalities in formula F_π^B which is defined dually to F_π^A as

$$F_\pi^B(x) \equiv \bigwedge_{\substack{k \in \text{Stores}(\pi) \\ i \neq k \ A\text{-local}}} x \neq k \ \wedge \bigwedge_{\substack{k \in \text{Stores}(\pi) \\ i \neq k \ \text{mixed}}} \text{EQ}(x_{ik}, x).$$

The interpolant is the conjunction of the path interpolants I_π and $F_\pi^B(x)$.

The interpolant contains only shared terms by construction, in particular, all auxiliary variables for disequalities appear under EQ predicates. It follows from the A-part of the conflict: the interpolant formula for a B-path is just the conjunction of the A-projections of A-local or mixed disequalities on this path, where the shared term x replaces index i and $i = x$ follows from the A-projection of $i = j$. For an A-path, $\neg F_\pi^A(x)$ with the A-projections of $i \neq k$ implies $x \neq k$ for $k \in \text{Stores}(\pi)$. Thus, the interpolant formula for an A-path follows from (read-over-weakeq). The interpolant contradicts the B-part: An A-path interpolant together with the B-parts of the corresponding index disequalities implies that the shared arrays at the path ends contain the same element at index i, and similarly for an F_π^B formula together with the corresponding B-path. Together with transitivity, this contradicts the main disequality.

For case (r-ii), a dual interpolant formula can be computed by replacing conjunctions by disjunctions and vice versa and equalities by disequalities and vice versa. The EQ predicates are unchanged because of the asymmetry of the projection functions.

In case (r-iii), where $i = j$ is B-local and no shared term for $i = j$ exists, we cannot summarise A-paths in the way described above. However, we know that the shared arrays only differ at the finitely many store indices and we can express in shared terms the formula that each index where they differ must satisfy. In order to capture the store indices, we build rewrite chains between the shared arrays at the path ends using the diff function.

We use a convenient notation from [15] for rewriting an array step by step into another array: for two arrays s_1, s_2 and $m \geq 0$, the term $s_1 \overset{m}{\leadsto} s_2$ denotes the array obtained by modifying s_1 at m indices to resemble array s_2, which is equal to array s_2 if s_1 and s_2 differ at m or less indices. It is defined inductively as

$$s_1 \overset{0}{\rightsquigarrow} s_2 := s_1 \qquad s_1 \overset{m+1}{\rightsquigarrow} s_2 := s_1 \langle \text{diff}(s_1, s_2) \lhd s_2[\text{diff}(s_1, s_2)] \rangle \overset{m}{\rightsquigarrow} s_2.$$

As an example, if $s_1 = s_2 \langle i \lhd v \rangle \langle j \lhd w \rangle$, then $s_1 \overset{2}{\rightsquigarrow} s_2 = s_2$, and $s_1 = s_2 \lor \text{diff}(s_1, s_2) = i \lor \text{diff}(s_1, s_2) = j$. Similarly for $\text{diff}(s_1 \overset{1}{\rightsquigarrow} s_2, s_2)$. To express that two arrays s_1 and s_2 differ at most at m indices that all satisfy a formula $F(\cdot)$ with one free parameter, a formula $\text{weq}(s_1, s_2, m, F(\cdot))$ is defined inductively over $m \geq 0$ as follows.

$$\text{weq}(s_1, s_2, 0, F(\cdot)) \equiv s_1 = s_2$$
$$\text{weq}(s_1, s_2, m + 1, F(\cdot)) \equiv (s_1 = s_2 \lor F(\text{diff}(s_1, s_2))) \land \text{weq}(s_1 \overset{1}{\rightsquigarrow} s_2, s_2, m, F(\cdot))$$

With this notation, we can summarise an A-path $\pi : s_1 \approx_i s_2$ by

$$I_\pi : \text{weq}(s_1, s_2, |\pi|, F_\pi^A(\cdot))$$

where $|\pi|$ is the number of stores on path π and $F_\pi^A(\cdot)$ is defined as above. For B-paths, there is nothing to do as all store disequalities are B-local as well. The interpolant is the conjunction of all path interpolants.

By construction, the interpolant contains only shared terms. It follows from the A-part: for an A-path $\pi : s_1 \approx_i s_2$, we know that s_1 and s_2 can differ at most at $|\pi|$ indices. If they differ, applying diff hits one of the store indices for which $C \restriction A$ contains the corresponding EQ predicate. The interpolant contradicts the B-part: the arrays at the ends of each B-path cannot differ at i because of $C \restriction B$. The arrays at the ends of each A-path can only differ at finitely many indices satisfying F_π^A. Because of the corresponding B-projections, i does not satisfy F_π^A and hence the arrays store the same value at i. Transitivity yields the contradiction to the main disequality.

For case (r-iv), one can again compute the dual interpolant, and a formula $\text{nweq}(s_1, s_2, m, F(\cdot))$ is defined dually to the weq formula:

$$\text{nweq}(s_1, s_2, 0, F(\cdot)) \equiv s_1 \neq s_2$$
$$\text{nweq}(s_1, s_2, m + 1, F(\cdot)) \equiv (s_1 \neq s_2 \land F(\text{diff}(s_1, s_2)))$$
$$\lor \text{nweq}(s_1 \overset{1}{\rightsquigarrow} s_2, s_2, m, F(\cdot))$$

A (weakeq-ext) conflict consists of a main path $a \overset{P}{\not\leftrightarrow} b$ and a weak path $a \sim_i b$ for every $i \in \text{Stores}(P)$ which ensure that a and b store the same element at each i, in contradiction to the main disequality $a \neq b$. We consider three cases: (e-i) $a \neq b$ in B, (e-ii) $a \neq b$ A-local, or (e-iii) $a \neq b$ mixed.

We shortly recapitulate the interpolant for (e-i). If $a \neq b$ is in B, the interpolant is built by summarising A-paths. For an A-path $s_1 \overset{A}{\leftrightarrow} s_2$ on the main path P, we compute for each store index $i \in \text{Stores}(\pi)$ the interpolant of $a \sim_i b$, as in case (r-i) for (read-over-weakeq) using a fresh variable $\cdot$ for the shared index. If

i itself is shared, then a conjunct $i = \cdot$ has to be added. We call this interpolant $I_i(\cdot)$. Then we summarise π by a weq formula that states that s_1 and s_2 only differ at most at $|\pi|$ indices and each index satisfies one of these interpolants:

$$I_\pi \equiv \text{weq}(s_1, s_2, |\pi|, I_i(\cdot)).$$

For every store index i on a B-path, we interpolate $a \sim_i b$ as in case (r-i) or (r-iii) and obtain I_i. The interpolant is then obtained as the conjunction of I_π for A-paths and I_i for store indices i on B-paths.

There is an important variation in the methods for (read-over-weakeq) if a weak congruence $a \sim_i b$ uses select equality $a'[j] = b'[k]$, which we call *select edge* and see it as an edge connecting a' and b'. If the select edge lies on a B-path $\pi : s_1 \sim_i s_2$, any A-path is still a weak equivalence on i, and therefore the A-path summaries can be built as before. If one of the index equalities $i = j$ or $i = k$ is A-local or mixed, a conjunct for the corresponding A-projection must be added to F_π^B. If the select edge is on an A-path $\pi : s_1 \sim_i s_2$, a weq formula cannot be built as it holds only for weak equivalences. But this is no problem: either we built an $I_i(\cdot)$-summary for an index i on an A-path of the main path P and the fresh variable $\cdot$ is a shared index term. Otherwise, the index i on a B-path of P is either itself shared, or, because the select edge is in A, j must be shared or $i = j$ must be mixed. Thus, in each case there is a shared index term and the A-path (and all other A-paths similarly) is summarised as in case (r-i), i.e., by $s_1[\cdot] = s_2[\cdot] \vee F_\pi^A(\cdot)$ where F_π^A also includes disjuncts for the negated B-projections of $i = j$, $i = k$ if these equalities are B-local or mixed. If the select edge is mixed, w.l.o.g. $a'[j]$ A-local and $b'[k]$ B-local, there is a shared index x for similar reasons. In this case, there is no shared array at the end of the A-path $s_1 \sim_i a'$. Instead, the auxiliary variable is used in the summary $s_1[x] = x_{a'[j]b'[k]} \vee F_\pi^A(x)$.

The interpolant for case (e-ii) is the dual obtained by swapping disjunctions with conjunctions and equalities with disequalities. The interpolant for case (e-iii) is complicated and requires an exponential case distinction. We refer the interested reader to [10].

4.2 Interpolants for Conflicts of Type (const-weakeq)

A (const-weakeq) conflict $\text{Cond}(\text{const}(v) \overset{P}{\Longleftrightarrow} \text{const}(w)) \wedge v \neq w$ consists of a weak equivalence path between two constant arrays $\text{const}(v)$ and $\text{const}(w)$ that describes that the two constant arrays must be equal at all positions except the store indices, which contradicts the disequality $v \neq w$. We distinguish three base cases for computing interpolants: $v \neq w$ is (c-i) in B, (c-ii) in A, or (c-iii) it is mixed.

(c-i) If $v \neq w$ is in B, the weak equivalence path $\text{const}(v) \overset{P}{\Longleftrightarrow} \text{const}(w)$ can be subdivided into A- and B-subpaths such that all A-paths start and end with shared arrays. An interpolant should state for each A-path $s_1 \overset{A}{\Longleftrightarrow} s_2$ that the arrays at the path ends, s_1 and s_2, differ at most at the number of store indices

$|\pi|$. This can be described by a weq formula, i.e., for an A-path $s_1 \overset{\pi}{\Leftrightarrow} s_2$ the interpolant formula is $I_\pi : \text{weq}(s_1, s_2, |\pi|, \top)$.

The interpolant of the conflict is the conjunction of all I_π for A-paths.

Lemma 1. *If $v \neq w$ is in B, then an interpolant of the conflict $\text{Cond}(\text{const}(v) \overset{P}{\Leftrightarrow} \text{const}(w)) \wedge v \neq w$ is given by*

$$I \equiv \bigwedge_{s_1 \overset{\pi}{\Leftrightarrow} s_2 \in A\text{-paths}} \text{weq}(s_1, s_2, |\pi|, \top).$$

Proof. By construction, the interpolant contains only the shared arrays at path ends, and diff and select terms constructed from these arrays. Hence, the symbol condition is fulfilled.

$C \restriction A$ implies I: Let $s_1 \overset{\pi}{\Leftrightarrow} s_2$ be an A-path. The path π witnesses that the arrays s_1 and s_2 can only differ at the store indices, i.e., at most at $|\pi|$ positions. Rewriting s_1 towards s_2 in $|\pi|$ steps therefore yields an array term that is equal to s_2, i.e., $s_1 \overset{|\pi|}{\leadsto} s_2 = s_2$ which is exactly the formula $\text{weq}(s_1, s_2, |\pi|, \top)$.

$C \restriction B \wedge I$ is unsatisfiable: Each pair of arrays at the ends of a B-path can only differ at finitely many indices. Because of I, each pair of arrays at the ends of an A-path can only differ at finitely many indices as well, and therefore by transitivity, $\text{const}(v)$ and $\text{const}(w)$ can only differ at finitely many indices. But then because of the axiom (infinity), there exists an index j that is different from all these indices and because of (read-over-write) the arrays store the same value at j, i.e., $v = \text{const}(v)[j] = \text{const}(w)[j] = w$. This contradicts the disequality $v \neq w$.   □

(c-ii) Similarly, if $v \neq w$ is in A, all B-subpaths of the weak equivalence path $\text{const}(v) \overset{P}{\Leftrightarrow} \text{const}(w)$ start and end with shared arrays. Each B-path $s_1 \overset{\pi}{\Leftrightarrow} s_2$ is summarised by $I_\pi : \text{nweq}(s_1, s_2, |\pi|, \bot)$ and the interpolant is the disjunction of all subpath interpolants.

Lemma 2. *If $v \neq w$ is in A, an interpolant of the conflict $\text{Cond}(\text{const}(v) \overset{P}{\Leftrightarrow} \text{const}(w)) \wedge v \neq w$ is given by*

$$I \equiv \bigvee_{s_1 \overset{\pi}{\Leftrightarrow} s_2 \in B\text{-paths}} \text{nweq}(s_1, s_2, |\pi|, \bot).$$

Proof. Again, by construction, I contains only shared arrays and diff and select terms constructed over these arrays. Thus, the symbol condition is fulfilled.

$C \restriction A$ implies I: For each A-path, $C \restriction A$ implies that the arrays at the path ends can only differ at finitely many indices. Because of the main disequality $v \neq w$, the constant arrays $\text{const}(v)$ and $\text{const}(w)$ must differ at all positions. This means that there must exist a B-path $s_1 \overset{\pi}{\Leftrightarrow} s_2$ such that the arrays s_1 and s_2 differ at almost all indices. Therefore, the weaker statement that s_1 and s_2 differ at more than $|\pi|$ indices also holds, i.e., $\text{nweq}(s_1, s_2, |\pi|, \bot)$. The disjunction of the nweq formulas results from the fact that it is not known for which B-path this holds.

$C \downharpoonleft B \wedge I$ is unsatisfiable: For each B-path $s_1 \overset{\pi}{\Leftrightarrow} s_2$, the B-projection $C \downharpoonleft B$ implies that the arrays s_1 and s_2 differ at most at $|\pi|$ indices, in contradiction to the corresponding nweq formula in the interpolant I.   □

(c-iii) If the atom $v \neq w$ is mixed, we assume w.l.o.g. that v is A-local and w B-local. All A-paths except the one starting at const(v) start and end with shared arrays. As in case (c-i), summarise inner A-paths $s_1 \overset{\pi}{\Leftrightarrow} s_2$ by weq$(s_1, s_2, |\pi|, \top)$.

In the interpolant the auxiliary variable x_{vw} for $v = w$ may only occur in EQ predicates. The difficulty is to express the value v of this variable as a shared term. The outer A-path const$(v) \overset{\pi_0}{\Leftrightarrow} s$ ensures that s stores v at all indices except those in the finite set Stores(π_0). We use diff to find an index where s stores v, and then we can express v as the corresponding select term. Note that any index that is not contained in Stores(π_0) works for this purpose.

We start by taking an arbitrary element $\tilde{v}_0$ of s, using $\tilde{v}_0 := s[\text{diff}(s, s)]$, which is a shared term. If this does not yield the right constant, diff(s, s) must be one of the store indices and const$(\tilde{v}_0)$ differs from s at all indices except diff(s, s) and possibly some of the other store indices. If we rewrite const$(\tilde{v}_0)$ towards s, then in each step the diff term either finds an index different from the store indices and hence a representation of const(v), or we find a store index, and obtain an array that does not differ from s at this index. Therefore, after $|\pi_0| - 1$ steps, either we have already found an index different from the store indices, or the obtained array const$(\tilde{v}_0) \overset{|\pi_0|-1}{\leadsto} s$ is equal to s at all store indices and $s[\text{diff}(\dots, s)]$ is a shared term for $\tilde{v}$.

For each of the candidate values $\tilde{v}$, we build a candidate interpolant $I_{\pi_0}^A(\tilde{v})$ of the outer path const$(v) \overset{\pi_0}{\Leftrightarrow} s$ that states that the constant array const$(\tilde{v})$ differs from s at most at $|\pi_0|$ indices, and that $\tilde{v}$ is the correct value for the auxiliary variable.

Lemma 3. *If $v \neq w$ is mixed where w.l.o.g. v is A-local, an interpolant of the conflict* Cond$(\text{const}(v) \overset{P}{\Leftrightarrow} \text{const}(w)) \wedge v \neq w$ *is given by*

$$I \equiv \left(I_{\pi_0}^A(\tilde{v}_0) \vee \bigvee_{m=0}^{|\pi_0|-1} I_{\pi_0}^A(s[\text{diff}(\text{const}(\tilde{v}_0) \overset{m}{\leadsto} s, s)]) \right)$$

$$\wedge \bigwedge_{\pi:s_1 \approx_i s_2 \text{ inner } A\text{-path}} \text{weq}(s_1, s_2, |\pi|, \top)$$

where the outer A-path is const$(v) \overset{\pi_0}{\Leftrightarrow} s$, *and* $\tilde{v}_0 := s[\text{diff}(s, s)]$, *and*

$$I_{\pi_0}^A(\tilde{v}) \equiv \text{EQ}(x_{vw}, \tilde{v}) \wedge \text{weq}(\text{const}(\tilde{v}), s, |\pi_0|, \top).$$

Proof. The symbol condition is met, in particular, only the shared array s is used to construct the interpolant formula for the outer A-path.

$C \downharpoonleft A$ implies I: The interpolant parts for the inner A-paths follow from $C \downharpoonleft A$ as in case (c-i). For the outer A-path const$(v) \overset{\pi_0}{\Leftrightarrow} s$, if $\tilde{v}$ is equal to v, then the weq formula $\text{weq}(\text{const}(\tilde{v}), s, |\pi_0|, \top)$ follows from A as in case (c-i). The EQ predicate follows by replacing v with $\tilde{v}$ in the A-projection of $v \neq w$. Thus, it remains to show that $\tilde{v}_0 = v$ or $s[\text{diff}(\text{const}(\tilde{v}_0) \overset{i}{\leadsto} s, s)] = v$ for some $m < |\pi_0|$.

If $\tilde{v}_0$ does not equal v, then $\text{const}(\tilde{v}_0)$ and s differ at infinitely many indices. We consider the sequence of diff terms for $d_0 := \text{diff}(s, s)$, $d_{m+1} := \text{diff}(\text{const}(\tilde{v}_0) \overset{m}{\leadsto} s, s)$. By construction, the arrays $\text{const}(\tilde{v}_0) \overset{m}{\leadsto} s$ and s cannot differ at positions $d_0, \ldots, d_m$. Hence, the indices $d_0, \ldots, d_{|\pi_0|}$ are all different and some d_{m+1} is not one of the store indices in π_0. But then $s[d_{m+1}]$ is equal to v.

$C \restriction B \wedge I$ is unsatisfiable: Each B-path implies that the arrays at the path ends differ at most at the finitely many store indices. Each interpolant part for an inner A-path implies that the arrays at these path ends also differ at most at finitely many indices. The interpolant part for the outer A-path $\text{const}(v) \overset{\pi}{\Leftrightarrow} s$ implies that there exists a constant array $\text{const}(\tilde{v})$ that differs from s at finitely many indices, and that the value $\tilde{v}$ of this constant array satisfies $\text{EQ}(x, \tilde{v})$. But then by transitivity, this $\text{const}(\tilde{v})$ and $\text{const}(w)$ can only differ at finitely many indices. Hence, $\tilde{v} = w$ as in the soundness proof for (const-weakeq). But then also $\text{EQ}(x_{vw}, w)$ must hold, in contradiction to the B-projection of $v \neq w$. □

Remark 2. The size of the interpolants in cases (c-i) and (c-ii) is linear in the size of the lemma: the formulas $\text{weq}(s_1, s_2, |\pi|, \top)$ and $\text{nweq}(s_1, s_2, |\pi|, \bot)$ are linear in the length of the subpath $s_1 \overset{\pi}{\Leftrightarrow} s_2$. The size of the interpolants in case (c-iii) is quadratic: the formula $I_{\pi_0}^A(\cdot)$ is linear in the size of π_0, and it occurs $|\pi_0|$ times in the interpolant.

The size of the interpolant in case (c-iii) can be reduced as follows. Compare the lengths of the outer A-path and the outer B-path. If the A-path is shorter than the B-path, compute the interpolant as described above. Otherwise, compute the dual interpolant by summarising the inner B-paths using nweq formulas as in case (c-ii), and the outer B-path $s \overset{\pi_0}{\Leftrightarrow} \text{const}(w)$ by

$$I_{\pi_0}^B(s[\text{diff}(s, s)], s, |\pi_0|, \bot) \wedge \bigwedge_{m=0}^{|\pi_0|-1} I_{\pi_0}^B(s[\text{diff}(\text{const}(s[\text{diff}(s, s)]) \overset{m}{\leadsto} s, s)])$$

with

$$I_{\pi_0}^B(\tilde{w}) \equiv \text{EQ}(x_{vw}, \tilde{w}) \vee \text{nweq}(s, \text{const}(\tilde{w}), |\pi_0|, \bot).$$

4.3   Interpolants for Conflicts of Type (read-const-weakeq)

A (read-const-weakeq) conflict is basically a (read-over-weakeq) conflict, with the particularity that one side is a constant array, i.e., the weak path $a \approx_i \text{const}(v)$ witnesses that a and $\text{const}(v)$ must store the same value at index i which contradicts the main disequality $a[i] \neq v$.

We focus on the case where $a[i] \neq v$ is mixed and where i is not shared. In all other cases, we can apply the algorithm for (read-over-weakeq) outlined in Sect. 4.1 with the following variations: there is a shared term for i only if i itself is shared, and if the interpolant would contain the select term $\mathrm{const}(v)[i]$, it is replaced by the value v which is justified by axiom (const).

The main disequality $a[i] \neq v$ is mixed and i is not shared. If i is B-local, then $a[i]$ is B-local and v is A-local. We summarise A-paths in weq formulas, similar to the B-local case (r-iii). But then we also need to build a weq formula over the outer A-path $\pi_0 : s \approx_i \mathrm{const}(v)$ ending with the A-local array $\mathrm{const}(v)$. The idea is the same as in case (c-iii) of Sect. 4.2: we use the array s to construct candidate shared terms $\tilde{v}$ for v. For each $\tilde{v}$ we summarise $\pi_0 : s \approx_i \mathrm{const}(v) = \mathrm{const}(\tilde{v})$ with $\mathrm{EQ}(x_{a[i]v}, \tilde{v})$ and the weq term for π_0 including $F^A_{\pi_0}$. If i is A-local, we build the dual interpolant by summarising B-paths.

Lemma 4. *If $a[i] \neq v$ is mixed and i is B-local, an interpolant of the conflict $\mathrm{Cond}(a \approx_i \mathrm{const}(v)) \wedge a[i] \neq v$ is given by*

$$I \equiv \left(I^A_{\pi_0}(\tilde{v}_0) \vee \bigvee_{m=0}^{|\pi_0|-1} I^A_{\pi_0}(s[\mathrm{diff}(\mathrm{const}(\tilde{v}_0) \overset{m}{\rightsquigarrow} s, s)]) \right)$$

$$\wedge \bigwedge_{\pi:s_1 \approx_i s_2 \text{ inner } A\text{-path}} \mathrm{weq}(s_1, s_2, |\pi|, F^A_\pi(\cdot))$$

where $\pi_0 : s \approx_i \mathrm{const}(v)$ is the outer A-path, $\tilde{v}_0 := s[\mathrm{diff}(s,s)]$, and

$$I^A_{\pi_0}(\tilde{v}) \equiv \mathrm{EQ}(x_{a[i]v}, \tilde{v}) \wedge \mathrm{weq}(s, \mathrm{const}(\tilde{v}), |\pi_0|, F^A_{\pi_0}(\cdot)).$$

and if i is A-local, an interpolant is given by

$$I \equiv \left(I^B_{\pi_0}(\tilde{v}_0) \wedge \bigwedge_{m=0}^{|\pi_0|-1} I^B_{\pi_0}(s[\mathrm{diff}(\mathrm{const}(\tilde{v}_0) \overset{m}{\rightsquigarrow} s, s)]) \right)$$

$$\vee \bigvee_{\pi:s_1 \approx_i s_2 \text{ inner } B\text{-path}} \mathrm{nweq}(s_1, s_2, |\pi|, F^B_\pi(\cdot))$$

where $\pi_0 : s \approx_i \mathrm{const}(v)$ is the outer B-path, $\tilde{v}_0 := s[\mathrm{diff}(s,s)]$, and

$$I^B_{\pi_0}(\tilde{v}) \equiv \mathrm{EQ}(x_{a[i]v}, \tilde{v}) \vee \mathrm{nweq}(s, \mathrm{const}(\tilde{v}), |\pi_0|, F^B_{\pi_0}(\cdot)).$$

Proof. We consider the case where the select index i is B-local, the interpolant for the case where i is A-local is just the dual interpolant.

By construction, the interpolant only contains the shared arrays separating A- and B-paths and diff terms over such arrays, and in the F^A_π or F^B_π formulas, shared indices of store index inequalities and auxiliary variables for inequalities under EQ predicates.

$C \downharpoonright A$ implies I: The interpolants for the inner A-paths follow as in case (r-iii) for (read-over-weakeq) interpolants. As in the proof of Lemma 3, it follows that $\tilde{v}_0$ or some $\tilde{v}_{m+1} := s[\mathrm{diff}(\mathrm{const}(\tilde{v}_0) \overset{m}{\rightsquigarrow} s, s)]$ is equal to v. This value $\tilde{v}$ satisfies $I^A_{\pi_0}(\tilde{v})$, because $\mathrm{EQ}(x_{a[i]v}, \tilde{v})$ follows from $(a[i] \neq v) \downharpoonright A$ and $\mathrm{weq}(s, \mathrm{const}(\tilde{v}), |\pi_0|, F^A_{\pi_0}(\cdot))$ follows as in case (r-iii).

$C \downharpoonright B \wedge I$ is unsatisfiable: For a B-path, $C \downharpoonright B$ and (read-over-weakeq) imply that the arrays at the path ends must store the same element at i. For an inner A-path $\pi : s_1 \approx_i s_2$, the interpolant states that s_1 and s_2 differ at most at $|\pi|$ indices and each index where they differ must satisfy formula F_π^A. But F_π^A contains the negated B-projection of each B-local or mixed store index disequality on π and therefore any index where s_1 and s_2 differ is different from i. Hence, $s_1[i] = s_2[i]$. The same argument holds for s and the value $\tilde{v}$ for which $I_{\pi_0}^A(\tilde{v})$ holds. One of the disjuncts must hold, and transitivity and axiom (const) yield $a[i] = \tilde{v}$. Together with the corresponding EQ predicate in $I_{\pi_0}^A(\tilde{v})$ this contradicts the B-projection of $a[i] \neq v$, i.e., $\neg \mathrm{EQ}(x_{a[i]v}, a[i])$. □

Remark 3. The size of the interpolants is worst-case cubic in the size of the lemma: the formula $I_{\pi_0}^A(\cdot)$ is quadratic in the size of π_0 because $F_{\pi_0}^A(\cdot)$ is linear. The formula $I_{\pi_0}^A(\cdot)$ occurs $|\pi_0|$ times in the interpolant.

4.4   Interpolants for Conflicts of Type (weakeq-ext)

In the presence of constant arrays, the index paths in (weakeq-ext) conflicts can contain select edges of the form $s[k] = v$. In the case that a select edge $s[k] = v$ is mixed, we can split it using the auxiliary variable into a select edge $s[k] = x_{s[k]v}$ (which is no longer mixed) and the equality edge $\mathrm{const}(x_{s[k]v}) = \mathrm{const}(v)$ on the weak congruence chain. Thus, we only need to handle non-mixed edges. If a select edge $s[k] = v$ is not mixed, we can handle it like a select edge $a'[j] = b'[k]$ that is not mixed, except that there is only one index equality $i = k$.

5   Evaluation

The algorithm was integrated into the interpolating SMT solver SMTINTER-POL. Since constant arrays are not part of the SMTLIB standard, there were no benchmarks. We manually created a few benchmarks that we obtained using a model checker for C programs and evaluated the possible performance improvement from using constant arrays.

To obtain interesting examples we used the ULTIMATE AUTOMIZER model checker on a real-world program[1]. We took a small C library from an embedded system, added a test harness, and used the model checker to prove that it has no out-of-bound memory writes. The model checker is based on CEGAR and needs five abstraction-refinement iterations to find an inductive invariant that proves the program correct. Each query requests interpolants for a path through the C program. We logged the queries to generate our benchmarks.

Because the C program uses a large static array (1024 bytes) that is implicitly initialised with zero and because the model checker does not support constant arrays yet, each query uses a large store chain to explicitly initialise the memory. We manually edited the queries to remove the store chain and replace it by a constant array. This manual step can be avoided, once the model checker

---

[1] https://ultimate.informatik.uni-freiburg.de/smtinterpol/vmcai2019.zip.

supports constant arrays. Both the original and the manually simplified query yield the same interpolants. The results can be found in Table 1. As one would expect, introducing constant arrays drastically decreased the size of the queries and the runtime of the solver.

The example was picked because it uses a large static array. We claim that this is not untypical, especially for embedded software where dynamic memory allocation is usually avoided. We expect similar savings for other programs in the same category. Note that the interpolation query is only a small part of the software model checker, but we expect that a model checker using constant arrays will also profit in other parts such as query generation, counterexample generation, and inductivity checks.

Table 1. Experimental results running verification problems for a drawing library. The left column gives the iteration number (the model checker needs five interpolation queries to find an inductive invariant). The next two columns give the size (in bytes) of the query and the runtime (wall time in ms) for each interpolation problem as provided by the model checker. The last two columns give the size and runtime of the same problems where the initialisation was manually replaced by a constant array.

Iteration	Store chain		Constant array	
	Size	Time	Size	Time
1	283486	352 ms	8991	7 ms
2	284796	368 ms	10109	9 ms
3	285268	620 ms	10581	12 ms
4	285214	487 ms	10524	6 ms
5	285232	371 ms	10545	9 ms

6 Related Work

Our work is based on our previous algorithm that does not include constant arrays, which mentions some related work on deciding and interpolation of the theory of arrays. Here we only focus on related work on constant arrays.

Decision procedures for constant arrays have been presented by several authors. To our knowledge the first procedure was in [14]. They have similar restriction to us, requiring an infinite index sort. One of their rules is even identical to our (const-weakeq) pattern. The solver z3 has a decision procedure for combinatory array logic (CAL) [7], which includes constant arrays. They do not require infinite index sort as they do not have an equivalent to the (const-weakeq) pattern. However, our experiments revealed a case where the solver was unsound and returned a false model for an unsatisfiable formula. We reported the bug and it was fixed, but it shows that the theory of constant arrays becomes tricky if the requirement of infinite index sort is removed. Constant arrays can also be seen as a very simple special case of the map property fragment [2]. While the authors do not explicitly mention it, their procedure also requires the key sort to be infinite (they assume there is a κ different from all keys occurring in select terms).

All these decision procedures create instances based on syntactic criteria. Their completeness proof requires that these instances are created, even if they are already true, because they may trigger new syntactic instances. In contrast, our decision procedure keeps track of a partial model and creates only instances that are not true in the current partial model. We presented an efficient algorithm, cubic in the size of the input formula, that generates these instances based on weak equivalence.

Furthermore, the previous decision procedures are not interpolation-friendly. They create new select terms where the array and index may come from different parts of the interpolation problem. These create difficulties for quantifier-free interpolation algorithms and cannot be handled by our proof tree preserving interpolation method. Also, the procedures create much more terms than necessary, while our decision procedure only creates a linear number of new terms in the preprocessing step and no new term during the main solving algorithm.

To our knowledge, this is the first published interpolation procedure for constant arrays.

7   Conclusion

We presented an algorithm to solve and interpolate quantifier free formulas in the theory of arrays with constant arrays. The solving algorithm can be easily integrated into DPLL(T) based solvers with Nelson–Oppen theory combination. It is efficient and only creates very few new terms. The interpolation algorithm is based on proof tree preserving interpolation and also works in combination with other equality interpolating theories. Our preliminary results show that constant arrays are useful for software model checking: they simplify the queries to the solver, which leads to a big speed-up for solving the queries. Constant arrays are currently integrated into the ULTIMATE framework for software model checking to profit from the simplified queries.

References

1. Beyer, D.: Software verification with validation of results - (report on SV-COMP 2017). In: Legay, A., Margaria, T. (eds.) TACAS 2017. LNCS, vol. 10206, pp. 331–349. Springer, Heidelberg (2017). https://doi.org/10.1007/978-3-662-54580-5_20
2. Bradley, A.R., Manna, Z., Sipma, H.B.: What's decidable about arrays? In: Emerson, E.A., Namjoshi, K.S. (eds.) VMCAI 2006. LNCS, vol. 3855, pp. 427–442. Springer, Heidelberg (2005). https://doi.org/10.1007/11609773_28
3. Bruttomesso, R., Ghilardi, S., Ranise, S.: Quantifier-free interpolation of a theory of arrays. Log. Methods Comput. Sci. 8(2), 1–39 (2012)

4. Christ, J., Hoenicke, J.: Weakly equivalent arrays. In: Lutz, C., Ranise, S. (eds.) FroCoS 2015. LNCS (LNAI), vol. 9322, pp. 119–134. Springer, Cham (2015). https://doi.org/10.1007/978-3-319-24246-0_8

5. Christ, J., Hoenicke, J., Nutz, A.: Proof tree preserving interpolation. In: Piterman, N., Smolka, S.A. (eds.) TACAS 2013. LNCS, vol. 7795, pp. 124–138. Springer, Heidelberg (2013). https://doi.org/10.1007/978-3-642-36742-7_9

6. Dangl, M., Löwe, S., Wendler, P.: CPACHECKER with support for recursive programs and floating-point arithmetic - (competition contribution). In: Baier, C., Tinelli, C. (eds.) TACAS 2015. LNCS, vol. 9035, pp. 423–425. Springer, Heidelberg (2015). https://doi.org/10.1007/978-3-662-46681-0_34

7. de Moura, L.M., Bjørner, N.: Generalized, efficient array decision procedures. In: Proceedings of 9th International Conference on Formal Methods in Computer-Aided Design, FMCAD 2009, Austin, Texas, USA, 15–18 November 2009, pp. 45–52 (2009)

8. Fuchs, A., Goel, A., Grundy, J., Krstić, S., Tinelli, C.: Ground interpolation for the theory of equality. In: Kowalewski, S., Philippou, A. (eds.) TACAS 2009. LNCS, vol. 5505, pp. 413–427. Springer, Heidelberg (2009). https://doi.org/10.1007/978-3-642-00768-2_34

9. Heizmann, M., et al.: Ultimate Automizer with an on-demand construction of Floyd-Hoare automata - (competition contribution). In: Legay, A., Margaria, T. (eds.) TACAS 2017. LNCS, vol. 10206, pp. 394–398. Springer, Heidelberg (2017). https://doi.org/10.1007/978-3-662-54580-5_30

10. Hoenicke, J., Schindler, T.: Efficient interpolation for the theory of arrays. In: Automated Reasoning - Proceedings of the 9th International Joint Conference, IJCAR 2018, Held as Part of the Federated Logic Conference, FLoC 2018, Oxford, UK, 14–17 July 2018, pp. 549–565 (2018)

11. McCarthy, J.: Towards a mathematical science of computation. In: IFIP Congress, pp. 21–28 (1962)

12. McMillan, K.L.: An interpolating theorem prover. Theor. Comput. Sci. **345**(1), 101–121 (2005)

13. Pudlák, P.: Lower bounds for resolution and cutting plane proofs and monotone computations. J. Symb. Log. **62**(3), 981–998 (1997)

14. Stump, A., Barrett, C.W., Dill, D.L., Levitt, J.R.: A decision procedure for an extensional theory of arrays. In: Proceedings of the 16th Annual IEEE Symposium on Logic in Computer Science, Boston, Massachusetts, USA, 16–19 June 2001, pp. 29–37 (2001)

15. Totla, N., Wies, T.: Complete instantiation-based interpolation. J. Autom. Reason. **57**(1), 37–65 (2016)

A Decidable Logic for Tree Data-Structures with Measurements

Xiaokang Qiu$^{(\boxtimes)}$ and Yanjun Wang$^{(\boxtimes)}$

Purdue University, West Lafayette, USA
{xkqiu,wang3204}@purdue.edu

Abstract. We present DRYAD$_{dec}$, a decidable logic that allows reasoning about tree data-structures with measurements. This logic supports user-defined recursive measure functions based on Max or Sum, and recursive predicates based on these measure functions, such as AVL trees or red-black trees. We prove that the logic's satisfiability is decidable. The crux of the decidability proof is a small model property which allows us to reduce the satisfiability of DRYAD$_{dec}$ to quantifier-free linear arithmetic theory which can be solved efficiently using SMT solvers. We also show that DRYAD$_{dec}$ can encode a variety of verification and synthesis problems, including natural proof verification conditions for functional correctness of recursive tree-manipulating programs, legality conditions for fusing tree traversals, synthesis conditions for conditional linear-integer arithmetic functions. We developed the decision procedure and successfully solved 220+ DRYAD$_{dec}$ formulae raised from these application scenarios, including verifying functional correctness of programs manipulating AVL trees, red-black trees and treaps, checking the fusibility of height-based mutually recursive tree traversals, and counterexample-guided synthesis from linear integer arithmetic specifications. To our knowledge, DRYAD$_{dec}$ is the first decidable logic that can solve such a wide variety of problems requiring flexible combination of measure-related, data-related and shape-related properties for trees.

1 Introduction

Logical reasoning about tree data-structures has been needed in various application scenarios such as program verification [4,14,24,26,32,42,49], compiler optimization [9,17,18,44] and webpage layout engines [30,31]. One particular class of desirable properties is the measurements of trees such as the size or height. For example, one may want to check whether a compiler optimizer always reduces the size of the program in terms of the number of nodes in the AST, or a tree balancing routine does not increase the height of the tree. These measurements are usually tangled with other shape properties and arithmetic properties, making logical reasoning very difficult. For example, an AVL tree should be sorted (arithmetic property) and height-balanced (shape property based on height), or a red-black tree of height 5 should contain at least 10 nodes (two measurements combined).

© Springer Nature Switzerland AG 2019
C. Enea and R. Piskac (Eds.): VMCAI 2019, LNCS 11388, pp. 318–341, 2019.
https://doi.org/10.1007/978-3-030-11245-5_15

Most existing logics for trees either give up the completeness, aiming at mostly automated reasoning systems [4,5,16,39], or disallow either data properties [28,32,58] or tree measurements [24,25]. There do exist some powerful automatic verification systems that are capable of handling all of data, shape and tree measurements, such as VCDryad [26,36,42] and Leon [49,50]. However, the underlying logic of VCDryad cannot reason about the properties of AVL trees or red-black trees in a decidable fashion. In other words, they can verify the functional correctness of programs manipulating AVL trees or red-black trees, but they do not guarantee to provide a concrete counterexample to disprove a defective program. Leon [49,50] does guarantee decidability/termination for a small and brittle fragment of their specification language, which does not capture even the simplest measurement properties. For example, consider a program that inserts a new node to the leftmost path of a full tree: Skipping lines 2 and 3, the program recursively finds the leftmost leaf of the input tree and inserts a newly created node to the left. The requires (line 2) and ensures (line 3) clauses describe the simplest properties regarding the size of the tree: if the input tree is a nonempty full tree, the returned tree after running the program should not be a full tree and should contain at least 2 nodes. Note that the full-treeness $full^*$ and the tree-size $size^*$ can be defined recursively in VCDryad or Leon in a similar manner. However, none of VCDryad or Leon can verify the program below in a decidable fashion (see explanation in Sect. 5).

```
1   loc insertToLeft(Node t)
2     requires full*(t) ∧ size*(t) ≥ 1
3     ensures ¬full*(ret) ∧ size*(ret) ≥ 2
4   {
5       if (t.l == nil) t.l = new Node();
6       else t.l = insertToLeft(t.l);
7       return t;
8   }
```

In this work, our aim is to develop a decidable logic for tree data-structures that combines shape, data, and measurement. The decidability for such a powerful logic is highly desirable, as the decision procedure will guarantee to construct either a proof or witness trees as a disproof, which can benefit a wide variety of techniques beyond deductive verification, e.g., syntax-guided synthesis or test generation.

The decidable logic we set forth in this paper stems from the DRYAD logic, an expressive tree logic proposed along with a proof methodology called Natural Proofs [26,42]. DRYAD allows the user to define recursive definitions that can be unfolded exhaustively for arbitrarily large trees. Natural proofs, as a lightweight, automatic but incomplete proof methodology, restricts the unfolding to the footprint of the program only, then encodes the unfolded formula to decidable SMT-solvable theories using predicate abstraction, i.e., treating the remaining recursive definitions as uninterpreted. The limited unfolding and predicate abstraction make the procedure incomplete.

In this paper, we identify DRYAD$_{dec}$, a fragment of DRYAD, and show that its satisfiability is decidable. The fragment limits both user-defined recursive definitions and formulae with carefully crafted restrictions to obtain the *small model property*. With a given DRYAD$_{dec}$ formula, one can analytically compute

$dir \in Loc$ Fields $G \in Loc$ Field Groups $x, y \in Loc$ Variables $K : Int$ Constant
$f \in Int$ Fields $r : Intermittence$ $j, k \in Int$ Variables $q \in Boolean$ Variables

$$\text{Increasing } Int \text{ function} : mif^*(x) \stackrel{def}{=} \text{ite}\Big(\text{isNil}(x), \ -\infty, \ \max\big(\{mif^*(x.dir)|dir \in Dir\} \cup \{it[x]\}\big)\Big)$$

$$\text{Decreasing } Int \text{ function} : mdf^*(x) \stackrel{def}{=} \text{ite}\Big(\text{isNil}(x), \ \infty, \ \min\big(\{mdf^*(x.dir)|dir \in Dir\} \cup \{it[x]\}\big)\Big)$$

$$\text{Increasing } IntSet \text{ function} : sf^*(x) \stackrel{def}{=} \text{ite}\Big(\text{isNil}(x), \ \emptyset, \ \big(\bigcup_{dir} sf^*(x.dir)\big) \cup ST[x]\Big)$$

$$\text{Measure function Max-based} : lif^*(x) \stackrel{def}{=} \text{ite}\Big(\text{isNil}(x), \ 0, \ \max_{dir \in Dir} lif^*(x.dir) \ + \text{ite}^r(v[x], 1, 0)\ \Big)$$

$$\text{Measure function Sum-based} : eif^*(x) \stackrel{def}{=} \text{ite}\Big(\text{isNil}(x), \ 0, \ \sum_{dir \in Dir} eif^*(x.dir) \ + \text{ite}^r(v[x], 1, 0)\ \Big)$$

$$\text{General predicate} : gp^*(x) \stackrel{def}{=} \text{ite}\Big(\text{isNil}(x), \ \text{true}, \ \big(\bigwedge_{dir} gp^*(x.dir)\big) \wedge \varphi[x.dir, \ x.f]\Big)$$

(φ may involve other general predicates or increasing functions that only have positive coefficients, or decreasing functions that only have negative coefficients.)

$$\text{Measure-related predicate} : mp^*(x) \stackrel{def}{=} \text{ite}\Big(\text{isNil}(x), \ \text{true}, \ \big(\bigwedge_{dir} mp^*(x.dir)\big) \wedge \varphi[x.dir, \ x.f]\Big)$$

(φ may involve anything allowed for general predicates and one Max-based measure function lif^* in the form of $lif^*(x.dir_1) - lif^*(x.dir_2) \geq K$)

Local Int Term: $\quad it, it_1, it_2, \ldots ::= K \mid x.f \mid t_1 + t_2 \mid -t \mid \text{ite}(v, t_1, t_2)$
Local Set Term: $\quad ST, ST_1, ST_2, \ldots ::= \emptyset \mid \{it\} \mid ST_1 \cup ST_2 \mid ST_1 \cap ST_2$
Local Formula: $\quad v, v_1, v_2, \ldots ::= it_1 \geq 0 \mid v_1 \wedge v_2 \mid v_1 \vee v_2 \mid \neg v$

Fig. 1. Templates of DRYAD$_{dec}$ functions and predicates

a bound up to which all recursive definitions should be unfolded, and the small model property ensures that a fixed number of unfolding is sufficient and guarantees completeness. The DRYAD$_{dec}$ logic features the following properties: (a) allows user-defined and mutually recursive definitions to describe the functional properties of AVL trees, red-black trees and treaps; (b) the satisfiability problem is *decidable*; (c) experiments show that the logic can be used to encode and solve a variety of practical problems, including *correctness verification, fusibility checking and syntax-guided synthesis*. To the best of our knowledge, DRYAD$_{dec}$ is the first decidable logic that can reason about a flexible mixture of sophisticated data, shape and measure properties of trees.

2   A Decidable Fragment of DRYAD

DRYAD is a logic for reasoning about tree data-structures, first proposed by Madhusudan *et al.* [26]. DRYAD can be viewed as a variant of first-order logic extended with least fixed points. The syntax of DRYAD is free of quantifiers but supports user-provided recursive functions for describing properties and measurements of tree data structures. Each recursive function maps trees to a boolean value, an integer or a set of integers, and is defined recursively in the following form: $F^*(x) \stackrel{def}{=} \text{ite}(\text{isNil}(x), \ F_{base}, \ F_{ind})$, where F_{base} stands for the value of the base case, i.e., x is *nil*, and F_{ind} recursively defines the value of $F^*(x)$ based on the local data fields and subtrees of x. DRYAD is in general undecidable and Madhusudan *et al.* [26] present an automatic but incomplete procedure for DRYAD based on a methodology called *Natural Proofs*.

$$
\begin{aligned}
\textit{Int Term:} \quad & t, t_1, t_2, \ldots ::= K \mid j \mid mif^*(x) \mid mdf^*(x) \mid t_1 + t_2 \mid -t \mid \mathtt{ite}(l, t_1, t_2) \\
\textit{IntSet Term:} \quad & S, S_1, S_2, \ldots ::= \emptyset \mid \{t\} \mid sf^*(x) \mid S_1 \cup S_2 \mid S_1 \cap S_2 \\
\textit{Measure-related Formula } \psi ::= {} & lif^*(x) - lif^*(y) \geq K \mid eif^*(x) - eif^*(y) \geq K \mid \\
& lif^*(y) \geq K \mid eif^*(y) \geq K \mid mp^*(x) \\
& (x \text{ is related to } lif^*, eif^*, \text{ or } mp^*, \text{ respectively.}) \\
\textit{Negatable Formula:} \quad & l ::= q \mid t \geq 0 \mid t \in S \mid \psi \mid \mathtt{isNil}(x) \mid gp^*(x) \mid \neg l \\
\textit{Formula:} \quad & \varphi, \varphi_1, \varphi_2, \ldots ::= l \mid S_1 \not\subseteq S_2 \mid \varphi_1 \wedge \varphi_2 \mid \varphi_1 \vee \varphi_2
\end{aligned}
$$

(Every variable x can be related to only one measure function.)

Fig. 2. Syntax of DRYAD$_{dec}$ logic

In this paper, we carefully crafted a decidable fragment of DRYAD, called DRYAD$_{dec}$, which is amenable for reasoning about the measurement of trees.

2.1 Syntax

The templates for recursive functions and predicates allowed in DRYAD$_{dec}$ are shown in Fig. 1 and the syntax of DRYAD$_{dec}$ is presented in Fig. 2. To simplify the presentation, these figures show unary functions and predicates only, i.e., those recursively defined over a single tree. DRYAD$_{dec}$ also supports recursive functions and predicates with multiple arguments, which are amenable to define data structures characterizing loop invariants, such as list segments, tree-with-a-hole, etc.

Overall, DRYAD$_{dec}$ allows seven categories of recursive functions or predicates with various types, constraints on their definitions and forms of occurrence in a formula. Figure 3 gives several common examples of recursive definitions expressible in DRYAD$_{dec}$. We explain the intuition behind each category below:

Increasing or decreasing *Int* function[1] defines the maximum or minimum value of $it[x]$, where x is the location being unfolded in the tree. The local term $it[x]$ is an integer term defined only based on the local data fields of x. The most common example is $it[x] = x$.key; then the function gives the maximum or minimum key stored in a tree. These increasing/decreasing functions can be combined using standard arithmetic connectives to form atomic formulae.

Increasing *IntSet* function defines the union of all set terms $ST[x]$ for any location x under the tree, where $ST[x]$ is a set of local integer terms defined only based on the local data fields of x. The most typical example is the function representing the set of all keys w.r.t. the data field key, where $ST[x] = \{x.\text{key}\}$. These *IntSet* functions can be combined with regular *Int* terms arbitrarily to form *IntSet* terms in DRYAD$_{dec}$, which can be further used to construct atomic formulae for set-inclusion and subset relationship. The only restriction is that the subset checking $S_1 \subseteq S_2$ can occur *negatively only*.

---

[1] Intuitively, a DRYAD$_{dec}$ function is increasing/decreasing if its value monotonically increases/decreases when the input tree expands. The monotonicity will be formally defined in Sect. 3.1.

There are two types of **measure functions**. Intuitively, they recursively define Max- and Sum-based measurements of a tree or tree segment, respectively. For each node x under the tree, it counts towards the measurement, i.e., the height/size being increased by 1, if and only if a local formula $v[x]$ is satisfied. In Fig. 1, this conditional value is written as $\mathtt{ite}^r(v[x], 1, 0)$, where r is an integer constant called *intermittence*. For example, the black height for red black trees can be defined with intermittence 2: $\mathtt{ite}^2(x.color = \mathtt{black}, 1, 0)$. The intermittence's semantics will be explained in Sect. 2.3. Specifically, when $v[x] \stackrel{def}{=} \mathtt{true}$ and $r = 1$, the corresponding Max- and Sum-based functions define the regular tree height and size, respectively. In this paper, we denote them as *height** and *size**.

A measure-related *Int* term can be a measure function $f^*(x)$ only, or a difference of form $f^*(x_1) - f^*(x_2)$. A measure-related *Int* term can be compared with a constant K. For example, one can specify two trees with the same height using $height^*(x_1) - height^*(x_2) = 0$.

General predicate is satisfied by trees (x) if and only if a local constraint φ is satisfied between any location in x. Notice that φ may involve other non-measure-related functions or predicates (with some restrictions as shown in Fig. 1). For example, the *sorted** property can be defined based on *max** and *min** (see the definition of *sorted** in Fig. 3).

Measure-related predicate is similar to general predicates. In addition to everything allowed in the definition of general predicates, a measure-related predicate is allowed to involve a single measure-related function in the difference form. For example, an *avl**-tree requires the *height**-difference between two subtrees is at most one (see the definition of *avl** in Fig. 3).

2.2   Syntactic Restrictions for Decidability

As we have mentioned before, the syntax of DRYAD$_{dec}$ is carefully crafted for decidability. Besides the specific syntactical restrictions delineated above for the definitions in each category of recursive functions or predicates, DRYAD$_{dec}$ also restricts how variables, functions and predicates can be related to each other. As shown in Fig. 2, a variable x is considered related to a measure function if x occurs in a measure-related predicate or in the difference form $f^*(x) - f^*(y)$. One important restriction of DRYAD$_{dec}$ is that a location variable can be related to only one measure function. For example, DRYAD$_{dec}$ cannot express a single-path tree: $height^*(x) = size^*(x)$.

Insight Behind the Syntax. Intuitively, the DRYAD$_{dec}$ syntax characterizes the class of formulae *independent* to the height/size of the tree. Hence non-measure functions such as *min** or *max** can occur unrestrictedly in the logic, as their values are only determined by the "witness nodes". For measure functions such as height or size, obviously they are determined by the height/size of the tree; that's why we allow only differences between measure functions such as $height^*(x_1) - height^*(x_2)$, as the difference is *unchanged* if we tailor both the two trees rooted by x_1 and x_2 at the same time. Likewise for subset relation, the negation of subset relation $S_1 \not\subseteq S_2$ can also be captured by a "witness node" which is in the set of S_1 but not in the set of S_2 whereas the subset relation $S_1 \subseteq S_2$ is determined by all elements in two sets. Therefore, $S_1 \not\subseteq S_2$ is allowed whereas $S_1 \subseteq S_2$ is not as $S_1 \subseteq S_2$ is not ensured to be unchanged through tailoring. To conclude, we try to maximize the logic without losing decidability.

Capabilities And Limitations. DRYAD$_{dec}$ can express all standard tree-based data structures such as lists, trees, lists of trees, etc., and some limited non-tree data structures such as doubly linked lists or cyclic lists. However, DRYAD (and inherently DRYAD$_{dec}$) is unable or not natural to express non-tree data structures, e.g., DAGs or overlaid data structures. The main restrictions from DRYAD to DRYAD$_{dec}$ are twofold. First, only Max- and Sum-based measure functions are allowed. For example, DRYAD$_{dec}$ cannot define the length of the leftmost path of a tree. Second, properties involving multiple measure functions are not allowed. For example, as red-black trees are defined using black-height, DRYAD$_{dec}$ cannot describe the real height of a red-black tree.

Category	Name	Definition
Measure Function (Max-based)	$height^*$	$\texttt{ite}\big(\texttt{isNil}(x), 0, \max\big(height^*(x.left), height^*(x.right)\big) + 1\big)$
	bh^*	$\texttt{ite}\big(\texttt{isNil}(x), 0, \max\big(bh^*(x.left), bh^*(x.right)\big) + \texttt{ite}^2(x.isBlack, 1, 0)\big)$
Measure Function (Sum-based)	$size^*$	$\texttt{ite}\big(\texttt{isNil}(x), 0, size^*(x.left) + size^*(x.right) + 1\big)$
Non-Measure Function	max^*	$\texttt{ite}\big(\texttt{isNil}(x), -\infty, \max\big(max^*(x.left), max^*(x.right), x.key\big)\big)$
	min^*	$\texttt{ite}\big(\texttt{isNil}(x), \infty, \min\big(max^*(x.left), min^*(x.right), x.key\big)\big)$
	$keys^*$	$\texttt{ite}\big(\texttt{isNil}(x), \emptyset, keys^*(x.left) \cup keys^*(x.right) \cup \{x.key\}\big)$
Measure-related Predicate	avl^*	$\texttt{ite}\big(\texttt{isNil}(x), \texttt{true}, avl^*(x.left) \wedge avl^*(x.right)$ $\wedge 1 \geq height^*(x.left) - height^*(x.right) \geq -1\big)$
	rbt^*	$\texttt{ite}\big(\texttt{isNil}(x), \texttt{true}, rbt^*(x.left) \wedge rbt^*(x.right)$ $\wedge bh^*(x.left) = bh^*(x.right)\big)$
General Predicate	$sorted^*$	$\texttt{ite}\big(\texttt{isNil}(x), \texttt{true}, sorted^*(x.left) \wedge sorted^*(x.right)$ $\wedge max^*(x.left) < x.key < min^*(x.right)\big)$
	$treap^*$	$\texttt{ite}\big(\texttt{isNil}(x), \texttt{true}, treap^*(x.left) \wedge treap^*(x.right)$ $\wedge max\_key^*(x.left) < x.key < min\_key^*(x.right)$ $\wedge max\_prt^*(x.left) < x.prt \wedge max\_prt^*(x.right) < x.prt\big)$

Fig. 3. List of recursive definitions

2.3 Semantics

The semantics of DRYAD$_{dec}$ is consistent with the semantics of DRYAD defined in [26], which is interpreted on program heaps. A heap consists of a finite set of locations with the same layout. Each location contains a set of pointer fields Dir and a set of data fields DF. In addition, there is a set of location variables LV, a set of integer variables IV, and a special location nil where the pointer fields can point to. We call $\Sigma = (Dir, DF, LV, IV)$ a signature for the DRYAD$_{dec}$ logic, and call the heap w.r.t. Σ a Σ-heap. The formal definition is as below:

Definition 1. *Let* $\Sigma = (Dir, DF)$. *A* Σ-*heap is a tuple* (N, pf, df) *where:*

- N *is a finite set of locations;* $nil \in N$ *is a special location;*
- $pf \colon (N \setminus \{nil\}) \times Dir \to N$ *is a function defining the pointer fields;*
- $df \colon (N \setminus \{nil\}) \times DF \to \mathbb{Z}$ *is a function defining the data fields.* □

A recursive definition $f^*(x)$ can be interpreted on a Σ-heap (N, pf, df) by mapping x to a location n_x in the heap. As f^* is a recursive definition, $f^*(x)$ is *undefined* if n_x is not the root of a tree; otherwise it is evaluated inductively using the recursive definition of f^*. Notice that the evaluation is only determined by a subset of N that is reachable from n_x. If a heap T's locations form a tree, we use $f^*(T)$ to represent the interpretation of $f^*(x)$ with x mapped to the root of T. We simply call T a Σ-*tree*. We denote n as $root(T)$, and the subtree rooted by $n.dir$ as $T.dir$.

A DRYAD_{dec} formula $\varphi(\bar{x}, \bar{j}, \bar{r})$ can be interpreted on a Σ-heap by mapping every *Loc* variable in $\bar{x}$ to a location in the heap and mapping every *Int* variable in $\bar{j}$ and *IntSet* variable in $\bar{r}$ to the corresponding sort. The mapping is valid only if every *Loc* variable maps to the root of a tree in the heap; otherwise the interpretation is undefined.

Most logical connectives and recursive functions/predicates are interpreted as one can expect. In addition, measure functions have a special intermittence constraint. Recall that any measure function f^*'s definition comes with an intermittence r occurred in form of $\text{ite}^r(v[x], 1, 0)$. The intermittence is a positive integer indicating *how often* the local formula $v[x]$ should be satisfied in the trees. Formally, f^* is defined on a tree T only if the following intermittence constraint is satisfied: for *any* node x in T and its $(r - 1)$ immediate ancestors, there is a node w within these r nodes such that $v[w]$ is true.

Notice that a satisfiable φ with m *Loc* variables $x_1, \dots, x_m$ can always be satisfied by a heap consisting of m disjoint trees $T_1, \dots, T_m$ by mapping every x_i to the root of T_i. In the rest of the paper, we focus on checking satisfiability and consider only these disjoint-tree models.

3   Proof of Decidability

In this section, we prove that the satisfiability problem of DRYAD_{dec} is decidable. The crux of the proof is the *small model property*: Given a DRYAD_{dec} formula φ, it is satisfiable only if it is satisfied by a model of bounded size. The main idea is to show that if φ is satisfied by a model larger than the bound, one can tailor the model to obtain a smaller model which preserves the satisfiability (Theorem 1).

Intuitively, the value of an increasing/decreasing *Int* function or increasing *IntSet* function always relies on a *witness node*. For example, if an increasing *Int* function mif^* is defined w.r.t. a local term it within any tree T, there is a witness node w s.t. $mif^*(T) = it[w]$ and $it[w] \geq it[u]$ for any other node u. Then these function values can be preserved as long as these witness nodes are retained in the tailored model (Lemma 6).

The most challenging part is that the value of a measure-related function will become smaller. Nonetheless, we prove that one can tailor the tree appropriately such that the height/size is reduced by exactly 1 while all relevant recursive predicates are still preserved. Then as these measure functions only occur in the form $f^*(x_1) - f^*(x_2)$, both $f^*(x_1)$ and $f^*(x_2)$ will be reduced by 1 simultaneously and the difference will remain unchanged. Moreover, we prove the tailoring guarantees that the evaluation of other functions and predicates are not affected (Lemmas 7 and 8).

3.1   Preliminaries

We start with some formal definitions and lemmas. The proofs for these lemmas can be found at the project website [1].

Normalization. We normalize a DRYAD$_{dec}$ formula φ through repeatedly applying the following steps until no rule can be applied:

1. For every ite-expression $E_{ite} = \text{ite}(l, t_1, t_2)$ in φ, rewrite φ to $(l \land \varphi[t_1/E_{ite}]) \lor (\neg l \land \varphi[t_2/E_{ite}])$;
2. For every literal $S_1 \not\subseteq S_2$, introduce a fresh integer variable w as a witness, and replace the literal with $w \in S_1 \land w \notin S_2$;
3. For every atomic formula of the form $t \in A \cap B$ or $t \in A \cup B$, replace it with $t \in A \land t \in B$ or $t \in A \lor t \in B$, respectively;
4. For every atomic formula of the form $t_1 \in \{t_2\}$, replace it with $t_1 = t_2$;
5. For every atomic formula $t \in S$ where t is a non-variable expression, introduce a fresh integer variable j and replace $t \in S$ with $j \in S \land j = t$;
6. For every literal $lif^*(x) - lif^*(y) \not\geq K$ or $eif^*(x) - eif^*(y) \not\geq K$, replace it with $lif^*(y) - lif^*(x) \geq 1 - K$ or $eif^*(y) - eif^*(x) \geq 1 - K$.

We denote the normalized formula constructed from φ as $Norm(\varphi)$. The first two steps remove the ite-expressions and the $\not\subseteq$ relations from the formula. Steps 3–5 make sure that set terms occur in the form of $j \in sf^*(x)$ only. Step 6 makes sure differences between measure functions occur positively only. To check the satisfiability of φ, one can always normalize the formula first, as the normalization process preserves satisfiability, which can be trivially proved:

Lemma 1. *For any* DRYAD$_{dec}$ *formula* φ, φ *and* $Norm(\varphi)$ *are equisatisfiable.*

$d : |Dir|$ $\qquad\qquad$ $n : \#$ *Int* Variables $\qquad\qquad$ $m : \#$ *Loc* Variables
$P : \#$ General Predicates $\quad M : \#$ lif^* -related Predicates $\quad C :$ Balance Bound
$D_{ht} :$ Height Bound $\qquad\quad D_{sz} :$ Size Bound $\qquad\qquad$ $D_{sub} :$ Subtractive Bound
$F : \#$ Increasing/Decreasing *Int* Fuctions $\quad E : \#$ Increasing *IntSet* Fuctions

Fig. 4. Denotations for metrics

Formula Metrics. The size bound for the small model property will be determined by a set of metrics regarding the signature Σ, the formula φ and the set of recursive definitions it relies on. For the rest of the paper, we fix the denotation for these metrics, as shown in Fig. 4. Besides simple counting of functions or predicates, these metrics also include the bounds on various kinds of constants involved in the formula. Specifically, we define the following four bounds:

Definition 2 (Balance Bound). *For any Max-based measure function lif^*, the balance bound C is the maximal constant in the set:* $\{\mathtt{ite}(K > 0, K, 1 - K) \mid lif^*(t) - lif^*(t') \geq K$ *occurred in the definition of a lif^*-related predicate*$\}$.

Definition 3 (Subtractive Bound). *The subtractive bound D_{sub} of a formula φ is the maximal constant in the set:* $\{\mathtt{max}(K, 0) \mid lif^*(x) - lif^*(y) \geq K$ *or $eif^*(x) - eif^*(y) \geq K$ occurred positively in φ*$\}$.

Definition 4 (Height Bound). *The height bound D_{ht} of a formula φ is the maximal constant in the set:* $\{rK \mid lif^*(y) \geq K$ *occurred positively in φ and r is the intermittence of lif^**$\}$.

Definition 5 (Size Bound). *The size bound D_{sz} of a formula φ is the maximal constant in the set:* $\{(\frac{d^r - 1}{d - 1}) \cdot K + 1 \mid eif^*(y) \geq K$ *occurred positively in φ and r is the intermittence of eif^**$\}$.

Remark: For all of the above bounds, if the corresponding set is empty, we define the bound to be 0.

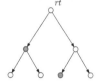
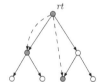

(a) T: a binary-tree heap S: the set of shaded nodes   (b) $tailor_S(T)$: the tailored tree represented by shaded nodes and dashed edges   (c) critical nodes and critical paths

Fig. 5. A binary tree example of tailored trees and critical nodes and paths

Tailored Tree and Monotonicity. As a key concept in the decidability proof, the small model is formalized via *tree tailoring*: a tree model can be tailored to obtain a smaller model.

Definition 6 (Tailored tree). *Let $T = (N, pf, df)$ be tree, and let $S \subset N$ be a subset, then the tailored tree $tailor_S(T)$ can be defined as (N', pf', df'), where (i) $N' = S \cup \{lca(S') \mid S' \subseteq S\}$ where $lca(S')$ is the lowest common ancestor of S'; (ii) $pf'(x, dir) = lca(N' \cap T_x.dir)$ for any $x \in N'$ and $dir \in Dir$, where $T_x.dir$ is the subtree of T rooted by $x.dir$; and (iii) $df' = df|_{N' \times DF}$.*

Note that N' is LCA-closed, the lowest common ancestor $lca(N' \cap T.dir)$ defined by $pf(x, dir)$ always belongs to N'. As an example, Fig. 5a shows a tree-shaped heap T and a subset S of nodes (the shaded ones); Fig. 5b shows the tailored tree $tailor_S(T)$ constructed from S. The edges of the tailored tree are represented using dashed edges.

Now with tailored tree formally defined, we can prove the *monotonicity* of non-measure functions/predicates, a very important property for our decidability proof. We prove the following three lemmas.

Lemma 2 (Monotonicity for increasing/decreasing function). *Let mif^* (or mdf^*) be an increasing (or decreasing) function w.r.t. Σ. Let T be a Σ-tree and let $tailor_S(T)$ be the tailored tree w.r.t. a subset of nodes S. Then $mif^*(T) \geq mif^*(tailor_S(T))$ (or $mdf^*(T) \leq mdf^*(tailor_S(T))$).*

Lemma 3 (Monotonicity for increasing *IntSet* function). *Let T be a Σ-tree and let $tailor_S(T)$ be the tailored tree w.r.t. a subset of nodes S. Then for any increasing set function sf^*, $sf^*(tailor_S(T)) \subseteq sf^*(T)$.*

Lemma 4 (Monotonicity for general predicate). *Let T be a Σ-tree and let $tailor_S(T)$ be the tailored tree w.r.t. a subset of nodes S. Then for any general predicate gp^*, $gp^*(T)$ implies $gp^*(tailor_S(T))$.*

Critical Path. While measure-related functions/predicates do not have witness nodes, their evaluation can be determined by a set of paths, which we call *critical paths*.

Definition 7 (Critical Node and Critical Path). *Let $T = (N, pf, df)$ be a nonempty Σ-tree and $y \in N$ be a node. Let lif^* be a Max-based measure function. Then y is a* critical node *of T w.r.t. lif^* if one of the following conditions holds:*

1. *$lif^*(y) \geq lif^*(z)$ for any other sibling node z;*
2. *there is a measure-related predicate mp^* whose recursive definition involves a subformula of the form $lif^*(x.dir_1) - lif^*(x.dir_2) \geq K$, and there is a node $x \in N$ such that:*
   - *either $K \geq 1$, $lif^*(x.dir_1) - lif^*(x.dir_2) = K$, $y = x.dir_2$ and $x.dir_1$ is a critical node;*
   - *or $K \leq 0$, $lif^*(x.dir_1) - lif^*(x.dir_2) = K - 1$, $y = x.dir_1$ and $x.dir_2$ is a critical node.*

For the second case, we also call y a critical child *of x. Moreover, a critical path w.r.t. lif^* is a path from a child of T to a leaf consisting of critical nodes only.*

As an example, Fig. 5c shows a binary tree rooted by x. The shaded nodes are critical nodes and curved edges are two critical paths w.r.t. $height^*$. (See definition of $height^*$ in Fig. 3.)

Lemma 5 (Length bound for critical paths). *Let lif^* be a Max-based function with intermittence r and with a local constraint v, let T be a d-ary tree. Then for any critical path of T w.r.t. lif^*, the number of nodes satisfying v on the path is at least $\lfloor \frac{lif^*(T) - 1}{(d-1)Cr + 1} \rfloor$, where C is the balance bound of lif^*.*

3.2 Tailorability

The tailorability of various functions/predicates is the crux of guaranteeing the small model property, which in turn guarantees the decidability. As mentioned before, non-measure functions/predicates can be easily preserved as long as the tailoring does not affect witness nodes.

Lemma 6 (Tailorability for non-measure functions and general predicates). *Let $T = (N, pf, df)$ be a tree, $S \subset N$ be a subset of nodes.*

Then if the height of T is greater than $P + F + |S|$, there is a tailored tree T' of T such that

(i) T' contains all nodes of S;
(ii) $f^*(T') = f^*(T)$ for any increasing/decreasing Int function f^*;
(iii) $gp^*(T') \leftrightarrow gp^*(T)$ for any general predicate gp^*.

Proof See [1].   □

For a Max-based function, a large tree can be tailored by removing exactly one node from every critical path; hence the function value is reduced by 1. Similarly, Sum-based functions can also be reduced by 1 through tailoring.

Lemma 7 (Tailorability for Max-based function). *Let $T = (N, pf, df)$ be a d-ary tree, $S \subset N$ be a subset of nodes. Let lif^* be a Max-based measure function with intermittence r and balance bound C. Then if $lif^*(T) > (P + M + F + |S| + 1) \cdot ((d-1)Cr + 1)$, there is a tailored tree T' of T such that*

(i) T' contains all nodes of S;
(ii) $f^*(T') = f^*(T)$ for any increasing/decreasing Int function f^*;
(iii) $gp^*(T') \leftrightarrow gp^*(T)$ for any general predicate gp^*;
(iv) $lif^*(T') = lif^*(T) - 1$;
(v) $mp^*(T') \leftrightarrow mp^*(T)$ for any lif^*-related predicate mp^*.

Proof. Let the definition of lif^* be $\mathtt{ite}\Big(\mathtt{isNil}(x),\ 0,\ \ldots\ +\ \mathtt{ite}^r(v[x], 1, 0)\Big)$
Consider an arbitrary critical path w.r.t. lif^* in T. By Lemma 5, the number of nodes in the path satisfying the local constraint v from the definition of lif^* is at least

$$\lfloor \frac{lif^*(T) - 1}{(d-1)Cr + 1} \rfloor \geq \lfloor \frac{(P + M + F + |S| + 1) \cdot ((d-1)Cr + 1)}{(d-1)Cr + 1} \rfloor = P + M + F + |S| + 1$$

Let $\mathcal{N}$ be the set including all these nodes. We denote a node in $\mathcal{N}$ as n_j if it is the j-th highest one in the set. For each j, consider the set of nodes $\mathcal{N}_j \overset{def}{=} \{n \mid n \prec n_j \wedge n \nprec n_{j+1}\}$, where $n \prec n_j$ denotes that n is a descendant of n_j. Intuitively, $\mathcal{N}_j$ is the root or a descendant of a sibling of n_{j+1}. Notice that there are at least $P + M + F + |S| + 1$ such sets and they are all disjoint, i.e., there is a set of at least $P + M + F + 1$ nodes such that for every node j in the set, $\mathcal{N}_j \cap S = \emptyset$. Furthermore, consider the witness node for every $f^*(T)$, where

f^* is an increasing or decreasing Int function, among the remaining at least $P + M + F + 1$ nodes, at least $P + M + 1$ ones are nodes for which corresponding set $\mathcal{N}_j$ does not contain any witness nodes. Moreover, as the number of all predicates is $P + M$, there is at least one node l such that n_l and n_{l+1} [2] agree on the evaluation of all general predicates and lif^*-related predicates.

Now we can replace the subtree rooted by n_l with the subtree rooted by n_{l+1} to form a tailored tree T_l. Notice that T_l holds the first three properties for the desired tailored tree:

1. T_l retains all nodes of S, as $\mathcal{N}_j \cap S = \emptyset$.
2. $f^*(T_l) = f^*(T)$ for any increasing or decreasing f^*.
3. $gp^*(T_l)$ if and only if $gp^*(T)$ for any general predicate gp^*.

The reason for properties (i) and (ii) to hold is straightforward. For property (iii), consider three situations:

1. if $gp^*(T)$ is true, so is $gp^*(T_l)$ by Lemma 4.
2. if $gp^*(T)$ is false and $gp^*(n_l)$ is true, then T does not satisfy gp due to a path not affected by the tailoring. Hence $gp^*(T_l)$ remains false.
3. if $gp^*(T)$ is false and $gp^*(n_l)$ is false, by our assumption about l, n_l and n_{l+1} agree on the evaluation of all general predicates. Hence $gp^*(n_{l+1})$ is also false. Then by Lemma 4, $gp^*(T_l)$ is also false.

Moreover, as n_l and n_{l+1} agree on all predicates, the tailoring also preserves any lif^*-related predicate mp.

This tailoring also removes exactly one node from $\mathcal{N}$ for the critical path we are considering. One can continue this tailoring for other critical paths until all critical paths have been shortened and the value of lif^* is reduced by 1. We claim that the resulting tree is just the desired tailored tree T'. As each tailoring guarantees the first three properties, we only need to show the last two properties. Property (iv) is obvious: all critical paths of z are shortened and $lif^*(z)$ is reduced by 1. For Property (v), we prove it by a bottom-up induction for any node z under which a tailoring took place. The evaluation of any lif^*-related predicate $mp^*(z)$ is not affected: if the subtree under z replaced another subtree rooted by z', $mp^*(z)$ if and only if $mp^*(z')$ is true; otherwise, there was a separate tailoring for each critical child of z. Therefore

- by induction hypothesis, $mp^*(z.dir)$ is preserved for any mp^* and any dir;
- local Int terms are not affected, as z is unchanged during the tailoring;
- for any increasing or decreasing function f^* and any child $T.dir$, the value of $f^*(T.dir)$ is preserved during every tailoring and still unchanged;
- similarly, $gp^*(T.dir)$ for any general predicate gp^* is unchanged;
- for any critical child $T.dir$, $lif^*(T.dir)$ only occurs in subtractive formulae in the recursive definition for $lif^*(x)$. Notice that $lif^*(T.dir)$ is decreased by 1 and so is any other critical $lif^*(T.dir')$, the evaluation of these subtractive formulae will be unaffected.   □

---

[2] Let n_{l+1} be nil if $|\mathcal{N}| \leq l$.

Lemma 8 (Tailorability for Sum-based function). *Let $T = (N, pf, df)$ be a d-ary tree, $S \subset N$ be a subset of nodes. Let eif^* be a Sum-based measure function with intermittence r. Then if $eif^*(T) > 2 \cdot (|S| + F + 2^P) - 1$, there is a tailored tree T' of T such that*

(i) T' retains all nodes of S;
(ii) $f^*(T') = f^*(T)$ for any increasing/decreasing Int function f^*;
(iii) $gp^*(T') \leftrightarrow gp^*(T)$ for any general predicate gp^*;
(iv) $eif^*(T') = eif^*(T) - 1$;

Proof. Let the definition of eif^* be $\texttt{ite}\Big(\texttt{isNil}(x),\ 0,\ \dots\ +\ \texttt{ite}^r(v[x], 1, 0)\Big)$. Let $\mathcal{N}$ be the set including all nodes satisfying v. Note that $|\mathcal{N}| = eif^*(T) \geq 2 \cdot (|S| + F + 2^P)$. Consider those nodes in $\mathcal{N}$ but not above two other nodes in $\mathcal{N}$ from two different branches: $\mathcal{N}' \overset{def}{=} \{n \mid n \in \mathcal{N}, \nexists n_1, n_2, dir_1, dir_2 : dir_1 \neq dir_2 \wedge n_1 \prec n.dir_1 \wedge n_2 \prec n.dir_2\}$. Similar to the proof of Lemma 7, for each node $n \in \mathcal{N}'$, T can be tailored by removing the subtree rooted by n or replaced with its subtree preserving all nodes from $\mathcal{N}'$. We denote the set of removed nodes $\mathcal{N}_n$. Moreover, it is not hard to see that $|\mathcal{N}'| \geq \lceil \frac{|\mathcal{N}|+1}{2} \rceil \geq |S| + F + 2^P + 1$.

Now we remove from $\mathcal{N}'$ every node n such that $\mathcal{N}_n \cap S \neq \emptyset$ or $\mathcal{N}_n$ contains the witness node for $f^*(T)$ for a increasing or decreasing Int function f^*. Let the set of the remaining nodes in $\mathcal{N}'$ be $\mathcal{N}''$. As the number of removed nodes from $\mathcal{N}'$ is at most $|S| + F$, $|\mathcal{N}''| \geq 2^P + 1$. Therefore there are at least two nodes $n_1, n_2 \in \mathcal{N}''$ such that n_1 and n_2 agree on all general predicates. If n_1 and n_2 are on the same path and n_1 is above n_2, then we tailor $\mathcal{N}_{n_1}$; otherwise we tailor $\mathcal{N}_{n_2}$. WLOG, assume the tailoring replaces n_2 with n_2' and forms T'. The tailoring satisfies all desired properties:

1. T' retains all nodes of S as $\mathcal{N}_{n_2}$ does not contain any node of S.
2. T and T' agree on all increasing/decreasing functions as all witness nodes are retained.
3. T and T' also agree on all general predicates: for any gp^*, if n_2 and n_2' agree on gp^*, the preservation can be propagated up to the root of T. Otherwise, $gp^*(n_2)$ is false and $gp^*(n_2')$ is true. Notice that n_1 and n_2 are not on the same path in this situation – otherwise n_2' is between n_2 and n_1 and does not satisfy gp^*. Then n_1 is not affected by the tailoring and $gp^*(n_1)$ remains false and propagates up to the root: $gp^*(T)$ remains false.
4. By the definition of $\mathcal{N}$, n_2 is the only node in $\mathcal{N}_{n_2}$ that satisfies the local constraint ϵ; hence $eif^*(T') = eif^*(T) - 1$.   □

3.3 Decidability

Now we are ready to show the small model property for $\textsc{Dryad}_{dec}$.

Theorem 1. *Let φ be a Σ-formula in $\textsc{Dryad}_{dec}$. Then there is a height bound h_φ such that φ is satisfiable if and only if it can be satisfied by trees with height at most h_φ.*

Proof. According to Lemma 1, we assume φ is normalized and satisfiable. Consider any m disjoint trees T_1 through T_m satisfying φ. For any T_i, we construct a subset of nodes S_i as follows: for every literal $j \in sf^*(x_i)$ where $sf^*(x)$ is an *IntSet* function recursively defined as $\mathtt{ite}\big(\mathtt{isNil}(x), \ \emptyset, \ \big(\bigcup_{dir} sf^*(x.dir)\big) \cup ST[x]\big)$, there must be a witness node y such that $j \in T_i[y]$. We add y to S_i. For a fixed location variable x_i, there are up to En atomic formulae of the form $j \in sf^*(x_i)$. Hence there are up to En nodes in the subset S_i constructed for T_i.

Now if x_i is related to a Max-based measure function, we claim the following height bound: $h_\varphi = (En+P+M+F+1)\cdot((d-1)Cr+2)+D_{ht}+(m-1)D_{sub}-1$. for a set of variables J including x_i. We define J recursively as the smallest set satisfying the following properties:

- x_i belongs to J;
- if $lif^*(x_1) - lif^*(x_2) \geq K$ occurs in φ and the inequation is tight, i.e., the model we are considering satisfies $lif^*(x_1) - lif^*(x_2) = K$, then x_2 belongs to J if x_1 does.

Similarly, if x_i is related to a Sum-based measure function eif^*, we claim the following size bound: $U_\varphi = 6(En + F + 2^P) - 3 + 2D_{sz} + 2(m-1)D_{sub}$. Note that the size bound is trivially a height bound as well. The proofs for the two bounds h_φ and U_φ can be found at [1].

If x_i is not related to any measure function, we claim a height bound $En + P + F$. When T_i's height is greater than the bound, by Lemma 6, it can be tailored to T_i' and have all set-inclusions, non-measure *Int* functions and general predicates preserved.

Now we obtain a tree T_i' with strictly fewer nodes. By assumption, T_i is the smallest model and T_i' should not satisfy φ. In the rest of the proof, we will show they do satisfy φ; and the contradiction concludes the proof.

As φ is quantifier-free, we only need to show that for any literal in φ, if T_i satisfies it, so does T_i'. We prove this for each type of literals:

Measure-Related Predicate. For any measure-related predicate $mp^*(x_j)$ in φ, x_j must be involved in a Max-based measure function lif^* or not involved in any measure function. Replacing T_j with T_j' guarantees that $lif^*(T_j') = lif^*(T_j) - 1$, and according to Lemma 7, $mp^*(T_j) = mp^*(T_j')$.

Measure-Related Inequation. For any atomic formula $f^*(x_i) - f^*(y) \geq K$ affected by the tailoring, the second rule for the construction of J guarantees that x_i is in J. If $f^*(x_i) - f^*(y)$ is strictly greater than K or less than K, as the value of $f^*(x_i)$ is reduced by only 1 in the course of shrinking, the inequation is still satisfied or unsatisfied. Otherwise, $f^*(x_i) - f^*(y) = K$, then y is also contained in J. In that case, $f^*(x_i)$ is also reduced by 1. Hence $f^*(x_i) - f^*(y) \geq K$ will remain satisfied or unsatisfied in T_i'.

For any atomic formula $f^*(x) \geq K$ affected by the tailoring, the tailoring only happens when $f^*(x) \geq K$ before the tailoring. We have shown above that $f^*(x) \geq K$ is still satisfied after each tailoring. Hence the satisfiability is preserved.

For any atomic formula $f^*(y) \leq K$, the tailorings will make it easier to be satisfied.

Non-measure Predicate or Function. By Lemmas 7 and 8, any tailoring described above does not affect the evaluation of any non-measure predicate or function, including any general predicate and increasing/decreasing function.

Set Inclusion. For any $j \in sf^*(x_j)$ in φ satisfied by T_j, if it occurs positively, the witness node is in S and will be preserved during the tailoring from T_j to T_j'; hence it is satisfied by T_j' as well. If T_j does not satisfy $j \in sf^*(x_j)$, as the set $sf^*(x_j)$ becomes smaller during the tailoring (by Lemma 3), T_j' does not satisfy $j \in sf^*(x_j)$.

isNil **predicate and other boolean variables.** These are not affected by tree tailoring and obviously unchanged.   □

Corollary 1. *The satisfiability problem of* DRYAD$_{dec}$ *is decidable. For a fixed signature Σ and a fixed set of recursive functions, the problem is in NEXPTIME.*

Proof. Given a DRYAD$_{dec}$ formula φ with maximum constant bound D (including subtractive, size and height bounds), by Theorem 1, a minimal satisfying model of the normalized formula consists of m disjoint trees, each of which has a bounded height $\mathcal{O}(n+mD)$, i.e., there are up to $2^{\mathcal{O}(n+mD)}$ nodes in the smallest model. Hence one can unfold every recursive function/predicate in the formula for $2^{\mathcal{O}(n+mD)}$ times and leave them uninterpreted. The resulting formula is equi-satisfiable with φ and obviously decidable as it is in the theory of quantifier-free uninterpreted functions and linear integer arithmetic (QF_UFLIA), which is NP-complete. As the size of the QF_UFLIA formula is $2^{\mathcal{O}(n+mD)}$, the satisfiability of DRYAD$_{dec}$ is decidable and is in NEXPTIME.

If Σ does not involve any Max-based measure function, then the size of the tree and the QF_UFLIA formula is bounded by $\mathcal{O}(n + mD)$, and the time complexity becomes NP-complete.   □

4   Experiments

To demonstrate the expressivity of DRYAD$_{dec}$ and the efficiency of the decision procedure, we implemented the decision procedure and solved 220+ DRYAD$_{dec}$ formulae. These formulae encode various problems from three verification/synthesis scenarios: natural proof verification, fusion of recursive tree traversals, and synthesis of CLIA functions. The implementation is SMT-based: for each formula, we first analytically computed the height bound; then the decision procedure encoded the DRYAD$_{dec}$ formula to a QF_UFLIA formula with the computed bound, and invoked an SMT solver to solve the formula.

Applications. The first set of 61 DRYAD$_{dec}$ formulae is for program verification. We aim to verify the functional correctness of five tree-manipulating programs, i.e., every routine should ensure that the returned tree after insertion remains a corresponding data-structure. We have described insertToLeft in Sect. 1; BST-insert, Treap-insert, AVL-insert and RBT-insert are self-explanatory. We manually broke down each program into basic blocks and wrote all of the Natural Proof Verification Conditions (NPVC) following the NPVC-generation algorithm adapted from [26]. For sanity checking, we also manually implanted some artificial bugs to the programs and created the corresponding NPVCs.

The second set of 48 formulae is for checking the fusibility of recursive tree traversals. Fusion of tree traversals arises in numerous settings [8,17,18,27,31, 37,43,44,47] for performance concern. One of the crucial parts for this fusion process is to check the *fusibility* of two traversals, i.e., if there exists a fused traversal that has identical behavior with the original two traversals. We used DRYAD$_{dec}$ to check all possible fusions of two pairs of traversals: a pair of height-based, mutually recursive traversals and another pair of a post-order traversal execute before a pre-order traversal. Neither can be handled by state-of-the-art checkers [48]. Please find more details of encoding fusibility to DRYAD$_{dec}$ at [1].

The last set of 112 formulae is for synthesizing Conditional Linear Integer Arithmetic (CLIA) functions. The goal is to synthesize a sequence of arithmetic operations that implements an unknown function described by a formula. DRYAD$_{dec}$ formulae are created by our in-house Syntax Guided Synthesis SyGuS synthesizer [13] as queries raised from the Counter-Example Guided Inductive Synthesis (CEGIS) algorithm. We adopted 23 benchmarks from the 2017 SyGuS [2] competition, for which the queries fall into DRYAD$_{dec}$. The detail of the CEGIS algorithm and the DRYAD$_{dec}$ encoding can be found at [1].

Table 1. Height/Size bounds for different scenarios (Metrics defined in Fig. 4)

Scenario	Signature	E	P	M	F	r	C	D_{sub}	Bound
BST mutation	$bst^*, keys^*, max^*, min^*$	1	1	0	2	0	0	0	$n+3$
Treap mutation	$treap^*, prts^*, max\_prt^*$ $keys^*, max\_key^*, min\_key^*$	2	1	0	3	0	0	0	$n+4$
AVL mutation	$height^*, avl^*$	0	0	1	0	1	2	3	$3m-2$
RBT mutation	bh^*, rbt^*	0	0	1	0	2	1	3	$3m-2$
CLIA	$\{exp^*_{spec_f, F} \mid \emptyset \subset F \subseteq G\}$	0	$2^{|G|}-1$	0	0	0	0	0	$|G| \cdot |spec_f|$
Fusion	$dp^*, schd^*$	0	2	0	F	0	0	0	$F+2$

Bound Optimization. We implemented the decision procedure with a set of optimizations. The height/size bound derived in Theorem 1 is general and loose, affecting the decision procedure's scalability. We developed many optimization strategies for different situations. Every strategy is automatically applied when the corresponding condition is satisfied. Table 1 shows the best bounds we obtain for each scenario after all applicable optimizations. Below we explain the main optimization strategies we developed.

To check the satisfiability of a formula φ, we first converted φ to the Disjunctive Normal Form (DNF) and computed the height/size bound for each disjunct separately, as φ is satisfiable if and only if one of the disjuncts is satisfiable. This helps us compute a better bound in many situations, as for each disjunct, at least one or more factors used in the bound computation, e.g., n, m, D_{ht}, D_{sz} and D_{sub}, can be reduced.

Analyzing how variables occur in φ can also be helpful. For example, the number of location variables m only contribute to the bound with the term $(m-1)D_{sub}$. This term is concise only if there is a chain of variables $x_1, \ldots, x_m$ such that for any $i < m$, there is a literal $lif^*(x_i) - lif^*(x_{i+1}) \geq K$ in φ with a positive K. Hence the number m can be improved to $|V| + 2$ where $V = \{x \mid$ there are y_1, y_2 and positive K_1, K_2 such that $lif^*(x) - lif^*(y_1) \geq K_1$ and $lif^*(y_2) - lif^*(x) \geq K_2$ occur in $\varphi\}$.

Moreover, when a location variable is involved in the regular $height^*$ function, the local constraint v is true and trivially satisfied by all nodes. Hence in the proof of Theorem 1, the claim $lif^*(x_i) - L \leq En + P + M + F$ can be improved to $lif^*(x_i) = 0$. As the intermittence r is trivially 1, the height bound can be improved to $(En + P + M + F + 1) \cdot ((d-1)C + 1) + D_{ht} + (m-1)D_{sub}$.

We also observed that the definitions of avl^* and rbt^* do not involve any positive constant, e.g., there is no formula $lif^*(x.dir) - lif^*(x.dir') \geq K$ with positive K. For these measure-related predicates, if they only occur positively in a DRYAD$_{dec}$ formula φ, the height bound computed in Lemma 7 can be improved, because we only need to tailor those paths with maximum number of nodes satisfying the corresponding measure function lif^*'s local constraint v. Once all of these paths are tailored, the value of lif^* is reduced by 1; moreover, these tailorings make the measure-related predicates easier to be satisfied. Hence the balancedness factor $(d-1)Cr + 1$ can be skipped and the height bound for Lemma 7 becomes $P + F + |S|$; the height bound for lif^*-related variables in Theorem 1 also can be improved to $(2En + 2P + 2F + 1) + D_{ht} + (m-1)D_{sub}$.

For CLIA synthesis, with a set of counterexamples G, there are $2^{|G|} - 1$ predicates and the height bound should be $2^{|G|} - 1$ according to Theorem 1. However, we can easily show an alternative bound which is usually better: $|G| \cdot |spec_f|$ where $|spec_f|$ is the number of distinct f-terms in φ, e.g., those terms of the form $f(v_1, \ldots, v_n)$: no matter how large a decision tree T is, concretizing the $|spec_f|$ terms for each counterexample will lead to up to $|spec_f|$ leaf nodes and the whole set G will lead to up to $|G| \cdot |spec_f|$ leaf nodes in T. Let this set of leaves be S and we can tailor T to $tailor_S(T)$, which is of height up to $|G| \cdot |spec_f|$ and does not affect the evaluation of any f-term.

Performance. Our implementation leverages Z3 [33], a state-of-the-art SMT solver as the backend QF_UFLIA solver. The experiments were conducted on a server with a 40-core, 2.2 GHz CPU and 128 GB memory running Fedora 26.

Table 2. Performance for program verification and fusibility checking

Category	Formulae	DRYAD$_{dec}$ size	Bound (Unoptimized)	Z3 size (KB)	Time (s) (Unoptimized)	Satisfiable?
BST_insert	nil, rec_l_pre, rec_r_pre rec_l_post, rec_r_post	≤48	5(11)	≤161	<1 (⊥)	N
	rec_r_post_bug	48	5(11)	161	0.3 (100.5)	Y
Treap_insert	nil, rec_l_pre, rec_r_pre, rec_l_prt_le, rec_r_prt_le, rec_l_r_rtt, rec_r_l_rtt	≤108	7(17)	≤1,696	<12 (⊥)	N
	rec_l_prt_le_bug,	88	7(17)	1,172	0.7 (89.8)	Y
AVL_insert (balancedness)	nil, rec_l_pre, rec_r_pre, rec_l_no_rtt, rec_l_r_rtt, rec_r_no_rtt, rec_r_l_rtt, rec_l_lr_rtt, rec_r_rl_rtt, rec_l_df_0, rec_r_df_0	≤197	7(10)	≤399	<1 (<6)	N
	rec_r_rl_rtt_bug	197	7(10)	399	2.7 (63.2)	Y
AVL_insert (sortedness)	nil, rec_l_pre, rec_r_pre, rec_l_no_rtt,, rec_r_no_rtt, rec_l_r_rtt, rec_r_l_rtt, rec_l_lr_rtt, rec_r_rl_rtt	≤134	5(11)	≤271	<1 (⊥)	N
RBT_insert (balancedness)	nil, rec_l_pre, rec_r_pre, rec_l_l_blk, rec_l_r_rd, rec_l_ll_rd, rec_l_all_blk, rec_r_r_blk, rec_r_l_rd, rec_r_rr_rd, rec_r_all_blk, rec_l_lr_rd, rec_r_rl_rd	≤150	7(10)	≤464	<1 (<6)	N
	l_r_rd_bug	142	7(10)	279	0.4 (9.4)	Y
RBT_insert (sortedness)	nil, rec_l_pre, rec_l_l_blk, rec_r_pre, rec_r_r_blk, rec_l_r_rd, rec_l_lr_rd, rec_l_ll_rd, rec_l_all_blk, rec_r_l_rd, rec_r_rl_rd, rec_r_rr_rd, rec_r_all_blk	≤136	5(11)	≤271	<1 (⊥)	N
InsertToLeft	nil, rec_pre, rec_post	≤28	7	≤216	<1	N
Fusion (post_pre)	schd_lrab, schd_rlab	4	5	84	<1	N
	schd_lrba, schd_rlba	4	5	84	<1	Y
	unfusible_schd(20)	4	6	<216	<1	Y
Fusion (mutl_rec)	schd_lra1b2, schd_rla1b2, schd_lrb2a1, schd_rlb2a1	4	7	604	<3	N
	unfusible_schd(20)	4	9	<3,304	<7	Y

Table 2 summarizes the experimental results on correctness verification and tree traversal fusion. For each DRYAD$_{dec}$ formula, we report the formula size, the analytically computed height bound, the size of the encoded Z3 constraint in KB, the time spent by Z3 in seconds (⊥ for timeout to 30 min) and the satisfiability result. Bounds computed from Theorem 1 and corresponding Z3 running time are shown in parentheses if Bounds computed from Theorem 1 are not equal to the optimized bounds. For the program verification examples, the NPVCs generated from different basic blocks vary in their sizes, but share the same height bound. Experiments show that the height bound is critical for the performance

Table 3. Performance for SyGuS benchmarks synthesis

Category	Formulae	DRYAD$_{dec}$ size	Time(s)
Multiple functions	fg_fivefuncs(3), fg_sixfuncs(3), fg_sevenfuncs(3), fg_eightfuncs(3), fg_ninefuncs(3), fg_tenfunc1(3), fg_tenfunc2(3)	<279	<1
Polynomial	fg_polynomial1(3), fg_polynomial2(3), fg_polynomial3(3), fg_polynomial4(4)	<60	<1
Other CLIA	fg_max2(7), fg_VC22_a(17)	<2,227	<1
INV	ex11-new(18), ex11(17), ex14_simp(3), ex14_vars(3), formula22(1), formula25(1), formula27(1), treax1(3), trex1_vars(3), vsend(4)	<936	<1

of our decision procedure. Our bound optimization can significantly decrease the bounds, making the decision procedure scale well to solve all benchmarks. Table 3 lists the names of CLIA synthesis problems, each followed by the number of formulae raised to solve it, the DRYAD$_{dec}$ formula size and synthesis time. All queries for CLIA synthesis are solved in negligible time.

5   Related Work

It is well known that the First-Order Logic (FOL) of finite graphs is undecidable [51], and the decidability can only be obtained by restricting the logic or the class of graphs. There is a rich literature on logics over tree-like structures [7,21].

PALE [32] has been developed to verify all structures that can be expressed using graph types [21], by reducing problems to the MONA system [12]. Nonetheless, PALE and other similar techniques [11,29,57] do not reason with the data stored in the structure. Separation logic [35,45] has been a popular logic for reasoning with heap structures. Many decidable fragments have been identified. There has been significant efforts on decidable logic for structure properties of list-like structures. SLP [34] and SeLoger [6,10] are designed to check validity of the entailment problem for separation logic over pointers and lists. Iosif *et al.* [14] extend separation logic with recursive definitions to define structures of bounded tree-width, and guarantee the decidability by classical MSO reasoning.

The last decade has seen logics for reasoning about both the structure properties and data properties. The LISBQ [22] logic used in the HAVOC system is a well known decidable logic; it obtains decidability by syntactically restricting the reachability predicates and universal quantification. The CSL [3] logic is designed in a similar vein, with a different set of syntactic restrictions that allow it to express doubly-linked lists. Neither LISBQ nor CSL can handle basic tree data-structures such as binary search trees. AF^R [15] is also a decidable fragment of first-order logic with transitive closure for list-like structures. The GRIT logic [40,41] is capable to handle tree structures; its decidability is obtained by reducing the separation logic to a decidable fragment of first order logic. GRIT is decidable for reasoning local data properties, such as sortedness, but measurements of trees cannot be expressed. The STRAND logic [24,25] combines a powerful tree logic with an arbitrary data-logic. If the underlying data-logic is decidable, a fragment of STRAND is also decidable. As the first decidable logic for binary search trees, a main limitation of STRAND is it cannot express any tree measurement. In other words, AVL trees or red black trees cannot be defined. The underlying logic in the type checker Catalyst [19] is decidable but Catalyst cannot handle measurements either. In contrast, combining term algebra and Presburger arithmetic [28,58] yields decidable theories that can model tree balancedness of red black trees, but not sortedness.

More recently, several automatic verification systems for heap-manipulating programs have been developed. Liquid Types [20,46] handle measurements by folding or unfolding the recursive definitions systematically and then treat the refined types as uninterpreted functions. As the number of unfolding or folding needed is unbounded, the system has to give up either termination or completeness. Inherited the approach from Liquid Types, LiquidHaskell [52–55] cannot guarantee termination and completeness at the same time either. Apart from DRYAD and natural proofs, by which our decidable logic is inspired, [49,50] and [4] exploit recursive definitions and proof tactics that unfold the definitions tactically. These approaches can handle arbitrary combinations of data, shape and measurement properties for trees, but give up general decidability, as mentioned in Sect. 1 and explained below.

Recall the insertToLeft example we described in Sect. 1. To reason about the recursively defined full-treeness and tree-size in Leon, one has to define an ad hoc abstraction function α that maps trees to the domain (Int, Boolean), whose first and second elements represent the tree size and full-treeness, respectively. Then Leon can decidably verify the insertToLeft example only if α is *sufficiently surjective* (see Definition 7 of [49]), which is not the case. To show α is not sufficiently surjective, it suffices to find a positive integer p such that for an arbitrarily large tree t with $\alpha(t) = (i, b)$, the property $|\alpha^{-1}(i, b)| > p$ cannot be characterized by a linear arithmetic formula $M_{i,b}(c)$. Now let t be an arbitrarily large non-full tree such that $\alpha(t) = (i, false)$. Notice that i, as the first part of the abstraction, represents the size of the tree t and is arbitrarily large, too. Then the term $|\alpha^{-1}(i, b)|$ essentially means the number of different non-full trees with size i. As the total number of binary trees of size i can be computed combinatorially as $\frac{(2i)!}{(i+1)!\cdot i!}$ and there is a single full tree when $i = 2^k - 1$ for some k. Hence, the property $|\alpha^{-1}(i, false)| > p$ can be essentially captured by the following formula

$$M_{i,false} \equiv \frac{(2i)!}{(i+1)!\cdot i!} - \text{ite}(\exists k : i = 2^k - 1, 1, 0) > p$$

Obviously, this $M_{i,false}$ is too complicated and not equivalent to any linear arithmetic formula. Therefore, the abstract domain (Int, Boolean) representing size and full-treeness is not sufficiently surjective and hence cannot be reasoned by Leon in a decidable fashion.

The more recent following work [23,38] either only handle tree with bounded size in a decidable fashion or can only verify the red-black properties and the black-height of the tree, i.e., they cannot verify the functional correctness of AVL or red-black trees manipulating programs. A more recent work [56] related to Liquid Types also shows decidability for transparent formulae; but the formulae handled in our experiments are usually non-transparent.

Acknowledgments. This material is based upon work supported by the National Science Foundation under Grant No. 1837023.

References

1. https://engineering.purdue.edu/~xqiu/dryad-dec
2. Alur, R., et al.: Syntax-guided synthesis. In: Formal Methods in Computer-Aided Design, FMCAD 2013, Portland, OR, USA, 20–23 October 2013, pp. 1–8 (2013)
3. Bouajjani, A., Drăgoi, C., Enea, C., Sighireanu, M.: A logic-based framework for reasoning about composite data structures. In: Bravetti, M., Zavattaro, G. (eds.) CONCUR 2009. LNCS, vol. 5710, pp. 178–195. Springer, Heidelberg (2009). https://doi.org/10.1007/978-3-642-04081-8_13
4. Chin, W.N., David, C., Nguyen, H.H., Qin, S.: Automated verification of shape, size and bag properties via user-defined predicates in separation logic. Sci. Comput. Program, 1006–1036 (2012)
5. Chlipala, A.: Mostly-automated verification of low-level programs in computational separation logic. In: PLDI 2011, pp. 234–245 (2011)
6. Cook, B., Haase, C., Ouaknine, J., Parkinson, M., Worrell, J.: Tractable reasoning in a fragment of separation logic. In: Katoen, J.-P., König, B. (eds.) CONCUR 2011. LNCS, vol. 6901, pp. 235–249. Springer, Heidelberg (2011). https://doi.org/10.1007/978-3-642-23217-6_16
7. Courcelle, B.: The monadic second-order logic of graphs. i. recognizable sets of finite graphs. Inf. Comput. **85**(1), 12–75 (1990)
8. Engelfriet, J., Maneth, S.: Output string languages of compositions of deterministic macro tree transducers. J. Comput. Syst. Sci. **64**(2), 350–395 (2002)
9. Goldfarb, M., Jo, Y., Kulkarni, M.: General transformations for GPU execution of tree traversals. In: Proceedings of the International Conference on High Performance Computing, Networking, Storage and Analysis (Supercomputing), SC 2013 (2013)
10. Haase, C., Ishtiaq, S., Ouaknine, J., Parkinson, M.J.: SeLoger: a tool for graph-based reasoning in separation logic. In: Sharygina, N., Veith, H. (eds.) CAV 2013. LNCS, vol. 8044, pp. 790–795. Springer, Heidelberg (2013). https://doi.org/10.1007/978-3-642-39799-8_55
11. Habermehl, P., Iosif, R., Vojnar, T.: Automata-based verification of programs with tree updates. Acta Informatica **47**(1), 1–31 (2010)
12. Heinze, T.S., Møller, A., Strocco, F.: Type safety analysis for Dart. In: Proceedings of 12th Dynamic Languages Symposium (DLS), October 2016
13. Huang, K., Qiu, X., Tian, Q., Wang, Y.: Reconciling enumerative and symbolic search in syntax-guided synthesis (2018)
14. Iosif, R., Rogalewicz, A., Simacek, J.: The tree width of separation logic with recursive definitions. In: Bonacina, M.P. (ed.) CADE 2013. LNCS (LNAI), vol. 7898, pp. 21–38. Springer, Heidelberg (2013). https://doi.org/10.1007/978-3-642-38574-2_2

15. Itzhaky, S., Banerjee, A., Immerman, N., Nanevski, A., Sagiv, M.: Effectively-propositional reasoning about reachability in linked data structures. In: Sharygina, N., Veith, H. (eds.) CAV 2013. LNCS, vol. 8044, pp. 756–772. Springer, Heidelberg (2013). https://doi.org/10.1007/978-3-642-39799-8_53
16. Jacobs, B., Smans, J., Philippaerts, P., Vogels, F., Penninckx, W., Piessens, F.: VeriFast: a powerful, sound, predictable, fast verifier for C and Java. In: Bobaru, M., Havelund, K., Holzmann, G.J., Joshi, R. (eds.) NFM 2011. LNCS, vol. 6617, pp. 41–55. Springer, Heidelberg (2011). https://doi.org/10.1007/978-3-642-20398-5_4
17. Jo, Y., Kulkarni, M.: Enhancing locality for recursive traversals of recursive structures. In: Proceedings of the 2011 ACM International Conference on Object Oriented Programming Systems Languages and Applications, OOPSLA 2011, pp. 463–482. ACM, New York (2011)
18. Jo, Y., Kulkarni, M.: Automatically enhancing locality for tree traversals with traversal splicing. In: Proceedings of the 2012 ACM International Conference on Object Oriented Programming Systems Languages and Applications, OOPSLA 2012. ACM, New York (2012)
19. Kaki, G., Jagannathan, S.: A relational framework for higher-order shape analysis. In: Proceedings of the 19th ACM SIGPLAN International Conference on Functional Programming, ICFP 2014, pp. 311–324. ACM, New York (2014)
20. Kawaguchi, M., Rondon, P., Jhala, R.: Type-based data structure verification. In: Proceedings of the 30th ACM SIGPLAN Conference on Programming Language Design and Implementation, PLDI 2009, pp. 304–315. ACM, New York (2009)
21. Klarlund, N., Schwartzbach, M.I.: Graph types. In: Proceedings of the 20th ACM SIGPLAN-SIGACT Symposium on Principles of Programming Languages, POPL 1993, pp. 196–205. ACM, New York (1993)
22. Lahiri, S., Qadeer, S.: Back to the future: revisiting precise program verification using SMT solvers. In: Principles of Programming Languages (POPL 2008), p. 16. Association for Computing Machinery, Inc., January 2008
23. Le, Q.L., Sun, J., Chin, W.-N.: Satisfiability modulo heap-based programs. In: Chaudhuri, S., Farzan, A. (eds.) CAV 2016. LNCS, vol. 9779, pp. 382–404. Springer, Cham (2016). https://doi.org/10.1007/978-3-319-41528-4_21
24. Madhusudan, P., Parlato, G., Qiu, X.: Decidable logics combining heap structures and data. In: POPL 2011, pp. 611–622. ACM (2011)
25. Madhusudan, P., Qiu, X.: Efficient decision procedures for heaps using STRAND. In: Yahav, E. (ed.) SAS 2011. LNCS, vol. 6887, pp. 43–59. Springer, Heidelberg (2011). https://doi.org/10.1007/978-3-642-23702-7_8
26. Madhusudan, P., Qiu, X., Stefanescu, A.: Recursive proofs for inductive tree data-structures. In: POPL 2012, pp. 123–136. ACM (2012)
27. Maletti, A.: Compositions of extended top-down tree transducers. Inf. Comput. 206(9–10), 1187–1196 (2008)
28. Manna, Z., Sipma, H.B., Zhang, T.: Verifying balanced trees. In: Artemov, S.N., Nerode, A. (eds.) LFCS 2007. LNCS, vol. 4514, pp. 363–378. Springer, Heidelberg (2007). https://doi.org/10.1007/978-3-540-72734-7_26
29. McPeak, S., Necula, G.C.: Data structure specifications via local equality axioms. In: Etessami, K., Rajamani, S.K. (eds.) CAV 2005. LNCS, vol. 3576, pp. 476–490. Springer, Heidelberg (2005). https://doi.org/10.1007/11513988_47
30. Meyerovich, L.A., Bodik, R.: Fast and parallel webpage layout. In: Proceedings of the 19th International Conference on World Wide Web, WWW 2010. pp. 711–720. ACM, New York (2010)

31. Meyerovich, L.A., Torok, M.E., Atkinson, E., Bodik, R.: Parallel schedule synthesis for attribute grammars. In: PPoPP 2013 (2013)

32. Møller, A., Schwartzbach, M.I.: The pointer assertion logic engine. In: PLDI 2001, pp. 221–231. ACM, June 2001

33. de Moura, L., Bjørner, N.: Z3: an efficient SMT solver. In: Ramakrishnan, C.R., Rehof, J. (eds.) TACAS 2008. LNCS, vol. 4963, pp. 337–340. Springer, Heidelberg (2008). https://doi.org/10.1007/978-3-540-78800-3_24

34. Navarro Pérez, J.A., Rybalchenko, A.: Separation logic + superposition calculus = heap theorem prover. In: PLDI 2011, pp. 556–566 (2011)

35. O'Hearn, P., Reynolds, J., Yang, H.: Local reasoning about programs that alter data structures. In: Fribourg, L. (ed.) CSL 2001. LNCS, vol. 2142, pp. 1–19. Springer, Heidelberg (2001). https://doi.org/10.1007/3-540-44802-0_1

36. Pek, E., Qiu, X., Madhusudan, P.: Natural proofs for data structure manipulation in C using separation logic. In: PLDI 2014, pp. 440–451. ACM (2014)

37. Petrashko, D., Lhoták, O., Odersky, M.: Miniphases: compilation using modular and efficient tree transformations. In: Proceedings of the 38th ACM SIGPLAN Conference on Programming Language Design and Implementation, PLDI 2017, pp. 201–216. ACM, New York (2017)

38. Pham, T., Gacek, A., Whalen, M.W.: Reasoning about algebraic data types with abstractions. CoRR abs/1603.08769 (2016)

39. Philippaerts, P., Mühlberg, J.T., Penninckx, W., Smans, J., Jacobs, B., Piessens, F.: Software verification with VeriFast: industrial case studies. Sci. Comput. Program. **82**, 77–97 (2014)

40. Piskac, R., Wies, T., Zufferey, D.: Automating separation logic using SMT. In: Sharygina, N., Veith, H. (eds.) CAV 2013. LNCS, vol. 8044, pp. 773–789. Springer, Heidelberg (2013). https://doi.org/10.1007/978-3-642-39799-8_54

41. Piskac, R., Wies, T., Zufferey, D.: Automating separation logic with trees and data. In: Biere, A., Bloem, R. (eds.) CAV 2014. LNCS, vol. 8559, pp. 711–728. Springer, Cham (2014). https://doi.org/10.1007/978-3-319-08867-9_47

42. Qiu, X., Garg, P., Stefanescu, A., Madhusudan, P.: Natural proofs for structure, data, and separation. In: PLDI 2013, pp. 231–242. ACM (2013)

43. Rajbhandari, S., et al.: A domain-specific compiler for a parallel multiresolution adaptive numerical simulation environment. In: Proceedings of the International Conference for High Performance Computing, Networking, Storage and Analysis, SC 2016, pp. 40:1–40:12. IEEE Press, Piscataway (2016)

44. Rajbhandari, S., et al.: On fusing recursive traversals of Kd trees. In: Proceedings of the 25th International Conference on Compiler Construction, pp. 152–162. ACM (2016)

45. Reynolds, J.: Separation logic: a logic for shared mutable data structures. In: LICS 2002, pp. 55–74. IEEE-CS (2002)

46. Rondon, P.M., Kawaguci, M., Jhala, R.: Liquid types. In: Proceedings of the 29th ACM SIGPLAN Conference on Programming Language Design and Implementation, PLDI 2008, pp. 159–169. ACM, New York (2008)

47. Saarikivi, O., Veanes, M., Mytkowicz, T., Musuvathi, M.: Fusing effectful comprehensions. SIGPLAN Not. **52**(6), 17–32 (2017)

48. Sakka, L., Sundararajah, K., Kulkarni, M.: Treefuser: a framework for analyzing and fusing general recursive tree traversals. Proc. ACM Program. Lang. **1**(OOPSLA), 76:1–76:30 (2017)

49. Suter, P., Dotta, M., Kuncak, V.: Decision procedures for algebraic data types with abstractions. In: POPL 2010, pp. 199–210 (2010)

50. Suter, P., Köksal, A.S., Kuncak, V.: Satisfiability modulo recursive programs. In: Yahav, E. (ed.) SAS 2011. LNCS, vol. 6887, pp. 298–315. Springer, Heidelberg (2011). https://doi.org/10.1007/978-3-642-23702-7_23

51. Trakhtenbrot, B.A.: The impossibility of an algorithm for the decision problem for finite domains. Doklady Akad. Nauk SSSR (N.S.) **70**, 569–572 (1950)

52. Vazou, N., Bakst, A., Jhala, R.: Bounded refinement types. In: Proceedings of the 20th ACM SIGPLAN International Conference on Functional Programming, ICFP 2015, pp. 48–61. ACM, New York (2015)

53. Vazou, N., Rondon, P.M., Jhala, R.: Abstract refinement types. In: Felleisen, M., Gardner, P. (eds.) ESOP 2013. LNCS, vol. 7792, pp. 209–228. Springer, Heidelberg (2013). https://doi.org/10.1007/978-3-642-37036-6_13

54. Vazou, N., Seidel, E.L., Jhala, R.: LiquidHaskell: experience with refinement types in the real world. In: Haskell (2014)

55. Vazou, N., Seidel, E.L., Jhala, R., Vytiniotis, D., Peyton-Jones, S.: Refinement types for haskell. In: Proceedings of the 19th ACM SIGPLAN International Conference on Functional Programming, ICFP 2014, pp. 269–282. ACM, New York (2014)

56. Vazou, N., et al.: Refinement reflection: complete verification with SMT. Proc. ACM Program. Lang. **2**(2), 53 (2017)

57. Yorsh, G., Rabinovich, A., Sagiv, M., Meyer, A., Bouajjani, A.: A logic of reachable patterns in linked data-structures. In: Aceto, L., Ingólfsdóttir, A. (eds.) FoSSaCS 2006. LNCS, vol. 3921, pp. 94–110. Springer, Heidelberg (2006). https://doi.org/10.1007/11690634_7

58. Zhang, T., Sipma, H.B., Manna, Z.: Decision procedures for term algebras with integer constraints. Inf. Comput. **204**(10), 1526–1574 (2006)

A Practical Algorithm for Structure Embedding

Charlie Murphy$^{(\boxtimes)}$ and Zachary Kincaid

Princeton University, Princeton, USA
{tcm3,zkincaid}@cs.princeton.edu

Abstract. This paper presents an algorithm for the *structure embedding problem*: given two finite first-order structures over a common relational vocabulary, does there exist an injective homomorphism from one to the other? The structure embedding problem is NP-complete in the general case, but for *monadic* structures (each predicate has arity ≤ 1) we observe that it can be solved in polytime by reduction to bipartite graph matching. Our algorithm, MatchEmbeds, extends the bipartite matching approach to the general case by using it as the foundation of a backtracking search procedure. We show that MatchEmbeds outperforms state-of-the-art SAT, CSP, and subgraph isomorphism solvers on difficult random instances and significantly improves the performance of a client model checker for multi-threaded programs.

1 Introduction

This paper introduces and addresses the *structure embedding problem*, an algorithmic problem in finite model theory. The task is to determine whether a given first-order structure contains an isomorphic copy of another (e.g., if both structures in question are graphs, this is exactly the subgraph isomorphism problem). The structure embedding problem is NP-complete in general, but applications in software model checking demand algorithms that work well on instances that arise in practice.

A *finite relational structure* (simply *structure* in the following) consists of a finite set (the structure's *universe*) and a collection of relations over that set. For example, a graph is a structure where the universe is the set of vertices and which has a single binary relation, incidence. Structures are objects of interest in the fields of finite model theory and the theory of databases. A *structure embedding* is an injective homomorphism from one structure to another, and the *structure embedding problem* is to determine whether such an embedding exists between two given structures.

In the context of model checking, the structure embedding problem arises in abstract state space exploration of parameterized concurrent programs—multi-threaded programs with arbitrarily many threads each running the same code. Analogously to the way that the state of a (non-parameterized) program can be modeled by a valuation of a finite set of predicates, the state of a parameterized

C. Enea and R. Piskac (Eds.): VMCAI 2019, LNCS 11388, pp. 342–362, 2019.
https://doi.org/10.1007/978-3-030-11245-5_16

program can be modeled by a structure: the universe of the structure is a set of threads, and each relation represents a collection of program properties that hold. For example, a structure with universe $\{1, 2, 3\}$ and two monadic relations $X = \{1\}$ and $Y = \{2, 3\}$ might represent a configuration with three threads $\{1, 2, 3\}$ where thread 1 is at location X and threads 2 and 3 are at location Y. Inter-thread relationships are represented with higher-arity predicates—e.g., a linear order on process identifiers might be represented by a binary relation $PidLt = \{\langle 1, 2 \rangle, \langle 1, 3 \rangle, \langle 2, 3 \rangle\}$. The structure embedding problem is exactly the problem of determining whether one such abstract state subsumes another (and so can be pruned from the state expiration).

Predicate automata are an automaton model that has been proposed for use in verification of multi-threaded programs [8,9], that utilizes structures to model program states. The state space of a predicate automaton is infinite, and the emptiness problem—the fundamental problem of interest for these automata — is not decidable in general. However, Farzan et al. [8] give a semi-algorithm that can determine emptiness of a predicate automaton without enumerating all reachable states, employing ideas from well-structured transition systems [1,10]. The idea is to exploit structure embeddings to prune the state space: if there is an embedding from a structure $\mathfrak{A}$ to another $\mathfrak{B}$ and $\mathfrak{A}$ cannot reach an accepting state, then neither can $\mathfrak{B}$. By retaining only those states in the search space that are minimal w.r.t. embedding, it is often possible to make the search space finite. In particular, for *monadic* predicate automata (in which each relation has arity ≤ 1, corresponding to a program property that refers to the local variables of only one thread), this is always the case.

A single predicate automaton emptiness problem can involve thousands of structure embedding queries, and each structure embedding query can potentially take exponential time. Fortunately, there are two properties that make the situation less dire: first, we expect each embedding query to be small (e.g., we would not expect to observe a configuration involving hundreds of threads); second, we can expect structures to be dominated by monadic predicates (i.e., the correctness argument of a multi-threaded program somewhat rarely requires inter-thread properties).

This paper presents MatchEmbeds, an algorithm for the structure embedding problem that is based on the observation that the embedding problem for *monadic* structures can be solved in polynomial time by reduction to bipartite graph matching. We develop a practical algorithm for general structure embedding that uses bipartite graph matching as the backbone of a backtracking search procedure. Graph matching is used to inform the backtracking search procedure both on which decision points to branch on and which decisions to make. We show that this algorithm is practical for both structure embedding problems that result from predicate automaton emptiness checking and difficult randomly generated instances.

Paper Organization. The remainder of the paper is structured as follows. Section 2 formalizes the structure embedding problem and presents the main contribution of this paper: an efficient algorithm for the structure embedding problem. Section 3 discusses various heuristics and implementation issues that are important for practical performance. Section 4 presents experimental results, which compares our embedding algorithm against state-of-the-art SAT, Constraint Satisfaction Problem (CSP), and subgraph isomorphism solvers. Section 5 discusses related work, and Sect. 6 concludes.

2   Structure Embedding

This section describes our algorithm for the structure embedding problem. We begin by formalizing finite relational structures and embeddings. We then describe a reduction of the special case of monadic structure embedding to bipartite graph matching. Finally, we show how to use bipartite graph matching as the core of a backtracking search algorithm for the general structure embedding problem.

2.1   Finite Relational Structures and the Embedding Problem

First we recall the definition of finite relational vocabularies and structures:

Definition 1 (Vocabulary, structure). *A **(finite relational) vocabulary** $\sigma = \langle Q, ar \rangle$ is a pair consisting of a finite set of predicate symbols $Q = \{q_1, \dots, q_n\}$ and a function $ar : Q \to \mathbb{N}$ associating an **arity** to each predicate symbol. We say that σ is **monadic** if for each predicate symbol $q \in Q$, the arity of q is at most 1.*

*A **(finite)** σ-**structure** $\mathfrak{A} = \langle A, \{q^{\mathfrak{A}}\}_{q \in Q} \rangle$ consists of a finite universe A together with an interpretation $q^{\mathfrak{A}} \subseteq A^{ar(q)}$ of each predicate symbol $q \in Q$ as a relation over A of arity $ar(q)$.*

Example 1. Consider the class of non-deterministic finite automata (NFA) over the alphabet $\Sigma = \{a, b\}$. This class of NFAs can be represented as $\sigma_{\text{NFA}(\Sigma)}$-structures, where $\sigma_{\text{NFA}(\Sigma)}$ is the vocabulary consisting of two monadic predicates *Start* and *Final* (representing the start and final states of an automaton, respectively), and two binary relations Δ_a and Δ_b (representing the transition relation on the letters a and b, respectively).

For example, the automaton pictured below to the left (which recognizes sequences consisting of pairs of a and b followed by an even number of as) can be represented by the $\sigma_{\text{NFA}(\Sigma)}$-structure $\mathfrak{F}$ pictured below to the right.

$$\mathfrak{F} \triangleq \langle \{1, 2, 3, 4, 5\}, Start^{\mathfrak{F}}, Final^{\mathfrak{F}}, \Delta_a^{\mathfrak{F}}, \Delta_b^{\mathfrak{F}} \rangle,$$
where:
$$Start^{\mathfrak{F}} \triangleq \{1\}$$
$$Final^{\mathfrak{F}} \triangleq \{4\}$$
$$\Delta_a^{\mathfrak{F}} \triangleq \{\langle 1, 2 \rangle, \langle 1, 5 \rangle, \langle 3, 1 \rangle, \langle 4, 5 \rangle, \langle 5, 4 \rangle\}$$
$$\Delta_b^{\mathfrak{F}} \triangleq \{\langle 1, 3 \rangle, \langle 1, 4 \rangle, \langle 2, 1 \rangle, \langle 4, 4 \rangle, \langle 5, 5 \rangle\}$$

Next, we define structure homomorphisms and embeddings. Intuitively, one structure embeds into another if a "copy" of it appears in the second structure (modulo renaming of universe elements). Formally,

Definition 2 (Homomorphism, embedding). *Let* $\sigma = \langle Q, ar \rangle$ *be a vocabulary, and let* $\mathfrak{A}$ *and* $\mathfrak{B}$ *be* σ-*structures. A* **homomorphism** *is a function* $h : A \rightarrow B$ *such that for all* $q \in Q$ *and all* $\langle a_1, \ldots, a_{ar(q)} \rangle \in q^{\mathfrak{A}}$, *we have* $\langle h(a_1), \ldots, h(a_{ar(q)}) \rangle \in q^{\mathfrak{B}}$. *We say that a homomorphism is an* **embedding** *if* h *is injective.*

Note that the usual notion of embedding from model theory additionally requires that a "reverse homomorphism" condition hold: if $\langle h(a_1), \ldots, h(a_{ar(q)}) \rangle \in q^{\mathfrak{B}}$ then we must have $\langle a_1, \ldots, a_{ar(q)} \rangle \in q^{\mathfrak{A}}$. This condition is not required within the scope of this paper, but if it is desired it can be encoded by introducing for each relation q in the vocabulary a second relation q^C that holds the complement of q: a function that is homomorphic w.r.t. q^C is reverse homomorphic w.r.t. q.

The **structure embedding problem** is as follows: *given two finite structures over a common relational vocabulary, determine whether there is an embedding from one to the other.* The structure embedding problem is NP-complete, following immediately from the fact that subgraph isomorphism is a special case.

2.2 Monadic Structure Embedding

Although the structure embedding problem is NP-complete in the general case, it can be solved in polytime for monadic structures. This section describes a polytime reduction from monadic structure embedding to bipartite graph matching, which can be solved in $O(N^{5/2})$ time (where N is the number of vertices) [13].

First, recall the definitions of bipartite graphs and matchings:

Definition 3 (Bipartite graph, matching). *A* **bipartite graph** $G = \langle U, V, E \rangle$ *consists of two sets of vertices* U *and* V *and a set of edges* $E \subseteq U \times V$. *A* **matching** *in* G *is a set* $M \subseteq E$ *of edges such that no two edges share a common vertex. A matching* M *is* **total** *if its cardinality is equal to that of* U. *A total matching defines an injective function* $f_M : U \hookrightarrow V$ *where for each* $u \in U$, $f_M(u)$ *is defined to be the unique* $v \in V$ *such that* $\langle u, v \rangle \in M$.

The reduction of the monadic structure embedding problem to bipartite graph matching is based on the observation that the homomorphism condition acts on each element of the universe independently. That is, a function $h : \mathfrak{A} \rightarrow \mathfrak{B}$ is a homomorphism of monadic structures iff for each $a \in \mathfrak{A}$, $h(a)$ satisfies all the monadic predicates in $\mathfrak{B}$ that a does in $\mathfrak{A}$ (and additionally, the nullary predicates that hold in $\mathfrak{A}$ also hold in $\mathfrak{B}$, which is trivially checked). To capture this idea, we introduce *signatures* and *signatures graphs*.

Definition 4 (Signature, Signature graph). *Let* $\sigma = \langle Q, ar \rangle$ *be a vocabulary, let* $\mathfrak{A}$ *be a* σ-*structure, and let* $a \in A$ *be a member of its universe. The signature* $sig(\mathfrak{A}, a)$ *of* a *in* $\mathfrak{A}$ *is defined to be*

$$sig(\mathfrak{A}, a) \triangleq \{ q \in Q : \exists \langle a_1, \ldots, a_n \rangle \in q^{\mathfrak{A}}. \exists i. a = a_i \}$$

Let $\mathfrak{A}$ *and* $\mathfrak{B}$ *be structures over a common vocabulary. The **signature graph** of* $\mathfrak{A}$ *and* $\mathfrak{B}$ *is a bipartite graph* $Sig(\mathfrak{A}, \mathfrak{B}) = \langle A, B, E \rangle$ *where the vertices* $E \triangleq \{ \langle a, b \rangle \in A \times B : sig(\mathfrak{A}, a) \subseteq sig(\mathfrak{B}, b) \}$.

The intuitive idea behind the above definition is that b is a candidate target of a homomorphism for a iff $sig(\mathfrak{A}, a) \subseteq sig(\mathfrak{B}, b)$. The signature graph $Sig(\mathfrak{A}, \mathfrak{B})$ draws an edge from each element of $\mathfrak{A}$'s universe to its candidate targets in $\mathfrak{B}$. There is an embedding from $\mathfrak{A}$ to $\mathfrak{B}$ precisely when it is possible to select a distinct candidate target for each element of the universe—that is, there exists a total matching for $Sig(\mathfrak{A}, \mathfrak{B})$. Summarizing:

Observation 1. *Let* $\mathfrak{A}$ *and* $\mathfrak{B}$ *be structures over a common vocabulary* σ.

1. *For any embedding* $f : A \hookrightarrow B$, *the graph of* f *(the set* $\{ \langle a, f(a) \rangle : a \in A \}$*) is a total matching in* $Sig(\mathfrak{A}, \mathfrak{B})$.
2. *If* σ *consists only of monadic predicates, then for every total matching* M *in* $Sig(\mathfrak{A}, \mathfrak{B})$, f_M *is an embedding.*

Example 2. Two monadic structures $\mathfrak{A}$ and $\mathfrak{B}$ over the vocabulary consisting of two monadic predicates q and r appears below to the left. In the center is the signature graph $Sig(\mathfrak{A}, \mathfrak{B})$; the signature of each element appears below it. To the right are the two total matchings of the signature graph (equivalently, the two embeddings of $\mathfrak{A}$ into $\mathfrak{B}$).

$\mathfrak{A} \triangleq \langle \{1, 2, 3\}, q^{\mathfrak{A}}, r^{\mathfrak{A}} \rangle$,
$\mathfrak{B} \triangleq \langle \{1, 2, 3\}, q^{\mathfrak{B}}, r^{\mathfrak{B}} \rangle$
where:

$q^{\mathfrak{A}} \triangleq \{1\}$
$r^{\mathfrak{A}} \triangleq \{2, 3\}$
$q^{\mathfrak{B}} \triangleq \{1, 2, 3\}$
$r^{\mathfrak{B}} \triangleq \{1, 3\}$

Total Matchings:
$M_1 = \{ \langle 1, 2 \rangle, \langle 2, 1 \rangle, \langle 3, 3 \rangle \}$
$M_2 = \{ \langle 1, 2 \rangle, \langle 2, 3 \rangle, \langle 3, 1 \rangle \}$

2.3   General Structure Embedding

This section presents the MatchEmbeds algorithm, the main contribution of this paper. MatchEmbeds is a backtracking search algorithm that uses bipartite graph matching to guide search. The algorithm is designed to be fast on monadic structures, and have good practical performance on general structures. In the case that MatchEmbeds is applied to monadic structures, it operates in polytime, effectively applying the reduction to matching described in the previous section. In general

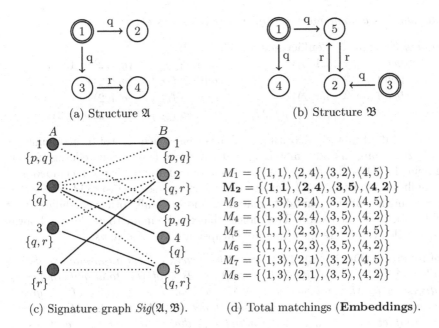

(a) Structure $\mathfrak{A}$

(b) Structure $\mathfrak{B}$

(c) Signature graph $Sig(\mathfrak{A}, \mathfrak{B})$.

$M_1 = \{\langle 1,1 \rangle, \langle 2,4 \rangle, \langle 3,2 \rangle, \langle 4,5 \rangle\}$
$\mathbf{M_2} = \{\langle \mathbf{1,1} \rangle, \langle \mathbf{2,4} \rangle, \langle \mathbf{3,5} \rangle, \langle \mathbf{4,2} \rangle\}$
$M_3 = \{\langle 1,3 \rangle, \langle 2,4 \rangle, \langle 3,2 \rangle, \langle 4,5 \rangle\}$
$M_4 = \{\langle 1,3 \rangle, \langle 2,4 \rangle, \langle 3,5 \rangle, \langle 4,2 \rangle\}$
$M_5 = \{\langle 1,1 \rangle, \langle 2,3 \rangle, \langle 3,2 \rangle, \langle 4,5 \rangle\}$
$M_6 = \{\langle 1,1 \rangle, \langle 2,3 \rangle, \langle 3,5 \rangle, \langle 4,2 \rangle\}$
$M_7 = \{\langle 1,3 \rangle, \langle 2,1 \rangle, \langle 3,2 \rangle, \langle 4,5 \rangle\}$
$M_8 = \{\langle 1,3 \rangle, \langle 2,1 \rangle, \langle 3,5 \rangle, \langle 4,2 \rangle\}$

(d) Total matchings (**Embeddings**).

Fig. 1. Running example.

(non-monadic structures) it can (in the worst case) take time proportional to the number of total matchings in the signature graph for the instance.

First, we give an example showing why the reduction to bipartite graph matching does not work for general structures:

Running Example 1. Consider a vocabulary σ consisting of one monadic relation p and two binary relations q, r, and the two σ-structures $\mathfrak{A}$ and $\mathfrak{B}$ visualized in Fig. 1(a) and (b). Members of the monadic relation p are illustrated with double circles; the binary relations are illustrated with labeled edges.

The signature graph $Sig(\mathfrak{A}, \mathfrak{B})$ is depicted in Fig. 1(c). All edges (dotted and solid) belong to $Sig(\mathfrak{A}, \mathfrak{B})$; the solid edges belong to an embedding, dotted do not. Observe while $Sig(\mathfrak{A}, \mathfrak{B})$ has eight total matchings, only one of them corresponds to an embedding.

Intuitively, the reason that the reduction to bipartite graph matching does not work for general structures is that the homomorphism condition for relations of arity greater than one is not captured by the signature graph. As a result, for a given candidate matching M there may be tuples belonging to relations of the source structure that have no corresponding tuple in the image of f_M. This idea is encapsulated by the following definition of *conflict*:

Definition 5 (Conflict set). *Let $\mathfrak{A}$ and $\mathfrak{B}$ be structures over a common vocabulary $\sigma = \langle Q, ar \rangle$, and let $f : A \to B$ be a function. The **conflict set** of f is the set*

$$conflict(f) \triangleq \{q(a_1, ..., a_n) : q \in Q, \langle a_1, ..., a_n \rangle \in q^{\mathfrak{A}}, \langle f(a_1), ..., f(a_n) \rangle \notin q^{\mathfrak{B}}\}.$$

Note that f is a homomorphism iff its conflict set is empty.

Running Example 2. Conflict sets for $M_1, \ldots, M_8$.

$conflict(f_{M_1}) \triangleq \{q(1,3)\}$ $conflict(f_{M_5}) \triangleq \{q(1,2), q(1,3)\}$

$conflict(f_{M_2}) \triangleq \emptyset$ $conflict(f_{M_6}) \triangleq \{q(1,2)\}$

$conflict(f_{M_3}) \triangleq \{q(1,2)\}$ $conflict(f_{M_7}) \triangleq \{q(1,2)\}$

$conflict(f_{M_4}) \triangleq \{q(1,2), q(1,3)\}$ $conflict(f_{M_8}) \triangleq \{q(1,2), q(1,3)\}$

The MatchEmbeds algorithm searches the space of total matchings of $Sig(\mathfrak{A}, \mathfrak{B})$, trying to find a matching that corresponds to an embedding (following point 1 of Observation 1). If a given candidate matching is *not* an embedding, its conflict set tells us *what went wrong*, which we can use to guide the search away from the current candidate matching and hopefully other candidates that will fail for the same reason. The choices that can be made to guide search away from a failed candidate matching are encapsulated by *decisions*:

Definition 6 (Decision). *Let $\mathfrak{A}$ and $\mathfrak{B}$ be structures over a common vocabulary σ, $G = \langle A, B, E \rangle$ a bipartite graph over A and B, and M a total matching on G. A **decision of** M is an edge $\langle a, b \rangle \in M$ such that (1) the degree of a is greater than one in G (i.e., there is some other choice available for a), and (2) there is some conflict $q(a_1, \ldots, a_{ar(q)}) \in conflict(f_M)$ that involves a ($a = a_i$ for some i).*

MatchEmbeds represents a search space of candidate matchings as a bipartite graph G. It can split the search space by choosing a decision $\langle a, b \rangle$ and either *committing* to it (by removing every edge incident to a and b in G excluding $\langle a, b \rangle$) or *eliminating* it (by removing $\langle a, b \rangle$ from G). But in either case, we would like to avoid exhaustively searching through all candidate matchings. Furthermore, when we explore the branch of the search space in which we commit to the decision $\langle a, b \rangle$ (which we know was part of a conflict in the "current" candidate matching) we would like to be able to make progress—to remove matchings from the search space that fail for the same essential reason. Both of these goals are accomplished by employing *constraint propagation*, a classic technique in CSP solving (more precisely, generalized arc consistency) [23, Chap. 6]. The idea is to identify edges in G that cannot be part of any embedding and to remove them (and thereby eliminate any matching that uses them). We formalize this idea with the notion of *consistent* graphs (which do not contain such edges):

Definition 7 (Consistency). *Let $\mathfrak{A}$ and $\mathfrak{B}$ be structures over a common vocabulary $\sigma = \langle Q, ar \rangle$. Given a bipartite graph $G = \langle A, B, E \rangle$, we say that an edge $\langle a, b \rangle \in E$ is **consistent with** $\langle a_1, \ldots, a_{ar(q)} \rangle \in q^{\mathfrak{A}}$ when for all positions $i \in [1, ar(q)]$ such that $a = a_i$, there is some $\langle b_1, \ldots, b_{ar(q)} \rangle \in q^{\mathfrak{B}}$ such that $b = b_i$ and for all positions $j \in [1, ar(q)]$, $\langle a_j, b_j \rangle \in E$. We say that G is **consistent** when for all $\langle a, b \rangle \in E$, all $q \in Q$, and all $\alpha \in q^{\mathfrak{A}}$, $\langle a, b \rangle$ is consistent with α.*

Definition 8 (Maximum Consistent Sub-graph). *Let $\mathfrak{A}$ and $\mathfrak{B}$ be structures over a common vocabulary σ. Given a bipartite graph $G = \langle A, B, E \rangle$, the **maximum consistent sub-graph** of G is a graph $G' = \langle A, B, E' \rangle$ such that*

(1) $E' \subseteq E$ *(2)* G' *is consistent (3) there is no* G'' *such that 1 and 2 hold and* $|G'| < |G''|$ *(*G'' *contains more edges than* G'*). For any* G*, we define* filter(G) *to be the maximum consistent sub-graph of* G*.*

Efficient implementation of *filter* is discussed in Sect. 3. The crucial property of filtering is that it preserves all embeddings:

Proposition 1. *Let* $\mathfrak{A}$ *and* $\mathfrak{B}$ *be structures and let* $G = \langle A, B, E \rangle$ *be a bipartite graph. For any embedding* $f : A \hookrightarrow B$ *such that* G *contains the graph of* f *(for all* $a \in A$*,* $\langle a, f(a) \rangle \in E$*),* filter($G$) *also contains the graph of* f*.*

Running Example 3. The picture to the right illustrates the maximum consistent subgraph of the signature graph from the running example (Fig. 1(c)). The edge $\langle 2, 1 \rangle$ is inconsistent with the constraint $q(1,2)$ (i.e., 2 cannot map to 1 because 2 has an incoming q-edge in $\mathfrak{A}$ and 1 has no incoming q-edge in $\mathfrak{B}$); similarly, the edge $\langle 2, 3 \rangle$ is inconsistent with the constraint $q(1,2)$. The edges $\langle 2, 1 \rangle$ and $\langle 2, 3 \rangle$ are removed from the signature graph, which eliminates half of the candidate total matchings (M_5 through M_8). The one total matching corresponding to an embedding (M_2) remains, along with three other candidate total matchings.

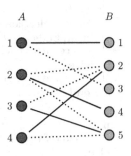

Now we have all of the machinery necessary to define our algorithm. We define MatchEmbeds in terms of the recursive sub-procedure **embeds** as shown in Algorithm 1. At a high-level, **embeds** explores the space of total matchings in the given bipartite graph G, searching for an embedding (G is initially the signature graph, $Sig(\mathfrak{A}, \mathfrak{B})$). We first try to compute a total matching on G. If we fail then we backtrack, returning false if no further decision is left to backtrack. Otherwise, we have a candidate total matching M and we check if f_M is an embedding. If so, we return true; otherwise, we select a decision $\langle a, b \rangle$ and branch on it.

Some more care is needed to understand how a decision $\langle a, b \rangle$ is selected from M. How can we be assured that there is some decision to select? When control reaches the decision selection point, we know that (1) G is consistent, (2) it contains a total matching M, and (3) f_M is not an embedding. Since f_M is not an embedding, it must have at least one conflict—say $q(a_1, \ldots, a_{ar(q)})$. Some $\langle a_i, f_M(a_i) \rangle$ must be a decision, because if none are then G is inconsistent with $\langle a_1, \ldots, a_{ar(q)} \rangle$. Thus, there is always at least *some* decision to choose. How do we choose which one? While any choice is enough to ensure correctness of MatchEmbeds, in practice we found that choosing a decision $\langle a, b \rangle$ that minimizes the degree of a works well (this is essentially the minimum remaining values heuristic in CSP literature).

Next, we remark on the design choice that MatchEmbeds explores the branch that *commits* to the decision $\langle a, b \rangle$ *first* (after all, we know that $\langle a, b \rangle$ is involved in a conflict). The reason is two-fold. First, observe that for a binary proposition $p(a_1, a_2)$ to be involved in a conflict, both $\langle a_1, f_M(a_1) \rangle$ and $\langle a_2, f_M(a_2) \rangle$ must

---

Algorithm 1. MatchEmbeds

Data: $\mathfrak{A}$ and $\mathfrak{B}$ finite structures over a relational vocabulary $\sigma = \langle Q, ar \rangle$.
Result: **true** $\iff$ there exists an embedding from $\mathfrak{A}$ to $\mathfrak{B}$.

Function embeds(G)
 $G \leftarrow \mathit{filter}(G)$
 $M \leftarrow \textbf{maximum\_matching}(G)$
 if $|M| \neq |G.A|$ **then**
  | **return false**
 end
 if f_M *is an embedding* **then**
  | **return true**
 end
 Select a decision $\langle a, b \rangle$ of M
 if **embeds**($G \setminus \{\langle u, v \rangle \in E : u = a \text{ xor } v = b\}$) **then**
  | **return true**
 else
  | **return embeds**($G \setminus \{\langle a, b \rangle\}$)
 end

if *there is some* $q \in Q$ *with* $ar(q) = 0$, $q^{\mathfrak{A}} \neq \emptyset$, *and* $q^{\mathfrak{B}} = \emptyset$ **then**
 | **return false**
else
 | **return** *embeds*($Sig(\mathfrak{A}, \mathfrak{B})$)
end

---

be decisions (otherwise, G is inconsistent)—we must change one of the decisions, but *which* one is arbitrary. In either case, the same matching M cannot be computed in the next recursive call to the algorithm. (For a conflict involving an n-ary predicate, we must decide on $n - 1$ decisions in the conflict to ensure we discard the candidate matching). Second, observe that we need not recompute a matching from scratch: many edges may be shared between the previous candidate and the next one. Our implementation uses the algorithm of Ford and Fulkerson [11] to compute matchings, which benefits from starting from a *partial matching* consisting of the edges of the previous candidate matching that were not removed by *filter*.

Running Example 4. Figure 2 illustrates the execution of MatchEmbeds on the embedding instance from the Running Example. We start by computing a total matching M on G. We observe that f_M is not an embedding, and compute its conflicts and decisions. We select the decision $\langle 3, 2 \rangle$ and filter the graph—the result is empty. Unable to compute a total matching, we backtrack and blame the decision $\langle 3, 2 \rangle$; we remove it from the graph and once again filter. We then compute another total matching on the graph. This matching corresponds to an embedding from $\mathfrak{A}$ to $\mathfrak{B}$, so we return **true**.

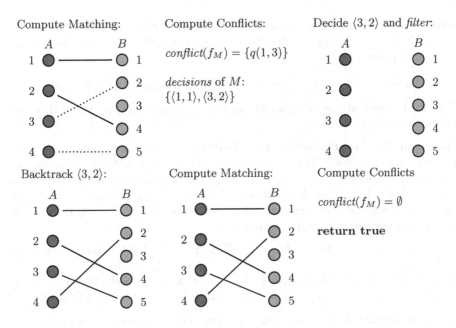

Fig. 2. The operation of MatchEmbeds on the running example.

3   Discussion

This section discusses some additional ideas that are important for the practical performance of MatchEmbeds. We also discuss a data structure for organizing a collection of structures for a multi-source single-target variation of the structure embedding problem, which is useful for our target application of testing emptiness of predicate automata.

Refined Signatures. Definition 4 shows how to associate a bipartite graph with a pair of structures $\mathfrak{A}$ and $\mathfrak{B}$ over a common vocabulary $\sigma = \langle Q, ar \rangle$ by drawing an edge from $a \in \mathfrak{A}$ to $b \in \mathfrak{B}$ iff the set of predicates that involve a in $\mathfrak{A}$—the *signature* of a in $\mathfrak{A}$—is a subset of the predicates that involve b in $\mathfrak{B}$. A simple generalization of this idea is to define a partial order $\langle P, \leq \rangle$ and a function $sig(\cdot, \cdot)$ that maps a structure and a member of its universe into P such that

1. If $h : \mathfrak{A} \hookrightarrow \mathfrak{B}$ is an embedding, then $sig(\mathfrak{A}, a) \leq sig(\mathfrak{B}, h(a))$, and
2. If $sig(\mathfrak{A}, a) \leq sig(\mathfrak{B}, b)$ then for all monadic $q \in Q$ such that $a \in q^{\mathfrak{A}}$ we have $b \in q^{\mathfrak{B}}$.

The associated bipartite graph for such a refined notion of signature is formed by drawing an edge from a to b iff $sig(\mathfrak{A}, a) \leq sig(\mathfrak{B}, b)$.

Signatures can be used to encode various properties that are monotone w.r.t homomorphism (e.g., the size of the connected component of a binary relation to which an element belongs). Using a more refined notion of signature can yield smaller signature graphs, which results in graph matching being a more informative heuristic. In our implementation of MatchEmbeds, we use the partial order $(Q \times \mathbb{N}) \rightarrow \mathbb{N}$ (i.e., multisets of predicates indexed by the position an element appears), with

$$sig(\mathfrak{A}, a)(q) \triangleq |\{(\langle a_1, \ldots, a_{ar(q)} \rangle, i) : \langle a_1, \ldots, a_{ar(q)} \rangle \in q^{\mathfrak{A}} \wedge a_i = a\}|$$

E.g., for the special case of a binary predicate e, $sig(\mathfrak{A}, a)(e)$ is the total degree of a in the graph $\langle A, e^{\mathfrak{A}} \rangle$.

An Algorithm for Enforcing Consistency. A crucial factor in the practical performance of MatchEmbeds is the algorithm *filter* that enforces consistency of a graph. To support this operation we make use of an auxiliary bipartite graph $G_q = \langle q^{\mathfrak{A}}, q^{\mathfrak{B}}, E_q \rangle$ for each predicate q of arity ≥ 2. Our implementation of *filter* repeatedly iterates over each G_q as well as the graph $G = \langle A, B, E \rangle$ while performing the following update rules:

1. If $(\langle a_1, \ldots, a_{ar(q)} \rangle, \langle b_1, \ldots, b_{ar(q)} \rangle) \in E_q$ and $\langle a_i, b_i \rangle \notin E$ for some i, remove it from E_q.
2. If $\langle a, b \rangle \in E$, $\langle a_1, \ldots, a_{ar(q)} \rangle \in q^{ar(q)}$ with $a = a_i$, and there is no edge $(\langle a_1, \ldots, a_{ar(q)} \rangle, \langle b_1, \ldots, b_{ar(q)} \rangle) \in E_q$ with $b = b_i$, remove $\langle a, b \rangle$ from E.

The *filter* algorithm keeps applying these two rules until no more apply (a fixed point is reached).

A Structure Embedding Database. In the context of predicate automaton emptiness checking, the problem of interest is to check whether any structure within a given set of structures (i.e., the states of the automaton that have already been explored) embeds into another given structure (i.e., some new candidate state). To solve this problem, we require a data structure that stores a set of structures, and that supports an embedding query operation that can test if any member of this set embeds into a given structure (ideally without simply testing embedding for each structure in the set).

We use k-d trees [2] to organize the database of structures, and use range queries to support multi-source single-target embedding problems. The idea is to associate each structure $\mathfrak{A}$ with a vector $v(\mathfrak{A}) \in \mathbb{N}^d$ (for some fixed dimension d) such that if $\mathfrak{A}$ embeds into $\mathfrak{B}$, then $v(\mathfrak{A}) \leq v(\mathfrak{B})$. By storing structures in a k-d-tree-based map that is keyed by these vectors, we can support multi-source embedding queries by using a range query to search for structures keyed by vectors less than a given target vector, and attempt structure embedding only for the subset of structures returned. In our implementation, we use $|Q|$-dimensional binary vectors where $v(\mathfrak{A})_q = 0$ if $q^{\mathfrak{A}} = \emptyset$ and $v(\mathfrak{A})_q = 1$ otherwise.

4   Experiments

In this section, we evaluate the performance of MatchEmbeds by comparing it against three CSP solvers (Gecode [24], HaifaCSP [27], and Google's or-tools [20]), two SAT solvers (Lingeling [3] and CryptoMiniSat [26]), and two subgraph isomorphism solvers (Boost's implementation of VF2 [19] and Glasgow [16]). Our experiments are designed to answer three questions:

1. Does MatchEmbeds improve the performance of its intended client application of subsumption checking in state-space exploration of parameterized concurrent programs?
2. Does the k-d tree data structure improve the performance of many-to-one structure embedding queries in predicate automata emptiness checking?
3. Is MatchEmbeds capable of solving difficult problem instances?

4.1   Predicate Automata Emptiness

We integrated MatchEmbeds into a prototype implementation of the software model checking algorithm proposed in [8]. The model checking algorithm operates by iteratively constructing a predicate automaton that recognizes a *safe* set of executions and checking whether all program traces are contained inside the safe one (so a single verification task involves many predicate automaton emptiness tests, each of which involves many structure embedding instances). We experimented with small synthetic benchmark programs that were designed to stress-test the structure embedding procedure. While these programs are small and synthetic it allows us to control both the universe and arity of predicates involved in any structure. We used the API provided with Gecode and Boost to integrate it into the prototype. We used the text interface provided by HaifaCSP, or-tools, Lingeling, and CryptoMiniSat which bears a performance penalty.

Count Threads: we consider a family of programs wherein the main thread spawns some number of threads N, each of which atomically increments a global variable count, and then finally asserts that count is no greater than N. We expect the count threads benchmark to produce monadic structures, but to vary in size with many structures having a universe size close to N, as we need to explore the execution of all threads to verify that the assertion holds.

```
main():                          thread():
    count = 0                        count = count + 1
    for i = 1 to N:
       fork thread
    assert(count <= N)
```

Secret Sharing: we consider a family of programs wherein all threads execute a protocol that results in having a shared secret. The significance is that the shared secret forces the use of a binary predicate that expresses that two threads have the same secret value. The correct protocol is shown in main_safe below: it allocates a secret positive number, spawns an arbitrary number of threads, sends it to each using the to variable, then checks if it has received a message in the from variable. If so, it asserts that the received message is equal to its secret. The incorrect protocol is shown in main_bug. It does the same, except that it computes a new secret for every N threads, where N is a parameter to the system. The assertion may fail if at least N threads are spawned. The correct version can be verified in 0.77 s with MatchEmbeds, 0.78 with VF2, 0.80 with Gecode, 5.36 with Lingeling, 11.02 with CryptoMiniSat, 30.99 with HaifaCSP, and 41.25 with or-tools.

```
main_safe():
  local secret = *
  assume(secret > 0)
  from = 0
  while (*):
    to = secret
    fork thread
    while (to > 0): skip
  if (from > 0):
    assert(from == secret)
```

```
main_bug():
  from = 0
  while (*):
    local secret = *
    assume(secret > 0)
    for (i = 1 to N):
      to = secret
      fork thread
      while (to > 0): skip
    if (from > 0):
      assert(from == secret)
```

```
thread():
  local m = to
  to = 0
  from = m
```

We expect the secret sharing benchmark to produce mostly binary structures, that form a hub-and-spoke topology, since the local threads only interact with the main thread.

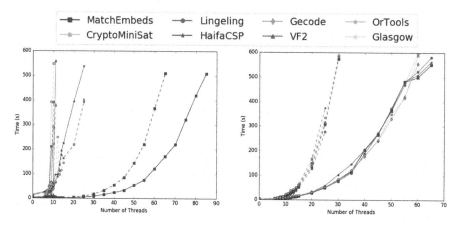

Fig. 3. Proof space benchmarks: count threads (Left), secret sharing (Right). Solid line indicates k-d tree, dashed line indicates list data structure.

In Fig. 3, we compare the results of each tool, with and without the use of the k-d tree data structure, on the *Count Threads* and *Secret Sharing* parametric benchmarks. In the *Count Threads* benchmark, MatchEmbeds substantially outperforms all other solvers, verifying up to 85 threads; HaifaCSP and Crypto-MiniSat, the two next closest, reached up to 25. In the *Secret Sharing* benchmark we see a different story: almost identical performance from each solver, but a large performance gain from the k-d tree. When using the k-d data structure, only a small fraction—less than 1/50th—of the time was spent on embedding queries. In contrast, without the k-d tree data structure almost the entirety of the verification task was spent solving embedding instances. We see similar improvements in the *Count Threads* benchmark when using MatchEmbeds. For the 30 thread secret sharing benchmark, we see that the k-d tree only performs 220 thousand embedding queries while the naive method explores 318 million embeddings. We note a similar reduction in number of embedding queries for all benchmarks. We suspect the similar performance of all solvers in the *Secret Sharing* benchmark is due to the topology of the structures resulting in easy embedding instances.

4.2 Hard Instances

The previous experiment demonstrates that MatchEmbeds is able to very quickly solve the (typically easy) embedding problems that arise in predicate automaton emptiness checking. The second question we would like to answer is whether MatchEmbeds also works well for larger, more difficult instances. To answer this question, we compared the performance of MatchEmbeds against SAT, CSP, and subgraph isomorphism solvers on a suite of *hard* randomly generated benchmarks.

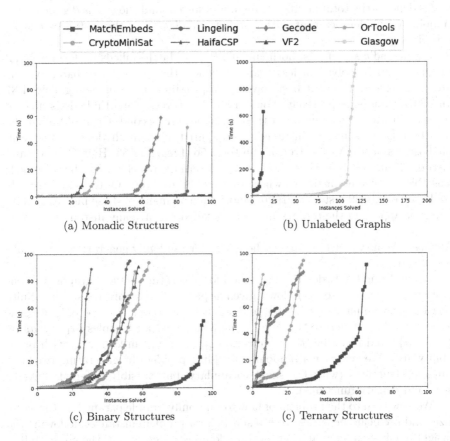

(a) Monadic Structures

(b) Unlabeled Graphs

(c) Binary Structures

(c) Ternary Structures

Fig. 4. Embedding instances solved within time for each benchmark.

4.3 Random Embedding

Results. We randomly generated a suite of difficult monadic, binary, and ternary structure embedding problems, pictured in Fig. 4. For each monadic instance, the source universe size is 40, target universe size is 50, and the vocabulary consists of 3 monadic predicates; the suite has 53 satisfiable and 47 unsatisfiable instances. For each binary instance, the source universe size is 20, target universe size is 30, and the vocabulary has 3 monadic and 3 binary predicates; the suite has 46 satisfiable, 49 unsatisfiable, and 5 unsolved instances. For each ternary instances, the source universe size is 10, the target universe size is 30, the vocabulary had 3 monadic, 3 binary, and 3 ternary predicates; the suite has 35 satisfiable, 32 unsatisfiable, and 33 unsolved instances.

Cactus plots comparing the performance of the structure embedding solvers on the random embedding instances are pictured in Fig. 4. In a cactus plot, the x-axis denotes the total number of instances solved, and the y-axis denotes time. A point (x, y) denotes that within a timeout of y, x of the instances can be solved.

For monadic structures, both HaifaCSP and MatchEmbeds perform well: all instances can be solved in less than a second—their graphs are barely visible above the x-axis; the next best solvers, CryptoMiniSat and lingeling, solved 87 and 86 instances respectively. For binary structures, MatchEmbeds is able to solve 95 instances, solving 60 of these in under one second. CryptoMiniSat,the next best solver, solved 64 instances and required substantially longer to solve 40 of those instances. VF2 solves 58, OrTools 56, Lingeling 53, HaifaCSP 31, and Gecode 27 in the 100s time limit. For the ternary benchmark, MatchEmbeds was able to solve 65 instances where the next best solvers, OrTools and Gecode could solve only 29 instances, taking more time on many of those instances. VF2 does not appear in the ternary figure as it failed to solve any instances.

Method. We now describe our methodology for randomly generating hard problem instances.

Generalizing the Erdős-Rényi method for generating random graphs, we generate random structures as follows: given as parameters a universe size n, a finite relational vocabulary $\sigma = \langle Q, ar \rangle$, and a density function $d : Q \to [0, 1]$, we generate a random structure $\mathfrak{A}(n, \sigma, d)$ by iterating over all k-tuples $(a_1, \ldots, a_k) \in \{1, \ldots, n\}^k$ and including the proposition $q(a_1, \ldots, a_n)$ in $\mathfrak{A}(n, \sigma, d)$ with probability $d(q)$. We generate a random embedding problem by generating two such random structures (with the same vocabulary, but possibly different universe sizes and density functions).

We now turn to the problem of how to randomly sample parameters (universe sizes and predicate densities) that result in *hard* problem instances, following the insight of Cheeseman et al. that hard random instances lie near the phase shift—the parameters used to generate the instances have probability ∼0.5 to produce satisfiable instances [5]. Similarly to McCreesh et al.'s method for generating hard subgraph isomorphism instances [17], we fix the source and target universe sizes and the vocabulary, and search only over densities. We aim to sample density functions that achieve near parity between the number of satisfiable and unsatisfiable embedding instances.

Our method is based on the assumption that parameters with similar expected number of solutions also have similar probabilities of there existing at least one solution. The expected number of solutions for a given set of parameters, which we denote $E(n, m, d^{\mathfrak{A}}, d^{\mathfrak{B}})$, has a simple closed form formula (which we derive below). Using this formula, we find a target expected number $T(n, m, d^{\mathfrak{A}}, d^{\mathfrak{B}})$ experimentally, using a binary search for an expected number such that the ratio between satisfiable and unsatisfiable instances, estimated by generating 10 instances at random, is nearly $1/2$ (there is a 5-5 or 6-4 split). We then generate a random hard instance as follows. First, we randomly sample parameters that achieve (nearly) the target number of solutions by using stochastic gradient decent to minimize $|T(n, m, d^{\mathfrak{A}}, d^{\mathfrak{B}}) - E(n, m, d^{\mathfrak{A}}, d^{\mathfrak{B}})|$. Specifically, we uniformly at random pick a parameter, and perform 1 iteration of stochastic gradient descent using the partial derivative w.r.t. the chosen parameter, and repeat this process until E converges (within 0.005) to T. We then use these parameters to produce random embedding problems until we find one that is non-trivial (at least one solver takes more than 1 s to solve). To generate the benchmark suites pictured in Fig. 4, we repeat this process 100 times.

We conclude with a derivation of a formula to calculate the expected number of embeddings for a random embedding problem. Observe that the number of injective functions from a set of size n to a set of size m is given by $m!/(m-n)!$. For any given injective function h, recall that an $ar(q)$-tuple belongs to $q^{\mathfrak{A}}$ with probability $d^{\mathfrak{A}}(q)$ and its image, $\langle h(a_1), \ldots, h(a_{ar(q)}) \rangle$, belongs to $q^{\mathfrak{B}}$ with probability $d^{\mathfrak{B}}(q)$; thus the probability that h satisfies the homomorphism condition for a given predicate q and $ar(q)$-tuple is $d^{\mathfrak{A}}(q)d^{\mathfrak{B}}(q) + (1 - d^{\mathfrak{A}}(a))$. Since there are $n^{ar(q)}$ such tuples and each event is independent, we raise the probability to the $n^{ar(q)}$ power to get the probability of all $ar(q)$-tuples satisfying the homomorphism conditions for q. Taking the product over all $q \in Q$, then gives the probability that h is a homomorphism. We can multiply this probability by the total number of injective functions to arrive at the function E that computes the expected number of embeddings for structures sampled using the given parameters:

$$E(n, m, d^{\mathfrak{A}}, d^{\mathfrak{B}}) = \frac{m!}{(m-n)!} \prod_{q \in Q} (d^{\mathfrak{A}}(q)d^{\mathfrak{B}}(q) + (1 - d^{\mathfrak{A}}(q)))^{n^{ar(q)}}$$

4.4 Unlabeled Subgraph Isomorphism

(Unlabeled) subgraph isomorphism is a special case of the structure embedding problem that has received considerable attention (see Sect. 5). Figure 4(b) compares the performance of CSP, SAT, and subgraph isomorphism solvers on a suite of 200 *hard* random subgraph isomorphism instances from [17]. We included the Glasgow subgraph isomorphism solver in this benchmark, as it was the leading solver in [17]; it is excluded from our other experiments because it does not support labeled subgraph isomorphism. In this benchmark, all source graphs consist of 30 vertices and all target graphs contain 150 vertices. Glasgow outperforms all other solvers on these instances, solving 118; MatchEmbeds performs second best, solving just 13 instances in the 1000 s time limit. All other solvers solved at most one instance. The poor performance of MatchEmbeds (relative to the previous experiments) is expected: MatchEmbeds matching-based heuristic search is uninformative in this setting. Since the signature of any vertex in an unlabeled graph is exactly the total degree of that vertex and random graphs are likely to have many vertices with similar degree, the expectation is that signature graphs will be dense and MatchEmbeds will have little information to exploit. We expect more informative signatures to result in MatchEmbeds performing better on unlabeled graphs.

4.5   Encoding Structure Embedding into CSP

A constraint satisfaction problem consists of a finite set of variables $X = \{x_1, \ldots, x_n\}$, with each variable $x_i \in X$ associated with a finite domain D_i that determines which values that x_i, and a finite set of constraints among those variables. Given two structures $\mathfrak{A}$ and $\mathfrak{B}$ over a common vocabulary $\langle Q, ar \rangle$, we construct the following CSP. We introduce a variable x_a for each $a \in A$ with domain $D_a = \{b \in B : sig(\mathfrak{A}, a) \subseteq sig(\mathfrak{B}, b)\}$. We add the constraint $\texttt{alldifferent}(X)$, which asserts that each a must map to a unique b (i.e. $\forall x_a, x_{a'} \in X. x_a \neq x_{a'}$). Then for each $\langle a_1, \ldots, a_n \rangle \in q^{\mathfrak{A}}$ we introduce a constraint $C_\alpha = \bigvee_{\langle b_1, \ldots, b_n \rangle \in q^{\mathfrak{B}}} (\bigwedge_i x_{a_i} = b_i)$ to ensure the homomorphism condition. The CSP is satisfiable iff $\mathfrak{A}$ embeds into $\mathfrak{B}$.

4.6   Encoding Structure Embedding into SAT

Let $\mathfrak{A}$ and $\mathfrak{B}$ be structures over a common vocabulary $\langle Q, ar \rangle$. For each edge $\langle a, b \rangle$ in the signature graph $\langle A, B, E \rangle = Sig(\mathfrak{A}, \mathfrak{B})$, we introduce one propositional variable $p_{a,b}$, with the interpretation that $p_{a,b}$ is set iff a maps to b in an embedding from $\mathfrak{A}$ to $\mathfrak{B}$. For each $a \in A$ we introduce a constraint $\bigvee_{\langle a,b \rangle \in E} p_{a,b}$ to encode that a must have an image. We encode that a has at most one image ensuring that for each $a \in A$, at most one of $\{p_{a,b} | b \in Adj(a)\}$ holds, using the sequential counter encoding of that at-most-1 constraint [25]. Similarly, we enforce injectivity by ensuring that for each $b \in B$, at most one of $\{p_{a,b} | a \in Adj(b)\}$ holds. Finally, for each $q \in Q$ and $\langle a_1, ..., a_n \rangle \in q^{\mathfrak{A}}$, we introduce a constraint $\bigvee_{\langle b_1, \ldots, b_n \rangle \in q^{\mathfrak{B}}} (p_{a_1, b_1} \wedge \cdots \wedge p_{a_n, b_n})$ to encode the homomorphism condition. The resulting formula is satisfiable iff $\mathfrak{A}$ embeds into $\mathfrak{B}$.

4.7   Encoding Structure Embedding into Labeled Subgraph Isomorphism

Given a structures $\mathfrak{A}$ with vocabulary $\langle Q, ar \rangle$, we generate a graph $G(\mathfrak{A})$. For each $q \in Q$ we introduce a vertex label, l_q and for each $i \in [1, ar(q)]$ we introduce an edge label l_{qi}. Then for each universe element, $a \in A$, we introduce a vertex a in G. Additionally, for each tuple $\alpha \in q^{\mathfrak{A}}$, we introduce a vertex v_α and for each $i \in [1, ar(q)]$ we introduce an edge $\langle v_\alpha, a_i \rangle$ with edge label l_{qi}. Note, for both the binary and monadic embeddings, the VF2 implementation allows labeling vertices and edges with sets of labels and using set inclusion for matching vertex and edge labels, we are able to directly encode monadic and binary structures without adding any additional vertices and edges (i.e. $l(v) = \{q : v \in q^{\mathfrak{A}}\}$ and $l(\langle u, v \rangle) = \{q : \langle u, v \rangle \in q^{\mathfrak{A}}\}$).

5   Related Work

Constraint Satisfaction Problems. Constraint satisfaction problems (CSPs) are a broad class of combinatorial problems that includes structure embedding. A good introduction appears in [23, Chap. 6]. MatchEmbeds employs several ideas that are commonly used in resolution algorithms for CSPs, including backtracking search, filtering (constraint propagation), and heuristics for decision selection (variable and value selection). The hypothesis of our work, validated in Sect. 4, was that by exploiting the injectivity feature of structure embedding we could outperform general-purpose CSP solvers.

Of particular relevance to structure embedding is work on the `alldifferent` constraint, which requires a specified subset of variables in the problem to be assigned distinct values (mirroring the injectivity condition of structure embeddings). The work most relevant to ours is Régin's domain consistency algorithm for `alldifferent`. Régin's algorithm uses biparite graph matching to discover all edges in a value graph of a CSP (analogous to the signature graph of a structure embedding problem) that do not belong to *any* total matching and deletes them. Efficient algorithms for weaker notions of consistency (namely bounds consistency) have also been developed [15,21]. A survey on the `alldifferent` constraint can be found in [12]. Considering the CSP solvers included in Sect. 4: HaifaCSP implements Régin's algorithm [22] and Gecode and or-tools implement the algorithm of Lopez-Ortiz et al. [15]. The superior performance of HaifaCSP (particularly for monadic structures) demonstrates the importance of the `alldifferent` constraint.

A commonality of these works is that they are *constraint propagation* techniques: they infer additional constraints on the problem that must be satisfied by any solution. In contrast, the algorithm presented in Sect. 2.3 uses graph matching as the central search mechanism, guiding both which decisions to make and when to make them (value and variable selection in the terminology of constraint programming). Our algorithm exploits the fact that structure embedding problems involve an `alldifferent` constraint on *all variables*, which makes matching more informative for structure embedding than it is for general CSPs.

Subgraph Isomorphism. Given two graphs G and H, the *subgraph isomorphism* problem is to determine if there exists a subgraph of H that is isomorphic to G, or equivalently, to determine whether there exists an injective homomorphism from G to H. Subgraph isomorphism has a number of applications, including subcircuit identification [18] and finding motifs in biochemical graph data [4]—see [6] for a broad survey of techniques for and applications of subgraph isomorphism. An accessible account describing the differences between some subgraph isomorphism algorithms and an experimental comparison between them can be found in [14].

The subgraph isomorphism problem is a special case of structure embedding, where the vocabulary of structures is fixed to the vocabulary of graphs consisting of a single binary incidence relation. A reduction from structure embedding to labelled subgraph isomorphism (wherein the signature consists only of monadic and binary predicates) is also possible through constraint binarization [23, Chap. 6]. However, the applications of subgraph isomorphism differ from the setting of this paper: typically, the source graph is small and the target is very large, and the problem of interest is to enumerate *all* injective homomorphisms. In this paper, the problem of interest is the decision problem to determine whether there is at least one injective homomorphism, and the expectation is that the source and target are of similar size.

A common theme in algorithms for subgraph isomorphism is to exploit local edge structure. In contrast, the algorithm we propose exploits the global structure of the problem by using graph matching as the foundation of the backtracking search. We are not aware of an existing algorithm for subgraph isomorphism that operates in polytime for labelled graphs without edges, which is the analogue of monadic structures. We see from Fig. 4 that VF2 is not competitive on monadic structures, unable to exploit any local edge structure.

6   Conclusion

In this paper we presented MatchEmbeds, a practical algorithm for the problem of testing whether one finite relational structure embeds into another. The core idea is to use bipartite graph matching to drive a backtracking search procedure. The algorithm operates in polytime for monadic structures, but may take exponential time for general structures. The procedure has been shown to be effective for problems that arise in practice and for difficult random instances.

It would be interesting to apply matching-based search to other problems where injectivity constraints are important. For instance, in entailment checking for separation logic formulas, separately conjoined heap cells in a source formula must map to separately conjoined heap cells in a target formula. Entailment checking for the list fragment can be done in polytime using graph homomorphism [7], but entailment checking for formulas with existential quantifiers may benefit from matching-based search.

References

1. Abdulla, P.A., Cerans, K., Jonsson, B., Tsay, Y.K.: General decidability theorems for infinite-state systems. In: LICS, pp. 313–321 (1996)
2. Bentley, J.L.: Multidimensional binary search trees used for associative searching. Commun. ACM **18**(9), 509–517 (1975)
3. Biere, A.: Lingeling, plingeling and treengeling entering the sat competition 2013. In: Balint, A., Belov, A., Heule, M.J., Järvisalo, M. (eds.) SAT Competition 2013, pp. 51–52. Department of Computer Science Series of Publications B (2013)
4. Bonnici, V., Giugno, R., Pulvirenti, A., Shasha, D., Ferro, A.: A subgraph isomorphism algorithm and its application to biochemical data. BMC Bioinform. **14**(7), S13 (2013)
5. Cheeseman, P.C., Kanefsky, B., Taylor, W.M.: Where the really hard problems are. In: IJCAI vol. 91, pp. 331–340 (1991)
6. Conte, D., Foggia, P., Sansone, C., Vento, M.: Thirty years of graph matching in pattern recognition. Int. J. Pattern Recognit. Artif. Intell. **18**(03), 265–298 (2004)
7. Cook, B., Haase, C., Ouaknine, J., Parkinson, M., Worrell, J.: Tractable reasoning in a fragment of separation logic. In: Katoen, J.-P., König, B. (eds.) CONCUR 2011. LNCS, vol. 6901, pp. 235–249. Springer, Heidelberg (2011). https://doi.org/10.1007/978-3-642-23217-6_16
8. Farzan, A., Kincaid, Z., Podelski, A.: Proof spaces for unbounded parallelism. In: POPL, pp. 407–420 (2015)
9. Farzan, A., Kincaid, Z., Podelski, A.: Proving liveness of parameterized programs. In: LICS, pp. 185–196 (2016)
10. Finkel, A., Schnoebelen, P.: Well-structured transition systems everywhere!. TCS **256**(1), 63–92 (2001)
11. Ford, L.R., Fulkerson, D.R.: Maximal flow through a network. Can. J. Math. **8**(3), 399–404 (1956)
12. van Hoeve, W.J.: The alldifferent constraint: a survey. In: 6th Annual Workshop of the ERCIM Working Group on Constraints (2001)
13. Hopcroft, J.E., Karp, R.M.: A $n^{5/2}$ algorithm for maximum matchings in bipartite graphs. In: SWAT, pp. 122–125 (1971)
14. Lee, J., Han, W.S., Kasperovics, R., Lee, J.H.: An in-depth comparison of subgraph isomorphism algorithms in graph databases. In: PVLDB, pp. 133–144 (2013)
15. Lopez-Ortiz, A., Quimper, C.G., Tromp, J., Van Beek, P.: A fast and simple algorithm for bounds consistency of the all different constraint. In: IJCAI, pp. 245–250 (2003)
16. McCreesh, C., Prosser, P.: A parallel, backjumping subgraph isomorphism algorithm using supplemental graphs. In: Pesant, G. (ed.) CP 2015. LNCS, vol. 9255, pp. 295–312. Springer, Cham (2015). https://doi.org/10.1007/978-3-319-23219-5_21
17. McCreesh, C., Prosser, P., Trimble, J.: Heuristics and really hard instances for subgraph isomorphism problems. In: IJCAI, pp. 631–638 (2016)
18. Ohlrich, M., Ebeling, C., Ginting, E., Sather, L.: SubGemini: identifying subcircuits using a fast subgraph isomorphism algorithm. In: DAC, pp. 31–37 (1993)
19. Cordella, L.P., Foggia, P., Sansone, C., Vento, M.: A (sub)graph isomorphism algorithm for matching large graphs. IEEE Trans. Pattern Anal. Mach. Intell. **26**(10), 1367–1372 (2004)
20. Perron, L.: Operations research and constraint programming at Google. In: Lee, J. (ed.) CP 2011. LNCS, vol. 6876, p. 2. Springer, Heidelberg (2011). https://doi.org/10.1007/978-3-642-23786-7_2. https://developers.google.com/optimization/

21. Puget, J.F.: A fast algorithm for the bound consistency of alldiff constraints. In: AAAI, pp. 359–366 (1998)
22. Régin, J.C.: A filtering algorithm for constraints of difference in CSPs. In: AAAI, pp. 362–367 (1994)
23. Russell, S.J., Norvig, P.: Artificial Intelligence - A Modern Approach. Prentice Hall Series in Artificial Intelligence, 3rd edn. Pearson, Prentice Hall (2009)
24. Schulte, C., Lagerkvist, M., Tack, G.: GECODE - an open, free, efficient constraint solving toolkit. www.gecode.org
25. Sinz, C.: Towards an optimal CNF encoding of boolean cardinality constraints. In: van Beek, P. (ed.) CP 2005. LNCS, vol. 3709, pp. 827–831. Springer, Heidelberg (2005). https://doi.org/10.1007/11564751_73
26. Soos, M., Nohl, K., Castelluccia, C.: Cryptominisat. SAT race solver descriptions (2010)
27. Veksler, M., Strichman, O.: Learning general constraints in CSP. In: Michel, L. (ed.) CPAIOR 2015. LNCS, vol. 9075, pp. 410–426. Springer, Cham (2015). https://doi.org/10.1007/978-3-319-18008-3_28. http://strichman.net.technion.ac.il/haifacsp/

EUFORIA: Complete Software Model Checking with Uninterpreted Functions

Denis Bueno$^{(\boxtimes)}$ and Karem A. Sakallah

University of Michigan, Ann Arbor, USA
{dlbueno,karem}@umich.edu

Abstract. We introduce and evaluate an algorithm for an IC3-style software model checker that operates entirely at the level of equality with uninterpreted functions (EUF). Our checker, called EUFORIA, targets control properties by treating a program's data operations/relations as uninterpreted functions/predicates. This results in an EUF abstract transition system that EUFORIA analyzes to either (1) discover an inductive strengthening EUF formula that proves the property or (2) produce an abstract counterexample that corresponds to zero, one, or many concrete counterexamples. Infeasible counterexamples are eliminated by an efficient refinement method that constrains the EUF abstraction until the property is proved or a feasible counterexample is produced. We formalize the EUF transition system, prove our algorithm correct, and demonstrate our results on a subset of benchmarks from the software verification competition (SV-COMP) 2017.

1 Introduction

Control properties are an integral part of software verification. The 2014 Apple Secure Transport "goto fail" bug [1] provides a compelling illustration:

```
extern int f();
int g() {
    int ret = 0;
    /* ... */
    goto out; /* this line was inadvertently added */
    ret = f();
out:
    return ret;
}
```

In this simplified version of the bug, the function f() implements a security check that returns 0 on success. g() is supposed to call f(); however, f() is never called because there is an (inadvertent) jump directly to g()'s return statement. To prove the absence of this bug, one would like to verify the property that every success path actually calls f() (i.e., that f() is called whenever g() returns 0). This property does not require reasoning precisely about what f() does with

© Springer Nature Switzerland AG 2019
C. Enea and R. Piskac (Eds.): VMCAI 2019, LNCS 11388, pp. 363–385, 2019.
https://doi.org/10.1007/978-3-030-11245-5_17

data; it only requires reasoning about control paths. Consequently, this property is a *control property*.

A variety of important properties are control properties. For instance, many operating systems require that secure programs drop elevated privileges as soon as those privileges are no longer needed. Such a rule is a control property because it has little to do with details about particular privileged operations. Instead, the rule only requires reasoning about when privilege drops occur relative to the unprivileged parts of a program [2]. Similarly, verifying a locking discipline does not require reasoning about the data being protected; it only requires reasoning about when locking and unlocking occurs relative to when data is accessed or modified [3]. Typestate properties [4] are also control properties.

The typical approach for verifying control properties is predicate abstraction [5,6], which casts the state space of a program into a Boolean space defined by a set of predicates over program variables. The primary challenge with predicate abstraction lies in the selection of predicates. All of the necessary information about data and control must be inferred using a finite set of predicates. Searching the predicate space has an exponential cost because adding a new predicate doubles the size of abstract state space. To make matters worse, predicate abstraction does not directly abstract operations, which can lead to time-consuming solver queries for complex operations – even though many complex operations are irrelevant for control properties.

Instead, we propose a more direct abstraction. Rather than projecting program state onto an interpreted predicate space, we syntactically abstract it into a set of constraints over the theory of equality with uninterpreted functions (EUF). This means that our abstraction can happen at the operation level (e.g., addition, subtraction, comparison, etc.) reducing the complexity of queries sent to the solver. Moreover, EUF reduces the number of bits in the search space (by abstracting bit vector terms), and has efficient implementations. The Averroes verifier [7] showed that such an approach works well for checking control properties in hardware designs.

This paper adapts IC3-style model checking with EUF abstraction to software. We find this gives performance benefits by reducing the number of refinement iterations in a counter-example-guided abstraction refinement (CEGAR) [8,9] loop, while keeping the Boolean state space smaller. We make the following contributions:

- EUFORIA, a ground-up implementation of a complete software model checking algorithm inspired by Averroes (Sect. 3);
- detailed descriptions of EUFORIA's novel cube expansion method (Sect. 3.1) and refinement (Sect. 3.2), including new proofs of correctness and termination for finite state systems (Sect. 3.3),
- experimental evaluation on 752 from SV-COMP '17 (Sect. 4), showing that EUFORIA outperforms a related predicate abstraction algorithm, IC3IA [10], on control property benchmarks.

2   Software Data Abstraction

Our goal is safety verification: showing that all reachable states of a program are safe, or producing a counterexample test case. Kesten and Pnueli [11] made a distinction between control abstraction and data abstraction: while the former abstracts observations of computation sequences, the latter abstracts data values. We are targeting properties that involve verifying the control flow of a program, not its data, and thus we focus on abstracting data values using EUF theory.

This section describes the logic of EUF, how we represent a program (precisely) as a concrete transition system, and how we create an (over-approximate) abstract transition system from that concrete transition system.

2.1   Background

Equality with Uninterpreted Functions   Our setting is standard quantifier-free, first-order logic (FOL) with the standard notions of theory, satisfiability, validity, entailment, and models. Inspired by Kroening's presentation in [12], we begin with a review of the EUF logic. The EUF logic grammar is presented here:

non-terminal	production	explanation
$term ::=$	$x \mid y \mid z \mid \cdots$	0-arity term, sans serif face
$\mid$	$F(term_1, term_2, \ldots, term_n)$	uninterpreted function (UF)
$\mid$	$ITE(formula, term_1, term_2)$	if-then-else
$atom ::=$	$term_1 = term_2$	equality atom
$\mid$	$x \mid y \mid z \mid \cdots$	Boolean atom
$\mid$	$P(term_1, term_2, \ldots, term_n)$	uninterpreted predicate (UP)
$formula ::=$	$atom$	
$\mid$	$\neg atom$	negation
$\mid$	$formula_1 \wedge formula_2$	conjunction
$\mid$	$formula_1 \vee formula_2$	disjunction

Atomic formulas (atoms) are made up of Boolean identifiers, uninterpreted predicates (UPs), and (possibly-negated) equalities between terms. Formulas are made up of terms combined with arbitrary Boolean structure. For simplicity, but without loss of generality, we only consider formulas in negation normal form. A *literal* is a (possibly-negated) atom containing no occurrences of ITE. A *clause* is a disjunction of literals. A *cube* is a conjunction of literals. $a \models b$ means that a entails b. We write uninterpreted objects – terms x, functions F, and predicates P – in sans serif face. The semantics of these formulas is standard.

Transition Systems. The front-end of our checker EUFORIA translates a C program into a bit-precise transition system. A *transition system* [13,14] is a tuple (X, Y, I, T) consisting of a (non-empty) set of *state variables* $X = \{x_1, \ldots, x_n\}$, a (possibly empty) set of *input variables* $Y = \{y_1, \ldots, y_m\}$, and two formulas: I, the *initial states*, and T, the *transition relation*. Formulas over state variables are identified with the sets of states they denote; for example, the formula $(x_1 = x_2)$

denotes all states where x_1 and x_2 are equal, and other variables may have any value. The set of *next-state variables* is $X' = \{x'_1, x'_2, \ldots, x'_n\}$. For a formula σ, the set $\text{Vars}(\sigma)$ denotes the set of state variables free in σ (respectively, $\text{Vars}'(\sigma)$ denotes set of next-state variables in σ). We may write σ as $\sigma(X)$ when we wish to emphasize that the free variables in σ are drawn solely from the set X, i.e., $\text{Vars}(\sigma(X)) \subseteq X$. Any formula $\sigma(X')$ (also written σ') refers to the result of substituting for the current-state variables in $\sigma(X)$ with the corresponding next-state variables from X', e.g., $(x_1 = x_2)'$ is $(x'_1 = x'_2)$. The system's *transition relation* T is a formula

$$T(X, Y, X') \equiv \bigwedge_{1 \leqslant i \leqslant n} (x'_i = f_i(X, Y)) \tag{1}$$

where $f_i(X, Y)$ is a term denoting the next-state function for $x_i \in X$.

We write $\sigma(X) \xrightarrow{T} \omega(X)$ if each state in σ transitions to some state in ω under T, i.e., $\sigma \wedge T \models \omega'$. An *execution* of a transition system is a (possibly-infinite) sequence of transitions $\sigma_0(X) \xrightarrow{T} \sigma_1(X) \xrightarrow{T} \sigma_2(X), \ldots$ such that $\sigma_0(X) \models I(X)$.

A *safety property* is specified by a predicate, $P(\text{X})$. The *model checking problem* is to check whether any state satisfying $\neg P(X)$ is reachable through an execution of T. A counterexample to a safety property $P(X)$ is a k-step execution such that $\sigma_k(X) \models \neg P(X)$.

A *concrete transition system* (CTS) is defined over bit vector state variables and operations in the quantifier-free logic of bit vectors (QF_BV from SMT-LIB [15]). EUFORIA encodes a C program into a CTS using standard methods [16,17].

2.2   EUF Transition Systems

Inspired by the work of Burch and Dill [18] for microprocessor verification, our approach is to abstract a program's concrete operations (resp. conditions) by uninterpreted functions (resp. predicates), and to replace constants by 0-arity terms (Kroening also gives a detailed overview of EUF abstraction [12], pp. 61ff). Concrete constants (e.g., 1, -3) are represented as unique uninterpreted 0-arity terms (K1, K-3); data operations such as addition, division, and bit-extraction are represented with correspondingly-named UFs; relational operators are represented as UPs; and bit-vector variables x are represented by 0-arity terms $\hat{x}$, and given a hat to distinguish them from constants. Boolean variables are represented directly in EUF. We abstract P into $\hat{P}$ and I into $\hat{I}$ in the same way as other formulas. For example, using state variables $X = \{x, a\}$, we represent the transition relation $T(X, \emptyset, X') \equiv (x' = \text{ITE}(x > a, x, 1 + a)) \wedge (a' = x)$ as $\hat{T}(\hat{X}, \emptyset, \hat{X}') \equiv (\hat{x}' = \text{ITE}(\text{GT}(\hat{x}, \hat{a}), \hat{x}, \text{ADD}(\text{K1}, \hat{a}))) \wedge (\hat{a}' = \hat{x})$, over state variables $\hat{X} = \{\hat{x}, \hat{a}\}$.

This abstraction can be formally defined by an *abstraction function* $\mathcal{A}[\![\cdot]\!]$ that performs a linear-time, syntax-directed, structure-preserving transformation of the CTS (described in [12]). The resulting *abstract transition system* (ATS)

$(\widehat{X}, \widehat{Y}, \widehat{I}, \widehat{T})$ consists of state variables $\widehat{X} = \{\widehat{x}_1, \widehat{x}_2, \dots, \widehat{x}_n\}$, input variables $\widehat{Y} = \{\widehat{y}_1, \widehat{y}_2, \dots, \widehat{y}_m\}$, initial state $\widehat{I}$, and transition relation $\widehat{T}$ defined by n next-state terms $\widehat{f}_1(\widehat{X}, \widehat{Y}), \dots, \widehat{f}_n(\widehat{X}, \widehat{Y})$ according to:

$$\widehat{T}(\widehat{X}, \widehat{Y}, \widehat{X}') \equiv \bigwedge_{1 \leqslant i \leqslant n} \left(\widehat{x}'_i = \widehat{f}_i(\widehat{X}, \widehat{Y}) \right) \tag{2}$$

Abstract formulas over-approximate their concrete counterparts. Recovering the concrete formulas is easy: 0-arity terms (which stand for concrete constants and variables) are mapped to their concrete countererparts; UFs and UPs are mapped to their concrete operations by name. Consider a concrete formula $\sigma(X)$ and its EUF abstraction $\widehat{\sigma}(\widehat{X})$. The relation of the concrete and abstract systems is $\models \widehat{\sigma} \implies \models \sigma$: the concretization σ of any valid EUF formula $\widehat{\sigma}$ is valid [12]. Therefore, if the abstract system cannot reach an unsafe state, then the concrete system will also never reach it. A concrete state is a complete assignment to bit vector and Boolean variables. An abstract state is a pair $\langle \pi, A \rangle$ where π is a partition of all the terms in the ATS and A is a complete assignment to the UPs and Boolean variables.

The EUF abstraction partitions the set of all concrete states. Each concrete state is represented by a single abstract state but abstract states may represent zero, one, or many concrete states. For instance, given a transition system with one 32-bit integer state variable, x, and a single transition equation,

$$x' = 1 + x \qquad \text{concrete transitions}$$
$$\widehat{x}' = \text{ADD}(K1, \widehat{x}) \qquad \text{abstract transitions}$$

the abstract state space is defined over the term set $\{\widehat{x}, K1, \text{ADD}(K1, \widehat{x})\}$ and consists of the following 5 states and their corresponding concrete states:[1]

Abstract state/partition	Concrete state(s)
$\pi_1 = \{\widehat{x} \mid K1 \mid \text{ADD}(K1, \widehat{x})\}$	$x \neq 1$ and $x \neq 0$
$\pi_2 = \{\widehat{x}, \text{ADD}(K1, \widehat{x}) \mid K1\}$	$\emptyset$ (infeasible)
$\pi_3 = \{\widehat{x} \mid K1, \text{ADD}(K1, \widehat{x})\}$	$x = 0$
$\pi_4 = \{\widehat{x}, K1 \mid \text{ADD}(K1, \widehat{x})\}$	$x = 1$
$\pi_5 = \{\widehat{x}, K1, \text{ADD}(K1, \widehat{x})\}$	$\emptyset$ (infeasible)

We should note that while the CTS is deterministic, the abstraction causes the ATS to be non-deterministic.

3 EUFORIA: Model Checking EUF Transition Systems

EUFORIA builds on the model checker IC3 [19] by extending it to EUF and wrapping it inside a CEGAR loop that refines the abstract transition system. The algorithm's main novelties are that it checks an entirely uninterpreted transition

EUFORIA(I, T, P):
Globals:
N current depth
F_i set of cubes, $i \in \{0, 1, \ldots, N, N + 1\}$ $(F_{N+1} = F_\infty)$
$R_i \equiv \bigwedge_{j=i}^{N+1} \bigwedge_{\hat{c} \in F_j} \neg \hat{c}$ reachable set (over-approximate)

1: $\hat{I}, \hat{T}, \hat{P} \leftarrow \text{abstract}(I, T, P)$ ▷ construct abstract transition system
2: $N = 0$ ▷ initialize global variables
3: push $F_\infty = true$, push $F_0 = \{\hat{I}(\hat{X})\}$ ▷ assume I is a cube
4: **while** true **do**
5:     **if** $\exists \hat{s} \models R_N \wedge \neg \hat{P}$ and BACKWARDREACHABILITY$(\hat{s})$ is true **then**
6:         **if** REFINECOUNTEREXAMPLE() is true **then**   ▷ found counterexample
7:             **return** BUILDCOUNTEREXAMPLE()
8:     **else**
9:         $N \leftarrow N + 1$, add new frame $F_N = true$
10:        **if** PROPAGATE() is true **then**   ▷ found inductive invariant
11:            **return** true

Fig. 1. Entry point to EUFORIA. I, T, and P define a model checking problem. Backward reachability is performed until it converges or discovers an abstract counterexample, which may trigger a refinement. BUILDCOUNTEREXAMPLE() constructs a concrete program trace from a feasible abstract counterexample. R_i is a global definition in terms of the individual frames, stored in F.

system, is guaranteed to terminate, and refines spurious counterexamples automatically. Our implementation is most closely related to PDR (Property Directed Reachability) [20], a popular variant of IC3.

EUFORIA's entry point is given in Fig. 1. We highlight algorithm components that EUFORIA introduces. As in IC3, the central object in EUFORIA is an iteratively-deepened sequence of reachable sets, R_i, each denoting an over-approximation of the set of states reachable in i transitions. The algorithm maintains the following invariants:

$$R_0 = \hat{I}(\hat{X}) \tag{3}$$

$$R_i \models R_{i+1} \tag{4}$$

$$R_i \models \hat{P}(\hat{X}) \quad (i < N) \tag{5}$$

$$R_{i+1} \text{ over-approximates the image of } R_i \tag{6}$$

Initially EUFORIA abstracts the concrete transition system and then loops over three distinct phases: backward reachability (Fig. 2), forward propagation (Fig. 3), and refinement (Fig. 6). This section will discuss the first two phases; refinement is discussed in Sect. 3.2.

Backward reachability (Fig. 2) attempts to prove that the property holds for N transitions or to construct a counterexample. It manages a queue of proof

---

[1] Vertical bars delineate the cells of a partition.

BACKWARDREACHABILITY($\widehat{s}$):
Precondition: cube $\widehat{s} \models \neg \widehat{P}$

1: push $\langle \widehat{s}, N \rangle$ onto Q
2: **while** $\langle \widehat{s}, i \rangle \leftarrow$ pop from Q **do**   ▷ states $\widehat{s}$ reach bad state
3:     **if** $i = 0$ **then**
4:         **return** true   ▷ found abstract counterexample
5:     **if** $\widehat{s} \wedge R_i$ is SAT **then**   ▷ $\widehat{s}$ might be reached in i transitions
6:         **if** $\neg \widehat{s} \wedge R_{i-1} \wedge \widehat{T} \wedge \widehat{s}'$ has model M **then**
7:             $\widehat{z} \leftarrow$ EXPANDPREIMAGE($\widehat{s}', M$)   ▷ $\widehat{z}$ reaches $\widehat{s}$ in one step
8:             push $\langle \widehat{z}, i-1 \rangle$ onto Q ▷ new part of partial counterexample
9:             push $\langle \widehat{s}, i \rangle$ onto Q ▷ may still be reachable
10:        **else**   ▷ $\widehat{s}$ is inductive relative to $\neg \widehat{s} \wedge \widehat{R}_{i-1}$
11:            $\langle \widehat{z}, m \rangle \leftarrow$ GENERALIZEBLOCKEDCUBE($\langle \widehat{s}, i \rangle$)   ▷ $m \geq i$
12:            **while** $m < N-1$ and $\neg \widehat{z} \wedge R_{m-1} \wedge \widehat{T} \wedge \widehat{z}'$ is UNSAT **do**
13:                $\langle \widehat{z}, m \rangle \leftarrow$ GENERALIZEBLOCKEDCUBE($\langle \widehat{z}, m \rangle$)   ▷
       attempt to block at later frame
14:            ADDBLOCKEDCUBE($\langle \widehat{z}, m \rangle$)
15:            **if** $m < N$ **then**
16:                push $\langle \widehat{z}, m+1 \rangle$ onto Q ▷ may still be reachable at $m+1$
17: **return** false

ADDBLOCKEDCUBE($\langle \widehat{s}, i \rangle$):

1: **for** $j \in \{1, 2, \ldots, i\}$ **do**   ▷ test whether $\widehat{s}$ subsumes a cube in an earlier frame
2:     **if** $\widehat{s} \subseteq \widehat{c}$ for any $\widehat{c} \in F_j$ **then**
3:         $F_j \leftarrow F_j \setminus \{\widehat{c}\}$
4: $F_i \leftarrow F_i \cup \{\widehat{s}\}$ ▷ record that $\widehat{s}$ is unreachable in i steps

Fig. 2. Proof obligations are represented as an abstract cube and frame index pair, $\langle \widehat{s}, i \rangle$. The proof obligation queue, Q, is a priority queue that orders cubes by frame index (earliest first) and breaks ties arbitrarily.

PROPAGATE():

1: **for** $i \in \{1, 2, \ldots, N-1\}$ **do**   ▷ Propagate at level i
2:     **for** $\widehat{s} \in F_i$ **do**
3:         **if** $R_i \wedge \widehat{T} \wedge \widehat{s}'$ is UNSAT **then**   ▷ $\widehat{s}$ is blocked at F_{i+1} or later
4:             $m \leftarrow$ maximum in $\{i+1, i+2, \ldots, N+1\}$ at which $\widehat{s}$ is blocked
5:             ADDBLOCKEDCUBE($\langle \widehat{s}, m \rangle$)   ▷ propagate cube $\widehat{s}$ to F_m
6:     **if** F_i is empty **then**
7:         **return** true   ▷ invariant found
8: **return** false

Fig. 3. Just prior to this phase of EUFORIA, $R_N \models \widehat{P}$. N is incremented and then PROPAGATE is called. In line 4, it is possible that a cube is blocked *beyond* the next frame ($i+1$). EUFORIA examines the unsat core given by the solver to see which frames were used in order to calculate m.

obligations that represent potential executions to $\neg \widehat{P}$. At each iteration, it chooses a proof obligation pair $\langle \widehat{s}, i \rangle$ and performs a counterexample-to-induction (CTI) query to see if cube $\widehat{s}'$ is reachable from the current i-step over-approximation (lines 2–6). If so, our new procedure EXPANDPREIMAGE (Sect. 3.1) generalizes the pre-state and adds it to the queue (lines 6–9). Otherwise, it generalizes the unreachable cube $\widehat{s}$ to refine the reachability frames (lines 11–14). Note that this over-approximation and refinement is a standard part of IC3 and is independent of our EUF abstraction and refinement.

Forward propagation (Fig. 3) pushes unreachable cubes forward, attempting to extend them over more transitions (lines 1–5). On line 6, if two (over-approximate) reachable sets become identical $R_i = R_{i+1}$ ($i < N$), the algorithm terminates having discovered an inductive invariant that proves the property by Eq. (5).

Generalizing Unsatisfiable CTI Queries If the CTI query (line 6 of Fig. 2) is unsatisfiable, then state $\widehat{s}$ is unreachable in i transitions. We want to generalize $\widehat{s}$ by finding a set of states (a cube) $\widehat{m} \supseteq \widehat{s}$ that is unreachable and covers more states than $\widehat{s}$, if possible. We use a simple greedy scheme for finding a minimal unsatisfiable set that is given in Fig. 4.

GENERALIZEBLOCKEDCUBE($\langle \widehat{s}, i \rangle$):

1: $\widehat{t} \leftarrow \widehat{s}, j \leftarrow i$
2: **for** $\widehat{l} \in \widehat{s}$ **do**
3:     $\widehat{m} \leftarrow \widehat{t} \setminus \widehat{l}$ ▷ test if $\widehat{m}$ unreachable if literal $\widehat{l}$ removed
4:     **if** $\widehat{m} \not\models I(\widehat{X})$ and $\neg \widehat{m} \wedge R_{j-1} \wedge \widehat{T} \wedge \widehat{m}'$ is UNSAT **then**
5:         $j \leftarrow$ frame $\geq j$ at which $\widehat{m}$ is still blocked
6:         $\widehat{t} \leftarrow \widehat{m}$ ▷ literal $\widehat{l}$ was not necessary
7: **return** $\langle \widehat{t}, j \rangle$

Fig. 4. Generalized blocked cube procedure. EUFORIA, like PDR, examines the unsat core of the query on line 4 in order to implement line 5.

3.1   Generalizing Satisfiable Counterexample-to-induction Queries

If the CTI query (line 6 of Fig. 2) is satisfiable, EUFORIA generalizes (expands) the preimage state to a cube that includes many states that satisfy the query. The purpose of generalization is efficiency: a bad state is often reached by many states and it is usually more efficient to find counterexamples if state sets contain as many states as possible.

Example 1. Consider the following transition relation on variables $\widehat{X} = \{\widehat{x}_1, \widehat{x}_2\}$:

$$\widehat{x}_1' = f_1 \text{ where } f_1 = \mathsf{ITE}(\widehat{x}_1 = \widehat{x}_2, \mathsf{ADD}(\widehat{x}_1, \mathsf{K1}), \mathsf{SUB}(\widehat{x}_1, \mathsf{K3})) \tag{7}$$

$$\widehat{x}_2' = f_2 \text{ where } f_2 = \widehat{x}_1 \tag{8}$$

EXPANDPREIMAGE($\hat{s}', M$):
1: $C \leftarrow \varnothing$ ▷ set of constraints
2: **for** $\hat{x}'_i \in \text{Vars}'(\hat{s}')$ **do**
3:     $c \leftarrow \text{COI}(f_i(\hat{X}, \hat{Y}), M)$ ▷ traverse f_i to collect M-relevant constraints
4:     $C \leftarrow C \cup c$
5: $\hat{g} \leftarrow$ restrict model M to variables, terms, and predicates in C
6: **return** $\hat{g}$

Fig. 5. Pre-image generalization procedure. M is the model for the CTI query. $\text{COI}(f, M)$ is a model-based cone of influence traversal.

Consider a proof obligation cube $\hat{s}' \equiv \text{GT}(\hat{x}'_1, \hat{x}'_2)$ and a model consisting of partition $\{\hat{x}_1, \hat{x}_2, \hat{x}'_2 \mid \text{K1}, \text{ADD}(\hat{x}_1, \text{K1}), \hat{x}'_1 \mid \text{K3}, \text{SUB}(\hat{x}_1, \text{K3})\}$ and assignment $\text{GT}(\hat{x}_1, \hat{x}_2) \wedge \text{GT}(\hat{x}'_1, \hat{x}'_2)$. EUFORIA performs a cone-of-influence (COI) traversal on f_1 and f_2 to find relevant constraints, terms, and variables; in this case, it finds the constraint $(\hat{x}_1 = \hat{x}_2)$, as well as terms $\text{K1}, \text{ADD}(\hat{x}_1, \text{K1})$, and variables $\hat{x}_1, \hat{x}_2$. It does not find the $\text{SUB}(\cdots)$ term because it only traverses the true branch of the ITE. Relating these constraints, terms, and variables according to the model yields our generalized pre-image cube: $(\hat{x}_1 = \hat{x}_2) \wedge (\text{ADD}(\hat{x}_1, \text{K1}) = \text{K1}) \wedge (\hat{x}_1 \neq \text{K1})$. This has the effect of generalizing away the predicate $\text{GT}(\hat{x}_1, \hat{x}_2)$. We omit the COI traversal details due to space constraints and because it is relatively straightforward: for each variable $\hat{x}'_i \in \text{Vars}'(\hat{s}')$, its next-state formula $f_i(X, Y)$ is traversed, collecting constraints required to satisfy the model. Then those constraints are used to form the pre-state cube.

EUFORIA's expansion procedure, given in Fig. 5, has two key properties: (1) it projects only onto constraints from $\hat{T}$ and (2) it exploits the fact that $\hat{T}$ represents each next-state relation as a function in order to perform a COI traversal on each next-state function $f_i(X, Y)$. This allows us to omit irrelevant state variables and constraints. Property (1) is important for guaranteeing termination and (2) is important for efficiency.

CTI expansion is common to many IC3-style checkers. CTIGAR [21] generalizes by examining the unsatisfiable core of a query that is unsatisfiable by construction: it asks whether a state has, under the same inputs, some other successor than the reached one [21]. EUFORIA can't use this method to generalize because such a query may be satisfiable over EUF (due to the non-deterministic nature of UFs). PDR performs generalization using ternary simulation at the bit level, which is not suitable for the word-level EUF abstract transition system. Other checkers have explored theory-specific generalization methods, such as for linear arithmetic [22,23] and for polyhedra [24]. Yet other checkers generalize by calculating the weakest precondition for the proof obligation [7,25]. Weakest preconditions (WP) are particularly problematic for EUF, as iterated applications of WP can cause EUF terms to grow arbitrarily large, leading to potential non-termination of EUF abstract reachability.

3.2   Refinement

When BACKWARDREACHABILITY finds an abstract counterexample, it must be checked for feasibility, potentially refining the abstract state space. An n-step abstract counterexample (ACX) is an execution $\widehat{A}_0 \xrightarrow{\widehat{T} \wedge \widehat{Y}_0} \widehat{A}_1 \xrightarrow{\widehat{T} \wedge \widehat{Y}_1} \cdots \xrightarrow{\widehat{T} \wedge \widehat{Y}_{n-2}}$ $\widehat{A}_{n-1} \xrightarrow{\widehat{T} \wedge \widehat{Y}_{n-1}} \widehat{A}_n$ where each $\widehat{A}_i$ ($0 \leq i \leq n$) is a state cube and $\widehat{Y}_i$ ($0 \leq i < n$) is a cube constraining input variables. An abstract formula $\widehat{\sigma}$ is *feasible* if its concretization σ is satisfiable over QF_BV. The ACX is spurious for any of the following reasons:

1. A_i is infeasible for some i, i.e., there are no concrete states that correspond to the abstract state cube $\widehat{A}_i$; or
2. $A_{i-1} \wedge Y_{i-1} \wedge T \wedge A_i$ is unsatisfiable for some i, i.e., there are no concrete transitions that correspond to the abstract state transition; or
3. the concretized counterexample is discontinuous. This will happen if all concretized cubes and transitions are feasible but the transitions "land" on distinct concrete states in a concretized cube. Below, the circles represent concrete cubes and the dots represent concrete states:

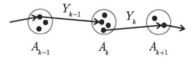

Figure 6 shows EUFORIA's refinement algorithm. REFINECOUNTEREXAMPLE first performs feasibility checks on individual transitions to address reasons 1 and 2 (Fig. 6a, lines 1–8), afterward performing symbolic simulation on the counterexample path to address reason 3 (Fig. 6b). If the counterexample is spurious, one of these feasibility checks will find an unsatisfiable subset of constraints. LEARN-LEMMA creates a *refinement lemma* by abstracting the unsatisfiable subset and asserting its negation in $\widehat{T}$.

The details of forward refinement are fiddly but the idea is simple: to determine if the counterexample is feasible, symbolically simulate the program along the concretized counterexample path. Beginning in the initial state, our implementation iteratively computes the next state in a manner reminiscent of image computation in BDD-based symbolic model checking. Note that there is no path explosion during this process because we only follow the path denoted by the concrete counterexample. If a contradiction is reached, then an unsatisfiable subset is found and used to learn a lemma.

Specifically, REFINEFORWARD (Fig. 6b) represents a symbolic state s_i as a pair $\langle v_i, pc_i \rangle$ where v_i represents a map of state variables to values, and pc_i is the path constraint represented as a set of cubes. One transition at a time, it asks whether the next transition in the abstract counterexample is concretely feasible. If it is, SIMULATE (Fig. 6c) computes the next state symbolically, in two steps: (1) updating variable assignments by symbolically evaluating each next-state function in T (as was done during cube expansion, Sect. 3.1), (2) updating the path constraint with any new input constraints, and (3) uniquely renaming all

REFINECOUNTEREXAMPLE($\widehat{A_0} \xrightarrow{\widehat{T} \wedge \widehat{Y_0}} \widehat{A_1} \xrightarrow{\widehat{T} \wedge \widehat{Y_1}} \cdots \xrightarrow{\widehat{T} \wedge \widehat{Y_{n-2}}} \widehat{A_{n-1}} \xrightarrow{\widehat{T} \wedge \widehat{Y_{n-1}}} \widehat{A_n}$):

1: **if** $n = 1$ **then**
2:     **if** A_0 is UNSAT, with unsat core c **then**   ▷ check for 0-step counterexample
3:         LEARNLEMMA(c)
4:         **return** false
5: **for** $i \in \{1, 2, 3, \ldots, n\}$ **do**   ▷ test cubes and transitions
6:     **if** $A_{i-1} \wedge T \wedge Y_{i-1} \wedge A_i$ is UNSAT, with unsat core c **then**
7:         LEARNLEMMA(c)
8:         **return** false
9: **return** REFINEFORWARD()

(a) Refinement entry point

REFINEFORWARD() :

1: **if** $I \wedge A_0$ is UNSAT, with unsat core c **then**   ▷ check initial state
2:     LEARNLEMMA(c)
3:     **return** false
4: $s_1 \leftarrow \langle$ concrete assignment for each state variable, $\{\}\rangle$
5: **for** $i \in \{2, 3, \ldots, n\}$ **do**   ▷ test cubes and transitions
6:     **if** $v_{i-1} \wedge pc_{i-1} \wedge T \wedge Y_{i-1} \wedge A_i'$ is UNSAT, with unsat core c **then**
7:         LEARNLEMMA(c)
8:         **return** false
9:     $s_i \leftarrow$ SIMULATE($M, s_{i-1}, T, Y_{i-1}, A_i$)   ▷ M is the model for the query
10: **return** true   ▷ feasible counterexample

(b) Symbolically simulate counterexample

SIMULATE($M, \langle v_{i-1}, pc_{i-1}\rangle, T, Y_{i-1}, A_i$) :

1: $v \leftarrow$ empty map
2: **for** $x_i \in X$ **do**
3:     update v with value $f_i[X/v_{i-1}] \downarrow M$ ▷ substitute last values, simplify with M
4: $pc \leftarrow Y_{i-1} \cup \{l[X/v] \mid l \in A_i$ and $l[X/v]$ contains inputs$\}$
5: **return** $\langle$RENAMEINPUTS(v), RENAMEINPUTS(pc)$\rangle$

(c) Steps a symbolic state $s_{i-1} = \langle v_{i-1}, pc_{i-1}\rangle$ forward one step by updating values (v) and path constraint (pc) using T

LEARNLEMMA(c) :

1: $\widehat{c} \leftarrow$ ABSTRACTANDNORMALIZE(c)   ▷ abstract and eliminate input variables
2: **if** c contains no inputs **then**
3:     **if** VARS(c) $\subseteq X$ **then**   ▷ only present-state vars
4:         Simplify and add lemma $\neg\widehat{c}(\widehat{X'})$
5:     **if** VARS(c) $\subseteq X'$ **then**   ▷ only next-state vars
6:         Simplify and add lemma $\neg\widehat{c}(\widehat{X})$
7: Simplify and add lemma $\neg\widehat{c}$

(d) Learns a lemma by abstracting the concrete core c and conjoining $\widehat{c}$ to $\widehat{T}$

Fig. 6. EUFORIA's refinement procedure, REFINECOUNTEREXAMPLE

input variables. The notation $f_i[X/v_{i-1}]$ denotes the simultaneous substitution of state variables in X for their values from v_{i-1} in f_i. For a formula g with model M, $g \downarrow M$ simplifies g to a literal (by removing any complex Boolean logic) using the model M, similar to our COI procedure (see Sect. 3.1).

As we have said, the symbolic formula created by this process represents a single execution path through the program being analyzed, with inputs remaining symbolic. If this formula is found to be unsatisfiable, then it is desirable to find an equivalent formula without symbolic input variables. A full-fledged quantifier elimination procedure is computationally expensive. Instead, LEARN-LEMMA (Fig. 6d) calls ABSTRACTANDNORMALIZE, which (1) performs some simple equality propagation (which often will eliminate the inputs) and (2) otherwise under-approximates by substituting for each input variable the last concrete value that was assigned during symbolic simulation.

EUFORIA's refinement lemmas fall into two categories: (1) *one-step lemmas* learned during individual transition checks (lines 1–8 in Fig. 6a); and (2) *forward lemmas* learned during the symbolic simulation of the concrete counterexample (Fig. 6b). The key fact is that one-step lemmas *do not increase* the size of the abstract state space; they merely constrain existing terms, similar to a blocking clause in IC3. One-step lemmas constrain the behavior of uninterpreted objects to be consistent with their concrete semantics, i.e., partially interpreting the uninterpreted operations. Forward lemmas, on the other hand, increase the size of the abstract state space, similar to predicates added by refinement in predicate abstraction.

There are many options for performing feasibility checks and deriving suitable refinements from them if one or more of them fail (e.g., [26–28]). We chose this refinement procedure because our focus is on assessing the suitability of EUF abstraction for control properties, and because it's simple.

3.3   Proof of Correctness

First, we prove that reachability for EUF transition systems terminates. Second, we show that EUFORIA's refinement will increase the fidelity of the abstract system until it represents all concrete states exactly. Since the concrete system is finite, EUFORIA must eventually terminate.

Theorem 1. BACKWARDREACHABILITY *terminates with an answer of* true *or* false.

Proof. Our proof relies on two facts: (1) the number of models for an abstract transition system is finite and (2) EUFORIA searches among these models only, eventually blocking all of them or producing an abstract counterexample.

The set of possible models for a given abstract transition system $\hat{T}$ is finite. In fact, if the system has k Boolean state variables and n terms, then the number of Herbrand models is bounded by $2^k \cdot B_n$, where 2^k is the number of possible Boolean assignments to k Boolean variables and $B_n = \sum_{i=0}^{n} S(n, i)$ is the number of ways to partition n objects into disjoint sets (the Bell number). $S(n, i)$

is the number of ways to partition a set of n objects into i non-empty subsets (Stirling number of the second kind).

EUFORIA's preimage generalization procedure, EXPANDPREIMAGE (Fig. 5), searches only among this bounded set of models, since it explicitly uses only terms from $\widehat{T}$ to construct its preimage cube. If a cube is subsequently blocked by GENERALIZEBLOCKEDCUBE (Fig. 4), those models will be infeasible. As there are finitely many models and frames, eventually all cubes will be blocked and BACKWARDREACHABILITY will terminate.

Theorem 2. EUFORIA*'s refinement procedure increases the fidelity of the abstract transition system (ATS), up to expressing all concrete* QF_BV *behavior.*

Proof. One-step lemmas do increase the fidelity of the ATS but do not increase the number of terms in the ATS. REFINEFORWARD may increase the number of terms in the ATS, resulting in an increased state space. If the state space size could grow without bound, EUFORIA would potentially not terminate.

We first show that we can guarantee termination by using a refinement method simpler than REFINEFORWARD. This method learns a lemma from a single concrete path. Recall that an n-step abstract counterexample is an execution $\widehat{A}_0 \xrightarrow{\widehat{T} \wedge \widehat{Y}_0} \widehat{A}_1 \xrightarrow{\widehat{T} \wedge \widehat{Y}_1} \cdots \xrightarrow{\widehat{T} \wedge \widehat{Y}_{n-2}} \widehat{A}_{n-1} \xrightarrow{\widehat{T} \wedge \widehat{Y}_{n-1}} \widehat{A}_n$ where each $\widehat{A}_i$ is an abstract state cube $(0 \leq i \leq n)$ and $\widehat{Y}_i$ is an abstract formula constraining input variables $(0 \leq i < n)$. Beginning in any single state $\sigma_0 \in A_1 \wedge I$, for all $1 \leq i \leq n$,

1. Check whether $\sigma_{i-1} \wedge T \wedge Y_{i-1} \wedge A_i'$ is satisfiable.
2. If so, form new state σ_i using the concrete assignments to all variables X'
3. If not, call LEARNLEMMA(c) where c is the unsat subset of the query (1.)

When step 1 is not satisfiable, this procedure will introduce *a new abstract constant* (from state σ_{i-1}) and *a new abstract UF/UP constraint* (due to the transition to A_i') on that constant. The number of constants is bounded by the size of bit vector words in the concrete transition system and the number of constraints is as well (up to modeling every concrete behavior of every UF/UP in the program).

REFINEFORWARD (Sect. 3.2) is essentially the same as this procedure, except REFINEFORWARD attempts to generate stronger lemmas that refute multiple spurious concrete paths at once.

4   Evaluation

EUFORIA is implemented in 13,700 lines of C++. It uses LLVM 5.0.1 as front-end for processing C programs, running various optimizations including inlining, dead code elimination, and promoting memory to registers. It uses Z3 4.5.0 [29] for EUF solving during backward reachability and Boolector 2.0 [30] for QF_BV solving during refinement. EUFORIA cannot yet process programs with memory allocation or recursion. EUFORIA also assumes that C programs do not exhibit undefined behavior (signed overflow, buffer overflow, etc.), and may give incorrect results if the input program is ill-defined.

We evaluated EUFORIA on 752 benchmarks containing safety property assertions from the SV-COMP'17 competition [31]. 516 are safe and 236 are unsafe. We ran all the benchmarks on 2.6 GHz Intel Sandy Bridge (Xeon E5-2670) machines with 2 sockets, 8 cores with 64 GB RAM. Each benchmark was assigned to one socket during execution and was given a one hour timeout. All the benchmarks are C programs in the ReachSafety-ControlFlow, ReachSafety-Loops, and ReachSafety-ECA sets. Although these sets contain 1,451 total benchmarks, we elided all the benchmarks that use pointers or arrays, as well as those that took more than 30 s to pre-process.[2] Some static characteristics of these benchmarks are presented in Fig. 7.

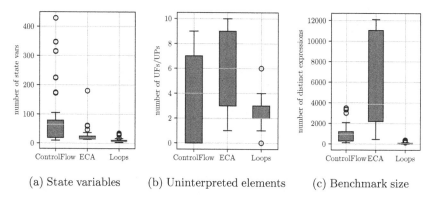

(a) State variables   (b) Uninterpreted elements   (c) Benchmark size

Fig. 7. Traditional box plots showing quartile ranges and outliers for all benchmark. Plot (a) shows that the ControlFlow class contains the instances with the most state variables. The y axis of plot (c) is the number of distinct expressions in $\widehat{T}$, indicating that the ECA instances can be huge. In particular, the ECA benchmarks are on average the largest-size benchmarks; followed by ControlFlow, followed by Loops.

We evaluated EUFORIA against IC3IA [10], an IC3-based checker that implements implicit predicate abstraction. We chose IC3IA largely because it is similar to EUFORIA, with one essential difference: it uses predicate abstraction instead of EUF abstraction. Moreover, as pointed out by Cimatti *et al.* [10], IC3IA is superior in performance to state-of-the-art bit-level IC3 implementations as well as other IC3-Modulo-Theories implementations; and it can support hundreds of predicates (around an order of magnitude more than what explicit predicate abstraction tools can practically compute). In order to ensure an apples-to-apples comparison, we run IC3IA on the exact same model checking problem as EUFORIA,

---

[2] Note that this is *pre-processing* time, which is the time to optimize and encode the instances. The instances that take more than 30 s to preprocess are multi-megabyte source files that come from the ECA set. They are so big that they time out on both checkers, so we excluded them from our evaluation.

by dumping the model checking instance (transition system and property encoding) into a vmt[3] file, which is readable by IC3IA. Currently, EUFORIA only supports LLVM bitcode as input, so our runtime numbers for EUFORIA include the time it takes to re-encode the transition system and property, but IC3IA does not need to do this; thus EUFORIA's numbers are slightly higher than they could be (up to 30 s).

Our evaluation sought answers to the following questions:

1. When EUFORIA performs relatively well, why?
2. When EUFORIA performs relatively poorly, why?
3. Does EUFORIA require more clauses than IC3IA to accomplish verification?
4. How does convergence depth compare?

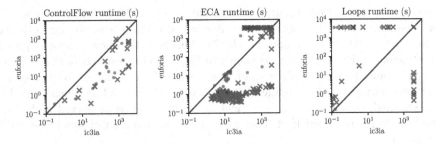

Fig. 8. Scatter plot of runtimes broken down by benchmark set. Timeout was set to one hour. Safe benchmarks show with green dots, unsafe with blue x's. (Color figure online)

Figure 8 shows our overall results on all benchmarks compared with IC3IA. EUFORIA and IC3IA are to a certain extent complementary in what they are able to solve within the timeout. IC3IA uniquely solves 62 benchmarks (17 from Loops and 45 from ECA, none from ControlFlow); all of these benchmark properties are about arithmetic and EUFORIA gets stuck inferring weak refinement lemmas. The properties involve things like proving sorting; complex state updates involving division, multiplication, and addition; and invariants involving relationships between addition and signed/unsigned integer comparison. These are benchmarks expected to be tough for EUFORIA, since we have explicitly abstracted these operations in order to target control properties. We believe this weakness can be addressed through a refinement algorithm that infers lemmas related to arithmetic facts, such as commutativity or monotonicity. These benchmarks help address research question 2.

EUFORIA's *uniquely solved benchmarks* EUFORIA uniquely solves 26 benchmarks; these cut across the benchmark sets: 9 in Loops, 5 ControlFlow, and 12 ECA. EUFORIA is on average spending only 13 s in refinement on these benchmarks, compared to 767 for IC3IA:

---

[3] https://es-static.fbk.eu/tools/nuxmv/index.php?n=Languages.VMT.

Refinement times on uniquely solved benchmarks

	EUFORIA	IC3IA (timeout)		EUFORIA (timeout)	IC3IA
average	12.98	766.57	average	937.65	154.27
median	0.11	135.95	median	975.41	81.59

On the ControlFlow set (which fits our property target best), EUFORIA solves 5 unique benchmarks and IC3IA solved no uniques. The ControlFlow benchmarks have the most state variables, moderate UF/UP use, and are medium-sized. Moreover, EUFORIA requires very little refinement time, supporting our hypothesis that EUFORIA's EUF abstraction provides a decent means for targeting control properties.

Benchmarks both solved. Figure 9 shows that, of the 249 benchmarks for which *both* checkers terminated, EUFORIA is able to solve the overwhelming majority faster than IC3IA. Surprisingly, nearly 200 benchmarks among these required no refinements from EUFORIA, as shown in Fig. 10. This result is perhaps unexpected because EUFORIA's abstraction removes nearly all behavior from program operators, suggesting that refinement is likely necessary. While much behavior is abstracted, equality, which is critical for verification, is preserved and some benchmarks simply need EUF reasoning (i.e., functional consistency), as we'll see shortly.

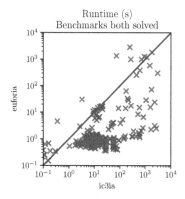

Fig. 9. Runtime of EUFORIA and IC3IA on 249 benchmarks for which both checkers terminated within an hour. EUFORIA solves most instances more quickly than IC3IA.

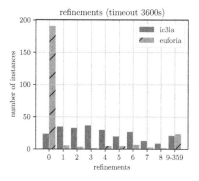

Fig. 10. Number of instances grouped by how many refinements were required to solve them, on benchmarks both checkers finished. The key take away is that EUFORIA is able to solve many instances with very few refinements.

It is interesting that for some relatively simple arithmetic benchmarks, IC3IA diverges and EUFORIA converges. IC3IA begins inferring predicates like ($k =$

$0), (k = 1), (k = 2), \ldots$ as well as $(1 < j), (2 < j), (3 < j), \ldots$ and will continue this until exhausting all possible values (on 32 bits). A sample program is shown below:

$$k = i = 0$$
while $i < n$ **do** $\triangleright k = i$ is invariant
$\quad i \leftarrow i + 1; \; k \leftarrow k + 1$
$j \leftarrow n$ $\triangleright k = j = n$
while $j > 0$ **do** $\triangleright k = j$ is invariant
$\quad \text{assert}(k > 0)$
$\quad j \leftarrow j - 1; \; k \leftarrow k - 1$

The second while loop's assertion holds because of the relatively simple property that $(k = j \land j > 0) \rightarrow (k > 0)$, which also holds in EUF. IC3IA was unable to discover the relevant predicates, underscoring that choice of predicates is crucial for predicate abstraction. Several other benchmarks follow a similar pattern.

We hypothesize that EUFORIA can take advantage of certain structure from the ControlFlow benchmarks. For example, many of the benchmarks implement a state machine that records its state in an integer state variable. Our abstraction will keep state machine states distinct, since equality is interpreted and integer terms are kept distinct. IC3IA on the other hand must learn predicates such as $(s = 4)$, $(s = 5)$, in order to reason about which state the state machine is in. Indeed, *all* predicates that IC3IA learns on this benchmark set are of the form $(x = y)$ where x is a state variable and y is a constant or a variable; in other words, it learns no predicates besides simple equalities that EUFORIA preserves intrinsically.

There are several other factors contributing to EUFORIA's relatively low runtime on these benchmarks. EUFORIA's SMT queries are roughly an order of magnitude faster than IC3IA's, due to the fact that it is reasoning using EUF and not bit vectors. EUFORIA's effort spent per lemma is consistently lower than IC3IA's effort spent per predicate: the time spent generating each new lemma is up to 10x faster than IC3IA. IC3IA performs bounded model checking on the concrete system to extract an interpolant to generate new predicates, which is more expensive than our approach of examining a single error path and finding an unsatisfiable constraint. For larger transition relations, the difference between query times increases steadily, and the performance advantage of EUFORIA's EUF reasoning becomes more evident. This difference comes out in driver benchmarks which implement several state machines at once. EUFORIA solves these benchmarks one or two orders of magnitude faster than IC3IA and finds smaller invariants. Both checkers refine similarly (i.e., number of refinement lemmas/predicates introduced is comparable) but EUFORIA exploits that information much more effectively, as evidenced by IC3IA requiring roughly an order of magnitude more blocking cubes than EUFORIA.

An interesting outcome of these experiments is that the vast majority of EUFORIA's refinement lemmas are one-step lemmas that merely constrain the behavior of the UFs and UPs in the abstract transition system. In contrast, every new predicate that is introduced by IC3IA doubles the size of the state space (i.e., it goes from size 2^n to 2^{n+1} when increasing the number of predicates from n to $n+1$).

Figure 11 shows the number of cubes blocked (i.e., clauses added) during solving. Generally, EUFORIA is able to complete with fewer blocked cubes than IC3IA, addressing research question 3.

We hypothesized that EUFORIA, due to its abstraction, may require fewer frames to converge than IC3IA; this is why we asked research question 4. Figure 12 shows the termination depths of EUFORIA and IC3IA. Generally, the termination depths of both checkers are comparable.

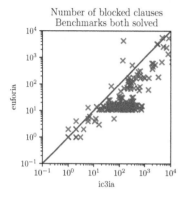

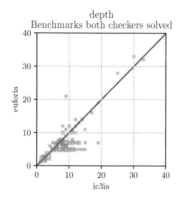

Fig. 11. Number of blocked clauses during solving for all benchmarks solved by EUFORIA and IC3IA. Overall, EUFORIA seems to add fewer cubes.

Fig. 12. Frame depth after convergence for both EUFORIA and IC3IA. The area of the squares is proportional to the number of different benchmarks terminating at the given depths.

Overall, EUFORIA performs well on benchmarks testing control properties. In aggregate, EUFORIA solved 275 out of 752 and timed out on 477. IC3IA solved 311 and timed out on 441.

5   Related Work

Since IC3's advent in 2011 [19], applications and extensions of the basic algorithm have flourished. Cimatti and Griggio [22] and Hoder and Bjørner [23] presented the first software model checkers built in IC3 style. More germane for this paper is how abstraction has been applied in IC3-style solvers. SPACER [32] is implemented in IC3 style using a Horn clause solver and linear rational arithmetic. It abstracts programs by dropping elements of the transition relation; it's a kind of generic abstraction support, but expressing EUF abstraction under such a model would require a significant amount of extra constraints (to encode functional consistency). IC3 has been adapted to use predicate abstraction, with a couple of different refinement schemes. CTIGAR's [21] refinement is triggered by individual queries during backward reachability. IC3IA's [10] refinement is triggered whenever an abstract counterexample is found and uses interpolation to derive new predicates. Bjørner and Gurfinkel [33] integrated polyhedral abstract interpretation with IC3 to compute safe convex polyhedral invariants. Our work abstracts using EUF, which is a different mechanism from each of these, and is bit-precise in its concrete representation.

Burch and Dill [18] introduced the use of EUF for pipelined microprocessor verification. For software, Babić and Hu [34,35] implemented Calysto, a CEGAR abstraction that uses EUF to abstract away internal function bodies. Calysto computes verification conditions (VCs) and function summaries for all the functions in the program. If the abstraction is too coarse to establish the property, Calysto finds abstract summaries that are responsible for the spurious counterexample, and refines them by removing EUF terms and making them bit-precise. Our refinement differs in that refinement lemmas are lifted to EUF instead of certain EUF terms becoming bit-precise; moreover, we do not unroll loops, as Calysto does.

EUF abstraction has been studied extensively, especially for translation validation and equivalence checking, but not for IC3/PDR applied to checking safety properties; see [12] for further discussion of EUF abstraction. Similar techniques to ours were developed by Andraus [36] for hardware verification, particularly using uninterpreted functions for abstracting wide datapaths. In the context of hardware model checking, Ho et al. [37] abstract difficult operations by turning them into inputs; they then use EUF to perform refinement of these previously-abstracted operations. Our work applies directly to software and abstracts uniformly in order to effectively target control properties.

Predicate abstraction [5] is the dominant technique in control property verification, e.g., as used in the tools SLAM [3], BLAST [28], and IC3IA [10]. SLAM's approach is to abstract the program into a program on Boolean variables alone, which preserves control and abstracts data with respect to a set of predicates. SLAM checks its Boolean program with pushdown techniques using Binary Decision Diagrams (BDDs). BLAST improves the SLAM scheme; it uses interpolants to discover relevant predicates locally and these predicates are only kept track of in the parts of the abstract state space where spurious counterexamples occurred. SLAM requires an exponential number of calls to the theorem prover in the worst case (or an approximation to the abstraction [38]). IMPACT demonstrated how to implicitly compute the predicate abstraction, to avoid this cost [39]. EUF abstraction is nearly "free" in that it does not require any calls to a theorem prover. Moreover, our approach directly abstracts operations as well as predicates, because we are targeting control properties.

Abstraction in general has been employed extensively to address verification complexity [9,40–42]. Counterexample-Guided Abstraction Refinement (CEGAR) was introduced by Kurshan [8] and refined and generalized by Clarke et al. [9].

6 Conclusions and Future Work

We presented an approach for the automatic verification of safety properties of programs using EUF abstraction. Our approach targets control properties by abstracting operations and predicates but leaving a program's control flow structure intact. EUF abstraction is syntactic; it preserves the structure of the concrete transition system and can be computed in linear time. We have integrated it with modern incremental inductive solving and proved that it terminates by producing a word-level inductive invariant demonstrating safety or a true concrete-level counterexample.

Our evaluation shows that EUFORIA is particularly effective on control-oriented benchmarks. In many cases EUFORIA completes without requiring any refinements even in the presence of arithmetic operations. In cases where refinement is required, most refinement lemmas are simply constraints on the abstract transition system that do not increase the size of the state space. This suggests that EUF abstraction is a natural over-approximation of program behavior when data state is mostly irrelevant to establishing the truth or falsehood of the desired safety property.

Going forward, we plan to demonstrate EUFORIA on larger and more diverse benchmarks. This requires modification to its front-end to add support for program constructs such as pointers and arrays, as well as modification to the back-end to support more efficient checking. We also plan to explore how to leverage loop identification inside the EUFORIA algorithm, specifically during refinement to find concrete counterexamples longer than the abstract counterexamples.

Some control properties require reasoning about relatively small amounts of data operations. Often, specific code fragments in a program are critical for verifying the property. It may be beneficial in these situations to modify the refinement procedure so that such fragments are *concretized* to avoid generating a large number of refinement lemmas.

During development, we noticed that the front-end is at times generating code that is sub-optimal for verification. We found a simple example that contains one state variable, and uses only assignments of constants and equality tests against constants. The property requires only equality reasoning and thus should not trigger any refinement. Nevertheless, LLVM's optimizer transforms this into code that uses a subtraction, and verifying the property requires a refinement. Moreover, recent work [43] has elucidated some drawbacks of static single assignment (SSA) form, specifically in its name management and input/output asymmetry. Besides complicating EUFORIA's encoder implementation, our SSA-based encoding introduces more state variables and leads to less understandable verification lemmas. Future work will explore using alternative front-ends tailored for verification.

Acknowledgements. We would like to thank Arlen Cox, Shelley Leger, Geoff Reedy, Doug Ghormley, Sean Weaver, Marijn Heule, and the anonymous reviewers for their incisive comments on previous drafts. Supported by the Laboratory Directed Research and Development program at Sandia National Laboratories, a multi-mission laboratory managed and operated by National Technology and Engineering Solutions of Sandia, LLC, a wholly owned subsidiary of Honeywell International, Inc., for the U.S. Department of Energy's National Nuclear Security Administration under contract DE-NA0003525.

References

1. Langley, A.: Apple's SSL/TLS bug (2014). https://www.imperialviolet.org/2014/02/22/applebug.html. Accessed 28 Sept 2018
2. Chen, H., Wagner, D.A.: MOPS: an infrastructure for examining security properties of software. In: Atluri, V. (ed.) Conference on Computer and Communications Security, pp. 235–244. ACM (2002). https://doi.org/10.1145/586110.586142
3. Ball, T., Rajamani, S.K.: The SLAM project: debugging system software via static analysis. In: Launchbury, J., Mitchell, J.C. (eds.) Symposium on Principles of Programming Languages, pp. 1–3. ACM (2002)
4. Strom, R.E., Yemini, S.: Typestate: a programming language concept for enhancing software reliability. IEEE Trans. Softw. Eng. **12**(1), 157–171 (1986). https://doi.org/10.1109/TSE.1986.6312929
5. Graf, S., Saidi, H.: Construction of abstract state graphs with PVS. In: Grumberg, O. (ed.) CAV 1997. LNCS, vol. 1254, pp. 72–83. Springer, Heidelberg (1997). https://doi.org/10.1007/3-540-63166-6_10
6. D'Silva, V., Kroening, D., Weissenbacher, G.: A survey of automated techniques for formal software verification. IEEE Trans. CAD Integr. Circ. Syst. **27**(7), 1165–1178 (2008)
7. Lee, S., Sakallah, K.A.: Unbounded scalable verification based on approximate property-directed reachability and datapath abstraction. In: Biere, A., Bloem, R. (eds.) CAV 2014. LNCS, vol. 8559, pp. 849–865. Springer, Cham (2014). https://doi.org/10.1007/978-3-319-08867-9_56
8. Kurshan, R.P.: Computer-aided Verification of Coordinating Processes: The Automata-theoretic Approach. Princeton University Press, Princeton (1994)
9. Clarke, E., Grumberg, O., Jha, S., Lu, Y., Veith, H.: Counterexample-guided abstraction refinement. In: Emerson, E.A., Sistla, A.P. (eds.) CAV 2000. LNCS, vol. 1855, pp. 154–169. Springer, Heidelberg (2000). https://doi.org/10.1007/10722167_15
10. Cimatti, A., Griggio, A., Mover, S., Tonetta, S.: IC3 modulo theories via implicit predicate abstraction. In: Ábrahám, E., Havelund, K. (eds.) TACAS 2014. LNCS, vol. 8413, pp. 46–61. Springer, Heidelberg (2014). https://doi.org/10.1007/978-3-642-54862-8_4
11. Kesten, Y., Pnueli, A.: Control and data abstraction: the cornerstones of practical formal verification. STTT **2**(4), 328–342 (2000). https://doi.org/10.1007/s100090050040
12. Kroening, D., Strichman, O.: Decision procedures - an algorithmic point of view. Texts in Theoretical Computer Science. An EATCS Series. Springer, Heidelberg (2008). https://doi.org/10.1007/978-3-540-74105-3
13. Clarke, E.M., Grumberg, O., Long, D.E.: Model checking and abstraction. ACM Trans. Program. Lang. Syst. **16**(5), 1512–1542 (1994)
14. Bradley, A.R., Manna, Z.: Checking safety by inductive generalization of counterexamples to induction. In: Formal Methods in Computer-Aided Design, pp. 173–180. IEEE Computer Society (2007)

15. Barrett, C., Stump, A., Tinelli, C.: The SMT-LIB standard: Version 2.0. In: Gupta, A., Kroening, D. (eds.) Workshop on Satisfiability Modulo Theories (2010)
16. Manna, Z., Pnueli, A.: Temporal Verification of Reactive Systems - Safety. Springer, Heidelberg (1995). https://doi.org/10.1007/978-3-540-74105-3
17. Beyer, D., Keremoglu, M.E., Wendler, P.: Predicate abstraction with adjustable-block encoding. In: Bloem, R., Sharygina, N. (eds.) Proceedings of International Conference on Formal Methods in Computer-Aided Design, pp. 189–197. IEEE (2010). http://ieeexplore.ieee.org/document/5770949/
18. Burch, J.R., Dill, D.L.: Automatic verification of pipelined microprocessor control. In: Dill, D.L. (ed.) CAV 1994. LNCS, vol. 818, pp. 68–80. Springer, Heidelberg (1994). https://doi.org/10.1007/3-540-58179-0_44
19. Bradley, A.R.: SAT-based model checking without unrolling. In: Jhala, R., Schmidt, D. (eds.) VMCAI 2011. LNCS, vol. 6538, pp. 70–87. Springer, Heidelberg (2011). https://doi.org/10.1007/978-3-642-18275-4_7
20. Een, N., Mishchenko, A., Brayton, R.: Efficient implementation of property directed reachability. In: Formal Methods in Computer-Aided Design, pp. 125–134. IEEE (2011)
21. Birgmeier, J., Bradley, A.R., Weissenbacher, G.: Counterexample to induction-guided abstraction-refinement (CTIGAR). In: Biere, A., Bloem, R. (eds.) CAV 2014. LNCS, vol. 8559, pp. 831–848. Springer, Cham (2014). https://doi.org/10.1007/978-3-319-08867-9_55
22. Cimatti, A., Griggio, A.: Software model checking via IC3. In: Madhusudan, P., Seshia, S.A. (eds.) CAV 2012. LNCS, vol. 7358, pp. 277–293. Springer, Heidelberg (2012). https://doi.org/10.1007/978-3-642-31424-7_23
23. Hoder, K., Bjørner, N.: Generalized property directed reachability. In: Cimatti, A., Sebastiani, R. (eds.) SAT 2012. LNCS, vol. 7317, pp. 157–171. Springer, Heidelberg (2012). https://doi.org/10.1007/978-3-642-31612-8_13
24. Welp, T., Kuehlmann, A.: QF_BV model checking with property directed reachability. In: Macii, E. (ed.) Design, Automation and Test, pp. 791–796. ACM DL, EDA Consortium, San Jose (2013)
25. Lange, T., Neuhäußer, M.R., Noll, T.: IC3 software model checking on control flow automata. In: Kaivola, R., Wahl, T. (eds.) Formal Methods in Computer-Aided Design, pp. 97–104. IEEE (2015)
26. Kroening, D., Groce, A., Clarke, E.: Counterexample guided abstraction refinement via program execution. In: Davies, J., Schulte, W., Barnett, M. (eds.) ICFEM 2004. LNCS, vol. 3308, pp. 224–238. Springer, Heidelberg (2004). https://doi.org/10.1007/978-3-540-30482-1_23
27. Ball, T., Bounimova, E., Kumar, R., Levin, V.: SLAM2: static driver verification with under 4% false alarms. In: Bloem, R., Sharygina, N. (eds.) Proceedings of International Conference on Formal Methods in Computer-Aided Design, pp. 35–42. IEEE (2010)
28. Henzinger, T.A., Jhala, R., Majumdar, R., Sutre, G.: Software verification with BLAST. In: Ball, T., Rajamani, S.K. (eds.) SPIN 2003. LNCS, vol. 2648, pp. 235–239. Springer, Heidelberg (2003). https://doi.org/10.1007/3-540-44829-2_17
29. de Moura, L., Bjørner, N.: Z3: an efficient SMT solver. In: Ramakrishnan, C.R., Rehof, J. (eds.) TACAS 2008. LNCS, vol. 4963, pp. 337–340. Springer, Heidelberg (2008). https://doi.org/10.1007/978-3-540-78800-3_24
30. Niemetz, A., Preiner, M., Biere, A.: Boolector 2.0 system description. J. Satisfiability Boolean Model. Comput. 9, 53–58 (2014)

31. Beyer, D.: Software verification with validation of results. In: Legay, A., Margaria, T. (eds.) TACAS 2017. LNCS, vol. 10206, pp. 331–349. Springer, Heidelberg (2017). https://doi.org/10.1007/978-3-662-54580-5_20

32. Komuravelli, A., Gurfinkel, A., Chaki, S., Clarke, E.M.: Automatic abstraction in SMT-based unbounded software model checking. In: Sharygina, N., Veith, H. (eds.) CAV 2013. LNCS, vol. 8044, pp. 846–862. Springer, Heidelberg (2013). https://doi.org/10.1007/978-3-642-39799-8_59

33. Bjørner, N., Gurfinkel, A.: Property directed polyhedral abstraction. In: D'Souza, D., Lal, A., Larsen, K.G. (eds.) VMCAI 2015. LNCS, vol. 8931, pp. 263–281. Springer, Heidelberg (2015). https://doi.org/10.1007/978-3-662-46081-8_15

34. Babić, D., Hu, A.J.: Structural abstraction of software verification conditions. In: Damm, W., Hermanns, H. (eds.) CAV 2007. LNCS, vol. 4590, pp. 366–378. Springer, Heidelberg (2007). https://doi.org/10.1007/978-3-540-73368-3_41

35. Babić, D., Hu, A.J.: Calysto: scalable and precise extended static checking. In: Schäfer, W., Dwyer, M.B., Gruhn, V. (eds.) International Conference on Software Engineering, pp. 211–220. ACM (2008)

36. Andraus, Z.S., Liffiton, M.H., Sakallah, K.A.: Reveal: a formal verification tool for verilog designs. In: Cervesato, I., Veith, H., Voronkov, A. (eds.) LPAR 2008. LNCS (LNAI), vol. 5330, pp. 343–352. Springer, Heidelberg (2008). https://doi.org/10.1007/978-3-540-89439-1_25

37. Ho, Y., Mishchenko, A., Brayton, R.K.: Property directed reachability with word-level abstraction. In: Stewart, D., Weissenbacher, G. (eds.) Formal Methods in Computer Aided Design, pp. 132–139. IEEE (2017). https://doi.org/10.23919/FMCAD.2017.8102251

38. Ball, T., Podelski, A., Rajamani, S.K.: Boolean and cartesian abstraction for model checking C programs. In: Margaria, T., Yi, W. (eds.) TACAS 2001. LNCS, vol. 2031, pp. 268–283. Springer, Heidelberg (2001). https://doi.org/10.1007/3-540-45319-9_19

39. McMillan, K.L.: Lazy abstraction with interpolants. In: Ball, T., Jones, R.B. (eds.) CAV 2006. LNCS, vol. 4144, pp. 123–136. Springer, Heidelberg (2006). https://doi.org/10.1007/11817963_14

40. Andraus, Z.S., Liffiton, M.H., Sakallah, K.A.: CEGAR-based formal hardware verification: a case study. Ann Arbor, vol. 1001, pp. 48 109–2122 (2008)

41. Ball, T., Majumdar, R., Millstein, T., Rajamani, S.K.: Automatic predicate abstraction of C programs. In: Conference on Programming Language Design and Implementation, PLDI 2001, pp. 203–213. ACM, New York (2001)

42. McMillan, K.L., Amla, N.: Automatic abstraction without counterexamples. In: Garavel, H., Hatcliff, J. (eds.) TACAS 2003. LNCS, vol. 2619, pp. 2–17. Springer, Heidelberg (2003). https://doi.org/10.1007/3-540-36577-X_2

43. Gange, G., Navas, J.A., Schachte, P., Søndergaard, H., Stuckey, P.J.: Horn clauses as an intermediate representation for program analysis and transformation. In: TPLP, vol. 15, no. 4–5, pp. 526–542 (2015). https://doi.org/10.1017/S1471068415000204

Fast BGP Simulation of Large Datacenters

Nuno P. Lopes$^{(\boxtimes)}$ and Andrey Rybalchenko

Microsoft Research, Cambridge, UK
{nlopes,rybal}@microsoft.com

Abstract. Frequent configuration churn caused by maintenance, upgrades, hardware and firmware failures regularly leads to costly outages. Preventing network outages caused by misconfigurations is important for ensuring high network availability. Dealing with production datacenters with thousands of routers is a major challenge.

Network verification inspects the forwarding tables of routers. These tables are determined by the so-called control plane, which is given by the steady state of the routing protocols. The ability to simulate routing protocols given router configuration files and thus obtain the control plane is a key enabling technology.

In this paper, we present FASTPLANE, an efficient BGP simulator. BGP support is mandated by modern datacenter designs, which choose BGP as the routing protocol. The key to FASTPLANE's performance is our insight into the routing policy of cloud datacenters that allows the usage of a generalized Dijkstra's algorithm. The insight reveals that these networks are monotonic, i.e., route advertisements decrease preference when propagated through the network.

The evaluation on real world, production datacenters of a major cloud provider shows that FASTPLANE (1) is two orders of magnitude faster than the state-of-the-art on small and medium datacenters, and (2) goes beyond the state-of-the-art by scaling to large datacenters. FASTPLANE was instrumental in finding several production bugs in router firmware, routing policy, and network architecture.

1 Introduction

Preventing network outages caused by misconfigurations is important for ensuring high network availability. It is particularly relevant for public cloud infrastructures where an outage can affect thousands of customers [35].

Computing the network control plane is a crucial building block to prevent outages, as it consists of routing tables (RIBs) that determine network connectivity. These tables can be automatically inspected to check validity of configuration intents related to connectivity, as well as fault-tolerance and performance.

The ability to compute control planes from router configuration files and topology information enables static, dynamic, and design-time verification scenarios. Statically, i.e., before deploying a configuration into production, we first

© Springer Nature Switzerland AG 2019
C. Enea and R. Piskac (Eds.): VMCAI 2019, LNCS 11388, pp. 386–408, 2019.
https://doi.org/10.1007/978-3-030-11245-5_18

compute the control plane and verify its properties. If all checks pass, the configuration can be deployed with increased confidence. Some configuration intents can also be validated when the network is designed. For example, the computed control plane can demonstrate whether the required level of fault-tolerance and load-balancing is achievable. Unfortunately, static checks are not sufficient, due to bugs in router firmware. Hence there is a need for dynamic checking as well, i.e., once a configuration is already deployed. Cross-checking the computed control plane with the one from production routers can uncover firmware bugs.

Due to lack of adequate validation tools, frequent configuration churn in datacenter networks caused by maintenance, upgrades, hardware and firmware failures regularly leads to costly outages. Scaling control plane computation to thousands of datacenter routers and network prefixes is still an open problem [42].

In this paper we present FASTPLANE, a tool for fast BGP simulation of large datacenters. Support for BGP is mandated by best practices in modern datacenter design, where BGP runs on each router [6,31,32]. The key to FAST-PLANE's scalability is our insight into the routing policy that is revealed through a study of production configurations deployed by a major cloud provider. The insight shows that the network is monotonic, i.e., route advertisements decrease preference when propagated through the network [44]. It allows the deployment of a generalized form of Dijkstra's algorithm. FASTPLANE executes Dijkstra's algorithm over route advertisements instead of numeric path weights.

We adapt Dijkstra's algorithm to directly perform route advertisement propagation. Instead of numeric weight addition when traversing a graph edge, we apply routing policy determined by configuration files. The order of priority queue is no longer arithmetic comparison, but route preference order determined by BGP RFC/vendor specifications. The result corresponds to the control plane of the datacenter network once it reached a stable state [25].

We evaluated FASTPLANE on all production datacenters of a major cloud provider, and compared it with the state-of-the-art control plane verifier Batfish. For small and medium datacenters, FASTPLANE is two orders of magnitude faster than Batfish. For large datacenters, FASTPLANE finishes in a few minutes while Batfish either times out after one CPU week or runs out of memory.

Control planes computed by FASTPLANE exposed several bugs. A bug in the redistribution policy of connected routes was discovered by comparing computed RIBs with expected entries specified by network operators. This bug was fixed in production. A firmware bug that caused the RIB to contain different next-hops than the forwarding table was caught by cross-checking production against computed control planes. By similar cross-checking we also discovered a bug in high level routing architecture that causes a non-deterministic drop in fault-tolerance and load-balancing. Mitigation measures for this bug are underway.

In summary, we contribute a scalable algorithm for fast BGP simulation of datacenter networks. It exploits monotonicity of datacenter routing policy, from which we derive the applicability of a shortest path-based characterization of the control plane, yet, for the first time, expressed over route advertisements instead of numeric weights. Our implementation scales to large production datacenters, which are out of reach for the state-of-the-art.

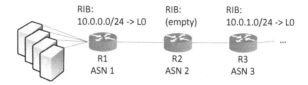

Fig. 1. Example network with three routers running BGP. We show the initial RIB of each router, i.e., before any information has been exchanged between neighbors.

```
! --------------- Router R1 ----------------------
interface Ethernet0               ! physical port connected to R2
  ip address 172.16.0.0/31

bgp router 1                      ! run BGP with ASN 1
  network 10.0.0.0/24             ! export prefix to neighbors
  neighbor 172.16.0.1 remote-as 2 ! peer with R2

! --------------- Router R2 ----------------------
interface Ethernet0               ! physical port connected to R1
  ip address 172.16.0.1/31

bgp router 2                      ! run BGP with ASN 2
  ! export prefix if any sub-prefix in RIB
  aggregate-address 10.0.0.0/16 summary-only
  neighbor 172.16.0.0 remote-as 1 ! peer with R1
  neighbor 172.16.0.3 remote-as 3 ! peer with R3
```

Fig. 2. Configuration fragments for routers R1 and R2 in Fig. 1. R1 exports the prefix used by directly connected servers. R2 aggregates and exports the prefix 10.0.0.0/16 whenever a more specific prefix exists in the RIB. At the same time, R2 blocks advertisement of the more specific prefixes.

2   Datacenters and BGP

Modern datacenter designs choose BGP as the routing protocol to compute RIBs [2,23,32]. By running BGP each datacenter router participates in a distributed best path computation, where information about the best paths is exchanged between direct neighbors. The cost metric is not, however, the number of hops in the path, but rather a lexicographic order of several path attributes.

Each router has an autonomous system number (ASN). ASNs are used to keep track of the path an advertisement has taken. Datacenter routers have different ASNs between layers such that external BGP (eBGP) is used.

We will now show how BGP propagates best path information. Figure 1 shows an example network with three routers and Fig. 2 shows fragments of two configuration files. RIBs are initialized with locally exported prefixes. For example, router R1 exports 10.0.0.0/24, and therefore this prefix is inserted in its RIB.

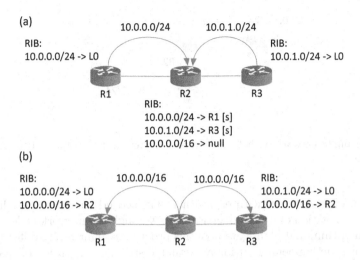

Fig. 3. Example of BGP running on the network of Fig. 1. [s] indicates a suppressed entry, which will not be advertised to the neighbors.

The second step of BGP is to continuously exchange information with neighbor routers about newly learnt prefixes and about prefixes that the router can no longer reach. In our example, R1 advertises 10.0.0.0/24 to R2 and, similarly, R3 advertises 10.0.1.0/24 to R2, as can be seen in Fig. 3(a). Since R2 does not block any advertisement from its neighbors, both of these prefixes are installed in the RIB of R2.

Router R2 has an "aggregate summary-only" command, which blocks any sub-prefix of 10.0.0.0/16 from being advertised to neighbors. Therefore, the prefixes received from R1 and R2 are marked with [s] in the RIB, meaning they are suppressed. Additionally, the aggregated prefix is installed in the RIB.

Router R2 then advertises the new entries in its RIB to its neighbors, as shown in Fig. 3(b). The only new non-suppressed entry is 10.0.0.0/16 and it is sent to both neighbors, which install it in their RIBs.

As a final step, routers R1 and R3 try to advertise the new prefix to their neighbor (R2), but since this prefix was sent to them by R2 and BGP does not send a prefix back to the router that advertised it, routers R1 and R3 do not advertise anything further. Therefore, the RIBs in Fig. 3(b) are the stable state of the network and no further communication occurs until some RIB changes.

Although we have presented the execution of BGP as a sequence of steps, the protocol does not run in a synchronous way: advertisements can be sent in any order.

3   Illustration

In this section we illustrate several key aspects of our algorithm. The first example introduces the algorithm through a simple step-by-step run and shows how

Fig. 4. Example network with four routers and prefixes they export. R2 aggregates 10.0.0.0/16.

different prefixes interact with each other. The second one focuses on how the order of propagation of route advertisements through the network is determined by our algorithm, and highlights how this order is fundamentally different from the propagation happening during an actual, distributed execution of BGP. The last example shows that preference decrease across route advertisement is a necessary condition, as otherwise our algorithm fails to compute a correct answer.

For each example we assume that a router named Ri is configured to have the AS number i and they run eBGP.

3.1   Prefix Interaction

First we show how our algorithm computes routing tables for the example network of Fig. 4.

Each router R1, R3, and R4 exports a single prefix. Router R2 aggregates sub-prefixes of 10.0.0.0/16. This prefix is initially not exported by R2 because R2 has no sub-prefix in its RIB to trigger the aggregation.

In the first step of the algorithm, we collect all seed advertisements, i.e., all advertisements that routers in the network export on their own. In this example, we have three such advertisements that we will represent as tuples ($router, prefix, AS\ path$). Note that in practice BGP advertisements have many more attributes, but for the sake of simplicity we omit them. We use $\langle\rangle$ to represent the empty AS path. The seed advertisements are $a_1 = (R1, 10.0.1.0/24, \langle\rangle)$, $a_3 = (R3, 10.0.0.0/24, \langle\rangle)$, and $a_4 = (R4, 10.0.1.0/24, \langle\rangle)$. These advertisements are then grouped by prefix as follows.

$$((10.0.0.0/24, \{a_3\}),\ (10.0.1.0/24, \{a_1, a_4\}))$$

Our algorithm will now iterate over this list of seeds and consume its elements. Later we will see how additional items are placed on the list.

Routes are computed for each prefix individually, since routing policies may differ for different prefixes. We need to start with more specific prefixes and continue with less specific prefixes, for reasons that will be explained later. In our example, the list only has two prefixes and they have equal prefix length, which is 24, so they are incomparable and hence we can pick either of them arbitrarily. We chose to start with 10.0.0.0/24.

After we picked the prefix, we consider the corresponding set of seed advertisements, $\{a_3\}$. Now we propagate this set of advertisements to every router. That is, every router needs to learn a best path to reach 10.0.0.0/24 at R3.

We show our adaptation of Dijkstra's shortest path algorithm for this task. First we initialize a work list WL with the seed advertisements, i.e., $WL = \{a_3\}$. Then the algorithm takes advertisements from the work list, one-by-one, processes them, and iterates until the work list becomes empty. So, we take the only present element in the work list, a_3, and re-advertise it to all neighbors of R3, which happens to be only router R2. To re-advertise, we create a new advertisement by copying a_3 and prepending R3's ASN to the AS path, and obtain $a_{2'} = (R2, 10.0.0.0/24, \langle 3 \rangle)$. This new advertisement is then added to the work list, hence we obtain $WL = \{a_{2'}\}$. After the first re-advertisement we obtain the following RIB entries.

R2	R3
$a_{2'} = (R2, 10.0.0.0/24, \langle 3 \rangle)$	$a_3 = (R3, 10.0.0.0/24, \langle \rangle)$

The algorithm then advertises $a_{2'}$ to R2's neighbors R1 and R4. Two new advertisements $a_{1'} = (R1, 10.0.0.0/24, \langle 2, 3 \rangle)$ and $a_{4'} = (R4, 10.0.0.0/24, \langle 2, 3 \rangle)$ are created. Note how R2's ASN is prepended to the AS path. The work list becomes $WL = \{a_{1'}, a_{4'}\}$.

We now reach a new case in our algorithm, in which the work list WL has more than one element. The choice of the next advertisement to process is important. Like in Dijkstra's algorithm we pick a vertex that is labeled with the smallest distance value: we need to visit a most preferred advertisement first. We assume that a partial order relation $\prec$ captures BGP's advertisement preference order. We can obtain $\prec$ from the description of the BGP's best path selection algorithm, which specifies that advertisements with shorter AS paths are preferable to advertisements with longer AS paths, among other criteria.

The order $\prec$ is partial, since BGP advertisements are not always comparable. One of the main reasons we particularly notice lack of totality is that the BGP best path selection algorithm was designed to be used within a single router, while our work list contains advertisements that reside at different routers. In our example, both advertisements in the work list have the same AS path length, so they are equally preferable. We will break the tie through an auxiliary lexicographic order on names of routers that store the advertisements, i.e., R1 and R4. As a result, our algorithm deterministically picks $a_{1'}$ from the work list.

Advertisement $a_{1'}$ can only be re-advertised back to R2 since R1 has no other neighbor. However, R2 rejects this advertisement because its own ASN occurs in the AS path $\langle 2, 3 \rangle$. A similar advertisement rejection happens with $a_{4'}$. Finally, the work list WL becomes empty and the advertisement propagation loop finishes. We computed four RIB entries, one for each of the routers in the network, since there are no policies in our example network that block advertisements of the considered prefix and all routers are reachable from R3.

Now we inspect if aggregation is configured on any of the routers. Router R2 has an aggregate for 10.0.0.0/16 which was not previously enabled since the

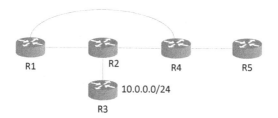

Fig. 5. Example network with five routers. Only R3 advertises a prefix.

RIB of R2 was empty. With the installation of $a_{2'}$ in R2's RIB, the aggregation becomes active because the prefix of $a_{2'}$ is a sub-prefix of the aggregate. Therefore, we generate a new advertisement $a_{2''} = (R2, 10.0.0.0/16, \langle\rangle)$, which tracks the enabled aggregate. The list with seed advertisements we had before is now extended to include the new advertisement and its prefix as follows.

$$((10.0.1.0/24, \{a_1, a_4\}), \ (10.0.0.0/16, \{a_{2''}\}))$$

We are now considering a case when it matters which prefix we take from the seed list to process next. Note that aggregate advertisements, like $a_{2''}$, are created and installed due to advertisements for sub-prefixes being installed in the RIB. The attributes of $a_{2''}$ are computed by applying appropriate aggregation functions on the attributes of sub-prefixes. Therefore, we advertise all sub-prefixes before advertising the aggregate, and hence avoid the problem of updating advertisement attributes and propagating the effect of such updates through additional route advertisements. This is why we iterate over the seed list by starting with more specific prefixes and proceeding with less specific prefixes.

The BGP RFC [41, Sect. 9.2.2.2] mandates that the aggregated AS path should be the largest common prefix of the AS paths of advertisements of sub-prefixes. In our example, we set the AS path of the aggregate to $\langle\rangle$, which is not what the BGP specification mandates, but it is how it is implemented by some relevant vendors, e.g., Cisco.

Our algorithm proceeds with a new run of the modified Dijkstra's algorithm that advertises 10.0.1.0/24. The only difference to what we described previously is that now we have two seed advertisements, a_1 and a_4. These are inserted in the work list WL and the rest of the algorithm proceeds as before. Finally, all advertisements for 10.0.0.0/16 are computed and our algorithm terminates.

The forwarding tables (FIBs) of the routers can be computed from the RIBs by taking the best advertisements for each prefix. In our example, each router only has one advertisement for each prefix, so all advertisements are propagated to the FIB.

3.2 Globally vs. Locally Preferred Advertisements

In this example we show how the order of propagation of route advertisements used by our algorithm differs from what a (distributed) execution of BGP in a real network can choose. This difference is important in ensuring that any propagated route advertisement will never be superseded by a better one.

To illustrate the above point, we change our example network to include an additional link from R1 to R4 and an extra router R5, as shown in Fig. 5. We also add a route map to router R2 that applies to advertisements going out to R4. This route map augments the AS path by prepending the AS number 2 twice. The configuration change in router R2 to include this route map is as follows.

```
route-map prepend permit 10
  set as-path prepend 2 2
!
router bgp 2
  neighbor 10.1.0.4 route-map prepend out  ! R4
```

In this example, we only have one seed advertisement $a_3 = (R3, 10.0.0.0/24, \langle \rangle)$. This propagates to R2 as $a_2 = (R2, 10.0.0.0/24, \langle 3 \rangle)$. Advertisement a_2 is then propagated to the neighbors of router R2, and so we obtain two new advertisements $a_1 = (R1, 10.0.0.0/24, \langle 2, 3 \rangle)$ and $a_4 = (R4, 10.0.0.0/24, \langle 2, 2, 3 \rangle)$. The work list becomes $WL = \{a_1, a_4\}$, together with the RIB entries shown below. Note that for brevity we only show the AS path in each of the advertisements.

R1	R2	R3	R4	R5
$a_1 = \langle 2, 3 \rangle$	$a_2 = \langle 3 \rangle$	$a_3 = \langle \rangle$	$a_4 = \langle 2, 2, 2, 3 \rangle$	

The next advertisement to explore is a_1, since it is more preferred than a_4, i.e., $a_1 \prec a_4$. Advertising a_1 to R1's neighbors results in a new advertisement $a_{4'} = (R4, 10.0.0.0/24, \langle 1, 2, 3 \rangle)$, while R2 drops the advertisement from R1 due to the occurrence of its ASN in the AS path of a_1. We now have two competing advertisements at R4. One was received from R1, $a_{4'}$, and the other from R2, a_4. A router only advertises a most preferred advertisement, which in this case is $a_{4'}$ since $a_{4'} \prec a_4$ as the AS path $\langle 1, 2, 3 \rangle$ for $a_{4'}$ is shorter than $\langle 2, 2, 2, 3 \rangle$ for a_4. Therefore, we replace a_4 with $a_{4'}$ in the work list to get $WL = \{a_{4'}\}$. We point out that advertisement a_4 is nevertheless stored in the RIB of R4, but is not advertised further. Finally, the algorithm computes $a_5 = (R5, 10.0.0.0/24, \langle 4, 1, 2, 3 \rangle)$ for R5. The final result is that each router has one entry in the RIB, except R4 which has two entries, where one is singled out as a best advertisement.

In this example we observed that since the work list stores advertisements across all routers, when we take the globally most preferred advertisement for exploration, the exploration of the most preferred advertisement within a given router may be delayed. Here we speak of a global preference order. It is essential for avoiding recomputation of advertisements due to arrival of more preferred ones, as it happens when BGP runs in a distributed setting over real networks in which a router propagates an advertisement that is most preferred among the locally present ones. In this case we speak of a local preference order.

In contrast, when running BGP on our example and following the local order on the RIBs containing advertisements $a_1, \ldots, a_5$, R4 may advertise a_4 before it receives $a_{4'}$, which leads to $a_{5'} = (R5, 10.0.0.0/24, \langle 4, 2, 2, 2, 3 \rangle)$. After the advertisement of a_4, R1 may advertise a_1 to R4 which results in $a_{4'}$ appearing on R4.

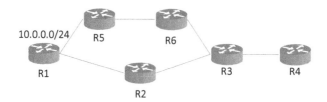

Fig. 6. Example network, where only router R1 advertises a prefix. R3 has a route map that increases local preference on incoming advertisements from R6.

At this point R4 discovers that a_4 is no longer the most preferred advertisement, while $a_{4'}$ is. So it needs to ask R5 to withdraw advertisement $a_{5'}$. In a larger network, by transitivity all advertisements that were sent out because of $a_{4'}$ would need to be withdrawn, which could be a significant effort.

By following the global order, instead of the local ones, our algorithm never withdraws advertisements, which helps in scaling to large datacenter networks.

3.3 Necessity of Monotonic Increase of Preference

We showed how our algorithm avoids recomputation of advertisements by propagating only globally optimal advertisements. However, this procedure is only correct if the routing policy produces advertisements that never increase in preference. This means that the preference of a route advertisement at the destination router cannot be higher than the preference of the originating advertisement at the source router. However, some features supported by BGP routing policies can lead to violation of this property.

The following example illustrates the necessity of the monotonic increase property, and shows that without it our algorithm computes an incorrect result.

We consider the network in Fig. 6. Router R3 has a route map that increases the local preference of advertisements incoming from R6 to 200, while the default value is usually 100. The route map is as follows.

```
route-map in_r6 permit 10
  set local-preference 200
!
router bgp 3
  neighbor 10.1.0.3 route-map in_r6 in
```

Note that the BGP best path selection algorithm states that the advertisement with the highest local preference is preferred. If advertisements have an equal value of the local preference attribute, then the advertisement with the shortest AS path is preferred.

Since we now need to track the local preference attribute, we will represent advertisement as tuples ($router, prefix, local\ pref, AS\ path$).

The seed advertisement is $a_1 = (R1, 10.0.0.0/24, 100, \langle\rangle)$. Our algorithm propagates a_1 from R1 to R2 and R5 resulting in $a_2 = (R2, 10.0.0.0/24, 100, \langle 1 \rangle)$ and $a_5 = (R5, 10.0.0.0/24, 100, \langle 1 \rangle)$. The resulting work list is $WL = \{a_2, a_5\}$.

As a_2 and a_5 are equally preferred, our algorithm picks the advertisement located at the router with the lowest identifier (in order to stay deterministic), which is a_2 in this case. We propagate a_2 to R3 and obtain $a_3 = (R3, 10.0.0.0/24, 100, \langle 2, 1 \rangle)$ and $WL = \{a_3, a_5\}$. We then take a_5 from the work list and compute $a_6 = (R6, 10.0.0.0/24, 100, \langle 5, 1 \rangle)$ and $WL = \{a_3, a_6\}$. Afterward we take a_3 and compute $a_4 = (R4, 10.0.0.0/24, 100, \langle 3, 2, 1 \rangle)$ and $WL = \{a_4, a_6\}$. The resulting RIBs (with just the local preference and AS path attributes) are shown below.

R1: $a_1 = (100, \langle\rangle)$	R2: $a_2 = (100, \langle 1 \rangle)$	R3: $a_3 = (100, \langle 2, 1 \rangle)$
R4: $a_4 = (100, \langle 3, 2, 1 \rangle)$	R5: $a_5 = (100, \langle 1 \rangle)$	R6: $a_6 = (100, \langle 5, 1 \rangle)$

We now arrive at the problematic part. When we take a_6 from the work list and advertise it to R3, the incoming route map at R3 sets the local preference of the incoming advertisement to 200. Therefore we obtain $a_{3'} = (R3, 10.0.0.0/24, 200, \langle 6, 5, 1 \rangle)$. This advertisement is more preferred than a_3 that was received previously from R2, i.e., $a_{3'} \prec a_3$ since $200 > 100$. This means that R3 now has a more preferred advertisement than the one previously present in its RIB and therefore the new advertisement needs to be propagated, with all the related withdrawals and re-advertisements, while a_3 is still kept in the RIB.

Unfortunately, we already propagated a_3 to R4 by following the global preference order. To fix the problem, we would need to remove a_4 from R4's RIB, as well as remove any advertisements transitively derived from a_4, potentially spanning the whole network. However, due to the monotonic increase assumption, our algorithm does not anticipate such an issue and hence is not able to delete RIB entries. As a consequence, we obtain a wrong result for this network.

To summarize, our algorithm only produces a correct result when the network's routing policies ensure monotonic increase of preference. Fortunately, several studies (including ours) confirm that industrial datacenter networks have this property.

4 Algorithms

In this section we describe an algorithm for efficient simulation of BGP in datacenter networks. Our algorithm is based on Dijkstra's shortest path algorithm, and adapts it to our setting by using BGP route advertisements to track distance, comparing distances using BGP path selection function, and updating distance using BGP route maps. We also show how to deal with equal-cost multi-path routing (ECMP) and aggregation.

4.1 Generalizing Dijkstra's Algorithm

We begin by revisiting Dijkstra's algorithm, in order to fix a particular version as there are different ways of setting up and maintaining the distance and work list data structures. See Fig. 7.

```
function DIJKSTRA
input
    E : V × V − set of edges
    v₀ : V − initial vertex
    length : V × V → ℕ − edge length
vars
    dist : V → ℕ − distance from source to other vertexes
    queue : 𝒫(V) − queue with vertexes pending processing
begin
1   dist(v₀) := 0
2   queue := {v₀}
3   while queue ≠ ∅ do
4       u = arg minᵂᵉ𐞥ᵘᵉᵘᵉ dist(w)
5       queue := queue \ {u}
6       for each v ∈ E(u) do
7           if v ∉ dom(dist) ∨ dist(u) + length(u,v) < dist(v) then
8               dist(v) := dist(u) + length(u,v)
9               queue := queue ∪ {v}
10      done
11  done
12  return dist
end
```

Fig. 7. DIJKSTRA computes the shortest path between a source vertex in the graph and all other vertexes. $E(u)$ is the set of neighbors of u. $\arg\min^<$ chooses a minimum with respect to the relation $<$.

Dijkstra's algorithm works as follows. It initializes the distance from the source vertex to itself as zero and adds the vertex to the queue (lines 1–2). Then it iterates over the queue until it is empty. At each iteration of the loop it picks the vertex u from the queue with the smallest distance from the source vertex (lines 3–5). The algorithm then iterates over each neighbor v of vertex u and updates the best known distance so far to v if it is the first path we discover to v or if the previously known path was longer (lines 6–10). When the queue becomes empty, the function returns function $dist$ which contains the shortest distance from vertex v_0 to all the other reachable vertexes in the graph (line 12).

We gave a brief description of how Dijkstra's algorithm works. It is important to note that the result is a labeling of vertexes with a natural number: the shortest distance from the source to that vertex. We will now consider a few operations in Dijkstra's algorithm in a more general setting. In particular, we will consider the labels of vertexes to be of an arbitrary type D, with the ordering $\prec$ between these labels. We assume that a function $trans$ can be used to compute labeling of a neighboring vertex. The generalized version of Dijkstra's algorithm is shown in Fig. 8.

The deviations from Dijkstra's algorithm are as follows. For initialization (lines 1–2), we now take the initial label of the source vertex d_0 as input, instead of setting it to zero. Secondly, the order of extraction of vertexes from the queue

```
        function GDIJKSTRA⟨D⟩
        input
            E : V × V – set of edges
            v₀ : V – initial vertex
            d₀ : D – initial label
            trans : D × V × V → D – transform label along an edge
            ≺ : P(D × D) – label ordering
        vars
            dist : V → D – distance from v₀ to other vertexes
            queue : P(V) – queue with vertexes pending processing
        begin
  1         dist(v₀) := d₀
  2         queue := {v₀}
  3         while queue ≠ ∅ do
  4             u = arg min≺_{w∈queue} dist(w)
  5             queue = queue \ {u}
  6             for each v ∈ E(u) do
  7                 if v ∉ dom(dist) ∨ trans(dist(u), u, v) ≺ dist(v) then
  8                     dist(v) := trans(dist(u), u, v)
  9                     queue := queue ∪ {v}
 10             done
 11         done
 12         return dist
        end
```

Fig. 8. GDIJKSTRA computes min. labels that reach each vertex from v_0 labeled by d_0.

is given by a label order $\prec$ given as input (line 4). Finally, the new label computed for a neighbor is computed by the *trans* function given as input instead of computing a path length explicitly (line 7–8). Old and new labels are compared with $\prec$ as well.

We relate Dijkstra's algorithm with the generalized version as follows.

$$\text{DIJKSTRA}(E, v_0, length) = \text{GDIJKSTRA}\langle\mathbb{N}\rangle(E, v_0, 0, \lambda d\, u\, v.d + length(u, v), <)$$

Here we set the initial label of the source vertex to zero. The label of a neighbor is the label of the current vertex u, i.e., the distance between source and u, plus the length of the path from u to v.

We now state the correctness of the generalized Dijkstra's algorithm.

Theorem 1. *If $\prec$ is a strict partial order and function trans is monotonically increasing, i.e.,*

$$\forall d\ \forall(u, v) \in E : \neg(trans(d, u, v) \prec d),$$

then GDIJKSTRA labels each vertex with a minimal label that can be computed by traversing the set of edges E starting at vertex v_0 with label d_0 and using function trans to label edges.

4.2   Advertising a Single Prefix

We now show how to simulate BGP for the advertisement of a single prefix using our generalized version of Dijkstra's algorithm.

Vertexes correspond to routers and edges the peering relations established between them. The label type D will be route advertisements. The source vertex will be the router that exports the prefix. The source label will be an initial advertisement as mandated by the BGP standard, e.g., with empty AS path, with the origin type indicating how this advertisement was produced, etc.

The order between advertisements is given by $\prec_{BGP}$. For example, $a \prec_{BGP} a'$ holds if the local preference of a is greater than that of a'. If $a \prec_{BGP} a'$ holds, we say that a is preferred to a'. Order $\prec_{BGP}$ corresponds to the best past selection algorithm of BGP, which is a lexicographic order on advertisement attributes.

The transform function $trans$ has to do several things. Firstly, it needs to check if the advertisement can be propagated any further. One example of an advertisement that is blocked is when there is a summary-only aggregate whose prefix intersects with the prefix being advertised. This type of aggregates blocks contributing advertisements (i.e., advertisements of more specific prefixes) from being propagated to neighbors. Secondly, this function needs to transform the advertisement for the given neighbor, e.g., prepend its own ASN to the AS path, and then apply the outgoing route map of the sender and the incoming route map of the neighbor (if any). Any of these route maps may rewrite some fields of the advertisement or even block it from being advertised or added to the RIB, respectively for outgoing and incoming route maps. We need to compute a new advertisement for each neighbor because routers can have different policies for different neighbors and incoming route maps may also differ between neighbors.

A simplified version of the transform function can be represented by the following pseudo code. We refer to [47] for an example of a formal discussion. In the pseudo code we use ∞ to denote a least preferred advertisement with respect to $\prec_{BGP}$. We use ∞ to model the case when a route map rejects an advertisement. Such advertisements can be ignored upon the termination of the algorithm, when installing advertisements into the RIBs of their respective routers.

$trans_{BGP}(a, u, v) :=$
    if u should not advertise a **then**
        return ∞
    $a' :=$ create advertisement for v from a
    $a'' :=$ OutRouteMap(u, a')
    if v should not accept a'' **then**
        return ∞
    return InRouteMap(v, a'')

In practice, function $trans_{BGP}$ can be quite complicated and needs to faithfully implement vendor-specific details. For example, there are more cases that block advertisements from being propagated besides summary-only aggregates, such as when an advertisement is tagged with the "no export" or "no advertise" communities, and when an advertisement is received from an iBGP peer it cannot be advertised to other iBGP peers. Also, some vendors do not support the advertisement of IPv4 prefixes to neighbor routers that are connected over IPv6.

A reason to reject an incoming advertisement is, e.g., if the AS path contains the ASN of the receiving router. This check can only be performed after the outgoing transformations, since outgoing route maps are allowed to change the AS path.

Putting everything together, we define a function BGP_{ONE} that computes a RIB for a given prefix. Here v_0 is the router that exports the initial advertisement d_0 for the prefix, and E is defined by the BGP peering between routers.

$$BGP_{ONE}(E, v_0, d_0) := GDIJKSTRA(E, v_0, d_0, trans_{BGP}, \prec_{BGP})$$

To be able to use GDIJKSTRA and obtain a correct result, we need to establish the two assumptions made by the algorithm: (1) $\prec_{BGP}$ is a strict partial order, and (2) $trans_{BGP}$ is monotonically increasing. Assumption (1) holds because $\prec_{BGP}$ is a lexicographic order on advertisement attributes.

In general, $trans_{BGP}$ is not monotonically increasing. For example, route maps may increase local preference, which ranks higher in the best path selection than the AS path length which usually increases by one when an advertisement is propagated to a neighbor. In this work, since we target datacenter networks, we deal with $trans_{BGP}$ that is monotonically increasing.

4.3   Computing All Advertisements for a Single Prefix

In the previous section, we showed how to use our generalized version of Dijkstra's algorithm to compute advertisements that are propagated to every router from a given prefix. This is very close to what BGP actually computes, but not exactly. BGP records at each router not only the most preferred advertisement it has received for a given prefix, but also all the received advertisements. This way the router can, e.g., promote the second best advertisement to become the most preferred one if the neighbor that sent the original most preferred advertisement becomes unreachable. As we have done, a router only propagates most preferred advertisements to its neighbors.

We need a further extension in Dijkstra's algorithm to keep track of all advertisements, including non-best ones. The new (and final) generalization is shown in Fig. 9. This algorithm tracks distance from the source as a set of labels instead of a single label. It stores at vertex v all labels computed by traversing paths from the neighbors of v to v, instead of keeping only the smallest label. The creation of a new label for a neighbor of vertex v continues to depend only on a minimal label of v as previously (c.f. arguments to $trans$ function).

We note that $\min^{\prec} dist(v)$ in this algorithm in line 7 is exactly the same value as $dist(v)$ in the previous algorithm GDIJKSTRA in line 7. Therefore, the only change in behavior of GDIJKSTRASET is in line 9. Previously we only stored the minimal label found so far, so the assignment of $dist(v)$ was inside the if statement. Now, we moved the assignment out of the if statement such that the assignment is executed regardless whether the new label is $\prec$-better than the previous one.

```
      function GDIJKSTRASET⟨D⟩
      input
        E : V × V – set of edges
        v₀ : V – initial vertex
        d₀ : D – initial label
        trans : D × V × V → D – transform label along an edge
        ≺ : 𝒫(D × D) – label ordering
      vars
        dist : V → 𝒫(D) – distance from v₀ to other vertexes
        queue : 𝒫(V) – queue with vertexes pending processing
      begin
1       dist(v₀) := {d₀}
2       queue := {v₀}
3       while queue ≠ ∅ do
4         u = arg min≺_{w∈queue}(min≺ dist(w))
5         queue := queue \ {u}
6         for each v ∈ E(u) do
7           if v ∉ dom(dist) ∨ trans(min≺ dist(u), u, v) ≺ (min≺ dist(v)) then
8             queue := queue ∪ {v}
9             dist(v) := {trans(min≺ dist(u), u, v)} ∪ (dist(v) if v ∈ dom(dist) else ∅)
10          done
11        done
12      return dist
      end
```

Fig. 9. GDIJKSTRASET computes a set of minimal labels at each vertex, as well as keeps track of all labels that are propagated to a vertex, a so called one-hop history.

We now define BGP tracking all advertisements in terms of the set-tracking generalization of Dijkstra's algorithm.

$$\mathrm{BGP_{ALL}}(E, v_0, d_0) := \mathrm{GDIJKSTRASET}(E, v_0, d_0, trans_{BGP}, \prec_{BGP})$$

The function $\mathrm{BGP_{ALL}}$ correctly computes propagation of a single prefix in an efficient way. The network must, however, respect the monotonic increase property we mentioned previously.

We now state the correctness of $\mathrm{BGP_{ALL}}$.

Theorem 2. *Given a monotonically increasing BGP network, BGP_{ALL} computes a stable state of RIBs in the network.*

In this section we assumed that there is only one source router for each prefix. This is not true in general, however. For example, we may want to load balance traffic for a service between different racks in a datacenter, and so the routers of all such racks have to advertise the same prefix corresponding to the service.

Extending the given algorithm for multiple sources is straightforward. Instead of taking a single source vertex and advertisement, the algorithm can take a set instead. Then the queue is populated with all the advertisements and these will be explored in order.

4.4   Computing RIBs for All Prefixes

In the previous section we presented an algorithm to compute BGP advertisements for a single prefix. We now show an algorithm that computes BGP advertisements for all prefixes originating in a monotonic network, and produces the RIBs for all the routers. The algorithm consists of a loop invoking the single prefix-propagating algorithm for each prefix and a prefix composition step.

We compute a separate control plane for each prefix since prefixes are exported at varying locations. Moreover, different routers in a network are often configured to accept and/or modify advertisements differently depending on the prefix. Therefore we cannot simply run the set-generalized Dijkstra algorithm for all prefixes at once.

The algorithm to compute the RIB for all routers is as follows.

$\text{RIB} := \emptyset$
$seeds := \text{INITSEEDS}()$

while $seeds \neq \emptyset$ **do**
    $(prefix, adverts) := $ take most specific prefix from $seeds$
    $\text{RIB} := \text{RIB} \cup \{(r, prefix) \mapsto a \mid (r, a) \in \text{BGP}_{\text{ALL}}(E, adverts)\}$
    $seeds := \text{UPDATESEEDS}(\text{RIB}, prefix, seeds)$
done
return RIB

The procedure starts by computing the set of seed advertisements. grouped by prefix. Seed adverts consist of the prefixes advertised by each router through, e.g., the `network` command, or via aggregation of locally installed routes.

The order of iteration through prefixes is relevant for features where there is a dependency between different prefixes, i.e., features that make advertisement of prefixes to not be independent of each other. For example, an aggregated prefix, say 10.0.0.0/8, depends on contributing prefixes, say 10.0.1.0/24. In this case we need to iterate through more specific prefixes before the less specific ones, e.g., we need to execute BGP_{ALL} on 10.0.1.0/24 before executing it on 10.0.0.0/8.

Function UPDATESEEDS creates and updates existing seed advertisements. These new and/or updated seeds need to be iterated over later. It is guaranteed, however, that any new seed is of a less specific prefix than any other already processed. Since we iterate from more specific to less specific prefixes, we never miss any update to a seed or explore the same prefix more than once.

4.5   Updating Seed Advertisements

Sometimes there are dependencies between different IP prefixes, and installing an entry in the RIB may automatically trigger the installation (or update) of an entry for another prefix.

One such case is aggregation. For example, if a router is configured to aggregate 10.0.0.0/16 but has no initial seed with a sub-prefix, initially 10.0.0.0/16 will not be installed in the RIB since there is no contributing advertisement. If later this router receives an advertisement for, e.g., 10.0.0.1/32, the aggregated prefix becomes active and thus it becomes a seed since it needs to be advertised to the neighbors.

Another case is when an aggregated prefix is already active and the router installs another sub-prefix. In this case, we may need to update the seed advertisement for the aggregated prefix since it depends on all contributing advertisements. For example, the origin type of an aggregated advertisement is the result of combining the origin type of all contributing advertisements. Other attributes of advertisements are often combined using vendor-specific functions.

Function UPDATESEEDS takes the last prefix that was advertised as input and checks if that prefix is a potential contributor to any aggregated prefix in the routers. If so, it creates a new seed advertisement for the aggregated prefix in case it does not exist yet, or updates the existing seed.

It is guaranteed that any created or updated seed advertisement has not been visited yet by the BGP_{ALL} algorithm. This is because the main loop traverses prefixes from more specific to less specific, and the created/updated seeds have a less specific address than in the current loop iteration, otherwise the advertisements created in the current iteration could not possibly be contributors to the created/updated seeds of aggregated prefixes.

5   Evaluation

To evaluate the proposed algorithm, we implemented a prototype called FAST-PLANE in C++17. It supports several router vendors, including Arista, Cisco (IOS and Nexus), Force10, and Juniper. The range of implemented features includes BGP (internal and external), communities, BGP multipath, route maps, prefix aggregation, ACLs, ECMP, static routes, IPv4, and IPv6.

We compare the running time of FASTPLANE with Batfish [20], which is the state-of-the-art tool for RIB computation supporting general networks (as opposed to FASTPLANE, which only supports monotonic ones). As far as we are aware, Batfish is the only publicly available tool that can parse significant portions of industrial router configurations and that scales to thousands of routers.

Setup. We took the configuration files for all datacenters (DCs) of a major public cloud provider. Overall we collected a few (single digit) GBs of configuration files containing hundreds of millions of lines.

The network architecture of these DCs is a fat-tree running eBGP between all routers [23]. The dataset contains DCs with several variants of the architecture, depending on the DC size and age (since the architecture keeps evolving). We validated that the monotonicity property holds for all DCs in our dataset.

The machine used to run the experiments had 2x Intel Xeon E5-2660 CPUs (16 cores total), with 112 GBs of RAM. We used Batfish revision b004dff from 11/Jan/2018, with a limit of 100 GBs of memory for the JVM.

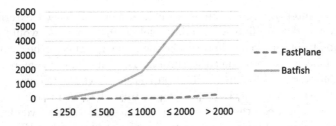

Fig. 10. CPU time (in seconds) to compute the RIBs and FIBs of all routers in each datacenter vs. datacenter size (number of routers).

Performance Results. For each datacenter, we computed RIBs and FIBs for all routers using FASTPLANE and Batfish, and measured the table size and the running time. The total number of entries in the RIBs of all devices of a single datacenter varied between several thousands and hundreds of millions.

We present the CPU time taken to compute the RIBs and FIBs in Fig. 10. Datacenters are grouped into five buckets, according to their number of routers. For each bucket we show the average time for the datacenters in that bucket.

Figure 10 shows that FASTPLANE is about two orders of magnitude faster than Batfish. Given 100 GBs of memory, Batfish does not scale beyond 2,000 routers. Moreover, Batfish only supports IPv4, while FASTPLANE supports IPv6 as well.

FASTPLANE only executes one round of BGP propagation, since it stratifies the computation. This is possible for monotonic networks. Batfish, on the other hand, does not pick any particular propagation order, which leads to several iterations. In our dataset, we see Batfish requiring up to eight BGP iterations. This shows that choosing the right propagation order has significant impact on the efficiency of the algorithm.

Besides the higher number of BGP rounds, Batfish is fundamentally slower than FASTPLANE for two other reasons: (1) Batfish supports generic BGP networks while FASTPLANE only supports monotonic networks, and (2) Batfish's fixed-point check resembles the so-called naive Datalog evaluation (as opposed to the more efficient semi-naive [13]).

Batfish does not simulate BGP through message passing like C-BGP. Instead, a router's RIB is computed by peeking into the neighbor's RIBs and importing those (subject to routing policies, and so on). Batfish keeps two sets of RIBs per router: one from the previous iteration and another for the current iteration, which is computed based on the neighboring RIBs from the previous iteration. Therefore, Batfish keeps two RIBs per router in memory at a time.

Validation of BGP Semantics. To increase confidence in our implementation of BGP, in particular in vendor-specific features, we compared the RIBs and FIBs computed by FASTPLANE with the ones from production routers in the datacenters.

Since datacenters operate in an open environment and receive external advertisements, we had to define a boundary delimiting what we would simulate. Routers outside of the given datacenter, i.e., the Internet, other datacenters, and load balancers, were modeled as dummy BGP neighbors that replayed the advertisements received by the production routers at the boundary.

This validation was effective. We found several bugs in our semantics of BGP, differences between the BGP implementations of different vendors, as well as bugs in the network. After validation, FASTPLANE computes FIBs and RIBs that are equivalent to those of several thousand routers we compared against.

One interesting bug we found was a difference in the behavior of BGP aggregation between Cisco and Arista: Arista follows the RFC and sets the AS path to the longest common prefix of the contributing advertisements' AS paths, while Cisco always creates aggregates with empty AS paths.

Production Bugs Found. We give a high-level description of some of the bugs found in datacenter networks while doing the cross-checking explained in the previous section.

One of the bugs was in the redistribution policy of connected routes. A network operator specified how the RIB of each device type is expected to look like. For example, ToRs must have all prefixes exported by load balancers. We then checked if the computed RIBs matched the expectations, and the check failed. In particular, there were unexpected advertisements. The routing policy was fixed to block them, and FASTPLANE was used to validate the fix before deployment.

We also found a bug in a router's firmware that resulted in the FIB's next-hops to be incorrect for some prefixes, due to a race condition in the code that updates the FIB. This bug would have been hard to find without FASTPLANE, which provides the ground truth for the router behavior.

Another type of bug was a problem with the network architecture. The architecture allows the network control plane to converge to different stable states, due to non-determinism. We found that some of these states have reduced load balancing and fault tolerance. We confirmed that the problem manifests in production and a fix is underway.

6   Related Work

Control plane verification is closely related to our work. Existing tools use a variety of techniques to compute the control plane, including simulation of message passing of routing protocols, Batfish [20] and C-BGP [40], and SMT encodings of BGP, Bagpipe [47], MineSweeper [8]. ERA [17] uses BDDs for reachability analysis between endpoints. ARC [22] and [48] compute an abstraction of the control plane. These tools are less scalable than FASTPLANE when applied to obtain the entire control plane, but they often support more BGP features and more complex interactions between routing protocols. We believe that our algorithm could be used to scale existing tools to large datacenters, while keeping the applicability of general methods when needed.

CrystalNet [34] uses the router's firmware in a virtualized environment to compute the control plane. It is bug-compatible with production networks, but it is significantly more resource intensive and slower than FASTPLANE.

There also exists static analysis of configuration files, similarly to compiler warnings. Such tools, e.g., rcp [18], do not compute the control plane.

Another area of network verification is data plane verification [52]. These tools operate over given FIBs, which can be either be computed from RIBs, or obtained directly from production routers, which unfortunately precludes verification before deployment. Tools for data plane verification employ a range of techniques including specialized algorithms and data structures, e.g., HSA [29], NetPlumber [28], VeriFlow [30], ddNF [12], TenantGuard [46], Datalog solvers, e.g., NoD [36], predicate abstraction, e.g., AP [49], SAT solvers, e.g., Anteater [37] and NetSAT [51], BDDs, e.g., FlowChecker [3], symmetry reduction [39], localized, per router, properties, e.g., SecGuru [11], and symbolic execution [14].

Software defined networks (SDNs) offer an alternative to BGP or OSPF, however they are not yet deployed at datacenter scale. There exist model checkering tools for SDN controllers, e.g., Kuai [38], VeriCon [7], and SDNRacer [16].

Correct by construction is an alternative approach to network reliability. Tools for configuration synthesis include Propane [9,10], and Genesis [45]. There is also work on synthesizing ACLs [27,50]. We anticipate that synthesis tools could improve scalability by applying our monotonicity observation.

There are new languages to declaratively specify routing behavior, e.g., NetKAT [5], and firewalls, e.g., Mignis [1].

There is related work in the area of routing algebras [4,24,25,44]. For example, [26] proves that monotonicity of the edge labeling function, which corresponds to our $trans_{BGP}$, with respect to the label order, which is our $\prec_{BGP}$, ensures convergence of the routing protocol. [43] gives a generalization of Dijkstra's algorithm, but using numerical weights, while the generalization in [33] is for arbitrary, totally ordered, cost functions. [15] also gives a generalization of Dijkstra's algorithm, but does not handle aggregation, unlike our algorithm.

[19] gives an algorithm to compute the control plane of an iBGP mesh with several routers peering with other ASs. [21] gives guidelines for configuring routers that peer with other organizations to ensure convergence of BGP.

7   Future Work

In this paper we presented an algorithm for computing routing tables that is applicable only when a certain subset of features of BGP is used. Further research is needed to broaden and precisely characterize what is the set (or sets) of features that can be used together and is still compatible with the proposed algorithm (or similar monotonic reasoning approach).

Dually, further research is needed to characterize protocol features to avoid in order to support efficient verification. Moreover, there is little understanding of if/how to replace non-monotonic features by monotonic ones. This could not only improve efficiency of network verification, but also speed up convergence time in production networks, since fewer advertisements would be withdrawn.

Another avenue is a study of non-determinism in control planes. $\prec$ is sometimes not a total order, which means there may exist different stable states in the network. This has disadvantages, such as making troubleshooting more difficult. Our current prototype deliberately computes a single stable state in a consistent, deterministic way so that the results are reproducible. However, this stable state may not be identical to the state in which the real network stabilizes.

8   Conclusion

We studied datacenter networks of a major cloud provider and confirmed their monotonicity. We then presented an efficient algorithm that leverages this fact to compute routing tables of that kind of networks. The evaluation shows that our prototype, FASTPLANE, scales to large production datacenters.

References

1. Adão, P., Bozzato, C., Rossi, G.D., Focardi, R., Luccio, F.L.: Mignis: a semantic based tool for firewall configuration. In: CSF (2014)
2. Al-Fares, M., Loukissas, A., Vahdat, A.: A scalable, commodity data center network architecture. In: SIGCOMM (2008)
3. Al-Shaer, E., Al-Haj, S.: FlowChecker: configuration analysis and verification of federated openflow infrastructures. In: SafeConfig (2010)
4. Alim, M.A., Griffin, T.G.: On the interaction of multiple routing algorithms. In: CoNEXT (2011)
5. Anderson, C.J., et al.: NetKAT: semantic foundations for networks. In: POPL (2014)
6. Andreyev, A.: Introducing data center fabric, the next-generation Facebook data center network (2014)
7. Ball, T., et al.: VeriCon: towards verifying controller programs in software-defined networks. In: PLDI (2014)
8. Beckett, R., Gupta, A., Mahajan, R., Walker, D.: A general approach to network configuration verification. In: SIGCOMM (2017)
9. Beckett, R., Mahajan, R., Millstein, T., Padhye, J., Walker, D.: Don't mind the gap: bridging network-wide objectives and device-level configurations. In: SIGCOMM (2016)
10. Beckett, R., Mahajan, R., Millstein, T., Padhye, J., Walker, D.: Network configuration synthesis with abstract topologies. In: PLDI (2017)
11. Bjørner, N., Jayaraman, K.: Checking cloud contracts in Microsoft Azure. In: Natarajan, R., Barua, G., Patra, M.R. (eds.) ICDCIT 2015. LNCS, vol. 8956, pp. 21–32. Springer, Cham (2015). https://doi.org/10.1007/978-3-319-14977-6_2
12. Bjørner, N., Juniwal, G., Mahajan, R., Seshia, S.A., Varghese, G.: ddNF: an efficient data structure for header spaces. In: Bloem, R., Arbel, E. (eds.) HVC 2016. LNCS, vol. 10028, pp. 49–64. Springer, Cham (2016). https://doi.org/10.1007/978-3-319-49052-6_4

13. Ceri, S., Gottlob, G., Tanca, L.: What you always wanted to know about datalog (and never dared to ask). IEEE Trans. Knowl. Data Eng. 1(1), 146–166 (1989)
14. Dobrescu, M., Argyraki, K.: Software dataplane verification. In: NSDI (2014)
15. Dynerowicz, S., Griffin, T.G.: On the forwarding paths produced by internet routing algorithms. In: ICNP (2013)
16. El-Hassany, A., Miserez, J., Bielik, P., Vanbever, L., Vechev, M.: SDNRacer: concurrency analysis for software-defined networks. In: PLDI (2016)
17. Fayaz, S.K., et al.: Efficient network reachability analysis using a succinct control plane representation. In: OSDI (2016)
18. Feamster, N., Balakrishnan, H.: Detecting BGP configuration faults with static analysis. In: NSDI (2005)
19. Feamster, N., Rexford, J.: Network-wide prediction of BGP routes. IEEE/ACM Trans. Netw. 15(2), 253–266 (2007)
20. Fogel, A., et al.: A general approach to network configuration analysis. In: NSDI (2015)
21. Gao, L., Rexford, J.: Stable internet routing without global coordination. In: SIG-METRICS (2000)
22. Gember-Jacobson, A., Viswanathan, R., Akella, A., Mahajan, R.: Fast control plane analysis using an abstract representation. In: SIGCOMM (2016)
23. Greenberg, A., et al.: Vl2: a scalable and flexible data center network. In: SIG-COMM (2009)
24. Griffin, T.G., Shepherd, F.B., Wilfong, G.: The stable paths problem and interdomain routing. IEEE/ACM Trans. Netw. 10(2), 232–243 (2002)
25. Griffin, T.G., Shepherd, F.B., Wilfong, G.T.: Policy disputes in path-vector protocols. In: ICNP (1999)
26. Griffin, T.G., Sobrinho, J.L.: Metarouting. In: SIGCOMM (2005)
27. Hallahan, W.T., Zhai, E., Piskac, R.: Automated repair by example for firewalls. In: FMCAD (2017)
28. Kazemian, P., Chang, M., Zeng, H., Varghese, G., McKeown, N., Whyte, S.: Real time network policy checking using header space analysis. In: NSDI (2013)
29. Kazemian, P., Varghese, G., McKeown, N.: Header space analysis: static checking for networks. In: NSDI (2012)
30. Khurshid, A., Zou, X., Zhou, W., Caesar, M., Godfrey, P.B.: VeriFlow: verifying network-wide invariants in real time. In: NSDI (2013)
31. Lahiri, P., et al.: Routing design for large scale data centers: BGP is a better IGP. In: NANOG'55 (2012)
32. Lapukhov, P., Premji, A., Mitchell, J.: RFC 7938: Use of BGP for Routing in Large-Scale Data Centers (2016)
33. Lengauer, T., Theune, D.: Efficient algorithms for path problems with general cost criteria. In: Albert, J.L., Monien, B., Artalejo, M.R. (eds.) ICALP 1991. LNCS, vol. 510, pp. 314–326. Springer, Heidelberg (1991). https://doi.org/10.1007/3-540-54233-7_144
34. Liu, H., et al.: CrystalNet: faithfully emulating large production networks. In: SOSP (2017)
35. Lloyd's. Failure of a top cloud service provider could cost US economy $15 billion (2018)
36. Lopes, N.P., Bjørner, N., Godefroid, P., Jayaraman, K., Varghese, G.: Checking beliefs in dynamic networks. In: NSDI (2015)
37. Mai, H., Khurshid, A., Agarwal, R., Caesar, M., Godfrey, P.B., King, S.T.: Debugging the data plane with anteater. In: SIGCOMM (2011)

38. Majumdar, R., Tetali, S.D., Wang, Z.: Kuai: a model checker for software-defined networks. In: FMCAD (2014)
39. Plotkin, G.D., Bjørner, N., Lopes, N.P., Rybalchenko, A., Varghese, G.: Scaling network verification using symmetry and surgery. In: POPL (2016)
40. Quoitin, B., Uhlig, S.: Modeling the routing of an autonomous system with C-BGP. IEEE Netw. **19**(6), 12–19 (2005)
41. Rekhter, Y., Li, T., Hares, S.: RFC 4271: A Border Gateway Protocol 4 (BGP-4) (2006)
42. Rusinovich, M.: TechEd 2013: Windows Azure Internals (2013)
43. Sobrinho, J.L.: Algebra and algorithms for QoS path computation and hop-by-hop routing in the internet. IEEE/ACM Trans. Netw. **10**(4), 541–550 (2002)
44. Sobrinho, J.L.: An algebraic theory of dynamic network routing. IEEE/ACM Trans. Netw. **13**, 1160–1173 (2005)
45. Subramanian, K., D'Antoni, L., Akella, A.: Genesis: synthesizing forwarding tables in multi-tenant networks. In: POPL (2017)
46. Wang, Y., et al.: TenantGuard: scalable runtime verification of cloud-wide VM-level network isolation. In: NDSS (2017)
47. Weitz, K., Woos, D., Torlak, E., Ernst, M.D., Krishnamurthy, A., Tatlock, Z.: Scalable verification of border gateway protocol configurations with an SMT solver. In: OOPSLA (2016)
48. Xie, G.G., et al.: On static reachability analysis of IP networks. In: INFOCOM (2005)
49. Yang, H., Lam, S.S.: Real-time verification of network properties using atomic predicates. In: ICNP (2013)
50. Zhang, S., Mahmoud, A., Malik, S., Narain, S.: Verification and synthesis of firewalls using SAT and QBF. In: ICNP (2012)
51. Zhang, S., Malik, S.: SAT based verification of network data planes. In: Van Hung, D., Ogawa, M. (eds.) ATVA 2013. LNCS, vol. 8172, pp. 496–505. Springer, Cham (2013). https://doi.org/10.1007/978-3-319-02444-8_43
52. Zhang, S., Malik, S., McGeer, R.: Verification of computer switching networks: an overview. In: Chakraborty, S., Mukund, M. (eds.) ATVA 2012. LNCS, pp. 1–16. Springer, Heidelberg (2012). https://doi.org/10.1007/978-3-642-33386-6_1

Verification of an Industrial Asynchronous Leader Election Algorithm Using Abstractions and Parametric Model Checking

Étienne André[1,2,3]([⊠]), Laurent Fribourg[4], Jean-Marc Mota[5], and Romain Soulat[5]

[1] Université Paris 13, LIPN, CNRS, UMR 7030, 93430 Villetaneuse, France
eandre93430@lipn13.fr
[2] JFLI, CNRS, Tokyo, Japan
[3] National Institute of Informatics, Tokyo, Japan
[4] LSV, ENS Paris-Saclay & CNRS & INRIA, U. Paris-Saclay, Paris, France
[5] Thales Research and Technology, Palaiseau, France

Abstract. The election of a leader in a network is a challenging task, especially when the processes are asynchronous, i.e., execute an algorithm with time-varying periods. Thales developed an industrial election algorithm with an arbitrary number of processes, that can possibly fail. In this work, we prove the correctness of a variant of this industrial algorithm. We use a method combining abstraction, the SafeProver solver, and a parametric timed model-checker. This allows us to prove the correctness of the algorithm for a large number p of processes ($p = 5000$).

Keywords: Leader election · Distributed algorithm · Model checking SaveProver · Parameterized verification · Parametric timed automata

1 Introduction

Distributed systems, where entities communicate with each other, are booming in our societies. Drones communicating with each other, swarms of various objects, intelligent cars... all may face communication and leadership issues. Therefore, the algorithm that all entities execute should be verified. Thales developed an industrial election algorithm with an arbitrary number of processes, that can possibly fail. We cannot describe the code of the actual algorithm for confidentiality issues. Therefore, we consider a modified variant of the algorithm. This

This work is partially supported by Institut Farman (ENS Paris-Saclay & CNRS), by the ANR national research program PACS (ANR-14-CE28-0002) and by ERATO HASUO Metamathematics for Systems Design Project (No. JPMJER1603), JST.

C. Enea and R. Piskac (Eds.): VMCAI 2019, LNCS 11388, pp. 409–424, 2019.
https://doi.org/10.1007/978-3-030-11245-5_19

algorithm focuses on the election of a leader in a distributed system with a potentially large number of entities or *nodes* in an *asynchronous* environment. Our main contribution is to perform a formal verification of the algorithm correctness for a large number of nodes. By correctness, we mean the actual election of the leader after a fixed number of rounds.

We consider here a special form of the general leader election problem [22]: we assume that, in the network, all the processes (or *nodes*) have a specific ID number, and they execute the same code (*symmetry*) in order to agree which ID number is the highest one. In the synchronous context where all processes communicate simultaneously, the problem is often solved using the "Bully algorithm" [18]. In the asynchronous context where each process communicates with a specific period possibly subject to delay variation (jitter), the problem is much more difficult. Periods can be all slightly different from each other, which makes the problem particularly complex. For example, a classical distributed leader election protocol, where the nodes exchange data using broadcasting, was designed by Leslie Lamport [20] in the asynchronous context. The correctness of this algorithm was proved mechanically many times using, e.g., TLA$^+$ tool [21], or, more recently, using the timed model checking tool UPPAAL [10]. However, these automated proofs work only for a small number p of processes, typically for $p \leq 10$. In this paper, we present a technique to prove the correctness of such a distributed leader election using automated tools for a large number of nodes (e.g., $p = 5000$). The principle of the method relies on the abstraction method consisting in viewing the network from the point of view of a specific (but arbitrary) node, say $node_i$, and considering the rest of the nodes of the network as an abstract environment interacting with $node_i$. In this abstract model, two basic properties of the algorithm can be proven. However, in order to prove the full correctness of the leader election algorithm, we will need an auxiliary model, where some timing information is added to (a raw form of) the abstract model. Using this auxiliary timed model, we are able to prove an additional property of the leader election algorithm. Thanks to the three aforementioned properties added as assumptions, we can then prove the full correctness of the leader election algorithm, using the bounded model checker SafeProver [16] on the abstract model.

The leader election algorithm we use is not Lamport's algorithm, but a simple asynchronous form of the Bully algorithm. We consider a specific framework of network structure and asynchronous form of communications. Basically, we assume that:

1. the graph is complete (every node communicate with all the other ones).
2. the communications are instantaneous (the time between the sending of a message and its reception is null), and the nodes exchange data via synchronous one-way unconditional value passing.
3. the processes are *visibly faulty*, i.e., they always execute the generic code of the algorithm, trying to elect the leader when they are non-faulty (mode On), and do nothing when they are faulty (mode Off).

1.1   Relationship with Thales' Actual Algorithm

As mentioned above, for confidentiality issue, we cannot reveal the original algorithm developed at Thales. Nevertheless, it is in essence the same as the one we present. Only the executed code has been modified. In addition, the technique presented in this paper was designed for and applied to the original algorithm. To summarize, we present exactly the methodology, up to the content of the *UpdateNode* code (that is still similar in spirit).

After its verification using the techniques we present here, the original algorithm has been implemented in C, and is nowadays running in one of the Thales products. This product embeds a standard processor (in the line of Intel X86), with some limited RAM, hard drive, Ethernet ports, etc.

1.2   Related Work

The method proposed here makes use of several powerful techniques such as counter abstraction, bounded model checking and parametric timed model checking for verifying distributed fault-tolerant algorithms, similarly to what has been recently described, e.g., in [19]. As said in [19]: "Symmetry allows us to change representation into a *counter representation* (also referred to as 'counter abstraction'): (...) Instead of recording which process is in which local state, we record for each local state, how many processes are in this state. Thus, we need one counter per local state ℓ, hence we have a fixed number of counters. A step by a process that goes from local state ℓ to local state ℓ' is modeled by decrementing the counter associated with ℓ and incrementing the counter associated with ℓ'. When the number p of processes is fixed, each counter is bounded by p." The work described in [19] makes use of SMT solvers [15] in order to perform finite-state model checking of the abstracted model.

Our work can be seen as a new application of such techniques to (a variant of) an industrial election algorithm. Another originality is to combine counter abstraction, bounded model checking, with *parametric timed* model checking.

In an orthogonal direction, the verification of identical processes in a network, i.e., a unknown number of nodes running the same algorithm, has been studied in various settings, notably in the long line of work around regular model checking [11,17], and in various settings in the *timed* case [1–3]. However, the focus of that latter series of works is on decidability, and they do not consider real-world algorithms, nor do they have tools implementing these results.

Finally, the line of works around the Cubicle model-checker [12–14] performs parameterized verification of cache memory protocols, that is also parameterized in the number of processes. However, timing parameters are not present in these works.

1.3   Outline

The rest of the paper is organized as follows. Section 2 introduces the variant of the leader election algorithm we consider. Section 3 presents our direct verification method for a small number of nodes. Section 4 presents our abstraction-based verification for a much larger number of nodes. Section 5 concludes the manuscript and outlines perspectives.

2   An Asynchronous Leader Election Algorithm

Thales recently proposed a leader election algorithm. This simple leader election algorithm is based on the classical Bully algorithm originally designed for the synchronous framework [18]. Basically, all nodes have an ID (all different), and the node with the largest ID must be elected as a leader. This algorithm is asynchronous. As usual, each node runs the same version of the code. We cannot describe the code of the actual algorithm for confidentiality issues, and we therefore consider and prove a modified variant of Thales' original algorithm, described throughout this section.

2.1   Periods, Jitters, Offset

The system is a fixed set of p nodes $\mathcal{N} = \{node_1, \ldots, node_p\}$, for some $p \in \mathbb{N}$. Each node $node_i$ is defined by:

1. its integer-valued *ID* $node_i.id \in \mathbb{N}$,
2. its rational-valued *activation period* $node_i.per \in [\mathsf{period_{min}}, \mathsf{period_{max}}]$,
3. its rational-valued *first activation time* $node_i.start \in [0, node_i.per]$ (which can be seen as an *offset*, with the usual assumption that the offset must be less than or equal to the period), and
4. its rational-valued *jitter* values represent a delay variation for each period belonging to $[\mathsf{jitter_{min}}, \mathsf{jitter_{max}}]$, which is a static interval defined for all nodes and known beforehand.

Observe that all periods are potentially different (even though they are all in a fixed interval, and each of them remains constant over the entire execution), which makes the problem particularly challenging. In contrast, the jitter is different at each period (this is the common definition of a jitter), and the jitter of node i at the jth activation is denoted by $jitter_i^j$. The jth activation of node $node_i$ therefore takes place at time $t_i^j = t_i^{j-1} + node_i.per + jitter_i^j$. We have besides: $t_i^0 = node_i.start$.

The concrete values for the static timing constants are given in Table 1.

Example 1. Assume the system is made of three nodes. Assume $node_1.per = 49$. Recall that a period is an arbitrary *constant* in a predefined interval. Assume $node_1.start = 0$.

Assume $node_2.per = 51$ and $node_2.start = 30$.

Assume $node_3.per = 49$ and $node_3.start = 0.1$.

Also assume the jitters for the first three activations of the nodes given in Table 2.

Table 1. Constants (in ms)

Constant	Value
$period_{min}$	49
$period_{max}$	51
$jitter_{min}$	−0.5
$jitter_{max}$	0.5

Table 2. Jitter values for Example 1

	$jitter^1$	$jitter^2$	$jitter^3$
Node 1	0.5	−0.5	0.5
Node 2	0	0.1	0
Node 3	0.1	0.3	0.5

We therefore have $t_1^0 = 0$, $t_1^1 = 49.5$, $t_1^2 = 97.5$, $t_1^3 = 147.5$, $t_2^0 = 30$, $t_2^1 = 81$, $t_2^2 = 132.1$, $t_2^3 = 183$, $t_3^0 = 0.1$, $t_3^1 = 48.6$, $t_3^2 = 98.4$, $t_3^3 = 147.6$. The first activations of the nodes are depicted in Fig. 1. Due to both uncertain periods and the jitters, it can happen that, between two consecutive activations of a node, another node may not be activated at all: for example, between t_3^0 and t_3^1, node 1 is never activated, and therefore node 3 will not receive a message from node 1 during this interval. Conversely, between two consecutive activations of a node, another node is activated twice: for example, between t_3^1 and t_3^2, node 1 is activated twice (i. e., t_1^1 and t_1^2), and therefore node 3 may receive two messages from node 1 during this interval.

Finally note that, in this example, the number of activations since the system start for nodes 1 and 3 is always the same at any timestamp, up to a difference of 1 (due to the jitters) because they have the same periods. In contrast, the number of activations for node 2 will be smaller than that of nodes 1 and 3 by an increasing difference, since node 2 is slower (period: 51 instead of 49). This phenomenon does not occur when periods are equal for all nodes, and makes this setting more challenging.

Remark 1. The rest of this paper assumes the constant values given in Table 1. However, our method remains generic for constants of the same order of magnitude. Here, the variability of the periods is reasonably limited (around 4 %). A variability of more than 40 % will endanger the soundness of our method, as our upcoming assumption that between any three consecutive activations of a node, all nodes execute at least once, would not hold anymore.

2.2 IDs, Modes, Messages

We assume that all the IDs of the nodes in the network are different. Each node executes the same code. Each node has the ability to send messages to all the

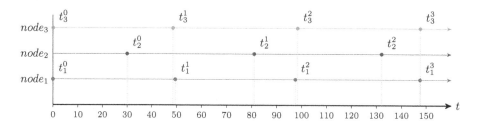

Fig. 1. Activation of three nodes with uncertain periods and jitters

nodes in the network, and can store (at least) one message received from any other node in the network. Nodes are either in mode On and execute the code at each activation time, or do nothing when they are in mode Off. (This models the fact that some nodes in the network might fail.) A node in mode On is in one of the following states:

– Follower: the node is not competing to become leader;
– Candidate: the node is competing to become leader;
– Leader: the node has declared itself to be the leader.

Each transmitted message is of the form: $message = (SenderID, state)$ where $state$ is the state of the sending node.

2.3   The Algorithm

At each new activation, $node_i$ executes the code given in Algorithm 1. In short, if the Boolean flag $node_i.EvenActivation$ (which we can suppose being initially arbitrary) is true, then the code line 1–line 15 is executed. In this code, the node first reads its mailbox, and checks whether any message contains a higher node ID than the node ID (line 3–line 7) and, if so, sets itself as a follower (line 6). If no higher ID was received, the node "upgrades" its status from follower to candidate (line 10), from candidate to leader (line 12), or remains leader if already leader (line 14).

Finally (and this code is executed at every iteration), the node swaps the Boolean flag $EvenActivation$ (line 16), prepares a message with its ID and current state (line 17) and sends this message to the entire network (line 18). We assume that the $Send\_To\_All\_Network$ function sends a message to all nodes—including the sender.

We can see that the significant part of the code (line 1–line 15) is only executed once every two activations (due to Boolean test $node_i.EvenActivation$). This is enforced in order to ensure that each node executes the code after receiving at least one message from all the other nodes (in mode On). However, note that each node sends a message at each iteration.

The order of magnitude of the constants in Table 1 gives the immediate lemma.

Algorithm 1. $UpdateNode(i)$

---

1 if $node_i.EvenActivation$ **then**
2      $allMessages \leftarrow ReadMailbox()$
3      $higherIDreceived \leftarrow$ false
4   **foreach** $message \in allMessages$ **do**
5   **if** $message.SenderID > node_i.id$ **then**
6              $state_{next} \leftarrow$ Follower
7              $higherIDreceived \leftarrow$ true

8   **if** $\neg\ higherIDreceived$ **then**
9   **if** $node_i.state =$ Follower **then**
10             $state_{next} \leftarrow$ Candidate
11   **else if** $node_i.state =$ Candidate **then**
12             $state_{next} \leftarrow$ Leader
13   **else if** $node_i.state =$ Leader **then**
14             $state_{next} \leftarrow$ Leader

15     $node_i.state \leftarrow state_{next}$

16 $node_i.EvenActivation \leftarrow \neg node_i.EvenActivation$
17 $message = \{node_i.id; node_i.state\}$
18 $Send\_To\_All\_Network(message)$

Lemma 1. *Assume a node i and activation times t_i^j and t_i^{j+2}. Then in between these two activations, node i received at least one message from all nodes.*

Proof. From Table 1 and Algorithm 1.

Remark 2. For different orders of magnitudes, we may need to execute the code once every more than two activations. For example, if we set $\text{jitter}_{min} = -25$ and $\text{jitter}_{max} = 25$ in Table 1, the code should be executed every three activations for our algorithm to remain correct.

2.4 Objective

We first introduce the following definitions.

Definition 1 (round). *A* round *is a time period during which all the nodes that are* On *have sent at least one message.*

Definition 2 (cleanness). *A round is said to be* clean *if during its time period no node have been switched from* On *to* Off *or from* Off *to* On.

The correctness property that we want to prove is:

> **"When, following a preliminary clean round, 4 new clean rounds occur, the node with the highest ID is recognized as the leader by all the nodes in modes On of the network."**

This property is denoted by (P) in the following.

Remark 3 (fault model). Our model does allow for faults but, according to Definition 2, only prior to the execution of the algorithm. That is, once it has started, all nodes remain in On or Off during its entire execution. If in reality there is a fault during the execution, it suffices to consider the execution of the algorithm at the next clean round.

3   Direct Verification of the Leader Election Algorithm

In this section, we first verify our algorithm for a fixed number of processes.

We describe here the results obtained by SafeProver on a model M representing directly a network of a fixed, constant number of p processes (without abstraction); for a small number p of nodes, we thus obtain a simple proof of the correctness of the algorithm. The model includes explicitly a representation of each node of $\mathcal{N}$ as well as their associated periods, first activation times, local memories, and mailboxes of received messages. The code is given in Algorithm 2. The mailbox is represented as a queue, initially filled with a message from oneself.[1]

During the initialization declaration, we set everything as free variables (with some constraints, e. g., on the periods) in order to have no assumptions on the state of the network at the beginning. This ensures that this model is valid whatever happened in the past, and this can be seen as a symbolic initial state: this notion of symbolic initial state was used to solve a challenge by Thales [23], also featuring uncertain periods. We also fully initialize the mailboxes of all the nodes since we are assuming that we are right after a clean round. The variable *Activation* is used as a variable to store how many times a node has been executed after the last clean round. The code of called function $UpdateNode(i)$ corresponds exactly to Algorithm 1.

The property (P) we want to prove is formalized as:
$$\big(\forall i \in \{1, \ldots, p\}, Activation(i) \geq 4 \big) \Rightarrow$$
$$\big(\forall j \in \{1, \ldots, p\}, j \neq maxId : node_j.state = \mathsf{Follower}$$
$$\wedge \; node_{maxId}.state = \mathsf{Leader} \big)$$
with $maxId = \arg\max(\{node_i.id \mid node_i.mode = \mathsf{On}\}_{i\in\{1,\ldots,p\}})$. Using this model and SafeProver [16], we obtain the proof of (P) with the times tabulated in Table 3.[2] While this method allows us to formally prove the leader election for up to 5 nodes, SafeProver times out for larger number of nodes. This leads us to consider another method to prove the correctness of our algorithm for larger numbers.

---

[1] An initial empty mailbox would do as well but, in the actual Thales system, this is the way the initialization is performed.

[2] All the experiments reported in this paper have been run on a machine with two Intel® Xeon® CPU E5-2430 at 2.5 GHz, with 164 GiB of RAM and running a Debian 9 Linux distribution.

Algorithm 2. SafeProver code for model M

```
 1  Activation[1, . . . , p] ← [0, . . . , 0]
    // Network initialization
 2  foreach i ∈ {1, . . . , p} do
 3  │   node_i.id ∈ ℕ
 4  │   node_i.per ∈ [period_min; period_max]
 5  │   node_i.start ∈ [0; node_i.per]
 6  │   node_i.state ∈ {Follower, Candidate, Leader}
 7  │   node_i.EvenActivation ∈ {true, false}
 8  │   node_i.mode ∈ {On, Off}
 9  └   nextActivationTime(i) ← node_i.start

    // Mailboxes initializations
10  foreach i ∈ {1, . . . , p} do
    │   // Arbitrary mailbox initialization with a message from oneself
11  └   node_i.mailbox ← [(node_i.id, Follower)]

12  foreach i ∈ {1, . . . , p} do
13  │   foreach j ∈ {1, . . . , p} do
14  │   │   if node_j.mode = On then
15  │   └   └   node_i.mailbox.enqueue(message_j)

    // Main algorithm
16  while true do
17  │   i ← arg min(nextActivationTime)
18  │   if node_i.mode = On then
19  │   │   UpdateNode(i)
20  │   │   Activation(i) ← Activation(i) + 1
21  │   │   jitter ∈ [jitter_min, jitter_max]
22  └   └   nextActivationTime(i) ← nextActivationTime(i) + node_i.per + jitter
```

---

4 Abstraction-Based Method

We now explain how to construct an abstract model $\widehat{M}$ of the original model M. This model $\widehat{M}$ clusters together all the p processes, except the process $node_i$ under study (where i is arbitrary, i.e., a free variable); $\widehat{M}$ also abstracts away the timing information contained in M. We then use SaveProver to infer two basic properties P1 and P2 for $\widehat{M}$.

In a second phase, we consider an auxiliary simple (abstract) model T of M which merely contains relevant timing information; we then use a parametric timed model checker to infer a third property (P3) for T. The parametric timed model checker is required due to the *uncertain* periods, that can have any value in [period_min, period_max] but remain constant over the entire execution.

In the third phase, we consider again the model $\widehat{M}$, and integrate P1–P3 to SafeProver as assumptions, which allows us to infer a fourth property P4. The properties P1 and P4 express together a statement equivalent to the desired correctness property P of the leader election algorithm. The advantage of reasoning

Table 3. Computation times

Nodes	Time (s)
$p = 4$	66.65
$p = 5$	215.61
$p = 6$	time out (> 3600)

with abstract models $\widehat{M}$ and T rather than directly to M, is to prove P for a large number p of processes.

We now describe our method step by step in the following.

4.1   Abstract Model $\widehat{M}$ and Proof of P1-P2

The idea is to model the system as one node $node_i$ (the node of interest) interacting with the rest of the network: $node_i$ receives messages from the other nodes which are clustered into a single abstract process (see Fig. 2). In the abstract model $\widehat{M}$, each node can take any state at any activation, with no regards to the parity ($node_i.EvenActivation$), what has been previously sent, what $node_i$ is sending. We only consider the activation of $node_i$. The rest of the network is abstracted by the messages contained in the mailbox of $node_i$. Since we assume that at least one clean round has passed, we always have a message from a working node in the mailbox. The code is given in Algorithm 3. (Note its analogy with the SafeProver code of Algorithm 2 for M.) The first four lines define free variables.

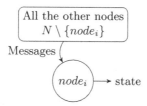

Fig. 2. Scheme of model $\widehat{M}$ with node i under study interacting with the cluster of all the other nodes

The list of assumptions that the solver can make on the messages received is denoted by $List\_of\_assumptions\_on\_message_j$. This list is initially empty, and augmented with "guarantees" (a.k.a. "proven properties") on the other nodes as they are iteratively generated by the solver. The first proven properties are:

- P1: $(Activation(j) \geq 2 \ \wedge \ node_j.id \neq maxId) \Rightarrow \ node_j.state = \mathsf{Follower}$
- P2: $(Activation(j) \geq 2 \ \wedge \ node_j.id = maxId)$
$$\Rightarrow node_j.state \in \{\mathsf{Candidate}, \mathsf{Leader}\}$$

Algorithm 3. SafeProver code for abstract model $\widehat{M}$

---

1 Assume $i \in \{1, \ldots, p\}$
2 Assume $node_i.id \in \mathbb{N}$
3 Assume $node_i.state \in \{\text{Follower, Candidate, Leader}\}$
4 Assume $node_i.EvenActivation \in \{\text{true, false}\}$
5 $Activation(i) \leftarrow 0$
6 **while** *true* **do**
7   **for** $j \in \{1, \ldots, p\}$ **do**
8          $message_j \in \{node_j.id\} \times \{\text{Follower, Candidate, Leader}\}$
9   **Assume:** $List\_of\_assumptions\_on\_message_j$
10         $node_i.mailbox.enqueue(message_j)$
11     $UpdateNode(i)$
12     $Activation(i) + +$
13     $Guarantee\_to\_prove$

In these properties, j is a free variable: therefore, it is "fixed" among one execution, but can correspond to any of the node IDs. The two properties state that, after two rounds, a node which has not the largest ID is necessarily a follower (P1), or a candidate or a leader if it has the largest ID (P2). As said before, P1 and P2 are then integrated to $List\_of\_assumptions\_on\_message_j$.

$Guarantee\_to\_prove$ contains iteratively P1, then P1 and P2, then P1, P2 and P4.

4.2 Abstract Model T and Proof of P3

To represent the timed abstract model T of M, we use an extension of the formalism of timed automata [5], a powerful extension of finite-state automata with clocks, i. e., real-valued variables that evolve at the same time. These clocks can be compared with constants when taking a transition ("guards"), or to remain in a discrete state ("invariants"). Discrete states are called *locations*. Timed automata were proven successful in verifying many systems with interactions between time and concurrency, especially with the state-of-the-art model-checker UPPAAL [10]. However, timed automata cannot model and verify arbitrary periods: while it is possible to model a different period at each round, it is not possible to first fix a period once for all (in an interval), and then use this period for the rest of the execution. We therefore use the extension "parametric timed automata" [6,8] allowing to consider *parameters*, i. e., unknown constants (possibly in an interval). IMITATOR [9] is a state-of-the-art model checker supporting this formalism.

In our method, the timed abstract model T of M is a product of two similar parametric timed automata representing the node i under study and a generic node j belonging to $\mathcal{N} \setminus \{i\}$ respectively. Each parametric timed automaton contains a single location. The parametric timed automaton corresponding to $node_i$ uses an activation period per_i that we model as a parameter. Indeed, recall that the period belongs to an interval: taking a value in the interval at each round would not be correct, as the period would not be constant. This is where we need parameters in our method. In addition, we constrain this parameter per_i to belong to $[\text{period}_{min}, \text{period}_{max}]$. Each automaton has its own clock c_i that is used to measure how much time has passed since the last activation. Each automaton has a discrete variable[3] $Activation(i)$ which is initialized at 0 and is used to count the number of activations for this node. We give the constraint on c_i at the beginning that $c_i \in [0, per_i + \text{jitter}_{max}]$. An activation can occur as soon as c_i reaches $per_i + \text{jitter}_{min}$. This is modeled by the guard $c_i \geq per_i + \text{jitter}_{min}$ on the transition that resets c_i and increment $Activation(i)$. An activation can occur as long as c_i is below or equal to $per_i + \text{jitter}_{max}$. This is modeled by the invariant $c_i \leq per_i + \text{jitter}_{min}$ on the unique location of the automaton. This invariant forces the transition to occur when c_i reaches its upper bound. This parametric timed automaton is represented in Fig. 3.[4] The other component representing the cluster of the rest of the nodes is modeled similarly as a generic component $node_j$.

Fig. 3. Component 1 of timed model T

For nodes $node_i$ and $node_j$, the property that we want to specify corresponds in the direct model M (without abstraction) of Sect. 3 to:

$$(Activation(i) \leq 13 \ \wedge \ Activation(j) \leq 13)$$
$$\Rightarrow \ | \ Activation(i) - Activation(j) \ | \ \leq \ 2.$$

In our timed abstract model T, such a property becomes:

$(P3) : \forall i \in \{1, \ldots, p\} \ Activation(j) \leq 13 \Rightarrow$
$- 2 \leq Activation(j) - Activation(i) \leq 1.$

where $Activation(i)$ denotes the number of activations of node i since the last clean round.

The value "13" has been obtained experimentally: smaller numbers led the algorithm to fail (the property was not satisfied). Intuitively, it consists in the number of activations by which we are sure the leader will eventually be elected.

---

[3] Discrete variables are global Boolean- or integer-valued variables, that can be read or written in transition guards. If their domain is finite they are syntactic sugar for a larger number of locations.

[4] The color code is that of IMITATOR automated LaTeX outputs: clocks are in blue, parameters in orange, and discrete variables in pink.

The proof of P3 is obtained by adding to the model an observer[5] automaton checking the value of the discrete variables $Activation(i)$ and $Activation(j)$, which goes to a *bad* location when the property is violated. The property is then verified by showing that the *bad* location is not reachable. For the values of the timing constants in Table 1, IMITATOR proves P3 (by showing the non-reachability of the bad location) in 12 s. Recall that, thanks to our assumption on the number of nodes, we only used two nodes in the input model for IMITATOR.

In the next part, we show how the addition of P3 as an assumption in the original abstract model allows to prove the desired property P for a large number of nodes.

4.3 Proof of P Using P1–P3 as Assumptions

In addition to P1-P2, we now put P3 $(Activation(j) \in [Activation(i) - 1; Activation(i)+2])$ as an element of $List\_of\_assumptions\_on\_message_j$ used in the SafeProver code of $\widehat{M}$ (see Algorithm 3). SafeProver is then able to generate the following property:

$$P4 : (Activation(i) \geq 4 \;\wedge\; node_i.id = maxId) \Rightarrow node_i.state = \text{Leader}$$

Property P4 states that the node with the highest ID will declare itself as Leader after at most 4 activations. Besides, property P1 states that a node, not having the highest ID, is in the state Follower within at most 2 activations. Properties P1 and P4 together thus express a statement equivalent to the desired correctness property P. The global generation of properties (P1), (P2) and (P4) by SafeProver takes the computation times tabulated in Table 4. As one sees, the computation time is now smaller by an order of magnitude than the ones given in Table 3, thus showing the good scalability of our method.

Table 4. Computation times

Nodes	Time (s)
$p = 500$	13.34
$p = 1000$	45.95
$p = 5000$	623.46

Remark 4. Note that verifying the model for 5,000 nodes also gives a guarantee for any smaller of nodes. Indeed, we can assume that an arbitrary number of nodes are in mode Off, and remain so, which is equivalent to a smaller number of nodes.

---

[5] An observer is an additional automaton that can synchronize with the system (using synchronized actions, clocks or discrete variables values), without modifying its behavior nor blocking it. See e. g., [4,7].

4.4   Discussion

Soundness We briefly discuss the soundness of the algorithm. First, note that the assumptions used above have been validated by the system designers (i.e., those who designed the algorithm). Second, SafeProver validated the assumptions, i.e., proved that they were not inconsistent with each other (which would result in an empty model).

Now, the abstraction used in Sect. 4.2, i.e., to consider only two nodes, is the one which required most human creativity. Let us briefly discuss its soundness. Our abstraction allows to model the sending of any message, which includes the actual message to be sent in the actual system. The fact that a message was necessarily received in the actual system between two (real) executions of the node under study is given by the fact that all nodes necessarily execute at least once in the last two periods (see Lemma 1). Of course, this soundness is only valid under our own assumptions on the variability of the period, considering the constants in Table 1: if the period of one node is 1 while the other is 100, our framework is obviously not sound anymore.

Parametric vs. parametrized model checking. As shown in Table 4, we verified the model for a *constant* number of nodes. This comes in contrast with the recent work on parameterized verification (e.g., [2,12,13]). However, while these latter consider a parameterized number of nodes, they consider *non-parametric* timed models; in contrast, we need here parametric timed models to be able to represent the uncertainty on the periods. Combining both worlds (parameterized number of nodes with parametric timed models) would be of interest—but remains a very challenging objective.

5   Conclusion

We described a method combining abstraction, SafeProver and parametric timed model-checking in order to prove the correctness of a variant of an asynchronous leader election algorithm designed by Thales. Our approach can efficiently verify the leader election after a fixed number of rounds for a large number p of processes (up to $p = 5000$). The method relies on the construction of two abstract models $\widehat{M}$ and T of the original model M. Although it is intuitive, it could be interesting to prove formally that each abstraction is *correct* in the sense that it *over-approximates* all the behaviors of M.

Perspectives

Many variants of the algorithm can be envisioned (loss of messages, non-instantaneous transmission, non-complete graph topology, ...). The fault model could also be enriched. It will then be also interesting to propose extensions of our abstraction-based method to prove the correctness of such extensions.

The correctness of the method relies on the order of magnitude of the constants used (Remark 1). For different intervals, it might be necessary to both adapt the algorithm (read messages only every k activations) but also the assumptions used in the proof using abstraction, a manual and possibly error-prone process. A more general verification method would be desirable.

In addition, the number of activations in our correctness property ("after 13 activations, the leader is elected") was obtained using an incremental verification (values of up to 12 all gave concrete counterexamples). As a future work, we would like to automatically infer this value too, i.e., obtaining the minimal value of activations before a leader is guaranteed to be elected.

Finally, adding probabilities to model the fault of nodes will be of interest.

Acknowledgment. We thank anonymous reviewers for very useful remarks and suggestions.

References

1. Abdulla, P.A., Delzanno, G., Rezine, O., Sangnier, A., Traverso, R.: On the verification of timed ad hoc networks. In: Fahrenberg, U., Tripakis, S. (eds.) FORMATS 2011. LNCS, vol. 6919, pp. 256–270. Springer, Heidelberg (2011). https://doi.org/10.1007/978-3-642-24310-3_18
2. Abdulla, P.A., Delzanno, G., Rezine, O., Sangnier, A., Traverso, R.: Parameterized verification of time-sensitive models of ad hoc network protocols. Theor. Comput. Sci. **612**, 1–22 (2016)
3. Abdulla, P.A., Jonsson, B.: Model checking of systems with many identical timed processes. Theor. Comput. Sci. **290**(1), 241–264 (2003)
4. Aceto, L., Bouyer, P., Burgueño, A., Larsen, K.G.: The power of reachability testing for timed automata. In: Arvind, V., Ramanujam, S. (eds.) FSTTCS 1998. LNCS, vol. 1530, pp. 245–256. Springer, Heidelberg (1998). https://doi.org/10.1007/978-3-540-49382-2_22
5. Alur, R., Dill, D.L.: A theory of timed automata. Theor. Comput. Sci. **126**, 183–235 (1994)
6. Alur, R., Henzinger, T.A., Vardi, M.Y.: Parametric real-time reasoning. In: Kosaraju, S.R., Johnson, D.S., Aggarwal, A. (eds.) Proceedings of the Twenty-Fifth Annual ACM symposium on Theory of Computing (STOC 1993), pp. 592–601. ACM, New York (1993)
7. André, É.: Observer patterns for real-time systems. In: Liu, Y., Martin, A. (eds.) Proceedings of the 18th IEEE International Conference on Engineering of Complex Computer Systems (ICECCS 2013), pp. 125–134. IEEE Computer Society, July 2013
8. André, É.: What's decidable about parametric timed automata? Int. J. Softw. Tools Technol. Transf. (2019, to appear)
9. André, É., Fribourg, L., Kühne, U., Soulat, R.: IMITATOR 2.5: a tool for analyzing robustness in scheduling problems. In: Giannakopoulou, D., Méry, D. (eds.) FM 2012. LNCS, vol. 7436, pp. 33–36. Springer, Heidelberg (2012). https://doi.org/10.1007/978-3-642-32759-9_6
10. Behrmann, G., David, A., Larsen, K.G.: A tutorial on UPPAAL. In: Bernardo, M., Corradini, F. (eds.) SFM-RT 2004. LNCS, vol. 3185, pp. 200–236. Springer, Heidelberg (2004). https://doi.org/10.1007/978-3-540-30080-9_7

11. Bouajjani, A., Jonsson, B., Nilsson, M., Touili, T.: Regular model checking. In: Emerson, E.A., Sistla, A.P. (eds.) CAV 2000. LNCS, vol. 1855, pp. 403–418. Springer, Heidelberg (2000). https://doi.org/10.1007/10722167_31
12. Conchon, S., Declerck, D., Zaïdi, F.: Compiling parameterized X86-TSO concurrent programs to Cubicle-$\mathcal{W}$. In: Duan, Z., Ong, L. (eds.) ICFEM 2017. LNCS, vol. 10610, pp. 88–104. Springer, Cham (2017). https://doi.org/10.1007/978-3-319-68690-5_6
13. Conchon, S., Declerck, D., Zaïdi, F.: Parameterized model checking modulo explicit weak memory models. In: Laleau, R., Méry, D., Nakajima, S., Troubitsyna, E. (eds.) Proceedings of the Joint Workshop on Handling IMPlicit and EXplicit Knowledge In Formal System Development (IMPEX) and Formal and Model-Driven Techniques for Developing Trustworthy Systems (FM&MDD), IMPEX/FM&MDD 2017. EPTCS, vol. 271, pp. 48–63 (2017)
14. Conchon, S., Goel, A., Krstić, S., Mebsout, A., Zaïdi, F.: Cubicle: a parallel SMT-based model checker for parameterized systems. In: Madhusudan, P., Seshia, S.A. (eds.) CAV 2012. LNCS, vol. 7358, pp. 718–724. Springer, Heidelberg (2012). https://doi.org/10.1007/978-3-642-31424-7_55
15. De Moura, L., Bjørner, N.: Satisfiability modulo theories: introduction and applications. Commun. ACM **54**(9), 69–77 (2011)
16. Étienne, J.F., Juppeaux, É.: SafeProver: a high-performance verification tool. ACM SIGAda Ada Lett. **36**(2), 47–48 (2017)
17. Fribourg, L., Olsén, H.: Reachability sets of parameterized rings as regular languages. Electron. Notes Theor. Comput. Sci. **9**, 40 (1997)
18. García-Molina, H.: Elections in a distributed computing system. IEEE Trans. Comput. **31**(1), 48–59 (1982)
19. Konnov, I.V., Veith, H., Widder, J.: What you always wanted to know about model checking of fault-tolerant distributed algorithms. In: Mazzara, M., Voronkov, A. (eds.) PSI 2015. LNCS, vol. 9609, pp. 6–21. Springer, Cham (2016). https://doi.org/10.1007/978-3-319-41579-6_2
20. Lamport, L.: The part-time parliament. ACM Trans. Comput. Syst. **16**(2), 133–169 (1998)
21. Lamport, L.: Specifying Systems: The TLA+ Language and Tools for Hardware and Software Engineers. Addison-Wesley Longman Publishing Co. Inc., Boston (2002)
22. Lynch, N.A.: Distributed Algorithms. Morgan Kaufmann Publishers Inc., San Francisco (1996)
23. Sun, Y., André, É., Lipari, G.: Verification of two real-time systems using parametric timed automata. In: Quinton, S., Vardanega, T. (eds.) Proceedings of the 6th International Workshop on Analysis Tools and Methodologies for Embedded and Real-time Systems (WATERS 2015), July 2015

Application of Abstract Interpretation to the Automotive Electronic Control System

Tomoya Yamaguchi[1]([✉]), Martin Brain[2], Chirs Ryder[3], Yosikazu Imai[4], and Yoshiumi Kawamura[1]

[1] Toyota Motor Corporation, 1200, Mishuku, Susono, Shizuoka, Japan
tomoya.yamaguchi@toyota.com, yoshiumi_kawamura@mail.toyota.co.jp
[2] University of Oxford, Wolfson Building, Parks Road, Oxford, UK
martin.brain@cs.ox.ac.uk
[3] Diffblue, 10 St. Ebbs Street, Oxford, UK
chris.ryder@diffblue.com
[4] Nu-soft, 3-24-2 Shinyokohama, Kouhoku, Yokohama, Kanagawa, Japan
imai@nu-soft.jp

Abstract. The verification and validation of industrial automotive systems is increasingly challenging as they become larger and more complex. Recent automotive Electric Control Units (ECUs) have approximately one half to one million of lines of code, and a modern automobile can contain hundreds of controllers. Significant work-hours are needed to understand and manage systems of this level of complexity. One particular challenge is understanding the changes to the software across development phases and revisions. To this end, we present a code dependency analysis tool that enhances designer understanding. It combines abstract interpretation and graph based data analysis to generate visualized dependency graphs on demand to support designer's understanding of the code. We demonstrate its value by presenting dependency graph visuals for an industrial application, and report results showing significant reduction of work-hours and enhancement of the ability to understand the software.

1 Introduction

In recent years, functional requirements for automotive control systems have become far more sophisticated. This necessitated the development of more complex and larger scale control software, which lead to a significant increase in work-hours. Figure 1 shows the amount of work-hours for control software development based on our project management data, which reveals that work hours almost doubled from 2012 to 2017. Based on this trend, the work-hours are expected to increase considerably in the near future.

One of the causes of the considerable increase in work-hours is that much time is spent understanding complex vehicle systems that are composed of many

© Springer Nature Switzerland AG 2019
C. Enea and R. Piskac (Eds.): VMCAI 2019, LNCS 11388, pp. 425–445, 2019.
https://doi.org/10.1007/978-3-030-11245-5_20

smaller subsystems, which we call *unit-systems*. The designer's interests are to grasp the vehicle system architecture, the unit-system architecture, and the impact of their revisions or extensions at the program level. Therefore, accurate and comprehensive visualization of abstractions of the software will help to increase the designer's understanding and will mitigate the increase in work-hours.

In this paper, we present a tool that provides various view graphs that can support the designer's understanding of the system by using a static analysis technology. Characteristics of our tool include the following: (1) ability to control the scalability and preciseness based on the designer's interest, and (2) a guarantee of soundness (there are no missed dependencies). Traditional code analysis does not guarantee absolute precision. On the other hand, legacy static analysis guarantees precision but is not scalable. Thus we developed an abstract interpretation technology, which is based on static analysis methods, to our tool. In addition, a graph-based data base is exploited to manage enormous dependency for large scale code.

Specific contributions of the paper are:

- Explaining background on automotive control system software and the corresponding industrial challenges that the support the designer's understanding to maintains our product quality under situation of increasing work-hours trend (Sect. 2).
- Algorithmic and implementation innovations needed for scalable and precise abstract interpretation (Sect. 3).
- An overview of the C Analysis Tool (CAT) developed (Sect. 4).
- Results of the application of our tool to the actual control system code (Sect. 5).

2   The Challenges of Modern Automotive Software

2.1   Architecture of Automotive Software

Figure 3 shows the software architecture of a modern vehicle. The vehicle system consists of several unit-systems, like the engine and the transmission, which have their own ECU; each ECU communicates via a CAN network. The majority of ECUs are implemented in C. The largest unit-system in the vehicle is the engine ECU, and we use it as a recurring example. The engine ECU has multiple features, such as ignition, injection, and variable valve control. Each feature contains program modules that are divided into functional units, each of which are collections of several functions. The functions that compose the modules are allocated to tasks for the Operating System (OS), which manages time driven and event driven tasks.

A key characteristic of the software is the scale; each ECU has up to half a million of lines of code (LoC). Several thousand global variables are used for inter-function communication, which results in module interdependency and a high level of code complexity. Pointer access is used as little as possible in the application layer, but many pointer accesses occur at the lower layer, like for sensor data, or ROM (Read Only Memory)/RAM (Random Access Memory) access. About five hundred such pointers are used in the lower layer.

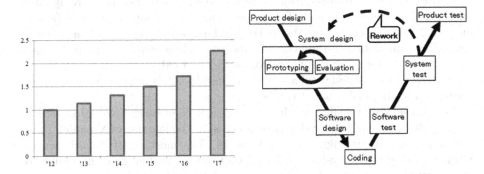

Fig. 1. Magnification of work-hour based on 2012.

Fig. 2. Design development of automotive software development.

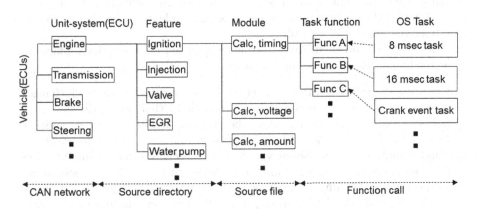

Fig. 3. Architecture of automotive control system.

2.2 Development Process

Figure 2 shows the automotive software development process for the Electronic Control Unit (ECU). Our process uses a version of the typical V-model design process. Since complex physical phenomena, such as the vehicle dynamics, are the target of the control algorithms, prototypes of the physical components are used to develop system software. The prototype development tends to be incremental, focused on components, while re-using, and extending legacy systems. The system design involves iterative development of the prototype, along with evaluation, while validating operation of the control system in actual usage environments. Due to the use of iterative prototypes and corresponding control algorithms, a spiral-up type process is incorporated into the system design process on the left side of the V-model.

Our development process involves various testing activities that are applied on the right side of V-model. Those tests include evaluation of the software on actual vehicles, engine test beds, HILS (Hardware-in-the-Loop-Simulation), and SILS (Simulation-in-the-Loop-Simulation). Those tests are more intense (demanding, in terms of system performance) and exhaustive than the evaluation at the system design phase and are employed to achieve and maintain quality up to the final product test phase.

A main source of inefficiency in our process is the rework involved to return to an earlier phase of the development process, in the left side of V-model, from a test process, in the right side of V-model. The most costly rework occurs when returning to the system design phase from the system test phase, due to the many development and testing steps that have already been performed to reach the testing phase. Thus making well defined system designs is important to reduce the amount of rework. In that sense, misunderstanding the system design is one of the significant causes of the rework. Accordingly, a good review process, founded on a firm understanding of the implementation, is required to help limit the amount of rework.

The designer will benefit from the following, either for a new development or for extending an existing system design.

1. Understanding the software architecture: It is important to decide which module or function should be revised beforehand. In that sense, the developer needs to understand the entirety of the program architecture on every level, such as the function, the module, the sub-system, and the system levels.
2. Impact analysis of the revised variables or the calibration parameters: The designer is interested in what kind of influence their own design revision has to the system. The impact analysis is necessary in the Design Review Based on Failure Mode (DRBFM) [1] to prevent the revision leading to unexpected behaviors when revising variables or re-calibration of parameters.

The review process is basically done in manual or semi-manual manner, such as reading a natural language of the specification or using the `grep` command in for C code. When considering the module or function level graph, this process can be sufficient, since the scale is small. However, if the system level graph is considered, the manual process becomes a development bottleneck, because the system scale is large, and the corresponding system graph is created manually.

2.3   Technical Issue and Approach

In order to automate the software architecture analysis and impact analysis, we present a method based on static analysis. The required functionality and challenges are as follows.

Program 1. Code example for struct/union.

```
1   struct st {
2     int m1;
3     int m2;
4   };
5
6   extern int g_in;
7   struct st g_st;
8   int g_out1, g_out2, g_out3;
9
10  void main(void){
11    if (g_in == 1)
12      g_st.m1 ++;
13
14    if (g_in == 2)
15      g_st.m2 ++;
16
17    g_out1 = g_st.m1;
18    g_out2 = g_st.m2;
19    g_out3 = g_st.m1 + g_st.m2;
20  }
```

Program 2. Code example for closed loop.

```
1   extern int g_in1;
2   extern int g_in2;
3   int g_x1;
4   int g_x2;
5
6   void main(void) {
7     if (g_in1)
8       g_x2 = 0;
9
10    g_x1 = g_x2;
11
12    if (g_in2)
13      g_x2 = g_x1;
14  }
```

Dependency Analysis. To understand the ECU program architecture, we need to generate the "unit-system dependency graph" by using exhaustive dependency analysis in the reviewing phase. This is like a map for software architecture, which aids in understanding the software. The software directory composition, shown in Fig. 3, is not sufficient because it does not contain essential program information like function calls or global variable reads/writes; program (Control and Data) dependencies are needed to make a more helpful graph [2]. Particular challenges are;

1. The analysis must scale to a half million lines of code and handle several thousand global variable.
2. At some levels of detail we require precise handling of nested struct and union variables. These often contain flags indicates important conditions, like whether the engine is idling or whether the engine is in a fuel-cut mode. Program 1 shows an example. It has **struct st** on L1 and the members are accessed in **main** function several times.
3. It is necessary to consider the software as a closed-loop system. In that case, the entry function is called repeatedly in the embedded controller; therefore, it is necessary to consider the previous status of global variables. Program 2 shows an example. When **main** on L6 is called repeatedly for the closed-loop system, 2nd call of L10 depends 1st call of L13 in specific case. We call this capability the periodic option, which is an option for our data dependency analysis.

Pointer Resolution. The dependency analysis must be able to handle both data and function pointers. Pointer analysis is challenging in general, but this functionality is a key requirement for static analysis tools and means that purely syntactic approaches to dependency analysis will not work. False negatives for pointer analysis are not allowed, because it results in missing important cases. We require flow, loop, array, and struct/union awareness.

Program 3. Code example for pointer.

```
1   #define ARRAY_SIZE   4
2   const int cAarray[ARRAY_SIZE] = { 10, 20, 30, 40};
3   int gArray1[ARRAY_SIZE];
4   int gArray2[ARRAY_SIZE];
5
6   void main(){
7     const int* p0 = cAarray;
8     int* p1 = gArray1;
9
10    for (int i=0; i<ARRAY_SIZE; i++){
11      *p1 = cAarray[i];
12      gArray2[i] = *p0;
13      p0++;
14      p1++;
15    }
16  }
```

Program 4. Code example for function pointer.

```
1   struct st {
2     int (*req)(char, char *);
3   };
4
5   int f1( char, char *);
6   int f2( char, char *);
7   const struct st fptbl1[]={
8     { f1 },
9     { f2 },
10  };
11
12  int g1(char, void*);
13  int g2(char, void*);
14  int (* const fptbl2[])(char, void *) = {
15    g1,
16    g2,
17  };
18
19  void func(int id, int len, char* buf ){
20    const struct st *p = &fptbl1[id];
21    p->req(len, buf);
22  }
```

Program 3 is an example demonstrating the variable pointer use-case. It has array on L2-4, and loop on L10, furthermore pointer accesses on L7 and L8. Program 4 demonstrates the function pointer use-case. It has function pointer on L20, and arrow access by using function pointer "p" on L21.

A designer can typically resolve a pointer manually within 15 min. Usually, the designer manually resolves only what they deem interesting, which usually exists at the module level. However, if the vehicle or system graph is considered in an initial phase of development, all pointers should be resolved to clarify all dependency. In this case, the work hours are estimated at about 125 h (=15 min * 500 pointers). This is an unreasonable amount of work-hours to spend resolving pointers.

The embedded ECU does not have un-resolvable pointers because it is a safety critical system and does not use dynamic memory allocation. Even considering pointers in loop statements, there are no unbounded loops because the number of loops are based on constant values, like the number of banks, cylinders, and the look-up table size.

Program Slicing. We attempt to apply program slicing [3] to the "unit-system dependency graph" for the impact analysis. This is similar to a path-planning problem. Often the generated graphs are too large to understand. To address that, we expect a kind of extraction functionality that allows the designer to focus on their interests. Program slicing is a kind of forward and backward analysis on dependency. Our expected use-case is impact analysis from the revised variables or the calibration parameters to understand the influence of their revisions. The challenging aspect is to handle enormous dependency from a half million lines of code and on-demand access for forward and backward analysis.

As many of these challenges require understanding parts of the semantics of the program, purely syntactic approaches to the dependency graph are not sufficient. To this end, we use abstract interpretation, which can produce scalable and precise results and further guarantee soundness regarding pointer and dependency analysis. To support the enormous information management on the slicing requirements, we use a non-relational database. In the next section, we describe the key technique: abstract interpretation.

3   Abstract Interpretation

Abstract Interpretation [4] is a mathematical framework for designing, developing and understanding static analysis techniques [5]. It provides general results, based on order theory, that guarantee soundness and termination of an analysis given a few basic properties of the data structures and functions used. These allow the development of a new analysis to be reduced to developing one data structure and two (optionally three) functions:

Domain. A domain is a mathematical object that *represents* a set of possible program states. The conventional approach to implementing abstract interpretation analyses to create a data-structure for the domain. Commonly this is a *non-relational* domain, a map from variable to an abstract representation of their possible values (for example intervals, or sets of dependencies).

Transform. A function that takes the domain representing the state before an instruction and generates the domain representing the possible program states after. This is the abstract version of executing one step of the program. The transform function covering all possibilities (in this case, tracking all dependencies) is one of the key criteria for a sound analysis. Obviously the details of transformation will depend on the domain, for example, if the domain uses intervals then the transform function will perform interval arithmetic.

Merge. A function that takes two domains and combines them into one that includes things represented by either (but may contain more). In the case of intervals, this would be merging the two intervals. Merge is the over-approximate version of a union and allows control-flow paths to be merged, a key criteria for termination.

Widen. A key result in abstract interpretation is that the fixed-point of an (over-)approximation is an (over-)approximation of a fixed-point. So just by iterating the analysis, loops can be handled in a correct and terminating manner. Depending on the domain, direct iteration can take too long, so a widening function is often used to accelerate the process. In the case of intervals this might be setting the upper or lower bounds to their max.

3.1 Variable-Sensitivity Domain

As this project needs to compute dependencies for each variable individually and does not need to track the relationships between them, it is sufficient to use a non-relational domain. This means that we can represent the state of a program a given location using one map which stores an object for each variable. Doing so allows us a uniform and simple way of handling one of the requirements – a variable level of sensitivity in the analysis depending on whether it is being analyses at feature, module or task function level.

By implementing a common object interface, we can use dynamic dispatch to control the objects, and thus the precision, used to track arrays, pointers, structs, unions and combinations of them. When the program is analysed at the large scale, we can smash arrays, tracking one dependency set per arrays, and switch seamlessly to per-element dependencies at smaller scales. Similarly, we can switch from just dependencies to tracking constant value or intervals for each variable as well to increase precision for more detailed analyses.

Although this approach is less general than conventional approaches using separate value, array and pointer analyses and reduced products or open combinations [14], it scales better and handles large, complex, global data-structures (for example, pointers to arrays that are members of structs) in a clean and simple manner. It also simplifies various implementation and algorithmic improvements discussed below.

3.2 Copy-on-Write Data Structures

As we need to generate dependencies for every location in the program and keep these in memory to handle periodic analysis as described above, memory is a significant concern. If we are to store 1,000,000 domains (one per line of code), each tracking up to 10,000 variables (not counting per-element analysis of arrays), then every byte required by a dependency set will need 10 GB of RAM.

Here the "one big map" approach of the variable sensitivity domain is of great use. Although we have to store domains for every program location, the majority of them are largely similar to the domains at preceding locations. By using a custom copy-on-write map data-structure, we only have to store the *difference* between two domains, which makes the memory consumption tractable. The authors believe a similar approach is implemented in Astrée [15] although the details are not public. This also gives a fast way of iterating across the differences between two domains.

Program 5. The need for three way merging

```
1   int gState;
2
3   void func (void) {
4     // Does not modify gState
5   }
6
7   void task(void) {
8     gState = INIT;
9     func();
10
11    // Other functionality
12
13    gState = FINAL;
14    func();
15  }
```

3.3 Three-Way Merge

Conventional abstract interpretation is *context-insensitive*, so each call to a function will merge the calling state with the starting state of the function. For programs with fixed and tight scoping rules, this is not necessarily a problem. However when handling a large number of global variables it causes an interesting problem.

Consider the Program 5. The first call to func will correctly track the dependencies and the constant value of gState. The second call to func will merge in its value of gState which causes a problem on function return: even though the function does not alter gState its value and dependencies will be set to the merge of *all possible calling locations*. In the case of low-level utility functions this can cause very significant loss of precision, particularly when unwinding loops.

To avoid this problem without the cost of performing full context-sensitive analysis, we use the dependencies and modification information implicitly stored in the copy-on-write data structures. On function return, rather than just merging the state at the end of the callee into the caller, we identify each of the variables (array elements, struct fields, etc. depending on the sensitivity) that has changed *between the start and end of the callee* and merge only those into the caller state, resulting in a three-way merge.

4 C Analysis Tool

Figure 4 shows the C Analysis Tool (CAT) architecture. The CAT basically consists of three components. The CPROVER [7] component compiles ECU code and executes the abstract interpretation and finally outputs the instruction level of dependency. The Orient-DB [8] component is a non-relational database and deals with the enormous dependency information and analyzes forward and backward analysis based on the dependency on demand to implement the slicing. The visualization component converts instruction-level of dependency to a more user-friendly level. The visualization back-ends can be accessed via a Java-API, and the user can operate it from their own environment or an Integrated Development Environment (IDE) like MATLAB ®, Eclipse ®, Visual Studio ®, Windows ®CMD and so on. Those components are explained in detail in following sections.

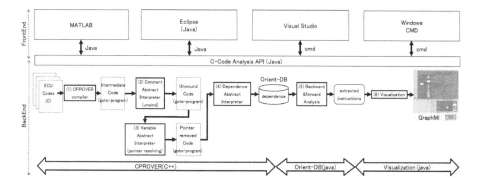

Fig. 4. C Analysis Tool architecture.

4.1   CPROVER

CPROVER [7] is an open-source C++ framework for building C, C++ and Java analysis and verification tools. It provides components for compilation, program transformation and analysis, abstract interpretation, symbolic execution and SMT solving. For instance, C Bounded Model Checker (CBMC) [9] is a well-known bounded model checker and is implemented using CPROVER.

goto-cc CPROVER has a compiler goto-cc which supports gcc [10] equivalent compiler options. This means goto-cc can compile C-code by just changing the command gcc to goto-cc in a make-file, which has a high advantage in industrial application. The goto-cc produces a "goto-program", which is a kind of intermediate representation (see Fig. 5). In our CAT tool, the goto-cc is used in **CPROVER compiler** ((1) in Fig. 4).

goto-analyzer is the abstract interpreter from CPROVER. It operates on goto-programs and thus is language independent. The goto-analyzer supports three types of abstract domain, which are the constant domain, the variable sensitivity domain, and the dependency domain.

Constant Domain ((2) in Fig. 4): Finds unwinding-bounds for the loops, then it unwinds the original code. The command is goto-analyzer --constant

Variable Domain ((3) in Fig. 4): Simplifies and removes the data and function pointers with array and struct/union awareness. The command is goto-analyzer --variable --structs --arrays

Example code

```
void func(void) {
    u1 * u1t_p;
    u1 u1t_x;
    u2 u2t_y;
    bitstr stt_s;

    u1t_x = u1g_x;
    u2t_y = u2g_y;
    stt_s = stg_s;
    u1t_p = &u1g_a[0];

    if (u1g_j == 0) {
        u1t_x++;
        u2t_y = u1g_a[0];
        stt_s.b1 = 1;
        u1t_p++;
    }
    else if (u1g_j == 1) {
        u2t_y = u1g_a[u1g_j];
        stt_s.b1 = 0;
        stt_s.b34 = 2;
    }

    u1g_x = u1t_x;
    u2g_y = u2t_y;
    stg_s = stt_s;
    *u1t_p = stt_s.b1;
    u1t_p++;
    *u1t_p = stt_s.b34;
}
```

goto-program

type	code / guard	target
DECL	unsigned char *u1t_p;	
DECL	unsigned char u1t_x;	
DECL	unsigned short int u2t_y;	
DECL	struct bitstr stt_s;	
ASSIGN	u1t_x = u1g_x;	
ASSIGN	u2t_y = u2g_y;	
ASSIGN	stt_s = stg_s;	
ASSIGN	u1t_p = &u1g_a[(signed long int)0];	
GOTO	!((signed int)u1g_j == 0)	
ASSIGN	u1t_x = u1t_x + 1;	
ASSIGN	u2t_y = (unsigned short int)u1g_a[(signed long int)0];	
ASSIGN	stt_s.b1 = (unsigned char : 1)(unsigned char)1;	
ASSIGN	u1t_p = u1t_p + 1;	
GOTO	GOTO 2	
GOTO	!((signed int)u1g_j == 1)	
ASSIGN	u2t_y = (unsigned short int)u1g_a[(signed long int)u1g_j];	
ASSIGN	stt_s.b1 = (unsigned char : 1)(unsigned char)0;	
ASSIGN	stt_s.b34 = (unsigned char : 2)(unsigned char)2;	
ASSIGN	stt_s.b34 = (unsigned char : 2)((unsigned char)stt_s.b34 + ..	
ASSIGN	u1g_x = u1t_x;	
ASSIGN	u2g_y = u2t_y;	
ASSIGN	stg_s = stt_s;	
ASSIGN	*u1t_p = (unsigned char)stt_s.b1;	
ASSIGN	u1t_p = u1t_p + 1l;	
ASSIGN	*u1t_p = (unsigned char)stt_s.b34;	

Fig. 5. Goto-program.

Dependency Domain ((4) in Fig. 4): Extracts the instruction level dependency from the pointer-resolved goto-program. It supports typical control dependency and data dependency with array and struct/union awareness. In addition, it supports the recurrent data dependency, which is an embedded specific option. Typically, the embedded controller calls a task repeatedly and considers the status of the previous control step as necessary. The command is goto-analyzer --dependence-graph-vs
--structs --arrays --periodic-task.

The CAT exploits the constant and variable sensitivity domains to handle loops and pointers and the dependency abstract interpreter for extracting program dependency. Finally, that outputs the dependency at the instruction-level to Orient-DB.

4.2   Orient-DB

The Orient-DB [8,11] handles the dependency information that comes from a half million lines of code and CPROVER's abstract interpreter (goto-analyzer). The sum of the control and data dependencies is approximately relations 445,000 from a half million lines of code. In general, applying a database is reasonable to handle such an enormous amount of information. One feature is that we apply the oriented graph based database "Orient-DB". This is because the code dependency is considered as a directed graph. Each instruction can be considered a

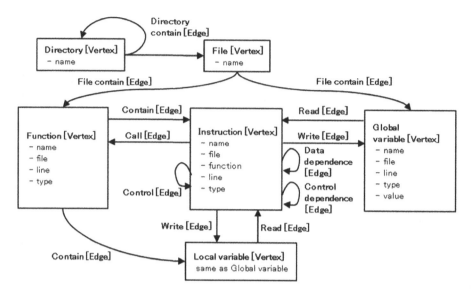

Fig. 6. Orient-DB data architecture.

"vertex", and each dependency can be considered an "edge". From that perspective, the impact analysis can be implemented as a backward and forward analysis from any slicing criterion.

Figure 6 shows the data structure that is stored in Orient-DB. The vertices represent the instruction, the function, the global variable, and the local variable. Those are based on the C-code intermediate format from the goto-program. In addition, the file directory and the file are included to support the directory and file-level merging in the visualization layer. The edges represent the call, the control that expresses the instruction ordering, variable read, and write as in a typical program data dictionary. In addition to that, the data and control dependency that come from the dependency abstract interpreter are registered.

The Orient-DB supports the edge based backward and forward analysis. CAT exploits that for **Backward and Forward Analysis** ((5) in Fig. 4).

4.3   Visualization

The visualization component relates **Visualization** ((6) in Fig. 4). The Orient-DB can extract the vertices that correspond to instructions from the goto-program with any Orient-DB commands. It is easy to imagine that such an instruction-level graph may be difficult to understand. In practice, it is more detail than required to understand the software architecture for most cases.

The designers need to understand the system-level, but they mainly focus on a particular module they are developing. Thus, the graph vertex that relates the module they are developing should be provided in detail; like the module or function-level, other vertices should be abstract like the sub-system or

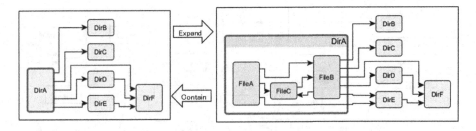

Fig. 7. Example of visualization process.

system-level. In that sense, this component is allowed to violate the CPROVER and Orient-DB's data-structure (Fig. 6) and generates the visualized graph so that it is easy to understand. In this layer, vertices can be merged or expanded to and level, like function, file, and folder-level, using a manual command. In accordance with the vertex merging, the edges that include the control, data dependency and the function call are merged as an edge automatically (See Fig. 7). The output graph format is GraphMl [12]. yEd Graph Editor [13] is used as a viewer, and the Graph layout is used independently from the CAT to show the result. This component is also implemented in Java.

5   Experiment of CAT with Automotive Unit-System

We evaluate the CAT's unit-system dependency graph generation and the impact analysis with actual code. We choose the engine ECU that is the largest scale in the vehicle system and has a half million of LoC. All experiments were run on a workstation computer with Intel® Xeon® CPU E5-2690, 2.9 GHz, 8 cores, 2 processor, and 256 GB RAM on OS Ubuntu 16.04.

5.1   Result of Analysis for Small Examples

This section explains the result of CPROVER `goto-analyzer` in Sect. 4.1.

Dependency Analysis. The result of dependency analysis `goto-analyzer --dependence-graph-vs` of Program 1 is shown in Fig. 8, which indicates the data dependency has offset of struct member.

The result of dependency analysis of Program 2 is also shown in Fig. 9, which indicates the control, data, and periodic dependency (shown as "later" on edge from L13 to L10 node) are extracted correctly. Above results indicate the requirements those are mentioned in Sect. 2.3 are satisfied. All those dependencies are exported in JSON format and stored to Orient-DB.

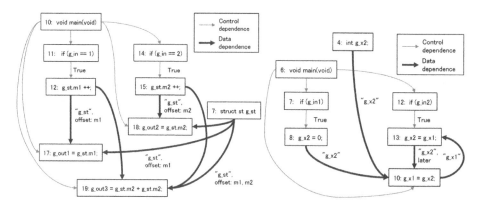

Fig. 8. Dependence result of Program 1   **Fig. 9.** Dependence result of Program 2

Program 6. Unwound code of Program 3.

```
1   const signed int cAarray[41]={ 10, 20, 30, 40 };
2   signed int gArray1[41];
3   signed int gArray2[41];
4
5   void main(){
6     const signed int *p0=cAarray;
7     signed int *p1=gArray1;
8     signed int i=0;
9     if(!(i >= 4)){
10      *p1 = cAarray[(signed long int)i];
11      gArray2[(signed long int)i] = *p0;
12      p0 = p0 + 1l;
13      p1 = p1 + 1l;
14      i = i + 1;
15      if(!(i >= 4)){
16        *p1 = cAarray[(signed long int)i];
17        gArray2[(signed long int)i] = *p0;
18        p0 = p0 + 1l;
19        p1 = p1 + 1l;
20        i = i + 1;
21        if(!(i >= 4)){
22          *p1 = cAarray[(signed long int)i];
23          gArray2[(signed long int)i] = *p0;
24          p0 = p0 + 1l;
25          p1 = p1 + 1l;
26          i = i + 1;
27          if(!(i >= 4)){
28            *p1 = cAarray[(signed long int)i];
29            gArray2[(signed long int)i] = *p0;
30            p0 = p0 + 1l;
31            p1 = p1 + 1l;
32            i = i + 1;
33            __CPROVER_assume(!(i < 4));
34          }
35        }
36      }
37    }
38  }
```

Pointer Resolution. The first step of pointer resolution using CAT is unwinding the loops. Program 6 shows the result of loop resolving `goto-analyzer --constant` of Program 3 in Sect. 2.3 by using the constant abstract interpreter. The `for` loop on L10 in Program 3 is unwound and converted to `if` statements. Program 7 shows the result of pointer resolving `goto-analyzer --variable`

Program 7. Pointer resolved code of Program 3.

```
1    const signed int cAarray[41]={ 10, 20, 30, 40 };
2    signed int gArray1[41];
3    signed int gArray2[41];
4
5    void main(){
6      const signed int *p0=cAarray;
7      signed int *p1=gArray1;
8      signed int i=0;
9      gArray1[01] = 10;
10     gArray2[01] = 10;
11     p0 = &cAarray[11];
12     p1 = &gArray1[11];
13     i = 1;
14     gArray1[11] = 20;
15     gArray2[11] = 20;
16     p0 = &cAarray[21];
17     p1 = &gArray1[21];
18     i = 2;
19     gArray1[21] = 30;
20     gArray2[21] = 30;
21     p0 = &cAarray[31];
22     p1 = &gArray1[31];
23     i = 3;
24     gArray1[31] = 40;
25     gArray2[31] = 40;
26     p0 = &cAarray[41];
27     p1 = &gArray1[41];
28     i = 4;
29     __CPROVER_assume((_Bool)1);
30   }
```

--structs --arrays of Program 6. This result shows the abstract interpreter can resolve complex pointer accesses that include loop and array access.

Program 8 also shows the result of function pointer resolving of Program 4. Actually because of implementation difficulties, it is solved by using a heuristic method goto-instrument --remove-function-pointers. The function pointer access p->req(len, buf) on L21 in Program 4 should be function f1 or f2. However, this heuristic method solves as all possible function; f1, f2, g1, or g2 in over-abstract (See L20–L50 in Program 8). Potentially the abstract interpreter can reduce the set of possibilities and it is one direction of future development.

5.2 Visualization for Automotive Unit-System

Figure 10 shows the engine unit-system dependency graph, where the red-line shows the extracted result of program slicing. The slicing criteria is an important variable for the engine control software and for the back-forward control and data-dependency analysis. The top segment of this figure shows the feature layer. The middle segment shows the module graph. The bottom segment shows the function and global variable graph. This figure shows the unit-system level, the feature level, and the module level hierarchically and with the designer preferred abstraction. The result shows that the program slicing gives the information the designer should focus on.

The time and memory consumption was evaluated while generating Fig. 10. First, the CAT compiling CPROVER compiler ((1) in Fig. 4) takes about 24 min.

Program 8. Pointer resolved code of program 4.

```
1   struct st;
2   signed int f1(char, char *);
3   signed int f2(char, char *);
4   void func(signed int id, signed int len, char *buf);
5   signed int g1(char, void *);
6   signed int g2(char, void *);
7
8   struct st{
9     signed int (*req)(char, char *);
10  };
11
12  const struct st fptbl1[21];
13  const struct st fptbl1[21]={ { .req=f1 }, { .req=f2 } };
14  signed int (* const fptbl2[21])(char, void *);
15  signed int (* const fptbl2[21])(char, void *)={ g1, g2 };
16
17  void func(signed int id, signed int len, char *buf){
18    const struct st *p=&fptbl1[(signed long int)id];
19    p->req;
20    if(!(p->req == f2))
21    {
22      if(p->req == (signed int (*)(char, char *))g1)
23        goto __CPROVER_DUMP_L2;
24
25      if(p->req == f1)
26        goto __CPROVER_DUMP_L3;
27
28      if(p->req == (signed int (*)(char, char *))g2)
29        goto __CPROVER_DUMP_L4;
30    }
31
32    f2((char)len, buf);
33    goto __CPROVER_DUMP_L5;
34
35  __CPROVER_DUMP_L2:
36    ;
37    g1((char)len, (void *)buf);
38    goto __CPROVER_DUMP_L5;
39
40  __CPROVER_DUMP_L3:
41    ;
42    f1((char)len, buf);
43    goto __CPROVER_DUMP_L5;
44
45  __CPROVER_DUMP_L4:
46    ;
47    g2((char)len, (void *)buf);
48
49  __CPROVER_DUMP_L5:
50    ;
51  }
```

The abstract interpreters, the constant abstract interpretation ((2) in Fig. 4), the variable abstract interpreter ((3) in Fig. 4), and Dependency Abstract Interpreter ((4) in Fig. 4), which are for the dependency analysis, take about 7 h and consumes a maximum of 198 GB memory. Forward and backward analysis ((5) in Fig. 4) and Visualization ((6) in Fig. 4) take up to a few minutes.

In total, the CAT takes about 8 h while consuming up to 198 GB RAM. It is done fully automatically and means the CAT can reduce work-hours dramatically compare with manual or semi-manual manner. Furthermore, it is practically impossible to extract such exhaustive dependency information manually.

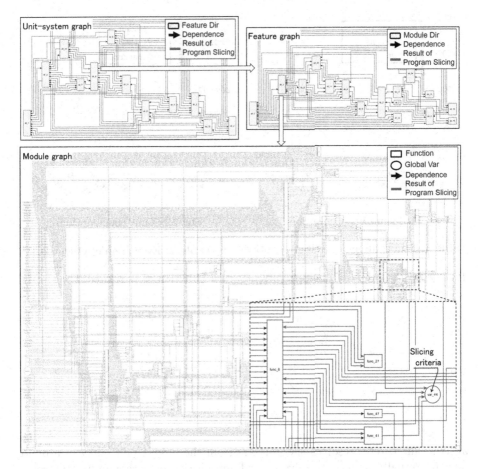

Fig. 10. Engine unit-system dependence graph. (Color figure online)

5.3 Examination of Preciseness and Scalability

In this section, we discuss the exhaustiveness of the abstract interpreter and the Orient-DB. Table 3 shows the scalability of the abstract interpretation. It shows the calculation time and memory consumption from several levels: task, module, and function. Every entry is the largest function in each levels. The related preciseness combinations are shown in Table 1. Each LoC refers to the scale of the code. The LoC is estimated from the goto-program, which completely resolves the loop and the context. Figure 11 shows the memory consumption Fig. 12 shows the trends of time and for each abstract interpreter.

This result illustrates the possibility that the abstract interpreter can coordinate the scalability and the preciseness according to the designers PC spec. One of contributions of CAT is the decrease in work-hours for pointer-resolving, which is expected to take about 125 h to resolve five hundred pointers manually (Sect. 2.3). As row "Unit #1-4" and column "Variable Time" shows, the variable

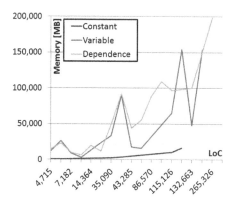

Fig. 11. Memory consumption.

Fig. 12. Time consumption.

Table 1. Combination of preciseness options.

Preciseness	Flow	Context	Loop	Recurrent
#1	✓			
#2	✓	✓		
#3	✓		✓	
#4	✓	✓	✓	
#5	✓		✓	✓
#6	✓	✓	✓	✓

Table 2. Evaluation of Orient-DB.

# Criterion	# Extracted instructions	Time [ms]
1	146	68
2	419	146
3	536	188
42	3,562	1,065
88	5,949	1,349

abstract interpreter resolves the pointers from the largest unit entry in around 50 min. Actually we need to solve several unit entries, even though it can resolve in about 2 h.

The program slicing is implemented using Orient-DB's backward and forward analysis on the oriented graph. There are 200 thousand instructions treated as vertices, 410 thousand control/data dependencies, which are treated as edges. We have not compared any data bases; however Table 2 shows Orient-DB can extract 5,949 instructions from 8 slicing criteria on a half million items related to dependency in 1,349 ms. The search speed is extremely fast and well satisfied our use-case.

5.4 Discussion of Preciseness and Scalability

As demonstrated above, CAT can provide the unit-system dependency graph (See Fig. 10). In this section, we discuss the CAT's components; CPROVER, Orient-DB, and Visualization.

CPROVER mainly provides the abstract interpreter, which is one of two key technical items. The abstract interpreter solves the pointer and the dependency

Table 3. Evaluation of abstract interpretation.

Entry	Pre.	LoC	Constant		Variable		Dependence	
			Memory [MB]	Time	Memory	Time	Memory	Time
Module	#1	4,715	540	00:00:04	12,015	00:04:45	14,395	00:04:42
	#2	5,766	558	00:00:04	26,460	0:0:5:45	22,849	00:05:02
	#3	7,182			8,843	00:03:49	10,137	00:03:19
	#4	8,779			3,158	00:01:07	6,280	00:01:30
	#5	14,364					19,740	00:07:10
	#6	17,558					11,975	00:02:50
Feature	#1	35,090	2,528	00:00:13	33,756	00:15:02	49,033	00:18:12
	#2	34,874	3,222	00:00:23	89,819	00:21:51	92,351	00:27:39
	#3	43,285			17,664	00:07:41	44,260	00:15:34
	#4	50,072			15,770	00:06:46	55,348	00:17:10
	#5	86,570					88,239	00:32:28
	#6	100,144					109,197	00:38:56
Unit	#1	115,126	10,200	00:00:50	64,753	00:53:01	96,699	00:47:14
	#2	123,881	16,390	00:02:06	154,118	00:49:36	Out of memory	
	#3	132,663			48,008	00:40:41	99,864	00:39:33
	#4	155,178			153,872	00:46:15	Out of memory	
	#5	265,326					198,149	01:16:06
	#6	310,356					Out of memory	

at the instruction level. Table 3 shows the possibility of coordinating the scalability and the preciseness; however, the scalability still remains an issue. The abstract interpreter consumes up to 198 GB of memory, furthermore, Unit #1, #4, and #6 are out of memory. Actually, Unit #5 satisfies our visualization usecase (the context sensitivity or more precise analysis is not needed.). In general, that is too heavy to perform on a standard desktop PC, but the performance requirement can be overcome by sharing the Orient-DB repository via a network as the host. In this case, the computing demand on the local PC is not as high.

From this experience, not only the large program scale (half million LoC) but also the many (several thousands of) global variable impacts the scalability. There are two main reasons for this. First, the domain information for each global variable cannot be released because they are "global" variables. Second, every global variable domain (status) needs to be stored for each instruction. This means the memory consumption is a multiplication of the number of global variables and LoC, approximately. The embedded controller cannot avoid using the global variable, and we typically cannot expect to decrease the LoC. The only way is to lessen the domain scale and update the domain objects.

The essential advantages of abstract interpretation are the soundness and the ability to trade off the preciseness with the computation time. The ideal usage is applying the abstract interpreter in a hierarchical fashion; meaning, in the early phase, use a less precise (scalable) abstract interpreter to simplify (erase dead code, simplify pointers), then in the later phase, gradually apply a precise (less scalable) abstract interpreter to the simplified code. The CAT exploits the abstract interpreter in this way; however, our design of data structures for the Orient-DB (Fig. 6) deals with the most precise instruction-level of the information and does not consider intermediate information like unwound-bounds and pointer simplifying. More sophisticated data-structures that can deal with the history of the result from the abstract interpreter are needed to better exploit the abstract interpreter.

In the visualization component, the on-demand access that is supported by the Orient-DB realizes a user preferred level for the graph (Fig. 7) to provide the enormous dependency information from a half million lines of code. On the other hand, the graph placement is a further issue related to the large size of the graph. The yEd Graph Editor is used in this paper separately from CAT and the default placement setting is used, but the preference for the placement depends on the domain. We need to consider those settings for each domain to deploy CAT. The yEd allows user specific placement settings. We expect it can implement this by using the yEd API.

5.5   Future Work

Authors think the CAT tool achieved a trial level, even though still there remain improvement items. The biggest advantage of the CAT is that is capable to extracting the exhausting dependence analysis which includes pointer analysis with just one night. We have already presented a demo to designers. They are also interested in the capabilities of scalability and, the result of program slicing; even though it is the function level graph, the slicer extracts well because of the statement level of dependence analysis is done in behind. (See bottom of Fig. 10, the slicer does not extract all of input edges at func_6.)

We are planning trial with 3 domains; Vehicle Control, Engine and Fuel Cell domain. The vehicle control domain is rapidly increasing the work-hours due to applying Automated Driving Technology. The engine still remains the largest scale of controller in automotive. The fuel cell system is also complex system which involves FC stack, Battery, and Electric motor. We expect the around 8,000 h reduction of work-hours per an ECU development when the CAT is deployed.

6   Conclusion

In this paper, we focus on the enhancement of control software development processes in the early development phases. The technical difficulty relates to the management of up to half a million lines of code per ECU. We applied an advanced static analysis method, abstract interpretation, to address function pointers and variable pointers and to extract an instruction-level of dependency. We systematize this process in the CAT tool, which uses CPROVER and Orient-DB. The CAT tool can handle a half million lines of code, resolve 500 pointers, and extract a half million dependencies within 8 h. CAT provides system graphs to understand software architecture on demand. CAT is a flexible and sophisticated tool for reviewing code in early development phases.

References

1. Haughey, B.: Design Review Based on Failure Modes (DRBFM) and Design Review Based on Test Results (DRBTR) Process Guidebook. SAE International, Warrendale (2012)
2. Cytron, R., et al.: An efficient method of computing static single assignment form. In: Proceedings of the 16th ACM SIGPLAN-SIGACT Symposium on Principles of Programming Languages, pp. 25–35. ACM (1989)
3. Weiser, M.: Program slicing. In: Proceedings of the 5th International Conference on Software Engineering. IEEE Press (1981)
4. Cousot, P., Cousot, R.: Abstract interpretation: a unified lattice model for static analysis of programs by construction or approximation of fixpoints. In: Proceedings of the 4th ACM SIGACT-SIGPLAN Symposium on Principles of Programming Languages, pp. 238–252. ACM (1977)
5. D'Silva, V., Kroening, D., Weissenbacher, G.: A survey of automated techniques for formal software verification. IEEE Trans. Comput.-Aided Des. Integr. Circ. Syst. **27**(7), 1165–1178 (2008)
6. Aho, A.V.: Compilers: Principles, Techniques and Tools (for Anna University), 2/e. Pearson Education India, Bengaluru (2003)
7. http://www.cprover.org/cbmc/
8. https://orientdb.com/
9. Kroening, D., Tautschnig, M.: CBMC – C bounded model checker. In: Ábrahám, E., Havelund, K. (eds.) TACAS 2014. LNCS, vol. 8413, pp. 389–391. Springer, Heidelberg (2014). https://doi.org/10.1007/978-3-642-54862-8_26
10. https://gcc.gnu.org/
11. Tesoriero, C.: Getting Started with OrientDB. Packt Publishing Ltd., Birmingham (2013)
12. http://graphml.graphdrawing.org/
13. https://www.yworks.com/products/yed?
14. Blazy, S., Bühler, D., Yakobowski, B.: Structuring abstract interpreters through state and value abstractions. In: Bouajjani, A., Monniaux, D. (eds.) VMCAI 2017. LNCS, vol. 10145, pp. 112–130. Springer, Cham (2017). https://doi.org/10.1007/978-3-319-52234-0_7
15. Blanchet, B., et al.: A static analyzer for large safety-critical software. In: PLDI 2003, pp. 196–207 (2003)

Syntactic Partial Order Compression for Probabilistic Reachability

Gereon Fox[1,2]($\boxtimes$), Daniel Stan[1], and Holger Hermanns[1]

[1] Saarland University, Saarland Informatics Campus, Saarbrücken, Germany
{fox,dstan,hermanns}@depend.uni-saarland.de
[2] Saarbrücken Graduate School of Computer Science, Saarbrücken, Germany

Abstract. The state space explosion problem is among the largest impediments to the performance of any model checker. Modelling languages for compositional systems contribute to this problem by placing each instruction of an instruction sequence onto a dedicated transition, giving concurrent processes opportunities to interleave after every instruction. Users wishing to avoid the excessive number of interleavings caused by this default can choose to explicitly declare instruction sequences as *atomic*, which however requires careful considerations regarding the impact this might have on the model as well as on the properties that are to be checked. We instead propose a preprocessing technique that automatically identifies instruction sequences that can safely be considered atomic. This is done in the context of concurrent variable-decorated Markov Decision Processes. Our approach is compatible with any off-the-shelf probabilistic model checker. We prove that our transformation preserves maximal reachability probabilities and present case studies to illustrate its usefulness.

Keywords: State space explosion · Atomicity
Partial order reduction · Concurrency · Interleavings · Model checking

1 Introduction

Concurrency problems are notoriously difficult to study. One important reason is that activities local to a single component can interleave in arbitrary order with those of others, which is a root cause of the state-space explosion problem.

One of the earliest attempts to alleviate this problem is a feature of Holzmann's language PROMELA [16], exploited in the model checker SPIN. PROMELA contains an `atomic` keyword, to be used by the modeller to group sequences of computations so that they are executed *atomically*, i.e. without the need to store intermediate states, which would otherwise contribute to state space explosion. Nowadays, model checkers like UPPAAL allow the modeller to place entire C-code fragments as effects on single transitions [4]. As another example, LNT, the modern language of the CADP model checking framework [10], provides a dedicated "procedure" construct, the semantics of which ensure that the effect

© Springer Nature Switzerland AG 2019
C. Enea and R. Piskac (Eds.): VMCAI 2019, LNCS 11388, pp. 446–467, 2019.
https://doi.org/10.1007/978-3-030-11245-5_21

of each procedure body does not span more than a single transition. Apart from interesting semantic questions (what if the body does not terminate, what if it cannot be made atomic?), these solutions burden the modeller with deciding which computations to group together.

Instead, partial order reduction techniques (POR) take over the task of identifying local computations that can be considered independent, and thus need to be explored in only *one* of their interleavings as opposed to *all* interleavings. POR techniques usually fall into one of two categories: *Static* POR [12,18,21], running mostly *before* state space exploration (hence the name "static"), computes so-called *persistent sets*, that are subsets of the transitions enabled in the different states of the system. Exploration then does not follow *all* the transitions enabled in a state, but only the ones in the persistent set of that state. *Dynamic* POR [1,9] on the other hand aims at materialising persistent sets *during* state space exploration, which promises to be more precise, as information about concrete executions is available and does not need to be overapproximated as much. POR has also been adapted to the probabilistic setting [2,3,7,8,11].

The present paper describes a technique that achieves reductions comparable to those of POR, but is actually geared towards automated placement of atomic's in the model source code. Executed as a preprocessing step prior to the actual model checking, our approach analyses the model statically, in order to identify instruction sequences inside components that can safely be made atomic. This places the instructions on a single transition in the state space, instead of taking multiple steps that would multiply when interleaved.

We present our technique for variable-decorated, concurrent probabilistic models and probabilistic model checking. In this setting, the model checker usually constructs a Markov decision process that needs to be stored explicitly and very often is of prohibitive size. Symbolic or SAT-based approaches do not work particularly well here [15,20], basically because numerical computations need to be performed at the end.

We call our approach "syntactic partial order compression", because it has the same goal as partial order reduction, i.e. to rule out redundant interleavings. In general, POR techniques appear more capable of reducing the number of interleavings than the placement of atomic's, because POR can freely choose between interleavings that involve several components of the system, whereas an atomic sequence is restricted to allowing only one component to make progress. We expect that the latter will often not suffice to preserve the property of interest, while the former still can, i.e. POR can still find opportunities for reduction when placing an atomic is just not sound anymore. In contrast to most POR techniques however, our approach does not require the model checker to cooperate (e.g. by pruning state space exploration) and thus can be used with any off-the-shelf tool. Furthermore, traditional POR techniques do not work well in our particular setting, rooted in the fact that probabilistic decisions (inside components) alternate with interleaving of components, and the resulting tree-shaped executions contain cross-dependencies that are difficult to account for [11]. Therefore, POR techniques have so far not delivered true success stories for probabilistic models. Recent work in this realm [8] did explore POR to find and syntactically enforce particular representative interleavings — but the results of this approach do not translate to atomic's, which we aim at.

Our main contribution is a perspicuous three-step approach that transforms a parallel composition of processes without ever materializing the product process: First, a *generation step* builds up a set of so-called *chains* for each process. A chain is a sequence of alternating nondeterministic and probabilistic decisions in one component, with the main requirement being that schedulers that never interrupt this sequence by any transitions from other components still achieve the same maximum reachability probability for the state-formula in question. We give a wellformedness condition for these chain sets, largely independent of how they are actually generated. Second, as a *filtering step* we describe an optimization problem aimed at finding a subset of the generated chains that admits as few interleavings as possible without changing said probability. Lastly, the *fusion step* turns the remaining chains into proper probabilistic transitions again, whereby sequences of decisions are compacted into atomic decisions, obtaining a syntactic representation of the transformed system.

2   Preliminaries

We start off by reviewing the basics of variable-decorated Markov decision processes in the style of MODEST [5,13], building upon [14], which we recommend for further details and elaborate discussions of the concepts.

Basic Structures. Throughout the paper we assume a finite set Var of variables with countable domains $\text{Dom}(x)$ for all $x \in Var$ and a set Exp of expressions over these variables, the detailed syntax and semantics of which are not of importance. We assume $Bxp \subseteq Exp$ to comprise boolean expressions ranging over $\{\text{tt}, \text{ff}\}$ and $Axp \subseteq Exp$ to denote arithmetic expressions ranging over $\mathbb{Q}$. The set $Val :=$ $Var \to \text{Dom}(Var)$ of valuations contains all mappings of variables to values of their domains, i.e. for each $v \in Val$ we have $\forall x \in Var : v(x) \in \text{Dom}(x)$.

For $x \in Var$ and $e \in Exp$ we call $x := e$ an *assignment*. Two assignments $x_1 := e_1$ and $x_2 := e_2$ are called *consistent* iff $x_1 \neq x_2$ or $[\![e_1]\!](v) = [\![e_2]\!](v)$ for all $v \in Val$, where $[\![e]\!](v) \in Val \to Val$ is the function that evaluates expression e given valuation v. The set Upd of all updates contains all sets of pairwise consistent assignments. Consistency allows the definition of a function $[\![u]\!] \in Val \to Val$ updating valuations after simultaneous evaluation of the assignments in u.

For a set S we call elements of $S \to Axp$ *symbolic probability distributions over* S and the values these functions return *weight expressions*. Given a function f the set $\text{Supp}\,(f)$ contains the arguments f is defined for. For all sets S of the form $S = A \times B$ we define $S^\perp := (A \times B)^\perp := A^\perp \times B^\perp$ and if S is not a cartesian product we set $S^\perp := S \cup \{\perp\}$, where $\perp \notin S$ is a distinct placeholder element. Tuples $(\perp, \ldots, \perp)$ will be abbreviated with $\perp$. For sequences $s, t \in S^*$ we call s a *prefix* of t and write $s \sqsubseteq t$ iff $\exists t' : t = s \cdot t'$.

For $a, b \in \mathbb{N}$ we define $[a : b] := \{i \in \mathbb{N} \mid a \leq i \leq b\}$ and for vector variables we usually use the notation $\vec{v} = (v_1, \ldots, v_n)$.

MDPs with Variables. Our models are based on parallel compositions of Markov Decision Processes (MDP), enhanced with variables, guards and probability expressions [13, 14]:

Definition 1 (VMDP). *A Markov decision process with variables (VMDP) is a tuple (Loc, A, E, l_{init}) where Loc is a finite set of locations, $A \supseteq \{\tau\}$ is a finite alphabet, including the silent action τ, and $l_{init} \in Loc$ is the initial location. Furthermore, $E \in Loc \rightarrow \mathscr{P}(Bxp \times A \times (Upd \times Loc \rightarrow Axp))$ maps each location to a set of transitions, which each consist of a guard $g \in Bxp$, a label $\alpha \in A$ and a symbolic probability distribution $m \in Upd \times Loc \rightarrow Axp$ that weighs pairs of updates and target locations. We denote the set of all transitions by $\mathbb{T} := \bigcup_{l \in Loc} E(l)$.*

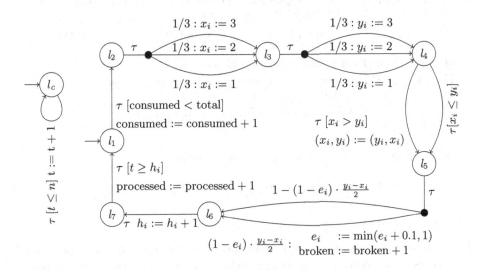

Fig. 1. A VMDP network modelling Example 1

As examples, consider the two processes depicted in Fig. 1: Locations are connected by transitions, which are decorated with their label and nontrivial guard. Distributions m with $|\mathrm{Supp}\,(m)| > 1$ are represented by splitting up transitions at • and labeling arcs with their probability expressions and updates. Each process transitions between locations: Given its current location l and a valuation v, a transition $(g, \alpha, m) \in E(l)$ is picked *nondeterministically*, under the condition that its guard expression is satisfied by v. Then, the weights assigned by m are evaluated over v, turning weight expressions into actual probabilities, based on which the new location l', along with an update u is chosen. The process then transitions to l' and updates v to v', according to u.

The fact that probability distributions are *symbolic* (i.e. probabilities depend on the current valuation of variables) contributes to the expressiveness of the formalism, as we will see in Example 1. For the purposes of this paper, we require that all symbolic probability distributions m be well-formed, i.e. they satisfy

$$\forall v \in Val, (u,l) \in \text{Supp}(m) : 0 \leq [\![m(u,l)]\!](v) \wedge \sum_{(u,l)\in\text{Supp}(m)}[\![m(u,l)]\!](v) = 1$$

Violations of this condition will be considered modelling errors in practise, causing MODEST to reject the model.

Networks of VMDPs. So far, we have not said a lot about the action labels $\alpha \in A$. They become significant when we consider *networks* of VMDPs. From now on we will deal with finite sets of VMDP's $\mathcal{C}_i = (Loc_i, A_i, E_i, l_{init_i})$:

Definition 2 (VMDP network semantics). *A VMDP network is a tuple* $\mathcal{N} = (\mathcal{C}, v_{init})$ *consisting of an initial valuation* $v_{init} \in Val$ *and a finite set* $\mathcal{C} = \{\mathcal{C}_1, \ldots, \mathcal{C}_N\}$ *of VMDP components. We call* $\mathbb{S} := (Loc_1 \times \ldots \times Loc_N) \times Val$ *the state space of* $\mathcal{N}$, *with* initial state $s_{init} := ((l_{init_1}, \ldots, l_{init_N}), v_{init}) \in \mathbb{S}$. *We write* $(\vec{l}, v) \xrightarrow{\vec{g},\vec{\alpha},\vec{p},\vec{u}} (\vec{l}', v')$ *iff there is* $\alpha \in A$ *and* $P \subseteq [1:N]$, *such that*

1. *If* $\alpha = \tau$, *then* $|P| = 1$, *otherwise* $P = \{i \mid \alpha \in A_i\}$.
2. *For all* $i \in P$ *we have* $\alpha_i = \alpha$ *and* $(g_i, \alpha, m) \in E_i(l_i)$ *for some* m *with* $m(u_i, l_i') = p_i$, *such that* $[\![g_i]\!](v) = tt$ *and* $[\![p_i]\!](v) > 0$.
3. *For all* $i \in [1:N] \setminus P$ *we have* $l_i = l_i'$ *and* $(g_i, \alpha_i, p_i, u_i) = \bot$
4. $v' = [\![\bigcup_{i\in P} u_i]\!](v)$

A (finite) path in $\mathcal{N}$ *to* s_n *is a sequence of the form*

$$\pi = s_{init} \xrightarrow{\vec{g}_0,\vec{\alpha}_0,\vec{p}_0,\vec{u}_0} s_1 \xrightarrow{\vec{g}_1,\vec{\alpha}_1,\vec{p}_1,\vec{u}_1} s_2 \ldots \xrightarrow{\vec{g}_{n-1},\vec{\alpha}_{n-1},\vec{p}_{n-1},\vec{u}_{n-1}} s_n \in \text{Paths}$$

and we set state$(\pi) := s_n$.

In a network, the executions of VMDPs interleave, i.e. the order in which they progress is chosen nondeterministically. Definition 2 however mandates common-alphabet synchronization in the style of Hoare [6], making steps in the network fall into one of two categories: Either a *silent* τ-step is made by one single process, or a different, *nonsilent* action label is chosen, requiring all processes with this label in their alphabet to participate and execute a step *synchronously*. In addition to communicating via synchronizing actions, processes also share all the variables in Var and can read and write them to exchange information. Similar to the wellformedness of symbolic probability distributions above we require that networks never lead to a state in which updates according to rule 4 would be inconsistent. Even after strengthening this condition to make it easily implementable (e.g. in MODEST), it remains a very light restriction and is relevant only for non-τ steps.

Example 1 (Factory). A factory receives a delivery of machine parts that are to be welded together in pairs. Part sizes are randomly distributed. A number of workers start out with a certain amount of experience with this type of task. Working in parallel, they grab pairs of parts and process them, which takes one hour per pair. The less experienced a worker is and the more two parts differ in size, the more likely it is that the worker makes a mistake and breaks the parts.

Figure 1 depicts a model for Example 1: A global clock keeps track of time during an n-hour day, while each worker is represented by a dedicated process (indexed with i): Starting in l_1, the worker obtains a pair of parts, unless all have been obtained already. From l_2 to l_4 he measures the parts. From l_4 to l_5 measures are sorted: x_i should refer to the shorter part length. Based on the difference in part lengths and his current level of experience, the worker will then either succeed or fail in welding parts together, the latter of which will make him gain experience. Both success and failure take one hour (l_6 to l_7) which is why the worker can obtain another job only after the clock has progressed.

Note that at each location l_i a worker process might be nondeterministically interrupted by others. To avoid the enormous number of interleavings that these locations give rise to the modeller might want to manually compact subsequent transitions into one. This error-prone transformation would require duplicating parts of the model and thus lead to a less concise representation, justifying the desire for a tool that performs such a transformation "under the hood".

Probabilistic Reachability. Model analysis is often concerned with the question of reachability, i.e. whether there is a path of the system such that at some point of the path the system state satisfies a given condition. We denote such queries by $\Diamond\,\varphi$, where φ is a predicate over states. By Paths($\Diamond\,\varphi$) we denote the set of finite paths containing a state s satisfying φ.

Since exploring paths of the system usually involves probabilistic choices it makes sense to not only ask for the existence of paths satisfying $\Diamond\,\varphi$, but for the probability $P(\Diamond\,\varphi)$ with which one of these paths is chosen. These probabilities depend on the way that nondeterministic choices are resolved and thus can be defined only given a *scheduler* $\mathfrak{S} \in Sched$ which is a function $\mathbb{S} \to \mathbb{T}_1^\perp \times \ldots \times \mathbb{T}_N^\perp$, such that whenever $\mathfrak{S}((\vec{l}, v)) = (g_1, \alpha_1, m_1, \ldots, g_N, \alpha_N, m_N)$ we have

$$(\vec{l}, v) \xrightarrow{\begin{pmatrix} g_1 \\ \vdots \\ g_N \end{pmatrix}, \begin{pmatrix} \alpha_1 \\ \vdots \\ \alpha_N \end{pmatrix}, \vec{p}, \vec{u}} (\vec{l}', v')$$

for some $\vec{p}, \vec{u}, \vec{l}', v'$ with $\forall i \in [1 : N] : m_i(u_i, l_i'') = p_i$.

Intuitively, a scheduler thus resolves nondeterministic choices by selecting transitions that are enabled in the current network state. We define Paths($\mathfrak{S}$) to be the smallest set satisfying the following conditions:

1. $s_{init} \in$ Paths($\mathfrak{S}$)

2. If $s_{init} \xrightarrow{\vec{g}_0,\vec{\alpha}_0,\vec{p}_0,\vec{u}_0} s_1 \ldots \xrightarrow{\vec{g}_{n-1},\vec{\alpha}_{n-1},\vec{p}_{n-1},\vec{u}_{n-1}} s_n \in \text{Paths}(\mathfrak{S})$ and we have $\mathfrak{S}(s_n) = (\vec{g},\vec{\alpha},\vec{m})$, then for all steps $s_n \xrightarrow{\vec{g},\vec{\alpha},\vec{p},\vec{u}} s_{n+1}$ we also have

$$s_{init} \xrightarrow{\vec{g}_0,\vec{\alpha}_0,\vec{p}_0,\vec{u}_0} s_1 \ldots \xrightarrow{\vec{g}_{n-1},\vec{\alpha}_{n-1},\vec{p}_{n-1},\vec{u}_{n-1}} s_n \xrightarrow{\vec{g},\vec{\alpha},\vec{p},\vec{u}} s_{n+1} \in \text{Paths}(\mathfrak{S})$$

Remark 1. In full generality, schedulers base their decisions not only on the current state, but the complete sequence of visited states and transitions, and can randomize their decision. In our context this does however not add any power [19], which is why we restrict to *pure memoryless* schedulers.

This is what we need to properly define reachability probabilities:
For $\pi = (\vec{l}_0,v_0) \xrightarrow{\vec{g}_0,\vec{\alpha}_0,\vec{p}_0,\vec{u}_0} (\vec{l}_1,v_1) \ldots \xrightarrow{\vec{g}_{n-1},\vec{\alpha}_{n-1},\vec{p}_{n-1},\vec{u}_{n-1}} (\vec{l}_n,v_n) \in \text{Paths}:$

$$\text{P}(\pi) := \prod_{0 \leq i < n} \prod_{1 \leq j \leq N} [\![p_{i,j}]\!](v_i) \quad \text{and} \quad \text{P}^{\mathfrak{S}}(\Diamond\,\varphi) := \sum_{\pi \in \text{Paths}(\mathfrak{S}) \cap \text{Paths}(\Diamond\,\varphi)} \text{P}(\pi)$$

$\text{P}(\pi)$ can be seen as a short-hand notation for the measure value $\text{P}(\text{Cyl}(\pi))$ of the cylinder $\text{Cyl}(\pi)$ composed of all maximal paths prefixed by π. It is easy to see that this definition meets Carathéodory's extension theorem so that P defines a unique *measure* over the σ-algebra generated by the finite paths. In particular, the set $\max_{\sqsubseteq}(\text{Paths}(\mathfrak{S}))$ of (possibly infinite) prefix-maximal paths is a measurable set and $\text{Paths}(\Diamond\,\varphi)$ identified as $\text{Cyl}(\text{Paths}(\Diamond\,\varphi))$ is also measurable. Moreover, $\text{P}^{\mathfrak{S}}(\cdot) = \text{P}(\max_{\sqsubseteq}(\text{Paths}(\mathfrak{S})) \cap \cdot)$ is a *probability* measure.
In this paper we will focus on *quantitative reachability properties*:

$$\text{P}_{\max}(\Diamond\,\varphi) := \max_{\mathfrak{S} \in Sched} \text{P}^{\mathfrak{S}}(\Diamond\,\varphi) \quad \text{or} \quad \text{P}_{\min}(\Diamond\,\varphi) := \min_{\mathfrak{S} \in Sched} \text{P}^{\mathfrak{S}}(\Diamond\,\varphi)$$

Example 2. For the scenario modelled in Fig. 1 interesting queries include the probability $\text{P}_{\max}(\Diamond(\text{processed} = \text{total} \wedge t \leq b))$ of finishing work within a certain time horizon and the probability $\text{P}_{\max}(\Diamond(\text{processed} = \text{total} \wedge \text{broken} = 0))$ of not breaking any parts. Since model checkers are able to output the schedulers that achieve extremal probabilities, these queries correspond to finding strategies of how to distribute work packages among the workers.

Chains. The key data structure of our approach is the concept of a *chain*:

Definition 3 (Branches, links and chains). *For a transition $t = (g,\alpha,m)$ we denote the* branches *of t by $\text{Br}(t) := \{(u,l',p) \mid m(u,l') = p\}$. Each branch $b \in \text{Br}(t)$ corresponds to a* link $t \cdot b$ *and we denote the set of all links in the network by $\mathbb{L}$. Two links $t_1 \cdot (u,l',p)$, $t_2 \cdot b_2$ are called* consecutive *iff $t_2 \in E(l')$. A* chain *is a finite sequence $t_0 \cdot b_0 \cdot t_1 \cdot b_1 \cdots t_n \cdot b_n$ of consecutive links.*

Example 3. Consider the arrows from l_2 to l_3 in Fig. 1: Together they depict a transition that we refer to as t. The three segments between $\bullet$ and l_3 represent the branches of t. Every route from l_2 to l_3 depicts a link. A link itself is already a chain. But also any finite route in Fig. 1 that starts at a location and ends at a location is a chain, as it is a sequence of links.

If $|\operatorname{Br}(t)| = 1$ we call t *Dirac* and write $t \in T_{\mathrm{nd}}$, omitting the $\bullet$ in the graphical representation. We call a location l *pure* iff $l \in Loc_p := \{l \in Loc \mid |E(l)| \leq 1\}$.

The goal of our approach is to identify certain chains as "uninterruptible", i.e. to establish that while a process is inside such a chain, one can refrain from switching control to a different process, without losing behavior relevant for the reachability property in question. By collapsing these chains into single transitions one obtains a new network that thus admits fewer interleavings than the original one, while preserving the property.

Mobility. To establish chains as "uninterruptible" we use the concept of mobility:

Definition 4 (Mobility). *Let* $i, j \in [1 : N]$ *with* $i \neq j$ *and* $t_1 \in E_i(l_1), t_2 \in E_j(l_2)$ *with* $b_1 \in \operatorname{Br}(t_1), b_2 \in \operatorname{Br}(t_2)$. *We say that* $t_1 \cdot b_1$ *is* forward-commutative *with* $t_2 \cdot b_2$ *iff for all states s and all step sequences* $s \xrightarrow{\vec{g}_1, \vec{\alpha}_1, \vec{p}_1, \vec{u}_1} s_1' \xrightarrow{\vec{g}_2, \vec{\alpha}_2, \vec{p}_2, \vec{u}_2} s''$ *that involve $t_1 \cdot b_1$ followed by $t_2 \cdot b_2$ (i.e. projecting the first step on process i gives $t_1 \cdot b_1$ and projecting the second step on process j gives $t_2 \cdot b_2$) we also have* $s \xrightarrow{\vec{g}_2, \vec{\alpha}_2, \vec{p}_2, \vec{u}_2} s_2' \xrightarrow{\vec{g}_1, \vec{\alpha}_1, \vec{p}_1, \vec{u}_1} s''$ *for some s_2' and*

$$\mathrm{P}\left(s \xrightarrow{\vec{g}_1, \vec{\alpha}_1, \vec{p}_1, \vec{u}_1} s_1' \xrightarrow{\vec{g}_2, \vec{\alpha}_2, \vec{p}_2, \vec{u}_2} s''\right) = \mathrm{P}\left(s \xrightarrow{\vec{g}_2, \vec{\alpha}_2, \vec{p}_2, \vec{u}_2} s_2' \xrightarrow{\vec{g}_1, \vec{\alpha}_1, \vec{p}_1, \vec{u}_1} s''\right).$$

If $s \not\models \varphi \wedge s_1' \models \varphi \wedge s'' \not\models \varphi$ *we also require* $s_2' \models \varphi$. Backward-commutativity *is defined by swapping 1 and 2 above.* $t_1 \cdot b_1$ *is called* mobile *iff it is forward-commutative and backward-commutative with* all *links from other processes.*

Mobility of links is what allows us to reorder paths such that the links of a chain appear as one contiguous sub-path in the proofs of Sect. 4. Since it ensures that we neither lose behavior, nor miss states that satisfy φ, we can be sure to preserve maximal reachability probabilities.

Remark 2. Definition 4 is related to the notion of independence usually found in POR literature [1,3,17]: Intuitively, two transitions t_1, t_2 are independent if for any *state* where they are both enabled, both executions $t_1 \cdot t_2$ and $t_2 \cdot t_1$ can be performed and lead to the same *state* distribution. The difference is that while mobility is defined on the syntactic level of links, independence talks about steps between concrete *states* (i.e. *vectors* of locations, paired with valuations).

3   Algorithm

Our syntactic partial order compression approach comprises three steps: In Step A we identify a set of candidate chains that are sufficient for spanning the relevant behavior. Since some of these chains are redundant, Step B is then concerned with selecting a subset of chains that eliminates a maximal number of interleavings. Finally Step C compiles the remaining chains into a new VMDP network. We assume a given input VMDP network $\mathcal{N}$ to start with.

Step A: Chain Generation

The objective of this step is to collect a finite set C of chains that can be turned into atomic transitions without altering probabilistic reachability. C should satisfy the following requirements:

Definition 5 (Chain set validity). *Given a property of the form* $\mathrm{P}_{\max}(\Diamond\,\varphi)$, *a chain set C is called* valid *iff it satisfies the following conditions:*

1. *For each chain $c = t_1 \cdot b_1 \cdots t_n \cdot b_n \in C$ we have:*
   (a) c does not contain any link more than once.
   (b) If $n > 1$, c comprises τ-actions only and all its links are mobile.
   (c) There is $k \in [1:n]$, s.t. $b_1, \ldots, b_{k-1}$ are Dirac and $l_k, \ldots, l_n \in Loc_p$.
   (d) For each state s with $s \nvDash \varphi$ and every path segment

$$s \xrightarrow{\vec{g}_0, \vec{\alpha}_0, \vec{p}_0, \vec{u}_0} s_1 \xrightarrow{\vec{g}_1, \vec{\alpha}_1, \vec{p}_1, \vec{u}_1} s_2 \ldots \xrightarrow{\vec{g}_{n-1}, \vec{\alpha}_{n-1}, \vec{p}_{n-1}, \vec{u}_{|c|-1}} s_{|c|}$$

   that involves c as a sequence of steps in one of the processes of $\mathcal{N}$, we have $s_{|c|} \nvDash \varphi \rightarrow \forall i \in [1:|c|-1]: s_i \nvDash \varphi$.
2. *For each process $\mathcal{C}_i$ and each sequence λ of consecutive links originating in l_{init_i}, there is $\gamma \in C^*$, s.t. $\lambda \sqsubseteq \gamma$.*
3. *For each chain $t_1 \cdot b_1 \cdots t_k \cdot b_k \cdot t_{k+1} \cdot b_{k+1} \cdots t_n \cdot b_n \in C$ and $b'_k \in \mathrm{Br}(t_k) \setminus \{b_k\}$, there is $t_1 \cdot b_1 \cdots t_k \cdot b'_k \cdot t'_1 \cdot b'_1 \cdots t'_m \cdot b'_m \in C$ for some $t'_1, b'_1, \ldots t'_m, b'_m$.*

Condition 1a ensures acyclicity of chains. Condition 1b allows us to reorder paths of $\mathcal{N}$ such that chain c emerges as one contiguous path segment, see Sect. 4. Condition 1c rules out chains that contain a probabilistic choice before a nondeterministic one. This is necessary because chains will eventually be turned into atomic transitions again, that according to Definition 2 need to be picked nondeterministically *before* their probabilistic choices are made, thus not allowing schedulers to base their nondeterministic decision on the outcome of the probabilistic choice, which is not yet available. This condition echoes the need to add additional conditions to Peled's ample set approach [18] to preserve all relevant schedulers in probabilistic partial order reduction [2,3,7]. Condition 1d rules out chains during the execution of which φ is briefly satisfied in some intermediate state, without being also satisfied upon entering or leaving the chain. This prevents such intermediate states from being lost when chains are converted to atomic links. Condition 2 makes sure that control flow inside components is preserved, i.e. all paths through the locations of a component can still be realized by sequences of chains. Together with Condition 3, that preserves the probabilistic branching structure of components, it ensures that we can produce a syntactically well-formed result in Step C. Notice that all links bearing a nonsilent label will only be represented in C as chains of length 1.

Example 4. In Fig. 1 the only link in the clock process, as well as the links from l_1 to l_2 and from l_7 to l_1 in the worker constitute chains of length 1. The 9 paths from l_2 to l_4 constitute chains of length 2. The 4 paths from l_4 to l_7 are chains of length 3. This chain set satisfies the conditions of Definition 5. Condition 1c rules out chains running through l_4.

Algorithm 1. Chain generation

---

  function COLLECTCHAINS(component $\mathcal{C}_i$)
    $C \leftarrow \emptyset$ ▷ Collected chains
    $T \leftarrow \{l_{init}\}$; $V \leftarrow \emptyset$ ▷ Locations to visit, locations visited
    function CONTINUE(*prefix*,*l*)
      terminal $\leftarrow$ tt   ▷ Is $|E(l)| = 0$?
      total $\leftarrow$ tt   ▷ Was *prefix* continued for all outgoing links of *l*?
      for all $t \in E(l)$, $b = (u, l', p) \in \mathrm{Br}(t)$ **do**
        terminal $\leftarrow$ ff
        if *valid*(*prefix*, *t*, *b*) **then** CONTINUE(*prefix* · *t* · *b*, *l'*)
        else *total* $\leftarrow$ ff
      if *prefix* $\neq \epsilon \wedge$ (*terminal* $\vee \neg total$) **then**   ▷ Yield *prefix* as chain?
        $C \leftarrow C \cup \{prefix\}$
        $T \leftarrow T \cup (\{l\} \setminus V)$
    while $T \neq \emptyset$ **do**
      $l \leftarrow pop(T)$; $T \leftarrow T \setminus \{l\}$
      $V \leftarrow V \cup \{l\}$
      CONTINUE(ϵ, l)
    return C

We give one possibility of generating a set C according to the above conditions in Algorithm 1: It basically performs a depth-first search through every component, extending chain prefixes as long as possible and starting new empty prefixes at locations where a chain ended. The latter already ensures condition 2.

The predicate $valid(c, t \cdot b)$ is implemented such that the concatenation $c \cdot t \cdot b$ satisfies conditions 1b, 1c, 1d and does not contain more than one link with the same source location, to satisfy 1a and ensure termination. Conditions 1a and 1c are local syntactic checks. Condition 1b can be conservatively overapproximated in many ways. Our implementation considers both orders in which two links can be combined and performs syntactic checks that imply the necessary conditions in Definition 4. Similarly, we overapproximate Condition 1d, by ensuring that chains contain at most one link that writes to variables occuring in φ.

A careful look at Condition 3 reveals that it is actually not ensured by Algorithm 1: For example, there might be a chain c covering a sequence of transitions, as depicted in Fig. 2. Since c contains the link $t \cdot b$, the condition requires a counterpart c' that agrees with c up to l and then contains the probabilistic alternative $t \cdot b'$. This counterpart is missing in Fig. 2. However, since Algorithm 1 starts new chains at exactly those locations where previously generated chains end and because it satisfies Condition 2, we know that chains c^1 and c^2 as in the figure must have been generated, which also entails the generation of c^3. Thus there is at least a subset of C that does preserve all conditions including 3, which is sufficient as an input for the next step.

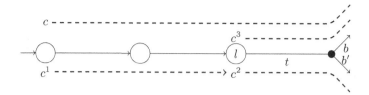

Fig. 2. c violates Condition 3, because $\neg valid(c^1, t \cdot b')$. Algorithm 1 thus generated c^1 as a chain, which put l into its agenda T and caused generation of c^2 and c^3.

Step B: Chain Filtering

The output of Step A is a chain set C that satisfies Definition 5, except for Condition 3. To enforce the latter we need to select a subset of C that satisfies it, a problem that can always be solved as we have argued in the previous section. Since we strive for the selection of a subset that reduces the number of interleavings as far as possible, we are dealing with an optimization problem that we cast as a $\{0, 1\}$-weighted MAX-SAT instance.

However, Condition 3 is not the only reason for optimizing a subset of C: A simple iteration over the syntax as in Algorithm 1 will generate redundant chains in C, because it has to start new chains in all directions at the end of *every* chain generated so far, unless sophisticated bookkeeping keeps track of the path-segments already covered, complicating step A significantly. As an example see Fig. 2, where c is subsumed by $c^1 \cdot c^3$. Experiments have shown that not eliminating these redundancies by optimization can not only prevent reduction of the number of interleavings but even increase it, because there are more nondeterministic choices to enumerate.

Constraints. We need to preserve the conditions of Definition 5. Condition 1 is trivially satisfied for all subsets of C and thus does not need to be encoded. Condition 3 can be encoded easily, because for every chain c the number of chains c' that need to be selected as a consequence of selecting c according to the condition is usually rather small.

Condition 2 does need to be encoded, because discarding chains in C might make certain control flow paths unrealizable. For this purpose we propose Algorithm 2. This algorithm attaches so-called *bundles* to the links of each process. A bundle B attached to a link $t \cdot b$ represents a set of finite paths that all start in the initial location and end with $t \cdot b$. A solution to the optimization problem must select a set S of chains that all contain $t \cdot b$. The chains selected in this way are the ones remaining at the end of step B.

The algorithm starts by attaching bundles to the initial links. For every newly created bundle attached to a link, successor bundles for all successor links are created, which is why branches and loops lead to links being attached more tha none bundle. The constraints generated for bundles make sure that the sets S for subsequent bundles "fit together": A chain c can be selected for a bundle attached to $t \cdot b$ only if c is select for the predecessor bundle as well ("continuation"), or if

$t \cdot b$ is the very first link in c and the predecessor bundle selected a chain ending in the link that it is attached to ("initiation"). Termination is guaranteed because for every link there is only a finite number of chains that contain it, bounding the number of bundles attached to it. Correctness of Algorithm 2 can be proven by structural induction over paths.

Algorithm 2. Generation of constraints that encode chain set invariant 2

---

for all $t \in \mathbb{T}$, $b \in \mathrm{Br}(t)$ **do** bundles$(t \cdot b) \leftarrow \emptyset$

for all $t \in E(l_{init})$, $b \in \mathrm{Br}(t)$ **do**

    $B \leftarrow \{c \in C \mid \exists c' : c = t \cdot b \cdot c'\}$

    bundles$(t \cdot b) \leftarrow$ bundles$(t \cdot b) \cup \{B\}$

    ADDCONSTRAINT$(\bigvee_{c \in B} u_{B,c})$ ▷ At least one chain must be used to cover $t \cdot b$

$k \leftarrow 0$

repeat

    for all consecutive links $t_i \cdot b_i$, $t \cdot b$ and $B \in$ bundles$(t_i \cdot b_i)$ **do**

        $B_T \leftarrow \{c \in B \mid \exists c' : c = c' \cdot t_i \cdot b_i\}$ ▷ Chains terminated with $t_i \cdot b_i$

        $B'_C \leftarrow \{c \in B \mid \exists \pi, \sigma : c = \pi \cdot t_i \cdot b_i \cdot t \cdot b \cdot \sigma\}$ ▷ Chains continued from $t_i \cdot b_i$

        $B'_I \leftarrow \{c \in C \mid \exists c' : c = t \cdot b \cdot c'\}$ ▷ Chains initiated with $t \cdot b$

        $B' \leftarrow B'_C \cup B'_I$

        bundles$(t \cdot b) \leftarrow$ bundles$(t \cdot b) \cup \{B'\}$

        ADDCONSTRAINT$(I_k \vee C_k)$ ▷ Initiate new chain, or Continue previous one

        ADDCONSTRAINT$(I_k \leftrightarrow \bigvee_{c \in B'_I} u_{B',c})$

        ADDCONSTRAINT$(C_k \leftrightarrow \bigvee_{c \in B'_C} u_{B',c})$

        ADDCONSTRAINT$(I_k \to \bigvee_{c \in B_T} u_{B,c})$

        ADDCONSTRAINT$(\forall c \in B'_C : u_{B',c} \to u_{B,c})$

        $k + +$

until fixpoint   ▷ Exists because there can be only finitely many B

Objective. Intuitively, the goal of Step B is to minimize the number of times a process can be "interrupted" by the scheduler, giving other processes opportunity to interfere and thus burdening the model checker with a great number of interleavings. More technically this means that when given the choice of how to "emulate" a path $\lambda \in \mathbb{L}^*$ by a concatenation $\gamma \in C^*$ of chains, we should attempt to pick γ such that it contains a minimal number of positions in which one chain ends and another begins, because these are exactly the positions where a scheduler might choose to interrupt a process. To encode this intuition, we chose the summation over all variables I_k generated by Algorithm 2 as the primary objective to be minimized. This choice is justified by the fact that setting a variable I_k to true basically means that there is a set of path prefixes that can only be continued by leaving one chain and entering into a new one. Of course counting interruptions with this heuristic is biased by being performed on the syntactic representation of the model, but we expect it to lead to reasonable results as long as the control flow of processes is not too unusual. As a secondary objective we minimize the total number of selected chains, hoping to obtain a compact syntactic representation of the transformation result.

Step C: Chain Fusion

Having obtained a chain set C that satisfies Definition 5, all that remains is to compile chains to a proper VMDP network again, for which we give Algorithm 3. Starting at the initial location, the algorithm follows chains to reachable locations, building up the transformed network along the way.

Algorithm 3. Compilation of a set of chains to a VMDP network

---

function COMPILE(component (Loc, A, E, l_{init}), chain set C)

   $T \leftarrow \emptyset$ ▷ Locations to visit

   $L \leftarrow \emptyset \; ; E' \leftarrow \emptyset$ ▷ New locations, New transitions

   function MAP(location l)

      $l' \leftarrow L[l]$

      if $l' = \perp$ **then**

         $l' = $ NEW LOCATION()

         $T \leftarrow T \cup \{l'\}$

      return l'

   $l'_{init} \leftarrow$ MAP(l_{init})

   while $T \neq \emptyset$ **do**

      $l \leftarrow pop(T); \; T \leftarrow T \setminus \{l\}$

      $l' \leftarrow$ MAP(l)

      $E(l') \leftarrow \{$ FUSE(MAP, cs) $\mid cs \in$ ndchoices(l)$\}$

   return $(\{L[l] \mid l \in Loc\}, A, E, l'_{init})$

---

ndchoices(l) contains subsets of the chains starting in location l. It reflects the possible control flow choices a scheduler can make inside a component: A subset cs is in ndchoices(l) iff there is a mapping of locations to transitions, such that cs is precisely the set of all chains starting in l that contain only selected transitions:

$$cs(S) := \quad \{t_0 \cdot b_0 \cdot \ldots t_n \cdot b_n \in C \mid t_0 \in E(l) \land \forall i \in [0 : n] : t_i \in S\}$$

$$\text{ndchoices}(l) := \quad \{cs(S) \mid S \subseteq \mathbb{T} \land \forall l \in Loc : |S \cap E(l)| = min(|E(l)|, 1)\}$$

FUSE(MAP, cs) converts each such subset cs into a transition of the new model: Every $c \in cs$ is traversed, maintaining a record of the updates seen so far, in order to substitute variables in guards, weight expressions and subsequent updates. In the case of guards, the results of the substitutions are then conjoined, while in the case of weight expressions they are multiplied. After all chains have been traversed in this fasion, for each chain there is thus one guard g, one combined update u and one weight expression p. The guard of the resulting transition is the conjunction of all g. Weight expressions need to be normalized before they can be combined with updates and target locations to form the branches of the new transition. Since all nonatomic chains contain only τ-labels synchronization does not complicate FUSE.

Remark 3. Instead of compiling a new model in this fashion, we could as well resort to the textual representation of the original model (if any), in order to declare instruction sequences along chains `atomic`. This, however, can turn out to be even more cumbersome than the very technical computation in Algorithm 3, depending on the generated chains and the syntactic structure of the modelling language. As an example, consider a piece of code like

```
a; b; if (c) then d else e; f; g;
```

If the sequence a b d f g can safely be made atomic, but a b e f g cannot, it is not clear what parts of the code to enclose in an `atomic` block. Chains that span across loops can be even harder to represent in syntax.

4   Correctness

In this section, we prove that the transformation given in the previous section is sound, i.e. that maximal reachability probabilities are preserved.

In the following, mathematical objects indexed by r will refer to the reduced network. Our goal in this section is to relate $P^{\mathfrak{S}}(\Diamond\varphi)$ and $P^{\mathfrak{S}_r}(\Diamond\varphi)$, respectively for $\mathfrak{S} \in Sched$ and $\mathfrak{S}_r \in Sched_r$. Note that despite its similar notation, $\Diamond\varphi$ refers to different sets of paths $\mathrm{Paths}(\Diamond\varphi)$ and $\mathrm{Paths}_r(\Diamond\varphi)$. The reduced system is composed of transitions built from the filtered chain set $C_f \subseteq C$.

For a transition $t \in \mathbb{T}_i$, we set $\downarrow t := (\bot,\dots,\bot,t,\bot\dots\bot) \in (\mathbb{T}_1^\bot \times \dots \times \mathbb{T}_N^\bot)^T$ and define $\downarrow b$ equivalently for branches b. We extend the notation to links and sets or sequences thereof. For any path π we denote similarly by $\downarrow\pi$ the underlying sequence of vectors of transitions and branches.

Finally, we extend this translation to the whole set C_f:

$$\Downarrow C_f = \{\downarrow c \mid c \in C_f \text{ with } \tau\text{-actions}\} \uplus$$
$$\{(t_1,\dots) \cdot (b_1,\dots) \mid \alpha \in A, (t_i, b_i) \in C_f \text{ if } \alpha \in A_i, (t_i, b_i) = \bot \text{ otherwise}\}$$

Note that special care has to be taken for chains of length 1 that represent non-silent actions, that have to be "synchronized" with each other in $\Downarrow C_f$.

Without loss of generality, and for the sake of clarity, we assume in this section that all schedulers are *history*-dependent. This means, that a scheduler $\mathfrak{S}$ is defined for a whole path π instead of only its last state. This assumption does not interfere with the optimal value of the reachability property, while at the same time allows us to reason and manipulate the sub-tree of a set of paths, without interfering with previous transitions taken by the scheduler.

Soundness. In order to establish correctness of the transformation, we want to simulate any run of the reduced network in the original one, which basically means that the transformation introduced no new behavior. However, we can already notice that our reduction may introduce new deadlock situations, that are fortunately harmless for the reachability properties we are considering:

Example 5. Composing the process on the left of Fig. 3 with itself (under synchronization over actions a and b) yields a system that is free of deadlocks. Reducing the depicted chain in both components results in a composition of the process on the right with itself. Here, deadlock is possible. Fortunately, because we are interested in reachability properties, this newly introduced deadlock doesn't influence the value of $P_{max}(\Diamond(x = 1))$.

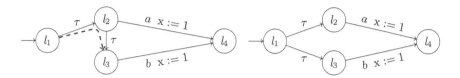

Fig. 3. Reducing the chain over $l_1 l_2 l_3$ turns the process on the left into the process on the right.

Lemma 1 (Simulation of the reduced system). *Let $\mathfrak{S}_r \in Sched_r$ a scheduler of the reduced system. We can construct $\mathfrak{S} \in Sched$ for the original system such that $P^{\mathfrak{S}}(\Diamond\varphi) = P^{\mathfrak{S}_r}(\Diamond\varphi)$.*

Proof. Basically, $\mathfrak{S}$ has to *follow* the moves made by $\mathfrak{S}_r$. For this purpose, we define $\mathfrak{S}(\pi)$ for any $\pi \in$ Paths by induction on $|\pi|$. The following invariant will hold during the induction:

Invariant 1. *If $P^{\mathfrak{S}}(\pi) > 0$ then $\pi = \pi' \cdot \rho$ for some π',ρ and there are $\pi_r \in$ Paths$_r$, cs returned from ndchoices and $c \in$ cs $\subseteq C_f$, s.t.*

$$\downarrow\pi' \in \Downarrow C_f^* \wedge \downarrow\rho \sqsubseteq \downarrow c \wedge |\rho| < |c| \wedge \text{state}(\pi_r) = \text{state}(\pi')$$
$$\wedge \ \mathfrak{S}(\pi_r) = t_{cs} \wedge P^{\mathfrak{S}}(\pi') = P^{\mathfrak{S}_r}(\pi_r)$$

where t_{cs} denotes the transition resulting from FUSE(MAP, cs).

   Intuitively, π' represents the already chain-reconstructed path in $\mathcal{N}$ matched by π_r in $\mathcal{N}_r$, while ρ is the next prefix of a valid chain to be added to π. The empty path starting in the initial state satisfies the invariant. Let us consider π satisfying the invariant.

- If $P^{\mathfrak{S}}(\pi) = 0$, we define $\mathfrak{S}(\pi)$ arbitrarily, and easily check that any successor of π still satisfies the invariant, since it is also not reachable.
  From now on, we assume that $P^{\mathfrak{S}}(\pi) > 0$ and define π', ρ, π_r as above.
- If $|\rho| = 0$ and $\mathfrak{S}_r(\pi_r)$ is a transition of the original system, we simply define $\mathfrak{S}(\pi) = \mathfrak{S}_r(\pi_r)$ and check that the invariant is still satisfied by all successors (we can add the same branch to π,π' and π_r).

– Otherwise, $\downarrow\rho \sqsubseteq \downarrow c$ which means a chain has to be continued. We define $\mathfrak{S}(\pi) = (\downarrow c)[|\downarrow\rho| + 2] = \vec{t}$ as the next transition vector to be played. For any branch $b \in Br(t)$, there exists $c' \in cs$ such that $\downarrow\rho \cdot \downarrow(t,b) \sqsubseteq \downarrow c'$. Moreover if the equality holds, the chain is over. In this case, in order to preserve the invariant, we define $\rho' = \epsilon$, and due to the way c' is compiled into a simple link in $\mathcal{N}_r$ by Algorithm 3, the probability stays equal to probability of the sequence of individual links in c' from state(π) in $\mathcal{N}$.

Completeness. We now establish that our transformation is *complete*, i.e. that any run in the initial network can still be reproduced in the reduced system, up to interleavings that do not contribute to the reachability property in question. This direction is more challenging, and essentially relies on the conditions in Definition 5. Most of all, the key ingredient is the ability for a scheduler to postpone any Dirac transition after a probabilistic one:

Lemma 2. *Let $\mathfrak{S} \in Sched$, $t \cdot b$ Dirac and mobile and $\pi \in Paths$. Let $s \in \mathbb{S}$ such that $\pi \xrightarrow{\downarrow t, \downarrow b} s$ and $\vec{t}' := \mathfrak{S}(\pi \xrightarrow{\downarrow t, \downarrow b} s)$. We can rewrite $\mathfrak{S}$ into $\mathfrak{S}'$ such that:*

– *For all $\pi' \in Paths$ with $\pi \not\sqsubseteq \pi'$, $\mathfrak{S}(\pi') = \mathfrak{S}'(\pi')$ and $P^{\mathfrak{S}}(\pi') = P^{\mathfrak{S}'}(\pi')$*
– *For all π', and for all $\vec{b}', s'$, $\mathfrak{S}'(\pi \xrightarrow{\vec{t}',\vec{b}'} s' \xrightarrow{\downarrow t, \downarrow b} \pi') = \mathfrak{S}(\pi \xrightarrow{\downarrow t, \downarrow b} s \xrightarrow{\vec{t}',\vec{b}'} \pi')$*
  and $P^{\mathfrak{S}}(\pi \xrightarrow{\downarrow t, \downarrow b} s \xrightarrow{\vec{t}',\vec{b}'} \pi') = \sum_{s'' \in \mathbb{S}} P^{\mathfrak{S}'}(\pi \xrightarrow{\vec{t}',\vec{b}'} s'' \xrightarrow{\downarrow t, \downarrow b} \pi').$

Proof. Intuitively, the state is already determined to be s after $\downarrow t$, so the scheduler can postpone this transition and play the (possibly) probabilistic one first, thanks to mobility.

Lemma 3. *Let $\mathfrak{S} \in Sched$. We can build $\tilde{\mathfrak{S}} \in Sched$ such that $P^{\mathfrak{S}}(\lozenge\varphi) \leq P^{\tilde{\mathfrak{S}}}(\lozenge\varphi)$ and such that $\forall\pi : P^{\tilde{\mathfrak{S}}}(\pi) > 0 \Rightarrow \downarrow\pi \in \Downarrow C_f^{*}.$*

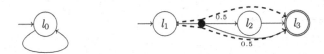

Fig. 4. Example of an increasing reachability probability after applying Lemma 3: Consider the scheduler running the second component once, then the first component forever. Probability of eventually reaching l_3 is 0.5 as the second component may remain in l_2 forever. After transformation, the scheduler has to follow each chain entirely which yields possible reachability probabilities 0 and 1.

Proof. We define $\tilde{\mathfrak{S}}(\pi)$ by induction on $|\pi|$. See Fig. 5 for illustration.

– If $\mathfrak{S}(\pi) = \vec{t}$ is a transition of the original system that was kept in the reduced one, we immediately define $\tilde{\mathfrak{S}}(\pi) = \vec{t}$ which satisfies the property.

– Otherwise, $\mathfrak{S}(\pi)$ is a transition that has now been subsumed by a set of chains. More precisely, for each $i \in [1 : N]$, the next transition run on component $\mathcal{C}_i$ will represent the beginning of a fixed given chain c_i. Let us consider the maximal extension $\pi\pi'$ such that π' contains only Dirac links from one of the c_i. (not necessarily from the same component). Two cases can occur:

- Either the system is deadlocked: $\pi\pi'$ has no successor. We swap the Dirac transitions, which are assumed to be mobile, in order to write $\downarrow\pi' = \downarrow c_1' \cdots \downarrow c_N'$ with for each i, c_i' a prefix of c_i. We then apply Condition 1d to show that if φ doesn't hold at state(π), it cannot hold anywhere in π' either, so that for any scheduler $\tilde{\mathfrak{S}}$ already defined up to π and arbitrarily defined later, $\mathrm{P}^{\mathfrak{S}}(\lozenge\varphi) \leq \mathrm{P}^{\tilde{\mathfrak{S}}}(\lozenge\varphi)$.

- Otherwise, we consider $i \in [1 : N]$ such that $\mathcal{C}_i$ is the first process to have fired the last Dirac transition of its current chain. Let us consider the set of chains $cs \subseteq C_f$ corresponding to the sequence of non-deterministic choice made by $\mathcal{C}_i$. The rest of the run for $\mathcal{C}_i$ is indeed determined: It consists in a finite sequence of probabilistic transitions according to the chains of cs. We apply Lemma 2 recursively on each link of cs to move it towards the beginning of the trace. This is possible because each link is assumed to be mobile and has to be swapped only with probabilistic transitions of other components. Thus, we have defined a scheduler $\tilde{\mathfrak{S}}$ such that $\mathrm{P}^{\tilde{\mathfrak{S}}}(\pi\pi')$ implies that there exists $c \in cs$ such that $\downarrow c \sqsubseteq \downarrow\pi'$.

Remark 4. The transformation as stated in Lemma 3 may strictly increase the reachability probability. As an example consider Fig. 4. We note however that this can only happen for non-optimal schedulers, as pointed out by Lemma 1 so maximal reachability probability is still preserved.

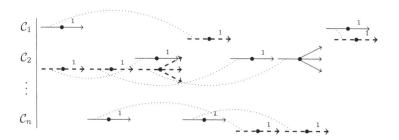

Fig. 5. Illustration of the proof strategy for Lemma 3. Here, the first component to terminate a chain is $\mathcal{C}_2$, represented by the first non-Dirac transition. All links of the chain are then "pulled" to the beginning of the run. This transformation is achieved by permuting links in $\mathcal{C}_2$ with links of the other components. The latter links are indeed assumed by minimality to be Dirac and so can always be postponed with Lemma 2.

Remark 5. The reduced model may lack deadlocks exhibited by the original system: Consider the network comprising only the process on the left of Fig. 6, with only one non-trivial chain going through $l_1 l_2 l_3$. Clearly, the system can deadlock in location l_2, which is why $P_{\min}(\Diamond(x = 2)) = 0$. After transformation (depicted on the right), the guard becomes ff which leads to $P_{\min}(\Diamond(x = 2)) = 1$. This is why we restrict ourselves to maximal reachability probabilities, where a scheduler has no incentive to trigger a deadlock as it will only reduce the reachability probability.

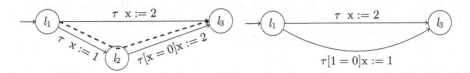

Fig. 6. A network comprising only a single process, with one nontrivial chain, before and after transformation

We conclude this section by establishing the correctness of our transformation:

Theorem 1. *The following equality holds for reachability objectives $\Diamond\varphi$:*

$$P_{\max,\mathcal{N}_r}(\Diamond\varphi) = P_{\max,\mathcal{N}}(\Diamond\varphi)$$

Proof. Lemma 1 ensures that our transformation does not introduce new behavior and thus $P_{\max,\mathcal{N}_r}(\Diamond\varphi) \leq P_{\max,\mathcal{N}}(\Diamond\varphi)$. Equality follows with Lemma 3, allowing us to convert any $\mathcal{N}$-scheduler into an $\mathcal{N}_r$-scheduler with a reachability probability at least as high as the one in the original system.

5   Case Studies

We have implemented our approach in the model-checking framework MOD-EST [5,13]. Experiments were conducted on an OpenSUSE Linux machine with an Intel Core i7-6700 CPU (3.40 GHz) and 32 GB of working memory. We considered two different exemplary cases: On the one hand, we looked at the Factory example, depicted in Fig. 1. This is a genuine VMDP network and it is not manually hand-optimized for model-checking, contrary to essentially all existing case studies around. In addition, we looked at an example on flow control, from the context of the SPIN model checker. This is a non-probabilistic case study, and we use it to demonstrate in how far our approach can place atomics mechanically.

Factory. To illustrate the nature of our transformation and its ability to reduce state space size, we applied it to instances of the network in Fig. 1. The algorithm generated the chain set described in Example 4. We had MODEST answer the query $P_{\max}(\Diamond(\text{processed} = 4 \wedge \text{broken} = 0))$ on both the original and the transformed model. Table 1 shows our results for different numbers of workers: While the exponential growth in both state space size as well as model-checking run-time caused by the additional interleavings that each new worker introduces can in principle not be avoided by our transformation, the reduction ratio increases with the number of workers. For more than 4 workers, MODEST gives up for lack of memory on the original system, while it still succeeds to answer the query on the transformed system for 5 and for 6 workers.

For 6 workers our algorithm took only about one second of runtime, including the optimization problem in step B, and used only negligible amounts of working memory. Even more encouraging, the performance of our algorithm would not be affected at all by changes to constants such as the total number of work items in the factory, that have a dramatic impact on the state space size.

Table 1. Resource usage for model checking the network from Fig. 1 before and after our transformation

	# Workers	1	2	3	4	5	6
Original	# States	1 558	164 264	5 207 980	59 873 864	?	?
	MC time	<1 s	1.2 s	48 s	10 m 50 s	?	?
Transformed	# States	719	56 291	1 187 248	9 994 337	38 657 750	104 937 279
	MC time	<1 s	0.7 s	16 s	2 m 19 s	9 m 07 s	25 m 25 s
Reduced by	# States	54%	66%	77%	83%	?	?
	MC time	0%	42%	67%	79%	?	?

Flow Control. The model checker SPIN comes, among others, with a PROMELA example file `pftp.pml`. In this model, a sender and a receiver communicate over a lossy channel, supported by a flow control layer that prevents message loss and reordering. Holzmann discusses the model in the original SPIN book [16] and notes that whenever possible, one should surround parts of the code by `atomic` blocks, to "reduce the complexity of the validation". Our goal in this case study was to omit the `atomic` keyword and have our algorithm infer the corresponding chains automatically.

We slightly modified the model: SPIN's special `timeout` predicate (that is used to resend messages when no other transition in the system is enabled) was replaced by a constant `true`, because its non-compositional semantics is difficult to capture in MODEST. Furthermore, we changed the model by disabling `white` messages, so as to have the MDP-focussed model-checking engine of MODEST scale better in the absence of (nontrivial) probabilities. We then translated the SPIN model to an isomorphic VMDP network, ignoring all the `atomic` keywords.

Applying our algorithm to the translated model had the expected effects: Most of the `atomic` blocks of the original could be recovered in the form of chains, with one restriction: Chains stop at channel accesses, because we had to model those by reads and writes to global variables. Notably, Holzmann's atomics can span across channel accesses, but lose atomicity (only) in case a channel access blocks (which again is a non-compositional feature). A small number of the chains we generate are hard to translate into PROMELA atomics, e.g. because they start in front of a loop and end inside it.

Despite not recovering the original atomics precisely, we achieve a dramatic reduction in state space size: Checking whether any assertions in the model are violated MODEST explored 15 922 533 states of the original model, but only 4 588 039 on the transformed one, a reduction by 70%. In total the algorithm generated 99 chains, all of which remained after filtering, which used 72 056 MAXSAT variables and 147 176 clauses. Again, steps A, B and C together took about one second of runtime and negligible amounts of memory.

For comparison we applied SPIN to our variants of pftp.pml. Table 2 shows that the atomic keywords we manually derived from the generated chains reduce state space considerably (about 24%), though not as much as the original atomic's in [16]. The first column shows that, surprisingly, SPIN benefits from atomic keywords far less than MODEST benefits from our transformation. This may again be rooted in the fact that MODEST is optimized for probabilistic model checking. The second column reveals that even under partial order reduction the usage of atomic keywords can reduce state space size considerably. This suggests that one should use our technique in addition to POR.

Table 2. SPIN state space sizes for our variants of pftp.pml, with and without POR

	Without POR	With POR
No atomics	97 652	15 062
Chain atomics	74 442	12 088
Holzmann's atomics	46 773	11 248

6 Conclusion

We have presented an automated approach to fusing transition executions prior to model checking, within models of concurrent probabilistic processes, so as to alleviate the state space explosion problem. The probabilistic setting makes this task particularly challenging, owed to the tree-shaped structure of probabilistic executions. However, our approach is readily applicable to the nonprobabilistic setting, too, where it effectively yet mechanically detects instruction sequences that can be made atomic without altering reachability properties, as demonstrated on Holzmann's flow control example. Furthermore, the *Factory* case study demonstrates that on concurrent probabilistic examples the state-space compression factor achieved becomes more drastic the larger the models get.

A comparison to SPIN's implementation of partial order reduction demonstrated that while our approach achieves less state space reduction than POR, using it in addition to existing POR implementations can still increase the reduction ratio considerably. Notably, we were unable to report successes of our techniques on established examples, mainly because those have been highly optimised by hand, leaving no room for detecting further transitions to fuse.

There are several avenues extending this first work on *syntactic partial order compression*. Condition 1b constraining chains in Definition 5 could for instance be relaxed by replacing it by a more precise analysis. As a matter of fact, some transitions may never happen concurrently so that less independence requirements have to be met in order to establish a chain. We are working on an abstract interpretation-based approach to collect state information statically and exploit it for justifying chains even across synchronizing actions and accesses to global variables. Furthermore, we plan to investigate how to extend beyond reachability properties. Our approach does at this point add deadlocks to the model (see Remark 5), which implies that minimum probabilities are not preserved.

Acknowledgments. This work is partly supported by the DFG as part of CRC 248 (see perspicuous-computing.science) and by the ERC Advanced Investigators Grant 695614 (POWVER).

References

1. Abdulla, P.A., Aronis, S., Jonsson, B., Sagonas, K.: Source sets: a foundation for optimal dynamic partial order reduction. J. ACM **64**(4), 25:1–25:49 (2017). https://doi.org/10.1145/3073408
2. Baier, C., Grosser, M., Ciesinski, F.: Partial order reduction for probabilistic systems. In: 2004 Proceedings First International Conference on the Quantitative Evaluation of Systems, QEST 2004, pp. 230–239, September 2004. https://doi.org/10.1109/QEST.2004.1348037
3. Baier, C., D'Argenio, P., Groesser, M.: Partial order reduction for probabilistic branching time. Electron. Notes Theor. Comput. Sci. **153**(2), 97–116 (2006). https://doi.org/10.1016/j.entcs.2005.10.034. Proceedings of the Third Workshop on Quantitative Aspects of Programming Languages (QAPL 2005)
4. Behrmann, G., David, A., Larsen, K.G., Håkansson, J., Pettersson, P., Yi, W., Hendriks, M.: UPPAAL 4.0. In: Third International Conference on the Quantitative Evaluation of Systems (QEST 2006), 11–14 September 2006, Riverside, California, USA. pp. 125–126. IEEE Computer Society (2006). https://doi.org/10.1109/QEST.2006.59
5. Bohnenkamp, H.C., D'Argenio, P.R., Hermanns, H., Katoen, J.: MODEST: a compositional modeling formalism for hard and softly timed systems. IEEE Trans. Softw. Eng. **32**(10), 812–830 (2006). https://doi.org/10.1109/TSE.2006.104
6. Brookes, S.D., Hoare, C.A.R., Roscoe, A.W.: A theory of communicating sequential processes. J. ACM **31**(3), 560–599 (1984). https://doi.org/10.1145/828.833
7. D'Argenio, P.R., Niebert, P.: Partial order reduction on concurrent probabilistic programs. In: 1st International Conference on Quantitative Evaluation of Systems (QEST 2004), 27–30 September 2004, Enschede, The Netherlands, pp. 240–249. IEEE Computer Society (2004). https://doi.org/10.1109/QEST.2004.1348038

8. Díaz, Á.F., Baier, C., Earle, C.B., Fredlund, L.: Static partial order reduction for probabilistic concurrent systems. In: Ninth International Conference on Quantitative Evaluation of Systems. QEST 2012, London, United Kingdom, 17–20 September 2012, pp. 104–113. IEEE Computer Society (2012). https://doi.org/10.1109/QEST.2012.22

9. Flanagan, C., Godefroid, P.: Dynamic partial-order reduction for model checking software. In: Palsberg, J., Abadi, M. (eds.) Proceedings of the 32nd ACM SIGPLAN-SIGACT Symposium on Principles of Programming Languages, POPL 2005, 12–14 January 2005, Long Beach, California, USA, pp. 110–121. ACM (2005). https://doi.org/10.1145/1040305.1040315

10. Garavel, H., Lang, F., Serwe, W.: From LOTOS to LNT. In: Katoen, J.-P., Langerak, R., Rensink, A. (eds.) ModelEd, TestEd, TrustEd. LNCS, vol. 10500, pp. 3–26. Springer, Cham (2017). https://doi.org/10.1007/978-3-319-68270-9_1

11. Giro, S., D'Argenio, P.R., Ferrer Fioriti, L.M.: Partial order reduction for probabilistic systems: a revision for distributed schedulers. In: Bravetti, M., Zavattaro, G. (eds.) CONCUR 2009. LNCS, vol. 5710, pp. 338–353. Springer, Heidelberg (2009). https://doi.org/10.1007/978-3-642-04081-8_23

12. Godefroid, P. (ed.): Partial-Order Methods for the Verification of Concurrent Systems - An Approach to the State-Explosion Problem. LNCS, vol. 1032. Springer, Heidelberg (1996). https://doi.org/10.1007/3-540-60761-7

13. Hahn, E.M., Hartmanns, A., Hermanns, H., Katoen, J.: A compositional modelling and analysis framework for stochastic hybrid systems. Formal Methods Syst. Des. $43(2)$, 191–232 (2013). https://doi.org/10.1007/s10703-012-0167-z

14. Hartmanns, A.: On the analysis of stochastic timed systems. Ph.D. thesis, Saarland University (2015). https://doi.org/10.22028/D291-26597

15. Hermanns, H., Kwiatkowska, M.Z., Norman, G., Parker, D., Siegle, M.: On the use of mtbdds for performability analysis and verification of stochastic systems. J. Log. Algebr. Program. $56(1–2)$, 23–67 (2003). https://doi.org/10.1016/S1567-8326(02)00066-8

16. Holzmann, G.J.: Design and Validation of Computer Protocols. Prentice-Hall, Englewood Cliffs (1991)

17. Katz, S., Peled, D.A.: Defining conditional independence using collapses. Theor. Comput. Sci. $101(2)$, 337–359 (1992). https://doi.org/10.1016/0304-3975(92)90054-J

18. Peled, D.: All from one, one for all: on model checking using representatives. In: Courcoubetis, C. (ed.) CAV 1993. LNCS, vol. 697, pp. 409–423. Springer, Heidelberg (1993). https://doi.org/10.1007/3-540-56922-7_34

19. Puterman, M.L.: Markov Decision Processes: Discrete Stochastic Dynamic Programming, 1st edn. Wiley, New York (1994). https://doi.org/10.1002/9780470316887

20. Teige, T.: Stochastic satisfiability modulo theories: a symbolic technique for the analysis of probabilistic hybrid systems. Ph.D. thesis, Carl von Ossietzky University of Oldenburg (2012). https://oops.uni-oldenburg.de/id/eprint/1389

21. Valmari, A.: Stubborn sets for reduced state space generation. In: Rozenberg, G. (ed.) ICATPN 1989. LNCS, vol. 483, pp. 491–515. Springer, Heidelberg (1991). https://doi.org/10.1007/3-540-53863-1_36

Termination of Nondeterministic Probabilistic Programs

Hongfei Fu[1][(✉)] and Krishnendu Chatterjee[2]

[1] Shanghai Jiao Tong University, Shanghai, China
fuhf@cs.sjtu.edu.cn
[2] IST Austria, Klosterneuburg, Austria
krish.chat@ist.ac.at

Abstract. We study the termination problem for nondeterministic probabilistic programs. We consider the bounded termination problem that asks whether the supremum of the expected termination time over all schedulers is bounded. First, we show that ranking supermartingales (RSMs) are both sound and complete for proving bounded termination over nondeterministic probabilistic programs. For nondeterministic probabilistic programs a previous result claimed that RSMs are not complete for bounded termination, whereas our result corrects the previous flaw and establishes completeness with a rigorous proof. Second, we present the first sound approach to establish lower bounds on expected termination time through RSMs.

1 Introduction

In this work we consider nondeterministic probabilistic programs and the termination analysis problem for them. We present results that show how martingale-based approaches provide sound and complete method for such analysis, and can also derive quantitative bounds related to termination time. We first present probabilistic programs, then the termination problems, next the previous results, and finally our contributions.

Probabilistic Programs. Probabilistic aspects in computation is becoming increasingly important, and analysis of programs with probabilistic aspects has received significant attention in the recent years [5,6,12,15,21,24,28,52,55]. In probabilistic programs the classical imperative programs are extended with *random value generators*. The random value generators produce random values according to some desired probability distribution. Probabilistic programs provide a flexible framework to model a wide variety of applications, such as analysis of stochastic network protocols [4,41], robot planning [35], etc. The formal analysis of probabilistic systems and probabilistic programs is an active research topic across different disciplines, such as probability theory and statistics [22,33,39,49,51], formal methods [4,41], artificial intelligence [35,36], and programming languages [5,6,12,15,21,23,24,28,52,55].

© Springer Nature Switzerland AG 2019
C. Enea and R. Piskac (Eds.): VMCAI 2019, LNCS 11388, pp. 468–490, 2019.
https://doi.org/10.1007/978-3-030-11245-5_22

Termination Problems. The most basic and fundamental notion of liveness for static analysis of programs is the *termination* problem. In the absence of probabilistic behavior, the termination problem asks whether a program always terminates. For nonprobabilistic programs, the proof of termination in finite time coincides with the construction of *ranking functions* [25]. Many different approaches exist for construction of ranking functions for termination analysis of nonprobabilistic programs [9,18,50,54]. In the presence of probabilistic behavior the notion of termination problem needs to be extended. Two natural and basic extensions are as follows: first, the *almost-sure* termination question asks whether the program terminates with probability 1; second, the *bounded* termination question asks whether the expected termination time of the program is bounded. While the bounded termination implies almost-sure termination, the converse is not true in general. In this work we focus on the bounded termination problem.

Previous Results: Nonrecursive Probabilistic Programs. We describe the most relevant previous results for termination of probabilistic nonrecursive programs.

- *Finite probabilistic choices.* First, in [43,44] quantitative invariants were used to establish termination for probabilistic programs with nondeterminism, but restricted only to finite probabilistic choices.
- *Infinite probabilistic choices without nondeterminism.* The approach of [43,44] was extended in [12] to *ranking supermartingales* to obtain a sound (but not complete) approach for almost-sure termination for infinite-state probabilistic programs with infinite-domain random variables. The above approach was for probabilistic programs without nondeterminism. The connection between termination of probabilistic programs without nondeterminism and *Lyapunov ranking functions* was considered in [8]. For probabilistic programs with countable state space and without nondeterminism, the Lyapunov ranking functions provide a sound and complete method to prove bounded termination [8,26].
- *Infinite probabilistic choices with nondeterminism.* In the presence of nondeterminism for bounded termination, the Lyapunov-ranking-function/ranking-supermartingale method were claimed to be incomplete, and a partial completeness results has been established for subclass of ranking supermartingales [24]. A proof-rule based approach has also been proposed for probabilistic programs with loops [38]. Automated approaches for synthesizing linear and polynomial ranking supermartingales have been established in [12,14,15]. A martingale based approach for high probability termination and nontermination has also been considered [16].

The problem of deciding termination of probabilistic programs is undecidable, and its precise undecidability characterization has been studied in [37].

Important Open Questions. Given the many important results established in the literature, there are still several fundamental open questions.

- A sound and complete martingale-based approach for bounded termination for nondeterministic probabilistic programs is an important open question.

- While ranking supermartingales can provide upper bounds for expected termination time, whether they can be used to derive lower bounds remains open.

We address these fundamental questions in this work.

Our Results. We consider probabilistic programs with nondeterminism. Our main contributions are as follows.

- *Bounded termination: soundness and completeness.* We show that a ranking-supermartingale based approach is both sound and complete for the bounded termination problem for probabilistic programs with nondeterminism. Note that [24, Theorem 5.7] claimed that ranking supermartingales are incomplete for probabilistic programs with nondeterminism. A counterexample was used as the witness for the incompleteness claim in [24]. We present an explicit ranking supermartingale for the counterexample (see Example 2) to show that the counterexample is invalid, and establish completeness for nondeterministic probabilistic programs for bounded termination. The significance of our result is as follows: it presents a sound and complete approach for nondeterministic probabilistic programs, thus clarifies the understanding of ranking-supermartingale approach in the presence of nondeterminism. Moreover, we also show that our results extend even in the presence of recursion (i.e., for recursive probabilistic programs with nondeterminism).
- *Quantitative bounds.* We present the first sound approach to obtain lower bounds on expected termination time of nondeterministic probabilistic programs using ranking supermartingales. In detail, we show that lowerly-bounded ranking supermartingales present the above sound approach, and demonstrate the necessity of the lowerly-bounded condition.

We note that previous works, such as [12,14,15], present algorithmic approaches to construct special classes (e.g. linear, polynomial) of ranking supermartingales. Thus ranking supermartingales often lead to automated approaches, and we establish that in general such approaches are both sound and complete.

2 Preliminaries

We first introduce some basic concepts in probability theory, and then present the syntax and semantics of nondeterministic probabilistic programs.

2.1 Basic Notations and Concepts

We denote by $\mathbb{N}$, $\mathbb{N}_0$, $\mathbb{Z}$, and $\mathbb{R}$ the sets of all positive integers, nonnegative integers, integers, and real numbers, respectively.

Probability Space. A *probability space* is a triple $(\Omega, \mathcal{F}, \mathbb{P})$, where Ω is a nonempty set (the so-called *sample space*), $\mathcal{F}$ is a *sigma-algebra* over Ω (i.e., a collection of subsets of Ω that contains the empty set $\emptyset$ and is closed under complementation and countable union), and $\mathbb{P}$ is a *probability measure* on $\mathcal{F}$, i.e., a function $\mathbb{P} \colon \mathcal{F} \to [0,1]$ such that (i) $\mathbb{P}(\Omega) = 1$ and (ii) for all set-sequences $A_1, A_2, \cdots \in \mathcal{F}$ that are pairwise-disjoint (i.e., $A_i \cap A_j = \emptyset$ whenever $i \neq j$) it holds that $\sum_{i=1}^{\infty} \mathbb{P}(A_i) = \mathbb{P}(\bigcup_{i=1}^{\infty} A_i)$. Elements $A \in \mathcal{F}$ are usually called *events*. An event $A \in \mathcal{F}$ is said to hold *almost surely* (a.s.) if $\mathbb{P}(A) = 1$.

Random Variables. A *random variable* X from a probability space $(\Omega, \mathcal{F}, \mathbb{P})$ is an $\mathcal{F}$-measurable function $X \colon \Omega \to \mathbb{R} \cup \{-\infty, +\infty\}$, i.e., a function satisfying the condition that for all $d \in \mathbb{R} \cup \{-\infty, +\infty\}$, the set $\{\omega \in \Omega \mid X(\omega) < d\}$ belongs to $\mathcal{F}$. By convention, we abbreviate $+\infty$ as ∞.

Expectation. The *expected value* of a random variable X from a probability space $(\Omega, \mathcal{F}, \mathbb{P})$, denoted by $\mathbb{E}(X)$, is defined as the Lebesgue integral of X w.r.t $\mathbb{P}$, i.e., $\mathbb{E}(X) := \int X \, d\mathbb{P}$; the detailed definition of Lebesgue integral is somewhat technical and is omitted here (cf. [57, Chap. 5] for a formal definition). In the case that range $X = \{d_0, d_1, \ldots, d_k, \ldots\}$ is countable with distinct d_k's, we have that $\mathbb{E}(X) = \sum_{k=0}^{\infty} d_k \cdot \mathbb{P}(X = d_k)$.

Characteristic Random Variables. Given random variables $X_0, \ldots, X_n$ from a probability space $(\Omega, \mathcal{F}, \mathbb{P})$ and a predicate Φ over $\mathbb{R} \cup \{-\infty, +\infty\}$, we denote by $\mathbf{1}_{\Phi(X_0,\ldots,X_n)}$ the random variable such that $\mathbf{1}_{\Phi(X_0,\ldots,X_n)}(\omega) = 1$ if $\Phi(X_0(\omega), \ldots, X_n(\omega))$ holds, and $\mathbf{1}_{\Phi(X_0,\ldots,X_n)}(\omega) = 0$ otherwise. By definition, $\mathbb{E}\left(\mathbf{1}_{\Phi(X_0,\ldots,X_n)}\right) = \mathbb{P}\left(\Phi(X_0, \ldots, X_n)\right)$. Note that if Φ does not involve any variable, then $\mathbf{1}_{\Phi}$ can be deemed as a constant whose value depends only on whether Φ holds or not.

Filtrations and Stopping Times. A *filtration* of a probability space $(\Omega, \mathcal{F}, \mathbb{P})$ is an infinite sequence $\{\mathcal{F}_n\}_{n \in \mathbb{N}_0}$ of sigma-algebras over Ω such that $\mathcal{F}_n \subseteq \mathcal{F}_{n+1} \subseteq \mathcal{F}$ for all $n \in \mathbb{N}_0$. A *stopping time* (from $(\Omega, \mathcal{F}, \mathbb{P})$) w.r.t $\{\mathcal{F}_n\}_{n \in \mathbb{N}_0}$ is a random variable $R \colon \Omega \to \mathbb{N}_0 \cup \{\infty\}$ such that for every $n \in \mathbb{N}_0$, the event $R \leq n$ belongs to $\mathcal{F}_n$.

Conditional Expectation. Let X be any random variable from a probability space $(\Omega, \mathcal{F}, \mathbb{P})$ such that $\mathbb{E}(|X|) < \infty$. Then given any σ-algebra $\mathcal{G} \subseteq \mathcal{F}$, there exists a random variable (from $(\Omega, \mathcal{F}, \mathbb{P})$), conventionally denoted by $\mathbb{E}(X|\mathcal{G})$, such that

(E1) $\mathbb{E}(X|\mathcal{G})$ is $\mathcal{G}$-measurable, and
(E2) $\mathbb{E}\left(|\mathbb{E}(X|\mathcal{G})|\right) < \infty$, and
(E3) for all $A \in \mathcal{G}$, we have $\int_A \mathbb{E}(X|\mathcal{G}) \, d\mathbb{P} = \int_A X \, d\mathbb{P}$.

The random variable $\mathbb{E}(X|\mathcal{G})$ is called the *conditional expectation* of X given $\mathcal{G}$. The random variable $\mathbb{E}(X|\mathcal{G})$ is a.s. unique in the sense that if Y is another random variable satisfying (E1)–(E3), then $\mathbb{P}(Y = \mathbb{E}(X|\mathcal{G})) = 1$. We refer to [57, Chap. 9] for more details.

Discrete-Time Stochastic Processes. A *discrete-time stochastic process* is a sequence $\Gamma = \{X_n\}_{n \in \mathbb{N}_0}$ of random variables where the X_n's are all from some probability space (say, $(\Omega, \mathcal{F}, \mathbb{P})$); we say that Γ is *adapted to* a filtration

$\{\mathcal{F}_n\}_{n \in \mathbb{N}_0}$ of sub-sigma-algebras of $\mathcal{F}$ if for all $n \in \mathbb{N}_0$, the random variable X_n is $\mathcal{F}_n$-measurable.

Difference-Boundedness. A discrete-time stochastic process $\Gamma = \{X_n\}_{n \in \mathbb{N}_0}$ is *difference-bounded* if there is $c \in [0, \infty)$ such that for every $n \in \mathbb{N}_0$, $|X_{n+1} - X_n| \leq c$ almost-surely.

Stopping Time Z_Γ. Given a discrete-time stochastic process $\Gamma = \{X_n\}_{n \in \mathbb{N}_0}$ adapted to a filtration $\{\mathcal{F}_n\}_{n \in \mathbb{N}_0}$, we define the random variable Z_Γ by $Z_\Gamma(\omega) := \min\{n \mid X_n(\omega) \leq 0\}$ where $\min \emptyset := \infty$. Note that by definition, Z_Γ is a stopping time w.r.t $\{\mathcal{F}_n\}_{n \in \mathbb{N}_0}$.

Martingales. A discrete-time stochastic process $\Gamma = \{X_n\}_{n \in \mathbb{N}}$ adapted to a filtration $\{\mathcal{F}_n\}_{n \in \mathbb{N}_0}$ is a *martingale* (resp. *supermartingale, submartingale*) if for every $n \in \mathbb{N}_0$, $\mathbb{E}(|X_n|) < \infty$ and it holds almost-surely that $\mathbb{E}(X_{n+1}|\mathcal{F}_n) = X_n$ (resp. $\mathbb{E}(X_{n+1}|\mathcal{F}_n) \leq X_n$, $\mathbb{E}(X_{n+1}|\mathcal{F}_n) \geq X_n$). We refer to [57, Chap. 10] for more details.

In this paper, we construct super/submartingales Γ from probabilistic programs and use them to prove termination and lower bound properties of the programs. In our setting, Z_Γ will correspond to termination time of a probabilistic program.

Discrete Probability Distributions over Countable Support. A *discrete probability distribution* over a countable set U is a function $q : U \to [0, 1]$ such that $\sum_{z \in U} q(z) = 1$. The *support* of q is defined as $\operatorname{supp}(q) := \{z \in U \mid q(z) > 0\}$. We use discrete probability distributions for samplings of values.

2.2   The Syntax for Nondeterministic Probabilistic Programs

Due to page limit, we present a brief description of our syntax. Our programming language involves two types of variables: *program variables* and *sampling variables*. Program variables are normal variables, while each sampling variable is bound to a discrete probability distribution. Statements in our language are similar to C programming language: assignment statements are indicated by ':='; 'skip' is the special statement that does nothing; if-branches (resp. while-loops) are indicated by 'if' (resp. 'while') together with a logical formula (as the condition) and possibly 'then' and 'else' branches; demonic nondeterministic branches are indicated by 'if', the special symbol '$\star$' and the two nondeterministic 'then' and 'else' branches. The detailed syntax that also covers recursion can be found in [13, p. 13].

Remark 1. The syntax of our programming language is quite general and covers major features of imperative probabilistic programming. For example, our syntax is the same as [37] considered for studying theoretical complexity on termination of probabilistic programs, as well as similar to the popular probabilistic programming language from [30] (the only difference is that the language of [30] has extra observe statements). Finally, we use standard control-flow graphs (CFGs) as the basis of our semantics and then present results directly on CFGs (see Sect. 2.3).

Thus our results are not specific to any syntax, but applicable to all probabilistic imperative programs with CFG-based semantics.   □

2.3   The Semantics for Nondeterministic Probabilistic Programs

We use control-flow graphs (CFGs) and discrete-time Markov decision processes (MDPs) to specify the operational semantics of nondeterministic probabilistic programs. To avoid measurability issues arising from real-valued variables, for simplicity we only consider integer-valued variables in our semantics.

We first introduce the notions of *valuations* and *propositional arithmetic predicates* as follows.

Valuations and Propositional Arithmetic Predicates. Let V be a finite set of variables. A *valuation* over V is a function ν from V into $\mathbb{Z}$. The set of valuations over V is denoted by Val_V. A *propositional arithmetic predicate* (over V) is a logical formula ϕ built from (i) atomic formulae of the form $\mathfrak{e} \bowtie \mathfrak{e}'$ where $\mathfrak{e}, \mathfrak{e}'$ are arithmetic expressions over V and $\bowtie \in \{<, \leq, >, \geq\}$, and (ii) logical connectives such as $\vee, \wedge, \neg$. The satisfaction relation $\models$ between a valuation ν and a propositional arithmetic predicate ϕ is defined through evaluation and standard semantics of logical connectives such that $\nu \models \phi$ holds iff ϕ holds when all variables in V are replaced by theirs corresponding values in ν.

Then we describe the notion of control-flow graphs (CFGs).

Definition 1 (Control-Flow Graphs (CFGs)). *A* control-flow graph *(CFG) is a tuple which takes the form*

$$(L, \ell_{\mathrm{in}}, \ell_{\mathrm{out}}, V_{\mathrm{p}}, V_{\mathrm{r}}, \rightarrow) \tag{1}$$

where:

- V_{p} *(resp. V_{r}) is a finite set of* program variables *(resp. sampling variables);*
- L *is a finite set of* labels *partitioned into the set L_{b} of* branching *labels, the set L_{a} of* assignment *labels and the set L_{d} of* nondeterministic *labels;*
- ℓ_{in} *(resp. ℓ_{out}) is the* initial label *(resp. terminal label);*
- $\rightarrow$ *is a relation whose every member is a triple of the form (ℓ, α, ℓ') for which $\ell \in L$ (resp. $\ell' \in L$) is the source label (resp. target label) of the triple and α is either a propositional arithmetic predicate ϕ over V_{p} if $\ell \in L_{\mathrm{b}}$, or an update function $u : Val_{V_{\mathrm{p}}} \times Val_{V_{\mathrm{r}}} \rightarrow Val_{V_{\mathrm{p}}}$ if $\ell \in L_{\mathrm{a}}$, or the nondeterminism symbol $\star$ if $\ell \in L_{\mathrm{d}}$.*

Informally, a CFG specifies how labels (program counters) and values for program variables change along the execution of a program. In addition, it is intuitively clear that every nondeterministic probabilistic program can be equivalently transformed into a CFG. Transformation from programs to CFGs can be found in e.g. [14,15].

Below we illustrate an example for probabilistic programs and CFGs.

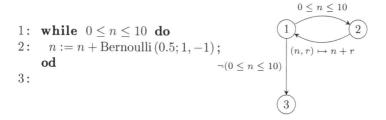

1: **while** $0 \le n \le 10$ **do**
2:      $n := n + \text{Bernoulli}\,(0.5; 1, -1)\,;$
    od
3:

Fig. 1. A probabilistic program (left) with its control-flow graph (right)

Example 1. Consider the program depicted in the left part of Fig. 1, where n is a program variable and Bernoulli $(0.5; 1, -1)$ is a sampling variable. Its CFG is given in the right part of the figure. We use "$0 \le n \le 10$" for a shorthand of "$n \ge 0 \wedge n \le 10$". The semantics of Bernoulli $(0.5; 1, -1)$ is a sampling from the two-point probability distribution q such that $q(1) = q(-1) = \frac{1}{2}$. Basically, the program executes around the value held by n. First, the program starts at the program counter 1. Second, if the value of n falls in $[0, 10]$ then the program enters the while loop (the arc from 1 to 2 in the CFG), otherwise the program terminates. Third, in the while loop, the value of n is incremented by a random value that observes the probability distribution of the sampling variable r, then the program goes back to the start (the program counter 1).   □

Based on CFGs, we illustrate the semantics of nondeterministic probabilistic programs as follows. Below we fix a nondeterministic probabilistic program W with its CFG taking the form (1). We first define the notion of *configurations*.

Definition 2 (Configurations $\mathcal{C}$). *A configuration $\mathfrak{c}$ is a pair (ℓ, ν) where $\ell \in L$ and $\nu \in Val_{V_p}$. We say that the configuration $\mathfrak{c}$ is terminal if $\ell = \ell_{\text{out}}$, and nondeterministic if $\ell \in L_d$. The set of configurations is denoted by $\mathcal{C}$.*

To demonstrate the formal semantics of probabilistic programs, we also need to assign exact probability distributions to sampling variables. To this purpose, we introduce the notion of sampling functions. A *sampling function* Υ is a function assigning to every sampling variable $r \in V_r$ a discrete probability distribution over $\mathbb{Z}$; the associated joint discrete probability distribution $\overline{\Upsilon}$ over Val_{V_r} is then defined by $\overline{\Upsilon}(\mu) := \prod_{r \in V_r} \Upsilon(r)(\mu(r))$ for $\mu \in Val_{V_r}$.

Now given a sampling function Υ, the semantics of a probabilistic program W is described by a Markov decision process (MDP) (cf. [4, Chap. 10]) $\mathcal{M}_W = (S_W, Act, \mathbf{P}_W)$ as follows. Informally, $\mathcal{M}_W$ describes the probabilistic execution of the program W such that (i) the states S_W of $\mathcal{M}_W$ are configurations reflecting both the current program counter and the values for program variables, (ii) the actions Act are either normal (i.e., absence of non-determinism) or the **then**/**else**-branch that refers to the choice at a non-deterministic label, and (iii) the probabilistic transition function $\mathbf{P}_W$ describes the probabilistic transitions between configurations. Due to lack of space, we put the detailed definition of the MDP $\mathcal{M}_W$ in [13, Definition 5].

Nondeterminism in MDPs are resolved by *schedulers*. To introduce the notion of schedulers, we first describe the notion of histories upon which schedulers make decisions.

Definition 3 (Histories). *A history is a finite sequence $\rho = c_0 \ldots c_n \ (n \geq 0)$ of configurations such that for all $0 \leq k < n$, we have $\mathbf{P}_W(c_k, a, c_{k+1}) > 0$ for some $a \in Act$. We denote the ending configuration c_n of the history ρ by $\rho\!\downarrow$.*

Below we present the standard notion of schedulers. Informally, a scheduler resolves nondeterminism at nondeterministic configurations by choosing a discrete probability distribution over actions that specifies the probabilities to take each action. In this paper, the schedulers are considered *demonic* in the sense that they always try to make the expected termination time longer.

Definition 4 (Schedulers). *A scheduler σ is a function which maps every history ρ to a discrete probability distribution $\sigma(\rho)$ over all possible successor configurations of $\rho\!\downarrow$.*

The Final Semantics. Based on schedulers, applying a scheduler σ to $\mathcal{M}_W$ yields an infinite-state discrete-time Markov chain $\mathcal{M}_{W,\sigma}$ where the state space is the set of all histories and the probability transition function is determined by the counterpart from $\mathcal{M}_W$ and the scheduler σ. With an *initial configuration* c, the semantics of the MDP $\mathcal{M}_W$ is then defined as the probability space $(\Lambda, \mathcal{H}, \mathbb{P}_c^\sigma)$ induced by the Markov chain $\mathcal{M}_{W,\sigma}$ where (i) the sample space Λ consists of all infinite sequences $\{\rho_n\}_{n \in \mathbb{N}_0}$ of histories such that (a) $\rho_0 = c$ and (b) for all $k \in \mathbb{N}_0$, there is some configuration c' such that $\rho_{k+1} = \rho_k \cdot c'$, (ii) the sigma-algebra $\mathcal{H}$ is generated by all *cylinder sets* for which a cylinder set consists of all infinite sequences of histories sharing a common prefix, and (iii) the probability measure $\mathbb{P}_c^\sigma$ is uniquely determined by the initial configuration c and the probability transition function from the Markov chain $\mathcal{M}_{W,\sigma}$ (which in turn depends on the MDP $\mathcal{M}_W$ and the scheduler σ). See [4, Chap. 10] for details.

Infinite Runs. We shall call elements from Λ *infinite runs*. By definition, each infinite run $\{\rho_n\}_{n \in \mathbb{N}_0}$ can be equivalently expressed as the unique infinite sequence $\{c_n\}_{n \in \mathbb{N}_0}$ of configurations such that $\rho_n = c_0 \ldots c_n$ for all $n \geq 0$. For the sake of technical convenience, we treat each infinite run $\{\rho_n\}_{n \in \mathbb{N}_0}$ as its corresponding infinite sequence $\{c_n\}_{n \in \mathbb{N}_0}$ of configurations. Intuitively, such a sequence $\{c_n\}_{n \in \mathbb{N}_0}$ describes an execution of the probabilistic program in the sense that the nth configuration in the execution is c_n.

Expectation for $(\Lambda, \mathcal{H}, \mathbb{P}_c^\sigma)$. We use the notation $\mathbb{E}_c^\sigma(-)$ to denote expectation for random variables over elements from Λ w.r.t the probability measure $\mathbb{P}_c^\sigma$ (with the initial configuration c and the scheduler σ).

Finally, we discuss other operational semantics for probabilistic programs that will be crucial to our completeness result.

Remark 2. There are two possible operational semantics for probabilistic programs.

- *Standard MDP Semantics.* In the MDP semantics, the probability space is defined over infinite runs. Moreover, each scheduler defines a probability measure. In this setting, there is only one termination time random variable T (cf. Definition 5), but each scheduler σ defines a probability measure $\mathbb{P}_{\mathfrak{c}}^{\sigma}$.
- *Alternative Semantics.* In an alternative semantics (cf. [24]) the probability space is defined directly over sampled values. In this setting, there is only one probability measure $\mathbb{P}$ (generated by the samplings) but many termination time random variables T^{σ} (each corresponds to a scheduler σ).

Although these two semantics seems similar, they are different. For example, in the standard MDP semantics, the assertion "the program terminates within a bounded amount of time" can be expressed as $\sup_{\sigma} \mathbb{E}^{\sigma}(T) < \infty$, while in the alternative semantics it is expressed as $\mathbb{E}(\sup_{\sigma} T^{\sigma}) < \infty$. In general, $\sup_{\sigma} \mathbb{E}^{\sigma}(T)$ can be smaller than $\mathbb{E}(\sup_{\sigma} T^{\sigma})$ and it is possible that the former is finite and the latter is infinite. The standard MDP semantics is also more applicable as it preserves the local information of nondeterminism by assigning to each scheduler a probability measure. In this work we follow the standard MDP semantics. $\square$

3 Termination Problems

In this section, we define the notions of finite and bounded termination over nondeterministic probabilistic programs. Below we fix a probabilistic program W with its associated CFG in the form (1) and a sampling function Υ. We recall the probability spaces (i.e., $(\Lambda, \mathcal{H}, \mathbb{P}_{\mathfrak{c}}^{\sigma})$'s) defined in the previous section where σ is a scheduler and $\mathfrak{c}$ is an initial configuration.

We first present two definitions of termination times of a probabilistic program.

Definition 5 (Termination-Time Random Variable and Function). *The termination-time random variable T is a random variable on Λ defined by:*

$$T(\{(\ell_n, \nu_n)\}_{n \in \mathbb{N}_0}) := \min\{n \in \mathbb{N}_0 \mid \ell_n = \ell_{\mathrm{out}}\}$$

for any infinite sequence $\{(\ell_n, \nu_n)\}_{n \in \mathbb{N}_0}$ of configurations (as an infinite run), where $\min \emptyset := \infty$ (this case corresponds to program nontermination where no ℓ_n is ℓ_{out}). The termination-time function $\overline{T} : \mathcal{C} \to [0, \infty]$ is given by $\overline{T}(\mathfrak{c}) := \sup_{\sigma} \mathbb{E}_{\mathfrak{c}}^{\sigma}(T)$ for all configurations $\mathfrak{c}$, where σ ranges over all schedulers.

Thus, T is the random variable that measures the amount of computational steps until termination, while $\overline{T}$ is the function that takes the supremum of expected termination times over all schedulers. Below we further define the notion of finite and bounded termination.

Definition 6 (Finite and Bounded Termination). *We say that the program W is:* finitely terminating *from an initial configuration $\mathfrak{c}$ if $\mathbb{E}_{\mathfrak{c}}^{\sigma}(T) < \infty$ for all schedulers σ; furthermore, it is* boundedly terminating *from an initial configuration $\mathfrak{c}$ if $\overline{T}(\mathfrak{c}) = \sup_{\sigma} \mathbb{E}_{\mathfrak{c}}^{\sigma}(T) < \infty$.*

Remark 3 (Finite vs Bounded Termination). We note that there is an important conceptual difference between finite and bounded termination. While finite termination requires the expected termination time to be finite for all schedulers, the bounded termination requires the supremum of the expected termination time to be finite. In other words, the bounded termination is the uniform bounded version of finite termination. Bounded termination implies finite termination, but not vice-versa. For example, there can be schedulers $\sigma_1, \sigma_2, \sigma_3, \ldots$, such that for σ_i the expected termination time is i; thus for every scheduler the expected termination time is finite, but the supremum is unbounded. For an explicit example see the example in the first paragraph, right column on Page 2 in [24]. Finite termination is also called *positive a.s. termination* in the literature. However, to clarify the important difference between finite vs bounded version of expected termination time we refer to them as finite and bounded termination, respectively. In this work we focus on bounded termination problem, consider ranking supermartingales (a special class of stochastic processes) and show that they are sound and complete for bounded termination. $\square$

4   Bounded Termination: Soundness and Completeness

In this section, we consider the notion of ranking supermartingales (RSMs) for proving bounded termination of probabilistic programs with nondeterminism. Our contributions for this section, which are the main results of this work, are two-fold: (i) we show that RSMs in general form are sound for proving bounded termination; (ii) we prove that RSMs in general form are complete for proving bounded termination, in contrast to the previous claim from [24]. In the whole section, we fix a nondeterministic probabilistic program W together with its CFG taking the form (1) and a sampling function Υ. We define $Val^r := \mathrm{supp}(\Upsilon)$.

4.1   The Soundness Result

We first recall the notion of RSMs. Intuitively, an RSM is a nonnegative stochastic process with decreasing conditional expectation until the value of the process becomes zero.

Definition 7 (Ranking Supermartingales [12,15,24]). *A discrete-time stochastic process $\Gamma = \{X_n\}_{n \in \mathbb{N}_0}$ adapted to a filtration $\{\mathcal{F}_n\}_{n \in \mathbb{N}_0}$ is a ranking supermartingale (RSM) if there exists $\epsilon \in (0, \infty)$ such that for all $n \in \mathbb{N}_0$, the following conditions hold:*

- *(integrability)* $\mathbb{E}(|X_n|) < \infty$;
- *(nonnegativity)* *it holds a.s. that* $X_n \geq 0$;
- *(ranking)* *it holds a.s. that* $\mathbb{E}(X_{n+1}|\mathcal{F}_n) \leq X_n - \epsilon \cdot \mathbf{1}_{X_n > 0}$.

Thus, an integrable stochastic process Γ is an RSM if it is nonnegative and its values decrease in conditional expectation when the step n increases. The following known result relates RSMs Γ with the bounded-terminating behaviour of the stopping times Z_Γ. It serves as an extension of Foster's Theorem [8,26].

Theorem 1 ([24, Lemma 5.5]). *Let $\Gamma = \{X_n\}_{n \in \mathbb{N}_0}$ be a ranking supermartingale adapted to a filtration $\{\mathcal{F}_n\}_{n \in \mathbb{N}_0}$ with ϵ given as in Definition 7. Then $\mathbb{P}(Z_\Gamma < \infty) = 1$ and $\mathbb{E}(Z_\Gamma) \leq \frac{\mathbb{E}(X_0)}{\epsilon}$.*

To apply Theorem 1, one needs to embed RSMs into probabilistic programs. To resolve this issue, the notion of linear/polynomial *ranking-supermartingale maps* (RSM-maps) (see [12, Definition 6] and [15, Definition 8]) plays a key role. Below we generalize linear/polynomial RSM-maps to RSM-maps in general form.

Definition 8 (RSM-maps). *A* ranking-supermartingale map *(RSM-map) is a function $h : \mathcal{C} \to [0, \infty]$ satisfying that there exists $\epsilon \in (0, \infty)$ such that for all configurations (ℓ, ν), the following conditions hold:*

(B1) if $\ell = \ell_{\mathrm{out}}$, then we have $h(\ell, \nu) = 0$;

(B2) if $\ell \in L_{\mathrm{a}} \setminus \{\ell_{\mathrm{out}}\}$ and (ℓ, u, ℓ') is the only triple in $\to$ with source label ℓ and update function u, then we have $\epsilon + \sum_{\mu \in Val^r} \Upsilon(\mu) \cdot h\left(\ell', u(\nu, \mu)\right) \leq h(\ell, \nu)$;

(B3) if $\ell \in L_{\mathrm{b}} \setminus \{\ell_{\mathrm{out}}\}$ and $(\ell, \phi, \ell_1), (\ell, \neg\phi, \ell_2)$ are the two triples in $\to$ with source label ℓ and propositional arithmetic predicate ϕ, then we have $\mathbf{1}_{\nu \models \phi} \cdot h(\ell_1, \nu) + \mathbf{1}_{\nu \models \neg\phi} \cdot h(\ell_2, \nu) + \epsilon \leq h(\ell, \nu)$;

(B4) if $\ell \in L_{\mathrm{d}} \setminus \{\ell_{\mathrm{out}}\}$ and $(\ell, \star, \ell_1), (\ell, \star, \ell_2)$ are the two triples in $\to$ with source label ℓ, then we have $\max\{h(\ell_1, \nu), h(\ell_2, \nu)\} + \epsilon \leq h(\ell, \nu)$.

($d \cdot \infty := \infty$ for $d \in (0, \infty]$, $0 \cdot \infty := 0$ by convention.)

Intuitively, an RSM-map is a function whose expected values decrease by a positive stepwise amount ϵ along the execution of a probabilistic program. For example, the condition (B2) means that the expected value taken by h after the execution of an assignment statement decreases by at least ϵ compared with the current value taken by h; (B3) means that the value taken by h after the conditional branch decreases by at least ϵ; (B4) means that the value taken by h after the nondeterministic branch decreases by at least ϵ no matter which branch is taken. We incorporate the infinity ∞ to cover the situation that the supremum of the expected termination time may not be finite.

Below we demonstrate the soundness of RSMs for bounded termination through RSM-maps. There is also a related soundness result established in [24], see Remark 5 below.

Lemma 1 (Soundness). *For all RSM-maps h with ϵ given as in Definition 8 and for all configurations $\mathfrak{c}$, we have that $\overline{T}(\mathfrak{c}) \leq \frac{h(\mathfrak{c})}{\epsilon}$.*

Proof (Proof Sketch for Lemma 1). We generalize the proof idea in [15]. Informally, the soundness result holds as the existence of an RSM-map leads to the existence of an RSM that witnesses the bounded termination of the program. First, we define the random variables lb_n, val_n^x for $n \in \mathbb{N}_0$, $x \in V_{\mathrm{p}}$ so that given any infinite run ω, $\mathsf{lb}_n(\omega)$ represents the label (i.e. the program counter) at the nth step, while $\mathsf{val}_n^x(\omega)$ represents the value of the program variable x at the nth step. We write $\mathsf{val}_n(\omega)$ for the valuation which maps every program variable x to $\mathsf{val}_n^x(\omega)$. Then we consider any RSM-map h with ϵ given as in Definition 8 and any initial configuration $\mathfrak{c} = (\ell, \nu)$. The case when $h(\mathfrak{c}) = \infty$ is straightforward. So the non-trivial case is that of $h(\mathfrak{c}) < \infty$. Let σ be any scheduler. Define the stochastic process $\Gamma = \{X_n\}_{n \in \mathbb{N}_0}$ by:

$$X_n(\omega) := h\left(\mathsf{lb}_n(\omega), \mathsf{val}_n(\omega)\right) \tag{2}$$

for all n and all infinite runs ω. By Definition 8, we have that for all ω, $X_n(\omega) > 0$ iff $\mathsf{lb}_n(\omega) \neq \ell_{\mathrm{out}}$; it follows immediately that $T = Z_\Gamma$. Thus, once we show that Γ is an RSM (under $\mathbb{P}_{\mathfrak{c}}^{\sigma}$), we can apply Lemma 1 and obtain the result. Intuitively, we have that Γ is an RSM since conditions (B2)–(B4) somehow specify the ranking condition of an RSM (see Definition 7). Then by applying Lemma 1, we obtain that $\mathbb{E}_{\mathfrak{c}}^{\sigma}(T) = \mathbb{E}_{\mathfrak{c}}^{\sigma}(Z_\Gamma) \leq \frac{\mathbb{E}_{\mathfrak{c}}^{\sigma}(X_0)}{\epsilon} = \frac{h(\mathfrak{c})}{\epsilon}$. Thus, $\overline{T}(\mathfrak{c}) \leq \frac{h(\mathfrak{c})}{\epsilon}$ by the arbitrary choice of σ. Note that each X_n is nonnegative so the integrability is equivalent to saying that $\mathbb{E}_{\mathfrak{c}}^{\sigma}(X_n) < \infty$. The integrability proof follows from an inductive argument saying that $\mathbb{E}(X_{n+1}) \leq \mathbb{E}(X_n)$, which in turn is derived from the decreasing amount ϵ. Then, we obtain directly from $\mathbb{E}(X_0) = h(\mathfrak{c}) < \infty$ that every X_n is integrable. The detailed proof that also works for recursion is available in [13, Lemma 1]. □

Remark 4 (RSM-maps and Bounded Termination). From Lemma 1 it follows that to prove that the program W is boundedly terminating from an initial configuration $\mathfrak{c}$, it suffices to construct an RSM-map h (possibly in a specific form) satisfying that $h(\mathfrak{c}) < \infty$. □

Remark 5 (Novelty of Our Soundness Result). In previous works such as [12,15], RSM-maps linear or polynomial in program variables serve as a sound approach for proving bounded termination of probabilistic programs. We present a general result to show that RSM-maps in general form are also sound for bounded termination. The main novelty is to ensure that general RSM-maps induce integrable stochastic processes, which naturally holds for linear and polynomial RSM-maps. We also note that there is a soundness result established in [24], however, it is orthogonal to our results as we follow different semantics (see Remark 2). □

4.2 The Completeness Result

Lemma 2 (Completeness). $\overline{T}$ *is an RSM-map with corresponding* $\epsilon = 1$ *(cf. Definition 8).*

Informally, our completeness result says that the termination time function itself is an RSM-map. This has the following consequence: if the program W is boundedly terminating from some initial configuration $\mathfrak{c}$ (i.e. $\overline{T}(\mathfrak{c}) < \infty$), then one can always find an RSM-map h (in general form) satisfying $h(\mathfrak{c}) < \infty$ by taking h simply to be $\overline{T}$. Note that the existence of such an RSM-map witnesses the bounded-terminating behaviour of the program W (cf. Remark 4). In this sense, Lemma 2 shows that RSMs are complete for proving bounded termination of probabilistic programs.

Proof. By the definition of RSM-maps, we need to prove that the function $\overline{T}$ satisfies the properties (B2)–(B4) for which $\epsilon = 1$. (Note that (B1) directly holds for $\overline{T}$ from definition.) This follows directly from the MDP semantics. In detail, the fact that (B2)–(B4) hold follows from the one-step properties of MDPs. For example, the condition (B2) holds since it is intuitive that the expected termination time is an averaged sum over all successor configurations; (B4) holds since the supremum expected termination time should be the maximum among the two nondeterministic branches.   □

Our completeness result is non-trivial as it corrects a previous incompleteness claim from [24, Theorem 5.7]. Below we compare our results with the previous incompleteness claim.

Remark 6 (Comparison with [24]). The result of [24, Theorem 5.7] claims that under the standard MDP semantics, RSMs are not complete for bounded termination over nondeterministic probabilistic programs. We proved that the claim is wrong and established the completeness of RSMs for bounded termination. Note that a relative completeness result is established in [24, Theorem 5.8] under their alternative semantics (cf. Remark 2). Since we consider the MDP semantics, this relative completeness result is orthogonal to the focus of our work.   □

In [24], the incompleteness claim was supported by a "counterexample". In the following example, we present however an explicit RSM-map for the "counterexample". This invalidates the incompleteness claim.

Example 2. Consider the probabilistic program depicted in Fig. 2 which results from adapting the example in [24, Figure 1] by using the parameters in the second paragraph on Page 2, right column of [24]. In the figure, n, i, c are program variables and Bernoulli (0.5) is a sampling variable that samples to either 0 or 1 both with probability $\frac{1}{2}$. In [24, Theorem 5.7], this program is used as the counterexample to witness the incompleteness of RSMs for proving bounded termination of nondeterministic probabilistic programs under standard MDP semantics. In contrast, we present an exponential RSM (as an RSM-map h) with corresponding $\epsilon = 1$ for this program in Fig. 3. In the table, the column "Invariant" specifies logical formulae at labels that reachable valuations satisfy when the program starts from label 1, while "The RSM-map h" presents an RSM-map h label by label, e.g., the RSM-map at the label 5 is specified by $h(5, n, i, c) = 2^{n+1} + 2 \cdot n + 13$. In the invariant column, we abbreviate "$i \geq 0 \wedge n \geq 0$" as "$i, n \geq 0$". With the help of the "invariant" column, one can verify from definition that h is an RSM-map. For example, at label 3 we have from the invariant $i = 0 \wedge n = 0$ that $16 = h(4, 0, 0, 0) + 1 \leq h(3, 0, 0, c) = 17$ which fulfills the (B2) condition; at label 6, we have $1 + 0.5 \cdot (2^{n+2} + 2 \cdot n + 18) + 0.5 \cdot (2 \cdot n + 4) \leq 2^{n+1} + 2 \cdot n + 12$ which fulfills the (B2) condition that $1 + 0.5 \cdot h(7, n, i, 0) + 0.5 \cdot h(7, n, i, 1) \leq h(6, n, i, c)$; from label 8 to label 4, we have $1 + h(4, n+1, i, 0) \leq h(8, n, i, 0)$ for (B2); at label 4 the condition (B3) holds directly from the function at label $5, 12$ in the table. Note that although we replace uniform distribution (in the original program) by Bernoulli distribution to fit our integer setting, the RSM-map given in Fig. 3 remains to be effective for the original program as it preserves probability value for the guard $c < 0.5$. □

1: $n := 0$; 2: $i := 0$;

3: $c := 0$;

4: **while** $c = 0$ **do**

5:    **if** $\star$ **then**

6:      $c :=$ Bernoulli (0.5);

7:      **if** $c = 0$ **then**

8:        $n := n + 1$

      else

9:        $i := n$

      fi

    else

10:    $i := 2^n$; 11: $c := 1$

    fi od;

12: **while** $i > 0$ **do**

13:    $i := i - 1$ **od**

14:

Label	Invariant	The RSM-map h
1	true	19
2	$n = 0$	18
3	$i = 0 \land n = 0$	17
4	$i, n \geq 0$	$1_{c=1} \cdot (2 \cdot i + 2) +$ $1_{c=0} \cdot (2^{n+1} + 2 \cdot n + 14)$
5	$i, n \geq 0 \land c = 0$	$2^{n+1} + 2 \cdot n + 13$
6	$i, n \geq 0 \land c = 0$	$2^{n+1} + 2 \cdot n + 12$
7	$i, n \geq 0$	$1_{c=0} \cdot (2^{n+2} + 2 \cdot n + 18) +$ $1_{c=1} \cdot (2 \cdot n + 4)$
8	$i, n \geq 0 \land c = 0$	$2^{n+2} + 2 \cdot n + 17$
9	$i, n \geq 0 \land c = 1$	$2 \cdot n + 3$
10	$i, n \geq 0 \land c = 0$	$2^n + 4$
11	$i, n \geq 0 \land c = 0$	$2 \cdot i + 3$
12	$i, n \geq 0$	$2 \cdot i + 1$
13	$i \geq 1 \land n \geq 0$	$2 \cdot i$
14	$i = 0 \land n \geq 0$	0

Fig. 2. The counterexample in [24]

Fig. 3. The RSM-map for Example 2

We summarize our soundness and completeness result as follows.

Theorem 2 (Soundness and Completeness). *RSM-maps are sound and complete for bounded termination over non-deterministic probabilistic programs.*

Remark 7 (Decidability). A sound and complete approach does not imply decidability as it only guarantees the existence of RSM-maps in general form for bounded termination. While termination of probabilistic programs is undecidable in general [37], yet RSMs present a sound and complete approach.   □

5   Quantitative Results on Bounded Termination

In this section, we present results showing how RSMs can establish quantitative results related to termination of probabilistic programs. Our main contribution of this section shows that *lowerly-bounded* RSMs, a subclass of RSMs, can be used to derive lower bounds on expected termination time.

Lower Bounds on Expected Termination Time. We first present a result (Proposition 1) which shows that difference-bounded RSMs Γ can derive lower bound on the expected value of the stopping time Z_Γ. This proposition serves as the theoretical backbone for deriving a lower bound for expected termination time. Moreover, we present an example (Example 3) showing that the difference-boundedness condition of Proposition 1 is necessary, and without such condition the desired result does not hold. Then we define the notion of lowerly-bounded RSM-maps, and in Theorem 3 show that they can derive tight lower bounds on expected termination time. Finally we present an example (Example 4) to illustrate the application of Theorem 3.

Proposition 1. *Consider any difference-bounded ranking supermartingale $\Gamma = \{X_n\}_{n \in \mathbb{N}_0}$ adapted to a filtration $\{\mathcal{F}_n\}_{n \in \mathbb{N}_0}$ with ϵ given as in Definition 7. If*

- *for every $n \in \mathbb{N}_0$, it holds for all ω that $X_n(\omega) = 0$ implies $X_{n+1}(\omega) = 0$, and*
- *The Lower Bound Condition. there exists $\delta \in (0, \infty)$ such that for all $n \in \mathbb{N}_0$, it holds a.s. that $\mathbb{E}(X_{n+1}|\mathcal{F}_n) \geq X_n - \delta \cdot \mathbf{1}_{X_n > 0}$,*

then $\mathbb{E}(Z_\Gamma) \geq \frac{\mathbb{E}(X_0)}{\delta}$.

Note that by definition, we have that $\delta \geq \epsilon$. Below we sketch the proof ideas for Proposition 1.

Proof (Proof Sketch for Proposition 1). The key idea is to construct a difference-bounded submartingale from Γ and apply Optional Stopping Theorem. We first define the stochastic process $\{Y_n\}_{n \in \mathbb{N}_0}$ by: $Y_n = X_n + \delta \cdot \min\{n, Z_\Gamma\}$, and prove that it is a difference-bounded submartingale from the Lower Bound condition. Then, we apply Optional Stopping Theorem to the supermartingale $\{-Y_n\}_{n \in \mathbb{N}_0}$ and the stopping time Z_Γ, and obtain that $-\mathbb{E}(X_{Z_\Gamma} + \delta \cdot Z_\Gamma) = \mathbb{E}(-Y_{Z_\Gamma}) \leq \mathbb{E}(-Y_0) = \mathbb{E}(-X_0)$. It follows from $X_{Z_\Gamma} = 0$ a.s. that $\mathbb{E}(Z_\Gamma) \geq \frac{\mathbb{E}(X_0)}{\delta}$. $\qquad \square$

In Proposition 1 the difference-bounded condition is a prerequisite, and in the following example we show that the prerequisite is a necessary condition.

Example 3 (Necessity of Difference-boundedness). The difference-bounded condition in Proposition 1 cannot be dropped. Consider the family $\{Y_n\}_{n \in \mathbb{N}_0}$ of independent random variables defined by: $Y_0 := 3$ and each Y_n $(n \geq 1)$ satisfies that $\mathbb{P}(Y_n = 2^{n-1}) = \frac{1}{2}$ and $\mathbb{P}(Y_n = -2^{n-1} - 2) = \frac{1}{2}$. Let the stochastic process $\Gamma = \{X_n\}_{n \in \mathbb{N}_0}$ be inductively defined by: $X_0 := Y_0$ and for all $n \in \mathbb{N}_0$, we have $X_{n+1} := \mathbf{1}_{X_n > 0} \cdot (X_n + Y_{n+1})$. Let $\{\mathcal{F}_n\}_{n \in \mathbb{N}_0}$ be the filtration such that each $\mathcal{F}_n$ is the smallest sigma-algebra that makes all $Y_0, \ldots, Y_n$ measurable, so that Γ is adapted to $\{\mathcal{F}_n\}_{n \in \mathbb{N}_0}$. Then we obtain that for all $n \in \mathbb{N}_0$, we have $\mathbb{E}(X_{n+1}|\mathcal{F}_n) - X_n = -\mathbf{1}_{X_n > 0}$. Moreover, for all n and ω, we have $X_n(\omega) = 0 \Rightarrow X_{n+1}(\omega) = 0$. However, $\mathbb{E}(Z_\Gamma) = 2 < \frac{\mathbb{E}(X_0)}{1}$. $\qquad \square$

Now we introduce the notion of lowerly-bounded RSM-maps which serve as the main technical notion for proving lower bounds on expected termination time.

Definition 9 (Lowerly-bounded RSM-maps). *An RSM-map $h : \mathcal{C} \to [0, \infty]$ is lowerly-bounded RSM-map if there exist $\delta, \zeta \in (0, \infty)$ such that for all configurations (ℓ, ν) satisfying $h(\ell, \nu) < \infty$, the following conditions hold:*

(B5) *if $\ell \in L_a \setminus \{\ell_{out}\}$ and (ℓ, u, ℓ') is the only triple in $\rightarrow$ with source label ℓ and update function u, then we have that $\delta + \sum_{\mu \in Val^r} \overline{\Upsilon}(\mu) \cdot h(\ell', u(\nu, \mu)) \geq h(\ell, \nu)$, and $|h(\ell', u(\nu, \mu)) - h(\ell, \nu)| \leq \zeta$ for all $\mu \in Val^r$;*

(B6) *if $\ell \in L_b \setminus \{\ell_{out}\}$ and $(\ell, \phi, \ell_1), (\ell, \neg\phi, \ell_2)$ are the two triples in $\rightarrow$ with source label ℓ and propositional arithmetic predicate ϕ, then we have that $\mathbf{1}_{\nu \models \phi} \cdot h(\ell_1, \nu) + \mathbf{1}_{\nu \models \neg\phi} \cdot h(\ell_2, \nu) + \delta \geq h(\ell, \nu)$;*

(B7) *if $\ell \in L_d \setminus \{\ell_{out}\}$ and $(\ell, \star, \ell_1), (\ell, \star, \ell_2)$ are the two triples in $\rightarrow$ with source label ℓ, then we have that $\max\{h(\ell_1, \nu), h(\ell_2, \nu)\} + \delta \geq h(\ell, \nu)$.*

Informally, an RSM-map h is lowerly-bounded if (i) its change on values between the current step and the next step is bounded by some real number ζ along all possible program executions and (ii) the gap between the expected value of the next step and the current value is no greater than δ. The constant ζ guarantees that the RSM induced by h is difference-bounded, while the constant δ is related to the Lower Bound condition in Proposition 1. For example, the condition (B5) means that the difference between the current value $h(\ell, \nu)$ and the next value $h(\ell', u(\nu, \mu))$ is bounded by ζ for any sampled values μ, while the gap between the expected next-step value $\sum_{\mu \in Val^r} \overline{\Upsilon}(\mu) \cdot h(\ell', u(\nu, \mu))$ and the current value $h(\ell, \nu)$ should be no greater than δ. In (B6), (B7) we only have the gap condition as the bound on value changes follows implicitly from the conditions (B3), (B4) for RSM-maps.

By Theorem 1, RSM-maps serve as a sound approach for proving bounded termination (cf. Lemma 1). Below we prove through Proposition 1 that lowerly-bounded RSM-maps serve as a sound approach for proving lower bounds on expected termination time. This extends the metering functions proposed in [29].

Theorem 3 (Lower Bounds on Expected Termination Time). *For any lowerly-bounded RSM-map h with δ, ζ given as in Definition 9, $\overline{T}(\mathfrak{c}) \geq \frac{h(\mathfrak{c})}{\delta}$ for all configurations $\mathfrak{c}$ such that $h(\mathfrak{c}) < \infty$.*

Proof (Proof Sketch). Fix an initial configuration $\mathfrak{c}$ such that $h(\mathfrak{c}) < \infty$. Consider any lowerly-bounded RSM-map h with corresponding δ, ζ. Define the stochastic process $\Gamma = \{X_n\}_{n \in \mathbb{N}_0}$ as in (2). From the proof of Lemma 1, we have that Γ is an RSM with $T = Z_\Gamma$ for any schedulers, thus $\overline{T}(\mathfrak{c}) \leq \frac{h(\mathfrak{c})}{\epsilon} < \infty$. By the bound ζ, we further have that Γ is difference-bounded under any schedulers. Pick a scheduler σ that always choose the nondeterministic branch ℓ' satisfying $h(\ell, \nu) = h(\ell', \nu)$ for any history ending in a nondeterministic configuration (ℓ, ν). Then from the constant δ and the conditions (B5)–(B7), we obtain that $\mathbb{E}(X_{n+1}|\mathcal{F}_n) \geq X_n - \delta \cdot \mathbf{1}_{X_n > 0}$. It follows that Γ satisfies the prerequisites of Proposition 1. Hence by applying Proposition 1, we obtain that $\mathbb{E}_{\mathfrak{c}}^{\sigma}(T) = \mathbb{E}_{\mathfrak{c}}^{\sigma}(Z_\Gamma) \geq \frac{\mathbb{E}_{\mathfrak{c}}^{\sigma}(X_0)}{\delta} = \frac{h(\mathfrak{c})}{\delta}$. Since $\overline{T}(\mathfrak{c}) \geq \mathbb{E}_{\mathfrak{c}}^{\sigma}(T)$, we have $\overline{T}(\mathfrak{c}) \geq \mathbb{E}_{\mathfrak{c}}^{\sigma}(T) \geq \frac{h(\mathfrak{c})}{\delta}$. $\square$

Remark 8. We consider the lower bound of $\overline{T}(\mathfrak{c})$ (i.e., the supremum of all expected termination times) instead of the infimum. This is because we have demonic nondeterminism which always tries to make the program nonterminating or the termination time longer. $\square$

Below we illustrate an example on how one can derive lower bounds on expected termination time. This example shows that we can derive *exact* lower bounds from Theorem 3.

Example 4. Consider the program in Example 1. To derive a lower bound on expected termination time, we construct a lowerly-bounded RSM-map h in Table 1. First, one can verify that h is an RSM-map with $\epsilon = 1$ (see Definition 8). This can be observed from the facts that (i) the condition (B3) holds at the label 1 as the loop guard is $0 \le n \le 10$, while (ii) the condition (B2) holds at the label 2 as for $0 \le n \le 10$, it holds that $1+0.5 \cdot h(1, n+1)+0.5 \cdot h(1, n-1) = h(2, n)$. (For $n \notin [0, 10]$, the value $h(2, n)$ is not relevant and we simply let this value to be the infinity.) Second, from the equality that $1 + 0.5 \cdot h(1, n + 1) + 0.5 \cdot h(1, n - 1) = h(2, n)$ for $0 \le n \le 10$, we can also set $\delta = 1$ for h in Definition 9. Finally, since the interval $[0, 10]$ is bounded, we can choose a sufficiently large ζ that fulfills the conditions in Definition 9. Thus, h is also lowerly-bounded. Hence by Theorem 3 and Lemma 1, we have that given any initial configuration $\mathfrak{c} = (1, n)$, $\frac{h(\mathfrak{c})}{\epsilon} \ge \overline{T}(\mathfrak{c}) \ge \frac{h(\mathfrak{c})}{\delta}$. Since $\delta = \epsilon$, we have $\overline{T}(\mathfrak{c}) = h(\mathfrak{c})$. Thus, our lower bound through Theorem 3 is tight on this example.   □

Table 1. A Lowerly-Bounded RSM-map h for Example 1

Label	The RSM-map h
1	$1 + \mathbf{1}_{-1 \le n \le 11} \cdot 2 \cdot (n + 1) \cdot (11 - n)$
2	$1 + \mathbf{1}_{0 \le n \le 10} \cdot (2 \cdot (n + 1) \cdot (11 - n) - 1) + \mathbf{1}_{n \le -1 \vee n \ge 11} \cdot \infty$
3	0

Remark 9 (Significance of lower bounds). While RSMs provide upper bounds on expected termination time (see Lemma 1), there has been no RSM-based techniques for lower bounds for expected termination time. The significance of lower bounds is that together with upper bounds they provide guarantees on expected termination time. In particular, if the lower and upper bounds are asymptotically same, then they provide tight (i.e., asymptotically optimal) bounds on expected termination time. Example 4 illustrates that there are examples where our approach provides such tight bounds for expected termination time. The lower bounds for expected termination time has been considered in other approaches (see Remark 10 below), and we present the first RSM-based approach for lower bounds for expected termination time for probabilistic programs.   □

Remark 10 (Proof-rule Based Approaches). As far as we know, the only known approach to derive lower bounds on expected termination time is based on the notion of proof rules [38,48]. Compared with their approaches, our approach based on RSMs.   □

6   Extensions: Continuous Sampling and Recursion

In this section we show that our soundness and completeness results extend in several directions. In particular we show extension to probabilistic programs with (a) continuous sampling and (b) recursion.

Continuous Sampling. The extension of our results to continuous sampling is simple and straightforward, but technical, has following three steps.

1. First, we use general state space Markov chains [46] as our semantics. To this end, we need to define *measurable* schedulers so that a scheduler is measurable if it is a measurable function from histories into actions (see e.g. standard textbooks [7, Chap. 2] for measurability). Then given any initial configuration and a measurable scheduler, we need to define measurable *kernel* functions that specify the probabilities from a current configuration to a region of next configurations. These kernel functions will determine a unique general state space Markov chain. This is standard measurability aspects for Markov chains.

2. Second, for soundness we need to define measurable RSM-maps so that an RSM-map is measurable if it is a measurable function from the measurable space of configurations into the Borel measurable space of real numbers, and change the infinite summation $\sum_{\mu \in Val^r} \overline{T}(\mu) \cdot h(\ell', u(\nu, \mu))$ in (B2) by the Lebesgue integral $\int h(\ell', u(\nu, \mu)) \, d\mu$, where the $d\mu$ here is the probability measure for samplings. By adopting this definition, our soundness proof directly extends to continuous sampling, for which we use Fubini's Theorem [7, Chap. 3] (for multidimensional integrals) to show that (E3) holds, i.e., the conditional expectation of $h(\ell', u(\nu, \mu))$ is $\int h(\ell', u(\nu, \mu)) \, d\mu$. Thus the only extension is to switch from sum to integrals, which is technical rather than conceptual.

3. Finally, for completeness we simply need to prove that the measurability of the termination time function $\overline{T}$, while the fact that $\overline{T}$ still satisfies the conditions (B1)–(B4) follows from applying Fubini's Theorem at (B2). This can be observed as follows. By definition, $\overline{T}(\mathfrak{c}) = \sup_\sigma \mathbb{E}^\sigma_{\mathfrak{c}}(T)$. Then there exists a sequence of measurable schedulers $\sigma_1, \sigma_2, \ldots$ such that $\overline{T}(\mathfrak{c}) = \lim_{n \to \infty} \mathbb{E}^{\sigma_n}_{\mathfrak{c}}(T)$. Note that for each measurable scheduler σ, the function $\mathfrak{c} \mapsto \mathbb{E}^\sigma_{\mathfrak{c}}(T)$ is measurable as we have (i) each function $\mathfrak{c} \mapsto \mathbb{E}^\sigma_{\mathfrak{c}}(\min\{m, T\})$ ($m \in \mathbb{N}_0$) is measurable since the function computes expected values in a bounded horizon (i.e., m), and (ii) $\lim_{m \to \infty} \mathbb{E}^\sigma_{\mathfrak{c}}(\min\{m, T\}) = \mathbb{E}^\sigma_{\mathfrak{c}}(T)$ (from Monotone Convergence Theorem). Thus we have $\overline{T}$ is measurable as measurability is preserved under limit. Again the extension is technical but straightforward application of standard results.

Theorem 4. *RSM-maps are sound and complete for bounded termination over nondeterministic probabilistic programs, even with continuous sampling.*

Recursion. Our results also extend to nondeterministic recursive probabilistic programs. We consider value passing recursive probabilistic programs (i.e., we have call-by-value setting and no return statements). In the presence of recursion, we extend RSM maps to recursive RSM maps. Intuitively, recursive RSM maps extend RSM maps by adding an additional condition that sum the values taken for the function calls. The soundness and completeness result also extends to the recursive case (detailed demonstration in [13, Theorem 1]).

Theorem 5. *Recursive RSM-maps are sound and complete for bounded termination over nondeterministic probabilistic programs with recursion.*

7 Related Works

Termination Approaches. In [53] the termination of concurrent probabilistic programs with finite state space was considered as a fairness problem, and the precise probabilities did not play a role in termination. A sound and complete method for proving termination of weakly finite state programs was given in [23]. The above approaches do not apply to programs with countable state space in general. For countable state space and almost-sure termination a characterization through fixed-point theory was presented in [31], which is irrelevant to our approach. The analysis of nonprobabilistic program and the termination problem has also been extensively studied [9,10,18,19,29,42,50,54].

Supermartingale Based Approach. The most relevant works related to supermartingale based approach and their predecessor, such as [8,12,14–16,24,43,44], has been discussed in the introduction (Sect. 1). Compared with those results, the most significant difference is that our result considered completeness of ranking supermartingales for proving bounded termination. Besides bounded termination, special classes of (ranking) supermartingales have also been considered as a sound approach for almost-sure termination [1,45], while a potential-function based sound approach similar to ranking supermartingales has also been proposed in [47] to derive upper bounds on expected cost.

Proof-Rule Based Approach. In this work we consider the supermartingale based approach for probabilistic programs. An alternative approach for termination analysis is based on the notion of proof rules [32,34,38,48]. For example, [38] presents a complete proof-rule based approach for probabilistic while loops, but no recursion, and [48] presents sound proof rules for probabilistic programs with recursion, but no completeness result. Both these works do not consider continuous sampling variables. In contrast, our completeness result extends to probabilistic programs with recursion and continuous variables. The proof-rule and martingale-based approaches complement each other, and has their own advantages. A detailed comparison is as follows. The proof-rule based approach itself does not depend on invariants (cf. e.g. [17,20]) and synthesize quantitative invariants, whereas the supermartingale approach usually require invariants (generated with approaches such as [12,14,15]). In contrast the advantage of the supermartingale-based approach are as follows: (a) the supermartingale-based approach leads to algorithmic results, such as polynomial-time algorithms [14,15], and (b) the supermartingale-based approach also yield results to reason about tail-bound on probabilities of termination [12,15,40]. A deep investigation of combining proof-rule based and supermartingale based approach is an interesting direction for future work.

Comparison with the Recent Work [2]. A recent work [2] studies termination for probabilistic term rewriting systems in the same principle of RSMs. The work considers only discrete probability setting and the bounded expected derivation height which is specialized for term rewriting systems. Instead our results can handle (i) both probability distribution over countable variables, as well as continuous variables, and (ii) the program termination problem. Moreover, our results that handle countable variables as well as recursion have already been announced in January, 2017 [13, Lemmas 1, 2 and Theorem 1] (before the results of [2] were announced in [3]), which subsumes the results of [2].

8   Conclusion and Future Work

In this work we studied termination of nondeterministic probabilistic programs. We show that RSMs are sound and complete for proving bounded termination; in particular, the completeness result corrects a previous incompleteness claim in [24]. Then, we showed that under additional restrictions, ranking supermartingales can serve as a sound approach for deriving lower bounds on expected termination time. An interesting direction is the deep investigation of combining the proof-rule based approach and the RSM based approach.

Acknowledgements. This work is partially funded by the National Natural Science Foundation of China (NSFC) Grant no. 61802254, Austrian Science Fund (FWF) grant S11407-N23 (RiSE/SHiNE) and Vienna Science and Technology Fund (WWTF) project ICT15-003.

References

1. Agrawal, S., Chatterjee, K., Novotný, P.: Lexicographic ranking supermartingales: an efficient approach to termination of probabilistic programs. PACMPL **2**(POPL), 34:1–34:32 (2018)
2. Avanzini, M., Dal Lago, U., Yamada, A.: On probabilistic term rewriting. In: Gallagher, J.P., Sulzmann, M. (eds.) FLOPS 2018. LNCS, vol. 10818, pp. 132–148. Springer, Cham (2018). https://doi.org/10.1007/978-3-319-90686-7_9
3. Avanzini, M., Lago, U.D., Yamada, A.: On probabilistic term rewriting. CoRR abs/1802.09774 (2018). http://arxiv.org/abs/1802.09774
4. Baier, C., Katoen, J.P.: Principles of Model Checking. MIT Press, Cambridge (2008)
5. Barthe, G., Espitau, T., Grégoire, B., Hsu, J., Strub, P.: Proving expected sensitivity of probabilistic programs. PACMPL **2**(POPL), 57:1–57:29 (2018)
6. Barthe, G., Grégoire, B., Hsu, J., Strub, P.: Coupling proofs are probabilistic product programs. In: Castagna and Gordon [11], pp. 161–174 (2017)
7. Billingsley, P.: Probability and Measure, 3rd edn. Wiley, Hoboken (1995)

8. Bournez, O., Garnier, F.: Proving positive almost-sure termination. In: RTA, pp. 323–337 (2005)
9. Bradley, A.R., Manna, Z., Sipma, H.B.: Linear ranking with reachability. In: CAV, pp. 491–504 (2005)
10. Bradley, A.R., Manna, Z., Sipma, H.B.: The polyranking principle. In: ICALP, pp. 1349–1361 (2005)
11. Castagna, G., Gordon, A.D. (eds.): Proceedings of the 44th ACM SIGPLAN Symposium on Principles of Programming Languages, POPL 2017, Paris, France, 18–20 January 2017. ACM (2017)
12. Chakarov, A., Sankaranarayanan, S.: Probabilistic program analysis with martingales. In: CAV, pp. 511–526 (2013)
13. Chatterjee, K., Fu, H.: Termination of nondeterministic recursive probabilistic programs. CoRR abs/1701.02944 (2017). http://arxiv.org/abs/1701.02944
14. Chatterjee, K., Fu, H., Goharshady, A.K.: Termination analysis of probabilistic programs through Positivstellensatz's. In: CAV, pp. 3–22 (2016)
15. Chatterjee, K., Fu, H., Novotný, P., Hasheminezhad, R.: Algorithmic analysis of qualitative and quantitative termination problems for affine probabilistic programs. In: POPL, pp. 327–342 (2016)
16. Chatterjee, K., Novotný, P., Zikelic, D.: Stochastic invariants for probabilistic termination. In: Castagna and Gordon [11], pp. 145–160 (2017)
17. Colón, M.A., Sankaranarayanan, S., Sipma, H.B.: Linear invariant generation using non-linear constraint solving. In: Hunt, W.A., Somenzi, F. (eds.) CAV 2003. LNCS, vol. 2725, pp. 420–432. Springer, Heidelberg (2003). https://doi.org/10.1007/978-3-540-45069-6_39
18. Colón, M., Sipma, H.: Synthesis of linear ranking functions. In: TACAS, pp. 67–81 (2001)
19. Cook, B., See, A., Zuleger, F.: Ramsey vs. lexicographic termination proving. In: TACAS, pp. 47–61 (2013)
20. Cousot, P.: Proving program invariance and termination by parametric abstraction, lagrangian relaxation and semidefinite programming. In: Cousot, R. (ed.) VMCAI 2005. LNCS, vol. 3385, pp. 1–24. Springer, Heidelberg (2005). https://doi.org/10.1007/978-3-540-30579-8_1
21. Cusumano-Towner, M., Bichsel, B., Gehr, T., Vechev, M.T., Mansinghka, V.K.: Incremental inference for probabilistic programs. In: Foster and Grossman [27], pp. 571–585 (2018)
22. Durrett, R.: Probability: Theory and Examples, 2nd edn. Duxbury Press, Boston (1996)
23. Esparza, J., Gaiser, A., Kiefer, S.: Proving termination of probabilistic programs using patterns. In: CAV, pp. 123–138 (2012)
24. Fioriti, L.M.F., Hermanns, H.: Probabilistic termination: soundness, completeness, and compositionality. In: POPL, pp. 489–501 (2015)
25. Floyd, R.W.: Assigning meanings to programs. Math. Asp. Comput. Sci. **19**, 19–33 (1967)
26. Foster, F.G.: On the stochastic matrices associated with certain queuing processes. Ann. Math. Stat. **24**(3), 355–360 (1953)
27. Foster, J.S., Grossman, D. (eds.): Proceedings of the 39th ACM SIGPLAN Conference on Programming Language Design and Implementation, PLDI 2018, Philadelphia, PA, USA, 18–22 June 2018. ACM (2018)
28. Foster, N., Kozen, D., Mamouras, K., Reitblatt, M., Silva, A.: Probabilistic netKAT. In: Thiemann [56], pp. 282–309 (2016)

29. Frohn, F., Naaf, M., Hensel, J., Brockschmidt, M., Giesl, J.: Lower runtime bounds for integer programs. In: Olivetti, N., Tiwari, A. (eds.) IJCAR 2016. LNCS (LNAI), vol. 9706, pp. 550–567. Springer, Cham (2016). https://doi.org/10.1007/978-3-319-40229-1_37

30. Gordon, A.D., Henzinger, T.A., Nori, A.V., Rajamani, S.K.: Probabilistic programming. In: Herbsleb, J.D., Dwyer, M.B. (eds.) Proceedings of the on Future of Software Engineering, FOSE 2014, Hyderabad, India, 31 May–7 June 2014, pp. 167–181. ACM (2014)

31. Hart, S., Sharir, M.: Concurrent probabilistic programs, or: How to schedule if you must. SIAM J. Comput. 14(4), 991–1012 (1985)

32. Hesselink, W.H.: Proof rules for recursive procedures. Formal Asp. Comput. 5(6), 554–570 (1993)

33. Howard, H.: Dynamic Programming and Markov Processes. MIT Press, Cambridge (1960)

34. Jones, C.: Probabilistic non-determinism. Ph.D. thesis, The University of Edinburgh (1989)

35. Kaelbling, L.P., Littman, M.L., Cassandra, A.R.: Planning and acting in partially observable stochastic domains. Artif. Intell. 101(1), 99–134 (1998)

36. Kaelbling, L.P., Littman, M.L., Moore, A.W.: Reinforcement learning: a survey. JAIR 4, 237–285 (1996)

37. Kaminski, B.L., Katoen, J.-P.: On the hardness of almost–sure termination. In: Italiano, G.F., Pighizzini, G., Sannella, D.T. (eds.) MFCS 2015. LNCS, vol. 9234, pp. 307–318. Springer, Heidelberg (2015). https://doi.org/10.1007/978-3-662-48057-1_24

38. Kaminski, B.L., Katoen, J., Matheja, C., Olmedo, F.: Weakest precondition reasoning for expected run-times of probabilistic programs. In: Thiemann [56], pp. 364–389 (2016)

39. Kemeny, J., Snell, J., Knapp, A.: Denumerable Markov Chains. D. Van Nostrand Company, New York City (1966)

40. Kura, S., Urabe, N., Hasuo, I.: Tail probabilities for randomized program runtimes via martingales for higher moments. CoRR abs/1811.06779 (2018). http://arxiv.org/abs/1811.06779

41. Kwiatkowska, M., Norman, G., Parker, D.: PRISM 4.0: verification of probabilistic real-time systems. In: Gopalakrishnan, G., Qadeer, S. (eds.) CAV 2011. LNCS, vol. 6806, pp. 585–591. Springer, Heidelberg (2011). https://doi.org/10.1007/978-3-642-22110-1_47

42. Lee, C.S., Jones, N.D., Ben-Amram, A.M.: The size-change principle for program termination. In: POPL, pp. 81–92 (2001)

43. McIver, A., Morgan, C.: Developing and reasoning about probabilistic programs in pGCL. In: PSSE, pp. 123–155 (2004)

44. McIver, A., Morgan, C.: Abstraction, Refinement and Proof for Probabilistic Systems. Monographs in Computer Science. Springer, Heidelberg (2005). https://doi.org/10.1007/b138392

45. McIver, A., Morgan, C., Kaminski, B.L., Katoen, J.: A new proof rule for almost-sure termination. PACMPL 2(POPL), 33:1–33:28 (2018)

46. Meyn, S., Tweedie, R.: Markov Chains and Stochastic Stability. Cambridge University Press, Cambridge (2009)

47. Ngo, V.C., Carbonneaux, Q., Hoffmann, J.: Bounded expectations: resource analysis for probabilistic programs. In: Foster and Grossman [27], pp. 496–512 (2018)

48. Olmedo, F., Kaminski, B.L., Katoen, J.P., Matheja, C.: Reasoning about recursive probabilistic programs. In: LICS, pp. 672–681 (2016)

49. Paz, A.: Introduction to Probabilistic Automata. Computer Science and Applied Mathematics. Academic Press, Cambridge (1971)
50. Podelski, A., Rybalchenko, A.: A complete method for the synthesis of linear ranking functions. In: VMCAI, pp. 239–251 (2004)
51. Rabin, M.: Probabilistic automata. Inf. Control. **6**, 230–245 (1963)
52. Sankaranarayanan, S., Chakarov, A., Gulwani, S.: Static analysis for probabilistic programs: inferring whole program properties from finitely many paths. In: PLDI, pp. 447–458 (2013)
53. Sharir, M., Pnueli, A., Hart, S.: Verification of probabilistic programs. SIAM J. Comput. **13**(2), 292–314 (1984)
54. Sohn, K., Gelder, A.V.: Termination detection in logic programs using argument sizes. In: PODS, pp. 216–226 (1991)
55. Staton, S., Yang, H., Wood, F.D., Heunen, C., Kammar, O.: Semantics for probabilistic programming: higher-order functions, continuous distributions, and soft constraints. In: Grohe, M., Koskinen, E., Shankar, N. (eds.) Proceedings of the 31st Annual ACM/IEEE Symposium on Logic in Computer Science, LICS 2016, 5–8 July 2016, pp. 525–534. ACM, New York (2016)
56. Thiemann, P. (ed.): ESOP 2016. LNCS, vol. 9632. Springer, Heidelberg (2016). https://doi.org/10.1007/978-3-662-49498-1
57. Williams, D.: Probability with Martingales. Cambridge University Press, Cambridge (1991)

Parametric Timed Broadcast Protocols

Étienne André[1,2,3(✉)], Benoit Delahaye[4], Paulin Fournier[4], and Didier Lime[5]

[1] Université Paris 13, LIPN, CNRS, UMR 7030, 93430 Villetaneuse, France
eandre93430@lipn13.fr
[2] JFLI, CNRS, Tokyo, Japan
[3] National Institute of Informatics, Tokyo, Japan
[4] Université de Nantes, LS2N UMR CNRS 6004, Nantes, France
[5] École Centrale de Nantes, LS2N UMR CNRS 6004, Nantes, France

Abstract. In this paper we consider state reachability in networks composed of many identical processes running a parametric timed broadcast protocol (PTBP). PTBP are a new model extending both broadcast protocols and parametric timed automata. This work is, up to our knowledge, the first to consider the combination of both a parametric network size and timing parameters in clock guard constraints. Since the communication topology is of utmost importance in broadcast protocols, we investigate reachability problems in both clique semantics where every message reaches every processes, and in reconfigurable semantics where the set of receivers is chosen non-deterministically. In addition, we investigate the decidability status depending on whether the timing parameters in guards appear only as upper bounds in guards, as lower bounds or when the set of parameters is partitioned in lower-bound and upper-bound parameters.

1 Introduction

The application of model-checking to real-life complex systems faces several problems, and for many of them the use of parameters, i.e., symbolic constants representing an unknown quantity can be part of the solution. First, for big systems, the so-called *state-space explosion* limits the practical applicability of model-checking. Such big systems however are in general specified as the composition of smaller systems. A particularly interesting setting is the one in which all the components are identical, such as in many communication protocols. The number of involved components can then be abstracted away as a *parameter*, with the hope of both overcoming the state-space explosion, and obtaining more useful answers from the model-checking process, such as "for which sizes of the system does some property hold?". Second, the earlier in the development phase verification can be applied, the less costly will fixing the problems be. On the other hand, the earlier the verification is applied, the less information we have

This work is partially supported by the ANR national research program PACS (ANR-14-CE28-0002) and by ERATO HASUO Metamathematics for Systems Design Project (No. JPMJER1603), JST.

C. Enea and R. Piskac (Eds.): VMCAI 2019, LNCS 11388, pp. 491–512, 2019.
https://doi.org/10.1007/978-3-030-11245-5_23

on the final system, in particular on many timing features, such as transmission times, watchdogs, etc. Parameters can also be useful here by abstracting away the precise values of some yet unknown features, and at the same time allowing their dimensioning.

In this paper, we propose to combine two different types of parameters, namely the *number of identical processes* and the *timing features*, and study the decidability of classic parametric decision problems in the resulting formalism. Both types of parameters, when introduced separately in timed automata-based formalisms, result in hard problems undecidable even in restricted settings.

Timed automata [5] extend finite-state automata with clocks, i.e., real-valued variables that can be compared to constants in guards, and reset along transitions. Parametric timed automata (PTA) [6] allow to replace constants with unknown parameters in timing constraints. The most basic verification question, "does there exist a value for the parameters such that some location is reachable" is undecidable with as few as 1 integer- or rational-valued parameter [11,23], or when only 1 clock is compared to a unique parameter [23] (with additional clocks); see [7] for a survey. The main syntactic subclass of PTA for which decidability is obtained is L/U-PTA [20], in which the set of parameters is partitioned into lower-bound parameters (i.e., parameters always compared as a lower bound in a clock guard) and upper-bound parameters (always as upper bounds). L/U-PTA have been shown [20] to be expressive enough to model classical examples from the literature, such as root contention or Fischer's mutual exclusion algorithm for instance.

Broadcast protocol networks [15–18], allow treating the size of a network as an unknown parameter. Here also the most simple basic verification question "does there exist a value for the parameter such that some location is reachable by a process" is undecidable when considering arbitrary communication topologies [16]. However one can regain decidability by considering different communication topology settings. One option is to limit the topologies to cliques (every process receives every message) [16–18]. Another is to consider reconfigurable broadcasts in which the set of receivers is chosen non-deterministically at each step [15]. A timed version of this broadcast protocol was studied in [2]. In the clique topology for this network, the reachability problem is decidable only when there is a single clock per process.

Contributions. In this work, we provide one more level of abstraction to the formalisms of the literature by proposing *parametric timed broadcast protocols* (PTBP), i.e., a new formalism made of an arbitrary number of identical timed processes in which timing parameters can be used. A combination of two kinds of parameters seems natural, for example when designing and verifying communication protocols. Indeed, those protocols are required to work independently of the number of participants (hence the parametric size of networks) and the time constraints in each process are of paramount importance and thus could be tweaked in early development thanks to timing parameters. This work is, up to our knowledge, the first to consider the combination of both a parametric network size and timing parameters in clock guard constraints. We consider the following problems: does there exist a number of processes for which the set of timing parameter valuations allowing to reach a given location for one run ("EF"), or for all runs ("AF") is empty (or universal)? This gives rise to 4 problems: EF-emptiness, EF-universality, AF-emptiness and AF-universality. As PTBP can be seen as an extension of both broadcast protocols and parametric timed automata, undecidability follows immediately from the existing undecidability results known for these two formalisms. However, combining decidable subclasses of both formalisms is challenging, and does not necessarily make the EF and AF problems decidable for PTBP.

The communication topology is of utmost importance in broadcast protocols, and we therefore investigate reachability problems depending on the broadcast semantics. In the reconfigurable semantics (where the set of receivers is chosen non-deterministically), AF-emptiness and AF-universality are decidable for 1-clock PTBP, and undecidable from 3 clocks even for L/U-PTBP with the same parameters partitioning as in L/U-PTA (the 2-clock case is equivalent to a well-known open problem for PTA). The AF results may not seem surprising, as they resemble equivalent results for PTA. However, EF-emptiness and EF-universality becomes undecidable even for 1-clock PTBP: this result comes in contrast with both non-parametric timed broadcast protocols and PTA for which the 1-clock case is decidable.

In the clique semantics (where every message reaches every process), we show that AF problems are undecidable even without any clock. Then, as it is known that 2 clocks (and no parameter) yield undecidability, we study EF problems over 1 clock. We investigate the decidability status depending on whether the timing parameters in guards appear only as upper bounds in guards (U-PTBP), as lower bounds (L-PTBP) or when the set of parameters is partitioned in lower-bound and upper-bound parameters (L/U-PTBP). We show that L/U-PTBP become decidable for EF-emptiness (but not universality) when the parameter domain is bounded. For EF-universality, decidability is obtained only for L-PTBP and U-PTBP for a parameter domain bounded with closed bounds. The decidability border between L/U-PTA with a bounded parameter domain with closed bounds, and L/U-PTA with closed bounds was already spotted in [10], for liveness properties. Our contributions are summarized in Table 1 (p. 20).

Related Work. The concept of identical processes has been addressed in various settings, such as regular model checking [12], or network of identical timed processes [1,3,4].

To the best of our knowledge, combining two types of parameters (i.e., discrete and continuous) was very little studied—with a few exceptions. In [13], an attempt is made to mix discrete and continuous timing parameters (in an even non-linear fashion, i.e., where parameters can be multiplied by other parameters). However, the approach is fully *ad-hoc* and addresses an extension of PTA, for which problems are already undecidable. In [14,22], security protocols are studied with unknown timing constants, and an unbounded number of participants. However, the focus is not on decidability, and the general setting is undecidable. In [9], action parameters (that can be seen as Booleans) and continuous timing parameters are combined (only linearly though) in an extension of PTA; the mere emptiness of the sets of action and timing parameters for which a location is reachable is undecidable. In contrast, we exhibit in this work some decidable cases.

Outline. We introduce necessary definitions in Sect. 2. We then study the emptiness and the universality problems for which a state is reachable and unavoidable respectively, in reconfigurable semantics (Sect. 3) and clique semantics (Sect. 4). We then investigate a restriction of the protocols, namely the L/U restriction (Sect. 5). We conclude in Sect. 6.

2   Definitions

We denote by $\mathbb{N}$, $\mathbb{Q}_+$, and $\mathbb{R}_+$ the sets of all natural, non-negative rational, and non-negative real numbers respectively. $[a, b]$ denotes the interval containing all rational numbers x such that $x \leq b$ and $x \geq a$. As usual, we write $(a, b]$ to exclude a from this set and $[a, b)$ to exclude b (in which case we allow $b = +\infty$). We denote by $\mathbb{I}_{\mathbb{Q}_+}$ the set of all rational intervals.

Given a set E, and an integer $n \in \mathbb{N}$ we denote $\mathbb{V}_n(E)$ the set of all vectors composed by n elements of E. We denote $\mathbb{V}(E)$ the set of all vectors i.e., $\mathbb{V}(E) = \cup_{n \in \mathbb{N}} \mathbb{V}_n(E)$.

Given a set of clocks $\mathbb{X}$, a valuation of $\mathbb{X}$ is a function of $\mathbb{X} \to \mathbb{R}_+$. We denote by $\mathcal{V}(\mathbb{X})$ the set of all valuations of $\mathbb{X}$ or just $\mathcal{V}$ when $\mathbb{X}$ is clear from the context. The valuation assigning 0 to all clock is written $\mathbf{0}$. Given a valuation $v \in \mathcal{V}$ and a real number t we denote by $v + t$ the valuation v' such that for all $x \in \mathbb{X}$, $v'(x) = v(x) + t$, and $v - t$ (if it exists) the valuation such that $(v - t) + t = v$. Given a set of clocks $\mathbb{X}$ and a set of parameters $\mathbb{P}$ we write $\mathcal{G}(\mathbb{X}, \mathbb{P})$ for the set of all sets of constraints of the form $x \bowtie a$ with $x \in \mathbb{X}$, $\bowtie \in \{<, \leq, =, \geq, >\}$ and $a \in \mathbb{Q}_+ \cup \mathbb{P}$.

We denote by $\text{Updates}(\mathbb{X})$ the set of updates of the clocks, where an update is a function $up : \mathcal{V} \to \mathcal{V}$ such that for all $x \in \mathbb{X}$, either $up(v)(x) = v(x)$ or $up(v)(x) = 0$. When convenient we represent the update function with the set $\{x_1, \dots, x_k\}$ representing that clocks x_1 to x_k are reset to 0 while other clocks (here x_i with $i > k$) are left unchanged.

Given a clock valuation $v \in \mathbb{X} \to \mathbb{R}_+$ and a rational valuation of the variables $p : \mathbb{P} \to \mathbb{Q}_+$ we say that the valuation v satisfies a guard $g \in \mathcal{G}(\mathbb{X}, \mathbb{P})$, written $v \models_p g$ if for all $x \bowtie a \in g$ either $a \in \mathbb{Q}_+$ and $v(x) \bowtie a$ or $a \in \mathbb{P}$ and $v(x) \bowtie p(a)$.

We now introduce parametric timed broadcast protocols (PTBP), which are timed broadcast protocols [1] extended with timing parameters in clock guards. Equivalently, PTBP can be seen as a PTA [6] augmented with communication features.

Definition 1 (Parameterized timed broadcast protocol). *A Parameterized timed broadcast protocol (PTBP) is a tuple* $\mathcal{N} = (Q, \mathbb{X}, \Sigma, \mathbb{P}, q_0, \Delta)$ *where:*

– *Q is a finite set of states;*

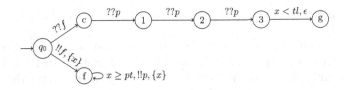

Fig. 1. Example of a (L/U-)PTBP

- $\mathbb{X}$ *is a finite set of clocks;*
- Σ *is the finite communication alphabet;*
- $\mathbb{P}$ *is a finite set of timing parameters;*
- $q_0 \in Q$ *is the initial state; and*
- $\Delta \subseteq Q \times \mathcal{G}(\mathbb{X}, \mathbb{P}) \times Act \times \mathrm{Updates}(\mathbb{X}) \times Q$ *is the edge relation, where Act is the set of actions composed of:*
  - *internal actions:* ϵ;
  - *broadcasts of a message* $m \in \Sigma$: $!!m$; *and*
  - *reception of a message* $m \in \Sigma$: $??m$.

A PTBP is a U-PTBP, L-PTBP, or L/U-PTBP if all timing parameters appear only as upper bounds in guards (i.e., of the form $x < \lambda$ or $x \leq \lambda$), only as lower bounds (i.e., of the form $x > \lambda$ or $x \geq \lambda$), or if the set of parameters $\mathbb{P}$ is partitioned into lower-bound and upper-bound parameters, respectively.

A *bounded* PTBP is a pair $(\mathcal{N}, bounds)$ where $\mathcal{N}$ is a PTBP and $bounds: \mathbb{P} \rightarrow \mathcal{I}_{\mathbb{Q}_+}$ are bounds on the parameters that assign to each parameter λ an interval $[inf, sup]$, $(inf, sup]$, $[inf, sup)$, or (inf, sup), with $inf, sup \in \mathbb{N}$. We use $inf(\lambda, bounds)$ and $sup(\lambda, bounds)$ to denote the infimum and the supremum of λ, respectively. A bounded PTBP is a *closed PTBP* if, for each parameter λ, its ranging interval $bounds(\lambda)$ is of the form $[inf, sup]$. Otherwise it is open bounded. Abusing notation we say that a parameter valuation p belongs to a bound *bounds*, written $p \in bounds$, if for all parameters λ, $p(\lambda) \in bounds(\lambda)$.

Example 1. An example of a PTBP is given in Fig. 1. This PTBP is composed of an initial state q_0, two states f and c representing a factory and a client, three counting states 1, 2 and 3 and a goal state g. The set of clocks is the singleton $\{x\}$ and the communication alphabet is composed of two messages p and f. There are two timing parameters pt and tl representing respectively the production time and the time limit. Notice that this PTBP is in fact an L/U-PTBP since the parameter pt appears only in guards as a lower bound and tl only as an upper bound.

We now define the semantics of parameterized networks of PTBP. This semantics is illustrated in Example 2 after the formal definition.

A network is composed of a multitude of processes all running the same protocol $\mathcal{N}$. Let N denote the number of processes, or *size* of the network.

Formally, a configuration γ of a network running a parametric timed broadcast protocol $\mathcal{N} = (Q, \mathbb{X}, \Sigma, \mathbb{P}, q_0, \Delta)$ is a vector $\gamma \in \mathbb{V}(Q \times \mathcal{V})$. Intuitively, a configuration γ with $\gamma[i] = (q, v)$ means that the process i is in state q and with clock valuation v.

Given a configuration γ with N processes and a process i, we write $state(\gamma[i])$ for the state and $val(\gamma[i])$ for the valuation such that $\gamma[i] = (state(\gamma[i]), val(\gamma[i]))$. Abusing notation we extend $state$ to the whole configuration i.e., $state(\gamma)[i] = state(\gamma[i])$ for $i \in \{1, \dots, N\}$.

Note that the representation of configuration as vectors is only for practical reasons, the processes are identical and do not have ids.

We say that a configuration γ is initial if all processes are in the initial state and their clocks are all set to 0 i.e., for all i, $\gamma[i] = (q_0, \mathbf{0})$.

Given a timing parameter valuation, the transition relation on configurations is intuitively defined as follows: First a delay is chosen and all the clocks in the network are increased by this delay. Then one of the processes performs a possible action i.e., an action for which the guard is satisfied given its clock valuation and the valuation of the timing parameter. Two cases follow. Either the action is internal and only this process moves and updates its clocks accordingly, or the action is a broadcast and a set of receivers is chosen. It this latter case, the sender moves and updates its clocks and all the chosen receivers also move and update their clocks accordingly.

More formally, given a timing parameter valuation p and a configuration $\gamma \in \mathbb{V}_N(Q \times \mathcal{V})$, there are transitions for all $t \in \mathbb{R}_+$, $i \in \{1, \dots, N\}$, $\delta = (q_1, g, a, up, q_2) \in \Delta$, and $R \subseteq \{1, .., N\}$ such that:

elapse of time there is a valuation $\gamma_t \in \mathbb{V}_N(Q \times \mathcal{V})$ such that $\forall j \in \{1, \dots, N\}$, $\gamma_t[j] = (q, v + t)$ where $(q, v) = \gamma[j]$, and
execution of the action the following conditions are satisfied:
    the action is enabled $state(\gamma_t[i]) = q_1$ and $val(\gamma_t[i]) \models_p g$, and
    execution of the action the transition leads to a configuration γ' such that
      – the active process performed the action: $\gamma'[i] = (q_2, up(val(\gamma_t[i])))$,
      – unconcerned processes are unaffected: $\forall j \in \{1, \dots, N\} \setminus (R \cup \{i\})$, $\gamma'[j] = \gamma_t[j]$, and
      – either
         • a is an internal action ($a = \epsilon$) and the receiving processes are unaffected: $\forall j \in R \setminus \{i\}$, $\gamma'[j] = \gamma_t[j]$; or
         • $a = !!m$ and $\forall j \in R \setminus \{i\}$, if there exists an edge $(state(\gamma_t[j]), g', ??m, up', q')$ such that $val(\gamma_t[j]) \models_p g'$, then the process receives the message and $\gamma'[j] = (q', up'(val(\gamma_t[j])))$. Otherwise the process is unaffected and $\gamma'[j] = \gamma_t[j]$.

When such a transition exists, it is written $\gamma \xrightarrow{t,i,\delta,R}_p \gamma'$ or simply $\gamma \to_p \gamma'$.

Notice that we consider non blocking broadcast i.e., if a process is in the receiver set but has no available reception edge, the process is unaffected and the network behaves as if this process was not in the receiver set.

An execution ρ is a sequence of transitions starting in an initial configuration γ_0, $\rho = \gamma_0 \to_p \gamma_1 \to_p \cdots$. An execution is maximal if it is infinite or if it ends in a configuration from which there is no possible transition.

Notice that once an initial configuration is fixed, the number of processes does not change along an execution. However the semantics is infinite for several reasons: first there is an infinite number of initial configurations (i.e., of network sizes); second, there is also an infinite number of possible parameter valuations; third, given a network size and parameter valuation, clock valuations assign real values to clocks and are thus uncountable.

Given PTBP $\mathcal{N}$, a network size N and a timing parameter valuation p, we denote by $\mathcal{E}(\mathcal{N}, N, p)$ the set of all maximal executions for the valuation p with N processes.

We say that a maximal execution $\rho = \gamma_0 \rightarrow_p \gamma_1 \rightarrow_p \cdots$ reaches a state q, written $\rho \models \Diamond q$, if there exists an index n such that $q \in state(\gamma_n)$.

Example 2. We give an example of a possible execution for a network composed of 4 processes running the protocol given in Example 1. In this example $tl = 9$ and $pt = 3$. The edge used during a transition is here only represented by the associated action for readability.

$$
\begin{pmatrix} q_0, 0 \\ q_0, 0 \\ q_0, 0 \\ q_0, 0 \\ q_0, 0 \end{pmatrix} \xrightarrow{0.1, 1, f, \emptyset} \begin{pmatrix} f, 0 \\ q_0, 0.1 \\ q_0, 0.1 \\ q_0, 0.1 \\ q_0, 0.1 \end{pmatrix} \xrightarrow{4.1, 2, f, \{3, 5\}} \begin{pmatrix} f, 4.1 \\ f, 0 \\ c, 4.2 \\ q_0, 4.2 \\ c, 4.2 \end{pmatrix} \xrightarrow{1.3, 1, p, \{5\}} \begin{pmatrix} f, 0 \\ f, 1.3 \\ c, 5.5 \\ q_0, 5.5 \\ 1, 5.5 \end{pmatrix} \xrightarrow{1.8, 2, p, \{1, 3, 4, 5\}}
$$

$$
\xrightarrow{1.8, 2, p, \{1, 3, 4, 5\}} \begin{pmatrix} f, 1.8 \\ f, 0 \\ 1, 7.3 \\ q_0, 7.3 \\ 2, 7.3 \end{pmatrix} \xrightarrow{1.2, 1, p, \{5\}} \begin{pmatrix} f, 0 \\ f, 1.2 \\ 1, 8.5 \\ q_0, 8.5 \\ 3, 8.5 \end{pmatrix} \xrightarrow{0, 5, \epsilon, \emptyset} \begin{pmatrix} f, 0 \\ f, 1.2 \\ 1, 8.5 \\ q_0, 8.5 \\ g, 8.5 \end{pmatrix}
$$

Remark 1. Notice that even if the notations are slightly different, PTBP networks fully extend both PTA [6] and timed broadcast protocols [1]. Indeed, PTA are PTBP networks of size one and timed networks are PTBP networks without timing parameters.

In this paper, we consider parameterized reachability problems: we ask whether there exists a network size N satisfying a given reachability property. We consider existential (EF) and universal (AF) reachability properties that ask, given goal state q_f, whether this state is reached by some (EF) or all (AF) executions. Moreover we also consider variants on the quantifier on timing parameters and ask whether the property holds for all parameter valuations (universality) or for none (emptiness).

Thus, given a bounded PTBP $(\mathcal{N}, bounds)$ and a state q_f we consider the following problems:

∃-**EF-emptiness** $\exists N \in \mathbb{N}, \nexists p \in bounds, \exists \rho \in \mathcal{E}(\mathcal{N}, N, p), \rho \models \Diamond q_f$
∃-**EF-universality** $\exists N \in \mathbb{N}, \forall p \in bounds, \exists \rho \in \mathcal{E}(\mathcal{N}, N, p), \rho \models \Diamond q_f$
∃-**AF-emptiness** $\exists N \in \mathbb{N}, \nexists p \in bounds, \forall \rho \in \mathcal{E}(\mathcal{N}, N, p), \rho \models \Diamond q_f$
∃-**AF-universality** $\exists N \in \mathbb{N}, \forall p \in bounds, \forall \rho \in \mathcal{E}(\mathcal{N}, N, p), \rho \models \Diamond q_f$

For convenience, we will omit the bounds when they are irrelevant and consider these problems in the case of general PTBP. In the following, the bounds will only be relevant in Sect. 5.

In the next section we investigate these problems in the general semantics defined above. This semantics is called *reconfigurable* since the communication topology (modeled by the reception sets) can be reconfigured at each step. However, in broadcast protocol networks with a parametric number of processes, the communication topology plays a decisive role on decidability status. We will thus investigate another communication setting, in Sect. 4, in which every message is received by all the other processes i.e., the reception set R is always equal to $\{1, \ldots, N\}$. These networks are called *clique* networks.

Example 3. Considering the PTBP given in Example 1 and the target state g. The execution presented in Example 2 shows that the answer for the $\exists$-EF-emptiness problem is positive whenever the bounds allow for $tl = 9$ and $pt = 3$ in the reconfigurable semantics. Notice that in the clique semantics, it is not possible to reach g unless $pt * 3 < tl$. Indeed in the clique semantics when a first process moves to f, all the other processes receive the message f and thus move to c. Thus, at least three pt time units are necessary in order to receive 3 messages p.

Notice also that in this example, in both semantics, both $\exists$-AF problems would give negative answers since there is always an execution that forever sends p in the bottom self-loop and never uses the internal transition leading to g. Thus such an execution never reaches g.

3   Reconfigurable Semantics

3.1   AF Problems in the Reconfigurable Semantics

The reconfigurable semantics of broadcast networks, where the set of receivers can be chosen non-deterministically, makes the AF problems equivalent to the same problems in networks of size 1. This is due to the fact that in the reconfigurable semantics nothing prevents messages to be sent to an empty set of receivers. The following theorem is a direct consequence of previous known results on parameterized timed automata and this previous remark.[1]

Theorem 1. $\exists$-*AF-emptiness and* $\exists$-*AF-universality are decidable for 1 clock PTBP but undecidable for (L/U)-PTBP with 3 clocks or more.*

3.2   EF Problems in the Reconfigurable Semantics

We start by recalling some known results on networks composed of an arbitrary number of timed processes. In [4] the authors considered timed networks and proved that the reachability problem ($\exists$-EF) is decidable with one clock per process and undecidable for two clocks per process [3]. Note that timed networks have a different semantics than the one we use in this paper since they use rules

---

[1] The proof of the results that can be obtained using existing techniques in a more or less straightforward manner can be found in the appendix.

and not broadcasts. However the reconfigurable semantics can be easily encoded in the rules of timed networks. This gives us the decidability of the ∃-EF problem (without timing parameters and with one clock per process).

Theorem 2 ([3,4]). *∃-EF is decidable for PTBP without parameters and with one clock per process and undecidable with two clocks per process.*

A direct consequence of this theorem is the undecidability of the ∃-EF problems for PTBP with two clocks.

Lemma 1. *The ∃-EF-emptiness and ∃-EF-universality problems are undecidable for PTBP with two clocks.*

Moreover, we show below that the undecidability even holds for PTBP with a single clock. This is a major difference with both parameterized networks and PTA, where the restriction to one clock leads to decidability [6]. Also observe that our result does not rely on the reconfigurable semantics particularly.

Theorem 3. *The ∃-EF-emptiness and ∃-EF-universality problems are undecidable for PTBP with one clock.*

Proof. The proof is by reduction of the halting and boundedness (respectively) problems for two-counter machines.

First, in this proof we will assume that the parameter λ only takes integer values. This is not a restriction since we can add a gadget at the beginning of the PTBP to check such property. This gadget is an adaptation of similar gadgets from the PTA community to the case of PTBP, and is given in [8].

Given a two-counter machine, we define a protocol $\mathcal{P}$ separated in three parts, the controller part (in charge of tracking the current instruction), the counters part (to model the counters behaviors) and an idle part that allows to use additional processes when needed.

The value of the counters is encoded (up to the value of parameter λ minus 1 here for technical reasons) by the difference between the clock value of the processes in states representing counters and the clock value of the processes in the controller part.

Formally, $\mathcal{P}$ is defined as follows:

- $Q = \{q_0, error, c_i, nc1_i, nc2_i, zt1_i^j, zt2_i^j, dec1_i^j, dec2_i^j, inc1_i^j, inc2_i^j, inc3_i^j, idle \mid j \in \{1, 2\}, i \in \{1, 2\}\} \cup \{k^j \mid \mathbf{k} \in \mathbf{K}, j \in \{1, 2, 3, 4\}\}$
- $\Sigma = \{tick, inc_i, dec_i, zt_i, c_i, oc_i, nc_i \mid i \in \{1, 2\}\}$
- $\mathbb{P} = \{\lambda\}$
- $\mathbb{X} = \{x\}$
- Δ is defined as described below.

Let us describe Δ: On every transition, there is a guard $x \leq \lambda$ which is omitted to clarify notations; similarly, when a guard is true or when there is no reset, we omit them in the transition. The construction is represented in Fig. 2. Δ is composed of the following transitions:

Initialization. $(q_0, x = 0, \epsilon, k_0^1)$, for $i \in \{1, 2\}$, $(q_0, x = 0, \epsilon, c_i)$, $(q_0, x = 0, \epsilon, idle)$

The processes can chose non-deterministically to either move to the controller part, the counters part, or the idle part (Fig. 2a).

Decrement of counter i. For a decrement instruction $\mathbf{k} : decr \; \mathbf{C}_i \; goto \; \mathbf{k}_1$, we define the following transitions in Δ (depicted in Fig. 2b):

- For the controller: $(k^1, x = 1, !!dec_i, k^2)$ $(k^2, x = \lambda, !!tick, \{x := 0\}, k_1^1)$
  The controller "announces" that the instruction is a decrement (using $!!dec_1$) when its clock is equal to 1 (guard $x = 1$) and then announces when its clock reaches the value of the parameter (guard $x = \lambda$).

- For the counter involved (i): $(c_i, x > 1, ??dec_i, dec1_i^i)$, $(dec1_i^i, x = \lambda, \epsilon, \{x := 0\}, dec2_i^i)$ $(dec2_i^i, x = 1, \epsilon, \{x := 0\}, dec3_i^i)$ $(dec3_i^i, ??tick, c_i)$
  When the processes representing the counter i receive the message corresponding to the decrement, they move to an intermediary state, then reset their clock when it reaches λ and reset it another time when the clock reaches 1. This way, the difference with the controller clock has decreased by one. Notice that, if $x = 1$ when they receive the decrement message (meaning that the counter has value 0), they cannot take the transition.

- For the counter not involved $(3-i)$: $(c_j, ??dec_i, dec1_i^j)$ $(dec1_i^j, x = \lambda, \{x := 0\}, decj2_i^j)$ $(dec2_i^j, ??tick, c_j)$.
  The processes encoding the counter not involved just reset their clock when it reaches λ, thus the difference remains constant.

Increment of counter i. For an increment instruction $\mathbf{k} : incr \; \mathbf{C}_i \; goto \; \mathbf{k}_1$, the construction is almost symmetric to decrement, but involves an additional technicality—and therefore we give it below. We define the following transitions in Δ (depicted in Fig. 2c):

- For the controller: $(k^1, x = 1, !!inc_i, k^2)$ $(k^2, x = \lambda, !!tick, \{x := 0\}, k_1^1)$
  The controller announces that the instruction is an increment when its clock is equal to 1 and then announces when its clock reaches the value of the parameter.

- For the counter involved:
  The clock value should be reset at $\lambda - 1$, but such a guard is not allowed and is not possible to encode with just one clock. As an additional technicality, we thus rely on a *non-deterministic guess*, that is the checked by a new process. This is done as follows:

  For the current counter processes $(c_i, x < \lambda, ??inc_i, inc1_i^i)$, $(c_i, x = \lambda, ??inc_i, error)$, $(inc1_i^i, !!nc_i, inc2_i^i)$ $(inc2_i^i, x = \lambda, !!oc_i, idle)$.
  The processes encoding the counter receive the increment message and then guess non-deterministically that their clock value is $\lambda - 1$ and send a message nc_i. In order to check that the guess was right, they then announce when their clock reaches λ by sending message oc_i, and the processes move to *idle*. The value of the counter will then be encoded by the new processes. Notice that if the clock value is already equal to λ, then we reached the maximal possible value, and the processes move to the error state *error*.

For the new counter process $(idle, ??nc_i, \{x := 0\}, nc1_i)$ $(nc_i, x = 1, ??oc_i, nc2_i)$ $(nc2_i, ??tick, c_i)$.

To check that the guess was right, we use the idle processes that when receiving the message nc_i reset their clock. They are then allowed to encode the counter if they receive the confirmation oc_i when their clock is equal to 1 (thus the guess was correct).

- For the counter not involved: $(c_j, ??inc_i, incl_i^j)$ $(incl_i^j, x = \lambda, \{x := 0\}, incj2_i^j)$ $(inc2_i^j, ??tick, c_j)$.

The processes encoding the counter not involved just reset their clock when it reaches λ.

Zero-test. For a zero-test instruction $\mathbf{k} : if\ \mathbf{C}_i = 0\ then\ goto\ \mathbf{k}_1\ else\ goto\ \mathbf{k}_2$, we define the following transitions:

- For the controller $(k^1, x = 1, !!zt_i, k^2)$ $(k^2, x = \lambda, ??c_i, k^3)$ $(k^2, x < \lambda, ??c_i, k^4)$ $(k^3, x = \lambda, !!tick, \{x := 0\}, k_1^1)$ $(k^4, x = \lambda, !!tick, \{x := 0\}, k_2^1)$.

The controller announces that the instruction is a zero-test when its clock is equal to 1, and then waits for a notification c_i from the counter. Depending when this notification arrives, when $x = \lambda$ (meaning the counter has value 0) or when $x < \lambda$ (meaning the counter has positive value), the controller moves to the corresponding intermediary states.

- For the counter involved $(c_i, ??zt_i, zt1_i^i)$ $(zt1_i, x = \lambda, !!c_i, \{x := 0\}, zt2_i^i)$ $(zt2_i^i, ??tick, c_i)$.

The processes encoding the counter involved, after receiving the instruction, send a notification c_i when their clock reaches λ.

- For the counter not involved $(c_j, ??zt_i, zt1_i^j)$ $(zt1_i, x = \lambda, \epsilon, \{x := 0\}, zt2_i^j)$ $(zt2_i^j, ??tick, c_j)$.

The processes encoding the counter not involved just reset their clock when it reaches λ.

Finally, there is an additional transition $(idle, \epsilon, \{x := 0\}, idle)$ used to keep the clock of idle processes below $p(\lambda)$.

Given a valuation p of the parameter, we say that a configuration γ of the network encodes a configuration (k, v_1, v_2) of the two-counter machine if for all i, $\gamma[i] = (q, x)$ then either $x > p(\lambda)$ or $q \in \{c_1, c_2, k^1, idle\}$. Moreover all processes with a clock lower than $p(\lambda)$ and not in state $idle$ must agree on their clock valuation if they have the same state. Finally, if $\gamma[i] = (k^1, z)$ then for all i' such that $\gamma[i'] = (c_1, y)$ we have $v_1 = y - z$ and similarly for v_2.

Given an execution ρ, and a time t we denote by $\rho_{T=t}$ the configuration obtained when considering ρ at global time t. Notice that $\rho_{T=t}$ may not be a configuration that appears in ρ since it can be a configuration obtain during the elapsing of time in a transition.

We will prove that, for any execution ρ, either $\rho_{T=k*p(\lambda)+1/2}$ is not defined (the execution time never reaches $k * p(\lambda) + 1/2$) or $\rho_{T=k*p(\lambda)+1/2}$ encodes s_k, i.e., the kth configuration of the two-counter machine.

We start by some remarks on the shape of possible executions.

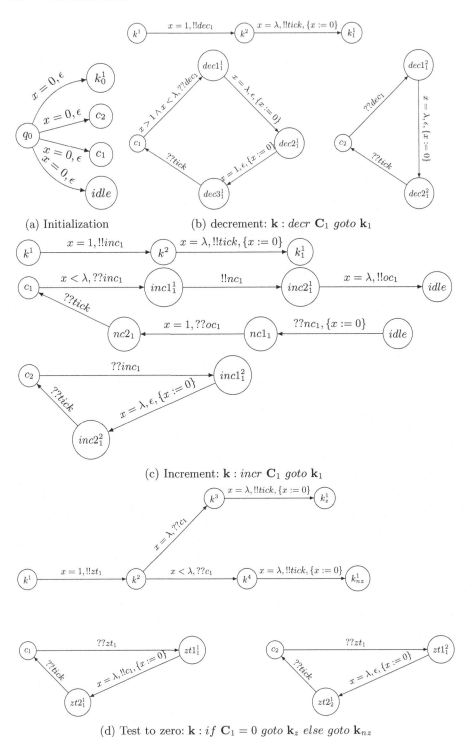

(a) Initialization

(b) decrement: **k** : *decr* **C**$_1$ *goto* **k**$_1$

(c) Increment: **k** : *incr* **C**$_1$ *goto* **k**$_1$

(d) Test to zero: **k** : *if* **C**$_1$ = 0 *goto* **k**$_z$ *else goto* **k**$_{nz}$

Fig. 2. Representation of the construction

1. If two processes are in the controller part, then their clocks are equal modulo $p(\lambda)$. Indeed, in the controller part, the clock is reset only when it reaches $p(\lambda)$.
2. It follows that, by definition of the protocol, the message *tick* is sent only at time units multiple of $p(\lambda)$.
3. Moreover, the instruction messages (inc_i, dec_i, zt_i) are only sent at global time units of the form $k * p(\lambda) + 1$.
4. Consider a process in state c_i with clock value lower than $p(\lambda)$. Assume that the global time is of the form $k * p(\lambda) + 1$. If this process does not receive an instruction message without delay, it will not be able to receive any before time $(k+1)*p(\lambda)+1$, thus it cannot take any transition before $(k+1)*p(\lambda)+1$. Note that at this time, its clock will be greater than $p(\lambda)$, thus the guard prevents it to take any transition for the rest of the execution.
5. With the same idea, if the process is in an intermediary state $nc2_i, dec2_i^j, dec3_i^j, inc2_i^j, zt2_i^i, zt2_i^j$ and does not receive a *tick* message at time $k * p(\lambda)$, we are certain that at time $(k+1) * p(\lambda)$ its clock will be above $p(\lambda)$ and it will thus be stuck forever.
6. Similarly if a process is in state $dec1_i^j, dec1_i^i, dec2_i^i, inc1_i^j, k^2$ and does not reset the clock when it is possible it will be stuck forever.
7. If an increment is requested by the controller part but the counter value is already equal to $p(\lambda) - 1$ i.e., the clock value of the counter process is equal to $p(\lambda)$, then the processes are sent to an error state and thus for the rest of the execution there will not be any processes in the counter part.
8. Similarly, if an increment is requested while no processes are left in the idle state, then the execution gets stuck in the next zero test.

In other words, if a process does not behave correctly, its clock will increase over $p(\lambda)$ and the process will be stuck forever.

Example 4. Before going further, let us first give some example of the behavior of the network encoding the two-counter machine.

Successful decrement k: *decr* c_1 *goto* $\mathbf{k}_1$ with $v_2 \geq v_1$ and $v_2 + 1 \leq p(\lambda)$ (those assumptions only matter for the order of the transitions).

$$
\begin{pmatrix} k^1, 0 \\ c_1, v_1 \\ c_2, v_2 \end{pmatrix} \xrightarrow{1,1,!!dec_1,\{2,3\}} \begin{pmatrix} k^2, 1 \\ dec1_1^1, v_1 + 1 \\ dec1_1^2, v_2 + 1 \end{pmatrix} \xrightarrow{\lambda-(v_2+1),3,\epsilon,\emptyset} \begin{pmatrix} k^2, \lambda - v_2 \\ dec1_1^1, v_1 + \lambda - v_2 \\ dec2_1^2, 0 \end{pmatrix}
$$

$$
\xrightarrow{v_2-v_1,2,\epsilon,\emptyset} \begin{pmatrix} k^2, \lambda - v_1 \\ dec2_1^1, 0 \\ dec2_1^2, v_2 - v_1 \end{pmatrix} \xrightarrow{1,2,\epsilon,\emptyset} \begin{pmatrix} k^2, \lambda - v_1 + 1 \\ dec2_1^1, 0 \\ dec2_1^2, v_2 - v_1 + 1 \end{pmatrix} \xrightarrow{v_1-1,1,!!tick,\{2,3\}} \begin{pmatrix} k_1^1, 0 \\ c_1, v_1 - 1 \\ c_2, v_2 \end{pmatrix}
$$

Failed decrement k: *decr* c_1 *goto* $\mathbf{k}_1$ with $v_2 \geq v_1$ and $v_2 + 1 \leq p(\lambda)$.

$$
\begin{pmatrix} k^1, 0 \\ c_1, 0 \\ c_2, v_2 \end{pmatrix} \xrightarrow{1,1,!!dec_1,\{2,3\}} \begin{pmatrix} k^2, 1 \\ c1_1, 1 \\ dec1_1^2, v_2 + 1 \end{pmatrix} \xrightarrow{\lambda-(v_2+1),3,\epsilon,\emptyset} \begin{pmatrix} k^2, \lambda - v_2 \\ c_1, \lambda - v_2 \\ dec2_1^2, 0 \end{pmatrix}
$$

Notice that for the rest of the execution the process 2 will be stuck in c_1, unable to perform any action, nor to receive any message.

Let us now show by induction on k that either $\rho_{T=(k+1)*p(\lambda)+1/2}$ is not defined or $\rho_{T=k*p(\lambda)+1/2}$ encodes $\mathbf{s}_k$.

The case $k = 0$ is direct. By definition it is easy to see that $\rho_{T=1/2}$ encodes γ_0.

Assume that the property holds for k. Let ρ be an execution such that $\rho_{T=k*p(\lambda)+1/2}$ encode $\mathbf{s}_k$. By the above remarks we have seen that if the network does not behave in the correct way it will get stuck before the next p time unit thus $\rho_{T=(k+2)*p(\lambda)+1/2}$. The only thing left to show that the reduction is correct is that the clocks are reset at the right time to correctly model increment and decrement and that zero tests are correct. For the latter, it is easy to see that by construction the controller part goes to the k_z instruction if and only if its clock is equal to the counter clock hence the counter is equal to 0, otherwise it moves to k_{nz}. For the former, the clocks evolve as in [21]. The only difference is for the increment where we need to introduce a new process used to guess when the clock value of the counter is equal to $p(\lambda) - 1$.

We thus obtain that if the controller part can reach k_{acc} then since the execution correctly encodes the run, the run must terminate. Conversely if the run is infinite, for any N and any p, any execution will either be infinite (and correct) thus never reaching k_{acc}, or eventually get stuck either because of an error in message, or because the counter clock is equal to 1 during an increment, or because there will not be enough processes in the idle state.

This concludes the proof that $\exists$-EF-emptiness is undecidable for 1-clock PTBP in the reconfigurable semantics.

For $\exists$-EF-universality, notice that the error state $error$ is reachable only if an increment is requested when the counter value is equal to $p(\lambda) - 1$. Thus if the error state is reached for all parameter valuations, this means that the run is unbounded. Conversely if the run is unbounded for all parameter valuations, at some point the counter value is equal to $p(\lambda) - 1$ during an increment and thus the error state is reachable. To conclude on the undecidability of $\exists$-EF-universality, we just have to recall that we consider rational valuations for the parameters, but in this proof we only used integer valuations. This does not harm the proof of undecidability since we can modify the aforementioned gadget given in [8] by replacing the state not integer by $error$. This modification ensures that $error$ is reachable for any non integer valuation and the above argument that it is reachable for all integer valuations if and only if the two-counter machine is unbounded. □

4   Clique

In broadcast protocol networks with a parametric number of processes, the topology of message communication plays a decisive role on the decidability status. In this section, we thus investigate a communication setting in which every message is received by all the other processes. We call these networks clique networks.

Formally, the semantics of a clique network is the restriction of the semantics given in Sect. 2 to internal transitions and broadcast transitions in which the set of receivers is always composed of all processes.

4.1   AF Problems in the Clique Semantics

We first rule out the ∃-AF problem for the clique semantics, as we can show from [19] that it is undecidable already without any clock.

Theorem 4. *The ∃-AF problem is undecidable for PTBP with no clock in the clique semantics.*

Proof. In [19, Chap. III, Theorem 3.5] it is shown that one can reduce the halting problem of a two-counter machine (which is undecidable [24]) to the AF problem in a clique network without clocks.

Intuitively the reduction goes as follows: the values of the counter are encoded by the number of processes in a given state. Increment and decrement of counter are easy to encode since in the clique semantics when one process sends a message everyone receives it, thus we can ensure that only one process performs the increment or decrement. The difficulty comes from the zero tests. Indeed, since we cannot force processes to answer we cannot differentiate between the case where there is no process encoding a counter and the case where the processes do not answer. To tackle this problem, zero tests are implemented non-deterministically: if we choose that the counter is zero, a message is sent. If it was not the case, then the processes encoding the counter value move to an error state. In the case we choose that the value is not zero, the network is locked until a process encoding the counter sends a message or a process moves to the error state. This encoding ensures that every run that does not encode truthfully the two-counter machine reaches the error state. Thus by adding a transition from the halting state of the counter machine toward the error state, we can ensure that every path reaches the error state if and only if the two-counter machine halts. □

4.2   EF Problems in the Clique Semantics

Recall that the proof of Theorem 3 does not rely on the reconfigurable semantics particularity. In fact the strong synchronization of processes in the clique semantics makes it even easier. We thus obtain the following lemma:

Lemma 2. *The   ∃-EF-emptiness   and   ∃-EF-universality   problems   are   undecidable for PTBP.*

This undecidability does not hold in the case where each parameter appears either always as an upper bound or always as a lower bound in guards (but not both). We thus consider in the following the case of L/U-PTBP.

5   1-Clock L/U-PTBP

Since the L/U restriction brings some decidability to PTAs, we focus in this section on L/U-PTBP. Recall that L/U-PTA are expressive enough to model classical examples from the literature [20], such as root contention or Fischer's mutual exclusion algorithm. As a consequence, L/U-PTBP make an interesting subclass of PTBP.

Due to the undecidability results of [1] for processes with 2 clocks (already without parameters), we consider in this section L/U-PTBP with one clock only. When considering L/U-PTBP, we can get the following monotonicity result on the timing parameter valuations.

Lemma 3. *Given $\mathcal{N}$ an L/U-PTBP with one clock, a network size $N \in \mathbb{N}$, and a parameter valuation p, for all valuations p' such that for all upper-bound parameters λ^u, $p(\lambda^u) \leq p'(\lambda^u)$ and for lower-bound parameters λ^l, $p(\lambda^l) \geq p'(\lambda^l)$ we have that $\forall \rho \in \mathcal{E}(\mathcal{N}, N, p)$, $\exists \rho' \in \mathcal{E}(\mathcal{N}, N, p')$ such that ρ is a prefix of ρ'.*

Proof. The proof is direct from the semantics definition. Notice that we do not have full inclusion of $\mathcal{E}(\mathcal{N}, N, p)$ in $\mathcal{E}(\mathcal{N}, N, p')$ since we consider maximal executions and it may be the case that some executions of $\mathcal{E}(\mathcal{N}, N, p)$ appear only as prefixes of executions of $\mathcal{E}(\mathcal{N}, N, p')$. Notice also that this holds in both semantics (reconfigurable and clique). □

A direct consequence of Lemma 3 and the decidability of the EF problem for PTBP with a single clock and without parameters is the decidability of the ∃-EF-emptiness problems for L/U-PTBP with one clock.

Lemma 4. *The ∃-EF-universality problem is decidable for closed bounded L/U-PTBP with one clock in both semantics.*

Proof. Let $\mathcal{N}$ be an L/U-PTBP with one clock, and *bounds* be the closed bounds on the parameters. Let p_{min} be the minimal permissive valuation i.e., the valuation such that for all upper-bound parameters λ^u, $p_{min}(\lambda^u) = inf(\lambda^u, bounds)$ and for all lower-bound parameters λ^l, $p_{min}(\lambda^l) = sup(\lambda^l, bounds)$. By definition we have $p_{min} \in bounds$.

We define the PTBP without parameters $\mathcal{N}_{min}$ as $\mathcal{N}$ but replacing each occurrence of an upper-bound parameter λ^u by $inf(\lambda^u, bounds)$ and each occurrence of a lower-bound parameter λ^l by $sup(\lambda^l, bounds)$. It is then easy to see that $\mathcal{E}(\mathcal{N}, N, p_{min}) = \mathcal{E}(\mathcal{N}_{min}, N)$.

Assume that for all N there is no execution reaching q_f in $\mathcal{E}(\mathcal{N}_{min}, N)$; then the above equality implies that the answer to ∃-EF-universality is false.

Conversely assuming that there exists an execution reaching q_f in $\mathcal{E}(\mathcal{N}_{min}, N)$ for some N, we obtain by the equality and the monotonicity Lemma 3 that this execution is a prefix of an execution of $\mathcal{E}(\mathcal{N}, N, p)$ for any valuation p.

Thus the ∃-EF-universality problem for $\mathcal{N}$ is equivalent to the ∃-EF problem for $\mathcal{N}_{min}$ and thus is decidable in the clique semantics (see [1]) and in the reconfigurable semantics (see Theorem 2). □

For the ∃-EF-emptiness problem, we can remove the assumption on the closed bounds.

Lemma 5. *The ∃-EF-emptiness problem is decidable for (open or closed) bounded L/U-PTBP with one clock in both semantics.*

Proof. Let $\mathcal{N}$ be an L/U-PTBP with one clock, and *bounds* be the bounds on the parameters. As for the $\exists$-EF-universality problem, we define a protocol $\mathcal{N}_{max}$ with the difference that non-strict guards involving open bounded parameters are changed to strict guards. We define the PTBP without parameters $\mathcal{N}_{max}$ as $\mathcal{N}$ but for all upper-bound parameters λ^u if $bounds(\lambda^u)$ is of the form $(inf, sup]$ or $[inf, sup]$ then every occurrence of λ^u is replaced by sup. Otherwise if $bounds(\lambda^u)$ is of the form (inf, sup) or $[inf, sup)$ then every guard of the form $x < \lambda^u$ or $x \leq \lambda^u$ is replaced by the guard $x < sup$. We operate similarly for lower-bound parameters.

Using the same argument as for the monotonicity Lemma 3 it is easy to see that for any valuation $p \in bounds$, any execution ρ in $\mathcal{E}(\mathcal{N}, N, p)$ is a prefix of some execution in $\mathcal{E}(\mathcal{N}_{max}, N)$. Thus if some execution reaches q_f for some N and some p in $\mathcal{E}(\mathcal{N}, N, p)$, there is also an execution reaching q_f in $\mathcal{E}(\mathcal{N}_{max}, N)$.

The other direction is more subtle. Assume that there exists an execution ρ reaching q_f in $\mathcal{E}(\mathcal{N}_{max}, N)$. Let ρ' be a finite prefix of ρ reaching q_f. We define a valuation $p \in bounds$ that contains an execution identical to ρ' as follows: Let λ^u be an upper-bound parameter. Either $bounds(\lambda^u)$ is of the form $(inf, sup]$ or $[inf, sup]$ and we define $p(\lambda^u) = sup$. Or $bounds(\lambda^u)$ is of the form (inf, sup) or $[inf, sup)$. In this case, let v_u be the maximal value of clock x along ρ' when x is compared in a guard which was formerly $x \bowtie \lambda^u$. By definition of $\mathcal{N}_{max}$ we know that $v_u < sup$. We thus define $p(\lambda^u) = v_u + \epsilon$ with $\epsilon > 0$, $\epsilon + v_u < sup$ and $\epsilon > inf - v_u$ (it exists since necessarily $inf < sup$).

We operate in a symmetrical way for lower-bound parameters: v_l is the minimal value of clock x along ρ' when x is compared in a guard which was formerly $x \bowtie \lambda^l$ and $p(u) = v_u - \epsilon$ with $v_u - \epsilon > inf$, $\epsilon > 0$ and $\epsilon < sup + v_u$ (it exists since necessarily $sup > inf$).

It is easy to see that for this valuation, ρ' is a prefix of some execution in $\mathcal{E}(\mathcal{N}, N, p)$. Hence, the $\exists$-EF-emptiness problem for $\mathcal{N}$ is equivalent to the EF problem for $\mathcal{N}_{max}$ and thus decidable in the clique semantics [1] and in the reconfigurable semantics (Theorem 2). □

In contrast with the $\exists$-EF-emptiness problem, the monotonicity result is not enough to show decidability of the $\exists$-EF-universality problem for L/U-PTBP with open bounds. In fact we can even show that the problem becomes undecidable for general L/U-PTBP in the clique semantics. More precisely it is undecidable for U-PTBP with one parameter with open left bound, and for L-PTBP with one unbounded parameter.

Theorem 5. *The $\exists$-EF-universality problem is undecidable for open bounded L/U-PTBP with one clock in the clique semantics.*

Proof. We reduce from the halting problem of two-counter machines. The idea is to encode a two-counter machine, the number of processes in a particular state is used to encode the counter value. Thanks to the clique semantics, increment and decrement of counters are easy to simulate. However, zero tests are not possible since there is no way to distinguish between the fact that no process is modeling a counter and the fact that they just do not send a message. We thus allow the simulation to guess whether the counter is zero or not zero non-deterministically; in case of a wrong guess we are able to detect it thanks to the clique semantics. In this case, at least one process is stuck in an error state, we then use the timing parameter to repeat the simulation an unbounded (but finite) number of times before moving to the target state. To be able to reach the target state, we thus have to be able to correctly simulate the two-counter machine without wrong guess.

Formally, given a two-counter machine $\mathbf{M} = (\mathbf{K}, \mathbf{k}_0, \mathbf{k}_{acc})$ we define a PTBP $\mathcal{P}$ as follows:

- $Q = \{q_0, idle, c_i, c_i^d, c_i^i, c_i^z, err, q_f \mid i \in \{1, 2\}\} \cup \{k, k' \mid k \in K\}$ where, q_0 is the initial state, $idle$ is a waiting state for the processes encoding the counters, c_i is the state used to encode the value of counter $\mathbf{C}_i$, c_i^i and c_i^d are intermediary states for increment and decrement of counter c_i, c_i^z is an intermediary state used for the zero test, a state k is used to encode that the simulation reached instruction k of the machine and k' is an intermediary state, err is a sink state used to detect error in the simulation, finally q_f is the target state.
- $\mathbb{X} = \{x\}$ and $\mathbb{P} = \{\lambda^u, \lambda^l\}$.
- $\Sigma = \{inc_i, dec_i, z_i, nz_i, ok, end \mid i \in \{1, 2\}\}$ where inc_i, dec_i, z_i, and nz_i stand respectively for increment, decrement, zero, and not zero of counter c_i, ok is a message to acknowledge that the action was performed correctly, and end is the message sent at the end of the simulation to either restart a simulation or reach the target state.
- Δ is defined as follows (for simplicity the guard and update of the clock are omitted when trivial, i.e., the true guard and no reset):

  Initialization. $(q_0, !!ok, k_0) \in \Delta$, $(q_0, ??ok, idle) \in \Delta$.

  Increment of counter i. For an increment instruction $\mathbf{k} : incr\ \mathbf{C}_i\ goto\ \mathbf{k}_1$, we add to Δ the transitions: $(k, !!inc_i, k')$, $(k', ??ok, k_1)$, $(idle, ??inc_i, c_i^i)$, $(c_i^i, !!ok, c_i)$ $(c_i^i, ??ok, idle)$.

  Decrement of counter i. For a decrement instruction $\mathbf{k} : decr\ c_i\ goto\ \mathbf{k}_1$, we add to Δ the transitions: $(k, !!dec_i, k')$, $(k', ??ok, k_1)$, $(c_i, ??dec_i, c_i^d)$, $(c_i^d, !!ok, idle)$ $(c_i^d, ??ok, c_i)$.

  Zero-test of counter i. For a zero-test instruction $\mathbf{k} : if\ c_i = 0\ goto\ \mathbf{k}_z\ else\ goto\ \mathbf{k}_{nz}$, we add to Δ the transitions: $(k, !!z_i, k_z)$, $(k, !!nz_i, k')$, $(k', ??ok, k_{nz})$, $(c_i, ??z_i, err)$, $(c_i, ??nz_i, c_i^z)$ $(c_i^z, !!ok, c_i)$, $(c_i^z, ??ok, c_i)$.

  End of simulation.

  $(k_{acc}, x < \lambda^u, !!end, \{x := 0\}, k_0)$ $(idle, x > \lambda^l, ??end, q_f)$ $(c_i, ??end, idle)$.

Given a configuration γ of the network, we say that it encodes a configuration (k, v_1, v_2) of the two-counter machine if there is one process in state k and v_i processes in states c_i for $i \in \{1, 2\}$. If we omit the *end of simulation* part, this reduction is similar to the one found in [19, Chap. III, Theorem 3.5]; we therefore proceed with less details on this part. In short, every execution of the network is of one of the three kinds:

Correct simulation. The execution correctly encodes the run of the two-counter machine.

Lack of processes. The controller is stuck in an intermediary state while performing an increment, *i.e.* there was no process left in the *idle* state when the controller sent the inc_i message, thus it is stuck waiting for an *ok* message that no one can send.

Wrong zero-test. Along the execution, the controller wrongly assumed the value of a counter. Either it guessed a non-zero value and it is stuck waiting for an *ok* message, or it guessed zero when it was not—in which case at least one process moved to the error state.

Notice now that to reach the target state q_f a process in *idle* must receive the message *end* after its clock value is greater than parameter λ^l. But the end of simulation part requires that the controller clock is lower than parameter λ^u. Thus when reaching state k_{acc}, in order to be able to let more time elapse, the controller has to send the message *end* which leads to a configuration where there is no process in the counter states and the controller is in the initial state of the two-counter machine. This configuration thus encodes the initial configuration of the two-counter machine. The controller then must simulate another time the two-counter machine before being able to send *end* again.

Thus, given a valuation p of the parameters, to reach q_f at least $p(\lambda^l)/p(\lambda^u)$ messages *end* must be sent by the controller. In other words, $p(\lambda^l)/p(\lambda^u)$ (correct or incorrect) simulations of the two-counter machine must be performed before reaching q_f. We have seen before that every incorrect simulation either gets stuck, or sends at least a process in the error state. Hence, given a network size N, if for a valuation p such that $p(\lambda^l)/p(\lambda^u) > N$ the state q_f is reached, then at least one simulation was correct, thus the two-counter machine halts.

This proves the undecidability of the EF-universality problem with 0 as an open lower bound for λ^u. Indeed, if there exists a network of size N which satisfies the EF-universality, then it is possible to reach q_f for all valuation and in particular for a valuation such that $p(\lambda^l)/p(\lambda^u) > N$. For the other direction, if the machine halts, there exists a size of network ($m + 2$ where m is the maximal sum of the two-counter value along the execution) that ensures that q_f is reachable for any valuation p with $p(\lambda^u) > 0$. Indeed, the controller can simulate the two-counter machine correctly (since it has enough processes to model the counters) in 0 time unit, wait a positive delay but less than λ^u time unit, and repeat this until the clock value of the processes in *idle* is greater than λ^l. This is possible since every time the controller sends the message *end* the configuration obtained is the same as the one obtained after the initialization (the first message *ok*). □

Lemma 6. *∃-EF-universality in the clique semantics is undecidable already with a single clock for U-PTBP with open bounds on the left, and L-PTBP with infinity as right bound.*

Proof. The proof of Theorem 5 uses an open bounded L/U-PTBP. Moreover we only used the fact for all size of network N there exists a valuation of the parameter p such that $p(\lambda^l)/p(\lambda^u) > N$. Thus the proof can be adapted with only one upper-bound parameter λ^u (resp. lower-bound parameter λ^l) by replacing

Table 1. Summary of our contributions (bold green: decidable; red italic: undecidable)

	1-c	2-c	3-c	1-L/U		2-L/U	3-L/U
				cb	ob		
∃-EF-empt.	*Th3*			**L5**		*L1*	
∃-EF-univ.	*Th3*			**L4**	*open*	*L1*	
∃-AF	**Th1**	*open*	*Th1*	**Th1**		*open*	*Th1*

(a) Reconfigurable semantics

	PTBP	L/U		L or U	
		cb	ob	cb	ob
∃-EF-empt.	*L2*	**L5**		**L5**	
∃-EF-univ.	*L2*	**L4**	*Th5*	**L4**	*L6*
∃-AF	*Th4*				

(b) Clique semantics for 1 clock

λ^l by 1 in the protocol (resp. λ^u by 1). This still ensures that there exists a valuation such that $1/p(\lambda^u) > N$ (resp. $p(\lambda^l) > N$). □

6   Conclusion

Up to our knowledge this work is the first to consider two different sets of parameters at the same time. Both parameterized number of processes and parametric clocks are difficult to deal with and number of problems are undecidable for each of these systems. However we have shown that the combination of the decidable subclasses leads to some decidable problems. Our contributions are summarized in Table 1; i-c (resp. i-L/U) denotes PTBP (resp. L/U-PTBP) with i clocks per process. In Table 1b, cb and ob denote formalisms with a closed bounded parameter domain and an open bounded parameter domain.

The open 2-clock case in the reconfigurable semantics is a well-known open problem, with connections to open problems of logic and automata theory [6]. The other open case in Table 1 we are interested in solving is ∃-EF-universality for 1-L/U-PTBP in the reconfigurable semantics with open bounds. In addition, EF problems are still open for bounded 1-clock PTBP (Theorem 3 requires unbounded parameters), and for 1-c L/U with unbounded parameters in the clique semantics. Finally, for the decidable subclasses we exhibited, it remains to be studied whether exact synthesis can be achieved, i.e., obtaining the set of sizes of processes and timing parameter valuations for which EF or AF holds.

More general future works include considering other semantics such as asynchronous broadcast or different communication topologies (reconfigurable under constraint, restricted to graph of bounded width, . . .), as well as the reachability problem for *all* sizes of networks (instead of the *existence* of a network size): while it seems straightforward for EF problems, it remains to be done for AF problems. Another quantifier of interest is the number of processes reaching the target: so far, we considered the existence of one process reaching the target. All processes reaching the target is also of interest.

Acknowledgement. The authors warmly thank Nathalie Bertrand for fruitful discussions on the topic of this paper.

References

1. Abdulla, P.A., Delzanno, G., Rezine, O., Sangnier, A., Traverso, R.: On the verification of timed ad hoc networks. In: Fahrenberg, U., Tripakis, S. (eds.) FORMATS 2011. LNCS, vol. 6919, pp. 256–270. Springer, Heidelberg (2011). https://doi.org/10.1007/978-3-642-24310-3_18

2. Abdulla, P.A., Delzanno, G., Rezine, O., Sangnier, A., Traverso, R.: Parameterized verification of time-sensitive models of ad hoc network protocols. Theor. Comput. Sci. **612**, 1–22 (2016)

3. Abdulla, P.A., Deneux, J., Mahata, P.: Multi-clock timed networks. In: LiCS, pp. 345–354. IEEE Computer Society (2004)

4. Abdulla, P.A., Jonsson, B.: Model checking of systems with many identical timed processes. Theor. Comput. Sci. **290**(1), 241–264 (2003)

5. Alur, R., Dill, D.L.: A theory of timed automata. Theor. Comput. Sci. **126**(2), 183–235 (1994)

6. Alur, R., Henzinger, T.A., Vardi, M.Y.: Parametric real-time reasoning. In: Kosaraju, S.R., Johnson, D.S., Aggarwal, A. (eds.) STOC, pp. 592–601. ACM (1993)

7. André, É.: What's decidable about parametric timed automata? Int. J. Softw. Tools Technol. Transf. (2018, to appear)

8. André, É., Delahaye, B., Fournier, P., Lime, D.: Parametric timed broadcast protocols (long version) (2018). http://arxiv.org/

9. André, É., Knapik, M., Penczek, W., Petrucci, L.: Controlling actions and time in parametric timed automata. In: Desel, J., Yakovlev, A. (eds.) ACSD, pp. 45–54. IEEE Computer Society (2016)

10. André, É., Lime, D.: Liveness in L/U-parametric timed automata. In: Legay, A., Schneider, K. (eds.) ACSD, pp. 9–18. IEEE (2017)

11. Beneš, N., Bezděk, P., Larsen, K.G., Srba, J.: Language emptiness of continuous-time parametric timed automata. In: Halldórsson, M.M., Iwama, K., Kobayashi, N., Speckmann, B. (eds.) ICALP 2015. LNCS, vol. 9135, pp. 69–81. Springer, Heidelberg (2015). https://doi.org/10.1007/978-3-662-47666-6_6

12. Bouajjani, A., Jonsson, B., Nilsson, M., Touili, T.: Regular model checking. In: Emerson, E.A., Sistla, A.P. (eds.) CAV 2000. LNCS, vol. 1855, pp. 403–418. Springer, Heidelberg (2000). https://doi.org/10.1007/10722167_31

13. D'Argenio, P.R., Katoen, J.-P., Ruys, T.C., Tretmans, J.: The bounded retransmission protocol must be on time! In: Brinksma, E. (ed.) TACAS 1997. LNCS, vol. 1217, pp. 416–431. Springer, Heidelberg (1997). https://doi.org/10.1007/BFb0035403

14. Delzanno, G., Ganty, P.: Automatic verification of time sensitive cryptographic protocols. In: Jensen, K., Podelski, A. (eds.) TACAS 2004. LNCS, vol. 2988, pp. 342–356. Springer, Heidelberg (2004). https://doi.org/10.1007/978-3-540-24730-2_27

15. Delzanno, G., Sangnier, A., Traverso, R., Zavattaro, G.: On the complexity of parameterized reachability in reconfigurable broadcast networks. In: FSTTCS. LIPIcs, vol. 18, pp. 289–300. Schloss Dagstuhl - Leibniz-Zentrum fuer Informatik (2012)

16. Delzanno, G., Sangnier, A., Zavattaro, G.: Parameterized verification of ad hoc networks. In: Gastin, P., Laroussinie, F. (eds.) CONCUR 2010. LNCS, vol. 6269, pp. 313–327. Springer, Heidelberg (2010). https://doi.org/10.1007/978-3-642-15375-4_22

17. Delzanno, G., Sangnier, A., Zavattaro, G.: On the power of cliques in the parameterized verification of ad hoc networks. In: Hofmann, M. (ed.) FoSSaCS 2011. LNCS, vol. 6604, pp. 441–455. Springer, Heidelberg (2011). https://doi.org/10.1007/978-3-642-19805-2_30

18. Delzanno, G., Sangnier, A., Zavattaro, G.: Parameterized verification of safety properties in ad hoc network protocols. arXiv preprint arXiv:1108.1864 (2011)

19. Fournier, P.: Parameterized verification of networks of many identical processes. Ph.D. thesis, Rennes 1 (2015)

20. Hune, T., Romijn, J., Stoelinga, M., Vaandrager, F.W.: Linear parametric model checking of timed automata. J. Log. Algebr. Program. **52–53**, 183–220 (2002)

21. Jovanović, A., Lime, D., Roux, O.H.: Integer parameter synthesis for timed automata. IEEE Trans. Softw. Eng. **41**(5), 445–461 (2015)

22. Li, L., Sun, J., Liu, Y., Dong, J.S.: Verifying parameterized timed security protocols. In: Bjørner, N., de Boer, F. (eds.) FM 2015. LNCS, vol. 9109, pp. 342–359. Springer, Cham (2015). https://doi.org/10.1007/978-3-319-19249-9_22

23. Miller, J.S.: Decidability and complexity results for timed automata and semi-linear hybrid automata. In: Lynch, N., Krogh, B.H. (eds.) HSCC 2000. LNCS, vol. 1790, pp. 296–310. Springer, Heidelberg (2000). https://doi.org/10.1007/3-540-46430-1_26

24. Minsky, M.L.: Computation: Finite and Infinite Machines. Prentice-Hall Inc., Upper Saddle River (1967)

Flat Model Checking for Counting LTL Using Quantifier-Free Presburger Arithmetic

Normann Decker[1](✉) and Anton Pirogov[2](✉)

[1] ISP, Universität zu Lübeck, Lübeck, Germany
decker@isp.uni-luebeck.de
[2] RWTH Aachen University, Aachen, Germany
pirogov@cs.rwth-aachen.de

Abstract. This paper presents an approximation approach to verifying counter systems with respect to properties formulated in an expressive counting extension of linear temporal logic. It can express, e.g., that the number of acknowledgements never exceeds the number of requests to a service, by counting specific positions along a run and imposing arithmetic constraints. The addressed problem is undecidable and therefore solved on flat under-approximations of a system. This provides a flexibly adjustable trade-off between exhaustiveness and computational effort, similar to bounded model checking. Recent techniques and results for model-checking frequency properties over flat Kripke structures are lifted and employed to construct a parametrised encoding of the (approximated) problem in quantifier-free Presburger arithmetic. A prototype implementation based on the z3 SMT solver demonstrates the effectiveness of the approach based on problems from the RERS Challange.

1 Introduction

Counting is a fundamental principle in the theory of computation and well-established in the study and verification of infinite-state systems. The concept is ubiquitous in programming, and counting mechanisms are a natural notion of quantitative measurement in specification formalisms. For example, they are useful for expressing constraints such as "the number of acknowledgements never exceeds the number of requests" or "the relative error frequency stays below some threshold". An established and well-studied framework for correctness specification is linear temporal logic (LTL) [30]. Therefore, various counting extensions were proposed [6,8,13,25] that allow for imposing constraints on the number of positions along a run that satisfy some property. These extensions target different kinds of system models, and vary in the type of events that can be counted and the constraints that can be expressed.

A. Pirogov—This author is supported by the German research council (DFG) Research Training Group 2236 UnRAVeL.

C. Enea and R. Piskac (Eds.): VMCAI 2019, LNCS 11388, pp. 513–534, 2019.
https://doi.org/10.1007/978-3-030-11245-5_24

This paper is concerned with verifying properties expressed in the counting temporal logic CLTL. This extension of LTL features a generalised *temporal until* operator $\mathbf{U}_{[.]}$ for evaluating a counting constraint within its scope. For example, consider the property that between two system resets, two events e_1 and e_2 (say, related sensor events) should be correlated linearly. The CLTL formula

$$\mathbf{G}(\neg reset\ \mathbf{U}_{[2e_1-e_2\geq-10]}\ reset)$$

would specify that there are not more than twice as many occurrences of e_1 than there are of e_2, with an absolute margin of 10. Notice that this property is not regular. The events e_1 and e_2 may be atomic or again characterised by some temporal (counting) property. The definition used[1] here extends that of [25] by admitting not only natural but arbitrary integer coefficients in constraints. Without this extension, the logic was shown to be more concise but not more expressive than LTL. Moreover, in the present work, CLTL is interpreted over *counter systems* instead of Kripke structures and allows for imposing arithmetic constraints also on (linear combinations of) the counter values, similar to the formalisms considered in [11,16,18].

Towards making the extended features of this specification language available for program verification, we propose an approach to the *existential model-checking problem* of CLTL over counter systems, i.e. deciding for some counter system whether it admits a run satisfying a given formula. Both system model and logic are very powerful, and the problem is undecidable. However, we avoid the often made compromise of recovering decidability by means of essential restrictions to the specification language. Instead, we use an approximation scheme based on an extension of recent work [13] that has laid the theoretical basis for a decision procedure in the special case of structures that are *flat*. Flatness demands, essentially, that cycles of the system cannot be alternated during an execution. It is thus a strong restriction but decreases the computational complexity of verification tasks significantly. To benefit from the improved complexity while being generally applicable, our approach verifies *flat under-approximations* of a specific depth given as parameter. Similarly to bounded model checking [4,5], the parameter allows the user to flexibly adjust the trade-off between exhaustiveness and computational effort. An essential advantage of flat under-approximations is that they represent sets of complete (infinite) runs instead of only a finite number of bounded prefixes. They can be understood as a bounded unfolding of loop alternations, represented symbolically. When increasing the approximation depth to include one more alternation, an infinite number of additional runs is represented, and verified at once. Considering first a small depth and increasing it only if no witness was found allows for finding "simple" witnesses quickly where they exist, even for complex path properties that cannot be evaluated on prefixes. The underlying theory provides a bound on the maximal depth that needs to be considered in the case of a flat system.

---

[1] To avoid cluttered notation when respecting various existing naming schemes, the denotation CLTL is reused, despite semantic differences.

The method is (necessarily) incomplete in the general case but can nevertheless be directly applied.

Contributions. As conceptual basis, we first extend the theory of model-checking counting logics on flat structures developed in [13], where only frequency constraints and Kripke structures were considered. Symbolic models called *augmented path schemas* were introduced to represent sets of runs. We extend the definitions and techniques to apply to more general counting constraints and flat counter systems while preserving the previous complexity bounds. This is a consequent continuation of the development of the theory. From the user perspective, it is a valuable extension, since CLTL provides a much more flexible specification language and counter systems an extended application domain. It is particularly important for the practical application of the method.

Subsequently, based on the lifted theory, we describe an explicit formulation of the (approximated) model-checking problem in quantifier-free Presburger arithmetic (QPA). Recall that Presburger arithmetic is first-order logic over the integer numbers with addition. Its satisfiability problem is decidable [31] and in the case of the quantifier-free fragment in NP [7]. Importantly, the theory of QPA is well-supported by a number of competitive SMT-solvers (cf. [10]). Our construction is parametrised by the depth of the flat approximation that is to be verified, and the resulting QPA formula is linear in the problem size and the chosen depth.

We have implemented the incremental model-checking procedure based on the QPA encoding and the z3 SMT solver [29]. Verification tasks of the RERS Challenge [22] and counting variations were used to evaluate the effectiveness of our approach.

Related Work. In [6] an LTL extension to express relative frequencies, called fLTL, was studied. It features a generalised until operator that can be understood as a variant of the $U_{[.]}$ operator restricted to a specific class of counting constraints. Various other classes were studied in the context of CTL [26]. One of the corresponding CTL variants, denoted $CCTL_{\pm}$, admits integer coefficients and thus represents the branching-time analog to CLTL, although interpreted over finite Kripke structures. The difference between linear and branching time is crucial, however. Satisfiability, and hence model checking Kripke structures, is undecidable for fLTL [6] (and hence for CLTL) but decidable for its branching-time analog fCTL and even $CCTL_{\pm}$ [13,26]. Counting extensions were also studied for regular expressions in [1,20]. The notion of flat (or *weak*) systems was investigated as a sensible restriction to reduce the computational complexity of various verification problems. Considering (finite) Kripke structures, model-checking LTL properties, which is PSPACE-complete [32], becomes NP-complete under the flatness condition [24]. It follows from [6] that model-checking fLTL, and thus all more expressive counting logics, is undecidable. Over flat Kripke structures, the problem is in NExp and even an extremely powerful counting extension of CTL* was shown to become decidable [13]. A similar impact is observable for (infinite state) counter systems. While reachability is already undecidable for two-counter systems [28], results from [12] provide that flatness recovers decidability with an arbitrary number of counters (see also [11]). Later, it was shown in [15] that LTL properties (including past) can generally be evaluated in NP (see also [17]). The authors also make the suggestion to consider flat systems as under-approximations, which is addressed here.

Increasing the depth of a flat under-approximation is similar to so-called *loop acceleration* in symbolic verification. It aims at stepping over an arbitrary number of consecutive iterations of a loop during state space exploration, by symbolically representing its effect. Since this is particularly effective for simple loops, flatness is a desired property [2] also in this setting. Unfortunately, acceleration typically concerns the computation of reachability sets [2,3,9,21,23] and is thus insufficient when analysing *path properties* as expressible in (extensions of) LTL. For accelerating the latter, flat systems, and path schemas in particular, provide a suitable symbolic model since they represent entire runs.

Outline. First, Sect. 2 provides basic definitions. In Sect. 3, a generalised notion of augmented path schemas is introduced and employed to lift the decidability results of [13]. It provides the basis for Sect. 4 describing the parametrised encoding of the model-checking problem into QPA. Section 5 reports on our implementation of the approach and Sect. 6 concludes.

2   Counting in Linear Temporal Logic

Constraints and Counter Systems. For $x, y \in \mathbb{Z}$ let $[x, y]$ denote the (potentially empty) interval $\{x, x+1, \ldots, y\} \subset \mathbb{Z}$. A *constraint* over a set X is a linear arithmetic inequation $\tau \geq b$ where $\tau = \sum_{i=0}^{n} a_i x_i$, $n \in \mathbb{N}$, $b, a_i \in \mathbb{Z}$, and $x_i \in X$ for $i \in [0, n]$. For convenience, we may use relation symbols $\leq, <$, and $>$, denoting arithmetically equivalent constraints, e.g. $2x_1 + x_2 < 3$ denotes $-2x_1 - x_2 \geq -2$. The *dual* of a constraint $\tau \geq b$ is denoted by $\overline{\tau \geq b}$ and defined as the equivalent of $\tau < b$. For a valuation $\theta : X \to \mathbb{Z}$, we denote by $[\![\tau]\!](\theta) := \sum_{i=0}^{n} a_i \theta(x_i)$ the arithmetic evaluation of τ. Satisfaction is defined as $\theta \models \tau \geq b$ if and only if $[\![\tau]\!](\theta) \geq b$. Constraint sets are interpreted as conjunction and satisfaction is defined accordingly. The set of all constraints over X is denoted $\mathfrak{C}(X)$. For convenience, arithmetic operations are lifted point-wise to integer-valued functions of equal domain.

Let Λ be a set of *labels* and $C_{\mathcal{S}}$ a finite set of *system counters*. A *counter system (CS)* over Λ and $C_{\mathcal{S}}$ is a tuple $\mathcal{S} = (S, \Delta, s_I, \lambda)$ where S is a finite set of *control states*, $s_I \in S$ is the *initial state*, $\lambda : S \to 2^{\Lambda}$ is a *labelling* function, and $\Delta \subseteq S \times \mathbb{Z}^{C_{\mathcal{S}}} \times 2^{\mathfrak{C}(C_{\mathcal{S}})} \times S$ is a finite set of *transitions* carrying an *update* $\mu : C_{\mathcal{S}} \to \mathbb{Z}$ to the system counters and a finite set of *guards* $\Gamma \subseteq \mathfrak{C}(C_{\mathcal{S}})$ over them. A *configuration* of $\mathcal{S}$ is a pair (s, θ) comprised of a state $s \in S$ and a *valuation* $\theta : C_{\mathcal{S}} \to \mathbb{Z}$. A *run* of $\mathcal{S}$ is an infinite sequence $\rho = (s_0, \theta_0)(s_1, \theta_1) \ldots \in (S \times \mathbb{Z}^{C_{\mathcal{S}}})^{\omega}$ such that $(s_0, \theta_0) = (s_I, \mathbf{0})$ and for all positions $i \in \mathbb{N}$ there is a transition $(s_i, \mu_i, \Gamma_i, s_{i+1}) \in \Delta$ such that $\theta_{i+1} = \theta_i + \mu_i$ and $\theta_{i+1} \models \Gamma_i$. The set of all runs of $\mathcal{S}$ is denoted $\mathrm{runs}(\mathcal{S})$.

Let $\lambda^\# : S^* \to \mathbb{N}^\Lambda$ denote the accumulation of labels in a multi-set fashion, counting the number of occurrences of each label on a finite state sequence $w \in S^*$ by $\lambda_{\mathcal{P}}^\#(w) : \ell \mapsto |\{i \in [0, |w| - 1] \mid \ell \in \lambda(w(i))\}|$ for all $\ell \in \Lambda$. The set of successors of a state $s \in S$ in $\mathcal{S}$ be denoted by $\mathrm{suc}_{\mathcal{S}}(s) := \{s' \in S \mid \exists_{\mu, \Gamma} : (s, \mu, \Gamma, s') \in \Delta\}$, and the corresponding transitive and reflexive closure by $\mathrm{suc}_{\mathcal{S}}^*(s)$. A (finite) *path* in $\mathcal{S}$ is a (finite) state sequence $w = s_0 s_1 \ldots$ with $s_{i+1} \in \mathrm{suc}_{\mathcal{S}}(s_i)$ for all $0 \leq i < |w|$. A finite path $w = s_0 \ldots s_n$ is *simple* if no state occurs twice, it is a *loop* if $s_0 \in \mathrm{suc}_{\mathcal{S}}(s_n)$, and a *row* if no state is part of any loop in $\mathcal{S}$. The counter system $\mathcal{S}$ is *flat* if for every state $s \in S$ there is at most one simple loop $s_0 \ldots s_n$ with $s_0 = s$. Let the size of $\mathcal{S}$ be denoted by $|\mathcal{S}|$ and defined as the length of its syntactic representation with numbers encoded binary.

Counting LTL. We consider linear temporal logic extended by counting constraints in the style of [25]. In contrast, however, we admit arbitrary *integer coefficients*. Moreover, the semantics is defined in terms of runs of *counter systems* and the logic provides access to the counter valuation by means of Presburger constraints. Let AP and C be fixed, finite sets of atomic propositions and counter names, respectively. The set of CLTL formulae (denoted simply by CLTL) is defined by the grammar

$$\varphi ::= \mathsf{true} \mid p \mid \gamma \mid \varphi \wedge \varphi \mid \neg\varphi \mid \mathbf{X}\,\varphi \mid \varphi\,\mathbf{U}_{[\tau \geq b]}\,\varphi$$
$$\tau ::= a \cdot \varphi \mid \tau + \tau$$

for atomic propositions $p \in AP$, guards over counter names $\gamma \in \mathfrak{C}(C)$ and integer constants $a, b \in \mathbb{Z}$. Additional abbreviations may be used with expected semantics, in particular $\mathsf{false} := \neg\mathsf{true}$, $\varphi\,\mathbf{U}\,\psi := \varphi\,\mathbf{U}_{[1\cdot\mathsf{true}\geq 0]}\,\psi$ and $\mathbf{F}_{[\tau \geq b]}\,\varphi := \mathsf{true}\,\mathbf{U}_{[\tau \geq b]}\,\varphi$. We may write $\mathsf{CLTL}(C')$ for the restriction to formulae that only use counter names from some specific set $C' \subseteq C$. By $\mathrm{sub}(\varphi)$ we denote the set of subformulae of φ (including itself).

Let $\mathcal{S} = (S, \Delta, s_I, \lambda)$ be a counter system over counters $C_{\mathcal{S}}$ with a run $\rho = (s_0, \theta_0)(s_1, \theta_1) \ldots$ and $i \geq 0$ a position on ρ. Observe that expressions of the form $\tau \geq b$ are in fact arithmetic constraints from the set $\mathfrak{C}(\mathsf{CLTL})$. The satisfaction relation $\models$ is defined inductively as follows. For plain LTL formulae, the usual definition applies. Additionally, for $(\tau \geq b) \in \mathfrak{C}(\mathsf{CLTL}(C_{\mathcal{S}}))$, $\gamma \in \mathfrak{C}(C_{\mathcal{S}})$, and $\varphi, \psi \in \mathsf{CLTL}(C_{\mathcal{S}})$ let

$$(\mathcal{S}, \rho, i) \models \gamma \qquad :\Leftrightarrow \theta_i \models \gamma$$
$$(\mathcal{S}, \rho, i) \models \varphi\,\mathbf{U}_{[\tau \geq b]}\,\psi :\Leftrightarrow \exists_{j \geq i} : (\mathcal{S}, \rho, j) \models \psi \text{ and } \llbracket \tau \rrbracket(\#_{i, j-1}^{\mathcal{S}, \rho}) \geq b$$
$$\text{and } \forall_{i \leq k < j} : (\mathcal{S}, \rho, k) \models \varphi$$

where $\#_{i,j}^{\mathcal{S},\rho} : \mathsf{CLTL} \to \mathbb{N}$ denotes the function mapping a CLTL formula χ to the number

$$\#_{i,j}^{\mathcal{S},\rho}(\chi) := |\{k \mid i \leq k \leq j, (\mathcal{S}, \rho, k) \models \chi\}|$$

of positions on ρ between i and j satisfying it. Notice that this is well-defined because the mutual recursion descends towards strict subformulae. We write $(\mathcal{S}, \rho) \models \chi$ if $(\mathcal{S}, \rho, 0) \models \chi$ and $\mathcal{S} \models \chi$ if there is $\rho \in \mathrm{runs}(\mathcal{S})$ with $(\mathcal{S}, \rho) \models \chi$.

The logic fLTL [6] features a dedicated *frequency-until* operator $\mathbf{U}^{\frac{a}{b}}$ for $a, b \in \mathbb{N}$ and $a \leq b > 0$ that can be considered as restricted variant of $\mathbf{U}_{[\cdot]}$. An fLTL formula $\varphi \, \mathbf{U}^{\frac{a}{b}} \, \psi$ specifies that a formula φ holds at least at a fraction $0 \leq \frac{a}{b} \leq 1$ of all positions before some position satisfying ψ. This is equivalently expressed in CLTL by $\mathrm{true} \, \mathbf{U}_{[b \cdot \varphi - a \cdot \mathrm{true} \geq 0]} \, \psi$.

Model Checking. We target the *existential model-checking problem* for CLTL. Given a counter system $\mathcal{S}$ and a CLTL formula Φ the task is to decide whether $\mathcal{S} \models \Phi$, i.e., to compute if $\mathcal{S}$ contains a run satisfying Φ. The problem is undecidable for two reasons: First, counter systems extend Minsky machines [28] and even LTL can express their undecidable (control-state) reachability problem. Second, CLTL extends fLTL and checking a universal Kripke structure encodes its undecidable satisfiability problem [6]. We therefore approach a parametrised approximation of the problem that considers only runs with a specific shape, namely those represented by so-called *path schemas*. A path schema [15,27] is characterised by a (connected) sequence $u_0 v_0 u_1 v_1 \ldots u_n v_n$ of paths u_i and cycles v_i of $\mathcal{S}$. It represents all those runs ρ of $\mathcal{S}$ that traverse a state sequence of the form $u_0 v_0^{\ell_0} \ldots u_{n-1} v_{n-1}^{\ell_{n-1}} u_n v_n^{\omega}$. Restricting the length of such a schema effectively controls how complicated the shape of the considered runs can be. In particular, it bounds the cycle alternation performed by a run.

Definition 1 (Flat model checking). *Let $\mathcal{S} = (S, \Delta, s_I, \lambda)$ be a counter system and $n \in \mathbb{N}$. The* flat approximation *of depth n of $\mathcal{S}$ is the set $\mathsf{FA}(\mathcal{S}, n) \subseteq \mathrm{runs}(\mathcal{S})$ such that, for all $\rho = (s_0, \theta_0)(s_1, \theta_1) \ldots \in \mathrm{runs}(\mathcal{S})$,*

$$\rho \in \mathsf{FA}(\mathcal{S}, n) \Leftrightarrow \exists_{u_0, v_0, \ldots, u_m, v_m \in S^*} : |u_0 v_0 u_1 v_1 \ldots u_m v_m| \leq n$$

$$\wedge \, \exists_{k_0, \ldots, k_{m-1} \in \mathbb{N}} : s_0 s_1 \ldots = u_0 v_0^{k_0} \ldots u_{m-1} v_{m-1}^{k_{m-1}} u_m v_m^{\omega}.$$

The flat model-checking problem *is to decide for a given CLTL formula φ, whether there is a run $\rho \in \mathsf{FA}(\mathcal{S}, n)$ with $(\mathcal{S}, \rho) \models \varphi$, denoted $\mathsf{FA}(\mathcal{S}, n) \models \varphi$.*

A flat approximation $\mathsf{FA}(\mathcal{S}, n)$ induces a flat counter system $\mathcal{F}$ such that $\mathsf{FA}(\mathcal{S}, n) = \mathrm{runs}(\mathcal{F})$ and thus a series $(\mathcal{F}_n)_{n \in \mathbb{N}}$ of flat counter systems representing an increasing number of runs of $\mathcal{S}$. Flat model checking can hence be understood as verifying the nth system in this series providing the computational benefits of flatness in the concrete case. As mentioned earlier, this is similar to bounded model checking, where the approximation is prefix-based and represents only a finite number of runs.

3 Model Checking CLTL over Flat Counter Systems

This section is dedicated to lifting the technique for model-checking fLTL over flat Kripke structures [13] to CLTL and flat counter systems. The central aspect is the definition of *augmented path schemas (APS)* and the notion of *consistency*. We observe that consistent APS are suitable witnesses for runs because they are of bounded size and exist if a formula is satisfied. The QPA encoding of the flat-model-checking problem presented in Sect. 4 builds on these definitions. To simplify notation, we fix in this section a counter system $S = (S_S, \Delta_S, s_I, \lambda)$ and a CLTL formula Φ, both over counters C_S. Augmented path schemas [13] extend path schemas by a labelling that provides additional information, as well as counters and guards to constrain the set of runs of an APS beyond a specific shape. The following definition extends that of [13] to take the counters and guards of S into account. See Fig. 1 for an example.

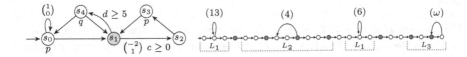

Fig. 1. A counter system S over propositions $AP = \{p, q\}$ as labels and counters $\{c, d\}$, and (a sketch of) an APS $\mathcal{P}$ in S that alternates the loops $L_1 = s_0$ and $L_2 = s_1 s_2 s_3$ of S. Associating with each loop of $\mathcal{P}$ a number of iterations (potentially) identifies one specific run of S that is represented by $\mathcal{P}$.

Definition 2 (APS). *An* augmented path schema (APS) *in S is a structure $\mathcal{P} = (Q, \Delta_\mathcal{P}, \lambda_\mathcal{P}, \text{org})$ where*

- *$(Q, \Delta_\mathcal{P}, q_0, \lambda_\mathcal{P})$ is a flat counter system over $Q = \{q_0, \ldots, q_n\}$, for some $n \in \mathbb{N}$, with labelling $\lambda_\mathcal{P} : Q \to 2^{\text{sub}(\Phi) \cup AP}$ and simple path $q_0 \ldots q_n$;*
- *$\text{org} : Q \to S_S$ maps every state to an origin such that $\lambda_\mathcal{P}(q) \cap AP = \lambda_S(\text{org}(q)) \cap AP$ and $\text{org}(q_0) = s_I$;*
- *for each transition $(q, \mu, \Gamma, q') \in \Delta_\mathcal{P}$ there is $(\text{org}(q), \hat{\mu}, \hat{\Gamma}, \text{org}(q')) \in \Delta_S$ with $\hat{\Gamma} \subseteq \Gamma$ and $\hat{\mu}(c) = \mu(c)$ for all $c \in C_S$;*
- *$\Delta_\mathcal{P} = \Delta_{fwd} \cup \Delta_{bwd}$ is comprised of* forward- *and* backward transitions *where*
  - *$\Delta_{fwd} = \{(q_0, \mu_0, \Gamma_0, q_1), \ldots, (q_{n-1}, \mu_{n-1}, \Gamma_{n-1}, q_n)\}$,*
  - *there is $(q_n, \mu_n, \Gamma_n, q_{n'}) \in \Delta_{bwd}$, for $n' \leq n$, closing the last loop, and*
  - *for all $(q_j, \mu, \Gamma, q_i), (q_k, \mu', \Gamma', q_h) \in \Delta_{bwd}$ we have $i \leq j, h \leq k$, and the corresponding loops $q_h q_{h+1} \ldots q_k$ and $q_i q_{i+1} \ldots q_j$ are disjoint; and*
- *for each loop $L = q_i q_{i+1} \ldots q_{i+\ell}$ there is a front row $F = q_{i-\ell-1} \ldots q_{i-1}$ and, if $i + \ell < n$, a rear row $R = q_{i+\ell+1} \ldots q_{i+2\ell+1}$ with identical labelling $\lambda_\mathcal{P}(q_{i-\ell-1}) \ldots \lambda_\mathcal{P}(q_{i-1}) = \lambda_\mathcal{P}(q_i) \ldots \lambda_\mathcal{P}(q_{i+\ell}) = \lambda_\mathcal{P}(q_{i+\ell+1}) \ldots \lambda_\mathcal{P}(q_{i+2\ell+1}).$*

The paths, loops, rows, and runs of $\mathcal{P}$ are those of the underlying counter system where the latter are restricted to those visiting the last state q_n of $\mathcal{P}$. The mapping org is lifted from states to paths and runs as expected, restricting the valuations to the counters C_S of S. Then, for every run ρ of $\mathcal{P}$, the sequence $\text{org}(\rho)$ is a run of S starting in $\text{org}(q_I) = s_I$. We denote by $\text{lastl}(\mathcal{P}) := q_{n'} \ldots q_n$

the last loop of $\mathcal{P}$. Observe that the definition requires each loop to be preceded and (except for $\mathrm{lastl}(\mathcal{P})$) succeeded by state sequences that may be considered as an *unfolding* regarding the labelling sequence. These front and rear rows are needed for technical reasons to cover edge-cases in reasoning on the first and last loop iteration, respectively.

We are interested in APS that provide a semantically correct labelling because they allow us to reason syntactically on where a particular formula is satisfied.

Definition 3 (Correctness). *A state* $q \in Q$ *of an APS* $\mathcal{P}$ *is correctly labelled with respect to a* CLTL *formula* $\varphi \in \mathrm{sub}(\Phi)$ *if for all runs* $\rho = (q_0, \theta_0)(q_1, \theta_1) \ldots \in$ $\mathrm{runs}(\mathcal{P})$ *and all positions* $x \in \mathbb{N}$ *with* $q_x = q$ *we have* $(\mathcal{S}, \mathrm{org}(\rho), x) \models \varphi \Leftrightarrow \varphi \in$ $\lambda_{\mathcal{P}}(q)$.

This notion is very strict in the sense that the annotation must *always* be in line with the CLTL semantics. Observe that there may not even exist a correct labelling for a particular state: if the latter resides on a loop it may occur more than once on some run and a formula Φ may hold at one of them but not at the other (e.g., because Φ imposes a minimal number of iterations to follow). However, an APS in $\mathcal{S}$ that is actually correctly labelled witnesses the existence of a run satisfying Φ in case it is non-empty and its initial state is labelled by Φ. In [13], the syntactic criterion called *consistency* was introduced in order to characterise APS that are labelled correctly with respect to fLTL formulae. We generalise the definition and the results to CLTL, i.e., from relative frequencies to arbitrary linear constraints and from Kripke structures to counter systems.

Consider an APS $\mathcal{P} = (Q, \Delta_{\mathcal{P}}, \lambda_{\mathcal{P}}, \mathrm{org})$ using counters $C_{\mathcal{P}} \supseteq C_{\mathcal{S}}$ where $q_0 \ldots q_n$ is the unique simple path traversing all states of $\mathcal{P}$. The criterion distinguishes the syntactical forms of a CLTL formula based on the top most operator and identifies for each case syntactical conditions that certify satisfaction or violation of a corresponding formula. Further subordinate cases formulate individual conditions to matching the various situations that may apply to a control state, e.g., whether it is on a loop or not. Before presenting the formal definition, let us discuss the rationale of the individual conditions.

Consistency for Non-until Formulae. The simplest case is that of propositions, because these labels are correct by definition. Recall that constraints $\gamma \in \mathfrak{C}(C_{\mathcal{S}})$ over system counters, e.g. $c_1 - 2c_2 \geq 0$, are not only valid atomic CLTL formulae but also valid transition guards. Therefore, the reasoning on their satisfaction can directly be moved to the level of the counter system. If all incoming transitions of a state $q \in Q$ are guarded by some constraint γ, then every valid run necessarily satisfies it whenever visiting q. Similarly, if these transitions are guarded by the dual constraint $\overline{\gamma}$, then γ can not hold at any occurrence of q on any run.

If Φ is a Boolean combination, correctness can be established locally for any state q when inductively assuming that q is labelled correctly by all the strict subformulae. For example, a negation $\neg\varphi$ holds on all runs at all positions of a state q if and only if on all runs φ does not hold at q. With the assumption that the labelling with respect to φ is correct, labelling q by $\neg\varphi$ is correct if and only if q is not labelled by φ, and vice versa. Similar reasoning applies to conjunctions and the temporal operator **X**.

Consistency for Until Formulae Using Balance Counters. For counted until formulae, we also make use of the counting capabilities of the system model, although the reasoning is more involved. Consider Φ to have the form $\varphi\, \mathbf{U}_{[\tau \geq b]}\, \psi$, and let $q, q' \in Q$ be row states such that $q' \in \mathrm{suc}^*_{\mathcal{P}}(q)$ is a successor of q and (correctly) labelled by ψ. Assume that the states in-between q and q' are correctly labelled by φ. In order to establish that Φ holds at state q on any run, it remains to enforce the counting constraint on the intermediate segment. To this end, also assume that $\mathcal{P}$ features a counter $c_{\tau,q}$ that tracks the value of the term τ as a *balance* that starts with zero at q and is updated according to the effect that each individual state would have on the value of τ. For example, if $\tau = p_1 - 2p_2$, then the counter is updated by $+1$ on every outgoing transition of a state labelled by p_1, because this is what each such state contributes to the term value. The counter would be update by -2 on the outgoing transitions, if the state is labelled by p_2, and consequently by $1 - 2 = -1$ if it carries both labels. Then, upon reaching q' along some run, the counter $c_{\tau,q}$ would hold precisely the value of the counting term τ evaluated on the intermediate path taken from q to q'. If the incoming (forward) transition of q' is now labelled by the guard $c_{t,q} \geq b$, then Φ can be assumed to hold whenever a valid run visits q because q' is certainly visited and will then serve as witness. Dually, if *all* such potential witness states q' are guarded instead by the dual constraint $c_{t,q} < b$, then there is no way a valid run could satisfy Φ when visiting q.

Definition 4 (Balance counter). *Let $\mathcal{P} = (Q, \Delta_{\mathcal{P}}, \lambda_{\mathcal{P}}, \mathrm{org})$ be an APS in $\mathcal{S}$ with counters $C_{\mathcal{P}}$. Let τ be a constraint term over $\mathrm{sub}(\Phi)$, and $q \in Q$ a row state in $\mathcal{P}$. A* balance counter *for τ and q in $\mathcal{P}$ is a counter $c_{\tau,q} \in C_{\mathcal{P}}$ that is updated, on all transitions $(q_1, \mu, \Gamma, q_2) \in \Delta_{\mathcal{P}}$, by*

$$\mu(c_{\tau,q}) = \begin{cases} 0 & \textit{if } q_1 \notin \mathrm{suc}^*_{\mathcal{P}}(q) \\ [\![\tau]\!](\lambda^{\#}_{\mathcal{P}}(q_1)) & \textit{otherwise.} \end{cases}$$

In combination with appropriately guarded states, balance counters allow us to reason syntactically about the satisfaction of Φ. Such counters are particularly useful to track the value of a term across an entire loop, even if some runs of $\mathcal{P}$ iterate it more often than others.

Static Consistency Conditions for Until Formulae. If there is no entire loop between two states q and q', using a counter is still possible but not necessary. Each run passes precisely once the (unique) path between q and q', so whether or not q' witnesses satisfaction of Φ at q can be determined statically, independently of the precise course of the run in other parts. While the existence of a balance counter and appropriate guards imply that a formula is satisfied, it would be too restrictive to consider this as only option. There are situations where satisfaction of a formula can not be witnessed by a balance counter. For example, if a witness state q' is part of a loop, a corresponding guard may be satisfied at one of its occurrences on a run but not at all of them. While the consistency criterion is intended to be strong enough to imply correctness, it shall also admit a sufficiently large class of APS to represent all reasons for satisfaction (and violation). Therefore, the definition admits also the static reasoning.

A further case treated explicitly concerns the effect of the *last loop*. If traversing it once exhibits a positive effect on the evaluation of τ, then it dominates the effects of all other loops, since it is traversed infinitely often. Therefore, if it can be reached from q and traversed once without violating φ, and contains some witness state labelled by ψ, then Φ is necessarily satisfied when a run reaches q.

Finally, the last case considered by the consistency criterion is concerned with the satisfaction of Φ when visiting states that are situated directly on a loops: If Φ holds at the first occurrence of a state q on a run *and* at the last, then the formula holds also at all occurrences of q in-between. The reason is, essentially, that the effect of one iteration of a loop on the value of the term τ is always the same (at least, if the labelling by all subformulae is correct, as we have assumed). Therefore, the worst (i.e., smallest) value of τ is encountered either in the first or the last iteration. Augmented path schemas are defined to feature for each loop a preceding and a succeeding row that are exact copies and can be considered as *unfoldings*. Hence, if these are correctly labelled with respect to Φ, then the loop labelling inherits their correctness.

Using the above reasoning, it can be shown that the following definition of consistency is a sufficient criterion for correctness. It extends that of [13] to the present context and accounts for the various subtleties arising from the different cases.

Definition 5 (Consistency). *Let $\mathcal{P} = (Q, \Delta_{\mathcal{P}}, \lambda_{\mathcal{P}}, \mathrm{org})$ be an APS in $\mathcal{S}$ with $|Q| = n$, simple path $q_0 \ldots q_{n-1}$, and φ a* CLTL *formula. A state $q_i \in Q$ is φ-consistent if $\varphi \in AP$ is an atomic proposition or*

(A) $\varphi = (\tau \geq b) \in \mathfrak{C}(C)$, all incoming transitions $(q, \mu, \Gamma, q_i) \in \Delta_{\mathcal{P}}$ are guarded by $\varphi \in \Gamma$ if $\varphi \in \lambda_{\mathcal{P}}(q_i)$ and by $\overline{\varphi} \in \Gamma$ otherwise, and if $i = 0$, then $\varphi \in \lambda_{\mathcal{P}}(q_i) \Leftrightarrow 0 \geq b$.

For non-atomic formulae φ, the state q_i is φ-consistent if for all $\psi \in \mathrm{sub}(\varphi) \backslash \{\varphi\}$ all states $q \in Q$ are ψ-consistent and one of the following condition B to D applies.

(B) $\varphi = \chi \wedge \psi$ and $\varphi \in \lambda_{\mathcal{P}}(q_i) \Leftrightarrow \chi, \psi \in \lambda_{\mathcal{P}}(q_i)$; or $\varphi = \neg\psi$ and $\neg\psi \in \lambda_{\mathcal{P}}(q_i) \Leftrightarrow \psi \notin \lambda_{\mathcal{P}}(q_i)$.

(C) $\varphi = \mathbf{X}\,\psi$ and $\mathbf{X}\psi \in \lambda_{\mathcal{P}}(q_i) \Leftrightarrow \psi \in \lambda_{\mathcal{P}}(q)$, for all $q \in \mathrm{suc}_{\mathcal{P}}(q_i)$.

(D) $\varphi = \chi\,\mathbf{U}_{[\tau \geq b]}\,\psi$ and one of the following holds:

*   1. $\varphi \in \lambda_{\mathcal{P}}(q_i)$, $[\![\tau]\!](\lambda_{\mathcal{P}}^{\#}(\mathrm{lastl}(\mathcal{P}))) > 0$, $\psi \in \lambda_{\mathcal{P}}(q)$ for some $q \in \mathrm{lastl}(\mathcal{P})$, and $\chi \in \lambda_{\mathcal{P}}(q')$ for all $q' \in \mathrm{suc}_{\mathcal{P}}^*(q_i)$.*

2. *The state q_i is not part of a loop. If $\varphi \notin \lambda_\mathcal{P}(q_i)$, then $\psi \notin \lambda_\mathcal{P}(q_i)$ or $0 < b$. Further, if $\varphi \notin \lambda_\mathcal{P}(q_i)$, then*

   (i) *there is some $k \geq i$ such that $\chi \notin \lambda_\mathcal{P}(q_k)$ and, for each $j \in [i,k]$, $|\mathrm{suc}_\mathcal{P}(q_j)| = 1$ and $\psi \in \lambda_\mathcal{P}(q_j) \Rightarrow [\![\tau]\!](\lambda_\mathcal{P}^\#(q_i \ldots q_{j-1})) < b$ or*

   (ii) *$\mathcal{P}$ contains a balance counter $c_{\tau,i} \in C_\mathcal{P}$ for τ and q_i, and the guard $(c_{\tau,i} < b) \in \Gamma$ for all $(q, \mu, \Gamma, q_j) \in \Delta_\mathcal{P}$ where $j > i$, $\psi \in \lambda_\mathcal{P}(q_j)$, and $\forall_{k \in [i,j-1]} : \chi \in \lambda_\mathcal{P}(q_k)$.*

   If $\varphi \in \lambda_\mathcal{P}(q_i)$, then there is $k \geq i$ with $\psi \in \lambda_\mathcal{P}(q_k)$, $\forall_{j \in [i,k-1]} : \chi \in \lambda_\mathcal{P}(q_j)$, and

   (iii) *$[\![\tau]\!](\lambda_\mathcal{P}^\#(q_i \ldots q_{k-1})) \geq b$ and $\forall_{j \in [i,k-1]} : |\mathrm{suc}_\mathcal{P}(q_j)| = 1$, or*

   (iv) *$k > i$ and $\mathcal{P}$ contains a balance counter $c_{\tau,i} \in C_\mathcal{P}$ for τ and q_i, and the unique transition from q_{k-1} to q_k has the form $(q_{k-1}, \mu, \Gamma \cup \{c_{\tau,i} \geq b\}, q_k) \in \Delta_\mathcal{P}$.*

3. *q_i is on some loop L of $\mathcal{P}$, and $q_{i-|L|}$ and $q_{i+|L|}$ (if $L \neq \mathrm{lastl}(\mathcal{P})$) are φ-consistent.*

The APS $\mathcal{P}$, a loop, or a row in $\mathcal{P}$ are φ-consistent if all their states are φ-consistent, respectively.

Using a structural induction on a CLTL formula φ we can show that if some state of an APS is φ-consistent, then the state is correctly labelled by that formula. The base cases those of atomic propositions and guards, concerning condition A of Definition 5. The remaining conditions cover the inductive cases for the potential shape of φ and rely on the fact that the definition demands all states to be consistent with respect to each strict subformula of φ. The proof relies on a thorough investigation of each syntactic case in combination with various specific situations that states can be found in, as discussed above. It has to deal with the sometimes quite subtle interplay between temporal counting constraints and iterated loops and we omit the technicalities of the proof here in favour of conciseness.

Theorem 6 (Correctness). *If a state q of an APS $\mathcal{P}$ in $\mathcal{S}$ is φ-consistent, then it is labelled correctly with respect to φ.*

Consequently, a non-empty APS in $\mathcal{S}$ of which the initial state is Φ-consistent and labelled by Φ witnesses that $\mathcal{S} \models \Phi$.

Existence of Consistent APS in Flat Systems. Although consistency imposes a very specific shape, it can be shown that for a significant class of systems there is always a Φ-consistent APS (of bounded size) if the formula Φ is satisfied. The construction for fLTL over flat Kripke structures [13] extends with Definition 5 to CLTL.

Assume $\mathcal{S}$ is flat and let $\sigma \in \mathrm{runs}(\mathcal{S})$ be a run that satisfies Φ. In the following we sketch how to construct a Φ-consistent APS in $\mathcal{S}$ that contains (a representation of) σ and is thus labelled by Φ at its initial state. It is known that each path in a flat structure can be represented by some path schema of linear size [2,15]. Hence, let $\mathcal{P}$ be an APS containing a run $\rho \in \mathrm{runs}(\mathcal{P})$ with

$\mathrm{org}_\mathcal{P}(\rho) = \sigma$ and thus satisfying Φ. The states of this APS can now recursively be labelled by the subformulae of Φ as semantically determined by ρ.

The conditions of Definition 5 can be realised for Φ under the assumption, that the labelling has been completed for each strict subformula. The construction distinguishes which case applies to Φ. If Φ is an atomic proposition, nothing needs to be done since the labelling is consistent by definition. Boolean combinations can be realised by simply adjusting the labelling locally for each state of $\mathcal{P}$, e.g., including $\Phi = \neg\varphi$ in the labelling of a state if and only if it is not labelled by φ. Assume Φ has the form $\mathbf{X}\,\varphi$. Depending on whether the successor states of a state q are labelled by φ or not, q is labelled by $\mathbf{X}\,\varphi$ or not. Notice that all successors of a state have the same labelling because either there is only one or the state is the last state of some loop. In the latter case, the successors are the first states of the loop and its rear copy and thus share the same labelling (cf. Definition 2).

For the remaining types of formulae, i.e., until formulae and constraints over system counters, the structure of $\mathcal{P}$ may have to be altered, in order to provide a consistent labelling *and* to retain a valid run ρ (as representation of σ). The essential difficulties concern loop states because these may occur at more than one position on ρ. A subformula φ may then be satisfied at some, but not all of these positions. For example, consistency for a constraint formula $\gamma = \tau \geq b$ and a state q demands to add γ or its dual to every incoming transition of q, depending on whether we want to label it by γ or not. Clearly, the guards can simply be added and this would settle consistency. However, if γ is satisfied at one occurrence of q on ρ but not at another, the guards would be violated at one of these positions and ρ would not be valid anymore. To establish consistency for until formulae, we may have to add a fresh balance counter to the system and similar issues may arise. It may therefore be necessary to introduce copies of a state in order to distinguish the positions of the state and label them differently in the APS. The important observation is that during the iteration of a loop the validity of a formula φ at some state switches at most once, assuming the APS is labelled consistently by all subformulae already. Therefore, loops may have to be *duplicated* once for each subformula, one copy where on all iterations φ holds and one where it does not. The recursive labelling procedure may therefore increase the size of $\mathcal{P}$ exponentially.

Theorem 7 (Existence). *If $\mathcal{S}$ is flat and $\mathcal{S} \models \Phi$ then there is a non-empty and Φ-consistent APS in $\mathcal{S}$ with initial state labelled by Φ and of at most exponential size in $\mathcal{S}$ and Φ.*

Notice that, even if $\mathcal{S}$ is *not flat*, each run contained in the flat approximation $\mathsf{FA}(\mathcal{S}, n)$ of $\mathcal{S}$ can by definition be represented by an APS in $\mathcal{S}$ of size n. Therefore, the construction applied to $\mathsf{FA}(\mathcal{S}, n)$ also yields an exponential witness.

Corollary 8. *If $\mathsf{FA}(\mathcal{S}, n) \models \Phi$ then there is a non-empty and Φ-consistent APS in $\mathcal{S}$ with initial state labelled by Φ and of at most exponential size in n and Φ.*

4   From Flat Model Checking to Presburger Arithmetic

For solving the flat model-checking problem of a counter system $\mathcal{S} = (S, \Delta, s_I, \lambda)$ over counters $C_{\mathcal{S}}$ and a $\mathsf{CLTL}(C_{\mathcal{S}})$ formula Φ, the developments in the previous section devise the search for an augmented path schema $\mathcal{P}$ in $\mathcal{S}$ that is Φ-consistent, labelled initially by Φ and non-empty. In the following we sketch a formulation of this search in quantifier-free Presburger arithmetic, aiming at an SMT-based implementation.

The idea is to encode an APS of size $n \in \mathbb{N}$ and a run of it as valuation of a set of first-order variables. We construct a formula $\mathrm{fmc}(\mathcal{S}, \Phi, n)$ that is satisfiable if there is a run $\rho \in \mathsf{FA}(\mathcal{S}, n)$ satisfying Φ and such that any solution represents a valid witness that $\mathcal{S} \models \Phi$. Without restriction, we need only to represent APS $\mathcal{P} = (Q, \Delta_{\mathcal{P}}, \lambda_{\mathcal{P}}, \mathrm{org})$ where the states are natural numbers $Q = [0, n - 1]$. The natural ordering implicitly determines the unique maximal simple path in $\mathcal{P}$. It hence suffices to encode explicitly the beginning and end of loops, the origin and labelling of each state, as well as a valid run. Further, the formula expresses the satisfaction of all encountered guards and the consistency criterion.

For convenience, we use not only first-order variables for integer numbers but also boolean, enumeration and natural number types (sorts). They can, theoretically, be encoded into integers but are more readable and directly supported by, e.g., the z3 SMT solver. We use notation of the form var $: X$ to denote that some variable symbol var is of some sort X. Mappings with some finite domain Y can be represented by variable vectors of length $|Y|$ that we denote concisely by single variable symbols var $: X^Y$. The shorthand $\mathrm{ite}(\mathrm{cond}, \mathrm{prop}, \mathrm{alt})$ represents the *if-then-else* construct. Figure 2 depicts an example of an APS $\mathcal{P}$ and its representation in terms of first-order variables and their valuation. For every state $i \in Q$, we encode the positions of loops in terms of a variable $\mathsf{typ}_i : \{⊟, ▷, ⊞, ◁\}$ that indicates whether it is outside ($⊟$), inside ($⊞$), the beginning ($▷$), or the end ($◁$) of a loop. We use $\diamond_i$ to abbreviate $\mathsf{typ}_i = \diamond$ for $\diamond \in \{⊟, ▷, ⊞, ◁\}$. The origin is represented by a variable $\mathsf{org}_i : S$ and the labelling by $\mathsf{lbl}_i : \{0,1\}^{\mathrm{sub}(\Phi)}$, describing the set $\lambda_{\mathcal{P}}(i) \subseteq \mathrm{sub}(\Phi)$. The formula

$$\mathrm{fmc}(\mathcal{S}, \Phi, n) := \mathrm{aps}(\mathcal{S}, n) \wedge \mathrm{run}(\mathcal{S}, n) \wedge \mathrm{consistency}(n, \Phi) \wedge \Phi \in \mathsf{lbl}_0$$

specifies the shape of $\mathcal{P}$, a run and that the initial state is labelled by Φ. The formula components are discussed next.

Basic Structure of APS. The basic structure is easily specified as QPA formula $\mathrm{aps}(\mathcal{S}, n)$. It states that s_I is the origin of the first state ($\mathsf{org}_0 = s_I$), that loops are delimited by $▷$ and $◁$, and that the labelling of states by propositions coincides with that of $\mathcal{S}$.

A way to express that the backward transitions from the last to the first state of the loops has a correspondence in $\mathcal{S}$ is to build a constraint over all pairs of states from Q. This is, however, quadratic in n and we therefore use a propagation scheme introducing n additional variables $\mathsf{orgAtEnd}_i : S$. We let them equal org_i where $\mathsf{typ}_i = ◁$ and otherwise be copied from $\mathsf{orgAtEnd}_{i+1}$,

Diagram (states 0–14 with transitions):

Above state 1 and 2: $\binom{1}{0}$; over state 2: $\binom{1}{0}$; between 3 and 7: $c\geq 0$ $\binom{-2}{1}$, $c\geq 0$, $d\geq 5$; above 8 and 9: $\binom{1}{0}$; $d\geq 5$ between 9–10; $d\geq 5$ loop at 13.

i	0	1	2	3	4	5	6	7	8	9	10	11	12	13	14
typ_i	⊟	▷	◁	⊟	▷	⊞	◁	⊟	▷	◁	⊟	⊟	⊟	▷	◁
org_i	s_0	s_0	s_0	s_1	s_2	s_3	s_1	s_4	s_0	s_0	s_1	s_4	s_0	s_1	s_4
itr_i		7	7		6	6	6		4	4				0	0
valFst_i	0	1	2		14	14	14		4	5				17	17
	0	0	0		0	0	0		5	5				5	5
lUpd_i		12	6		−10	0	0		12	6					
		0	0		5	0	0		0	0					
valLst_i	13	14	14	4	4	4	4	4	16	17	17	17	17	17	17
	0	0	0	5	5	5	5	5	5	5	5	5	5	5	5
lbl_i	p,φ	p,φ	p,φ	$\emptyset$	φ	p,φ	φ	q,φ	p,φ	p,φ	$\emptyset$	q,φ	p,φ	$\emptyset$	q,φ
maxFst_i^φ	14	13	12	−1	0	1	0	6	7	6	−1	0	0	−1	0
updFst_i^φ	14	13	12	−1	0	1	0	6	7	6	−1	−1	0	−1	
sumEff_i^t			2·6					−1·5		2·3					
maxLst_i^φ	14	1	0	−1	5	6	5	6	1	0	−1	0	0		
updLst_i^φ	14	1	0	−1	5	6	5	6	1	0	−1	−1	0		

Fig. 2. Example of the encoding of the run and path schema from Fig. 1 with consistent labelling by $\varphi = \text{true}\ \mathbf{U}_{[p-\neg p\geq 0]}\ q$. It demonstrates propagation of counter values and the maximal witness position for φ. Some variables are omitted for conciseness.

thus propagating backward the origin of the last state of every loop. The formula $\bigwedge_{i=0}^{n-1} \triangleright_i \rightarrow \bigvee_{(s,\mu,\Gamma,s')\in\Delta} \text{orgAtEnd}_i=s \wedge \text{org}_i=s'$ then guarantees that all backward transitions exist in $\mathcal{S}$. Forward transitions are specified similarly. We assume a minimal loop length of 2 due to distinct positions for the first ($\triangleright$) and the last ($\triangleleft$) state of each loop but single-state loops can still be represented (cf. Fig. 2) while increasing the upper bound for the size of path schemas only by one state per loop. Definition 2 demands that loops be surrounded by identical rows which are not represented explicitly in the encoding. Instead, runs are required to traverse each representation of a loop at least three times, the first representing the front, the last representing the rear and the remaining representing the actual loop traversals. The construction distinguishes between the first, second, and last iteration where necessary.

To allow for a simplified presentation, let us assume that there is at most one transition between every two states of $\mathcal{S}$, thus being uniquely identified by org_i and org_{i+1}. The assumption could be eliminated by adding $2n$ additional variables determining explicitly which transition is selected for the represented APS.

Runs. The formula $\text{run}(\mathcal{S}, n)$ specifies the shape and constraints of a run in the encoded schema. Variables $\text{itr}_i : \mathbb{N}$ indicate how often state $i \in Q$ is visited and are thus constraint to equal 1 outside loops and to stay constant inside each loop. Infinite iteration of the last loop is represented by the otherwise unused value 0.

To ensure that the represented run is valid it has to satisfy all the guards at any time. The variables $\mathsf{valFst}_i, \mathsf{valSec}_i, \mathsf{valLst}_i : \mathbb{Z}^{Cs}_\infty$ hold the counter valuations at state $i \in Q$ when the represented run visits it for the first, the second and the last time, respectively. Due to flatness each loop is entered and left only once. Since the guards of the counter system are linear inequalities and the updates are constant, it suffices to check them in the first and last iteration of a loop. For a term $\tau = \sum_{j=0}^{\ell} a_j c_j$ and a variable symbol var $: \mathbb{Z}^{Cs}$ let $\tau[\mathsf{var}] := \sum_{j=0}^{\ell} a_j \cdot \mathsf{var}(c_j)$ denote the substitution of the counter names by the variable symbol (representing the value of) $\mathsf{var}(c_j)$. The formula

$$\bigwedge_{i=1}^{n-1} \bigwedge_{(s,\mu,\Gamma,s')\in\Delta} \mathsf{org}_{i-1} = s \wedge \mathsf{org}_i = s'$$
$$\rightarrow \bigwedge_{(\tau\geq b)\in\Gamma} \tau[\mathsf{valFst}_i] \geq b \wedge (\neg\triangleright_i \rightarrow \tau[\mathsf{valLst}_i] \geq b)$$

then specifies that the encoded run satisfies the guards whenever taking a forward transition. Notice that the (forward) transition from state $i-1$ to state i is not taken at the beginning of the last iteration of a loop and thus, its guard must not be checked for the corresponding valuation. Instead, the guards of the *backward transition* pointing to i must be satisfied from the second iteration on, and are expressed similarly.

It remains to actually specify the counter valuations along the run. By definition, $\mathsf{valFst}_0 = 0$. Outside of loops ($\boxminus$) we impose $\mathsf{valFst}_i = \mathsf{valSec}_i = \mathsf{valLst}_i = \mathsf{valLst}_{i-1}+\mu$ where μ is the update of the transition from $i-1$ to i. Inside ($\boxplus$, $\triangleleft$) we let $\mathsf{valFst}_i = \mathsf{valFst}_{i-1} + \mu$, $\mathsf{valSec}_i = \mathsf{valSec}_{i-1} + \mu$ and $\mathsf{valLst}_i = \mathsf{valLst}_{i-1} + \mu$. At the beginning ($\triangleright$) of a loop the value in the first iteration is propagated as outside ($\mathsf{valFst}_i = \mathsf{valLst}_{i-1} + \mu$), but for the second iteration we impose $\mathsf{valSec}_i = \mathsf{valFstAtEnd}_i + \mu$ where μ comes from the incoming *backward transition* and is applied to the last value of the previous iteration propagated as above using variables $\mathsf{valFstAtEnd}_i$.

Having a direct handle on the valuations in the first and second iteration (in terms of the variables valFst_i and valSec_i) as well as the total number of loop iterations (itr_i), it is tempting to specify the valuations in the last iteration simply by
$$\mathsf{valLst}_i = \mathsf{valFst}_i + (\mathsf{valSec}_i - \mathsf{valFst}_i) \cdot (\mathsf{itr}_i - 1).$$

Unfortunately, this formula uses multiplication of variables and hence exceeds Presburger arithmetic. Instead, the updates over the second to last loop iteration are accumulated in an explicit variable lUpd_i such that valLst_i can be set to $\mathsf{valFst}_i + \mathsf{lUpd}_i$. We express this accumulation by the formula

$$\bigwedge_{\substack{i\in[1,n-2]\\(s,\mu,\Gamma,s')\in\Delta}} \left(\begin{array}{ll} (\triangleleft_i \wedge \mathsf{org}_{i-1} = s \wedge \mathsf{org}_i = s' & \rightarrow \mathsf{lUpd}_i = \mu \cdot \mathsf{itr}_i - \mu) \\ \wedge\ (\boxplus_i \wedge \mathsf{org}_{i-1} = s \wedge \mathsf{org}_i = s' & \rightarrow \mathsf{lUpd}_i = \mu \cdot \mathsf{itr}_i - \mu + \mathsf{lUpd}_{i+1}) \\ \wedge\ (\triangleright_i \wedge \mathsf{orgAtEnd}_i = s \wedge \mathsf{org}_i = s' \rightarrow \mathsf{lUpd}_i = \mu \cdot \mathsf{itr}_i - \mu + \mathsf{lUpd}_{i+1}) \end{array} \right).$$

Essentially, the multiplication by itr_i is distributed over the individual transition updates along the loop. This is admissible because the individual updates μ appear in the formula not as variables but as constants. In the formulation above,

lUpd_i is always zero for states i on the last loop but this is no problem because this particular situation can be handled using valFst_i and valSec_i. Observe also that the variable lUpd_i holds only intermediate results inside and at the end of loops and is undefined outside. Only for states i that are the beginning of a loop, it holds the precise accumulated loop effect and this value is used for propagation as above.

Using lUpd_i, the calculation of the valuations in the last iteration of a loop is now specified by $\mathsf{valLst}_i = \mathsf{valFst}_i + \mathsf{lUpd}_i$. In the infinitely repeated last loop of the schema, there is no actual last iteration, but the variables are nevertheless used to indicate the limit behaviour by specifying

$$\bigwedge_{c \in C_S} \quad (\mathsf{valFst}_i(c) = \mathsf{valSec}_i(c) = \mathsf{valLst}_i(c))$$
$$\vee \, (\mathsf{valFst}_i(c) > \mathsf{valSec}_i(c) \wedge \mathsf{valLst}_i(c) = -\infty)$$
$$\vee \, (\mathsf{valFst}_i(c) < \mathsf{valSec}_i(c) \wedge \mathsf{valLst}_i(c) = \infty).$$

Consistency. The formulae constructed above describe a non-empty augmented path schema in $\mathcal{S}$ of which the first state is labelled by $\varPhi$. In the following, we develop the components of the formula $\mathsf{consistency}(\mathcal{S}, n, \varPhi)$ expressing the different cases of Definition 5. Consistency for Boolean combinations (condition B) can almost literally be translated to QPA. Concerning condition A, constraints of the form $\tau \geq b$ are not modelled explicitly. Rather, the formula

$$(\tau \geq b) \in \mathsf{lbl}_i \leftrightarrow \tau[\mathsf{valFst}_i] \geq b \wedge \tau[\mathsf{valLst}_i] \geq b$$

imposes for each i that the represented run satisfies the constraints as if they were guards on all incoming transitions on any state labelled by an atomic constraint. To express condition C, variables $\mathsf{lblAtBeg}_i : 2^{\mathrm{sub}(\varPhi)}$ propagate labelling information from the start of a loop towards the end. The condition for formulae $\mathbf{X}\varphi \in \mathrm{sub}(\varPhi)$ is then specified by $(\mathbf{X}\varphi \in \mathsf{lbl}_{n-1} \leftrightarrow \varphi \in \mathsf{lblAtBeg}_{n-1})$ and for $0 \leq i \leq n-2$ by

$$\mathsf{ite}\big(\, \mathbf{X}\,\varphi{\in}\mathsf{lbl}_i, \; \varphi{\in}\mathsf{lbl}_{i+1} \wedge (\triangleleft_i \rightarrow \varphi{\in}\mathsf{lblAtBeg}_i), \; \varphi{\notin}\mathsf{lbl}_{i+1} \wedge (\triangleleft_i \rightarrow \varphi{\notin}\mathsf{lblAtBeg}_i)\big).$$

Until Condition D1. Consider a formula $\varphi = \chi \, \mathbf{U}_{[\tau \geq b]} \, \psi \in \mathrm{sub}(\varPhi)$. We first set up some propagations to be able to express condition D1. To access the accumulated value of τ on a single iteration of the last loop we introduce variables acc_i^τ for $i \in Q$. Let the formula $\mathsf{accu}(n, \tau)$ be defined as

$$(\mathsf{acc}_{n-1}^\tau = \tau[\mathsf{lbl}_{n-1}]) \wedge \bigwedge_{i=0}^{n-2} \mathsf{ite}(\mathsf{itr}_i = 0, \; \mathsf{acc}_i^\tau = \mathsf{acc}_{i+1}^\tau + \tau[\mathsf{lbl}_i], \; \mathsf{acc}_i^\tau = \mathsf{acc}_{i+1}^\tau).$$

It implies that acc_0^τ holds the effect of the last loop on the value of τ. Condition D1 requires that χ holds globally at all reachable states. For loop states this concerns not only larger states (with respect to $\geq$). The whole loop must be labelled by χ. Using variables prpg_i^χ and glob_i^χ for $i \in Q$ the formula

$$\mathsf{glob}(n, \chi) := (\mathsf{prpg}_{n-1}^\chi \leftrightarrow \chi \in \mathsf{lbl}_{n-1}) \wedge \left(\bigwedge_{i=0}^{n-2} \mathsf{prpg}_i^\chi \leftrightarrow \mathsf{prpg}_{i+1}^\chi \wedge \chi \in \mathsf{lbl}_i \right)$$
$$\wedge (\mathsf{glob}_0^\chi \leftrightarrow \mathsf{prpg}_0^\chi) \wedge \bigwedge_{i=1}^{n-1} \mathsf{glob}_i^\chi \leftrightarrow \mathsf{ite}(\boxminus_i \vee \triangleright_i, \, \mathsf{prpg}_i^\chi, \, \mathsf{glob}_{i-1}^\chi)$$

propagates this information through the structure by implying that glob_i^χ is true if and only if χ is labelled at all states reachable from i. The information whether ψ holds somewhere on the last loop is made available in terms of the variable onLast^ψ by

$$\mathrm{fin}(n, \psi) := \mathsf{onLast}^\psi \leftrightarrow \bigvee_{i=0}^{n-1} \mathsf{itr}_i = 0 \wedge \psi \in \mathsf{lbl}_i.$$

Then, condition (D1) is expressed by

$$\mathsf{conD1}(\varphi, i) := \varphi \in \mathsf{lbl}_i \wedge \mathsf{acc}_0^\tau > 0 \wedge \mathsf{onLast}^\psi \wedge \mathsf{glob}_i^\chi.$$

Until Condition D2. Condition D2 demands the existence or absence of a witness state proving that $\varphi = \chi \, \mathbf{U}_{[\tau \geq b]} \, \psi$ holds. As before, it would be inefficient to model balance counters and the guards required by the criterion explicitly. Instead, a formulation is developed that assures that the encoded APS can be assumed to have the necessary counters and guards. For example, assume some state i is to be labelled by φ and consider the best (maximal) value of the term τ on a path starting at state i and leading to some state satisfying ψ, without violating χ in between. If that value is at least b, then there is a state at which a balance counter $c_{\tau,i}$ for i and τ would have precisely that value and checking the constraint $c_{\tau,i} \geq b$ would succeed. On the other hand, if the best value is below b, then there is no such state. Even, the dual constraint could be added to any potential witness state and the encoded run would still be valid.

We introduce variables $\mathsf{maxFst}_i^\varphi : \mathbb{Z}_\infty$ and $\mathsf{maxLst}_i^\varphi : \mathbb{Z}_\infty$ for each $i \in Q$. For the first and last occurrence of state i, respectively, they are supposed to hold the maximal value possibly witnessing satisfaction of the constraint, the symbolic value $-\infty$ expressing non-existence. Recall that these positions represent only rows as the first and last iteration of loops represent their front and rear, respectively. Notice also that the latter value is not defined for positions belonging to the last loop. Then, condition D2 can be expressed for state i in terms of the formula $\mathsf{conD2}(\varphi, i)$ defined as

$$(\varphi \in \mathsf{lbl}_i \leftrightarrow \mathsf{maxFst}_i^\varphi \geq b) \wedge ((\varphi \in \mathsf{lbl}_i \leftrightarrow \mathsf{maxLst}_i^\varphi \geq b) \vee \mathsf{itr}_i = 0).$$

Maximal Witness. The optimal witness value is obtained by a suffix optimum backward propagation from the end to the start of the represented schema. Its QPA formulation $\mathsf{witnessMax}(n, \varphi)$ is comprised of three parts: the *computation* of the potentially propagated value, the calculation of the accumulated *loop effect* on the value of τ as necessary part of that, and the actual *selection*. Concerning the selection, the best value is propagated backwards, as long as χ holds. When the chain breaks, no witness position is properly reachable and the best value is set to $-\infty$. Each state of the schema where ψ holds is a potential witness for preceding states. Thus, if the propagated value is less than 0, this state will generally provide a better value for τ than any of its successors. For example, for the case $\chi, \psi \in \mathsf{lbl}_i$ the formula specifies that $\mathsf{maxLst}_i^\varphi = \max(\mathsf{updLst}_i^\varphi, 0)$ where variables $\mathsf{updLst}_i^\varphi$ are assumed to hold the value propagated from state $i + 1$.

The overall effect of (all iterations of) a loop on the value of τ is made accessible in terms of variables sumEff_i^τ where i is the first state of a loop. It is obtained by summing up the individual contribution $\tau[\mathsf{lbl}_i] \cdot (\mathsf{itr}_i - 3)$ of each loop state i bound to variables eff_i^τ. The effect is multiplied only by $\mathsf{itr}_i - 3$ since the first (front), second (auxiliary), and last (rear) iteration is already accounted for explicitly. In order to circumvent multiplication of variables in the formula, the variables eff_i^τ are themselves defined by distributing the factor $(\mathsf{itr}_i - 3)$ over the sum of monomials of the term τ. Assuming τ to have the form $\tau = \sum_{k=0}^{m} a_k \chi_k$ the loop effect is hence specified by

$$\left(\bigwedge_{i=1}^{n-2} \mathsf{ite}(\triangleright_i, \mathsf{sumEff}_i^\tau = \mathsf{eff}_i^\tau, \mathsf{sumEff}_i^\tau = \mathsf{sumEff}_{i-1} + \mathsf{eff}_i^\tau)\right)$$
$$\wedge \bigwedge_{i=0}^{n-1} \mathsf{ite}(\chi_0 \in \mathsf{lbl}_i, \mathsf{eff}_i^{t,0} = a_0 \cdot \mathsf{itr}_i - 3a_0, \mathsf{eff}_i^{t,0} = 0)$$
$$\wedge \bigwedge_{k=1}^{m} \mathsf{ite}(\chi_k \in \mathsf{lbl}_i, \mathsf{eff}_i^{t,k} = \mathsf{eff}_i^{t,k-1} + a_k \cdot \mathsf{itr}_i - 3a_k, \mathsf{eff}_i^{t,k} = \mathsf{eff}_i^{t,k-1})$$

where the variables $\mathsf{eff}_i^\tau = \mathsf{eff}_i^{t,m}$ are to be considered identical. Then, we can formulate the actual computation of the (potentially) propagated optimum using

$$(\boxminus_i \rightarrow \mathsf{updFst}_i^\varphi = \mathsf{updLst}_i^\varphi = \mathsf{maxFst}_{i+1}^\varphi + \tau[\mathsf{lbl}_i])$$
$$\wedge(\triangleleft_i \rightarrow \mathsf{updLst}_i^\varphi = \mathsf{maxFst}_{i+1}^\varphi + \tau[\mathsf{lbl}_i] \wedge \mathsf{updFst}_i^\varphi = \mathsf{maxAuxAtBeg}_i^\varphi + \tau[\mathsf{lbl}_i]$$
$$\wedge \mathsf{updAux}_i^\varphi = \mathsf{maxLst}_i^\varphi + \mathsf{sumEff}_i^\tau)$$
$$\wedge(\triangleright_i \vee \boxminus_i \rightarrow \mathsf{updLst}_i^\varphi = \mathsf{maxLst}_{i+1}^\varphi + \tau[\mathsf{lbl}_i] \wedge \mathsf{updFst}_i^\varphi = \mathsf{maxFst}_{i+1}^\varphi + \tau[\mathsf{lbl}_i]$$
$$\wedge \mathsf{updAux}_i^\varphi = \mathsf{maxAux}_{i+1}^\varphi + \tau[\mathsf{lbl}_i]).$$

To evaluate condition D(2)i and D(2)iii an additional set of auxiliary variables $\mathsf{maxAux}_i^\varphi$ and $\mathsf{updAux}_i^\varphi$ is used that represents, intuitively, the first real iteration of a loop. The maximal value is, effectively, propagated through the rear of the loop, then extrapolated over all iterations to the last position on the auxiliary iteration (by adding the accumulated loop effect) and finally through the front row. Since the value at the last state at the auxiliary iteration depends on that at the first state in the last iteration, the latter is propagated from the beginning to the end of the loop using variables $\mathsf{maxAuxAtBeg}_i^\varphi$, similar to the origin above.

Finally, the discussed parts can be combined to express consistency for a formula $\chi \, \mathbf{U}_{[\tau \geq b]} \psi$ by

$$\mathsf{glob}(n, \chi) \wedge \mathsf{accu}(n, t) \wedge \mathsf{fin}(n, \psi) \wedge \mathsf{witnessMax}(n, \chi \, \mathbf{U}_{[\tau \geq b]} \psi)$$
$$\wedge \bigwedge_{i=0}^{n-1} \mathsf{conD1}(\chi \, \mathbf{U}_{[\tau \geq b]} \psi, i) \vee \mathsf{conD2}(\chi \, \mathbf{U}_{[\tau \geq b]} \psi, i).$$

The structure of the encoding assures that the actual loops are always identically labelled to their front and rear rows. Thus, by assuring those are consistent, all loops automatically satisfy condition D3. This completes the construction of the formula $\mathsf{consistency}(\mathcal{S}, n, \Phi)$ and thereby that of $\mathsf{fmc}(\mathcal{S}, n, \Phi)$.

Properties of the Encoding. A solution to $\mathsf{fmc}(\mathcal{S}, \Phi, n)$ yields a Φ-consistent APS in $\mathcal{S}$ and a run, implying by Theorem 6 that $\mathcal{S} \models \Phi$. Corollary 8 implies that if the flat approximation $\mathsf{FA}(\mathcal{S}, n)$ contains any run satisfying Φ, then $\mathsf{fmc}(\mathcal{S}, \Phi, 2^{p(n)})$ is satisfiable (for a fixed polynomial p) at latest.

Theorem 9. *(i) If* $\mathrm{fmc}(\mathcal{S}, \Phi, n)$ *is satisfiable, then* $\mathcal{S} \models \Phi$. *(ii) If* $\mathsf{FA}(\mathcal{S}, n) \models \Phi$, *then* $\mathrm{fmc}(\mathcal{S}, \Phi, 2^{p(n)})$ *is satisfiable.*

The encoding hence provides an effective means to solve the flat model-checking problem based on QPA satisfiability checking. A major concern of our construction is to keep the formula as small as possible. Examining the indexing scheme of variables, we observe that their number is linear in $|\Phi| + |\mathcal{S}|$ and n. The length of most parts of the formula $\mathrm{fmc}(\mathcal{S}, \Phi, n)$ only depends linearly on n or $n \cdot |\Delta| \leq n \cdot |\mathcal{S}|$. The parts encoding the guards in $\mathcal{S}$ further depend (linearly) on the size of the guard sets associated to the transitions, more precisely, linearly on the total length of all guards. The components of $\mathrm{consistency}(\mathcal{S}, n, \Phi)$ are of linear size in $n \cdot |\mathcal{S}|$ or $n \cdot |\mathrm{sub}(\Phi)|$. Those concerning atomic constraints and until formulae depend on the length of the constraint terms present in Φ.

Theorem 10 (Formula size). *The length of* $\mathrm{fmc}(\mathcal{S}, \Phi, n)$ *is in* $\mathcal{O}(n(|\mathcal{S}| + |\Phi|))$.

5 Evaluation

In order to evaluate whether flat model checking and the QPA-based encoding can be used to perform verification tasks, we have implemented the procedure and applied it to a set of problems provided by the RERS Challenge [22].

The tool `flat-checker`[2] takes a CLTL specification, a counter system to be verified in DOT format [19] and the approximation depth (schema size) and performs the translation of the verification problem to a linear arithmetic formula. The SMT solver z3 [29] is used to compute a solution of the formula, if possible, that is subsequently interpreted as satisfying run and presented adequately to the user. The tool is developed in Haskell and provides a search mode that automatically increases the depth up to a given a bound, in order to potentially find a small witness quickly, before investing computation time in large depths. A successful search can be continued to find a witness of smallest depth.

The RERS Challenge 2017[3] poses problems as C99 and Java programs that provide output depending on read input symbols and internal state. The programs have a regular structure but are inconceivable with reasonable effort. It features a track comprising 100 LTL formulas to be checked on a program (Problem 1) that is representable as a counter system by treating integer variables as counters. The counting mechanism of CLTL admits a more specific formulation of a correctness property, making it more restrictive or permissive than a plain LTL formula. For example, a typical pattern in the RERS problem set has the form $\neg p\, \mathbf{U}\, q$, stating q occurs before p. It can be relaxed to state, e.g., p occurs at most 5 times ($\mathbf{F}_{[p \leq 5]}\, q$) or less often than r ($\mathbf{F}_{[p-r<0]}\, q$). A stronger formulation would be that q must occur more often before p ($\neg p\, \mathbf{U}_{[q \geq 5]}\, q$ or $\neg p\, \mathbf{U}_{[r-q \geq 5]}\, q$). To evaluate our procedure on counting properties, we constructed variations of formulae from the LTL track that express relaxed or strengthened versions of the properties.

---

[2] https://github.com/apirogov/flat-checker.

[3] http://www.rers-challenge.org/2017/.

By checking negated properties, counterexamples were found at an approximation depth of at most 128 for all violated formulae, while most formulae could be falsified quickly. From the original 52 falsifiable LTL formulae, 43 were falsified after less than 200 seconds per formula at depth at most 64, the remaining 9 took at most 32 min per formula and depth 128. A batch analysis of the whole set of 100 formulae at depth 200 took a total of four days running time (Desktop PC, Intel i5-750 CPU, 4 GB RAM). Some derived CLTL formulae took significantly longer to be evaluated than the original LTL formulation. However, in most cases, the introduction of counting constraints did not increase the evaluation effort significantly.

6   Conclusion

The concise representation of runs in terms of augmented path schemas allows for an accelerated evaluation of complex path properties expressed in a powerful specification framework with counting as first-class feature. We therefore believe that flat approximation provides a promising technique that deserves further investigation. The underlying theory provides that the procedure is complete on flat systems and, practically, an existing witness will be found eventually unless all of them have an infinitely aperiodic shape. It can also be used as (incomplete) approach to the satisfiability and synthesis problems of CLTL.

Although it may eventually hinder problem-specific optimisations, the SMT-based implementation benefits from the engineering effort put into solvers. The configurability of, e.g., z3 using specific tactics, provides potential for future improvements. It remains to develop and compare different encoding variants. Especially, formulations that admit incremental solving could speed up the verification process. The primary ambition of our approach is to verify the expressive class of CLTL properties. Our evaluation suggests that this is feasible and, moreover, that flat model checking is well applicable in a general verification context such as the RERS Challenge.

Lifting the theoretical foundation to linear constraints and counter systems as a class of infinite-state models is a consequent advancement of the theory of path schemas. Characterising CLTL model-checking over flat systems in Presburger arithmetic fills a gap between corresponding results for temporal logics with and without counting [13–15].

Acknowledgement. We thank Daniel Thoma for valuable technical discussions.

References

1. Abdulla, P.A., Atig, M.F., Meyer, R., Salehi, M.S.: What's decidable about availability languages? In: FSTTCS. LIPIcs, vol. 45, pp. 192–205 (2015)
2. Bardin, S., Finkel, A., Leroux, J., Schnoebelen, P.: Flat acceleration in symbolic model checking. In: Peled, D.A., Tsay, Y.-K. (eds.) ATVA 2005. LNCS, vol. 3707, pp. 474–488. Springer, Heidelberg (2005). https://doi.org/10.1007/11562948_35

3. Beyer, D., Henzinger, T.A., Majumdar, R., Rybalchenko, A.: Path invariants. In: PLDI, pp. 300–309. ACM (2007)
4. Biere, A.: Bounded model checking. In: Handbook of Satisfiability. Frontiers in Artificial Intelligence and Applications, vol. 185, pp. 457–481. IOS Press (2009)
5. Biere, A., Cimatti, A., Clarke, E., Zhu, Y.: Symbolic model checking without BDDs. In: Cleaveland, W.R. (ed.) TACAS 1999. LNCS, vol. 1579, pp. 193–207. Springer, Heidelberg (1999). https://doi.org/10.1007/3-540-49059-0_14
6. Bollig, B., Decker, N., Leucker, M.: Frequency linear-time temporal logic. In: TASE, pp. 85–92. IEEE (2012)
7. Borosh, I., Treybig, L.B.: Bounds on positive integral solutions of linear Diophantine equations. Proc. Am. Math. Soc. **55**(2), 299–304 (1976)
8. Bouajjani, A., Echahed, R., Habermehl, P.: On the verification problem of nonregular properties for nonregular processes. In: LICS, pp. 123–133. IEEE (1995)
9. Caniart, N., Fleury, E., Leroux, J., Zeitoun, M.: Accelerating interpolation-based model-checking. In: Ramakrishnan, C.R., Rehof, J. (eds.) TACAS 2008. LNCS, vol. 4963, pp. 428–442. Springer, Heidelberg (2008). https://doi.org/10.1007/978-3-540-78800-3_32
10. Cok, D.R., Stump, A., Weber, T.: The 2013 evaluation of SMT-COMP and SMT-LIB. J. Autom. Reason. **55**(1), 61–90 (2015)
11. Comon, H., Cortier, V.: Flatness is not a weakness. In: Clote, P.G., Schwichtenberg, H. (eds.) CSL 2000. LNCS, vol. 1862, pp. 262–276. Springer, Heidelberg (2000). https://doi.org/10.1007/3-540-44622-2_17
12. Comon, H., Jurski, Y.: Multiple counters automata, safety analysis and presburger arithmetic. In: Hu, A.J., Vardi, M.Y. (eds.) CAV 1998. LNCS, vol. 1427, pp. 268–279. Springer, Heidelberg (1998). https://doi.org/10.1007/BFb0028751
13. Decker, N., Habermehl, P., Leucker, M., Sangnier, A., Thoma, D.: Model-checking counting temporal logics on flat structures. In: CONCUR. LIPIcs, vol. 85, pp. 29:1–29:17. Schloss Dagstuhl - Leibniz-Zentrum fuer Informatik (2017)
14. Demri, S., Dhar, A.K., Sangnier, A.: Equivalence between model-checking flat counter systems and Presburger arithmetic. In: Ouaknine, J., Potapov, I., Worrell, J. (eds.) RP 2014. LNCS, vol. 8762, pp. 85–97. Springer, Cham (2014). https://doi.org/10.1007/978-3-319-11439-2_7
15. Demri, S., Dhar, A.K., Sangnier, A.: Taming past LTL and flat counter systems. Inf. Comput. **242**, 306–339 (2015)
16. Demri, S., D'Souza, D.: An automata-theoretic approach to constraint LTL. Inf. Comput. **205**(3), 380–415 (2007)
17. Dhar, A.K.: Algorithms for model-checking flat counter systems. Ph.D. thesis, Université Paris Diderot (2014)
18. Čerāns, K.: Deciding properties of integral relational automata. In: Abiteboul, S., Shamir, E. (eds.) ICALP 1994. LNCS, vol. 820, pp. 35–46. Springer, Heidelberg (1994). https://doi.org/10.1007/3-540-58201-0_56
19. Gansner, E.R., North, S.C.: An open graph visualization system and its applications to software engineering. Softw. Pract. Exp. **30**(11), 1203–1233 (2000)
20. Hoenicke, J., Meyer, R., Olderog, E.-R.: Kleene, Rabin, and Scott are available. In: Gastin, P., Laroussinie, F. (eds.) CONCUR 2010. LNCS, vol. 6269, pp. 462–477. Springer, Heidelberg (2010). https://doi.org/10.1007/978-3-642-15375-4_32
21. Hojjat, H., Iosif, R., Konečný, F., Kuncak, V., Rümmer, P.: Accelerating interpolants. In: Chakraborty, S., Mukund, M. (eds.) ATVA 2012. LNCS, pp. 187–202. Springer, Heidelberg (2012). https://doi.org/10.1007/978-3-642-33386-6_16

22. Howar, F., Isberner, M., Merten, M., Steffen, B., Beyer, D., Pasareanu, C.S.: Rigorous examination of reactive systems - the RERS challenges 2012 and 2013. STTT **16**(5), 457–464 (2014)
23. Kroening, D., Weissenbacher, G.: Verification and falsification of programs with loops using predicate abstraction. Formal Asp. Comput. **22**(2), 105–128 (2010)
24. Kuhtz, L., Finkbeiner, B.: Weak Kripke structures and LTL. In: Katoen, J.-P., König, B. (eds.) CONCUR 2011. LNCS, vol. 6901, pp. 419–433. Springer, Heidelberg (2011). https://doi.org/10.1007/978-3-642-23217-6_28
25. Laroussinie, F., Meyer, A., Petonnet, E.: Counting LTL. In: TIME, pp. 51–58. IEEE (2010)
26. Laroussinie, F., Meyer, A., Petonnet, E.: Counting CTL. Log. Methods Comput. Sci. **9**(1), 1–34 (2012)
27. Leroux, J., Sutre, G.: On flatness for 2-dimensional vector addition systems with states. In: Gardner, P., Yoshida, N. (eds.) CONCUR 2004. LNCS, vol. 3170, pp. 402–416. Springer, Heidelberg (2004). https://doi.org/10.1007/978-3-540-28644-8_26
28. Minsky, M.L.: Computation: Finite and Infinite Machines. Prentice-Hall Inc., Upper Saddle River (1967)
29. de Moura, L., Bjørner, N.: Z3: an efficient SMT solver. In: Ramakrishnan, C.R., Rehof, J. (eds.) TACAS 2008. LNCS, vol. 4963, pp. 337–340. Springer, Heidelberg (2008). https://doi.org/10.1007/978-3-540-78800-3_24
30. Pnueli, A.: The temporal logic of programs. In: FOCS, pp. 46–57. IEEE (1977)
31. Presburger, M.: Über die Vollständigkeit eines gewissen Systems der Arithmetik ganzer Zahlen, in welchem die Addition als einzige Operation hervortritt. In: Comptes Rendus du premier congrès de mathématiciens des Pays Slaves, Warszawa, pp. 92–101 (1929)
32. Sistla, A.P., Clarke, E.M.: The complexity of propositional linear temporal logics. J. ACM **32**(3), 733–749 (1985)

A Parallel Relation-Based Algorithm for Symbolic Bisimulation Minimization

Richard Huybers and Alfons Laarman$^{(\boxtimes)}$

LIACS, Leiden University, Leiden, The Netherlands
richardhuybers22@gmail.com, a.w.laarman@liacs.leidenuniv.nl

Abstract. Symbolic computation using BDDs and bisimulation minimization are alternative ways to cope with the state space explosion in model checking. The combination of both techniques opens up many parameters that can be tweaked for further optimization. Most importantly, the bisimulation can either be represented as equivalence classes or as a relation. While recent work argues that storing partitions is more efficient, we show that the relation-based approach is preferable. We do so by deriving a relation-based minimization algorithm based on new coarse-grained BDD operations. The implementation demonstrates that the relational approach uses fewer memory and performs better.

Keywords: Bisimulation minimization · Symbolic model checking BDDs · Decision diagrams · Parallel computing

1 Introduction

Model checking [1] proves a system's correctness by analyzing its behavior as a transition system, i.e., taking a model theoretical view of the system. As the size of the transition system, or state space, is the bottleneck in this technique, many reduction methods are used to manage large state space. In the current paper, we combine bisimulation minimization [3] with symbolic representations [6] in binary decision diagrams (BDDs) [5].

The state spaces of systems typically contain many states that have different in data valuations, yet identical behavior. This notion of "bisimilar" states is defined as an equivalence relation, which in turn induces a partition of (coarsest) blocks of bisimilar states. Bisimulation minimization algorithms reduce the size of the transition systems by merging bisimilar states.

Bisimulation minimization algorithms can thus represent the bisimulation relation as either a (coarsest) partition or an equivalence relation. Fisler and Vardi [13] argue that symbolic relation-based algorithms are not feasible, because

---

The second author is funded by the research program VENI with project number 639.021.649 of the Netherlands Organization for Scientific Research (NWO).

in practice the BDD that represents the equivalence relation grows too large. For this reason, the latest research gravitated towards the partition-based approach. For instance, Van Dijk and Van de Pol [11] present a parallel symbolic partition-based bisimulation algorithm. They state that partition BDDs, like the one used in their algorithm, should in practice remain smaller than equivalence relation BDDs.

The current paper presents a relation-based algorithm, which is derived from first principles. Our algorithm is similar to the algorithm proposed by Ciardo [19], but was found independently. We present the derivation of the key symbolic operations offering more details of its inner workings. Moreover, the derived operations are coarse, avoiding BDD unique and cache table pollution by skipping intermediary results, similar to what has been done before for image computation [24]. Additionally, we present a parallel version in the spirit of Van Dijk and Van de Pol [11]. The algorithm is used to compare for the first time the relation-based approaches to the partition-based approaches.

Surprisingly, the experimental results show that the relation-based approaches use less memory and perform better than the partition-based approaches. We argue that the variable interleavings allowed in the relational approach can explain these unexpected results.

The current paper is structured as follows. In Sect. 2 we will explain the notions of transition systems, bisimulation minimization, and BDDs in more detail. Section 3 presents the parallel relation-based symbolic bisimulation algorithm, along with its derivation. Related work, and in particular Van Dijk's algorithm, are discussed in Sect. 4. Our experiments and their results are presented in Sect. 5. Section 6 concludes this thesis with a discussion.

2   Background

Labelled transition systems. A labelled transition system, or LTS for short, is a directed graph with labelled edges. LTSs are commonly used in model checking to model different kinds of systems. The nodes of an LTS represent the system's states. The labelled edges represent actions or events which cause the system to transition to another state.

Definition 1. *A labelled transition system (LTS) is a tuple $(S, A, \rightarrow)$ consisting of a set of states S, a set of action labels A, and a transition relation $\rightarrow \subseteq S \times A \times S$. Instead of $(s, a, t) \in \rightarrow$, we write $s \xrightarrow{a} t$.*

Example 1. A sliding tile puzzle is a combination puzzle in which the player has to construct an image by rearranging square tiles that depict parts of the image. The tiles are lain on a rectangular grid in which one space is left empty. The player can rearrange the tiles by sliding adjacent tiles into the empty space. The sliding tile puzzle considered in this example consists of a 2 by 2 grid and three identical tiles. The tiles can be lain in four different arrangements, as shown in Figure 1a. Each arrangement may be seen as a different state of the puzzle. In each state one tile can be slid horizontally (h) and one tile can be slid vertically (v). By sliding a tile, the state of the puzzle changes. The LTS which models this puzzle is shown in Figure 1b. Each state of the puzzle is represented by a node and each move is represented by a labelled transition. Formally, the LTS consists of the following sets:

$S = \{s_1, s_2, s_3, s_4\}$

$A = \{h, v\}$

$\rightarrow \; = \{(s_1, h, s_2), (s_1, v, s_3), (s_2, h, s_1), (s_2, v, s_4), (s_3, h, s_4), (s_3, v, s_1), (s_4, h, s_3), (s_4, v, s_2)\}$

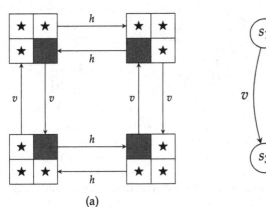 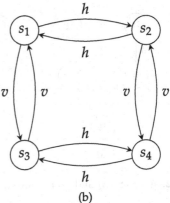

Fig. 1. The four arrangements of a simple sliding tile puzzle (a) and its LTS (b).

Bisimulation. Due to concurrent behavior, an LTS typically contains multiple (distinct) states with the same behavior. Fortunately, we can find and remove these redundant nodes by computing a bisimulation relation.

Definition 2. *A binary relation* $R \subseteq S \times S$ *over the set of states of an LTS* $(S, A, \rightarrow)$ *is a bisimulation relation if whenever* $(s, t) \in R$ *and* $a \in A$,

1. *for all* s' *with* $s \xrightarrow{a} s'$, *there exists a* t' *such that* $t \xrightarrow{a} t'$ *and* $(s', t') \in R$
2. *for all* t' *with* $t \xrightarrow{a} t'$, *there exists a* s' *such that* $s \xrightarrow{a} s'$ *and* $(s', t') \in R$

We say that s *is bisimilar to* t *and write* $s \sim t$ *if there exists a bisimulation* R *with* $(s, t) \in R$.

Corollary 1. *The bisimilarity relation* $\sim$ *is an equivalence relation.*

To obtain reduction through *bisimulation minimization*, two bisimilar states can be merged, preserving a well-defined subset of all branching-time behavior of the system [9,15,18,21]. The bisimilarity relation $\sim$ is the largest possible bisimulation relation over an LTS, and is more commonly known as the *maximal bisimulation*. Because the maximal bisimulation is an equivalence relation, the size of an LTS can be minimized by computing the maximal bisimulation and merging all states that are in the same equivalence class.

Example 2. Consider the LTS shown in Fig. 2a. First off, note that every state is always bisimilar to itself. Consequently, states s_3 and s_4 are also bisimilar, as their outgoing transitions, (s_3, c, s_5) and (s_4, c, s_5), have the same label and $s_5 \sim s_5$. Thus, it is possible to merge these two states. This is done by first adding all incoming transitions of s_4 to s_3 and then removing s_4 from the LTS. The result is depicted in Fig. 2b. Observe that the incoming transitions of a state do not affect its behavior.

Example 3. Figure 2c shows the bisimulation minimization of Fig. 1b.

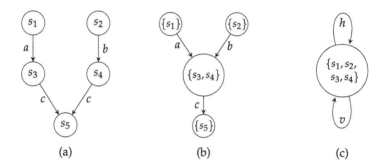

Fig. 2. An LTS (a) and its minimized equivalent (b) And the minimization of Fig. 1b.

Binary decision diagrams. BDDs were introduced by Bryant [5] as canonical representations of Boolean functions that can easily be manipulated. A Boolean function $f : \mathbb{B}^n \to \mathbb{B}$ takes $n \geq 0$ arguments $x_1, x_2, \ldots, x_n \in \{0, 1\}$ and returns either a 1 or a 0 (true or false). We can restrict f with respect to one of its arguments x_i by assigning the value 0 or 1 to it, notation $f_{\overline{x}_i}$ and f_{x_i} respectively. These so-called cofactors are defined as follows.
$f_{\overline{x}_i}(x_1, \ldots, x_n) = f(x_1, \ldots, x_{i-1}, 0, x_{i+1}, \ldots, x_n)$ and
$f_{x_i}(x_1, \ldots, x_n) = f(x_1, \ldots, x_{i-1}, 1, x_{i+1}, \ldots, x_n)$
The Shannon decomposition [22] of f can now be defined as follows.

$$f(x_1, \ldots, x_n) = \overline{x}_i \cdot f_{\overline{x}_i} + x_i \cdot f_{x_i}$$

Definition 3. *A binary decision diagram (BDD) is a rooted directed acyclic graph comprising internal decision nodes and leaves with value 0 or 1. Internal nodes have as attributes a variable label and two child nodes called its "low" and "high" child.*

Definition 3 defines the BDD data structure. A BDD is called *ordered* if the variable labels are encountered in the same order for every directed path down the root. A BDD is called *reduced* if it contains no redundant nodes (nodes with the same low and high child) and no duplicate nodes (two nodes with the same label, low child, and high child). Given a fixed variable ordering, a *reduced ordered BDD* is a canonical representation of a Boolean function. From this

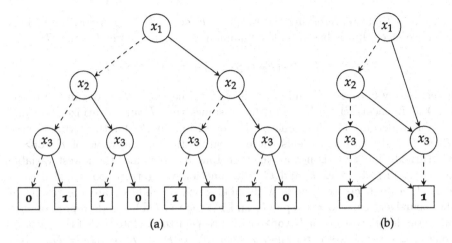

Fig. 3. A non-reduced (a) and reduced (b) BDD representing the function $f(x_1, x_2, x_3) = \overline{x}_1\overline{x}_2x_3 + \overline{x}_1x_2\overline{x}_3 + x_1\overline{x}_2\overline{x}_3 + x_1x_2\overline{x}_3$

point forward we will use the term BDD to refer to reduced ordered BDDs, as is common in the literature.

Figure 3 shows an example of a non-reduced BDD and its reduced equivalent. The low and high child of an internal node can be found by following the dashed and solid arrows originating in the node respectively. Paths which go from the root of a BDD down to a leaf specify different variable assignments. Whenever we traverse from a node to its low (or high) child, we assign 0 (or 1) to the variable contained in the node. The bottom nodes (rectangles) represent the function evaluation.

In essence, non-reduced BDDs are binary trees which enumerate all possible variable assignments of a Boolean function. Reduced BDDs remove from this binary tree all isomorphic subgraphs and all nodes for which the low and high edges point to the same node. The variables over which a BDD is defined are usually expressed using a vector notation: $x = x_1, \ldots, x_n$, where we assume the order $x_1 < \ldots < x_n$. If a path jumps over a certain variable, then it does not matter which value is assigned to the variable. For instance, in the BDD shown in Fig. 3b the edge from x_1 to x_3 skips variable x_2, hence both $1, 0, 0$ and $1, 1, 0$ are assignments to x_1, x_2, x_3 evaluating to 1 according to this BDD.

Viewed conversely, a BDD represents a set of assignments to its variables. For instance, the BDD in Fig. 3b assigns to x_1, x_2, x_3 the set $\{001, 010, 100, 110\}$.

BDD Operations. Besides concise representations of Boolean functions, BDDs also provide efficient implementations of Boolean operations, such as disjunction $\vee$ (union $\cup$) and conjunction $\wedge$ (intersection $\cap$). *These Boolean operations can even be realized in time linear to the number of nodes in the BDD (whereas the BDD might represent exponentially many assignments in the number of variables).* Given two BDDs F and G, and a binary set operation `<op>`, we can compute a BDD representing the result of F <op> G using Algorithm 1. This recursive algorithm is based on the Shannon decomposition of F <op> G

$$F \text{ <op> } G = \overline{x} \cdot (F_{\overline{x}} \text{ <op> } G_{\overline{x}}) + x \cdot (F_x \text{ <op> } G_x)$$

It recursively traverses F and G at the same time, creating nodes in the result BDD as it backtracks. The algorithm assumes that F and G utilize the same variable ordering. The first line in the algorithm checks for the terminal case where F and G are both leafs. Here a leaf containing the value of F <op> G is returned. If F or G is not a leaf, then Line 3 determines the lowest variable label x (min) of nodes F and G (the function var returns ∞ if called on a leaf). Lines 4–6 create a node with label x whose children are the results of the recursively calls to $F_{\overline{x}}$ <op> $G_{\overline{x}}$ and F_x <op> G_x. This node represents the Shannon decomposition of F <op> G with respect to x. Note that if the variable label of F (or G) is greater than x, then $F_{\overline{x}} = F_x = F$ (or $G_{\overline{x}} = G_x = G$) because the BDD contains no nodes with label x. In summary, this algorithm builds up a BDD which follows the structure of the Shannon decomposition of F <op> G and has the same variable ordering as F and G.

To merge duplicate nodes, a *unique table* is used to store every created node. The call to BDD_node at Line 6 checks whether the node that needs to be created already exists in the unique table before constructing a new one. It also makes sure that the low and high child are not the same, by returning either high or low if this is the case. These checks assure that the result BDD is reduced.

Dynamic programming is used to make the BDD operations polynomial in the number of BDD nodes. A separate *operation cache* is used to store the result of every function call. Line 2 checks whether the result of the current call has already been computed and Line 7 stores a new result in the cache. Due to dynamic programming, the apply operation is linear in the number of nodes.

Given an LTS $(S, A, \rightarrow)$, the complement of BDD $B(x)$ is defined as $S - B$. Complements can even be computed in constant time [4]. Furthermore, through the following identities, existential/universal quantification can also be implemented in BDDs in polynomial time (in the number of nodes) as well.

$$\exists x : F = F_{\overline{x}} \cup F_x \qquad \forall x : F = F_{\overline{x}} \cap F_x$$

Algorithm 1. apply($F, G,$ <op>)

1: **if** $(F = 0 \vee F = 1) \wedge (G = 0 \vee G = 1)$ **then return** F <op> G
2: **if** $(F, G,$ <op>$)$ in **cache then return** cache$[(F, G,$ <op>$)]$
3: $x \leftarrow \text{min}(\text{var}(F), \text{var}(G))$
4: $low \leftarrow \text{apply}(F_{\overline{x}}, G_{\overline{x}},$ <op>$)$
5: $high \leftarrow \text{apply}(F_x, G_x,$ <op>$)$
6: $result \leftarrow \text{BDD\_node}(x, low, high)$
7: cache$[(F, G,$ <op>$)] \leftarrow result$
8: **return** $result$

Symbolic Model Checking with BDDs. Model checkers automatically prove that a system M satisfies a specification φ, by analyzing the LTS of M according to the propositions in φ. McMillan et al. [6] were the first to introduce a symbolic algorithm for model checking by representing the system's LTS as a BDD. States of the system are represented as assignments to Boolean variables $\boldsymbol{x} := x_1, \ldots, x_n$ (after bit blasting), and can therefore be represented by a BDD over those variables (an assignment evaluates to 1 when the state is in the LTS). Transitions can be represented as a relation, by copying all variables in the system to a primed version: $\boldsymbol{x}, \boldsymbol{x}' := x_1, \ldots, x_n, x_1', \ldots, x_n'$.

Given BDDs $S(\boldsymbol{x})$ and $R(\boldsymbol{x}, \boldsymbol{x}')$, representing a subset of LTS states (initial states or those satisfying some proposition in the specification φ) and the transition relation, the model checker then has to compute fix points to prove it satisfies φ. This is done using *image computation* of the set S under a relation R:

$$\exists \boldsymbol{x} : (S \cap R)[\boldsymbol{x}' := \boldsymbol{x}]$$

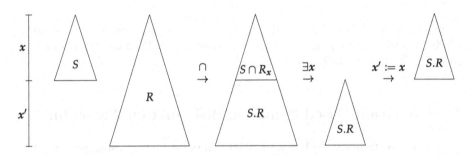

Fig. 4. The three steps performed in the image computation of S under R ($S.R$).

This operation consists of three steps as illustrated in Fig. 4. First, the intersection of S and R is determined. This results in a BDD containing all transitions in R with a source in S. Next, the source states are removed from this BDD by existential quantification over $\boldsymbol{x}$. The result of this abstraction is a BDD containing the image of S under R. As a last step, the $\boldsymbol{x}'$ variables are renamed to $\boldsymbol{x}$ variables by the relabelling operation ($[\boldsymbol{x}' := \boldsymbol{x}]$). In practice, the three steps can be combined into one operation with a worst case linear runtime in the number of nodes.

Example 4. Consider a sliding tile puzzle which consists of just one tile and a 2 by 1 grid. This puzzle can be represented by an LTS with $S = \{s_1, s_2\}$ and (unlabelled) transition relation $\to\ =\ \{(s_1, s_2), (s_2, s_1)\}$. Thus, the puzzle can only go back and forth between two states. The states are encoded by a string of two variables, $x_1 x_2$, which represent the two grid positions with $x_i = 1$ iff a tile is at grid position 1. We encode s_1 by 10 and s_2 by 01. The transitions are encoded by concatenating the source state with the target state.

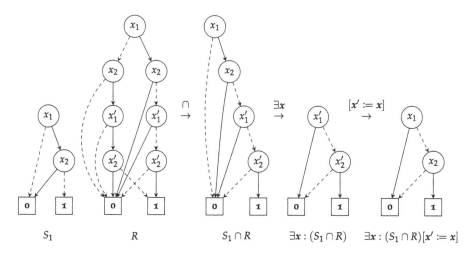

Fig. 5. The five BDDs that are involved in the computation of the image of S_1 under R.

Let S_1 be a BDD which encodes $\{s_1\}$ over $\boldsymbol{x} = x_1, x_2$, and let R be a BDD which encodes $\to$ over $\boldsymbol{x}$ and $\boldsymbol{x}'$. Figure 5 shows the image computation of $\{s_1\}$ under $\to$. The final BDD represents $\{s_2\}$.

3 A Relation-Based Symbolic Bisimulation Algorithm

The current section first derives a fix point computation that establishes the bismilarity relation. It then goes on to derive coarse BDD operations to implement the algorithm more efficiently. Finally, the algorithm is parallelized.

The Relational Fix Point Computation. Given an LTS $(S, A, \to)$, our algorithm computes a non-bisimilarity relation $\not\sim$, i.e., the complement of the relation defined in Definition 2, similar to Liu and Smolka [17]. In order to construct $\not\sim$, the algorithm maintains a relation R which contains all pairs of non-bisimilar states that have been found thus far. R is initialized as the empty set. Pairs of non-bisimilar states are iteratively added to R until a fix point is reached, at which point R equals $\not\sim$. For this purpose, the following functions are used

$$f_a(R) := \{(s,t) \mid \exists s' \in S : (s \xrightarrow{a} s' \wedge \nexists t' \in S : (t \xrightarrow{a} t' \wedge (s',t') \notin R))\} \ \cup$$
$$\{(s,t) \mid \exists t' \in S : (t \xrightarrow{a} t' \wedge \nexists s' \in S : (s \xrightarrow{a} s' \wedge (s',t') \notin R))\}, \text{and}$$
$$f(R) := \bigcup_{a \in A} f_a(R)$$

R is called a *fix point* of f if $f(R) = R$. The function f is a monotonic with respect to $\subseteq$ and $(\mathcal{P}(S \times S), \subseteq)$ forms a complete lattice. Therefore, according to the Knaster-Tarski Lemma [16], there exists a (unique) least fix point of f.

In order to compute f_a two sets of pairs of states need to be determined. Let

$$Y_a := \{(s,t) \mid \exists s' \in S : (s \xrightarrow{a} s' \land \nexists t' \in S : (t \xrightarrow{a} t' \land (s',t') \notin R))\}, \text{and}$$

$$Z_a := \{(s,t) \mid \exists t' \in S : (t \xrightarrow{a} t' \land \nexists s' \in S : (s \xrightarrow{a} s' \land (s',t') \notin R))\}$$

such that $f_a(R) := Y_a \cup Z_a$. R is initially symmetric, as the empty set is a symmetric relation. If R is symmetric then $Z_a = Y_a^{-1}$, and thus the result of $f_a(R)$ is also symmetric. Therefore, R is symmetric during every step of the construction of $\not\sim$. Furthermore, this means that Z_a can be determined by taking the converse of Y_a.

Algorithm 2 presents our symbolic bisimulation algorithm *bisim*. As input, *bisim* takes a BDD S and a set of relational BDDs T, indexed by the action labels $a \in A$, splitting the transition relation on the actions. At Line 1, R is initialized to the empty set. The algorithm then computes the least fix point in the loop starting at Line 2. Line 3 stores a copy of R, Lines 4–7 extend R using a chaining approach, and Line 8 checks if a fix point is reached. After a fix point is found, the complement of R is returned by Line 9.

Algorithm 2. bisim$(S, A, (T_a)_{a\in A})$

1: $R \leftarrow \emptyset$
2: **repeat**
3:     $R' \leftarrow R$
4:     **for all** $a \in A$ **do**
5:         $X_a \leftarrow \{(s',t) \mid \nexists t' : ((t,t') \in T_a \land (s',t') \notin R)\}$
6:         $Y_a \leftarrow \{(s,t) \mid \exists s' : ((s,s') \in T_a \land (s',t) \in X)\}$
7:         $R \leftarrow R \cup Y_a \cup Y_a^{-1}$
8: **until** $R = R'$
9: **return** $\overline{R}$

The rest of this section explains how the operations at Line 5 and 6 can be implemented as two single coarse-grained BDD operations. We omit the well-known implementation of the converse relation Y^{-1} at Line 7, that is required as the last step for computing $f_a(R)$.

Note that Algorithm 2 uses a *chaining* approach [23] to implement the union over all actions, instead of a strict breadth-first search (BFS). Chaining immediately adds new results to R for each action (as on Line 7), using these results for the next action (see Fig. 6), whereas BFS would first store those sub-results in a queue. For BDDs, chaining can be much more efficient [23].

BDD Operations for Computing Non-Bisimilar States. New pairs of non-bisimilar states are determined in two steps. First, we derive the BDD operation which computes a relation: $X_a := \{(s',t) \mid \nexists t' : ((t,t') \in T_a \land (s',t') \notin R)\}$.

This BDD operation is called the $\forall$preimage operation, as $(s',t) \in X_a$ implies that $\forall t' \in \{t' \mid (t,t') \in T_a\} : (s',t') \in R$. It takes as arguments two BDDs R and T, which are both defined over variables $\boldsymbol{x}$ and $\boldsymbol{x}'$. Its result BDD X should again be defined over $\boldsymbol{x}$ and $\boldsymbol{x}'$. Note that the source states of T, which are defined

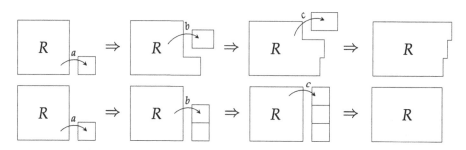

Fig. 6. The extension of R using chaining (above), as used by Algorithm 2, vs BFS (below).

over x, form the target states of X, which are defined over x'. The source states of T cannot be redefined over x', as these variables are already used to encode the target states of R and T. The source states of T must therefore be relabelled to a new set of variables x''. As a final step, the operation relabels these states once more to x' in order to define the result over the desired variables. We find the following operation:

$$\forall\mathrm{preimage}(R, T) := (\not\exists x' : (T[x := x''] \wedge \neg R))[x'' := x']$$

To derive the recursive BDD algorithm, we abstract a single variable x from the formula using Shannon decomposition and rewrite until recursive calls can be identified. As x can be a part of either x, x', or x'', we identify three cases.

$Case\ x \in x :$ $\quad \forall\mathrm{preimage}(R, T) := (\not\exists x' : (T[x := x''] \wedge \neg R))[x'' := x']$

$= \overline{x}((\not\exists x' : (T[x := x''] \wedge \neg R))[x'' := x'])_{\overline{x}} \vee x((\not\exists x' : (T[x := x''] \wedge \neg R))[x'' := x'])_x$

$= \overline{x}((\not\exists x' : (T[x := x''] \wedge \neg R_{\overline{x}}))[x'' := x']) \vee x((\not\exists x' : (T[x := x''] \wedge \neg R_x))[x'' := x'])$

$= \overline{x} \cdot \forall\mathrm{preimage}(R_{\overline{x}}, T) \vee x \cdot \forall\mathrm{preimage}(R_x, T)$

$Case\ x' \in x' :$ $\quad \forall\mathrm{preimage}(R, T) := (\not\exists x' : (T[x := x''] \wedge \neg R))[x'' := x']$

$= (\not\exists x' : ((T[x := x''] \wedge \neg R)_{\overline{x}'} \vee (T[x := x''] \wedge \neg R)_{x'}))[x'' := x']$

$= (\not\exists x' : ((T_{\overline{x}'}[x := x''] \wedge \neg R_{\overline{x}'}) \vee (T_{x'}[x := x''] \wedge \neg R_{x'})))[x'' := x']$

$= (\neg(\exists x' : (T_{\overline{x}'}[x := x''] \wedge \neg R_{\overline{x}'}) \vee \exists x' : (T_{x'}[x := x''] \wedge \neg R_{x'})))[x'' := x']$

$= (\not\exists x' : (T_{\overline{x}'}[x := x''] \wedge \neg R_{\overline{x}'}) \wedge \not\exists x' : (T_{x'}[x := x''] \wedge \neg R_{x'}))[x'' := x']$

$= (\not\exists x' : (T_{\overline{x}'}[x := x''] \wedge \neg R_{\overline{x}'}))[x'' := x'] \wedge (\not\exists x' : (T_{x'}[x := x''] \wedge \neg R_{x'}))[x'' := x']$

$= \forall\mathrm{preimage}(R_{\overline{x}'}, T_{\overline{x}'}) \wedge \forall\mathrm{preimage}(R_{x'}, T_{x'})$

$Case\ x'' \in x'' :$ $\quad \forall\mathrm{preimage}(R, T) := (\not\exists x' : (T[x := x''] \wedge \neg R))[x'' := x']$

$= (\overline{x}''(\not\exists x' : (T[x := x''] \wedge \neg R))_{\overline{x}''} \vee x''(\not\exists x' : (T[x := x''] \wedge \neg R))_{x''})[x'' := x']$

$= (\overline{x}''(\not\exists x' : (T[x := x'']_{\overline{x}''} \wedge R)) \vee x''(\not\exists x' : (T[x := x'']_{x''} \wedge \neg R)))[x'' := x']$

$= (\overline{x}''(\not\exists x' : (T_{\overline{x}}[x := x''] \wedge \neg R)) \vee x''(\not\exists x' : (T_x[x := x''] \wedge \neg R)))[x'' := x']$

$= (\overline{x}''(\not\exists x' : (T_{\overline{x}}[x := x''] \wedge \neg R)))[x'' := x'] \vee (x''(\not\exists x' : (T_x[x := x''] \wedge \neg R)))[x'' := x']$

$= \overline{x}'(\not\exists x' : (T_{\overline{x}}[x := x''] \wedge \neg R))[x'' := x'] \vee x'(\not\exists x' : (T_x[x := x''] \wedge \neg R))[x'' := x']$

$= \overline{x}' \cdot \forall\mathrm{preimage}(R, T_{\overline{x}}) \vee x' \cdot \forall\mathrm{preimage}(R, T_x)$

The terminal cases of $\forall$preimage are found by assigning values 0 or 1 to R and T: $\forall$preimage$(0,1) = 0$ and $\forall$preimage$(1,T) = \forall$preimage$(R,0) = 1$. The algorithm which results from these derivations is shown in Algorithm 3. (The parallel call structure is discussed in Sect. 5.)

Algorithm 3. $\forall$preimage(R,T)

1: **if** $R = 0 \wedge T = 1$ **then return** 0
2: **if** $R = 1 \vee T = 0$ **then return** 1
3: **if** $(R, T, \forall$preimage$)$ in **cache then return cache**$[(R, T, \forall$preimage$)]$
4: $x \leftarrow \min(\text{var}(R), \text{var}(T))$
5: **if** $x \in \boldsymbol{x} \wedge x = \text{var}(R)$ **then**
6:     **do in parallel:**
7:         $low \leftarrow \forall$preimage$(R_{\overline{x}}, T)$
8:         $high \leftarrow \forall$preimage(R_x, T)
9:     $result \leftarrow$ BDD_node$(x, low, high)$
10: **else if** $x \in \boldsymbol{x} \wedge x = \text{var}(T)$ **then**
11:     **do in parallel:**
12:         $low \leftarrow \forall$preimage$(R, T_{\overline{x}})$
13:         $high \leftarrow \forall$preimage(R, T_x)
14:     $result \leftarrow$ BDD_node$(\boldsymbol{x}'(x), low, high)$
15: **else**
16:     **do in parallel:**
17:         $low \leftarrow \forall$preimage$(R_{\overline{x}}, T_{\overline{x}})$
18:         $high \leftarrow \forall$preimage(R_x, T_x)
19:     $result \leftarrow$ apply$(low, high, \cap)$
20: **cache**$[(R, T, \forall$preimage$)] \leftarrow result$
21: **return** $result$

Lines 1 and 2 check for terminal cases. Line 4 selects the lowest variable label x of nodes R and T. As stated before, x can be a part of either $\boldsymbol{x}$, $\boldsymbol{x}'$, or $\boldsymbol{x}''$. The use of $\boldsymbol{x}''$ variables can be avoided by distinguishing the source states of R and T with a simple check. This is done by changing the case $x \in \boldsymbol{x}$ to $x \in \boldsymbol{x} \wedge x = \text{var}(R)$ and changing the case $x \in \boldsymbol{x}''$ to $x \in \boldsymbol{x} \wedge x = \text{var}(T)$. Lines 5–19 create nodes in the result BDD according to the three recursive definitions of $\forall$preimage which follow from the derivations. The expression $\boldsymbol{x}'(x)$ in Line 14 maps the variable x to its primed equivalent in $\boldsymbol{x}'$, e.g. $\boldsymbol{x}'(x_i) = x_i'$. Lines 3 and 20 add the usual caching to the BDD operation. Line 21 returns the result.

Next, we derive a BDD operation for: $Y := \{(s,t) \mid \exists s' : ((s,s') \in T \wedge (s',t) \in X)\}$. The operation computes the composition of the relations T and X, and is thus named the relcomp operation. It takes as arguments the BDDs T and X, which are both defined over variables $\boldsymbol{x}$ and $\boldsymbol{x}'$. The result is a BDD which represents Y and which is defined over variables $\boldsymbol{x}$ and $\boldsymbol{x}'$. The operation matches the target states of T with the source states of X. Thus, these should be defined over the same variables. Both the target states of T and the source states of X are therefore relabelled to $\boldsymbol{x}''$. We find the following operation and again derive an algorithm for the operation by abstracting a single variable from this formula. Again, there are three cases.

$$\mathrm{relcomp}(T, X) := \exists \boldsymbol{x}'' : (T[\boldsymbol{x}' := \boldsymbol{x}''] \wedge X[\boldsymbol{x} := \boldsymbol{x}''])$$

Case $x \in \boldsymbol{x}$: $\mathrm{relcomp}(T, X) := \exists \boldsymbol{x}'' : (T[\boldsymbol{x}' := \boldsymbol{x}''] \wedge X[\boldsymbol{x} := \boldsymbol{x}''])$

$$= \overline{x}(\exists \boldsymbol{x}'' : (T[\boldsymbol{x}' := \boldsymbol{x}''] \wedge X[\boldsymbol{x} := \boldsymbol{x}'']))_{\overline{x}} \vee x(\exists \boldsymbol{x}'' : (T[\boldsymbol{x}' := \boldsymbol{x}''] \wedge X[\boldsymbol{x} := \boldsymbol{x}'']))_x$$

$$= \overline{x}(\exists \boldsymbol{x}'' : (T_{\overline{x}}[\boldsymbol{x}' := \boldsymbol{x}''] \wedge X[\boldsymbol{x} := \boldsymbol{x}''])) \vee x(\exists \boldsymbol{x}'' : (T_x[\boldsymbol{x}' := \boldsymbol{x}''] \wedge X[\boldsymbol{x} := \boldsymbol{x}'']))$$

$$= \overline{x} \cdot \mathrm{relcomp}(T_{\overline{x}}, X) \vee x \cdot \mathrm{relcomp}(T_x, X))$$

Case $x' \in \boldsymbol{x}'$: $\mathrm{relcomp}(T, X) := \exists \boldsymbol{x}'' : (T[\boldsymbol{x}' := \boldsymbol{x}''] \wedge X[\boldsymbol{x} := \boldsymbol{x}''])$

$$= \overline{x}'(\exists \boldsymbol{x}'' : (T[\boldsymbol{x}' := \boldsymbol{x}''] \wedge X[\boldsymbol{x} := \boldsymbol{x}'']))_{\overline{x}'} \vee x'(\exists \boldsymbol{x}'' : (T[\boldsymbol{x}' := \boldsymbol{x}''] \wedge X[\boldsymbol{x} := \boldsymbol{x}'']))_{x'}$$

$$= \overline{x}'(\exists \boldsymbol{x}'' : (T[\boldsymbol{x}' := \boldsymbol{x}''] \wedge X_{\overline{x}'}[\boldsymbol{x} := \boldsymbol{x}''])) \vee x'(\exists \boldsymbol{x}'' : (T[\boldsymbol{x}' := \boldsymbol{x}''] \wedge X_{x'}[\boldsymbol{x} := \boldsymbol{x}'']))$$

$$= \overline{x}' \cdot \mathrm{relcomp}(T, X_{\overline{x}'}) \vee x' \cdot \mathrm{relcomp}(T, X_{x'}))$$

Case $x'' \in \boldsymbol{x}''$: $\mathrm{relcomp}(T, X) := \exists \boldsymbol{x}'' : (T[\boldsymbol{x}' := \boldsymbol{x}''] \wedge X[\boldsymbol{x} := \boldsymbol{x}''])$

$$= \exists \boldsymbol{x}'' : ((T[\boldsymbol{x}' := \boldsymbol{x}''] \wedge X[\boldsymbol{x} := \boldsymbol{x}''])_{\overline{x}''} \vee (T[\boldsymbol{x}' := \boldsymbol{x}''] \wedge X[\boldsymbol{x} := \boldsymbol{x}''])_{x''})$$

$$= \exists \boldsymbol{x}'' : ((T[\boldsymbol{x}' := \boldsymbol{x}'']_{\overline{x}''} \wedge X[\boldsymbol{x} := \boldsymbol{x}'']_{\overline{x}''}) \vee (T[\boldsymbol{x}' := \boldsymbol{x}'']_{x''} \wedge X[\boldsymbol{x} := \boldsymbol{x}'']_{x''}))$$

$$= \exists \boldsymbol{x}'' : ((T_{\overline{x}'}[\boldsymbol{x}' := \boldsymbol{x}''] \wedge X_{\overline{x}}[\boldsymbol{x} := \boldsymbol{x}'']) \vee (T_{x'}[\boldsymbol{x}' := \boldsymbol{x}''] \wedge X_x[\boldsymbol{x} := \boldsymbol{x}'']))$$

$$= \exists \boldsymbol{x}'' : (T_{\overline{x}'}[\boldsymbol{x}' := \boldsymbol{x}''] \wedge X_{\overline{x}}[\boldsymbol{x} := \boldsymbol{x}'']) \vee \exists \boldsymbol{x}'' : (T_{x'}[\boldsymbol{x}' := \boldsymbol{x}''] \wedge X_x[\boldsymbol{x} := \boldsymbol{x}''])$$

$$= \mathrm{relcomp}(T_{\overline{x}'}, X_{\overline{x}}) \vee \mathrm{relcomp}(T_{x'}, X_x)$$

Algorithm 4. relcomp(T, X)

1: **if** $T = 0 \vee X = 0$ **then return** 0
2: **if** $T = 1 \wedge X = 1$ **then return** 1
3: **if** $(T, X, \mathrm{relcomp})$ in **cache then return** $\mathtt{cache}[(T, X, \mathrm{relcomp})]$
4: $x \leftarrow \min(\mathtt{var}(T), \mathtt{var}(X))$
5: **if** $x \in \boldsymbol{x} \wedge x = \mathtt{var}(T)$ **then**
6:     **do in parallel:**
7:         $low \leftarrow \mathrm{relcomp}(T_{\overline{x}}, X)$
8:         $high \leftarrow \mathrm{relcomp}(T_x, X)$
9:     $result \leftarrow \mathtt{BDD\_node}(x, low, high)$
10: **else if** $x \in \boldsymbol{x}' \wedge x = \mathtt{var}(X)$ **then**
11:     **do in parallel:**
12:         $low \leftarrow \mathrm{relcomp}(T, X_{\overline{x}})$
13:         $high \leftarrow \mathrm{relcomp}(T, X_x)$
14:     $result \leftarrow \mathtt{BDD\_node}(x, low, high)$
15: **else**
16:     $x \leftarrow \boldsymbol{x}(x), x' \leftarrow \boldsymbol{x}'(x)$
17:     **do in parallel:**
18:         $low \leftarrow \mathrm{relcomp}(T_{\overline{x}'}, X_{\overline{x}})$
19:         $high \leftarrow \mathrm{relcomp}(T_{x'}, X_x)$
20:     $result \leftarrow \mathrm{apply}(low, high, \cup)$
21: $\mathtt{cache}[(T, X, \mathrm{relcomp})] \leftarrow result$
22: **return** $result$

The terminal cases of relcomp are: $\text{relcomp}(T, 0) = \text{relcomp}(0, X) = 0$ and $\text{relcomp}(1, 1) = 1$. Algorithm 4 constructs Y using these derivations. The use of the variables x'' can be avoided by changing the case $x \in x$ to $x \in x \wedge x = \text{var}(T)$ and changing the case $x \in x'$ to $x \in x' \wedge x = \text{var}(X)$.

Both the $\forall$preimage and relcomp operation require one symbolic step, i.e., $\cap$ and $\cup$, as witnessed by the call to apply in the recursion. This follows from the existential quantifier in their definition and makes the complexity of the operations quadratic in the number of BDD nodes (as for $\exists$).

Parallel Fix Point Computation. The *bisim* algorithm can be further parallelized by concurrently performing the computation of f_a for each action a, instead of looping over all actions. This approach employs a BFS extension of R, rather than an extension by chaining (which is inherently sequential). Algorithm 5 displays the version of *bisim* which implements this approach.

The parallelization of the loop which computes f_a is handled by the function *parLoop*, shown in Algorithm 6. It takes similar inputs as the *bisim* algorithm: a BDD R which represents non-bisimilar state pairs and a list T of BDDs representing transition relations which are separated on action labels.

Instead of considering each transition relation in T sequentially, the algorithm decomposes T into two halves. It then recursively calls itself on both halves, and computes the results in parallel. This takes place on Lines 6–8. The union of the two results is returned at Line 9. When T only contains one transition relation, the recursive procedure is stopped. Lines 2–5 return the result of $f_a(R)$ for the action corresponding to the transition relation contained in T.

The recursive decomposition applied in *parLoop* yields a task dependency graph as shown in Fig. 7. It is not immediately clear if the *bisimP* algorithm is more efficient than the standard *bisim* algorithm. The parallelization of the extension of R should cause *bisimP* to have a better scalability than *bisim*, but chaining is usually the more efficient approach [23]. The two algorithms are therefore compared empirically in Sect. 5.

Algorithm 5. bisimP(S, T)

1: $R \leftarrow \emptyset$
2: **repeat**
3:      $R' \leftarrow R$
4:      $R \leftarrow R \cup \text{parLoop}(R, T)$
5: **until** $R = R'$
6: **return** $\overline{R}$

Algorithm 6. parLoop(R, T)

1: $n \leftarrow |T|$
2: **if** $n = 1$ **then**
3:      $X \leftarrow \forall$preimage(R, T[1])
4:      $Y \leftarrow$ relcomp(T[1], X)
5:      **return** $Y \cup Y^{-1}$
6: **do in parallel:**
7:      $L \leftarrow$ parLoop(R, T[1 : $\lfloor \frac{n}{2} \rfloor$])
8:      $H \leftarrow$ parLoop(R, T[$\lfloor \frac{n}{2} \rfloor + 1 : n$])
9: **return** $L \cup H$

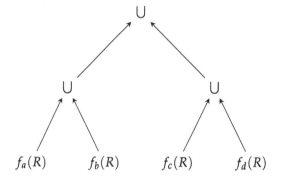

Fig. 7. A task dependency graph of parLoop for an input LTS with $A = \{a, b, c, d\}$.

4 Related Work

The *relation-based* approach used in Algorithm 2/5 was pioneered by Boauli and de Simone [3] and later generalized by Liu and Smolka [17]. Their results showed small improvements over the existing explicit methods. Another symbolic relation-based algorithm was introduced by Mumme and Ciardo [19]. Their algorithm functions much like our *bisim* algorithm, although found independently. Mumme and Ciardo's algorithm differs from Algorithm 2 (*bisim*) in four ways. First, the algorithm does not employ high-level BDD operations, requiring intermediate symbolic computations which pollute the cache. Second, the algorithm is sequential. Third, the algorithm does not apply the converse operation utilized in *bisim* (see Line 7). As a consequence, the computation of non-bisimilar pairs of states requires two extra symbolic steps. Fourth, the algorithm improves on chaining by implementing saturation [7].

Also, Dalsgaard et al. [8] use Liu and Smolka's general approach [17] to distribute the computation of bisimulation minimization. In essence, this algorithm therefore is also relation-based.

The second approach to bisimulation minimization uses signatures to iteratively refine a partition representing the bisimilar equivalence classes. This *partition-based* approach is used in explicit algorithms by Paige and Tarjan [20], and in symbolic algorithms by Wimmer et al. [25] and Van Dijk [11] among others. The algorithm presented by van Dijk is, as far as we are aware, the only parallel symbolic bisimulation algorithm.

The algorithm maintains a partition π initialized with a single block containing S before it is refined using the transition relation. The partition π is represented by a BDD $P(s, b)$, which encodes a state s followed by a block number (= equivalence class label) b. The symbolic partition refinement operation efficiently reuses block numbers to avoid trashing the BDD cache, a solution that improved over the state of the art by up to a factor 50 for the considered inputs.

It is stated by Van Dijk and by Fisler and Vardi [13] that partition-based BDDs form a smaller representation of the maximal bisimulation than relation-based BDDs. This statement is based on the number of variables which are used in partition- and relation-based BDDs. If an LTS contains n states, then a relation-based R will require $\lceil 2 \cdot \log_2 n \rceil$ variables to encode all pairs of states. The number of variables used in partition-based BDD P depends on the number of equivalence classes in the partition, but is always in between $\lceil \log_2(n) \rceil$ and $\lceil 2 \cdot \log_2(n) \rceil$. The number of nodes in a BDD can grow exponentially in the number of used variables. Therefore, the researchers concluded that partition-based BDDs are generally smaller.

The benefits of bisimulation minimization in the context of state space reduction prior to or during the verification of invariance properties are examined by Fisler and Vardi in [13]. They compare three algorithms which verify the invariance properties of a model while computing its maximal bisimulation on-the-fly (or online). Thus, if the input does not verify, the model checking process can be stopped prematurely (without even exploring, minimizing and storing all reachable states). Fisler and Vardi found in previous work [14] that the cost of bisimulation minimization often exceeds the cost of model checking by a considerable margin. They hoped that their new approach would be more efficient than model checking without the use of bisimulation minimization. Unfortunately, the results show that using bisimulation minimization as either a part of, or as a preprocessor to, model checking invariant properties is not profitable. However, this does not mean that bisimulation minimization can not be beneficial in other verification contexts, such as offline distributed verification [2].

5   Experimental Evaluation

We repeated the experiment ran by Van Dijk and Van de Pol in [11] to study the difference in performance between *bisim*, *bisimP* and Van Dijk's state-of-the-art algorithm. In the experiment, the maximal bisimulation is computed for six LTS models which portray Kanban production systems [25]. The smallest model contains 256 states and 904 transitions, while the largest model contains 264,515,056 states and 1,689,124,864 transitions.

The experiment was performed on a machine that contains two Intel Xeon E5-2630v3 CPUs with eight cores each. To evaluate the parallel speedup of each algorithm, the experiment was run once using only one core and once using all sixteen cores. At the start of the experiment, 2.625 GB of memory space is allocated for the two hash tables which contain the unique table and the operation cache. The maximum size of each hash table was limited to 84 GB.

Implementation. The *bisim* and *bisimP* algorithms (Algorithms 2 and 5) and the ∀preimage and relcomp BDD operations were implemented in Sylvan [10], a parallel BDD library written in C. Sylvan offers (internally) parallel BDD operations, by splitting the recursive calls into fine-grained tasks, which are scheduled by Lace [12]. We used the same approach to implement the recursive calls listed in Algorithms 3 and 4 as parallel calls. Thus, all BDD operations performed in our two algorithms are fully parallel.

The *bisimP* algorithm also features high-level parallelism by creating a task dependency graph of BDD operations themselves. We implemented these parallel calls as separate tasks in Lace, which ensures that the fine-grained internal tasks and the high-level (external) calls are all executed in parallel, while maintaining the partial order stipulated by the dependency graphs.

We did not succeed with implementing the *bisim* and *bisimP* without the coarse-grained BDD operations from Algorithms 3 and 4. Therefore, we could not compare the individual gains achieved by the development of these coarse operations. Since [24] showed an up to 40% percent performance and space savings improvement for an integrated image BDD operation (`RelProdS`), we can reasonably expect at least a similar improvement from our coarse BDD operations. In fact, the benefit likely exceeds that amount, because the bisimulation computation in small steps requires the introduction of doubly primed variables (and `RelProdS` does not).

Results. The results of the experiment are presented in Table 1. The run times shown in the table are the averages of 16 runs. Entries containing a dashed line (-) went over the time limit, which was set to 2400 s. The number behind the algorithm name in the column header indicates the number of cores that were used in the experiment. The speedup of each algorithm is determined per model by dividing the sequential run time by the parallel run time.

Table 1. Results of the experiments. The shown run times are the average of at least 16 runs. The timeout is set to 2400 s.

Model	Time (s)						Speedups		
	Van Dijk 1	Van Dijk 16	*bisim* 1	*bisim* 16	*bisimP* 1	*bisimP* 16	Van Dijk	*bisim*	*bisimP*
kanban01	0.07	0.09	0.02	0.08	0.03	0.11	0.78	0.25	0.27
kanban02	0.17	0.61	0.72	1.93	1.42	1.71	0.28	0.37	0.83
kanban03	3.66	3.18	7.14	5.83	18.67	7.18	1.15	1.22	2.60
kanban04	53.84	24.60	42.81	18.38	194.17	39.45	2.19	2.33	4.92
kanban05	549.47	201.82	216.82	55.44	1223.02	157.65	2.72	3.91	7.76
kanban06	-	1758.71	724.84	147.12	-	576.85	-	4.93	-

For the three largest models *bisim* provides the best results. The parallel execution of *bisim* on the kanban06 model is almost 4 times faster than the parallel execution of *bisimP* and almost 12 faster than the parallel execution of Van Dijk's algorithm. Also, *bisim* is the only algorithm that can compute the maximal bisimulation of the kanban06 model within the time limit using only one core. The speedups of both *bisim* and *bisimP* are higher than the speedup of Van Dijk's algorithm, indicating a better scalability. As expected, *bisimP* does have a better speedup than *bisim*. For kanban01 and kanban02 the speedup is less than 1, thus here the overhead of parallelizing is greater than the benefits.

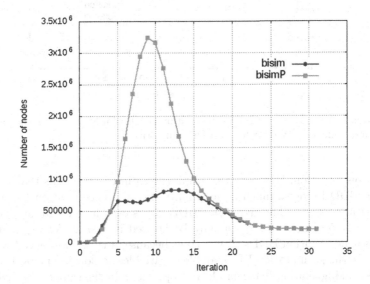

Fig. 8. Number of nodes contained in R per iteration for the execution of *bisim* and *bisimP* on the kanban05 model.

Longer run times of symbolic algorithms are generally caused by BDDs that grow larger. The graphs in Fig. 8 depicts the number of nodes in R during the execution of *bisim* and *bisimP*. At its peak, the BDD used in *bisimP* is about 4 times as large as the BDD used in *bisim*. It appears that the chaining heuristic used in *bisim* keeps R much smaller than the breadth first heuristic employed in *bisimP*. We also measured the peak size of the BDDs X and Y, which are used to compute the pairs of non-bisimilar states with which R is extended. For *bisim*, X contains 1,965,391 nodes and Y contains 1,165,512 at its peak. The peak sizes of *bisimP* are much higher, with 11,405,465 nodes for X and 16,761,754 nodes for Y.

The kanban05 model contains 16,772,032 states, which, after bisimulation, are divided over 5,033,631 equivalence classes. We therefore expected that the permutation BDD used in Van Dijk's algorithm would be smaller than the equivalence relation BDD used in *bisim*, as it requires less variables to represent the

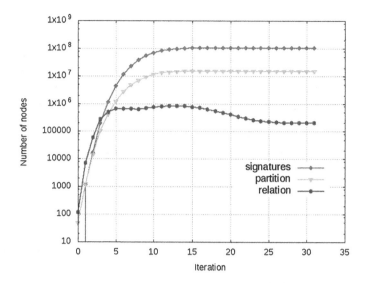

Fig. 9. Number of nodes contained in the relation BDD R for $bisim$ and in the partition BDD P and signatures BDD σ for Van Dijk's algorithm.

maximal bisimulation. However, the graph shown in Fig. 9 reveals that the permutation BDD becomes much larger than the equivalence relation BDD (note the logarithmic scale). The signatures BDD grows even larger still, and is at its peak at least 50 times as large as any BDD used in $bisim$. We presume that the equivalence relation BDDs stay smaller because of their interleaved variable ordering. In the permutation BDD, all block variables are located below the state variables making sharing between blocks impossible. In the signatures BDD, the action variables are located in between the state and block variables as well. Encoding different objects underneath each other in a BDD typically causes the BDD to blow up in size. So, even though the permutation BDD contains less variables, it still grows much larger than the equivalence relation BDD. Also, the permutation and signatures BDDs do not decrease in size at any time during the execution of the algorithm. This is likely caused by the fact that Van Dijk's algorithm adds new block variables at the bottom of the BDDs during its execution.

The size of the signatures BDD is crucial for the time efficiency of Van Dijk's algorithm, as it is used in both the permutation refinement and the signature computation step. One iteration of Van Dijk's algorithm takes one symbolic step, while a single iteration in $bisim$ could require at most $2 \cdot |A|$ symbolic steps. Coincidentally, both algorithms terminate after 31 iterations for the kanban05 model. Thus, the difference in size between the BDDs used in the two algorithms seems to outweigh the difference in symbolic steps.

To validate our results, we converted the partitions of Van Dijk's algorithm to an equivalence relation. Unfortunately, this conversion was too time consuming to verify the results of the two largest models. All other results were successfully validated.

6 Conclusions

We have presented an algorithm for parallel symbolic bisimulation minimization, which stores the bisimilar states in a relation rather than as a partition of equivalence classes. We realized key parts of the algorithm through novel coarse-grained BDD operations derived from the specification using the Shannon decomposition. The correctness of derived algorithms follows therefore immediately. Moreover, our coarse-grained BDD operations increase performance by avoiding pollution in the computer and unique tables, especially since an algorithm using fine-grained operations would require additional doubly primed variables.

We have compared the performance of our algorithm to that of the state-of-the-art parallel symbolic bisimulation algorithm, which is partition-based. The surprising result is that our relation-based algorithm outperforms the partition-based algorithm by at least one order of magnitude for large models. The consensus in the literature is that partition-based algorithms require fewer variables and should therefore also result in smaller BDDs. However, our results suggest that the opposite is true. We hypothesize that the interleaving of (primed and unprimed) variables in the BDD representing the bisimulation relation results in more sharing than partition-based approaches can deliver.

As future work, we advocate an investigation of the other bisimulation approaches discussed in Van Dijk and Van de Pol [11]. Furthermore, we are interested in the application of the saturation heuristic on BDDs. We suspect also that the number of symbolic steps in our algorithms can be reduced by encoding transition labels in the BDD, as Van Dijk does.

References

1. Baier, C., Katoen, J.: Principles of Model Checking. MIT Press, Cambridge (2008)
2. Blom, S., Orzan, S.: Distributed branching bisimulation reduction of state spaces. Electron. Notes Theor. Comput. Sci. **89**(1), 99–113 (2003)
3. Bouali, A., de Simone, R.: Symbolic bisimulation minimisation. In: von Bochmann, G., Probst, D.K. (eds.) CAV 1992. LNCS, vol. 663, pp. 96–108. Springer, Heidelberg (1993). https://doi.org/10.1007/3-540-56496-9_9
4. Brace, K.S., Rudell, R.L., Bryant, R.E.: Efficient implementation of a BDD package. In: 27th ACM/IEEE Design Automation Conference, pp. 40–45 (1990)
5. Bryant, R.E.: Graph-based algorithms for boolean function manipulation. IEEE Trans. Comput. **C–35**(8), 677–691 (1986)
6. Burch, J., Clarke, E., McMillan, K., Dill, D., Hwang, L.: Symbolic model checking: 1020 states and beyond. Inf. Comput. **98**(2), 142–170 (1992)
7. Ciardo, G., Lüttgen, G., Siminiceanu, R.: Saturation: an efficient iteration strategy for symbolic state—Space generation. In: Margaria, T., Yi, W. (eds.) TACAS 2001. LNCS, vol. 2031, pp. 328–342. Springer, Heidelberg (2001). https://doi.org/10.1007/3-540-45319-9_23

8. Dalsgaard, A.E., Enevoldsen, S., Larsen, K.G., Srba, J.: Distributed computation of fixed points on dependency graphs. In: Fränzle, M., Kapur, D., Zhan, N. (eds.) SETTA 2016. LNCS, vol. 9984, pp. 197–212. Springer, Cham (2016). https://doi.org/10.1007/978-3-319-47677-3_13

9. De Nicola, R., Vaandrager, F.: Three logics for branching bisimulation. J. ACM (JACM) **42**(2), 458–487 (1995)

10. van Dijk, T.: Sylvan: multi-core decision diagrams. Ph.D. thesis, University of Twente (2016). https://doi.org/10.3990/1.9789036541602

11. van Dijk, T., van de Pol, J.: Multi-core symbolic bisimulation minimisation. Int. J. Softw. Tools Technol. Transf. **20**(2), 157–177 (2018)

12. van Dijk, T., van de Pol, J.C.: Lace: non-blocking split deque for work-stealing. In: Lopes, L., et al. (eds.) Euro-Par 2014. LNCS, vol. 8806, pp. 206–217. Springer, Cham (2014). https://doi.org/10.1007/978-3-319-14313-2_18

13. Fisler, K., Vardi, M.Y.: Bisimulation and model checking. In: Pierre, L., Kropf, T. (eds.) CHARME 1999. LNCS, vol. 1703, pp. 338–342. Springer, Heidelberg (1999). https://doi.org/10.1007/3-540-48153-2_29

14. Fisler, K., Vardi, M.Y.: Bisimulation minimization in an automata-theoretic verification framework. In: Gopalakrishnan, G., Windley, P. (eds.) FMCAD 1998. LNCS, vol. 1522, pp. 115–132. Springer, Heidelberg (1998). https://doi.org/10.1007/3-540-49519-3_9

15. Hennessy, M., Milner, R.: Algebraic laws for nondeterminism and concurrency. J. ACM (JACM) **32**(1), 137–161 (1985)

16. Huth, M., Ryan, M.: Verification by model checking, chap. Logic in Computer Science, p. 241. Cambridge University Press, Cambridge (2004)

17. Liu, X., Smolka, S.A.: Simple linear-time algorithms for minimal fixed points. In: Larsen, K.G., Skyum, S., Winskel, G. (eds.) ICALP 1998. LNCS, vol. 1443, pp. 53–66. Springer, Heidelberg (1998). https://doi.org/10.1007/BFb0055040

18. Milner, R.: Communication and Concurrency. Prentice Hall, Upper Saddle River (1989)

19. Mumme, M., Ciardo, G.: An efficient fully symbolic bisimulation algorithm for non-deterministic systems. IJFCS **24**(02), 263–282 (2013)

20. Paige, R., Tarjan, R.E.: Three partition refinement algorithms. SIAM J. Comput. **16**(6), 973–989 (1987). https://doi.org/10.1137/0216062

21. Park, D.: Concurrency and automata on infinite sequences. In: Deussen, P. (ed.) GI-TCS 1981. LNCS, vol. 104, pp. 167–183. Springer, Heidelberg (1981). https://doi.org/10.1007/BFb0017309

22. Shannon, C.E.: A symbolic analysis of relay and switching circuits. Electr. Eng. **57**(12), 713–723 (1938). https://doi.org/10.1109/EE.1938.6431064

23. Solé, M., Pastor, E.: Traversal techniques for concurrent systems. In: Aagaard, M.D., O'Leary, J.W. (eds.) FMCAD 2002. LNCS, vol. 2517, pp. 220–237. Springer, Heidelberg (2002). https://doi.org/10.1007/3-540-36126-X_14

24. Van Dijk, T., Laarman, A., Van De Pol, J.: Multi-core BDD operations for symbolic reachability. Electron. Notes Theor. Comput. Sci. **296**, 127–143 (2013)

25. Wimmer, R., Herbstritt, M., Hermanns, H., Strampp, K., Becker, B.: SIGREF – a symbolic bisimulation tool box. In: Graf, S., Zhang, W. (eds.) ATVA 2006. LNCS, vol. 4218, pp. 477–492. Springer, Heidelberg (2006). https://doi.org/10.1007/11901914_35

Combining Refinement of Parametric Models with Goal-Oriented Reduction of Dynamics

Stefan Haar[1], Juraj Kolčák[1,2(✉)], and Loïc Paulevé[3,4]

[1] LSV, CNRS & ENS Paris-Saclay, Université Paris-Saclay, Cachan, France
{stefan.haar,juraj.kolcak}@lsv.fr
[2] National Institute of Informatics, Tokyo, Japan
[3] LRI UMR 8623, Univ. Paris-Sud – CNRS, Université Paris-Saclay, Orsay, France
[4] Univ. Bordeaux, Bordeaux INP, CNRS, LaBRI, UMR5800, 33400 Talence, France
loic.pauleve@labri.fr

Abstract. Parametric models abstract part of the specification of dynamical models by integral parameters. They are for example used in computational systems biology, notably with parametric regulatory networks, which specify the global architecture (interactions) of the networks, while parameterising the precise rules for drawing the possible temporal evolutions of the states of the components. A key challenge is then to identify the discrete parameters corresponding to concrete models with desired dynamical properties. This paper addresses the restriction of the abstract execution of parametric regulatory (discrete) networks by the means of static analysis of reachability properties (goal states). Initially defined at the level of concrete parameterised models, the goal-oriented reduction of dynamics is lifted to parametric networks, and is proven to preserve all the minimal traces to the specified goal states. It results that one can jointly perform the refinement of parametric networks (restriction of domain of parameters) while reducing the necessary transitions to explore and preserving reachability properties of interest.

1 Introduction

Various cyber and physical systems are studied by the means of discrete dynamical models which describe the possible temporal evolution of the state of the components of the system. Defining such models requires extensive knowledge on the underlying system for specifying the rules which generate the admissible state transitions over time. Usually, and especially for physical systems, such as biological networks for which discrete models are extensively employed

This work has been partly funded by ANR-FNR project "AlgoReCell" ANR-16-CE12-0034, by Labex DigiCosme (project ANR-11-LABEX-0045-DIGICOSME) operated by ANR as part of the program "Investissement d'Avenir" Idex Paris-Saclay (ANR-11-IDEX-0003-02), and by ERATO HASUO Metamathematics for Systems Design Project (No. JPMJER 1603), JST.

C. Enea and R. Piskac (Eds.): VMCAI 2019, LNCS 11388, pp. 555–576, 2019.
https://doi.org/10.1007/978-3-030-11245-5_26

[1,8,9,12,18,24], it is common to lack such precise knowledge, making an accurate specification of discrete models challenging.

With *parametric* models, part of the specification of the rules for generating the discrete transitions is encoded as (integral) parameters. Thus, a parametric model abstracts a set of concrete *parameterised* models, this set being characterised by the domain of parameter values.

In this paper, we focus on *Parametric Regulatory Networks* (PRNs), also known as Thomas Networks [2,4,15,23], which are commonly employed for modelling qualitative dynamics of biological systems. PRNs allow separating biological knowledge on the pairwise interactions (the architecture of the network) from the rules of interplay between the interactions, usually less known.

In the literature, PRNs are mainly used as a basic framework for identifying fully parameterised models (i.e., Boolean and multilevel networks) which satisfy dynamical properties typically generated from experimental data. This identification task, related to so-called model inference and process mining [5,16,17,21], consists in transforming an abstract parametric model into a set of concrete parameterised models verifying desired dynamical properties. For PRNs, state-of-the-art methods rely on parameter enumeration [13], coloured model-checking [14], logic programming and Boolean satisfiability [10,19], and Hoare logic [3].

However, the exhaustive identification of parameters is often limited to small models, as the set of parameterised models can turn out to be too large to be exhaustively enumerated and further analysed.

In [15], we introduced a semantics of PRNs enabling the *refinement* of a PRN by restricting the domain of its parameters without having to enumerate concrete models, keeping them in a compact abstract representation instead. The refinement is performed according to concrete discrete state transitions: the domain of parameters is restricted so that it abstracts all the concrete models in which the state transition is admissible. Essentially, such semantics of PRNs enable efficient exploration of dynamics of a set of parameterised models.

This exploration suffers from the same bottleneck as individual parameterised models: the number of reachable states grows exponentially with the number of components and thus, becomes intractable for large networks. The exploration of the reachable state space is usually performed to verify dynamical properties. Consequently, various *model reduction* methods have been designed on concrete parameterised models to enhance the tractability of their verification [6,11,20,22]: by reducing the transitions to consider, these methods limit the reachable state space to explore while guaranteeing the correctness of the verification.

In this paper, we address the combination of refinement operations on parametric models with model reductions initially defined at the level of concrete individual models. Essentially, the challenge consists in lifting up such model reductions so they can be performed at the abstract level of parametric models, while ensuring the correctness of their refinement.

We focus on reachability properties, i.e., starting in an initial configuration, the ability to eventually reach a given (partial) configuration. On the one hand, we are interested in refining PRNs to accurately identify concrete parameterised discrete network models that verify the reachability property; on the other hand, we want to take advantage of goal-driven exploration of dynamics of parameterised models to ignore transitions which do not influence the reachability of the goal, enhancing the tractability of the analysis.

The refinement of PRNs we consider for reachability properties has been introduced in [15]. It consists in dynamically drawing transitions allowed by at least one concrete model, and subsequently restricts the domain of parameters to exclude models which do not allow the drawn transition. The generation of transitions is done directly from the abstract representation of the set of concrete models, and therefore involves no enumeration of parameterised models.

The goal-oriented model reduction we consider has been introduced in [20] at the level of parameterised network models. Given a reachability property (goal), the method relies on static analysis by abstract interpretation to identify transitions which are not involved in any minimal trace leading to the goal. Here the minimality refers to the absence of a sub-trace. Whereas deciding reachability properties in parametrised models (namely automata networks) is a PSPACE-complete problem [7], the goal-oriented model reduction has a complexity polynomial in the number of components and exponential in the in-degree of components in the networks (components having a direct influence on a single one).

In this article we present a lifting of the goal-oriented reduction from parametrised models to sets of models with shared architecture, represented by parametric models. To this end, we introduce a directed version of PRNs which allow us to efficiently capture model reduction without the need to explicitly enumerate all possible transitions. We conduct the reduction itself on abstract dynamics of PRNs where instead of enumerating all enabled transitions, we only consider the minimal necessary condition for each component to change value.

The introduced reduction method can be applied on-the-fly to speed up reachability checking in parametric models. Thanks to the preservation of *all* minimal traces, it is guaranteed to capture all parametrised models capable of reproducing the coveted behaviour.

Outline. Section 2 recalls the definition of parametric regulatory networks, their dynamics, constraints on influences and finally presents a generalised parametrisation set semantics. In Sect. 3, the goal-oriented model reduction procedure is extended from parametrised models to parametric models. Directed version of PRNs is introduced for this purpose alongside an abstraction of dynamics designed to alleviate the reduction complexity. Section 4 supplies an algorithm for computing a suitable abstraction of PRN dynamics used in the reduction procedure. Finally, Sect. 5 summarises the results and possible extensions.

Notations. We use $\prod$ to build Cartesian products between sets. As the ordering of components matters, $\prod$ is not commutative. Hence, we write $\prod_{x \in X}^{\leq}$ for the product over elements in X according to a total order $\leq$. To ease notations, when the order is clear from the context, or when either X is a set of integers, or a set of integer vectors, on which we use the lexicographic ordering, we simply write

$\prod_{x \in X}$. Given a sequence of n elements $\pi = (\pi_i)_{1 \le i \le n}$, $\widetilde{\pi} \overset{\Delta}{=} \{\pi_i \mid 1 \le i \le n\}$ is the set of its elements. Given a vector $v = \langle v_1, \ldots, v_n \rangle$, $v_{[i \mapsto y]}$ is the vector equal to v except on the component i, which is equal to y.

2   Parametric Regulatory Networks

Regulatory networks are finite discrete dynamical systems where the components evolve individually with respect to the value of (a few) other components, their regulators. The value of components in regulatory networks ranges in a finite discrete domain, usually represented as $\{0, \ldots, m\}$ for some $m \in \mathbb{N}$, thus extending Boolean networks [24]. The evolution of components is then defined by discrete functions which associate to the global states of the network the value towards which each component tends.

Thus, defining regulatory networks requires knowledge on which components influence each others, and how the value of each component is computed from the value of its regulators. *Parametric* Regulatory Networks (PRNs) allow to decouple this specification by having on the one hand a fixed architecture of the network, so-called *influence graph*, and on the other hand discrete parameters, which when instantiated specify the functions of the regulatory network.

2.1   Influence Graph and Constraints

The influence graph encodes the directed interactions between the components of the regulatory networks: a component u having a direct influence on component v means that in some states of the regulatory network, the computation of the value of node v *may* depend on the value of u. Importantly, if the component w has no direct influence of v, then the computation of the value on v never depends on the value of w.

Definition 1 (Influence Graph). *An* influence graph G *is a tuple* (V, I) *where* V *is a finite set of* n *nodes (components) and* $I \subseteq V \times V$ *is a set of directed edges (influences).*

For each $v \in V$ *we denote the set of its* regulators *by* $n^-(v) \overset{\Delta}{=} \{u \in V \mid (u, v) \in I\}$.

Besides the existence/absence of direct influences between components, it is usual to have some knowledge about the nature of the influences. Two kinds of constraints are generally considered: *signs* and *observability*.

Influence signs are captured by monotonicity constraints. An influence $(u, v) \in I$ is *positive-monotonic*, denoted $+$, if the sole increase of the value of the regulator u cannot cause a decrease of the computed value of the target v. Symmetrically, an influence $(u, v) \in I$ is *negative-monotonic*, denoted $-$, if the sole increase in the value of u cannot cause an increase in the computed value of v. An influence $(u, v) \in I$ is *observable*, denoted o, if there exists a state in which the sole change of the value of u induces a change of the computed value of v. Thus observability enforces that u does have an influence on the value of v, in some states of the regulatory network. Remark that observability does not imply positive/negative monotonicity – e.g., when the value of v is computed as the exclusive disjunction XOR between its own value and the value of u.

Let us denote a set of influence constraints for an influence graph (V, I) as $R \subseteq I \times \{+, -, \mathrm{o}\}$. An example of influence constraint set is given in Fig. 1(a) as labels on edges of the influence graph.

2.2   Parametrisation

Let us consider an influence graph $G = (V, I)$ among n components and a set of influences constraints R. Let us denote by $m \in \mathbb{N}^n$ the vector specifying the maximum discrete value of each component: the states of the regulator networks span $\prod_{v \in V}\{0, \ldots, m_v\}$. The computation of the value of each component of a regulatory network is constrained by G, R and m. In particular, G imposes that the value of a component depends only on its regulators.

A *regulator state* ω of a component $v \in V$ is a vector specifying the value of each regulator of v. We denote the set of all regulator states of a component as $\Omega_v \triangleq \prod_{u \in n^-(v)}\{0, \ldots, m_u\}$. Intuitively, a regulator state of a component v is a projection of a global state of the network (states of all components) to just the regulators of v, that fully determine its evolution.

A *parameter* $\langle v, \omega \rangle$ then represents a target value towards which component $v \in V$ evolves in regulator state $\omega \in \Omega_v$. We denote the set of all parameters as $\Omega \triangleq \bigcup_{v \in V}\{v\} \times \Omega_v$.

A *parametrisation* P is a vector assigning a value to each parameter. The set of all parametrisations associated to an influence graph G and a maximum value vector m is therefore given by $\mathbb{P}(G_m) = \prod_{\langle v, \omega \rangle \in \Omega}^{\trianglelefteq}\{0, \ldots, m_v\}$ where $\trianglelefteq$ is an arbitrary, but fixed total order on parameters. The set of all parametrisations satisfying both the influence graph $G = (V, I)$ and influence constraints R with maximum value vector m is then defined as:

$$\mathbb{P}(G_m^R) \triangleq \{P \in \prod_{\langle v, \omega \rangle \in \Omega}^{\trianglelefteq}\{0, \ldots, m_v\} \mid \forall u, v \in V,$$

$$(u, v, +) \in R \Rightarrow \forall \omega \in \Omega_v, \forall k \in \{1, \ldots, m_u\} : P_{v, \omega_{[u \mapsto k]}} \geq P_{v, \omega_{[u \mapsto k-1]}}$$

$$(u, v, -) \in R \Rightarrow \forall \omega \in \Omega_v, \forall k \in \{1, \ldots, m_u\} : P_{v, \omega_{[u \mapsto k]}} \leq P_{v, \omega_{[u \mapsto k-1]}}$$

$$(u, v, \mathrm{o}) \in R \Rightarrow \exists \omega \in \Omega_v, \exists k \in \{1, \ldots, m_u\} : P_{v, \omega_{[u \mapsto k]}} \neq P_{v, \omega_{[u \mapsto k-1]}}\}$$

2.3   Parametric Regulatory Networks

A *Parametric Regulatory Network* (PRN) gathers an influence graph G, influence constraints R, and maximum value vector m, to which can then be associated a subset of parametrisations $\mathbb{P}(G_m^R)$. A (*parametrised*) regulatory network can then be defined by a couple (G_m^R, P) where $P \in \mathbb{P}(G_m^R)$.

Definition 2. *A parametric regulatory network (PRN) is a tuple (G, m, R), written G_m^R, where G is an influence graph between n components, R is a set of influence constraints, and $m \in \mathbb{N}^n$ is a vector of the maximum values of each component.*

The set of states of G_m^R is denoted by $S(G_m^R) \triangleq \prod_{v \in V}\{0, \ldots, m_v\}$.

The set of (local) transitions of G_m^R is denoted by: $\Delta(G_m^R) \triangleq \{(v_i \to v_j, \omega) \mid v \in V \land \omega \in \Omega_v \land i, j \in \{0, \ldots, m_v\} \land |i - j| = 1\}$. We use $V((v_i \to v_j, \omega)) = v$ to denote the component whose value is changed by transition $(v_i \to v_j, \omega) \in \Delta(G_m^R)$. Furthermore, $s((v_i \to v_j, \omega)) = s(v_i \to v_j) = j - i$ denotes the sign of the transition (value change).

A transition $(v_i \to v_j, \omega) \in \Delta(G_m^R)$ is *enabled* in state $x \in S(G_m^R)$ if $x_v = i$ and $\omega_v(x) = \omega$, where $\omega_v(x)$ is the projection of state x to the regulators of v. Given a state x and a transition t enabled in x, $x \cdot t$ denotes the state $x_{[v \mapsto j]} \in S(G_m^R)$ obtained by firing transition t in x.

Finally, a transition $(v_i \to v_j, \omega) \in \Delta(G_m^R)$ is *enabled* by a parametrisation set $\mathcal{P} \subseteq \mathbb{P}(G_m^R)$ if there exists a parametrisation $P \in \mathcal{P}$ such that the parameter value $P_{v,\omega} = j + a \cdot s(v_i \to v_j)$ for some $a \in \mathbb{N}_0$.

Example 1. An example of a PRN G_m^R composed of an influence graph $G = (V, I)$ and vector $m = \{1\}^{|V|}$ is depicted in Fig. 1. Based on the influences in G and maximum values in m, all regulator states of each component, which correspond to parameters of G_m^R are determined. The table in Fig. 1(b) lists all the parameters alongside an example parametrisation $P \in \mathbb{P}(G_m^R)$. G_m^R combined with P identifies a unique parametrised network (G_m^R, P). The dynamics of (G_m^R, P) are given in Fig. 1(c).

We capture the basic semantics of a PRN by traces, which correspond to different possible behaviours of the network.

Definition 3 (Trace). *Given a PRN G_m^R and set of parametrisations $\mathcal{P} \subseteq \mathbb{P}(G_m^R)$, a finite sequence $\pi = (\pi_1, \ldots, \pi_{|\pi|})$ of transitions in $\Delta(G_m^R)$ is a trace of G_m^R starting in state $x \in S(G_m^R)$ iff $\forall i \in \{1, \ldots, |\pi|\} : \pi_i$ is enabled in state $x \cdot \pi_1 \cdot \ldots \cdot \pi_{i-1}$ and by parametrisation set $\mathcal{P}$.*

To simplify notation, we use $^\bullet\pi = x$ and $\pi^\bullet = x \cdot \pi_1 \cdot \ldots \cdot \pi_{|\pi|}$. Moreover, let $\pi^{:i} = (\pi_1, \ldots, \pi_i)$, $\pi^{i:} = (\pi_i, \ldots, \pi_{|\pi|})$ and $\pi^{i:j} = (\pi_i, \ldots, \pi_j)$ denote the prefix, suffix and infix sub-traces of π respectively.

With $P \in \mathbb{P}(G_m^R)$ and $\mathcal{P} = \{P\}$, the above definition gives the traces of the parametrised regulatory network (G_m^R, P). In the general case, each transition is independently enabled with respect to any parametrisation in $\mathcal{P}$.

2.4   Parametrisation Set Semantics

With the basic PRN semantics (Definition 3), two transitions are allowed to fire consequently in a single trace despite no single parametrisation enabling both of them. To forbid such behaviours, semantics have been introduced for PRNs that associate each trace (set of transitions) with a set of parametrisations [15]. Said trace can then be extended only by transitions enabled under some parametrisation from the associated set.

The purpose of parametrisation set semantics is to discriminate transitions based on their causal history. This is done by progressive restriction of the set of parametrisations to *admissible* parametrisations. Following [15], we consider a parametrisation P to be admissible if all transitions in the set (causal history) are enabled under P. However, we allow for a more lenient definition to make room for over-approximation.

Definition 4 (Parametrisation Set Semantics). *Given a PRN G_m^R, a function $\Psi : 2^{\Delta(G_m^R)} \rightarrow 2^{\mathbb{P}(G_m^R)}$ is a* parametrisation set semantics *of G_m^R iff:*

1. $\forall T \subseteq \Delta(G_m^R) : \{P \in \mathbb{P}(G_m^R) \mid \forall t \in T : P$ *enables* $t\} \subseteq \Psi(T)$,
2. $\forall T, T' \subseteq \Delta(G_m^R) : T \subseteq T' \Rightarrow \Psi(T') \subseteq \Psi(T)$.

A trace π of the PRN G_m^R is realisable *according to the parametrisation set semantics if and only if $\Psi(\widetilde{\pi}) \neq \emptyset$.*

A best abstraction Ψ_C producing parametrisation sets of exactly all the parametrisations that allow each transition in the input set has been defined in [15]. To facilitate practical application, as the number of parametrisations may be in the worst case double exponential in the number of components, [15] has tackled the semantics Ψ_A over-approximating parametrisation sets by convex covers, keeping track of only a maximal and minimal element and thus avoiding the need to enumerate parametrisations explicitly. More formally, let us first reintroduce the *parametrisation order*.

Definition 5. *The* parametrisation order *on vectors of length k is the partial order $\leq$ defined as follows:*

$$a \leq b \overset{\Delta}{\Leftrightarrow} \forall i \in \{0, \ldots, k-1\} : a_i \leq b_i$$

The parametrisation set given by Ψ_A is a couple of parametrisations (L, U) representing the lower and upper bound. Formally, $(L, U) = \{P \in \mathbb{P}(G_m^R) \mid L \leq P \wedge U \geq P\}$ is a bounded convex sublattice of all vectors of length $|\Omega|$ with the parametrisation order. In [15], a method has been provided to compute *the tightest lower and upper bounds* for a given set of transitions and influence constraints without the need to explicitly enumerate the parametrisations.

Naturally, checking whether a particular parametrisation belongs to the abstracted set can be done simply by comparing it with the bounds. Similarly, determining whether a transition is enabled (by any parametrisation) can be done without explicit enumeration of the parametrisations. In fact, it is enough to compare against the corresponding parameter value of the relevant bound, e.g. $U_{v,\omega} \geq k+1$ is the sufficient and necessary condition for the transition $(v_k \rightarrow v_{k+1}, \omega)$ to be enabled.

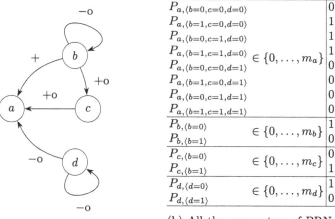

(a) The influence graph G.

(b) All the parameters of PRN G_m^R with an example parametrisation P.

(c) States and transitions of (G_m^R, P) depicted as nodes and edges of a state space graph respectively. Since components b and d may update values independently of other components (i.e. in any state), their value changes are only displayed schematically to improve readability.

Fig. 1. Influence graph with influence constraints as labels, parameters and dynamics of a possible parametrisation of PRN G_m^R.

In this article, we consider any parametrisation set semantics compatible with Definition 4, however, special attention is given to Ψ_A as it can be used with the restriction method without the need to enumerate the parametrisations explicitly.

3   Goal-Oriented Reduction

In this section, we extend the goal-oriented model reduction procedure from parametrised models (in particular, automata networks) [20] to the parametric models.

3.1   Minimal Traces

Given a PRN G_m^R and a state $x \in S(G_m^R)$, we say a value $\top \in \{0, \dots, m_g\}$ of a component $g \in V$ is *reachable* from x iff either $x_g = \top$ or there exists a realisable trace π with ${}^\bullet\pi = x$ and $\pi^\bullet{}_g = \top$.

We are interested in reachability by *minimal* traces. Adapted from [20], a realisable trace is minimal for $g_\top$ reachability if there exists no other realisable trace reaching $g_\top$ with a subsequence of transitions.

Definition 6 (Minimal Trace). *Given a parametrised PRN (G_m^R, P), a trace π of (G_m^R, P) is minimal w.r.t. reachability of goal $g_\top$ from state x if and only if there exists no other trace ρ satisfying $x = {}^\bullet\rho$, $\rho^\bullet{}_g = \top$, $|\rho| < |\pi|$ and existence of an injection $\phi : \{1, \dots, |\rho|\} \to \{1, \dots, |\pi|\}$ such that $\forall i, j \in \{1, \dots, |\rho|\} : i \leq j \Rightarrow \phi(i) \leq \phi(j)$ and $\rho_i = \pi_{\phi(i)}$.*

An important property of minimal traces is their independence on the exact parametrisation. More precisely, using parametrisation set semantics, if a trace is minimal for at least one parametrisation, then it is minimal for any other parametrisation under which it is enabled.

Property 1 (Parametrisation Independence of Minimal Traces). Let G_m^R be a PRN and π a realisable trace minimal in (G_m^R, P) for some $P \in \Psi(\widetilde{\pi})$. Then, π is minimal in any (G_m^R, P') where $P' \in \Psi(\widetilde{\pi})$.

Proof. $P' \in \Psi(\widetilde{\pi})$ guarantees π is a proper trace of (G_m^R, P'). We conduct the rest of the proof by contradiction. Let thus ρ be a trace in (G_m^R, P') satisfying the conditions in Definition 6. From the existence of the injection ϕ we get $\widetilde{\rho} \subseteq \widetilde{\pi}$ and from the definition of parametrisation set semantics $\Psi(\widetilde{\pi}) \subseteq \Psi(\widetilde{\rho})$. ρ is therefore realisable in (G_m^R, P) meaning that π is not minimal in (G_m^R, P) which is a contradiction.

Property 1 allows us to speak of a realisable trace of a PRN as minimal without the need to explicitly state the parametrisation which is witness to the minimality.

3.2   Directed Parametric Regulatory Networks

The goal-oriented reduction for parametrised models is facilitated by pruning transitions which are guaranteed to not be used by any minimal trace reaching the goal [20]. The PRN definition could be extended to allow for pruning the transition set to subsets $T \subseteq \Delta(G_m^R)$. Unlike the case of general parametrised models, however, the transitions of a PRN only allow to change the value of a component by steps of size 1. As such, if a transition increasing the value of a component $v \in V$ to $k \in \{0, \dots, m_v\}$ is to be pruned, all transitions increasing the value of v beyond k can surely be pruned as well, and symmetrically for decreasing transitions. Thus, instead of removing individual transitions of PRNs, we disable increasing, respectively decreasing, value of a component in a given regulator state beyond a certain value (or entirely). This is facilitated by keeping record of the activation (increase) and inhibition (decrease) limits for each component in vectors l^A and l^I respectively.

Definition 7 (Directed Parametric Regulatory Network). *A directed parametric regulatory network (DPRN) is a tuple* $\mathcal{G} = (G_m^R, l^A, l^I)$*, where* G_m^R *is a parametric regulatory network,* $l^A \in (\mathbb{N} \cup \{-\infty\})^{|\Omega|}$ *is a vector of activation limits for each regulator state* $\omega \in \Omega_v$ *and* $l^I \in (\mathbb{N}_0 \cup \{\infty\})^{|\Omega|}$ *is a vector of inhibition limits for each regulator state* $\omega \in \Omega_v$*.*

The set of states of $\mathcal{G}$ *is equal to the set of states of the underlying PRN:* $S(\mathcal{G}) = S(G_m^R)$*.*

The set of transitions of $\mathcal{G}$ *is a subset of the PRN transitions satisfying the activation and inhibition limits* l^A *and* l^I *respectively. Formally,* $\Delta(\mathcal{G}) \subseteq \Delta(G_m^R)$ *such that:*

$$\forall t = (v_i \to v_j, \omega) \in \Delta(G_m^R) : t \in \Delta(\mathcal{G}) \overset{\triangle}{\Leftrightarrow} \begin{cases} i < l^A{}_\omega & \text{if } s(t) = +1 \\ i > l^I{}_\omega & \text{if } s(t) = -1 \end{cases}$$

One may remark that by using parametrisation set semantics, it is already possible to restrict the activation or inhibition of components in individual regulator states while just using PRNs. While it is true that an equivalent set of enabled transitions can be achieved both by restricting the parametrisation set and by DPRN, the semantics of the two restrictions are different.

The parametrisation set semantics serves primarily to keep track of parametrisations capable of reproducing certain behaviour(s), and thus restrict the set of enabled transitions based on their causal history. On the other hand, the l^A and l^I of DPRN mark components whose activation or inhibition (beyond a certain value) is not necessary to reach a given goal (via a minimal trace). A parametrisation that allows changing a component value beyond the limit, thus allowing behaviour which does not lead to the established goal may still allow a different sequence of transitions leading to the goal. We want to retain such parametrisations, thus the "useless" behaviour which does not lead to the goal cannot be restricted in the parametrisation set semantics. Therefore, keeping the information about parametrisations and about the activation and inhibition limits independently is key.

The complete independence of parametrisation set semantics and the limit vectors l^A and l^I allows us to employ both in parallel. The extension of both traces (Definition 3) and parametrisation set semantics (Definition 4) from PRNs to DPRNs is thus natural.

3.3   Objectives

The reduction for parametrised models relies on identifying sub-goals, or *objectives*, local in terms of individual components. We reintroduce the concept of a (local) objective for the parametric model.

Definition 8 (Objective). *Given an DPRN $\mathcal{G}$, an objective $v_i \rightsquigarrow v_j$ is a pair of values $i, j \in \{0, \ldots, m_v\}$ of a component $v \in V$.*

An objective $v_i \rightsquigarrow v_j$ is valid in a starting state $x \in S(\mathcal{G})$ iff $i = j$ or a realisable trace π of the parametrised DPRN exists, such that $^{\bullet}\pi = x$, $\pi^{\bullet}{}_v = j$ and $\exists k \in \{0, \ldots, |\pi| - 1\} : {}^{\bullet}\pi_{kv} = i$.

$i \rightsquigarrow j$ is used to denote $v_i \rightsquigarrow v_j$ if the component $v \in V$ is obvious from the context.

Each objective $v_i \rightsquigarrow v_j$ captures either increase or decrease of the value of the component. Formally, the sign of an objective $s(v_i \rightsquigarrow v_j) \overset{\Delta}{=} \mathrm{SIGN}(j - i)$.

By requiring the witness of objective validity to be a realisable trace instead of just a trace of enabled transitions, we retain only behaviours which are present in at least one parametrised model.

The objective represents a change of value of only one component $v \in V$. A realisable trace reproducing such a change may, however, require to also change value of other components, namely the regulators of v. Each objective is thus associated to a set of transitions which may be used to complete it, and from which the required regulator values can be obtained.

3.4 Regulation Cover Sets

Depending on the parametrisation set semantics, it may be a common occurrence for a particular value change to be enabled by numerous regulator states (recall that enabling is existential w.r.t. parametrisations). Such cases lead to a substantial redundancy in individual transition enumeration as the value of only a subset of regulators may be enough to determine whether a value change is enabled or not. To this end we introduce a definition of a partial regulator state, which is used to represent a (minimal) condition for a value change to be enabled.

Definition 9 (Partial Regulator State). *A partial regulator state $\aleph$ of component $v \in V$ is a vector $\aleph \in \prod_{u \in n^-(v)} \{0, \ldots, m_u\} \cup \{*\}$ assigning a value or a wildcard character $*$ to each regulator u of v. By abuse of notation, $\aleph$ is also a set of regulator states, more precisely $\aleph \subseteq \Omega_v$ such that for all $\omega \in \Omega_v$:*

$$\omega \in \aleph \overset{\Delta}{\Leftrightarrow} \forall u \in n^-(v) : \omega_u = \aleph_u \vee \aleph_u = *$$

The set of all partial regulator states of $v \in V$ is denoted as $\mathcal{A}_v$.

Partial regulator states can be utilised to abstract the DPRN dynamics while minimising the number of repetitions of each value of each regulator. We capture these abstractions by the means of sets of partial regulator states, called *regulation cover sets*, representing the enabling condition of a given value change. We impose two conditions on regulation cover set of value change c. First, the set has to cover all regulator states ω such that (c, ω) is enabled. In other words, for each such regulator state there must exist one or more partial regulator states which specify the value of each regulator in ω. Second, no bad regulator state ω such that (c, ω) is not enabled is subsumed by any of the partial regulator states in the cover set. These two conditions not only guarantee that the abstract dynamics enable exactly the same value changes as the concrete dynamics, but also preserve the regulator information, i.e. each value of each regulator that appears in the enabling conditions. The regulator information is necessary to accurately determine which regulator values are necessary to complete an objective.

Definition 10 (Regulation Cover Set). *Let $\mathcal{G}$ be a DPRN and $\mathcal{P}$ a parametrisation set from the parametrisation set semantics, and let $c = v_i \rightarrow v_j$ be an arbitrary value change of a component $v \in V$. A set of partial regulator states $\mathcal{A}_c \subseteq \mathcal{A}_v$ is a cover set of c iff the following is satisfied:*

- *$\forall \omega \in \Omega_v : (c, \omega)$ is enabled under $\mathcal{P}: \forall u \in n^-(v) : \exists \aleph \in \mathcal{A}_c : \omega \in \aleph \wedge \omega_u = \aleph_u$.*
- *$\forall \omega \in \Omega_v : (c, \omega)$ is not enabled: $\forall \aleph \in \mathcal{A}_c : \omega \notin \aleph$.*

Any regulation cover set, including the concrete regulation cover set $\{\omega \mid \omega \in \Omega_v : (c, \omega)$ is enabled$\}$, may be used for the purposes of the reduction procedure. The aim of the regulation cover set being to minimise the number of individual regulator values which appear across all of the partial regulator states, an algorithm that computes regulator cover sets with no more regulator value specifications than the concrete regulation cover set is introduced in Sect. 4.

3.5   Reduction of Directed Parametric Regulatory Networks

Our reduction procedure essentially relies on associating to objectives the set of (partial) transitions which are necessary to realise the objective within the corresponding components of the PRN. Starting from the final (goal) objective, the procedure then recursively collects objectives related to the identified transitions.

Since PRNs allows only unitary value changes, the realisation of an objective $v_i \rightsquigarrow v_j$ involves a monotonic change of value of component v from i to j, where each change of value depends on specific (partial) regulator state. This coupling of a value change with a corresponding partial regulator state is referred to as a *partial transition*.

Definition 11 (Objective Transition Set). *Let $\mathcal{G}$ be an DPRN parametrised by $\mathcal{P}$, and let $v_i \rightsquigarrow v_j$ be an objective for $v \in V$. The objective transition set $\tau(v_i \rightsquigarrow v_j)$ is defined as $\tau(v_i \rightsquigarrow v_j) \overset{\Delta}{=} \emptyset$ whenever $i = j$, otherwise,*

$$\tau(v_i \rightsquigarrow v_j) \overset{\Delta}{=} \{(v_k \rightarrow v_q, \aleph) \mid s(v_k \rightarrow v_q) = s(v_i \rightsquigarrow v_j) \wedge \aleph \in \mathcal{A}_{v_k \rightarrow v_q}$$
$$\wedge \text{MAX}\{k, q\} \leq \text{MAX}\{i, j\} \wedge \text{MIN}\{k, q\} \geq \text{MIN}\{i, j\}\}$$

Given an initial state $x \in S(\mathcal{G})$, the valid objective transition set *of an objective $v_i \rightsquigarrow v_j$ in state x is a subset of the objective transition set $\tau_x(v_i \rightsquigarrow v_j) \subseteq \tau(v_i \rightsquigarrow v_j)$ such that: $(c, \aleph) \in \tau_x(v_i \rightsquigarrow v_j) \overset{\Delta}{\Leftrightarrow} \forall u \in n^-(v) : \aleph_u \neq * \Rightarrow x_u \rightsquigarrow \aleph_u$ is valid in state x.*

The (valid) objective transition sets extend to sets of objectives in the natural manner: $\tau(\mathcal{O}) = \bigcup_{O \in \mathcal{O}} \tau(O)$.

Remark that the definition of a valid objective transition set benefits from the use of partial regulator states. Indeed, instead of having to check validity of an objective for each regulator, only the minimal necessary subset of regulators is considered. Checking objective validity consists of searching for a realisable trace, which translates to finding all possible extensions (enabled transitions) of a trace. As enabled transitions can be retrieved using Ψ_A without explicitly enumerating the parametrisations, the validity check is compatible with Ψ_A.

The goal-oriented reduction of DPRNs can then be defined by recursively collecting objectives from partial transitions ($\mathcal{B}$) and refining the component activation and inhibition limits accordingly.

Definition 12 (Reduction Procedure). *The goal-oriented reduction of a DPRN $\mathcal{G} = (G_m^R, l^A, l^I)$ for an initial state $x \in S(\mathcal{G})$ and a goal $g_\top$ is the DPRN $\mathcal{G}' = (G_m^R, l^{A'}, l^{I'})$ with $l^{A'}$ and $l^{I'}$ being defined as follows, $\forall v \in V, \forall \omega \in \Omega_v$:*

$$l^{A'}_\omega = \mathrm{MAX}(\{k \in \{0, \dots, m_v\} \mid \exists(v_{k-1} \to v_k, \aleph) \in \tau_x(\mathcal{B}) : \omega \in \aleph\} \cup \{-\infty\})$$

$$l^{I'}_\omega = \mathrm{MIN}(\{k \in \{0, \dots, m_v\} \mid \exists(v_{k+1} \to v_k, \aleph) \in \tau_x(\mathcal{B}) : \omega \in \aleph\} \cup \{\infty\})$$

where $\mathcal{B}$ is the smallest set of objectives satisfying the following:

1. $x_g \rightsquigarrow \top \in \mathcal{B}$
2. $\forall O \in \mathcal{B} : \forall (v_k \to v_q, \aleph) \in \tau_x(O) : \forall u \in n^-(v) \setminus \{v\} : \aleph_u \neq * \Rightarrow x_u \rightsquigarrow \aleph_u \in \mathcal{B}$
3. $\forall O \in \mathcal{B} : \forall (v_k \to v_q, \aleph) \in \tau_x(O) : \forall v_i \rightsquigarrow v_j \neq O \in \mathcal{B} : v_q \rightsquigarrow v_j \in \mathcal{B}$.

Example 2. Consider the parametric regulatory network G_m^R introduced in Example 1 converted to a DPRN $\mathcal{G} = (G_m^R, l^A, l^I)$ in an unrestrictive manner ($l^A = \{1\}^V$ and $l^I = \{0\}^V$), and a parametrisation set containing only two parametrisations $\mathcal{P} = \{P, P'\}$, where P is the parametrisation from Example 1 and P' differs from P only in value of $P'_{a, \langle b=1, c=0, d=0 \rangle} = 0$. Furthermore, let $a = 1$ be a goal and $x = \langle a = 0, b = 0, c = 0, d = 0 \rangle$ an initial state.

In Fig. 2 we recall the dynamics of $\mathcal{G}$ given as a state space graph. Note that the second parametrisation P' is also shown within the graph as opposed to the one in Example 1.

In our example, there are three minimal traces from the initial state x reaching the goal $a = 1$:

$$\langle 0000 \rangle \xrightarrow{b+, \langle 0 \rangle} \langle 0100 \rangle \xrightarrow{a+, \langle 100 \rangle} \langle 1100 \rangle$$

$$\langle 0000 \rangle \xrightarrow{b+, \langle 0 \rangle} \langle 0100 \rangle \xrightarrow{c+, \langle 1 \rangle} \langle 0110 \rangle \xrightarrow{a+, \langle 110 \rangle} \langle 1110 \rangle$$

$$\langle 0000 \rangle \xrightarrow{b+, \langle 0 \rangle} \langle 0100 \rangle \xrightarrow{c+, \langle 1 \rangle} \langle 0110 \rangle \xrightarrow{b-, \langle 1 \rangle} \langle 0010 \rangle \xrightarrow{a+, \langle 010 \rangle} \langle 1010 \rangle$$

All the listed traces share a common prefix, however, they are all minimal as a different regulator state is used to activate a each time, thus each of the

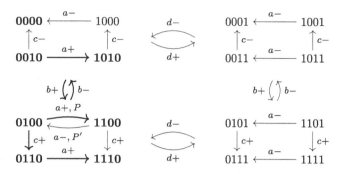

Fig. 2. States and transitions of $(\mathcal{G}, \{P, P'\})$ depicted as nodes and edges of a state space graph respectively. Transitions changing the value of b and d are displayed schematically. Transitions only enabled by a single of the parametrisations are marked accordingly. Bold font and lines indicate states and transitions used by at least one minimal trace from the initial state to the goal.

traces has at least one unique transition. One may further remark that the first (shortest) minimal path is only available under parametrisation P, however, thanks to Property 1 this has no impact on the reduction procedure itself.

Observe that node d never activates in any of the minimal traces. This follows from the fact that a is never allowed to activate while d is active. Thus, if d activates it has to deactivate again before the goal can be reached. As d has no impact on the value of the other components besides a, such an activation and deactivation loop can always be stripped from the trace to obtain a smaller trace, unlike the loop by b in the third (longest) trace, which is necessary for the activation of c. One might thus expect the activation of d to be pruned during the reduction procedure, which is, indeed the case:

We start with $\mathcal{B} := \{a_0 \rightsquigarrow a_1\}$ according to rule (1) of Definition 12.

Inference of the regulator cover set used for $\tau_x(a_0 \rightsquigarrow a_1) = \{(a_0 \rightarrow a_1, \aleph) \mid \aleph \in \mathcal{A}_{a_0 \rightarrow a_1}\} = \{(a_0 \rightarrow a_1, \langle 100 \rangle), (a_0 \rightarrow a_1, \langle 010 \rangle), (a_0 \rightarrow a_1, \langle 110 \rangle)\}$ is illustrated in Example 3. Then, by rule (2) of Definition 12, the following objectives are included in $\mathcal{B} := \mathcal{B} \cup \{b_0 \rightsquigarrow b_0, b_0 \rightsquigarrow b_1, c_0 \rightsquigarrow c_0, c_0 \rightsquigarrow c_1, d_0 \rightsquigarrow d_0\}$.

For arbitrary component v, the objective $v_0 \rightsquigarrow v_0$ has an empty valid transition set $\tau_x(v_0 \rightsquigarrow v_0) = \emptyset$ and thus neither of rules (2) or (3) are applicable. For the remaining $b_0 \rightsquigarrow b_1$ and $c_0 \rightsquigarrow c_1$ rule (2) produces only duplicate objectives ($b_0 \rightsquigarrow b_0$ and $b_0 \rightsquigarrow b_1$, respectively). Rule (3), however, may be applied to $b_0 \rightsquigarrow b_1$ and $c_0 \rightsquigarrow c_1$ to bridge them to $b_0 \rightsquigarrow b_0$ and $c_0 \rightsquigarrow c_0$, respectively, to include objectives $\mathcal{B} := \mathcal{B} \cup \{b_1 \rightsquigarrow b_0, c_1 \rightsquigarrow c_0\}$.

Only duplicate objectives are obtained by application of either rule (2) or (3) on the newly added $b_1 \rightsquigarrow b_0$ and $c_1 \rightsquigarrow c_0$. Thus, the reduction concludes with $\mathcal{B} = \{a_0 \rightsquigarrow a_1, b_0 \rightsquigarrow b_0, b_0 \rightsquigarrow b_1, b_1 \rightsquigarrow b_0, c_0 \rightsquigarrow c_0, c_0 \rightsquigarrow c_1, c_1 \rightsquigarrow c_0, d_0 \rightsquigarrow d_0\}$, with valid transition set $\tau_x(\mathcal{B}) = \{(a_0 \rightarrow a_1, \langle 100 \rangle), (a_0 \rightarrow a_1, \langle 010 \rangle), (a_0 \rightarrow a_1, \langle 110 \rangle), (b_0 \rightarrow b_1, \langle 0 \rangle), (b_1 \rightarrow b_0, \langle 1 \rangle), (c_0 \rightarrow c_1, \langle 1 \rangle), (c_1 \rightarrow c_0, \langle 0 \rangle)\}$. One may observe that the computed transition set indeed covers all the transitions used by any of the minimal traces (thick edges in Fig. 2).

Finally, the limit vectors for the new DPRN $\mathcal{G}' = (G_m^R, l^{A'}, l^{I'})$ are computed as follows:

$$l^{A'} = \langle a = 1, b = 1, c = 1, d = -\infty \rangle$$

$$l^{I'} = \langle a = \infty, b = 0, c = 0, d = \infty \rangle$$

Observe that component d is indeed completely forbidden from acting in the reduced model, considerably decreasing the reachable state space that has to be explored. Notice that deactivation of a is also disabled, however, in our Boolean case this has no practical effect w.r.t. reachability of $a = 1$.

3.6 Correctness

Following the interpretation of the reduction procedure and thanks to the monotonicity of value updating, a transition (c, ω) remains enabled in $\mathcal{G}'$ iff at least one partial transition $(c, \aleph)$ exists in $\tau_x(\mathcal{B})$ with $\omega \in \aleph$. This leads us to formulate the soundness theorem of the reduction procedure, guaranteeing that all transitions of all minimal traces are preserved and thus, in turn, all minimal traces are preserved.

Theorem 1. *Let $\mathcal{G}$ be a DPRN, and let a realisable trace π of $\mathcal{G}$ be minimal for an initial state $x \in S(\mathcal{G})$ and goal $g_\top$. Then, for any transition $(c, \omega) \in \tilde{\pi}$ there exists at least one partial transition $(c, \aleph) \in \tau(\mathcal{B})$ such that $\omega \in \aleph$, where $\mathcal{B}$ is constructed according to Definition 12.*

The proof of the theorem relies on showing that any transition which is not preserved is part of a cycle on any trace leading to the goal, and as a consequence does not belong to any minimal trace. The formal proof is given in the appendix available at https://arxiv.org/src/1811.12377/anc/appendix.pdf.

4 Regulation Cover Set Inference

In this section we introduce a heuristic for construction of regulation cover sets whose size, w.r.t. specified regulator values across all partial regulator states, does not exceed the size of the concrete regulation cover set.

Let $\mathcal{A}_{\text{ENA}} = \{\aleph \in \mathcal{A}_v \mid \forall \omega \in \aleph : (c, \omega) \text{ is enabled}\}$ be the set of all partial regulators states which contain no bad regulator states. For each $i \in \{0, \ldots, |n^-(v)|\}$ let $\mathcal{A}_i = \{\aleph \in \mathcal{A}_v \mid |\{u \in n^-(v) \mid \aleph_u = *\}| = i\}$ to be the set of all partial regulator states with exactly i regulator values equal to $*$.

The algorithm consists of choosing partial regulator state set, $\mathcal{A}_{\text{EXT}}$, to cover each (concrete) regulator state enabling the value change. This is done separately for each regulator state in an increasing order of a weight function. The weight function represents flexibility of covering the regulator state, i.e. there are

---

Algorithm 1. Pseudocode of the algorithm computing regulation cover set.

---

function WEIGHT(ω)

    return $|\{\aleph \in (\mathcal{A}_1 \cap \mathcal{A}_{\text{ENA}}) \setminus \mathcal{A}_{\text{RMV}} \mid \omega \in \aleph\}| + \frac{|\{\aleph \in \mathcal{A}_1 \cap \mathcal{A}_{\text{ENA}} \mid \omega \in \aleph\}|}{|n^-(v)|+1}$

end function

function COMPUTECOVERSET($c = v_k \rightarrow v_q$)

    $\mathcal{A}_c \leftarrow \emptyset$

    $\mathcal{A}_{\text{RMV}} \leftarrow \emptyset$

    while $\mathcal{A}_0 \neq \emptyset$ **do**

        $\omega \leftarrow \omega' \in (\mathcal{A}_0 \cap \mathcal{A}_{\text{ENA}}) \setminus \mathcal{A}_{\text{RMV}}$

            with WEIGHT(ω') = MIN$\{$WEIGHT(ω'') $\mid \omega'' \in (\mathcal{A}_0 \cap \mathcal{A}_{\text{ENA}}) \setminus \mathcal{A}_{\text{RMV}}\}$

        $\mathcal{A}_{\text{EXT}} \leftarrow \emptyset$

        $i \leftarrow |n^-(v)| - 1$

        while ω is not covered by $\mathcal{A}_c \cup \mathcal{A}_{\text{EXT}}$ **do**

            $\mathcal{A}_{\text{EXT}} \leftarrow (\mathcal{A}_i \cap \mathcal{A}_{\text{ENA}}) \setminus \mathcal{A}_{\text{RMV}}$

            $i \leftarrow i - 1$

        end while

        $\mathcal{A}_c \leftarrow \mathcal{A}_c \cup \mathcal{A}_{\text{EXT}}$

        $\mathcal{A}_{\text{RMV}} \leftarrow \mathcal{A}_{\text{RMV}} \cup \{\aleph \in \mathcal{A}_v \mid \omega \in \aleph\}$

    end while

    return $\mathcal{A}_c$

end function

---

more partial regulator states in $\mathcal{A}_{\text{ENA}}$ containing a regulator state with a larger weight than the ones covering regulator state with smaller weight. The weights are dynamic as the partial regulator states get removed ($\mathcal{A}_{\text{RMV}}$) throughout the algorithm. The $\mathcal{A}_{\text{EXT}}$ for each regulator state is computed by testing candidate sets of partial regulator states from $\mathcal{A}_i$ in decreasing order on i. A cover set for each regulator state is guaranteed to exist as for $i = 0$ the candidate set is a singleton set containing the regulator state itself. Once a suitable cover set is found for a particular regulator state, it is included in the regulation cover set $\mathcal{A}_c$ and all partial regulator states containing the regulator state are excluded from further computation.

As the weight function gives only a partial order on the regulator states, the algorithm is forced to make nondeterministic choices. This occurs, however, only in cases when the choices are isomorphic. As such, the partial order given by weights can be extended to a total order arbitrarily, e.g. by underlying lexicographic order. The pseudocode of the algorithm to construct regulation cover sets is given in Algorithm 1.

The correctness of the algorithm comes directly from the construction. No bad states may be included as the algorithm works only with the set of partial regulator states which include no bad states. On the other hand, all regulator states which enable the value change are fully covered as the algorithm ensures this for each of them individually.

The resulting cover set computed by Algorithm 1 contains no more explicit regulator value specifications than the concrete regulation cover set. This is a consequence of the order of regulator states covering. Suppose a regulator state ω is covered by several partial regulator states which contain more regulator value specifications than ω itself. Each partial regulator state $\aleph \in \mathcal{A}_1$ with $\aleph_u = *$ is shared with exactly $m_u - 1$ other regulator states. Thus, the partial regulator states included to cover ω can be utilised while covering $m_u - 1$ other regulator states. Finally, since WEIGHT(ω) ≥ 2 is the smallest weight among all uncovered regulator states, all the other uncovered regulator states are also sharing partial regulator states among themselves, thus closing the loop and guaranteeing the regulator value specification debt eventually gets "payed off".

The fractional part of the weight function is included to introduce bias towards states that have less partial regulator states in the beginning (due to sharing with more bad states). If there are two regulator states ω and ω' such that $\lfloor$WEIGHT(ω)$\rfloor = \lfloor$WEIGHT(ω')$\rfloor$ but WEIGHT(ω) $<$ WEIGHT(ω'), we know that both of them have equally many partial regulator states to choose from for their respective cover sets. However, more of the partial regulator states containing ω' have been removed and thus, quite possibly included in the regulation cover set $\mathcal{A}_c$. ω' is therefore in all likelihood already covered to a higher degree than ω and possibly, has more covering options. The bias thus ensures ω is covered first in order to avoid introducing potentially redundant partial regulator states into the regulation cover set.

Both principles making up the weight function are illustrated in Example 3.

Example 3. Consider the same directed parametric regulatory network $\mathcal{G}$ as in Example 2.

We now show the regulation cover set computation for value changes of component a. Let us start with $a_0 \rightarrow a_1$. The initial configuration and first two iterations, consisting of covering of the first two regulator states, of the algorithm are schematically depicted in Fig. 3.

Figure 3 lists all regulator states of component a as nodes in a graph. Bold font indicates the three regulator states which enable the increase of a. The partial regulator states from $\mathcal{A}_1$ correspond to edges in the graph, connecting contained regulator states. Thick edges indicate partial regulator states which contain no bad regulator states. Partial regulator states from $\mathcal{A}_2$ could in turn be viewed as squares in the diagram, all of them containing at least one bad regulator state in our case. In the graphical representation of regulator states, a partial regulator state belonging to $\mathcal{A}_i$ is a i-dimensional hypercube in the Boolean case, or a i-dimensional hyper-rectangular cuboid in the general case.

The graph representation in Fig. 3 allows for easy visualisation of the weight function. The weight corresponds to number of thick, non-dashed edges plus, the number of thick edges divided by $|n^-(a)| + 1$, in our case 4. Consequently, in the initial configuration (Fig. 3(a)) the regulator states $\langle 100 \rangle$ and $\langle 010 \rangle$ have equal (minimal) weight. This is justified by their perfectly symmetrical position.

Figure 3 illustrates the run of the algorithm assuming lexicographic order is used to distinguish between regulator states with equal weights. In the first iteration $\langle 010 \rangle$ is covered using itself for the extension set $\mathcal{A}_{\text{EXT}} = \{\langle 010 \rangle\}$ as the only partial regulator state with more unspecified regulator values, $\langle *10 \rangle$,

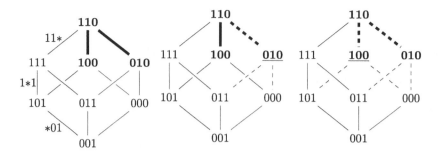

(a) Initial configuration

(b) Configuration after one iteration.

(c) Configuration after two iterations.

Fig. 3. Regulator states of component a during computation of regulation cover set for value change $a_0 \to a_1$. Only the leftmost edges in (a) are labelled by the corresponding partial regulator states $11*, 1*1$ and $*01$ for the sake of readability. Bold text and lines indicate (partial) regulator states which enable the value change ($\mathcal{A}_{\mathrm{ENA}}$). Underlined regulator state is the state covered in the respective iteration and dashed lines represent removed partial regulator states ($\mathcal{A}_{\mathrm{RMV}}$).

alone does not fully cover $\langle 010 \rangle$. Figure 3(b) depicts the situation after the first iteration, including the removed partial regulator states (dashed lines).

In the second iteration $\langle 100 \rangle$ is covered in the exact same fashion, owning to the symmetric position w.r.t. $\langle 010 \rangle$. The result is shown in Fig. 3(c).

No partial regulator states remain for the last regulator state $\langle 110 \rangle$ except the regulator state itself. Thus, $\langle 110 \rangle$ also gets covered explicitly. The algorithm therefore concludes with the concrete regulation cover set $\mathcal{A}_{a_0 \to a_1} = \{\langle 010 \rangle, \langle 100 \rangle, \langle 110 \rangle\}$, which, in fact, is the optimal solution in our case.

Let us now consider also the decreasing case $a_1 \to a_0$. Again, we illustrate the running of the algorithm using graph representation of the regulator states of a. All iterations up to the final one of the algorithm using lexicographic order on regulator states of equal weight are given in Fig. 4.

The algorithm begins with covering the regulator state $\langle 000 \rangle$. Unlike in the case of increasing a, a nonempty candidate extension set exists for partial regulator states on level $\mathcal{A}_2$ containing a single element $\{\langle *0* \rangle\}$. This partial regulator state alone, however, does not suffice to cover $\langle 000 \rangle$ and extension set $\{\langle 00* \rangle, \langle *00 \rangle\}$ is used instead as indicated by double lines in Fig. 4(b). Notice that in this case, the node $\langle 000 \rangle$ gets covered by two partial regulator states having one more regulator value specification (a total of 4 specifications against the explicit 3).

According to the weight function, $\langle 100 \rangle$ gets covered next. $\langle *0* \rangle$ is no longer available, thus the first nonempty candidate extension set is $\{\langle 10* \rangle\}$. Although $\langle 10* \rangle$ alone is not enough to fully cover $\langle 100 \rangle$, the cover set $\mathcal{A}_{a_1 \to a_0}$ already contains $\langle *00 \rangle$ which covers $\langle 100 \rangle$ completely in combination with $\langle 10* \rangle$. Thus,

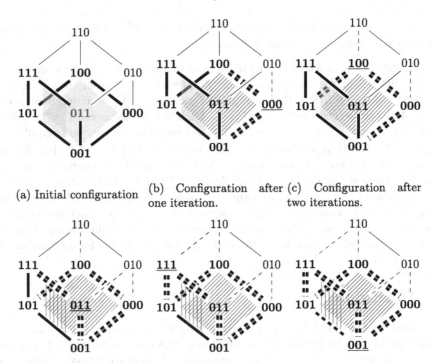

(a) Initial configuration

(b) Configuration after one iteration.

(c) Configuration after two iterations.

(d) Configuration after three iterations.

(e) Configuration after four iterations.

(f) Configuration after five iterations.

Fig. 4. Regulator states of component a during computation of regulation cover set for value change $a_1 \to a_0$. Bold text, lines and shaded areas indicate (partial) regulator states which enable the value change ($\mathcal{A}_{\mathrm{ENA}}$). The underlined regulator state is the state covered in the respective iteration. Dashes represent removed partial regulator states ($\mathcal{A}_{\mathrm{RMV}}$) and double lines represent partial regulator states included in the regulation cover set ($\mathcal{A}_{a_1 \to a_0}$).

$\langle 100 \rangle$ gets covered by including only 2 additional regulator value specifications, effectively "paying-off" the depth incurred while covering $\langle 000 \rangle$.

Covering $\langle 011 \rangle$ and subsequently $\langle 111 \rangle$ is identical to that of $\langle 000 \rangle$ and $\langle 100 \rangle$. Both of them thus get covered by three partial regulator states $\langle 0*1 \rangle$, $\langle *11 \rangle$ and $\langle 1*1 \rangle$ as shown in Fig. 4(d) and (e). Furthermore, $\langle 00* \rangle$ and $\langle 0*1 \rangle$, fully cover $\langle 001 \rangle$ and $\langle 10* \rangle$, $\langle 1*1 \rangle$ fully covers $\langle 101 \rangle$. As such, the remaining two regulator states are covered with empty extension sets and the final solution uses 12 regulator value specifications as opposed to the 18 required by the explicit representation.

The fractional part of the weight function is crucial to distinguish between $\langle 001 \rangle$, $\langle 101 \rangle$ and $\langle 011 \rangle$, $\langle 111 \rangle$ after the second iteration (Fig. 4(c)). Covering $\langle 001 \rangle$ or $\langle 101 \rangle$ before $\langle 011 \rangle$ and $\langle 111 \rangle$ would include either $\langle **1 \rangle$ or $\langle *01 \rangle$, depending on the exact order, in the final regulation cover set. As both of them are redundant, this would lead to a suboptimal solution.

Algorithm 1 is quasilinear in the number of regulator states and quadratic in the number of regulators. Its main complexity comes from computing the extension sets $\mathcal{A}_{\mathrm{EXT}}$. Whether a regulator state $\omega \in \Omega_v$ is covered by some $\mathcal{A}_c \cup \mathcal{A}_{\mathrm{EXT}}$ can be checked in $\mathcal{O}(|n^-(v)|)$. Each ω requires at most $|n^-(v)|$ such tests (but usually much less). As such, the extension set can be computed in $\mathcal{O}(|n^-(v)|^2)$ and thus, for all the regulator states: $\mathcal{O}(|\Omega_v| \cdot |n^-(v)|^2)$. Finally, the quasilinear complexity comes from the need to keep the regulator states in a priority queue giving us the final complexity of $\mathcal{O}(|\Omega_v| \cdot (\mathrm{LOG}(|\Omega_v|) + |n^-(v)|^2))$.

Algorithm 1 does not require explicit enumeration of parametrisations when coupled with the parametrisation set semantics Ψ_A. The parametrisation set is only used to determine which regulator states enable the value change (queries to $\mathcal{A}_{\mathrm{ENA}}$). This information is readily available using Ψ_A in the form of parameter values of the relevant bound.

5   Discussion

The goal-oriented model reduction procedure for parametrised models has been extended to parametric regulatory networks. The parametric reduction procedure is compatible with a large family of parametrisation set semantics functions, including the over-approximating semantics introduced for PRNs in [15], without the need to enumerate the parametrisations explicitly.

The reduction method can be applied alongside the model refinement procedure based on unfolding [15]. The parametric reduction can be applied on-the-fly within PRN unfolding in the same fashion the reduction procedure for parametrised networks is applied in Petri net unfoldings [6]. The application to PRN unfoldings suffers from the same challenge with cut-off events as the parametrised version with Petri net unfoldings. The challenge arises from the need to keep track of the transition set as the model evolves (transitions are pruned) by the reduction procedure along the unfolding process. Moreover, a similar challenge is already present in PRN unfoldings due to parametrisation sets [15]. Two different methods are used to tackle the issue. In [6], if more transitions are encountered during the unfolding, the respective branch is reiterated with the new transition set. In [15], a new branch is introduced into the unfolding for the new parametrisation set instead. Both of the methods are applicable for transitions (respectively, l^A and l^I) in PRN unfoldings with model reduction.

The parametric reduction is an independent procedure and can be applied in any other setting besides the mentioned coupling with model refinement. Moreover, should complexity be a concern, several possibilities to abstract the procedure exist. The regulation cover set allows for a different algorithm, or even to relax the definition itself. Or, the condition for a trace to be realisable can be dropped from the validity criterion for objectives to avoid having to check against parametrisation sets. Both of the suggested approximations are sound as adding new transitions has no effect on minimal traces.

Future work includes the refinement of the interplay between parametric model reduction and model refinement, further applications and extensions of the parametric model reduction itself and application of goal-oriented reduction to a wider variety of parametric models.

References

1. Bartocci, E., Lió, P.: Computational modeling, formal analysis, and tools for systems biology. PLOS Comput. Biol. **12**(1), 1–22 (2016). https://doi.org/10.1371/journal.pcbi.1004591
2. Bernot, G., Comet, J.-P., Khalis, Z.: Gene regulatory networks with multiplexes. In: European Simulation and Modelling Conference Proceedings, pp. 423–432 (2008)
3. Bernot, G., Comet, J.-P., Khalis, Z., Richard, A., Roux, O.: A genetically modified hoare logic. Theor. Comput. Sci. (2018). https://doi.org/10.1016/j.tcs.2018.02.003
4. Bernot, G., Cassez, F., Comet, J.-P., Delaplace, F., Müller, C., Roux, O.: Semantics of biological regulatory networks. Electron. Notes Theor. Comput. Sci. **180**(3), 3–14 (2007). https://doi.org/10.1016/j.entcs.2004.01.038
5. Chatain, T., Carmona, J.: Anti-alignments in conformance checking – the dark side of process models. In: Kordon, F., Moldt, D. (eds.) PETRI NETS 2016. LNCS, vol. 9698, pp. 240–258. Springer, Cham (2016). https://doi.org/10.1007/978-3-319-39086-4_15
6. Chatain, T., Paulevé, L.: Goal-driven unfolding of Petri nets. In: Meyer, R., Nestmann, U. (eds.) 28th International Conference on Concurrency Theory (CONCUR 2017). Leibniz International Proceedings in Informatics (LIPIcs), vol. 85, pp. 18:1–18:16. Schloss Dagstuhl-Leibniz-Zentrum fuer Informatik, Dagstuhl (2017). https://doi.org/10.4230/LIPIcs.CONCUR.2017.18
7. Cheng, A., Esparza, J., Palsberg, J.: Complexity results for 1-safe nets. Theor. Comput. Sci. **147**(1&2), 117–136 (1995). https://doi.org/10.1016/0304-3975(94)00231-7
8. Cohen, D.P.A., Martignetti, L., Robine, S., Barillot, E., Zinovyev, A., Calzone, L.: Mathematical modelling of molecular pathways enabling tumour cell invasion and migration. PLoS Comput. Biol. **11**(11), e1004571 (2015). https://doi.org/10.1371/journal.pcbi.1004571
9. Collombet, S., et al.: Logical modeling of lymphoid and myeloid cell specification and transdifferentiation. Proc. Natl. Acad. Sci. **114**(23), 5792–5799 (2017). https://doi.org/10.1073/pnas.1610622114
10. Corblin, F., Fanchon, E., Trilling, L., Chaouiya, C., Thieffry, D.: Automatic inference of regulatory and dynamical properties from incomplete gene interaction and expression data. In: Lones, M.A., Smith, S.L., Teichmann, S., Naef, F., Walker, J.A., Trefzer, M.A. (eds.) IPCAT 2012. LNCS, vol. 7223, pp. 25–30. Springer, Heidelberg (2012). https://doi.org/10.1007/978-3-642-28792-3_4
11. Haddad, S., Pradat-Peyre, J.-F.: New efficient Petri nets reductions for parallel programs verification. Parallel Process. Lett. **16**(1), 101–116 (2006). https://doi.org/10.1142/S0129626406002502
12. Helikar, T., et al.: The cell collective: toward an open and collaborative approach to systems biology. BMC Syst. Biol. **6**, 96 (2012). https://doi.org/10.1186/1752-0509-6-96

13. Khalis, Z., Comet, J.-P., Richard, A., Bernot, G.: The SMBioNet method for discovering models of gene regulatory networks. Genes Genomes Genomics **3**(1), 15–22 (2009). http://www.globalsciencebooks.info/Online/GSBOnline/OnlineGGG_3_SI1.html

14. Klarner, H., Streck, A., Šafránek, D., Kolčák, J., Siebert, H.: Parameter identification and model ranking of thomas networks. In: Gilbert, D., Heiner, M. (eds.) CMSB 2012. LNCS, pp. 207–226. Springer, Heidelberg (2012). https://doi.org/10.1007/978-3-642-33636-2_13

15. Kolčák, J., Šafránek, D., Haar, S., Paulevé, L.: Parameter space abstraction and unfolding semantics of discrete regulatory networks. Theor. Comput. Sci. (2018). https://doi.org/10.1016/j.tcs.2018.03.009

16. Koutny, M., Desel, J., Kleijn, J. (eds.): Transactions on Petri Nets and Other Models of Concurrency XI. LNCS, vol. 9930. Springer, Heidelberg (2016). https://doi.org/10.1007/978-3-662-53401-4

17. Mokhov, A., Carmona, J., Beaumont, J.: Mining conditional partial order graphs from event logs. In: Koutny, M., Desel, J., Kleijn, J. (eds.) Transactions on Petri Nets and Other Models of Concurrency XI. LNCS, vol. 9930, pp. 114–136. Springer, Heidelberg (2016). https://doi.org/10.1007/978-3-662-53401-4_6

18. Naldi, A., et al.: The CoLoMoTo interactive notebook: accessible and reproducible computational analyses for qualitative biological networks. Front. Physiol. **9**, 680 (2018). https://doi.org/10.3389/fphys.2018.00680

19. Ostrowski, M., Paulevé, L., Schaub, T., Siegel, A., Guziolowski, C.: Boolean network identification from perturbation time series data combining dynamics abstraction and logic programming. Biosystems **149**, 139–153 (2016). https://doi.org/10.1016/j.biosystems.2016.07.009

20. Paulevé, L.: Reduction of qualitative models of biological networks for transient dynamics analysis. IEEE/ACM Trans. Comput. Biol. Bioinform. (2017). https://doi.org/10.1109/TCBB.2017.2749225

21. Ponce-de-León, H., Rodríguez, C., Carmona, J., Heljanko, K., Haar, S.: Unfolding-based process discovery. In: Finkbeiner, B., Pu, G., Zhang, L. (eds.) ATVA 2015. LNCS, vol. 9364, pp. 31–47. Springer, Cham (2015). https://doi.org/10.1007/978-3-319-24953-7_4

22. Talcott, C., Dill, D.L.: Multiple representations of biological processes. In: Priami, C., Plotkin, G. (eds.) Transactions on Computational Systems Biology VI. LNCS, vol. 4220, pp. 221–245. Springer, Heidelberg (2006). https://doi.org/10.1007/11880646_10

23. Thieffry, D., Thomas, R.: Dynamical behaviour of biological regulatory networks–II. Immunity control in bacteriophage lambda. Bull. Math. Biol. **57**, 277–297 (1995). https://doi.org/10.1007/BF02460619

24. Thomas, R.: Boolean formalization of genetic control circuits. J. Theor. Biol. **42**(3), 563–585 (1973). https://doi.org/10.1016/0022-5193(73)90247-6

Mechanically Proving Determinacy of Hierarchical Block Diagram Translations

Viorel Preoteasa[1,3]([✉]), Iulia Dragomir[2]([✉]), and Stavros Tripakis[3,4]([✉])

[1] Space Systems Finland, Espoo, Finland
`viorel.preoteasa@gmail.com`
[2] Univ. Grenoble Alpes, CNRS,
Grenoble INP (Institute of Engineering Univ. Grenoble Alpes),
VERIMAG, 38000 Grenoble, France
`iulia.dragomir@univ-grenoble-alpes.fr`
[3] Aalto University, Espoo, Finland
`stavros.tripakis@aalto.fi`
[4] Northeastern University, Boston, USA

Abstract. Hierarchical block diagrams (HBDs) are at the heart of embedded system design tools, including Simulink. Numerous translations exist from HBDs into languages with formal semantics, amenable to formal verification. However, none of these translations has been proven correct, to our knowledge.

We present in this paper the first mechanically proven HBD translation algorithm. The algorithm translates HBDs into an algebra of terms with three basic composition operations (serial, parallel, and feedback). In order to capture various translation strategies resulting in different terms achieving different tradeoffs, the algorithm is nondeterministic. Despite this, we prove its *semantic determinacy*: for every input HBD, all possible terms that can be generated by the algorithm are semantically equivalent. We apply this result to show how three Simulink translation strategies introduced previously can be formalized as determinizations of the algorithm, and derive that these strategies yield semantically equivalent results (a question left open in previous work). All results are formalized and proved in the Isabelle theorem-prover and the code is publicly available.

1 Introduction

Dozens of tools, including Simulink [28], the most widespread embedded system design environment, are based on *hierarchical block diagrams* (HBDs). Being a graphical notation (and in the case of Simulink a "closed" one in the sense that

This work has been partially supported by the Academy of Finland and the U.S. National Science Foundation (awards #1329759 and #1801546). V. Preoteasa—Partially supported by the ECSEL JU MegaM@Rt2 project under grant agreement #737494. I. Dragomir—Partially supported by the the European Union's Horizon 2020 research and innovation programme under grant agreement #730080 (ESROCOS).

C. Enea and R. Piskac (Eds.): VMCAI 2019, LNCS 11388, pp. 577–600, 2019.
https://doi.org/10.1007/978-3-030-11245-5_27

the tool is not open-source), such diagrams need to be translated into other formalisms more amenable to formal analysis. Several such translations exist, e.g., see [2,12,24,29,30,34,39,41,43,44] and the related discussion in Sect. 2. To our knowledge, none of these translations has been formally verified. This paper aims to remedy this fact.

Our work builds upon the Refinement Calculus of Reactive Systems (RCRS), a publicly available compositional framework for modeling and reasoning about reactive systems [17,18]. RCRS is itself implemented on top of the Isabelle theorem prover [31].

RCRS uses Simulink as one of its front-ends, and includes a tool that translates Simulink diagrams to RCRS theories [16]. This *Translator* implements three translation strategies from HBDs to an algebra of components with three basic composition operators: serial, parallel, and feedback. The several translation strategies are motivated by the fact that each strategy has its own pros and cons. For instance, one strategy may result in shorter and/or easier to understand algebra terms, while another strategy may result in terms that are easier to simplify by manipulating formulas in a theorem prover. But a fundamental question is left open in [16]: are these translation strategies *semantically equivalent*, meaning, do they produce semantically equivalent terms? This is the question we study and answer (positively) in this paper.

The question is non-trivial, as we seek to prove the equivalence of three complex algorithms which manipulate a graphical notation (hierarchical block diagrams) and transform models in this notation into a different textual language, namely, the algebra mentioned above. Terms in this algebra have intricate formal semantics, and formally proving that two given specific terms are equivalent is already a non-trivial exercise. Here, the problem is to prove that a number of translation strategies $T_1, T_2, \ldots, T_k$ are equivalent, meaning that for *any* given graphical diagram D, the terms resulting from translating D by applying these strategies, $T_1(D), T_2(D), \ldots, T_k(D)$, are all semantically equivalent.

This equivalence question is important for many reasons. Just like a compiler has many choices when generating code, a HBD translator has many choices when generating algebraic expressions. Just like a correct compiler must guarantee that all possible results are equivalent (independently of optimization or other flags/options), the translator must also guarantee that all possible algebraic expressions are equivalent. Moreover, the algebraic expressions constitute the formal semantics of HBDs, and hence also those of tools like Simulink. Therefore, this determinacy principle is also necessary in order for the formal Simulink semantics to be well-defined.

In order to formulate the equivalence question precisely, we introduce an *abstract* and *nondeterministic* algorithm for translating HBDs into an abstract algebra of components with three composition operations (serial, parallel, feedback) and three constants (split, switch, and sink). By *abstract algorithm* we understand an algorithm that produces terms in this abstract algebra. Concrete versions for this algorithm are obtained when using it for concrete models of the algebra (e.g., *constructive functions*). The algorithm is *nondeterministic* in the sense that it consists of a set of basic operations (transformations) that can be applied in any order. This allows to capture various deterministic translation strategies as determinizations (*refinements* [5]) of the abstract algorithm.

The main contributions of the paper are the following:

1. We formally and mechanically define a translation algorithm for HBDs.
2. We prove that despite its internal nondeterminism, the algorithm achieves deterministic results in the sense that all possible algebra terms that can be generated by the different nondeterministic choices are semantically equivalent.
3. We formalize two translation strategies introduced in [16] as refinements of the abstract algorithm.
4. We formalize also the third strategy (feedbackless) introduced in [16] as an independent algorithm.
5. We mechanically prove the equivalence of these three translation strategies.
6. We make our results publicly available at https://github.com/hbd-translation/TranslateHBD.

To our knowledge, our work constitutes the first and only mechanically proven hierarchical block diagram translator. Moreover, our method is compositional and our abstract algorithm can be instantiated in many different ways, encompassing not just the three translation strategies of [16], but also any other HBD translation strategy that can be devised by combining the basic composition operations defined in the abstract algorithm.

2 Related Work

Model transformation and the verification of its correctness is a long standing line of research, which includes classification of model transformations [3] and the properties they must satisfy with respect to their intent [26], verification techniques [1], frameworks for specifying model transformations (e.g., ATL [19]), and various implementations for specific source and target meta-models. Extensive surveys of the above can be found in [1,3,11].

Several translations from Simulink have been proposed in the literature, including to Hybrid Automata [2], BIP [39], NuSMV [29], Lustre [41], Boogie [34], Timed Interval Calculus [12], Function Blocks [24], I/O Extended Finite Automata [43], Hybrid CSP [44], and SpaceEx [30]. It is unclear to what extent these approaches provide formal guarantees on the determinism of the translation. For example, the order in which blocks in the Simulink diagram are processed might a-priori influence the result. Some works fix this order, e.g., [34] computes the control flow graph and translates the model according to this computed order. In contrast, we prove that the results of our algorithm are equivalent for any order. To the best of our knowledge, the abstract translation proposed hereafter for Simulink is the only one formally defined and mechanically proven correct.

The focus of several works is to validate the preservation of the semantics of the original diagram by the resulting translation (e.g., see [9,24,35,36]). In contrast, our goal is to prove equivalence of all possible translations. Given that Simulink semantics is informal ("what the simulator does"), ultimately the only way to gain confidence that the translation conforms to the original Simulink model is by simulation (e.g., as in [16]).

In general, our approach can be considered as a means in the certification and qualification of compilers by mechanical formal verification. Several works tackle the formal verification of compilers for programming languages: COMPCERT [25] is a verified compiler for a subset of C with the COQ interactive theorem prover [40], while the verification of a compiler for Lustre with COQ is considered in [4,10]. The aim of these works is to show that the semantics of the original program is preserved during the different compilation phases until the generated assembly code, while we provide a semantics for HBDs and we prove it correct with respect to the different translation choices.

Further comparison of our approach to additional related works and in particular works on category theory such as [6,13,21–23,37,38,42] is included in [32] and is omitted from here due to space limitations. To our knowledge, none of these works has been mechanically formalized nor verified.

3   Preliminaries

For a type or set X, X^* is the type of finite lists with elements from X. We denote the empty list by ϵ, $(x_1, \ldots, x_n)$ denotes the list with elements $x_1, \ldots, x_n$, and for lists x and y, $x \cdot y$ denotes their concatenation. The length of a list x is denoted by $|x|$. The list of common elements of x and y in the order occurring in x is denoted by $x \otimes y$. The list of elements from x that do not occur in y is denoted by $x \ominus y$. We define $x \oplus y = x \cdot (y \ominus x)$, the list of x concatenated with the elements of y not occurring in x. A list x is a *permutation* of a list y, denoted $\mathsf{perm}(x, y)$, if x contains all elements of y (including multiplicities) possibly in a different order. For a list x, $\mathsf{set}(x)$ denotes the set of all elements of x.

In the sequel we refer to *constructive functions* as used in the *constructive semantics* literature [8,20,27]. Constructive functions enjoy important properties, in particular with respect to feedback composition, and are one of the concrete models for the abstract algebra of HBDs introduced in Sect. 5. The formal definition of constructive functions is omitted due to lack of space and the reader is referred to [32].

4   Overview of the Translation Algorithm

A *block diagram* N is a network of interconnected blocks. A block may be a basic (*atomic*) block, or a *composite* block that corresponds to a *sub-diagram*. If N contains composite blocks then it is called a *hierarchical block diagram* (HBD); otherwise it is called *flat*. An example of a flat diagram is shown in Fig. 1a. The connections between blocks are called wires, and they have a source block and a target block. For simplicity, we will assume that every wire has a single source and a single target. This can be achieved by adding extra blocks. For instance, the diagram of Fig. 1a can be transformed as in Fig. 1b by adding an explicit block called *Split*.

Let us explain the idea of the translation algorithm. We first explain the idea for flat diagrams, and then we extend it recursively for hierarchical diagrams.

A diagram is represented in the algorithm as a list of elements corresponding to the basic blocks. One element of this list is a triple containing a list of input variables, a list of output variables, and a *function*. The function computes the values of the outputs based on the values of the inputs, and for now it can be thought of as a constructive function. Later this function will be an element of an abstract algebra modeling HBDs. Wires are represented by matching input/output variables from the block representations.

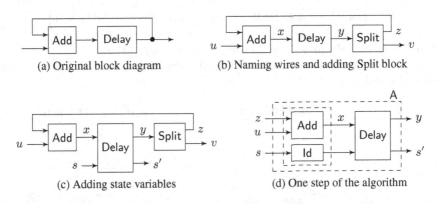

(a) Original block diagram   (b) Naming wires and adding Split block

(c) Adding state variables   (d) One step of the algorithm

Fig. 1. Running example: diagram for summation.

A block diagram may contain *stateful* blocks such as delays or integrators. We model these blocks using additional state variables (wires). In Fig. 1, the only stateful block is the block **Delay**. We model this block as an element with two inputs (x, s), two outputs (y, s') and function $(y, s') := (s, x)$ (Fig. 1c). More details about this representation can be found in [16].

In summary, the list representation of the example of Fig. 1 is the following:

$(\mathsf{Add}, \mathsf{Delay}, \mathsf{Split})$, where: $\mathsf{Add} = ((z, u),\ x,\ [z, u \rightsquigarrow z + u])$,
$\mathsf{Delay} = ((x, s),\ (y, s'),\ [x, s \rightsquigarrow s, x])$, $\mathsf{Split} = (y,\ (z, v),\ [y \rightsquigarrow y, y])$.

The algorithm works by choosing nondeterministically some elements from the list and replacing them with their appropriate composition (serial, parallel, or feedback). The composition must connect all the matching variables. Let us illustrate how the algorithm may proceed on the example of Fig. 1; for the full description of the algorithm see Sect. 6. Symbols ∘, ∥ and feedback used below denote serial, parallel and feedback compositions, respectively, and they will be formally introduced in Sect. 5.1.

Suppose the algorithm first chooses to compose Add and Delay. The only matching variable in this case is x, between the output of Add and the first input of Delay. The appropriate composition to use here is serial composition. Because Delay also has s as input, Add and Delay cannot be directly connected in series. This is due to the number of outputs of Add that need to match the number of inputs of Delay. To compute the serial composition, Add must first be composed in parallel with the identity block Id, as shown in Fig. 1d. Doing so, a new element A is created:

$$A = ((z, u, s),\ (y, s'),\ \text{Delay} \circ (\text{Add} \parallel \text{Id}))$$

Next, A is composed with Split. In this case we need to connect variable y (using serial composition), as well as z (using feedback composition). The resulting element is A′:

$$A' = \Big((u, s),\ (v, s'),\ \text{feedback}\big((\text{Split} \parallel \text{Id}) \circ \text{Delay} \circ (\text{Add} \parallel \text{Id})\big)\Big)$$

where we need again to add the Id component for variable s'.

As a different nondeterministic choice, the algorithm may first compose Split and Add into B:

$$B = ((y, u),\ (x, v),\ (\text{Add} \parallel \text{Id}) \circ (\text{Id} \parallel [v, u \rightsquigarrow u, v]) \circ (\text{Split} \parallel \text{Id}))$$

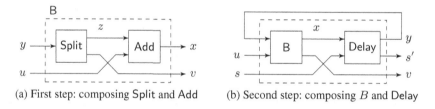

(a) First step: composing Split and Add   (b) Second step: composing B and Delay

Fig. 2. A different composition order for the example from Fig. 1.

In this composition, shown in Fig. 2a, we now need in addition to the Id components, a switch $([v, u \rightsquigarrow u, v])$ for wires v and u. Next the algorithm composes B and Delay (Fig. 2b):

$$B' = \Big((u, s),\ (s', v),\ \text{feedback}\big((\text{Delay} \parallel \text{Id}) \circ (\text{Id} \parallel [v, s \rightsquigarrow s, v]) \circ (\text{B} \parallel \text{Id})\big).\Big)$$

As we can see from this example, by considering the blocks in the diagram in different orders, we obtain different expressions. On this example, expression A′ is simpler (it has less connectors) than B′. In general, a diagram, being a graph, does not have a predefined canonical order, and we need to show that the result of the algorithm is *the same* regardless of the order in which the blocks are considered.

We make two remarks here. First, the final result of the algorithm is a triple with the same structure as all elements on the original list: (input variables, output variables, function), where the function represents the computation performed by the entire diagram. Therefore, the algorithm can be applied recursively on HBDs. Second, the variables in the representation occur at most twice, once as input, and once as output. The variables occurring only as inputs are the inputs of the resulting final element, and variables occurring only as outputs are the outputs of the resulting final element. This is true in general for all diagrams, due to the representation of splitting of wires. This fact is essential for the correctness of the algorithm as we will see in Sect. 6.

5   An Abstract Algebra for Hierarchical Block Diagrams

We assume that we have a set of Types. We also assume a set of *diagrams* Dgr. Every element $S \in$ Dgr has input type $t \in$ Types* and output type $t' \in$ Types*. If $t = t_1 \cdots t_n$ and $t' = t'_1 \cdots t'_m$, then S takes as input a tuple of the type $t_1 \times \ldots \times t_n$ and produces as output a tuple of the type $t'_1 \times \ldots \times t'_m$. We denote the fact that S has input type $t \in$ Types* and output type $t' \in$ Types* by $S : t \xrightarrow{\circ} t'$. The elements of Dgr are abstract.

5.1   Operations of the Algebra of HBDs

Constants. Basic blocks are modeled as constants on Dgr. For types $t, t' \in$ Types* we assume the following constants:

$$\mathsf{Id}(t) : t \xrightarrow{\circ} t \quad \mathsf{Split}(t) : t \xrightarrow{\circ} t \cdot t \quad \mathsf{Sink}(t) : t \xrightarrow{\circ} \epsilon \quad \mathsf{Switch}(t, t') : t \cdot t' \xrightarrow{\circ} t' \cdot t$$

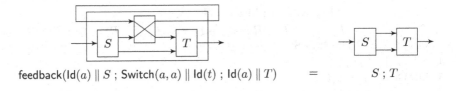

$$\mathsf{feedback}(\mathsf{Id}(a) \parallel S \,;\, \mathsf{Switch}(a, a) \parallel \mathsf{Id}(t) \,;\, \mathsf{Id}(a) \parallel T) \quad = \quad S \,;\, T$$

Fig. 3. Two flat diagrams and their corresponding terms in the abstract algebra.

Id corresponds to the identity block. It copies the input into the output. In the model of constructive functions $\mathsf{Id}(t)$ is the identity function. $\mathsf{Split}(t)$ takes an input x of type t and outputs $x \cdot x$ of type $t \cdot t$. $\mathsf{Sink}(t)$ returns the empty tuple ϵ, for any input x of type t. $\mathsf{Switch}(t, t')$ takes an input $x \cdot x'$ with x of type t and x' of type t' and returns $x' \cdot x$. In the model of constructive functions these diagrams are total functions and they are defined as explained above. In the abstract model, the behaviors of these constants is defined with a set of axioms (see below).

Composition Operators. For two diagrams $S : t \xrightarrow{\circ} t'$ and $S' : t' \xrightarrow{\circ} t''$, their *serial composition*, denoted $S \; ; S' : t \xrightarrow{\circ} t''$ is a diagram that takes inputs of type t and produces outputs of type t''. In the model of constructive functions, the serial composition corresponds to function composition $(S \; ; S' = S' \circ S)$. Please note that in the abstract model we write the serial composition as $S \; ; S'$, while in the model of constructive functions the first diagram that is applied to the input occurs second in the composition.

The *parallel composition* of two diagrams $S : t \xrightarrow{\circ} t'$ and $S' : r \xrightarrow{\circ} r'$, denoted $S \parallel S' : t \cdot r \xrightarrow{\circ} t' \cdot r'$, is a diagram that takes as input tuples of type $t \cdot r$ and produces as output tuples of type $t' \cdot r'$. This parallel composition corresponds to the parallel composition of constructive functions.

Finally we introduce a *feedback composition*. For $S : a \cdot t \xrightarrow{\circ} a \cdot t'$, where $a \in \mathsf{Types}$ is a single type, the feedback of S, denoted $\mathsf{feedback}(S) : t \xrightarrow{\circ} t'$, is the result of connecting in feedback the first output of S to its first input. Again this feedback operation corresponds to the feedback of constructive functions.

We assume that parallel composition operator binds stronger than serial composition, i.e. $S \parallel T \; ; R$ is the same as $(S \parallel T) \; ; R$.

Graphical diagrams can be represented as terms in the abstract algebra, as illustrated in Fig. 3. This figure depicts two diagrams, and their corresponding algebra terms. As it turns out, these two diagrams are equivalent, in the sense that their corresponding algebra terms can be shown to be equal using the axioms presented below.

5.2   Axioms of the Algebra of HBDs

In the abstract algebra, the behavior of the constants and composition operators is defined by a set of axioms, listed below (f^n denotes n applications of function f, so for example $\mathsf{feedback}^2(\cdot) = \mathsf{feedback}(\mathsf{feedback}(\cdot))$):

1. $S : t \xrightarrow{\circ} t' \implies \mathsf{Id}(t) \; ; S = S \; ; \mathsf{Id}(t') = S$
2. $S : t_1 \xrightarrow{\circ} t_2 \wedge T : t_2 \xrightarrow{\circ} t_3 \wedge R : t_3 \xrightarrow{\circ} t_4 \implies S \; ; (T \; ; R) = (S \; ; T) \; ; R$
3. $\mathsf{Id}(\epsilon) \parallel S = S \parallel \mathsf{Id}(\epsilon) = S$
4. $S \parallel (T \parallel R) = (S \parallel T) \parallel R$
5. $\mathsf{Id}(t) \parallel \mathsf{Id}(t') = \mathsf{Id}(t \cdot t')$
6. $S : s \xrightarrow{\circ} s' \wedge S' : s' \xrightarrow{\circ} s'' \wedge T : t \xrightarrow{\circ} t' \wedge T' : t' \xrightarrow{\circ} t''$
   $\implies (S \parallel T) \; ; (S' \parallel T') = (S \; ; S') \parallel (T \; ; T')$
7. $\mathsf{Switch}(t, t' \cdot t'') = \mathsf{Switch}(t, t') \parallel \mathsf{Id}(t'') \; ; \mathsf{Id}(t') \parallel \mathsf{Switch}(t, t'')$
8. $S : s \xrightarrow{\circ} s' \wedge T : t \xrightarrow{\circ} t' \implies \mathsf{Switch}(s, t) \; ; T \parallel S \; ; \mathsf{Switch}(t', s') = S \parallel T$
9. $\mathsf{feedback}(\mathsf{Switch}(a, a)) = \mathsf{Id}(a)$
10. $S : a \cdot s \xrightarrow{\circ} a \cdot t \implies \mathsf{feedback}(S \parallel T) = \mathsf{feedback}(S) \parallel T$
11. $S : a \cdot s \xrightarrow{\circ} a \cdot t \wedge A : s' \xrightarrow{\circ} s \wedge B : t \xrightarrow{\circ} t'$
    $\implies \mathsf{feedback}(\mathsf{Id}(a) \parallel A \; ; S \; ; \mathsf{Id}(a) \parallel B) = A \; ; \mathsf{feedback}(S) \; ; B$
12. $S : a \cdot b \cdot s \xrightarrow{\circ} a \cdot b \cdot t$
    $\implies \mathsf{feedback}^2(\mathsf{Switch}(b, a) \parallel \mathsf{Id}(s) \; ; S \; ; \mathsf{Switch}(a, b) \parallel \mathsf{Id}(t)) = \mathsf{feedback}^2(S)$
13. $\mathsf{Split}(t) \; ; \mathsf{Sink}(t) \parallel \mathsf{Id}(t) = \mathsf{Id}(t)$

14. $\mathsf{Split}(t) \mathbin{;} \mathsf{Switch}(t, t) = \mathsf{Split}(t)$
15. $\mathsf{Split}(t) \mathbin{;} \mathsf{Id}(t) \parallel \mathsf{Split}(t) = \mathsf{Split}(t) \mathbin{;} \mathsf{Split}(t) \parallel \mathsf{Id}(t)$
16. $\mathsf{Sink}(t \cdot t') = \mathsf{Sink}(t) \parallel \mathsf{Sink}(t')$
17. $\mathsf{Split}(t \cdot t') = \mathsf{Split}(t) \parallel \mathsf{Split}(t') \mathbin{;} \mathsf{Id}(t) \parallel \mathsf{Switch}(t, t') \parallel \mathsf{Id}(t')$.

Due to space limitations, the intuition behind these axioms is explained and illustrated with figures in [32].

6 The Abstract Translation Algorithm and Its Determinacy

6.1 Diagrams with Named Inputs and Outputs

The algorithm works by first transforming the graph of a HBD into a list of basic components with named inputs and outputs as explained in Sect. 4. For this purpose we assume a set of names or variables Var and a function $\mathsf{T} : \mathsf{Var} \to \mathsf{Types}$. For $v \in \mathsf{Var}$, $\mathsf{T}(v)$ is the type of variable v. We extend T to lists of variables by $\mathsf{T}(v_1, \dots, v_n) = (T(v_1), \dots, T(v_n))$.

Definition 1. *A diagram with named inputs and outputs or io-diagram for short is a tuple (in, out, S) such that $in, out \in \mathsf{Var}^*$ are lists of distinct variables, and $S : \mathsf{T}(in) \xrightarrow{\ \circ\ } \mathsf{T}(out)$.*

In what follows we use the symbols $A, A', B, \dots$ to denote io-diagrams, and $\mathsf{I}(A)$, $\mathsf{O}(A)$, and $\mathsf{D}(A)$ to denote the input variables, the output variables, and the diagram of A, respectively.

Definition 2. *For io-diagrams A and B, we define $\mathsf{V}(A, B) = \mathsf{O}(A) \otimes \mathsf{I}(B) \in \mathsf{Var}^*$.*

$\mathsf{V}(A, B)$ is the list of common variables that are output of A and input of B, in the order occurring in $\mathsf{O}(A)$. We use $\mathsf{V}(A, B)$ later to connect for example in series A and B on these common variables, as we did for constructing A from Add and Delay in Sect. 4.

6.2 General Switch Diagrams

We compose diagrams when their types are matching, and we compose io-diagrams based on matching names of input and output variables. For example if we have two io-diagrams A and B with $\mathsf{O}(A) = u \cdot v$ and $\mathsf{I}(B) = v \cdot u$, then we can compose in series A and B by switching the output of A and feeding it into B, i.e., $(A \mathbin{;} \mathsf{Switch}(\mathsf{T}(u), \mathsf{T}(v)) \mathbin{;} B)$.

In general, for two lists of variables $x = (x_1 \cdots x_n)$ and $y = (y_1 \cdots y_k)$ we define a *general switch diagram* $[x_1 \cdots x_n \rightsquigarrow y_1 \cdots y_k] : \mathsf{T}(x_1 \cdots x_n) \xrightarrow{\ \circ\ } \mathsf{T}(y_1 \cdots y_k)$. Intuitively this diagram takes as input a list of values of type $\mathsf{T}(x_1 \cdots x_n)$ and outputs a list of values of type $\mathsf{T}(y_1 \cdots y_k)$, where the output value corresponding to variable y_j is equal to the value corresponding to the first x_i with $x_i = y_j$ and it is arbitrary (unknown) if there is no such x_i. For example in the constructive functions model $[u, v \rightsquigarrow v, u, w, u]$ for input (a, b) outputs $(b, a, \perp, a)$.

To define $[\_ \rightsquigarrow \_]$ we use Split, Sink, and Switch, but we need also an additional diagram that outputs an arbitrary (or unknown) value for an empty input. For $a \in$ Types, we define $\mathsf{Arb}(a) : \epsilon \xrightarrow{\circ} a$ by $\mathsf{Arb}(a) = \mathsf{feedback}(\mathsf{Split}(a))$. The diagram Arb is represented in Fig. 4.

We define now $[x \rightsquigarrow y] : \mathsf{T}(x) \xrightarrow{\circ} \mathsf{T}(y)$ in two steps. First for $x \in \mathsf{Var}^*$ and $u \in \mathsf{Var}$, the diagram $[x \rightsquigarrow u] : \mathsf{T}(x) \xrightarrow{\circ} \mathsf{T}(u)$, for input $a_1, \ldots, a_n$ outputs the value a_i where i is the first index such that $x_i = u$. Otherwise it outputs an arbitrary (unknown) value.

Fig. 4. The diagram Arb.

$$
\begin{aligned}
[\epsilon \rightsquigarrow u] &= \mathsf{Arb}(\mathsf{T}(u)) \\
[u \cdot x \rightsquigarrow u] &= \mathsf{Id}(\mathsf{T}(u)) \parallel \mathsf{Sink}(\mathsf{T}(x)) \\
[v \cdot x \rightsquigarrow u] &= \mathsf{Sink}(\mathsf{T}(v)) \parallel [x \rightsquigarrow u] \qquad \text{(if } u \neq v) \\
[x \rightsquigarrow \epsilon] &= \mathsf{Sink}(\mathsf{T}(x)) \\
[x \rightsquigarrow u \cdot y] &= \mathsf{Split}(\mathsf{T}(x)) \, ; \, ([x \rightsquigarrow u] \parallel [x \rightsquigarrow y])
\end{aligned}
$$

6.3   Basic Operations of the Abstract Translation Algorithm

The algorithm starts with a list of io-diagrams and repeatedly applies operations until it reduces the list to only one io-diagram. These operations are the extensions of serial, parallel and feedback from diagrams to io-diagrams.

Definition 3. *The named serial composition of two io-diagrams A and B, denoted $A \, ; ; \, B$ is defined by $A \, ; ; \, B = (in, out, S)$, where $x = \mathsf{I}(B) \ominus \mathsf{V}(A, B)$, $y = \mathsf{O}(A) \ominus \mathsf{V}(A, B)$, $in = \mathsf{I}(A) \oplus x$, $out = y \cdot \mathsf{O}(B)$ and*

$$
S = [in \rightsquigarrow \mathsf{I}(A) \cdot x] \, ; \, \mathsf{D}(A) \parallel [x \rightsquigarrow x] \, ; \, [\mathsf{O}(A) \cdot x \rightsquigarrow y \cdot \mathsf{I}(B)] \, ; \, [y \rightsquigarrow y] \parallel \mathsf{D}(B).
$$

The construction of A from Sect. 4 can be obtained by applying the named serial composition to Add and Delay.

Figure 5a illustrates an example of the named serial composition. In this case we have $\mathsf{V}(A, B) = u$, $x = (a, b)$, $y = (v, w)$, $in = (a, c, b)$, and $out = (v, w, d, e)$. The component A has outputs u, v, w, and u is also input of B. Variable u is the only variable that is output of A and input of B. Because the outputs v, w of A are not inputs of B they become outputs of $A \, ; ; \, B$. Variable a is input for both A and B, so in $A \, ; ; \, B$ the value of a is split and fed into both A and B. The diagram for this example is:

$$
[a, c, b \rightsquigarrow a, c, a, b] \, ; \, A \parallel \mathsf{Id}(\mathsf{T}(a, b)) \, ; \, [u, v, w, a, b \rightsquigarrow v, w, a, u, b] \, ; \, \mathsf{Id}(\mathsf{T}(v, w)) \parallel B
$$

The result of the named serial composition of two io-diagrams is not always an io-diagram. The problem is that the outputs of $A \, ; ; \, B$ are not distinct in general. The next lemma gives sufficient conditions for $A \, ; ; \, B$ to be an io-diagram.

Lemma 1. *If A, B are io-diagrams and $(O(A) \ominus I(B)) \otimes O(B) = \epsilon$ then $A \;;; B$ is an io-diagram. In particular if $O(A) \otimes O(B) = \epsilon$ then $A \;;; B$ is an io-diagram.*

The named serial composition is associative, expressed by the next lemma.

Lemma 2. *If A, B, C are io-diagrams such that $(O(A) \ominus I(B)) \otimes O(B) = \epsilon$ and $(O(A) \otimes I(B)) \otimes I(C) = \epsilon$, then $(A \;;; B) \;;; C = A \;;; (B \;;; C)$.*

Next we introduce the corresponding operation on io-diagrams for the parallel composition.

Definition 4. *If A, B are io-diagrams, then the named parallel composition of A and B, denoted $A \;|||\; B$ is defined by*

$$A \;|||\; B = (I(A) \oplus I(B), \;\; O(A) \cdot O(B), \;\; [I(A) \oplus I(B) \rightsquigarrow I(A) \cdot I(B)] \;; (A \,\|\, B)).$$

Figure 5b presents an example of a named parallel composition. The named parallel composition is meaningful only if the outputs of the two diagrams have different names. However, the inputs may not necessarily be distinct as shown in Fig. 5b.

As in the case of named serial composition, the parallel composition of two io-diagrams is not always an io-diagram. Next lemma gives conditions for the parallel composition to be io-diagram and also states that the named parallel composition is associative.

Lemma 3. *Let A, B, and C be io-diagrams, then*

1. $O(A) \otimes O(B) = \epsilon \;\Rightarrow\; A \;|||\; B$ *is an io-diagram.*
2. $(A \;|||\; B) \;|||\; C = A \;|||\; (B \;|||\; C)$.

Next definition introduces the feedback operator for io-diagrams.

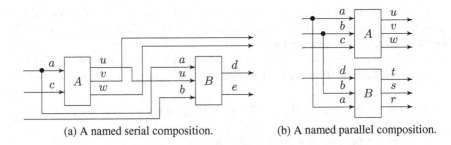

(a) A named serial composition.   (b) A named parallel composition.

Fig. 5. Examples of named compositions.

Definition 5. *If A is an io-diagram, then the named feedback of A, denoted $FB(A)$ is defined by (in, out, S), where $in = I(A) \ominus V(A, A)$, $out = O(A) \ominus V(A, A)$ and*

$$S = \mathsf{feedback}^{|V(A,A)|}([V(A, A) \cdot in \rightsquigarrow I(A)] \;; S \;; [O(A) \rightsquigarrow V(A, A) \cdot out]).$$

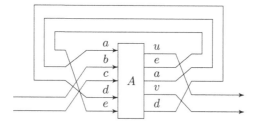

Fig. 6. Example of named feedback composition.

The named feedback operation of A connects all inputs and outputs of A with the same name in feedback. Figure 6 illustrates an example of named feedback composition. The named feedback applied to an io-diagram is always an io-diagram.

Lemma 4. *If A is an io-diagram then* $\mathsf{FB}(A)$ *is an io-diagram.*

6.4   The Abstract Translation Algorithm

We have now all elements for introducing the abstract translation algorithm. The algorithm starts with a list $\mathcal{A} = (A_1, A_2, \ldots, A_n)$ of io-diagrams, such that for all $i \neq j$, the inputs and outputs of A_i and A_j are disjoint respectively ($\mathsf{I}(A_i) \otimes \mathsf{I}(A_j) = \epsilon$ and $\mathsf{O}(A_i) \otimes \mathsf{O}(A_j) = \epsilon$). We denote this property by $\mathsf{io-distinct}(\mathcal{A})$. The algorithm is given in Algorithm 1. Formally the algorithm is represented as a monotonic predicate transformer [15], within the framework of refinement calculus [5].

Computing $\mathsf{FB}(A)$ in the last step of the algorithm is necessary only if $\mathcal{A}$ contains initially only one element. However, computing $\mathsf{FB}(A)$ always at the end does not change the result since, as we will see later in Theorem 1, the FB operation is idempotent, i.e. $\mathsf{FB}(\mathsf{FB}(A)) = \mathsf{FB}(A)$. In the presentation of the algorithm, we have used the keyword **choose** for the nondeterministic choice $\sqcap$, to emphasize the two alternatives.

Note that, semantically, choice (b) of the algorithm is a special case of choice (a), as shown later in Theorem 1. But syntactically, choices (a) and (b) result in

> input: $\mathcal{A} = (A_1, A_2, \ldots, A_n)$ (list of io-diagrams)
> **while** $|\mathcal{A}| > 1$:
>   **choose** between options (a) and (b) :
>   (a) $[\,\mathcal{A} := \mathcal{A}' \mid \exists\, k, B_1, \ldots, B_k, \mathcal{C} : k > 1 \;\wedge$
> $\mathsf{perm}(\mathcal{A}, (B_1, \ldots, B_k)\!\cdot\!\mathcal{C}) \wedge \mathcal{A}' = \mathsf{FB}(B_1 \,|||\, \ldots \,|||\, B_k)\!\cdot\!\mathcal{C}\,]$
>   (b) $[\,\mathcal{A} := \mathcal{A}' \mid \exists\, A, B, \mathcal{C} : \mathsf{perm}(\mathcal{A}, (A, B) \cdot \mathcal{C}) \;\wedge$
> $\mathcal{A}' = \mathsf{FB}(\mathsf{FB}(A) \,;;\, \mathsf{FB}(B)) \cdot \mathcal{C}\,]$
> $A := \mathsf{FB}(A')$ (where A' is the only remaining element of $\mathcal{A}$)

Algorithm 1. Nondeterministic algorithm for translating HBDs.

different expressions that achieve different performance tradeoffs as observed in Sect. 4 and as further discussed in [16]. The point of the Translator is to be indeed able to generate semantically equivalent but syntactically different expressions, which achieve different performance tradeoffs [16].

The result for the running example from Sect. 4 can be obtained by applying the second choice of the algorithm twice for the initial list of io-diagrams ([Add, Delay, Split]), first to Add and Delay to obtain A, and next to A and Split to obtain

$$\Big((u, s), \ (v, s'), \ \mathsf{feedback}\big((\mathsf{D(Add)} \parallel \mathsf{Id}) \ ; \ \mathsf{D(Delay)} \ ; \ ((\mathsf{Split}) \parallel \mathsf{Id})\big)\Big)$$

As opposed to the example from Sect. 4, the elements are composed serially in the order occurring in the diagram.

6.5 Determinacy of the Abstract Translation Algorithm

The result of the algorithm depends on how the nondeterministic choices are resolved. However, in all cases the final io-diagrams are equivalent modulo a permutation of the inputs and outputs. To prove this, we introduce the concept *io-equivalence* for two io-diagrams.

Definition 6. *Two io-diagrams A, B are io-equivalent, denoted $A \sim B$ if they are equal modulo a permutation of the inputs and outputs, i.e., $\mathsf{I}(B)$ is a permutation of $\mathsf{I}(A)$, $\mathsf{O}(B)$ is a permutation of $\mathsf{O}(A)$ and*

$$\mathsf{D}(A) = [\mathsf{I}(A) \rightsquigarrow \mathsf{I}(B)] \ ; \ \mathsf{D}(B) \ ; \ [\mathsf{O}(B) \rightsquigarrow \mathsf{O}(A)]$$

Lemma 5. *The relation io-equivalent is a congruence relation, i.e., for all io-diagrams A, B, C:*

1. $A \sim A$
2. $A \sim B \Rightarrow B \sim A$
3. $A \sim B \wedge B \sim C \Rightarrow A \sim C$.
4. $A \sim B \Rightarrow \mathsf{FB}(A) \sim \mathsf{FB}(B)$.
5. $\mathsf{O}(A) \otimes \mathsf{O}(B) = \epsilon \Rightarrow A \parallel\!\parallel B \sim B \parallel\!\parallel A$.
6. *If* $\mathsf{io-distinct}(A_1, \ldots, A_n)$ *and* $\mathsf{perm}((A_1, \ldots, A_n), (B_1, \ldots, B_n))$ *then*

$$A_1 \parallel\!\parallel \ldots A_n \sim B_1 \parallel\!\parallel \ldots B_n.$$

To prove correctness of the algorithm we also need the following results:

Theorem 1. *If A, B are io-diagrams such that $\mathsf{I}(A) \otimes \mathsf{I}(B) = \epsilon$ and $\mathsf{O}(A) \otimes \mathsf{O}(B) = \epsilon$ then*

(1) $\mathsf{FB}(A \parallel\!\parallel B) = \mathsf{FB}(\mathsf{FB}(A) \ ;; \ \mathsf{FB}(B))$ *and*   (2) $\mathsf{FB}(\mathsf{FB}(A)) = \mathsf{FB}(A)$.

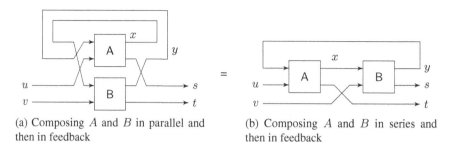

(a) Composing A and B in parallel and then in feedback

(b) Composing A and B in series and then in feedback

Fig. 7. Named feedback of parallel composition is equivalent to named feedback of serial composition.

The proof of Theorem 1 is quite involved and requires several properties of diagrams (see the RCRS formalization [18] for details). Figure 7 illustrates a simplified application of Theorem 1 (1). In the general case of this theorem there are possibly multiple wires between A and B. There may also be wires between the outputs and inputs of A, and B, and these wires may also be inter-mixed.

We can now state and prove one of the main results of this paper, namely, determinacy of Algorithm 1.

Theorem 2. *If $\mathcal{A} = (A_1, A_2, \ldots, A_n)$ is the initial list of io-diagrams satisfying* io$-$distinct$(\mathcal{A})$, *then Algorithm 1 terminates, and if A is the io-diagram computed by the algorithm, then*

$$A \sim \mathsf{FB}(A_1 \,|||\, \ldots \,|||\, A_n)$$

7   Proving Equivalence of Two Translation Strategies

To demonstrate the usefulness of our framework, we return to our original motivation, namely, the open problem of how to prove equivalence of the translation strategies introduced in [16]. Two of the translation strategies of [16], called *feedback-parallel* and *incremental* translation, can be seen as a determinizations (or refinements) of the abstract algorithm of Sect. 6, and therefore can be shown to be equivalent and correct with respect to the abstract semantics. (The third strategy proposed in [16], called *feedbackless*, is significantly different and is presented in the next section.)

The feedback-parallel strategy is the implementation of the abstract algorithm where we choose $k = |\mathcal{A}|$. Intuitively, all diagram components are put in parallel and the common inputs and outputs are connected via feedback operators. On the running example from Fig. 1c, this strategy will generate the following component:

$$((u, s), \ (v, s'), \ \mathsf{feedback}^3([z, x, y, u, s \rightsquigarrow z, u, x, s, y]$$
$$; \mathsf{D}(\mathsf{Add}) \,\|\, \mathsf{D}(\mathsf{Delay}) \,\|\, \mathsf{D}(\mathsf{Split}) \,;\, [x, y, s', z, v \rightsquigarrow z, x, y, v, s']))$$

The switches are ordering the variables such that the feedback variables are first and in the same order in both input and output lists.

The incremental strategy is the implementation of the abstract algorithm where we use only the second choice of the algorithm and the first two components of the list $\mathcal{A}$. This strategy is dependent on the initial order of $\mathcal{A}$, and we order $\mathcal{A}$ topologically (based on the input - output connections) at the beginning, in order to reduce the number of switches needed.

Again on the running example, assume that this strategy composes first Add with Delay, and the result is composed with Split. The following component is then obtained:

$$((u, s), (v, s'), \mathsf{feedback}(\mathsf{D}(\mathsf{Add}) \parallel \mathsf{Id} ; \mathsf{D}(\mathsf{Delay}) ; \mathsf{D}(\mathsf{Split}) \parallel \mathsf{Id})$$

The Add and Split components are put in parallel with Id for the unconnected input and output state respectively. Next all components are connected in series with one feedback operator for the variable z.

The next theorem shows that the two strategies are equivalent, and that they are independent of the initial order of $\mathcal{A}$.

Theorem 3. *If A and B are the result of the feedback-parallel and incremental strategies on $\mathcal{A}$, respectively, then A and B are input - output equivalent $(A \sim B)$. Moreover both strategies are independent of the initial order of $\mathcal{A}$.*

Since both strategies are refinements of the nondeterministic algorithm, they both satisfy the same correctness conditions of Theorem 2.

8   Proving Equivalence of A Third Translation Strategy

The abstract algorithm for translating HBDs, as well as the two translation strategies presented in Sect. 7, use the feedback operator when translating diagrams. As discussed in [16], expressions that contain the feedback operator are more complex to process and simplify. For this reason, we wish to avoid using the feedback operator as much as possible. Fortunately, in practice, diagrams such as those obtained from Simulink are *deterministic* and *algebraic loop free*. As it turns out, such diagrams can be translated into algebraic expressions that do not use the feedback operator at all [16]. This can be done using the third translation strategy proposed in [16], called *feedbackless*.

While the two translation strategies presented in Sect. 7 can be modeled as refinements of the abstract algorithm, the feedbackless strategy is significantly more complex, and cannot be captured as such a refinement. We therefore treat it separately in this section. In particular, we formalize the feedbackless strategy and we show that it is equivalent to the abstract algorithm, namely, that for the same input, the results of the two algorithms are io-equivalent.

8.1   Deterministic and Algebraic-Loop-Free Diagrams

Before we introduce the feedbackless strategy, we need some additional definitions.

Definition 7. A *diagram* S *is* deterministic *if* $[x \rightsquigarrow x, x] \; ; (S \parallel S) = S \; ; [y \rightsquigarrow y, y]$. *An io-diagram* A *is* deterministic *if* $\mathsf{D}(A)$ *is deterministic.*

The definition of deterministic diagram corresponds to the following intuition. If we execute two copies of S in parallel using the same input value x, we should obtain the same result as executing one S for the same input value x.

The deterministic property is closed under the serial, parallel, and switch operations of the HBD algebra.

Lemma 6. *If* $S, T \in \mathsf{Dgr}$ *are deterministic and* x, y *are lists of variables such that* x *is distinct and* $\mathsf{set}(y) \subseteq \mathsf{set}(x)$, *then* $[x \rightsquigarrow y]$, *and* $S \; ; T$, *and* $S \parallel T$ *are also deterministic.*

It is not obvious whether we can deduce from the axioms that the deterministic property is closed under the feedback operation. However, since we do not use the feedback operation in this algorithm, we do not need this property.

Definition 8. *The* output input dependency relation *of an io-diagram* A *is defined by*

$$\mathsf{oi\_rel}(A) = \mathsf{set}(\mathsf{O}(A)) \times \mathsf{set}(\mathsf{I}(A))$$

and the output input dependency relation *of a list* $\mathcal{A} = [A_1, \ldots, A_n]$ *of io-diagrams is defined by*

$$\mathsf{oi\_rel}(\mathcal{A}) = \mathsf{oi\_rel}(A_1) \cup \ldots \cup \mathsf{oi\_rel}(A_n)$$

A list $\mathcal{A}$ *of io-diagrams is* algebraic loop free, *denoted* $\mathsf{loop\_free}(\mathcal{A})$, *if*

$$(\forall x : (x, x) \notin (\mathsf{oi\_rel}(\mathcal{A}))^+)$$

where $(\mathsf{oi\_rel}(\mathcal{A}))^+$ *is the reflexive and transitive closure of relation* $(\mathsf{oi\_rel}(\mathcal{A}))$.

If we apply this directly to the list of io-diagrams from our example $\mathcal{A} = [\mathsf{Add}, \mathsf{Delay}, \mathsf{Split}]$ we obtain

$$\mathsf{oi\_rel}(\mathcal{A}) = \{(x, u), (x, z), (y, x), (y, s), (s', x), (s', s), (z, y), (v, y)\}$$

and we have that $(z, z) \in (\mathsf{oi\_rel}(\mathcal{A}))^+$ because $(z, y), (y, x), (x, z) \in \mathsf{oi\_rel}(\mathcal{A})$, therefore $\mathcal{A}$ is not algebraic loop free. However, the diagram from the example is accepted by Simulink, and it is considered algebraic loop free. In our treatment $\mathsf{oi\_rel}(\mathcal{A})$ contains pairs that do not represent genuine output input dependencies. For example output y of Delay depends only on the input s, and it does not depend on x. Similarly, output s' of Delay depends only on x.

Before applying the feedbackless algorithm, we change the initial list of blocks into a new list such that the output input dependencies are recorded more accurately, and all elements in the new list have one single output. We split a basic block A into a list of blocks $A_1, \ldots, A_n$ with single outputs such that $A \sim A_1 \lvert\lvert\lvert \ldots \lvert\lvert\lvert A_n$. Basically every block with n outputs is split into n single output blocks.

We can do the splitting systematically by composing a block A with all projections of the output. For example if $A = (x, (u_1, \ldots, u_n), S)$, then we can split A into $A_i = (x, u_i, S \; ; [u_1, \ldots, u_n \rightsquigarrow u_i])$. Such splitting is always possible:

Lemma 7. *If A is deterministic, then $A_1, \ldots, A_n$ is a splitting of A, i.e.*

$$A \sim A_1 \,|||\, \cdots \,|||\, A_n.$$

However, this will still introduce unwanted output input dependencies. We solve this problem by defining the splitting for every basic block, such that it accurately records the output input dependency. For example, we split the delay block into Delay_1 and Delay_2:

$$\mathsf{Delay}_1 = (s, y, [s \rightsquigarrow s]) = (s, y, \mathsf{Id}) \quad \text{and} \quad \mathsf{Delay}_2 = (x, s', [x \rightsquigarrow x]) = (x, s', \mathsf{Id})$$

The Split block is split into Split_1 and Split_2:

$$\mathsf{Split}_1 = (y, z, [y \rightsquigarrow y]) = (y, z, \mathsf{Id}) \quad \text{and} \quad \mathsf{Split}_2 = (y, v, [y \rightsquigarrow y]) = (y, v, \mathsf{Id})$$

The blocks Delay_1, Delay_2, Split_1, and Split_2 are all the same, except the naming of the inputs and outputs. The Add block has one single output that depends on both inputs, so it remains unchanged.

After splitting, the list of single output blocks for our example becomes

$$\mathcal{B} = \big(\mathsf{Add}, \mathsf{Delay}_1, \mathsf{Delay}_2, \mathsf{Split}_1, \mathsf{Split}_2\big)$$

and we have

$$\mathsf{oi\_rel}(\mathcal{B}) = \{(x, u), (x, z), (y, s), (s', x), (z, y), (v, y)\}.$$

Now $\mathcal{B}$ is algebraic loop free.

Definition 9. *A block diagram is algebraic loop free if, after splitting, the list of blocks is algebraic loop free.*

We assume that every splitting of a block A into $B_1, \ldots, B_k$ is done such that $A \sim B_1 \,|||\, \cdots \,|||\, B_k$.

Lemma 8. *If a list of blocks $\mathcal{A} = (A_1, \ldots, A_n)$ is split into $\mathcal{B} = (B_1, \ldots, B_m)$, then we have*

$$A_1 \,|||\, \cdots \,|||\, A_n \sim B_1 \,|||\, \cdots \,|||\, B_m.$$

For the feedbackless algorithm, we assume that $\mathcal{A}$ is algebraic loop free, all io-diagrams in $\mathcal{A}$ are single output and deterministic, and all outputs are distinct. We denote this by $\mathsf{ok\_fbless}(\mathcal{A})$.

Definition 10. *For $\mathcal{A}$, such that $\mathsf{ok\_fbless}(\mathcal{A})$, a variable u is internal in $\mathcal{A}$ if there exist A and B in $\mathcal{A}$ such that $O(A) = u$ and $u \in \mathsf{set}(\mathsf{I}(B))$. We denote the set of internal variables of $\mathcal{A}$ by $\mathsf{internal}(\mathcal{A})$.*

Definition 11. *If A and B are single output io-diagrams, then their internal serial composition is defined by*

$$A \rhd B = \mathsf{if}\ \mathsf{set}(O(A)) \subseteq \mathsf{set}(\mathsf{I}(B))\ \mathsf{then}\ A \mathbin{;;} B\ \mathsf{else}\ B$$

and

$$A \rhd (B_1, \ldots, B_n) = (A \rhd B_1, \ldots, A \rhd B_n)$$

We use this composition when all io-diagrams have a single output, and for an io-diagram A, we connect A in series with all io-diagrams from $B_1, \ldots, B_n$ that have $O(A)$ as an input.

The internal serial composition satisfies some properties that are used in proving the correctness of the algorithm.

Lemma 9. *If* ok_fbless(A, B, C) *then* $((A \triangleright B) \triangleright (A \triangleright C)) \sim ((B \triangleright A) \triangleright (B \triangleright C))$

Lemma 10. *If* ok_fbless$(\mathcal{A})$ *and* $A \in$ set$(\mathcal{A})$ *such that* $O(A) \in$ internal$(\mathcal{A})$ *then*

ok_fbless$(A \triangleright (\mathcal{A} \ominus A))$ *and*   internal$(A \triangleright (\mathcal{A} \ominus A)) =$ internal$(\mathcal{A}) - \{O(A)\}$.

8.2   Functional Definition of the Feedbackless Strategy

Definition 12. *For a list x of distinct internal variables of $\mathcal{A}$, we define by induction on x the function* fbless$(x, \mathcal{A})$ *by*

$$\text{fbless}(\epsilon, \mathcal{A}) = \mathcal{A} \quad and \quad \text{fbless}(u \cdot x, \mathcal{A}) = \text{fbless}(x, A \triangleright (\mathcal{A} \ominus A))$$

where A is the unique io-diagram from $\mathcal{A}$ with $O(A) = u$.

Lemma 10 shows that the function fbless is well defined.

The function fbless is the functional equivalent of the feedbackless iterative algorithm that we introduce in Sect. 8.3.

Theorem 4. *If $\mathcal{A} = (A_1, \ldots, A_n)$ is a list of io-diagrams satisfying* ok_fbless$(\mathcal{A})$, *x is a distinct list of all internal variables of $\mathcal{A}$ (set$(x) =$ internal$(\mathcal{A})$), and $(B_1, \ldots, B_k) =$ fbless$(x, \mathcal{A})$ then*

$$\text{FB}(A_1 \,|||\, \ldots \,|||\, A_n) \sim (B_1 \,|||\, \ldots \,|||\, B_n).$$

This theorem together with Lemma 8 show that the result of the fbless function is io-equivalent to the results of the nondeterministic algorithm. This theorem also shows that the result of fbless is independent of the choice of the order of the internal variables in x.

The proof of Theorem 4 is based on Lemmas 9 and 10, and is available in the RCRS formalization – https://github.com/hbd-translation/TranslateHBD.

8.3   The Feedbackless Translation Algorithm

The recursive function fbless calculates the feedbackless translation, but it assumes that the set of internal variables is given at the beginning in a specific order. We want an equivalent iterative version of this function, which at every step picks an arbitrary io-diagram A with internal output, and performs one step:

$$\mathcal{A} := A \triangleright (\mathcal{A} \ominus A)$$

The feedbackless algorithm is given in Algorithm 2.

input: $\mathcal{A} = (A_1 \ldots, A_n)$ (list of io-diagrams satisfying ok_fbless($\mathcal{A}$))
while internal($\mathcal{A}$) $\neq \emptyset$:
$\quad [\, \mathcal{A} := \mathcal{A}' \mid \exists\, A \in \mathsf{set}(\mathcal{A}) : O(A) \in \mathsf{internal}(\mathcal{A}) \land \mathcal{A}' = A \rhd (\mathcal{A} \ominus A) \,]$
$A := B_1 \,|||\, \ldots \,|||\, B_k$ (where $\mathcal{A} = (B_1, \ldots, B_k)$)

Algorithm 2. Feedbackless algorithm for translating HBDs.

The feedbackless algorithm is also nondeterministic, because it allows choosing at every step one of the available io-diagrams with internal output. As we will see in Sect. 8.4, this nondeterminism allows for different implementations regarding the complexity of the generated expressions.

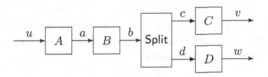

Fig. 8. Example for efficient implementation of feedbackless.

Theorem 5. *If $\mathcal{A} = (A_1 \ldots, A_n)$ is a list of io-diagrams satisfying* ok_fbless($\mathcal{A}$), *then the feedbackless algorithm terminates for input $\mathcal{A}$, and if A is the output of the algorithm on $\mathcal{A}$, then*

$$\mathsf{FB}(A_1 \,|||\, \ldots \,|||\, A_n) \sim A.$$

Theorem 6. *For a deterministic and algebraic loop free block diagram, the feedbackless algorithm and the nondeterministic algorithm are equivalent.*

8.4 On the Nondeterminism of the Feedbackless Translation

We have seen already that different choices in the nondeterministic abstract algorithm result in different algebraic expressions, e.g., with different numbers of composition operators. We show in this section that the same is true for the feedbackless translation algorithm. In particular, consider a framework like the Refinement Calculus of Reactive Systems [16], where the intermediate results of the algorithm are symbolically simplified at every translation step. Different choices of the order of internal variables could result in different complexities of the simplification work. We illustrate this with the example from Fig. 8.

After the splitting phase, the list of blocks for this example is

$$\mathcal{A} = \big((u,a,A),\ (a,b,B),\ (b,c,\mathsf{Id}),\ (b,d,\mathsf{Id}),\ (c,v,C),\ (d,w,D)\big)$$

and the set of internal variables is

$$\mathsf{internal}(\mathcal{A}) = \{a,b,c,d\}.$$

If we choose the order (c, d, b, a), then after first two steps (including intermediate simplifications) we obtain the list:

$$((u, a, A),\ (a, b, B),\ (b, v, C),\ (b, w, D))$$

After another step for internal variable b we obtain:

$$((u, a, A),\ (a, v, \mathsf{simplify}(B\ ;\ C)),\ (a, w, \mathsf{simplify}(B\ ;\ D)))$$

where the function $\mathsf{simplify}$ models the symbolic simplification. Finally, after applying the step for the internal variable a we obtain:

$$((u, v, \mathsf{simplify}(A\ ;\ \mathsf{simplify}(B\ ;\ C))),\ (u, w, \mathsf{simplify}(A\ ;\ \mathsf{simplify}(B\ ;\ D)))) \quad (1)$$

In this order, we end up simplifying A serially composed with B twice. This is especially inefficient if A and B are complex. If we choose the order (c, d, a, b), then in the first three steps we obtain:

$$((u, b, \mathsf{simplify}(A\ ;\ B)),\ (b, v, C),\ (b, w, D))$$

At this point the term $A\ ;\ B$ is simplified, and the simplified version is composed with C and D to obtain:

$$((u, v, \mathsf{simplify}(\mathsf{simplify}(A\ ;\ B)\ ;\ C)),\ (u, w, \mathsf{simplify}(\mathsf{simplify}(A\ ;\ B)\ ;\ D))) \quad (2)$$

If we compare relations (1) and (2) we see the same number of occurrences of $\mathsf{simplify}$, but in relation (2) there are two occurrences of the common subterm $\mathsf{simplify}(A\ ;\ B)$, and this is simplified only once.

As this example shows, different choices of the nondeterministic feedbackless translation strategy result in expressions of different quality, in particular with respect to simplification. It is beyond the scope of this paper to examine efficient deterministic implementations of the feedbackless translation. Our goal here is to prove the correctness of this translation, by proving its equivalence to the abstract algorithm. It follows that every refinement/determinization of the feedbackless strategy will also be equivalent to the abstract algorithm, and therefore a correct implementation of the semantics. Once we know that all possible refinements give equivalent results, we can concentrate in finding the most efficient strategy. In general, we remark that this way of using the mechanisms of nondeterminism and refinement are standard in the area of correct by construction program development, and are often combined to separate the concerns of correctness and efficiency, as is done here.

9   Implementation in Isabelle

Our implementation in Isabelle uses locales [7] for the axioms of the algebra. We use locale interpretations to show that these axioms are consistent. In Isabelle locales are a powerful mechanism for developing consistent abstract theories (based on axioms). To represent the algorithm we use monotonic predicate transformers. To prove correctness of the algorithm we use Hoare total correctness rules.

The formalization contains the locale for the axioms, a theory for constructive functions, and one for proving that such functions are a model for the axioms. An important part of the formalization is the theory introducing the diagrams with named inputs and outputs, and their operations and properties. The formalization also includes a theory for monotonic predicate transformers, refinement calculus, Hoare total correctness rules for programs, and a theory for the nondeterministic algorithm and its correctness.

In total the formalization contains 14797 lines of Isabelle code of which 13587 lines of code for the actual problem, i.e., excluding the code for monotonic predicate transformers, refinement calculus, and Hoare rules. The formalization is available at https://github.com/hbd-translation/TranslateHBD.

10   Conclusions and Future Work

We introduced an abstract algebra for hierarchical block diagrams, and an abstract algorithm for translating HBDs to terms of this algebra. We proved that this algorithm is correct in the sense that no matter how its nondeterministic choices are resolved, the results are semantically equivalent. As an application, we closed a question left open in [16] by proving that the Simulink translation strategies presented there yield equivalent results. Our HBD algebra is reminiscent of the algebra of flownomials [14] but our axiomatization is more general, in the sense that our axioms are weaker. This implies that all models of flownomials are also models of our algebra. Here, we presented constructive functions as one possible model of our algebra.

Our work applies to hierarchical block diagrams in general, and the de facto predominant tool for embedded system design, Simulink. Proving the HBD translator correct is a challenging problem, and as far as we know our work is the only one to have achieved such a result.

We believe that our results are reusable in other contexts as well, in at least two ways. First, every other translation that can be shown to be a refinement/special case of our abstract translation algorithm, is automatically correct. For example, [34,44] impose an order on blocks such that they use mostly serial composition and could be considered an instance of our abstract algorithm. Second, our algorithms translate diagrams into an abstract algebra. By choosing different models of this algebra we obtain translations into these alternative models.

As future work we plan to investigate further HBD translation strategies, in addition to those studied above. Currently the RCRS Translator can only partially handle diagrams with algebraic loops, i.e., with instantaneous circular dependencies. Fully dealing with diagrams with algebraic loops is a non-trivial problem, because of the subtleties of instantaneous feedback for non-deterministic and non-input-receptive systems [33]. For deterministic and input-receptive systems, however, the model of constructive functions should be sufficient. Another future research goal is to unify the proof of the third translation strategy with that of the other two which are currently modeled as refinements of the abstract translation algorithm.

This work covers hierarchical block diagrams in general and Simulink in particular. Any type of diagram can be handled, however, we do assume a *single-rate* (i.e., synchronous) semantics. Handling multi-rate or event-triggered diagrams is left for future work. Handling hierarchical state machine models such as Stateflow is also left for future work.

As mentioned in Sect. 2, there are many existing translations from Simulink to other formalisms. It is beyond the scope of this paper to define and prove correctness of those translations, but this could be another future work direction. In order to do this, one would first need to formalize those translations. This in turn requires detailed knowledge of the algorithms or even access to their implementation, which is not always available. Our work and source code are publicly available and we hope can serve as a good starting point for others who may wish to provide formal correctness proofs of diagram translations.

Acknowledgments. We would like to thank Gheorghe Ştefănescu for his help with the algebra of flownomials.

References

1. Rahim, L.A., Whittle, J.: A survey of approaches for verifying model transformations. Softw. Syst. Model. **14**(2), 1003–1028 (2015)
2. Agrawal, A., Simon, G., Karsai, G.: Semantic translation of Simulink/stateflow models to hybrid automata using graph transformations. Electron. Notes Theor. Comput. Sci. **109**, 43–56 (2004)
3. Amrani, M., et al.: Formal verification techniques for model transformations: a tridimensional classification. J. Object Technol. **14**(3), 1:1–43 (2015)
4. Auger, C.: Compilation certifiée de SCADE/LUSTRE. (Certified compilation of SCADE/LUSTRE). Ph.D. thesis, University of Paris-Sud, Orsay, France (2013). (in French)
5. Back, R.-J., von Wright, J.: Refinement Calculus: A Systematic Introduction. Springer, New York (1998). https://doi.org/10.1007/978-1-4612-1674-2
6. Baez, J.C., Erbele, J.: Categories in control. CoRR, abs/1405.6881 (2015)
7. Ballarin, C.: Locales: a module system for mathematical theories. J. Autom. Reason. **52**(2), 123–153 (2014)
8. Berry, G.: The constructive semantics of pure Esterel (1999)
9. Bouissou, O., Chapoutot, A.: An operational semantics for Simulink's simulation engine. SIGPLAN Not. **47**(5), 129–138 (2012)
10. Bourke, T., Brun, L., Dagand, P.É., Leroy, X., Pouzet, M., Rieg, L.: A formally verified compiler for lustre. SIGPLAN Not. **52**(6), 586–601 (2017)
11. Calegari, D., Szasz, N.: Verification of model transformations. Electron. Notes Theor. Comput. Sci. **292**, 5–25 (2013)
12. Chen, C., Dong, J.S., Sun, J.: A formal framework for modeling and validating Simulink diagrams. Form. Asp. Comput. **21**(5), 451–483 (2009)

13. Courcelle, B.: A representation of graphs by algebraic expressions and its use for graph rewriting systems. In: Ehrig, H., Nagl, M., Rozenberg, G., Rosenfeld, A. (eds.) Graph Grammars 1986. LNCS, vol. 291, pp. 112–132. Springer, Heidelberg (1987). https://doi.org/10.1007/3-540-18771-5_49

14. Ştefănescu, G.: Network Algebra. Springer, London (2000). https://doi.org/10.1007/978-1-4471-0479-7

15. Dijkstra, E.W.: Guarded commands, nondeterminacy and formal derivation of programs. Commun. ACM **18**(8), 453–457 (1975)

16. Dragomir, I., Preoteasa, V., Tripakis, S.: Compositional semantics and analysis of hierarchical block diagrams. In: Bošnački, D., Wijs, A. (eds.) SPIN 2016. LNCS, vol. 9641, pp. 38–56. Springer, Cham (2016). https://doi.org/10.1007/978-3-319-32582-8_3

17. Dragomir, I., Preoteasa, V., Tripakis, S.: The refinement calculus of reactive systems toolset. In: Beyer, D., Huisman, M. (eds.) TACAS 2018. LNCS, vol. 10806, pp. 201–208. Springer, Cham (2018). https://doi.org/10.1007/978-3-319-89963-3_12

18. Dragomir, I., Preoteasa, V., Tripakis, S.: The refinement calculus of reactive systems toolset - February 2018. Figshare. https://doi.org/10.6084/m9.figshare.5900911. Accessed Feb 2018

19. Eclipse: ATL - a model transformation technology. http://www.eclipse.org/atl/

20. Edwards, S., Lee, E.A.: The semantics and execution of a synchronous block-diagram language. Sci. Comput. Prog. **48**, 21–42(22) (2003)

21. Ghica, D.R., Jung, A.: Categorical semantics of digital circuits. In: Piskac, R., Talupur, M. (eds.) 2016 Formal Methods in Computer-Aided Design, FMCAD 2016, Mountain View, CA, USA, 3–6 October 2016, pp. 41–48. IEEE (2016)

22. Ghica, D.R., Jung, A., Lopez, A.: Diagrammatic semantics for digital circuits. In: Goranko, V., Dam, M. (eds.) 26th EACSL Annual Conference on Computer Science Logic, CSL 2017, LIPIcs, Stockholm, Sweden, vol. 82, pp. 24:1–24:16. Schloss Dagstuhl - Leibniz-Zentrum fuer Informatik (2017)

23. Ghica, D.R., Lopez, A.: A structural and nominal syntax for diagrams. In: Coecke, B., Kissinger, A. (eds.) Proceedings 14th International Conference on Quantum Physics and Logic, QPL 2017, EPTCS, Nijmegen, The Netherlands, 3–7 July 2017, vol. 266, pp. 71–83 (2017)

24. Yang, C., Vyatkin, V.: Transformation of Simulink models to IEC 61499 function blocks for verification of distributed control systems. Control Eng. Pract. **20**(12), 1259–1269 (2012)

25. Leroy, X., Blazy, S., Kästner, D., Schommer, B., Pister, M., Ferdinand, C.: CompCert - a formally verified optimizing compiler. In: 8th European Congress on ERTS 2016: Embedded Real Time Software and Systems, Toulouse, France, January 2016. SEE

26. Lúcio, L., et al.: Model transformation intents and their properties. Softw. Syst. Model. **15**(3), 647–684 (2016)

27. Malik, S.: Analysis of cyclic combinational circuits. IEEE Trans. Comput.-Aided Des. **13**(7), 950–956 (1994)

28. MathWorks: Simulink. https://www.mathworks.com/products/simulink.html

29. Meenakshi, B., Bhatnagar, A., Roy, S.: Tool for translating Simulink models into input language of a model checker. In: Liu, Z., He, J. (eds.) ICFEM 2006. LNCS, vol. 4260, pp. 606–620. Springer, Heidelberg (2006). https://doi.org/10.1007/11901433_33

30. Minopoli, S., Frehse, G.: SL2SX translator: from Simulink to SpaceEx models. In: Proceedings of the 19th International Conference on Hybrid Systems: Computation and Control, HSCC 2016, pp. 93–98. ACM, New York (2016)

31. Nipkow, T., Paulson, L.C., Wenzel, M.: Isabelle/HOL – A Proof Assistant for Higher-Order Logic. LNCS, vol. 2283. Springer, Heidelberg (2002). https://doi.org/10.1007/3-540-45949-9

32. Preoteasa, V., Dragomir, I., Tripakis, S.: Mechanically proving determinacy of hierarchical block diagram translations. CoRR, abs/1611.01337 (2018)

33. Preoteasa, V., Tripakis, S.: Towards compositional feedback in non-deterministic and non-input-receptive systems. In: Proceedings of the 31st Annual ACM/IEEE Symposium on Logic in Computer Science, LICS 2016, pp. 768–777. ACM, New York (2016)

34. Reicherdt, R., Glesner, S.: Formal verification of discrete-time MATLAB/Simulink models using Boogie. In: Giannakopoulou, D., Salaün, G. (eds.) SEFM 2014. LNCS, vol. 8702, pp. 190–204. Springer, Cham (2014). https://doi.org/10.1007/978-3-319-10431-7_14

35. Ryabtsev, M., Strichman, O.: Translation validation: from Simulink to C. In: Bouajjani, A., Maler, O. (eds.) CAV 2009. LNCS, vol. 5643, pp. 696–701. Springer, Heidelberg (2009). https://doi.org/10.1007/978-3-642-02658-4_57

36. Schlesinger, S., Herber, P., Göthel, T., Glesner, S.: Proving transformation correctness of refactorings for discrete and continuous Simulink models. In: ICONS 2016, The Eleventh International Conference on Systems, EMBEDDED 2016, International Symposium on Advances in Embedded Systems and Applications, pp. 45–50. IARIA XPS Press (2016)

37. Schmeck, H.: Algebraic characterization of reducible flowcharts. J. Comput. Syst. Sci. 27(2), 165–199 (1983)

38. Selinger, P.: A survey of graphical languages for Monoidal categories. In: Coecke, B. (ed.) New Structures for Physics. LNP, vol. 813, pp. 289–355. Springer, Heidelberg (2011). https://doi.org/10.1007/978-3-642-12821-9_4

39. Sfyrla, V., Tsiligiannis, G., Safaka, I., Bozga, M., Sifakis, J.: Compositional translation of Simulink models into synchronous BIP. In: SIES, pp. 217–220, July 2010

40. The Coq Development Team: The Coq proof assistant reference. INRIA, 2016. Version 8.5 (2016)

41. Tripakis, S., Sofronis, C., Caspi, P., Curic, A.: Translating discrete-time Simulink to Lustre. ACM Trans. Embed. Comput. Syst. 4(4), 779–818 (2005)

42. Zanasi, F.: Interacting Hopf algebras - the theory of linear systems. (Interacting Hopf Algebras - la théorie des systèmes linéaires). Ph.D. thesis, École normale supérieure de Lyon, France (2015)

43. Zhou, C., Kumar, R.: Semantic translation of Simulink diagrams to input/output extended finite automata. Discret. Event Dyn. Syst. 22(2), 223–247 (2012)

44. Zou, L., Zhany, N., Wang, S., Franzle, M., Qin, S.: Verifying Simulink diagrams via a hybrid Hoare logic prover. In: EMSOFT, pp. 9:1–9:10, September 2013

Author Index

Printed in the United States
by Baker & Taylor Publisher Services

Printed in the United States
By Bookmasters